AN
INTRODUCTION
TO THINKING
LIKE A
SOCIOLOGIST
16.
11.
9.
6.
14.
5.
15.
2.
17.
7.
3.
18.
10.
8.
13.
1.
12.
4.

RECENT SOCIOLOGY TITLES FROM W. W. NORTON

Code of the Streets by Elijah Anderson

The Cosmopolitan Canopy by Elijah Anderson

Social Problems, 2nd Edition by Joel Best

The Real World: An Introduction to Sociology, 3rd Edition by Kerry Ferris and Jill Stein

Essentials of Sociology, 4th Edition by Anthony Giddens, Mitchell Duneier, Richard P. Appelbaum, and Deborah Carr

Introduction to Sociology, 8th Edition by Anthony Giddens, Mitchell Duneier, Richard P. Appelbaum, and Deborah Carr

Mix it Up: Popular Culture, Mass Media, and Society by David Grazian

The Contexts Reader, 2nd Edition edited by Douglas Hartmann and Christopher Uggen

When Sex Goes to School by Kristin Luker

Inequality and Society by Jeff Manza and Michael Sauder

Doing Race by Hazel Rose Markus and Paula M. L. Moya

Readings for Sociology, 7th Edition edited by Garth Massey

Families as They Really Are edited by Barbara J. Risman

Sociology of Globalization by Saskia Sassen

The Sociology of News, 2nd Edition by Michael Schudson

The Social Construction of Sexuality, 2nd Edition by Steven Seidman

The Corrosion of Character by Richard Sennett

Biography and the Sociological Imagination by Michael J. Shanahan and Ross Macmillan

A Primer on Social Movements by David Snow and Sarah Soule

Six Degrees by Duncan J. Watts

More than Just Race by William Julius Wilson

American Society: How it Really Works by Erik Olin Wright and Joel Rogers

Third Edition

You May Ask Yourself

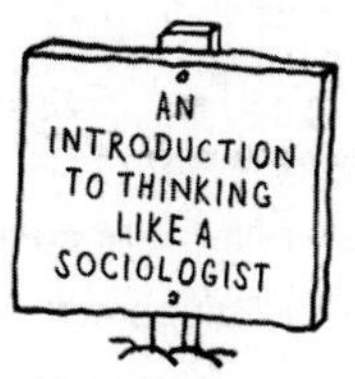

Dalton Conley

NEW YORK UNIVERSITY

W. W. NORTON
NEW YORK | LONDON

W. W. Norton & Company has been independent since its founding in 1923, when William Warder Norton and Mary D. Herter Norton first published lectures delivered at the People's Institute, the adult education division of New York City's Cooper Union. The firm soon expanded its program beyond the Institute, publishing books by celebrated academics from America and abroad. By mid-century, the two major pillars of Norton's publishing program—trade books and college texts—were firmly established. In the 1950s, the Norton family transferred control of the company to its employees, and today—with a staff of four hundred and a comparable number of trade, college, and professional titles published each year—W. W. Norton & Company stands as the largest and oldest publishing house owned wholly by its employees.

Printed in the United States of America
Third Edition

Editor: Karl Bakeman
Project editor: Kate Feighery
Editorial assistants: Rebecca Charney, Alicia Gonzalez-Gross, and Jennifer Barnhardt
Media editor: Eileen Connell
Associate media editor: Laura Musich
Production managers, College: Jane Searle and Eric Pier-Hocking
Photo research: Trish Marx
Marketing manager: Natasha Zabohonski
Book designer: Kiss Me I'm Polish LLC, New York
Design director: Rubina Yeh
Composition: Jouve
Manufacturing: Courier Kendallville

Library of Congress Cataloging-in-Publication Data

Conley, Dalton, 1969–
You may ask yourself : an introduction to thinking like a sociologist / Dalton Conley.—3rd ed.
p. cm.
Includes bibliographical references and index.
ISBN 978-0-393-91299-9 (pbk.)
1. Sociology—Methodology. 2. Sociology—Study and teaching. I. Title.
HM511.C664 2013
301—dc23

2012013752

W. W. Norton & Company, Inc., 500 Fifth Avenue, New York, N.Y. 10110
www.wwnorton.com
W. W. Norton & Company Ltd., Castle House, 75/76 Wells Street, London W1T 3QT

1 2 3 4 5 6 7 8 9 0

BRIEF CONTENTS

PART I
USING YOUR SOCIOLOGICAL IMAGINATION 1

PART II
FAULT LINES . . . SOCIAL DIVISION AND INEQUALITY 237

PART III
BUILDING BLOCKS: INSTITUTIONS OF SOCIETY 449

CONTENTS

HOT DATE
MARIA
JOB REFERRAL
TYLER

HUMANS

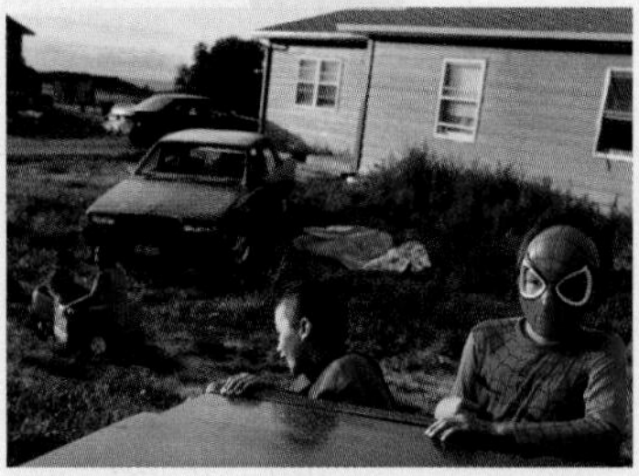

ME, MYSELF AND I
AMA
U.S. CITIZEN
MUSLIM
STUDENT

PREFACE

I came to sociology by accident, so to speak. During the 1980s, there were no sociology courses at the high-school level, so I entered college with only the vaguest notion of what sociology—or even social science—was. Instead, I headed straight for the pre-med courses. But there was no such thing as a pre-med major, so I ended up specializing in the now defunct "humanities field major." This un-major major was really the result of my becoming a junior and realizing that I was not any closer to a declared field of study than I had been when arriving two years earlier. So I scanned a list of all the electives I had taken until then—philosophy of aesthetics, history of technology, and so on—and marched right into my advisor's office, declaring that it had always been my lifelong dream to study "art and technology in the twentieth century." I wrote this up convincingly enough, apparently, because the college allowed me to write a senior thesis about how the evolution of Warner Brothers' cartoon characters from the stuttering, insecure Porky Pig to the militant Daffy Duck to the cool, collected, and confident Bugs Bunny reflected the self-image of the United States on the world stage during the Depression, World War II, and the postwar period, respectively. Little did I know, I was already becoming a sociologist.

After college, I worked as a journalist but then decided that I wanted to continue my schooling. I really was drawn to the critical stance and reflexivity that I had learned in my humanities classes. But I knew that I didn't want to devote my life to arcane texts. What I wanted to do was take those skills—that critical stance—and apply them to everyday life, to the here and now. I also was rather skeptical of the methods that humanists used. What texts they chose to analyze always seemed so arbitrary. I wanted to systematize the inquiry a bit more; I found myself trying to apply the scientific method that I gotten a taste of in my biology classes. But I didn't want to do science in a lab. I wanted to be out in the proverbial real world. So when I flipped through a course catalog with these latent preferences somewhere in the back of my head, my finger landed on the sociology courses.

Once I became a card-carrying sociologist, the very first course I taught was Introduction to Sociology. I had big shoes to fill in teaching this course at Yale.

Kai Erikson, the world-renowned author of *Wayward Puritans* and *Everything in Its Path* and son of the psychologist Erik Erikson, was stepping down from his popular course, "The Human Universe," and I, a first-year assistant professor, was expected to replace him.

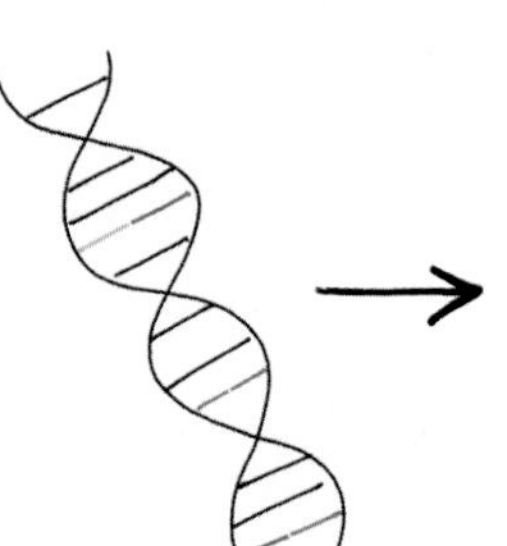

I had a lot of sociology to learn. After all, graduate training in sociology is spotty at best. And there is no single theory of society the same way one might learn, for example, micro and macro as core courses in economics or the biochemistry of DNA translation and transcription as the central dogma of molecular biology. We talk about the sociological imagination as an organizing principle. But even that is almost a poetic notion, not so easily articulated. Think of sociology as more like driving a car than learning calculus. You can read the manual all you want, but that isn't going to teach you how to do it. Only by seeing sociology in action and then trying it yourself will you eventually say, "Hey, I've got the hang of this!"

Hence the title of this book. In *You May Ask Yourself,* I show readers how sociologists question what most others take for granted about society, and I give readers opportunities to apply sociological ways of thinking to their own experiences. I've tried to jettison the arcane academic debates that become the guiding light of so many intro books in favor of a series of contemporary empirical (gold) nuggets that show off sociology (and empirical social science more generally) in its finest hour. Most students who take an introductory sociology class in college will not end up being sociology majors, let alone professional sociologists. Yet I aim to speak to both the aspiring major and the student who is merely fulfilling a requirement. So rather than having pages filled with statistics and theories that will go out of date rather quickly, *You May Ask Yourself* tries to instill in the reader a way of thinking—a scientific approach to human affairs that is portable, one that students will find useful when they study anything else, ranging from history to medicine.

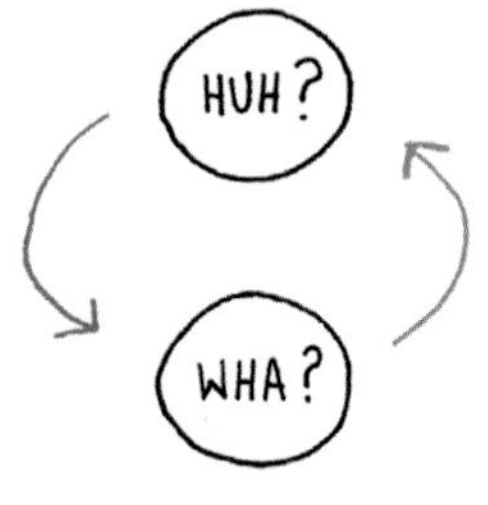

To achieve that ambitious goal, I tried to write a book that was as "un-textbook"-like as possible, while covering all the material that a student in sociology needs to know. In this vein, each chapter is organized around a motivating paradox, meant to serve as the first chilling line of a mystery novel that motivates the reader to read on to find out (or rather, figure out, because this book is not about spoon-feeding facts) the nugget, the debate, the fundamentally new way of looking at the world that illuminates the paradox. Along with a paradox, each chapter begins with a profile of a relevant "person" who speaks to the core theme of the chapter. These range from myself to the Obama family to a guy who declared himself king of an offshore platform, battling the British government for sovereignty. In addition, in order to show the usefulness of sociological knowledge in shaping the world around us, each chapter also culminates in a policy discussion and Practice section where the reader gets a chance to show his or her sociological imagination in action (rather than just regurgitate facts).

WHAT'S NEW IN THE THIRD EDITION

While the Second Edition involved some major fixes of some things we tried in the first that had fallen flat, the Third Edition involved delving into whole new media. Higher education is rapidly in transition, with online instruction expanding rapidly both at traditional institutions, in the ever-expanding for-profit sector, and in the new, open-courseware movement. With these changes, textbooks must also reinvent and reorient themselves. Students now expect—I believe—an entire multimedia experience when they purchase a text. So in addition to the lecture slides and interview videos we provided with the Second Edition (more of which have been included for the Third), we have added what was the most fun project I've perhaps ever worked on: animated short films illustrating the central themes and paradoxes of each chapter. There was something so exciting about trying to make the sometimes abstract concepts of sociological theory and practice understandable with squiggly little lines in three minutes. But this brings a long American tradition into sociology. Not only was the comic book invented here, the use of animated shorts to convey important academic information was particularly imprinted on me during my childhood that was infused with Schoolhouse Rock. I only hope that "Sociological Rock" (sorry, no music though) is half as successful as those 1970s shorts were at teaching me about Congress, adverbs, and conjunctions. I helped write, develop, and narrate these film clips along with Karl Bakeman, the book's editor at W. W. Norton, but the bulk of the creative and production work fell upon the folks at the creative studio Kiss Me I'm Polish (who along with Kirsten Livingston are also responsible for the new look of the text itself). These include Agnieszka Gasparska, Mattias Mackler, and their animator, Aaron Hughes. Sound was engineered by Kevin Scott. These were so fun to make, I'm not sure how we can top them for the Fourth Edition. (At least we've got some time before we have to figure that out—sociological holograms perhaps?)

In addition to the new animations, we revised every chapter in the book. Here are some of the highlights:

Chapter 3

WikiLeaks is used as an example of how the secret documents released on the Internet were prescreened by hackers and researchers in a similar manner to how news is also selectively chosen. A new section on consumer culture, with interview excerpts from Allison Pugh, is included, in addition to a new section on children and advertising. Pugh speaks to the result of advertising in the creation of a self-sustaining consumer culture among children and how that plays out differently for low income and high income families. The policy box has been updated with George W. Bush's 2002 public relations campaign launched in the Middle East to improve the U.S.'s image problem.

Chapter 4

Chapter 4 features an interview by Annette Lareau about how different parenting strategies based on socioeconomic backgrounds may or may not affect the long term outcomes of children. The policy box on Harlem Children's Zone has been updated.

Chapter 7

A new example of the power elite focuses on former White House budget director Peter Orzsag's move to Citibank after working for the Obama administration. His replacement Jacob Lew also has ties to the Clinton administration and Citibank. The links between government and finance are explored through the lens of the financial crisis. New data on the growing wealth disparities in the United States are included.

Chapter 8

A new chapter opener features Deirdre McCloskey, who went through sex reassignment surgery and chronicled her journey in the book, *Crossing*. The Great Recession has helped accelerate gender equality in the workforce, with employed women at one point outnumbering employed men. New data on sexual assaults in the military has been included.

Chapter 9

Statistics on the population, health, and socioeconomic status of the Native American population have been updated. Demographic information for Black, Latino, Asian, and Middle Eastern populations in the U.S. has been updated. The economic gap between different racial groups is explored through the lens of the Great Recession and housing crash. New discussion of structural racism has been included in the chapter.

Chapter 10

An excerpt from an interview with David Grusky, director of Stanford University's Center for the Study of Poverty and Inequality, discusses perverse incentives and the question that if we had an attractive alternative to the labor market, in the form of very substantial safety net resources, would people opt for the safety net instead of the labor market. Grusky also speaks about delegitimating residential segregation. The recession's effect on the net worth of families by race has been updated. Updates on the disparity between the richest and poorest in America are included.

Chapter 11

The section on the social construction of illness has been rewritten, featuring Ka Liu's research on autism. Statistics on infant mortality by race, gender, and life expectancy have been updated.

Chapter 12

Family demographic statistics in the U.S. have been updated. A new section on intimate partner violence includes contemporary data. The percentage of babies born to unwed mothers by race has also been updated. New information on same-sex marriage reflects the most recent legal status and American public opinion. Intermarriage rates are updated and broken down by race and gender.

Chapter 13

An interview excerpt from sociologist Shamus Khan is now included. The discussion explores his research on elite educational institutions like St. Paul's, the subject of his book *Privilege: The Making of an Adolescent Elite at St. Paul's School.* Educational attainment and poverty statistics by race have been updated. Notably, as of 2010, more women earned high school and college degrees than men.

Chapter 14

The chapter opener describes the challenges the Obamas face with negotiating the roles of parenthood and work. Statistics on mothers in the workforce have been updated, along with the increased hours and unused vacation time Americans have collected. The section on globalization has been rewritten to show how technology has influenced trade worldwide. An excerpt from an interview with Nitsan Chorev points out that globalization is not inevitable and features research from her book *Remaking U.S. Trade Policy: From Protectionism to Globalization.*

Chapter 15

During Arab Spring, clashing forces in Yemen led to violence targeted toward peaceful protesters and a neutral military unit. The disintegration of Yemen's state monopoly affected its relationships with other states.

Chapter 16

The commercialization of religion through Christian merchandise sold at Wal-Mart and movies like *The Passion of the Christ* is explored. New information on the growth and influence of megachurches is also included. Rates of religious affiliation are updated with data about adherents in the U.S. and abroad.

Chapter 17

China is now the largest emitter of greenhouse gasses, with the United States the second largest producer. The concept of a "gay gene" is discussed.

Chapter 18

The Tea Party and Occupy Wall Street movements are explored as new social movements that developed from the current political and economic climate.

ACKNOWLEDGEMENTS

You May Ask Yourself originated in the Introduction to Sociology course that I have taught on and off since the mid-1990s at New York University, Yale University, and Columbia University. However, the process of writing it made me feel as if I were learning to be a sociologist all over again. For example, I never taught religion, methodology, or the sociology of education. But instructors who reviewed the manuscript requested that we cover these topics here, so with the assistance of an army of graduate students who really ought to be recognized as coauthors, I got to work. That was four years ago. The experience was invaluable, and in a way, I finally feel like a card-carrying sociologist, having acquired at last a bird's-eye view of my colleagues' work. I consider it a great honor to be able to put my little spin (or filter) on the field in this way, to be able not just to influence the few hundred intro students I teach each year, but to excite (I hope) and instill the enthusiasm I didn't get to experience until graduate school in students who may even be just a few months out of high school (if that).

I mentioned that the graduate students who helped me create this book were really more like coauthors, ghost writers, or perhaps law clerks. Law clerks do much of the writing of legal opinions for judges, but only a judge's name graces a decision. I asked Norton to allow more coauthors, but they declined—perhaps understandably, given how long such a list would be—so I will take this opportunity to thank my students and hope that you are still reading this preface.

The original transcribing of my lectures that formed the basis of this text was completed by Carse Ramos, who also worked on assembling the glossary and drafted some parts of various chapters, such as sections in the economic sociology chapter, as well as some text in the chapters on authority and deviance. She also served as an all-around editor. Ashley Mears did the heavy lifting on the race, gender, family, and religion chapters. Amy LeClair took the lead on methods, culture, groups and networks, socialization, and health. Jennifer Heerwig cobbled together the chapter on authority and the state and deviance (a nice combo), while her officemate Brian McCabe whipped up the chapter on science, technology, and the environment and the one on social movements. Melissa Velez wrote the first draft of the education chapter (and a fine one at that). Michael McCarthy did the same for the stratification chapter. Devyani Prabhat helped revise the social movements chapter. My administrative assistant Amelia Branigan served as fact checker, editor, and box drafter while running a department, taking the GREs, and writing and submitting her own graduate applications. When Amelia had to decamp for Northwestern University to pursue her own doctorate, Lauren Marten took over the job of chasing down obscure references, fact-checking, and proofreading. Alexandre Frenette drafted the questions and activities in the Practice sections at the end of each chapter.

For the Second Edition, much of the work to integrate the interview transcripts and update material based on reviewer feedback fell to a great extent on the shoulders of Laura Norén, a fantastic New York University graduate student who has worked on topics as far ranging as public toilets (with my colleague Harvey Molotch) to how symphonies and designers collaborate (as part of her dissertation). I hope Laura will find her crash-course overview of sociology useful at some point in what promises to be a productive and exciting scholarly career.

When it was time to begin the Third Edition, the updating of all the statistics, fact-checking, and so on that is the bread and butter of a revision fell upon the capable shoulders of Emi Nakazato, who though trained as a social worker in graduate school, adeptly pivoted to that field's cousin, sociology.

In addition to the students who have worked with me on the book, I need to give shouts out to all the top-notch scholars who found time in their busy schedules to sit down with me and do on-camera interviews: Andrew Cherlin, Nitsan Chorev, Mitchell Duneier, Paula England, John Evans, David Grusky, Michael Hout, Shamus Khan, Annette Lareau, Jennifer Lee, Ka Liu, Douglas McAdam, Steven Morgan, Alondra Nelson, Devah Pager, Nathan Palmer, C. J. Pascoe, Frances Fox Piven, Allison Pugh, Jen'nan Read, Victor Rios, Jeffrey Sachs, and Duncan Watts. And the filmmaking, editing, and post-production were done by Erica Rothman at Nightlight Productions with the assistance of Jim Haverkamp, Kevin Wells, Saul Rouda, Dimitriy Khavin, and Arkadiy Ugorskiy. This was no easy task since we wanted a bunch of cuts ranging from 30-second sound bites through to 3 minutes on the way up to 22-minute, television show length. While a bunch of interviews with academic social scientists on topics ranging from estimating the effects of Catholic schools on student outcomes to the political economy of global trade to the social contagion of autism are not likely to win any Emmys or rock the Nielsens (with the possible exception of the last one on college sex), it was certainly one of the most exciting moments of my sociological career to host this makeshift talk-show of sorts on this wide range of interesting topics. (If only more of our public discourse would dig into issues in a way that we did in these interviews, our society and governance would be in better shape—if I do say so myself!)

Meanwhile, many thanks to Kendall and Annie Madden, who did the transcriptions of the interviews so that they could seamlessly migrate from video to the pages herein.

I also relied on a number of scholars who generously read chapters of this book and offered valuable feedback, criticisms, and suggestions:

REVIEWERS FOR THE THIRD EDITION

Orit Avishai, Fordham University
Carl Backman, Auburn University
Nielan Barnes, California State University, Long Beach
Renee Beard, College of the Holy Cross
Gayle Gordon Bouzard, Texas State University
Andrea Brenner, American University
Jeneve Brooks, Troy University
Victoria Carty, Chapman University
Susan Cody-Rydzewski, Georgia Perimeter College
Carolyn Corrado, State University of New York–Albany
John Curra, Eastern Kentucky University
Gayle D'Andrea, J. Sargeant Reynolds Community College
Regina Davis-Sowers, Santa Clara University
Sophia DeMasi, Montgomery County Community College
Daniel Dexheimer, Santa Clara University
Lynda Dickson, University of Colorado
Gianna Durso-Finley, Mercer County Community College
Kathryn Fox, University of Vermont
Duane Gill, Oklahoma State University
Keisha Goode, City College of New York
Heather Griffiths, Fayetteville State University
Charles Hanna, Duquesne University
Bruce Haynes, University of California, Davis
Kalynn Heald, Northwest Arkansas Community College
Druann Heckert, Fayetteville State University
Larry Hunt, University of Maryland, College Park
Jack King, Northern Illinois University
Roger Klomegah, Fayetteville State University
Rosalind Kopfstein, Western Connecticut State University
Jamee Kristen, Portland Community College
Timothy Kubal, California State University, Fresno
Liza Kuecker, Western New Mexico University
Jenifer Kunz, West Texas A&M University
Jennifer Lerner, Northern Virginia Community College
Ho Hon Leung, State University of New York–Oneonta
Carlos Lopez, Chemeketa Community College
Clara Magliola, Chapman University
Helen Mederer, University of Rhode Island
Joan Meyers, Rutgers University
Linda Morrison, Duquesne University
Geoffrey Moss, Temple University
Ryan Orr, Millersville University
Aurea Osgood, Winona State University
Joshua Packard, Midwestern State University
Nathan Palmer, Georgia Southern University
Paul Prew, Minnesota State University, Mankato
Rachel Zimmer Schneider, University of Akron
Jerald Schrimsher, Southern Illinois University Carbondale
Ben Shirley, Alamance Community College
Sheryl Skaggs, University of Texas at Dallas
Carrie Smith, Millersville University
Tomecia Sobers, Fayetteville Technical Community College
Ann Stein, College of Charleston
Cat Steinhauer, South Plains College
Ann Strahm, California State University, Stanislaus
Steven Vassar, Minnesota State University, Mankato
Linda Vang, Fresno City College
Robert Wahl, Pennsylvania State University
Angela Ware, Auburn University
Sharon Weiss, Truckee Meadows Community College
KC Williams, Coastal Carolina University
Robert Wonser, College of the Canyons
James Wright, Chattanooga State College
Luis Zanartu, Sacramento City College

REVIEWERS FOR THE SECOND EDITION

Christopher Armstrong, Bloomsburg University
Ingrid Castro, Northeastern Illinois University

Jennifer Chernega, Winona State University
Stacia Creek, Southern Illinois University
Michael Cuckler, Asbury College
Marianne Cutler, East Stroudsburg University
Martine Delannay, Madison Area Technical College
James Dowd, University of Georgia
Mark Edwards, Oregon State University
James Elliott, University of Oregon
Colleen Eren, Hunter College
Sally Gallagher, Oregon State University
Fang Gong, Ball State University
Edward Gott, Northeast Wisconsin Technical College
Jennifer Hartsfield, University of Oklahoma
Bruce Haynes, University of California, Davis
Gesine Hearn, Idaho State University
Teri Hibbert, University of Texas, El Paso
Lori Hunter, University of Colorado, Boulder
Susan Janssen, University of Minnesota, Duluth
Laura Jennings, University of South Carolina, Upstate
Ellis Jones, University of California, Davis
Eric Kaldor, State University of New York–Brockport
Rosalind Kopfstein, Western Connecticut State University
Annette Lareau, University of Pennsylvania
Kevin Leicht, University of Iowa
Jennifer Lena, Vanderbilt University
Steve Lippman, Miami University
D. A. Lopez, California State University, Northridge
Robert Mackin, Texas A&M University
Cheryl Maes, University of Nevada, Reno
Joan Manley, Florida Gulf Coast University
Joan Meyers, University of California, Davis
Wendy Moore, Texas A&M University
David Nicholson, University of Oklahoma
Donald Nielsen, College of Charleston
Marjukka Ollilainen, Weber State University
Michael Perez, California State University, Fullerton
Richard Petts, Ball State University
Nancy Plankey Videla, Texas A&M University
John Poindexter, West Shore College
Gabrielle Raley, University of California, Los Angeles
Julie Rauli, Wilson College
Alden Roberts, Texas Tech University
Olga Rowe, Oregon State University
Jennifer Schultz, University of Arizona
Julie Setele, University of California, Davis
Linda Sibler, Union College
Kathleen Slevin, College of William and Mary
Marshall Smith, University of Colorado, Boulder
Katherine Stovel, University of Washington
Steve Swinford, Montana State University
Ronald Thrasher, Oklahoma State University
Amy Traver, Queensborough Community College
Diana Tumminia, California State University, Sacramento
Glenda Walden, University of Colorado, Boulder
Melissa Weiner, Quinnipiac University
Susan Wortmann, University of Nebraska, Lincoln

REVIEWERS FOR THE FIRST EDITION

Rebecca Adams, University of North Carolina–Greensboro
Robert Aponte, Indiana University–Purdue University Indianapolis
Nina Bandelj, University of California–Irvine
Donna Barnes, University of Wyoming
Nielan Barnes, California State University–Long Beach
Marshall Battani, Grand Valley State University
Joel Best, University of Delaware
Melissa Bonstead-Bruns, University of Wisconsin–Eau Claire
Dan Brook, San José State University
Ernesto Bustillos, Pasadena City College
Patricia Campion, Tennessee Tech University
Victoria Carty, Chapman University
Ursula Castella, Ohio University
Pam Chao, American River College

Brenda Chappell, University of Central Oklahoma
Theresa Davidson, Samford University
Patricia Ewick, Clark University
Kathleen J. Fitzgerald, Columbia College
Nicole Flynn, University of South Alabama
Doug Forbes, University of Wisconsin–Stevens Point
David Friedrichs, University of Scranton
Bob Girvan, Clarion University of Pennsylvania
Jeremy Hein, University of Wisconsin–Eau Claire
Christopher Henke, Colgate University
Terrence Hill, University of Miami
Sue Hinze, Case Western Reserve
Robert Hironimus-Wendt, Western Illinois State University
Abdy Javadzadeh, Florida International University
Robert Keel, University of Missouri–St. Louis
Markus Kemmelmeier, University of Nevada–Reno
Jerry Koch, Texas Tech University
Samantha Kwan, University of Houston
Bill Lockhart, New Mexico State University at Alamogordo
Gerardo Marti, Davidson College
Michael Massoglia, Pennsylvania State University
Dennis Mcgrath, Community College of Philadelphia
Edward Morris, Ohio University
Michael Oldani, University of Wisconsin–White Water
Kirsten Olsen, Anoka-Ramsey Community College
Colin Olson, University of New Mexico
Paul Olson, Briar Cliff University
Krista Paulsen, University of North Florida
Christine Plumeri, Monroe Community College
Brian Powell, Indiana University–Bloomington
Ralph Pyle, Michigan State University
John S. Rice, University of North Carolina, Wilmington
Bryan Robinson, State University of New York–Albany
Sarah Rusche, North Carolina State University
Luis Salinas, University of Houston
Lafleur Small, Wright State University
Regina Smardon, University of Pennsylvania
Travis Vande Berg, Ithaca College
Sandra Way, New Mexico State University
Michael Weissbuch, Xavier University
William J. Weston, Centre College
Jerry Williams, Stephen F. Austin University
Howie Winant, University of California–Santa Barbara
Rowan Wolf, Portland Community College
Robert Wood, Rutgers University–Camden
Matt Wray, University of Nevada–Las Vegas
Richard Zamoff, George Washington University

As you can see, it took a village to raise this child. But that's not all. At Norton, I need to thank, first and foremost, Karl Bakeman, the editor into whose lap this project landed (after having passed through the hands of Steve Dunn and Melea Seward). He deserves even more credit for this edition—brainstorming with me how to do something novel for this edition (hence the animations) and then convincing the Norton board to dive headfirst into this multimedia experiment of sorts. I am also indebted to the keen eye of Harry Haskell, who served as development editor. In addition, I am grateful to editorial assistants Becky Charney and Alicia González-Gross, project editor Kate Feighery, and production managers Jane Searle and Eric Pier-Hocking, who handled every stage of the manuscript and managed to keep the innumerable pieces of the book moving through production. I also must thank Norton sociology's marketing manager Natasha Zabohonski and the social science sales specialist Julie Sindel. Much of *You May Ask Yourself*'s success is due to their boundless energy and enthusiasm. Finally, I owe a special thanks to Eileen Connell, Laura Musich, Jen Barnhardt, Kathryn Young, and Alice Garrard. They are responsible for putting together all of the electronic resources that accompany *You May Ask Yourself*. When it comes to developing new digital products to help instructors teach in the classroom or teach online, they are the most creative and resourceful folks working in college publishing today.

PART I
USING YOUR
SOCIOLOGICAL
IMAGINATION

Thinking like a sociologist means looking at the world around you in a new way. Challenge conventional wisdom and question what most people take for granted.

1 The Sociological Imagination: An Introduction

PARADOX

A SUCCESSFUL SOCIOLOGIST MAKES THE FAMILIAR STRANGE.

If you want to understand sociology, why don't we start with you. Why are you taking this class and reading this textbook? It's as good a place to start as any—after all, sociology is the study of human society, and there is the sociology of sports, of religion, of music, of medicine, even a sociology of sociologists. So why not start, by way of example, with the sociology of an introduction to sociology?

For example, why are you bent over this page? Take a moment to write down the reasons. Maybe you have heard of sociology and want to learn about it. Maybe you are merely following the suggestion of a parent, guidance counselor, or academic advisor. The course syllabus probably indicates that for the first week of class, you are required to read this chapter. So there are at least two good reasons to be reading this introduction to sociology text.

Let's take the first response, "I want to educate myself about sociology." That's a fairly good reason, but may I then ask why you are taking the class rather than simply reading the book on your own? Furthermore, assuming that you're paying tuition, why are you doing so? If you really are here for the education, let me suggest an alternative: Grab one of the course schedules at your college, decide which courses to take, and just show up! Most introductory classes are so large that nobody notices if an extra student attends. If it is a smaller, more advanced seminar, ask the professor if you can audit it. I have never known a faculty member who checks that all class attendees are legitimate students at the college—in fact, we're happy when students *do* show up to class. An auditor, someone who is there for the sake of pure learning,

Sociology the study of human society.

and who won't be grade grubbing or submitting papers to be marked, is pure gold to any professor interested in imparting knowledge for learning's sake.

You know the rest of the drill: Do all the reading (you can usually access the required texts for free at the library), do your homework, and participate in class discussion. About the only thing you won't get at the end of the course is a grade. So give yourself one. As a matter of fact, once you have compiled enough credits and written a senior thesis, award yourself a diploma. Why not? You will probably have received a better education than most students—certainly better than I did in college.

But what are you going to do with a homemade diploma? You are not just here to learn; you wish to obtain an actual college degree. Why exactly do you want a college degree? Students typically answer that they have to get one in order to earn more money. Others may say that they need credentials to get the job they want. And some students are in college because they don't know what else to do. Whatever your answer, the fact that you asked yourself a question about something you may have previously taken for granted is the first step in thinking like a sociologist. "Thinking like a sociologist" means applying analytical tools to something you have always done without much conscious thought—like opening this book or taking this class. It requires you to reconsider your assumptions about society and question what you have taken for granted in order to better understand the world around you. In other words, thinking like a sociologist means *making the familiar strange*.

This chapter introduces you to the sociological approach to the world. Specifically, you will learn about the *sociological imagination*, a term coined by C. Wright Mills. We'll return to the question "Why go to college?" and apply our sociological imaginations to it. You will also learn what a social institution is. The chapter concludes by looking at the sociology of sociology—that is, the history of sociology and where it fits within the social sciences.

The Sociological Imagination

Sociological imagination the ability to connect the most basic, intimate aspects of an individual's life to seemingly impersonal and remote historical forces.

More than 50 years ago, the sociologist C. Wright Mills argued that in the effort to think critically about the social world around us, we need to use our sociological imagination, the ability to see the connections between our personal experience and the larger forces of history. That is just what we are doing when we question this textbook, this course, and college in general. Writes Mills in *The Sociological Imagination* (1959), "The first fruit of this imagination—and the first lesson of the social science that embodies it—is the idea that the individual can understand his own experience and gauge his own fate only by locating himself within his period, that he can know his own chances in life only by becoming aware of those of all individuals in his circumstances. In many ways it is a terrible lesson; in many ways a magnificent one." The terrible part of the lesson is to make our own lives ordinary—that is, to see our intensely personal, private experience of life as typical of the period and place in which we live. This can also serve as a source of comfort, however, helping us to realize that we are not alone in our experiences, whether they involve our alienation from the increasingly dog-eat-dog capitalism of modern America, the peculiar combination of intimacy and dissociation that we may experience on the Internet, or the ways that nationality or geography affect our life choices. The sociological imagination does not just leave us hanging with these feelings of recognition, however. Mills writes that it also "enables [us] to take into account how individuals, in the welter of their daily experience, often become falsely conscious of their social positions." The sociological imagination thus allows us to see the veneer of social life for what it is, to step outside the "trap" of rapid historical change in order to comprehend what is occurring in our world and the social foundations that may be shifting right under our feet. As Mills wrote after World War II, a time of enormous political, social, and technological change, "The sociological imagination enables us to grasp history and biography and the relations between the two within society. That is its task and its promise. To recognize this task and this promise is the mark of the classic social analyst."

Mills offered his readers a way to stop and take stock of their lives in light of all that had happened in the previous decade. Of course, we almost always

Sociologist C. Wright Mills commuting to Columbia University on his motorcycle. How does Mills's concept of the sociological imagination help us make the familiar strange?

HOW TO BE A SOCIOLOGIST ACCORDING TO QUENTIN TARANTINO: A SCENE FROM PULP FICTION

Have you ever been to a foreign country, noticed how many little things were different, and wondered why? Have you ever been to a church of a different denomination—or a different religion altogether—from your own? Or have you been a fish out of water in some other way? The only guy attending a social event for women, perhaps? Or the only person from out of state in your dorm? If you have experienced that fish-out-ofwater feeling, then you have, however briefly, indulged the sociological imagination. By shifting your social environment enough to be in a position where you are not able to take everything for granted, you are forced to see the connections between particular historical paths taken (and not taken) and how you live your daily life. You may, for instance, wonder why there are bidets in most European bathrooms and not in American ones. Or why people waiting in lines in the Middle East typically stand closer to each other than they do in Europe or America. Or why, in some rural Chinese societies, many generations of a family sleep in the same bed. If you are able to resist your initial impulses toward xenophobia, feelings that may result from the discomfort of facing a different reality, then you are halfway there. If you then use these cases of other people's daily living to reexamine your own way of life, you have truly adopted the sociological imagination, which allows you to start questioning the links between your personal experience and the particulars of a given society without ever leaving home.

In the following excerpt of dialogue from Quentin Tarantino's 1994 film Pulp Fiction, the character Vincent tells Jules about the "little differences" between life in the United States and life in Europe.

VINCENT: It's the little differences. A lotta the same shit we got here, they got there, but there they're a little different.

JULES: Example?

VINCENT: Well, in Amsterdam, you can buy beer in a movie theater. And I don't mean in a paper cup either. They give you a glass of beer, like in a bar. In Paris, you can buy beer at McDonald's. Also, you know what they call a Quarter Pounder with Cheese in Paris?

JULES: They don't call it a Quarter Pounder with Cheese?

VINCENT: No, they got the metric system there, they wouldn't know what the fuck a Quarter Pounder is.

JULES: What'd they call it?

VINCENT: Royale with Cheese.

Vincent Vega (John Travolta) describes his visit to a McDonald's in Amsterdam to Jules Winnfield (Samuel L. Jackson).

JULES: (repeating) Royale with Cheese. What'd they call a Big Mac?
VINCENT: Big Mac's a Big Mac, but they call it Le Big Mac.
JULES: What do they call a Whopper?
VINCENT: I dunno, I didn't go into a Burger King. But you know what they put on french fries in Holland instead of ketchup?
JULES: What?
VINCENT: Mayonnaise.
JULES: Goddamn!
VINCENT: I seen 'em do it. And I don't mean a little bit on the side of the plate, they fuckin' drown 'em in it.
JULES: Uuccch!

Your job as a sociologist is to get into the mindset that mayonnaise on french fries, while it might seem disgusting at first, is not strange after all, certainly no more so than ketchup.

feel that social change is fairly rapid, getting ahead of us. Think of the 1960s or even today, with the rise of the Internet and global terror threats. In retrospect, we consider the 1950s, the decade when Mills wrote his seminal work, to be a relatively placid time, when Americans experienced some relief from the change and strife of World War II and the Great Depression. But Mills believed the profound sense of alienation experienced by many during the postwar period was a result of the change that had immediately preceded it.

Another way to think about the sociological imagination is to ask ourselves what we take to be natural that actually isn't. For example, let's return to the question "Why go to college?" Sociologists and economists have shown that the financial benefits of education—particularly higher education—appear to be increasing. They refer to this as the "returns to schooling." In today's economy (2010 data), the median (i.e., typical) annual income for a high-school graduate is $30,048; for those with a bachelor's degree, it is $49,824 (Bureau of Labor Statistics, 2011a). That $19,776 annual advantage seems like a good deal, but is it really? Let's shift gears and do a little math.

What Are the True Costs and Returns of College?

Now that you are thinking like a sociologist, let's compare the true cost of going to college for four years to calling the whole thing off and taking a full-time job right after high school. First, there is the tuition to consider. Let's assume for the sake of argument you are paying $8,000 per year for tuition and another $9,000 for fees and room and board. That's a lot less than what most private four-year colleges cost, but slightly more than the in-state tuition at many state schools. (Community colleges, by contrast, are usually much cheaper, especially because they tend to be commuter schools in which many students live with family, but they typically do not offer a four-year bachelor's degree.)

In making the decision to attend college, you are agreeing to pay $17,000 this year, something like $17,680 next year, 4 percent more the following year, and another 4 percent on top of that amount in your senior year. The $17,000 you have to pay right now is what hurts the most, because costs in the future are worth less than expenses today. Money in the future is worth less than money in hand for several reasons. The first is inflation. We all know that money is not what it used to be. In fact, taking into account the standard inflation rate—as measured by the government's Consumer Price Index—it took about $16 in 2011 to equal the buying power of a single dollar back in 1940 (Sahr, 2010). The second reason that money today is worth more than money tomorrow is that we could invest the money today to make more tomorrow.

Using a standard formula for bringing future amounts into current dollars, adjusting for inflation, we can determine that paying out $17,000 this year and the higher amounts over the next three years is equivalent to paying $70,023 in one lump sum today; this would be the direct cost of attending college. Indirect costs, so-called opportunity costs, exist as well—namely, the costs associated with the amount of time you are devoting to school. Taking into account the typical wage for a high-school graduate, not counting differences by gender, age, or level of experience, we calculate that if you worked full-time instead of going on to college, you would make $30,048 this year. Thus, we find that the present value of the total wages lost over the next four years by choosing full-time school over full-time work is $120,192. Add these opportunity costs to the direct costs of tuition and we get $190,215.

Next we need to calculate the "returns to schooling." For the sake of simplicity, we will ignore the fact that the differences between high-school graduates and college graduates change over time—given years of experience and the ups and downs of the economy. Instead, we will regard the $49,824 annual earnings figure for college graduates as fixed and subtract from that amount the $30,048 earned by the typical high-school graduate, to yield a net difference of $19,776. But remember, you would not start earning this money for four years. So the real difference is $19,776 four years from now plus $19,776 five years from now and so on, until you leave the labor force. Assuming that you attend college for only four years and will retire at 65, you will have worked 43 years (high-school grads will be in the work force for 47 years because they got a four-year head start). When we compare your college-degree-holding lifetime earnings to the lifetime earnings of someone who has only a high-school education, we find that with a college degree you will make $730,176 more than someone who went straight to work after high school (see Figure 1.1). (We are conveniently ignoring the fact that future money is inherently worth less than present ones in economic decision making to make matters more straightforward.) On top of this substantial financial return to schooling, one economist found that those with college degrees were happier, healthier, and less likely to get divorced than their high-school-educated peers even after controlling for income (Oreopoulos & Salvanes, 2009).

But wait a minute: How do we know for sure that college really mattered in the equation? Individuals who finish college might earn more because they actually learned something and obtained a degree, or—a big or—they might earn more regardless of the college experience because people who stay in school (take your pick) (1) are innately smarter, (2) know how to work the system, (3) come from wealthier families, (4) can delay gratification, (5) are more efficient at managing their time, or (6) all of the above. In other words, Yale graduates might not have needed to go to college to earn higher wages; they might have been successful anyway.

Maybe, then, the success stories of Mark Zuckerberg, Steve Jobs, Lady Gaga, and other college dropouts don't cut against the grain so sharply after all. Maybe they were the savvy ones: Convinced of their ability to make it on their own, thanks to the social cues they received (including the fact that they had

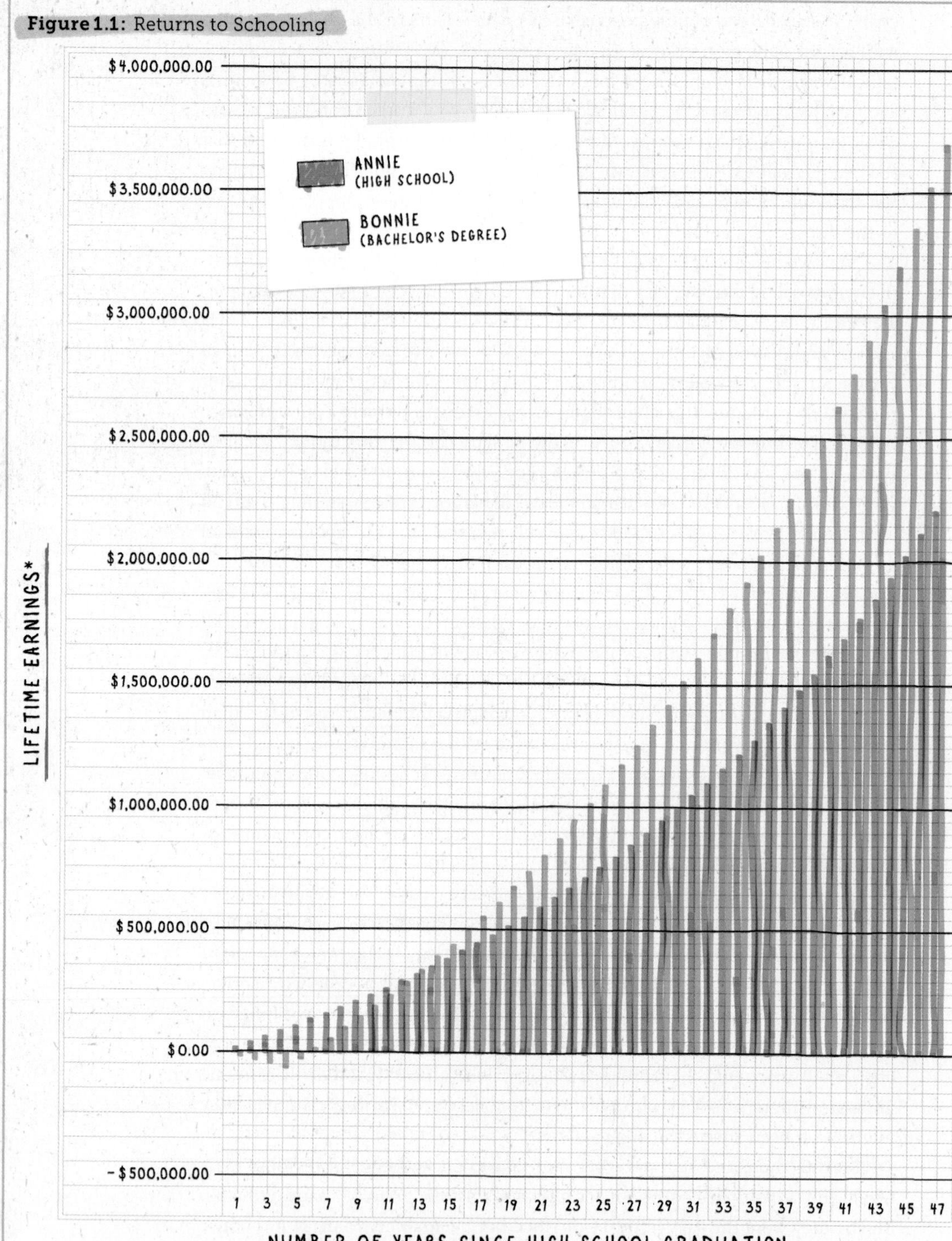

Figure 1.1: Returns to Schooling

* This set of hypothetical women—Annie and Bonnie—live in a world that is not quite like reality. We did not flatten Annie's trajectory to account for the fact that high school diploma holders are more likely to experience periods of forced part-time work and/or unemployment. We also assumed the same rate of income increase over time (i.e.,raises) for these two, although high school diploma holders are more likely to experience wage stagnation than college degree holders.

Source: Murray, 2009.

Two famous college dropouts. Facebook CEO Mark Zuckerberg (left) attended Harvard but dropped out before graduating. John Mackey (right) quit university before founding Whole Foods.

been admitted to college), they decided that they wouldn't wait four years to try to achieve success. They opted to just go for it right then and there. College's "value added," they might have concluded, was marginal at best.

Getting That "Piece of Paper"

Even if college turns out to matter in the end, does it make a difference because of the learning that takes place there or because of our credentialist society that it aids and abets? The answer to this question has enormous implications for what education means in our society. Imagine, for example, a society where people become doctors not by doing well on the SATs, going to college, taking premed courses, acing the MCATs, and then spending more time in the classroom. Instead, the route to becoming a doctor, among the most prestigious and highly paid occupations in our society, starts with emptying bedpans as a nurse's aide and working your way up through the ranks of registered nurse, apprentice physician, and so forth; finally, after years of on-the-job training, you achieve the title of doctor. Social theorist Randall Collins has proposed just such a medical education system in the controversial *Credential Society: A Historical Sociology of Education and Stratification* (1979), which argues that the expansion of higher education has merely resulted in a ratcheting up of credentialism and expenditures on formal education rather than reflecting

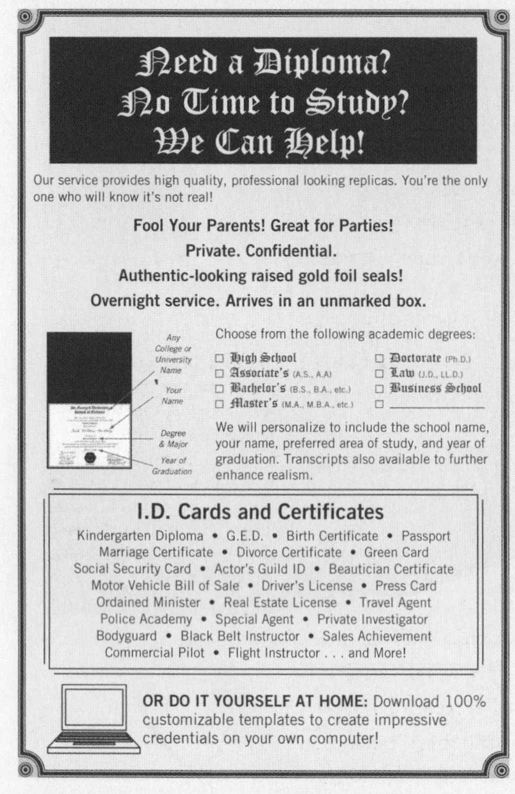

College-campus bulletin boards are covered with advertisements like this promoting Web sites that generate diplomas. Why are these fake diplomas not worth it?

any true societal need for more formal education or opening up opportunity to more people.

If Collins is correct and credentials are what matter most, then isn't there a cheaper, faster way to get them? In fact, all you need are $29.95 and a little guts, and you can receive a diploma from one of the many online sites that promise either legitimate degrees from nonaccredited colleges or a college diploma from any school of your choosing. Thus, why not save four years and lots of money and obtain your credentials immediately?

Obviously, universities have incentives to prevent such Web sites from undermining their monopoly on degree-conferring ability. So they rely on a number of other social institutions, ranging from copyright law to the local police force, to enforce this monopoly power. However, I have no knowledge of anyone—employer, school, landlord—ever verifying my educational claims. That is, no one has ever checked to see that I attended college or graduate school. They have taken my résumé at face value. (On the other hand, colleges do check that applicants have completed high school.)

But there are also informal mechanisms by which universities are protected that may be more important than any formal checks. First, there is the alumni network at a university. Potential employers rarely call a university's registrar to make sure you graduated, but they will expect you to talk a bit about your college experience. If your interviewer is an alumnus or otherwise familiar with the institution, you might also be expected to talk about what dorm you lived in, reminisce about a particularly dramatic homecoming game, or gripe about one slave-driving professor. If you slip up on any of this information, suspicions will grow, and then people might call to check on your graduation status. Perhaps there are some good reasons not to opt for that $29.95 degree and to pay the costs of college after all.

→ What is a Social Institution?

The university, then, is more than just a printing press that churns out diplomas, and, for that matter, it does not merely impart formal knowledge. It fulfills a variety of roles and provides links to many other societal institutions. For example, a college is an institution that acts as a gatekeeper to what are considered legitimate forms of educational advantage by certifying what is legitimate knowledge. It is an institution that segregates great swaths of our population by age. (You won't find a more age-segregated environment than a four-year college; it even beats a retirement home in having the smallest amount of age variation in its client population.) A college is a proprietary brand that is marketed on sweatshirts and mugs and through televised sporting events. Last but not least, it is an informal set of stories told within a social network of students, faculty, administrators, alumni, and other relevant individuals.

This last part of the definition is key to understanding one of sociology's most important concepts, the social institution. A social institution is a complex group of interdependent positions that, together, perform a social role and reproduce themselves over time. A way to think of these social positions is as a set of stories we tell ourselves; social relations are a network of ties; and the social role is a grand narrative that unifies these stories within the network. In order to think sociologically about social institutions, you need to think of them not as monolithic, uniform, stable entities—things that "just are"—but as institutions constructed within a dense network of other social institutions and meanings. Sound confusing? Bear with me as I provide an example: I teach at New York University, or NYU. What exactly is the social institution known as NYU? It is not the collection of buildings I frequent. It certainly cannot be the people who work there (or even the students), because we change over time, shifting in and out through recruitment and retirement, admission and graduation. We might thus conclude that a social institution is just a name. However, an institution can change its name and still retain its social identity. Duke University was once called Normal College and then Trinity College, yet it remains the same institution.

Social institution a complex group of interdependent positions that, together, perform a social role and reproduce themselves over time; also defined in a narrow sense as any institution in a society that works to shape the behavior of the groups or people within it.

Of course, all such transitions involving a change of name, location, mission, and so on require a great deal of effort and agreement among interested parties. In some cases, changes in personnel, function, or location may be too much for a social institution to sustain, causing it to die out and be replaced by something that is considered new. Sometimes institutions even try to rupture their identity intentionally. The Philip Morris Company had received such bad press as a cigarette manufacturer for so long that it changed its name to Altria, hoping to start fresh and shake off the connotations of its previous embodiment. For that effort to succeed, the narrative of Philip Morris circulating in social networks had to die out without being connected to Altria.

This grand narrative that constitutes social identity is nothing more than the sum of individual stories told between pairs of individuals. Think about your relationship to your parents. You have a particular story that you tell if asked to describe your relationship with your mother. She also has a story. Your story may change slightly, depending on whom you are talking to; you may add some details or leave out others. Your other relatives have stories about your mother and her relationship to you. So do her friends and yours. Anyone who

Tobacco company Philip Morris changed its name to Altria at a stockholders' meeting in January 2003.

knows her contributes to her social identity. The sum total of stories about your mom is the grand narrative of who she is.

All of this may seem like a fairly flimsy notion of how things operate in the social world, but even though any social identity boils down to a set of stories within a social network, that narrative is still hearty and robust. Imagine what it would take to change an identity. Let's say your mom is 50 years old. You want to make her 40 instead. You would not only have to convince her to refer constantly to herself as ten years younger; you would also have to get your other relatives and her friends to abide by this change. And it wouldn't stop there. You'd have to change official documents as well—her driver's license, passport, and so on. This is not so easily done. Even though your mother's identity (in this case her age, although the same logic can be extended to her name, ethnicity, and many other aspects of her identity) could be described as nothing more than an understanding between her, everyone who knows her, and the formal authorities, the matter is a fairly complicated one. If that sounds hard, just think about trying to change the identity of a major institution such as your university. You'd have to convince the board of directors, alumni, faculty, students, and everyone else who has a relationship to the school of the need for a change. Altering an identity is fairly difficult, even though it is ultimately nothing more than an idea.

I mentioned that if you wanted to change your mother's age, name, or race, you'd have to convince not only her friends but also the formal authorities, which are social institutions with their own logics and inertias. Let's take the example of college once again. Other than the informal ties of people who have a relationship to the grand narrative of a particular college, a number of social structures exist that make colleges, which are themselves made up of a series of stories within social networks, possible:

1. The *legal system* enforces copyright law, making fake diplomas illegitimate.
2. The *primary and secondary educational system* (i.e., K–12 schooling) prepares students both academically and culturally for college as well as acting as

an extended screening and sorting mechanism to help determine who goes to college and to which one.

3. The *Educational Testing Service* (ETS) is a private company that has a virtual monopoly on the standardized tests that screen for college admission.

4. The *wage labor market* encompasses the entire economy that allows your teacher to be paid, not to mention the administrators, staff, and other outside contractors who maintain the intellectual, fiscal, and physical infrastructure of the school you attend.

5. *English*, although not the official language of the United States (there isn't one!), is the language in which instruction takes place at the majority of U.S. colleges. Language itself is a social phenomenon; some would argue that it is the basis for all of social life. But a given language is a particular outcome of political boundaries and historical struggles among various populations in the world. It is often said the only difference between a language and a dialect is that a language has an army to back it up. In other words, deciding whether a spoken tongue is a language or merely a dialect is a question of power and legitimacy.

Trying to understand social institutions such as the legal system, the labor market, or language itself is at the heart of sociological inquiry. Although social institutions shape every aspect of our behavior, they are not monolithic. In fact, every day we construct and change social institutions through ordinary interactions and the meanings we ascribe to them. By becoming aware of the intersections between social institutions and your life, you are already thinking like a sociologist.

The Sociology of Sociology

Now that we have an idea of how sociologists approach their analysis of the world, let's turn that lens, the sociological imagination, to sociology itself. As a formal field, sociology is a relatively young discipline. Numerous fields of inquiry exist, such as molecular genetics, radio astronomy, and computer science, that could not emerge until a certain technology was invented. Sociology might seem to fall outside this category, but to study society, we need not only a curious mind and a certain willingness but also the specific frame of reference—the lens—of the sociological imagination. The sociological imagination is a technology of sorts, a technology that could have developed only during a certain time. That time was, arguably, the nineteenth century, when the French scholar Auguste Comte (1798–1857) invented what he called "social physics" or "positivism."

Auguste Comte and the Creation of Sociology

According to Comte, positivism arose out of a need to make moral sense of the social order in a time of declining religious authority. Comte claimed that a secular basis for morality did indeed exist—that is, we could determine right and wrong without reference to higher powers or other religious concepts. And that was the job of the sociologist: to develop a secular morality. Comte further argued that human society had gone through three historical, epistemological stages. In the first, which he referred to as the theological

TWO CENTURIES OF SOCIOLOGY

1780 1785 1790 1795 1800 1805 1810 1815

1776–81
American War of Independence

1789–99
French Revolution

1802
Harriet Martineau born

1780s
Industrial Revolution begins

1798
Auguste Comte born

American War of Independence

Industrial Revolution

French Revolution

stage, society seemed to be the result of divine will. If you wanted to understand why kings ruled, why Europe used a feudal and guild system of labor, or why colonialism took root, the answer was that it was God's plan. To better understand God's plan and thus comprehend the logic of social life, scholars of the theological period might consult the Bible or other ecclesiastical texts. During stage two, the metaphysical stage according to Comte, Enlightenment thinkers such as Jean-Jacques Rousseau, John Stuart Mill, and Thomas Hobbes saw humankind's behavior as governed by natural, biological instincts. To understand the nature of society—why things were the way they

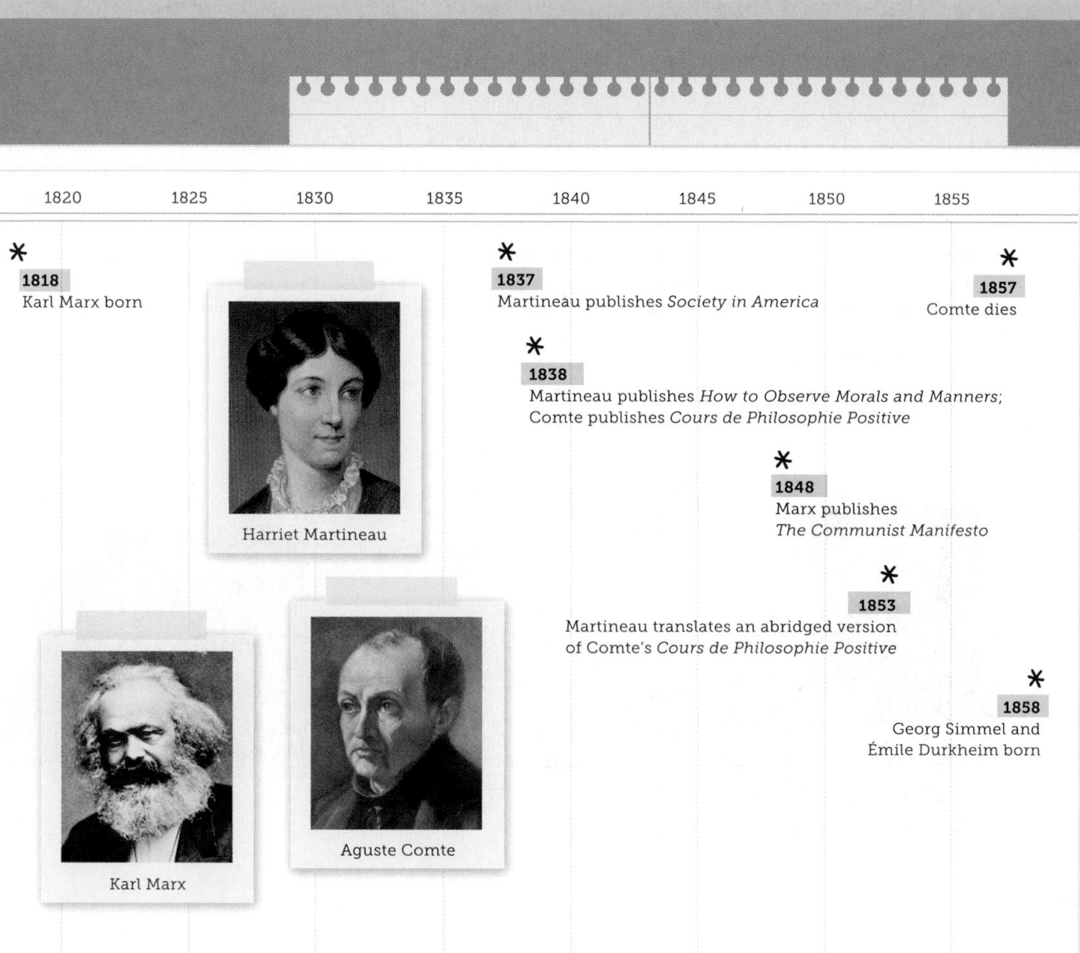

were—we needed to strip away the layers of society to better comprehend how our basic drives and natural instincts governed and established the foundation for the surrounding world. Comte called the third and final stage of historical development the scientific stage. In this era, he claimed, we would develop a social physics of sorts in order to identify the scientific laws that govern human behavior. The analogy here is not theology or biology but rather physics. Comte was convinced that we could understand how social institutions worked (and didn't work), how we relate to one another (whether on an individual or group level), and the overall structure of societies if we

TWO CENTURIES OF SOCIOLOGY

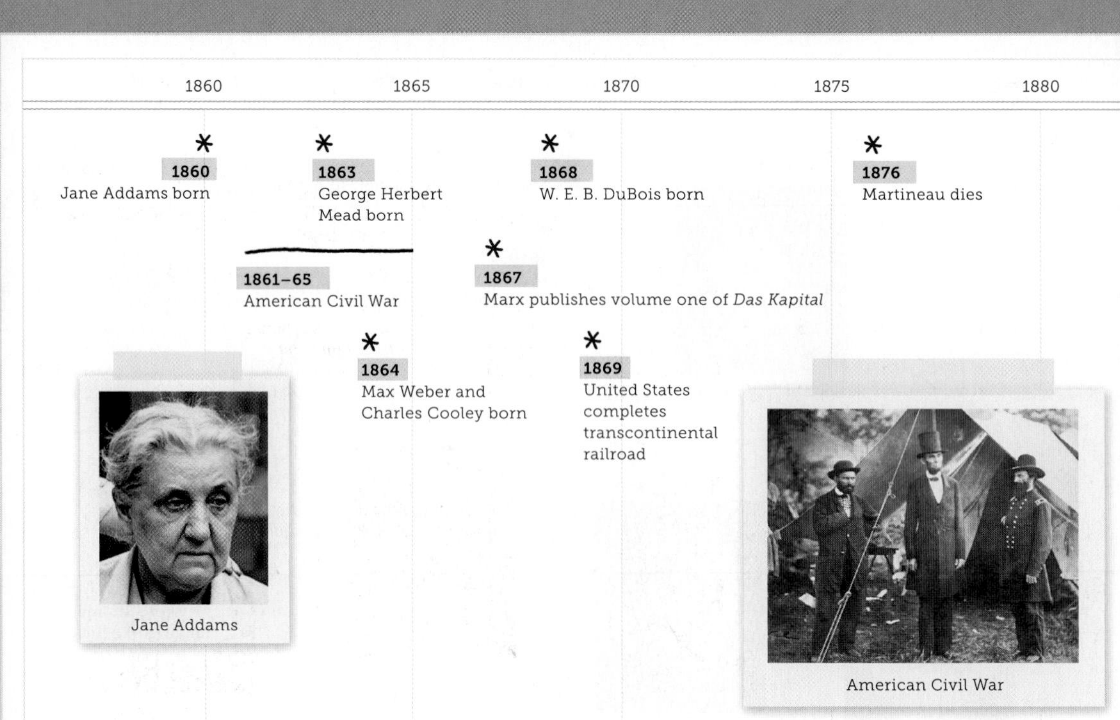

Jane Addams

American Civil War

merely ascertained their "equations" or underlying logic. Needless to say, most sociologists today are not so optimistic.

Harriet Martineau Harriet Martineau (1802–1876), an English social theorist, was the first to translate Comte into English. In fact, Comte assigned her translations to his students, claiming that they were better than the original. She also wrote important works of her own, including *Theory and Practice of Society in America* (1837), in which she describes our nation's physical and social aspects. She addressed topics ranging from the way we educate children (which, she

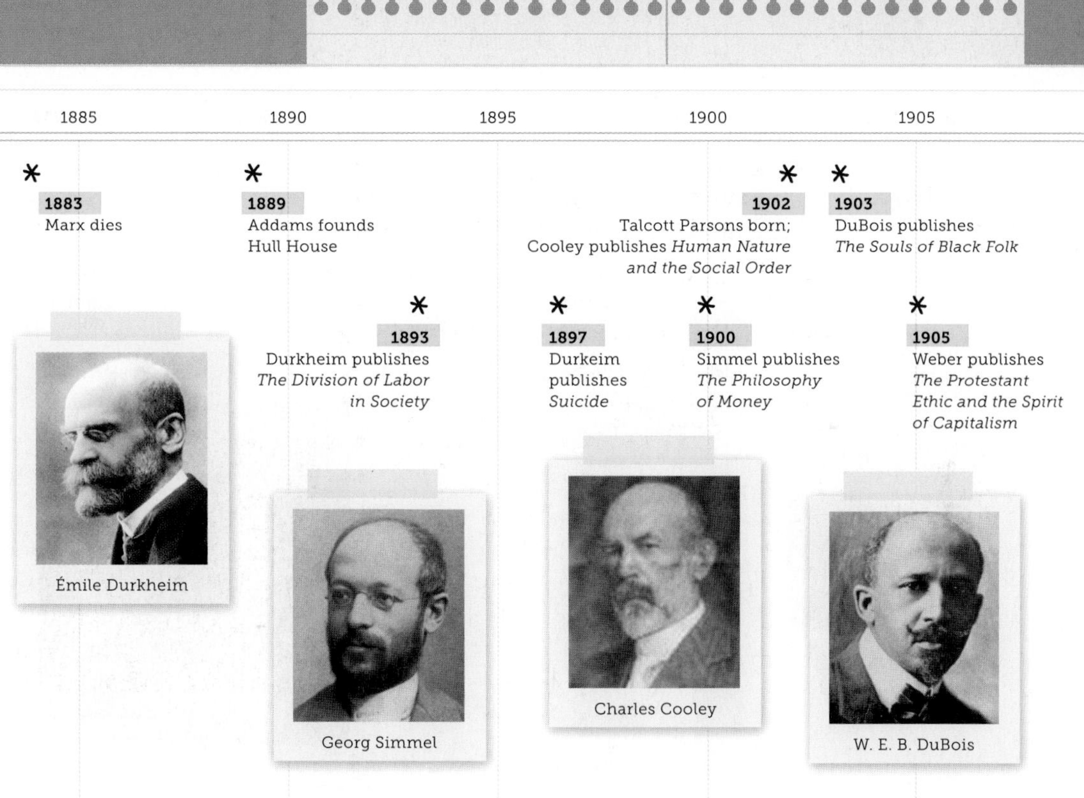

attests, affords parents too much control and doesn't ensure quality) to the relationship between the federal and state governments. She was also the author of the first methods book in the area of sociology, *How to Observe Morals and Manners* (1838), in which she took on the institution of marriage, claiming that it was based on an assumption of the inferiority of women. This critique, among other writings, suggests that Martineau should be considered one of the earliest feminist social scientists writing in the English language.

TWO CENTURIES OF SOCIOLOGY

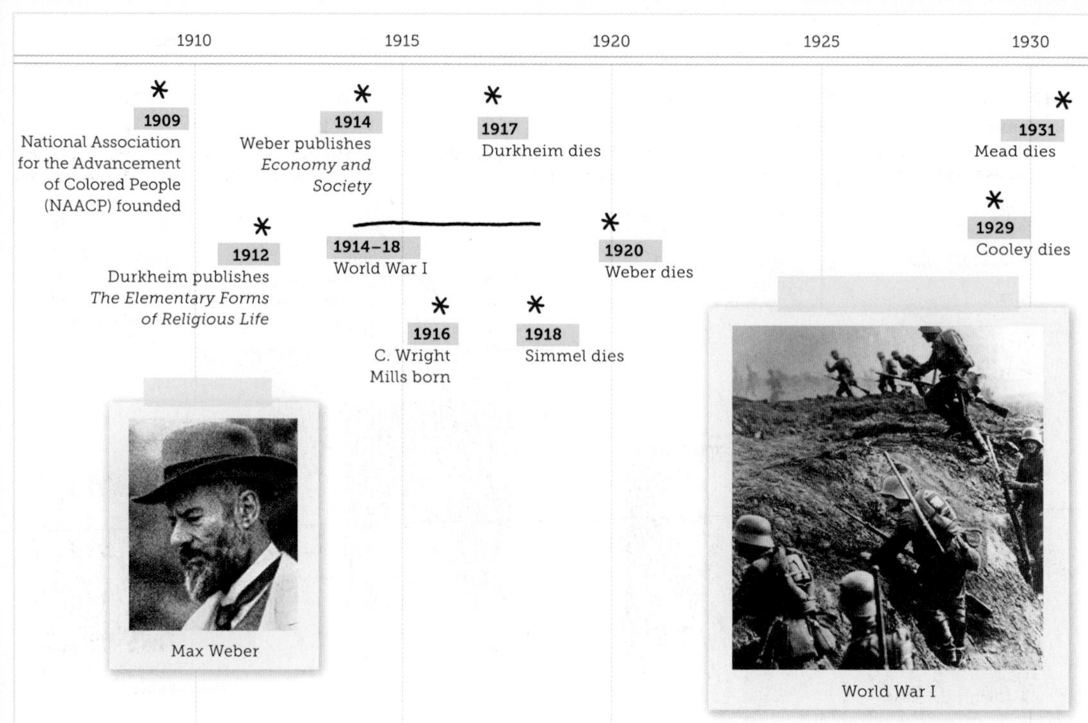

Max Weber

World War I

Classical Sociological Theory

Although Comte and Martineau preceded them, Karl Marx, Max Weber, and Émile Durkheim are often credited as the founding fathers of the sociological discipline. Some would add a fourth classical sociological theorist, Georg Simmel, to the triumvirate. A brief overview of each of their paradigms follows; we will return to the work of these thinkers throughout the book.

1935 1940 1945 1950 1955

1934
Mead's *Mind, Self, and Society* is published

1935
Addams dies

1937
Parsons publishes *Structure of Social Action*

1939–45
World War II

1943
William Foote Whyte publishes *Street Corner Society*

1951
Parsons publishes *The Social System*

1956
Mills publishes *The Power Elite*

1957
Robert Merton publishes *Social Theory and Social Structure*

George Herbert Mead

Talcott Parsons

World War II

Robert Merton

Karl Marx Karl Marx (1818–1883) is probably the most famous of the three early sociologists; from his surname the term *Marxism* (an ideological alternative to capitalism) derives, and his writings provided the theoretical basis for Communism. When Marx was a young man, he edited a newspaper that was suppressed by the Prussian government for its radicalism. Forced into exile, Marx settled in London, where he wrote his most important works. Marx was essentially a historian, but he did more than just chronicle events. He elaborated a theory of what drives history, now called historical materialism. Marx believed that it was primarily the conflicts between classes that drove social change throughout

TWO CENTURIES OF SOCIOLOGY

1960 | 1965 | 1970 | 1975

1959
Erving Goffman publishes *Presentation of Self in Everyday Life*; Mills publishes *The Sociological Imagination*

Erving Goffman

C. Wright Mills

1962
Mills dies

1963
DuBois dies; the March on Washington; Betty Friedan publishes *The Feminine Mystique*

March on Washington

1966
Equality of Educational Opportunity (the Coleman Report) is published.

1967
Elliott Liebow publishes *Tally's Corner*; Peter M. Blau and Otis Dudley Duncan publish *The American Occupational Structure*

1969
Woodstock

1972
Ann Oakley publishes *Sex, Gender, and Society*

Ann Oakley

1973
Daniel Bell publishes *The Coming of the Post-Industrial Society*

1977
Paul Willis publishes *Learning to Labor*

history. Marx saw history as an account of man's struggle to gain control of and later dominate his natural environment. However, at a certain point—with the Industrial Revolution and the emergence of modern capitalism—the very tools and processes that humans embraced to survive and to manage their surroundings came to dominate humans. Instead of using technology to master the natural world, people became slaves to industrial technology in order to make a living. In Marx's version of history, each economic system, whether small-scale farming or factory capitalism, had its own fault lines of conflict. In the current epoch, that fault line divided society into a small number of capitalists and a

1980 1985 1990 1995

1978
William Julius Wilson publishes *The Declining Significance of Race*

1979
Parsons dies

William Julius Wilson

1984
Pierre Bourdieu publishes *Distinction;* Anthony Giddens publishes *The Constitution of Society*

Anthony Giddens

1989
Arlie Hochschild publishes *The Second Shift: Working Parents and the Revolution at Home*

Arlie Hochschild

1991
James Coleman publishes *Foundations of Social Theory*

1993
Douglas S. Massey and Nancy A. Denton publish *American Apartheid*

James Coleman

large number of workers (the proletariat) whose interests were opposed. This political struggle, along with escalating crises within the economic system itself, would produce social change through a Communist revolution. In the ensuing Communist society, private property would be abolished and the resulting ideology governing the new economy would be "from each according to his abilities, to each according to his needs" (Marx & Engels, 1848/1998). We will explore Marx's theories in depth in Chapter 7 on social stratification.

Max Weber If Marx brought the material world back into history, which had been thought of as mostly idea-driven until then, Max Weber (1864–1920), writing shortly after Marx, is said to have brought ideas back into history. Weber and others believed Marx went too far in seeing culture, ideas, religion, and the like as merely an effect and not a cause of how societies evolve. Specifically, Weber criticized Marx for his exclusive focus on the economy and social class, advocating sociological analysis that allowed for the multiple influences of culture, economics, and politics. Weber is most famous for his two-volume work *Economy and Society* (published posthumously in 1922), as well as a lengthy essay titled "The Protestant Ethic and the Spirit of Capitalism" (1904/2003). In the latter, he argued that the religious transformation that occurred during the Protestant Reformation in the sixteenth and early seventeenth centuries laid the groundwork for modern capitalism by upending the medieval ethic of virtuous poverty and replacing it with an ideology that saw riches as a sign of divine providence. *Economy and Society* also provided the theories of authority, rationality, the state (i.e., government), and status and a host of other concepts that sociologists still use today.

Verstehen German: understanding. The concept of *Verstehen* forms the object of inquiry for interpretive sociology—to study how social actors understand their actions and the social world through experience.

One of Weber's most important contributions was the concept of *Verstehen* ("understanding" in German). By emphasizing *Verstehen*, Weber was suggesting that sociologists approach social behavior from the perspective of those engaging in it. In other words, to truly understand why people act the way they do, a sociologist must understand the meanings people attach to their actions. Weber's emphasis on subjectivity is the foundation of interpretive sociology, the study of social meaning.

Émile Durkheim Across the Rhine in France, the work of Émile Durkheim (1858–1917) focused on themes similar to those studied by his German colleagues. He wished to understand how society holds together and the ways that modern capitalism and industrialization have transformed how people relate to one another. Durkheim's sociological writing began with *The Division of Labor in Society* (1893/1997). The division of labor refers to the degree to which jobs are specialized. A society of hunter-gatherers or small-scale farmers has a low division of labor (each household essentially carries out the same tasks to survive);

today the United States has a high degree of division of labor, with many highly specialized occupations. What made the substance of Durkheim's work sociology, rather than economics, was the fact that he argued (and substantiated through legal evidence) that the division of labor didn't just affect work and productivity but had social and moral consequences as well. Specifically, the division of labor of a given society helps to determine its form of social solidarity—that is, the way social cohesion among individuals is maintained. Durkheim followed this work with *Suicide* (1897/1951), in which he shows how this individual act is, in reality, conditioned by social forces: the degree to which we are integrated into group life (or not) and the degree to which our lives follow routines. Durkheim argues that one of the main social forces leading to suicide is the sense of normlessness resulting from drastic changes in living conditions or arrangements, which he calls anomie. He also wrote about the methods of social science as well as religion in *The Elementary Forms of Religious Life* (1917/1995). Although the concept originated with Comte, Durkheim is often considered the founding practitioner of positivist sociology, a strain within sociology that believes the social world can be described and predicted by certain describable relationships.

Anomie a sense of aimlessness or despair that arises when we can no longer reasonably expect life to be predictable; too little social regulation; normlessness.

Positivist sociology a strain within sociology that believes the social world can be described and predicted by certain describable relationships (akin to a social physics).

Georg Simmel Historically, Georg Simmel (1858–1918) has received less credit as one of the founders of sociology, although as of late he is gaining wider recognition. In a series of important lectures and essays, Simmel established what we today refer to as formal sociology—that is, a sociology of pure numbers. For example, among the issues he addressed were the fundamental differences between a group of two and a group of three or more (independent of the reasons for the group or who belongs to it). His work was influential in the development of urban sociology and cultural sociology, and his work with small-group interactions served as an intellectual precedent for later sociologists who came to study microinteractions. He provided formal definitions for small and large groups, a party, a stranger, and the poor. (These are antecedents of network theory, which emerged in the latter half of the twentieth century.)

American Sociology

Throughout the history of sociology the pendulum has tended to swing back and forth between a focus on big, sweeping theories and on more focused empirical research. The emergence of American sociology was characterized by the latter, applied perspective, and was best embodied by what came to be referred to as the Chicago School, named for many of its proponents' affiliation with the University of Chicago. If the Chicago School had a basic premise, it was that humans' behaviors and personalities are shaped by their social and physical environments, a concept known as social ecology.

Chicago, which had grown from a middle-sized city of 109,260 in 1860 to a major metropolis by the beginning of the twentieth century, when these scholars were writing, served as the main laboratory for the Chicago School's studies. Chicago proved to be fertile ground for studying urbanism and its many discontents. Immigration, race and ethnicity, politics, and family life all became topics of study, primarily through a community-based approach (i.e., interviewing people and spending time with them). Robert Park (1864–1944), for example, exhorted scholars to "go and get the seat of [their] pants dirty in real research." This was a time of rapid growth in urban America thanks to a high rate of foreign immigration as well as the Great Migration of African Americans from the rural South to the urban North. The researchers of the Chicago School were concerned with how race and ethnic divisions played out in cities: how Polish peasants and African American sharecroppers adapted to life in a new, industrialized world, or how the anonymity of the city itself contributed to creativity and freedom on the one hand, and to the breakdown of traditional communities and higher rates of social problems on the other. For example, in the classic Chicago School essay "Urbanism as a Way of Life" (1938), Louis Wirth—himself an immigrant from a small village in Germany—described how the city broke down traditional forms of social solidarity while promoting tolerance, rationality (which led to scientific advances), and individual freedom. Much of the work was what would be called cultural sociology today. For example, in their studies of ethnicity, Park and others challenged the notion inherited from Europe that ethnicity was about bloodlines and instead showed ethnicity "in practice" to be more about the maintenance of cultural practices passed down through generations. Likewise, the stages of immigrant assimilation into American society (contact, then competition, and finally assimilation), which are today regarded as common knowledge and indeed part of our national ideology, were first described by Park.

If there was a theoretical paradigm that undergirded much of the research of the Chicago School, it would be the theory of the "social self" that emerged from the work of the social psychologists Charles Horton Cooley (1864–1929) and George Herbert Mead (1863–1931). Taking up the theme, manifest in the Chicago School's community studies, of how the social environment shapes the individual, Cooley and Mead incorporated some of the key ideas of the pragmatist school of philosophy (which argues that inquiry and truth cannot be understood outside their environment—i.e., that environment affects meaning). Cooley, who taught at the University of Michigan, is best known for the concept of the "looking-glass self." He argued that the self emerges from an interactive social process. We envision how others perceive us; then we gauge the responses of other individuals to our presentation of self. By refining our vision of how others perceive us, we develop a self-concept that is in constant interaction with the surrounding social world. Much of Cooley's work described the important role that group dynamics played in this process. (See Chapter 5 on groups and networks.)

In his classic *Mind, Self, and Society* (1934), George Herbert Mead, a social psychologist and philosopher at the University of Chicago, described how the "self" itself (i.e., the perception of consciousness as an object) develops over the course of childhood as the individual learns to take the point of view of specific others in specific contexts (such as games) and eventually internalizes what Mead calls the "generalized other"—our view of the views of society as a whole that transcends individuals or particular situations. (Mead's theories are discussed in depth in Chapter 4 on socialization.) Key to both Cooley's and Mead's work is the notion that it is through social interaction that meaning emerges. This theoretical paradigm is perhaps best summarized by another Chicago scholar, W. I. Thomas, who stated that "if men define situations as real they are real in their consequences" (Thomas & Thomas, 1928, p. 572). This was an important precursor to the notion of the social construction of reality.

W. E. B. Dubois However, even as the Chicago School questioned essentialist notions of race and ethnicity (and even the self), the community of scholars was still dominated by white men. The most important black sociologist

W. E. B. DuBois (second from right) at the office of the NAACP's *Crisis* magazine.

Double consciousness a concept conceived by W. E. B. DuBois to describe the two behavioral scripts, one for moving through the world and the other incorporating the external opinions of prejudiced onlookers, which are constantly maintained by African Americans.

of the time, and the first African American to receive a PhD from Harvard, W. E. B. DuBois (1868–1963) failed to gain the renown he deserved. The first sociologist to undertake ethnography in the African American community, DuBois made manifold contributions to scholarship and social causes. He developed the concept of double consciousness, a mechanism by which African Americans constantly maintain two behavioral scripts. The first is the script that any American would have for moving through the world; the second is the script that takes the external opinions of an often racially prejudiced onlooker into consideration. The double consciousness is a "sense of always looking at one's self through the eyes of others, of measuring one's soul by the tape of a world that looks on in amused contempt and pity" (1903, p. 2). Without a double consciousness, a person shopping for groceries moves through the store trying to remember everything on the list, maybe taste-testing the grapes, impatiently scolding children begging for the latest sugary treat or snacking on some cookies before paying for them at the register. With a double consciousness, an African American shopping for groceries is aware that he or she might be watched carefully by store security and makes an effort to get in and out quickly. He or she does not linger in back corners out of the gaze of shopkeepers and remembers not to reach into a pocket lest this motion be perceived as evidence of shoplifting. Snacking on a bag of chips before reaching the register or sampling a tasty morsel from the bulk bins is totally out of the question. Those operating with a double consciousness risk conforming so closely to others' perceptions that they are fully constrained to the behaviors predicted of them. DuBois was also interested in criminology, using Durkheim's theory of anomie to explain crime rates among African Americans. Specifically, DuBois theorized that the breakdown of norms resulting from the sudden and newfound freedom of former slaves caused high crime rates among blacks (at least in the South). He also analyzed the social stratification among Philadelphia's black population and argued that such class inequality was necessary for progress in the black community. African Americans, he argued, would be led by what he coined "the talented tenth," an elite of highly educated professionals. In addition to being a major academic sociologist, DuBois worked to advance a civil rights agenda in the United States. To this end, he cofounded the National Association for the Advancement of Colored People (NAACP) in 1909.

Jane Addams Among sociologists, women, much like African Americans, didn't always receive the respect they deserved. For example, Jane Addams (1860–1935) was considered a marginal member of the Chicago School, yet many of the movement's thinkers drew some of their insights from her applied work. Addams founded the first American settlement house, Hull House, an institution that attempted to link the ideas of the university to the poor through a full-service community center, staffed by students and professionals, which offered educational services and aid and promoted sports and the arts. It was at Hull House in Chicago that the ideas of the Chicago School were put into practice and tested. Although many of Addams's observations and experiences at Hull House were influential in the development of the Chicago School's theories and Addams herself was a prolific author on both the substance and methodology of community studies, she was regarded as a social worker by the majority of her contemporaries. This label, which she rejected, partly resulted from the applied nature of her work, but undoubtedly gender also played a role in her marginalization: Many of the men of the Chicago School also engaged in social activism yet retained their academic prestige.

Modern Sociological Theories

Although it was born in a tradition of community studies that avoided grand theory and drew its insights from the careful observation of people in their environments, American sociology was largely characterized by the concept of functionalism for much of the twentieth century. Drawing on the ideas of Durkheim and best embodied by the work of Talcott Parsons (1902–1979), functionalism derived its name from the notion that the best way to analyze society was to identify the roles that different aspects or phenomena play. These functions may be manifest (explicit) or latent (hidden). This lens is really just an extension of a nineteenth-century theory called *organicism*, the notion that society is like a living organism, each part of which serves an important role in keeping society together. The state or government was seen to be the brain; industry was the muscular system; media and mass communications were the nervous system; and so on.

Functionalism the theory that various social institutions and processes in society exist to serve some important (or necessary) function to keep society running.

Twentieth-century sociologists had moved beyond such simplistic biological metaphors, yet the essential notion that social institutions were present for a reason persisted. Hence, analysis by Parsons and others sought to describe how the various parts of the whole were integrated with, but articulated against, one another. Almost every social phenomenon was subjected to functionalist analysis: What is the function of schooling? The health-care system? Even crime and the Mafia were seen to play a role in a functioning society. For example, functionalists view social inequality as a "device by which societies ensure that the most important positions are conscientiously filled by the most qualified persons" (Davis & Moore, 1944).

Although associated with mid-twentieth-century sociology, the functionalist impulse originated in the nineteenth century, most notably in the work of Durkheim, who in 1893 wrote, "For, if there is nothing which either unduly hinders or favours the chances of those competing for occupations, it is inevitable that only those who are most capable at each type of activity will move into it. The only factor which then determines the manner in which work is

Female textile workers struggle with a national guardsman during a 1929 strike in Gastonia, North Carolina. How might a conflict theorist interpret labor unrest?

divided is the diversity of capacities" (1972). Functionalism was still being applied into the late twentieth century by Richard J. Herrnstein and Charles Murray, who argued in *The Bell Curve* that "no one decreed that occupations should sort us out by our cognitive abilities, and no one enforces the process. It goes on beneath the surface, guided by its own invisible hand" (1994, p. 52).

Conflict Theory Even though functionalism continues to reappear in many guises, its fundamental assertions have not gone unchallenged. Sociologists such as C. Wright Mills, writing from 1948 through 1962, criticized Parsons and functionalist theory for reinforcing the status quo and the dominant economic system with its class structures and inequalities rather than challenging how such systems evolved and offering alternatives. Functionalism also took a beating in the turbulent 1960s, when its place was usurped by a number of theories frequently subsumed under the label Marxist theory or conflict theory. Whereas functionalists painted a picture of social harmony as the well-oiled parts of a societal machine working together (with some friction and the occasional breakdown), conflict theory viewed society from exactly the opposite perspective. Drawing on the ideas of Marx, the theory—as expressed by Ralph Dahrendorf, Lewis Coser, and others—stated that conflict among competing interests is the basic, animating force of any society. Competition, not consensus, is the essential nature, and this conflict at all levels of analysis (from the individual to the family to the tribe to the nation-state), in turn, drives social change. And such social change occurs only through revolution and war, not evolution or baby steps.

Conflict theory the idea that conflict between competing interests is the basic, animating force of social change and society in general.

According to conflict theorists, inequality exists as a result of political struggles among different groups (classes) in a particular society. Although functionalists theorize that inequality is a necessary and beneficial aspect of society, conflict theorists argue that it is unfair and exists at the expense of less powerful groups. Thus, functionalism and conflict theory take extreme (if opposing) positions on the fundamental nature of society. Today most sociologists see societies as demonstrating characteristics of both consensus and conflict and believe that social change does result from both revolution and evolution.

Feminist Theory Emerging from the women's movement of the 1960s and 1970s, feminist theory shares many ideas with Marxist theory—in particular, the Marxist emphasis on conflict and political reform. Feminism is not one idea but a catchall term for many theories. What all have in common is an emphasis on women's experiences and a belief that sociology and society in general subordinate women. Feminist theorists emphasize equality between men and women and want to see women's lives and experiences represented in sociological studies. Early feminist theory focused on defining concepts such as sex and gender, and on challenging conventional wisdom by questioning the meanings usually assigned to these concepts. In *Sex, Gender, and Society* (1972), sociologist Ann Oakley argued that much of what we attribute to biological sex differences can be traced to behaviors that are learned and internalized through socialization (see Chapter 8 on gender).

In addition to defining sex and gender, much feminist research focuses on inequalities based on gender categories. Feminist theorists have studied women's experiences at home and in the workplace. They have also researched gender inequality in social institutions such as schools, the family, and the government. In each case, feminist sociologists remain interested in how power relationships are defined, shaped, and reproduced on the basis of gender differences.

Symbolic interactionism a micro-level theory in which shared meanings, orientations, and assumptions form the basic motivations behind people's actions.

Symbolic Interactionism A strain of thought that developed in the 1960s was symbolic interactionism, which eschewed big theories of society

Las Vegas, the ultimate postmodern city, borrows from various regions, times, and cultures to shape its constantly changing landscape.

(macrosociology) and instead focused on how face-to-face interactions create the social world (microsociology). Exemplified most notably by the work of one of Mead's students, Herbert Blumer, this paradigm operates on the basic premise of a cycle of meaning, namely, the idea that people act in response to the meaning that signs and social signals hold for them (e.g., a red light means stop). By acting on perceptions of the social world in this way and regarding these meanings as *sui generis* (i.e., appearing to be self-constituting rather than flimsily constructed by ourselves or others), we then collectively make their meaning so. In other words, John G. Roberts, Jr. is Chief Justice of the U.S. Supreme Court because we all act as if he is and believe that it is an objective fact he is (even if that belief is the creation of our somewhat arbitrary collective thinking). We then act in ways that reify, or make consequential, this consensus and arrive at our calculations based on the supposed objectivity of this "fact."

The groundwork for symbolic interactionism was laid by Erving Goffman's dramaturgical theory of social interaction. Goffman had used the language of theater to describe the social facade we create through such devices as tact, gestures, front-stage (versus backstage) behavior, props, and scripts. For example, in *The Presentation of Self in Everyday Life* (1959), Goffman explored how our everyday personal encounters shape and reinforce our notions about class and social status. According to Goffman, we make judgments about class and social status based on how people speak, what they wear, and the other tiny details of how they present themselves to others, and at the same time, they rely on the same information from our everyday interactions with them to classify us, too.

Postmodernism If symbolic interactionism emphasizes the meanings negotiated through the interaction of individuals, postmodernism can perhaps be summarized succinctly as the notion that these shared meanings have eroded. A red light, for instance, may have multiple meanings to different groups or individuals in society. There is no longer one version of history that is correct. Everything is interpretable within this framework; even "facts" are up for debate. It's as if everyone has become a symbolic interactionist and decided that seemingly objective phenomena are social constructions, so that all organizing narratives break down. Postmodernists may not feel compelled to act on these shared meanings as seemingly objective, because the meanings aren't, in fact, objective. The term itself derives from the idea that the grand narratives of history are over (hence, "after" modernism, *postmodernism*).

Postmodernism a condition characterized by a questioning of the notion of progress and history, the replacement of narrative within pastiche, and multiple, perhaps even conflicting, identities resulting from disjointed affiliations.

Social construction an entity that exists because people behave as if it exists and whose existence is perpetuated as people and social institutions act in accordance with the widely agreed-upon formal rules or informal norms of behavior associated with that entity.

Midrange Theory Although many sociologists have taken to the postmodernist project of deconstructing social phenomena (i.e., showing how they are created arbitrarily by social actors with varying degrees of power), most sociologists have returned, as the pendulum swings yet again, to what sociologist Robert Merton called for in the middle of the last century.: midrange theory. Midrange theory is neither macrosociology (it doesn't try to explain all of society) nor microsociology. Rather, midrange theory attempts to predict

Midrange theory a theory that attempts to predict how certain social institutions tend to function.

how certain social institutions tend to function. For example, a midrange theorist might develop a theory of democracy (under what political or demographic conditions does it arise?), a theory of the household (when do households expand to include extended kin or nonkin and when do they contract to the nuclear family unit or the individual?), or a theory explaining the relationship between the educational system and the labor market. The key to midrange theory is that it generates falsifiable hypotheses—predictions that can be tested by analyzing the real world. (Hypothesis generation is covered in Chapter 2.)

Sociology and Its Cousins

We have already noted that a sociology of sports exists, as can a sociology of music, of organizations, of economies, of science, and even of sociology itself. What then, if anything, distinguishes sociology from other disciplines? Certainly overlap with other fields does occur, but at the same time, there is something distinctive about sociology as a discipline that transcends the sociological imagination discussed earlier. All of sociology boils down to comparisons across cases of some form or another, and perhaps the best way to conceptualize its role in the landscape of knowledge is to compare it with other fields.

History

Let's start with history. History is concerned with the *idiographic* (from the Greek *idio*, "unique," and *graphic*, "depicting"), meaning that historians, at least traditionally, have been concerned with explaining unique cases. Why did Adolf Hitler rise to power? What conditions led to the Haitian slave revolt 200 years ago (the first such rebellion against European chattel slavery)? How did the Counter-Reformation affect the practices of lay Catholics in France? What was the impact of the railroad on civilization's sense of time? How did adolescence arise as a meaningful stage of life? Historians' research questions center on the notion that by understanding the particularity of certain past events, individual people, or intellectual concepts, we can better understand the world in which we live.

Italian dictator Benito Mussolini (on the left) and Nazi leader Adolf Hitler at a 1937 rally in Munich. How do different disciplines provide various tools to analyze the rise of fascism under these leaders?

Sometimes historians use comparative frameworks to situate their analysis—for example, comparing Hitler's rise and Mussolini's to examine why the Third Reich pursued a genocidal agenda, whereas the Italian fascists had no such agenda and, in fact, somewhat resisted cooperating with Germany's deportation of Jews. Another strategy historians often use, although it is sometimes frowned on, is the notion of the counterfactual: What would have happened had Hitler been killed rather than wounded in World War I? Would World War II have been inevitable even if the victors in World War I had not pursued such a punitive reparations policy after defeating Germany?

The preceding description is, of course, an oversimplification of a diverse field. History runs the gamut from "great man" theories (a focus on figures like Hitler) to people's histories (a focus on the lives of anonymous, disempowered people at various epochs or on groups traditionally given short shrift in historical scholarship, such as women, African Americans, and subaltern colonials) to historiography (in essence, metahistory examining the intellectual assumptions and constraints on knowledge entailed by the subjects and methods historians choose).

Sociology, by contrast, is generally not concerned with the uniqueness of phenomena but rather with commonalities that can be abstracted across cases. This is called a nomothetic approach (from the Greek root meaning "custom"—norm or pattern). So if the unique case is the staple of the historian, the comparative method is the staple of sociologists. Whether looking at contemporary American life, the formation of city-states in medieval Europe, or the origins of unequal economic development thousands of years ago, sociologists formulate hypotheses and theorems about how social life works or worked.

Instead of inquiring why Hitler rose to power, the sociologist might ask what common element allowed fascism to arise during the early to mid-twentieth century in Germany, Italy, Spain, and Japan and not in other countries such as France, Great Britain, or the Scandinavian nations. Of course, sociologists recognize that there is no one-size-fits-all hypothesis that will explain all these cases perfectly, but the exercise of considering competing explanations is illuminating in and of itself. Instead of asking what specific conditions led to the Haitian slave revolt in 1791, the sociologist might ask under what general conditions uprisings have occurred among indentured populations. Instead of asking how the Counter-Reformation affected the practices of lay Catholics in one region of Europe, the sociologist might ask what aspects of the conditions in various regions of Europe made the reaction to the Catholic Church's reforms different. This is a subtle but important difference in focus. Instead of examining the impact of the railroad on our sense of time, the sociologist might compare the railroad to other forms of transportation that both collapsed distances and opened up the possibility of more frequent and longer migrations. And finally, instead of asking how adolescence arose as a meaningful stage of life, the sociologist might compare various societies that have distinct roles for individuals ages 13 to 20 to examine how those labor markets, educational systems, family arrangements, life expectancies, and so on lead to different experiences for that age group.

Whether sociologists are comparing two tribes that died out 400 years ago, two countries today, siblings within the same family, or even changes in the

How does anthropologist Natasha Schull's research on slot-machine gamblers challenge the traditional boundaries between anthropology and sociology?

same person over the course of his or her life, they are always seeking a variation in some outcome that can be explained by variation in some input. This holds true, I would argue, whether the methods are interviews, research using historical archives, community-based observation studies of participants, or statistical analyses of data from the U.S. census. Sociologists are always at least implicitly drawing comparisons to identify abstractable patterns.

Anthropology

The field of anthropology is split between physical anthropologists, who resemble biologists more than sociologists, and cultural anthropologists, who study human relations similarly to the way sociologists do. Traditionally, the distinction was that sociologists studied "us" (Western society and culture), whereas anthropologists studied "them" (other societies or cultures). This distinction was helpful in the early to mid-twentieth century, when Margaret Mead studied rites of passage in Samoa and sociologists interviewed Chicago residents, but it is less salient today. Sociologists increasingly study non-Western social relations, and anthropologists do not hesitate to tackle domestic social issues.

Take two recent examples that confound this division from either side of the metaphorical aisle: Caitlin Zaloom is a cultural anthropologist whose "tribe" (she likes to joke) is the commodities traders on the floor of the Chicago Mercantile Exchange. Natasha Schull, another anthropologist, has studied gamblers in Las Vegas and how they relate to the slot machines into which they pour their hopes and money. Meanwhile, recent sociological scholarship includes Stephen Morgan's study of African status attainment and patronage relations. Another project, spearheaded by business-school professor Doug Guthrie in 2006, investigated the way informal social connections facilitate business in China. Given the era of globalization we have entered, it is appropriate that division on the basis of "us" and "them" has diminished. Many scholars now question the legitimacy of such a division in the first place, asking whether it served a colonial agenda of dividing up the world and reproducing social relations of domination and exclusion—accomplishing on the intellectual front what European imperialism did on the military, political, and economic fronts.

What then distinguishes sociology from cultural anthropology? Nothing, some would argue. However, although certain aspects of sociology are almost indistinguishable from those of cultural anthropology, sociology as a whole has a wider array of methods to answer questions, such as experimentation and statistical data analysis. Sociology also tends more toward comparative case study, whereas anthropology is more like history in its focus on particular circumstances. This does not necessarily imply that sociology is superior; a wider range of methods can be a weakness as well as a strength, because it can lead to irreconcilable differences within the field. For example, demographic and ethnographic studies of the family may employ different definitions of what a household is. This makes meaningful dialogue between the two subfields challenging.

The Psychological and Biological Sciences

Social, developmental, and cognitive psychology often address many of the same questions that sociologists do: How do people react to stereotypes? What explains racial differences in educational performance? How do individuals respond to authority in various circumstances? Ultimately, however, psychologists focus on the individual, whereas sociologists focus on the supra-individual (above or beyond the individual) level. In other words, psychologists focus on the individual to explain the phenomenon under consideration, examining how urges, drives, instincts, and the mind can account for human behavior, whereas sociologists examine group-level dynamics and social structures.

Biology, especially evolutionary biology, increasingly attempts to explain phenomena that once would have seemed the exclusive dominion of social scientists. There are now biological (evolutionary) theories of many aspects of gender relations—even rape and high-heeled shoes (Posner, 1992). Medical science has claimed to identify genes that explain some aspects of social behavior, such as aggressiveness, shyness, and even thrill seeking. Increasingly, social differences have been medicalized through diagnoses such as attention-deficit hyperactivity disorder (ADHD) and the autistic spectrum of diseases. The distinction between these areas of biology and the social sciences lies not so much in the topic of study (or even the scientific methods in some cases), but rather in the underlying variation or causal mechanisms with which the disciplines are concerned. Sociology addresses supra-individual-level dynamics that affect our behavior, psychology addresses individual-level dynamics, and biology typically deals with the intra-individual-level factors (those within the individual) that affect our lives, such as biochemistry, genetic makeup, and cellular activity. So if a group of biologists attempted to explain differences in culture across continents, they would typically analyze something like local ecological effects or the distribution of genes across subpopulations.

Economics and Political Science

The quantitative side of sociology shares many methodological and substantive features with economics and political science. Economics traditionally has focused on market exchange relations (or, simply, money). More recently, however, economics has expanded to include social realms such as culture, religion, and the family—the traditional stomping ground of sociologists. What distinguishes economics from sociology in these contexts is the underlying view of human behavior. Economics assumes that people are rational utility maximizers: They are out to get the best deal for themselves. Sociology, on the other hand, has a more open view of human motivation that includes selfishness, altruism, and simple irrationality. (New branches of economics are moving, however, into the realm of the irrational.) Another difference is methodological: Economics is a fundamentally quantitative discipline, meaning that it is based on numerical data.

Similarly, political science is almost a subsector of sociology that focuses on only one aspect of social relations—power. Of course, power relations take many forms. Political scientists study state relations, legal structure, and the nature of civic life. Like sociologists, political scientists deploy a variety of methods, ranging from historical case studies to abstract statistical models. Increasingly, political science has adopted the rational actor model implicit in economics in an attempt to explain everything from how lobbyists influence legislators to the recruitment of suicide bombers by terrorist groups.

Having explained all of these distinctions, we should keep in mind that disciplinary boundaries are in a constant state of flux. For example, Stanford English professor Franco Moretti argues that books should be counted, mapped, and graphed. In his research Moretti statistically analyzes thousands of books by thematic and linguistic patterns. Economist Steven Levitt has explored how teachers teach to the test (and sometimes cheat) and how stereotypically African American names may or may not disadvantage their holders. Historian Zvi Ben-Dor Benite has assembled a global, comparative history of how different societies execute criminals. It all sounds like sociology to me! For now, let's just say that significant overlap exists between various arenas of scholarship, so that any divisions are simultaneously meaningful and arbitrary.

Divisions within Sociology

Even if sociologists tend to leverage comparisons of some sort, significant fault lines still persist within sociology. Often, the major division is perceived to exist between those who deal in numbers (statistical or quantitative researchers) and those who deal in words (qualitative sociologists). Another split exists between theorists and empiricists. These are false dichotomies, however; they merely act as shorthand for deeper intellectual divisions for which they are poor proxies. A much more significant cleavage exists between interpretive and positivist sociology. Positivist sociology is born from the mission of Comte—that mission being to reveal the "social facts" (to use the term Durkheim later coined) that affect, if not govern, social life. It is akin to uncovering the laws of "social physics," although most sociologists today would shun Comte's phrase because it implies an overly deterministic sense of unwavering, time-transcendent laws.

To this end, the standard practice is to form a theory about how the social world works—for instance, that members of minorities have a high degree of group solidarity. The next task is to generate a hypothesis that derives from this theory, perhaps that minority groups should demonstrate a lower level of intragroup violence than majority groups. Next, we make predictions based on our hypotheses. Both the hypotheses and predictions have to be falsifiable by an empirical, or experimental, test; in this case, it might involve examining homicide rates among different groups in a given society or in multiple societies. And last comes the acceptance or rejection of the hypothesis and the revision (or extension) of the theory (in the face of contradictory or confirming evidence). These scientific methods are the same as in any basic science. For that reason, positivism is often called the "normal science" model of sociology.

Normal science stands in contrast to interpretive sociology, which is much more concerned with the meaning of social phenomena to individuals (remember Weber's *Verstehen*). Rather than make a prediction about homicide rates, the interpretive sociologist will likely seek to understand the experience of solidarity among minority groups in various contexts. An interpretive sociologist might object to the notion that we can make worthwhile predictions about human behavior—or more precisely, might question whether such an endeavor is worth the time and effort. It is a sociology premised on the idea that situation matters so much that the search for social facts that transcend time and place may be futile. Why measure the number of friends we have by the number of people we see face to face every day, given the existence of the Internet and how it has redefined the meaning of social interaction so completely?

Microsociology and Macrosociology

A similar cleavage involves the distinction between *microsociology* and *macrosociology*. Microsociology seeks to understand local interactional contexts—for example, why people stare at the numbers in an elevator and are reluctant to make eye contact in this setting. Microsociologists focus on face-to-face encounters and the types of interactions between individuals. They rely on data gathered through participant observations and other qualitative methodologies (for more on these methods, see Chapter 2).

Microsociology seeks to understand local interactional contexts; its methods of choice are ethnographic, generally including participant observation and in-depth interviews.

Macrosociology is generally concerned with social dynamics at a higher level of analysis—across the breadth of a society (or at least a swath of it). A macrosociologist might investigate immigration policy or gender norms or how the educational system interacts with the labor market. Statistical analysis is the most typical manifestation of this kind of research, but by no means the only one. Macrosociologists also use qualitative methods such as historical comparison and in-depth interviewing. They may also resort to large-scale experimentation. That said, a perfect overlap does not exist between methodological divisions and level of analysis. For example, microsociologists might use an experimental method such as varying the context of an elevator to see how people react. Or they might use statistical methods such as conversation analysis, which analyzes turn taking, pauses, and other quantifiable aspects of social interaction in localized settings.

Macrosociology generally concerned with social dynamics at a higher level of analysis—that is, across the breadth of a society.

→ CONCLUSION

The bottom line is that anything goes; as long as you use your sociological imagination, you will be asking important questions and seeking the best way to answer them. As you read the subsequent chapters, keep in mind that a sociologist "makes the familiar strange." I have divided this book into three parts. The first six chapters introduce the methodological and theoretical tools that you need in order to think like a sociologist. The second part, Chapters 7 through 11, asks you to study the inequalities and differences that divide people in our society. The third part, Chapters 12 through 18, gives you an overview of the social institutions that are the building blocks of our society.

ASSIGNMENT

Keep a journal for a day; document ten social phenomena that you generally perceive as natural in your everyday life. Your journal could include notes on the way people greet each other, share public space, eat, and so on. Pick one and discuss alternative ways your daily life might proceed if this element had been different throughout history. (Example: What if racial divisions in America were based on eye color rather than skin tone?)

QUESTIONS FOR REVIEW

1. Some people accuse sociologists of observing conditions that are obvious. How does looking at sociology as "making the familiar strange" help counter this claim? How does sociology differ from simple commonsense reasoning?
2. What is the sociological imagination, and how do history and personal biography affect it? If a sociologist studies the challenges experienced by students earning a college degree, how could the lessons gained be described as "terrible" as well as "magnificent"?
3. What is a social institution, and how does it relate to social identity? Choose a sports team or another social institution to illustrate your answer.
4. A sociologist studies the way a group of fast-food restaurant employees do their work. From what you read in this chapter, how would Weber and Durkheim differ in their study of these workers?
5. Compare functionalism and conflict theory. How would the two differ in their understanding of inequality?
6. You tell a friend that you're taking a class in sociology. There's a chance they know about sociology and are quite jealous. There's also a chance they're confusing sociology with the other social sciences. How would you describe sociology? How does sociology differ from history and psychology?
7. Sociology, like any discipline, features some divisions. What are some of the cleavages in the field, and why might these be described as false dichotomies?
8. Why do people go to college, and how does Randall Collins's book *Credential Society* make the familiar reality of college education seem strange?

PARADOX

A SUCCESSFUL SOCIOLOGIST MAKES THE FAMILIAR STRANGE.

WATCH THE ANIMATED SHORT ABOUT THE SOCIOLOGICAL IMAGINATION PARADOX AT

WWNORTON.COM/STUDYSPACE

The Robert Taylor homes, the site where Sudhir Venkatesh did the research featured in *Gang Leader for a Day*.

2 Methods

PARADOX

IF WE SUCCESSFULLY ANSWER ONE QUESTION, IT ONLY SPAWNS OTHERS. THERE IS NO MOMENT WHEN A SOCIAL SCIENTIST'S WORK IS DONE.

"I woke up at about 7:30 A.M. in a crack den, Apartment 1603 in Building Number 2301 of the Robert Taylor Homes. . . . The activities of the previous night—smoking crack, drinking, having sex, vomiting—had peaked at about 2:00 A.M. . . . I hadn't come for the crack; I was here on a different mission. I was a graduate student at the University of Chicago and for my research I had taken to hanging out with the Black Kings, a local crack-selling gang" (Venkatesh, 2008, pp. xiii–xiv).

Sudhir Venkatesh, a graduate student at the University of Chicago who had grown up in the suburbs, set out to study poor black folks in the Robert Taylor Homes, a now-demolished public housing project on the South Side of Chicago. At first, he arrived with a survey mounted to a clipboard and approached residents by knocking on doors and asking a series of questions: "'How does it feel to be black and poor?' I read. Then I gave the multiple-choice answers: 'Very bad, somewhat bad, neither bad nor good, somewhat good, very good'" (p. 14).

As you might imagine, Venkatesh did not get very far with this technique. Right away, he was detained by members of the Black Kings and introduced to the local kingpin, J.T. After a tense moment of rapid explanation and sizing up, Venkatesh was invited to come back and see J.T. another day if he wanted to know what it was like to be black and poor. That invitation lasted the duration of his graduate-school career.

From Venkatesh's perspective, the failed survey attempt represented not his own shortcomings, but a broader problem with survey-based sociological inquiry. Thinking things over on the way back from the Robert Taylor Homes, he began fuming about the fact that sociologists and social scientists "were not really seeing this world or [were] choosing to ignore it and were really not taking the time to figure out exactly what was going on in these inner-city communities. You know, most of them would, in a responsible way, ask a survey here and there, ask [a] few hundred people, and then, turn their backs. And I struggle to figure out what value I could offer if I didn't spend the time" (Simon, 2008).

But this isn't a sociological romantic comedy where researcher and subject meet and get to know each other amid hilarious antics until they fade into the happy ever-after of great book sales (for the sociologist) and new successful community interventions (for the subject population). Venkatesh did spend time in the Robert Taylor Homes. He spent so much time that he left only to go to class, if that. He slept on people's couches, hung out with J.T., J.T.'s mom, gang members, and other residents. The closeness of his relationships yielded rich sociological data, but these same relationships eventually presented a series of ethical challenges that tend to arise when researchers get *too* deeply involved in a sociological field site.

Venkatesh explains how he knew he was getting too close. A woman whom he had become friends with was badly beaten—her modeling career obviously ended—by her boyfriend, Bee-Bee. Because the police were afraid to respond to calls from this community, the residents gathered a group of squatters to find Bee-Bee and beat him up. Venkatesh went along with the group, who eventually caught up with Bee-Bee in a stairwell. But Bee-Bee was a big, strong man who was able to get one of his three (much smaller) assailants in a choke hold. At this place, Venkatesh remembers, "I'm the only one who sees this and 'I'm observing this.' I'm a neutral, [im]partial observer. And that line was crossed immediately when I kicked Bee-Bee in the stomach . . . so that he let go of this guy" (Simon, 2008).

From his original disgust with the survey method, Venkatesh learned firsthand that spending much time in the community and getting the full story came with dilemmas of their own. In an interview with National Public Radio, Venkatesh remembered thinking, "Okay. Now, I'm spending the time and now, I'm just trying to get involved and this—these lines I have to cross. And I struggle to figure out exactly what my contribution could be. And it's taken me a long time. And I still struggle with that question of exactly how to be a good sociologist" (Simon, 2008). Venkatesh's internal debates about how to be an ethical, responsible sociologist with sound, relevant research methods are not his alone.

Research methods approaches that social scientists use for investigating the answers to questions.

Quantitative methods methods that seek to obtain information about the social world that is already in or can be converted to numeric form.

As social scientists, we have a set of standard approaches that we follow in investigating our questions. We call these rules research methods. They're the tools we use to describe, explore, and explain various social phenomena in an ethical fashion. There are two general categories of methods for gathering sociological data:

Quantitative methods seek to obtain information about the social world that is already in or can be converted to numeric form. This methodology then uses statistical analysis to describe the social world that those data represent. Some of this analysis attempts to mimic the scientific method of using treatment and control (or placebo) groups to determine how changes in one factor affect another social outcome, while factoring out every other simultaneous event. Such information is often acquired through surveys like the one Venkatesh tried to administer at first but may also include data collected by other means, ranging from sampling bank records to weighing people on a scale.

Qualitative methods, of which there are many, attempt to collect information about the social world that cannot be readily converted to numeric form. The information gathered with this approach is often used to document the meanings that actions engender in social participants or to describe the mechanisms by which social processes occur. Qualitative data are collected in a host of ways, from spending time with people and recording what they say and do (participant observation) to interviewing them in an open-ended manner to reviewing archives.

Qualitative methods methods that attempt to collect information about the social world that cannot be readily converted to numeric form.

Both quantitative and qualitative research approaches provide ways to establish a causal relationship between social elements. Researchers using quantitative approaches, by eliminating all other possibilities through their study's design, hope to state with some certainty that one condition causes another. Qualitative methodology describes social processes in such detail as to rule out competing possibilities.

This chapter gives examples of sociological research conducted using different methods, starting with the various theoretical viewpoints from which social scientists approach research. We'll then examine some techniques used by researchers to tell causal stories and give examples of specific studies that have employed these methods. Finally, we'll talk about the ways that social research can be used for ends other than filling textbooks and keeping sociologists busy.

Research 101

The general goal of sociology is to allow us to see how our individual lives are intimately related to (and, in turn, affect) the social forces that exist beyond us. Good sociological research begins with a puzzle or paradox and asks, "What causes such and such a thing to happen?" Once you pick a question to investigate, there are two ways to approach research: *deductively* and *inductively*. A deductive approach starts with a theory, forms a hypothesis, makes empirical observations, and then analyzes the data to confirm, reject, or modify the original theory. Conversely, an inductive approach starts with empirical observations and then works to form a theory. These different approaches are represented in the research cycle shown in Figure 2.1.

Deductive approach a research approach that starts with a theory, forms a hypothesis, makes empirical observations, and then analyzes the data to confirm, reject, or modify the original theory.

Inductive approach a research approach that starts with empirical observations and then works to form a theory.

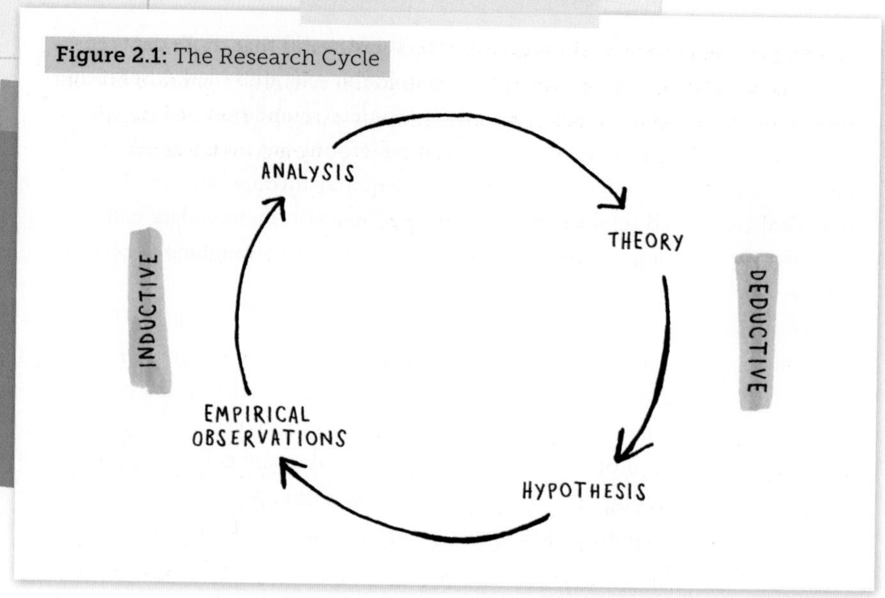

Figure 2.1: The Research Cycle

Causality versus Correlation

Correlation or **association** simultaneous variation in two variables.

Regardless of which method we use, social research is about telling a story. The goal is to recount the story as completely as possible so we're fairly certain it can't be told any other way. Let's take an example of something we'll examine more closely in Chapter 11: the relationship between income and health. We know that a correlation (or association) exists between income and health; that is, they tend to vary together. For example, people with higher levels of income tend to enjoy better overall health. But to say two things are correlated is very different from stating that one causes the other. In fact, there are three possible causal stories about the relationship between income and health. We might reasonably assert that bad health causes you to have a lower income—you get sick and can't work, you lose your job, and so forth. If we drew a diagram of such a scenario, it would look like this:

POORER HEALTH ⟶ LOWER INCOME

However, we could just as easily tell the opposite story—that higher income leads to better health. You can afford better doctors, you have access to fresh, healthful foods in your upscale neighborhood, and there's a gym at the office. The diagram of this story would resemble the following:

POORER HEALTH ⟵ LOWER INCOME

Finally, we could conclude that a third factor causes both income and health to vary in the same direction. For the sake of argument, we will call this factor "reckless tendencies"—a love of fast cars, wine, and late nights. Such shortsighted behavior could negatively affect our health (especially the wine). And it could also affect our income. Maybe we are unable to get to work on time or are spending too much money on those fast cars instead of investing it in the stock market. In that case, the causal diagram would look like this:

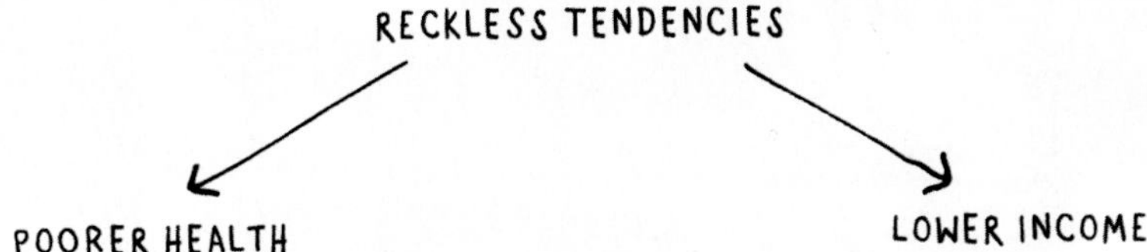

In this scenario, if we merely observe health and income, it may appear as if one causes the other, but the truth of the matter is that they are not related in the slightest apart from being connected through a third factor.

How can we arrive at any conclusions with respect to the health–income correlation? We can't randomly assign people to different jobs at various pay levels and see what happens, nor can we independently affect people's health and (ethically) observe what happens to their income, and it is certainly difficult to curb or instill reckless tendencies on a random basis. Thus, we can't really rule out any of the arrows, but we can confirm some of them. We can rule out many third factors by measuring them and then comparing individuals who are similar in that particular respect (like education level) but differ in other key regards (say, income). Other factors may not be so easy to measure, and in these cases we might look for a natural experiment, that is, an event or change in the real world that affects the factor we believe causes an outcome but does not affect the outcome in any way other than through that factor. For example, some researchers have used lottery winnings as a natural experiment, comparing the health of winners who won a significant sum with those who won only a token amount. The assumption, based on how lotteries work, is that the amount won is not determined by the winner's health, but that subsequent changes in health may well be driven by the money won.

Although few certain answers exist in social science, we can safely conclude that low income does contribute to poor health, at least to some extent in specific contexts. (We can also be fairly sure that bad health has a negative effect on our income.) However, our case would be stronger if we knew exactly what effect low income has on health. In other words, we don't know the causal mechanism. Is it that low-wage jobs are stressful? (It is well known that certain types of chronic stress are bad for you.) If so, does such stress cause these workers' behavior to change, perhaps by increasing their consumption of fast food, smoking rates, or alcohol intake? Or is there a more direct, psychobiological pathway—say, the stress of a verbally abusive boss that can cause higher corticosteroid levels in the bloodstream? Or is it all of these factors and more? The more dots we can connect, the stronger our causal story becomes and the better prepared we are to intervene.

How did studying lottery winners help sociologists understand the relationship between wealth and health?

Causality the notion that a change in one factor results in a corresponding change in another.

Remember, it is very difficult, especially in social science, to assert causality, that change in one factor causes a change in another. It's much easier to say two things are correlated, which just means that we observe change in both. For example, as race varies (across individuals), so does average life expectancy. Likewise, as nutrition changes across or within populations, so does average height, but can we say that better nutrition causes some populations to be taller? Maybe, but maybe not. Let's further examine this.

To establish causality, three factors are needed: correlation, time order, and ruling out alternative explanations. We've already covered correlation. We notice variations in nutrition across countries and simultaneously observe different average heights across the same countries that tend to correspond statistically to those differences in nutrition. Now we need to establish time order. Have people in country A always been taller than those in country B (a bad sign for the "better nutrition causes height" case)? Or, did changes in nutrition occur before increases (or decreases) in height? We can imagine a situation where a drought, flood, frost, or some other environmental factor destroyed a main food source in country B, leading to dramatic changes in people's diet and altering average heights in that nation. Finally, we have to rule out alternative explanations for the variations observed in both nutrition and height. Is a third factor responsible for changes in both? The groundwater supply perhaps? Groundwater supply could lead to better nutrition through higher crop yields (which turns out not to matter for height, let's say), but it could also lead to cleaner drinking water and thus less infection (which turns out to matter for height, again for the sake of argument). If this were the case, then the relationship between nutrition and height would be termed spurious or false, whereas the relationship between infection and height might be described as a "true" causal relationship. Figure 2.2 illustrates this possibility.

The Problem of Reverse Causality Reverse causality is just what it sounds like: You think A is causing B when, in fact, B is causing A. Let's look at the relationship between income and health. We know that people who are sick often have less income. But which one is causing the other to happen? Is it that when you're sick, you miss lots of school, don't receive as much education, must take off more time from work, are passed over for promotions, and ultimately remain stuck in a lower-level job and therefore have a lower income than your comparatively healthy neighbor? Or is it that when you're employed in a lower-paying job, you may experience more on-the-job stress and more stress as a result of worrying about money, which has a negative impact on your health by putting you at higher risk for cardiovascular disease? On top of that, you can't afford good health care, a gym membership, or fresh, nutritious food. The problem of reverse causality is why it's so important to establish time order. If a person's income drops only after they get sick, we can be surer that it was sickness that led to decline in income.

Reverse causality a situation in which the researcher believes that A results in a change in B, but B, in fact, is causing A.

However, we should also note that time order is no guarantee by itself: People may alter their current behavior based on future expectations. Perhaps, for example, I choose to save less today because I assume that my children will become rich adults on their own and support me in my old age. Strict reliance on time order—observing current savings behavior and children's income 30 years later—would lead me to the wrong conclusion, namely, that all the things I bought for my kids which put me into debt caused my children's success later in life, when it was actually the other way around. Their future success caused me to spend wantonly, assuming that they would bail

Figure 2.2: The Charge of Spuriousness

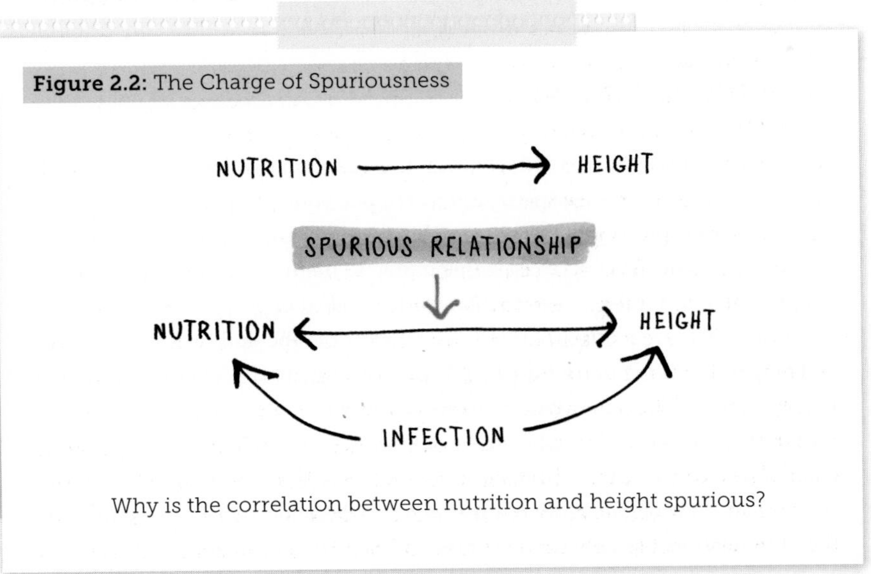

Why is the correlation between nutrition and height spurious?

me out once they got their six-figure salaries. One way to fix this, of course, would be to directly measure my expectations for my children's future income to resolve the matter of time order.

Variables

Dependent variable the outcome that the researcher is trying to explain.

Independent variable a measured factor that the researcher believes has a causal impact on the dependent variable.

In research we talk a great deal about variables. Simply put, you should always have one dependent variable, which is the outcome you are trying to explain, and one or more independent variables, which are the measured factors that you believe have a causal impact on the dependent variable. Because it's possible to have more than one independent variable, we will call the most important one the *key independent variable.* The difference between the independent and the dependent is that change in your dependent variable depends on change in your independent variable. Knowing which variable is which is important for complying with mandates for establishing causality. Often, when we establish correlation but can't do the same for causality, it's because we don't know which variable is causing change in the other—we can't establish time order, for example, so we don't know which variable is the independent and which is the dependent.

Hypothesis a proposed relationship between two variables.

In high-school science class, you may have learned that a hypothesis is an educated guess. In social research, we use the term *hypothesis* to refer to a proposed relationship between two variables, usually with a stated direction. The *direction* of the relationship refers to whether your variables move in the same direction (positive) or in opposite directions (negative).

Let's take some examples. We know that income is positively related to education: As people's education increases, usually so too does their income. Overt prejudice, on the other hand, is negatively related to education: As people's educational levels increase, generally their levels of expressed prejudice decrease.

Hypothesis Testing

Are you starting to see how these pieces fit together in the design of a research project? Perhaps we have a special interest in one concept, say, poverty. Poverty is a broad concept, so we need to specify what we mean by poverty in this particular study. The process of assigning a precise method for measuring a term being examined for use in a particular study is called operationalization. When you read a study, it's important to understand how the author is operationalizing his or her concept. If I do a study on poverty among Americans who fall below the official poverty line, and someone else completes a study that examines poverty using the United Nations definition of it—namely, subsistence on less than $1.25 per day—we're discussing two very different concepts of poverty. As the old adage says, we're comparing apples and oranges. Once I decide how I'm defining poverty, I can begin to consider all the variables related to my

Operationalization the process of assigning a precise method for measuring a term being examined for use in a particular study.

concept. In the case of poverty, we might take a look at education, employment status, race, or gender.

It's time to make some decisions. First of all, is poverty my dependent or independent variable? Am I thinking about poverty as the cause of something else (poor health) or its result (lack of formal education)? Let's say I want to examine the factors that cause poverty, and I'm especially interested in the effect of parental education on children's poverty levels, because theory tells me that a link exists. Assuming that I've defined educational level (number of years in school? grades or degrees completed? scores on a certain test? prestige of any college attended?), now I'm ready to pose my research question: What effect do parents' educational levels have on children's chances of living in poverty as adults? And I can form a hypothesis:

> Hypothesis: The lower the educational level of the parents, the greater the chance that their children will be poor as adults.

Also for each hypothesis, an equal and opposite alternative hypothesis exists:

> Alternative hypothesis: There is a positive relationship between parental education and children's likelihood of living in poverty as adults.

Parental education is my key independent variable, but I also believe that race and family structure may affect how my independent variable matters. In this example, race and family structure would be moderating variables—that is, they affect the relationship between my independent and my dependent variables. (Children's education or test scores in this example would be mediating variables that are positioned between the independent and dependent variables but do not interact with either to affect the relationship between them.)

I am not quite ready to test my hypotheses, however. First, I need to tell stories—that is, causal stories about why I would expect the hypotheses to be true. In support of the hypotheses, I might say that parents who are more educated have acquired more confidence and skills for succeeding in our economy and that they are then more likely to pass on some of this knowledge and positive outlook to their kids at home. In support of my alternative hypothesis, parents who have spent a great deal of money on their own education may have less left over to help their children. Establishing the groundwork for a reasonably "fair fight" between main and alternative hypotheses is important so we do not spend time discovering trivialities that are already well known (e.g., low-income individuals tend to be poor). So how good were my guesses or hypotheses?

Validity, Reliability, and Generalizability

Validity, reliability, and generalizability are simple but important concepts. To say a measure has validity means that it measures what you intend it to. So if you step on a scale and it measures your height, it's not valid. Likewise, if

Validity the extent to which an instrument measures what it is intended to measure.

I ask you how happy you are with your life in general, and you tell me how happy you are with school in particular, at this exact moment my question isn't a valid measure of your life satisfaction. Reliability refers to how likely you are to obtain the same result using the same measure the next time. A scale that's off by ten pounds might not be totally valid—it will not give me my actual weight—but the scale is reliable if every time I step on it, it reads exactly ten pounds less than my true weight. Likewise, a clock that's five minutes fast is reliable but not valid. But if I ask you to rate your overall satisfaction with your life so far, and you honestly tell me you would give yourself a 10 out of 10, and then a week from now I ask you to rate your overall satisfaction with life so far, and you honestly tell me you'd give yourself a 7 out of 10 (because that first time you had just found $10 on the floor), then that measure (my question) is valid but not reliable. Ideally, we'd like our measures to be both valid and reliable, but sometimes we have to make trade-offs between the two. Keep this in mind as we discuss the various methods of data collection.

Reliability likelihood of obtaining consistent results using the same measure.

Finally, generalizability is the extent to which we can claim that our findings inform us about a group larger than the one we studied. Can we generalize our findings to a larger population? And how do we determine whether we can?

Generalizability the extent to which we can claim our findings inform us about a group larger than the one we studied.

Role of the Researcher

Experimenter Effects As if social research weren't hard enough already (because we don't have placebos and double-blind studies with which to work), there are also "white coat" effects—that is, the effects that researchers have on the very processes and relationships they are studying by virtue of being there. Often, subjects change their behavior, consciously or not, just because they are part of a study. Have you ever been in a classroom when the teacher is being observed? It might prove to be the best class the teacher has ever taught, even if she didn't mean to put on the charm for the observer.

Placebo a simulated treatment given to a control group in an experimental study to factor out the effect of merely being in an experiment from the effect of the actual treatment under consideration.

Double-blind study an experimental study where neither the subjects nor the researchers know who is in the treatment group and who is in the control (placebo) group.

When we do qualitative fieldwork (interviews, ethnography, or participant observation) we talk about reflexivity, which means analyzing and critically considering the white coat effects you may be inspiring with your research process. What is your relationship to your research subjects? Frequently, research focuses on groups that are disadvantaged relative to the researcher in one way or another. Researchers might have more money, more education, or more resources in general. How does that shape the interactions between researcher and subjects and, ultimately, the findings?

Reflexivity analyzing and critically considering our own role in, and effect on, our research.

Urban ethnographer Mitchell Duneier spent five years hanging out with booksellers on the sidewalks of Sixth Avenue in Manhattan. He wanted to understand how these street vendors and their groups of friends, many of them homeless, functioned in the community. During the course of his research, Duneier became friends with many of these people, which was apparent when

What is the white coat effect? Sociologist Mitch Duneier (center), who studied street-side book vendors for his book *Sidewalk*, talks with a police officer. To see an interview with Duneier, go to wwnorton.com/studyspace.

he and I talked about how he made sure he was not exploiting his subjects. Duneier's firm belief in the researcher's responsibility to his or her subjects is not always easy for him. He told me that "in the process of doing my research, before I publish my work, I make an effort to try to show the research that I'm going to publish to the people who are depicted in it. . . . Doing this is a very stressful process. Sometimes you have to read people things that are very unflattering to them. And for me, it has taken a lot of courage to sit in a room with someone, with a manuscript, and to read those things to them. Sometimes I can be shaking when I do it because I'm so afraid of the way people are going to respond. But I feel that if I am going to be writing something about people, and I'm going to be putting it out there for the public to read, whether it's with their name on it or not, then they deserve the basic respect of hearing it from me in advance." Even after the private reading and scrutiny of the work for its most important audience—the subject—Duneier notes that the researcher must show ongoing respect for subjects:

> One of the most basic things that one can do, is to try really hard, to make sure that people don't feel used by you, after you leave the field. It's very easy given the constraints of our lives and the academy, and the great pressures we are under within our own universities, running departments, engaging in

> teaching, supervising students in research, it's very possible that given those demands that when we leave the field site that we can walk away from our subjects' lives and not stay in touch with them. Not ever send them any acknowledgment of the time that they spent with us. Not ever send them the results of the research. Especially if we end up moving to other parts of the country from where they live, and it's hard to stay in touch with them. It's very easy for them to get the impression that we have just walked away, benefited at their expense. They have given us their emotions, we have appropriated their lives for our sociological purposes, and then have gone on with ours. (Conley, 2009a)

As researchers, we're supposed to remain objective, but even if you want to (and some people may not want to remain impartial in certain situations), it's not always possible. One day an incident occurred between the police and the street vendors, and Duneier was there (with his tape recorder running in his shirt pocket, unbeknownst to the police). He defended his friends to the officers. Because he was a white, well-spoken, and highly educated professional, his interactions with police probably differed significantly from those between the typical African American street vendor and the police—Duneier could speak his mind with a bit less fear of arrest and with the knowledge that he could afford a competent lawyer to defend himself. How did Duneier's presence change the interaction that transpired? Most social scientists would argue that once subjects become accustomed to the researcher's presence, they again behave as normal, but we don't have any real way to determine this. When we're engaged in qualitative research, we may find ourselves in situations where we have to choose whether objectivity and distance are more important than standing up for what we believe is right. At these times, we need to take a step back and think about our own role as both researcher and participant, because it is our perception and experience of events that eventually become the data from which we make our claims. Duneier acknowledges that ethnographers are not perfect observer-reporters whose presence has absolutely no effect on subjects' attitudes and behavior. The ethnographer, like any other scientist, has a responsibility to readers to make his or her data collection methods public. Furthermore, readers "have to have a sense for how the conclusions were drawn . . . by making the lens through which the reality is being refracted apparent. That means telling them something about who we are, not only our race, not only our class or our gender, but a number of other fundamental things."

Power: In the Eyes of the Researcher, We're Not All Equal

Along these lines, it is worth asking the following: What role does power play in research? As social researchers, we're not supposed to make value judgments; we should put aside our personal biases, strive for neutrality, and remain impartial and objective. The truth, however, is that we make judgments all the time, beginning at the most basic level of deciding what to study. What does the field in general deem worthy of scholarly attention? What topics am I sufficiently interested in to spend two, five, or ten years, or my entire career studying? What research do grant-making institutions regard as important enough to fund? What does the social scientific community more broadly view as problematic or interesting and in need of explanation?

Historically, sociology, like most sciences, has been male dominated. But it's also a discipline founded on the idea of making the natural seem unnatural, so it's a good place from which change can percolate. Following the feminist movement of the late 1960s, a growing stream of thought within sociology sought to turn a critical, feminist lens on the discipline itself. Because research ultimately forms the foundation of our work, methods became a key site of debate, and thus the concept of feminist methodology was born. What do feminist research methods look like? First, it's important to understand that there is no one feminist research method, just as there is no single school of feminism. Feminist researchers use the same techniques for gathering data as other sociologists, but they employ those techniques in ways that differ significantly from traditional methods. As Sandra Harding explains it, feminist researchers

Feminist methodology a set of systems or methods that treat women's experiences as legitimate empirical and theoretical resources, that promote social science *for* women (think public sociology, but for a specific half of the public), and that take into account the researcher as much as the overt subject matter.

> listen carefully to how women informants think about their lives and men's lives, and critically to how traditional social scientists conceptualize women's and men's lives. They observe behaviors of women and men that traditional social scientists have not thought significant. They seek examples of newly recognized patterns in historical data. (1987, p. 2)

The feminist part doesn't lie in the method per se, or necessarily in having women as subjects. Rather, Harding proposes three ways to make research distinctly feminist. First, treat women's experiences as legitimate empirical and theoretical resources. Second, engage in social science that may bring about policy changes to help improve women's lives. Third, take into account the researcher as much as the overt subject matter. When we enter a research situation, an imbalance of power usually exists between the researcher and the research subjects, and we need to take this power dimension seriously. The point of adopting feminist methods isn't to exclude men or male perspectives: It's not *instead of*; it's *in addition to.* It means taking all subjects seriously rather than privileging one type of data, experience, or worldview over another.

Creating and Testing Theory

Good research is usually guided by theory, but there are different types of theories. Which theory best fits your subject? In Chapter 1, I described the differences between positivist and interpretive sociology. As distinct as they are in

SAMPLES: THEY'RE NOT JUST THE FREE TASTES AT THE SUPERMARKET

People use the word sample in many different ways, but in social research it has a very specific and important meaning. You are always studying a population. That population could be the entire U.S. population, gay fathers, public schools in the rural South, science textbooks, gangs, Fortune 500 companies, or middle-class, Caucasian single mothers. Most of the time it's too time consuming and expensive to collect information about the entire population you want to study, so instead you focus on a sample. Your sample then is the subset of the population from which you are actually collecting data. (If you do collect information on the entire population, it's called a census.)

Population an entire group of individual persons, objects, or items from which samples may be drawn.

How you go about collecting your sample is probably one of the most important steps of your research. Let's say I want to study attitudes toward underage drinking in the United States and hand out a survey to your sociology class. Based on the findings of that survey, I make claims on how the entire U.S. population feels about underage drinking: They're in favor of it. Would you believe my claims? I hope not! Your sociology class is probably not representative of the U.S. population as a whole. Age would be the most important factor, but differences in socioeconomic status, education, race, and the like would exist. In other

Sample the subset of the population from which you are actually collecting data.

Volunteer Phyllis Evans (center) questions a homeless man about his living situation and encourages him to seek help while conducting a survey with team members in New York City.

words, the results I would obtain from a survey of a college sociology class would not be generalizable to the U.S. population and probably not even to college students as a whole—maybe not even to students at your school (the students next door in organic chemistry might have very different thoughts about underage drinking). I would be "speaking beyond my data."

Census taker talking with Charles F. Piper as he works on his car.

Although the issues of generalizability are always at play, they become particularly acute when social scientists use case studies. A case study, often used in qualitative research, is an in-depth look at a specific phenomenon in a particular social setting. If we wanted to understand the interaction among parents, teachers, and administrators in the American public school system, we might do a case study of your high school. How representative of all U.S. high schools do you think your school is? Does your town have a higher or lower average household income than the United States as a whole? Is the PTA particularly vocal? Is yours a regional high school whose students travel long distances to attend? All these factors—these variables—are important, and if your town isn't typical (statistically speaking), we'd question the usefulness of the findings. This is perhaps the main drawback of the case study method. The findings have very low generalizability. One benefit, however, is that we typically obtain very detailed information. So there is often a trade-off between breadth (i.e., generalizability) and depth (i.e., amount of information and nuanced detail). A case study can serve as a useful starting point for exploring new topics. For example, researchers often use case studies to develop hypotheses, and generate and refine survey questions that the researchers will then administer to a much larger sample. Likewise, qualitative case studies are sometimes used to try to understand causal mechanisms that have been indicated in large-scale survey studies.

Case study an intensive investigation of one particular unit of analysis in order to describe it or uncover its mechanisms.

Feminist sociologist France Winddance Twine (right) interviews Sharon Elizabeth Dawkins for an ethnography on interracial intimacy.

their focus, they also lend themselves to different methodological approaches to research. Because positivists are concerned with the factors that influence social life, they tend to rely more heavily on quantitative measures. If, however, you're more concerned with the meanings actors attach to their behavior, as interpretive sociologists are, then you'll likely be drawn to more qualitative measures.

Ultimately, the distinction between quantitative and qualitative methods is a false dichotomy: The most important thing is to determine what you want to learn and then contemplate the best possible way to collect the empirical data that would answer your question—that is, deploy whatever tool or set of tools is called for by the present research problem. That's why getting the research question right is so important to the entire endeavor. Once the question is precisely operationalized, the method to answer the question should be obvious. If the question still could be approached in several ways, then you probably haven't refined it enough. Figure 2.3 gives an overview of the entire process.

Data Collection

Remember that social science research is largely about collecting empirical evidence to generate or test empirical claims. So how do we go about collecting the evidence needed to support our claims? Let's use case studies—that is, particular examples of good research—and see what these researchers wanted to know, how they obtained their data, and what they found.

Figure 2.3: The Research Process

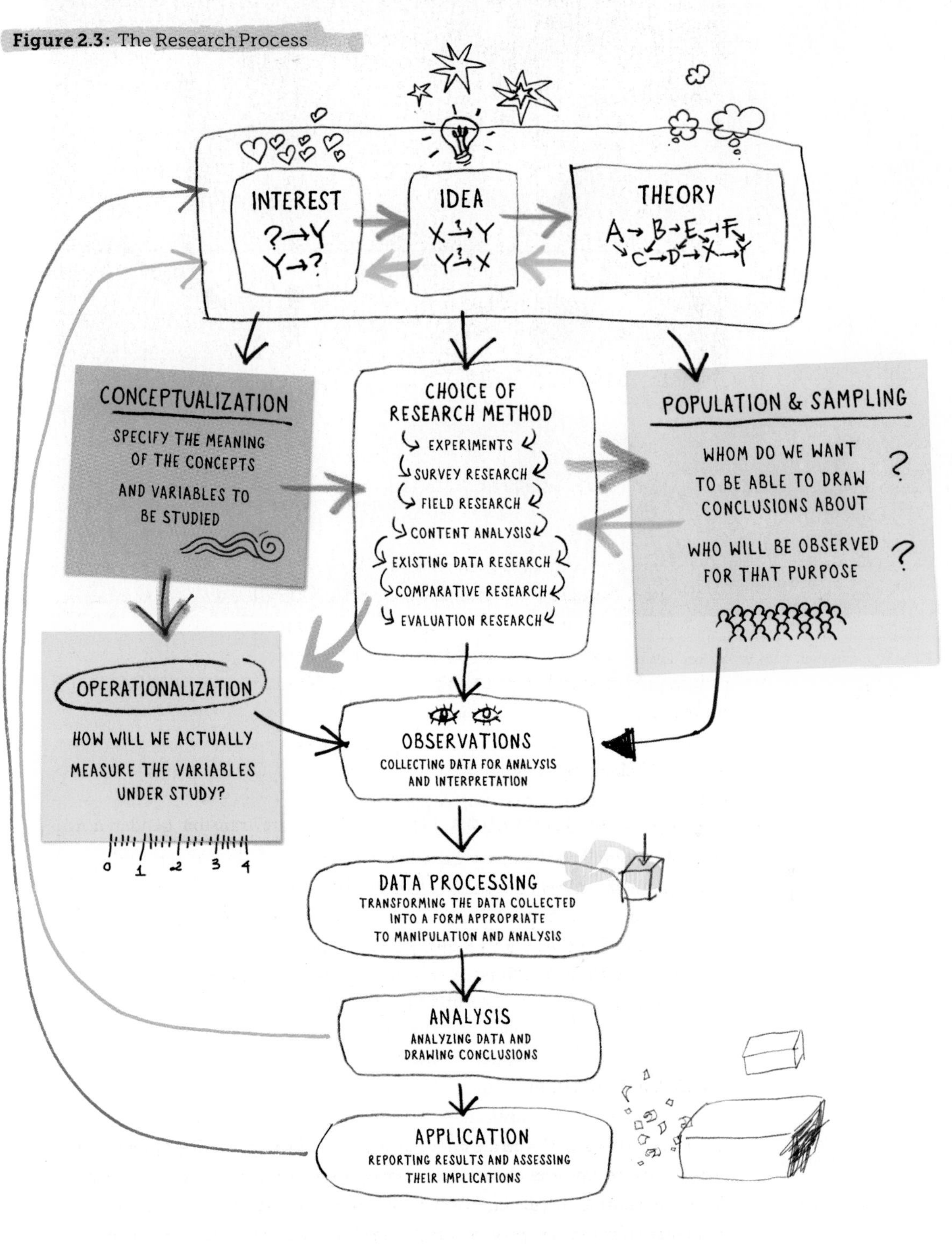

Source: Babbie, 2007.

Three young women study in San Jose Juvenile Hall in California. How did data from Lynne Haney's participant observation challenge conventional wisdom about the experience of young women in the juvenile justice system?

Participant Observation How does the state transmit gender norms in its attempts to reform deviant girls? This is one of the key questions guiding the analysis that sociologist Lynne Haney presents in an article titled "Homeboys, Babies, Men in Suits: The State and the Reproduction of Male Dominance" (1996). Taking a highly theoretical approach, Haney wanted to test feminist theories of the state (i.e., the government). Macro-level theories generally treat the state as a uniform structure that operates in the same way in all places on all people all of the time, but Haney had a hunch that these theories were too simplistic. People aren't just passive subjects acted on by a greater entity called the state.

To test these assumptions, Haney examined the state at the institutional level in a 10-month study using a technique called participant observation, which aims to uncover the meanings people give to their behavior by observing their actions in practice. What this usually entails is "hanging out" and documenting people's practices in a given society. Some participant observation focuses more heavily on the participating, and some concentrates on the

Participant observation a qualitative research method that seeks to uncover the meanings people give their behavior by observing social actions in practice.

observing, depending on the interests of the researcher and the appropriateness of actually "participating" in the given setting. The contexts in which the observations occur form the *sites* for ethnographic researchers. Haney chose as her sites a probation center and a group home for incarcerated teen mothers. These sites allowed her to compare different institutional settings within the juvenile justice system. In both sites, she began her research by interviewing key officials. She then worked as an assistant to a parole officer in one site and as a tutor in the other. She attended meetings between clients and staff, spent time with the girls, and accompanied them on shopping trips.

By engaging in all these activities at her sites, Haney was able to establish relationships with both the girls and the staff. This gave her access to a wide variety of information. Prevailing theories argued that the state (the government) imposed a monolithic, patriarchal agenda on women. But that's not what Haney found. She discovered conflicts and contradictions between the specific institutions she studied and the larger justice bureau (an arm of the state), among the staff, and between state workers and clients. The staff wanted to empower the girls, make them less dependent on public (through welfare and the state) and private (through their boyfriends) patriarchy. The girls, however, often used these very factors to defy their parole officers and case workers. For example, when the officer would forcibly separate (through assignment into juvenile detention) the girls from their "homeboys," in hopes of breaking their dependence, the girls would often bring the men in question to the next meeting. By doing her research where the action was, Haney complicated the preexisting feminist theory of the state and suggested a more complex and nuanced way of viewing it.

Interviews Interviews are another form of gathering qualitative data. For *Money, Morals, and Manners*, sociologist Michèle Lamont interviewed upper-middle-class men in France and the United States about their tastes. She chose the men in her sample based on their social status—they were employed as managers, professionals, and entrepreneurs—arguing that these people hold enormous power in their jobs and communities, and consequently their tastes are influential in shaping the culture around them. Lamont conducted more than 160 interviews, trying to determine how the people in her sample defined what it means to be a "worthy person" and analyzing "the relative importance attached to religion, honesty, low moral standards, cosmopolitanism, high culture, money, [and] power" (Lamont, 1992). The comparative aspect of her research design allowed her to identify some of the cultural differences between American and French tastes. For example, she ascertained that the French men valued art more than their American counterparts, whereas the Americans cared more about money than their French counterparts.

By using unstructured, open-ended interviews, Lamont allowed the subjects to go off on tangents, to vent, to share intimacies that might not appear at first glance to be related to the study. But she also did probe—that is, she pushed subjects past their initial, comfortable answers on somewhat delicate, controversial issues. Knowing how and when to probe and when to back off is part of the art of interviewing that results from practice. Other researchers may rely on semistructured or structured interviews—that is, interviews in which the researchers have more than just a set of topics to cover in no preset order; rather, the researchers develop a specific set of questions to address with all respondents in a relatively fixed sequence. If an interview becomes very structured, it falls into the next category: survey research.

Survey Research Chances are you've filled out a survey at some point. One customarily receives them from the manufacturers and retailers of electronics and from restaurants and hotels. Surveys are an ordered series of questions intended to elicit information from respondents, and they can be powerful methods of data collection. Surveys may be done anonymously and distributed widely, so you reach a much larger sample than if you relied solely on interviews. At the same time, however, you have to pay attention to your response rate. Out of all the surveys you distributed, how many were actually completed and returned to you? Lately, we have been bombarded with more and more surveys soliciting our opinions about everything from what soap we prefer to how to stop global warming. It has become increasingly difficult for researchers to get their surveys answered amid the din of the information society, and response rates, in general, continue to fall.

Survey an ordered series of questions intended to elicit information from respondents.

Why does this matter? If who answered your survey or tore it up was merely random, then the only concern would be the cost in time and money to obtain, say, 200 completed surveys. But, as it turns out, who responds and who doesn't is not random. As a researcher, you need to consider the ways that selection bias can enter your sample. Are the people who completed the survey different in some significant way from the people who didn't complete it? If your survey is about the sacrifices respondents would be willing to make to slow global warming and the only folks who bother to respond are environmentalists, your results will likely indicate that the population is willing to sacrifice far more than it actually would. In fact, the nonrespondents were not even willing to sacrifice the ten minutes to take the survey. Surveys can also be done in person or over the phone. This method of survey design differs from interviews in that a set questionnaire exists. Surveys are generally converted into quantitative data for statistical analysis—everything from simple estimates (How many gay policemen are there in America?) to comparisons of averages across groups (What proportion of gay policemen support abortion rights, and what proportion of retired female plumbers do?) to complex techniques such as multiple regression, where one measured factor (such as education level) is held constant, or statistically removed from the picture, to pin down the effect of another factor (such as total family income) on, say, reported levels of happiness.

The General Social Survey (GSS) run by the National Opinion Research Center of the University of Chicago is one of the premier surveys in the United States. Since 1972, the GSS has asked respondents a battery of questions about their social and demographic characteristics and their opinions on a wide range of subjects. Conducted every other year, the GSS includes some new questions, but many are the same from one survey to the next. This has allowed researchers to track American attitudes about a range of important issues, from race relations to abortion politics to beliefs about sexual orientation, and to see how the beliefs of different demographic subgroups have converged or diverged over four decades. The GSS is an example of a repeated cross-sectional survey. That is, it samples a new group of approximately 2,000 Americans in each yearly survey wave. Each sample should represent a cross-section of the U.S. population of that particular survey year.

A cross-sectional study stands in contrast to a panel survey, also known as a longitudinal study, which tracks the same individuals, households, or other social units over time. One such survey, the Panel Study of Income Dynamics (PSID) run by the Institute for Social Research at the University of Michigan, has followed 5,000 American families each year since 1968. (Recently, the PSID had to trim back to every other year because of budget cutbacks.) It even tracks family members who have split off and formed their own households and families. In this way, the survey has taken on the structure of a family tree. The PSID has contributed to important research on questions about how families transition in and out of poverty, what predicts if marriages will last, and how much economic mobility exists in the United States across generations—just to name a few of the topics that PSID analysis has illuminated.

Historical Methods How do we study the past? We can't interview or survey dead people, and we certainly can't observe institutions or social settings that no longer exist. What researchers employing historical methods do is collect data from written reports, newspaper articles, journals, transcripts, television programs, diaries, artwork, and other artifacts that date to the period they want to study. Researchers often study social movements using historical methods, because the full import of the movement may not be apparent until after it has ended.

Historical methods research that collects data from written reports, newspaper articles, journals, transcripts, television programs, diaries, artwork, and other artifacts that date to a prior time period under study.

How did America end up with a relatively weak welfare state and a high tolerance for inequality, particularly in the context of race, compared with other industrialized democracies? To answer that question, sociologist Jill Quadagno went back to the archives to research what had been said officially (in regulations and other government documents) and unofficially (in the press) about the passage and implementation of the New Deal in the 1930s and the War on Poverty in the 1960s (Quadagno, 1996).

Quadagno took into account many different explanations: timing (the United States industrialized early, before the adequate development of protective political institutions), institutions (the United States has one of the most fragmented political systems in the developed world, making it comparatively difficult to marshal large-scale government programs), and "American exceptionalism" (the notion that our culture, lacking a history of feudalism, was uniquely individualistic and nonpaternalistic).

Children of a plantation sharecropper preparing food on a wood stove in a sparsely furnished shack in 1936. How did Jill Quadagno use historical methods to analyze the ways that people like these children were excluded from the benefits of the New Deal?

Finally, the issue on which Quadagno focused her research was the looming shadow of racism in America. According to Quadagno, in order to prevent blacks from participating fully in the American social contract, authority devolved from the federal government to state and local authorities, which could then exclude blacks overtly or covertly. The result was a much weaker safety net and one that, for a long time, excluded minorities disproportionately. For example, to ensure that congressional committees controlled by racist southern Democrats passed Social Security, President Franklin D. Roosevelt had to agree to exclude agricultural and domestic workers when the system was established in 1935. This exception was made purposely to exclude African Americans, who were disproportionately employed in these two sectors. Thus, by conducting historical, archival research, Quadagno and others have been able to show the relevance of race in explaining the particularities of the social safety net in the United States.

Comparative Research Whereas the example above focuses on one case, sometimes sociologists compare two or more historical societies; we call this "comparative historical" research. For example, Roger Brubaker compared the conceptions of citizenship and nationhood in France and Germany (Brubaker, 1992). Comparative research is a methodology by which a researcher compares two or more entities (usually countries or cultures) with the intent of learning more about the factors that differ between them. By examining official documents and important texts over a period of many years leading up to, during, and after the formation of the German state and the French state, Brubaker showed that fundamentally different historical circumstances led to very different visions of citizenship in each nation.

Comparative research a methodology by which two or more entities (such as countries), which are similar in many dimensions but differ on one in question, are compared to learn about the dimension that differs between them.

France was formed from a loosely knit group of powerful duchies and principalities. There was no preexisting French nation or nationality before the creation of the French government. The idea of nationhood—that is, of French identity—had to be forged by the state itself, and this led to a very inclusive notion of citizenship. Germany, by contrast, grew out of an already well-refined, tribal sense of Prussian nationality. Thus, Germany's citizenship policy was based on excluding others rather than including them. In the early 1990s, when Brubaker was writing, the results of these different historical starting points could be seen in the two countries' immigration policies. In France, birth in French territory was sufficient for a claim on citizenship. But in Germany, it was difficult to become a citizen unless you were born to a German citizen—a catch-22 for multiple generations of guest workers who had known no other homeland but failed to become German. In recent years, these policies have converged significantly because of European integration, falling more toward the French model.

Greek miners seeking work in the German Ruhr Basin in 1960 after West Germany began a guest worker program. What did Roger Brubaker's comparative research about European immigration policies reveal about definitions of citizenship?

The general approach to comparative research is to find cases that match on many potentially relevant dimensions but vary on just one, allowing researchers to observe the effect of that particular dimension. Although all social science research makes inferences based on implicit or explicit comparison, comparative research usually refers to cross-national studies. For example, if you wanted to determine the effect of polygamy on gender relations, it would be a good idea to compare provinces of Mali, West Africa, that have different rates of polygamy and monogamy but similar cultures. It would be a bad idea to compare Mali with Massachusetts, because other than names that start with the same first two letters, these settings have little in common. Likewise, in studying the effects of universal health care, it would be better to compare the United States (which has not had such a health-care system in its recent history [though it should kick in over the next few years]) with Canada (which does) than to compare South Africa (which doesn't) with Sweden (which does), because the latter two countries are so different from each other geographically and culturally.

Experimentation Because social scientists deal with people, the controlled environment of a laboratory-based experiment is not always an option. For example, I dream of randomly assigning the students in one of my classes to married or single life in order to examine marital status on some dimension. Assuming seating is random, I'd just draw a line straight down the middle of the lecture hall; all the students on one side would have to marry, while those on the other side would have to remain single. Think of the possibilities! For better or worse, however, I'm not allowed to perform such experiments.

Experimental methods methods that seek to alter the social landscape in a very specific way for a given sample of individuals and then track what results that change yields; often involve comparisons to a control group that did not experience such an intervention.

Some sociologists do use experimental methods, however. For instance, sociologist Duncan Watts conducted an experiment to find out the extent to which taste in cultural products like music and movies is determined by what

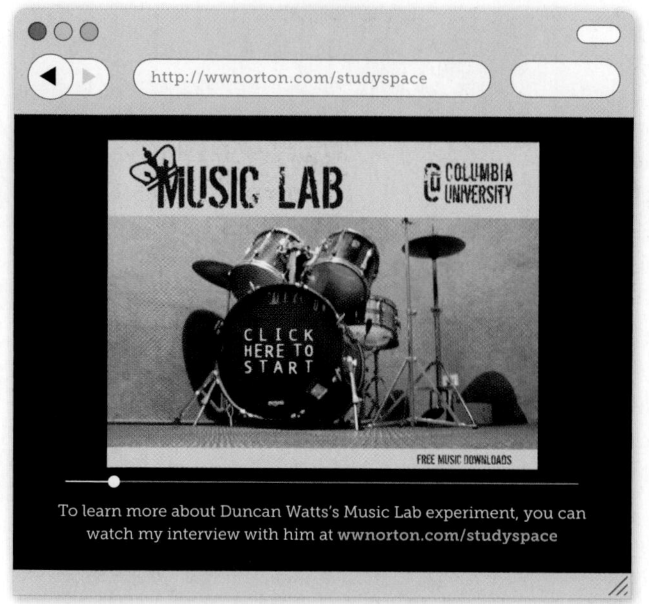

To learn more about Duncan Watts's Music Lab experiment, you can watch my interview with him at wwnorton.com/studyspace

other people think. Watts speculated that "when we look at cultural markets it's very clear that the successful ones are many times more successful than average, so you see things like Harry Potter books have sold probably about 400 million copies around the world. . . . What was puzzling to us about this fact, is that nobody seems to be able to predict which movies, books, albums, etc., are going to be these massive hits" (Conley, 2009b). Watts hypothesized that it was not just the innate cultural quality of a product but the luck of catching on via peer-to-peer influence that determined success in film, music, or publishing. Along with his co-researchers Matthew Salganik and Peter Dodds (2006), Watts tested his hypothesis by creating an online site called Music Lab where they posted mp3s from unknown bands. Visitors to the site could download songs and rate how much they liked the music. Some of the 14,341 downloaders saw how many times these previously unheard-of songs from unknown bands had been downloaded by the previous downloaders; some were unable to see download traffic; and still others could see the song rankings but they had been altered, unbeknownst to the subjects. What the researchers found was that the best songs in one condition rarely did poorly in another condition and the worst rarely did well but that the songs in the middle could be heavily influenced by how they were rated (if, that is, others could see those ratings). I asked Duncan Watts if his Music Lab experiment could explain other social phenomena. He explained that we can see the same kinds of social influence in the recent housing bubble and recession. According to Watts, "if you look at the recent financial crisis many things went wrong, right? But, the big things that went wrong on the way up, were this belief that housing prices could not go down and on the way down, a real collapse of our trust in the financial system. Both of them are driven by people thinking whatever they think because of what other people think. These are not fundamentally financial phenomena or economic phenomena even, they're really social phenomena" (Conley, 2009b).

Content Analysis You may have heard the common criticism that the media depict only exceptionally thin female bodies (and furthermore that the pervasiveness of such images is harmful to women and girls in our society).

What empirical evidence would we need to test the claim that the media have a bias toward thinness in women? We might start by choosing one type of media—movies, advertisements, or magazines—and counting the images of skinny women. This would be a type of content analysis, a systematic analysis of the content rather than the structure of a communication, such as a written work, speech, or film.

Content analysis a systematic analysis of the content rather than the structure of a communication, such as a written work, speech, or film.

Race scholar Ann Morning (2004) used content analysis to investigate depictions and discussions of race in American textbooks across academic disciplines and over time. Morning analyzed both manifest and latent content on race in 92 high-school textbooks in the fields of biology, anthropology, psychology, sociology, world culture, and world geography. *Manifest content* refers to what we can observe; Morning's study included overt discussions and definitions of race and images of different races. *Latent content* refers to what is implied but not stated outright, so Morning looked for sections of the texts where race was directly implied, even if the word *race* wasn't used. She chose her sample from all high-school textbooks published in the United States between 1952 and 2002.

Ultimately, Morning's analysis disputed earlier findings that biology textbooks no longer discuss race. Her findings showed that only social sciences texts employed constructivist approaches (i.e., the belief that race is a social construct), whereas biology books reinforced essentialist conceptualizations (i.e., the belief that race is innate and genetic). However, contrary to her original hypotheses, social sciences textbooks also used biological components in their definitions of race, and only the fields of anthropology and sociology critiqued the traditional concept of race. Why does all this matter? As Morning points out, if textbooks aren't changing, how are students supposed to learn new concepts or viewpoints? Anthropology and sociology aren't widely taught at the high-school level, whereas biology is mandatory in most public school systems. In fact, Morning's content analysis suggests that high-school students are likely to know more about the supposed links between some genetic diseases and certain races than they are about changing definitions of race over time.

Ethics of Social Research

At the beginning of this chapter, I mentioned the contributions feminists made to research methods with their emphasis on examining relationships between power and the process of knowledge generation. Today, we have more codified standards that must be met by all researchers. Many professional associations have their own ethical standards—doctors, lawyers, journalists, psychologists, and sociologists, just to name a few. Colleges and universities, too, often have guidelines for research conducted with humans (as well as animals, particularly vertebrates). As a professional sociologist, I am beholden to the ethical guidelines established by my peers and the American Sociological Association. As a professor, I am also responsible to my home institution. And as a researcher, I am ultimately responsible to my research subjects. I work with already-collected statistical information (or secondary data) for the most part, which makes the process a little easier, but that doesn't mean I don't have to pay careful attention to the ethical standards of my discipline.

A few golden rules exist in research. The first is "Do no harm." This may seem obvious; you don't want to cause physical harm to your subjects. But what about psychological or emotional harm? What if you want to interview men and women on their attitudes toward abortion, and a respondent becomes very upset because he or she cares deeply about the subject? The initial charge not to do harm seems a little more complicated now. Often, we tell research subjects that by participating in the study, they will encounter no more harm than they are likely to experience in everyday life.

The second rule is informed consent. Subjects have a right to know they are participating in a study and what that study will consist of. If you're interviewing people or asking them to complete a survey, this makes sense. But how far do you take the rule of informed consent in participant observation? Generally, you have to obtain permission to be at your chosen site, but do you remind every person you bump into that you're doing research? What's more, sometimes even mild forms of deception are necessary for the sake of research. You just need to periodically recall the first rule—if you're deceiving people, it had better be absolutely necessary, and you had better make sure they're safe.

The third rule is voluntary participation, which usually goes hand in hand with informed consent. People have a right to decide if they want to participate in your study. They can also stop participating at any point with no penalty. If you're interviewing someone who doesn't want to answer a question, he or she doesn't have to; if the interviewee becomes upset and wants to stop, that's his or her prerogative. There are also certain protected populations—minors, prisoners and other institutionalized individuals, pregnant women and their unborn fetuses, people with disabilities—whom you often need additional approval to study. As Lynne Haney's research shows, it's not impossible to study these populations. Haney, in fact, had a trifecta: Her subjects were underage, incarcerated, and pregnant. Such research just requires additional effort and caution.

Find out if your college or university has an institutional review board and what the requirements are to gain approval for a research project before you start your budding career as a sociologist. And then, never forget, question everything, and make the familiar strange. Good luck!

Social Science and Public Policy—Do the Twain Ever Meet?

Much debate has occurred throughout the history of sociology over the relationship between social science and public policy. The term public sociology is used to describe social research whose aims include sharing its findings with a wider audience in order to influence society instead of just studying it. Knowledge that stays locked up in books, journals, and libraries and that is read and understood only by those creating it, the argument goes, does little good for the general public.

Public sociology the practice of sociological research, teaching, and service that seeks to engage a wide audience for a normative, productive end.

The Role of the Public Intellectual

What good is all this research if no one pays any attention to it? Much of sociology does involve preaching to the choir. We write journal articles, which have to follow a very specific format. Few sociologists may read them because we focus on and speak to our own subfields. Some sociologists assert that the lack of attention from the media may be a good thing. We're not pressured by outside forces to pursue certain research agendas and forsake others, and we're not sanctioned when our findings don't support a specific political platform. Sociologist William Julius Wilson finds some merit in this argument but ultimately regards it as short-sighted:

> The more sociology is ignored by the media and policy makers, the less attention it receives as an academic discipline and therefore the more removed it is from the decision-making arena, the fewer students it attracts, and the more difficulty it has in trying to obtain funding from private foundations and government agencies. (Wilson, 1998, p. 436)

Wilson's own work focuses on the black underclass and on racial and class issues surrounding unemployment and economic depression. Because these are pressing national issues (even if they're not often acknowledged as such), Wilson has made a conscious effort to get his work out into public debate, to prompt the media and politicians to take notice of what his research finds.

The call for researchers to contribute their research to debates in the public arena has gone out, and Judith Stacey, like many, has answered. She hasn't

Judith Stacey at a gay rights rally in Colorado. How is her research an example of public sociology?

always liked the conversation, however. Much of her work focuses on gay families and their children—a hot-button topic in the United States at the moment and for the foreseeable future. Stacey has appeared on television talk shows and radio programs, and has even testified in court cases about the well-being of children with same-sex parents (Stacey & Biblarz, 2001). Wanting to do some good with her research, Stacey was dismayed when her findings were twisted, taken out of context, and ultimately used to support the very agenda she was seeking to dispel. Likewise, researchers Peter Bearman and Hannah Brückner discovered that teenagers who took a "virginity pledge" did on average delay their first sexual intercourse (Bearman & Brückner, 2001; Brückner & Bearman, 2005). However, they also found that "pledgers" were more likely to have unprotected, risky sex when that first encounter finally occurred. Bearman and Brückner may have been surprised to find that their research was cited on a presidential campaign Web site in 2000 as evidence supporting the efficacy of "abstinence-only" sexual education. Only the first half of their findings was reported: that the pledge delayed sexual activity. The politico chose to ignore the other half of the story—namely, that the pledge likely was broken in an unplanned moment of passion, which, in turn, led to greater risk of unwed pregnancy and STDs.

Stories like these don't mean that we shouldn't attempt to reach a broader audience with our research or be policy oriented, but we have to remember that ultimately we can't control how people interpret our research. We can just make our best effort in terms of research design, data collection, and the actual explanation of our findings. And then we cross our fingers.

→ CONCLUSION

Sociology is a field that deploys a variety of methodologies from survey research to participant observation to historical approaches. Therefore, we sociologists often feel that we have to defend our very identity as scientists. Indeed, even some sociologists would argue that sociology is not a science. I would assert, however, that sociology is among the most difficult sciences of all. Sociology is a science in which you can't complete controlled experiments—the treatment and control group staple of most bench science. Perhaps zoology and paleontology are other examples of fields in which the scientist is called on to piece together observational data without the ability to run experiments. Nonetheless, sociologists also must face the task of imputing causal processes, not just describing or classifying the world.

How does one assess causality with only observational data to go by, especially when there are multiple factors to analyze, factors that may all interact with one another? And add to that this complication: Reality changes as you study it and by virtue of the fact that you study it. Our basic units of analysis, such as the family, and our conceptual frameworks, such as race and class, are always shifting as we study them. On top of that, the fact remains that many of the topics we study—gender and sexuality, race and class, family life, politics, and so on—are, by design, the most politically charged and most personally sensitive topics in our society. That doesn't make research easy. So what we sociologists are trying to do in this difficult field is to inch our way toward causality.

ASSIGNMENT

Create a research design to collect empirical data to either support or disprove one of the following claims: People on welfare are lazy and don't want to work; women are worse drivers than men; or blacks are naturally more athletic.

Remember to think about the different variables involved, whether you're aiming to establish correlation or causality, and what method of data collection is best suited for your research question.

QUESTIONS FOR REVIEW

1. What is the difference between causality and correlation? Use the example from the beginning of the chapter, on the link between health and income, to illustrate this difference.
2. Describe one of the studies discussed in this chapter, its methodology (e.g., interviews), and general findings. Then imagine how an additional study using a different methodology (e.g., comparative research) might build on these findings and generate new questions.
3. A sociologist observes the work-seeking habits of welfare recipients. After weeks of observation, trends emerge and the researcher forms a theory about the behaviors of this group. Is the sociologist in this example using a deductive or inductive approach? How would the sociologist study this phenomenon using the other approach?
4. Participant observation research is often long, painstaking, and personally demanding for the sociologist. Why bother with this data collection method? Use the example of Lynne Haney's research to support your answer.
5. Surveys are complicated to design and costly to administer, and potentially suffer from response bias with respect to who answers them. Why use this data collection method? Draw on the case of the General Social Survey to support your answer.
6. Why do sociologists have to run their projects by institutional review boards? What are the "golden rules" sociologists should keep in mind when conducting research?

PARADOX

IF WE SUCCESSFULLY ANSWER ONE QUESTION, IT ONLY SPAWNS OTHERS. THERE IS NO MOMENT WHEN A SOCIAL SCIENTIST'S WORK IS DONE.

WATCH THE ANIMATED SHORT ABOUT THE METHODS PARADOX AT

WWNORTON.COM/STUDYSPACE

How does culture simultaneously reflect and create our world? Protests by Israeli religious leaders resulted in a more modest version of actor Sarah Jessica Parker's dress for this Tel Aviv billboard.

3 Culture and Media

PARADOX

DO MASS MEDIA CREATE SOCIAL NORMS OR MERELY REFLECT THEM? CULTURE IS LIKE TWO MIRRORS FACING EACH OTHER: IT SIMULTANEOUSLY REFLECTS AND CREATES THE WORLD WE LIVE IN.

Jill Peterson and Kevin Heinz were married on June 20, 2009 at Christ Lutheran Church in St. Paul, Minnesota. The event was filmed, and their processional—a rocking dance number in which all the attendants, the groom, and the satin-clothed bride shook their stuff down the aisle to hip-hop artist Chris Brown's "Forever"—was posted to YouTube (TheKheinz, 2009). The video received 12 million hits in ten days, making it the most viewed and most discussed. The total views six months later were at 31 million and still climbing. The entire wedding party was invited to be on the *Today* show on NBC, where they once again performed their routine to Chris Brown's song. Their popularity was covered in the *New York Times*, the *Washington Post*, and the *Wall Street Journal*, and the television show *The Office* scripted the wedding of its two main characters—Pam and Jim—to copy Jill and Kevin's wedding processional right down to the song (Daniels & Kaling, 2009).

Chris Brown's song moved up all the way to number four on iTunes and number three on Amazon.com's best-selling mp3 list. This spike in popularity is nearly unheard of for a song that has been available for seven months. YouTube's owner, Google, admitted that the wedding clip made YouTube profitable for the month of July but declined to reveal just how much they had made from Jill and Kevin's wedding (Taylor, 2009).

Criticism came from all sides. Some YouTube commenters griped that Jill and Kevin shouldn't have chosen a song by a man convicted of domestic abuse to celebrate their wedding. Jill and Kevin couldn't change their song at that point, but they did use their newfound celebrity to raise money for the Sheila Wellstone Institute, an advocacy group fighting family violence (Walsh,

Jill and Kevin head down the aisle to Chris Brown's "Forever."

2009). Other critics suggested that Jill and Kevin might have been paid by the Wrigley Company, which had commissioned the music to Chris Brown's song for a Doublemint gum advertisement. He reused the music and wrote new lyrics to make "Forever" while he was still in the same studio session paid for by Wrigley (Van Buskirk, 2009).

When it comes to questions about the relationship between culture and media, determining which comes first is like untangling a kite line that's been unspooled and left in the garage for a season or two. Is the relationship between media consumption and human behavior like "Monkey see, monkey do"? I see a happy wedding and want to go out and have one of my own because my reality is just like TV? Was *The Office* spoof of Jill and Kevin's wedding funny mostly because they did exactly that—directly copied what they had seen on YouTube? Is it more realistic to see the relationship between culture and media as a continuous process of reframing, much the way Jill and Kevin disregarded the gum-shilling, domestic abuse–tainted, "just for one night" lyrics of "Forever" to reshape the song as their own anthem of newly wedded bliss? Though Jill and Kevin's wedding dance is evidence that media consumers participate in a remix culture, made possible in part by tools like YouTube and blogging software, it was Google that probably made the biggest profit from their video. Further, while many have argued that with the Internet and free tools for making media public, everyone can shape the media discourse, traditional media are now owned by six huge companies that produce the majority of books, newspapers, radio and television programs, and movies that make up the media stream.

In this chapter we first take a look at culture to explain what this sometimes slippery term has meant for social scientists. Then we look at how culture and the media intersect to shape values, beliefs, and practices in contemporary America.

Definitions of Culture

Culture is a rather vague term that we use to describe and often rationalize a lot. We talk about a culture of poverty in the United States (see Chapter 10). We hear about corporate cultures and subcultures, culture wars, the clash of cultures, culture shock, and even cultural conflicts on a global scale. Culture is casually used as shorthand for many things, ranging in meaning from innate biological tendencies to social institutions—and everything in between.

Culture = Human – Nature

We might say that culture is the sum of the social categories and concepts we recognize in addition to our beliefs, behaviors (except the instinctual ones), and practices. In other words, culture is everything but nature.

Culture a set of beliefs, traditions, and practices; the sum total of social categories and concepts we embrace in addition to beliefs, behaviors (except instinctual ones), and practices; that which is not the natural environment around us.

The last sentence captures exactly how culture has been defined through the ages—in opposition to nature. The word *culture* derives from the Latin verb *colere* ("to cultivate or till"), suggesting the refinement of crops to meet human needs. (We still use *culture* as a verb in a similar sense, as when we culture bacteria in a petri dish.) The more common meaning of *culture* as a noun developed from the same kind of human control and domination over nature. We could say that culture began when humans started acting as the architects of nature by growing crops rather than hunting and gathering, hence the terms *agriculture* and *aquaculture* (growing fish and other aquatic organisms for human consumption). Dating back centuries, the term *culture* has referred to the distinction between what is natural, what comes directly from the earth and follows the laws of physics, and what is modified or created by humans and follows (or breaks) the laws of the state. That said, culture is both the technology by which humans have come to dominate nature and the belief systems, ideologies, and symbolic representations that constitute human existence.

In the fifteenth century, when European nations organized expeditions to extend commerce and establish colonies in North America, Africa, and Asia, Western peoples confronted non-Western natives. The beliefs and behaviors of these peoples served as a foil to European culture. Today, we recognize that culture is always relative. We cannot talk about culture without reference to the global world, but the definitions, practices, and concepts that we use in this chapter largely emanate from a Western viewpoint. It may also be easier to identify cultural elements when they are different from our own. The challenge in this chapter will be to take what we see as natural and view it as a product of culture. We'll also explore the media and the role they play in the birth and dissemination of culture.

Culture = (Superior) Man – (Inferior) Man

As colonialism led to increased interaction with non-Westerners, Europeans came to recognize that much of what they took for granted as natural was not. Alternative ways of living existed, as manifested in a variety of living arrangements and marital rules, different styles of dress (or lack thereof), other ways of

A sixteenth-century Aztec's drawing of the conquistador Hernán Cortés. Why did Western definitions of culture change during the age of exploration?

building cities, and other kinds of foodstuffs. Take, for example, the fact that American architecture of the nineteenth and twentieth centuries tended to use the three major Greek styles of columns: Doric, Ionic, and Corinthian. This was merely a product of tradition: There's nothing natural about these columnar styles that made them the dominant choices in the American architecture of those centuries. And if you traveled to non-Western cities, you would encounter examples of other columnar styles—for instance, the columns in the Blue Mosque in Istanbul, Turkey, or the Toltec columns in Tula, Mexico (see photos on next page). Such differences may not seem so striking to us now, but think about what it was like for Westerners who rarely came into contact with non-Westerners.

In the wake of these colonial encounters with the New World, philosophers began to define culture in contrast not just to nature but also to what other peoples do, realizing that the way they performed tasks or lived life was a historical product of specific cultural influences. People started to contemplate why their traditions, beliefs, styles of art, and other ways of living arose. There was nothing inevitable about them, and valid alternative approaches to interacting with the world existed. Coming face to face with these alternative ways of living caused Westerners to question the culture that they had so far taken for granted. Philosophers such as Jean-Jacques Rousseau idealized non-Western "savages" in contrast to corrupt and debased Europeans; others declared their own culture superior, going so far as to claim that non-Western peoples didn't have culture. Ethnocentrism is a term that encapsulates the sense of taken-for-granted superiority in the context of cultural practices and attitudes. It is the belief that one's own culture or group is superior to others and the tendency to view all other cultures from the perspective of one's own. At the time, some even believed that non-Westerners did not have souls and weren't human, and this notion was used to justify slavery, violence, and oppression. Such claims obviously weren't true (and we owe a lot to anthropologists for disproving them), but the long history of racism with which we still struggle does have some of its roots in these ideas.

Ethnocentrism the belief that one's own culture or group is superior to others and the tendency to view all other cultures from the perspective of one's own.

Culture = Man − Machine

Not long after European empires began to emerge and spread, new technologies and forms of business upended European definitions of culture at home. Beginning in the eighteenth and nineteenth centuries, goods that were

U.S. Capitol, Washington, D.C.

Lincoln Memorial, Washington, D.C.

Toltec columns, Tula, Mexico

Blue Mosque, Istanbul, Turkey

previously expensive and handcrafted began to be mass-produced and priced within the reach of the average European. New industries and a growing middle class of merchants and industrialists started to transform the political and social climate of Europe, particularly in Great Britain. In response to these rapid social changes, the poet and cultural critic Matthew Arnold (1822–1888) redefined culture as the pursuit of perfection and broad knowledge of the world in contrast to narrow self-centeredness and material gain. Intellectual refinement was the "pursuit of our natural perfection by means of getting to know, on all the matters which most concern us, the best which has been thought and said in the world." Arnold's definition of culture in his essay "Culture and Anarchy" (1869) elevates it beyond dull, middle-class institutions such as religion, liberal economics, and political bureaucracy.

Arnold's definition of culture was an extension of views advanced in Plato's *Republic*, which argues that culture is an ideal standing in opposition to the real world. Plato argues that God is the ideal form of anything. A carpenter, for example, tries to construct a material embodiment of that ideal form. He starts with a vision, the divine vision of what a chair or table should look

Ingres' *La Grande Odalisque* (1814)

like, and he works his hardest to bring that vision to fruition. Of course, it can never be perfect; it can never approximate the platonic ideal.

The artist's job, in contrast, is to *represent* the ideal within the realm of the real. In fact, there's a long history of artists attempting to represent the ideal female in sculpture and painting, but in reality, no woman could ever exist as a flawless object, content to be gazed upon. Jean Auguste Dominique Ingres' *Grande Odalisque* has an unrealistically long spine, allowing her to appear smooth, supple, and gracefully elegant as she shows us her backside but turns her face to meet the viewer's gaze with a hint of a smile. In this conception of art—and this understanding of culture—there is a single, best example of any element in the world, from the ideal woman to the ideal form of government to the ideal citizen, which humanity ought to emulate. Furthermore, we see that the ideal woman (and meal and family and governmental structure) is a fluid notion, changing from one place to another and across time periods. Can an ideal be discovered, as Plato believed, or is it constructed?

Material versus Nonmaterial Culture

Today, we tend to think that everything is a component of culture. Culture is a way of life created by humans, whatever is not natural. We can divide culture into nonmaterial culture, which includes values, beliefs, behaviors, and social norms, and material culture, which is everything that is a part of our constructed, physical environment, including technology. Well-known monuments, such as the Statue of Liberty or Mount Rushmore, are part of our culture, but so are modern furniture, books, movies, food, magazines, cars,

Nonmaterial culture values, beliefs, behaviors, and social norms.

Material culture everything that is a part of our constructed, physical environment, including technology.

and fashion. Of course, a relationship exists between nonmaterial culture and material culture, and that can take many forms. When someone conjures up a concept like a portable computer, such an invention flows directly from an idea into a material good. Other times, however, it is technology that generates ideas and concepts, values and beliefs. Take, for example, the invention of emoticons or other slang used in instant messaging. *ROFL* (rolling on the floor laughing) and *POS* (parent over shoulder) are part of the Internet lexicon, as are emoticons—symbols constructed from colons, semicolons, parentheses, dashes, and other marks of punctuation (Table 3.1).

Language, Meaning, and Concepts

Another way to contemplate culture is the following: It is what feels normal or natural to us but is, in fact, socially produced, like saying "bless you" when someone—even a stranger—sneezes. Another way to put it is this: Culture is what we do not notice at home but would spot in a foreign context (although remember, the sociologist's job is to notice these things at home, too). In France, no one says "*santé*" when a stranger sneezes in the grocery store. In meeting someone for the first time, but holding packages in your right hand, have you instead extended your left in greeting? In Saudi Arabia, this action would be construed as highly disrespectful. Have you ever taken public transportation during rush hour? Do the passengers waiting to board generally move aside to let people off the train first? In Moscow, nobody steps aside; in Japan, people

Table 3.1: Emoticons

:-)	=]	:)	=)	:]	:^)	:D	(^.^)	**Smile or happy**
:-(	:(	=(	(<_>)					**Frown or sad**
;-)	:P							**Wink and tongue sticking out (used to show a joke or sarcasm)**
>:0	:-@							**Yelling**
\(^o^)/								**Very excited**
%-(	:-S							**Confused**
~(_8^(I)								**Homer Simpson**

There are no inherent meanings behind a red light; its symbolism varies depending on context.

wait so long that they practically miss the train! In England, pants are called "trousers," women's underwear "pants," suspenders "braces," and garter belts "suspenders." You can imagine the confusion that would ensue if an American businessman told his English client he needed to find a shop where he could buy new pants and suspenders because his luggage had been lost. The Englishman would either assume the American was a cross-dresser or send him to a lingerie shop to buy something special for his wife. Even your sociology class probably has a different culture—language, meanings, symbols—from a biology or dance class.

Another way to think about culture is that it is a way of organizing our experience. Take our symbols, for example. What does a red light mean? It could mean that an alarm is sounding. It could mean that something is X-rated (the "red-light" district in Amsterdam, for instance). It could mean "stop." There is nothing inherent about the meaning of the red light. It is embedded within our larger culture and therefore is part of a web of meanings. You cannot change one without affecting the others.

Culture even includes our language. According to the Sapir-Whorf thesis in linguistics, the language we speak directly influences (and reflects) the way we think about and experience the world. On a more concrete level, if you speak another language, you understand how certain meanings can become lost in translation—you can't always say exactly what you want. Many English words have been adopted in other languages, often as slang, such as *hamburger* and *le weekend* in French. Some staunch traditionalists are opposed to such borrowing because they regard it as a threat to their culture. How many words do we have for college? How central does that make higher education to our society? Many words describe the state of being intoxicated. What does that say about our culture?

Concepts such as race, gender, class, and inequality are part of our culture as well. If you try to explain the American understanding of racial differences to someone from another country, you might feel frustrated, because it may not resonate with him or her. That's because meanings are embedded in a wider sense of cultural understanding; you cannot just extract concepts from their context and assume that their meanings will retain a life of their own. In some cases, when opposing concepts come into contact, one will necessarily usurp the other. For example, when Europeans first encountered them, Native Americans believed that owning land was similar to the way Americans now feel about owning air—a resource that was very difficult to put a price on and best understood as a collective responsibility. From a real-estate perspective, the Europeans must have been very excited. ("All this land and *nobody* owns it?") The issue was not a language barrier: Native Americans had a social order that had nothing to do with assigning ownership to pieces of the earth. Acting on their concepts of ownership, Europeans thus began the process of displacing native peoples from their homelands and attacking them when they resisted.

Ideology

Nonmaterial culture, in its most abstract guise, takes the form of ideology. Ideology is a system of concepts and relationships, an understanding of cause and effect. For example, generally on airplanes you're not allowed to use the toilets in first class if you have a coach ticket. Why not? It's not as if the bathrooms in first class are that much better. What's the big deal? We subscribe to an ideology that the purchase of an airline ticket at the coach, business, or first-class fare brings with it certain service expectations—an expensive first-class ticket would entitle a passenger to priority access for the bathroom, more leg room, and greater amenities, such as warm face towels. The ideology is embedded within an entire series of suppositions, and if you cast aside some of them, they will no longer hold together as a whole. If everyone flying coach started to hang out in first class, chatting with the flight attendants and using the first-class bathrooms, the system of class stratification (in airplanes at least) would break down. People would not be willing to pay extra for a first-class ticket; more airlines might go bankrupt, and the industry itself would erode.

Ideology a system of concepts and relationships, an understanding of cause and effect.

Even science and religion, which may seem like polar opposites, are both ideological frameworks. People once believed that the sun circled around the earth, and then, in the late fifteenth and early sixteenth centuries, along came Copernicus, Kepler, and Galileo, and this system of beliefs was turned inside out. The earth no longer lay at the center of the universe but orbited the sun. This understanding represented a major shift in ideology, and it was not an easy one to make. In a geocentric universe, humans living on earth stand at its center, and this idea corresponds to Christian notions that humans are the lords of the earth and the chosen children of God. However, when we view the earth as a rock orbiting the sun, just like seven other planets and countless subplanetary bodies, we may feel significantly less special and have to adjust our notion of humanity's special role in the universe. People invest a lot in their belief systems, and those who go against the status quo and question the prevailing ideology may be severely punished, as was Galileo.

Some concepts and beliefs can be disproved without engendering major ripple effects, however. One of the legends of the American political system is that the taller candidate usually wins the presidency. Believing this, we would have predicted John Kerry's victory in the 2004 election, but the shorter George W. Bush won reelection. Did devout Democrats mope for several days? Probably. But was people's understanding of the world shattered by the disruption of the documented pattern on presidential height? No. Did this shake people to their ideological core? Nah. Deep down, those who subscribe to the shorter/taller rule recognize that it's just a superstition; the rule of thumb was not a core principle of a systemic ideology.

The 2000 presidential election, by contrast, had the potential to shatter the ideology of democracy—that is, the belief that the candidate who receives the most votes ascends to power. The winner of the popular vote, Al Gore, was in fact defeated by George W. Bush, who accumulated the requisite number of Electoral College votes after the Supreme Court interceded on the matter of voter irregularities in Florida, the tie-breaker state. The concept of the Electoral College soon became a hot topic of debate, but the final election result did not prompt riots in the street. As it turned out, the entire ideology of American democracy did not crumble.

Of course, on occasion ideologies do shatter. The fall of the former Soviet Union, for example, marked not just a transition in government but the shattering of a particular brand of Communist ideology. Similarly, when apartheid was abolished in South Africa, more than just a few laws changed; a total reorganization of ideas, beliefs, and social relations followed.

The High/Low Culture Debate

A distinction is often made between high culture and low, or pop, culture. Our society tends to value the paintings of Rembrandt and Van Gogh over graffiti or comic book art, for example, and classical music over rock or hip-hop. Generally speaking, academics try to steer away from this kind of debate nowadays, because it's not terribly productive. What's the cultural value of an opera versus Xbox? We can't really answer that. In our society, however, the distinction between high and low culture is dredged up every so often. Take the example of Jonathan Franzen. Usually, authors are thrilled to be chosen for Oprah's Book Club. For starters, their books receive national attention, they're guaranteed tons of readers (generally at least a half-million), and they become instant best sellers. But when Oprah Winfrey selected Franzen's novel *The Corrections* in September 2001, Franzen did not have the anticipated reaction. Oprah's audience, he claimed, wasn't his intended audience. He wanted his writing to be seen as high art and suggested that the mass readership, consisting mainly of middle-class white women, who follow Oprah's recommendations are not high-art aficionados.

Oprah Makes A Correction

Oprah Winfrey recently withdrew her selection of Jonathan Franzen's *The Corrections* for her book club. What did Franzen do to get dropped?

- Kept calling it "Oprah's Book Cult"
- In NPR interview, described Winfrey as resembling a "chocolate-covered bulldozer"
- Let slip that he was a straight, white male who had never been sexually abused
- Expressed eagerness to appear on *The Oprah Winfrey Show* "the minute it stops sucking"
- Kept stopping by Barnes & Noble and ripping the Oprah's Book Club seals off copies of the book
- Refused to cry during appearance on show
- Wasn't sure if depressed, alienated housewives would understand novel about depressed, alienated people
- *New Yorker* editor David Remnick warned Franzen that if he went on *Oprah*, he couldn't be in the Big Brainy Writers' Club anymore
- Kept making the sort of non-groveling remarks to which Winfrey is unaccustomed

A page from the satirical newspaper *The Onion* that appeared after Jonathan Franzen criticized Oprah Winfrey's book club as middlebrow.

Studying Culture

The scholarly study of culture began in the field of anthropology in the United States. Franz Boas founded the first PhD program in anthropology at Columbia University in the early 1930s and developed the concept of cultural relativity. Ruth Benedict, following Boas, her teacher and mentor, coined the term *cultural relativism* in her book *Patterns of Culture* (1934). Cultural relativism means taking into account differences across cultures without passing judgment or assigning value. For example, in the United States you are expected to look someone in the eye when you talk to him or her, but in China this is considered rude, and you generally divert your gaze as a sign of respect. Neither practice is inherently right or wrong. By employing the concept of cultural relativism, we can understand difference for the sake of increasing our knowledge about the world. Cultural relativism is also important for businesses that operate on a global scale.

Cultural relativism taking into account the differences across cultures without passing judgment or assigning value.

But what should one's position be when local traditions conflict with universally recognized human rights? For example, should Western businesspeople condone the cutting of the clitoris in young girls as a local cultural practice, something to be respected, as they go about their business in parts of Africa? There are, of course, limits to cultural relativism. In some countries, it is both legal and socially acceptable for a man to beat his wife. Should we accept that wife beating is part of the local culture and therefore conclude we are not in a position to judge those involved? In the United States, some Jehovah's Witnesses reject blood transfusions because they believe blood to be sacred and not for "consumption" by Christians. If parents refuse a potentially lifesaving surgery for their child because it will require a transfusion, do we respect their right to religious freedom or arrest them for neglect? Where we draw the lines is a difficult matter to decide and sparks a great deal of political debate on topics such as domestic violence, female genital mutilation, and medical practices versus religious beliefs in treating the critically ill.

Margaret Mead, Benedict's student, wrote *Coming of Age in Samoa*, which has become part of the canon of anthropology and cultural studies. Based on her ethnographic fieldwork among a small group of Samoans, she concluded that women there did not experience the same emotional and psychological turmoil as their American counterparts in the transition from adolescence to

Margaret Mead with two Samoan women, 1926.

adulthood. She found that young women engaged in and enjoyed casual sex before they married and reared children. The book, published in 1928, caused quite an uproar in the United States and eventually contributed to the feminist movement. The validity of Mead's findings has been disputed, but her work continues to be a landmark of early anthropology for introducing the idea that cultural scripts, modes of behavior and understanding that are not universal or natural, shape our notions of gender. This concept stands in opposition to the belief that such ideas derive from biological programming.

Cultural scripts modes of behavior and understanding that are not universal or natural.

Cockfighting and Symbolic Culture Clifford Geertz, another American anthropologist, was famous for his studies of and writings on culture, one of which concerned the meaning of cockfighting in Bali. Cockfighting involves placing two roosters together in a cockpit, a ring especially designed for the event, and watching them fight. The meaning of cockfighting varies, however. Some see it as one of the basest forms of cruelty to animals. Others attach religious and spiritual meaning to the event. In the Balinese village where Geertz lived, cockfighting was primarily a vehicle for gambling, but it was also an important cultural event. Very few men are allowed to referee these fights, and their decisions are treated with more regard than the law. People bet a lot of money, often forming teams that pool their resources. Bettors profess themselves to be "cock crazy."

The owners of the prized cocks expend an enormous amount of time caring for them. They feed them special diets, bathe them with herbs and flowers, and insert hot peppers in their anuses to give them "spirit." The cock takes on larger symbolic meaning within Balinese society. According to Geertz,

> The language of everyday moralism is shot through, on the male side of it, with roosterish imagery. *Sabung*, the word for cock, is used metaphorically to mean "hero," "warrior," "champion," "man of parts," "political candidate," "bachelor," "dandy," "lady-killer," or "tough guy." . . . Court trials, wars, political contests, inheritance disputes, and street arguments are all compared to cockfights. Even the very island itself is perceived from its shape as a small, proud cock, poised, neck extended, back taut, tail raised, in eternal challenge to large, feckless, shapeless Java. (1973, pp. 412, 454)

In the United States, cocks do not have much symbolic meaning. A more central metaphor in American society is baseball. According to anthropologist Bradd Shore (1998), baseball serves a function in the United States similar to cockfighting's in Bali. We call baseball America's favorite pastime and regularly use baseball metaphors in our daily conversations. If your parents inquire about how you're doing in school this semester, you might say you're "batting a thousand." If you ask your friend how it went the other night at a party when she spoke to the smart guy from your sociology class, and she says she "struck out," you know not to ask, "So when's your first date?" We could learn a lot

A cockfight in Bali, Indonesia. How are roosters central to Bali's symbolic culture?

about American culture by studying baseball, how people watch the game, and what symbolic meanings they attach to it, just as Geertz learned such things about the Balinese by using cockfights as the center of his analysis.

In *The Interpretation of Cultures* (1973), perhaps his most famous book, Geertz wrote, "Culture is a system of inherited conceptions expressed in symbolic forms by means of which people communicate, perpetuate, and develop their knowledge about and attitudes toward life" (p. 89). He was trying to get away from a monolithic definition of culture. So for some, culture is watching players hit a small, hard ball into a field and run around a diamond; for others, it's squatting down in the dust beside a ring and watching two roosters go at it. One pastime isn't inherently better than the other. They're both interesting in their own right, and by understanding the significance of these events for the local people, we can better understand their lives.

Subculture the distinct cultural values and behavioral patterns of a particular group in society; a group united by sets of concepts, values, symbols, and shared meaning specific to the members of that group distinctive enough to distinguish it from others within the same culture or society.

Subculture

Like culture, subculture as a concept can be a moving target: It's hard to lock into one specific definition of the term. Historically, subcultures have been defined as groups united by sets of concepts, values, symbols, and shared meaning specific to the members of that group. Accordingly, they frequently are

WHAT'S IN A NAME?

Kim Novak and James Stewart in Alfred Hitchcock's *Vertigo*.

Stanley Lieberson, a sociology professor at Harvard, studies culture using first names. Why names? Names reflect cultural trends and fashions and are unique in important ways. Lieberson's biographical note on Harvard's Department of Sociology Web page provides an overview of his reasoning:

> First, there are good data based on births that permit relatively rigorous analysis over long spans of time and, moreover, allow for cross-national considerations. Second, these tastes are unaffected by the powerful commercial forces operating to influence most domains of taste. Manufacturers and retailers, for example, have no vested interest in the choice of names, but only in products purchased for children. Third, many tastes are affected by economic factors, but all parents can and do give their children names.

Lieberson uses names as a way of looking at a cultural phenomenon that is not mediated through formal institutions. Let's take an example. My daughter's name is E (just the letter). In France, I wouldn't be allowed legally to give her that name. A list of first names exists from which you must choose, and you are out of luck if the name you like is not on that list. (The French government may now be relaxing these restrictions, given mounting pressure from immigrant groups.) In the United States, however, there's no legal limit to your creativity, no formal institutions to which you must apply for permission to name your child, no agency that generates a list of approved names. Here, parents think of choosing a name as one of the most important, strictly personal decisions that they make at the birth of their child.

And yet, baby names follow certain socially structured patterns, some of which Lieberson has uncovered. One is related to the androgyny of names—the crossover of names between male and female. In American society a very strong pattern of names crossing from men to women exists—but not the reverse. For example, Figure 3.1 illustrates the popularity of the name Kim; the orange line represents females named Kim and the green line males named Kim. Notice that both lines rose until 1958, the year Alfred Hitchcock's Vertigo was released; the film's lead actress, Kim Novak, had by then become a huge star, even gracing the cover of Time. The name choice immediately became less popular for males, because it was now clearly demarcated as a feminine name. Its popularity spiked for women, and the name never recovered its androgyny. Similarly, Cary Grant became a cinema icon, and his fame led to an increase in both boys and girls being named Cary. Eventually, this name choice tapered off for men, because it became too popular as a women's name.

Figure 3.1: Popularity of the Name *Kim*

Cary Grant

By now you're possibly asking yourself, "Should I name my baby Cameron?" That is, what are the consequences of the gendering of names? In a 2005 paper titled "Boys Named Sue" (just like the Johnny Cash song), economist David Figlio found that boys with feminine names perform well until the sixth grade, at which point they tend to get into more trouble than the rest of their peers. Presumably, they are busy defending their masculinity. The end result is more academic problems, not just for them but for their classmates, too. (It must be very distracting to have to beat up Sue every day.) And here's the catch: Few parents would intentionally give their son a girl's name. The name only became a girl's in the popular culture after the boy had been named.

Names involve not only gender but also race. Two other economists conducted an experiment in which they sent out job applications that contained exactly the same information, except that some used the name Emily, whereas others used LaTisha. The LaTishas received far fewer callbacks for interviews. Why? LaTisha is understood to be an African American name and is racially marked in a way that Emily is not. Discrimination was obviously at work (Bertrand & Mullainathan, 2003). The relationship might not be so straightforward, however. An other pair of economists at tempted to build on this study, and their research indicated that the race associated with particular names didn't affect how people fare economically, at least in California (Fryer & Levitt, 2003). Whose research do we believe? The final word on the subject, for the time being, may be derived from the work of Figlio, who in a second study in 2005 compared black siblings using the same Florida school data he had utilized in researching the "Boys Named Sue" paper. Figlio ascertained that teachers had lower expectations for siblings with more African American–sounding names—they were less likely to be referred to classes for gifted students and more likely to be socially promoted (the practice of promoting schoolchildren to the next grade, to keep them with their peers, regardless of whether they are capable of completing gradelevel work). Names that are racially coded can make people targets for discrimination.

Goths in Germany (left) and Japan. What characteristics of Goth culture make it a subculture?

seen as vulgar or deviant and are often marginalized. Part of the original impetus behind subculture studies was to gain a deeper understanding of individuals and groups who traditionally have been dismissed as weirdos at best and deviants at worst.

For example, many music genres have affiliated subcultures: hip-hop, hardcore, punk, Christian rock. High-school cliques may verge on subcultures—the jocks, the band kids, the geeks—although these groups don't really go against the dominant society, because athleticism, musical talent, and intelligence are fairly conventional values. But what about the group of kids who dress in black and wear heavy eyeliner? Maybe teachers simply see them as moody teenagers with a penchant for dark fashion and extreme makeup just seeking to annoy the adults in their life, but perhaps their style of self-presentation means more to them.

Goth culture has its roots in the United Kingdom of the 1980s. It emerged as an offshoot of post-punk music. Typified by a distinctive style of dress—namely, black clothing with a Victorian flair and a general affinity for gothic and death rock—goth culture has evolved over the last three decades, with many internal subdivisions. Some goths are more drawn to magical or religious aspects of the subculture, whereas others focus mainly on the music. Even the term *goth* has different meanings to people within the subculture: Some see it as derogatory, some appropriate it for their own personal meaning. An internal struggle has grown over who has the right to claim and define the label.

What makes today's goths a subculture? They are not just a random group of people in black listening to music (classical musicians usually wear black when they perform, but we don't consider them gothic). Certain words and phrases are unique to goth communities, such as *baby bat* (young goth poseur) and *weekend goth* (someone who dresses up and enters the subculture only on the weekends). Goths in Germany may look very different from those in the United Kingdom, and norms even differ among U.S. cities, so each is a distinct branch of the subculture. Yet as a whole, goths do have their own shared symbols, especially with regard to fashion, so they are visible as a subculture. (Not all subcultures, however, adopt characteristic dress or other easily identifiable features. For example, black men on the down low [DL], secretly seeking sex with men, by definition do not want to be identifiable.)

Cultural Effects: Give and Take

How does culture affect us? As we've discussed, culture may be embedded in ideologies. Our understanding of the world is based on the various ideologies we embrace, and ideologies tend to be culturally specific. Culture also affects us by shaping our values, our moral beliefs. The concept of equal opportunity is a good example of this. The majority of us have been taught that everybody should have an equal shot at the "American dream": going to college, obtaining a job, and becoming economically self-sufficient. That is a relatively recent cultural conception. In England 600 years ago, there was no such culture of equal opportunity but rather a feudal system. If you had asked someone in the government of that period, a social elite, if he (and it would definitely have been a man) believed that everyone should have equal opportunity, he would probably have rejected such a claim. He would have likely insisted that the elite, the nobles, should have more rights, privileges, and opportunities than everybody else. Class mobility simply wasn't a concept that existed. Similarly, the way the concept of equal opportunity is expressed in the contemporary United States has a particularly American flavor. We have a very individualistic culture, meaning that we hold dear the idea that everyone should have the opportunity to advance, but we believe people should do it on their own—"pull yourself up by your bootstraps," as we say. Americans hold tightly to the rags-to-riches dream of triumph over adversity, of coming from nothing and becoming a success despite hardship. The problem with this cultural trope is that, as sociologists like to point out, the larger, structural, macro-level forces—general social stratification, racial segregation, sexism, differential access to health care, and education—keep the concept of equal opportunity more fiction than reality. As a culture, Americans tend to suffer a bit from historical amnesia. Slavery was abolished in 1863, and legal segregation lasted until the 1960s. Historically speaking, this is not very long ago. Our notion of equal opportunity often fails to take into account the very unequal starting positions from which people set out to achieve their goals.

Values moral beliefs.

If values are abstract cultural beliefs, norms are how values are put into play. We value hygiene in our society, so it is a norm that you wash your hands after going to the bathroom. When you are little, your parents and teachers must remind you, because chances are you haven't yet fully internalized this norm. Once you're an adult, however, you are in charge of your own actions, yet others may still remind you of this norm by giving you a dirty look if you walk from a stall straight past the sinks and out the door of a public restroom. In an office, people might gossip about the guy who doesn't wash his

Norms how values tell us to behave.

hands—they are shaming him for not following this norm. When you arrive at college, you enter a new culture with different norms and values, and you must adjust to that new environment. If you're attending a school with a major emphasis on partying, you might be reading this textbook secretly because the cultural norm in that kind of environment is not to buy the assigned books or even go to class on a regular basis. If you are enrolled at a community college, commuting may be the main cultural practice. You go there for class and then leave shortly thereafter.

Reflection Theory

Socialization the process by which individuals internalize the values, beliefs, and norms of a given society and learn to function as members of that society.

Reflection theory the idea that culture is a projection of social structures and relationships into the public sphere, a screen onto which the film of the underlying reality or social structures of our society is projected.

Culture affects us. It's transmitted to us through different processes, socialization—our internalization of society's values, beliefs, and norms—being the main one. But how do we affect culture? Let's start with reflection theory, which states that culture is a projection of social structures and relationships into the public sphere, a screen onto which the film of the underlying reality or social structures of our society is shown. For example, some people claim that there is too much violence in song lyrics, particularly in rap music. How do hip-hop artists often respond? "I live in a violent world, and I'm like a reporter. I'm telling it like it is; so if you want to fix that, then fix the problems of violence in my community. I'm just the messenger." They are invoking reflection theory.

A different version of reflection theory derives from the Marxist tradition, which says that cultural objects reflect the material labor and relationships of production that went into them. Earlier in this chapter, we discussed the distinction between material and nonmaterial culture. Karl Marx asserted that it is a one-way street—from technology and the means of production to belief systems and ideologies. According to Marx's view of reflection theory, our norms, values, sanctions, ideologies, laws, and even language are outgrowths of the technology and economic means and modes of production. Likewise, for Marx, ideology has a very specific definition: culture that justifies given relations in production.

By way of example, consider the creation of limited liability partnerships. The concept of limited liability emerged in the nineteenth century during the Industrial Revolution, when new technologies enabled the growth of factories and long-distance travel. At the same time, European countries such as Great Britain were colonizing regions all over the world and establishing large global trade networks. As

Why might performers like Lil' Wayne use reflection theory to defend their lyrics? What are some of the limitations to this theory?

merchants and factory owners tried to expand, they needed more capital from investors. To attract the most money, they came up with the idea of limited liability partnerships. Limited liability means that when you invest money in a publicly traded corporation, you are not responsible for their debt (you can't lose more than what you paid for your shares) or their actions (unless you are on the board of directors). So if you have stock in a cereal company and it goes bankrupt, the farmers who supply the grain can't hit you up for unpaid bills. Likewise, if several small children choke on the secret prize included in boxes of cereal, you cannot be held personally responsible for this tragedy. All you lose is the money you invested in the shares. Even if you didn't know what limited liability meant before you read this paragraph, the legal concept is something we take for granted as part of our common understanding of how capitalism works. Historically, however, it arose from a choice made in England in a specific context. Marx would argue that the combination of factory labor and global trade relations between England and its colonies necessitated and inevitably led to these kinds of legal structures.

Like most theories, reflection theory has its limitations. It does not explain why some cultural products have staying power, whereas others fall by the wayside. Why is it that one book hits the best-seller list and is number one for a week or two weeks only, whereas other books, such as *The Girl with the Dragon Tattoo* by Stieg Larsson, remain number one on the best-seller list for over a year? Conversely, Wolfgang Amadeus Mozart was a popular composer in his own day. Why is he still so popular today? Clearly, the relations of production and underlying social structures—indeed, Western society as a whole—have drastically changed since the late eighteenth century, yet the appeal of Mozart's music is as strong as ever. If culture is just a reflection of the state of society in a given epoch, then Mozart should have fallen completely out of favor and we would no longer be interested in him or his music, but this doesn't seem to be the case.

Likewise, if reflection theory is true, why do some products change their meaning over time? Shakespeare is a good example. In nineteenth-century America, Shakespeare was the poet of the people, the playwright for the common man. Scenes from various Shakespearean plays were performed during the intermissions of other events. Conversely, during the intermissions for a full-length Shakespearean play, spectacles, carnival-like entertainment for the masses, would be presented. He was the most widely performed playwright in England's former colonies, but not revered in terms of high culture. This is not quite what we associate Shakespeare with today, correct? It's just the opposite, in fact: His work is now considered high art. In this instance, the same product changed its meaning over time, and reflection theory doesn't help us understand that change.

Most importantly, reflection theory has been rejected largely because it is unidirectional—that is, it basically buys the rappers' defense that culture has no impact on society. Do we really believe that the media have no impact on the

How has the cultural significance of Shakespeare's plays changed over the last 400 years? Compare the poster for an 1884 performance of *Macbeth* (left) with a 1944 photo of Laurence Olivier as Henry V.

way we live or think? Do we really believe that ideologies have no effect on the choices we make? No. Most people now understand that an interactive process exists between culture and social structure. Most would agree that culture has an impact on society and is not just a unidirectional phenomenon.

Media

Media any formats or vehicles that carry, present, or communicate information.

Among the most pervasive and visible forms of culture in modern societies are those produced by the mass media. We might define media as any formats or vehicles that carry, present, or communicate information. This definition would, of course, include newspapers, periodicals, magazines, books, pamphlets, and posters. But it would also include wax tablets, sky writing, Web pages, and the children's game of telephone. We'll first discuss the history of the media and then tackle theory and empirical studies.

From the Town Crier to the Facebook Wall: A Brief History

When we talk about the media, we're generally talking about the mass media. The first form of mass media was the book. Before the invention of the printing press the media did exist—the town crier brought news, royal messengers traveled by horseback, every now and then hopping off to read a scroll—but they did not exactly reach the masses. People passed along most information by word of mouth. After the 1440s, when Johannes Gutenberg developed movable type for the printing press, text could be printed much more easily. Books and periodicals were produced and circulated at much greater rates and began to reach mass audiences. Since that time the terms *media* and *mass media* have become virtually synonymous.

The innovations didn't stop there, however. In the 1880s along came another invention: the moving picture or silent film. Its quality was not the best at first, but that improved over time. In the 1920s sound was added to films. For many, this represented an improvement over the radio, which had come along about the same time as the silent film. In the 1930s television was invented, although this technology didn't make its way into most American homes until after World War II. During the postwar period, new forms of media technology quickly hit the market, and the demand for media exploded: glossy magazines; color televisions; blockbuster movies; Betamax videos, then VHS videos, then DVDs; vinyl records, then eight-track tapes, then cassette tapes, then CDs—and once the Internet came along, the sky was the limit! In 2009, 66 percent of the American population had broadband at home, with access clustered among the younger, wealthier, and better educated.

You're well aware of all the forms the media come in, but let's stop for a minute and contemplate the impact certain forms, such as television, have had on society. Again, televisions didn't become household items in the United States until after World War II. From 1950, the year President Harry S. Truman first sent military advisors to South Vietnam, to 1964, when Congress approved the Tonkin Gulf Resolution calling for victory by any means necessary, the share of American households with television sets increased from 9 to 92 percent. During the Vietnam War, the American public witnessed military conflict in

Innovations in mass media include the invention of the printing press and movable type in the fifteenth century, the creation of moving pictures at the turn of the twentieth century, and the adoption of the scrolling ticker by today's 24-hour news channels.

In 1963, for the first time televisions beamed images such as this photo of police officers attacking a student in Birmingham, Alabama. How did television influence the reaction to events such as the civil rights movement?

a way they never had before, and these images helped fuel the antiwar movement. Likewise, television played a large role in the civil rights movement of the 1950s and 1960s. It was one thing to hear of discrimination secondhand, but quite another to sit with your family in the living room and watch images of police setting attack dogs on peaceful protesters and turning fire hoses on little African American girls dressed up in their Sunday best.

Hegemony: The Mother of All Media Terms

All of us might be willing to agree that, on some level, the media both reflect culture and work to produce the very culture they represent. How does this dynamic work? Antonio Gramsci, an Italian political theorist and activist, came up with the concept of hegemony to describe just that. Gramsci, a Marxist, was imprisoned by the Fascists in the 1920s and 1930s; while in jail, he attempted to explain why the working-class revolution Marx had predicted never came to pass. He published his findings in his "prison notebooks" of 1929–35 (Gramsci, 1971). In this vein, then, hegemony "refers to a historical process in

Hegemony a condition by which a dominant group uses its power to elicit the voluntary "consent" of the masses.

which a dominant group exercises 'moral and intellectual leadership' throughout society by winning the voluntary 'consent' of popular masses" (Kim, 2001). This concept of hegemony stands in contrast to another of Gramsci's ideas, *domination*. If domination means getting people to do what you want them to by force, hegemony means getting them to go along with the status quo because it seems like the best course or the natural order of things. Although domination generally involves an action by the state (such as the Fascist leaders who imprisoned those who disagreed with them), "hegemony takes place in the realm of private institutions . . . such as families, churches, trade unions, and the media" (Kim, 2001). For example, if free-market capitalism is the hegemonic economic ideology of a given society, then the state does not have to explicitly work to inculcate that set of principles into its citizenry. Rather, private institutions, such as families, do most of the heavy lifting in this regard. Ever wonder why children receive an allowance for taking out the trash and doing other household chores? Gramsci might argue that this is the way capitalist free-market ideology is instilled in the individual within the private realm of the family.

The concept of hegemony is important for understanding the impact of the media. It also raises questions about the tension between structure and agency. Are people molded by the culture in which they live, or do they actively participate in shaping the world around them? As we discussed earlier in the chapter, it's not an either/or question. Below we'll talk about some of the debates between structure and agency with regard to the media, look at some examples of hegemony in practice, and discuss the possibilities for countercultural resistance.

The Media Life Cycle

We live in a media-saturated society, but one of the most exciting aspects of studying the media is that it allows us to explore the tensions and contradictions created when large social forces conflict with individual identity and free will. We see how people create media, how the media shape the culture in which people live, how the media reflect the culture in which they exist, and how individuals and groups use the media as their own means to shape, redefine, and change culture.

Texts

Why do the adventures in a fairy tale often begin once a mother dies? Are blacks more often portrayed as professionals or criminals in television sitcoms? How often are Asians the lead characters in mainstream films? Who generally initiates conversation, men or women, in U.S. (or Mexican) soap operas? These questions are all examples of textual analysis, analysis of the content of media in its various forms, one of the important strands of study to materialize in the wake of Gramsci's work.

During the 1960s and 1970s academic studies focused almost solely on texts—television talk shows, newspapers, magazine pages. Finally, scholars recognized the importance of finding out how people read and interpret, and are affected by, these texts: Audience studies were born. The field of psychology has expended a lot of time investigating claims about the effects of television on children, and the debate continues. Sociologists have explored the way women read romance novels or how teenage girls interpret images of super-thin models in magazines. For example, in *Reading the Romance: Women, Patriarchy, and Popular Literature* (1987), Janice Radway argues that women exhibit a great deal of individual agency when reading romance novels, which helps them cope with their daily lives in a patriarchal society by providing both escapes from the drudgery of everyday life and alternative scripts to their readers. We are not just passive receptors of media; as readers or viewers, we experience texts through the lens of our own critical, interpretive, and analytical processes.

Back to the Beginning: Cultural Production

The media don't just spontaneously spring into being. They aren't organic; they're produced. You may have heard the expression "History is written by the winners." Well before something becomes history, it has to happen in the present. Who decides what's news? How are decisions made about the content of television shows? To write his classic *Deciding What's News* (1979a), Herbert Gans went inside the newsrooms at *CBS Evening News*, *NBC Nightly News*, *Newsweek*, and *Time* in the late 1970s. He paid careful attention to the processes by which these news outlets made their decisions on editorial content, "writing down the unwritten rules of journalism," because rules, sociologists know, contain values. Journalists are supposed to be objective, but Gans illustrated the ways in which the mainstream American values journalists had internalized biased the finished product—the news. The notion of "the facts, just the facts, and nothing but the facts" is a worthy idea but to a large degree a farce. Powerful boards of directors regulate the various media; writers, casting agents, directors, and producers decide what goes into sitcoms, soap operas, and after-school specials. Even the huge cache of secret government documents made available on the Internet by WikiLeaks in 2010 were prescreened by individual hackers and researchers. The media are produced by human beings, all of whom have their own biases. Professional journalists may try to minimize the extent to which their own beliefs affect their work, but it is important to keep in mind these "invisible" influences on the media.

In studying newsrooms, Herbert Gans found that many players influenced news production and analyzed how journalists internalized those unspoken rules.

Media Effects

In considering the media, mass culture, and subcultures, we can plot the media's effects in a two-dimensional diagram, as shown in Figure 3.2. The vertical dimension indicates if the effect is intended (i.e., deliberate) or unintended. The horizontal axis depicts whether it is a short- or long-term effect. A short-term, deliberate media effect (section A in the illustration) would be advertising. As a kid, you may have watched Saturday morning cartoons; watch them now and keep track of the number of advertisements for children's food. A child today might see an ad for Cocoa Puffs and that same afternoon go grocery shopping with his or her parents. That child is possibly on a sugar crash from an early-morning bowl of Super Frosted Mega Marshmallow Crackle Blasts and is really clamoring for a box of Cocoa Puffs. The advertisers timed it just right, with the pressure on mom or dad to buy that cereal.

Section B of Figure 3.2, on the other hand, represents a deliberate, long-term media campaign. Here, a single theme is reinforced through repeated exposure, as in public service announcements (PSAs). These are generally used by not-for-profit organizations to educate the public. Classic examples include Smokey the Bear (created in 1944, "Only you can prevent forest fires"), Woodsy Owl (created in 1970, "Give a hoot, don't pollute"), and the "This is your brain on drugs" commercials from the Partnership for a Drug-Free America (the original fried egg

THE RACE AND GENDER POLITICS OF MAKING OUT

"When I'm good, I'm very good, but when I'm bad, I'm better." —ACTRESS MAE WEST

The movie industry's Production Code enumerated three "general principles":

1. No picture shall be produced that will lower the moral standards of those who see it. Hence the sympathy of the audience should never be thrown to the side of crime, wrong–doing, evil, or sin.
2. Correct standards of life, subject only to the requirements of drama and entertainment, shall be presented.
3. Law, natural or human, shall not be ridiculed, nor shall sympathy be created for its violation.

Specific restrictions were spelled out as "particular applications" of these principles:

- Nudity and suggestive dances were prohibited.
- The ridicule of religion was forbidden, and ministers of religion were not to be represented as comic characters or villains.
- The depiction of illegal drug use was forbidden, as well as the use of liquor, "when not required by the plot or for proper characterization."
- Methods of crime (e.g., safe-cracking, arson, smuggling) were not to be explicitly presented.
- References to "sex perversion" (such as homosexuality) and venereal disease were forbidden, as were depictions of childbirth.
- The language section banned various words and phrases considered to be offensive.
- Murder scenes had to be filmed in a way that would not inspire imitation in real life, and brutal killings could not be shown in detail. "Revenge in modern times" was not to be justified.
- The sanctity of marriage and the home had to be upheld. "Pictures shall not infer that low forms of sex relationship are the accepted or common thing." Adultery and illicit sex, although recognized as sometimes necessary to the plot, could not be explicit or justified; they were never to be presented as an attractive option.
- Portrayals of interracial relationships were forbidden.
- "Scenes of passion" were not to be introduced when not essential to the plot. "Excessive and lustful kissing" was to be avoided, along with any other physical interaction that might "stimulate the lower and baser element."
- The flag of the United States was to be treated respectfully, as were the people and history of other nations.
- "Vulgarity," defined as "low, disgusting, unpleasant, though not necessarily evil, subjects," must be treated "subject to the dictates of good taste." Capital punishment, "third-degree methods," cruelty to children and animals, prostitution, and surgical operations were to be depicted with similar sensitivity and discretion.

Lucille Ball and Desi Arnaz in the 1950s hit television comedy *I Love Lucy*. Even though their characters were married, they still did not share a bed.

"Rules were made to be broken," the old saying goes, and the film industry did its best to prove the maxim true. Filmmakers like Alfred Hitchcock pushed the boundaries of a 10-second time limit for kisses by filming a lip-lock for the maximum allotted time, panning away, and then returning to the couple still passionately embracing. Rules such as this were slow to change, but not as slow as others. For one thing, you can be sure that the people kissing were a man and a woman, and they were both white. In fact, in the beginning they would have been married, too, but that ideology—the sanctity of marriage—fell away more quickly on the silver screen than did notions about racial and gender hierarchies and stereotypes. The first onscreen interracial kiss, between Sidney Poitier and Katharine Houghton in *Guess Who's Coming to Dinner*, didn't occur until 1967, the same year the U.S. Supreme Court ruled that state laws preventing interracial marriage were unconstitutional. And in a 1968 episode of *Star Trek*, William Shatner and Nichelle Nichols boldly ventured where no one had gone before with the first black–white lip-lock televised in the United States. The first homosexual kiss hit prime time in 2000 (between the characters Will and Jack on *Will & Grace*), and the first same-sex kiss between two women didn't occur until 2003, when two characters on ABC's popular daytime soap opera *All My Children* puckered up. The number of homosexual kisses is still quite small in comparison to the number of lesbian kisses: The ratio is about 1 to 5. Prime time doesn't seem quite ready for interracial, homosexual kisses just yet (although cable programs like *The L Word*, *Queer as Folk*, and *Six Feet Under* portray sexually active homosexual characters in lead roles). Furthermore, gay men, particularly members of minorities, frequently serve as comic relief, and lesbian women are often portrayed as sex objects of male desire rather than as women who love women. Homosexual and interracial relationships are much less likely to be depicted as loving, functional, and healthy. Change in the media takes time; as society's ideologies about what constitutes good and bad love change, the media will reflect those changes by portraying more positive images of people loving whomever they choose.

Jesse Tyler Ferguson and Eric Stonestreet play gay parents Mitchell and Cameron on ABC's *Modern Family*.

Figure 3.2: Media Effects

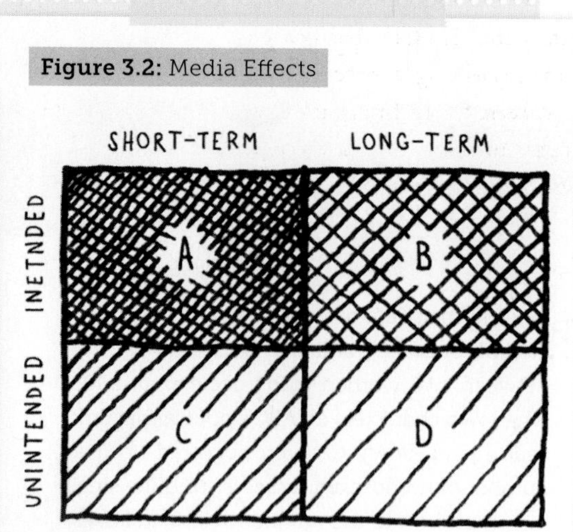

aired in 1987, and the sequel frying pan smash aired a decade later). In a current public service campaign the New York City Department of Public Health asks, "Are you pouring on the pounds?" next to an image of a glass full of human fat in an attempt to fight obesity (2009). There also have been long-standing campaigns against drug use and smoking. Of course, not all attempts at deliberate long-term effects are a success. For example, early into President George W. Bush's second term, the administration worked hard through the bully pulpit of the presidency to promote the idea of privatizing Social Security, but that concept did not go far. Part of the problem was the fact that the campaign to overhaul the existing system had not been around long enough. The American public has yet to embrace the idea that the Social Security system needs to be changed. Often, an issue must be framed as a problem before solutions can be advocated, and that can take a long time in a media campaign. Although conservative factions have been talking about privatizing Social Security for many years, they have not completed the work in the public media that would be necessary to lay the foundation for such change.

Section C of Figure 3.2 represents media with short-term, unintended consequences. An example might be when teenagers play violent video games and then go out and commit crimes almost identical to those portrayed in the game, or when a kid listens to heavy metal music with violent lyrics and then commits a school shooting. You hear of such events every so often, and sometimes the media's creator will use the defense that the short-term response was not intended. In an interview, for example, the software producer or musician might be asked, "Did you know that your music is causing teenage boys to commit violent crimes?" And the response will be, "That is not my intention at all. I use violence as a metaphor." Scientific research hasn't yet ruled definitively one way or the other on this controversial subject, but many believe that the media occasionally have short-term unintended effects.

Finally, section D of the illustration represents the long-term, unintended effects of the media. Many people, not just cultural conservatives, argue that we have been desensitized to violence, sexual imagery, and other content that some people consider inappropriate for mass audiences. In the film industry, for example, the Production Code, also known as the Hays Code, was a set of standards created in 1930 (although it wasn't officially enforced until 1934) to protect the moral fabric of society. The guidelines were fairly strict, and they were a testament to the mainstream ideologies of the time (see the box on pages 100–101). Slowly, however, the power of the code began to erode, because of the influence of television, foreign films, and the fact that being condemned as immoral didn't prevent a film from becoming a success. In 1967 the code was abandoned for the movie rating system. Over time, we have grown accustomed to seeing sexually explicit material in films, on television, and on the Internet. Those who lament this desensitization seek to reinstitute controls over media content.

Mommy, Where Do Stereotypes Come From?

Racism in the Media

On December 22, 1941, two weeks after the Japanese attack on Pearl Harbor, *Time* magazine ran an article titled "How to Tell Your Friends from the Japs." There were annotated photographs to help readers identify characteristics that would distinguish, for instance, friendly Chinese from the Japanese, America's enemies during World War II. The magazine offered the following rules of thumb, although admitting that they were "not always reliable":

- Some Chinese are tall (average: 5 ft. 5 in.). Virtually all Japanese are short (average: 5 ft. 2-½ in.).
- Japanese are likely to be stockier and broader-hipped than short Chinese.
- Japanese—except for wrestlers—are seldom fat; they often dry up and grow lean as they age. The Chinese often put on weight, particularly if they are prosperous (in China, with its frequent famines, being fat is esteemed as a sign of being a solid citizen).
- Chinese, not as hairy as Japanese, seldom grow an impressive mustache.
- Most Chinese avoid horn-rimmed spectacles.
- Although both have the typical epicanthic fold of the upper eyelid (which makes them look almond-eyed), Japanese eyes are usually set closer together.
- Those who know them best often rely on facial expression to tell them apart: the Chinese expression is likely to be more placid, kindly, open; the Japanese more positive, dogmatic, arrogant.

How can Gramsci's concept of hegemony help us understand this piece from *Time*? Does this article tell us more about the physical differences between Japanese and Chinese, or about the state of mind of the American public at the time? What values are reflected and projected? Are the descriptors empirical (based on fact) or normative (based on opinion)? This is what racism looks

The controversial O.J. Simpson arrest photo. *Time* magazine was accused of darkening his features for their cover.

like on paper, and it clearly illustrates America's fear and hatred of the Japanese at that time.

The media continue to reflect and perpetuate racist ideologies, even if such examples are not usually as blatant as the 1941 article in *Time*. Sometimes, the racism is obvious, and these instances present us with the opportunity to discuss racism in the media. In June 1994 the front cover of both *Time* and *Newsweek* showed the police mug shot of former NFL star O.J. Simpson, who had been arrested for allegedly killing his ex-wife and her friend. *Time* was accused of darkening its image, perhaps implying that those with darker skin are more dangerous, criminal, and evil. In a case whose trial months later would prove to be a racially charged event—Simpson's ex-wife was white, and the police detective overseeing the case had a long history of racial prejudice—the media added fuel to the fire. What purpose was served by darkening Simpson's image? Did the stir surrounding these photos affect the eventual outcome of the trial? Again, we can't state with certainty how one questionable instance in the media affects society, but we can look at the continued negative portrayals of minorities and hypothesize about the cumulative effects of those images.

In early September 2005, just days after Hurricane Katrina had devastated the areas surrounding the Mississippi River basin, two photos quickly began to circulate on the Internet amid discussion of racism and the role it played in the reaction (or inadequate government response) to the catastrophe. The first photo, published by the Associated Press, showed a young African American wading through chest-high water toting groceries; the caption proclaimed that the man had just been "looting a grocery store." The second, which pictured a Caucasian couple doing the same thing, stated that the two were photographed "after finding bread and soda at a local grocery store" (Ralli, 2005). The conclusion these images and their captions conveyed was this: White looters, in their struggle to survive the catastrophe, were not committing a crime, whereas blacks resorting to the same behavior were. Indeed, much of the coverage in the wake of Katrina focused on the crime, looting, and vandalism that took place. What critics have pointed out, however, is that these people did what most of us would logically do—try to obtain food and water for our suffering families in the absence of competent government assistance and disaster relief. Because the city of New Orleans, which received the majority of the media attention, was 78 percent nonwhite, the victims were frequently portrayed as criminals.

The coverage of Hurricane Katrina, which was exceptional in the amount of criticism that was publicly levied against such racially charged portrayals (unlike, for example, the December 1941 *Time* piece), supports the main thesis of Barry Glassner's *The Culture of Fear: Why Americans Are Afraid of the Wrong Things* (1999). Namely, Glassner asserts that as a culture, we grossly exaggerate the frequency of rarely occurring events, often via amplification of a single instance through media repetition. We tend to divert or redirect our attention from political, economic, and cultural issues that are either taboo or simply too

The photo above, published by the Associated Press, showed a young African American wading through chest-high water toting groceries; the caption proclaimed that the man had just been "looting a grocery store." The second, which pictured a Caucasian couple doing the same thing, stated that the two were photographed "after finding bread and soda at a local grocery store."

difficult to talk about toward sensational, but rare, events like school shootings and terrorist attacks. The media are the main vehicles through which this process occurs. In the case of Katrina, we blame the victims, the poorest of the poor, for not leaving the city, rather than asking how the government could leave its own citizens stranded like refugees without access to life's basic necessities.

Sexism in the Media

A frequent critique of the media centers on the representation of women. American media in particular, and Western media more generally, are charged with glamorizing and perpetuating unrealistic ideals of feminine beauty. Some argue that repetitive bombardment by these images decreases girls' self-esteem and contributes to eating disorders. Women's magazines have been heavily criticized, although some researchers (such as Angela McRobbie from the United Kingdom) have taken care to show that women who are active, critical readers still enjoy reading women's magazines. However, as the Canadian sociologist Dawn Currie points out (1999), although girls can choose which magazines, if any, to read and how to critically read them, they can't control the images available to them in those and other texts.

Another focus of feminist media critiques has been images of violence against women. Jean Kilbourne has become one of the most popular lecturers at college and university campuses across America. In 1979 she released a film titled *Killing Us Softly: Advertising's Image of Women*, in which she examines the

ways in which women are maimed, sliced, raped, and otherwise deformed in advertising images. One classic example is a photo that shows the image of a woman's body in a garbage can, with only her legs and a fantastic pair of high heels on her feet visible. The message is clear: These shoes are, literally, to die for. Kilbourne's point is clear, too: Such images help sustain a kind of symbolic violence against women. In this critique, advertising does not just reflect the underlying culture that produced it but also creates desires and narratives that enter women's (and men's) lives with causal force.

Of course, there's always room for innovation. Some girls (with the help of their parents) have responded by creating their own magazines that focus on topics other than makeup, clothing, and boys, as mainstream teenage magazines do. For example, *New Moon Girls* is written and edited by girls aged 8 to 13 and contains no advertisements. Likewise, magazines exist for adult women that have more pro-woman messages; *Ms. Magazine* was founded in 1971 during the feminist movement to give voice to women and explore women's issues. Because such magazines don't accept advertising from huge makeup companies and designer fashion houses, however, they are often less economically viable than mainstream women's magazines, which contain as much as 50 percent ads. *Bitch* magazine ("It's a noun; it's a verb; it's a magazine"), which has been around since 1996, is a self-declared feminist response to pop culture. It is supported by advertisers but is a not-for-profit publication.

Some advertisers have responded to feminist critiques of the media with new approaches. In 2005 Dove, a manufacturer of skin-care products, launched a new series of ads, backed by a social awareness program, called the Campaign for Real Beauty. The ads featured not models but "real" women, complete with freckles, frizzy hair, wrinkles, and cellulite. The images intentionally meant to offer a contrast to the images we're accustomed to seeing. And, as Dove's advertisers have said, "firming the thighs of a size 2 supermodel is no challenge" (Triester, 2005). Whether this media campaign will spark a trend in using "real beauty" in advertising remains to be seen—although this is now one of Dove's stated missions.

A 2005 billboard from Dove soap's advertising campaign featuring women who are not professional models.

On the one hand, a pessimist might point out that these ads use real people as a way to be novel; models are all so uniformly perfect, they've become boring. Also, Dove isn't telling women that they're beautiful whether or not they have dimpled thighs and therefore they don't need firming lotion. Rather, the manufacturer's message is that it's okay to need firming lotion because you're not the only one who does. Furthermore, the women in the campaign are not overweight even though 67 percent of Americans are overweight or obese (CDC, NCHS 2008). An optimist, on the other hand, might view this ad campaign as Dove's effort to be socially responsible and to provide alternative images of beauty that aren't based on the stick-thin, supermodel ideal. Because you're an active, critical reader, not a passive receptor of the media, I'll let you decide.

Political Economy of the Media

In the United States, we (politicians especially) spend a lot of time talking about freedom, particularly freedom of the press. The freedom to say whatever you want is often upheld as one of the great markers of the "land of the free." The press, however, is hardly free. Most broadcasting companies are privately owned in the United States, are supported financially by advertising, and therefore are likely to reflect the biases of their owners and backers. (Compare this with the United Kingdom, where the British Broadcasting Company cannot accept private funding; households must pay fees for owning television sets; and these fees help cover the BBC's operating costs. This system is beginning to change, however, because of increasing economic pressures, such as competition from satellite television.)

In the United States today, six major companies—Disney, Viacom, Time Warner, News Corporation, CBS, and General Electric—own more than 90 percent of the media. Ownership alone does not equal censorship, but when the majority of the media lie in the hands of a few players, it is easier to ignore or purposely suppress messages that the owners of the media don't agree with or support. For example, a radio station can refuse to play certain artists who express ideas with which the station disagrees. One band, the Dixie Chicks, learned this the hard way in 2003. Ten days before the United States invaded Iraq, the lead singer of the band made a critical remark about President George W. Bush while on stage in London. Backlash led not only to boycotts, particularly by country music radio stations, but also to the public destruction of the band's CDs and threats against the lives of its members and their families. Stores can refuse to carry a CD because they object to the cover art, and many musicians, including the Goo Goo Dolls, John Mellencamp, Nirvana, and others, have had their CDs rejected for this reason. Is this freedom of expression or censorship? As corporate control of the media becomes more and more centralized (owned by fewer and fewer groups), the concern is that the range of opinions available will decrease and corporate censorship (the act of suppressing facts or stories that may reflect negatively on certain companies and/or their affiliates) will further compromise the already-tarnished integrity of the mainstream media.

The Internet, to some extent, has balanced out communications monopolies. It's much easier to put up a Web site expressing alternative views than it is to broadcast a television or radio program suggesting the same. The MIT Center for Future Civic Media, led by Chris Csikszentmihályi and Mitchel Resnick, works to leverage the Internet for the promotion of local activism. One of their projects—VGAZA or Virtual Gaza—allows Palestinians in the Gaza Strip to document crises and share local stories globally, even while under embargo. But not even the Internet is beyond the realm of political economy. Smaller sites, for example, cannot afford to have sponsored links on the sidebar of Google.com.

Consumer Culture

America is often described as a consumer culture, and rightly so. Sociologist Allison Pugh pointed out in our discussion that the "corporate marketing to children is a 22 billion dollar industry." She paused. "That's an annual figure. Children 8 to 11," she added, "ask for between two and four toys [for Christmas], and they receive eleven on average!" Sales on major patriotic holidays (Veteran's Day, Memorial Day, Presidents' Day) thrive as a result of the notion that it is our duty as American citizens to be good shoppers. As Sharon Zukin points out in her book on shopping culture, *Point of Purchase: How Shopping Changed American Culture* (2003), 24 hours after the terrorist attacks of September 11, 2001, Mayor Rudy Giuliani urged New Yorkers to take the day off and go shopping. It's the tie that binds our society; everyone's got to shop. Malls are our modern-day marketplaces—they are where teenagers hang out, where elderly suburbanites get their exercise, and where Europeans come as tourists to see what American culture is all about. The term *consumerism*, however, refers to more than just buying merchandise; it refers to the belief that happiness and fulfillment can be achieved through the acquisition of material possessions. Versace, J. Crew, and realtors in certain hip neighborhoods are not just peddling shoes, jeans, and apartments. They are also selling a self-image, a lifestyle, and a sense of belonging and self-worth. The media, and advertising in particular, play a large role in the creation and maintenance of consumerism.

Consumerism the steady acquisition of material possessions, often with the belief that happiness and fulfillment can thus be achieved.

Advertising and Children

The rise of the consumer-citizen has met with increasing criticism, but how does our society produce these consumer-citizens? The Canadian author and activist Naomi Klein published *No Logo: Taking Aim at the Brand Bullies* in 2000; in this book Klein analyzes the growth of advertising in schools. Pepsi and Coca-Cola now bargain for exclusive rights to sell their products within schools, and brand-name fast foods are often sold in cafeterias. The logos of companies that sponsor athletic fields are displayed prominently. This has been commonplace in many colleges and universities for some time now, but the increasing presence of advertising in middle and high schools should also be noted.

One striking example is Channel One, which has been airing in schools around the United States since 1990 (Rhode Island was the only state to refuse Channel One funding). In exchange for television sets, video equipment, and satellite dishes, schools are required to show 12 minutes of prepackaged programming every day. Although Channel One provides news and public affairs information, its programming also includes two minutes of commercials per 12-minute segment. One analysis found that only 20 percent of airtime is devoted to "recent political, economic, social, and cultural stories"; the remaining 80 percent of the prepackaged programming includes sports, weather, and other topics, as well as advertisements for Channel One itself. Studies have found that Channel One cost taxpayers $1.8 billion a year in lost school time; of that amount, $300 million was lost to commercials alone (Molnar & Sawicky, 1998). Meanwhile, Channel One charges advertisers almost $200,000 for each 30-second segment. Channel One is disproportionately found in lower-income school districts that struggle with funding for books and technology, meaning disadvantaged students in these schools are exposed to more advertisements and fewer academic lessons than their peers in systems that can afford to forgo this kind of sponsorship.

To see my interview with Allison Pugh, go to **wwnorton.com/studyspace**.

The result of all of this advertising is the creation of a self-sustaining consumer culture among children—albeit one that plays out differently for low-income and high-income families. Let's hear Pugh discuss her research with me again on this point:

> I found, for low-income parents, a practice of what I ended up calling "symbolic indulgence." They couldn't afford everything that a middle-class family might consider part of an adequate resource to childhood. So, they might not have blocks, or a bike. They might not have those basics, but they would have the thing that kind of gave the child something to talk about at school [such as a Gameboy]. And so it would be these highly [socially] resonant items [that parents would purchase]. (Conley 2011a)

In other words, these highly symbolic purchases of "in" toys or devices gave low-resource families an avenue to feel as though they were able to participate in the broader American consumer culture. Meanwhile, ironically, middle-class parents downplayed their consumerism:

> "I'm not materialistic. I'm not one of those bad parents you read about on TV . . . never being able to say no to my kids," [they would say]. So what I found for them is the systematic practice of "symbolic deprivation." The

kid would have an enormous amount of stuff. There would be mostly yeses in that child's life. But there would be particular things that that child didn't have, so that they [the parents] could really kind of convince me, convince themselves that they were honorable people. (Conley 2011a)

Pugh emphasizes that these dynamics are not just about corporate advertising but about the local social systems in which kids and their families find themselves. So to fix the problem, we have to change that dynamic by (somehow) making folks less afraid of being different, or perhaps more realistically by diminishing difference itself through sameness through, for example, school uniforms.

Culture Jams: Hey Calvin, How 'Bout Giving That Girl a Sandwich?

Culture jamming the act of turning media against themselves.

People can take back the media, or use them to their own ends. In that sense, Jill and Kevin, the newlyweds we met at the beginning of this chapter, were *culture jammers*. Culture jamming (a term that evolved from radio jamming, another form of guerrilla cultural resistance that involves seizing control of the frequency of a radio station) is the act of turning media against themselves. Part of a larger movement against consumer culture and consumerism, it's based on the notion that advertisements are basically propaganda. Culture jamming differs from appropriating advertisements for the sake of art and sheer vandalism (where the sole goal is destruction of property), although advertisers probably don't care too much about this latter distinction. Numerous anticonsumerist

Two satirical ads from *Adbusters* magazine. How do these ads critique or subvert the tobacco and fashion industries?

activist groups have sprung up, such as *Adbusters*, a Canadian magazine that specializes in spoofs of popular advertising campaigns. For example, it parodied a real Calvin Klein campaign (which advanced the career of Kate Moss and ushered in an age of ultra-thin, waiflike models) with a presumably bulimic woman vomiting into a toilet. *Adbusters* also sponsors an annual Buy Nothing Day (held, with great irony, on the day after Thanksgiving, known in retail as "Black Friday," the busiest shopping day of the year), which encourages people to do just that—buy nothing on this specific day of the year, encouraging them to reclaim their buying power and focus on the noncommercial aspects of the holiday, such as spending time with family and friends.

Another *Adbusters* spoof caricatured the legendary Joe Camel, the anthropomorphic advertising icon of Camel cigarettes from 1987 until 1997, when R. J. Reynolds, the tobacco firm that conjured up Joe Camel, voluntarily stopped using his image after receiving complaints from Congress and various public-interest groups that its ads primarily targeted children. (In 1991, a *Journal of the American Medical Association* study found that more 5- and 6-year-old kids recognized Joe Camel than Mickey Mouse or Fred Flintstone [P. M. Fischer et al., 1991].) In the *Adbusters* spoof, "Joe Chemo" is walking down a hospital hallway with an IV, presumably dying of cancer caused by smoking.

Globalization, Culture, and the Media

Dateline: Doha, Qatar. Shortly after the Gulf War in 1991, I visited Syria, where the warmth of the Syrian people stood in stark contrast to the imposing portraits of Hafez Assad, then the Syrian president, that lined the streets. After a day of sipping tea and wandering through Damascus marketplaces, my friends announced that they wanted to take me to a "very special" restaurant. Expecting a rich meal of Middle Eastern cuisine, I hid my disappointment when we arrived at Burger King (which I later learned to be the handiwork of a local entrepreneur who may have "borrowed" the franchise without the mother company's knowing). Over possibly faux-Whoppers, these Syrian university students told me how, if they were really lucky, Damascus might hit the mother lode: McDonald's was considering opening a local franchise there. Enjoying a Big Mac would mean that they had arrived in the economy of global culture.

That evening in 1991 was a manifestation of what political scientist Joseph Nye calls American "soft power," cultural and diplomatic dominance that persuades, rather than forces, others to do one's bidding. Soft power, he argues, is the necessary complement to "hard power," otherwise known as coercion and the projection of military force. Traveling in the region more recently, I determined

As anti-American sentiments increase in the Middle East, new regional brands such as Mecca-Cola are replacing American commercial products like Coca-Cola or Pepsi.

that my friends' dreams have indeed come true. McDonald's operates in almost every Arab country. Many other American fast-food companies also have franchises. Starbucks is the latest brand to infiltrate, adding an American twist to the coffee-drinking tradition, which began on the Arabian Peninsula about 12 centuries ago. Meanwhile, local papers advertise satellite TV systems with more than 800 channels. It would seem that American soft power has only risen in the years since I ate my Syrian Whopper: The best estimates are that Arabs spend more than $20 billion a year on U.S. products, and the real potential remains untapped—more than 300 million potential consumers live in the region.

The Arab market will probably remain untapped for the time being, however. Of late, the news has not been good for American companies located there. Since the most recent intifada in the Palestinian territories, many Arabs have joined a boycott of American goods, seeing this as a logical extension of the boycott of Israeli products that began in 1951. The boycott has intensified as a result of the war in Iraq and U.S. support for Israel's 2006 bombing of Hezbollah in southern Lebanon. Major U.S. exporters report that regional sales are down. McDonald's, in fact, has announced plans to pull back from the region. The company will shut 175 restaurants in ten countries, pulling out of three countries altogether—reversing a 20-year policy of global expansion. Coca-Cola's revenues also have fallen as the popularity of Muslim-owned Mecca-Cola and its Iranian equivalent, Zam Zam Cola, has risen at staggering rates, even outstripping supply.

Yes, 800 satellite channels are now available, but many of them carry Arabic programming that presents points of view that stand in direct opposition to what is commonly considered American propaganda. For example, the dateline for Israel is "Occupied Palestine." The same goes for the Internet. Islamic fundamentalism has risen, not decreased, with prolonged exposure to American culture. The Arab boycott and retreat of McDonald's are important indicators of long-term American prospects in the Middle East. A poll conducted in Egypt, Pakistan, Jordan, and Turkey before the U.S. invasion of Iraq in 2003 found that 78 percent of the Muslim population in these ally nations of the United States believed "the spread of American ideas and customs is a bad thing."

Anti-Americanism is growing partly because of the paradox that the combination of hard and soft power presents. With the incursion of U.S. military power into the region, the sales of Mecca-Cola rise further. In 2002, the George W. Bush administration decided to address the country's image problem by launching a public relations campaign in the Middle East led by Charlotte Beers, a former advertising executive-turned-undersecretary of state for public diplomacy and public affairs. Beers's diplomatic efforts included broadcasting positive messages about the United States over the radio, publishing an Arabic-language "consumer lifestyle" magazine, organizing a Middle East book tour for popular American authors, and dropping leaflets over Iraq.

These activities were greeted with widespread skepticism in the Muslim world, and were even criticized by many American government officials. In any case, they seem obsolete and insufficient in a world linked by multilingual 24-hour news channels, the Internet, wireless telecommunications, and global air travel. A few leaflets are not going to counter the already-negative local image of the United States that was in place even before the Abu Ghraib prison scandal. Viewed in this light, the retreat of the Big Mac might do the United States some good. After all, there are better ways to cultivate soft power, like President Obama's vow to close the Guantánamo Bay detention center. We might also learn to respect international agreements such as the Kyoto Protocol on global warming and fully support the International Criminal Court. Just maybe we will deal with the Israeli–Palestinian conflict before it deals with us.

→ CONCLUSION

The chapter opened with a description of how a song commissioned by a candy company helped elevate an unknown couple to YouTube stardom and even raised money to fight domestic violence. Now perhaps you can see why that circuitous story is part of a discussion of culture and media. But the fact that YouTube's parent company, Google, and Chris Brown's record label made the most off Jill and Kevin's wedding speaks to the fundamental nature of media and culture in our society. Remember that one job of the sociologist is to see what is usually taken for granted as constructed. In a way, Jill and Kevin disrupted the media flow. Their wedding dance had nothing to do with gum, the original financial motivation that got Brown to write the song. Are Jill and Kevin just cultural dupes, using a song written by a man convicted of domestic violence to promote their own domestic bliss? Or are they savvy consumers of culture, reshaping and remixing the messages and materials available to them to produce their own, wholly new, noncommercial message?

This chapter has presented some new ways of looking at culture: how we construct it, how it affects us, and what this means for understanding ourselves and the world in which we live. Do you now have a new understanding of culture? Can you now see your own culture through a critical lens? What have you previously taken for granted that you can now view as a product of our culture? Can you now look at the media in a different way? Don your critical thinking cap and put some of the stuff you've just learned into practice.

ASSIGNMENT

Think about the multiple uses of the concept of *culture*. Keep a journal for the next three days and document the ways in which the concept of culture comes up in your day-to-day life. If by day three you're short on examples, ask five people you know what they think when they hear the word *culture*. Which definitions occur most frequently? Has this exercise (and chapter) changed how you think about culture?

QUESTIONS FOR REVIEW

1. Keeping in mind the story of Jill and Kevin's wedding dance or recent "reality" television shows, define *celebrity* and *cultural icon*. Are people celebrities because they are talented, or can anyone achieve this status? How might this question parallel debates about high culture versus low culture?
2. The experience of eating at an American fast-food chain in Qatar has seemingly changed over the last few years. Using this example, how would you describe the relationship between "soft power" and consumerism?
3. How does Herbert Gans's *Deciding What's News* (1979) help us understand the way that cultural production simultaneously reflects and creates our world?
4. Goths are visible as a subculture, in part because of their taste in music and fashion. Using these criteria, identify another subculture. In which ways might this group's values oppose dominant culture?
5. A student holds the widespread cultural belief in upward social mobility through education and therefore studies thoroughly before an upcoming sociology exam. How might this represent an example of hegemony?
6. The term *culture* is complex, in part because it is used in numerous (sometimes contradictory) ways. Use three of the definitions of culture from this chapter to illustrate how a Shakespearean play might be considered "culture."
7. Let's consider how we are part of a consumer culture. Think about a consumer good you recently acquired and care about, for example, an item of clothing. Does this item in any way help establish or demonstrate who you are, what you are about, and how you perceive yourself?
8. How do blogs and YouTube potentially change the dynamics of media coverage in the context of a system controlled by a few large companies? Could bloggers and YouTube posters like Jill and Kevin be considered culture jammers?

PARADOX

DO MASS MEDIA CREATE SOCIAL NORMS OR MERELY REFLECT THEM? CULTURE IS LIKE TWO MIRRORS FACING EACH OTHER: IT SIMULTANEOUSLY REFLECTS AND CREATES THE WORLD WE LIVE IN.

WATCH THE ANIMATED SHORT ABOUT THE CULTURE AND MEDIA PARADOX AT

WWNORTON.COM/STUDYSPACE

How do socializing factors like friends, family, school, and the media shape our behavior?

4 Socialization and the Construction of Reality

PARADOX

THE MOST IMPORTANT ASPECTS OF SOCIAL LIFE ARE THOSE CONCEPTS WE LEARN WITHOUT ANYONE TEACHING US.

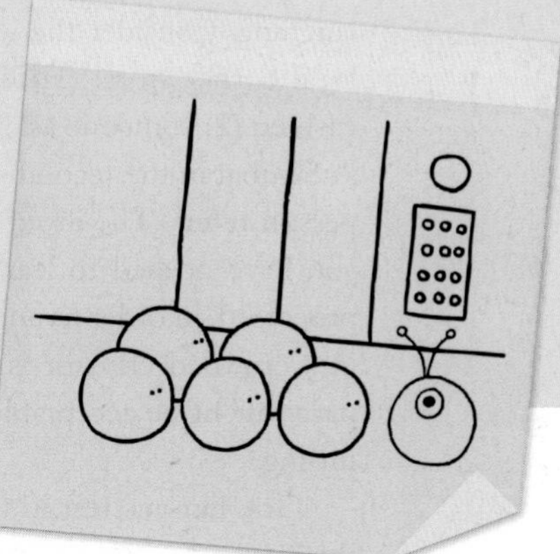

Think back to your first day of college. What did you do upon arriving at the classroom? Presumably, you sat in a chair. You probably opened a notebook and took out either a pen or a pencil, or maybe you fired up a laptop. When the professor walked in and called the class to attention, you stopped talking to the person next to you (or, if you didn't, you at least knew that you should). When handed a stack of syllabi, you took one and passed along the rest. You did not sit on anyone's lap. A million dollars says that you were wearing clothes. Another safe bet is that you did not physically assault anyone. Is all of this an accurate description of what occurred? Congratulations! You've been properly socialized.

So how did I know what you did, and, more important, how did you know what to do? Why did you sit in a chair and not on the floor? What if no furniture had been in the room? If a blackboard hung on one wall, you probably sat facing it in the absence of desks. Why? How did you know enough to bring paper and something with which to write? Did you receive an e-mail earlier in the week with explicit instructions telling you to do so? Why did you put on clothes this morning? When someone hands you a stack of papers, he or she might say, "Take one and pass them along," but even if that person doesn't, you still know what to do. You've internalized many unwritten rules about social behavior and public interaction. We call the process by which you learn how to become a functioning member of society socialization.

Imagine Mr. Spock, Tarzan, or an android trying to disguise himself as a college freshman. The droid would have to be programmed in minute detail with an endless list of possible reactions to potential situations. Think for a

Socialization the process by which individuals internalize the values, beliefs, and norms of a given society and learn to function as members of that society.

moment about the differences between your knowledge of how to respond to the following situations versus the responses of our droid: knowing how to answer when someone asks, "What's up?"; knowing to shift one's knees when someone else needs to slip in or out of a row of seats in the lecture hall; knowing to wait your turn when asking a question in the lecture or discussion section; knowing how to react when someone yells "Fire!" during class and screams versus a student shouting the same during a final exam and then laughing. Consider the difference between these two possible scenarios at a local corner store: (1) Someone asks for bread, holding out a $5 bill to the cashier; (2) someone asks for "bread," pointing a gun at the same cashier. You know that in the second scenario it is not a wheat-based product to which that person refers. The droid doesn't. He hasn't been socialized. Think how much you have needed to learn, how much knowledge you have internalized and processed, in order to understand that making direct eye contact with someone in a crowded elevator is inappropriate, whereas such behavior at a crowded party might be acceptable. The former might be considered creepy, the latter flirting.

One famous test in the computer science field of artificial intelligence is the Turing Test, in which a subject is asked to have two parallel conversations. One exchange occurs with an actual human, the other with a computer. Both are conducted by instant messaging or some other text-based platform. If the subject can't reliably distinguish the computer from the living human, then the computer is said to have passed the Turing Test (named for the scientist Alan Turing, who first proposed the test in a 1950 research paper). No computer has yet passed the test for very long. Now imagine adding facial expressions, body language, and other nonverbal communication cues to the test criteria. It quickly becomes clear why to be human is to be socialized and that true "artificial intelligence" is still a long way off.

Socialization: The Concept

Socialization, then, as defined by Craig Calhoun in the *Dictionary of the Social Sciences*, is "the process through which individuals internalize the values, beliefs, and norms of a society and learn to function as its members" (2002, p. 47). Starting from when you were born, the interactions between you and the rest of the world have shaped who you are. Presumably, as a baby, you were wrapped in either a pink or a blue blanket to signify your being a girl or a boy. At some point, you were potty trained—a critical expectation of our society. For babies, the primary unit of socialization is generally the family. As children grow older and enter the educational system, school becomes a key location in their socialization. This is where you probably learned to sit facing the front of the classroom. You learned to raise your hand before asking or answering a question. You learned not to talk when the teacher was speaking and what the punishment would be if you failed to follow this rule. By the time you entered college, you did not have to be told explicitly to do these things because you had *internalized* the rules that govern situations in which the people we designate students and teachers operate. As the examples that open this chapter illustrate, however, we learn more than explicit sets of rules. We learn how to interact on myriad levels in an endless number of situations.

Early in elementary school you were taught to raise your hand to speak in class. Can you think of other examples of internalized behavior?

You recognize the limits of your socialization when you find yourself in a new situation and aren't quite sure how to behave. If you've been shy and bookish in high school and you find yourself among a new set of party-going friends at a raucous fraternity party in college, you may not know just what to wear or how to behave. You may take as your model what you've seen on television and in the movies, but the party you are attending may not be quite the same. If, on the other hand, you've been going along to similar parties, maybe even at this very fraternity, with an older brother or sister for the past year or two, this particular party will not present any sort of anxiety. You'll know what to wear, which bathroom to use, whether or not it is cool to post photos of the event on Facebook, what music to like, and which songs deserve an eye rolling. Your previous experience as a tag-along may now make you a leader among your freshman peers.

Limits of Socialization

Although socialization is necessary for people to function in society, they are not simply blank slates onto which society transcribes its norms and values. Twins are often used to support one or the other side of the nature-versus-nurture debate, because they allow us to factor out genetics. Twins living hundreds or even thousands of miles apart may simultaneously experience the same pain in their right arms—score one point for nature. Take another set of twins, however, who were separated at birth in the early 1900s. One of them was raised as a Jew and the other became a Nazi—one for nurture. So which theory is correct? Both and neither. In sociology, we tend to think less about right and wrong and more about which theories are more or less helpful in explaining and understanding our social world. The concept of socialization is useful for understanding how people become functioning members of society. Like most theories, however, socialization can be limited in its explanatory power. Have you ever heard someone discussing a "problem child?" The conversation might go something like this: "I just don't know what's wrong with him. He comes from such a nice family. And his older brothers are such nice, respectful boys." How did this child go astray? The primary unit of socialization, the family, seems to have been functional. The other children went on to lead happy and productive lives. What else might explain the youngest son's delinquency? For starters, human beings have agency. This means that, while we operate within limits that largely are not of our own making (e.g., U.S. law requires that all children receive schooling), we also make choices about how to interact with our environment. We can physically walk out of the school, fall asleep in class, or refuse to take a test.

"Human" Nature

Is there such a thing as human nature? It's physiology that prompts you to urinate, but it's socialization that tells you where and when to do so. We are largely shaped by interaction, such that without society the human part of human nature would not develop. We can observe this in children raised by animals or denied human contact. Take the case of "Anna," a young girl whose true age was unknown but estimated at about five years who had been found in torturous conditions, bound to a chair in an attic, where she had been left almost completely alone in the dark since birth. Her nutritional requirements had been minimally met and it is believed that her only regular human contact was when her mother delivered these small meals. She could not properly speak or use her limbs, even walk when she was discovered. She did not respond to light or sounds the way children normally do. With some care and attention, the nurses at the treating hospital were able to provoke some giggles and coos by tickling her. Eventually, she was able to make speechlike sounds and gain more control of her body, but she never developed to the level of most children her age and died a few years later. Some of the doctors examining her wondered if she had been born mentally retarded, but ultimately, they opined that she could not have survived such an environment unless she had been healthy at birth.

The professionals who cared for Anna and followed her case reached five general conclusions:

1. Her inability to develop past an "idiot level of mentality . . . is largely the result of social isolation."
2. "It seems almost impossible for any child to learn to speak, think, and act like a normal person after a long period of isolation."
3. When she is compared with other cases of isolated children, the similarities "seem to indicate that the stages of socialization are to some extent necessarily related to the stages of organic development."
4. "Anna's history . . . seems to demonstrate that human nature is determined by the child's communicative social contacts as much as by his organic equipment and that the system of communicative symbols is a

highly complex business acquired early in life as the result of long and intimate training."

5. Theories of socialization are neither right nor wrong in this case, "but simply inapplicable." (Davis, 1940, pp. 554–65)

What this case illustrates is that "human nature" is a blend of "organic equipment," the raw materials we are physically made of, and social interaction, the environment in which we are raised. In what other ways can we look at the role of socialization and social structures in shaping our behaviors?

Theories of Socialization

Now that we have identified this process called socialization, we can turn to some of the theories about how it works.

Me, Myself, and I: Development of the Self and the Other

Self the individual identity of a person as perceived by that same person.

I one's sense of agency, action, or power.

Me the self as perceived as an object by the "I"; the self as one imagines others perceive one.

Have you ever seen a little girl cover her eyes with her hands and declare, "You can't see me now!" She does not realize that just because she cannot see you doesn't mean you cannot see her. She is incapable of distinguishing between *I* and *you* and has not yet formed an idea of her individual self. How does the concept of the self develop? Sociologists would argue that it emerges through a social process. Perhaps the first full theory of the social self was developed by Charles Horton Cooley, who coined the term *the looking glass self*. According to Cooley in *Human Nature and the Social Order* (1902/1922), the self emerges from our ability to assume the point of view of others and thereby imagine how they see us. We then test this "theory" of how we are perceived by gauging others' reactions and revise our theory by fine-tuning our "self concept."

George Herbert Mead further elaborated the process by which the social self develops in the 1930s (see Figure 4.1). Infants only know the I, that is, one's sense of agency, action, or power. Through social interaction, however, they learn the me, that is, the self as a distinct object to be perceived by others (and by the I). Imagine, for example, that you are taking care of your two-year-old cousin, Joey. He wants a cookie. You explain to him that you will happily give him a cookie just as soon as you go to the bathroom. He starts shouting, "I want cookie! I want cookie!" And you are ready to scream, "But I have to pee!" In a more rational moment, you might argue with your adorable cousin: "How would you feel if I demanded a cookie immediately when you entered

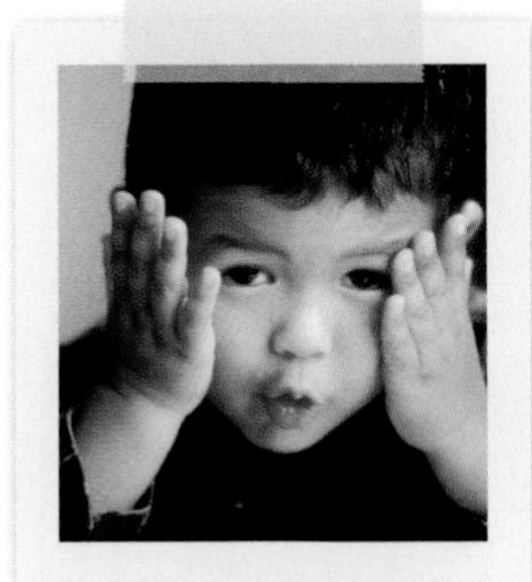

How does a small child playing peekaboo demonstrate the social process of creating the self?

Figure 4.1: Mead's Stages of Social Development

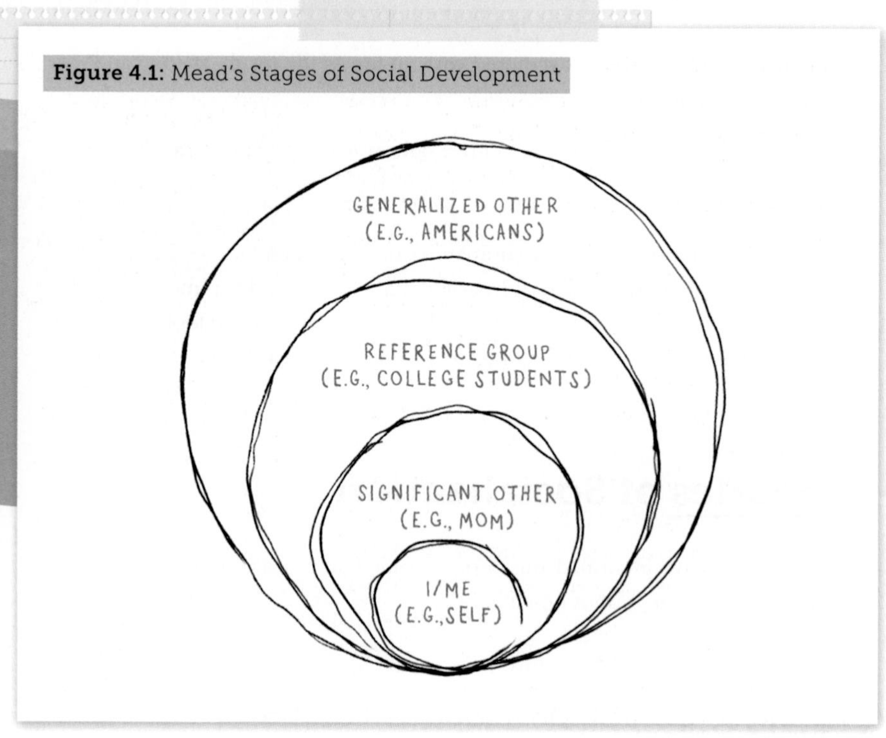

the house after a six-hour car ride with no rest stops along the way and your bladder was about to explode?" Although such a line of logic might work with your cousin's seven-year-old sister, it will not work with little Joey because he has yet to develop a sense of the other, that is, someone or something outside of oneself. In Joey's mind, there is no *other*, the *you* who hasn't seen a toilet in six hours; there is only the *self* who wants a cookie. This is why we allow children a certain amount of leeway. If your best friend behaved like this, however, you would accuse him or her of being childish, and you would be correct.

Other someone or something outside of oneself.

How do we move beyond the self? To function as fully adult members of society, we need to be able to recognize the other. Thus, imitation, play, and games are important components of childhood development. When a child imitates, he or she is just starting to learn to recognize an other. That's what peekaboo is all about. Eventually, kids understand that you are still there when they cover their eyes. They can then advance to play, according to Mead. During play, children are able to make a distinction between the self and the other. Suppose that you are playing with your cousin Joey, who is now five years old, and he says, "I'll be the cop, and you be the bad guy." He's recognizing you as the other, the bad guy, who has a different set of motives, responses, and actions from the good guy, the cop. Eventually, children move beyond play to formal games.

Games involve a more complex understanding of multiple roles; indeed, you must be able to recognize and anticipate what many other players are going to do in a given situation. Have you ever watched a swarm of toddlers try to play soccer? It's a mess. They're content to kick the ball; that's enough for them. They can't pass, let alone coordinate an offensive attack on an empty goal. It takes an understanding of the other to coordinate passing: You have to consider where to place the ball and calculate whether your teammate can make it to that spot in time for the pass to occur. Games such as soccer involve more than just hand-eye (or foot-eye) coordination. They involve a sophisticated understanding of the various positions others can occupy—that is, they require a theory of social behavior, knowing how others are likely to react to different situations. The goalie is not likely to leave the box in front of the goal, even if I tempt him or her with the ball. But a defender or midfielder is likely to pursue me if I am not controlling the ball very well. We have learned to anticipate these behaviors from repeated experience in the context of a particular sort of constrained social interaction—namely, a soccer game.

Why are games an important part of child development? What do team sports like soccer teach us about multiple roles?

As our parents, siblings, friends, teachers, and Little League coaches socialize us, we learn to think beyond the self to the other. According to Mead, however, that brings us only halfway to being socialized. The final step is developing a concept of the generalized other, which represents an internalized sense of the total expectations of others in a variety of settings—regardless of whether we've encountered those people or places before. In this way, we should be able to function with complete strangers in a wide range of social settings. For example, it is the perception of the generalized other that keeps you from taking off your pants to more comfortably lounge in the park on hot summer days, that keeps you from singing on the bus no matter how much you are enjoying the song on your iPod, and that keeps you from extracting an uncomfortable wedgie in public. We can, and do, continually update our internal sense of the generalized other as we gather new information about norms and expectations in different contexts.

Generalized other an internalized sense of the total expectations of others in a variety of settings—regardless of whether we've encountered those people or places before.

For instance, as a child, you may have been chided by your parents not to pick your nose. You have to be taught that this is unacceptable behavior, because otherwise it might seem perfectly reasonable. You have something in your nose, it's bothering you, you want to remove whatever is stuck there, and, lo and behold, your finger is just the right size. It's remarkably convenient. However, you learn not to pick your nose because it's a socially unacceptable action. But wait! Sometimes, you might catch your dad picking his nose. Now you revise the original lesson and realize what is most important: not to pick your nose in public. You may even have been taught explicitly that certain activities that are acceptable in private are unacceptable in public. The concept of the generalized other shapes our actions by our internalization of what is, and is not, acceptable in different social situations. Some of us may have internalized the notion that nose picking is inherently disgusting and should never be done anywhere. Some of us may have internalized the notion that nose picking is a little gross but believe it's okay when done in private; the action should just not be performed in public. If you walked outside right now and saw a child picking his nose, you might think, "Eww," but laugh because he is, after all, a child. On the other hand, if his mom was picking her nose, too, you might give her a look of disapproval for violating an established social norm.

People may also intentionally violate established norms. It is not uncommon for children to touch their genitalia in public (watch any group of four- or five-year-olds and you will quickly spot who needs to go to the bathroom). As a society, however, not touching or exposing your genitals in public is a well-established norm (a law, in fact). The exhibitionist who flashes himself or masturbates in public does so not because he was poorly socialized. He has a keen understanding of the generalized other and violates the norm with the explicit purpose of soliciting a reaction from a generalized other (or a very specific other, in some cases).

Agents of Socialization

Families

For most individuals, the family is the primary unit of socialization. If you have siblings, you may develop the sense that older and younger children are treated differently. The general impression is that the younger siblings get away with more. Parents, having already gone through the experience of child rearing, may relax their attitudes and behaviors toward later children (even if unconsciously). Note, too, that socialization can be a two-way street. Information doesn't always flow from the older to the younger family members. As computers and other technology become more and more ubiquitous in our society, children may need to socialize their parents in terms of how to use such technology. For example, the children of immigrants—who are immersed in the U.S. school system while their parents may maintain less contact with mainstream American communities—are likely to take on the role of an agent of socialization instead of the other way around, teaching their parents the language and other tools of cultural assimilation. In a similar vein, a study by economist Ebonya Washington (2008) showed that members of Congress who had daughters were more likely to vote for feminist measures. Perhaps daughters socialize their parents into being more sensitive to women's concerns. Alternatively, it could be that when legislators have their own daughters' future to worry about, they vote for legislative changes that will help them (and, by extension, women in general). So it's hard to say whether this is really socialization at work or merely a change in rational, selfish calculations.

The socialization that occurs within the family can be affected by various demographics. Parents of different social classes socialize their children differently. For example, when asked what values they want their children to have, middle-class parents are more likely to stress independence and self-direction, whereas working-class parents prioritize obedience to external authority (Kohn & Schooler, 1983). Indeed, sociologists have long recognized that parents' social class matters, but how exactly this privilege is transmitted to children (beyond strictly monetary benefits) has been less clear. To better understand this process, ethnographer Annette Lareau spent time in both black and white households with children approximately ten years of age. She found that middle-class parents, both black and white, are more likely to engage in what she calls "concerted cultivation." They structure their children's leisure time with formal activities (such as soccer leagues and piano lessons) and reason with them over decisions in an effort to foster their kids' talents.

According to Annette Lareau, how do working-class and middle-class families structure their children's free time differently? What are the results of these different socializing behaviors?

Working-class and poor parents, in contrast, focus on the "accomplishment of natural growth." They give their children the room and resources to develop but leave it up to the kids to decide how they want to structure their free time. A greater division between the social life of children and that of the adults exists in such households (Lareau, 2002). Whereas middle-class parents send their kids off to soccer leagues, music lessons, and a myriad of other after-school activities, kids in poor families spend a disproportionate amount of time "hanging out," as has been observed by Jason DeParle in *American Dream* (2004), his chronicle of three families on public assistance struggling through the era of welfare reform in Milwaukee. Likewise, a 2006 study by Annette Lareau, Eliot Weingarter, and this author shows the same statistical results: Outside of school, disadvantaged children spend 40 percent more time in unstructured activities than their middle-class counterparts.

Middle-class kids, on the other hand, spend their days learning how to interact with adult authority figures, how to talk to strangers, and how to follow rules and manage schedules. From a very young age, they are taught to use logic and reason to support their choices by mirroring their parents' explanations of why they can or cannot get what they want. Low-income parents, Lareau found, were more likely to answer their children with "because I said so," instilling respect for authority but missing an opportunity to help their children develop logical reasoning skills commonly used in adult interactions. Middle-class kids discover the confidence that comes with achievements such as learning to play the piano or mastering a foreign language. Whether they actually have fun is unknown, but they are certainly socialized into the same kind of lifestyles that their parents hope them to have as adult professionals. In fact, it should be no surprise that the rise of the "overscheduled" child comes during a period when, for the first time in history, higher-income Americans work more hours than lower-income Americans. Professional parents familiarize their children with the kind of lives they expect them to lead as adults.

http://wwnorton.com/studyspace

Annette Lareau. To see my interview with Lareau about *Unequal Childhoods*, go to **wwnorton.com/studyspace**.

An important question, however, is how these different parenting strategies may or may not affect the long-term outcomes of kids. Luckily, I was able to speak to Annette Lareau upon the publication of her updated edition of *Unequal Childhoods* (2003), for which she went back and followed up with many of the families she had originally studied. Here's what she told me:

> There really were no surprises. I would say it was sad. Many of the working-class and poor children had wanted to do well, their parents had wanted them to do well, but things had not worked out. So many of them dropped out of high school, some of them had graduated from high school, but they were all in blue-collar jobs or unemployed. Not one was in the professional sector. [For] the middle-class families, it wasn't always easy sailing [either]. Garrett Talinger got his heart broken. Melanie Hamlin had a friend killed in a car accident. It's not that bad things don't happen to middle-class kids; they do. But in terms of being launched, in terms of their life chances, they were much more likely to go to college, and their parents helped them, and supervised them in college. So their parents helped them choose their college classes, they gave them advice on their majors, and so the parents continued to provide guidance and help as they went into adulthood. Alexander Williams, the middle-class African American boy, is now going to become a doctor. Garrett Talinger became a high-level manager. He has a suit and tie, his face is shining. (Conley, 2011b)

This was so interesting, so I probed by asking: What exactly happened in the poor and working-class families' lives that caused the kids, despite their high aspirations, to drop out of high school or go no further than a high-school diploma?

> Well, one thing that was very important was the schools that they attended. Schools are very unequal in America. And they [working-class parents] tried to get them into other [better] high schools, but that often didn't work out. And private school is expensive, and they [had] scarce resources. The other thing that happened is that many of the parents wanted their children to go to college. But college [involves] a very complicated set of institutions. To apply to college involves many, many, many steps. If they wanted to go to college, did you take, say, advanced algebra? Did you take the [other] classes you needed to apply to college? Then did they take the SAT and the ACT? Did they apply to college? And if they got in, did they go? And so by the end you have these diversion in pathways between the parents who are middle class and the parents who are working class, despite the aspirations.

Lareau went on to provide a concrete example of these hurdles:

> One of the girls who was actually not featured in the book, named Tara Carroll, was dropped for space reasons. She is an African American young woman. Her mother dropped out of high school, [and was from a] deeply religious family, raised by a grandmother. She really wanted to go to college. She applied to eight colleges, but her SAT scores under the old system were a combined score of 700. So, they were really about as low as you can get. But that's a very typical SAT score in urban America. And then she applied

> to colleges, but she applied to colleges that were two and three hundred points above her SAT. Now, if she had been my daughter, could I have gotten her into a school? Probably. I would have found a school that would have taken a child who had a learning disability, or had low scores, and I could have placed her in college. It would have taken a lot of work. But in her system, her mother depended on the [high] school to help her daughter go to college. So the mother didn't see the applications, and the mother had a car, but she didn't go on college tours. It was up to her daughter and the school. And that is a reasonable decision. Her daughter was rejected everywhere, and she ended up going to community college for a semester and dropping out. And [her experience follows] a very typical pattern for working-class families.

Though Lareau can't definitively discern cause and effect here—what if Tara's SAT scores had been higher? Or if she had lucked out with a fabulous guidance counselor? Things might have turned out differently for her, despite the "natural growth" strategy her mother followed. But by showing how social stratification actually worked on the ground, Lareau tells a pretty convincing—if depressing—story.

School

When children enter school, the primary locus of socialization largely shifts. In addition to helping you learn the three *R*s, one of the teacher's main goals is to properly socialize you—teaching you to share, take turns, resolve conflict with words, be quiet when necessary, and speak when appropriate. Walk into any kindergarten classroom and compare it with a third-grade class. What are the main differences? For starters, there is probably a lot more order, and less noise, among the third graders. When you were young and needed to leave the classroom as a group (whether for recess, gym, or music class), you probably had to line up and follow your teacher. Did you have to do this in high school? Highly unlikely, because teenagers are able to get themselves from one classroom to the next, whereas five-year-olds are not. Think about how all those years prepared you for college: Your teachers taught you that you need to have something to take notes on and with, whether it be a pen and notebook or a laptop. You learned to sit at a desk and, if there was a clear front of the room, to face it.

Schools, however, teach us more than how to show up prepared for class, and all schools are not created equal. In *Preparing for Power*, Peter W. Cookson, Jr. and Caroline Hodges Persell explore how private prep schools indoctrinate the students who attend them into a world of social status and privilege. The researchers "document how the philosophies, programs, and lifestyles of boarding schools help transmit power and privilege and how elite families use

What advantages do students at elite private schools, such as the young men pictured above in this 1964 Philips Academy yearbook photo, have over those who attend public schools? How do elite schools prepare students differently?

these schools to maintain their social class" (1985). Admission to these schools is highly competitive and far from democratic. "Legacies" (children who come from families where at least one other member has attended the same school) make up more than half (54 percent) of the attendees on average and as many as 75 percent at some schools. The nonacademic part of the curriculum ranges from upper-class sports such as crew and sailing to cultural education in the form of study abroad and smaller field trips overseas. Probably the most important aspect of prep-school education is that it links students into social networks—helping them get into the top colleges and hobnob with students from wealthy and powerful families—that they will have access to and benefit from for the rest of their lives.

Peers

Once we reach school age, peers become an important part of our lives and function as agents of socialization. Adolescents, in particular, spend a great deal of their free time in the company of peers. Peers can reinforce messages taught in the home (even the most liberal of friends will probably expect you to wear clothing when you hang out with them after school) or contradict them. Either way, conformity is generally expected; hence, the term *peer pressure*. Walk into any high-school cafeteria and you'll observe the power of conformity among peer groups. If you have ever tried drugs or alcohol, did you do so by yourself? Probably not. Even when we are being deviant, we often do so in the company (and often at the suggestion) of others. This is why parents express

Research on television shows such as *Sesame Street* shows that they help children develop math and verbal skills.

concern about their children hanging out with the "wrong crowd." They're not just being paranoid.

Adolescents do tend to be more open to their friends' advice than to their parents'. A 2002 study of young adolescents (by Wood et al.) found, on the one hand, that friends were a major source of information on dating and sex. This makes sense. No matter how cool your parents are (or try to be), when you're 15, you probably don't want to talk to them about your love life. On the other hand, the same study found that even though adolescents obtained much of their information on sex from friends, they didn't necessarily believe it. In fact, they were less likely to believe what they learned from friends and the media and more likely to name parents and sex educators as sources of reliable information. It seems as if most adolescents have already learned that they shouldn't believe everything they hear.

Media

Ongoing is a debate about the impact the media have on us. Do violent video games desensitize children to violence and socialize them to become criminals? The jury is still out on that question, but the media can indeed serve as socializing agents. Some television shows are designed with that explicit purpose. *Sesame Street* was created with the intent of providing educational programming for low-income children who didn't have the same opportunities for day care and preschool as their wealthier peers. Guess what—this approach works!

Adult Socialization

The socialization we receive as children can never fully prepare us for the demands that we will face as adults. *Adult socialization* simply refers to the ways in which you are socialized as an adult. When you work at a restaurant, you learn, for instance, what your job responsibilities are, how to take orders and place them in the kitchen, and how to carry a tray full of drinks. As a result of your prior socialization, you probably already knew that you should not talk back to customers. Similarly, your plans upon graduation from college might include moving out of your parents' house, finding a job, and maybe starting a family. Right now, you may not know everything you need to in order to function in each of those situations, but you will learn. Some roles, like some jobs, take more preparation than others—you have to go to law school to become an attorney and medical school to become a doctor. Did you ever wonder why parenting schools don't exist?

Resocialization is a more drastic form of adult socialization. When you change your environment, you may need some resocialization. If you plan to live in another country, you may have to learn a new language and new ways of eating, speaking, talking, listening, or dressing. If you went to a single-sex high school and are attending a co-ed college or university, this change will probably require some resocialization, depending on the extent to which you interacted with the opposite sex during your high-school years. The most drastic case of resocialization would be that necessary if you had suffered a terrible accident and lost all of your memory. You would need to relearn everything—how to hold a fork and knife, how to tie your shoes, how to engage in conversation. You would be completely childlike once again—any inappropriate nose picking would be forgiven.

Resocialization the process by which one's sense of social values, beliefs, and norms are reengineered, often deliberately through an intense social process that may take place in a total institution.

Total Institutions

The term total institution refers to an institution that controls all the basics of day-to-day life. Members of the institution eat, sleep, study, play, perhaps even bathe and pray together. Boarding schools, colleges, monasteries, the army, and prisons are all total institutions to varying degrees—prisons being the most extreme (see Chapter 6). Sociologist Gwynne Dyer's *War* (1985) provides some insight into the total institution of the U.S. Marine Corps. Marine boot camp strips down much of the prior socialization of recruits and resocializes them to become Marines. Think about how boot camp treats new male enlistees: Certain parts of their identity are erased. Their heads are shaved and uniforms handed to them. Enlistees live, eat, sleep, bathe, exercise, and study together. Their every move is watched and critiqued, from how they hold a weapon to how they tuck in the corners of their bedsheets. New Marines—and recruits in all branches of the armed forces—also must be resocialized to accept the notion that it is okay, even necessary, to kill. Most of us have learned quite the opposite, of course—that under no circumstances should we kill another person. Basic training is not only about teaching recruits new skills; it's about changing them so that they can perform tasks they wouldn't have dreamed of doing otherwise. It works by applying enormous physical and mental pressure on men and women who have been isolated from their normal civilian environment and constantly placed in situations where the only right way to think and behave is that espoused by the

Total institution an institution in which one is totally immersed and that controls all the basics of day-to-day life; no barriers exist between the usual spheres of daily life, and all activity occurs in the same place and under the same single authority.

Marines training at Parris Island. How is Marine boot camp an example of a total institution?

Marine Corps. For people to be effective soldiers, they must learn a new set of rules about when it is okay and/or necessary to kill (that is, when they are on active duty, not on leave and at the pizza parlor with their family).

Social Interaction

Status a recognizable social position that an individual occupies.

Role the duties and behaviors expected of someone who holds a particular status.

Role strain the incompatibility among roles corresponding to a single status.

To talk about how institutions and society as a whole socialize us, we need a language to describe social interaction. Robert Merton's role theory provides just such a vocabulary. The first key concept for an understanding of role theory is status, which refers to a recognizable social position that an individual occupies. The person who runs your class and is responsible for grading each student has the status of professor. Roles, then, refer to the duties and behaviors associated with a particular status. You can reasonably expect your professor to show up on time, clothed, and prepared for class. You can also expect that he or she has a fair amount of education, often a PhD, and is knowledgeable about the material. This may not always be true, but it is a fairly standard set of role expectations for someone with the status of professor. Roles are complicated, however, and relatively few of them materialize with handbooks and clear sets of expectations. Sometimes, we experience role strain, the incompatibility among roles corresponding to a single status. An example of this is the old dictum for university faculty, particularly young professors, to publish or perish. On the one hand, they need to stay on top of their research, write articles, give lectures, and attend conferences to stay abreast of current topics and remain active in the academic world. On the other hand, they have to teach and perform all the teaching roles that come with the status of professor—preparing lectures, running class sections, meeting with students, grading papers, and writing letters of recommendation.

When your professor arrives at class tomorrow morning with bags under her eyes and a look on her face that seems to say, "No amount of coffee will help me at this point," you may be tempted to conclude, "Oh, she's experiencing

role strain." But what if her exhaustion results not from the time demands of simultaneously correcting her midterms and preparing for an upcoming research conference, but rather from the turmoil that ensued last night when the family dog destroyed her daughter's biology project and she had to stay up all night helping her daughter redo it? In this case, role conflict is the culprit. It is not the roles within her status as professor that are the root of her problems, but rather the tensions between her role as professor and her role as mother. Whereas *role strain* refers to conflicting demands within the same status, *role conflict* describes the tension caused by competing demands between two or more roles within different statuses. Each one of us, at any given time, enjoys numerous statuses. These statuses (and their corresponding roles) can and do change over time and between places. When you started college, how did your status change? The obvious answer is that you went from being either a high-school student or perhaps an unskilled worker to becoming a college student. If you graduated from high school and went straight to college, you traded in one status for another. If you still maintain a full- or part-time job, you have added another status. The term status set refers to all the statuses you have at any given time.

Role conflict the tension caused by competing demands between two or more roles pertaining to different statuses.

Status set all the statuses one holds simultaneously.

To obtain a better sense of how roles and statuses function, try the following experiment: Write down as many answers to the question, "Who am I?" as you can. Compare your answers with your classmates'. With remarkable similarity, the lists will include statuses such as brother, sister, daughter, boyfriend, student, lifeguard, babysitter, roommate, and so forth. This occurs because we know ourselves in our social roles, in the ways in which we relate to others. You most likely will have listed the key components of your status set.

There are some other key terms that you must learn to understand role theory. Sociologists often make a distinction between an ascribed status and an achieved status, which basically amounts to what you are born with versus what you become. Another way to think about it is in terms of involuntary versus voluntary status. Your age, race, and sex are all largely *ascribed statuses*, whereas your status as a juggler, drug dealer, peace activist, or reality television

Ascribed status a status into which one is born; involuntary status.

Achieved status a status into which one enters; voluntary status.

Who are you? What are the different roles in your status set? For example, singer Beyonce's statuses include mother, daughter, and partner.

junkie is an *achieved status*. Sometimes, one status within our status set stands out or overrides all the others. This is called a master status. Examples might include being unemployed, being lesbian, being disabled, or any status that overshadows other statuses. Master status roles can be ascribed, like disability, or achieved, like being a celebrity. The key characteristic of a master status is that people tend to interact with you on the basis of that one status alone.

Master status one status within a set that stands out or overrides all others.

Gender Roles

One of the most popular strains of thought to evolve from role theory has been the concept of gender roles, sets of behavioral norms assumed to accompany one's status as male or female. In their critiques of role theory, gender theorists such as Candace West and Don Zimmerman (1987) have argued that the statuses of boy/girl and man/woman have distinct power and significance which role theory doesn't adequately capture (you can read more about this in Chapter 8 on sex and gender). If we were to put West and Zimmerman's ideas into the language of role theory, we could argue that sex constitutes a master status in our society. We can see how this fits into larger theories of socialization. From the moment they leave the womb, babies usually wear either pink or blue to designate their sex. There are signs, balloons, greeting cards, and e-cards announcing, "It's a boy!" or "It's a girl!" Little boys' clothes are often decorated with baseballs, cars, or tools, whereas girls' clothes tend to feature flowers, bows, and lace. Similarly, studies (Lewis et al., 1992) have shown that people interact with babies differently based on whether they are boys or girls, commenting on how "big" and "strong" baby boys are and how "pretty" baby girls may be, or by closely snuggling with female babies rather than holding them outwardly, as with male babies so that they might see the world.

Gender roles sets of behavioral norms assumed to accompany one's status as male or female.

How do the displays at this New York City toy store serve as an example of the ways that we learn gender roles through socialization?

Not just family members but the larger social world interact with boys and girls very differently and, consequently, socialize them into different roles. Take a stroll through your local toy store, and you will glimpse the function of toys and play—both very important to the development of children—in creating and maintaining gender roles. The toys for playing house will likely be displayed in boxes showing images of little girls pushing and pulling pink irons and purple vacuum cleaners. The boxes for toy stoves will depict girls cooking. Baby dolls will be wrapped in pastel colors, and their packaging will show little girls cradling them. Now meander through the section of the store displaying tool sets, workbenches, and toys related to outdoor activities. On the packages, you will note little boys dressed in bright primary colors, wielding hammers and fishing poles. The action-figure aisle will be similarly gendered (think Barbie versus G.I. Joe). (Admittedly, these are generalizations. Some images will show boys playing house and girls constructing a bridge, but the vast majority will adhere to what we perceive as traditional gender roles.)

In high school, gender-role socialization continues as peers police each other. Sociologist C. J. Pascoe spent a year in a working-class high school in California finding out just how teens enforce gender norms on one another. She discovered what she calls "fag discourse," a term that describes the near-continuous use of the term *fag* or *faggot* as an insult teenage boys use against one another to curtail improper behavior. She explained in a recent interview how it worked. Someone could get called a fag "if you danced, if you cared about your clothing, if you were too emotional, or if you were incompetent." What's more, actually being gay turned out to be beside the point. Again, Pascoe stepped in to explain: "What I came to realize was that they used *fag* as an insult to police the boundaries of masculinity. It wasn't about same-sex desire. In fact when I asked them about same-sex desire one boy said, 'Well being gay is just a lifestyle; you can still throw a football around and be gay.'" This "masculinity policing" is no joking matter. A boy she called Ricky was "targeted so relentlessly that he dropped out of school" (Conley, 2009c).

If boys are constantly policing the boundaries of masculinity with homophobic insults, how are girls being socialized into their gender roles? At the school in Pascoe's study, girls did not insult each other. Instead they had to put up with constant sexual harassment from the boys. As the boys looked for behaviors that would prove they were not "fags," they used girls as unwitting resources with which to perform aggressive sexuality by describing to one another either how they could "get" girls or the outlandish and often violent sexual escapades that would then follow. Further, they engaged in rituals of forceful touching, often physically constraining girls' movements. Pascoe describes one hallway scene in which she "watched one boy walk down the hallway jabbing a girl in the crotch with his drum stick yelling, 'Get raped, get raped'" (Conley, 2009c). In this case, gender socialization looks a lot like gender-based bullying. Do these scenes remind you of high school? Was your gender performance policed by your peers?

C. J. Pascoe. To see my interview with Pascoe about *Dude, You're a Fag*, go to wwnorton.com/studyspace.

For some, constant gender-boundary policing has catastrophic effects. Ricky was subject to the steadiest, most virulent "fag discourse" in Pascoe's study and he dropped out. An 11-year-old in Massachusetts committed suicide after being relentlessly teased; many of the insults he received were part of "fag discourse." And Pascoe points out that 90 percent of school shooters who go on rampage school shootings have been subject to homophobic harassment and teasing (Conley, 2009c).

The Social Construction of Reality

In a February 19, 2006, *New York Times* op-ed essay titled "Mind over Splatter," Vassar professor Don Foster commented on the debate surrounding a Jackson Pollock painting that was recently alleged to be a fake. Is the painting any less artistic for not being a real Pollock when it was, after all, good enough to fool so many people for so long? In a similar vein, Shakespeare's Juliet once inquired, "What's in a name? That which we call a rose by any other name would smell as sweet." The implication is that something is what it is, apart from what we call it or who made it. But do we agree? This question speaks less to the essential nature of things and more to the social construction of reality. Something is real, meaningful, or valuable when society tells us it is.

So what does it mean to say that something is socially constructed? This question is less a debate about what is real versus fake and more an explanation of how we give meanings to things or ideas through social interaction. Two good ways of understanding how we socially construct our reality are to compare one society over different time periods and to compare two contemporary societies. Let's look at some examples.

In U.S. society we take for granted that childhood is a developmental stage. It wasn't always considered so, however; this view came about through a series of cultural, political, and economic changes. In preindustrial times children were expected to care for younger siblings and contribute to the household in other ways as soon as they were physically capable. Toys specifically for children, one of the cultural markers of childhood, did not exist. The early years of one's life were not regarded as a time for play and education. They represented a time of work and responsibility, like most of life's course. However, the development of the industrial factory led to the need for schools, a place where children might spend their days, because parents now left home to go to work. This change in parents' lifestyles meant that a separate sphere had to be created for children. People's lives became more segregated by age, and because of this separation, childhood began to be taken seriously and protected. For example, child labor laws sprang up to protect children from hazardous working conditions.

Adolescence has had a similar history. The notion that a distinct phase exists between childhood and adulthood is relatively new. This important change evolved during the 1950s. After decades of financial hardship and war, America's booming economy led to a new freedom in the popular culture. Access to higher education broadened as well. For many Americans, this extension of educational opportunity delayed the onset of adult responsibilities—such as employment and raising families. With the possibility of an extended adolescence, teenagers (biologically able to reproduce but delayed in their assumption of adult sexual roles) emerged as a discrete social category. Concurrently, cultural changes were marked by the advent of rock and roll, doo-wop, and other popular forms of music. With more access to radios and, to a lesser extent, televisions, and with more free hours after school, teens found the time and means to consume this emerging music culture. Today we can see the life course becoming even further subdivided, with the advent of terms such as *tween*, which refers to the time between childhood and one's teenage years (roughly, ages 10–12).

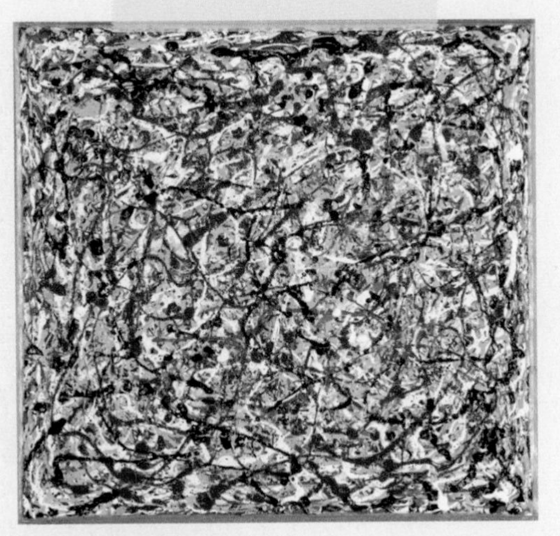

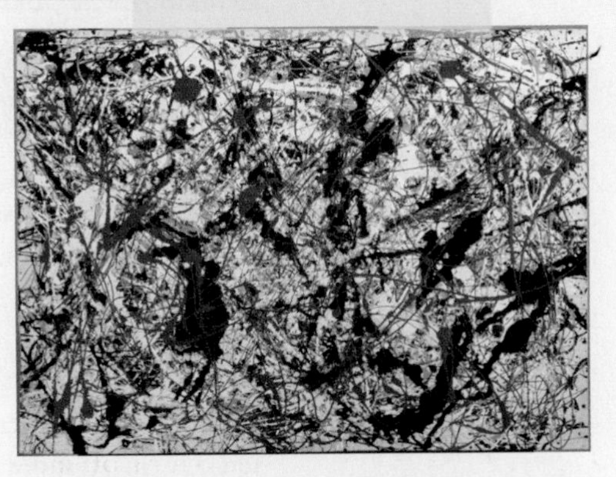

Which one of these paintings is a "real" Jackson Pollock? Does it matter? (For the record, the real one is on the bottom.) How is the controversy over the Pollock paintings an example of the social construction of reality?

As an example of cross-cultural differences in the social construction of reality, consider the following question: What constitutes food? We tend to think of insects as interesting, necessary to the ecosystem, annoying, or maybe simply gross. However, we generally do not regard them as food. In other cultures, dishes such as fried grasshoppers and chocolate-covered ants are considered a delicacy. Which perspective is "right"? In fact, Americans may be an exception in not eating insects, which, I am told, are delicious. Insects are nutritious (high in protein, low in fat and calories, and a good source of many vitamins and minerals) and economical, but they are inherently neither gross nor delicious. The point is that foods, which we take for granted as natural or self-evident, are assigned meanings and values in different cultural contexts.

We might call the process by which things—ideas, concepts, values—are socially constructed symbolic interactionism (see Chapter 1), which suggests that we interact with others using words and behaviors that have symbolic meanings. This theory has three basic tenets:

Symbolic interactionism a micro-level theory in which shared meanings, orientations, and assumptions form the basic motivations behind people's actions.

1. Human beings act toward ideas, concepts, and values on the basis of the meaning that those things have for them.

Lunch? Cicadas, grasshoppers, and other insects on skewers for sale in Donghaumen Night Market in Beijing, China.

2. These meanings are the products of social interaction in human society.
3. These meanings are modified and filtered through an interpretive process that each individual uses in dealing with outward signs.

Symbolic interactionism can be very useful in understanding cultural differences in styles of social interaction. A classic example of this would be the proximity in which two people stand to each other when conversing. Just because these boundaries are symbolic does not mean that they aren't real. In an interaction between a tourist and a local, standing too close or too far away may make one of the parties feel uncomfortable, but in an international business meeting or in peace talks between nations, symbolic interactions take on a greater level of importance. Similarly, in our culture, we generally believe that looking someone in the eye while talking to them indicates respect and sincerity. In some other cultures, however, it is considered extremely rude to look someone directly in the eye. When you raise your glass in a toast with others and say, "Cheers," you can generally focus your eyes wherever you want. In many European countries, however, it is highly impolite and may be regarded as a sign of dishonesty not to establish eye contact while touching glasses.

Comprehending the three basic tenets of symbolic interactionism listed above is key to seeing how the process of social construction is both ongoing and embedded in our everyday interactions. Symbolic interactionism as a theory is a useful tool for understanding the meanings of symbols and signs and the way shared meanings—or a lack thereof—facilitate or impede routine

How does symbolic interactionism help us understand the differences in greetings among various cultures? Pictured here are Bedouins touching noses, Malian men with their arms around each other, and the Belgian royal family celebrating the prince's 18th birthday.

interactions. Let's look at another theory of human interaction, Erving Goffman's dramaturgical theory of society, which laid the groundwork for symbolic interactionism by using the language of theater as a paradigm to formally describe the ways in which we interact to maintain social order.

Dramaturgical Theory

All the world's a stage,
And all the men and women merely players.

—William Shakespeare, *As You Like It*

We might say that the dramaturgical theory of society has its roots in William Shakespeare, but we generally credit Goffman with expounding this theory in *The Presentation of Self in Everyday Life* (1959). He argued that life is essentially a play—a play with a moral, of sorts. And that moral is what Goffman and social psychologists call "impression management." That is, all of us actors on the metaphorical social stage are struggling to make a good impression on our audience (who also happen to be actors). What's more, the goal is not just to make the best impression on others; we often actively work to ensure that others will believe they are making a good impression as well. This helps keep

Dramaturgical theory the view (advanced by Erving Goffman) of social life as essentially a theatrical performance, in which we are all actors on metaphorical stages, with roles, scripts, costumes, and sets.

society and social relations rolling along smoothly (without the need for too many retakes).

Because we are all actors with roles, according to Goffman's dramaturgical theory, we also need scripts, costumes, and sets. Think again about your first day in this college classroom. You knew your role was student, and presumably the professor understood his or her role as well. The professor handed out the syllabus (a prop), talked about the general outline of the class for the semester (a script), and maybe gave a short lecture (a performance). What if he had instead started talking about his love for Batman and all things related to Batman? You might have indulged him briefly, thinking that he seemed a bit loony but would eventually relate this tangent to sociology. If your professor, however, had spent the entire lecture talking about Batman, how would you feel? Shocked? Confused? The professor would have deviated from the script generally followed in a college classroom. Was anyone wearing a tuxedo or dressed like an action hero? Probably not, because those are not the costumes we wear to a sociology lecture. Think back to your status set for a minute and ask yourself what the stages, costumes, scripts, and other props associated with each of your roles are. For some, the answer is fairly clear.

We act out some of our roles much more intentionally than others, such as when we are a member of a sports team. If you are on the basketball team, you play on a basketball court (the stage or set), wear a uniform (the costume), follow the rules (the script), and play with a ball (a prop). Often, we play several roles simultaneously, and, if we have been properly socialized and don't suffer from too much role conflict, we can transition in and out of roles with a certain amount of ease. Presumably, you understand that the classroom is not the appropriate stage on which to act out an intimate scene with your partner. If you did, one of your classmates might heckle you: "Get a room." In dramaturgical theory, the translation would be, "This is the wrong stage. Find the right one."

Another important part of Goffman's theory is the distinction between front-stage and backstage arenas. If you've ever participated in a school play or some other type of performance, you know all about front stage and backstage. Here the meanings are quite literal—a curtain separates these areas, so the border between the front stage and the backstage is clearly delineated. If you've ever worked in a restaurant, you see very clearly a similar line of demarcation. As a waiter, out in the dining room, you are all smiles. Whenever the customer asks for something, you reply politely with a "Yes, ma'am" or "Right away, sir." Back in the kitchen, however, you might complain loudly to the rest of the staff, criticizing your customer's atrocious taste for ordering escargot with his cheeseburger.

For people in certain professions, the front stage/backstage distinction is more literal. In the news we sometimes hear about celebrities who have been caught saying something inappropriate because they thought the camera or microphone was off—they believed they were comfortably backstage. Whoops! The higher your profile, particularly if you have a master status such as a celebrity or politician, the greater the portion of your daily world that takes on the designation of front stage. You are always under close scrutiny, so you are always expected to perform your role. In other situations, the lines between front stage and backstage become more blurred. Has a professor ever caught you off-guard while you were talking with friends about her class? You might have thought that you were backstage when joking with your friends in the student union, but the unfortunate, unexpected appearance of your professor turned the situation into a front-stage experience.

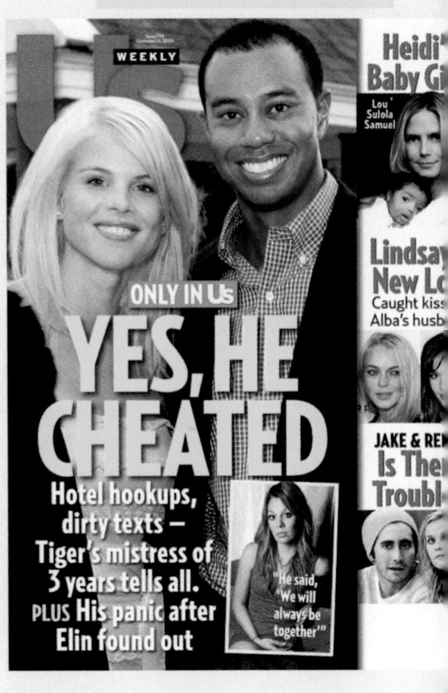

Celebrities such as Tiger Woods suffer from tabloid scandals when their backstage lives become public, but we all make distinctions in our lives between front-stage and backstage behaviors.

Face, according to Goffman, is the esteem in which an individual is held by others. We take this notion very seriously; hence, the idea of saving face, which is essentially the most important goal of impression management. If your best friend walked into the classroom right now and sat down beside you with a big smear of chocolate on his face, you would tell him. If the professor walked in sporting the same chocolate smear, however, you might not say anything. Because of the difference in status, and therefore power, between you and the professor, you may decide it's not your place, your role, to say something. If few students are in the class and the professor is your advisor with whom you have a fairly amicable relationship, you might indicate to him that he's got a little something on his cheek. Have you ever encountered a stranger with toilet paper stuck to the bottom of her shoe or with the fly of his pants unzipped? Did you say something? If you did, you were probably motivated by the thought that, if it were you, you would want someone to say something. If you didn't, perhaps you thought calling attention to the toilet paper or exposed underwear would embarrass the person. Or maybe you just simply felt it wasn't any of your business to interfere with a stranger. So you can see how no absolute, fixed scripts exist. (That said, one common rule of thumb is to speak up if the person can do something about it. For example, you would tell a man that he has chocolate on his face because he can wipe his face and remove the chocolate. On the other hand, you would not tell him that his shirt is ugly, because he probably cannot change his shirt at that moment.)

Face the esteem in which an individual is held by others.

Similarly, if your professor walked in tomorrow with a black eye, you might ask him what happened. Not wanting to admit he fell asleep grading papers and smacked his face on the desk, he might simply say, "You should see the other guy." This is a common joke people make to save face in light of injuries about which they do not wish to speak. There are many subtleties to learn in life, and nobody explicitly teaches us all of these things. Like driving a car, we generally learn by doing and by sometimes making mistakes.

Indeed, mistakes, called breaches, are themselves an important part of the game. When there's a breach in an established script, we work hard to repair it and move forward. Humor is a useful tool in getting the script back in place. So if your professor lets out an enormous belch in the middle of a lecture, how would you react? You might be horrified; you might laugh nervously. You might delight a little because she has been so arrogant all semester and you are pleased to see her off script, not the perfectly polished professor. If the professor manages to recover and says, "Note to self: Skip the Mountain Dew before lecture next time!" it may smooth over the situation a little (but just a little because, let's face it, what happened was funny) and allow class to continue without a hitch. If the same thing happens during your next class, however, you are just going to assume that your professor either is poorly socialized and extremely uncouth or has severe gastrointestinal problems and needs to scale back on carbonated beverages.

Sometimes, the stakes are so high or the situation is so new that we seek explicit guidance. People can and do make careers out of negotiating social scripts and methods for saving face—think about Miss Manners, Emily Post, or Dear Abby. Not wanting to act inappropriately but unsure of how to behave in situations where we lack a script, we may appeal to professional etiquette experts to coach us through a scene and give stage directions. The truth is, however, that human social interaction is too complex for a single script to work universally.

The art of tact even involves, on occasion, breaking the rules to make others feel comfortable. One particular fable tells the story of a peasant who is invited to the palace for dinner. Unknowingly, she picks up the bowl of water meant for hand washing and begins to drink from it. Many of the nobles at the table chuckle and mutter disparaging comments under their breath. But the queen, who invited the poor woman to dine with her, instead picks up her own silver finger bowl and drinks the water from it. She breaks a formal rule to preserve the face of the invited guest. Moreover, the social situation dictates that only the queen herself, as the most powerful figure at the table, can do that to repair the situation and save face for everyone.

There are some ways to generalize, however. For example, we almost always need to begin our scripts in specific ways; we generally can't just plunge into our lines. (Imagine a colleague getting on the elevator, not saying hello or even looking directly at you, but launching straight into the story of what happened to her on the way to work that day while staring up at the floor number indicators.) Goffman uses the term *opening* to signal the start of an encounter—that is, the first bracket. The closing bracket marks the end of an encounter. Sometimes, we need a nonverbal bracket to commence an encounter, a signal to cease our civic inattention. *Civic inattention* means refraining from directly interacting with someone, even someone you know, until an opening bracket has been issued. For example, you might clear your throat before speaking to somebody. You might catch his or her eye. You might stand up. You might purposely go to the bathroom first, so you can pass that person on the way back and start a conversation. You hope that you will bump into the person and catch his or her eye. We have to signal to people; we have to warn them that we are going to break civic inattention and initiate an encounter.

Openings can be awkward, but it may be even more difficult to end situations. How many times have you gotten off the phone saying, "I should get going." Where? To do what? Or you may say, "Well, I should let you go." Maybe you do hear sirens and screams in the background and you are genuinely concerned that your conversation is keeping the person on the phone from more pressing matters. Under less extreme circumstances, you may be phrasing your desire to end the conversation as a kind gesture to your interlocutor. Sometimes, we resort to formal closings. A ringing bell often indicates the end of a class period. In the absence of a bell, or even prior to its ringing, however, you may close your notebook, start to pack your books, and pick up your coat to signal to the professor that, although the lecture on socialization is fascinating, you have another class in 10 minutes that is a 15-minute walk away. There are *given gestures* that signal a closing, such as putting on your coat. Or, at the end of a meal, you may rub your stomach and say, "Boy, that was delicious. I'm stuffed!" to indicate that you have finished eating but did very much enjoy the food. However, *given off gestures* also exist, unconscious signals of our true feelings. If you grimace every time your fork reaches your mouth, you communicate something else entirely regarding your thoughts about the meal. Many of our gestures and brackets are nonverbal. This is why it is often more difficult to end a conversation on the phone than in person: Much of our toolbox is not available to us.

Ethnomethodology

At this point, you should be *thinking* more critically about the everyday interactions that we often (necessarily) take for granted. In the 1950s and 1960s Harold Garfinkel developed a method for studying social interactions, ethnomethodology (Garfinkel, 1967), that involves *acting* critically about them. Ethnomethodology literally means "the methods of the people" (from *ethnos*, the Greek word for "people"). Garfinkel and his followers became famous for their "breaching experiments." He would send his students into the social world to see what happened when they breached social norms. In one example, Garfinkel sent his students home for the weekend and told them to behave as if their parents' home were a rooming house where they paid rent. Imagine what would happen if you sat down at the kitchen table and demanded to know when dinner was typically served and what days of the week the bed linens were changed. Similarly, a New York City professor instructed his students to ask people on the subway for their seats without offering any reason. Some students simply could not take this action. Others did it, but lied and said that they were not feeling well when they asked for the seat. Try your own breaching experiments. What do you normally do when you get in an elevator? You face forward and watch the numbers above the door. Next time you get into

Ethnomethodology literally "the methods of the people," this approach to studying human interaction focuses on the ways in which we make sense of our world, convey this understanding to others, and produce a shared social order.

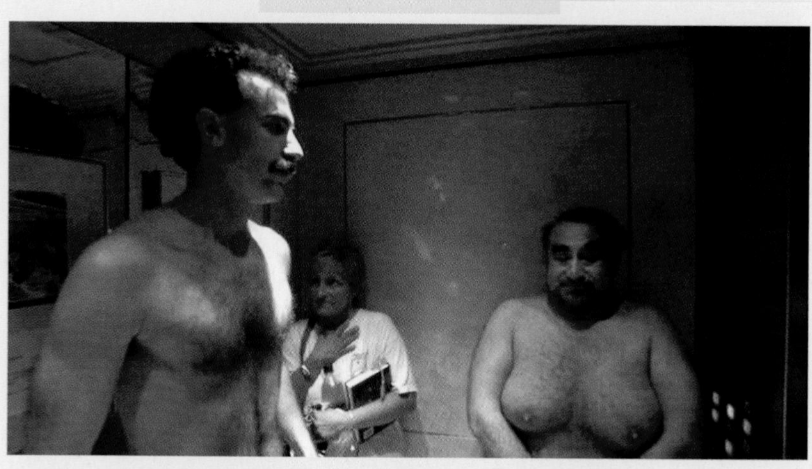

A scene from the film *Borat.* What established scripts did Sacha Baron Cohen's character Borat violate by going on an elevator naked? How did the unsuspecting woman on the elevator try to cope with the breach?

an elevator, face backward. See how the other people in the elevator react. A few weeks into the semester, students tend to sit in the same seats in the same class, particularly if it's a small group, even if they do not have assigned seats. The next time you are in such a situation, take someone else's usual seat and see how he or she reacts. (Come on, that's an easy one!)

Let's think through some of the reactions to breaches. Take the example of the student on the subway asking a stranger to give up his seat. What would you do if this happened to you? Would you give up your seat to the student? You might just get up and offer it to him, because you assume he would not ask for it unless he had a good reason (even if you don't see a cast on his leg). If the stranger were elderly, on crutches, or pregnant or had a small child, you might be more willing to get up—in fact, on most forms of public transportation, seats are marked as reserved for exactly these kinds of people. When this class assignment was originally handed out, note that some of the students simply could not bring themselves to do it. Others lied, saying they were sick, because being ill provides a valid excuse to sit down. Why is that? What's the big deal in asking someone to give you a seat? Well, you might decide, you just don't typically do such a thing. It's not normal behavior. But note that as a society, we construct rules and meanings for what constitutes normal.

Now contemplate the previously mentioned elevator scenario. How would you react if you stepped into an elevator and the only other person inside was facing away from the door (assuming the elevator only opens on one side)? You might look at the wall to see if something is there at which the person is looking and that you can't see. You might try to stand farther away from that person. If someone else gets on the elevator, maybe you would gauge her reaction. If she gave you a look that said, "What's this guy doing?" you might give a sympathetic look, even the hint of a smile, to indicate your agreement: "Yeah, crazy, huh?" Then you could breathe a little easier, knowing that the guy facing backward in the elevator is abnormal, and you, the other passenger, and anyone else who steps inside and is facing forward are normal, although there's no social imperative to face forward rather than backward in an elevator.

If you walked into the classroom today and someone was sitting in the seat you consider yours, how would you feel? Maybe you wouldn't think twice about it, but chances are you would notice, have an emotional reaction—be it annoyance, confusion, even anger—and get to class earlier the next time to claim what's rightfully yours.

New Technologies: What Has the Internet Done to Interaction?

What happens when we are faced with entirely new situations? We have no rules, no scripts, no established social norms. How do people know what to do, or what constitutes appropriate behavior? Usually, some continuity exists between situations, so we can draw on our previous knowledge (just as you could anticipate the norms of a college classroom even though you had never been in one before). But what about something like the Internet, something that humans created, which in turn creates social situations never before possible? Let's think about what happens.

Take online chat rooms, for example. Chat rooms present an interesting test of the dramaturgical model. The potential anonymity of the Internet allows us to present ourselves however we choose. Online I can play the role of a 57-year-old stay-at-home dad who was an international college badminton champ and who enters semiannual pesto-making competitions. Is that who I am? Some online dating and networking websites allow us to craft our own presentation of self, alter our identities, and thereby create new "realities." We've largely removed the stage, costumes, props, vocal inflections, and other nonverbal cues, so we must depend entirely on the scripts with which we are presented. We even develop new ways of communicating. Typing in capital letters can constitute online "yelling." New lexicons are developed: LOL (laugh out loud) and BRB (be right back) are semiverbal cues to our cyber interlocutor. But the technology may also, like the phone, make it difficult to deploy end brackets, to close interactions.

The Internet has changed society in other ways, such as forcing us to develop new technologies to prevent identity theft and create secure online transactions for shopping and banking. Certain aspects of the Internet have also altered the nature and details of crime. Software that allows for music sharing necessitates the development of a new set of ethics. Is it okay to download music free from the Internet? It's illegal in most cases, for sure, but is it unethical? Are there certain circumstances in which it might be okay? For example, when Radiohead made its album *In Rainbows* available for download and left the amount of payment up to customers, should folks have paid or was it just fine to download without donating? The new technologies are changing what we as a society mean by the term *stealing*. Other websites, such as eBay, allow for the sale of stolen goods in ways previously unforeseen. Intentionally or not, people may foster underground economies by purchasing stolen goods in a way not possible before the advent of online auctions. Clicking on an item and entering your credit card number is a completely different social interaction than walking into a dark alley and buying something that literally fell off the back of a truck. (Some of the other changes that the Internet is facilitating are discussed in Chapter 17.)

The Harlem Children's Zone

In a 2008 speech, President Obama addressed the problem of poverty in America: "If poverty is a disease that infects an entire community in the form of unemployment and violence, failing schools and broken homes, then we can't just treat those symptoms in isolation. We have to heal the entire community. We have to focus on what actually works" (Obama, 2008). But do we know what "actually works" in the war against poverty? Was Obama just saying what people wanted to hear—it was a campaign speech after all—or are there programs that have been shown to effectively combat poverty? One of his solutions is to clone a comprehensive set of programs that have been implemented in a 97-square-block area in upper Manhattan called the Harlem Children's Zone (HCZ) and implant it in 20 cities across the country (Harlem Children's Zone, Inc., 2011).

The HCZ refers to both the area being served and the service programs themselves. The programs range from education to social services to health care, recruit the very poorest people, target youth, and aim to get them enrolled before they are even born and keep them in the network until they have graduated from college. Harlem is a typical impoverished urban area: It has experienced the symptoms of impoverishment across generations; the unemployment rate is twice that of the city average; the chance that a male born in Harlem will be incarcerated is higher than the chance he will go to college; public schools consistently rank below citywide averages on standardized test scores; there are relatively large numbers of new immigrants. In the face of all these challenges, the leader of HCZ, former teacher Geoffrey Canada, decided that all of the children in the programs' geographical target area (not just the

Two teachers work with students in a Harlem Children's Zone program. The HCZ school day is 1.5 hours longer than public-school days and includes many special activities and clubs that most impoverished schools cannot offer.

best and brightest) would need to grow up with a seamless stream of comprehensive support in order to bring the neighborhood out of poverty.

The programs are inspired in part by Head Start, a classroom-based prekindergarten program offered to low-income students to make sure they are ready for kindergarten. Head Start is good at improving short-term cognitive and educational goals (Currie, 2000; Currie & Thomas, 1995, 1999). But researchers also found that these effects fade over time. By third grade, Head Start kids were no different from their low-income peers in terms of math scores, repeating a grade, or getting suspended (Aughinbaugh, 2001). And by high-school graduation, Head Starters had no advantages when it came to graduation rates or college attendance rates (Garces et al., 2002). The HCZ takes the classroom-based educational approach of Head Start, adds a medical service component, and then extends it from prenatal care all the way through college. HCZ programming is extensive both at the macro level, across the lifespan, and at the micro level: Each school day is 1.5 hours longer than public-school days, the school year lasts all the way through July, and extracurricular trips and clubs fill in many of the intervening weeks and hours.

In 2010 HCZ had an operating budget of over $75 million, which is paid for through a mixture of public and private funding (Spector, 2009). Much of the private funding comes directly from wealthy individual donors who made their fortunes on Wall Street. It costs tens of thousands of dollars more to send a child through all of HCZ's programming than to send him or her to traditional public schools. On the other hand, it is cheaper in the long run to send kids to college and on to middle-class taxpaying lives than to have them drop out of high school. High-school dropouts have a 1-in-10 chance of ending up in prison (Dillon, 2009), and each prisoner costs taxpayers $50,000 annually. Compare this to the 1-in-35 chance facing high-school graduates and the even lower chance college graduates have of ending up incarcerated (Sum et al., 2009). Obama has proposed that the federal government invest several billion dollars per year to cover half of the costs of each new implementation, with philanthropists, states, cities, and special grants making up the rest (Obama, 2009).

Journalist Paul Tough followed the progress of the first cohorts of children at the HCZ Promise Academy public charter school. One group started in kindergarten and the other started as sixth graders (Tough, 2008). The kindergarteners did well; their scores on reading and math tests were far higher than city averages in both reading comprehension and math by the time they took citywide standardized tests in third grade. But the entering sixth graders weren't as successful. In their two years at Promise Academy they made academic improvements but were still scoring below city averages, especially in English language arts. Newer data for cohorts of students who have been in HCZ programs over longer periods of time show that math and English language arts scores for elementary students and math scores for middle schoolers are "enormously" better than the scores of the kids who wanted to attend Promise Academy but had bad luck in the admissions lottery (Dobbie & Fryer, Jr., 2009). Right now, the HCZ is still so new that we will not know how babies who start in Baby College and stick with the program all the way through fare once they hit college and beyond. It remains to be seen if the first Baby College babies go to college.

Should Obama rush to replicate the HCZ across the country? What are the potential costs of waiting, and imperiling another generation of poor young folks, versus the risk that the HCZ may be good at getting kids to score well on standardized tests but may not be so good at helping those students become successful adults? And are there enough wealthy donors in each target city to make up the budget gap between real costs and promised federal funding? Not every city has a wealthy pool of Wall Street–enriched, big-hearted donors. Further, is there something special about Harlem or about Geoffrey Canada and his staff that means the program may not be so easy to clone and drop into new cities with the same level of success?

→ CONCLUSION

Paramedics try to resuscitate professional wrestler Owen Hart after a deadly fall in Kansas City, Missouri.

In the nature-versus-nurture debate, sociologists have generally fallen firmly on the side of nurture. At least that's what most of us study. Socialization helps us understand and explain how it is that babies—those wrinkled, sometimes alien-looking creatures newly emerged from their mothers' wombs—become people who attend college. How much stake do we put in preserving normality, the status quo? We already talked about tact. Little children are tactless all the time. I once handed my grandfather a wrapped present and said, "Happy Father's Day! It's a shirt!" It was cute because I was 5, but what if I had done the same thing at 15? Would it have been cute? Somewhere along the way, we learn the unwritten rules.

On May 23, 1999, the World Wrestling Federation (WWF) aired a live pay-per-view event called "Over the Edge." When a harness malfunctioned, wrestler Owen Hart, who was being lowered into the ring, fell 78 feet to his death. Although television viewers did not see the live footage of his death, once Hart was removed and sent to the hospital (he was pronounced dead upon arrival), the program continued. The decision to go forward with the event sparked conversation and criticism far beyond the wrestling world. Some were shocked, even outraged, that the producers did not cancel the program, whereas others stood by the old adage, "The show must go on." Why the radically different reactions? Well, for starters, we do not have a social script for this type of incident. Death is a serious matter, to be sure, but how should death be handled when it occurs on live television? We tend to seek a return to normalcy when things do not go as planned. Trying to quickly transition the situation back to normal (and probably to keep their paying customers happy), the WWF continued the live event. Others were disgusted by this seeming insensitivity. The following night the association aired a two-hour tribute to the fallen wrestler.

This is an extreme example and a tragic one, but we witness more mundane, even comical, breaches on a fairly regular basis. When someone important commits them, they draw yet more attention. The point is that we all have a stake in things going a certain way. When things don't go according to plan, depending on the severity, nature, and context of the deviation, we must find some way to recover, and recover we usually do. Whether it is a small breach in our shared understanding of turn-taking etiquette or a major rupture to the fabric of society, people work hard to broker consensus with respect to shared meaning. The alternative is nothing less than chaos and social insanity.

PRACTICE

ASSIGNMENT

Go to a fast-food restaurant and order an item made notable by a competing restaurant (e.g., order a Big Mac at Burger King or a Whopper at McDonald's). Make sure you order from a cashier, face to face (not from a car). How does the cashier respond? How do the people behind you in line respond? What does this experiment teach us about shared rules and meanings?

QUESTIONS FOR REVIEW

1. How does George Herbert Mead's concept of "generalized other" explain why, at the beginning of class, you became silent when your professor started speaking?
2. How does the case of "Anna" affect your assessment of early-socialization programs like Head Start?
3. School plays an important role in our socialization. Think about the way socialization works: What are some of the things we learn from schooling (e.g., the first years in elementary school), and how does this learning differ from what we are taught by our teacher? How are things like gender performance shaped in school?
4. Parents of different social classes socialize children differently. For example, middle-class parents are more likely to stress independence and self-direction, whereas working-class parents prioritize obedience to external authority. Using this example, how does socialization through families potentially reproduce social inequality?
5. You are a university student, but you also wait tables at a restaurant. One evening, one of your professors happens to come in for a meal (seemingly, on a date!). Use role theory to describe the interaction (and possible role conflict) that ensues.
6. What do sociologists mean by "social construction of reality"? How does the idea of social construction bring into question certain elements of everyday life, like gender roles?
7. Let's imagine you use file-sharing networks for music downloading and discuss your favorite music subgenres with people throughout the world. How does this differ from, for example, speaking only with employees at your local music store? Think about the way technology affects how you interact, the characteristics of the people with whom you're interacting, and how different ways of interacting might affect socialization.

PARADOX

THE MOST IMPORTANT ASPECTS OF SOCIAL LIFE ARE THOSE CONCEPTS WE LEARN WITHOUT ANYONE TEACHING US.

WATCH THE ANIMATED SHORT ABOUT THE SOCIALIZATION PARADOX AT

WWNORTON.COM/STUDYSPACE

An Internet café in Hanover, Germany. How has technology transformed social interaction?

5 Groups and Networks

PARADOX

THE STRENGTH OF WEAK TIES: IT IS THE PEOPLE WITH WHOM WE ARE THE LEAST CONNECTED WHO OFFER US THE MOST OPPORTUNITIES.

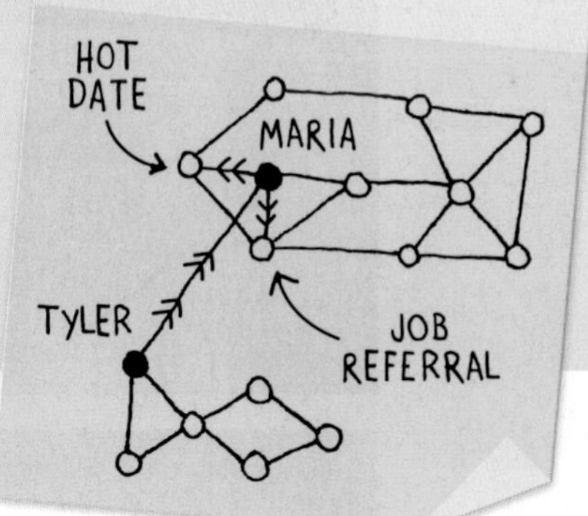

It would seem that we are living in the age of social networks. Facebook, Orkut, Twitter, and other social networking sites suck an ever-increasing proportion of the world's population into their virtual landscape, along with, of course, more and more of our free time, as social life and leisure move online. But other than getting in touch with long-lost high-school buddies, what good are social networks anyway? Sure, you might be able to use Evite or Facebook as a virtual social secretary if you are organizing a baby shower or dorm party. But a good old-fashioned address book and rotary phone could have done the trick (even if it took longer).

Kate Rich, an Australian artist who has made a habit of digging tunnels through the invisible social structures most of us take for granted, has found a practical application for social networks. When she's not working for an anonymous, multinational collective with the ominous title The Bureau of Inverse Technology (BIT), she's climbing trees with friends in the English countryside. Or perhaps she's perfecting the recipe for Cube-Cola (**http://sparror.cubecinema.com/cube/cola/**), an open-source cola whose motto is "Standing on the hands of giants." The beverage takes its name from the Cube Cinema, a workers' collective located in downtown Bristol, United Kingdom, where it is served to patrons.

As manager of the Cube's bar and café since 2003, Kate first looked into ordering only "Fair Trade" products when confronted with the need for a reliable source of good coffee for their patrons. But she found herself "unsure about the promises and threats made on the packet, almost inevitably happy farmers testifying as if at gunpoint that they use the money for their children's

Infused grappa from local vineyards in Croatia, distributed through Feral Trade.

education" (Conley, 2010). So she decided to put her own social networks to work and created what would soon become Feral Trade (www.feraltrade.org). The premise is simple. Pulling it off was not. The basic idea is that while we cannot quite trust packaging labels, we should be able to trust the firsthand reports of our close friends and colleagues.

To solve her coffee problem, she got in touch with fellow artist Amy Balkin, who was living in San Francisco and who had a sister working in the Peace Corps in El Salvador. The sister, in turn, put Kate in touch with a coffee co-op for which she could vouch. It took about three months to negotiate the first shipment of 30 bags of coffee (the chain of e-mails is documented on the Feral Trade website). From there the business slowly moved into import and distribution of other food products and utilities: tea from Bangladesh, sweets from Iran, Turkish delight from Montenegro, electric rice-cookers, and so on.

Kate explains her hand-to-hand shipping methodology:

> People sometimes point to the similarities between Feral Trade and the drug trade: some methods might be similar but the structures of economy and ownership are totally different. Drug running being more or less a mafia version of normal corporate relations, workers alienated from production etc. With Feral Trade, the couriers are exclusively unpaid; they are peers; they are uncontrollable: coaxed, convinced and occasionally spontaneously offering their services. I have entirely no leverage over them, other than their own interest or investment in the shipment. (Conley, 2010)

Though Feral Trade has been up and running for almost a decade and Kate has carefully documented every transaction and shipment online for public consumption, it took almost that long for the "authorities" to notice and contact her. Some officials from the U.K. government's Trading Standards Service Public Protection Group and its Environmental Health office dropped by the Cube unannounced. Kate explained to them that there was actually no consumer for them to protect, that this was the peer-to-peer transactions of the social economy that most people enact when they bring gifts back from vacation for their friends and family, with the key differences that cash is exchanged and that everything is publicly documented. They shifted their questions to the fact that many of the products depicted on the Feral Trade website appeared to be "brightly coloured" and therefore might involve dyes that are banned in the U.K. They also admitted that they had made inquiries to Her Majesty's Custom and Excise on the legality of commercial use of personal import food products and had been "unable to get a straight answer"—which Kate, of course, took as a clear precedent to continue trading.

Kate finds these interactions with official bureaucracies slightly terrifying, even if they make for great web documentation after the fact. The folks she actually finds more frustrating are "clients" who think she can take very specific retail-level orders.

> It's not about providing a global service to bring in desired items to an individual consumer. It's about coordinated social movement. Can I shift 20 boxes of Iranian sweets from Yazd to Bristol to distribute them amongst friends pre-Xmas? These went fridge-to-fridge—the couriers were me, an Egyptian musician friend, an Iranian art student I met at a party, a Russian professor I know in London and her four-year-old kid, and an IT guy from Hewlett Packard I'd never met before, along with various onlookers and companions. (Conley, 2010)

To the folks who request one very specific tee shirt from Ecuador, she says, "Get your own extended social network!"

> There's a moment where you're in the canopy suspended with your weight spread out over 10 or 20 twiglets of one tree and reaching for a handful of tendrils of the neighbouring tree, that's all your means of support. It always seems impossible, totally terrifying, then you just have to move and you're suddenly safe, grabbing onto one of tree two's branches. The shipping manoeuvres are like that, at their best. Total hazard then the thrill of things moving and cooperating in un-plannable ways. (Conley, 2010)

This chapter will explore some of the basic theories about group interaction and how it shapes our social world. We'll look at the connections between groups: how size and shape matter, what roles group members play, and how the power of groups works compared with individuals and other institutions. We'll also discuss organizations and how they both react to and create social structure.

Social Groups

Unless you live alone in the woods, and perhaps even then, you are a member of many social groups. Social groups form the building blocks for society and most social interaction. In fact, even the self evolves from groups. Let's start by talking about the various types and sizes of groups. In his classic work "Quantitative Aspects of the Group," sociologist Georg Simmel (1950) argues that without knowing anything about the group members' individual psychology or the cultural or social context in which they are embedded, we can make predictions about the ways people are going to behave based solely on the number of members, or "social actors," in that group. This theory applies not just to groups of people but also to states, countries, firms, corporations, bureaucracies, and any number of other social forms.

Just the Two of Us

Dyad a group of two.

Triad a group of three or more.

Simmel advances the notion that the most important distinction is that between a relationship of two, which he calls a dyad, and a group of three or more, which he calls a triad. This is the fundamental distinction among most social relations, he argues, and it holds regardless of the individual characteristics of members. Of course, personality differences will influence social relations, but there are numerous social dynamics about which we can make predictions that have nothing to do with the content of the social relations themselves.

The dyad has several unique characteristics. For starters, it is the most intimate form of social life, partly because the two members of the dyad are mutually dependent on each other. That is, the continued existence of the group is entirely contingent on the willingness of both parties to participate in the group; if either person leaves, the dyad ceases to be. This intimacy is enhanced by the fact that no third person exists to buffer the situation or mediate between the two. Meanwhile, the members of a dyad don't need to be concerned about how their relationship will be perceived by a third party.

For example, we might consider a couple the most intimate social arrangement in our society. Both people must remain committed to being in the dyad for it to exist, and if one partner leaves, the couple no longer exists. There can be no secrets—if the last piece of chocolate cake disappears and you didn't eat it, you know who did. You could withhold a secret from your dyadic partner, but in terms of the actions of the group itself, no mystery lingers about who performs which role or who did what. Either you did it, or the other person did.

In a dyad, symmetry must be maintained. There might be unequal power relations within a group of two to a certain extent, but Simmel would argue that in a group of two an inherent symmetry exists because of the earlier stipulation of mutual dependence, namely, that the group survives only if both members remain. Even in relationships where the power seems so clearly unequal—think of a master and a servant or a prisoner and his captor—Simmel argues that there's an inherent symmetry. Yes, the servant may be completely dependent on the master for his wages, sustenance, food, and shelter, but what happens to the master who becomes dependent on the labor that the servant performs? Of course, forcible relationships might develop in which one of two parties is forced to stay in the dyad, but to be considered a pure dyad, the relationship has to be voluntary. Because a dyad could fall apart at any moment, the underlying social relation is heightened.

Dyads are the foundation of all social relationships. Why are they the most intimate relationship, according to Georg Simmel?

The dyad is also unique in other ways. Because the group exists only as long as the individuals choose to maintain it in a voluntary fashion, the group itself exerts no supra-individual control over the individuals involved. For example, whereas a child might claim, "She made me do it" and shamelessly tell on her older sister, a member of a dyad is less likely to say, "I was just following orders" or "The whole group decided to go see *Mission: Impossible 7*, and I really didn't want to, but I went anyway." The force of a group is much stronger when three or more individuals are part of the group.

Let's take a real-life example of how the characteristics of a dyad play out and see why they matter. Think about divorce. One point in a marriage at which the divorce rate is especially high is when a first child is born (and not just because of the parental sleep deprivation that arrives with a newborn). The nature of the relationship between the two adults changes. They have gone from being a dyad to becoming a triad. Perhaps the parents feel a sudden lack of intimacy, even though the baby is not yet a fully developed social actor. On the flip side, a husband or wife might begin to feel trapped in a marriage specifically because of a child. All of a sudden, group power exists—a couple has evolved into a family, and with that comes the power of numbers in a group.

And Then There Were Three

This brings us to the triad, distinguished by characteristics you can probably infer by now. In a triad, the group holds supra-individual power. In other words, in a group of three or four, I can say, "I'm really unhappy, I hate this

In what ways are triads more complex than dyads? What are the possible roles of triad members?

place, I hate you, and I'm leaving," but the group will go on. The husband may walk out on his wife and children, but a family still exists that he's abandoning. He's ending his participation in the group, but the group is going to outlast his decision to leave it. Therefore, the group is not dependent on any one particular member.

What's more, in a triad, secrets can exist. Who left the cap off the toothpaste? If more than two people live under the same roof, you can't be sure. Politics is another aspect inherent in a group of three or more. Instead of generating consensus between two individuals, now you have multiple points of view and preferences that need to be balanced. This allows for power politics among the group's members (Figure 5.1). Simmel refers to three basic forms of political relations that can evolve within a triad depending on what role the entering third party assumes. The first role is that of mediator, who tries to resolve the conflict between the other two and is sometimes brought in for that explicit purpose. A good example would be a marriage counselor. Rather than go to therapy, couples will often start a family when having marital problems because they believe a baby will bring them back together. Unfortunately, as most couples come to realize sooner rather than later, that baby does not play the role of a mediator. Rather, the dynamics of the unhappy family may turn into a game of chicken: Which parent is more devoted to the child? Which dyad forms the core of the group, and which person will be left out or can walk away more easily?

Mediator member of a triad who attempts to resolve conflict between the two other actors in the group.

A second possible role for the incoming third member of a triad is that of *tertius gaudens* (Latin for "the third that rejoices"). This individual profits from the disagreement of the other two, essentially playing the opposite role from the mediator. Someone in this position might have multiple roles. In the previous example, the marriage counselor plays the part of the mediator, but she is also earning her wages from the conflict between the couple. Maybe she encourages continued therapy even after the couple appear to have resolved all their issues, or perhaps she promotes their staying together even though they've already decided to get a divorce.

Tertius gaudens the new third member of a triad who benefits from conflict between the other two members of the group.

The third possible role that Simmel identifies for a third party is *divide et impera* (Latin for "divide and conquer"). This person intentionally drives a wedge between the other two parties. This third role is similar to *tertius gaudens*, the difference between the two being a question of intent and whether the rift preexisted. (If you've ever seen or read Shakespeare's *Othello*, there is no better example of *divide et impera* than the way that Iago, counselor to Othello, uses the Moor's insecurities to foster a rift between him and his wife Desdemona, in order to strengthen Iago's own hand in court politics. The play ends tragically, of course.)

Divide et impera the role of a member of a triad who intentionally drives a wedge between the other two actors in the group.

To take an example with which millions of Americans are familiar, let's return to the case of the triad formed when a romantic couple has a child

Figure 5.1: Political Relations within a Triad

MEDIATOR
The mediator attempts to resolve conflict between the other two members of the triad, and is sometimes brought in for that explicit purpose.

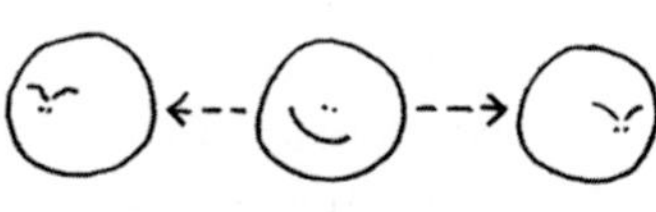

TERTIUS GAUDENS
Latin for "the third that rejoices." This individual profits from the disagreement of the other two actors, essentially playing the opposite role from the mediator.

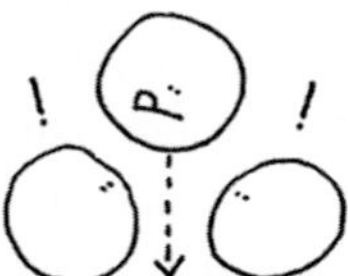

DIVIDE ET IMPERA
Latin for "divide and conquer." This person intentionally drives a wedge between the other two parties.

but experiences strife and separates. What happens when the couple divorces? What role does the child play? A child could play any of the roles mentioned above. In the original dyad of the biological parents, the child can be a mediator, forcing his or her parents to work together on certain issues pertaining to his or her care. A child can be "the third who rejoices" from the disagreement of the two, profiting from the fact that he or she might receive two allowances or extra birthday presents because each parent is trying to prove that he or she loves the child more. A complicated *divide et impera* situation could develop if one of the child's parents enters into a second marriage, in which the kid remains the biological child of one parent and becomes the stepchild of the other. All sorts of politics will arise because of the biological connection between the one parent and the child versus the marital love relationship between the two parents. The relationship between the nonbiological parent and the stepchild, who have the weakest bond, may be difficult. The situation could unfold in any number of ways. Many domestic comedies (think *The Parent Trap*) are based on the premise of a young, angst-ridden prankster playing the role of *divide et impera* between his or her parent and the new stepmother or -father.

When contemplating how these theoretical concepts work within actual social interaction, keep in mind that these groups—dyads and triads—don't exist in a vacuum in real life. In discussing the politics of a stepfamily, we're talking about a household where there's a stepparent, a biological parent, and a child. Beyond our textbook example, in real life, this triad probably doesn't function so independently. There is probably another biological parent living elsewhere, maybe another stepparent, maybe siblings. Most social groups are very complex, and we need to take that into consideration when we attempt to determine how they operate. This is why we start with Simmel's purest forms. The interactions that take place in groups of two and three become the building blocks for those in much larger groups.

Size Matters: Why Social Life Is Complicated

One key insight is that as the number of people in the group increases geometrically (2 + 1 = 3; 3 + 1 = 4; 4 + 1 = 5), the complexity of analyzing that group's ties increases exponentially (2 × 2 = 4; 4 × 4 = 16; 5 × 5 = 25). A two-person group has only one possible and necessary relationship; it must exist for there to be a group. In a triad, a sum of three relationships exists, with each person within the group having two ties. And again, for it to be a group of three, we're talking about not possible connections but actual ones. When you move beyond triads to groups of four or more, something different happens. To create a group of four, there must be at least four relationships, but you can have as many as six. Figure 5.2 shows this exponential rise in possible relationships graphically.

In a diagram with four people (A, B, C, and D), we can cross out the diagonals and the group will still exist. Everyone may have only two relationships

Figure 5.2: Relationship between Group Size and Complexity

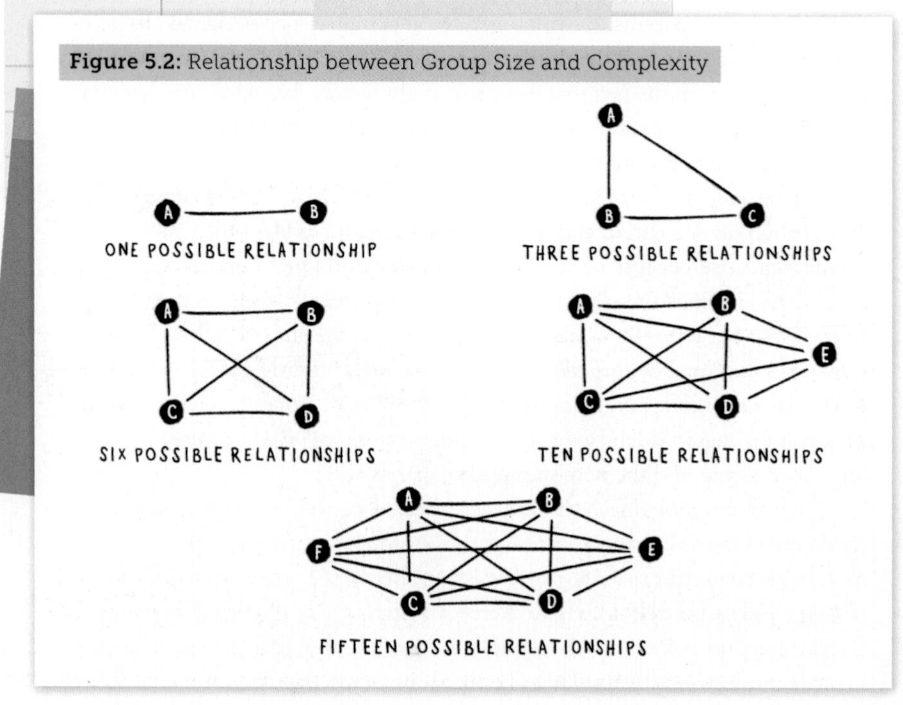

as opposed to three (the number of possible relationships). A and D might never have spoken to each other, but the group will continue to function. The tendency, however, is for these possible relationships to become actual relationships. You and your roommate are in separate chemistry classes, but your lab partners happen to be roommates. If you both become friendly with your lab partners outside of class, chances are that you will meet your roommate's lab partner and vice versa. Such social pathways tend to fill in. This can be good or bad. You may form a study group and, if your roommate's lab partner's boyfriend is a chemist, you (and everyone else) may benefit from his help. On the other hand, if the two break up and you start dating the chemist, it might make future labs a little uncomfortable for your roommate.

Let's Get This Party Started: Small Groups, Parties, and Large Groups

Groups larger than a dyad or triad, according to Simmel, can be classified into one of three types: *small groups*, *parties*, and *large groups*. A small group is characterized by four factors. The first is *face-to-face interaction*; all the members of the group at any given time are present and interact with one another. They are not spread out geographically. Second, a small group is *unifocal*, meaning that there's one center of attention at any given time. Turn taking among speakers occurs. A classroom, unless it's divided and engaged in group work, should be unifocal.

Small group a group characterized by face-to-face interaction, a unifocal perspective, lack of formal arrangements, and a certain level of equality.

Classes usually don't qualify as small groups because a third characteristic of small groups is a *lack of formal arrangements* or *roles*. A study group, though, might qualify if you decide shortly before an exam to meet with some of your

What makes the study group on the left a small group, and how is it different from the cocktail party on the right?

How is this classroom an example of a large group?

classmates. You need to agree on a place and time to meet, but otherwise there is no formal arrangement. In the classroom, however, a professor is in attendance, as are teaching assistants and students—all of whom play official roles in the group. The roles generally encountered in classes also contradict the fourth defining characteristic of a small group, *equality*. After all, you won't be giving your professor a grade, nor will she get into trouble, as you might, for arriving late at a planned lecture. Yours isn't a reciprocal and equal relationship. Within a small group, as in a dyad, there is a certain level of equality. Only in a dyad can pure equality exist, because both members hold veto power over the group. However, in a small group, even if the group will continue to exist beyond the membership of any particular member, no particular member has greater sway than the others. No one member can dissolve the group. If someone in your study group gets tired and falls asleep on his book, you and your classmates can continue to study without him.

When does a small group become a party? If you have ever hosted a party, you know that the worst phase is the beginning. You're worried that people might not show up: The party has started, only three people are there (everyone, after all, tends to arrive fashionably late), and you start to wonder, "Is this going to be it?" You have to keep a conversation going among three people; you refill their glasses as soon as they take one sip. If you're drinking alcohol (only if you're of legal drinking age, of course), you may consume more at the beginning of the party because you are nervous about it not going well. When does your small gathering officially evolve into a party, so that you can relax and enjoy yourself? Simmel would say that a party, like a small group, is characterized by face-to-face interaction but differs in that it is *multifocal*. Going back to the example of your sociology study group, if two people begin to talk about Margaret Mead's theory of the self while the rest of you discuss the differences between role conflict and role strain, then it is bifocal; if another subgroup splits off to deliberate on reference groups, then it has become multifocal. According to Simmel, you've got yourself a party! So when you're hosting your next party, you'll recognize when it has officially started.

Party a group that is similar to a small group but multifocal.

The last type of group to which Simmel makes reference is the large group. The primary characteristic of a large group is the presence of a *formal structure* that mediates interaction and, consequently, *status differentiation*. When you enter a classroom, it should be clear who the teacher is, and you comprehend that she has a higher status than you have in that specific social context.

Large group a group characterized by the presence of a formal structure that mediates interaction and, consequently, status differentiation.

The professor is an employee of the university, knows more than you know about the subject being taught, and is responsible for assigning you a grade based on your performance in the course. You might be asked to complete a teacher evaluation form at the end of the semester, but it's not the same thing as grading a student. You and your professor aren't equals. The point is that the inherent characteristics of a group are determined not just by its size but also by other aspects of its form. Whether a group stays small, becomes a party, or evolves into a large group may depend on numbers, but it also may depend on the size and configuration of the physical space in which the social actors are assembled, preexisting social relationships, expectations, and the larger social context in which that group is embedded.

Primary and Secondary Groups

Simmel wasn't the only one who tried to describe the basic types of groups. The sociologist Charles Horton Cooley (1909) emphasized a distinction between what he called primary and secondary groups. Primary groups are limited in the number of members, allowing for face-to-face interaction. The group is an end unto itself, rather than a means to an end. This is what makes your family different from a sports team or small business: Sure, you want the family to function well, but you're not trying to compete with other families or manufacture a product. Meanwhile, primary groups are key agents of socialization. Most people's first social group is their family, which is a primary group. Your immediate family (parents and siblings) is probably small enough to sit down at the same dinner table or at least gather in the same room at the same time. Loyalty is the primary ethic here. Members of a primary group are noninterchangeable—you can't replace your mother or father. And while you have strong allegiances to your friends, your primary loyalty is likely to be to your family. Finally, the relationships within a primary group are enduring. Your sister will always be your sister. Another example of a primary group might be the group of your closest friends, especially if you've known each other since your sandbox years.

Primary groups social groups, such as family or friends, composed of intimate face-to-face relationships that strongly influence the attitudes and ideals of those involved.

The characteristics of secondary groups, such as a labor union, stand in contrast to those of primary groups. The group is impersonal; you may or may not know all the members of your union. It's also instrumental. The group exists as a means to an end, in this case for organizing workers and lobbying for their interests. In a secondary group, affiliation is contingent. You are only a member of your union so long as you hold a certain job and pay your dues. If you change jobs or join another union, your membership in that earlier group ends. Because the members of a secondary group change, the roles are more important than the individuals who fill them. The shop steward, the person chosen to interact with the company's management, may be a different person every year, but that position carries the same responsibilities within the group regardless of who fills it. A sports team is another example of a secondary group, although if you're also close friends with your teammates and socialize with them when you're not playing sports, the line between a primary and secondary group can become blurred.

Secondary groups groups marked by impersonal, instrumental relationships (those existing as a means to an end).

Figure 5.3: The Asch Test

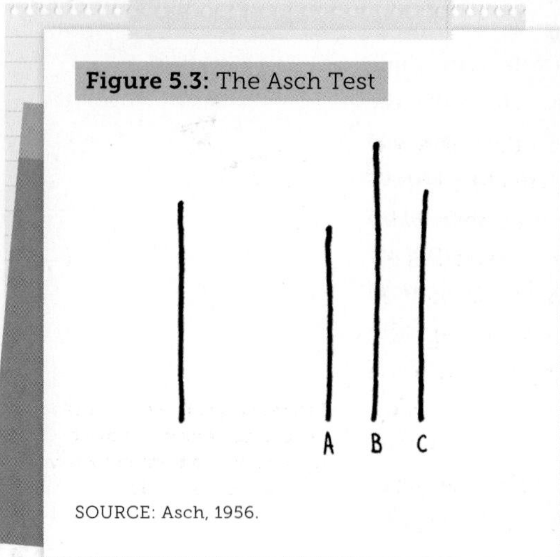

SOURCE: Asch, 1956.

Group Conformity

Although we tend to put a high value on individuality in American culture, our lives are marked by high levels of conformity. That is, groups have strong influences over individual behavior. In the late 1940s the social psychologist Solomon Asch carried out a now-famous series of experiments to demonstrate the power of norms of group conformity. He gathered subjects in a room under the pretense that they were participating in a vision test, showed them two images of lines, and asked which ones were longer than the others and which were the same length (Figure 5.3).

The trick was that only one person in each room was really a research subject; the rest of the people had been told ahead of time to give the same incorrect answer. While a majority of subjects answered correctly even after they listened to others give the wrong answer, about one-third expressed serious discomfort—they clearly struggled with what they thought was right in light of what everyone else was saying. Subjects were the most confused when the entire group offered an incorrect answer. When the group members gave a range of responses, the research subjects had no trouble answering correctly. This experiment demonstrates the power of conformity within a group. More troubling instances of group conformity may be seen in cases of collective violence such as gang rape, which tends to occur among tightly knit groups like sports teams or fraternities (Sanday, 1990).

In-Groups and Out-Groups

In-group another term for the powerful group, most often the majority.

Out-group another term for the stigmatized or less powerful group, the minority.

In-groups and out-groups are another broad way of categorizing people. The in-group is the powerful group, most often the majority, whereas the out-group is the stigmatized or less powerful group, usually the minority (though the numbers don't have to break down this way). For example, in the United States, heterosexuals are the in-group in terms of sexuality (both more powerful and numerically greater), whereas homosexuals, bisexuals, and those who have other nonnormative sexual identities fall into the out-group. However, in South Africa, despite being a minority group, whites are the in-group because of their enormous political and economic power (the legacy of colonialism and apartheid), whereas blacks are the out-group despite their greater numbers. The significance of in-groups and out-groups lies in their relative power to define what constitutes normal versus abnormal thoughts and behavior.

Reference Groups

We often compare ourselves to other groups of people we do not know directly in order to make comparisons. For example, your class might compare itself to another introduction to sociology class, which has a take-home midterm and an optional final. If your class has a 20-page term paper and a 2-hour comprehensive final exam, you might feel as if you face an unfair amount of work. If your class has no external assignments, however, and your final grades are based on self-assessment, you might feel comparatively lucky. In either case, the other class serves as a reference group. Reference groups help us understand or make sense of our position in society relative to other groups. The neighboring town's high school or even another socioeconomic class can serve as a reference group. In the first instance, you might compare access to sporting facilities; in the second, you might compare voting patterns.

Reference group a group that helps us understand or make sense of our position in society relative to other groups.

From Groups to Networks

Dyads, triads, and groups are the components of social networks. A social network is a set of relations—a set of dyads, essentially—held together by *ties* between individuals. A tie is the content of a particular relationship. One way to think about "the ties that bind" is as a set of stories we tell each other that explain a particular relationship. If I ask you how you know a specific person, and you explain that she was your brother's girlfriend in the eighth grade, and the two of you remained close even after her relationship with your brother ended, that story is your tie to that person. For every person in your life, you have a story. To explain some ties, the story is very simple: "That's the guy I buy my coffee from each morning." This is a uniplex tie. Other ties have many layers. They are multiplex: "She's my girlfriend. We have a romantic relationship. We also are tennis and bridge partners. And now that you mention it, we are classmates at school and also fiercely competitive opponents in Trivial Pursuit."

Social network a set of relations—essentially, a set of dyads—held together by ties between individuals.

Tie a set of stories that explains our relationship to the other members of our network.

A narrative is the sum of stories contained in a set of ties. Your university or college is a narrative, for example. Every person with whom you have a relationship at your university forms part of that network. For all your college-based relationships—those shared with a professor, your teaching assistant, or classmates—your school is a large part of the story, of the tie. Without the school, in fact, you probably wouldn't share a tie at all. When you add up the stories of all the actors involved in the social network of your school—between you and your classmates, between the professors and their colleagues, between the school and the vendors with whom it contracts—the result is a narrative of what your college is. Of course, you may have other friends, from high school or elsewhere, who have no relationship to your school, so your college is a more minor aspect of those relationships.

Narrative the sum of stories contained in a set of ties.

In Chapter 4 we talked about the power of symbols. What would you need to do if you wanted to change the name of your school? You and your friends could just start calling it something else. But you'd probably have to hire a legal team to alter the contracts (a form of tie that is spelled out explicitly in a written "story") that the school maintains with all its vendors. You alert alumni. You advise the departments and staff at school to change their stationery, websites, and any marketing materials. You advise faculty to use the new name when citing their professional affiliation. You contact legacy families (let's say a family whose last seven generations have attended this college) and inform them of the name change. Do you now have a sense of how complicated it would be to change this narrative? If you try to make a change that involves a large network, the social structure becomes very powerful. Ironically, something abstract like a name can be more robust than most of the physical infrastructure around us.

Embeddedness: The Strength of Weak Ties

Embeddedness the degree to which ties are reinforced through indirect paths within a social network.

Strength of weak ties the notion that relatively weak ties often turn out to be quite valuable because they yield new information.

One important dimension of social networks is the degree to which they are embedded. Embeddedness refers to the degree to which ties are reinforced through indirect paths within a social network. The more embedded a tie is, the stronger it is. That is, the more indirect paths you make to somebody, the stronger the relationship. It may feel less dramatic and intimate, but it's robust and more likely to endure simply by virtue of the fact that it's difficult to escape. You will always be connected to that person—if not directly, then through your "mutual" friends. However, the counterpoint to this dynamic lies in what sociologist Mark Granovetter (1973) calls the strength of weak ties, referring to the fact that relatively weak ties, those not reinforced through indirect paths, often turn out to be quite valuable because they bring novel information. Let's say you're on the track team and that's your primary social group. An old classmate from high school whom you didn't really know (or run in the same circles with) back then, you now see occasionally because he also attends your college—but he's on the volleyball team. If the track team isn't doing anything on Friday night but the volleyball team is having a party, you've got an "in" through this relationship that's much weaker than the ones you've got with the other members of the track team. That "in" is the strength of the weak tie you maintain with the classmate from home. If you end up taking your friends from the track team to the volleyball party and they become friends with your old friend, the tie between you and your old classmate is no longer "weak" because it is now reinforced by the ties between your old friend and your new track friends—regardless of whether you are actually more intimate with him or not. This example helps explain why the structure of the network is more complicated than the tie from one individual to another. Even though your friendships did not change at the volleyball party, the fact that people in your social network befriended others in your social network strengthens the ties between you and both of the individuals.

The strength of weak ties has been found especially useful in job searches (Granovetter, 1974). In a highly embedded network, all the individuals probably know the same people, hear of the same job openings, maintain the same contacts, and so on. However, your grandparents' neighbor, whom you see every so often, probably has a completely different set of connections. The paradox is that this weak tie provides the most opportunities. When Granovetter interviewed professionals in Boston (1973), he determined that among his 54 respondents who found their employment through personal network ties, more than half saw this contact person "occasionally" (less than once a week but more than once a year). Perhaps even more surprising was the fact that the runners-up in this category were not people whom the respondents saw "often" (once a week or more); it was those they saw "rarely" (once a year or less) by a factor of almost two to one. Additional research finds that weak ties offer the greatest benefits to job seekers who already have high-status jobs, suggesting that social networks combine with credentials to sort job applicants and that strong ties may be more useful in low-status, low-credential job markets (Wegener, 1991).

Jena McGregor (center) takes part in a speed networking event in New York City. Participants chat about their businesses and make contacts with as many people as they can in multiple four-minute sessions.

In Figure 5.4, by linking two otherwise separate social networks, the weak tie between Natalie and Emily provides new opportunities for dating—not only for them but for their friends as well. Their tie bridges what we call a structural hole between the two cliques, a gap between network clusters, where a possible tie could become an actual tie or where an intermediary could control the communication between the two groups on either side of the hole. In the figure, Jenny is a social entrepreneur bridging a structural hole because the people on the left side of the network diagram (Emily and Jason) have no direct ties with the people on the right (Michael, Doug, and Jeff). Their ties are only indirect, through Jenny. Assuming that the two sides have resources (romantic or otherwise) that would complement each other's, Jenny is in a position to mediate by acting as a go-between for the groups. When a third party connects two groups or individuals who would be better off in contact with each other, that third party is an "entrepreneur," and he or she can profit from the gap. (Sound like the *tertius gaudens* in the triad? It should.)

Structural hole a gap between network clusters, or even two individuals, if those individuals (or clusters) have complementary resources.

When sociologist Ronald Burt studied managers in a large corporation (1992), he found that those with the most structural holes in their social networks were the ones who rose through the company ranks the fastest and farthest. This notion can be expanded to explain how a great deal of profit making occurs in today's economy. At one extreme is the totally free market, in

Figure 5.4: The Strength of Weak Ties

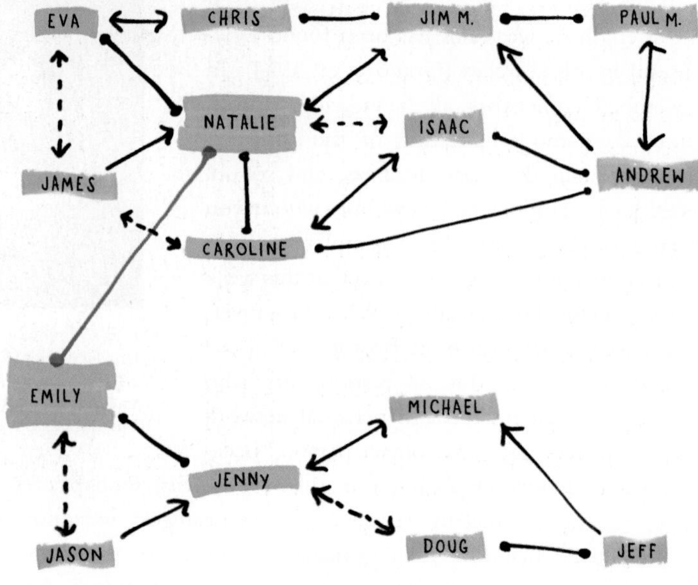

Natalie and Emily are social entrepreneurs; they command information to which the rest of their respective social networks do not have access.

which there are no structural holes; no restriction on information exists, and all buyers and sellers can reach one another—think eBay. At the other extreme is the monopoly, in which one firm provides necessary information or resources to a multitude of people (that is, maintains and profits from a gaping structural hole). And then there is everything in between these extremes: everyone from shipping magnates to spice traders to mortgage brokers to feral traders. Take real estate agents as an example. They earn their money by contractually maintaining (or creating) a structural hole. By signing up sellers, the real estate agents prevent the sellers from directly engaging in a transaction with potential buyers. Recently, the social network possibilities facilitated by the Internet (discussed below) have done much to erode the power of brokers—for example, by driving once-powerful travel agents into near extinction (ditto for stockbrokers).

Six Degrees

You have probably heard the term "six degrees of separation" and wondered if it is really true that each one of us is connected to every other person by social chains of no more than six people. The evidence supporting the six degrees theory came out of research undertaken in the 1960s by Stanley

Milgram, whose colleagues were pestering him about why it always seemed like the strangers they met at cocktail parties turned out to be friends of a friend. Milgram decided to test the reach of social networks by asking a stockbroker in Boston to receive chain letters from a bunch of folks living in Lincoln, Nebraska. The Lincolnites could only send letters to friends or relatives who they believed would be likely to know someone who might know someone who might know the guy in Boston. About 20 percent of the letters eventually made it to Boston, and the average trip length was just over five people, hence the summary that in the United States there are no more than five people between any set of strangers, or six degrees of separation.

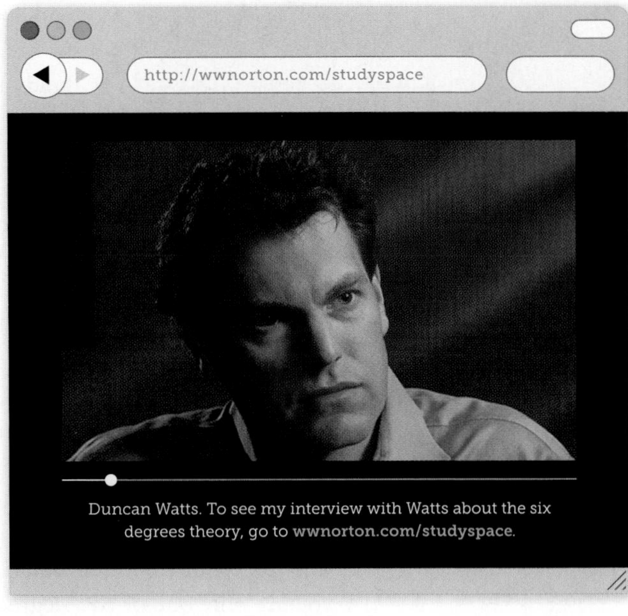

Duncan Watts. To see my interview with Watts about the six degrees theory, go to **wwnorton.com/studyspace**.

Duncan Watts (2003) noticed that Milgram's findings applied only to the letters that made it to their final destination. What about the letters that did not complete the journey? Were their chains quite a bit longer than six steps, thus making our six-degree theory more like a twelve-degree theory? Watts set up a similar, this time worldwide, experiment using e-mail and statistical models to estimate global connectedness and found that Milgram was not quite right. In Watts's words, "it's not true that everyone is connected to everyone else, but at least half the people in the world are connected to each other through six steps which is actually kind of surprising" (Conley, 2009b). Furthermore, Watts was able to test the commonsense notion that there are some people out there who just seem to know everyone and that it must be through these superconnected people that the rest of us are able to say we're only six degrees from Kevin Bacon (or whomever). But instead he found that when it comes to whom we know, "the world's remarkably egalitarian" and that superconnectors played almost no role in getting the e-mail forwarded all the way to its destination (Conley, 2009b).

Social Capital

Having many weak ties is one form of what sociologists call *social capital.* Like human capital, the training and skills that make individuals more productive and valuable to employers, social capital is the information, knowledge of people or things, and connections that help individuals enter preexisting networks or gain power in them. Consider the importance of networking in

Social capital the information, knowledge of people, and connections that help individuals enter, gain power in, or otherwise leverage social networks.

Neighbors in the Central City section of New Orleans gather for their weekly domino game. Communities with thick webs of connection tend to thrive, with lower crime rates and more volunteer involvement.

endeavors such as preventing neighborhood crime or obtaining a good job. As it turns out, the cliché holds a lot of truth: It's not just what you know but whom you know. But whereas weak ties may be the most advantageous for an individual, for a community, many dense, embedded ties are generally a sign of high levels of social capital.

This concept makes sense when you think about it. Dense social capital means that people are linked to one another through a thick web of connections. As a result of these connections, they will feel inclined—perhaps even impelled—to help each other, to return favors, to keep an eye on one another's property. The more connections there are, the more norms of reciprocity, values, and trust are shared. After all, there is no such thing as total anonymity: Even if you don't know someone directly, chances are that you are only one or two degrees removed from him or her.

In this way, strong social capital binds people together; it weaves them into a tight social fabric that can help a community thrive. "You tell me how many choral societies there are in an Italian region," notes social capital scholar Robert Putnam, "and I will tell you plus or minus three days how long it will take you to get your health bills reimbursed by its regional government" (Edgerton, 1995). After years of research in Italy, Putnam determined that different regions of the country varied widely in their levels of participation in voluntary associations. As it turns out, the strength of participation in a region was a fairly good predictor of the quality and efficiency of its regional government (and, in turn, its economic growth).

The United States and Social Capital If it's true that social capital is correlated with economic and political health, some critics will say that America is in big trouble. Voluntary participation in civic life has taken a turn for the worse and, as a result, the nation's stock of social capital is at risk. In his best seller *Bowling Alone: The Collapse and Revival of American Community* (2000), Putnam traces the decline of civic engagement in the last third of the twentieth century. We are more loosely connected today than ever before, he says, experiencing less family togetherness, taking fewer group vacations, and demonstrating little civic engagement.

For example, more and more people are bowling alone. Actual bowling activity was on the rise at the end of the twentieth century, when Putnam was writing—the total number of bowlers in America increased by 10 percent from 1988 to 1993—but *league* bowling dropped a whopping 40 percent in the same time frame. This is bad news for bowling lane owners, because league bowlers consume three times as much beer and pizza as lone bowlers.

Owners make most of their profits on these items, rather than on lane fees and shoe rentals (Edgerton, 1995). More important perhaps is the fact that it's also bad news for democracy in America, because it's part of a more general trend of civic disengagement and a decline in social capital. It's happening in PTAs, the Red Cross, local elections, community clean-ups, and labor unions. Even membership in the Boy Scouts has decreased by 26 percent since the 1970s. More people live alone. Some go so far as to say that friendships have become shallower, and the phenomenon of BFF (best friends forever) is an increasing rarity (Wuthnow, 1998). As civic participation withers, activities once performed by communities have moved toward private markets. In *Habits of the Heart* (1985), Robert Bellah argues that community in America is breaking down.

Bowling alone? Although the overall number of bowlers has increased, the number of people bowling in groups has dropped. Are we seeing a decline in social engagement?

Who's to blame for America's fading civic life? The social entrepreneur who has too many structural holes to maintain? Parents? Our school systems, television, the Internet? A combination of all these and other factors works in conjunction with broad social trends, creating an increasingly differentiated, specialized, urbanized, and modern world. Social institutions must adjust to the flexibility, sometimes called the liquidity, of modernity by becoming more fragmented, less rigid, and more "porous" (Wuthnow, 1998). It becomes easier to come and go, to pass through multiple social groups such as churches, friends, jobs, and even families. Gone is the rigid fixity of finding and holding onto a lifelong "calling." Similarly, a majority of graduating college students (60 percent) attend more than one school before receiving a degree (Zernike, 2006).

This mobility and flexibility take a toll on people's lives. More than in previous eras, people report feeling rushed, disconnected, and harried, so it's no surprise that civic responsibilities are pushed aside. It's not that Americans don't care. In fact, they join more organizations and donate more money than ever before. They just don't give their time or engage in face-to-face activities (Skocpol, 2004). But before we blame the Internet, note that the trend toward giving more but showing up less predates the web. It is probably more a result of increased work hours and other pressures to keep up in an age of rising inequality.

Indeed, a considerable majority of Americans believe that their communities are weaker than ever before (Wuthnow, 1998). Without communal ties of civic and religious participation, Americans have lost trust in their neighbors. Interpersonal trust matters; it is essential for building the complex social structures necessary for a functioning democracy and economy. In *Loose Connections: Joining Together in America's Fragmented Communities* (1998), Robert Wuthnow finds

CASE STUDY: SURVIVAL OF THE AMISH

Pennsylvania's Lancaster County attracts more than 5 million visitors a year with its Pennsylvania Dutch country charm. Horsedrawn wagons carry visitors over covered bridges toward historic museums, colonial homes, and restaurants. Lancaster thrives on tourists' curiosity about the Amish, who first settled the land in 1693. Today about 59,350 Amish live in nearby homogenous farm communities. As far as appearances go, they certainly meet tourists' expectations.

Wearing straw hats and black bonnets, riding horse-drawn buggies, the Amish provide great photo opportunities. Children are taught in private schoolhouses, typically one room, only until the eighth grade, at which point they work full time on the family farm. The lives of the Amish revolve around going to church, tilling the earth, and working for the collective good. They value simplicity and solidarity. How, visitors wonder, have Amish communities in Pennsylvania and other states survived in our fast-paced society?

The Amish certainly appear to be relics of the past, but looks can be deceiving. Although the Amish place primary importance on agriculture, they do so in anything but a premodern fashion. The Amish, especially those living close to urban areas, have adopted farming innovations such as the use of insecticides and chemically enhanced fertilizers. Their homes are stylishly modern, with sleek kitchens and natural gas–powered appliances.

Because Lancaster County has experienced a certain degree of urban growth and sprawl, the Amish are not immune to the hustle and bustle of commerce. In fact, many Amish are savvy business owners. The number of Amish-owned microenterprises more than quadrupled between 1970 and 1990. By 1993 more than one in four Amish homes had at least one nonfarm business owner (Kraybill and Nolt, 1995). The result of this economic growth is a curious mix of profit-seeking entrepreneurship with a traditional lifestyle. Imagine finding out that your local rabbi, priest, or imam doubled as a high-rolling stock trader during the week.

How can these seemingly incompatible spheres of religious tradition and commerce coexist? This is the question Donald Kraybill set out to answer when he studied 150 Amish business entrepreneurs in Lancaster County (1993; in 1995 with Nolt). Not only do the Amish trade with outsiders, Kraybill documented, but they do so quite successfully: About 15 percent of the businesses he studied had annual sales exceeding half a million dollars. Their success rate is phenomenal: Just 4 percent of Amish startups fail within a decade, compared with the 75 percent of all new American firms that

An Amish barn raising in Tollesboro, Kentucky.

fail within three years of opening. That is, in a time when the majority of new American business ventures flop, virtually all Amish businesses succeed. Are the Amish just naturally better at conducting commerce? Is it something in their faith, self-discipline? Perhaps the answer lies in the community's hand-pumped water?

The answer is, none of the above. The secret to Amish success turns out to be the way they strategically combine their traditions with the rest of the modern world. As the Amish have become increasingly entangled in the economic web of contemporary capitalism, they have held onto their cultural traditions by maintaining an ideologically integrated and homogenous community. They are distinctly premodern and un-American in that they believe in the subordination of the individual to the community. They have rejected the prevalent American culture of rugged individualism, the notion of "every man for himself," often said to be the basis for successful entrepreneurship, in favor of "every man for the greater good." Individuals are expected to submit not only to God but also to teachers, elders, and community leaders. Their social fabric firmly binds people together. Whereas fashion for many people is a means of self-expression, the dark, simple clothing of the Amish signals membership in and subordination to the community. They have no bureaucratic forms of government or business; rather, they operate in a decentralized, loose federation of church districts. They reject mass media and automobiles and limit their exposure to diverse ideas and lands. The outcome is homogeneity of belief, unified values, and, not surprisingly, dense social capital. Amish businesses, like the people themselves, are tightly enmeshed in social networks, such as church and kinship systems, that provide economic support. The typical Amish person has more than 75 first cousins, most of whom shop in the same neighborhood. Add to that the taboo on bankruptcy within the community, and Amish businesses would be a dream come true for investors—that is, if the Amish were to accept outside capital (they don't).

Kimberly Hamme works on billing for her online business, Plainly Dressed, in her Paradise Town, Pennsylvania, home office. Hamme sells what most people would call Amish clothing. She does most of her business over the Internet.

Rather than marvel at how this culture maintains its centuries-old traditions while functioning in the business world, we should look at how they succeed in business regardless of being Amish. Kraybill and Nolt found that the cultural restraints of being Amish do indeed thwart business opportunity to some extent. Amish business owners aren't allowed to accept financial capital from outsiders or to prosecute shoplifters (to do so would single out lawbreakers and go against community solidarity). The success of Amish entrepreneurship is a telling example of the power of social capital.

Volunteers build an elementary school playground in New Orleans, Louisiana. After Hurricane Katrina devastated the Gulf Coast in 2005, thousands of college volunteers participated in the rebuilding efforts.

that people are worried about what they see as a breakdown of families and neighborliness and a concurrent rise in selfishness. When Wuthnow surveyed a random sample of Americans, fewer than half believed that their fellow citizens genuinely cared about others. Even worse, some studies suggest that more and more people think their neighbors are inherently untrustworthy (Lasch, 1991).

But the news may not be all bad on the social capital front: Following September 11, 2001, Putnam noticed a revival of civic engagement among young people who were at or near college age during the terrorist attacks. He found that among 18- to 24-year-olds, voting rates have increased by 23 percent since 2001, following a quarter-century of declining participation in national politics. Another positive sign is that college freshmen are increasingly talking about politics and volunteering in their communities. As a "teachable moment," Putnam argues, 9/11 revealed how interconnected our individual fates are—a point often missed in the anonymity of the daily grind. "We learned that we need to—and can—depend on the kindness of strangers who happen to be near us," he writes (Sander & Putnam, 2005).

Understandably, Putnam's claims have ignited much controversy. Some researchers have noted that even if an increase in participation occurred after 9/11, it was short-lived among adults (Sander & Putnam, 2010). Others claim the opposite, insisting that social capital never declined as Putnam declared. Rather, it has simply become more informal. Wuthnow, for example, argues that modernization brings about new forms of "loose connection" but hardly a disappearance of all connection. Nor does it necessarily follow that modern Americans are any worse off than when connections were tight. Things change, but that does not always mean they change for the worse. While Putnam laments the loss of face-to-face communal ties, we've witnessed an explosion in the past three decades of non-place-based connections: Think of the rich social life ongoing at social networking websites such as MySpace, Friendster, and Facebook.

With the exit of the old (such as the Elks, Rotary, and other fraternal and civic organizations), in have come new kinds of clubs—large national groups like the National Organization of Women, which one can join by mail or online, and informal support groups like Weight Watchers. Furthermore, the trend of declining social capital is falsely linear, as if from the 1970s to today civic society has moved in one simple direction (downhill). More probable is that civic engagement moves like a pendulum, swinging back and forth between privatism, as in the 1920s, and heightened public consciousness, as in the 1930s. Right now may feel like the end of social capital, but perhaps we're just at a low point on a constantly shifting trend line. The calls to save social capital may be a form of projected nostalgia, a misplaced romanticizing of the past.

The picture we've arrived at is that of a complex social world, where the decay of some forms of civic life is accompanied by the eventual emergence of new ways of building communities. Americans, living in modern, urban, anonymous, and loosely connected communities, carve out new social spaces, in turn creating a different kind of social fabric that holds together our republic. People adapt to what's new, retain what they can of the old, and negotiate within global forces and local communities.

→ Network Analysis in Practice

Researchers take the concepts we've discussed so far—embeddedness, the iron law of the triad, and network position—and apply them to real-world contexts in order to understand how group life shapes individual behavior. Network analysts also map out social relationships to better understand transmission phenomena such as the spread of disease, the rise and fall of particular fads, the genesis of social movements, and even the evolution of language itself.

The Social Structure of Teenage Sex

According to a *New York Times Magazine* article (Denizet-Lewis, 2004), contemporary American teenagers supposedly approach their love lives with a blasé attitude. "Hooking up" has replaced going steady; "friends with benefits" are preferred over girlfriends and boyfriends, with all their attendant demands and the corresponding commitment. The good news is that more reputable studies, including one using network analysis, refute this image of 1970s hedonism being re-created in the contemporary American high school. The bad news is that, even so, the sexual mores of American adolescents are putting them at greater risk of contracting sexually transmitted infections (STIs) than ever before.

Here are some more trustworthy numbers: About 50 percent of American teenagers over the age of 15, when interviewed by researchers, have admitted to engaging in sexual intercourse. (Boys probably tend to exaggerate their sexual experience, and girls probably downplay it.) A good number of those who have not yet had intercourse are still sexually active in other ways: Approximately one-third have "had genital contact with a partner resulting in an orgasm in the past year." Bluntly put, what this means is that a good two-thirds of American teens are having sex or participating in some form of sexual activity. Teenagers' romantic relationships tend to be short-term compared with adults', averaging about 15 months, so there is a fair amount of partner trading. Survey research among college students where "hookup culture" is prevalent found that 70 percent use condoms when they engage in vaginal/penile intercourse. That 70 percent is "a lot less than a hundred, but a lot more than zero," notes principal investigator Paula England (Conley, 2009d). To top that off, most adolescents with a sexually transmitted infection "have no idea that they are infected." All these factors combine to make American teenagers a breeding ground for STIs, which have increased dramatically in this age group in the last decade.

Despite sensational media reports about teenage hookups, monogamous couples such as J.D. and Elysia, both 14, of Yorktown High School in Arlington, Virginia, are more typical. What else does research reveal about high-school sexual relationships?

So what's a public health officer to do? During the administration of George W. Bush, the religious right and conservative policy makers suggested the "virginity pledge" and other abstinence policies as a solution. As it turns out, the pledge does delay the onset of sexual activity on average, but when the teenagers who take it eventually do have sex, they are much more likely to practice unsafe sex (Bearman & Brückner, 2001; Brückner & Bearman, 2005). Among the many problems in designing safe-sex or other programs to reduce the rate of STIs among teenagers is the fact that we knew very little about the sexual networks of American adolescents until quite recently. It would not be far off to say that we knew more about the sexual networks of aboriginal tribes on Groote Island than we did about those of American teenagers.

One component of the National Longitudinal Survey of Adolescent Health (AddHealth)

Figure 5.5: Analysis of High-School Sexual Relationships

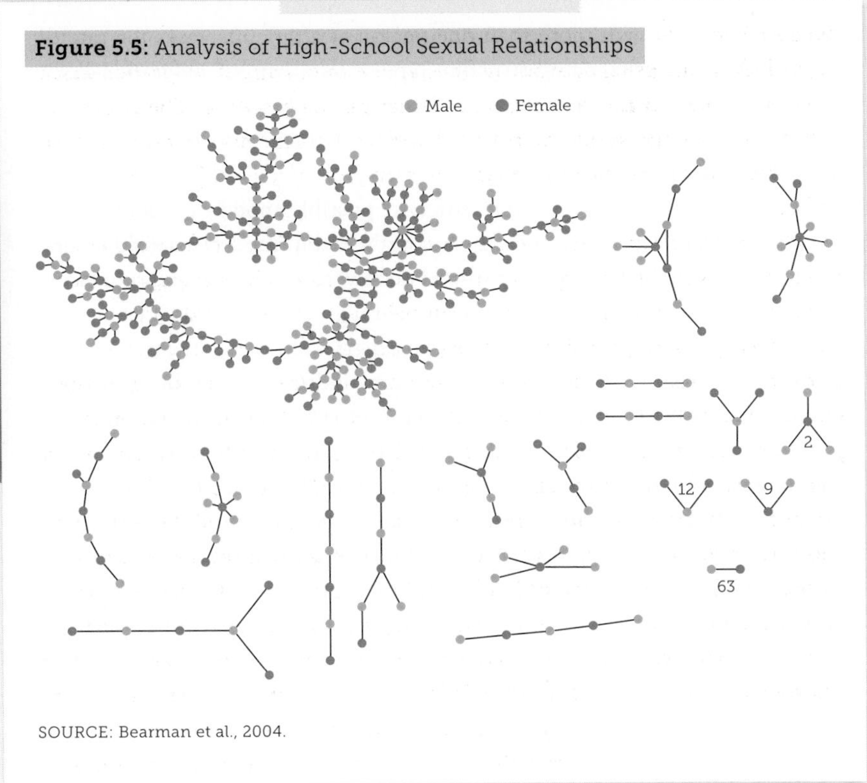

SOURCE: Bearman et al., 2004.

conducted by J. Richard Udry, Peter Bearman, and others from 1994 to 1996 investigated the complete sexual network at 12 high schools across the nation, including the pseudonymous Jefferson High School, whose 1,000-person student body is depicted in Figure 5.5 (Bearman et al., 2004). They focused their analysis on Jefferson, because its demographic makeup, although almost all white, is fairly representative of most American public high schools and, more important, it is in a fairly isolated town, so less chance exists of the sexual networks spilling over to other schools.

The pink dots represent girls and the blue ones boys. The dyad in the lower right-hand corner near the legend tells us that there are 63 couples in which the partners have only had sex with each other. There are small, comparatively isolated networks consisting of ten or fewer people and then one large ring that encompasses hundreds of students. Preventing the transmission of infection in the small networks is much simpler than preventing the spread in the large ring. One young man in the ring has had nine partners, but even if you persuaded him to use condoms or practice abstinence, you still wouldn't address most of the network. Your action might positively impact the people immediately around him. But to the extent other origin points of infection exist within the network, it is going to be very difficult to stop transmission. One practice that would slow the spread of STIs is lengthening the gap between partners: sleeping with more than one person at a time increases the rate of transmission. The fuzzy ring structure represents a type of network called a circular spanning tree—a spanning tree being one of four ideal types of sex networks hypothesized by Peter Bearman and other epidemiologists (scientists who study the spread of diseases).

Figure 5.6 illustrates the four different possible models of contact and spread for STIs. Panel A represents a core infection model, where the dark, filled-in circles (which represent infected people) are all connected to this core group. Therefore, the infection circulates through everyone in the group, but they're also connected outward to other partners. If you mapped out a sexual network like this, with the objective of stopping diseases from being sexually transmitted, you would try to isolate that core network and either cut them off from sexual relations with others or at least ensure that when they came into contact with uninfected partners, they practiced safe sex. Panel B shows a possible structural hole. Imagine an infected group and an uninfected group, but one person bridges them. Theoretically, such a circumstance is fairly easy to address, in that all you have to do is cut the tie or persuade that one person to engage in safe sex, and you've thus protected the uninfected population. Panel C depicts an inverse core model, representing the way much of the AIDS transmission occurs in Africa. Men go to prostitutes in the city, acquire the

Figure 5.6: Models for Spread of Sexually Transmitted Infections

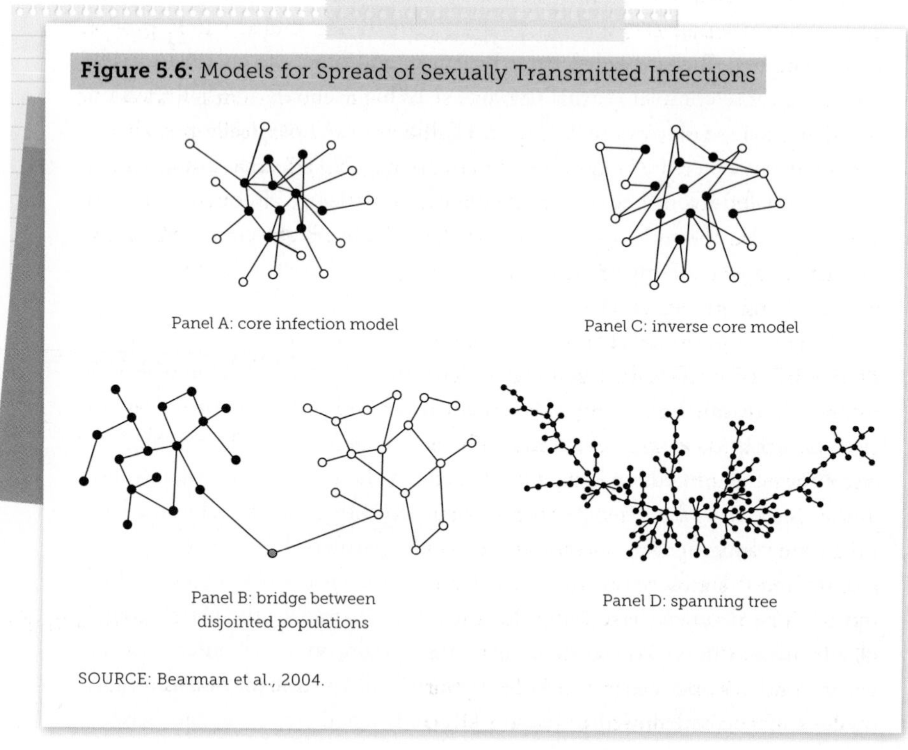

SOURCE: Bearman et al., 2004.

virus from them, and then bring the virus back to their villages. The infected members are not connected directly with one another (that is, the prostitutes are not having sex with each other); rather, the individuals at the periphery of the core (the men who solicit the prostitutes) connect the core members to each other and possibly beyond the group to other populations. The last network model, illustrated in panel D, is the spanning tree model, in linear rather than circular form. This is essentially how power grids are laid out: There's a main line, and branches develop off of that line. It is difficult to completely stop transmission along a spanning tree model. That's why we design electrical grids to be a series of spanning trees so that if one circuit fails the power can continue to flow around it, although as anyone who has experienced a blackout knows, specific sections can be left without power if they are severed from the rest of the tree. In terms of STI transmission, you could initiate some breaks that would split the tree into two groups, but that's not going to completely isolate the infection. If you attack something on a branch, you're not doing anything to the rest of the network. There's no key focal point that allows you to stop the spread.

Romantic Leftovers

When Peter Bearman and his colleagues analyzed the sexual habits of teenagers, they uncovered another rule that governed this social network. They found lots of examples of triads, where partners are traded within groups. But the main rule that seemed to govern these relationships was "no cycles of four," which means you do not date the ex of your ex's current boyfriend or girlfriend. The most interesting aspect of the rule, sociologically speaking, is that no one was consciously aware of this pattern. The researchers interviewed many students, and not one of them did directly state, "Of course not, man, you don't date the ex of your ex's new flame." Yet it's the single taboo that governs everyone. Figure 5.7 illustrates this rule of thumb graphically.

At time 1, Matt and Jennifer are dating, as are Jareem and Maya. At time 2, Jennifer and Jareem date. The rule suggests that Matt and Maya will never date. Why is that? Once Jennifer and Jareem start dating, if Matt and Maya decide to date each other, they are relegating themselves to secondary social status, as if they were "leftovers." The practical, take-home lesson in all of this is that if you want to date the ex of your ex's new crush, act before your ex does. If you're Jennifer and you wish to

Figure 5.7: Romantic "Leftovers"

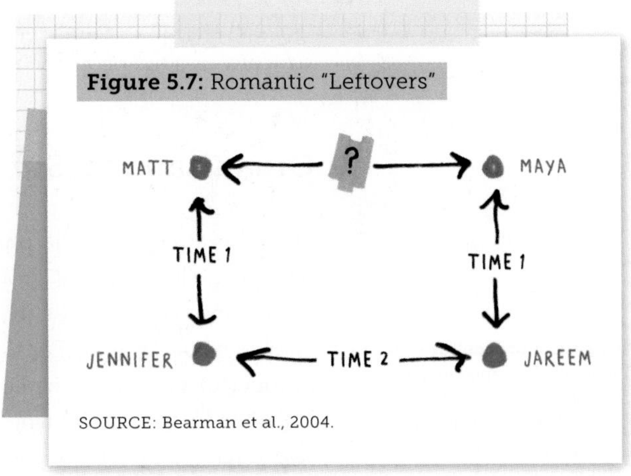

SOURCE: Bearman et al., 2004.

prevent your old boyfriend Matt from going out with Maya, quickly start dating Jareem, because then Maya and Matt will never date. But extend the "no seconds" rule to thirds or more, and the taboo erodes. The fact that no students in the high school studied were aware of the rule is what makes this kind of social norm possible: It's not conscious. This is a good example of how social structures govern individual-level behavior, and it speaks to some of the limitations of interpretive sociology. If the researchers had taken a more Weberian approach and asked students how they choose partners and, more important, why they don't date certain people, they probably wouldn't have discovered this rule. The researchers could see it only by taking a bird's-eye view and analyzing this structure with mathematical tools.

Organizations

I've mentioned several times that sociology—here network analysis—can be applied not just to individuals but to all social actors, which may include school systems, teams, states, and countries. In the contemporary United States, companies and organizations are important social actors. In fact, thanks to the Fourteenth Amendment, they have identities as legal persons: They sponsor charitable causes, they can sue and be sued; they even have birthdays.

Organization any social network that is defined by a common purpose and has a boundary between its membership and the rest of the social world.

Organization is an all-purpose term that can describe any social network, from a club to a Little League baseball team to a secret society to your local church to General Motors to the U.S. government, that is defined by a common purpose and that has a boundary between its membership and the rest of the social world. *Formal* organizations have a set of governing structures and rules for their internal arrangements (the U.S. Army, with its ranks and rules), whereas *informal* organizations do not (the local Brangelina fan club). Of course, a continuum exists, because no organization has absolutely no rules, and no organization has a rule for absolutely everything. Therefore, the study of organizations focuses mainly on the social factors that affect organizational structure and the people in those organizations.

Organizational Structure and Culture

Organizational culture the shared beliefs and behaviors within a social group; often used interchangeably with *corporate culture*.

Have you ever heard the phrase the "old boys' club"? The term is used to refer to exclusive social groups and derives literally from fraternities, businesses, and country clubs that allowed only men—specifically, certain groups of elite men—to join. These groups have their own customs, traditions, and histories that make it difficult for others to join and feel as if they belong, even when the "boys" aren't being deliberately hostile. The term organizational culture refers to the shared beliefs and behaviors within a social group and is often used interchangeably with *corporate culture*. The organizational culture at a slaughterhouse—where pay is low, employees must wear protective gear, the environment is dangerous, and animals are continuously being killed—is probably very different from the organizational culture at a small, not-for-profit community law center. The term organizational structure refers to the ways in which power and authority are distributed within an organization. The slaughterhouse probably has a hierarchical structure, with a clear ranking of managers and supervisors who oversee the people working the lines. The law center, however, might be more decentralized and cooperative, with five partners equally co-owning the business and collaborating on decisions. How an organization is structured often affects the type of culture that results. If a business grants both parents leave when a new child enters the home, allows for flextime or telecommuting, or has an on-site childcare center, those structural arrangements will be much more conducive to creating a family-friendly organizational culture than those of a company that doesn't offer such benefits.

Organizational structure the ways in which power and authority are distributed within an organization.

The growth of large multinational corporations over the course of the last 100 years has affected organizational structure. One example of this impact can be seen in *interlocking directorates*, the phenomenon whereby the members of corporate boards often sit on the boards of directors for multiple companies. A 2002 article in *USA Today* found that "eleven of the fifteen largest companies . . . have at least two board members who sit together on another board" (Krantz, 2002). (The website www.theyrule.net allows you to create an interactive map of companies' and institutions' boards of directors.) Does it matter that these people sit together on the same boards? The problem, critics argue, is that we then allow a select group of people—predominantly rich, white men—to control the decisions made in thousands of companies. Such people also have ties to research institutions and elected officials that may compromise their objectivity and create conflicts of interest. Capitalism, after all, is based on competition, but if board members on interlocking directorates favor the other companies to which they are connected, suppliers may not be competing on a level playing field when bidding for contracts. Or worse, take the situation that might develop when a board member of a cereal company asks his friend and fellow board member at a computer company, who is also an economic advisor to a newly elected senator, to support grain subsidies. This type of situation can lead to what sociologist C. Wright Mills called a "power elite" or aristocracy. (Concern over the consolidation of control in the media industry, for example, is discussed in Chapter 3.)

Institutional Isomorphism: Everybody's Doing It

Networks can be very useful. They provide information, a sense of security and community, resources, and opportunities, as we saw illustrated by Granovetter's concept of weak ties. Networks can also be constraining, however. Paul

DiMaggio and Walter Powell, focusing on businesses, coined the phrase *institutional isomorphism* to explain why so many businesses that evolve in very different ways still end up with such similar organizational structures (1983). Isomorphism, then, is a "constraining process that forces one unit in a population to resemble other units that face the same set of environmental conditions" (Hawley, 1968). With regard to organizations, this means that those facing the same conditions (say, in industry, the law, or politics) tend to end up like one another.

Isomorphism a constraining process that forces one unit in a population to resemble other units that face the same set of environmental conditions.

Let's consider a hypothetical case, a new organization that enters into a fairly established industry but wants to approach it differently, perhaps a bank that wants to distinguish itself from other banks by being more casual or more community oriented. The theory of isomorphism suggests that such a bank, when all is said and done, will wind up operating as most other banks do. It's locked into a network of other organizations and therefore will be heavily influenced by the environment of that network. The same is true for new networks of organizations. A group of not-for-profits might spring up in a specific area. Because all will face the same environmental conditions, they will likely be, in the final analysis, more similar than different, no matter how diverse their origins. DiMaggio and Powell are part of a school of social theory referred to as the new institutionalism, which essentially tries to develop a sociological view of institutions (as opposed to, say, an economic view). In this vein, networks of connections among institutions are key to understanding how the institutions look and behave. These theorists would argue that all airlines raise and lower their fares at the same time, for example, not because they are independently reacting to pure market forces but because symmetry, peer pressure, social signaling, and network laws all govern the organizational behavior of these *Fortune* 500 companies to the same extent that these forces affect the sex lives of seniors at Jefferson High School. Pretty scary, huh?

The 1965 Hart-Cellar Act

Since 1921 the United States has maintained strict quotas on the number of legal immigrants from specific countries. These quotas were originally based on the proportion of non-U.S.-born residents from each country of origin at the time of the 1910 Census. That original system evolved over the course of the twentieth century. For example, a law passed in 1924 shifted the basis for quotas from the 1910 Census to the 1890 Census, thereby curtailing the numbers of Eastern and Southern Europeans who could enter the United

States. That same law capped overall immigration from the Eastern Hemisphere at about 150,000, essentially cutting off immigration for many years. During the Great Depression, government officials also limited the number of immigrants to avoid competition in the labor market, given the high rates of domestic unemployment. The law was tweaked again in the 1950s. However, it was the Immigration and Nationality Act Amendments of 1965, otherwise known as the Hart-Cellar Act, that changed the face of immigration as we know it today.

Most important, the Hart-Cellar Act eliminated quotas on national origin, replacing this approach with a system of family preferences. Immigrants could sponsor their family members, so immigration suddenly became a network phenomenon. At the time, Senator Edward M. Kennedy of Massachusetts (then in his first term of office) said, "The bill will not flood our cities with immigrants. It will not upset the ethnic mix of our society. It will not relax the standards of admission. It will not cause American workers to lose their jobs" (U.S. Senate, 1965). Although many have debated in the years since whether our cities have become flooded with immigrants, standards of admission have been relaxed, or immigration has caused American workers to lose their jobs, no doubt exists that the ethnic mix of society has changed as a result. How might family networks have shifted the makeup of the immigrant population? And how has this changed national and local politics as of late?

→ CONCLUSION

What do we learn from the formal analysis of group characteristics and social networks? Simply knowing the formal characteristics of a group helps us understand much of the social dynamics within it. Is it a dyad or a triad? What is the proper reference group for a particular social process? Is this group a primary or secondary group—and what does that mean for my obligations to it? Likewise, we can use network analysis in micro- and macro-level studies. You could carefully weigh the potential consequences of dating your best friend's ex by mapping out your social network and anticipating shifts in ties that might transpire. Or you could analyze President Nixon's strategy of "triangulation" of the Soviet Union and communist China during the early 1970s using the iron law of the triad. Sociologists use network analysis to study everything from migration to social movements to cultural fads to global politics.

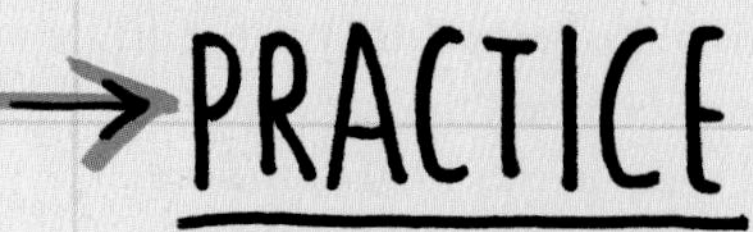

PRACTICE

ASSIGNMENT

Map out a network of your friendships and analyze it using the terms of network analysis. Are there any weak ties? If so, what are their relative strengths? How have these situations possibly resolved themselves? How embedded is your network? Do structural holes exist?

QUESTIONS FOR REVIEW

1. Consider Feral Trade—do you think it relies more on strong or weak ties? Why?
2. The Hart-Cellar Act brought a system of family preferences to the immigration process. Why might a network of family members make it easier for new immigrants to support themselves in the new country they call home?
3. If getting a job is "all about connections," how does the work on "the strength of weak ties" round out our understanding of this phenomenon? How does nepotism fit into this discussion?
4. An undecided voter who knows little about the political candidates reads the result of the latest poll on voting day and sees that other voters seem inclined to choose one of the candidates. According to Asch's work on conformity, how might the poll affect the voter's behavior? Do you think media sources should release polls shortly before an election?
5. If you could choose your position in a social network, would you want to bridge a structural gap? Why might the manager of a company try to prevent the development of structural gaps between the company's various departments? Would a high-school nurse be more likely to encourage or discourage structural gap formation?
6. What is an organizational structure? Describe the organizational structure at your school or workplace and determine how this structure might affect the organizational culture.
7. A new coffee shop opens in your neighborhood, which already has two other coffee shops. The new coffee shop offers free Internet access to customers. Within a few weeks, the two other shops offer free Internet access as well. Explain how this example might illustrate Paul DiMaggio and Walter Powell's concept of institutional isomorphism.

PARADOX

THE STRENGTH OF WEAK TIES: IT IS THE PEOPLE WITH WHOM WE ARE THE LEAST CONNECTED WHO OFFER US THE MOST OPPORTUNITIES.

WATCH THE ANIMATED SHORT ABOUT THE GROUPS AND NETWORKS PARADOX AT

WWNORTON.COM/STUDYSPACE

This New York City street poster refers to oppressive surveillance in George Orwell's novel *1984*. What are the social consequences of this sort of social control?

6 Social Control and Deviance

PARADOX

IT IS THE DEVIANTS AMONG US WHO HOLD SOCIETY TOGETHER.

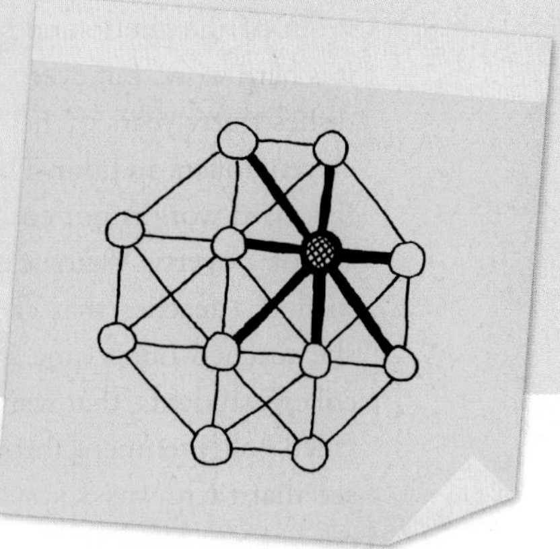

Smiley got his nickname because he always smiled at the most improbable times. When teachers yelled at him because he had trouble paying attention, he smiled. When his smile upset the teachers and incited more yelling, he kept smiling. When he and a friend broke into a car for a place to sleep after his abusive parents kicked him out, he smiled. He was surely smiling at the pretty girls with lipstick-reddened lips and poofy Aquanet pompadours he and a couple of homies decided to visit in the neighborhood of a rival gang. He was likely still smiling when eight rival gang members showed up, bringing guns to what might have been a fist fight. Smiley was shot in the head. His homie Victor scooped him off the pavement, bits of fresh brain matter clinging to his new sneakers. Victor cradled the dying Smiley in the back seat on the way to the emergency room; there was no time to wait for an ambulance that might never show up at their ghetto address.

When the police arrived at the hospital, they assigned partial blame to Victor, threatening to charge him as an accessory to murder for being present at the scene. Victor, in anger and disbelief, instead demanded that the police find the real shooter. "What for?" one of them replied, "We want you to kill each other off."

Homeboy Victor is now Associate Professor Victor Rios at U.C.-Santa Barbara. The other 67 homies from the original gang have not had Victor's success: four were murdered; nine were permanently injured, most with handguns; a dozen became addicted to drugs, sometimes living on the streets and panhandling to survive. Just two graduated from high school; only Victor went on to college. If it is surprising that Victor, a gang member son of a single welfare mother in an impoverished neighborhood, made it into one of the most heavily credentialed occupations, what does that tell us about the relationship between deviance and social mobility?

Because Victor is now a sociologist, I asked him what he has to say about getting out of the ghetto and into the ivory tower. He explains, "A lot of times people say to me, 'Oh, Professor Rios, you're so unique. You have all these qualities, you made it out. You pulled yourself up by the bootstrap. You made it out of the ghetto and now you are here.' And my response is, 'Well, part of it is hard work, but everyone works hard.' For example, my mom, she's washed dishes thirty years of her life working ten hours a day and she still makes ten, eleven dollars an hour. That's hard work. But she never progressed." He argues that hard work is not enough; there must be an opportunity trajectory leading out of poverty. Victor clearly recalls where his path started: "I was fortunate to find a teacher that cared, and she heard what happened [to Smiley], and she reached out to me and got me mentors from the university—students, college students, that wanted to go help the ghetto kids." These students provided enlightenment through the sociological imagination; they helped Victor see that there was a system at work larger than himself, larger even than his community. He saw "that I was actually living in a world of poverty that wasn't necessarily just produced by the way that people in my community acted, but it was also produced by a larger system of racism, classism and segregation" (Conley, 2009e).

In his book *Punished: Policing the Lives of Black and Latino Boys* (2011), Rios examines the way the current aggressive policing strategies have effectively criminalized young boys in poor neighborhoods. Police and parole officers are stationed in schools and community centers, the spaces in which education and mentoring traditionally occur, creating a self-fulfilling prophecy where teens are assumed to be criminals, treated with suspicion bordering on aggression, and watched closely until caught in some criminal act. Is flooding crime-ridden neighborhoods with aggressive policing the right thing to do? Or does sending more police to a neighborhood where criminal activity is concentrated simply increase the number of people who get caught, closing routes out of that neighborhood by saddling folks with criminal records?

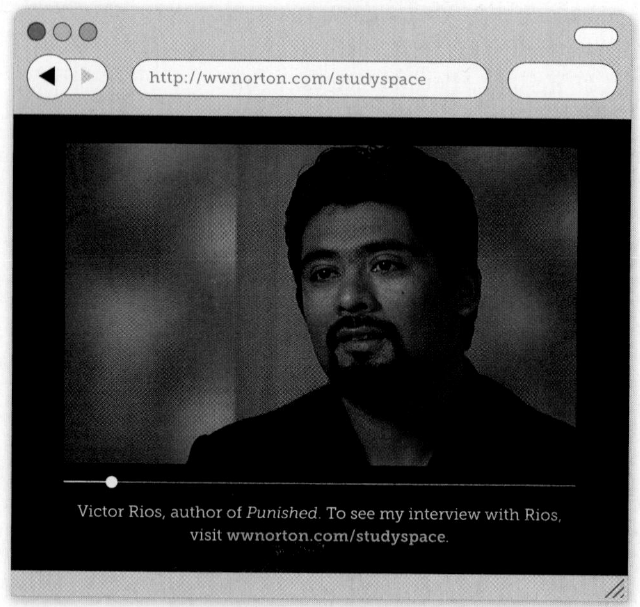

Victor Rios, author of *Punished*. To see my interview with Rios, visit wwnorton.com/studyspace.

The goal of this chapter will be to examine how society coheres and why some people transgress the boundaries of normality. For starters, how do people who presumably started life as innocent little kids end up in prison? How did Rios, an impoverished gang member growing up amid violence and theft, end up getting a PhD and becoming a professor? We can then turn to broader questions: Why doesn't society at large look like the violence-ridden Oakland neighborhood of Victor's youth? Why do most of us choose to sacrifice some of our personal interests for the sake of the social whole? How can we explain how society achieves predictable order, and what role does the criminal justice system play? Theorists of social deviance have produced various answers to these questions, which will be the subject of this chapter.

What is Social Deviance?

Social deviance, loosely understood, can be taken to mean any transgression of socially established norms. It can be as minor as farting in church or as serious as murder, so long as it consists of breaking the rules by which most people abide. Minor violations are acts of informal deviance, like picking your nose. Even if no one will punish you, you sense it is somehow wrong. At the other end of the continuum, we have formal deviance or crime, which is the violation of laws enacted by society. When deviant persons are caught in deviant acts, depending on the seriousness of the offense, they are subject to punishment. For instance, farting in church might result in glares from your fellow churchgoers, whereas crime, such as theft, may result in formal state-sanctioned punishments such as fines or community service or, for more severe violations, imprisonment, death, or even torture.

Social deviance any transgression of socially established norms.

Crime the violation of laws enacted by society.

Because social norms and rules are fluid and subject to change, the definitions of what counts as deviance are likely to vary across contexts. Even seemingly obvious cases of deviance, like killing another person, may not be so clear upon further investigation. When a soldier kills an enemy combatant, that act is considered heroic. But if the same soldier kills his or her spouse, the act is considered heinous and punishable by a long prison sentence. Persons and behaviors have been variously called deviant depending on what culture and historical period they happen to fall in. When women engaged in premarital sex in the Puritan colonies, they were subject to social exile; when women do so today in some Islamic countries, they risk public execution by stoning. In contemporary American society, however, sex outside of marriage is common and largely accepted. Similarly, 50 years ago, it was a crime for African Americans to share water fountains and swimming pools with white citizens; most people would consider such legislation unthinkable bigotry today. Just four decades ago, homosexuality was illegal nationwide. Gay bars were frequent targets of police raids, and sexual orientation was grounds for excluding immigrants (a rule that held until the Immigration Act of 1990; see Foss, 1994). As recently as 2003, the U.S. Supreme Court struck down Texas's criminalization of homosexual sex in *Lawrence v. Texas*; before the ruling, it was punishable by

arrest and a $500 fine. Changes in laws signal shifting social values and changes in social norms, such as increased tolerance of sexual and racial diversity.

In the popular conception, deviance typically takes the form of blatant rule breaking or lawlessness. But deviance does not necessarily require outlandish activity on the part of social misfits. Deviance is a broad concept covering everything from answering your cell phone during a lecture to murder. Both formal deviance and informal deviance are collectively defined and often subject to a range of punishments. For example, transgender persons—those who do not have a categorical masculine or feminine identity—are often subject to informal and formal punishments for their gender deviance, although most are perfectly law-abiding citizens. The same goes for ethnic minorities, people who bike down crowded city streets, and those who sing along with their iPods on the subway or bus. Even reserved, soft-spoken people, if they find themselves in a noisy crowd, may find that because their behavior goes against the grain, they become, for the moment, social deviants. Yet, deviance is sticky; it cannot be turned off and on so easily. Deviance can be a powerful label, capable of reproducing the entrenched social inequalities that punishment is often supposed to correct.

Functionalist Approaches to Deviance and Social Control

Imagine that society is a single, complex organism with many internal organs that perform specific tasks. The state is society's brain, its decision-making center where legislators contemplate the morality of laws and communicate legislative decisions to other social organs charged with implementation. All society's organs are necessary to keep the social organism alive and healthy, and these organs are composed of groups of individuals or cells. A functionalist approach explains the existence of social phenomena by the functions they perform. In this framework, the state develops because society needs a

Social norms and the punishments for violating them change over time and from place to place. Whether it was executing women as witches in the seventeenth century, enforcing Jim Crow laws in the segregated South, or prosecuting John Geddes Lawrence and Tyron Garner for engaging in a same-sex relationship, our definitions of what constitutes deviance change.

decision-making center to help organize and direct social life. All of society's various parts, or organs, are defined by their functions and are arranged as they are due to the needs of the social organism.

Émile Durkheim, author of *The Division of Labor in Society* (1893/1997), utilized such a functionalist approach to explain social cohesion, the way people form social bonds, relate to each other, and get along on a day-to-day basis. Durkheim's thesis is that there are two basic ways society can hold together or cohere, which he called mechanical and organic solidarity. Mechanical or segmental solidarity—which characterized premodern society—was based on the sameness of the individual parts. In this model, the functional units are like cargo containers—each container is like all the others and can perform the same function as the next. Cohesion stems from the reliable similarity of the parts. In a state of organic solidarity—which characterizes modern society—social cohesion is based on interdependence because the members in this type of social body perform different, specialized functions, and this increased mutual dependence among the parts is what allows for the smooth functioning of the whole. The physical analogy here is a machine in which each part is different and none would be so meaningful outside the context of the machine.

Social cohesion social bonds; how well people relate to each other and get along on a day-to-day basis.

Mechanical or **segmental solidarity** social cohesion based on sameness.

Organic solidarity social cohesion based on difference and interdependence of the parts.

In premodern society, people were held together by sameness. A peasant farmer in feudal times might have eked out a living by tilling a small plot of land, planting seeds, and then harvesting crops. The peasant next door also eked out a living by first tilling the land, planting seeds, and then harvesting crops. Slight variations might have existed in what farmers grew, but chances are that the farmers' life conditions, and particularly their day-to-day experiences in the field, were roughly the same. The farmers' conversations probably would not have been strained or awkward; the two neighbors would likely have had plenty of gardening tips to share. Such a situation would be an example of mechanical solidarity.

As Western society became more industrialized in the late eighteenth and nineteenth centuries, however, workers developed specialized skills, allowing them to perform particular tasks better and more quickly. This division

Farmers in premodern society would not have struggled to relate to one another; their sense of sameness bred mechanical solidarity. In contrast, most workers in the industrial and postindustrial economy perform such specialized tasks that they relate to one another through organic solidarity.

of labor resulted in a dramatic increase in productivity, but with the efficiency and high productivity of specialization come some negative consequences. Specialized workers have less and less in common with one another, and they may be less and less able to understand one another. For example, if you held a highly specialized position within the economy as, say, a techno-artist punk rocker, you might find yourself thinking that no one understands what it's like to be you. As a techno-artist punk rocker, you are isolated and alienated because your highly specialized position—your roles within the economy and society more generally—makes it difficult to find common ground with others. If you sit down on a commuter train next to an investment banker and try to talk with her, an awkward conversation might ensue, in which each of you tries to comprehend the daily activities of the other. You may share your morning commute and nothing more. Labor specialization divides us, pulls us apart by making it more difficult to form social bonds. However, the specialization of each task enables everyone to do something best. Maybe you are *the best* Japanese humane-certified chicken farm sex determiner (actually called a chick sexer, and yes, they make six figures) around because, among other reasons, you don't really have much competition. And this high degree of labor specialization makes us all interdependent, creating organic cohesion.

Distinguishing between these two types of social solidarity leads us to our first insight into social deviance. When individuals commit acts of deviance, they offend what Durkheim calls the collective conscience, meaning the common faith, or set of social norms by which a society and its members abide. Without a collective conscience, a set of common assumptions about how the world works, there would be no sense of moral unity, and a society would quickly dissolve into chaos. So when individuals break from the collectively produced moral fabric, societies are faced with the task of repairing the gash in the fabric by realigning the deviant individual through either punishment or rehabilitation.

The way in which social realignment is achieved, Durkheim concludes, depends on the type of solidarity holding that particular society together. Premodern societies, where people are united by sameness, tend to be characterized by punitive justice: making the offender suffer and thus defining the boundaries of acceptable behavior. Such punishment might involve collective vengeance. If someone in a medieval village committed adultery, stole vegetables, or murdered someone, the villagers would gather together, perhaps in a rowdy, pitchfork-wielding mob, to punish the criminal who had offended the collective conscience. The act of collective, group punishment might have culminated in storming the offender's house or hanging the poor sap in public. In either case, the group punishes the criminal in an act of collective vengeance. The collective probably wasn't interested in hearing the criminal's side of the story: the facts of his personal life, his possible motivations for committing the crime, or the details of his regrettable childhood. Mechanical social sanctions both reinforce the boundaries of acceptable behavior and unite collectivity through actions such as hanging, stoning, or publicly chastising a former member of the community. It is important to note that it is this collective action of vengeance that, by uniting the group through its perpetration and associated emotions of revenge, guilt, and so on, is key to the production of cohesion and unity. (Of course, there are always exceptions, such as the premodern Amish [see Chapter 5] who don't even bother to prosecute shoplifters.)

A similar form of justice can be administered by the state through a more formal process. When the infamous Oklahoma City bomber

A crowd marches two women accused of collaborating with the Nazis through the streets of Paris in summer 1944. The mob ripped the women's clothes, then painted swastikas on their shorn heads in order to punish them. How is this an example of a mechanical social sanction?

Eric Todaro (left) and Richard Grooms, inmates at a state penitentiary in Oregon, work on a General Education Diploma (GED) test. According to Durkheim, why would prisons provide educational programs and other rehabilitative tools?

Timothy McVeigh was put to death, he was, in effect, murdered by the collectivity, by the citizenry of the United States. To opponents of the death penalty, McVeigh's execution amounted to state-sponsored murder. To others, however, his death signaled that killing innocent people is not acceptable behavior. Although only a small team actually carried out McVeigh's execution, his death was an act in which—theoretically at least—we all participated. When we collectively and publicly put McVeigh to death, we were united in our reinforcement of social norms: Paradoxically, his deviance helped keep our society together.

Organic solidarity, in contrast, by differentiating individuals, produces social sanctions that focus on the individual; that is, they are tailored to the specific conditions and circumstances of the perpetrator. This response to deviance is rehabilitative, meaning that the response is designed to transform the offender into a productive member of society. In the modern mind-set, we care about the rapist's or murderer's motivations and regrettable childhood. We treat the criminal as an individual who can be "fixed" if we can root out the causes of, and triggers for, his or her criminality. For example, what happens if a drug addict steals car radios to support her cocaine habit? The court may order the addict into rehab in hopes of reintegrating her into the productive mainstream.

Punishments may also be restitutive—that is, they attempt to restore the status quo that existed prior to an offense or event. Tort law is an example of restitutive social sanctions. For instance, let's say a negligent contractor doesn't bother to install grating at the bottom of a swimming pool. A little girl playing at the edge of the pool is sucked into the drain, almost drowns, and ends up with brain damage. Restitutive social sanctions, or tort law, force the contractor (or his insurance company) to pay millions of dollars to the parents of the little girl. The money attempts to reestablish social equilibrium by repaying the parents for what they have lost. (Of course, in this case at least, money is a wholly inadequate salve.)

In the United States, we consider ourselves a modern society, yet both forms of social sanctions, mechanical and organic, still lurk within the U.S. justice system. We don't only try to rehabilitate our criminals and reimburse victims. We also still employ the death penalty in many states. Does Texas, where approximately one-third of the executions in the United States have taken place, have a more premodern division of labor than Wisconsin, which does not punish crimes with the death penalty? Probably not. Did the division of labor revert to primitive, subsistence levels all of a sudden in 1976, when the Supreme Court reinstated the legality of the death penalty? Of course not. Furthermore, some traditionally liberal states such as California and Connecticut still have the death penalty on their books. At the same time, we also have a signature form of modern, organic social sanctions as embodied by our elaborate court system. Durkheim doesn't argue that these forms of social sanctions are mutually exclusive, that they can't exist together. In fact, he would expect to find much more of one form of social sanction but not only one form. Both forms, however, help hold us together by reinforcing the boundaries of normal, socially acceptable behavior.

To make his case, Durkheim analyzed different historical penal and moral codes to discern the ratio of premodern sanctions to modern sanctions throughout history. He examined the Code of Hammurabi in Babylon dating back to 1750 B.C. as well as the Pentateuch, the first five books of the Old Testament. He studied more recent sanctions in the Magna Carta, the Napoleonic Code in France, and the South American Drago Doctrine. He argued that, as history progressed and the division of labor developed, the ratio of premodern to modern sanctions changed to favor modern, less punitive sanctions. So although the United States may still permit its states to apply the death penalty, Durkheim would hypothesize that as our labor market changes to favor even more specialization, we might expect the death penalty to fizzle out. In fact, approximately a dozen states have repealed the death penalty in recent decades, but we should be cautious in drawing overall conclusions about the relationship between division of labor and forms of punishment by focusing on one particular form of sanction.

Social Control

We have explored the paradox of deviance in Durkheim's *Division of Labor in Society*—the idea that deviance, and specifically the act of collective punishment, holds us together. But what makes us good, law-abiding citizens in the

Social control those mechanisms that create normative compliance in individuals.

Formal social sanctions mechanisms of social control by which rules or laws prohibit deviant criminal behavior.

Informal social sanctions the usually unexpressed but widely known rules of group membership; the unspoken rules of social life.

first place? Social control is what sociologists refer to as the set of mechanisms that create normative compliance, the act of abiding by society's norms or simply following the rules of group life. Other sociologists have tried to explain how social control works on individuals to induce compliance to social norms.

Sociologists classify mechanisms of social control into two categories. The first are called formal social sanctions. In most modern societies, these formal sanctions would be rules or laws prohibiting deviant criminal behavior such as murder, rape, and theft. These sanctions are formal, overt "expressions of official group sentiment" (Meier, 1982). Informal social sanctions are based on the usually unexpressed but widely known rules of group membership. Have you ever heard someone use the expression "an unwritten rule"? Informal social sanctions are the unwritten rules of social life. So, hypothetically, if you loudly belch in public, you will probably be the object of scowls of disgust. These gestures of contempt at your socially illicit behavior are examples of informal social sanctions, the ways we keep each other in check by watching and judging those around us. As discussed in Chapter 4, the process of socialization is largely responsible for our acquisition and understanding of these unspoken rules of group social life. Through years of trial and error, we have internalized the rules of the social game.

The idea behind informal social sanctions is that we are all simultaneously enforcing the rules of society and having them enforced upon us. How does

Renoir's *Luncheon of the Boating Party* (1881).

this work? At the same time that we are watching or observing others, others are watching us, too. All of us are both spectators and objects of spectacle. We are all the agents of a diffuse, watchful gaze, as in the painting *Luncheon of the Boating Party* by Pierre-Auguste Renoir, where everyone is gazing at someone else, but no two people make direct eye contact. And beyond watching, all of us can grant rewards for others' good behavior in the form of smiles and encouragement, but we can also sanction with dirty looks, snide comments, and worse. In this way, we are all chipping in our small contributions to the construction of the social whole.

Think about the neighborhood watch groups that preceded the widespread adoption of electronic home security systems. People in a community banded together and agreed to keep out an eye for trespassers, burglars, and suspicious strangers. The idea behind these groups was that neighborhoods could maintain social order by overtly declaring their intention to visually monitor their turf. Sometimes, such groups issued signs or decals for doors and windows to signal to unsavory characters that the neighborhood was being "protected" by watchful eyes. But this kind of activity doesn't have to be that formalized. The urban theorist Jane Jacobs coined the term the *eyes and ears of the street* to describe the fact that, ideally, in mixed-use (that is, commercial and residential) neighborhoods, the thread of social control is implicitly woven into daily life (Jacobs, 1961). Through their windows grandmothers watch children playing baseball on the street below, on the alert for any trouble. During the course of a busy weekday, a shopkeeper might notice a group of teenagers, who should be at school, loitering outside his store and report this to parents or the school.

In any society, many agents of both formal and informal social control exist. Our local neighbors act as the primary agents of informal social control, whereas the state, or the government, often has a hand in the construction of formal social sanctions by making laws. The police are an obvious example of an agent of state social control formed for the protection of the public. The police patrol public parks and neighborhoods after nightfall and contain public protests to ensure social order.

Informal social control is the bedrock on which formal social control must rest. If the police go on strike, for example, whether chaos will ensue depends on the degree of social cohesion in a given community. Likewise, without strong informal social norms, the police are relatively helpless. Consider the difficulty police officers have tracking down and arresting those who loot and commit acts of vandalism during an urban riot. Or the difficulty in solving or prosecuting a crime if witnesses are not willing to step forward and testify. If an entire community relaxes its informal social control, formal social control inevitably fails. Lately, the boundary between informal and formal social control is perhaps blurring a bit with the proliferation of surveillance cameras installed by private and public entities. (See box on page 220–21.)

A Normative Theory of Suicide

After making his observations on social solidarity and social control in *The Division of Labor in Society*, Durkheim next applied his ideas to the sociological study of suicide, perhaps the most striking act of deviance. If you were asked to explain what causes a person to commit suicide, you might say mental illness, depression, alcohol or drug addiction, or perhaps a catastrophic event such as a divorce, job loss, or bankruptcy. These are all common, intuitive explanations for suicide. They reflect our automatic perception of suicide as something intensely personal, mediated by individual life circumstances or caused by chemical imbalances and emotional disorders. And all these explanations may contain a piece of the complex answer. However, Durkheim believed these individualistic accounts of suicide were inadequate. What better challenge to a sociologist than taking the most personal act imaginable and explaining it as a "social fact" rather than a result of anguished individual circumstance?

There is something curiously social about suicide. Killing oneself is considered a sin in many religions and a violation of social norms besides. In his 1897 book *Suicide*, Durkheim sought to prove that the act of killing oneself cannot be explained solely by individual psychological characteristics; rather, suicide is also a product of social forces. According to Durkheim, suicide is, at its root, an instance of social deviance. By observing patterns in suicide rates across Europe (just as he had previously discerned patterns in penal codes), Durkheim developed a normative theory of suicide. His hypothesis is that the social norms of particular social groups—the conditions of group life—generate variations in group suicide rates.

Social integration how well you are integrated into your social group or community.

Social regulation the number of rules guiding your daily life and, more specifically, what you can reasonably expect from the world on a day-to-day basis.

What are the social mechanics that cause suicide rates to vary? Durkheim proposed that by plotting social integration on the *y*-axis and social regulation on the *x*-axis of a Cartesian coordinate system, we can construct a theory about how social forces influence suicide rates (Figure 6.1). Social integration refers to the degree to which you are integrated into your social group or community. A tightly knit community in which members interact with each other in a number of different capacities—say the coach of your child's Little League team is also your dentist and you are the dentist's mechanic—is more socially integrated than one in which people do not interact at all or interact in only one role. Social regulation refers to how many rules guide your daily life and what you can reasonably expect from the world on a day-to-day basis. To be at low risk for suicide (and other deviant behavior), you need to be somewhere in the middle: integrated into your community with a reasonable (not oppressive) set of guidelines to structure your life. If you go too far in either direction along either axis, you have either too much or too little of some important facet of "normal" life.

Let's say you drop down the *y*-axis significantly in the direction of egoism. You are not very well integrated into your group. What happens as a result? Durkheim argues that, because others give your life meaning, you would feel

Figure 6.1: A Normative Theory of Suicide

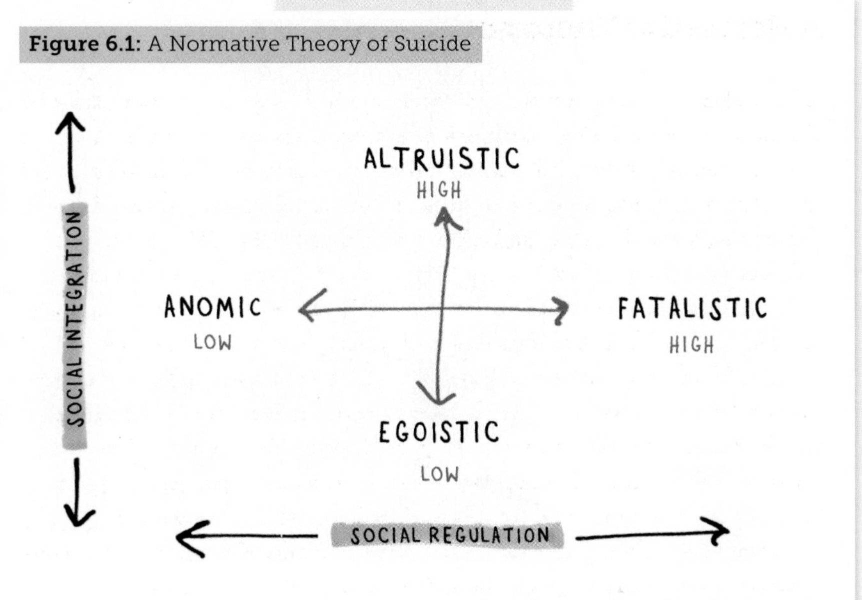

hopeless. You wouldn't be part of some larger long-term project, would feel insignificant, and would be at risk of committing egoistic suicide. We all need to feel as if we have made a difference to other people or produced something for their good that will endure after we have died. Durkheim demonstrated the prevalence of this phenomenon by using statistics about suicide rates across different religious groups.

Egoistic suicide suicide that occurs when one is not well integrated into a social group.

Although many western religions formally prohibit suicide, rates varied substantially across religious affiliations. Durkheim found that throughout Europe, Protestants killed themselves most often, followed by Catholics and then Jews. Why? Protestantism is premised on individualism. When Martin Luther nailed his 95 Theses to the door of the Castle Church, he was directly challenging the authority of the Catholic clergy. As a result of this antiauthoritarian tradition, an elaborate church hierarchy does not encumber most Protestant denominations, and Protestants are encouraged to maintain a direct personal relationship with God. By changing the relationship of the individual to God (and therefore of the individual to the church), Protestantism also stripped away many of the integrative structures of Catholicism. Without the sense of community engendered by the elaborate, communal church rituals, the Protestants slowly drifted down the *y*-axis of social integration, increasing the chances that individual Protestants might commit egoistic suicide. (More recent research shows that today the greater distinction is between people who are religiously affiliated and those who are not, the latter experiencing significantly higher levels of suicide.)

In Durkheim's era Catholics killed themselves less often than Protestants, but why did Jews have the lowest suicide rate of any major European

A Japanese man performs hara-kiri in this staged photograph from the 1880s. What makes this action altruistic suicide?

religious group, if all these religions prohibited suicide? Judaism may be less structured than Catholicism, but historically speaking, Jews have remained a persecuted minority group. When a social group is persecuted or rejected by the so-called mainstream, its members often bond together for protection from persecution. For example, in the United States today, African Americans have one of the lowest suicide rates, probably as a result of their bonding as a minority group, united in a common struggle against a history of oppression.

Altruistic suicide suicide that occurs when one experiences too much social integration.

Too little social integration increases the risk of suicide, but too much social integration can lead to the same result. A person who strays too far up the *y*-axis might commit altruistic suicide, because a group dominates the life of that individual to such a degree that he or she feels meaningless aside from this social recognition. Think about Japanese ritual suicide, sometimes called seppuku (sometimes colloquially known as hara kiri). In this scenario, samurai warriors who had failed their group in battle would disembowel themselves with a sword rather than continue to live as a disgrace in the community. Similarly, during World War II, with their country facing imminent defeat, Japanese kamikaze pilots deliberately crashed their planes into Allied warships. Durkheim uses the example of Hindu widows in some castes and regions of India, who were expected to throw themselves on their husbands' funeral pyre to prove their devotion. This practice, called suttee or sati, symbolized that a woman properly recognized that her life was meaningless outside her social role as a wife. (Official efforts to ban suttee commenced as early as the sixteenth century, and it is now illegal and extremely rare in India.)

In the preceding examples, the individuals who committed suicide were under some social pressure to do so, but altruistic suicide can be a more personal choice, too. For example, do you think that higher suicide rates exist among enlisted soldiers or officers in the military? Enlisted soldiers might be the obvious choice because they experience a lower standard of living and less social prestige, but statistics show that the suicide rate is, in fact, higher among officers. Why? Too much social integration. The identity of the officer, his sense of honor and self-worth, is more completely linked to his role in the military. Enlisted soldiers, in contrast, are not as responsible for group performance. More likely, these soldiers perceive their military service as a job and still identify strongly with their other, civilian roles, so they have a lower risk of altruistic suicide.

As we move to the *x*-axis, social regulation, why or how would social regulation influence the suicide rate? Imagine you commute to school every day. You rise at approximately 7:00 A.M., leave the house by 8:00 A.M., and take the 8:15 A.M. bus to school. But now imagine that some days the bus is late, some days the bus is early, and sometimes it just doesn't come at all. You have no way of knowing when or if the bus will come. You get tired of standing on a cold, lonely corner waiting for a bus that may never come, and after a while you might just stop trying to get to class at all. What's the point of waking up if you won't make it to class on time despite your effort? You have developed a sense of learned helplessness, a depressed outlook in which sufferers lack the will to take action to improve their lives, even when obvious avenues are present.

At the heart of learned helplessness is the sense that we are unable to stave off the sources of our pain, that we have no control of our own well-being. Durkheim studied a similar condition, which he termed *anomie*. Literally meaning "without norms," anomie is a sense of aimlessness or despair that arises when we can no longer reasonably expect life to be more or less predictable. Our sense of normalcy is eroded, because too little social regulation exists. Durkheim labeled suicide that resulted from the insufficient social regulation anomic suicide. For example, after the stock market crashed in 1929, it became common for businessmen to jump out of skyscraper windows. These stockbrokers and investors felt as if their lives were forever ruined and would never be the same again. For them, daily life had been irrevocably disrupted, and they had no idea how to cope with the changes.

Anomie a sense of aimlessness or despair that arises when we can no longer reasonably expect life to be predictable; too little social regulation.

Anomic suicide suicide that occurs as a result of insufficient social regulation.

Durkheim's argument about anomic suicide seems intuitive when it refers to negative events rupturing our everyday lives, but the same principles also hold for positive life events. For example, many lottery winners report spells of severe depression after winning millions of dollars, providing another case of what Durkheim would call anomie (Nissle & Bshor, 2002). If a very poor, frugal man wins the lottery, all of his money-saving habits instantaneously become irrelevant, unnecessary, even a bit silly. Maybe he previously structured his Sundays this way: Walk down to the corner store just as it's about to close to pick up a cast off of the Sunday paper, painstakingly cut coupons from the circulars for hours, and then plan a visit to each of three local grocery stores to find the best deals throughout the week. Maybe he always took lunch to work in reused brown paper bags to save money. Now he has $5 million in his checking account and no behavioral template (something that social processes yield) for life as a wealthy man. His difficulties do not revolve around the quantity of material resources or standard of living suddenly available to him. They revolve around the now-absent rules he previously used to order his life and the limits they placed on his expectations.

Fatalistic suicide suicide that occurs as a result of too much social regulation.

The final coordinate is fatalistic suicide, which occurs when a person experiences too much social regulation. Instead of floundering in a state of anomie with no guiding rules, you find yourself doing the same thing day after day, with no variation and no surprises. In 10 years, what will you be doing? The same thing. In 20 years? The same thing. You have nothing to look forward to because everything already has been planned. This type of suicide usually occurs among slaves and prisoners. You might imagine that slaves and prisoners would commit suicide because of the physical hardship of their conditions, but Durkheim's research suggested that they do so, at least in part, because of the mental torture of monotony.

Early feminists wrote of the "problem that has no name": that life as a 1950s suburban stay-at-home mother was a stifling routine, the same every day, for as long as the imagination could conjure. Sylvia Plath, a feminist poet and writer, committed suicide in 1963 shortly after the publication of her novel *The Bell Jar*, in which the semi-autobiographical character Esther's fatalism is palpable: "I saw the days of the year stretching ahead like a series of bright white boxes, and separating one box from another was sleep, like a black shade. Only for me, the long perspective of shades that set off one box from the next had suddenly snapped up, and I could see day after day after day glaring ahead of me like a white, broad, infinitely desolate avenue" (1963/1971, p. 143). Women's roles in society were tightly controlled, and thus they were at higher risk for fatalistic suicide.

The thought that an intensely personal act like suicide is, in fact, something social may seem strange, even jarring, but Durkheim found that the differences among group suicide rates cannot be accounted for by individual, psychological explanations alone. Are we to believe that suicide rates among Jews are lower because they as a group are simply immune to depression? Or that women in the 1950s and early 1960s were psychologically unstable compared to contemporary women? According to many theories of deviance, what happens at the group level affects what happens at the individual level. For example, Durkheim hypothesized that members of minority groups were more socially integrated within their group, and therefore Jews in Europe had lower suicide rates. Perhaps minority solidarity inspires feelings of belonging and love between family and nonfamily alike within the group. Because feeling loved and wanted is generally regarded as a good thing, we could say that this solidarity makes group members happy or at least staves off depression. Less

Conformist

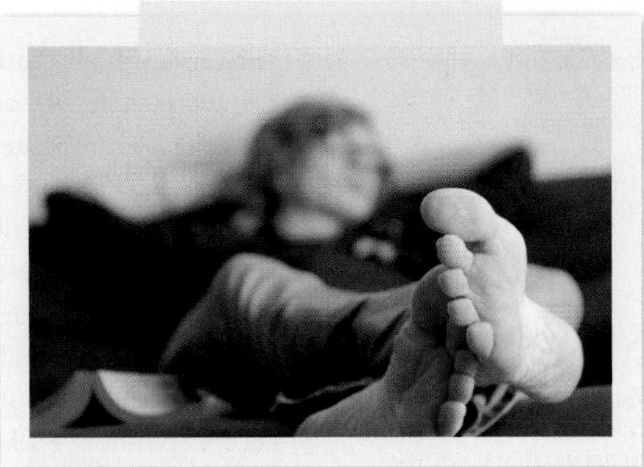

Ritualist

Innovator

Retreatist

Rebel

Which type are you? Do you follow socially accepted means and goals? According to Robert Merton, you're a conformist. Doing the bare minimum? You're probably a ritualist. If you're like WorldCom CEO Bernard Ebbers and want to earn big rewards but have few scruples about how you reach them, you're an innovator. You're a retreatist if you reject all means and goals of society. You're a rebel, like Che Guevara, if you not only reject social means and goals but also want to destroy society itself.

depressed, happier people commit suicide less often than those who feel unimportant, worthless, and sad. Because Jews are happier (because they feel loved and wanted by their group), they commit suicide less. These group dissimilarities start at the macro level (group solidarity), filter down to the individual level (feelings of depression or happiness), and then can be detected again in the aggregate (differential suicide rates).

Social Forces and Deviance

In keeping with Durkheim's attempt to discover the social roots of suicide and other forms of deviance, sociologist Robert Merton pioneered a complementary theory of social deviance. Instead of stressing the way sudden social changes lead to feelings of helplessness, Merton argued that the real problem behind anomie occurs when a society holds out the same goals to all its members but does not give them equal ability to achieve these goals. Merton's

Strain theory Merton's theory that deviance occurs when a society does not give all its members equal ability to achieve socially acceptable goals.

strain theory, advanced in 1938, explains how society gives us certain templates for acting correctly or appropriately. More specifically, we learn what society considers appropriate goals and appropriate means of achieving them. The strain in strain theory arises when the means don't match up to those ends; hence, Merton's theory is also called the "means-ends theory of deviance." When someone fails to recognize and accept either socially appropriate goals or socially appropriate means (or both), he or she becomes a social deviant.

Conformist individual who accepts both the goals and strategies to achieve them that are considered socially acceptable.

If you have decided to pursue a college education, presumably to land a decent job, you are probably what Merton terms a conformist. A conformist accepts both the goals and strategies to achieve those goals that are considered socially acceptable. Your goal is to earn a good living, maybe start a family, and take long, exotic vacations where you will take photos with a fancy camera and then post them online to impress your friends. You've decided to pursue this lifestyle through a better education, deliberate cultivation of the right social network, and hard work.

Now let's say that you go to class every day, take minimal notes, and read just enough to earn a passing grade. All you want is to get by and be left alone. You don't care how much money you will earn, as long as it's enough to pay for your studio apartment and other small monthly bills. You've accepted society's acceptable means (you're still going to college, after all), but you've rejected society's goals (the big house, the 2.3 kids, and the new car). You've rejected the idea of getting ahead through hard work, the American dream. You are a ritualist, a person who rejects socially defined goals but not the means.

Ritualist individual who rejects socially defined goals but not the means.

Innovator social deviant who accepts socially acceptable goals but rejects socially acceptable means to achieve them.

If, however, you yearn to be rich and famous but don't have the scruples, patience, or economic resources to get there by using socially acceptable means, you may be an innovator. Let's say you are particularly interested in buying a mansion and expensive jewelry, and marrying a gorgeous husband or wife. Instead of slaving away on Wall Street for years, you sell drugs, fence stolen goods, and make a few friends in the Mafia.

Retreatist one who rejects both socially acceptable means and goals by completely retreating from, or not participating in, society.

Rebel individual who rejects both traditional goals and traditional means and wants to alter or destroy the social institutions from which he or she is alienated.

Among those who reject *both* means and goals are retreatists and rebels, although the boundaries between the two are not always so cut and dried. Retreatists completely stop participating in society. This type is perhaps illustrated by adventurer Christopher Johnson McCandless, the main character of the best-selling 1997 book and 2011 film *Into the Wild*, who simply decided not to play the game and moved to the woods where he lived without running water or electricity. (I won't tell you what happens to him in case you plan on reading the book.) A rebel also rejects both traditional goals and traditional means but wants to change (or destroy) the social institutions from which he or she is alienated. One example is Ernesto "Che" Guevara, the Argentine Marxist who famously fought for communism in Cuba. His disgust at the impoverished conditions he encountered as a doctor traveling through Latin America led to the formation of a guerrilla group. Che chose to fight the government rather than, say, propose new legislation or raise money for a new hospital.

Symbolic Interactionist Theories of Deviance

Whereas Durkheim and Merton focused on the ways different parts of the organic social body function together, another school of sociologists in the 1960s and 1970s took a different approach to the study of deviance. Working in the tradition of symbolic interactionism (see Chapters 1 and 4), a term coined by Herbert Blumer, these sociologists stressed the particular meanings individuals bring to their actions, rather than the broader social structures of which they are unwittingly a part (Blumer, 1969). To determine why people commit crimes or the root causes of deviance in a given society, a symbolic interactionist would look at the small and subtle particulars of a social context, and the beliefs and assumptions people carry into their everyday interactions. Functionalist theories, such as Durkheim's and Merton's, are sometimes called macro theories because they seek to paint the social world in wide brushstrokes: generalizable trends, global or national forces, and broad social structures. At the opposite end of the spectrum, micro theories such as symbolic interactionism zoom in on the individual. Symbolic interactionism takes seriously our inner thoughts and everyday interactions with one another, including how others see us and how we respond to our surroundings.

Symbolic interactionism a micro-level theory in which shared meanings, orientations, and assumptions form the basic motivations behind people's actions.

Labeling Theory

As a child, did you ever shoplift, trespass, or forge a document? If you were slow and tactless enough to get caught, your parents probably gave you a stern lecture and maybe grounded you. Chances are, however, that over time the incident slowly faded into the background and you stopped feeling guilty. You probably never came to think of yourself as a shoplifter or trespasser, as a criminal or social deviant. You simply made a stupid mistake, never to be repeated. Let me give you an example from my own past. One afternoon when I was in junior high school, a friend and I decided to play "fireman, waterman," a game that required one person (the fireman) to flick lit matches into the air, while the waterman tried to extinguish them with a plant mister. To make a long story short, I was the fireman and I won. As you might expect, the incident ended badly—specifically, one of the stray, airborne matches set my friend's apartment on fire. After extinguishing the blaze, fire department officials questioned me about my role in starting the fire, but ultimately, I was absolved from blame and the fire was declared an accident. My parents, although obviously shaken and disappointed, never formally punished me. The trauma of the incident, they said, was lesson enough. Now imagine that, instead of being pardoned, I was held accountable for my role in starting the fire and sent to a juvenile corrections facility. Do you think I still would have followed the same life trajectory, eventually going to college and graduate school, and becoming a sociology professor and textbook author?

Labeling theory the belief that individuals subconsciously notice how others see or label them, and their reactions to those labels, over time, form the basis of their self-identity.

The labeling theory of social deviance offers insight into how people become deviants. According to this theory, individuals subconsciously notice how others see or label them, and their reactions to those labels over time form the basis of their self-identity. It is only through the social process of labeling that we create deviance by assigning shared meanings to acts. We all know that stealing, trespassing, and vandalizing are wrong, abnormal, and criminal behavior, but these acts are considered deviant only because of our shared meanings about the sanctity of private property and our rules about respecting that property. Although the fire caused by my unfortunate stint in pyrotechnics was labeled an accident, it might have been termed a crime just as easily. There was and is nothing inherently deviant about setting an apartment on fire, accidentally or otherwise. In 1963, Howard S. Becker, a proponent of labeling theory, made precisely this point, arguing that individuals don't commit crimes. Rather, social groups create deviance, first by setting the rules for what's right and wrong, and second by labeling wrongdoers as outsiders. Offenders are not born; they are made. They are a consequence of how other people apply rules and sanctions to them.

Social groups create rules about the correct or standard mode of conduct for social actors. When these rules are broken, society's reaction to the act determines if the offense counts as deviance. Becker also argues that not only are deviant acts created by a process of labeling but *deviants* are also created by a process of labeling. If you break a rule—say, accidentally burn down an apartment—but your violation is not labeled a crime or otherwise recognized as deviant, then *you* are not recognized as a criminal or deviant. We become (or don't become) deviant only in interaction with other social actors. It is this social reaction to an act and the subsequent labeling of that act and offender that create social deviance.

How did Howard Becker apply labeling theory to the use of marijuana?

To illustrate this process of becoming deviant, Becker interviewed fifty marijuana users in "Becoming a Marihuana User" (1953). He began his study with a simple inquiry: Are marijuana users different from nonusers? Is there something about the individual psychology of marijuana users that causes them to smoke marijuana? The answer given by most scientists, politicians, and parents in the 1950s, when Becker was writing, was a hearty *yes.* Certainly, the commonsense conception of marijuana use today assumes that marijuana users are somehow different from nonusers. But Becker argues that chronic marijuana use results from a process of social learning. Before people light up, they must first learn how to smoke marijuana. More important, they must then redefine the sensations of marijuana use as "fun" and desirable. Just as setting an apartment on fire is not inherently a crime, getting high is not "automatically or necessarily pleasurable" (Becker, 1963). According to one novice user in Becker's study, "It started taking effect and I didn't know what was happening, you know, what it was, and I was very sick. I walked around the room, walking around the room trying to get off, you know; it just scared me at first, you know. I wasn't used to that sort of thing" (p. 239). Another user never could learn to enjoy pot:

> It [marijuana] was offered to me, and I tried it. I'll tell you one thing. I never did enjoy it at all. I mean it was just nothing that I could enjoy. [Becker: Well, did you get high when you turned on?] Oh, yeah, I got definite feelings from it. But I didn't enjoy them. I mean I got plenty of reactions, but they were mostly reactions of fear. [You were frightened?] Yes. I didn't enjoy it. I couldn't seem to relax with it, you know. If you can't relax with a thing, you can't enjoy it, I don't think. (p. 240)

A person trying marijuana is usually able to redefine the experience when smoking with long-term users who assure the novice that the physical effects are normal, even enjoyable. One of Becker's interviewees, a veteran smoker, recalled how a beginner "became frightened and hysterical" after smoking for the first time. An older user told the newbie, "I'd give anything to get that high myself" (Becker, 1963). This comment and others like it apply new meaning to the sensations of getting high. Marijuana smoking becomes pleasant through a social process, and marijuana becomes an object of desire. How objects and sensations become meaningful (or pleasant) through social processes is the focus of Becker's study, in contrast to explanations that focus on what objects *are*. Similarly, the taste of alcohol probably didn't appeal to your palate when you first tried it; however, because alcohol had a certain social allure, being associated with either adulthood or rebellion, you may have learned to appreciate its taste (even before you reached the legal drinking age of 21).

Another example of a social process may help illustrate the power of labeling theory. As part of a psychology experiment, a group of eight adults with no history of mental illness and steady employment presented themselves at different psychiatric in-patient hospitals and complained of hearing voices (Rosenhan, 1973). Each of the pseudo-patients was admitted after describing the alleged voices, which spoke words like "thud," "empty," and "hollow." In all cases, the pseudo-patients were admitted with a diagnosis of schizophrenia. The researchers instructed the pseudo-patients, once they were hospitalized, to stop "simulating any symptoms of abnormality." Each pseudo-patient "behaved on the ward as he 'normally' behaved." Still, the doctors and staff did not suspect that the pseudo-patients were imposters. Instead, the treating psychiatrists changed their diagnosis of schizophrenia to "schizophrenia in remission." Something even more troubling than the misdiagnosis occurred. Once the pseudo-patients had been labeled insane, all their subsequent behavior was

THE STANFORD PRISON EXPERIMENT AND ABU GHRAIB

The force of labels and roles can affect us very quickly. The Stanford Prison Experiment, conducted by Philip Zimbardo in 1971, provides insight into the power of such social labels and how they might explain the incredibly inhumane acts of torture, most involving violence and humiliation, committed at Abu Ghraib, the American-run prison in Iraq. Zimbardo, a psychology professor at Stanford, rounded up some college undergraduate men to participate in an experiment about "the psychology of prison life." Half the undergraduates were assigned the role of prisoner, and half were assigned the role of prison guard. These roles were randomly assigned, so there was nothing about the inherent personalities of either group that predisposed them to prefer one role over the other.

To simulate the arrest and incarceration process, the soon-to-be prisoners were taken from their homes, handcuffed, and searched by actual city police. Then all the prisoners were taken to "prison"—the basement of the Stanford psychology department set up with cells and a special solitary confinement closet. The guards awaited their prisoners in makeshift uniforms and dark sunglasses to render their eyes invisible to inmates. Upon arrival at the prison, all the criminals were stripped, searched, and issued inmate uniforms, which were like short hospital gowns. The first day passed without incident, as prisoners and guards settled into their new roles. But on the morning of the second day, prisoners revolted, barricading themselves in their mock cells and sparking a violent confrontation between the fictitious guards and prisoners that would ensue for the next four days. From physical abuse, such as hour-long counts of push-ups, to psychological

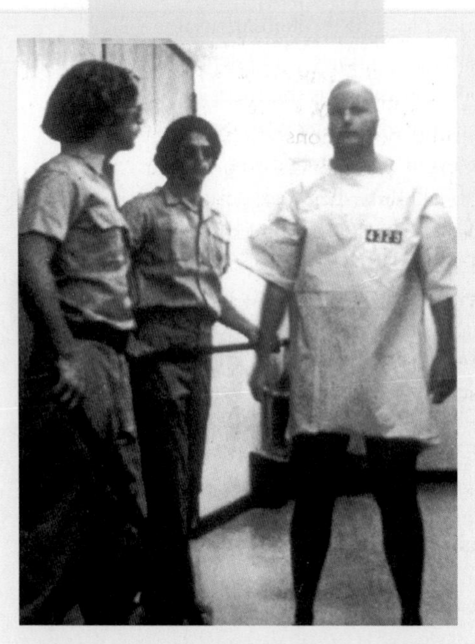

Philip Zimbardo's Stanford Prison Experiment.

violence, such as degradation and humiliation, the guards' behavior verged on sadism, although just days before these same young men were normal Stanford undergrads. The prisoners quickly began "withdrawing and behaving in pathological ways," while some of the guards seemed to relish their abuse. The original plan was for the experiment to last 14 days, but after only 6 days it spiraled out of control and had to be aborted.

This Iraqi detainee in Abu Ghraib prison was hooked up to wires after American soldiers made him stand on a box. How can Zimbardo's experiments help us understand the torture at Abu Ghraib?

The lesson, claims Zimbardo, is that good people can do terrible things, depending on their social surroundings and expectations. When thrown into a social context of unchecked authority, anonymity, and high stress, average people can become exceptional monsters. It's a phenomenon Zimbardo calls the "Lucifer effect," and it offers insights into how the atrocities at Abu Ghraib prison in Iraq became possible (Zimbardo, 2007). In 2005, when the media made public horrifying images of Iraqi prisoners being degraded and abused—some naked and on their knees inches from barking dogs, some wearing hoods and restrained in painful, grotesque positions, some forced to lie atop a pile of other naked prisoners—with grinning American soldiers looking on, many commentators (and military officials) sought to explain the abuses as a case of "bad apples" among otherwise good soldiers. Bad apples don't just arise out of nowhere, however, nor are people inherently malicious or brutal by nature. When given limitless power under the high stakes of uncertainty, as happened to the soldiers at Abu Ghraib, abuse becomes the norm, and people who are otherwise good can do evil things.

In experiments such as David L. Rosenhan's or films like *Shock Corridor* (above), people with no history of mental illness are admitted into psychiatric hospitals. These examples raise questions about the stickiness of labels. What are some of the consequences of being labeled a deviant?

interpreted accordingly. One male pseudo-patient, for example, gave the hospital staff a truthful account of his personal history. During his childhood he had been close to his mother but not his father. Later in life, he became close with his father and more distant from his mother. His marriage was "characteristically close and warm," with no persistent problems. He reported rarely spanking his children. Sounds like a fairly typical guy, right? This is how the hospital record described the pseudo-patient's personal history:

> This white 39-year-old male . . . manifests a long history of considerable ambivalence in close relationships, which begins in early childhood. A warm relationship with his mother cools during adolescence. A distant relationship to his father is described as becoming very intense. Affective stability is absent. His attempts to control emotionality with his wife and children are punctuated by angry outbursts and, in the case of his children, spankings. And while he says that he has several good friends, one senses considerable ambivalence embedded in those relationships also. (Rosenhan, 1973, p. 253)

Even though the pseudo-patient was acting "normally" shortly after his admission, the "abnormal" label stuck and continued to color the staff's perceptions and diagnoses. Just in case you are curious, the pseudo-patients were kept by the hospitals for 7 to 52 days, with an average stay of 19 days. Sticky label, indeed.

Labeling theorists believe the fact that deviant labels stick no matter what the circumstances has important consequences for behavior. If, after committing a crime or hearing voices, you were labeled deviant and people treated and thought about you differently, how would you feel? Like the same person but just someone who, say, was arrested for possessing drugs? Or would the criminal label become part of the way you thought about yourself? Labeling theorists call the first act of rule breaking (which can include experiences or actions such as hearing voices, breaking windows, or dyeing one's hair neon orange) primary deviance. After you are labeled a deviant (a criminal, a drug addict, a shoplifter, even a prostitute), you might begin behaving differently as a result of the way people think about and act toward you. Others' expectations about how you *will* act affect how you *do* act. Secondary deviance refers to deviant acts that occur after primary deviance and as a result of your new deviant label. For example, a deviance researcher interviewed a woman in her sixties who had been under psychiatric care for some 20 years (Glassner, 1999). This is how she recalls the process of becoming mentally ill:

Primary deviance the first act of rule breaking that may incur a label of "deviant" and thus influence how people think about and act toward you.

Secondary deviance subsequent acts of rule breaking that occur after primary deviance and as a result of your new deviant label and people's expectations of you.

> The first time I was taken to a psychiatrist for help was when I was getting depressed over a miscarriage. I had tried for many years to have that baby, and finally I was pregnant and planning to be a mother and all, and then I lost it. Anyhow, they told me I was "deeply depressed," but it didn't really mean much to me. I figured I'd get over it once I got pregnant again or something. But when I went home, everybody treated me differently. My husband and my mother had met with the social worker, who explained that I had this problem, with depression and all. From then on I was a depressive. I mean, that's the way everyone treated me, and I thought of myself in the same way after a while. Maybe I am that way, maybe I was born that way or grew up like that, but anyhow, that's what I am now. (p. 73)

First, the woman sees her experience with depression as a passing phase, something she will recover from in time. Then a psychiatrist labels her "deeply depressed." When she arrives home, family members treat her differently, and "from then on" she is "a depressive." You can see how the woman's initial experience is redefined by her interaction with the psychiatrist and how the psychiatrist's label eventually becomes an integral part of the woman's identity. Of course, these labels themselves are socially structured by group stereotypes that can often serve as default cognitive categories.

Stigma

We've seen how primary deviance can snowball into secondary deviance, whereby a few initial wrong steps or unlucky breaks can define a person's future actions and reactions. It doesn't end there. Secondary deviance can quickly become social stigma. A stigma is a negative social label that not only changes others' behavior toward a person but also alters that person's self-concept and social identity. We frequently say that certain behaviors, groups, identities, and even objects are stigmatized. Mental illness still carries a stigma in our society. Pedophilia carries a bigger one.

Stigma a negative social label that not only changes others' behavior toward a person but also alters that person's own self-concept and social identity.

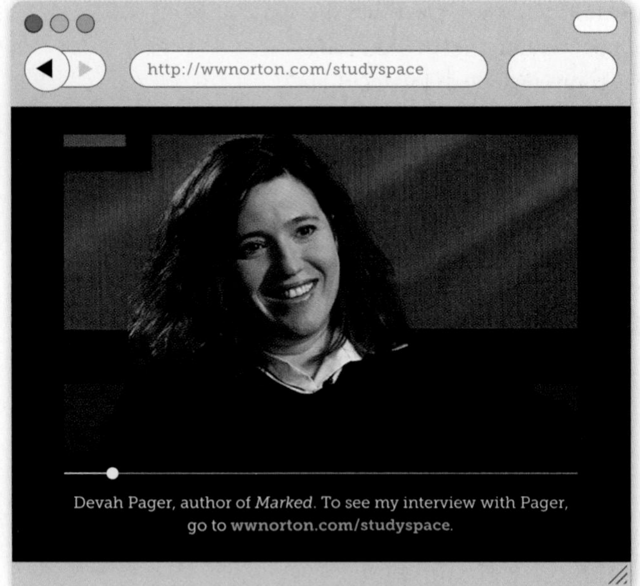

Devah Pager, author of *Marked*. To see my interview with Pager, go to **wwnorton.com/studyspace**.

Having a criminal record can also carry a stigma, as can a person's race. In 2001 Devah Pager, then a graduate student in sociology, conducted a study to determine the effects of race and a criminal record on employment opportunities (Pager, 2003). She dispatched potential job candidates (African American and Caucasian male college students who had volunteered for the experiment) with similar résumés to apply for entry-level service positions. Half the participants of each race were told to indicate a prior felony conviction on their job applications. Pager found not only that of those with no criminal record the white applicants were more likely to get a response (34 percent compared with 14 percent) but also that the white men with a supposed felony conviction were more likely to be called back than the black men who did not report a criminal record (17 percent compared with 14 percent). The employers in Pager's study were slightly more willing to consider a white applicant with a felony record than a black applicant with a clean history. So not only is a criminal record a stigma that deters potential employers, but the race of a job applicant continues to matter. One possible explanation, reasoned Pager, is that

> employers are attempting to select the best candidate for the job, but are affected by all kinds of pervasive and largely unconscious stereotypes that result in privileging or preferring a white candidate to a black candidate. . . . Employers have these negative stereotypes based on really pervasive media imagery, for example, of young black men involved with the criminal justice system or acting out in some negative way. There's lots of information we get about all of the negative characteristics that we might attribute to the African American population. . . . They talked about black men as being lazy and dangerous and criminal and dressing poorly; they were very candid about all of these negative characteristics that they attributed to black men. But then, right after that, when I asked them about their experiences over the past year with black applicants or black employees, they had a much harder time coming up with concrete examples of those general attitudes, and for the most part, employers reported having very similar kinds of experiences with their black and white employees. (Conley, 2009f)

Pager's research reveals how stigmas have real consequences, shaping the map of opportunities for men with criminal records, and illuminates the challenges faced by black men, whose skin carries a stigma of deviance into the labor market, whether they've been in prison or not. Of course, in this case, because the testers were trained with a script, the issue of internalized self-stigma doesn't come up to influence their interactions. But such internalized stigma is itself an important source of disadvantage and stress for marginalized groups. (See discussion of stereotype threat on page 526.)

Broken Windows Theory of Deviance

As labeling theory predicts, the ways other people see you affect your behavior and overall life chances. So, too, does the way you see your social surroundings, according to the broken windows theory. In 1969 Zimbardo conducted another experiment in which he and his graduate students abandoned two cars, leaving them without license plates and with their hoods propped up, in two different neighborhoods (Wilson & Kelling, 1982). The first car was abandoned in a seemingly safe neighborhood in Palo Alto, California, where Stanford University is located. The second car was left in the South Bronx in New York City, then one of the most dangerous urban ghettoes in the country. Unsurprisingly, the abandoned car in Palo Alto remained untouched, whereas the car deposited in the South Bronx lost its hubcaps, battery, and any other usable parts almost immediately. However, it was the next stage in the experiment that offers valuable insight into how social context affects social deviance. Zimbardo went back to the untouched car in Palo Alto and smashed it with a sledgehammer. He and his graduate students shattered the windshields, put some dents in the car's sides, and again fled the scene. What do you think happened to the smashed and dented car in the "safe," rich neighborhood? Passersby began stopping their cars and getting out to further smash the wreck or tag it with graffiti. The social cues, or social context, influenced the way people, even in a rich neighborhood, treated the car.

Broken windows theory of deviance theory explaining how social context and social cues impact whether individuals act deviantly; specifically, whether local, informal social norms allow deviant acts.

In the South Bronx, the overall social context—involving many broken windows, graffiti, and dilapidated buildings—encouraged deviant acts at the outset because the neighborhood setting of decay and disorder signaled to residents that an abandoned car was fair game for abuse. In Palo Alto, where neighborhood conditions were clean and orderly, people were unlikely to vandalize an abandoned car. However, when the vehicle was already mangled, that cue of turmoil signaled to people that it was okay to engage in the otherwise deviant act of vandalism. The broken windows theory of deviance explains how social context and social cues impact the way individuals

People inspect an abandoned car in the South Bronx. Philip Zimbardo placed this car in New York City and left another near Stanford University in Palo Alto, California. The car near Stanford went untouched for days, but the car pictured above was relieved of its hubcaps and other parts almost immediately.

act; specifically, whether local, informal social norms allow such acts. When signals seem to tell us that it's okay to do the otherwise unthinkable, sometimes we do. The broken windows theory of deviance has inspired some politicians to institute policies that target the catalysts for inappropriate behavior (vandalism, burglary, and so forth). In fact, one of Zimbardo's graduate students who participated in the car experiment, George Kelling, later worked as a consultant for the New York City Transit Authority in 1984, devising a plan to crack down on graffiti. The underlying assumption of the plan was that the continued presence of graffiti-covered cars served as a green light for more graffiti and perhaps even violent crimes. The Transit Authority then launched a massive campaign to clean up graffiti, car by car, in order to erase the signs of urban disorder, in the hope of reducing subway crime. In the mid-1990s New York City Mayor Rudy Giuliani also initiated a campaign of "zero tolerance" for petty crimes such as turnstile jumping, public urination, the drinking of alcohol in public, and graffiti. Today, the city's newer subway cars are "graffiti-proof," meaning that spray paint doesn't adhere to the metal exterior of the cars. Indeed, both petty and serious crimes have dropped dramatically in New York City since the 1990s (Kelling & Sousa, 2001), although some criminologists dispute the causal impact of the Giuliani strategy.

Crime

As noted above, crime is a more formal sort of deviance, not only subject to social sanction but also punishable by law. Sometimes, an act falls clearly at one end of the spectrum or another. Situations of self-defense aside, killing a person is generally agreed to be criminal; nose picking, however unpalatable, isn't. In other cases, though, the distinction is not so clear. Whereas you might get strange looks for wearing aluminum-foil hot pants to class, if you show up with no clothes on at all, you will likely be sent to a mental health care provider for assessment or arrested and thrown in jail for indecent exposure. But what if your hot pants weren't foil at all but just silver paint? Would this be indecent exposure?

Crime runs the gamut in type and degree. Most of us think of violence or drugs when we contemplate crime, but there are many other ways of breaking the law.

Street Crime

You don't make up for your sins in church. You do it in the streets.

—"Johnny Boy" Civello in *Mean Streets*

Street crime crime committed in public and often associated with violence, gangs, and poverty.

Street crime generally refers to crime committed in public. The term invokes specific images, however, of violent crime, typically perpetrated in an urban landscape. Both historically and today, street crime is often associated with gangs and currently with both disadvantaged minority groups and poverty. Just why people are drawn to a career of street crime has long been a favorite question of social scientists and is still a matter of heated debate. Explanations for the fluctuations and trends in violent crime rates also vary widely. One theory, for example, posits that street crime rises and falls in relation to the availability of opportunity within the legitimate economy. When this is lacking, people turn elsewhere. Expanding on Merton's strain theory and the idea of anomie, sociologists Richard Cloward and Lloyd Ohlin (1960) developed differential opportunity theory, which states that in addition to the legitimate economic structure, an illegitimate opportunity structure also exists that is unequally distributed across social classes. Hence, crime should rise or fall according to the relative returns on opportunities in the legitimate and illegitimate economies.

One way, then, to reduce crime would be to raise the costs in the illegitimate economy, thereby lowering the net returns. Such a strategy lies behind tougher sentencing policies, such as "three strikes" laws (if you are convicted of three felony crimes, you are imprisoned for life), which aim simultaneously to deter criminals and to incarcerate habitual offenders. The focus of such policies tends to be violent crime; lately, however, such laws have been extended to nonviolent crimes, such as drug dealing. Another strategy would be to increase the returns to entry-level opportunities in the legitimate economy; raising the minimum wage is one way to do this. Either strategy—decreasing the returns to the illegitimate economy or increasing the returns to the legitimate economy—shortens the distance, or differential, between the two economies.

Many people attribute the decrease in crime rates to the adoption of a community policing ideology, in which police officers are viewed (and view themselves) as members of the community they serve. Rather than enforce laws from the outside in, members of the police force work to develop reliable relationships and bonds of trust with community residents. On a practical level, this means that greater police presence is felt in areas where community policing is in effect. (However, convincing evidence on this causal claim is still lacking; that said, community policing probably doesn't hurt.)

White-Collar Crime

Bernard L. Madoff rose through the social ranks of wealth on Long Island, then Manhattan, then London, and eventually his name was known in major financial centers around the world. In 2009, he was sentenced to 150 years in prison—a life sentence for the then-71-year-old. His crime was taking money from investors and fabricating great return rates to pump up his reputation and keep money coming in when, in fact, his funds were losing money. Returns

Bernie Madoff

to investors were paid not from any actual gains their initial investments were accruing, but from the new money coming in the door. Madoff lived an opulent lifestyle, employing well-connected friends and family to keep a steady stream of new investments coming in. During the economic downturn in 2008, Madoff could not keep up with investors' demands to cash out. An investigation by the Federal Bureau of Investigation (FBI) led to his arrest. Madoff estimated that he had lost $50 billion, making this the largest fraud in American history.

Infractions such as fraud are called white-collar crime, a term coined by sociologist Edwin Sutherland in 1939. It is typically committed by a professional (or professionals) in his or her (or their) capacity in the professional world against a corporation, agency, or other professional entity. According to the FBI,

> [w]hite-collar crimes are categorized by deceit, concealment, or violation of trust and are not dependent on the application or threat of physical force or violence. Such acts are committed by individuals and organizations to obtain money, property, or services, to avoid the payment or loss of money or services, or to secure a personal or business advantage. (2003)

White-collar crime offense committed by a professional (or professionals) against a corporation, agency, or other institution.

Although street crime is the most prevalent type of crime, looking strictly at the numbers, white-collar crime has greater financial impact. It has been estimated in one Cornell University study to cost the United States more than $300 billion a year. In contrast, the FBI has estimated that in 2001 the total loss from robbery, burglary, larceny-theft, and motor vehicle theft was $17.2 billion (2002).

Corporate crime a particular type of white-collar crime committed by the officers (CEOs and other executives) of a corporation.

A particular type of white-collar crime is corporate crime, offenses committed by the officers (CEOs and other executives) of a corporation. In late 2005 an enormous criminal bust came in the form of the Enron scandal. High-level executives at the company and other financial services institutions were frequent guests on television news segments; the use of ordinarily innocuous pieces of office machinery was called into question; mundane lives suddenly seemed outrageous. Kenneth Lay, the company's now-infamous CEO, hadn't injured or threatened anyone. No one had been murdered or assaulted. What Lay and his colleagues did was misappropriate funds, issue false reports, and destroy evidence. The biggest criminal scandals of this century (so far) involved accounting fraud.

Interpreting the Crime Rate

Although it may seem, after a glance at the newspaper's gruesome headlines, that crime is only growing progressively worse, the truth is that deviance has always been present. Kai Erikson, in *Wayward Puritans*, demonstrates how even America's seemingly most upstanding and God-fearing community, the Puritans, produced some bad apples—drunkards, adulterers, and thieves (1966/2005). Erikson's point, however, was that while what is defined as deviant may change over history, deviance is forever with us. For example, Erikson found "crimes against the Church," particularly by Quakers in the late 1650s, to be of central concern to the Puritan community. Religious or moral offenses, such as drunkenness and adultery, were of primary concern over economic or political ones—at least those were the crimes taken most seriously and probably reported most frequently during the Puritan era. Erikson's central thesis is that a relatively stable amount of deviance may be expected in a given community, but what counts as deviance evolves depending on the type of society or historical period we examine. Think back to our early definition of social deviance; it is, after all, a social construct and subject to change over time and across cultural values.

If the definitions of deviance and crime are always changing, how can we discern if the crime rate is going up or down? In 1969, the total crime rate was around 160.9 per 100,000 people. By 1992, that number had soared to a little over 757. Figure 6.2 shows the violent crime rate in the United States from 1960 to 2010.

How can so much change occur in the crime rate in so little time? Is the situation really rapidly degenerating into complete chaos? Probably not. To make a statement about the crime rate going up or down, we have to know what is factored into the crime rate. For instance, the definition of assault may change to include more minor offenses. Recently, one local government proposed including brawls at sporting events in the assault category. And if the classifications of violent crimes are changing, it's difficult to compare the crime rate over time. It is also possible that levels of crime reporting by victims

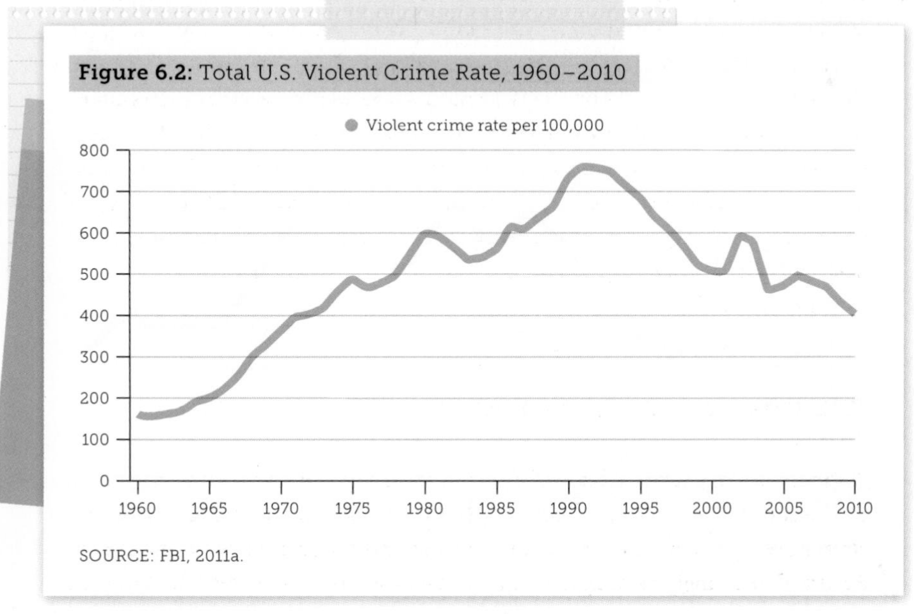

Figure 6.2: Total U.S. Violent Crime Rate, 1960–2010

SOURCE: FBI, 2011a.

fluctuate. In times of economic recession, people might be less likely to report crime because they feel helpless, depressed, or apathetic. Alternatively, a presidential address on fighting terrorism or injustice might make us more diligent in defending the social order.

The point is that the crime rate changes in response to fluctuations in how society classifies and reacts to deviance. In fact, reporting bias may work in the opposite direction from the actual crime rate. Imagine a neighborhood where crime is common. People might be reluctant to report being pick-pocketed on the subway when they have just read about three murders the same day. Conversely, in a situation where crime rates are perceived to be low, like at the opera house, you might be more likely to report a missing wallet. In this way, the reporting of petty crimes may vary inversely to the rate of serious crimes. For these reasons, criminologists, experts trained in studying crime, usually reject the overall crime rate as a reliable indicator of trends in crime. Instead, criminologists use the murder rate to make statements about the overall health of society. Why do they use these statistics instead of violent crime rates? For one thing, it's difficult to fake a murder—either there is a body or there isn't. The murder rate is the best indicator we have of crime in general (Figure 6.3), but even it is not immune to broader changes in society.

For example, if you were shot today in the United States, you would have a much better chance of surviving the gunshot injury than you would have had in 1960. It could be that many more people are arriving at the hospital with bullet wounds, but far fewer of those victims are dying on the operating table thanks to advances in medical technology. The greater survival rate

Figure 6.3: Homicide Victimization Rate, 1950–2010

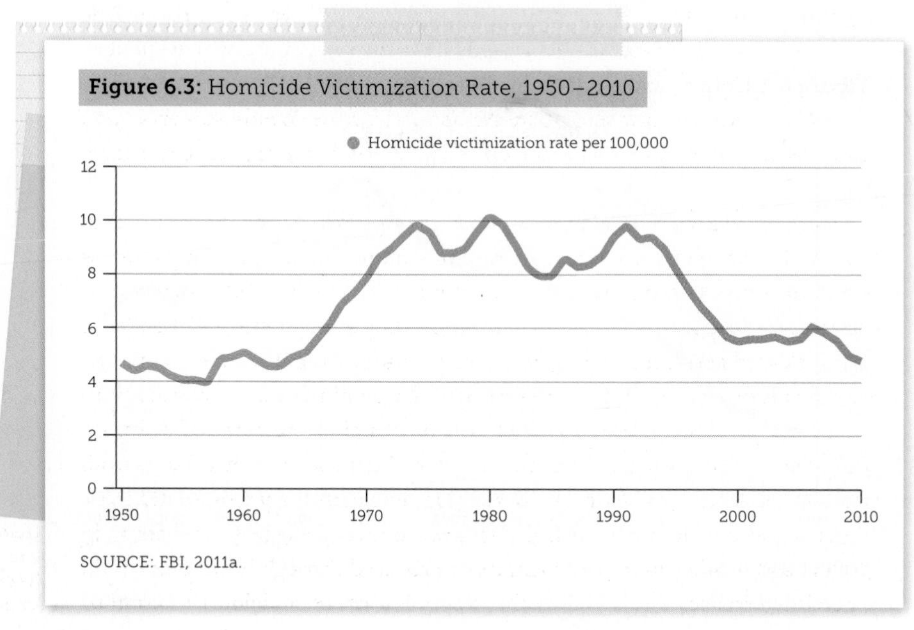

SOURCE: FBI, 2011a.

complicates our interpretation of the murder rate (Harris et al., 2002). Has there been a decline in the number of murder attempts, or are doctors just better able to treat bullet wounds? It's difficult to say definitively. We can use the murder rate as a gauge to gain a general sense of crime fluctuations, but precise statistics are practically impossible.

Crime Reduction

Thus far, we have studied some of the functions and social origins of criminal behavior, as well as the prevalent methods of measuring crime. So how do crime fighters fight crime?

Deterrence Theory of Crime Control

In 1971 President Richard M. Nixon ushered in America's first War on Drugs. Linking drug use to violent crimes and the decay of social order, the federal and state governments instituted an array of harsher penalties for the possession or sale of illegal substances. The philosophy of deterrence, or deterrence theory, suggests that "crime results from a rational calculation of the costs and benefits of criminal activity" (Spohn & Holleran, 2002). If you know you can make a quick buck by selling cocaine (maybe enough to pay your rent, say, or put food on the table), you might be tempted to engage in such illicit activities. But what if, instead of a slap on the wrist, a person caught with small quantities of cocaine is sentenced to a minimum of 15 years in prison? The temptation to sell cocaine might be reduced because you know that the cost of getting caught is higher than the potential benefits of selling drugs. Let's say you are arrested and wind up in prison for 15 years. Would you choose to sell cocaine again? How might the criminal justice system prevent you from doing so?

Deterrence theory philosophy of criminal justice arising from the notion that crime results from a rational calculation of its costs and benefits.

Specific deterrence is what the system attempts when it monitors and tries to prevent known criminals from committing more crimes. An example would be the prison parole system, because the criminal remains under supervision and is being specifically deterred from committing another crime. When he or she is released and freed from direct control after parole has ended, however, the effect is one of general deterrence, whereby criminals who have been punished for a previous offense may opt not to commit more crimes for fear of going back to jail. Another example of general deterrence would be if, from word on the street, you learn that dealing cocaine carries a prison sentence of 15 years and decide not to risk it. Deterrence theory suggests that crime in general, and recidivism in particular, can be reduced through both specific and general deterrence. Recidivism is the "reversion of an individual to criminal

Recidivism when an individual who has been involved with the criminal justice system reverts to criminal behavior.

PATHS OF LEAST SURVEILLANCE

Are Foucault's concerns about the panopticon (see page 228) just hysterical social theory in an age of the GPS, Google tracking, and voluntary uses of Foursquare, or does empirical evidence exist to support his claims? An ongoing effort in New York aims to coordinate the feeds from over 3,000 public and private surveillance cameras below Canal Street and between 34th Street and 59th Street in the city's business and financial centers. Google holds approximately 66 percent of the search engine market and captures almost every search term and subsequent mouse click, providing a virtual tracking device for online activity. Facebook and Yahoo do the same. Mobile phones often come equipped with a GPS, allowing applications and phone companies to track users. We may not expect privacy online, but perhaps some of us (not just Luddites like me) still expect to be able to walk down the street without being watched and recorded constantly. There is, however, an emerging resistance to the proliferation of surveillance. Researchers Brandon Welsh and David Farrington (2008) looked at 44 studies of London's CCTV installations and found them to be effective—but mostly only against vehicle theft in parking lots. And because new camera installations require excellent lighting, the researchers could not tell whether it was the cameras or the brighter lights that deterred car thefts.

Activists have also mobilized. The Institute of Applied Autonomy (IAA), a group of researcher-activists dedicated to developing technology for "average citizens, political protesters, and the functionally paranoid" to defend democratic institutions, launched an "inverse surveillance" project in 2001. The project, called iSee, allows users in urban centers (notably New York City) to access maps showing the locations of closed-circuit television surveillance cameras, represented by bright red squares, used in public spaces to monitor and track the movements of the public. The iSee project also allows users to generate a "path of least surveillance" that displays the walking route least densely populated by surveillance cameras between two points on a map. In some areas of Manhattan, avoiding surveillance cameras is almost impossible, requiring a long and circuitous journey. Another like-minded group, the New York Surveillance Camera Players, offers outdoor surveillance camera walking tours of Manhattan neighborhoods. Such groups are dedicated to subverting the visible and unverifiable watchful eye.

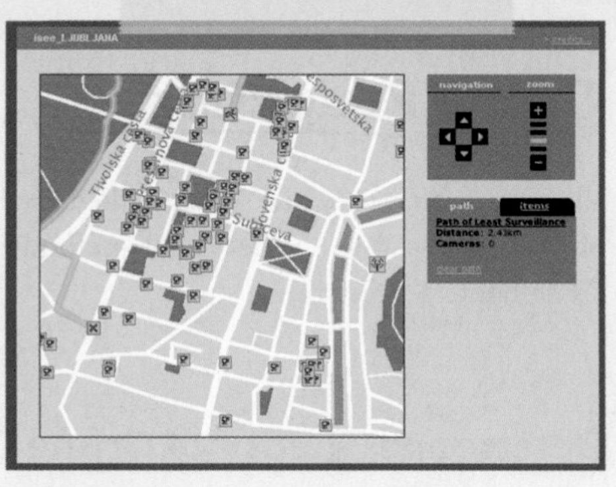

A surveillance camera map from the iSee project.

Other than placement, what turns a video camera into a surveillance camera? According to information engineer Natalie Jeremijenko, it's much more about who's pointing the camera at whom—that is, the structure of participation in the data it collects—than anything inherent about the technology itself. Any camera can become a surveillance camera if it meets four criteria:

1. It records you without your explicit per mission. For example, since when did entering a shopping mall mean that you signed a contract to star in a private movie of sorts? In most cases, surveillance cameras are hidden from the view of the subject.

2. There is an asymmetry of access to the images (and the archive of the images) the camera produces. Try going to the central security office of your university and asking to review the videotape of the campus security cameras so you can see how you are depicted. You'll have a fairly hard time convincing anyone to give you access, I'm willing to bet.

3. In addition to asymmetry of access, there is also an asymmetry of interpretation. If you are being prosecuted for shoplifting, for example, no one is likely to believe your claim that you were stuffing a shirt into your bag just to free your hands or to save plastic. In a court, experts regularly testify that when someone puts an item in his or her bag, 99 percent of the time that person's intent is to steal it.

A 2003 performance by the Surveillance Camera Players in New York's Times Square. They are trying to raise awareness of the density of public and private surveillance cameras.

4. An imbalance of power exists in terms of who is watching whom. Security cameras are deployed against the less powerful (think of a nanny cam). Often, this means that cameras survey from the vantage point of a private institution and record the actions of individuals exposed in public space. And often they are deployed by large institutions—the government or corporations—toward individual citizens. If an individual is pointing a camera at a fellow citizen, we call it voyeurism. If a corporation or state, it's called espionage.

Figure 6.4: National Recidivism Rates for Prisoners Released in 1983 and 1994

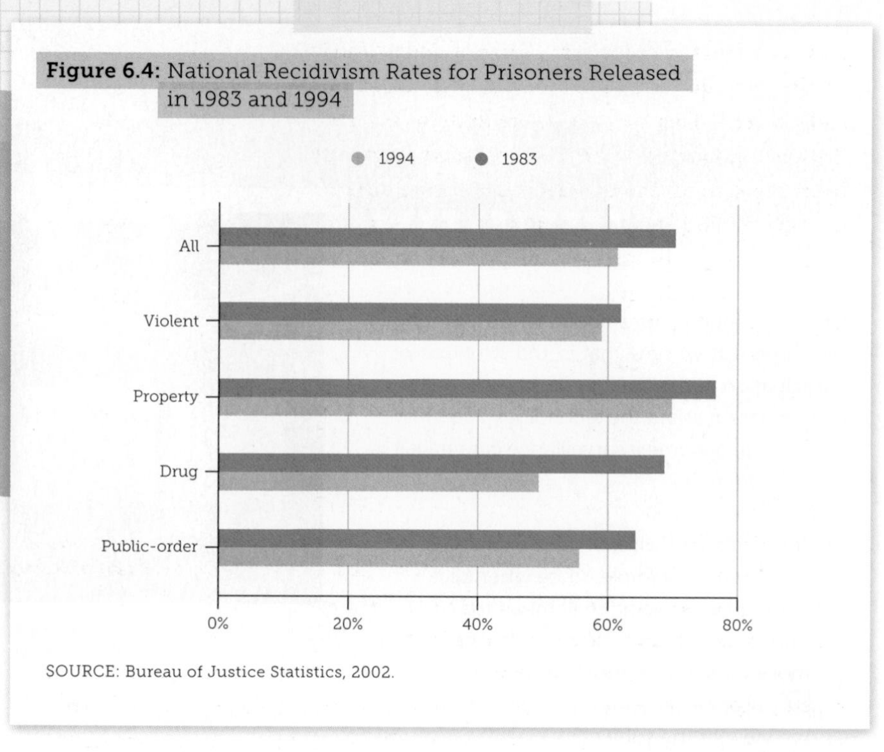

SOURCE: Bureau of Justice Statistics, 2002.

behavior" after involvement with the criminal justice system (Maltz, 2001). Recidivism rates by offense type are shown in Figure 6.4.

However, deterrence theory—in practice—has other, unintended consequences that may lead to more crime. For one thing, increased supervision and stricter parole codes have made it more likely that offenders will commit technical violations against their parole terms. Because the system has increased its surveillance of former prisoners, requiring time-consuming meetings with parole officers, the system creates better odds for technical slip-ups and for catching and punishing them. This is suggested by studies showing that rates of new criminal offenses (as opposed to technical violations) for parolees tend to resemble those of people with comparable sociodemographic characteristics who have never been incarcerated. In addition, the prison experience might not have the intended rehabilitative effect. Could prisons make it more difficult for offenders to return to the "straight and narrow"?

Let's first think back to Durkheim and his theory of anomie, which affirms that when our normal lives are disrupted and we can no longer rely on things being relatively stable, we are more likely to commit suicide or engage in other deviant acts. Going to prison for 10 or 15 years might have just this effect; it would be very difficult to "find stable employment, secure suitable housing, or reconcile with . . . family" afterward. Also, reintegration into a community after release from prison is extremely difficult because of "the absence of . . . informal social controls and strong social bonds" (Spohn & Holleran, 2002).

Furthermore, while in prison, drug offenders rarely receive the kind of substance abuse treatment that addicts need. They are thus more likely to revert to drug use upon release. Therefore, imprisonment may be particularly counterproductive for drug offenders, and getting tough on crime may inadvertently breed criminals. In addition, as low-level offenders interact daily with serious criminals in prison, they may become socialized by these new peers, adopting their attitudes and behaviors.

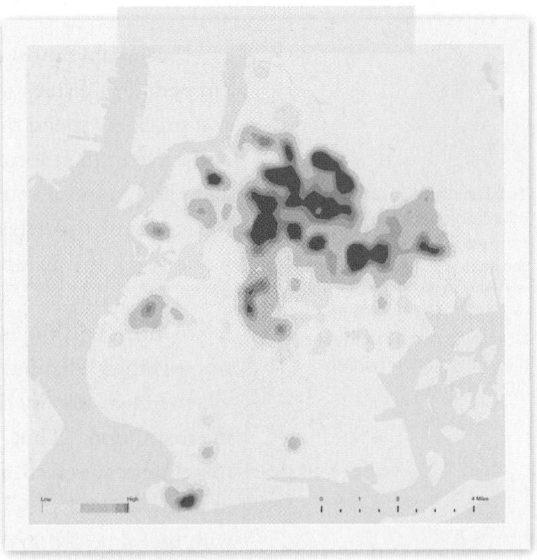

This map of Brooklyn, New York, shows the density of prison admissions in 2003.

Sociologists and geographers have also examined the impact of incarceration on the communities prison inmates call home (Fagan et al., 2003; Williams, 2005). In New York City the incarcerated population is disproportionately drawn from a small handful of neighborhoods, a pattern that is sustained even as crime rates have dropped dramatically. Inmates cannot make positive contributions to the community in terms of providing steady incomes, starting families, or building up social networks that lead to employment in legitimate industries while they are in prison. At the community level, high rates of incarceration among community members create conditions for continued poverty as those left behind must support families on fewer salaries both during and after incarceration. From Pager's research earlier in the chapter, we know that former felons have a difficult time finding employment. Blocked access to legitimate employment creates conditions for sustained poverty. At the same time, historic crime rates are used to determine current police involvement, which means that once-crime-ridden neighborhoods will continue to receive disproportionate formal surveillance and a higher likelihood that their residents will be arrested.

Goffman's Total Institution

The high rates of recidivism in the United States bring us back to labeling theory, which suggests that the process of becoming a deviant often involves contact with, even absorption into, a special institution such as a prison or mental health institution. And as labeling theorists have shown, our interaction with others very significantly impacts the formation of our personal identity. Erving Goffman, writing in the symbolic interactionist tradition, theorized about how institutions like prisons and mental health hospitals often become breeding grounds for secondary deviance, providing an important link in the reproduction of deviance through their effects on inmates and patients (Goffman, 1961).

Presumably, most of us sleep, play, and work in different places, with different people and rules structuring our interactions at each location. For example, you probably spend the evening in your home or dorm, relatively undisturbed, and leave in the morning for class, where you are expected to dress appropriately and respect your professors. Total institutions are distinguished by "a breakdown of the barriers separating" these "three spheres of life" (sleep, work, play). In total institutions, "all aspects of life are conducted in the same place and under the same single authority" (Goffman, 1961). Life is highly regimented, and the inmates at an institution take part in all scheduled activities together. The inmates have no control over the form or flow of activities, which are chosen by the institutional authorities to "fulfill the official aims of the institution." Thus, if the official aim of prisons is rehabilitation, prisoners might be required to attend at least one self-improvement class a day or engage in some sort of productive labor. All these activities occur in the same place with the same group of people every day.

Total institution an institution in which one is totally immersed and that controls all the basics of day-to-day life; no barriers exist between the usual spheres of daily life, and all activity occurs in the same place and under the same single authority.

In Chapter 4 we examined the various theories of socialization and the development of the self through our interactions with other social actors. All your life you have been slowly accumulating knowledge about who you are in the world. Once you enter a total institution such as a prison, a process that strips away your sense of self begins. As Goffman puts it, "a series of abasements, degradations, humiliations, and profanations" quickly commences. Once people enter a prison or a mental institution, they are closed off from

Inmates in an Arizona jail. The local sheriff requires all of the county's inmates to work seven days a week. They are fed only twice a day, are denied recreation, and receive no coffee, cigarettes, salt, pepper, or ketchup.

their normal routines and cease to fulfill their usual social roles. Because the roles people play are important to the way they perceive themselves, this separation from the world erodes that sense of identity. In the Stanford Prison Experiment, what first occurred when the "inmates" arrived at the "prison" in the basement of the psychology department? They were issued uniforms and given numbers in place of names. The mandated homogeneity of prisoners (and patients) results in an erasure of self. The total institution simultaneously strips away clothes, personal belongings, nicknames, hairstyles, cosmetics, and toiletries—all the tools that people use to identify themselves. The inmates no longer have control over their environment, peer group, daily activities, or personal possessions. It's not hard to see how this process leads to a sense of helplessness. The total institution rapidly destroys a prisoner's sense of self-determination, self-control, and freedom.

The authorities in these total institutions are given the unenviable duty of "showing the prisoners who's boss" and expediting the process of prisoner degradation to ensure "co-operativeness" (Goffman, 1961). Wardens must "socialize" inmates into compliance through informal "obedience test[s]" or "will-breaking contest[s]" until the inmate "who shows defiance receives immediate visible punishment, which increases until he openly 'cries uncle' and humbles himself." When Zimbardo locked a group of seemingly normal college kids into the basement of a Stanford building (discussed in the box on pages 208–9), he found that not only were the inmates affected but the guards also felt impelled to use increasingly violent and inhumane means to solidify their authority and keep the prisoners in check. We can see these patterns in everyday life, too. When given the responsibility of watching younger siblings, have you ever secretly (or not so secretly) delighted in bossing them around? Because the roles we play are important to how we think about ourselves, it is hardly possible for the self-images of both guards and prisoners to remain unaffected by the prison environment.

Foucault on Punishment

> On March 2, 1757, Damiens the regicide was condemned "to make the amende honorable [a kind of ritual abasement] before the main door of the Church of Paris," where he was to be "taken and conveyed in a cart, wearing nothing but a shirt, holding a torch of burning wax weighing two pounds"; then, "in the said cart, to the Place de Greve, where, on a scaffold that will be erected there, the flesh will be torn from his breasts, arms, thighs, and calves with red-hot pincers, his right hand, holding the knife with which he committed the said parricide, burnt with sulfur, and, on those places where the flesh will be torn away, poured molten lead, burning oil, burning resin, wax and sulfur melted together and then his body drawn and quartered by four horses and his limbs and body consumed by fire, reduced to ashes and his ashes thrown to the winds." (Foucault, 1977, p. 1)

Besides possibly turning your stomach, the above passage vividly illustrates the dramatic shift in penal practices from the eighteenth century to the present day. How do we conceive of punishment nowadays? We usually think of prisons, juvenile detention centers, and probation. In *Discipline and Punish* (1977), the French theorist Michel Foucault examines the emergence of the modern penal system and how this system represents a transformation in social control. How did the modern prison system emerge? And what functions does it serve in the disciplining of modern life?

When Damiens the regicide was publicly tortured and then eventually drawn and quartered for trying to kill King Louis XV, the target of punishment was Damiens' body. The entire public spectacle revolved around Damiens suffering for his wrongdoing, culminating in his death. Damiens was even put to death holding the same knife he used to attack the king. According to Foucault, this gruesome "violence against the body" (1977) exemplifies a premodern form of punishment, which is concentrated on the body and associated with the crime committed. So, for example, if you kill someone, you are publicly executed. If you steal something, perhaps your fingers or hand will be cut off. This "eye for an eye" mentality is similar to that represented by Durkheim's mechanical social sanctions.

We might like to believe that modern punishment came about because prison reformers lobbied for more humane penal tactics that aimed to reform the criminal through rehabilitation. We no longer (with the exception of the

The execution of Robert François Damiens, a French servant who attempted to assassinate King Louis XV at Versailles in 1757.

death penalty) publicly violate the criminal's body by, for example, pouring molten lead on his excoriated body. Punishment takes place in private, away from the public eye, and it leaves the criminal's body intact. (Although much violence, including rape, does occur inside prison walls, the state does not formally sanction it and is supposed to protect prisoners from such attacks.) Foucault claims that modern punishment has as its target what he calls "the soul" of the prisoner. The soul, for Foucault, is the sum of an individual's unique habits and peculiarities: what makes me *me* and you *you.* Such a penal system tries to understand the individual and his or her abnormalities to correct or reform bad habits. (Again, this is a highly stylized view of the history of criminal justice, given that in the United States, some jurisdictions still impose the death penalty and our government has even tortured political detainees. At the very least, we have witnessed an incomplete Foucaultian transformation.)

By "reforming the soul," Foucault means the use of experts such as social workers, psychologists, and criminologists to analyze and correct individual behavior. How does a prisoner become eligible for parole? The *New York State Parole Handbook* (New York State Division of Parole, 2007) indicates that "parole 'readiness'" depends on the inmate's "good prison behavior," involvement in "prison programming" for education and skills acquisition, and substance abuse counseling, all to "make important strides in self-improvement." After a criminal leaves prison on parole, the newly released prisoner is assigned a field parole officer who is in charge of monitoring the whereabouts of the parolee and guiding his or her reentry into community life. The handbook also indicates that a parole officer must help parolees "develop positive attitudes and behavior" and "encourage participation in programs for self-improvement." Parolees are, in principle, scrupulously supervised by parole officers and sometimes subject to unscheduled visits at work or home. This is all part of what Foucault would consider the modern face of penal practices.

How does the transformation in penal practice, from punishment targeted at the body to reform of the soul, take place? Foucault believes that this transformation is linked to changes in how social control operates more generally, which in turn leads to innovations in penal practices. Foucault uses the following example to illustrate the way modern punishment is organized and its implications for modern social control:

> The prisoners' day will begin at six in the morning in winter and at five in the summer. They will work for nine hours a day throughout the year. Two hours a day will be devoted to instruction. Work and the day will end at nine o'clock in winter and at eight in summer. . . . At the first drum-roll, the prisoners must rise and dress in silence, as the supervisor opens the cell doors. At the second drum-roll, they must be dressed and make their beds. (Foucault, 1977, p. 6)

Foucault's example, extracted from a contemporary prisoners' timetable in France, contrasts strikingly with the way poor Damiens was punished several centuries earlier. Foucault's point, however, is that this sort of regimentation happens in not only prisons but also society at large. Penal practices are indicative of how social control is exercised outside prison walls. Disciplinary techniques are modes of monitoring, examining, and regimenting individuals that are diffused throughout society. Foucault gives many examples of where and how this discipline takes place both in and out of prisons—in the military, in schools, in medical institutions, and so forth. For example, when you first entered school, perhaps even when you entered college, you were probably required to take a series of standardized tests. You were also required to visit your pediatrician for shots and a checkup in which he or she meticulously documented your growth and health. Once in school, you were made to sit in straight, orderly rows (so the teacher could see all students at all times) and then were issued a report card every term. If you were chronically disruptive or inattentive in class, you might have been sent for special testing by experts to determine if you had a learning or behavioral disorder. These are all examples of how you have been subjected to various modes of discipline that monitor, examine, and regiment individuals.

Panopticon a circular building composed of an inner ring and an outer ring designed to serve as a prison in which the guards, housed in the inner ring, can observe the prisoners without the detainees knowing whether they are being watched.

Foucault articulated the diffusion of disciplinary techniques in society through the concept of panopticism. Jeremy Bentham, an English philosopher, devised the panopticon as an architectural design for a prison. The panopticon is a circular building composed of an inner ring and an outer ring. Prisoners' cells are located in the peripheral outer ring, and large windows compose the front and back of each cell, allowing ample natural light to flood the rooms. The inner ring is a guards' tower, which also has large windows that open onto the windows of prisoners' cells. The cells "induce in the inmate a state of conscious and permanent visibility." The guards can always see the prisoners, regardless of where they are in their cells, but the prisoners do not know when they are being watched (although the visibility of the central tower serves as a reminder that they are always under scrutiny). Foucault asserts that the "power" of the guards is both "visible and unverifiable" (1977).

The Stateville Penitentiary in Illinois was built along the principles of Bentham's panopticon, a model for a prison in which inmates would always be visible.

Foucault uses the panopticon as a metaphor for the general functioning of disciplinary techniques in society. Therefore, when the modern prison system emerged, based on monitoring, examining, and regimenting individual prisoners, there was a "gradual extension of the mechanisms of discipline," and they "spread throughout the whole social body," which led to "the formation of what might be called in general the disciplinary society." Remember all the steps you had to go through to gain entrance to kindergarten? The tests and checkups? And then the report cards, the parent–teacher conferences, the tidy rows of desks? These are the sorts of panoptic (literally, "all-seeing") disciplinary techniques diffused throughout the social body. In Foucault's words, "our society is one not of spectacle, but of surveillance."

The U.S. Criminal Justice System

At various points in history, the U.S. criminal justice system has fluctuated between two approaches to handling criminals: rehabilitation and punishment. Since the 1890s, argues Frank Allen, the rehabilitative ideal has lost most of its significance and appeal because of shifting cultural values among Americans. Despite what Durkheim predicted, the concept of punishment ("lock 'em up and throw away the key") has largely replaced rehabilitation, winning political and popular favor and influencing criminal justice policy (Allen, 1981).

Today we have the highest rates of incarceration than ever before in American history. At the start of 2002, approximately 5.6 million adults at some point had served time in state or federal prison. That's about 2.7 percent of American adults, up from 1.3 percent in 1974, a difference of 3.8 million people. If these incarceration rates remain unchanged, according to estimates, about 1 in every 15 Americans will serve time in prison at some point during his or her life. What accounts for the increase? According to the Bureau of

Figure 6.5: Size of Prison Population since 1980

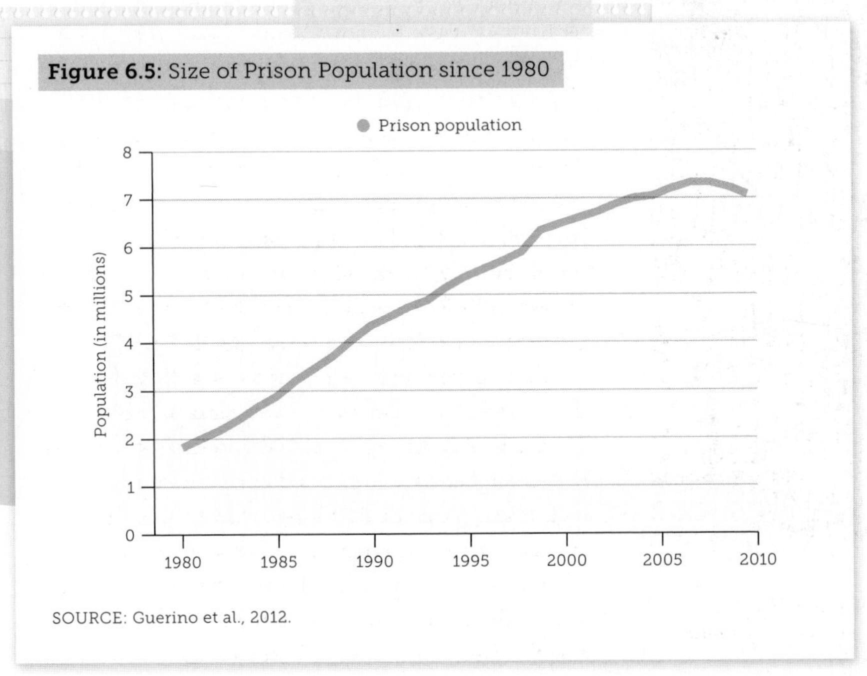

SOURCE: Guerino et al., 2012.

Justice Statistics, about two-thirds of the increase occurred as a result of first-incarceration rates, meaning that the system has expanded as a result of arresting first-time offenders, mostly caught in violation of tough new penal codes, such as those expanded in the War on Drugs.

Not all Americans have been affected equally by the tougher laws, however. Among black men, 16.6 percent were current or former prisoners in 2002, compared with 7.7 percent of Hispanic men and 2.6 percent of white men. Among women, a similar pattern holds, although far fewer women are incarcerated (1.7 percent of black women, 0.7 percent of Hispanic women, and 0.3 percent of white women). The lifetime chances of imprisonment for men and women combined are 3.4 percent for whites, 10 percent for Hispanics, and 11.3 percent for blacks. If current incarceration rates don't change, a whopping 32 percent of black males are estimated to serve time in a state or federal prison during their lifetime, compared with 17 percent of Hispanic men and 5.9 percent of white men. These numbers of prisoners are strikingly high for an industrialized democracy, and the United States is the only industrialized nation in the world to use capital punishment (U.S. Department of Justice, 2007).

Similar to imprisonment rates, justice on death row is not color-blind (see Figure 6.6). In 1998 a study of Philadelphia death penalty cases revealed ample

Figure 6.6: Number of Executions and Race of Prisoners Executed, 1976–2010

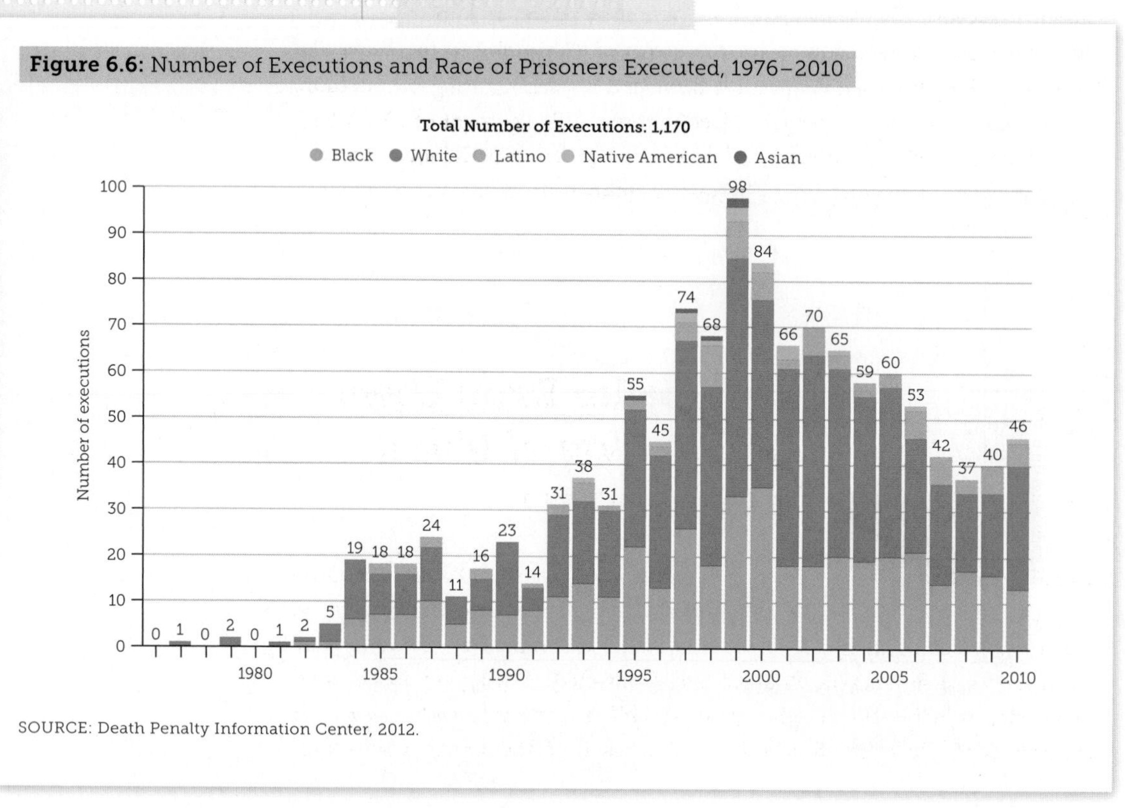

SOURCE: Death Penalty Information Center, 2012.

evidence of some form of racial discrimination: Either the race of the defendant or the race of the victim came to bear on the outcome of the case (Baldus et al., 1998). First, the race of the murder victim matters. For example, in a study of the North Carolina justice system, researchers found that the odds of a murderer receiving a death sentence rose three and a half times if the victim was white, holding constant other relevant factors (Unah & Boger, 2001). Second and more obviously, the race of the accused matters. Contrary to popular belief about black-on-white violence, interracial murders are fairly rare. Out of 1,170 executions carried out in the United States since 1976 (when the Supreme Court reinstated the death penalty), just 221 involved cases of black-on-white or white-on-black murder. Of those 221 persons, 209 were black defendants convicted of murdering white victims, whereas just 12 white defendants were executed for murdering black victims. One hypothesis would assert that these statistics could result from African Americans committing disproportionately more crime than whites while receiving, on average, appropriate penalties for their criminal behaviors. To make this sort of claim, we would need to have faith in the criminal justice system as a sound entity that generally delivers fair and accurate punishment. However, more than enough data to the contrary exist. Between 1973 and 2009, 138 people were exonerated from death row: 71 of them were black, 53 white, and 12 Latino. In 2004 alone six persons were released from death sentences, some after years behind bars, their careers and families having been permanently altered by the disruption. Many of these exonerations resulted from new DNA evidence. In a sense, the new technology has shed light on the flaws in the system, raising the question: "How many cases were wrongly judged before the deployment of DNA testing?" Evidently enough to convince the former governor of Illinois to impose a moratorium on executions and a growing number of other states to consider doing the same.

Rockefeller Drug Laws and the Age of Mass Incarceration

In 1973 the New York State legislature enacted the draconian Rockefeller Drug Laws, named for Governor Nelson Rockefeller. Designed to crack down on the use and sale of drugs, the legislation mandated an increase in prison time for drug possession or sale. A defendant "convicted of selling two ounces, or possessing four ounces of [a] 'narcotic drug'" is sentenced with a *mandatory minimum* of 15 years to life in prison. As a result of the stringent legislation (which has been amended only modestly since 1973), the New York State prison population has skyrocketed, more than tripling after 1980 (Wilson, 2000). The percentage of prison inmates convicted of drug felonies has increased from 11 percent in 1980 to almost 38 percent in 2005 (Correctional Association of New York, 2007). The costs of mass incarceration are staggering. An additional 46,000 prison beds cost New York State an estimated $4.5 billion dollars, and additional yearly operating costs are estimated at $2 billion (Abramsky, 2002). These costs are increasingly crowding out by spending on other social goods such as education.

The staggering rates and costs of incarceration are not unique to New York State. On the whole, America has witnessed an unprecedented increase in its prison population. Deviance is always with us, but our classifications and reactions change over time. Throughout most of the twentieth century the American incarceration rate hovered around 110 per 100,000 Americans. But starting in the 1970s, the incarceration rate grew steadily, increasing by 300 percent between 1980 and 1996 alone (Blumstein & Beck, 1999). The national costs of mass incarceration are enormous—approximately $20,000 per prisoner per year, amounting to a national total of $25 billion. The rigorous and unparalleled War on Drugs has caused an almost tenfold increase in the drug incarceration rate (p. 21) since 1980. By 1999, "the incarceration rate for drug offenses alone" was comparable to the total incarceration rate "that prevailed in the United States for fifty years" (p. 53). Incarceration for "drug offenses account[s] for 17 percent of the [incarceration] increase among whites compared with 36 percent among blacks and 32 percent among Hispanics" (p. 26). Clearly, the War on Drugs has disproportionately affected black and Hispanic communities.

In many ways, the War on Drugs looks like a war on the black family. Mass incarceration of African American men has created what Harvard sociologist William Julius Wilson, in *When Work Disappears: The World of the New Urban Poor* (1996), describes as a shortage of marriageable black men. According to Wilson, there simply are not enough employed black men available for women to marry and with whom to form stable family and community units. Wilson sees the problem as a condition of postindustrial urban change, in which the flight of manufacturing jobs, formerly the bedrock of black employment, has created joblessness, female-headed households, children born out of wedlock, and all the accompanying social ills of ghetto life.

Mass incarceration also plays a role. With so many young black men locked up—fathers and would-be fathers alike—it is no wonder black families account for disproportionate rates of single-mother households and children born out of wedlock. In what was known as the Fragile Families Study, researchers found only 46 employed African American males per 100 females in 20 observed cities. Compare that with 80 employed men in Hispanic and white communities (Fragile Families, 2004). More black males receive their GED in prison than graduate from high school on the outside (Hymowitz, 2004). Furthermore, think back to labeling theory and the work of Devah Pager on criminal records and employment. According to Pager, men with criminal records face discrimination in the labor market: Employers are not inclined to hire ex-cons, especially not black ex-cons. In the aftermath of their imprisonment, black men must overcome the stigma of their deviant label to get a job. This typically means working low-wage, dead-end jobs; experiencing limited opportunities; and finding greater appeal in rejoining the illegal economy. Such is the irony of the criminal justice system. It doesn't correct deviance, it breeds it. If you weren't a criminal going in, you are likely to be one coming out—a striking example of how secondary deviance and stigma operate. The situation that Goffman theorized about in 1961 has become an indisputable reality.

Another consequence of mass incarceration and the War on Drugs has been the disenfranchisement of millions of former felons. In 1974 disenfranchised felons constituted about 1.0 percent of the voting-age population. By 2004 this number had soared to nearly 2.5 percent of the voting-age population. As sociologists Jeff Manza and Christopher Uggen (2006) have documented, this mass disenfranchisement of American citizens has dire consequences for the proper functioning of democracy. The United States is "virtually the only nation" among similar postindustrial democracies (such as the United Kingdom, Canada, and Italy) "to permanently disenfranchise ex-felons." In a country with below-average political participation rates and even more abysmal voter turnout rates, Manza and Uggen estimate that granting former felons the right to vote again would have significantly affected the outcome of at least one presidential election and as many as seven Senate elections. Party affiliations aside, the disenfranchisement of felons has "impeded, and perhaps reversed, the historic extension of voting rights." In light of our new understanding of social deviance, and as Manza and Uggen conclude, the disenfranchisement of felons and mass incarceration are conspicuous and troubling factors "within a broader model of social control."

→ CONCLUSION

Training a sociological lens on deviance requires a careful and slow review of not only the immediate causes and effects of deviance but also the broader social forces that undergird and define it. Sometimes, doing so takes us to paradoxical places, such as Durkheim's finding that some degree of crime is healthy for a society, insofar as crime unites the social body by allowing us all to rally against a common enemy. Sometimes, doing so reveals the unintended consequences of labels like "deviant." And quite often, sociologists study tragedies—seeking the social answers to violence and death. Sociology does not hope to provide comprehensive accounts of criminal acts or injustice, but it does seek to dig deeper for concrete answers in our social world.

ASSIGNMENT

Find an article about the 2007 Boston Mooninite scare. Describe what happened and explain how this example demonstrates the way something that seems to be normal (advertising) can become deviant.

QUESTIONS FOR REVIEW

1. How does Philip Zimbardo's Stanford Prison Experiment help explain the behavior documented at Abu Ghraib prison?
2. Describe differential opportunity theory and deterrence theory. How do these two theories apply to the Rockefeller Drug Laws? Does current evidence show that the War on Drugs is working?
3. Explain the difference between mechanical and organic solidarity. How do deviants hold us together in both types of society?
4. We usually think of suicide as solely the result of an intensely personal decision. What is Émile Durkheim's explanation for suicide? Define egoistic suicide and describe why, according to Durkheim, more Protestants commit suicide than Catholics.
5. A student wants to achieve good grades but is not interested in studying for exams; instead, the student finds various ways to cheat. How does Robert Merton's strain theory explain this behavior, and which "type" does the student exemplify?
6. How does the broken windows theory of deviance support the claim that the definition of *deviant* depends on social context? What happened to social control mechanisms like formal and informal social sanctions in Philip Zimbardo's study involving cars?
7. Why don't criminologists use the crime rate as an indicator of crime trends? What do they use instead, and why?
8. Describe Émile Durkheim's theory of the collective conscience and explain how it is related to punishment. How does Michel Foucault's focus in *Discipline and Punish* (1977) differ from Durkheim's work regarding punishment in premodern and modern societies?
9. Explain how a fraternity house could be considered a total institution.

PARADOX

IT IS THE DEVIANTS AMONG US WHO HOLD SOCIETY TOGETHER.

WATCH THE ANIMATED SHORT ABOUT THE SOCIAL CONTROL AND DEVIANCE PARADOX AT

WWNORTON.COM/STUDYSPACE

CURIOUS ABOUT SOCIOLOGY?

NO.

WHY ARE YOU STILL HERE READING THIS?

YES.

NOW READ THIS TEXTBOOK.

UFF, THAT'S ENOUGH – MY BRAIN IS FULL.

I SEE THE WORLD VERY DIFFERENTLY.

I THINK THERE'S SOMETHING WRONG WITH MY EYES.

I'M HUNGRY FOR MORE!

GO TO THE FRIDGE.

GO TO THE INFORMATION SUPERHIGHWAY.

GET SIDETRACKED WATCHING VIDEOS OF CUTE KITTENS.

CONNECT WITH SOCIOLOGISTS AND OTHER STUDENTS WHO ARE READING ***YOU MAY ASK YOURSELF.***

YOU TUBE

NORTONSOC

NORTON SOCIOLOGY

@WWNSOC

GO BACK INTO SOCIETY A WISER, MORE KNOWLEDGABLE PERSON WHO UNDERSTANDS THEIR FELLOW HUMAN BEINGS A LITTLE MORE.

PART II

FAULT LINES... SOCIAL DIVISION AND INEQUALITY

Climatrol
I WANT MORE AND I
WANT IT NOW

7 Stratification

PARADOX

INEQUALITY IS THE RESULT OF ABUNDANCE.

Carlos Slim Helú is the wealthiest man in the world. With over US$74 billion, he is ranked way ahead of Bill Gates and Warren Buffett in the "world's wealthiest man" lineup (*Forbes*, 2011b). Many of you are probably wondering who the heck this guy is and why he isn't an American household name like Buffett and Gates. Son of Lebanese immigrants and trained as an engineer, he is a widower in his early seventies with six children who lives in Mexico City. He built his fortune slowly at first by buying faltering companies and turning them around. Then his wealth mushroomed when he bought the Mexican telephone monopoly, Teléfonos de México (Telmex), from the government in 1990.

Slim's anonymity stems in part from the fact that he is from Mexico and his holdings are in companies like Telmex (telecommunications), Inbursa (a bank), Sanborns (grocery stores), Volaris (an airline), Mexican construction and insurance companies, and the Mexican division of Sears, which are not part of the daily rounds of most Americans. The rest of his anonymity is quite deliberate. Even though he now owns a substantial portion of the *New York Times*, he refused an interview with the paper, assigning his nephew to fill in. If you lived in Mexico, though, it would be hard to get through a day without making a contribution to Slim or his six children—who all work for him—because his holdings are both vast and diverse. You may also know little about Slim because he is not a flashy character. He does not control a large charitable fund like the Bill and Melinda Gates Foundation, nor is he a sought-after financial oracle like Warren Buffett (Wright, 2009).

Slim is a billionaire many times over while his fellow citizens make about US$15,000 per year, on average. Another way to look at the distance between

Carlos Slim Helú

Stratification structured social inequality or, more specifically, systematic inequalities between groups of people that arise as intended or unintended consequences of social processes and relationships.

Slim and average Mexican citizens is to look at the proportion of the wealth held by the top 10 percent of Mexicans, including Slim, and the bottom 10 percent of Mexicans. In an economy of perfect equality, the top and bottom 10 percent would each control 10 percent of the country's wealth. But in Mexico, the bottom 10 percent holds less than 2 percent of the wealth while the top 10 percent controls about 40 percent (Central Intelligence Agency, 2010).

How can we view Slim's financial position as part of a wider social system? Sociologists use the term stratification to describe structured social inequality or, more specifically, systematic inequalities among groups of people that arise as intended or unintended consequences of social processes and relationships. When sociologists ask, for instance, what effect being born into the working class has on life chances and upward mobility, how race and ethnicity affect incomes, how gender affects occupational prestige, and more broadly, why some groups in society are more disadvantaged than other groups, they are essentially asking questions about stratification.

Consider the following folk statistics, widely circulated on the Internet (although the accuracy of some is questionable): If the world were reduced to 100 people, what would it be like? 60 Asians, 13 Africans, 12 Europeans, 10 Latin Americans and Caribbeans, 5 North Americans; 14 of the 100 would reside in the Western Hemisphere; 51 of the 100 would be female; 30 would be Christians; 70 would be illiterate; 50 would be malnourished; 1 would be near death at that very moment, 1 just born; only 1 would be college educated, and 0 (rounding down) would own computers; 6 people would own half the world's wealth. Such statistics present a glance at global inequalities, a microcosm of stratification.

Let's read into the numbers a little more closely. It is true that roughly half the hypothetical 100 composite people would be malnourished and only 1 would be college educated. But we also need to consider the interaction between those two classifications: How likely is it that the 1 percent of the world's population that is college educated is also among the malnourished? How many of the 51 females would be among the malnourished? Would it be approximately the same for males, or would the figure be a bit more lopsided? What are the consequences of 6 percent of the world owning half the world's wealth? As this example illustrates, the study of stratification is not just about how resources and outcomes are distributed among different groups but also about how those inequalities overlap, interact with, and reinforce each other. In summary, stratification is the study of who gets what (and why).

Views of Inequality

To answer such questions about stratification, we need a conceptual framework through which to view inequality. In the following section, I will present you with three possible frameworks and leave it to you to decide which you think is most appropriate to explain the intersection of various dimensions of stratification. We'll start with the Enlightenment in the eighteenth century and move forward from there.

Jean-Jacques Rousseau

Jean-Jacques Rousseau

Writing prolifically from 1750 to 1782, Jean-Jacques Rousseau greatly influenced the political ideas of the French Revolution and the development of socialist thought. Seeing humankind as naturally pure and good, Rousseau appealed to biology and human instincts to explain social outcomes. For Rousseau, it is only through the process of building society and repressing this pure natural character that social problems develop. Specifically, Rousseau sees the emergence of private property, the idea that a person has the right to own something, as the primary source of social ills. If we were to strip away the elements of society that result from the institution of private property—the competition, isolation, aggression, and hierarchical organization—only social equality, a condition in which no differences in wealth, power, prestige, or status based on nonnatural bases exist, would remain. According to Rousseau, there are two forms of inequality: physical (or natural), which "consists in a difference of age, health, bodily strength, and the qualities of the mind or of the soul," and social (or political), which

Social equality a condition whereby no differences in wealth, power, prestige, or status based on nonnatural conventions exist.

> depends on a kind of conventional inequality and is established or at least authorized by the consent of men. This latter consists of the different privileges which some men enjoy to the prejudice of others, such as that of being more rich, more honored, more powerful, or even in a position to exact obedience. (Rousseau, 1754/2004, p. 15)

Rousseau acknowledges that a certain amount of natural inequality will always exist between people: Someone is always going to be better than someone else at kicking a ball, hunting large game, doing math, or seeing long distances. Some of these inequalities are a simple result of aging, as a basketball player in his twenties will almost certainly have greater physical abilities than a basketball player in his eighties. In contrast, social inequality is a result of privileges and uneven access to resources (that is, private property) and will eventually lead to social ills. There are only so many resources available in any society and, more broadly, in the world as a whole.

Imagine that all the resources available in a given society are represented in a single pizza, cut into ten slices, and ten hungry people are sitting around the pie. In Rousseau's ideal natural world, where people are inherently good, lacking any notion of personal ownership, each individual would get one slice. But in a world where private property is the norm, the division is likely to be significantly less equitable. For whatever reason—maybe some of the ten have more guile, maybe some paid more than others, maybe one person's family owns the pizza parlor—the pie is distributed unevenly among the ten. Rousseau sees such inequality as ultimately detrimental and as a catalyst for social conflict.

Imagine yourself as one of the people who get no pizza, even though there are ten of you and ten slices. Imagine further that you have a hungry family who would certainly have appreciated that slice of pizza. Now imagine watching the person sitting across from you slowly enjoying five steaming slices, one by one. Would this make you jealous? Would it make you spiteful? Would it make you subvert your essentially good nature in trying to steal a slice? Might you even be willing to hurt the pizza hoarder to feed yourself and your family? Might the pizza hoarder then defend his personal property and maybe even hurt you to keep your hands off it? According to Rousseau, he might also buy off the biggest and strongest of those who have no pizza with two slices in order to protect his rights.

The Scottish Enlightenment and Thomas Malthus

Rousseau saw this move away from the pure state of nature as an extremely negative historical development, complaining that "man was born free, and he is everywhere in chains." But thinkers of the later Enlightenment, including Adam Ferguson and John Millar of Scotland and Thomas Robert Malthus of England, saw inequality as good—or at least necessary. These three agreed that inequality arises when private property emerges and that private property emerges when resources can be preserved, as it is only through surpluses that some people are able to conserve and increase their bounty. This leads to the paradox of inequality and of this chapter: Inequality is a result of surplus.

When individuals or groups in society become more efficient on a daily basis, they can gather, hunt, plant, or harvest more than they themselves can consume at a given time. They can then conserve such a surplus, whether that means turning milk into cheese, making berries into preserves, or putting their money into a hedge fund. In whatever way they choose, they can preserve current resources and transform them into assets, a form of wealth that can be stored for the future. (In fact, the word *asset* comes from the French legal expression *aver assetz*, meaning "to have enough.") Whereas previously the incentive might have been to share the wealth when you couldn't store it—to generate reciprocal goodwill for the rainy day when you don't have enough to eat and your neighbor does—now when property can be preserved, the incentive is for individuals to hoard all of it, so that when a rainy day comes along, personal savings are available. Alternatively, if a resource-rich individual decides to distribute surplus wealth, he or she might decide to extract power, promises, and rewards in return for what he or she provides.

For Ferguson and Millar, such social developments resulting from the establishment of private property represent a huge improvement in society, because private property leads to higher degrees of social organization and efficiency: If an individual can preserve and accumulate resources and become more powerful by storing up assets (that is, private property), he or she will have much more incentive to work. Thanks to personal incentives, people won't just slack off after they have accumulated what they need for the day's survival but will instead work to build up society, and as a by-product they will improve civilization. For the Scottish Enlightenment thinkers, inequality was a prerequisite for social progress, and social progress was a prerequisite for the development of civilization—the greatest goal toward which humankind could strive.

Thomas Robert Malthus also had a positive view of inequality, but for a different reason. In 1798, Malthus published an anonymous treatise titled "An Essay on the Principle of Population as It Affects the Future Improvement of Society," arguing that human populations grow geometrically (multiplicatively, like rabbits), while our ability to produce food increases only arithmetically (much more slowly). Simply put, his theory suggests that a rising number of people on the planet will eventually use up all the available resources and bring about mass starvation and conflict. Take the pizza example from above: With 10 people and 10 slices, the pie could be divided evenly. But what if there were 20 people or 50 people? Or 100 people? As the number of people increases, each person gets less and less, even if the pie is divided evenly. Humankind, Malthus believed, was similarly destined to live in a state of constant near-death misery, as population growth always pushed society to the limits of food availability.

Because of these dire trends, Malthus believed inequality was good or at least necessary for avoiding the problem of massive overpopulation and hence starvation. Inequality, from his perspective, kept the population in check. After all, for Malthus, the main problem with the world, especially with England, was the number of people in it, and anything that tended to restrain population growth was supremely good. In this vein, he denounced soup kitchens and early marriages while defending the effects of smallpox, slavery, and child murder (Heilbroner, 1999). Malthus believed that overpopulation would create more and more human misery, and therefore the most logical solution would be to allow the population to thin itself out naturally rather than to exacerbate the problem by reducing the levels of inequality, a measure that would "temporarily" ease the condition of the "masses," thereby causing their numbers to swell even more. Such a condition is today called a Malthusian poverty trap.

In an interview for this book, I asked Jeffrey Sachs of the Earth Institute at Columbia University if he thought that Africa might be facing a Malthusian trap as the per capita land available for farming dwindles and, if so, what can be done to get out of the trap. Sachs captured the complexity of the big picture, so I'll let him speak for himself:

> In Africa there's been a partial transition from high mortality to low mortality, from maybe 600 of every 1,000 children dying before their fifth

Farmworker Stella Machara and her sons Kudakwachi and Simbaracha in front of their home in Zimbabwe. According to Jeffrey Sachs, why is sub-Saharan Africa stuck in a Malthusian population trap? To see more of the conversation with Sachs, visit wwnorton.com/studyspace.

birthday to a situation where it's perhaps around 150 per 1,000 dying. Still remarkably high by global standards, but way down from what it was. But the fertility rates especially in the rural areas remain high—as many as five or six, sometimes even seven per woman. That means rapid population growth. The woman that has six children, [of whom] two die, has on average four children who grow up to adulthood. Two of those will be daughters. Each woman is replacing herself with two daughters in the next generation. That's a doubling of the population from one generation to the next, called a gross population number. That's extraordinary. You can't keep ahead of that in terms of economic development, and certainly not in ecology. So what do you do about that? What do you do to accelerate the reduction of fertility? Save the children. It seems paradoxical. But when the children are staying alive, the families say, "Ah! It's safe to have fewer children. I don't need to have six for insurance. My children will survive."

Make sure the girls stay in school, especially secondary school. A girl who has a chance to go to secondary school will get married several years later. By then she will be more empowered, have a market value in the economy, say, "I'm gonna go out and get a job. I don't want to get married, and also I'm not gonna let my father choose to marry me at age twelve," which is how it might be normally. Make sure there are contraceptives available. Family planning is not a freebie. It absolutely requires training, skilled community work, health workers, the physical availability of contraception; and that's more than an impoverished woman, in a patriarchal setting, with lots of children dying in a rural area, is going to somehow find her way to on her own. She may have zero cash. History has shown free availability of family planning and contraceptive services is part of the set of things that are necessary to lower fertility that also includes child survival, girls' education, women's awareness, and community health workers. That can lead to a remarkably accelerated demographic transition, and that's the kind of holistic approach that successful societies have done. (Conley, 2009g)

Florencia Molina, a victim of human trafficking, became virtually enslaved at a dressmaking shop on the outskirts of Los Angeles, where she worked up to 17 hours a day, seven days a week, and lived there, too, without the option of showering or washing her clothes.

Georg Wilhelm Friedrich Hegel

A third view of inequality comes from the German philosopher Georg Wilhelm Friedrich Hegel, who viewed history in terms of a master–slave (sometimes called a master–servant) dialectic. The word dialectic means a two-directional relationship, one that goes both ways, like a conversation between two people. One person talks, putting out an idea or thesis. Then the other responds, pointing out some problems with the thesis or posing a counterposition, an antithesis. Then the original speaker responds, and so on.

Dialectic a two-directional relationship, one that goes both ways.

In Hegel's master–slave dialectic, the slave is dependent on the master because the master provides food, shelter, and protection. In this way, the slave is akin to a child raised by the master. However, as Hegel observed, the master is also dependent on the slave, who performs the basic duties of survival until the master can no longer function on his own. He doesn't remember how to grow his own food, drive a car, or even go to the bathroom or get dressed without help. Basically, the master would not be able to function if left to fend for himself. Thus, the master–slave nexus becomes a relationship of mutual dependency.

But Hegel was writing in the early nineteenth century. There really aren't masters and slaves today, are there? In fact, while we think of slavery as a dreadful practice left on the ash heap of the past, researchers of modern human trafficking believe that there are actually more enslaved people now—estimates suggest 27 million people—than there were at the height of the transatlantic slave trade (De Baca, 2011). And, according to the CIA, the United States is no exception to this phenomenon, with forced laborers constituting tens of thousands of entrants to the country each year. Modern human trafficking often involves females who are kept as domestic workers and/or sex workers in cities around the world, but some tomato pickers in Florida and construction workers in Dubai may also be considered part of the modern trade in humans (Ehrenreich & Hochschild, 2004; Estabrook, 2009; Human Rights Watch, 2006). The path to becoming a slave is often paved with a mixture of deceit and desperation. Poor families in rural areas are perhaps too eager to believe the promises of men traveling through their villages, offering to find good, safe work for their daughters in the city. Once the girls arrive, they are often raped by these men to "teach" them how to serve clients, given a meager room watched over to prevent escape, and told they must work to repay the cost of their travel and lodging. Some end up staying this way for life—the stigma of prostitution is something they cannot bear to take back to their families and they have no other way to make money. In the case of the tomato pickers, the crew bosses who exploit them would simply go out of business if they paid their work forces minimum wage because 90 percent of the tomatoes grown in America are harvested by underpaid, illegal immigrant workers who risk beatings and deportation if they try to leave (Comisi, 2011). In this sense, the exploited people need their abusers for lodging and protection from the authorities and the abusers need their work forces to remain captive to ensure the continuation of their way of life.

Hegel views history as marching steadily forward from a situation of few masters and many servants or slaves—such as monarchies and empires, not to mention the entire feudal system—to a society with more and more free men and women, a situation of democracy and equality. His was an optimistic view of history, to say the least. According to Hegel, notions of inequality are constantly evolving in a larger historical arc. He saw this as a trajectory that would eventually lead to equality for all (or very nearly all). We will see later that many sociologists have had a bone or two to pick with this position, as well as with those laid out by Rousseau, Ferguson, Millar, and Malthus.

Standards of Equality

Assuming for the moment that we do value equality in society, what kind of equality do we want? There are different ideologies or belief systems regarding equality, so it's important to recognize that when various groups use the rhetoric of equality, particularly in the political sphere, they may be talking past each other or jostling for advantage. What did Thomas Jefferson mean when he declared in the Declaration of Independence that "all men are created equal"? And what exactly do we mean by equality in the twenty-first century?

Ontological Equality

The first standard of equality—one not often invoked in policy debates these days—is ontological equality. This is the Jeffersonian notion that everyone is created equal at birth (although, as we know, Jefferson and most of his eighteenth-century contemporaries turned a blind eye to slavery). Legitimated by theology, this notion is often used to justify material inequality by asserting that the distribution of power and resources here on earth does not matter, because all of us are equally children of God and will have to face our maker upon dying. In fact, ontological equality is sometimes used to put forth the notion that poverty is a virtue. Take the oft-quoted passage from the Gospel of Matthew in the Christian Bible: "It is easier for a camel to pass through the eye of a needle than for a rich man to enter into the kingdom of heaven."

Ontological equality the notion that everyone is created equal at birth.

Equality of Opportunity

A second standard of equality is termed equality of opportunity. Let's think of society as a game of Monopoly, in which all the players try to maximize their holdings of wealth (the game's houses and hotels) and their income (the rent collected from other players who land on their properties after an unfortunate roll of the dice). In this game, the person with the most money in the end is the winner. Monopoly follows the rules of equality of opportunity. Sure, one player may wind up flat broke and another player may control 95 percent of the wealth, but the rules were fair, right? Everyone had an equal chance at the start. Assuming nobody cheated, any differences were a result of luck (the dice) and skill (the players' choices). The same goes for society. The mere existence of inequality is not at issue here. Some people have more wealth and income than others, and some people enjoy greater social prestige or power than others, but the rules of the game are still fair. We all go into the game of society, as we do into a game of Monopoly, knowing the rules, and therefore any existing inequality is fair as long as everyone plays by the rules.

Equality of opportunity the idea that everyone has an equal chance to achieve wealth, social prestige, and power because the rules of the game, so to speak, are the same for everyone.

This is the standard model for what equality means in a bourgeois society, such as modern capitalist society. Although the word *bourgeois* is often used pejoratively, here I mean it as a neutral description—a society of commerce in which the maximization of profit is the primary business incentive. Almost all modern capitalist societies purport to follow an ideology of equal opportunity. The equal opportunity ideology was adopted by civil rights activists in the 1960s, who argued that the rules were unfair. For instance, the segregation of public spaces and other Jim Crow laws (a rigid set of antiblack statutes that relegated African Americans to the status of second-class citizens through educational, economic, and political exclusion) were seen as incompatible with the bourgeois notion of fairness or equality of opportunity.

Bourgeois society a society of commerce (modern capitalist society, for example) in which the maximization of profit is the primary business incentive.

Civil rights activists in San Francisco demonstrate against Jim Crow laws in 1964. Why did the demand for equal opportunity resonate with most Americans?

The rallying cry for equality of opportunity resonates with our overall capitalist ideology. Unequal opportunity clearly stifles meritocracy (a system in which advancement is based on individual achievement or ability). For example, if you were to have a heart transplant, would you not want the most knowledgeable heart surgeon with the most dexterous hands? Or would you settle for the one born to rich parents who finagled their child's way into medical school? Under a system of equal opportunity, everyone who is willing can compete to become a heart surgeon, and eventually the most talented will rise in the most demanding, important positions.

Equality of Condition

Equality of condition the idea that everyone should have an equal starting point.

A third standard of equality is a bit more progressive and is termed equality of condition. Going back to our Monopoly analogy, imagine if at the beginning of the game, two players started out with $5,000 extra and already owned hotels on Boardwalk and Park Place, and Pennsylvania and North Carolina Avenues, respectively, while the other two players started out with a $5,000 deficit and owned no property. Some would argue that the rules of the game need to be altered in order to compensate for inequalities in the relative starting positions. This is the ideology behind equality of condition. An example of this ideology is affirmative action, which involves preferential selection to increase the representation of women and minorities in areas of employment, education, and business from which they have historically been excluded (for a more thorough discussion, see Chapters 8 and 9). Here social actors know that the playing field is uneven, so they try to make it slightly more level. Sometimes these policies can enhance efficiency if they result in fairer competition; other times they may result in a trade-off between efficiency and equality in favor of the latter. We may accept that certain groups with slightly lower SAT scores are admitted to colleges because they faced much greater obstacles to attain those SAT scores than other groups of test takers who enjoyed more advantages. Such "social engineering" may be based on race, class, gender, or any other social sorting category, as long as the proponents can make a justifiable claim that the existing playing field is tilted against them.

Equality of Outcome

Equality of outcome a position that argues each player must end up with the same amount regardless of the fairness of the "game."

The final and most radical (or rather most antibourgeois and anticapitalist) form of equality is equality of outcome, a position that argues each player should end up with the same amount regardless of the fairness of the "game." This admittedly would make for a dull round of Monopoly: In this scenario, the players on Baltic Avenue would make just as much as those on Boardwalk, and some mechanism in the game—say, a central banker or all the players pooling their resources—would ensure game play that lived up to Karl Marx's maxim in the *Critique of the Gotha Programme* (1890–91/1999), "From each according to his ability, to each according to his needs." This standard is concerned less with the rules of the game than with the distribution of resources; it is essentially a Marxist (or communist) ideology. Like Rousseau's idea that there will always be physical inequalities—some will be better at math, others will be better at physical work, and so on—here the idea is that everyone contributes to society and to the economy according to what they do best. For instance, someone who is naturally gifted at math might become an engineer or a mathematician, whereas someone better at physical work might build infrastructure such as roads and bridges. A centrally organized society calls on its citizens to contribute to the best of their ability, yet everyone receives the same rewards. The median income is everyone's income regardless of occupation or position.

Under equality of outcome or result, the individual incentives touted by the Scottish Enlightenment thinkers are eliminated. Nobody will earn more power, prestige, and wealth by working harder. In this system, the only incentive is altruistic; you are giving to society for the sake of its progress and not merely for your own betterment (although arguably, it may be in the self-interest of the individual to see society progress as a whole). Bill Gates would probably have to give up his $125 million estate and take a big step

Middlebury College student Laura Blackman received help from the Posse Foundation, which recruits inner-city kids for elite colleges. How are affirmative action policies an example of equality of condition?

down, whereas a single mother working two jobs in order to provide food, shelter, and day care for her children is likely to take a bit of a step up. She might even end up being Bill Gates's neighbor. Critics worry that without the selfish incentives of capitalism, all progress would halt, and sloth might take over. Unless an oppressive rule emanated from some central agency, collective endeavors would be doomed to failure on account of the free rider problem, the notion that when more than one person is responsible for getting something done, the incentive is for each individual to shirk responsibility and hope others will pull the extra weight. (You might have encountered this sort of situation while collaborating on group projects for school.) Critics of this system argue that even when there is a relatively strong central planning agency to assign each worker a task and enforce productivity, such an administrative mechanism cannot efficiently make decisions and allocate resources as a more free-market approach does.

Free rider problem the notion that when more than one person is responsible for getting something done, the incentive is for each individual to shirk responsibility and hope others will pull the extra weight.

Forms of Stratification

Thus far we have discussed standards of equality and inequality only in general terms, but there are many dimensions and forms by which this equality or inequality can emerge in a given society. For example, a society can be stratified based on age. In many tribes, for instance, age determines the social prestige and honor that the group accords an individual. (By contrast, some argue that in the youth-obsessed culture of the United States, age is a source of dishonor.) Those younger than you would place great weight on your words and in some cases treat them as commands. Furthermore, birth order can be the basis of inequality. Such a system was prevalent as late as the nineteenth century in European society, where the first-born male typically inherited the family estate; however, in certain parts of the world, birth order still plays a role in resource distribution. Gender or race and ethnicity also can be the predominant forms social stratification takes. Ultimately, many dimensions exist within which inequality can emerge, and often these dimensions overlap significantly.

In Western Australia, Aboriginal elder Brandy Tjungurrayi wears a pencil through his nose—a sign of his senior status.

Stratified societies are those where human groups within them are ranked hierarchically into strata, along one or more social dimensions. Many sociologists and philosophers believe that there are four ideal types of social stratification—estate system, caste system, class system, and status hierarchy system—although all societies have some combinations of these forms and no type ever occurs in its pure form. In addition to these, some sociologists propose a fifth ideal type, an elite-mass dichotomy. Each system has its own ideology that attempts to legitimate the inequality within it.

Estate System

The first ideal type of social stratification is the estate system. Primarily found in feudal Europe from the medieval era through the eighteenth century and in the American South before the Civil War, social stratification in estate systems has a political basis. That is, laws are written in a language in which rights and duties separate individuals and distribute power unequally. For example, in the antebellum American South, many states required land ownership for voting privileges. Europe also historically restricted voting rights to land owners. Before reforms, political participation depended on the social group (that is, the estate) to which you belonged. There was limited mobility among the three general estates—the clergy, the nobility, and the commoners (the commoners were typically further divided into peasants and city dwellers)—and each group enjoyed certain rights, privileges, and duties. In certain eras, it was possible for a rich commoner to buy a title and become a member of the nobility. And often one son or daughter of a noble family would join the clergy and become part of that estate. Therefore, there was some mobility, but generally social reproduction prevailed—you are what your parents were and what your children will be. (We'll examine the concept of social mobility more closely below.)

Estate system politically based system of stratification characterized by limited social mobility.

Caste System

Another type of stratification is a caste system. As opposed to having a political basis, the caste system is religious in nature. That is, caste societies are stratified on the basis of hereditary notions of religious and theological purity. Today the caste system is primarily found in South Asia. For instance, in India the historical legacy of the caste system, also known as the *varna* system, still dominates. The *varna* system is composed of four main castes: Brahmin, Kshatriya, Vaishya, and Shudra (the Dalits or "untouchables" are a lower order of the Shudra). These divisions correspond loosely to priests, warriors, traders, and workers, respectively. However, over the past 5,000 years the caste system in India has evolved into a complex matrix of thousands of subcastes. Each of the major castes is allowed to engage in certain ritual practices from which the others, for better or worse, are excluded. For instance, the Dalits or untouchables are excluded from the performance of *any* rituals that confer purity, which places them at the bottom of the caste system and typically leaves them with occupations seen as impure—such as the cremation of corpses or disposal of sewage.

Caste system religion-based system of stratification characterized by no social mobility.

Islamic law prohibits Muslims from serving or imbibing alcohol, so the Christian Vaishya handle beer distribution in Pakistan. This employee inspects a bottle of vodka at the Murree Brewery Company, Pakistan's oldest public company and only brewery.

The castes in India have historically been endogamous, communities in which members generally marry within the group. Although the caste system there remains very powerful at many levels, intermarriage between castes (or exogamy) has begun to erode the system. Because of the resulting problems with classifying children, the caste system would simply fall apart if high levels of exogamy occurred. The strict divisions would begin to look more like a spectrum and would eventually fade away. An additional method of securing the caste hierarchy is *social closure* within Indian society. This means that there has been little to no individual mobility within the caste ranks. If you are born an untouchable, you remain an untouchable, you marry an untouchable, your children are untouchables, and you die an untouchable.

Although there is little to no individual mobility in caste systems, an entire caste can leapfrog over another and obtain a higher position in the hierarchy. This process is called sanskritization. Sometimes such an attempt works, and sometimes it doesn't. During the colonial period, when the British governed South Asia, the Vaishya, the second lowest caste in Pakistan, adopted Christianity, the religion of the British, in an attempt to jump ahead in the hierarchy. Their attempt was not successful. However, by becoming Christian, the Vaishya caste did enjoy a unique fate after the partition of Pakistan from India. Pakistan became a Muslim state in which Islamic law (the shar'ia) was enforced. One of the rules of the shar'ia is that Muslims are forbidden from imbibing or serving alcohol (or any mind-altering substances). So who got the jobs serving foreigners in the hotel bars? The Vaishya, who were now Christian. Their efforts to jump ahead in the caste system may have failed, but they ended up with fairly decent jobs in a relatively impoverished country.

Class System

Class system an economically based hierarchical system characterized by cohesive, oppositional groups and somewhat loose social mobility

A third type of stratification is the class system, an economically based hierarchical system characterized by cohesive, oppositional groups and somewhat loose social mobility. Class means different things to different people, and there is no consensus among sociologists as to the term's precise definition. For instance, some might define class primarily in terms of money, whereas others see it as a function of culture or taste. Some people barely even notice it (consciously at least), whereas others feel its powerful effects in their daily lives. So what is class? Is it related to lifestyle? Consumption patterns? Interests? Attitudes? Or is it just another pecking order similar to the caste system?

Some controversy has existed about whether class is a real category or a category that exists in name only. As in the caste and estate systems, the lines that separate class categories in theory should be clearly demarcated, but there have been problems in drawing boundaries around class categories—for instance, upper class, middle class, and so on. Some scholars have even argued that class should be abandoned as a sociological concept altogether. So let us try to clear up some of the misconceptions.

Why is the concept of class problematic? For example, Oseola McCarty, of Hattiesburg, Mississippi, worked as a washerwoman and had only a sixth-grade education. However, she donated $150,000 to the University of Southern Mississippi from her savings.

Unlike other systems, a class system implies an economic basis for the fundamental cleavages in society. That is, class is related to position in the economic market. Notions of class in sociological analysis are heavily influenced by two theorists, Karl Marx and Max Weber. In Marxist sociological analyses, every mode of production—from subsistence farming to small-scale cottage industries to modern factory production to the open-source information economy—has its own unique social relations of production, basically the rules of the game for various players in the process. Who controls the use of capital and natural resources? How are the tasks of making and distributing products divided up and allocated? And how are participants compensated for their roles? In tips? Hourly wages? In-kind goods? Profit or rent? Thus, to talk about class in this Marxist language is to place an individual into a particular group that has a particular set of interests that often stand opposite to those of another group. For example, workers want higher wages. Employers (specifically, capitalists) wish to depress wages, which come largely out of profits.

In this sense, class is a relational concept. That is, one can't gain information about a person's class by simply looking at his or her income (as in, "that person made only $13,000 last year; therefore, she is working class"). Class identity, in fact, does not correspond to an individual at all but rather to a role. A person may pull in a six-figure salary, but as long as she owns no capital (that is, stock or other forms of firm ownership) and earns her salary by selling her labor to someone else, she finds herself in the same category as the lowest-paid wage laborer and antagonistic to "owners," who may net a lot less income than she does. And an individual may, over the course of her career, change class positions as that career evolves. The class positions, the roles with respect to the production process, do not change, however.

Indeed for Marx, it all boils down to two antagonistic classes in a fully mature capitalist society: the employing class (the bourgeoisie or capitalist class) and the working class (the proletariat). The proletariat sells its labor to

Proletariat the working class.

Bourgeoisie the capitalist class.

the bourgeoisie in order to receive wages and thereby survive. But, according to Marx, the bourgeoisie extract surplus value from the proletariat, even when a few of the proletarians make high incomes. As this is a fixed-pie or zero-sum view of economic production, an exploitative and hence inherently conflict-ridden relationship exists between the two classes. The central aspect of Marxist class analysis is this exploitation—capitalists taking more of the value of the work of laborers than they repay in wages.

Contradictory class locations the idea that people can occupy locations in the class structure that fall between the two "pure" classes.

Because the two-class model does not appear to adequately describe the social world as we find it in most modern capitalist economies, more recent Marxist theorists such as Erik Olin Wright have elaborated this basic model with the concept of contradictory class locations. Wright suggests that people can occupy locations in the class structure that fall between the two "pure" classes. For instance, managers might be perceived as both working class and capitalist class: They are part of the working class insofar as they sell their labor to capitalists in order to live (and don't own the means of production), yet they are in the capitalist class insofar as they control (or dominate) workers within the production process. Conversely, the petit bourgeoisie, a group including professionals, craftsmen, and other self-employed individuals or small-business owners, according to Wright, occupy a capitalist position in that they own capital in the form of businesses, but they aren't fully capitalist because they don't control other people's labor. The issue of class definition could also be further complicated by multiple class locations (multiple jobs), mediated class locations (the impact of relationships with family members, such as spouses, who are in different class locations), and temporally distinct class locations (for instance, many corporations require that all their managers spend a couple of years as a shop floor worker before becoming a manager). Marxists use these distinctions to analyze how various classes rise and fall under the capitalist system.

Weber takes an alternative view of class. He argues that a class is a group that has as its basis common life chances or opportunities available to it in the marketplace. In other words, what distinguishes members of a class is that they have similar value in the commercial marketplace in terms of selling their own property and labor. Thus, for Weber, property and lack of property are the basic categories for all class situations. If you have just graduated from law school, you may have no current income or wealth, but you enjoy a great deal of "human capital," skills and certification, to sell in the labor market, so you would clearly be in a different class from someone else with little education but a similar current economic profile. But if you owned a company that you inherited, for instance, you would belong to yet another (higher) class. Weber's paradigm is distinct from the Marxist class framework, where the basic framework is antagonistic and exploitative; rather, for Weber, class is gradated, not relational. Put another way, your class as a newly minted attorney does not affect or determine my class as an accountant, computer programmer, or day laborer.

Status Hierarchy System

The fourth type of stratification system, a status hierarchy system, has its basis in social prestige, not in political, religious, or economic factors. In classical sociology, Weber contributed most heavily to the modern-day sociologist's understanding of status. For Weber, status groups are communities united by either a positive or negative social estimation of their honor. Put more simply, status is determined by what society as a whole thinks of the particular lifestyle of the community to which you belong. In this sense, those with and without property can belong to the same status group if they are seen to live the same lifestyle. Let's use the example of professors. There are certain things that professors typically do in common: They attend conferences to discuss scholarly issues, they teach college courses, and they tend to read a lot. This leads society as a whole to confer a certain status on professors, without placing the sole focus on income, which can vary widely among professors. Likewise, various individuals in a society who earn similar incomes may not have much in common in terms of lifestyles (and therefore status).

Status hierarchy system a system of stratification based on social prestige.

Although a status group can be defined by something other than occupation, such as a claim to a specific lifestyle of leisure (skate punks) or membership in an exclusive organization that defines one's identity (the Daughters of the American Revolution), much work by sociologists has been related to occupational status. After all, work is one of the most centrally defining aspects of our lifestyle. In the 1960s, for example, Peter M. Blau and Otis Dudley Duncan created the Index of Occupational Status by polling the general public about the prestige of certain occupations (1967; an abbreviated version based on 2001 data appears in Table 7.1). Many folks have since refined this rank ordering, but the story is much the same. What is particularly interesting is that the hierarchy is largely stable over time and across place. Occasionally, new jobs need to be slotted in (there were no Web designers in the 1960s), but they generally are slotted in fairly predictable ways based on the status of similar occupations and do not create much upheaval within the overall rank ordering. The scores on the Duncan scale (as it is known) range from 0 to 96, with 0 being the least prestigious and 96 the most prestigious.

Table 7.1 shows that occupations with very different characteristics may have similar prestige scores. For instance, college presidents are given the same occupational status as instructors despite the huge salary discrepancy between the two. Blau and Duncan observed that five-sixths, just over 83 percent, of the explanation for people's status ratings of occupations was attributed to the education necessary for the position and not the income corresponding to that position.

Although we have emphasized that status may have its basis in occupation, it can also be formed through consumption and lifestyle, though these factors are often closely linked. This means that there should be a tendency for status differences between groups to be finely gradated and not

Table 7.1: The Relative Social Prestige of Selected U.S. Occupations

OCCUPATION	Prestige Score	White-Collar Occupation	Blue-Collar Occupation	OCCUPATION	Prestige Score	White-Collar Occupation	Blue-Collar Occupation
Physician	86	X		Bank teller	43	X	
Lawyer	75	X		Welder	42		X
Architect	73	X		Farmer	40		X
Dentist	72	X		Carpenter	39		X
Member of the clergy	69	X		Child-care worker	36		X
Registered nurse	66	X		File clerk	36	X	
Secondary-school teacher	64	X		Bulldozer operator	34		X
Veterinarian	62	X		Auto body repairperson	31		X
Sociologist	61	X		Retail apparel salesperson	30	X	
Police officer	60		X	Truck driver	30		X
Actor	58	X		Cashier	29	X	
Aircraft Mechanic	53		X	Taxi driver	28		X
Firefighter	53		X	Waiter/waitress	28		X
Realtor	49	X		Bartender	25		X
Machinist	47		X	Door-to-door salesperson	22		X
Musician/composer	47	X		Janitor	22		X

SOURCE: National Opinion Research Center, 2001.

relational: Fundamentally antagonistic status groups such as capitalists and laborers or owners and renters do not exist. Rather, people exist along a status ladder, so to speak, on which there is a lot of social mobility. Often, individuals seek to assert their status or increase their status not just through their occupation but also through their consumption, memberships, and other aspects of how they live. They might try to generate social prestige by driving a fancy car, living in a gated community, wearing stylish clothes, or using a certain kind of language.

Elite-Mass Dichotomy System

Elite-mass dichotomy system system of stratification that has a governing elite, a few leaders who broadly hold power in society.

The final stratification system is the elite-mass dichotomy system, with a governing elite, a few leaders who broadly hold the power in society. Vilfredo Pareto, in *The Mind and Society* (1935/1983), took a positive view of elite-mass dichotomies, whereas C. Wright Mills saw much to dislike in such systems. For Pareto, when a select few elite leaders hold power—as long as the elites are the most able individuals and know what they are doing—the masses are all the better for it. This imbalance—where a small number of people (say 20 percent) cause a disproportionately large effect (more like 80 percent)—has come to be known as the Pareto Principle or the 80/20 rule. The basis for Pareto's argument is that individuals are unequal physically, intellectually, and morally. He suggests that those who are the most capable in particular groups and societies should lead. In this way, Pareto believes in a meritocracy, a society where status and mobility are based on individual attributes, ability, and achievement. Pareto opposed caste systems of stratification that create systematic inequality on the basis of birth into a specific group. He criticized societies based on strict military, religious, and aristocratic stratification, arguing that these systems will naturally tend to collapse. Concerning such systems, he argues that aristocracies do not last, and that, in fact, history is a "graveyard of aristocracies" (Pareto & Finer, 1966).

Meritocracy a society where status and mobility are based on individual attributes, ability, and achievement.

Along these lines, the ideal governing elite for Pareto is a combination of foxes and lions—that is, individuals who are cunning, unscrupulous, and innovative along with individuals who are purposeful and decisive, using action and force. This applies not only to the political realm but also to the economic realm, and the masses will be better off for it. The whole system works over time, in Pareto's view, when there are enough opportunity and social mobility to ensure that the most talented individuals end up in the elite and that it does not become a rusty aristocracy.

C. Wright Mills takes a much more negative view of the elite-mass dichotomy, arguing that it is neither natural nor beneficial for society. In Mills's view, the elite do not govern the way Pareto claims they do. Mills argues in *The Power Elite* (1956/2000) that there are three major institutional forces in modern American society where the power of decision making has become centralized: *economic institutions* (with a few hundred giant corporations holding the keys to economic decisions), the *political order* (once decentralized to states and localities, the increasing concentration of power in the federal government has led to a centralized executive establishment that affects every cranny of society), and the *military order* (the largest and most expensive feature of government). According to Mills, "Families and churches and schools adapt to modern life; governments and armies and corporations shape it; and, as they do so, they turn these lesser institutions into means for their ends." The elite for Mills are simply those who have most of what there is to possess: money, power, and prestige. But they would not have the most were it not for their positions within society's great institutions. Whereas Pareto views elite status as the reward for the talent that helped certain individuals rise through the ranks of society, Mills sees the unequal power and rewards as determining the positions. And whereas Pareto sees a benefit in having power centralized in a large, otherwise ungovernable society, Mills warns of the dangers. For Mills, such a system hurts democracy by consolidating the power to make major decisions into the hands (and interests) of the few.

The power elite is further stratified for Mills; at the inner core of the power elite are those individuals who interchange commanding roles at the top of one

How does Timothy Geithner embody C. Wright Mills's definition of a power elite?

dominant institutional order with those in another. In Mills's view, as the interactions among the big three power elites increase, so does the interchange of personnel among them. For example, after serving as President Obama's budget director, Peter Orszag took a top management position at Citigroup, a firm that benefited substantially from the government bailout after the 2008 financial crisis. Who replaced him in the White House? Jacob Lew, who was budget director under Clinton and later worked for Citigroup himself. Likewise, back in 1961, Robert McNamara left the presidency of Ford Motor Company to serve as secretary of defense under President John F. Kennedy. The list of people who have gone through the revolving doors of power goes on. This is of central importance to Mills, because as the elite increasingly assume positions in one another's domains, the coordination among the elite becomes more and more entrenched.

The inner core also includes the professional go-betweens of economic, political, and military affairs. These include individuals at powerful legal firms and financial institutions, such as corporate lawyers and investment bankers. The outer fringes of the power elite, which change more readily than the core, are individuals who count in the decisions that affect all of us but who don't actually make those decisions.

Let's take, for example, the business sector in America. Although the White House asserted that corrupt businesses such as Enron and WorldCom were simply isolated "bad apples," this assertion becomes suspect if we analyze the close personal networks and overlap of board members within the American business elite. For instance, more than 80 percent of the 1,000 largest corporations shared at least one director with another large company, and on average any two of the corporations were connected by fewer than four degrees of separation (Davis, 2003). Wall Street is particularly densely connected. Most troubling is the fact that many Treasury Secretaries have come from a single firm: the investment bank Goldman Sachs. As a result of these networks, which Mills both saw and predicted, decisions by various companies become increasingly similar. Many studies have suggested that these elite networks spread practices, principles, and information that account for some of the surprising conformity in approaches to corporate governance and ethics. Rather than "a few bad apples," a better analogy is perhaps a brush fire, where morals, practices, and decisions spread easily across corporate America—especially when like-minded people hold the power in government agencies that are meant to monitor business practices. For example, evidently, the response to the 2008 financial crisis was mapped out in a room with a dozen or so top bankers and the president of the New York

Income versus Wealth

Most people, when they consider economic status, think of **income**: money received by a person for work, from transfers (gifts, inheritances, or government assistance), or from returns on investments. Recent trends in earnings in the United States suggest that there is an increasing divergence or inequality between the bulk of the people and the rich, but especially between the super-rich and the merely rich. For instance, from 1950 to 1970, for every dollar earned by the bottom 90 percent of the American population, those in the top 0.01 percent earned an additional $162. If that sounds like a big distinction, that's nothing compared with more recent data. Between 1990 and 2002, for every dollar earned by those in the bottom 90 percent, each taxpayer at the top (and this would include Bill Gates) took home $18,000 (Johnston, 2005).

A recent trend in sociological analysis, however, is to analyze stratification in terms of wealth ownership. What is wealth in relation to income? Wealth is a family's or individual's net worth (total assets minus total debts). For the majority of American families, assets include homes, cars, other real estate, and business assets along with financial forms of wealth such as stocks, bonds, and mutual funds. Put simply, wealth is everything you own minus debts such as mortgages on homes, credit card debt, and, as most of you will probably have, debt from student loans. One way to think about the difference between income and wealth is to imagine income as a stream or river of money flowing through a family's hands. Wealth, by contrast, is a pool of collected resources that can be drawn on at specific times, a financial reservoir.

Federal Reserve, Tim Geithner, who later became U.S. Treasury Secretary in the Obama administration.

Again, because the stratification systems discussed above are all ideal types, these systems are not mutually exclusive. That is, they can overlap in a given society and almost always do, and it would be highly unlikely to find a modern society that is stratified by only one of the systems.

How Is America Stratified Today?

Sociologists often use the phrase socioeconomic status (SES) to describe an individual's position in a stratified social order. When sociologists talk about socioeconomic status, they are referring to any measure that attempts to classify groups, individuals, families, or households in terms of indicators

Socioeconomic status (SES) an individual's position in a stratified social order.

Income money received by a person for work, from transfers (gifts, inheritances, or government assistance), or from returns on investments.

Wealth a family's or individual's net worth (that is, total assets minus total debts).

such as occupation, income, wealth, and education. Although the boundaries between socioeconomic categories are not sharply defined, the lay public generally divides society into the upper class, the middle class, the working class, and the poor. Because these are common terms, we need to take them seriously, even if they are not of scientific origin and lack sufficient rigor.

The Upper Class

Upper class a term for the economic elite.

Generally, the upper class refers to the group of individuals at the top of the socioeconomic food chain. In practice, however, the term is used to describe diverse and complex concepts. Historically, the upper class was often distinguished by not having to work. (The economist and social critic Thorstein Veblen dubbed them the leisure class.) They were able to maintain their lifestyle by collecting rent and/or other investment returns. Its members were the aristocracy, the wealthy, the elite, the land owners. The only way to join this sphere was by birth or (occasionally) marriage. The upper class was the basis for Marx's capitalist class.

In the United States, "upper class" is associated with income, wealth, power, and prestige. According to some sources, the primary distinguishing characteristic of upper-class individuals is their sources of income—generally more from returns on investments rather than wages. Although estimates vary, approximately 1 percent of the U.S. population is considered to fall in this stratum. Over the decade leading up through 2008, this group saw its income rise 18 percent, while the average American worker experienced stagnant

Figure 7.1: Distribution of Net Worth, 2007

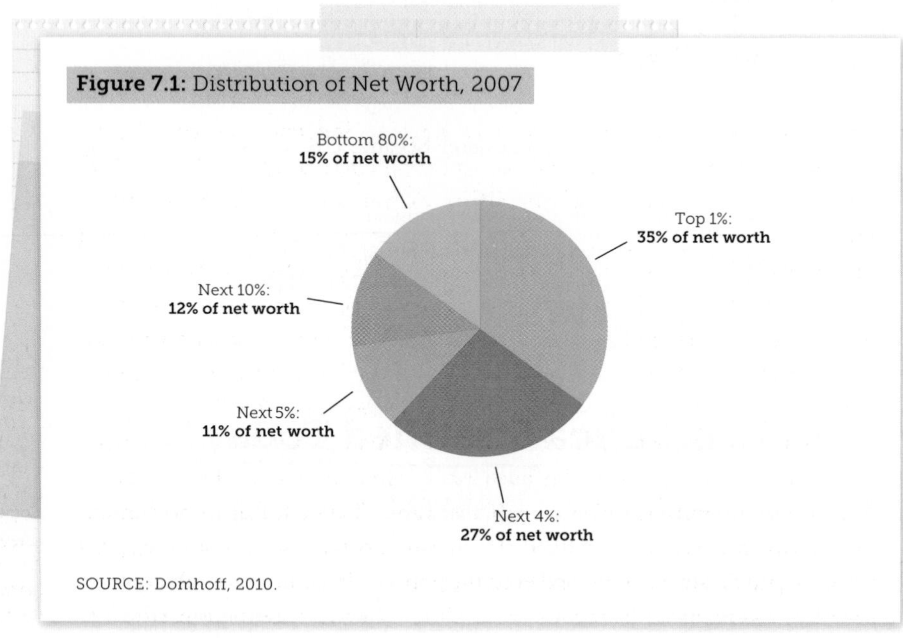

SOURCE: Domhoff, 2010.

wages (Saez, 2010). By 2009, the top 1 percent enjoyed a net worth that was 225 times greater than that of the median American family—the highest ratio ever recorded (Allegretto, 2011). Even in 2010—in the midst of an economic slump—the Forbes 400 list of wealthiest Americans managed to achieve a 12 percent increase in their collective net worth. Further, that year, CEO salaries averaged 263 times that of the average American worker (Anderson et al., 2010). Meanwhile, the nation saw its highest poverty rate in 2010 since 1993 (U.S. Census Bureau, 2011a). Over and above income levels, the upper class is also distinguished by prestige and power, which can be used to promote personal agendas and influence everything from political decisions to consumer trends. This is of particular importance because, as noted above, members of the upper class often wear many hats. As Dennis Gilbert states in *The American Class Structure in an Age of Growing Inequality* (1998),

> The members of the tiny capitalist class at the top of the hierarchy have an influence on economy and society far beyond their numbers. They make investment decisions that open or close employment opportunities for millions of others. They contribute money to political parties, and they often own media enterprises that allow them influence over the thinking of other classes. (p. 286)

Recently we have seen how top bankers' decisions to invest in risky mortgage practices have decimated the net worth of those—mostly in the middle and working classes—who have lost their homes (and home equity) to foreclosure (see Figure 7.2).

The Middle Class

Although those in the upper class have very real influence and control, the effects of this are sometimes limited in the public perception. In the 2007 article "The American People: Social Classes" published in the online magazine *Life in the USA* (a "complete guide to American life for Immigrants and Americans"), Elliot Essman speaks for much of the mainstream media when he asserts that the implications of such power are not far-reaching in our daily lives. "The very rich control corporations and have some political power, but the lifestyle and values of the very wealthy do not have much impact on the country in general," he states. "America is a middle class nation."

The United States is often thought of as a middle-class nation—so much so that depending on how the question is phrased, almost 90 percent of Americans have self-identified with this stratum. That said, there is no consensus on what the term middle class really means. Sociologists, economists, policymakers, think tank analysts, and even the public at large all work with different operating assumptions about the term. The categories become particularly

Middle class a term commonly used to describe those individuals with nonmanual jobs that pay significantly more than the poverty line—though this is a highly debated and expansive category, particularly in the United States, where broad swathes of the population consider themselves middle class.

Figure 7.2: CEO Compensation, 1970–2011

	Name	Company	Compensation
	1970		
1	**Henry Ford II**	*Ford Motor Co.*	$2,318,000
2	**Philip Hofmann**	*Johnson & Johnson*	$2,364,000
3	**Harold Geneen**	*IT & T*	$3,555,000
	1980		
4	**F. Hartley**	*Union Oil Co. of CA*	$2,762,000
5	**T. Wyman**	*CBS Inc.*	$2,971,000
6	**D. Kelly**	*Esmark Inc.*	$3,596,000
	1990		
7	**M. S. Davis**	*Paramount Comm.*	$15,666,000
8	**P. B. Fireman**	*Reebok International*	$18,750,000
9	**F. G. Wells**	*Walt Disney*	$27,278,000
	2000		
10	**S. I. Weill**	*CitiGroup*	$167,913,000
11	**C. B. Wang**	*Computer Associates International*	$243,137,000
12	**M. D. Eisner**	*Walt Disney*	$243,447,000
	2011		
13	**Robert Iger**	*Walt Disney*	$53,320,000
14	**Edward Mueller**	*Quest Communications*	$65,800,000
15	**Stephen Hemsley**	*UnitedHealth*	$101,960,000

Source: BusinessWeek, 1971, 1981, 1991, 2001; Forbes, 2011.

blurry when we attempt to separate the middle class from the working class (or "working families," to use the political campaign euphemism).

So what is middle class? If you look up the term in various dictionaries, you'll encounter myriad definitions. Some refer explicitly to position (that is, below upper, above lower); others speak to shared vocational characteristics and values. Still others mention principles. One of the most interesting comes from *Merriam-Webster's Collegiate Dictionary,* which indicates that the middle-class is "characterized by a high material standard of living, sexual morality, and respect for property."

The Middle Class and Working Class: Expansion and Retrenchment In the United States, the middle class has historically been composed of white-collar workers (office workers) and the working class of those individuals who work manually (using their hands or bodies). However, this distinction eroded with two trends. First, the post–World War II boom led to the enrichment of many manual workers. In those days, most working-class whites, ranging from factory workers to firemen to plumbers, were able to buy their own homes, afford college for their children, and retire comfortably. The working class became the newly expanded middle class.

From the post–World War II era of the late 1940s through the oil crisis of 1973, this middle class was a large and fairly stable group, maintained by corporate social norms emphasizing equality in pay and salary increases (Krugman, 2005). From 1947 through 1979, the average salary increase was fairly stable across all household income levels—in fact, the lowest-earning 20 percent of households showed the highest average earnings increase, 116 percent.

A second, countervailing trend has also eroded the traditional manual–nonmanual distinction between the working and middle classes: the rise of the low-wage service sector. Since 1973, manufacturing has steadily declined in the United States, and the service jobs replacing factory work have generally been either very high skilled (and rewarded) or relatively low skilled (and therefore not paid very well). This new and expanding group of low-wage service workers challenges the notion that working-class status arises from physical labor. Data entry clerks, cashiers, paralegals, and similar occupations are technically white-collar yet pull in working-class wages.

Over the past three decades, the income gap between a corporate CEO and a single-mother waitress has grown exponentially, and the relatively stable middle class of previous decades has become increasingly stratified (Figure 7.3). For example, a CEO who makes at least $184,500 is in the top 5 percent of households, and his or her average expected salary increase since 1979 (adjusted for inflation) is an impressive 81 percent. On the other end of the scale, a waitress who makes only $25,600 is in the bottom 20 percent of households, and her income will have decreased by 1 percent over the same time period. And if we consider an average family—say, a two-parent household with two kids and a middle-range annual income of $68,000—then this family

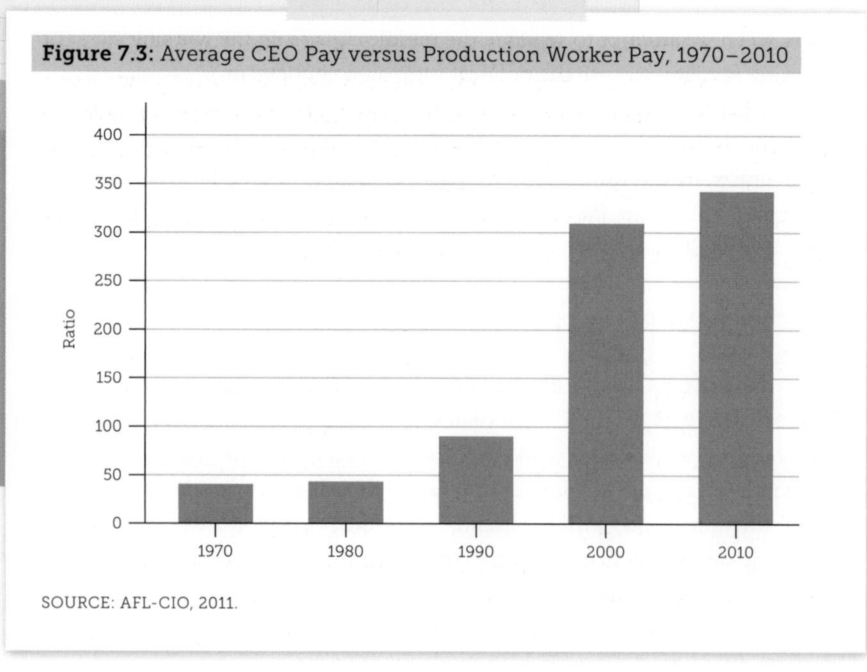

Figure 7.3: Average CEO Pay versus Production Worker Pay, 1970–2010

SOURCE: AFL-CIO, 2011.

would probably have experienced an income increase of 15 percent since 1979. (Go to www.inequality.com for more information.)

How and why has this differential income growth happened? One factor may be the changing nature of available employment. As the technological sector expands, the majority of jobs are being created either at very high skill levels with correspondingly high salaries (engineers and hedge fund managers) or at very low levels with little room for upward mobility (baristas at Starbucks who serve lattes to those hedge fund managers). And the fastest-growing job category for those with no more than a high-school education is food preparation and service.

Furthermore, this bifurcated job growth is reflected in the change in educational expectations of potential employers. Whereas for much of the post–World War II period, a high-school diploma could earn a person (a white man, specifically) enough to support a family, a college degree is now often a minimum requirement for decent employment. (We'll examine the phenomenon of credentialism in Chapter 13 on education.) But although the number of high-school graduates going to college has increased (to roughly 50 percent), bachelor's degree completion rates still stand at approximately 50 percent nationally (i.e., lots of folks are not finishing) (Bowen et al., 2009). If a college education is the gateway to becoming middle class and only a quarter of the American population has at least a four-year degree, we can expect the percentage of middle-class Americans to shrink.

In an interview for this book, sociologist Michael Hout helped explain that even though there has been stagnation in the number of people receiving bachelor's degrees, the value of those degrees is increasing. Hout pointed out that part of what is holding students back from getting the degree is that the cost of college is increasing and a larger proportion of the cost is borne by individuals and families rather than states. The University of California system—one of the biggest and best—announced a tuition hike of 32 percent for the academic year starting in 2010 that was swiftly followed by another 9.6 percent rise in 2011 (McMillan, 2011). Hout goes on to describe the way that sacrificing to pay for college plays out differently across social classes. He explains,

> There is a class-specific preference for these kinds of risks. The sons and daughters of college graduates see the benefit of a college education more clearly. They have had it drummed into them since they could talk. . . . Sons and daughters of people who haven't been to college can exercise a certain skepticism about it, and they see in their neighborhoods evidence that it might not pay off. Who leaves the neighborhood? Somebody who has reaped the full benefit of the college education. They're out of sight and out of mind. Who's back in the neighborhood? That kid who maybe dropped out after three years, with a three figure loan debt, six figure loan debt. And the presence of those people makes it look like college doesn't pay off. (Conley, 2009h)

Some argue that along with income inequality, income insecurity (or volatility) for the middle classes has also increased. In *The Great Risk Shift* (2006), Jacob Hacker asserts that the chances of an American family experiencing a 50 percent drop in their annual income from one year to the next were 17 percent in 2002, up from around 7 percent in 1970. A 50 percent salary cut would still leave the CEO mentioned above in the top 40 percent of household incomes, but how about our waitress and our middle-income family? Cutting their salary by half would send either into a major financial crisis, maybe even bankruptcy. However, other researchers argue that income instability is not the result of fluctuating earnings or job insecurity but rather stems from two major changes in family dynamics. First, there are more changes to household structure today because of divorce and remarriage; second, women now play a greater role in breadwinning (at one point during the recent recession even exceeding men as a proportion of the workforce), but they also enter and exit the workforce with greater frequency than men. (See Chapters 8 and 14 for more about women in the workforce.)

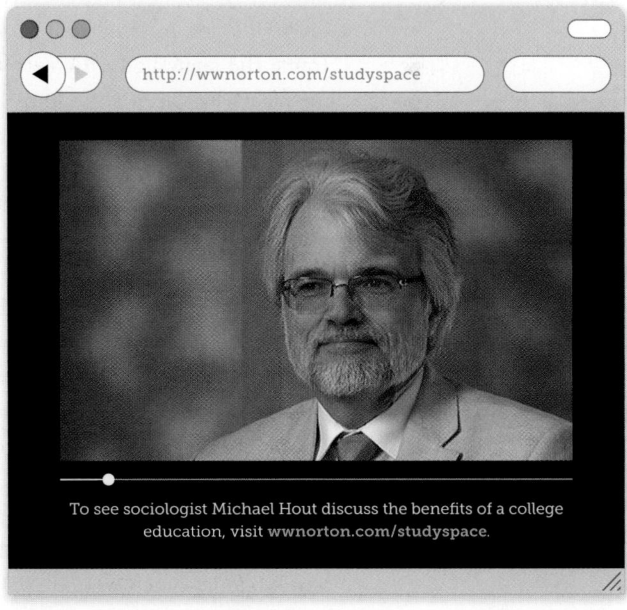

To see sociologist Michael Hout discuss the benefits of a college education, visit wwnorton.com/studyspace.

The Poor

Unlike the fuzzy definitions of other classes, poverty (covered in Chapter 10) has an official, government definition. In 2011, the poverty line for a family of four was $22,350 (U.S. Department of Health and Human Services, 2011b). The poor are, ironically, often said to resemble the rich in being more oriented toward the present and therefore less worried about the future than their middle-class and working-class counterparts (although this is highly debated). Day-to-day survival keeps the poor clearly planted in the present. Of course, like any class, the poor are not a unified group. In fact, one distinction often made in political speeches is that between the "working poor" (those who deserve our assistance) and the "nonworking poor" (those who can work but don't and therefore have a weaker moral claim on assistance). This latter group is sometimes called the "underclass." Of course, even these two categories obscure huge distinctions within either group; in fact, poverty is a state that families usually shift in and out of throughout their history, and often a clear distinction does not exist between the working class and the poor.

Global Inequality

One of the main reasons cited for rising income and wealth inequality in the United States is globalization—the rise in the trade of goods and services across national boundaries, as well as the increased mobility of multinational businesses and migrant labor. (See Chapter 14 for an extended discussion of globalization.) If the effect of globalization in the United States has been to bifurcate labor into high-skilled and low-skilled jobs, what has been the effect on worldwide inequality? The answer to that question depends on how you frame the analysis. In the long view, there is no question that global income inequality has been steadily rising over the last few centuries. At the start of the agricultural and industrial revolutions, almost the entire population of the world lived in poverty and misery (see the discussion of Malthus above). Birthrates were high, but so was mortality. Most people barely survived, no matter where they lived.

But then, thanks to technological innovations, food production started to increase dramatically in some areas of Europe (see Chapter 14 on the economy). Soon after—during the Industrial Revolution—large-scale factory production took the place of small cottage industries, resulting in the creation of vast, unequally distributed wealth. Simultaneously, European powers began to explore, conquer, and extract resources from other areas of the globe. Fast-forward a few hundred years to the mid-twentieth century, when the world and most of its wealth were carved up and ruled by major Western powers. Enormous global inequalities had emerged through the combination of colonialism and unequal development. Since around 1950, many of these former colonies have gained

Figure 7.4: Income Ratios

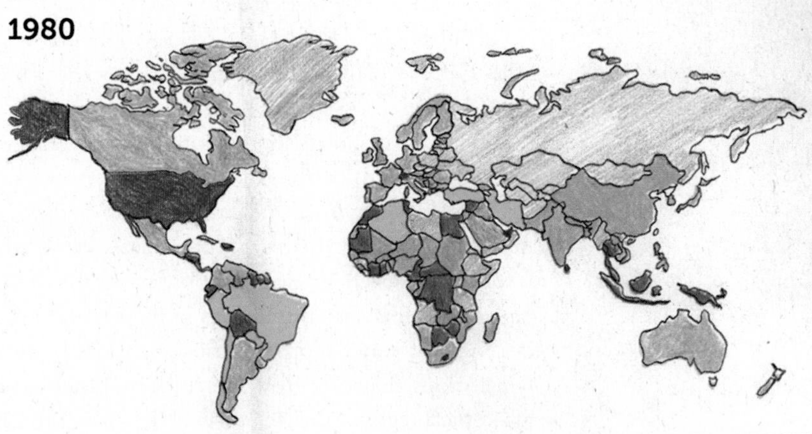

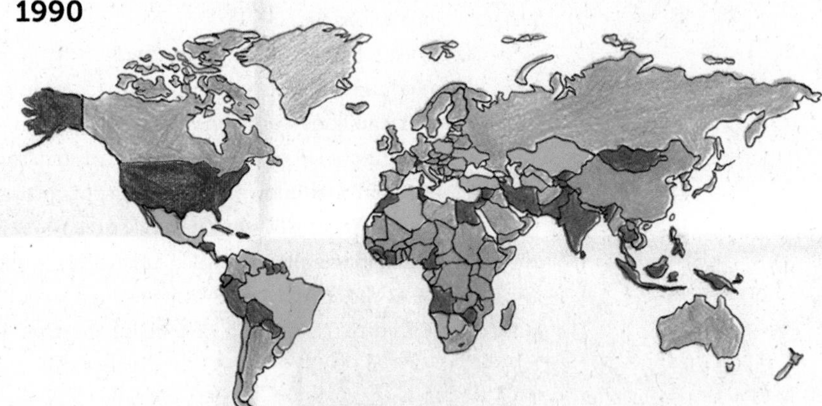

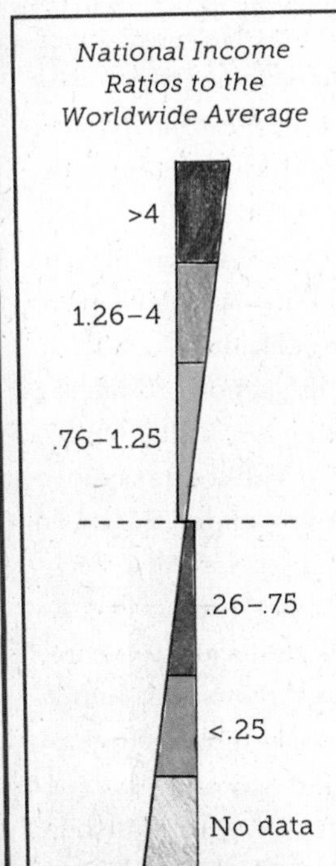

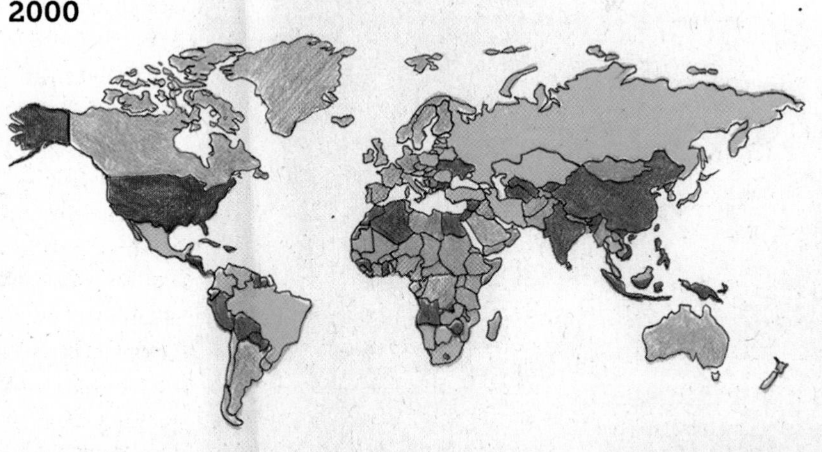

Source: UC Atlas of Global Inequality, 1980, 1990, 2000.

political independence, but they have lagged well behind the West in terms of income per capita. Figure 7.4 shows the ratios of national income to the worldwide average over three decades.

Scholars have long been trying to figure out why Europe developed first. Early explanations, dating back to the French essayist Montesquieu (1748/1750), focused on geographic differences between the peoples of Europe and the global south (as the less developed regions of the world are sometimes called). Perhaps because of the south's heat or humidity, Montesquieu associated virtue and rationality with the north; the south he associated with vice and passion. Montesquieu's views are now discarded as a racist account of uneven development, but more recent versions of the geographical explanation focus on differences in the length of growing seasons, the higher variability of water supply (because of more frequent droughts), the types of cereal crops that can grow in temperate zones compared with tropical and subtropical regions, the lack of coal deposits (the first fuel that drove industrialization, long before oil), and perhaps most important, the disease burden in warmer climates (Sachs, 2001).

Economist Jeffrey Sachs explains that Africa's geography made it much more difficult for an agricultural revolution to occur. He prods us to understand the complexity of the constraints on Africa's development before pointing fingers: "Africa is a continent largely of that rain-fed agriculture, whereas the Green Revolution was based first and foremost on irrigation agriculture. Now is that bad governance that Africa does not have vast river systems? Or is that a matter of the Himalayan Tibetan plateau which creates the Indus, the Punjab (meaning five rivers after all), the Ganges, the Yangtze, and so forth? These are functions of physical geography. Africa has a savannah region, which means a long dry season together with a single wet season typically" (Conley, 2009g). So Africa was not fortunate when it came to physical geography and it missed out on the Green Revolution because it could not easily implement irrigation agriculture. But that's not all. If you recall from our discussion of Malthus, Africa also carried a higher disease burden because of the way malaria is transmitted through animal hosts—more deadly in Africa than in Asia. Even with that, Sachs is not through explaining just how Africa came to be so disadvantaged compared with other regions of the world. Important impacts of colonialism would be easy to overlook if we focused only on geography and infectious disease transmission, he says.

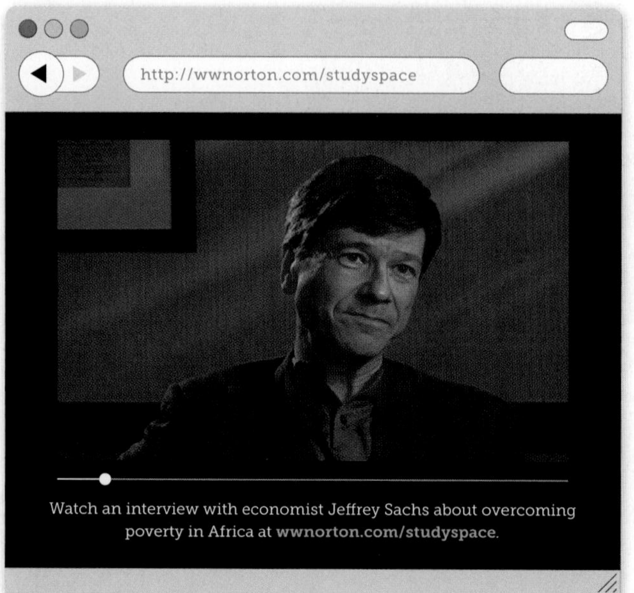

Watch an interview with economist Jeffrey Sachs about overcoming poverty in Africa at **wwnorton.com/studyspace**.

> Let's talk more about Africa. Racism. Absolutely pervasive. The slave era, the treatment of white people in the rich north Atlantic vis-à-vis the black people. Let's face it: we want to pretend that's not part of our society, part of our history, part of our view of the hopelessness of regions, part of the way that they were treated unfairly. If you look through the colonial-era memos in Africa about the repression of education levels and so forth by colonial powers, that's also part of the history. Then you come to infrastructure, you come to physical geography, you come to history and you come to an odd historical context. (Conley, 2009g)

Was the atrocious treatment by colonial powers somehow the fault of African leaders? Does this ever-so-brief primer on the history of African development help you to understand that the sociological imagination cannot function properly without a wide array of information about everything from epidemiology to history to geography and beyond?

Others argue that geography doesn't matter as much as social institutions do. In one version of this line of reasoning, it is a strong foundation of property rights, incorruptible judiciaries, and the rule of law in general that predict economic development (Easterly & Levine, 2002). These, in turn, were institutions

Tremendous global inequalities have emerged through the combination of colonialism and unequal development. What are some of the ways that social scientists explain the gap between rich and poor regions of the world?

"native" to Europe and were transferred to the areas where European colonists settled and lived in significant numbers (Acemoglu et al., 2001), spurring later development in areas such as India and Latin America (compared with much of Africa, where Europeans did not settle, which has lagged in development). Other scholars argue that the types of relationships different colonized regions had with the European powers largely determined their fate today: For example, under the rule of the British Raj, India was endowed with a huge network of railways to move cotton, tea, and other products to market. This network, in turn, helped spur economic growth once India got over the rocky transition to self-government after gaining its independence. By contrast, because of the disease burden in most sub-Saharan African countries, Europeans didn't stay and invest but rather focused on extractive industries, building railways that ran just to and from mines instead of extensive networks of roads and train tracks.

Today that legacy of unequal starting places and economic potentials means that the latest spurt of globalization has engendered an even greater level of income inequality across the north–south divide while creating huge differences within developing countries. Indeed, some regions, like sub-Saharan Africa and eastern Europe, have become poorer over the last 25 years, whereas in some previously poor regions, such as South and East Asia, income levels have risen. Considering the net change, the economist Xavier Salai-i-Martin estimates that there were around half a billion fewer poor people in the world by the turn of the twenty-first century than there were in the 1970s (Salai-i-Martin, 2002). Likewise, he claims, "all indexes show a reduction in global income inequality between 1980 and 1998." There have indeed been global reductions in population-weighted between-country differences, which can largely be attributed to the rapid growth of the Chinese and Indian economies over this time period. Within individual countries, however, inequality has generally risen over the same time period. The story of globalization and inequality is thus a complex and constantly changing one.

Social Reproduction versus Social Mobility

Once we begin to understand the basics of stratification—how members of a society are hierarchically organized along different lines—the next issue is the possibility of those members' changing their social position in the hierarchy. This is generally referred to as social mobility, the movement between different positions within a system of social stratification in any given society. Pitirim A. Sorokin (1927/1959) emphasized the importance of not just looking at the mobility of individuals but also examining group mobility. For example, rather than just asking why Ugo, cashier at Sears, was promoted to regional manager, thereby increasing his income and status, Sorokin suggests we also look at why

Social mobility the movement between different positions within a system of social stratification in any given society.

the group Ugo belongs to—black males of Nigerian descent in their mid-twenties—does or does not appear to be generally mobile.

Sorokin noted that social mobility can be either horizontal or vertical. *Horizontal social mobility* means a group or individual transitioning from one social status to another situated more or less on the same rung of the ladder. Examples of this might be a secretary who changes firms but retains her occupational status, a Methodist person who converts to Lutheranism, a family that migrates to one city from another, or an ethnic group that shifts its typical job category from one form of unskilled labor to another. *Vertical social mobility*, in contrast, refers to the rise or fall of an individual (or group) from one social stratum to another. We can further distinguish two types of vertical mobility, *ascending* and *descending* (more commonly termed *upward* and *downward*). An individual who experiences ascending vertical mobility either rises from a lower stratum into a higher one or creates an entirely new group that exists at a higher stratum. Ugo's promotion to regional manager at Starbucks is an example of rising from a lower stratum to a higher one. By becoming a manager, he has changed his class position, a change that confers both a higher salary and more prestige. Conversely, imagine that for some reason there was an immediate need for translators of Igbo (or Ibo, the language spoken by the Igbo people based in southeast Nigeria) in the United States. Ugo, who speaks Igbo, along with many other Nigerians who speak the language, will then find better jobs and thereby enjoy higher social status. This would be an example of a new group, Igbo translators, existing in a higher stratum.

Descending vertical mobility can similarly take either of two forms: individual or group. One way to think of these forms is as the distinction between a particular person falling overboard from a ship and the whole ship sinking. Sorokin asserted that "channels of vertical circulation necessarily exist in any stratified society and are as necessary as channels for blood circulation in the body" (1927).

Most sociologists concerned with studying mobility focus on the process of individual mobility. These studies generally fall into two types: mobility tables (or matrices) and status attainment models. Constructing a mobility table is easy, although making sense of it is much more difficult (see Table 7.2 for an example). Along the left-most column of a grid, list a number of occupations for people's fathers (it was traditionally done for males only). Across the top, list the same occupational categories for the sons (the respondents). There can be as many or as few categories as you see fit, so long as they are consistent for the parental and child generations. For example, a five-category analysis might include upper nonmanual occupations (managers and professionals), lower nonmanual occupations (administrative and clerical workers, low-level entrepreneurs, and retail salespeople), upper manual occupations (skilled workers who primarily use physical labor, such as plumbers and electricians), lower manual (unskilled physical laborers), and farmworkers. The number of categories can be expanded, and it is not uncommon to see seven-, nine-, or even fourteen-category tables. The key is filling in the boxes. Probably not many people fall into the cell where the father is upper nonmanual and the son is a

Table 7.2: Mobility Table: Father's Occupation by Son's First Occupation

FATHER'S OCCUPATION	SON'S OCCUPATION					
	Upper nonmanual	Lower nonmanual	Upper manual	Lower manual	Farm	Total
Upper nonmanual	**1,414**	521	302	643	40	2,920
Lower nonmanual	724	524	254	703	48	2,253
Upper manual	798	648	**856**	1,676	108	4,086
Lower manual	756	**914**	771	**3,325**	237	6,003
Farm	409	357	441	1,611	**1,832**	4,650
Total	4,101	2,964	2,624	7,958	2,265	19,912

SOURCE: Hout, 1983.

Structural mobility mobility that is inevitable from changes in the economy.

Exchange mobility mobility in which, if we hold fixed the changing distribution of jobs, individuals trade jobs not one-to-one but in a way that ultimately balances out.

farmer. However, because of the decline in the agricultural workforce over the course of the twentieth century, you are likely to observe (at least in the United States) a fair bit of movement from farmwork in the parental generation to other occupations in the children's generation. Changes in the distribution of jobs lead to what sociologists call structural mobility, mobility that is inevitable from changes in the economy. With the decline of farmwork because of technology, the sons and daughters of farmers are by definition going to have to find other kinds of work. This type of mobility stands in contrast to exchange mobility, in which, if we hold fixed the changing distribution of jobs, individuals trade jobs not one-to-one but in a way that ultimately balances out.

As most measures of economic inequality have risen each year since the 1960s, Americans have comforted themselves with the thought that they still live in the land of opportunity. Rates of occupational (and income) mobility in the United States have long been thought to have dwarfed those of European societies with their royalty, aristocracies, and long histories. However, recent research suggests that this may be cold comfort: Some economists have argued that U.S. mobility rates have declined significantly since the 1960s. Others go so far as to say that Americans now enjoy less mobility than their European counterparts. A fierce debate has ensued, because many of these studies compare apples and oranges—different measures, different data, different years. However, a consensus seems to be slowly emerging that mobility rates should be broken down into the two components discussed above, structural and exchange mobility. When we do this, it turns out that rates of "trading places" are fairly fixed across developed societies. By contrast, historically the United

States has enjoyed an advantage in growth-induced upward mobility; as the farm and blue-collar sectors withered and white-collar jobs expanded, sons and daughters of manual workers have, by necessity, experienced a degree of upward occupational mobility. However, sociologists and economists debate whether economic growth still drives upward mobility, or whether bifurcated job growth means intergenerational stagnation.

Another common methodology for studying social mobility is the status-attainment model. This approach ranks individuals by socioeconomic status, including income and educational attainment, and seeks to specify the attributes characteristic of people who end up in more desirable occupations. The occupational status research of Peter M. Blau and Otis Dudley Duncan (1967), who ranked occupations into a status hierarchy to study social attainment processes, is generally seen as the paradigmatic work in this tradition. Unlike mobility tables, the status-attainment model allows sociologists to study some of the intervening processes. For example, how important is education to facilitating upward occupational shifts in status? How critical is the prestige of a person's first job out of school? How does IQ relate to the chances for upward or downward mobility? The status-attainment model is an elastic one that allows researchers to throw in new factors as they arise and see how they affect the relationships between existing ones, generally ordered chronologically over a typical life course. Generally, it is thought that education is the primary mediating variable between parents' and children's occupational prestige. That said, recent research shows that parental education and net worth, not occupation or income, best predict children's educational and other outcomes (Conley, 1999). Blau and Duncan didn't measure net worth, but by now it has become a fairly standard factor in many socioeconomic surveys.

Status-attainment model approach that ranks individuals by socioeconomic status, including income and educational attainment, and seeks to specify the attributes characteristic of people who end up in more desirable occupations.

Although there is increasing consensus on what aspects of class background matter (and how much they do), there is relatively little understanding of the multiple mechanisms by which class is reproduced (or how mobility happens). For instance, a family with a higher socioeconomic status is likely to have more success in preparing their children for school, entry exams, and ultimately the job market because they have greater access to resources that promote and support their children's development. These might include educational toys when the children are very young, tutors in grade school, and expensive test-preparation courses for exams such as the SAT, GRE, LSAT, MCAT, and so on. Once again, let us compare the CEO of a large, profitable U.S. corporation with a single mother working as a waitress at the local diner. The status of the CEO's occupation and his disproportionate income and wealth in relation to the waitress's easily put his socioeconomic status leaps and bounds ahead of hers. Because of this disparity, he can send his children to the top private schools, where they will be funneled toward highly paid positions. In contrast, assuming that the single mother has no other source of income, her children are likely to get a public education without all the extras. This by no means mandates that they are destined for lower-level occupations, but it certainly suggests that if this were a race, the CEO's children started several miles ahead. (See Chapters 10, 11, and 13 on the various ways that these factors act as agents of class reproduction.)

The Death Tax

The U.S. estate tax, sometimes called (especially by Republican politicians) the "death" tax, is one that affects stratification and mobility. It is levied after the death of an individual, aimed at estates that have a net worth over a certain amount; currently, only estates with a gross value of more than $675,000 are taxed. However, the cutoff point for the estate tax, the line below which an estate is not taxed, has regularly increased since the 1960s. And in 2010 there was no tax whatsoever on estates. Opponents of the estate tax argue that taxing accumulated wealth discourages would-be entrepreneurs from taking risks and, as a result, reduces innovation and growth. However, proponents of the estate tax assert that the tax hits hardest at the people who have the most money, provides an important source of government revenue, bolsters the nonprofit industry because it allows deductions for charitable donations, and catches those who avoid paying income taxes on capital gains (money made from investments increasing in value) by not liquidating their assets during their lifetime. Most important, proponents suggest that the estate tax facilitates a move away from an aristocracy based on inheritance and propels us toward a meritocracy based on individual drive and skill. Michael J. Graetz and Ian Shapiro, the authors of a book on the estate tax, *Death by a Thousand Cuts* (2005), have referred to its repeal as the "Paris Hilton Benefit Act."

Opponents of the estate tax have consistently portrayed farmers as its undeserving victims. President George W. Bush, shortly after taking office, stated, "To keep farms in the family we are going to get rid of the death tax" (Johnston, 2003). The idea has been that to save the family farm, the tax had to be abolished. However, only 2 percent of the 2.4 million people who died in 2000 left an estate that owed any taxes. Furthermore, of the 52,000 estates that did, only 2,765 owned any farm assets, and the average value of farms was $149,000, far below the estate tax threshold. Throughout the 1990s, half of estate taxes were paid from estates valued at more than $5 million, families in the top 1 percent of wealth holders in the United States.

At the heart of the debate over the estate tax is the issue of stratification and inequality in the United States. Specifically, should people be able to transfer large sums of money across generations without interference by the government and thereby transfer social stratification as well? Some argue that the rights of private property (including the right to decide who gets it when you die) are fundamental to civilization and to a functioning capitalist economy. However, many wealthy Americans, including Warren Buffett, George Soros, Bill Gates, Jr., and Bill Gates, Sr., support the estate tax. Without the estate tax, these rich men believe, there will be, in America, an ever-growing concentration of power among those whose only virtue is that they were born to certain parents and stayed in their good graces. Such a system is essentially an aristocracy of wealth. Soros, for instance, has suggested that repealing the estate tax would result in higher taxes on earnings, thereby shifting the tax burden onto people with less money. When people like Bill Gates, whose families have the most to lose from the estate tax, speak out against its abolition, one has to question whose interests it is serving.

Why do billionaires such as Warren Buffett (left) or Bill Gates (right) support the estate tax?

→ CONCLUSION

Horatio Alger, Jr. (1832–99) was an American author of dime novels that told rags-to-riches stories. The narratives typically depicted a plucky young downtrodden boy who eventually achieved the American dream of success and fortune through tenacious hard work, while maintaining a genuine concern for the well-being of others. Alger wrote more than 130 novels with titles such as *Sink or Swim* (1870), *Up the Ladder* (1873), *From Boy to President* (1881), *Making His Way* (1901), *A New Path to Fortune* (1903), and *Finding a Fortune* (1904). Works like these contributed to the national ideology that all Americans could make it if they only pulled themselves up by their own bootstraps.

Although more than 100 years old, Alger's novels still resonate with a faith in mobility that is woven into the national fabric and self-image of Americans. Today the majority of Americans remain very positive about the possibility of upward mobility despite the economic damage of the Great Recession. A 2011 poll by the Pew Charitable Trusts found that more than two-thirds of Americans (68 percent) still thought that their children would be better off than they were and seven out of ten Americans believe they themselves have achieved (or will achieve) the American dream. What is so striking is that more and more Americans are buying into the Alger myth—more Americans than 20 years ago believe it possible to start at the bottom and work your way to the top. People generally believe that hard work and education are more important than social connections or a wealthy background. Are Americans overly optimistic, or are sociologists just being naysayers? Only more research will tell us for sure.

This Horatio Alger novel features a newsboy who rises to newspaper editor. Are most Americans today likely to achieve upward mobility?

PRACTICE

ASSIGNMENT

Why do sociologists build "mobility tables"? Create a mobility table for your family, starting with your parents and grandparents. Add your parents' siblings to the table and/or family friends (basically, any parent and child, where the child is no longer in school). What occupations are represented? Do you see any trends from one generation to the next? If the United States is a meritocracy, why does a relationship seem to exist between the occupational categories of parents and their children?

QUESTIONS FOR REVIEW

1. How does the case of Carlos Slim Helú, the richest person on the planet, resemble a Horatio Alger story? How does Slim's story simultaneously point to what is "wrong" about the way resources are distributed?
2. How does *The Power Elite* by C. Wright Mills help explain the repeal of the 2010 estate tax?
3. Whereas inequality is the result of abundance, how does the relationship between the bourgeois and proletariat suggest that abundance is the result of inequality?
4. To talk about the rich, the poor, and the way society is economically stratified sounds like the job of economists. Why should sociologists be interested in stratification? How does a better understanding of stratification potentially contribute to the well-being of society?
5. Why, according to Adam Ferguson and John Millar, is inequality necessary? In what way does their argument anticipate the "free rider problem"?
6. What is "equality of condition" and why did Thomas Malthus argue against striving for this form of equality?
7. What are the ideal types of social stratification and how do they differ? Which one, in your opinion, best describes stratification in the United States?
8. What is the difference between income and wealth? Why might certain sociologists prefer to measure inequality based on wealth instead of income?
9. What is "structural mobility" and how does this concept describe the decline of manufacturing jobs in the United States since the early 1970s?
10. According to Max Weber, what do being a teacher, having a cool car, and being a member of a prestigious association have in common?

PARADOX

INEQUALITY IS THE RESULT OF ABUNDANCE.

WATCH THE ANIMATED SHORT ABOUT THE STRATIFICATION PARADOX AT

WWNORTON.COM/STUDYSPACE

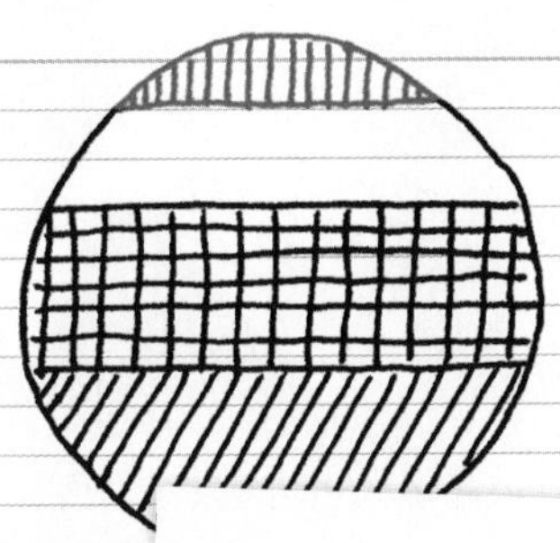

Rosia Rezaee is a member of the Afghan Women's Boxing Club. This organization's twenty members have challenged conservative gender ideology in Afghanistan through their passion for boxing and advocacy for women's freedom to equally participate in society.

8 Gender

PARADOX

THE BIOLOGICAL CATEGORIES OF SEX STRONGLY INFLUENCE THE SOCIAL DYNAMICS OF GENDER; HOWEVER, THE SOCIAL CATEGORIES OF GENDER CAN SOMETIMES DETERMINE THE BIOLOGY OF SEX.

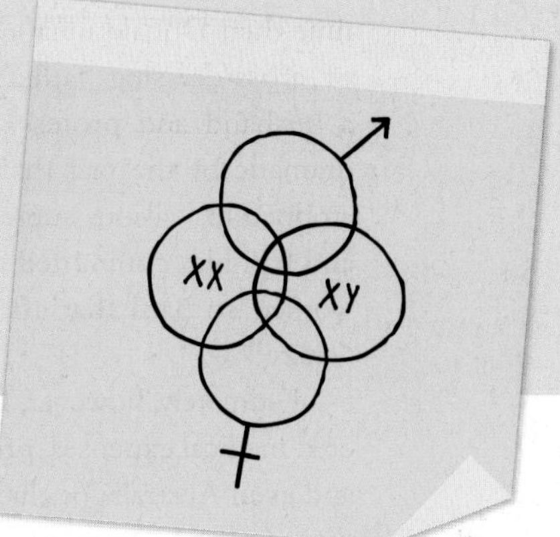

In social science, there is a statistical technique called "individual fixed effects." Basically it boils down to comparing an outcome across time as some factor changes. So, for example, if we want to know whether having kids makes folks happier and more fulfilled, we might ask them before they have their first child and then again afterward. Fixed effects can be used to look at the effect of marriage and divorce on health; of education on wages; of home ownership on savings rates; and of family income on kids' test scores. However, there are certain key sociological variables that resist fixed effects, simply because they don't change over time. Think race. Think birth cohort. Think parents' age. And, of course, think sex. Very few folks get to experience life in both locker rooms, so to speak. Sex isn't a boundary we typically flip back and forth across. However, it has been known to happen. Among the estimated 25,000 or so Americans who have undergone sexual reassignment surgery, few are probably better positioned to report with a scientific eye than Deirdre McCloskey, a Harvard-trained world-renowned economist who used to be named Donald.

Perhaps it was the combination of her gifts of economic science and beautiful writing style that made McCloskey destined to be the one who would prominently (and touchingly) describe effects of gender (and her associated border crossing) to a wide readership in her memoir, *Crossing*.

"It's strange to have been a man and now to be a woman," she admits. "But it's no stranger perhaps than having been a West African and now being an American, or once a priest and now a businessman. Free people keep deciding to make strange crossings, from storekeeper to monk or from civilian to soldier or from man to woman. Crossing boundaries is a minority interest, but human" (p. xii).

Written in the third person—certainly rare if not totally unique among memoirs—in order to reconcile the multiple selves that McCloskey experienced over the course of his/her adulthood, *Crossing* details the harrowing journey across the invisible yet robust boundary of sex/gender. This voyage was made all the more improbable by McCloskey's advanced age (52) at the time then-Donald initiated the biological process of the change after decades of cross-dressing, fathering and providing for two children, and serving as a husband and professionally active man: Made not only improbable but dramatic by the fact that McCloskey's sister—a professional psychologist—stopped his various surgeries several times by threatening to sue the surgeons and had him committed to a mental hospital against his will. Indeed, she had worked so hard that after his penile removal surgery, he feared waking up "crazy."

Ultimately, however, Deirdre triumphed: After almost $100,000 of uncovered medical expenses, procedures that were performed across North America and even Australia (including facial bone surgery, voice surgery, and hormone therapy, just to name a few), Deirdre emerged happy, if weatherworn, to document the process while beginning a new life. Estranged from his ex-wife and kids, she nonetheless was relieved (not crazy) to engage in the painful process of stretching his neovagina—fashioned from some of his small intestine—for thirty minutes each day, to continue the laborious (and also painful) electrolysis treatments, and otherwise continue the journey into womanhood—a continent she had previously visited as a cross-dressing tourist, hoping to pass for a native in Donald's dresses.

What does economist Deirdre McCloskey's experiences on both sides of the sex/gender divide tell us about the differences between sex, gender, and sexuality?

Along the way, McCloskey indeed chronicles a number of changes that she experienced before and after, as man and then as woman. It's too bad that his ex-wife couldn't stay married to the female McCloskey, because Deirdre speculates that she might, in fact, like this version better: "His wife would become angry if he talked of his Chicago doubt [back when he was deciding whether to leave his faculty position at the prestigious University of Chicago economics department], for it was tedious after a while to listen to the whining. My ex-wife would like Deirdre better if she knew her, she reflected. No angst" (p. 149).

McCloskey also wrote down 41 differences between Donald and Deirdre, some of which fall into the realm of well-worn gender stereotypes. (McCloskey is the first to note that however rigid and defended the boundary of sex is, the experience of gender operates along a continuum and consists of a culturally instantiated grab-bag of characteristics that are found among individuals of both sexes in varying degrees.) Below are twenty of those differences:

- She cries.
- She sweats less.
- She loses weight less easily.
- Her color memory and color vocabulary are a little better.
- She works at remembering what people wear.
- She likes cooking.
- She listens intently to stories people tell of their lives, and craves detail.
- She is more alert to relational details in stories: Ah, I see, she's his cousin by marriage. She finds herself remembering the family trees, the ex-boyfriends, the big events.
- She is less impatient.
- She drives more slowly and less aggressively.
- She can't remain angry for long.
- She feels duty bound to wash the dishes.
- She loves, just loves, the little favors of womankind, getting a card for someone, making meatloaf for Charles up the street, helping someone through a day of his life.
- She assumes a less confident mask for dealings with salespeople and auto mechanics.
- She is uninterested in sports and finds the sports pages pointless.
- She no longer thinks of social life as strict exchange.
- She dotes on every child she meets.
- She has more friends.
- She thinks less about sex.
- She gets as much pleasure from loving as from being loved.

All we need now is a whole group of social scientists to go through this form of participant observation in order that we can obtain a statistical distribution of effects! Or maybe not. Actually, sometimes what is gained in narrative is lost in numbers.

Mars and Venus

If you think Deirdre McCloskey's list of differences between herself and her male predecessor is long, that's just a drop in the bucket when it comes to the divergence of men and women, or so says pop psychologist John Gray. Gray argues that men and women differ so fundamentally in their values, attitudes, thought processes, preferences, and behavior patterns that they might as well be from different planets altogether. (Interplanetary travel might explain the exhaustion McCloskey felt after his journey into she.) Gray writes that men and women don't even speak the same language, but have distinct biologically and psychically driven styles of communication, feeling, and action.

Gray's relationship guidebook *Men Are from Mars, Women Are from Venus* (1992) was a number-one best seller for a decade. It sold more than 14 million copies and inspired nearly a dozen spin-offs, from *Mars and Venus on a Date* to a diet and health book with such recipes as the Mars–Venus supershake. So widely recognized is the book's title that by now, when the tricky issue of gender relations rises to the fore, as it so often does in America, we often discuss the matter in terms of the innate differences between Martians and Venusians.

When you deal with the stress of dating and breakups, you might be tempted to use the Mars–Venus framework. It offers the appeal of easy-to-grasp, commonsense generalizations. Men and women are different biological organisms, according to Gray, and their biological differences manifest themselves in the ways men and women behave. By nature, allegedly, men don't like to express their feelings but instead retreat to their "caves" after a hard day at the office. Women are just more expressive and relational, always communicating about their feelings. These things are just biological givens, so individuals must take personal action to navigate what nature's given us, or so the self-help books would have us believe.

Why would a sociologist disagree with the arguments about gender that John Gray poses in *Men Are from Mars, Women Are from Venus?*

If you're a sociologist, this kind of thinking won't get you too far in explaining concepts such as sex, sexuality, gender, and the many messy complications, exceptions, and social patterns that beg for explanations beyond the individual, psychical, or biological levels. In the marketplace of ideas, sociological explanations are always at a disadvantage compared to pop psychological explanations of complex social phenomena. People prefer quick, easy answers to the long and often arduous sociological route. After all, they make more intuitive sense at first blush, they're easier to grasp, and we're accustomed to them. Unfortunately, they are often wrong. On the sociologist's path, you'll have to leave behind your Mars–Venus guidebooks (including the shortened, illustrated version) and instead take up the sociological imagination. Sex and gender may, in fact, be the most difficult areas to remember that what seems natural is often anything but. The seemingly rigid and innate differences between the "opposite sexes" can turn out to be fluid.

In applying our sociological imaginations to sex and gender, we will come across many feminist strands of thought. Feminism was at first embraced as a consciousness-raising movement to get people to understand that gender is an organizing principle of life; gender matters because it structures relations between people. Further, as gender structures social relations, it does this on unequal ground, so there are real powers and privileges at stake in gender ideology. Neoconservative talk show host Rush Limbaugh would have you believe that feminism "was established to allow unattractive women easier access to the mainstream" (Media Matters, 2005). In fact, the basic idea behind feminism is that women and men should be accorded equal opportunities and respect—a position that almost anyone in the contemporary United States would be hard pressed to criticize. Feminists tend to be less interested in erasing the differences between men and women than in uncovering the power stakes behind the socially constructed differences between the genders.

Feminism a consciousness-raising movement to get people to understand that gender is an organizing principle of life. The underlying belief is that women and men should be accorded equal opportunities and respect.

The sociologist's first task is to disentangle the terms *sex, sexuality,* and *gender.* Sex is typically used to describe the biological differences that distinguish males from females. Sexuality refers to desire, sexual preference, sexual identity, and behavior. Far from being strictly natural, how we have sex and with whom vary by time and place. Gender denotes a social position, the set of social arrangements that are built around normative sex categories. It is, you could say, what people do with the physical materials of sex.

Sex the biological differences that distinguish males from females.

Sexuality desire, sexual preference, sexual identity, and behavior.

Gender a social position, the set of social arrangements that are built around normative sex categories.

No one can dispute that biological differences exist between men and women. However, what we make of those differences does not inevitably arise out of the biological. Gender is one set of stories we tell each other and believe in to get by in the world. It's a collectively defined guidebook that humans use to make distinctions among themselves, to separate one being from another, and to comprehend an otherwise fuzzy mass of individuals. But the gender story can change, and we'll see how it has done so throughout history and across cultures. To grasp this insight takes sociological imagination, and it brings us a step further toward understanding the power of ideas. We tell each other over and over again that women act a certain way that is distinct from the behavior of men, until that notion becomes experienced as real. Herein lies the paradox: Gender is a social construction, but it is so deeply rooted and seemingly natural that it is a major structure organizing our everyday lives—our goals, our desires, even our bodies. And if gender is a human invention, we have to take it as seriously as we would any other institution, as Judith Lorber argues. In *Paradoxes of Gender* (1994), Lorber claims that gender is a social institution that "establishes patterns of expectations for individuals, orders the social processes of everyday life, is built into the major social organizations of society, such as the economy, ideology, the family, and politics, and is also an entity in and of itself." Although gender is a social construction, it matters in the real world, organizing our day-to-day experiences and having profound consequences for the life chances of men and women. Gender is ultimately about power struggles and how they organize daily life, from household economies and wage labor to birth control and babies' names.

Sex: A Process in the Making

We make sense of much variation between men and women by referring to their biological differences. This can range from the behavioral consequences of hormones (such as premenstrual syndrome), relative physical strength of bodies ("real" versus "girl" push-ups), brain architecture (subsequent rational or irrational action), and chromosomes (XX or XY). But in so doing, we tend to miss a crucial link between nature and nurture. The study of gender boils down to seeing how the two spheres, nature and nurture, overlap, penetrate, and shape each other. The biological world of sex and bodies does not exist outside of a social world, and the social world of human beings is always made up of human bodies. Studying the links between the two allows us to see the social construction of both gender and sex.

Gayle Rubin, in her influential essay "The Traffic in Women: Notes on the 'Political Economy' of Sex" (1975), called the social construction of gender categories based on natural sex differences the "sex/gender system." Rubin claimed that in every society, a division of labor by gender occurred, one in which men universally performed the kinds of tasks accorded higher value than those done by women. Men did the hunting and the fighting; they ran corporations and governments. But a decade later, scholars paused to consider that perhaps Rubin got it wrong. What's so natural about a sexed body in the first place?

This might strike you as a strange question. Bodies are, so we think, natural, God-given, sacred, hardwired. Human babies come equipped with a set of male or female organs, hormones, and chromosomes—what we might call "the plumbing" that you're equipped with at birth. We think of sex as an either/or binary. You're either male or female. But in fact, there are some peculiar exceptions and blurred lines that have led sociologists to view this model of natural sex as more of an ideal than an absolute.

Consider the story of David Reimer, otherwise known as "John/Joan." In 1976, Reimer was an average baby boy who, at eight months of age, suffered a botched circumcision that left him with virtually no penis. Under the guidance of Dr. John Money at Johns Hopkins University, Reimer's parents agreed to have their son undergo sex reassignment surgery. David was surgically made into a girl, Brenda, who would go on to endure one heck of a tough childhood.

John Money claimed for years that Brenda was a success story of his approach to dealing with intersex children, those who are born with a reproductive or sexual anatomy that doesn't seem to fit the typical definitions of female or male. Here was proof that nurture trumped nature in sexual identity; you could raise a genetic male as a girl and she'd turn out just fine. Sex reassignment surgery was the best solution to cases like David Reimer's, Money argued. As it turns out, Money was wrong. Despite the hormone treatments, her frilly dresses and curly hair, Brenda never did feel comfortable as a girl. When Reimer learned the truth in his adolescence, he made several suicide attempts before eventually changing his sex identity back to that of a male. Later, he underwent reconstructive surgery that enabled him to have a normal sex life (Colapinto, 2000).

John/Joan's story has had little effect on the way physicians treat intersex children. Most notable has been the founding of the Intersex Society of North America (ISNA) in 1993, which advocates reform in the medical practice of sex reassignment (ISNA, 2006). Surgeons today still recommend quick and often secretive surgery to make intersex children conform to an ideal of normal genitalia. About 90 percent of these surgeries reassign an ambiguous male anatomy into a female one because, in the disquieting phrase of the surgical world, "It's easier to make a hole than build a pole." A 2000 American Academy of Pediatrics policy statement on intersex surgery states that "the birth of a child with ambiguous genitalia constitutes a social emergency." To quickly resolve the emergency, doctors are advised to examine external genitalia "to determine the degree of masculinization." Furthermore, the statement continues, "The size of the phallus and its potential to develop at puberty into a sexually functional penis are of paramount importance." So size does matter, it seems, at least to doctors.

A general rule among doctors is that a phallus less than 2 centimeters in length constitutes a "micropenis" (although that standard changes from time to time), and a male infant would be better off raised as a female rather than suffer the shame of a small penis. While physicians claim to have the interests of the child and the parents at heart, what else is at stake in intersex births? The social notion of a binary sex is also being protected. A binary sex system imposes order in the world and helps us makes sense of an otherwise complicated mass of populations. Yet it also limits our ability to accept difference. It is the goal of ISNA to reduce embarrassment and secrecy over intersex conditions.

David Reimer was subjected to gender reassignment surgery at 18 months old. What does his story tell us about the relationship between biological sex and gender identity?

Most people think—if they think about it at all—that the medical construction of sex applies only to a handful of individuals. Based on a review of medical literature from 1955 to 1998, Brown University biology researcher Anne Fausto-Sterling estimates that the number of deviations from the binary of male or female bodies may be as high as 2 percent of live births, and the number of people receiving "corrective" genital surgery runs between 1 and 2 in every 1,000 births (Fausto-Sterling, 2000). Human variation within and across the two sexes is surprisingly high, and intersex activists point to the fact that social discomfort and fear of difference, rather than medical necessity, may be what pushes parents and surgeons to the operating table.

Surgeons medically construct their version of "proper" or "normal" sex, in conjunction with one on which most of us also agree. What makes a male a male and not a female? To answer this, many people would unhesitatingly mention the presence of a penis. But consider for a moment that the answer to this question has varied throughout history. If you're hesitant to accept the modern medical construction of sex, then perhaps the Greeks can persuade you to consider the sociohistorical production of sex. Our present-day understanding of sex, in fact, has a very long history.

Sexed Bodies in the Premodern World

Whereas Dr. John Money operated on a mutually exclusive two-sex model of human body types, a lesser known but equally plausible "one-sex" model dominated Western biological thought from the ancient Greeks until the mid-eighteenth century (Laqueur, 1990). In the old one-sex way of thinking, there was only one body—a male body—and the female body was regarded as its inversion, that is, as a male body whose parts were flipped inside rather than hanging on the outside. People believed that women were a lesser but not so radically different version of men.

Not until the two-sex model of human bodies gained ground did women and men become such radically different creatures in the popular conception. Incidentally, historian Thomas Laqueur shows us that this differentiation of bodies prompted changes in ideas about the female orgasm. In the one-sex model, it was believed that both a man's orgasm and a woman's were requirements for conception. But by the mid-1800s, female orgasm was considered unnecessary. Whereas seventeenth-century (female) midwives advised would-be mothers that the trick to conceiving lay in an orgasm, nineteenth-century (male) doctors debated whether it was even possible for women to experience orgasm.

Contemporary Concepts of Sex and the Paradoxes of Gender

The point of all this sex talk is to challenge our tendency to think of bodies as wholly deterministic. This is not to say that biology isn't a driving force, but merely to acknowledge that our understandings of, categorizations of, and behavior toward bodies are not set in stone. By contrast, essentialist arguments, also called essentialism, explain social phenomena in terms of natural ones. The hallmarks of essentialism are fixity, lack of history, absolutism, and biological determinism—meaning that what you do in the social world should be a direct result of who you are in the natural world. If you are born with male parts, essentialists believe, you are essentially and absolutely a man, and you will be sexually attracted to women only, as preordained by nature. Medical experts today maintain the ideal of a dimorphic or binary (either male or female) model of sex by tweaking babies who blur the boundaries. The trick is to recognize that the very boundaries separating male and female bodies are themselves somewhat contested.

Essentialism a line of thought that explains social phenomena in terms of natural ones.

Biological determinism a line of thought that explains social behavior in terms of who you are in the natural world.

This is not to say that there is no biological reality or that everything is a social construction. However, a common assumption we make is that biology comes before or dictates behavior, but sociologists now think of the nature–behavior relationship as a two-way street. Confused yet? Feminist philosopher Elizabeth Grosz (1994) proposes that we view the relationship between the natural and the social (in this case, sex and gender) as existing on a Möbius strip. The Möbius strip is an old math puzzle that looks like a twisted ribbon loop, yet it has just one side and one edge. Biological sex, the plumbing, makes up the inside of the strip, whereas the social world—culture, experience, and gender—make up the outside. But as happens in the contours of gender, the inside and outside surfaces are inseparable. In thinking or talking about sex and gender, we often switch from one to the other without even noticing that we've changed our focus (Fausto-Sterling, 2000). Some societies in various historical periods have made sense of the plumbing in different ways, and these explanations become the social construction of gender.

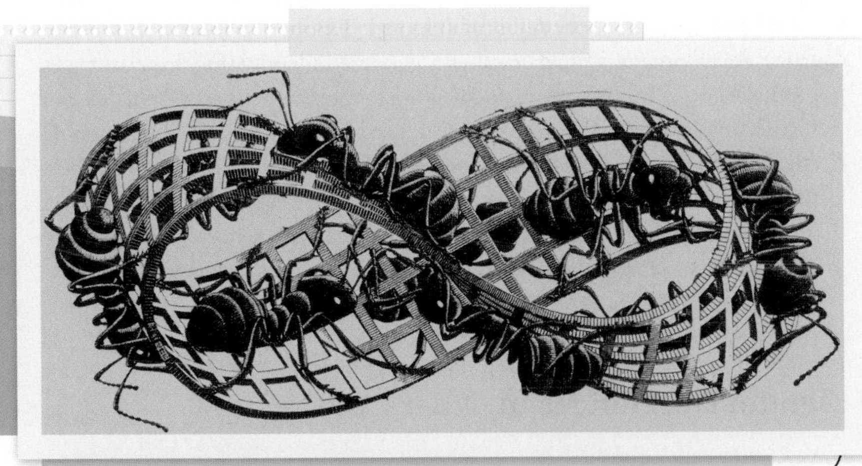

Elizabeth Grosz uses a Möbius strip, such as this one drawn by M. C. Escher, as a model for sex and gender. Even though the ants appear to be above or below each other, they are really on the same side of the strip.

Gender: What Does It Take to Be a Woman (or a Man)?

You have now learned about a case in which sex was conferred rather than innate. Medically and historically, biological sex does not exist in the world in some fixed, natural state. Our next step is to trace the different social senses that humans have taken from sex. There are many historical and cross-cultural meanings, roles, and scripts for behavior that we like to think correspond to more or less fixed biological categories. This complete set of scripts is what sociologists refer to as gender, or the division of people, behaviors, and institutions into two categories: male and female.

Much like sex difference, people tend to think that gender difference is a natural cleavage between two static groups—you're either a man or a woman. Why do men tend to fight one another, dominate the hard sciences, and outnumber women in the top political offices? Why do women tend to mother, stay more connected with their families, and outnumber men in occupations that involve caring for others? The short (essentialist) answer is that men and women are naturally (that is, biologically) different, so they behave differently.

The longer, sociological answer is that gender differences are much more fluid and ambiguous than we care to admit. They cannot be so easily explained by appeals to natural differences between the sexes, because gender isn't natural: It's a social institution, as Judith Lorber claimed (1994). Gender establishes patterns of expectations for people, orders our daily lives, and is one of the fundamental building blocks of society—law, family, education, the economy, everything. Gender is also a crucial part of how we define ourselves; it frames our identity. The process of forming a gendered identity starts before a person is even born, as soon as the fetus is identified. Through socialization and personality development, a child acquires a gendered identity that, in most cases, reproduces the attitudes, values, and actions that his or her social milieu deems suitable for a boy or girl. (Recall our discussion of gender roles in Chapter 4.) We impose rigid boundaries to maintain a gender order, but if we look at how gender systems vary, we can expose those boundaries as social constructions. If gender is a set of stories we tell ourselves to get through the complications of living, those stories are subject to change, but they do have real consequences for us, the actors who star in that story.

Gender Differences in Other Cultures

One crucial part of the story we hear about gender is that only two genders exist, just like our idea about sex. John Gray would surely have been writing a very different book if the title had been *Men Are from Mars, Women*

Are from Venus, and Everyone in Between Is from Earth. Many Western cultures struggle to divide the world neatly between men and women with correspondingly clear male and female bodies. Not so, however, for the Navajo society of Native Americans. In Navajo tribes, there are not two but three genders: masculine men, feminine women, and the *nadle*. The *nadle* might be born with ambiguous genitalia at birth or they may declare a *nadle* identity later on regardless of genitalia. The *nadle* perform both masculine and feminine tasks and dress for the moment, according to whatever activity they're doing. Although they are often treated like women, they have the freedom to marry people of any gender, "with no loss of status" (Kimmel, 2000).

Gender scholars have grown somewhat uncomfortable with the search for occurrences of "third genders" among ethnic others, pointing out that gender frameworks can be hard to shake. Serena Nanda (1990) and Gayatri Reddy (2005) studied *hijras* in India, a group that is often included in textbooks like this one to stand in as proof that a binary either/or gender system is not so natural after all. From Reddy we know that "hijras are phenotypic men who wear female clothing and ideally, renounce sexual desire and practice by undergoing a sacrificial emasculation—that is, an excision of the penis and testicles" (Reddy, 2005). To our Western ears, then, these men who renounce manhood but who are not women are actively staking a claim for a third gender. But Reddy goes on to develop the definition of what it means to be a *hijra*, which includes behaviors that may have little to do with gender: dedication to the goddess Bedhraj Mata, conferring fertility to newlyweds and newborns; a sometimes reluctant, sometimes quite dedicated entry into prostitution; communal living; self-sacrifice; and poverty. Thus *hijra* identity is a master status, but it is not experienced by the *hijras* as a fight for turf between gender categories. Like Don Kulick's Brazilian *travesti* (see pages 305–6), the *hijra* may have few qualms about the balance they've struck between gender and sexuality and more fears about the way their poverty will shape their chances in life. To be sure, the widespread stigmatization—both groups are believed to be violent and untrustworthy—is likely related to their transgression of the boundaries shaping and containing gender and sexuality practices, but using these two groups as measuring sticks against which the Western sex and gender binaries can be dismantled is a short-sighted exercise of the sociological imagination.

Hijras embracing at a wedding.

The Toilette of Venus by Peter Paul Rubens. What explanations do sociologists offer for changing ideals of beauty?

Gender Differences across History

Within a two-gender system, there is enormous variation of what counts as a good or bad woman. For example, how the ideal man or woman looks is itself historically contingent. Specifically, ideal feminine beauty has been a continuous site of change and contestation. Look at the seventeenth-century Rubenesque women, the voluptuous beauties who by contemporary standards are simply fat. In traditional economies where food was scarce, a plump woman was a sign of good health, wealth, and attractiveness. The long-standing preference for a robust female body has changed as industrialized societies moved from relative scarcity of food to plentifulness. Today cheaper foods are the fattening ones, and gym membership is only for those with enough disposable income. Contrary to the slogans, bigger isn't better in this economy—not if you're a woman, at least.

Accompanying this economic expansion, the transition to modern Western society also brought advances in medical knowledge and scientific discourse. By the 1920s, the female figure was standardized by the development of norms for healthy weights according to height. The fleshy Rubenses no longer fit a beauty ideal; they don't even look healthy.

Gender Differences Today

Today's idealized (white, middle-class) standards for feminine beauty in the United States present a dilemma for millions of women and girls. Approximately 3 percent of this country meets the diagnostic criteria for an eating disorder and 90 percent of that population is female (Swanson et al., 2011). In 2010, women had approximately 8.6 million cosmetic procedures. The top five cosmetic surgical procedures for women were liposuction (also the most popular procedure for men), breast augmentation, eyelid surgery, tummy tucks, and breast reduction. Americans spent almost $12.7 billion on cosmetic procedures in 2010, yet their quest for ideal beauty was likely the pursuit of an illusion. That is, women may come close but will never attain it, as the ideal itself is always evolving (ASAPS, 2011).

Dominant or "emphasized" definitions of femininity—as embodied by looks—are always undergoing change as well, from the hysterical Victorian housewife to the sporty working girl of the 1980s to today's heroically impossible supermom. This might be an easy point to grasp about femininity, but most people think that masculinity is less subject to such trends and fashions. It is always harder to denaturalize the dominant category; being the norm, it often is invisible. Among social categories, those who go unquestioned tend to be most privileged.

Hegemonic masculinity the condition in which men are dominant and privileged, and this dominance and privilege is invisivble.

In addition to a dominant image of femininity, some theorists argue that today there exists a hegemonic masculinity as well (Connell, 1987). Hegemony is the complete dominance of a group of people, a type of power so complete that it goes unnoticed by the people who are dominated. Hegemonic masculinity is so dominant that it easily escapes our attention and is regarded as the norm against which all others are judged. Erving Goffman (1963) describes this masculine ideal as a young man who is "married, white, urban, northern, heterosexual, Protestant, father, of college education, fully employed, of good complexion, weight and height, and [with] a decent record in sports."

Today's ideal man has not always been the hegemonic definition. In *Manhood in America* (1996), Michael Kimmel traces the development of masculinity in the West and finds that in the eighteenth century, the ideal man was not associated with physical fitness, money-making endeavors, or sports. Business endeavors were the boorish concerns of the rude trade classes, and physical strength undermined one's gentlemanly dispositions. Ideal masculinity in the 1700s went hand in hand with kindness and intellect, preferably a little poetry, a very different image from the modern-day ideal of the "man's man."

Over time and from place to place, gender roles are fluid, changing, and context-specific. Chapter 4 on socialization stated that gender roles are sets of behavioral norms assumed to accompany one's status as a male or female. Many of the differences we observe between men and women do not have much to do with gender differences at all; instead, the behaviors arise as a result of the different positions men and women occupy. Sociologist Cynthia Fuchs Epstein calls these "deceptive distinctions" that grossly exaggerate the actual differences between men and women (1988). What makes a man a man and not a woman? The sociological answer begins with, "It depends."

Gender roles sets of behavioral norms assumed to accompany one's status as a male or female.

Many sociologists think of gender as a major building block in the social order and as an integral element in everyday life. It is so fundamental to the way our lives go that it is often viewed as an organizing principle of everyday life, itself in need of explanation (Stacey & Thorne, 1985). That is, all social institutions and practices—education, marriage, law, the economy, health care, even baby names—are in some way tied up with gender norms and expectations. And gender crosses paths with other social statuses, such as race, class, nation, and even body type, in significant and materially consequential ways. To speak of gender as a social construction is to say that it isn't a given. Gender is a phenomenon that shapes reality and organizes our lives even if we don't realize it, or even when we wish it didn't. Therefore, it has been central to the feminist movement to unpack and understand what gender is, how it was constructed, and why it takes the forms it does.

The Woman Question

Rubin's Sex/Gender System

At the start of the feminist movement in the 1960s, theorists scrambled to find an answer to the "woman question": What explains the nearly universal dominance of men over women? What is the root of patriarchy, a system

Patriarchy a nearly universal system involving the subordination of femininity to masculinity.

involving the subordination of femininity to masculinity? Anthropologist Gayle Rubin was one of the first in a long string of thinkers to argue that the nearly universal oppression of women was in need of an explanation. In the field of anthropology, most scholars studying societies around the world had previously assumed that women's subordination was a given. If such subordination occurred everywhere, it must be fulfilling some function, and it could just as well be passed over in favor of more novel research questions.

Rubin challenged this notion and proposed the "sex/gender system" in which, she argued, every society participates in some form or other (1975). In this system, the raw materials of biological sex are transformed through kinship into asymmetrical gender statuses. She used the structural perspective of Claude Lévi-Strauss, a French anthropologist, to suggest that because of the universal taboo against incest, women are traded around kinship networks like property, and this "traffic in women" gives men certain rights over their female kin. The resulting sex/gender system, she argued, was not a given; it was the result of human interaction.

Rubin's theories made waves. Feminist thinkers widely agreed that the task at hand was to explain universal male dominance. Why were women—despite a few token examples of matrifocal or women-led tribes in the anthropology books—always on the bottom of stratification systems? Why did women in almost every society seem to get short shrift? Anthropologist Michelle Rosaldo (1974) answered that it must be women's universal association with the private sphere. Because women give birth and then rear children, they become identified with domestic life, which universally is accorded less prestige, value, and rewards than men's public sphere of work and politics. Another plausible answer to the "woman question" came from fellow anthropologist Sherry Ortner (1974), who claimed that women are furthermore identified with something that every culture defines as lower than itself—nature. A woman, she reasoned, comes to be identified with the chaos and danger of nature because of her bodily functions such as lactation and menstruation (what feminist philosopher Simone de Beauvoir [1952] has poetically described as "woman's enslavement to the species").

Parsons's Sex Role Theory

Structural functionalism theoretical tradition claiming that every society has certain structures (the family, the division of labor, or gender) that exist in order to fulfill some set of necessary functions (reproduction of the species, production of goods, etc.).

Ortner's answer to the "woman question" sounds like a plausible one. But note the binary logic at work in these anthropological accounts: culture versus nature, private versus public, man versus woman. However, the world is less rigid, more nuanced, and certainly less easily molded into binary categories than these theories suggest. What underlies these theoretical approaches is structural functionalism. This theoretical tradition dominated early anthropological thought, and it assumed that every society had certain structures (such as the family, the division of labor, or gender) that existed to fulfill some set of necessary functions. Talcott Parsons, an influential American sociologist of the 1950s, offered a widely accepted functionalist account of gender relations (Parsons, 1951). According to Parsons's sex role theory, the nuclear family is the ideal arrangement in modern societies because it fulfills the function of reproducing workers. With a work-oriented father in the public sphere and a domestic-oriented mother in the private sphere, children are most effectively reared to be future laborers who can meet the labor demands of a capitalist system. Sex, sexuality, and gender are taken to be stable and dichotomous, meaning that each has two categories. Each category is assigned a role and a given script that actors carry out according to the expectations of those roles, which are enforced by social sanctions to ensure that the actors do not forget their lines. Women and men play distinctive roles that are functional for the whole of society; a healthy, harmonious society exists when actors stick to their normal roles. Generally speaking, according to Parsons, social structures such as gender and the division of labor are held in place because they work to ensure a stable society.

In the 1950s, Talcott Parsons advanced the idea that the nuclear family effectively reared children to meet the labor demands of a capitalist system.

Sex role theory Talcott Parsons's theory that men and women perform their sex roles as breadwinners and wives/mothers, respectively, because the nuclear family is the ideal arrangement in modern societies, fulfilling the function of reproducing workers.

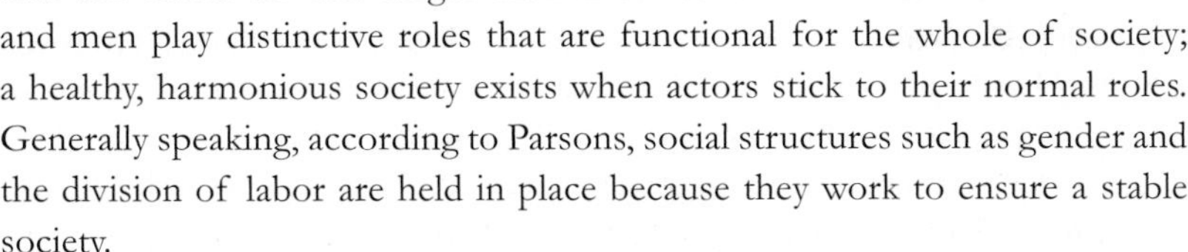

Functionalism was a hit in the 1950s; it makes intuitive sense and conveniently explains away otherwise difficult social facts fraught with exceptions. But Parsons's sex role theory falls short on several points. For starters, the argument is tautological—that is, it explains the existence of a structure in terms of its function, essentially claiming that things work the way they do because they work. In explaining a phenomenon in terms of its function, functionalists relied on the presumption that the need for the function preexists the phenomenon, a tricky leap of logical faith. Furthermore, they glossed over the possibility that other structures could fulfill the same functions.

The functionalist sex role story also does not explain how and why structures change throughout history. If traditional husband and wife sex roles were so functional, why did they change drastically in the 1970s? In Parsons's account, gender roles appear to be a matter of voluntarism, as if women and men choose, independently of external power constraints, to be housewives and breadwinners. Finally—and this is a problem with much early feminist thinking as well—sex and gender are regarded as being composed of dichotomous roles, when these categories are, in fact, fuzzy, flexible, and variable in combination with other social positions, such as race and class.

Psychoanalytic Theories

Where functionalism focuses too much, perhaps, on society as a whole, Freudian theorists have provided an overly individualistic, psychoanalytic account of sex roles. The father of psychoanalysis, Sigmund Freud (1856–1939), famously quipped, "Anatomy is destiny." Although biological determinism plays a major role in Freudian theory, so does the idea that gender develops through family socialization.

According to Freud's developmental psychology, girls and boys develop masculine and feminine personality structures through early interactions with their parents. Boys, so the story goes, have a tormented time achieving masculinity because they must resolve the oedipal complex. In this stage of development, around age 3, every normal boy experiences heterosexual love for his attentive mother. But he realizes quickly that he will be castrated (psychologically, not literally) by his father if he continues to fancy his mother. To resolve the oedipal stage, the boy rejects his mother, in turn emulating his emotionally distant father and developing rigid ego boundaries.

Girls do not experience quite the same resolution to their analogous "penis envy." When a little girl realizes that she lacks the plumbing to have sexual relations with her mother, she experiences penis envy toward her father. However, she ultimately realizes that one day she too can have a baby, thus providing feminine gratification. Girls end up identifying with their mothers, growing up with less rigid ego boundaries and more easily connecting with others than boys do.

Feminist psychoanalyst Nancy Chodorow (1978) applied Freud's theory to answer a particular version of the "woman question"—namely, why are women predominantly the caregivers? She reasoned that parents' unequal involvement in child rearing was a partial cause for the universal oppression of women. Her answer was that mothering by women is reproduced in a cycle of role socialization, in which little girls learn to identify as mothers and little boys as fathers. Social structures such as gender roles and the division of labor induce the psychological process of forming a gender identity, and they in turn reproduce themselves when women raise children and men work outside the home. Chodorow argued that egalitarian relations between the sexes would be possible if men shared the mothering.

Carol Gilligan (1982) also adapted Freudian psychology to make the case that men and women have different ways of thinking. By her account, women make major life decisions (such as choosing whether or not to have an abortion) based on what she calls an "ethics of care." Women, she claimed, tend to view the world as composed of human connections and relationships. In contrast, men make decisions by adhering to a system of rules. For them, the world is governed by impersonal, abstract rules and notions of justice.

Gilligan found evidence of men's and women's "different voices" in the playground observations of sociologist Janet Lever. Little boys, observed Lever, tend to play competitive, rule-intensive games (like war), whereas little girls play cooperative and people-based games (like house). Lever also found that when a conflict erupted on the playground, boys argued with appeals to the rules of the game. They made and judged claims such as "It's not fair!" and then were able to continue their game. Girls, however, played shorter and less complex games. When a conflict broke out, they were more likely to bend the rules to spare each other's feelings, or they would just give up and quit (Lever, 1976).

What did sociologist Janet Lever observe about the difference between the types of games that boys play versus those favored by girls?

If the "different" theoretical approaches of Chodorow and Gilligan sound reasonable, let's look at two variations on Freudian explanations for why girls and boys turn out the way they do. Melanie Klein (1882–1960) expanded Freud's account of child development to emphasize the importance of the mother's role. She claimed that boys suffer breast envy (Klein, 1949). Jacqueline Stevens went further, arguing that boys suffer from pregnancy envy on their way to acquiring a masculine identity that focuses on the acquisition of property and territory, through finance and war, in lieu of the baby they secretly lament not being able to have (Stevens, 2006).

Before you see a psychoanalyst to discuss your own penis or pregnancy envy, consider the biological reductionism in all these psychological accounts. For starters, Freud's theories lacked empirical evidence and were based on the model of a two-parent nuclear family. Most of you reading this probably did not grow up in the traditional family setting on which Chodorow and Gilligan based their research—a white, middle-class, nuclear family with a working father and stay-at-home mother. Sociologist Carol Stack underscored this point in her ethnography of a poor black community. In *All Our Kin* (1974), she finds that the division between male and female roles and attitudes is not as clear-cut as Freud would have us think. Caregiving is a valued responsibility for both men and women, who are oriented toward a larger network of community and family.

Moreover, Chodorow, Gilligan, Klein, and Stevens take for granted a binary sex/gender system, whereas we know that those categories are much more fluid in real life. These psychological theories of gender development contain elements of essentialist thinking as well. Recall that in essentialist arguments, social behavior is reduced to natural, biologically determined behavior. On the extreme end of essentialist thought is Freud, who claimed that "anatomy is destiny." Although Chodorow and Gilligan move away from such a reductionist stance by locating the root of gender differences in the household division of labor, they both treat men and women as agents who have inherent and necessary personality traits. Gilligan argues that not only are men and women inherently different, but women are so much the better because they're more relational and connected to others. Feminist historian Joan W. Scott (1988) calls this the "herstory" approach in women's history, in which feminists try so hard to include women's experiences that they end up assessing everything women do as superb. Such theorists fail to recognize that not all women adopt an ethics of care or relational orientation.

Conflict Theories

By the 1980s, another wave of thinkers began to tackle an issue missing from earlier discussions of the "woman question": power. Conflict theorists mixed old-school Marxism with feminism to claim that gender, not class, was the driving force of history. Socialist feminists, also known as radical feminists, claimed that the root of all social relations, including relations of production, stemmed from unequal gender relations.

Economist Heidi Hartmann (1981) and legal theorist Catharine MacKinnon (1983), for example, both analyzed how capitalism combines with patriarchy to make women economically dependent on men's incomes. This means that in a capitalist society, women have a disadvantaged position in the job market and within the family. Capitalists (that is, men) in turn reap all the benefits of women's subordination. When women are subordinate, men benefit. To radical feminists, gender inequality is first and foremost about power inequalities, and gender differences (as in personality development) emerge from there. However, what lies beneath these conflict theories is yet another variant of essentialism. They basically posited that the world is divided into two groups: men and women (red flag number one). These two groups are necessarily pitted against each other in a struggle for resources (red flag number two). Again, men and women are reduced to automatons in a static battle, which women always lose.

"Doing Gender": Microinteractionist Theories

A social theory is useful only if it helps you understand the social world in which you live. Of course, there are power differentials and forces of socialization that operate in the world. But men and women act and interact in a variety of ways and with unlimited possibilities for outcomes. Gender is also a process, as social constructionists have argued. Candace West and Don H. Zimmerman, for example, argue in their influential article "Doing Gender" (1987) that gender is not a fixed identity that we take with us into our interactions. Rather, it is the product of those interactions. In this framework, gender is a matter of active doing, not simply a matter of natural being. To be a man or a woman, they argue, is to perform masculinity or femininity constantly.

Many conflict theorists argue that patriarchal capitalists benefit through systems that subordinate women. For instance, many cotton mills in the nineteenth and early twentieth centuries hired young, unmarried women and required them to live in company boarding houses in order to regulate their behavior.

The "doing gender" perspective is rooted in Erving Goffman's dramaturgical theory, symbolic interactionism, and ethnomethodology. That is, West and Zimmerman argue that people create their social realities and identities through interactions with one another. Unlike the structural functionalists, psychoanalysts, and conflict theorists, however, social constructionists view gender roles as having open-ended scripts. Perhaps individuals come to the stage situated differently according to their place in power hierarchies or personality development, but their lines and gestures are far from being predetermined. Regardless of social location, individuals are always free to act, sometimes in unexpected ways that change the course of the play. But by and large, as a result of "doing gender," people contribute to, reaffirm, and reproduce masculine dominance and feminine submissiveness.

Black Feminism

If gender is a performance, it is much more than a set of neutral scripts that we voluntarily follow. Our actions are influenced by structural forces that we might not even be aware of, such as class or race privilege. As Patricia Hill Collins (1990) claims, we "do" a lot more than gender; gender intersects with race, class, nation, religion, and so forth. Black feminists have made the case that early liberal feminism was largely by, about, and for white middle-class women. In trying to answer the "woman question" and explain women's oppression, early feminists assumed that all women were in the same oppressed boat. In so doing, they effaced multiple lines of fragmentation and difference into one simple category: woman. For example, by championing women's rights to work outside the home in *The Feminine Mystique*, leading second-wave feminist Betty Friedan (1963/1997) ignored the experiences of thousands of working-class and nonwhite women who were already working, sometimes holding down two jobs to support their families.

"Woman" is not a stable or obvious category of identity. Rather, women are differentially located in what Collins calls a "matrix of domination." A 40-year-old poor, black, and straight single mother living in rural Georgia will not have the same conception of what it means to be a woman as a 25-year-old professional, white, single lesbian in Chicago. More fundamentally, she argues, black women face unique oppressions that white women don't. For instance, black women experience motherhood in ways that differ from the white masculinist ideal of the family, as "bloodmothers," "othermothers," and "community othermothers," thus revealing that white masculine notions of the world are sometimes irrelevant to the daily lives of black women (Collins, 1990).

Gender, sexual orientation, race, class, nation, ability, and other factors all intersect. Just as some women enjoy privilege by virtue of their wealth, class, education, and skin color, some men are disadvantaged by their lack of these same assets. As bell hooks (1984) noted, if women's liberation is aimed at

Patricia Hill Collins criticized feminist leaders such as Betty Friedan (pictured above in the red dress), Billie Jean King (in tan pants and a blue shirt on the left), or Bella Abzug (in gray dress, with the hat) for ignoring the experiences of thousands of working-class and nonwhite women.

making women the social equals of men, women should first stop and consider which men they would like to equal. Certainly, not all men are privileged over all women. Making universal comparisons of men to women misses these nuances and implicitly excludes marginally positioned people from the discussion.

Power comes from many different angles; it doesn't sit evenly on a plane for all women. When the black activist Sojourner Truth (1797–1883) asked, "Ain't I a woman?" (1851), she summed up some elusive philosophical questions: What is woman? Who counts as a woman and why?

Postmodern Theories

As perspectives have expanded and previously rigid categories have begun to crumble, the validity of the "woman question" is itself now in question. For instance, anthropologist Oyèrónké Oyˇewùmí argues that the "woman question" is a product of uniquely Western thought and cannot be applied to African societies. In *The Invention of Women* (1997), she presents ethnographic research of Yoruban society in West Africa, which she claims was once a genderless society. In Yoruba, before the arrival of anthropologists, villagers did not group themselves as men or women or use body markers at all. Rather, they ranked themselves into strata by seniority. When Western feminist scholars arrived on the scene, presuming the preexistence of gender relations, they, of course, found a system of gender. But this system of categories, distinct males and females, indicates a Western cultural logic, what Oyˇewùmí has termed "bio-logic."

Bio-logic runs deep in our cultural experiences and understandings of gender. It acts as a sort of filter through which all knowledge of the world runs, but in fact there may be different ways of knowing outside such a paradigm. But if "woman" is such an unstable category—one that is merely "performed," as postmodern theorist Judith Butler says, one that is so fragmented and trapped in discourse—how are we supposed to study it? Feminists must have some sturdy ground on which to unite, build coalitions, and tackle injustice. Philosopher Susan Bordo (1990) provides a pragmatic buoy by arguing that there are hierarchal and binary power structures out there that do still oppress women. The postmodern emphasis on fragmented identity, blurring of sex and gender boundaries, and gender skepticism won't get gender theory anywhere when it comes to addressing issues such as the wage gap, eating disorders, or rape. (See Chapter 18 for a fuller discussion of postmodernism.)

Middle-Range Approaches

You have now traveled the full Möbius strip in gender theory. From deterministic structural functionalism at the start all the way to free-floating deconstruction of identity at the finish, these are the basics of the history of feminist thought. Where do we go from here? Theories of gender relations range from macro to micro, deterministic to playful, rooted in the body to uprooted entirely, but the test of a good theory always lies in its usefulness: How useful is this theory for discovering the world and explaining our lived experiences and practices? Using this measure, you'll probably find that the most useful theories are what sociologist Robert Merton called "middle-range" theories, which connect our lived day-to-day experiences to larger social forces. Robert Connell, in *Gender and Power* (1987), takes a middle-range approach to gender by using Anthony Giddens's structuration theory to claim that the social and the personal always depend on each other. Connell formulates gender structures as a kind of feedback loop (like the Möbius strip), weaving individual practice back into social institutions, which in turn influence and socialize individuals into gendered beings. In this light, gender is a process linking individuals and structures into unequal but changeable social relations. The "woman question" becomes less a matter of trying to explain universal (and seemingly inevitable) male dominance and more a matter of attempting to account for how people navigate within structures like gender.

Sociology in the Bedroom

Sex. You think it's the most personal, intimate act. The bedroom is surely the one place where the sociological imagination is the last thing you'll need. But a sociological approach can reveal some startling insights about the social construction of sexuality. Connections may be found between the sheets and history, desire and science, how we do it and how it, in turn, organizes what we do, as well as with whom and with what meanings. As expected, an excavation into the social construction of sexuality divulges a surprising amount of variation in what is considered normal bedroom behavior. By exposing different social patterns of sexuality, throughout history and across cultures, the sociologist can trace unequal power relations and show how sexuality expresses, represses, and elucidates those relations.

Sexuality in Other Times and Places

Among the ancient Greeks, for example, homosexual relationships were accepted and supposed to be patterned on an active–passive distinction (although historians have shown that many exceptions existed). The active partner was supposed to be older or higher in status than the passive partner. To flip the rules was a violation, and it was considered shameful for a master or noble to be penetrated by a younger man. A more extreme and brutal example of sexual relations founded on power relations can be found today in the social orders in U.S. prisons, where rape is about power: who is in charge, who is being penetrated, and who is normal versus deviant. Prison rape may not be primarily about seeking sexual gratification; it is reported that few prison rapists climax during the act. In prison, the homosexual act is often seen as something altogether distinct from homosexual identity.

Or, consider sexual normality among the Sambia, a mountain people in Papua New Guinea. Anthropologist Gilbert Herdt (1981) reported that fellatio played a significant role in a boy's transition into manhood. Young boys are initiated into manhood by a daily ritual of fellatio on older boys and men. By taking in the vital life liquid (semen) of older men, boys prepare themselves to be warriors and sexual partners with women. Fellatio, for Sambia boys, then, is the only way to become "real" men.

An ancient Greek image of two male lovers. How can comparing social patterns of sexuality across cultures and throughout history help sociologists understand modern sexuality?

Other cultures' attitudes toward homosexuality are on a whole different level. Both the Siwans of North Africa and the Keraki, also in New Guinea, prefer homosexuality to heterosexuality, for fairly straightforward, practical reasons (Kimmel, 2000). Because every male is homosexual during his adolescence and then bisexual after heterosexual marriage, the limited straight sex keeps down the birthrate. In these cultures with scant resources, homosexuality makes practical sense to limit the chances of teen pregnancy and overpopulation.

There is enormous variation in how humans have sex and what it means to them. Mouth-to-mouth kissing, common in Western cultures, is unthinkable among the Thonga and Sirono cultures: "But that's where you put food!" (Kimmel, 2000). American middle-class couples have sex a few nights a week for about 15 minutes a pop; the people of Yapese cultures near Guam engage in sex once a month. Marquesan men of French Polynesia are said to have anywhere from 10 to 30 orgasms a night! Which of these is "normal"?

The Social Construction of Sexuality

By treating sexuality as a social construction—that is, as always shaped by social factors—the sociologist would argue that the notion of normal, especially behind closed bedroom doors, is always contested. In other words, there is no natural way of doing it. If an essentially right way existed, we wouldn't be able to find such wild and woolly variation throughout history and across cultures. Starting from the view that sex itself is a social creation, sociologists tend to argue that humans have sexual plumbing and potential but no sexuality until they are located in a social environment. The range of normal and abnormal is itself a construction, a production of society. The study of this range can lead the willing sociologist into an exploration of the social relations on which sex is built.

Sexuality and Power Marxist feminists, for instance, argue that sexuality in America is an expression of the unequal power balance between men and women. Catharine MacKinnon (1983) argued that in male-dominated societies, sexuality is constructed as a gender binary, with men on top and women on the bottom (literally and figuratively). To MacKinnon, sexuality is the lynchpin of gender inequality, an expression of male control. In a male-dominated state, where men have the power to create the world from their allegedly more objective point of view, says MacKinnon, sex is rape and rape is sex: "Man fucks woman; subject verb object."

Adrienne Rich (1980) called sexuality in America a "compulsory heterosexuality." This "political institution," at least for some women, is not a preference but something that has been imposed, managed, organized, and enforced to serve a male-dominated capitalist system. According to Rich, women come to see heterosexuality as the norm, when it is, in fact, a mechanism integral to sustaining women's social subordination. Although these arguments are provocative (and strongly worded), in the end, they also reflect essentialist and reductionist views of sex. Surely not all women are mere objects or are duped into exploitative relations with their oppressive male partners.

Sexuality: Middle-Range Approaches University of Michigan anthropologist Ann Stoler takes a middle-range theoretical approach to show how sexual desire was constructed in the nineteenth-century Dutch East Indies and French Indochina colonies. Most people take it for granted that the categories of colonized and colonizer were sharp and clear. But as Stoler finds in *Carnal Knowledge and Imperial Power* (2002), a lot of work went into maintaining those often blurry categories, and sex was a key marker of boundaries. According to early Dutch colonial policy, for instance, European men could legally couple with native prostitutes or concubines. But when the imperialist agenda came under threat of rebellion, concubinage ended, racial boundaries hardened, and the colonies prohibited social or sexual relations between natives and colonizers. Previously desirable natives, earlier the stuff that colonial fantasies were made of, were recast as off-limits and deviant "others." Sexuality is often the most salient marker of otherness. Who is allowed to do what, when, and to whom reveals much about the kinds of social relations that structure a society.

Homosexuality The connections between sex and power are best exemplified in the social construction of the homosexual, the social identity of a person who has sexual attraction to and/or relations with other persons of the same sex. This is indeed a curious phrase, "the making of" a person. For most of the past century, the dominant view has been that individuals are born either

Homosexual the social identity of a person who has sexual attraction to and/or relations with other persons of the same sex.

homosexual or heterosexual, gay or straight, queer or normal. Sexual orientation was thought of as a kind of personhood automatically acquired at birth or something carried in our genes (despite documented cases of identical twins, one of whom is straight and the other gay). But recall the Greeks' homosexual love, prison rape, and the Sambian rites of manhood. Men in these cultures engage in homosexual acts without adopting a homosexual identity. When do acts, behaviors, or desires crystallize into identities?

Before 1850, there was no such thing as a homosexual. Sure, people engaged in homosexual behaviors. But around 1850, the homosexual identity was born. The French philosopher Michel Foucault (1926–84) led the way to poststructuralist notions of the body and sexuality as historical productions. In *The History of Sexuality* (1978), Foucault made the case that the body is "in the grip" of cultural practices. That is, there is no presocial or natural body; instead, culture is always already inscribed on our bodies. It's a by now familiar stance on the social construction of the body and on the permanent intermingling of the biological and the social. But Foucault further argued that the way we know our bodies is linked to power, and knowledge and power go hand in hand. As the population expanded in nineteenth-century Europe, newly formed states and their administrators developed a concern for population

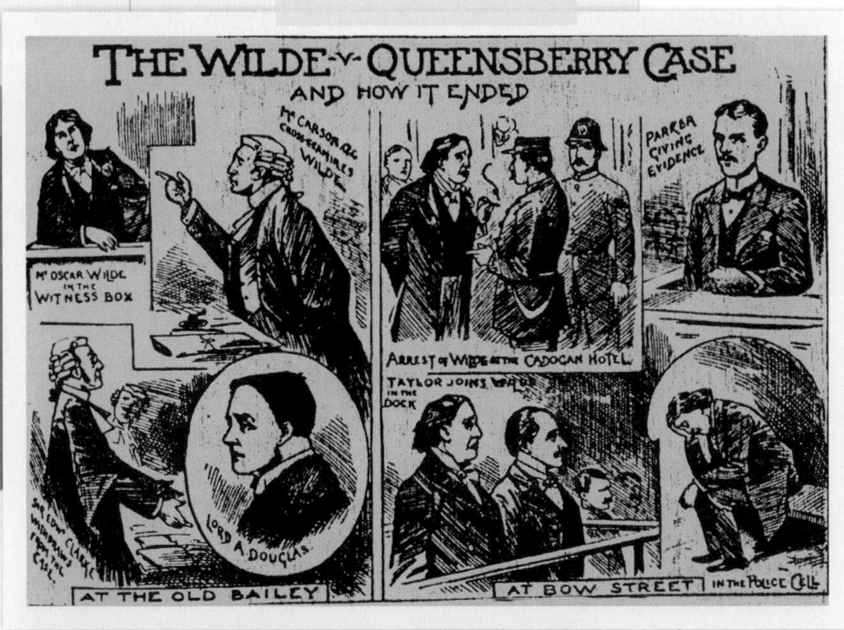

An 1895 cartoon illustrating Oscar Wilde's sodomy trial. Wilde was convicted of gross indecency for his homosexual relationship with Lord Alfred Douglas. He served two years of hard labor in prison.

management. The rise of scientific ways of thinking at the time led to the creation of what Foucault calls "bio-power," the observation of populations.

Discourses of sexuality had by then surfaced. People talked about sex, scientists studied it, and government officials tried to regulate it, whereas a century before all this sex talk did not exist. With the development of the biological and human sciences in the nineteenth century, doctors wanted to know which kinds of sex were normal and which were deviant, and new attention was paid to policing those differences. By the late 1800s, "Homosexuality appeared as one of the forms of sexuality when it was transposed from the practice of sodomy onto a kind of interior androgyny, a hermaphrodism of the soul" (Foucault, 1978). In Foucault's account, homosexuality comes back to the efforts of government bureaucrats trying to assert their power (that of the state) over human populations.

This new homosexual body that had been constructed became a personality type, and a deviant one at that. The American Psychiatric Association and the American Psychological Association listed homosexuality on their list of mental disorders until 1973. Homosexuals were regarded as needing to be regulated, observed, studied, and most important, controlled. Because everyone was capable of, or in danger of, sexual deviance, the urgency to confess one's sexuality grew, as did the scientific need for public surveillance. Who was gay? How could a homosexual be detected? Anyone could be a pervert—the person next to you, even you!

To regulate potentially perverse bodies, new modes of social control emerged in the transition to modern structures of state power. Coercion and direct force were replaced with more efficient forms of restraint: self-surveillance and what Foucault called *normalization*. Under a sovereign king (that is, before the modern state), discipline was administered on a scaffold or stockade, by direct punitive physical force. In modern society, discipline was administered by the self: "There is no need for arms, physical violence, material constraints. Just a gaze. An inspecting gaze, a gaze which each individual under its weight will end by interiorizing to the point that he is his own overseer, each individual thus exercising this surveillance over, and against, himself." It was, Foucault adds, "a superb formula" (Foucault, 1980).

The act of sodomy became synonymous with the person who performs it. Even our language reflects the way sexual behavior becomes more than a single event among the many other behaviors that make up an individual's life. Here's what I mean. If a man roasts a whole pig—a serious, time-consuming undertaking that requires research, dedication, and planning—he is not known ever after as a "pig roaster" or even as a gourmand. He's still just Bob from down the block who hosted one heck of a barbeque. But if a man has anal sex with another man—something that takes less time and probably less dedication and research than roasting a pig—he becomes a sodomite, a homosexual, gay, or whatever terminology might fit the context. This was not always so. At one point, what happened in the bedroom stayed there. But over the last century what happened behind closed doors was outed and a whole new body and being were produced. Today our society places a huge emphasis—our entire selfhood, according to Foucault—on sexuality. Now what you do (and with whom) defines who you are: not just how others see you, but how you experience yourself. The framing of homosexuality as a comprehensive social identity, in fact, produced homosexuals, so that today 9 million Americans identify themselves as homosexual or bisexual (Gates, 2011). There are hundreds of gay pride parades every year all over the country, and gay marriage legislation has been hotly debated in all 50 states.

Thousands participate in a 2003 gay pride parade.

Consider the widely used argument against lesbian and gay couplings: "It's unnatural," meaning that sex is supposed to be about reproduction. This is a popular argument against same-sex marriages, that such couples are underproductive. However, homosexuality occurs widely in the animal kingdom; one of our closest primate cousins, the bonobo, practices homosexuality (Parker, 2007). Though based on questionable data, Alfred Kinsey's 1948 study *Sexual Behavior in the Human Male* suggested that at least 10 percent of men were homosexual. He challenged the psychiatric model of homosexuals as perverse and abnormal and instead viewed sexuality as a continuum (Kinsey, 1948). Most people, he claimed, experience both heterosexual and homosexual feelings and behaviors. Kinsey's figures have since been disputed—his sampling was not representative of the U.S. population as a whole—but the basic idea holds. Across the globe and throughout history, there has been more or less the same degree of homosexual behavior. Social perceptions of homosexuals, however, are in flux.

Studies of homosexuality today approach the phenomenon not as being located in a unified, stable, or even identifiable type of person, "the homosexual." Rather, this fluid identity intersects with other social positions, such as class, race, age, location, ability, and gender. But how does gender influence sexuality? We've seen already how sex and gender do not match up; female plumbing does not always neatly correspond to a feminine gendered identity. Yale historian George Chauncey makes the case in *Gay New York* (1994) that in early-twentieth-century New York, an emerging working-class gay world was split between masculine men and the effeminate men who solicited them. As long as men stuck to their masculine gender scripts, no matter how often they engaged in gay sex, they were not considered abnormal like the girly men, who were derided for their effeminacy.

The reverse is true among the *travesti,* transgender prostitutes in Brazil. Anthropologist Don Kulick conducted an ethnography of the *travesti*, males

How do *travesti* challenge common binary models of understanding gender and sexuality?

who adopt female names, clothing styles, hairstyles, cosmetic practices, and linguistic pronouns; ingest female hormones; and inject industrial silicone directly into their bodies to give themselves breasts and round buttocks or *bunda* (Kulick, 1998). They display all the stereotypically feminine traits, yet they do not self-identify as women. In fact, they think it is both repugnant and impossible for men to try to become women. Kulick argues that in Brazil, gender is determined by sexual practice; "what one does in bed has immediate and lasting consequences for the way one is perceived (and the way one can perceive oneself) as a gendered being. If one penetrates, in this particular configuration of sexuality and gender, one is a 'man.' If one expresses interest in the penis of a male, and especially if one 'gives'—allows oneself to be penetrated by a male—then one is no longer a man." However, the *travesti* do not think they are women, they think of themselves as *travesti,* men who emulate women, but are not women. The primacy of penetration as a determinant of gender is common across cultures and challenges Americans to look beyond chromosomes and hormones to practices and cultural context.

Why Not Talk about Teen Sex?

The many ways of doing it—over time and across cultures—complicate the romantic ideal of love in modern America. Arguably, a glaring discrepancy exists between this ideal and reality. In 1948, Kinsey found high rates of bisexual activity—as many as 46 percent of males and between 6 and 14 percent of females engaged in it. He also documented a wide variety of sexual positions, preferences, desires, and extramarital activity among men and women. The Reverend Billy Graham denied the findings and claimed that Kinsey "certainly could not have interviewed any of the millions of born-again Christian women in this country who put the highest price on virtue, decency and modesty." Indeed, Kinsey's sample was biased by the willingness of those who participated. Although this bias calls the exact figure into question, his study was a landmark for bringing to light a wide range of sexual practices and preferences in the U.S. population.

Federal funding for studies of sexual activity has since come under attack in the name of decency. Witness the defunding of the American Teenage Study in 1992, which some politicians called one of those "reprehensive sex surveys undertaken to legitimize homosexuality and other sexually promiscuous lifestyles" (Remez, 2000).

From Hooking up to Virginity Pledges Sometimes, the policies meant to achieve one end backfire and cause the opposite outcome, despite the best intentions. Government efforts about teen sex provide one example. Recent studies have described the blasé attitude that contemporary American teenagers supposedly bring to their love lives. When sociologist Paula England surveyed students at one Midwestern university about their sex lives, half reported that their previous sexual partner was someone they had slept with only once. Here's how she explained hook-up culture, which has replaced dating as the route to romance on college campuses around the country. She did her first surveys at Northwestern where, "before people ever go on a date they hook up." Lest there be any confusion: a hook-up is not sex . . . unless it is. A hook-up means, "Something sexual happens, that 'something sexual' is not always intercourse, often in fact [in] the majority of cases it isn't, and there is no necessary implication that anybody's interested in a relationship, but they *might* be interested." Dating is infrequent, but it is not dead. It is "charged with more meaning now, and it's more likely to be leading to a relationship." Furthermore, "there's a strong norm that relationships should be monogamous and marriages should be monogamous and that people eventually want to get to monogamy and a marriage. They're just putting it off a lot longer. That's really what's changed I think" (Conley, 2009d).

Why so many short-lived hook-ups instead of longer-term relationships? For one thing, the students are not looking to begin families anytime soon. For another, relationships are just more work. England found that heterosexual males are not necessarily expected to sexually satisfy the women they hook up with, but the opposite is true when they are in relationships. In a hook-up, "a real gender inequality is if there's oral sex but they didn't have intercourse, sometimes it's reciprocal, but if it is not reciprocal it's much more likely that the woman is servicing the guy than vice versa. So it seems like the hook-ups are prioritizing male pleasure" (Conley, 2009d). In a hook-up culture, what might determine whether a pair continues to hook up or moves on to new partners? England has a theory that goes like this:

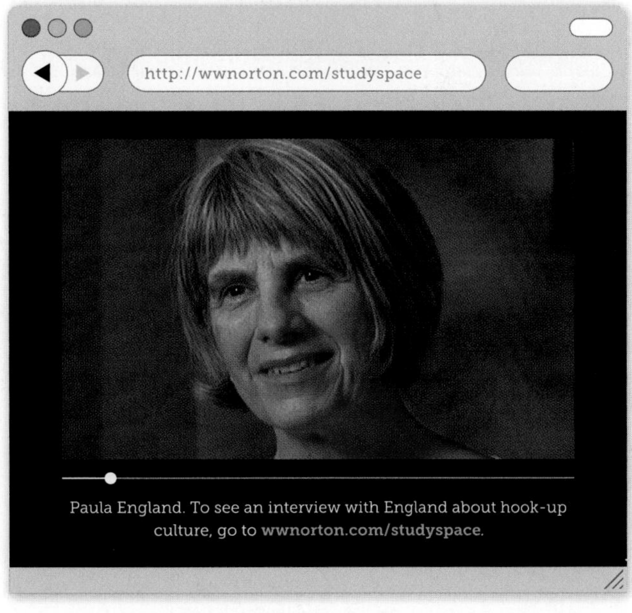

Paula England. To see an interview with England about hook-up culture, go to **wwnorton.com/studyspace**.

> Partner-specific investment may well be important. In other words, you know, our ability to please partners may not just be

generally what have we learned from a lifetime of experience but what have we actually learned about this particular partner and what works for them and what they like and what they need . . . if it's hook-up number two she's more likely to have an orgasm than if it's one, and if it's three more likely, and if it's four even more likely. (Conley, 2009d)

She also noted that these hook-ups rarely produce babies—70 percent of students used a condom the last time they had vaginal sex.

Here are more numbers: Just fewer than 50 percent of American teenagers over the age of 14 tell surveyors that they have had sexual intercourse (Figure 8.1), but this rate is not growing; it has remained more or less steady since 2003 (CDC, 2010a). Boys probably lie more often about the extent of their sexual experience (citing the proverbial girlfriend in a different state), and girls possibly downplay their sexual activity. Many of those who have not had intercourse are still sexually active in other ways. As we learned in Chapter 5, a good two-thirds of American teens are already having sex or are very close to doing it. Teenagers' romantic interludes last about 15 months on average, leaving them plenty of time before marriage (average age 25 for women and 27 for men) to have many partners. To top it off, most adolescents with a sexually transmitted disease don't know that they are infected. All these factors combine to put American teenagers at high risk for STDs, which have been increasing dramatically since the 1970s.

So what's a public health officer to do? During its years in office, the Bush administration (2001–09) advocated a "virginity pledge" and other abstinence policies, and the abstinence advocacy group True Love Waits says that

Figure 8.1: Percentage of High School Students Who Have Had Sex, 1991–2009

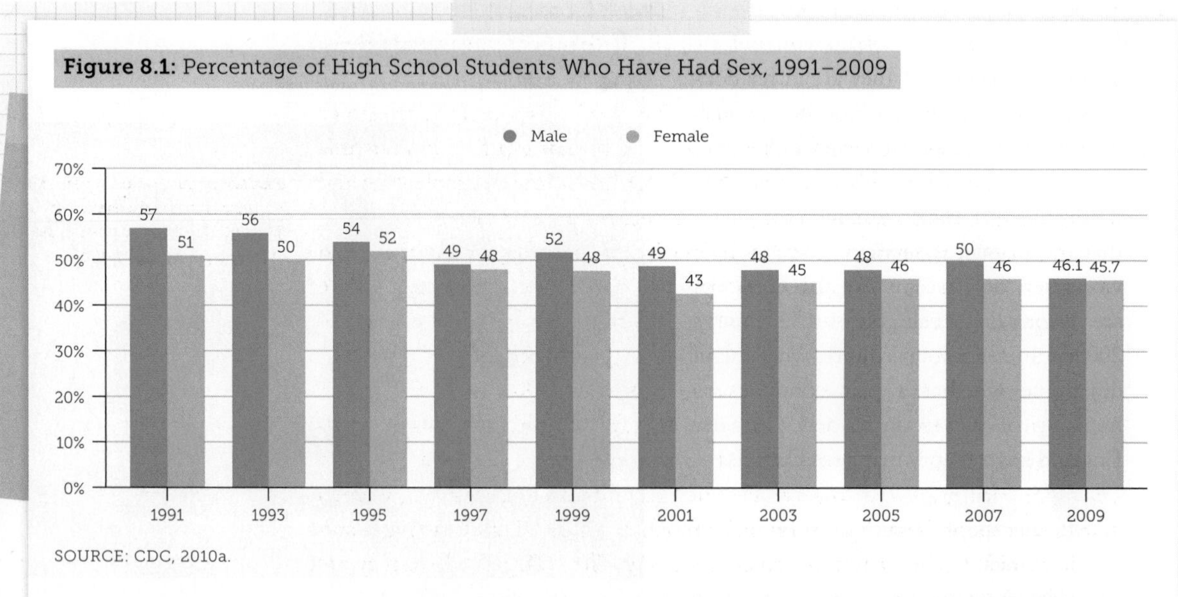

SOURCE: CDC, 2010a.

2.5 million young people have made the virginity pledge since 1993 (Herbert, 2011). As it turns out, the pledge does, on average, delay the onset of sexual activity as well as reduce a teenager's number of sexual partners, according to the National Longitudinal Study of Adolescent Health (Brückner & Bearman, 2005). The study, funded by the Centers for Disease Control and Prevention and the National Science Foundation, followed the sexual activity of 12- to 18-year-olds for six years. It found that teenagers who took the virginity pledge had about the same rates of sexually transmitted diseases as those who never made the pledge. So when sex happens (as it inevitably does), it's much more likely to come in a fit of irresponsible, unexpected passion. Among the pledgers, only 40 percent ended up using a condom during sex, compared with 60 percent of teens who had not pledged.

Teenagers at Silver Ring Thing, a faith-based abstinence-only program held at a church in Canton, Ohio. According to research by social scientists, what are the results of abstinence-only programs?

Growing Up, Getting Ahead, and Falling Behind

In January 2005, Harvard President Larry Summers was a guest speaker at a conference called "Diversifying the Science and Engineering Work Force." He was invited to deliver a provocative address, and indeed, his speech was so provocative that it sparked a media frenzy termed "Gendergate" by journalists. Summers stated that at the highest levels of performance, men might have an innate advantage over women in scientific aptitude and that genetic differences could explain the scarcity of female "hard" scientists at elite universities (Atlas, 2005). Critics referred to the speech as a blatant example in academia of sexism, in which a person's sex is the basis for prejudicial discrimination and where sex may matter more than a person's performance or merits.

Sexism occurs when a person's sex or gender is the basis for judgment, discrimination, and hatred against him or her.

Summers's explanation threw his university into turmoil and eventually led to his resignation, but the general problem he described is a real one. In 2000, although 48.2 percent of students who graduated with a bachelor's degree in math from a university ranked in the top 50 were female, only 8.3 percent of math faculty members were women (Nelson & Rogers, 2004). A flip side to this controversy is that women are overtaking men in college enrollment (Figure 8.2). Fifty-five percent of college students in 2006 were women (Wang & Parker, 2011). However, despite their increased enrollment, women remain over-represented in traditionally feminine fields of study: the arts and the humanities. Men also outnumber women at elite colleges, where they are groomed for high-power professions in finance, law, or politics.

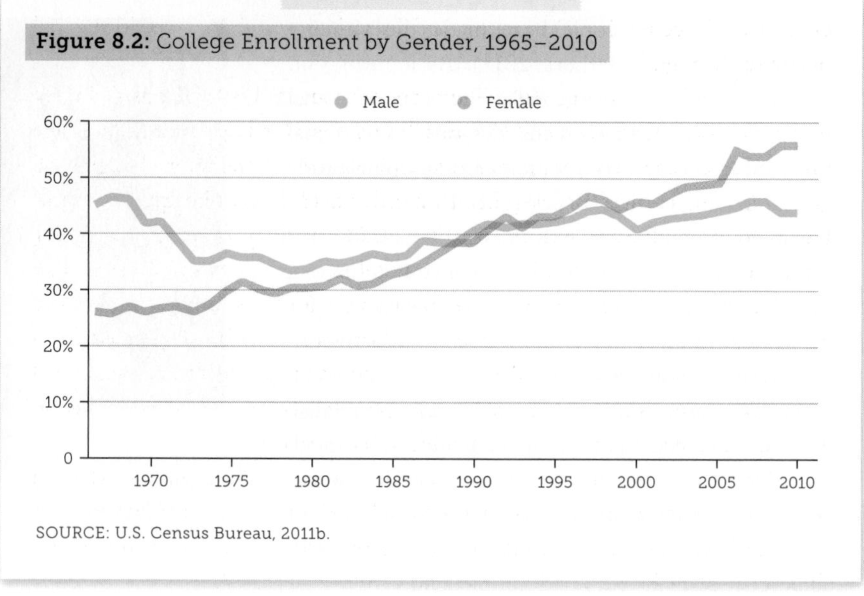

Within academia, men dominate traditionally masculine fields such as math and physics. Not surprisingly, positions in these "hard" sciences pay more than those in "soft" ones. The average physics college professor begins with a starting salary of about $55,000; the average social scientist starts out at $39,000 (*sigh*) (American Association of University Professors, 2007). Do men become mathematicians and women literary critics because they are hardwired to do so? Not even Larry Summers would attribute gender segmentation in education entirely to genes. He suggested that it may be one of many factors, and even that got him into trouble. In fact, what he argued was that there was greater variance (not a higher average) in math scores for boys. Because the very highest math scorers end up at the top, and because boys had a bigger spread, the very few at the top tended to be male (as well as the few at the bottom end), even if average scores were similar across gender.

Whether or not Summers's argument holds water, we do know that men and women vary in thousands of major and minor measures. It starts at birth. The average male newborn weighs 2 ounces more than the average female newborn. For infant death rates, however, the disadvantage is tilted against males, who are at higher risk of death than females. Psychologist Carol Gilligan contends that by adolescence, the disadvantages are stacked against girls, who "lose their voices" as they suffer blows to their self-confidence. Eating disorders disproportionately affect girls in adolescence compared with their male peers. More than half of teenaged girls are on diets or think they should be. What's more, girls more frequently report low self-esteem, more girls attempt suicide, and more girls report experiencing some form of sexual harassment in school. Psychologist Mary Pipher's *Reviving Ophelia* (1994) details the fiery demise of adolescent girls: "Something dramatic happens to girls in early adolescence. . . . They crash and burn in a social and developmental Bermuda Triangle."

Psychologist Christina Hoff Sommers challenges this "girl crisis" in *The War against Boys: How Misguided Feminism Is Harming Our Young Men* (2000). She finds that because they are inadvertently penalized for the shortchanging of girls, boys are the ones suffering in education and adolescent health. For example, although females in general attempt suicide twice as frequently as males, boys ages 15 to 19 succeed in killing themselves four times more often than girls. Teenaged girls may sneak more cigarettes than boys, but boys are more likely to be involved in crime, alcohol, and drugs and to be suspended from school or drop out. Male teens are also 40 percent more likely to be victimized by violent crime, and that's even taking rape into account. It seems being an adolescent stinks, no matter what gender (or sex) you are.

What accounts for the wide range of statistical differences that exist between men and women? Essentialists might refer to natural sex differences, but sociologists are apt to call these same differences "deceptive distinctions," those that arise because of the particular roles individuals come to occupy (Epstein, 1988). Why do men think in the abstract terms of rationality and justice? Because their employment possibilities are more likely to include jobs with these demands. Why are women so good at mothering? Because their bleak employment prospects encourage them to accept domestic roles and rely on a male's salary. Who is more relational and who is more rational? Anthropologists William and Jean O'Barr find that the true test of what type of language an individual uses during testimony in court is the witness's occupation, not gender (O'Barr, 1995; Kimmel, 2000). Physicists tend to speak in more abstract terms, teachers in more relational ones, regardless of gender. Once such deceptive distinctions are revealed, it is easy to flip the essentialist rhetoric to see that gender differences are a product of gender inequality, not the cause. Physicists speak in more abstract terms, teachers in more rational ones because their jobs demand it. The question then shifts to, Why do men and women end up disproportionately split into occupations by gender? We need to peel back another layer of the gender onion.

Gender Inequality in the Classroom

We can find one answer (or onion layer) in the educational system. As we saw in our discussion of gender-role socialization in Chapter 4, the classroom functions as a sort of gender training ground for boys and girls. Not only does the classroom begin training children how to act properly gendered (which toys to play with, what colors to wear), but this is the place where children learn quickly about gender inequality. In *Failing at Fairness,* education professors Myra and David Sadker (1994) report that boys are called on more in class, they interrupt girls (and get away with it) more often than the reverse, and their

Who Can Work?

Dick said, "See me work.
I can help Father.
I can get something.
Something for Father."

A 1975 survey of children's books found that boys played active roles but girls were frequently passive. What messages about gender roles might readers learn from this *Dick and Jane* book?

teachers expect them to be better at math and worse at reading. Girls, the authors show, are frequently bullied out of classroom discussion, put down by their male classmates, and effectively silenced. Boys and girls may share one classroom, but they receive two separate educations. (See Chapter 13 for more on the boy-girl achievement gap.)

When students open their schoolbooks or turn on the television set, they may find further representations of gender inequalities. In 1975, when the U.S. Department of Health, Education, and Welfare surveyed children's books, it found that active boys, shown outdoors having exciting and important adventures, populated textbooks. When shown at all, girls remained passive, dependent, and bored (and usually boring). Since then, some changes have been made. For example, representations in the popular media, once highly reflective of the same stereotypes as in textbooks, have increasingly shown more girls in active roles—engaged in sports, holding careers, and defying traditional stereotypes of homemaking femininity. Girls, so it appears in the media, are catching up. But representations of masculine roles have remained defiantly distant from child rearing, housework, and nurturance.

Inequality at Work

The same trend holds fast in the real world of work and family, where women's roles have expanded into paid work while men's have hardly budged toward more involvement in the domestic sphere (see Chapter 12). The past few decades have brought arguably the biggest change in American gender relations. Since the 1970s, almost 37 million more women have entered the labor force, from 31.5 million in 1970 to 72 million in 2008 (Figure 8.3). Of course, the overall population has increased by 50 percent in that time period as well, accounting for part of the rise, but the percentage of women ages 16 to 64 who are in the workforce has risen from approximately 43 to 60 percent. In fact, since the Great Recession hit male-dominated industries the hardest (such as construction), it helped accelerate the trend toward gender equality in labor force participation. Today there are about the same number of women and men in the workforce. Women even exceeded men for a brief moment at the depth of the economic crisis, though the recovery in male sectors has since outpaced that in predominantly female ones—notably since women are disproportionately employed in the public sector and state governments have yet

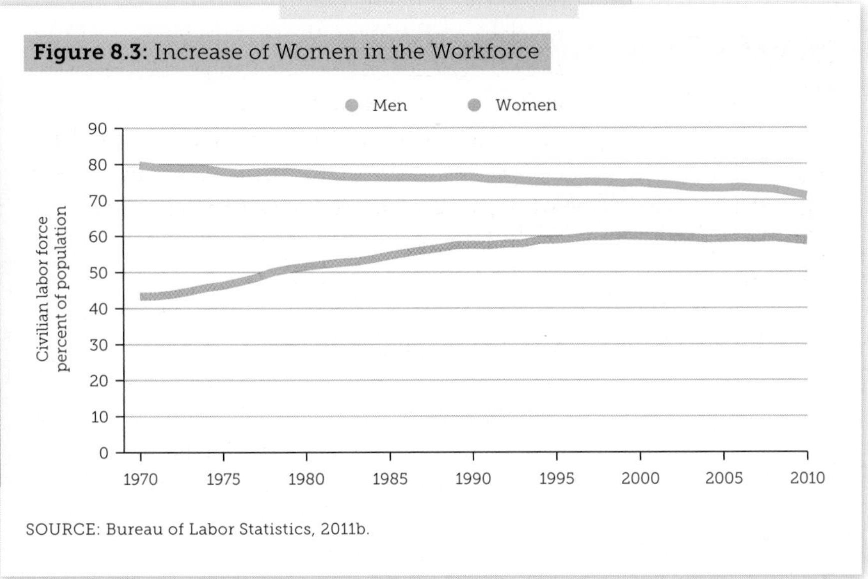

Figure 8.3: Increase of Women in the Workforce

SOURCE: Bureau of Labor Statistics, 2011b.

to recover from the twin challenges of economic woes and ballooning budgets (Covert, 2011).

However, the greater entry of women into the labor force has not catapulted them to equality with their male peers in the workplace (see Chapter 14). Despite the passage of Title VII of the 1964 Civil Rights Act, which declared it unlawful for employers to discriminate on the basis of a person's race, nationality, creed, or sex, women have continued to fare much worse than their male counterparts in the workforce. Although legally entitled to enter all lines of work, women routinely face sexual harassment, an illegal form of discrimination that runs the gamut from inappropriate jokes on the job to outright sexual assault to sexual "barter," in which women workers give sexual favors under the threat of punishment (Kimmel, 2000). Intended to make women feel uncomfortable and unwelcome, sexual harassment occurs across many settings and in all kinds of relationships—walking down the street and having to listen to "Whooo, baby!" is just one annoying everyday example. In the workplace, some argue, sexual harassment is one of the chief ways in which men resist gender equality. In 1982, the U.S. Court of Appeals ruled that sexual harassment is a violation of the Civil Rights Act, because it is a form of discrimination against an individual on the basis of sex. But sexual harassment takes insidious forms not easily detected by everyone or verifiable in court. Most commonly, sexual harassment takes the form of "hostile environments" in which women feel unsafe, excluded, singled out, and mocked.

Sexual harassment an illegal form of discrimination, involving everything from inappropriate jokes on the job to outright sexual assault to sexual "barter"—all intended to make women feel uncomfortable and unwelcome, particularly on the job.

In addition to working in such hostile environments, women have consistently been paid less than their male peers, earning about 81 cents to every $1 of a man's wage (BLS, 2006; Figure 8.4). (In some large, economically successful cities, however, the gender gap may be shrinking or even reversing among

Figure 8.4: Pay Discrepancy Based on Gender

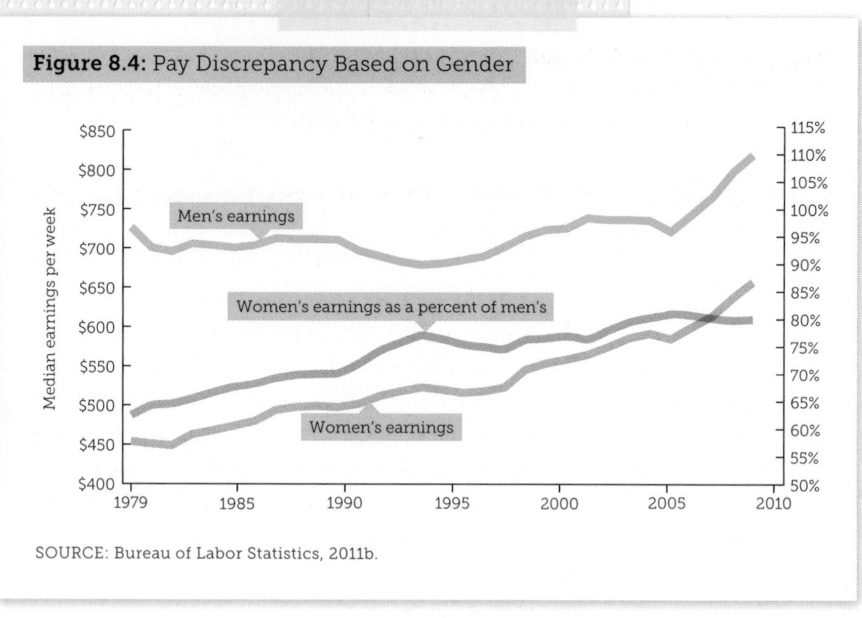

SOURCE: Bureau of Labor Statistics, 2011b.

young adults.) The media touted women's gains in the 1970s and 1980s, when masses of women entered the U.S. labor force. Yet women entered disproportionately the lower rungs of the occupational hierarchy. These feminized jobs, what Louise Howe (1977) calls "pink-collar" jobs, are low-paid secretarial or service industry jobs. Cleaning buildings, filing papers, and making coffee are hardly what women imagine when they dream of independence.

Many new women workers find themselves shuffled into occupations dominated by other women, and women who go into a male-dominated field often find that, soon enough, they are surrounded by women. Like names, jobs become feminized when too many women hit the scene. This has happened in fields such as real estate sales, clerical work, pharmacy, public relations, bartending, bank telling, and, more recently, sociology. In *Job Queues, Gender Queues* (1990), sociologists Barbara Reskin and Patricia Roos argue that women end up in lower-paid jobs because these occupations lose (or have lost) their attractiveness for white men. When a job becomes deskilled and less autonomous, earnings decline, and work conditions in general deteriorate, men flee to better positions, leaving (typically white) women next in line to shuffle into the ranks of men's cast-off work.

Take book editing, which changed from a "gentlemen's profession" to a virtual female ghetto in the mid-twentieth century. Formerly the high-cultural mission of men with elite academic records, book editing evolved into a more commercial enterprise in the 1960s and 1970s. The result was that editorial work took a downturn in autonomy, job security, and importance. As the job lost its attractiveness to male candidates, the female labor supply was increasing on the crest of second-wave feminism. Thus, book editing jobs, like the other fields that optimists point to as women's inroads into traditionally male-dominated work, became resegregated and ghettoized as women's work. And anything categorized as women's work tends to yield lower pay, prestige, and benefits such as health coverage than men's.

Glass Ceilings When women do enter more prestigious corporate worlds, they often encounter gendered barriers to reaching the very top: the so-called glass ceiling, which effectively is an invisible limit on women's climb up the occupational ladder. Sociologist Rosabeth Moss Kanter argues in her classic study *Men and Women of the Corporation* (1977) that the dearth of women in top corporate positions results from a cultural conflation of authority with masculinity. In Indesco, the fictitious name of the corporation Kanter studied, she found another case of deceptive distinctions at work: Most people believe that men and women come to occupy the kinds of jobs for which they are naturally best suited. Secretaries are predominantly women (98.6 percent), according to this belief, because women seem to act the feminine part better than they play the masculine managerial role.

Glass ceiling an invisible limit on women's climb up the occupational ladder.

To the contrary, Kanter showed, job segregation often works the other way around: The job makes the person; the person doesn't make the job. Employee behavior tends to be determined by job requirements and the constraints of the organizational structure of the company. At Indesco, secretarial positions derived status from that of the boss. The job was also based on principled arbitrariness, meaning that there were no limits to the boss's discretion as to what his secretary should do (type, fax, pick up his dry cleaning, look after his dog when he's away). Furthermore, secretarial work was characterized by fealty, the demand of personal loyalty and devotion of secretary to boss. Under these conditions, secretaries adopted certain behaviors to get through a day's work, including timidity and self-effacement, addiction to praise, and displays of emotion—all qualities that Indesco bosses tended to think of as just the way women are.

What happens when a woman breaks into a top managerial position? She becomes a numerical minority, what Kanter calls a token, a stand-in for all women. Because tokens have heightened visibility, they experience greater performance pressures. Male peers tend to rely on gender stereotypes when interpreting a token's behavior, seeing female managers as "seductresses, mothers, pets," or tough "iron maidens." When a token female manager botches the job, it just goes to show that women can't handle the corporate world and should be kept out of it.

Fourth-grade teacher Ryan Fittje is the only male teacher at his Fremont, Nebraska, school.

Similarly, Jennifer L. Pierce's study of law firms (1995) showed that sexual stereotypes, as much as organizational structure, are underlying causes of job segregation. Paralegals make up a feminized "semi-profession": About 86 percent of them are women, according to the Bureau of Labor Statistics. Meanwhile, women account for only 16 percent of law firm partners, even though, for the last two decades, the number of women graduating from law school was about 39 to 49 percent of all graduates (Scharf & Flom, 2010).

Paralegals are expected to be deferential (that is, they should not stick up for themselves), caring, and even motherly toward the trial lawyers for whom they work. Given the adversarial model of the U.S. legal system, trial lawyers, in contrast, perform what Pierce (1995) calls masculine emotional labor. To excel in the job takes aggression, intimidation, and manipulation. When a woman joins the higher ranks of trial lawyering, she's likely to face exclusion from informal socializing with her colleagues (no drinks after work), deflation of her job status (frequently being mistaken for a secretary), sexual harassment, and difficulty bringing clients into the firm. Female litigators find themselves in a double bind not experienced by their male counterparts. When deploying courtroom tactics of aggression and intimidation—the very qualities that make a male lawyer successful and respected—women litigators find themselves being called "bitches," "obnoxious," and "shrill." But when they fail to act like proper "Rambo litigators" in the courtroom, women are equally chided for being "too nice" and "too bashful." The trade-off between being a good woman and being a successful lawyer adds yet another obstacle for women to make it to the top in male-dominated jobs.

Glass Escalators Just as the odds are stacked against female tokens, they tilt in favor of men in female-dominated jobs. In *Still a Man's World* (1995), Christine Williams found that male nurses, elementary school teachers, librarians, and social workers inadvertently maintain masculine power and privilege. Specifically, when token men enter feminized jobs, they enjoy a quicker rise to the leadership positions on the aptly named glass escalator. Even when such male workers don't want to advance up the job ladder, they are more likely than women to experience camaraderie with male bosses and "tracking" into leadership positions. (On the flip side, they are more likely to be the objects of sexual suspicions, such as homophobic charges against male child-care workers.)

Glass escalator the promotional ride men take to the top of a work organization, especially in feminized jobs.

The same forces operate in law firms, where male paralegals, themselves tokens in the overwhelmingly female semiprofession, reap benefits from their heightened visibility (Pierce, 1995). Male paralegals are said to enjoy preferential treatment over their female peers, such as promotions and even the simple (but substantial) benefit of being invited to happy hour with the litigators. It's no wonder that even in female-dominated occupations, men tend to occupy the top positions of authority. Just think of your typical public high school in America: Approximately 75 percent of teachers are female, but just 50 percent of principals are female, though the proportion of female principals has been increasing (NCES, 2009).

Opting Out

Faced with bleak employment prospects and glass ceilings and stereotyped into what is considered women's work, some women may prefer marriage and the domestic life over careers. Recently, a flood of media attention has been paid to married women opting out of the labor force and returning to full-time motherhood. According to the *New York Times,* successful working women are retreating en masse to the domestic sphere. Female Yale graduates are willing to put aside their fast-track careers to keep a home and husband. As Louise Story reports (2005), "Many women at the nation's most elite colleges say they have already decided that they will put aside their careers in favor of raising children." *New York Times* columnist Maureen Dowd (2005) asks, "So was the feminist movement some sort of cruel hoax?" On the other hand, only married, relatively well-off women can afford to make this choice. A middle-class American lifestyle all but requires two full-time salaries.

These stories—overwhelmingly middle-class anecdotes—of women "opting out" of their high-powered careers are only slightly supported by statistical trends. But even the home is no haven in a changing gendered world. Family life is rife with struggles over the gendered division of labor. When the responsibility of mothering and housework falls on the shoulders of women alone, workplace gender inequality is perpetuated and reproduced. Is this a purely voluntary preference for the woman faced with lower wages, job segregation, a glass ceiling, and family-unfriendly work policies? Despite the media attention given to women's personally motivated pursuit of traditionally feminine roles, these social structures of gender inequality probably matter much more than journalists give them credit for. Ultimately, it's a chicken-and-egg question that's hard to resolve: Are women more likely to deemphasize work because the opportunities simply aren't there in the male-dominated labor market, or do women often achieve lower status and pay because they opt for less demanding roles at the office? Are they skipping happy hour? Or were they not asked because they had to run home to childrearing responsibilities? Or was that just assumed on the part of their colleagues? As with most social structures, the origin is difficult to assess.

Women in Combat

The media made a lot of noise about who was fit to fight in the armed forces during the 1990s. From Bill Clinton's 1993 "Don't ask, don't tell" solution to gays in the military to Barack Obama's repeal of this policy in 2011 and beyond, debates over women in combat and about sex in the military have been a heated issue. As the policy landscape shifts, the issue is coming back onto the media radar, and it's still a gendered battleground out there.

In 1994, the U.S. Department of Defense enacted a new policy that opened up an array of positions to women, from fighter piloting to commanding warships. But women were, and still are, barred from ground combat

A U.S. soldier prepares to distribute water to Iraqis in Al Faw, Iraq.

units, such as infantry, armor, and field artillery. That is, women can serve close to the front lines in support units, but not in actual combat units. So far, more than 160,000 female soldiers have been deployed to Iraq and Afghanistan—far more than the 7,500 who served in Vietnam and the 41,000 who fought in the first Gulf War. During the Iraq conflict, 1 in every 10 U.S. soldiers was female (Corbett, 2007). The trouble is, in a counterinsurgency operation like that in the Iraqi theater, where mortar attacks and roadside bombings occur just about anytime or anywhere, the distinction between combat and support units is virtually nonexistent. Women were essentially serving in combat operations throughout the Iraqi campaign, with some shocking outcomes and implications.

Unofficially, American women have been in combat since the War of Independence, when Margaret Corbin (Molly Pitcher) took over loading a cannon after her husband was shot. Even formally, women have long held dangerous roles in the military. Some 30 military nurses were held as prisoners of war for three years in World War II. About 1,000 women have been killed in action since the Spanish American War (Wilgoren, 2003). But there is something that makes us uncomfortable about women in the military, and the source of our unease boils down to a few potential concerns.

In 1979, Virginia's now-Senator Jim Webb wrote an article titled "Women Can't Fight," the central argument of which was that women are weak. They have less bodily strength, they can become pregnant, and they can't emotionally handle the calculated violence of war, thus making them a liability to their units. Second, and related, the presence of women was thought to jeopardize military goals by distracting male soldiers, either through sexual attraction or, more likely, through men's paternal instincts to protect female soldiers from danger and, particularly, rape by the enemy. Women, Webb thought, would make the masculine military organization crumble.

Even though Webb later apologized and proclaimed that "women *can* fight," the pregnancy controversy has continued. An order on November 4, 2009, from Major General Anthony Cucolo threatened court-martial for any soldiers and civilians under his command who become pregnant or caused someone else to become pregnant while serving a tour of duty. General Cucolo was later forced to rescind the threat of court-martial, but he and the Pentagon believe that pregnancy had threatened the mission in Iraq and will punish, though not imprison, pregnant soldiers. In other news around the military, recent reports of female veterans reveal that war is especially dangerous for women, not just on the battlefield but also in the barracks. According to studies of female veterans, women are more likely than men to develop post-traumatic stress disorder (PTSD). As of 2007, the Veterans Administration had diagnosed possible PTSD in some 34,000 Iraq and Afghanistan veterans, and nearly 3,800 of them were women (Corbett, 2007). A debilitating condition that combines depression, anxiety, emotional numbness, and sleeplessness, PTSD can develop after exposure to extreme stress and trauma. The principal source of trauma for male veterans is combat. For women, it is believed, there are two sources of trauma in the military: combat and sexual assault. Women are at high risk of rape or the threat of rape, not just by enemy forces but by their fellow soldiers.

Molly Pitcher at the battle at Monmouth.

According to researchers at the Veterans Affairs Medical Center in Iowa, 79 percent of female veterans in one reliable study reported being sexually harassed during their military service. Fully 30 percent of the women reported an attempted or completed rape (Sadler et al., 2003). In the Iowa study, among those who reported rape, 14 percent reported that they had been gang raped, and 37 percent said they had been raped more than once. In general, sexual assaults are reported in much higher numbers to organizations for veterans, as victims are less likely to deal with retaliation for speaking up. The 2010 Overview Report on sexual assault in the military by the Department of Defense states that only 4.4 percent of women and 0.9 percent of men have experienced some form of unwanted sexual contact (Rock & Lapari, 2011).

What makes the military an especially dangerous place for women? For one thing, it is a male-dominated organization with a masculine culture. This atmosphere puts newcomer women at an outsider disadvantage. As combat-support specialist Abbie Pickett told the *New York Times,* "You're one of three things in the military—a bitch, a whore, or a dyke. . . . As a female, you get classified pretty quickly" (Corbett, 2007). In addition, the military teaches core values of aggression, insensitivity, and obedience to carry out the violence of war. Add to that the stressful uncertainties of the battlefield, and sexual assault is just a short step up from routine harassment.

Finally, rape is not primarily about sex, pleasure, or desire but power. In the military, women hold less power than men. As subordinates, women enter this male-dominated field already having lesser authority, which increases the likelihood of what is sometimes called "command rape," in which men of rank assault their juniors (Benedict, 2007).

As hundreds more women soldiers have returned from battle showing the effects of trauma from both sexual assault and combat, the issue of women in the military is not likely to remain a quiet one. Ironically, the old debate has taken a new unfortunate turn: Women are indeed exposed to greater perils of war—not necessarily the danger of sexual predators across enemy lines but rather the risk of sexual predators among their own comrades.

→ CONCLUSION

During World War II, America got a gender makeover. When 6 million American women flooded the factory labor force in response to the nation's call for help, they were galvanized by the now-familiar Rosie the Riveter image. Hollywood discovered Rose Monroe in the 1940s, when she was working at an aircraft parts factory in Michigan; she was quickly remade into a female hero, espousing such empowering slogans as "We can do it!" (Enloe, 2000). Most women taking on men's jobs such as skilled factory work were eager to acquire the new skills and living wages that women's pink-collar jobs had not offered. Some of them were coaxed to the factories by offers of child care and ready-made meals they could take home to their families at the end of the workday. But as Ruth Milkman (1987) argues, the increase in female employment did not lead to gender equity. Far from it. Job segregation by sex did not break down; it just took new forms, redefining women's wartime work as an extension of domesticity, the new but temporary "woman's place." The work of women in factories was revised to be "women's work." It was supposedly light and less strenuous, clean, and even glamorous. Furthermore, it was still segregated by sex, and women earned less than male factory workers.

At the end of the war, husbands, brothers, and sons returned, and the nation called on women yet again to make a sacrifice—this time to return to the domestic life. In just four years, millions of women went from their homes to the factories and back again. Occupational segregation by sex persisted throughout, as it still does today. Did Rosie's dramatic moment amount to nothing? Maybe not, as it turns out.

A mother's employment outside the home is known to affect kids in surprising ways. In families where the mother works, even part-time, brothers and sisters are more likely to end up as economic equals down the road (Conley, 2004) and adopt more egalitarian attitudes toward gender roles (Kimmel, 2000). The kids may even spend fewer hours watching television

(Bianchi & Robinson, 1997). Regardless of early sex role socialization, Rosie's factory days made a ripple in the prevailing gender norms. This ripple was surely felt by her children, who had been exposed to new definitions of what a woman could be. This is just one sociological explanation of women's gains in equality today. Another interpretation is offered by Robert Jackson (1998), who makes the case that women are destined for equality because in a modern economy with rationalized, bureaucratic organizations, it just doesn't make strategic sense to be prejudiced against women. There's something irrational and inefficient, it seems, about sex discrimination. It doesn't make economic sense.

A World War II poster featuring Rosie the Riveter.

What both explanations underscore is the potential of sociology to account for changes in social structures like gender that too often we take as given and fixed. In the study of sex and gender (as in other "sociologies"), social structures and context matter. What seems to be normal or natural often turns out to be fluid and contingent. The stuff we build up around the plumbing—roles, expectations, psyches, institutions—is not essential. These are socially constructed facts, built less on the biological and more on the existing social structures of relations.

We've traced the intricate details through which a system of sexes, genders, and sexualities has evolved. Can we "undo gender," or are we stuck in the paradox of reproducing our own creation, even if we recognize its inequalities? If we humans have constructed gender as a way to organize, simplify, and control a messy social world, then indeed we can deconstruct it. Judith Lorber (1994) argues that only when we stop using gender as a basis for dividing up the world—in terms of which jobs people hold, what rights they exercise, how much money they earn, how much control they have over their bodies, and with whom they can have sex—will we find true equality in the world.

ASSIGNMENT

Have you ever been to a store and started to look at items of clothing, then realized you might be in the "wrong" department (i.e., clothes for the other sex)? Did you ever walk into the wrong restroom? Make a list of gender-inappropriate behaviors you have encountered. How did people react to these incidents? Would you feel weird at all if you considered buying a jacket meant for the other sex? How do these examples—for example, the separation of stores into "women's" and "men's" sections—demonstrate the way gender is socially constructed and enacted?

QUESTIONS FOR REVIEW

1. How does Gayle Rubin's "sex/gender system" help us understand the differences listed between Donald and Deirdre that economist McCloskey describes at the beginning of the chapter?
2. Women represent a minority group in the military. Men are in the minority as nurses and paralegals. How are women and men treated differently in these positions, and what does this suggest about the way gender structures social relations?
3. How do the cases of the *hijra* and the *travesti*, as described in this chapter, challenge our understanding of sex and gender?
4. How does the case of John/Joan support the view of sex as a category based on nature? How does the case of John/Joan support the view of sex as socially constructed and enforced?
5. What is "essentialism"? Explain how John Gray's book *Men Are from Mars, Women Are from Venus* could be described as essentialist.
6. How does Talcott Parsons describe the role of men and women in his "sex role theory"? Explain how conflict theories can be seen as a critique of structural functionalism and describe some limitations of each approach.
7. What is the difference between homosexual "acts" and a homosexual "identity"? How did the historical development of the latter, according to Michel Foucault, affect how one sees oneself?
8. More differences seem to exist among boys and girls than between them. Nonetheless, we tend to think of them as different. What are "deceptive distinctions" and how do they create gender differences? Use an example from Rosabeth Kanter's work to support your answer.

PARADOX

THE BIOLOGICAL CATEGORIES OF SEX STRONGLY INFLUENCE THE SOCIAL DYNAMICS OF GENDER: HOWEVER, THE SOCIAL CATEGORIES OF GENDER CAN SOMETIMES DETERMINE THE BIOLOGY OF SEX.

WATCH THE ANIMATED SHORT ABOUT THE GENDER PARADOX AT

WWNORTON.COM/STUDYSPACE

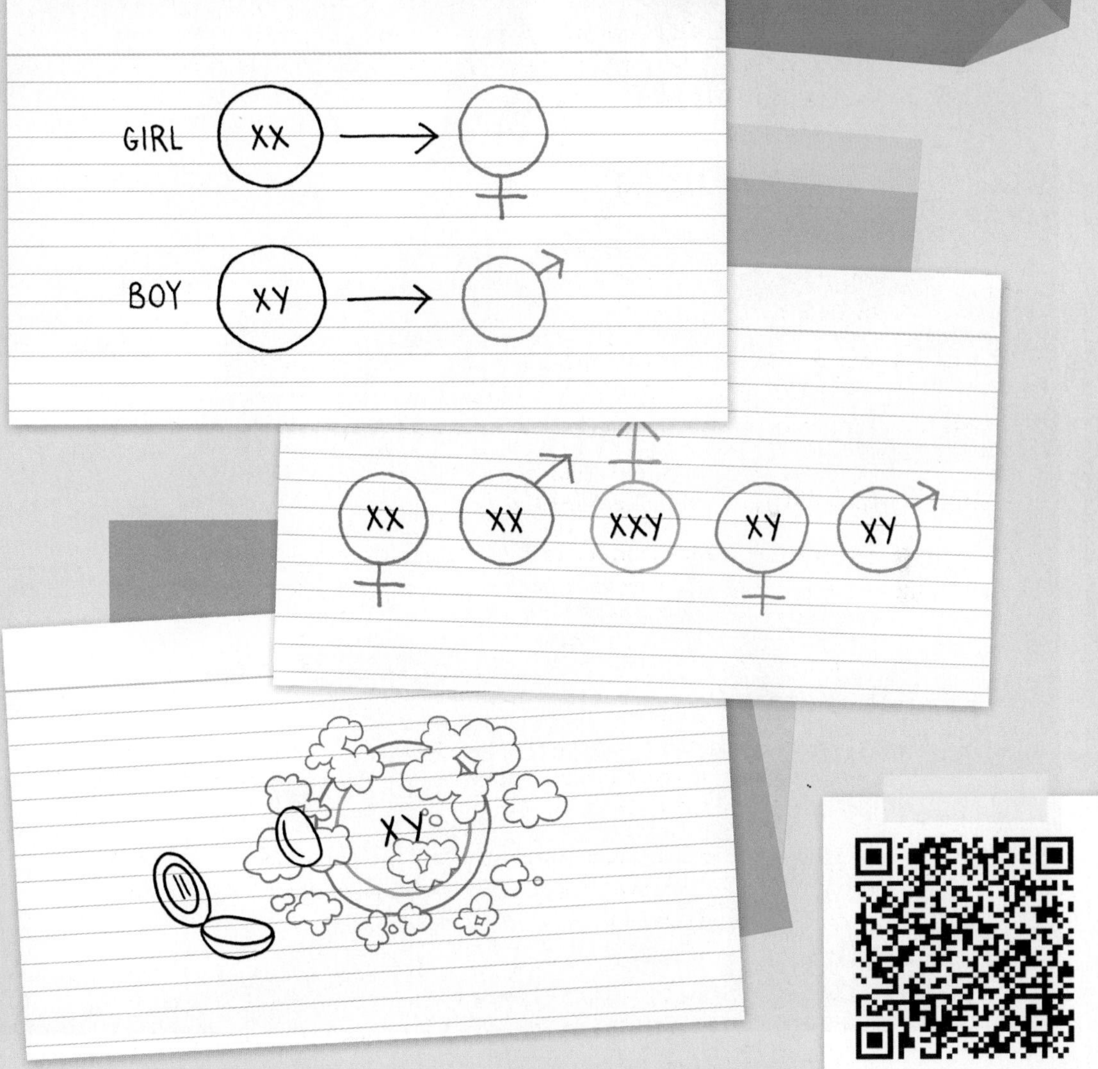

9 Race

PARADOX

RACE AS WE KNOW IT HAS NO DETERMINISTIC, BIOLOGICAL BASIS: ALL THE SAME, RACE IS SO POWERFUL THAT IT CAN HAVE LIFE-OR-DEATH CONSEQUENCES.

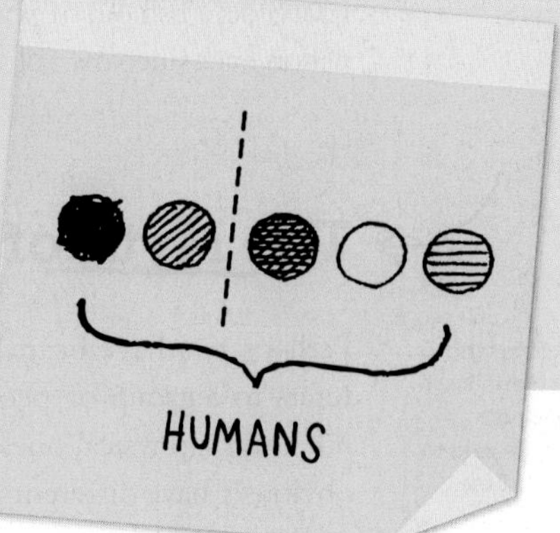

"I found my baby sister!" I declared to my mother, wheeling a carriage around for her to see the newest member of our family whom I had just kidnapped. I was not quite three years old, and the toddler was only a few months younger than that, with cornrows braided so tightly on her little head that they pulled the brown skin of her face tautly upward. I remember that she was smiling up at me, and I must have taken her smile as permission to swipe the unattended stroller from the courtyard of our housing complex.

"No, you haven't!" my mother gasped, putting a hand over her open mouth. The child was quickly returned to her frantically searching mother, despite my tearful protests.

This story fascinates me today: I wanted a baby sister so badly that I kidnapped a black child, not realizing that race is a primary way we divide families. How could I be so oblivious to the meaning of race—something that years later feels so natural, so innate? To my childhood self, race was neither a meaningful category nor a too obvious one. In the largely minority housing project where I grew up in the 1970s, race was not something mutable, like a freckle or hairstyle; it defined who looked like whom, who was allowed to be in the group, and who wasn't. But for my sister and me, as whites, race was turned inside out. We had no idea that we belonged to the majority group, the privileged one. We just thought we didn't belong.

Is race real? You might consider this a paradoxical question. After all, how is a huge part of your identity *not* real? The sociological study of race treats it as a social phenomenon that seems natural but isn't. That is, race is a real social distinction, and people around the world and throughout history have drawn sharp lines between "us" and "them" on the basis of race. But as a biological, genetic, geographic, or cultural category, race has fluid and changeable boundaries. In this sense, race is constructed in the interests of groups that wish to maintain power and social exclusion. To the sociologist, understanding racial differences—including income, educational attainment, crime rates, and teen pregnancy—means treating differences not just as personal matters but as pieces of a larger social picture. Having grown up as a "honky" in the housing projects of New York City's Lower East Side, a fish out of water, I've been looking at race with the sociological imagination ever since my failed kidnapping. Now it's your turn.

The Myth of Race

Race a group of people who share a set of characteristics—typically, but not always, physical ones—and are said to share a common bloodline.

Perhaps you have heard claims that race is fake, that it's "just a myth." Race refers to a group of people who share a set of characteristics—typically, but not always, physical ones—and are said to share a common bloodline. People obviously have different physical appearances, including eye color, hair texture, and skin color, so it's perhaps puzzling to hear that (biological) racial differences somehow do not exist. To speak of the myth of race is to say that it is largely a social construction, a set of stories we tell ourselves to organize reality and make sense of the world, rather than a fixed biological or natural reality. In this sense, it resembles the socially constructed notions of childhood and adolescence that we discussed in Chapter 4. We tell the set of stories over and over and, collectively, believe in it and act on it, therefore making it real through such practices as largely separate marriage and reproductive communities. But we could organize our social distinctions a different way (for example, based on foot size or hair color), and indeed, throughout history, we have told this set of stories in myriad ways.

Take, for example, the following excerpt from an 1851 issue of *Harper's Weekly Magazine*, in which the author describes the physiognomy of a certain racial group. Try to guess which race the author is describing:

> [They are] distinctly marked—the small and somewhat upturned nose, the black tint of the skin. . . . [They] are ignorant, and as a consequence thereof, are idle, thriftless, poor, intemperate, and barbarian. . . . Of course they will violate our laws, these wild bisons leaping over the fences which easily restrain the civilized domestic cattle, will commit great crimes of violence, even capital offences, which certainly have increased as of late.

Most people would guess that the minority group in question here is African Americans. This passage was written, in fact, about Irish immigrants, who in late-nineteenth-century America struggled to assimilate amid fierce and widespread racism (Knobel, 1986). It was believed that the Irish were a distinct category of people who carried innate differences in their blood, differences that made them permanently inferior to their white American neighbors.

When the term *race* comes up in America today, we usually think in two colors: black and white. But, at the turn of the twentieth century, Americans categorized themselves into anywhere from 36 to 75 different races that they organized into hierarchies, with Anglo-Saxon at the top followed by Slav, Mediterranean, Hebrew, and so on down the list (Jacobson, 1998). Even though the United States was a nation of immigrants, many Americans doubted whether "ethnic stock," such as the Irish, were fit for self-governance in the new democracy.

An anti-immigration cartoon from an 1871 issue of *Harper's Weekly*. How have attitudes about race changed over the course of American history?

In 1790, Congress passed the first naturalization law, limiting the rights of citizenship to "free white persons." This law strikes us today as both restrictive and inclusive. It was restrictive because it granted naturalization only to free whites, thereby coloring American citizenship. Yet it also set up an initially broad understanding of "whiteness," an umbrella term that in common parlance could include not just Anglo but also Slavic, Celtic, and Teutonic (German) Europeans. However, as millions of immigrants surged to the shores of America—between 1880 and World War I, 25 million European immigrants arrived—the notion of "free white persons" was reconsidered. With an Irish-born population of more than 1 million in 1860, Americans began to theorize racial differences within the white populace. Questions arose in the popular press and imagination, such as "Who should count as white?" "Whom do we want to be future generations of Americans?" "Who is fit for self-governance?" The inclusiveness of "white persons" splintered into a range of Anglos and "barbarous" others, and Americans began to distinguish among Teutons, Slavs, Celtics, and even the "swarthy" Swedes. The Immigration Act of 1924 formalized the exclusive definition of whiteness by imposing immigration restrictions based on a quota system that limited the yearly number of immigrants from each country. The law set an annual ceiling of 18,439 immigrants from eastern and southern Europe, following the recommendation of a report stating that northern and western Europeans were of "higher intelligence" and thus ideal "material for American citizenship" (Jacobson, 1998).

A racist ideology can be seen in this early line of thinking about whiteness. Racism is the belief that members of separate races possess different and unequal traits. Racist thinking is characterized by three key beliefs: that humans are divided into distinct bloodlines and/or physical types; that these bloodlines or physical traits are linked to distinct cultures, behaviors, personalities, and intellectual abilities; and that certain groups are superior to others.

Racism the belief that members of separate races possess different and unequal traits.

European immigration slowed during World War I and essentially came to a halt as a result of the 1924 National Origins Act, while internal African American migration from the rural South to the industrial North skyrocketed. These shifts, along with the solidification of the one-drop rule (see below), shifted national attention away from white–nonwhite relations toward white–black relations. Whites of "ethnic stock" were drawn back into the earlier, broad category of white, thereby reuniting Anglos and other Europeans. Public horror at Nazi crimes following the conclusion of World War II further strengthened the idea of whiteness as an inclusive racial category.

Today being of Irish descent is a matter of ethnic—not racial—identification, a reason to celebrate on St. Patrick's Day. I know this firsthand: Being one-eighth Irish and having an Irish-WASP name like Dalton Conley entitles me to free drinks on the Irish holiday. Irish American is no longer considered a restrictive racial category, as once was the case. Whiteness today is something we take for granted, a natural part of the landscape. But dig just a hundred years back into the unnatural history of race, and you might not even recognize it. Not only have groups of people been categorized differently over time, showing that there is nothing natural about how we classify groups into races today, but the very concept of what a race is has changed over time.

The Concept of Race from the Ancients to Alleles

The idea of race, some scholars have claimed, did not exist in the ancient world (Fredrickson, 2002; Hannaford, 1996; Smedley, 1999; Snowden, 1983). Well, it did and it didn't. It did in the sense that the ancients recognized physical differences and grouped people accordingly. In ancient Egypt, for example, physical markers were linked to geography. Believing that people who looked a certain way came from a certain part of the world, the Egyptians spoke for instance of the "pale, degraded race of Arvad," whereas their darker-skinned neighbors were designated the "evil race of Ish." The Chinese also linked physical variation to geography, as laid out in a Chinese creation myth. As the ancient tale goes, a goddess cooked human beings in an oven. Some humans were burnt black and sent to live in Africa. The underdone ones turned out white and were sent to Europe. Those humans cooked just right, a perfect golden brown, were the Chinese.

However, in the ancient worlds of Greece, Rome, and early Christendom, the idea of race did not exist as we know it today, as a biological package of traits carried in the bloodlines of distinct groups, each with a separate way of being (culture), acting (behavior), thinking (intelligence), and looking (appearance). The Greek philosopher Hippocrates, for instance, believed that physical markers such as skin color were the result of different environmental factors, much as the surface of a plant reflects the constitution of its soil and the amount of sunlight and water it receives. To be sure, the Greeks liked the looks of their fellow Greeks the best, but the very notion of race goes against Aristotle's principle of civic association, on which Greek society was based. The true test of a person was to be found in his (women were excluded) civic actions. Similarly, the Romans maintained a brutal slavery system, but their slaves, as well as their citizens, represented various skin colors and geographic origins. The ancients may have used skin color to tell one person from the next—they weren't color-blind—but they didn't discriminate in the sense of making judgments about people on the basis of their racial category without regard to their individual merit (Hannaford, 1996). The notion has been so thoroughly displaced by racialized thinking that to us moderns, it is impossibly idealistic to imagine a society without our race concept.

Race in the Early Modern World

Modern racial thinking developed in the mid-seventeenth century in parallel with global changes such as the Protestant Reformation in Europe, the Age of Exploration, and the rise of capitalism. For example, European colonizers, confronted with people living in newly discovered lands, interpreted human physical differences first with biblical and later with scientific explanations, and race proved to be a rather handy organizing principle to legitimate the imperial adventure of conquest, exploitation, and colonialism. To make sense of what they considered the "primitive" and "degraded" races of Africa, Europeans turned to a story in the book of Genesis 9, the curse of Ham. According to this obscure passage, when Noah had safely navigated his ark over the flood, he got drunk and passed out naked in his tent. When he woke from his stupor, Noah learned that his youngest son, Ham, had seen him naked, whereas his other sons had respectfully refused to behold the spectacle. Noah decided to curse Ham's descendants, saying, "A slave of slaves shall he be to his brothers" (Gourevitch, 1998). European Christians and scientists interpreted this tale to mean that Ham was the original black man, and all black people were his unfortunate, degraded descendants. For an

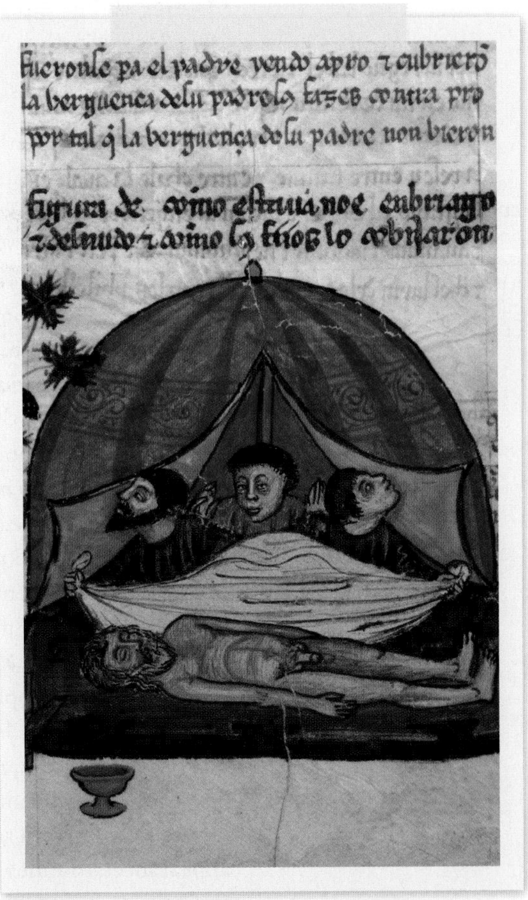

A medieval illustration depicting Ham as a black man. How did Europeans use the biblical story to defend colonialism?

expanding Europe and America, the Hamitic myth justified colonialism and slavery.

When the divine right of conquest lost its sway, science led the way as an authority behind racial thinking, legitimating race by scientific mandate. Scientific racism, what today we call the nineteenth-century theories of race, brought a period of feverish investigation into the origins, explanations, and classifications of race. In 1684, François Bernier (1625–88) proposed a new geography based not on topography or even political borders but on the body, from facial lineaments to bodily configurations. Bernier devised a scheme of four or five races based on the following geographic regions:

Scientific racism nineteenth-century theories of race that characterize a period of feverish investigation into the origins, explanations, and classifications of race.

- *Europe* (excluding Lapland), *South Asia, North Africa,* and *America:* people who shared climates and complexions
- *Africa proper:* people who had thick lips, flat noses, black skin, and a scanty beard
- *Asia proper:* people who had white skin, broad shoulders, flat faces, little eyes, and no beard
- *Lapps* (small traditional communities living around the northern regions of Finland and Russia): people who were ugly, squat, small, and animal-like

Scientific racism sought to make sense of people who were different from white Europeans—who constituted the norm, according to the French scientist Comte de Buffon (1707–88). This way of thinking, called ethnocentrism, the judgment of other groups by one's own standards and values, has plagued scientific studies of "otherness." In Buffon's classification schemes, anyone different from Europeans was a deviation from the norm. His pseudoscientific research, like all racial thinking of the time, justified imperial exploits by automatically classifying nonwhites as abnormal, improper, and inferior.

Ethnocentrism the belief that one's own culture or group is superior to others and the tendency to view all other cultures from the perspective of one's own.

With the publication of *On the Natural Varieties of Mankind* in 1775, Johann Friedrich Blumenbach (1752–1840), widely considered the founder of anthropology, cataloged variation by race, including differences in head formation, a pseudoscience called phrenology. Blumenbach's aim was to classify the world based on the different types of bumps he could measure on people's skulls. Based on these skull measurements, he came up with five principal varieties of humans: Caucasian, Mongoloid, Ethiopian, American, and Malay. Caucasians (named after the people who live in the southern slopes of the Georgian region of eastern Europe), he decided, were the superlatives of the races based on their excellent skull qualities.

Another eighteenth-century thinker, the Swiss theologian Johann Caspar Lavater (1741–1801), popularized physiognomy, which correlated outside appearances to inner virtues. Not surprisingly, light skin and small features signified high intellect and worthy character. Political philosophers were also on board with racial thinking. Charles de Secondat, Baron de Montesquieu,

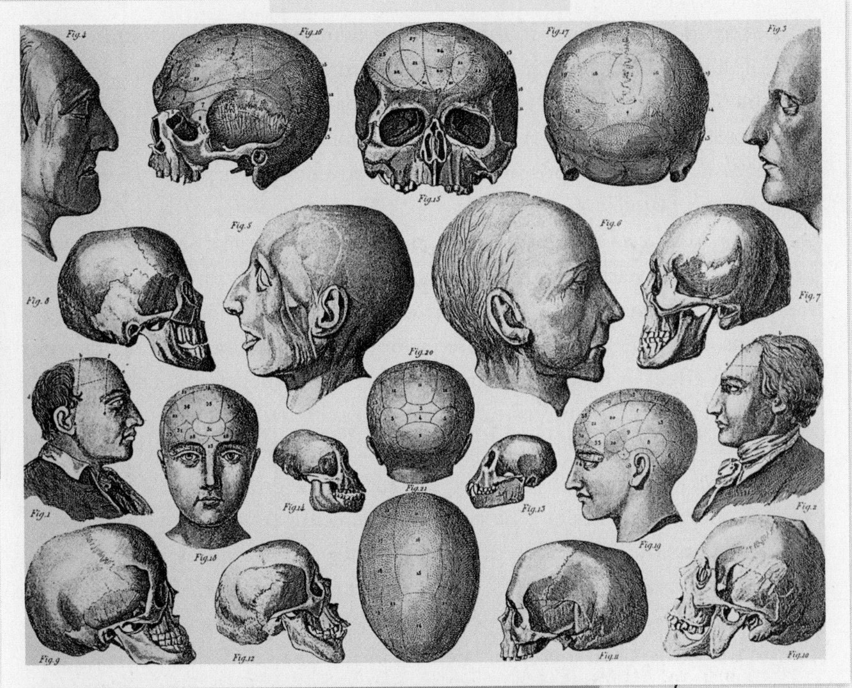

Charts like this one helped phrenologists interpret the shapes of human skulls. How did nineteenth-century theorists use this sort of pseudoscience to justify racism?

had already made the connection between climate and certain forms of government in *The Spirit of the Laws* (1748/1750).

Race was now considered not just a set of physical traits but something that comes with social implications. Immanuel Kant (1724–1804) argued for a link between inner character and outside physiognomy and further claimed that these individual markers were also imprinted on an entire nation's moral life.

However, racial differences were still believed by many to be the product of climate (and therefore not immutable or innate to the soul). In fact, in 1787 the Reverend Minister Samuel Stanhope Smith, who was president of what is now Princeton University, wrote an essay in which he proposed that dark skin should be thought of as a "universal freckle." Differences in skin shade, he maintained, were really just like different levels of suntans. It was his belief that if an African from the sub-Sahara were transplanted to Scandinavia, his dark-brown skin would turn lighter over the course of generations (and perhaps the underlying social and cognitive characteristics associated with race would change as well). Notice how Smith's pliable view of race captures the spirit of ontological equality: We are all the same deep beneath our skin; it just so happens that some of us have been out in the sun a bit longer than others. As we saw in Chapter 7, ontological equality is the philosophical and religious notion that all people are created equal.

Ontological equality the philosophical and religious notion that everyone is created equal.

Herbert Spencer coined the term *survival of the fittest*. How did Spencer draw from the work of Darwin to justify racism?

Social Darwinism the application of Darwinian ideas to society, namely, the evolutionary "survival of the fittest."

Reverend Smith's line of thinking also demonstrates the scientific influence of Lamarckism, now a discredited footnote in the history of scientific thought. The basic tenet of Lamarckism is that acquired traits can be passed down across generations. For example, an acquired attribute such as flexibility, language skill, or sun exposure can be passed down to a person's offspring, affecting generations to come.

Lamarckism was debunked by Charles Darwin, who in 1859 published his theory of natural selection. Darwin argued that acquired attributes could not be transmitted; instead, change can occur only through the positive selection of mutations. Darwin's theory had an enormous impact on how people thought of race. In effect, it called into question the popular belief that climate influenced racial difference and instead offered an account in which racial lineages were much more deeply rooted and long-standing. What's more, humankind was now seen as being on a trajectory in which some groups have advanced (or evolved) more than others. The popular nineteenth-century notion of social Darwinism was the application of Darwinian ideas to society, namely, the evolutionary "survival of the fittest." Social theorist Herbert Spencer (1820–1903) promulgated the idea that some people, defined by their race, are better fit for survival than others and therefore intended by nature to dominate inferior races. A new puzzle arose with Darwinian ideas: What, if not inherited climate change, could explain the development of humans along such radically different lines?

Eugenics

Scientists now had to arrive at a new explanation of physical difference among humans, and the scientific community confronted a growing debate: monogenism versus polygenism. The notion of ontological equality had faded in the late nineteenth century; now the debate turned on the origins of the various races of humans. Were humans a united species, or did we come from separate origins? Monogenists, including religious traditionalists, believed that humans were one species, united under God. Polygenists believed that different races were, in fact, distinct species. Darwin sided with the monogenists, claiming that the notion of different species was absurd. (Politics, it is said, makes for strange bedfellows. It certainly did in this case, as Darwinists and religious traditionalists, usually opposed, became allies in arguing that all humans were one species.)

Even though the monogenists won the debate, the notion of separate roots and distinct reproductive genetic histories has had a lasting impact on how we think of human difference. Under the model of natural selection, human difference must have evolved over tens or hundreds of thousands of years (if not millions), not just over a few generations in relative sun or shade. Such a vast timeframe was used as evidence that races were very different (and not simply superficially so).

Howard Knox (left), the creator of intelligence test puzzle questions, examines an immigrant (far right) at Ellis Island in 1910.

A new movement, eugenics, took the idea of very distant origins and ran with it. Eugenicists, led by Sir Francis Galton (1822–1911), claimed that each race had a separate package of social and psychological traits transmitted through bloodlines. Eugenics literally means "well born"; it is the pseudoscience of genetic lines and the inheritable traits they pass on from generation to generation. Everything from criminality and feeblemindedness to disease and intelligence, Galton asserted, could be traced through bloodlines and selectively bred out of or into populations. One of his followers, the American psychologist H. H. Goddard (1866–1957), applied eugenic thinking to generalize findings from his intelligence tests in America. He tested a handful of immigrants arriving at Ellis Island in the early twentieth century and generalized their test scores to whole populations, claiming—and garnering many believers, too—that around 70 percent of the immigrants sailing from eastern and southern Europe were, in his phraseology, "morons" who posed a serious threat to the good of the nation. Goddard supported the immigration exclusion acts that in 1924 largely blocked non-Anglos from immigrating, intended to improve the "stock" of the nation. This concern about the new and objectionable stock of immigrants, as opposed to "native," more desirable immigrants of an earlier epoch, was the crux of nativism, the movement to protect and preserve indigenous land or culture from the allegedly dangerous and polluting effects of new immigrants. Madison Grant (1865–1937), an influential writer, epitomized the spirit of nativism when he argued that not restricting the immigration of southern and eastern Europeans was "race suicide" for the white race (1916/1936).

Eugenics literally meaning "well born"; the theory of controlling the fertility of populations to influence inheritable traits passed on from generation to generation.

Nativism movement to protect and preserve indigenous land or culture from the allegedly dangerous and polluting effects of new immigrants.

The problem with race, for eugenicists, scientists, and politicians, has always been that if race is such an obvious, natural means of dividing the world, why does no foolproof way of determining racial boundaries exist?

Bhagat Singh Thind

According to the social historian Ian Haney López, the U.S. Supreme Court grappled with this question in the late nineteenth and early twentieth centuries (Haney López, 1995). In a landmark case in 1923, for example, Dr. Bhagat Singh Thind, a high-caste Hindu of full Indian blood, was denied American citizenship. The Supreme Court ruled that he did not qualify as a "free white person," despite being the first Indian Sikh to be inducted into the U.S. Army in World War I. In previous cases, the Court relied on a combination of scientific evidence and "common knowledge" to decide who counted as white. But the Thind case posed a particular challenge because leading anthropologists at the time uniformly classified Asian Indians as members of the Caucasian race. The very notion of whiteness was at stake: If the anthropologists were right, then the commonly accepted conception of whiteness would be radically changed to include dark-skinned immigrants like Thind. The Court therefore decried science as failing to distinguish human difference sufficiently, relying on common knowledge alone to deny Thind's claims to whiteness. As the Court put it, "The words 'free white persons' are words of common speech, to be interpreted in accordance with the understandings of the common man" (Haney López, 1995).

Twentieth-Century Concepts of Race

The judges in the Thind case were not the only people who attempted to define whiteness and nonwhiteness in the absence of a stable scientific taxonomy of race. In Nazi Germany, for example, race posed certain key questions: How can Jewishness be detected? Are Jews a race or a religious group? Both, actually: They are a religious group that has been racialized. Scholars have pointed out that the seeds of racism may be traced to anti-Judaism among early Christians, who forced Jews to convert. Anti-Semitism grew in the eleventh century and was based on the belief that getting rid of Jews was preferable to converting them. But Jewishness was still a social identity at this point—a matter of having religious beliefs that differed from the norm. Anti-Semitism did not turn into racism until the idea took hold that Jews were intrinsically inferior, having innate differences that separated them from their Christian neighbors (Fredrickson, 2002; Smedley, 1999). In Nazi Germany, where Jews were believed to have such innate and inherited differences, the problem remained: How can a person be identified as Jewish? This became an obsession during the Nazis' program of racial purification. They devised a "scientific" way to detect Jewishness by measuring ratios of forehead to nose size to face length, but they had little luck in nailing down a reliable strategy for making such a determination (hence, Jews in Nazi-occupied countries were forced to wear a yellow Star of David as a marker of their identity).

In the 1960s, many whites in rural parts of America similarly failed in trying to distinguish themselves from their mixed Native American and black neighbors (known as "tri-racial isolates") by searching for distinguishing signs on the body, such as differences in fingernails, feet, gums, and lines on the palm of a hand. In exasperation, some whites reported just having to rely on good, old-fashioned "instinct" to distinguish themselves from nonwhites (Berry, 1963).

One means (but still not foolproof) of drawing sharp racial boundaries in America was the one-drop rule, asserting that just "one drop" of black blood makes a person black. The rule developed out of the laws throughout the United States forbidding miscegenation or interracial marriage. By 1910, most whites in the United States had accepted this doctrine. The one-drop rule was integral in maintaining the Jim Crow system of segregation upheld in the 1896 Supreme Court decision in *Plessy v. Ferguson.* In the American South, it was clear that anyone of black lineage fell on the unfortunate side of the racial divide, and the rule essentially cleaved America into two societies: one black, one white. This meant again clumping together all "white ethnics" into one united category. As F. James Davis notes (1991), the one-drop rule was highly efficient, not least because it completely erased stratification *within* the black community that had previously been based on skin tone.

One-drop rule the belief that "one drop" of black blood makes a person black, a concept that evolved from U.S. laws forbidding miscegenation.

Miscegenation the technical term for interracial marriage; literally meaning "a mixing of kinds"; it is politically and historically charged—sociologists generally prefer *exogamy* or *outmarriage*.

Scientific racial thought slowly passed out of vogue as theories of cultural difference gained momentum among American intellectuals from the 1920s to the 1940s. Anthropologist Franz Boas dismissed the biological bases of discrete races, and sociologists such as Robert Park advanced new ideas about culture's importance in determining human behavior. Race, these thinkers argued, was less about fixed inherited traits than about particular social circumstances. Furthermore, when World War II exposed the kind of atrocities to which scientific racism could lead, it became socially and scientifically inappropriate to discuss race in biological terms, and eugenics came to be considered a dangerous way of thinking. With the decline of scientific racism and the shift toward cultural theories of race and ethnicity, the Immigration Act of 1924 was gradually chipped away at starting in 1959 and then completely repealed in 1965. Don't let the formal denouncement of racial thinking fool you, however. Cultural explanations of race often reflect a disguised racist ideology just as much as biological ones do.

Despite the ideas of scholars such as Boas and Park, the old idea of fixed, biological racial differences remains alive and well today, although in modified form. The search for racial boundaries continues in the twenty-first century with the rise of molecular genetics. DNA research now allows us to look deeper than the bumps on our heads, deeper than skin tone or palm lines. Today you can

Marion West (center) embraces Vy Higgensen (right). The distant cousins discovered their relationship after results of separate DNA tests were entered into a database.

find a number of DNA testing companies offering you an inside look at your heritage. You send in $100 to $200; the testing kit arrives in the mail; you swab your mouth according to the directions and then send the swab to the company. Your "real" identity comes back from the lab in about seven weeks. (See Chapter 17 for more on race and genetics.)

Wayne Joseph, a 53-year-old Louisiana high-school principal with Creole roots, did just that. Born and raised black, but having light skin, Joseph was mildly curious about the percentages in his veins. He received some unexpected results: His genetic make-up is 57 percent Indo-European, 39 percent Native American, 4 percent East Asian, and zero percent African (Kaplan, 2003). Despite the findings, Joseph continues to embrace his ethnic identity as black. As he put it to reporters, "The question ultimately is, are you who you say you are, or are you who you are genetically?"

Cells, alleles, and gene sequences have become the new tools of science that promise to reveal our racial truths, but the old idea hasn't much changed—that there is a biological and social package of traits inside our bodies that can be traced through our lineage—despite our knowledge that humans are biologically one species. There is no doubt that there exists genetic variation that corresponds to the general geographic origins of what we call race, but the amount of variation is nowhere near as great as most people believe. Further, the relationship between genes and complex social behavior (i.e., intelligence) is not very well understood. Yet when the 2004 General Social Survey asked respondents why, on average, African Americans have worse jobs, income, and housing than white people, about 80 of the 888 respondents, or 9 percent, responded that blacks "have less in-born ability to learn." (Moreover, a whopping 49.7 percent of respondents believed that blacks are worse off because they "just don't have the motivation or will power to pull themselves up out of poverty.") The historical search for difference affects our belief system today.

Racial Realities

The biological validity of discrete racial categories—be it the bumps on your skull or the DNA in your blood—may be debatable, but in social life, race is real, with real consequences. Just ask someone of the Burakumin race in Japan. Today approximately 3 percent of the Japanese population, the Burakumin originated as a group of displaced people during fourteenth-century feudal wars. With no connection other than being Japanese, the Burakumin suddenly shared something undesirable—they were homeless, destitute, and forced to wander the countryside together. Imagine all the homeless people today in Miami or Los Angeles suddenly uniting. The Burakumin formed a distinct social category, with complete social closure, their own reproductive pool, their own occupational pool, and so on, although they were not a distinct group genetically. Today, however, it is commonly believed that the Burakumin "are descendants of a less human 'race' than the stock that fathered the Japanese nation as a whole" (De Vos & Wagatsuma, 1966). Six hundred years later, the Burakumin still display no physical distinctions from their fellow Japanese citizens. For those people in Japan wishing to avoid interrelations with the Burakumin, this lack of distinctiveness poses a dilemma. So for a hefty price, there are private investigators for hire who will confirm the pedigree of your prospective employee, tenant, or future son-in-law.

The Burakumin are a minority who can be distinguished from the rest of the Japanese population only by genealogical detectives. Prejudice against this group often leads to homelessness.

In Japan, the Burakumin live in ghettos, called *burakus,* and score lower on health, educational achievement, and income compared with their fellow Japanese citizens. Yet when Japanese and Burakumin immigrate to America, the scoring gap narrows dramatically. The distinction between Burakumin and other Japanese is meaningless outside of the significance bestowed on it in their home country. Again, we see that race is not necessarily just about physical or biological differences.

To take an example of racial realities closer to home, consider the consequences of being Arab—or perhaps I should say being perceived as Muslim—in post-9/11 America. In an interview for this text, Jen'nan Read used the image of a Venn diagram to explain that "Arab is an ethnicity; being a Muslim is a religious categorization. In the U.S. context a lot of Muslims and Arabs seem to be the same group. In fact, most Arabs in the United States are Christians who immigrated prior to World War One. And most Muslims are actually not Arab . . . one third are South Asian, one third are Arab, and about a quarter are African Americans who have converted to the religion" (Conley, 2009i). In the United States, Muslims are often identified with Islamo-terrorists. Followers of Islam these days are often lumped into a fixed racial category as a dangerous and undemocratic "other," seen as separate from, and inferior and hostile to, Christians.

In the first year post 9/11 the number of anti-Muslim hate crimes shot up 1,600 percent (Read, 2008). And more than a decade later, while reported crimes have dropped, backlash has continued, as in the story of Zaid Ismail, a car salesman in Florida. Things were going fine for Ismail until his new manager took to calling him "little terrorist." One day, while in the restroom, Ismail heard someone knock on the door, asking, "Hey, are you making bombs in there?" Ismail, a Palestinian American, even found a note on his car telling him to go back to the Middle East or face death. "I'm an American like everyone else," he told reporters. "It's not right" (Moskovitz, 2006).

Racialization the formation of a new racial identity in which ideological boundaries of difference are drawn around a formerly unnoticed group of people.

In the wake of terrorist anxiety, and several years into the war on terror, Muslims in America have undergone what scholars call racialization, the formation of a new racial identity, in which ideological boundaries of difference

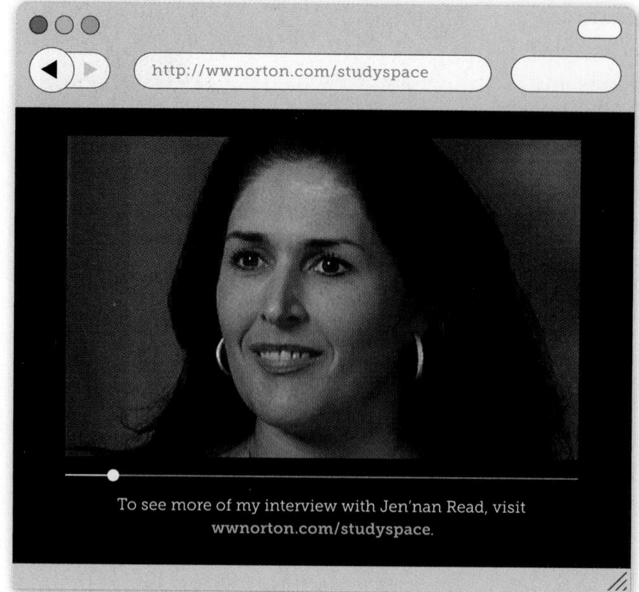

To see more of my interview with Jen'nan Read, visit wwnorton.com/studyspace.

are drawn around a formerly unnoticed group of people. These days, any brown-skinned man with a beard or woman with a headscarf is subject to threats, violence, and harassment. And men with turbans bear some of the worst discrimination, although nearly all men who wear turbans in the United States are Sikh or Punjabi, members of one of the world's largest religious groups, which originated in India. Four days after 9/11, Balbir Singh Sodhi, a Sikh living in Mesa, Arizona, was shot five times and killed in the gas station he owned. He was the first victim of an anti-Muslim epidemic, and he wasn't even Muslim. In one representative Harvard study, 83 percent of Sikhs interviewed said they or someone they knew personally had experienced a hate crime or incident, and another 64 percent felt fear or danger for their family and themselves (Han, 2006). Even more striking is what happens to Caucasian Americans who convert to Islam. One woman, despite having fair skin and green eyes, when she wears the Muslim headscarf, called the *hijab,* has been categorized by people as Palestinian. She's even been told, "Go back to your own country," although she was born and raised in California (Kuruvil, 2006; Spurlock, 2008). The frequency of such incidents is likely to increase as more people convert to Islam in the United States (Read, 2008).

The racialization of Muslims operates on several flawed assumptions. First, people make stereotyped assumptions based on physical traits (turban = Osama bin Laden), even if in their own personal experience they know better (not everyone wearing a turban is in cahoots with bin Laden). Second, making snap judgments about Muslims requires a gross caricaturization of Islam's followers. For instance, most Arabs in the United States are not Muslim but Christian, and about 23 percent of U.S. Muslims are African American (Pew Research Center, 2011a).

As it turns out, American Muslims are both a highly diverse population and a very mainstream one. About 37 percent of Muslims were born in America, and some Muslims have been in North America since the seventeenth century, when they were transported from Africa as slaves (Pew Research Center, 2011a). As a group, they are assimilated with the mainstream, having income and education levels similar to those of the rest of the population. By and large, they hold fast to the ideas that education is important and that hard work pays off in a successful career. Doesn't sound too radical, does it? That's because the overwhelming majority of Muslims in America and throughout the world strongly disagree with Islamic extremism (Pew Research Center,

2011a). Of course, no racial boundaries are drawn along accurate lines or real differences, but again, once racialized, a group faces real social consequences.

A group of Sikhs protest after the murder of Balbir Singh Sodhi.

Race versus Ethnicity

What's the difference between race and ethnicity anyway? Some books use the terms interchangeably; most subsume race under the umbrella label of ethnicity. Today's understanding of race is that it is

- *Externally imposed:* Someone *else* defines you as black, white, or other.
- *Involuntary:* It's not up to you to decide to which category you belong; someone else puts you there.
- *Usually based on physical differences:* Those unreliable bumps on your head.
- *Hierarchal:* Not white? Take a number down the ranks.
- *Exclusive:* You don't get to check more than one box.
- *Unequal:* It's about power conflicts and struggles.

This last point is important for making sense of the Burakumin and Muslim Americans. Racial groupings are about domination and struggles for power. They are organizing principles for social inequality and a means of legitimating exclusion and harassment.

Ethnicity, one's ethnic affiliation, is by contrast

Ethnicity one's ethnic quality or affiliation. It is voluntary, self-defined, nonhierarchal, fluid, and multiple, and based on cultural differences, not physical ones per se.

- *Voluntary:* I choose to identify with my one-eighth Irish background (it makes me feel special, so why not?).
- *Self-defined:* It is embraced by group members from within.
- *Nonhierarchal:* Hey, I'm Irish, you're German. *Great!*
- *Fluid and multiple:* I'm Irish *and* German. *Even better!*
- *Cultural:* Based on differences in practices such as language, food, music, and so on.
- *Planar:* Much less about unequal power than race is.

Ethnicity can be thought of as a nationality, not in the sense of carrying the rights and duties of citizenship but in the sense of identifying with a past

Crowds line the streets at the St. Patrick's Day Parade in New York City. How is this an example of symbolic ethnicity?

or future nationality. For Americans, Herbert Gans (1979a) called this identification symbolic ethnicity. Symbolic ethnicity today is a matter of choice for white middle-class Americans. It has no risk of stigma and confers the pleasures of feeling like an individual. For example, from 2000 to 2003 the fastest-growing ethnic group in the United States was Native Americans. According to the U.S. Census, the American Indian and Alaska Native population grew by 123,000, about 4.6 percent, whereas the entire U.S. population grew during that same time by 3.3 percent. These numbers are not the outcome of a Native American baby boom (although the birthrate among Indians is comparatively high), but instead reflect a growing interest in claiming one's heritage, so long as it's not too stigmatizing and brings just the right amount of uniqueness.

Symbolic ethnicity a nationality, not in the sense of carrying the rights and duties of citizenship but of identifying with a past or future nationality. For later generations of white ethnics, something not constraining but easily expressed, with no risks of stigma and all the pleasures of feeling like an individual.

These differences between race and ethnicity underscore the privileged position of whites in America, who have the freedom to pick and choose their identities, to wave a flag in a parade, or to whip up Grandma's traditional recipe and freely show their ethnic backgrounds. The surge of ethnic pride among white Americans today implies a false belief that all ethnic groups are the same, but in the very way that symbolic ethnicity is voluntary for white ethnics, it is not so for nonwhite ethnic Americans such as Latinos and Asians. As soon as someone classifies you as different on the basis of your phenotypical (racial) features, you lose the ability to choose your ethnic identity. It becomes racialized—subsumed under a forced identifier, label, or racial marker of "otherness" that you cannot escape. Thus, although it is common to use the term *ethnicity* across the board to refer to Latino, black, Asian, or Irish backgrounds, being Irish in America is something that a person can turn on or off at will. You can never *not* be Asian or black: Your body gives away your otherness, no matter how much you want to blend in.

To be black in America is to be just that—black. Some scholars argue that this is the fundamental issue about race in America. Blacks were considered, until recently, a monolithic group. They were unique among racial groups in that their ethnic (tribal, language group, and national) distinctions were deliberately wiped out during the slave trade in order to prevent social organization and revolt (Eyerman, 2001). Alex Haley's landmark novel *Roots* (1976) raised an awareness among African Americans about tracing their ethnic rather than racial identity. This is changing now as more and more African Americans trace back their roots to specific places in Africa through genealogical research or DNA testing. Likewise, immigration from Africa and the Caribbean has created distinctly recognizable national groups of origin among the U.S. black population. Finally, the presidential campaign of Barack Obama led, perhaps, to a symbolic expansion of who counts as black within the African American community: even the son of a white, Kansan mother and Kenyan father who has half-Asian and fully African half-siblings. Though some African Americans were initially uncomfortable with embracing Obama and his mixed heritage as black like them, their attitudes would have had little impact on the wider perception of Obama as a black man because of the continuing significance of the one-drop rule in America. In the end, these initial misgivings faded and Americans of all races celebrated the inauguration of America's first black President.

Ethnic Groups in the United States

The United States is home to countless ethnicities today. It has such a heterogeneous population, in fact, that it is on its way to having no single numerically dominant group. Until the mid-nineteenth century, ethnic diversity was minimal because immigration rates were relatively low until about 1820. Early in the country's formation, white Anglo-Saxon Protestants dominated over Native Americans as well as black slaves. From that point forward, Anglos secured their place at the top of the cultural, political, and economic hierarchy, prevailing over other immigrant populations. As exemplified in the following snapshot of ethnic groups in America today, these historical hierarchies have remained relatively stable and intact despite drastically changing demographics.

Native Americans

According to archaeological findings, the original settlers of the North American continent arrived anywhere between 12,000 and 50,000 years ago from Northeast Asia, traveling by foot on glaciers. This is disputed by some tribes like the Ojibwe, who believe that their ancestors came from the east, not the west. Before European explorers arrived in significant numbers for extended periods in the fifteenth century (there is evidence that the Vikings had reached North America before then), the indigenous population was anywhere between 10 and 100 million. Native Americans were a geographically, culturally, and physically diverse group, but they were categorically viewed as a single uncivilized group by arriving Spanish, French, and British explorers. Confronted with foreign diseases and unfamiliar military technology, the Indians were quickly dominated by white invaders. In Central and South America, the Spanish brutally enslaved them as labor for the mining industry. In the northern parts of North America, French colonialists nurtured their relationships with the Indians in order to cultivate a profitable fur trade. The British, chiefly concerned with acquiring land, settled colonies with the long-term goals of expanding the British state, dispossessing and "civilizing" America's indigenous population in the process (Cornell, 1988).

The Oglala Nation Pow Wow and Rodeo parade is a bright spot for the Pine Ridge Indian Reservation, which, like many federal reservations, is plagued by problems linked to low socioeconomic status.

American Indians' way of life was completely obliterated by the European settlements, from their obviously vital land, which was taken from them, to their communal infrastructure. Most devastating were diseases such as smallpox and cholera, against which the Indians were virtually defenseless, having no native immunity. There were also grueling forced marches from native lands to dedicated reservations. By the end of the 1800s, the Native American population had dwindled to approximately 250,000 (U.S. Census Bureau, 1993). The Indian Bureau (later called the Bureau of Indian Affairs) was established as part of the War Department in 1824 to deal with the remaining "Indian problem," and its chief means was "forced assimilation." This involved placing Native American children in government-run boarding schools that taught the superiority of Anglo culture over "primitive" Native culture and religion. Children who refused to adopt Western dress, language, and religion met with harsh physical and emotional punishment (Cornell, 1988). (A similar project was undertaken in British-ruled Australia with the native Aboriginal tribes.) Despite this poor treatment, Navajo men served the United States in World War II, in which 29 "code talkers" used the Navajo language, creating additional words to describe military terms that were used in lieu of cryptography to protect the secrecy of American communications. The work of the code talkers was critically instrumental in the American victory at Iwo Jima and many other battles throughout the war (Bixler, 1992). Today Native Americans number about 2.78 million (U.S. Census Bureau, 2011c). Only about one-third of Native Americans live on one of the 278 federal reservations. The largest reservation, Navajoland or Diné Bikéyah, covers approximately 16 million acres of Arizona, New Mexico, and Utah. Reservations are generally impoverished and rife with health problems, domestic abuse, substance abuse, poor infrastructure, and high crime. In fact, Native Indians as a whole are plagued by the lowest average socioeconomic status. They rank among the worst in terms of high school drop-out rates and unemployment, which go hand in hand with poor health outcomes such as alcoholism, suicide, and premature death. Suicide rates are double that of the general population and are the second leading cause of death for teens (CDC, 2010b). Around 33 percent of Native Americans die before age 45, compared with 11 percent of the U.S. population as a whole (Garrett, 1994). As an ethnic group, Native Americans have grown by 18.4 percent in the last ten years (U.S. Census Bureau, 2011c). This increase has resulted from the high birthrate among Native Americans and the increased tendency among whites to embrace their Native roots. Declaring your newfound Native roots is at once a case of symbolic ethnicity and a pragmatic act: Native Americans are eligible for numerous types of federal assistance, ranging from health-care services to preferential admission rates at colleges, though a 2004 Civil Rights Commission report found that the federal government spends more per capita for health care for prisoners than for Native Americans (Ho, 2009).

African Americans

The first black people in North America arrived not as slaves but as indentured servants contracted by white colonialists for set periods. They were in the same boat as poor, nonfree whites such as those from Ireland or Scotland (Franklin, 1980). The system of slavery, however, evolved to meet colonial labor needs, and the slave trade was a fixed institution by the end of the seventeenth century. African Americans have been, all in all, on the bottom of the racial hierarchy ever since.

Just before the American Revolution, slaves made up more than 20 percent of the colonial population (Dinnerstein et al., 1996). Today about 14 percent of the American population is black (U.S. Census Bureau, 2011d). Like the Japanese Burakumin, this minority group has high rates of poverty, health

Wiley College student body president Kabamba Kiboko dances at a pep rally. Her family came to the United States from the Congo. For the first time, more Africans are entering the country than during the slave trade.

problems, unemployment, and crime. According to the U.S. Census Bureau, the median income of African Americans as a group is roughly 64 percent that of whites. In 2009, more than 7.2 million people in the United States were on probation or parole, in jail, or in prison—that's 3.1 percent of all U.S. adult residents, or 1 in every 32 adults (Bureau of Justice Statistics, 2010). Among black men ages 20–29, 1 in every 9 is behind bars (Pew Center on States, 2008). Among white men in the same age group only 1 in 106 was behind bars; Hispanics were somewhere in between with 1 in 36 behind bars (Bureau of Justice Statistics, 2010).

Sociologists and demographers today are beginning to study how new black immigrants are fracturing the holistic conception of "African American." For the first time, more Africans are entering the country than during the slave trade. More than 8 percent of the black population is foreign born (U.S. Census Bureau, 2010a). Afro-Caribbeans such as Cubans, Haitians, and Jamaicans resent being unilaterally categorized as African American, because each of these immigrant groups enjoys a unique history, culture, and language that do not correspond to the American stereotypes of black skin. For this reason, new black immigrant groups would rather not assimilate but instead retain their distinctive immigrant status, setting themselves apart from the lowest status group in America, blacks (Greer, 2006).

Latinos

Latino, like the term *Hispanic* (the two are often used interchangeably), refers to a diverse group of people of Latin or Hispanic origin. In 2010, the majority of Latinos in the United States were from Mexico (about 63 percent), Puerto Rico (about 9.2 percent), Cuba (3.5 percent), and the Dominican Republic (2.8 percent). They are a huge and rapidly expanding segment of the American population; in 2010 they made up approximately 16 percent of the population, surpassing African Americans. Latinos also live in a wide array of locations, although they have clustered on the West Coast and in the South and Midwest (U.S. Census Bureau, 2011e).

Hispanics are often called an "in between" ethnic group because of their intermediate status, sandwiched between Caucasians and African Americans. Unlike African Americans, the majority of Latinos in America today have come by way of voluntary immigration, particularly during the last four decades of heavy, second-wave immigration. (Figure 9.1 provides a breakdown of the U.S. Hispanic population by region of origin.) Puerto Ricans are the exception, because they have been able to travel freely to the United States since 1917, when Puerto Rico became an American territory and its inhabitants U.S. citizens. The chief motivation for Latino immigration is economic, because of America's high demand for cheap labor, such as in the service, agriculture, and construction industries.

Figure 9.1: Hispanic Population by Region of Origin, 2010

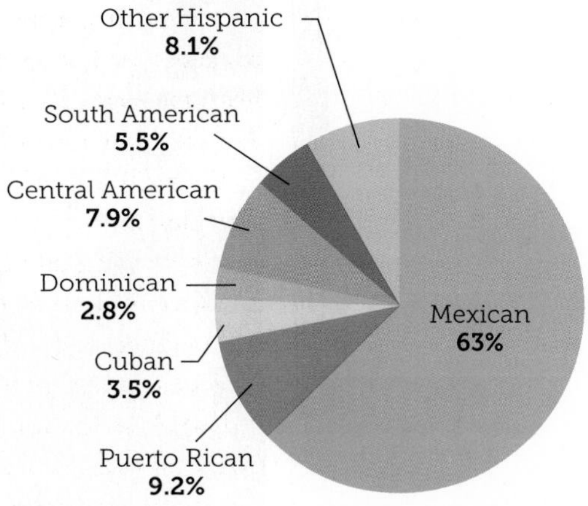

Other Hispanic **8.1%**
South American **5.5%**
Central American **7.9%**
Dominican **2.8%**
Cuban **3.5%**
Puerto Rican **9.2%**
Mexican **63%**

SOURCE: U.S. Census Bureau, 2011e.

Mexicans, Puerto Ricans, and Cubans all have diverse phenotypical traits that make racial distinctions of a unified Latino type nearly impossible. Mexicans are generally classified as "mestizos," a term referring to a racially mixed heritage that combines Native American and European traits. For instance, Puerto Ricans are often a mixture of African, European, and Indian backgrounds. So ambiguous is the Latino label that at various times the U.S. Census has classified them as part of the white race and as a separate race.

Most Cubans, meanwhile, "pass" as white, although their immigration status has changed drastically in recent years. Following the Communist revolution led by Fidel Castro, the first large wave of Cuban immigrants arrived in southern Florida in the 1960s. These immigrants were upper- or middle-class, and educated, and perceived as the victims of a Communist regime that came to power during the Cold War. As such, they were welcomed enthusiastically to this country, and their assimilation started smoothly (Portes, 1969). By 1995, however, that warm welcome had faded. The U.S. federal government terminated its 35-year "open door" policy toward Cuban refugees, and the heavy media coverage of Cubans arriving since then in small boats has led to stereotypes of a desperate "wetback" invasion. Arrivals since the 1970s—who generally are from lower socioeconomic backgrounds in Cuban society—have met more resistance from their host society, consequently experiencing higher rates of unemployment, low-wage work, and dependence on welfare and charity than whites and previous Cuban émigrés (Portes et al., 1985).

Asian Americans

Like *Latino,* the term *Asian American* is very broad, encompassing diverse and sometimes clashing peoples from China, Korea, Japan, and Southeast Asia. The first wave of Asians to arrive in the United States in the mid-nineteenth century were predominantly laborers of Chinese, then Japanese, then Korean and Filipino origin. A second large wave of immigration is currently underway, mostly made up of well-educated and highly skilled people from all over Asia.

Early Asian immigrants were perceived as a labor threat and therefore met with extreme hostility. The Chinese Exclusion Act of 1882, which led to a ban against the Chinese in 1902, marked the first time in American history in which a group was singled out and barred entry. Urban "Chinatowns"

Diners eat at a restaurant in Lowell, Massachusetts, which has the second-largest concentration of Cambodian immigrants in the United States. The area has become a tourist draw and economic engine for the old mill city.

developed out of ghettos in which marginalized Chinese workers, mostly men, were forced to live. Japanese immigrants faced similar hostilities and were formally barred entry by the Oriental Exclusion Act of 1924. By 2010, Asian and mixed Asian U.S. residents amounted to 4.8 percent of the population. This was a 43.3 percent increase over a decade, making Asian Americans the fastest growing racial group (U.S. Census Bureau, 2011f). They are most heavily concentrated in California, Hawaii, New York, Illinois, and Washington.

Asian Americans are unique among ethnic minorities because of their high average socioeconomic status, surpassing that of most other ethnic minorities and most whites as well in terms of educational attainment. For example, the median family income for the U.S. population as a whole in 2010 was $49,445, whereas for Asian Americans it was $64,308 (U.S. Census Bureau, 2011g). That said, despite the overall success of Asian Americans, certain groups—notably Cambodians and Hmong (from Laos and Vietnam)—experience very high poverty rates.

Furthermore, Asian Americans overall disproportionately find it difficult to be reemployed once they lose a job. In 2010, the Asian American unemployment rate for those with bachelor degrees or higher was 1.3 percentage points higher than the rate for whites (U.S. Equal Employment Opportunity Commission, 2011), and Asian Americans and blacks suffer from the longest average duration of unemployment spells. In 2011, unemployed Asian Americans experienced a median 28.2 weeks before they found work again. For blacks that year, the figure was 26.8. (Whites and Latinos had 20.9 and 20.1 week median durations in 2011.) However, these black-Asian and white-Latino similarities obscure different reasons for the long duration for the various groups. While blacks typically face barriers to employment, Asians have more family support and savings and thus are able to wait out a bad labor market for the best possible job.

In recent years, Asians have been applauded for their smooth assimilation as the "model minority," the implication being that if only other ethnic groups could assimilate so well, America would have fewer social problems. Such a view, however, effaces the rather unsmooth history Asian immigrants have faced in this country, as well as the continuing poverty and discrimination faced by some Asian ethnics. Furthermore, "positive" stereotypes of high achievement are not always beneficial and can place enormous pressure on Asian youths to measure up to an impossibly high ideal.

Middle Eastern Americans

Middle Easterners come from places as diverse as the Arabian Peninsula, North Africa, Iran, Iraq, and the Palestinian territories. They established communities in the United States as far back as the late 1800s, but their numbers have swelled since the 1970s as part of the rising tide of non-European immigration. Middle Easterners in this second wave of immigration often arrive from politically tumultuous areas seeking refuge in the United States.

Today about 3.5 million Americans report some Arab origins, and even more Americans have a Middle Eastern heritage, because not all Middle Easterners are Arabic (Arab American Institute, 2011), despite the fact that most Americans regard anyone from the Middle East as Arab and Muslim. In fact, the largest Middle Eastern population in the United States today is from Iran, and they are Persians, not ethnic Arabs, and do not generally speak Arabic. Similarly, although the majority of new Middle Eastern Americans are Muslim, many of them are Christian, and a small number Jewish (Bozorgmehr et al., 1996).

Widespread misunderstandings about Middle Easterners derive, in part, from their negative stereotyping in the mainstream media. In one study of television portrayals of Arabs, researchers found four basic myths that continue to surround this ethnic group. First, they are often depicted as fabulously wealthy—as sultans and oil tycoons. Second, they are shown as uncivilized and barbaric. Third, they are portrayed as sex-crazed, especially so that they can be used as underage white sex slaves. Fourth, they are said to revel in acts of terrorism, desiring to destroy all things American (Shaheen, 1984). Little has changed since this study came out nearly 30 years ago, although after 9/11, the emphasis shifted away from stereotypes of Arabs as extremely rich and toward one of Middle Easterners as terrorists.

The Importance of Being White

We've seen some of the trajectories of various ethnic and racial groups in America, but what about the largest racial population, whites? Scholars have begun to pay more attention to what it means to be a white person. Every year on the first day of my introduction to sociology class, I ask my 200 or so students to write down the five social categories that best describe who they are. Black students almost always put their race at or near the top of the list. Latino and Asian American students usually list their ethnicity as well. Until recently, I could be fairly confident that whites would not list their race. Some might identify Polish, German, or another ethnic or national origin, but not one white student would write down Caucasian, white, or even Euro-American. And that was the point of my experiment.

We have already seen how the category of whiteness is socially constructed—first inclusively defined as all "free white persons" in 1790, then restrictively defined as only northern and western European whites in the early twentieth century, and reformulated back to an umbrella category by the mid-twentieth century. We know now that this category, which seems so natural and innate, is actually a flexible label that has expanded over time to include many formerly nonwhite groups such as Jews, Irish, and Italians. Today most white people have little awareness of the meaning of whiteness as a category. As Nell Irvin Painter, the author of *The History of White People,* says, "The foundation of white identity is that there isn't any. You're just an individual" (Schackner, 2002).

Whiteness, argues Peggy McIntosh (1988), is an "invisible knapsack of privileges" that puts white people at an advantage, just as racism places nonwhites at a disadvantage. In her now classic essay "White Privilege: Unpacking the Invisible Knapsack," McIntosh catalogs more than 50 "Daily Effects of White Privilege," ranging from the mundane to the major. Here are just a few McIntosh notices:

- I can go into a music shop and count on finding the music of my race represented, into a supermarket and find the staple foods which fit with my cultural traditions, into a hairdresser's shop and find someone who can cut my hair.
- I can arrange to protect my children most of the time from people who might not like them.
- I do not have to educate my children to be aware of systemic racism for their own daily physical protection.
- I am never asked to speak for all the people of my racial group.
- I am not made acutely aware that my shape, bearing, or body odor will be taken as a reflection on my race.
- I can choose blemish cover or bandages in "flesh" color and have them more or less match my skin. (pp. 3–5)

Whiteness, then, is about not feeling the weight of representing an entire population with one's successes or failures. It's about not having to think about race much at all.

In recent years, however, awareness of whiteness has been on the rise, as evidenced by the profusion of scholarship on whiteness, the goal of which is to call attention to the social construction and ensuing privilege of the category. Calling attention to whiteness helps whites understand how slanted the playing field really is. It also helps rectify something wrong with the way we study race in America: By traditionally focusing on minority groups, the implicit message that scholarship projects is that nonwhites are "deviant," to borrow from the Comte de Buffon, and that's why we study them. Even popular culture has caught on with Web sites like stuffwhitepeoplelike.com offering humorous, pointed critiques of the habits of white people in America.

Former Klansman David Duke stands under a Confederate battle flag. How was Duke able to cast the NAAWP as a pro-white movement instead of a racist organization?

But white consciousness may have another, more troubling side. In 1980, before white studies got underway in universities, the white supremacist David Duke left his position as the grand wizard of the Knights of the Ku Klux Klan and founded the National Association for the Advancement of White People (NAAWP), attempting to sugarcoat his racist movement with a seemingly more politically correct approach. In this new framework, Duke presented whites as a besieged minority, writes sociologist Mitch Berbrier (2000), defining the NAAWP's mission as a pro-white heritage movement as opposed to an anti-black one. Sociologist Abby Ferber has analyzed the clever appropriation of civil rights language in Duke's white supremacist discourse. For example, in an article by Duke in the *White Patriot,* Ferber finds the rhetoric of reverse discrimination, victimhood, and the right to cultural difference:

> [O]ur race and all others should have the right to determine their own destiny through self-determination and rule. . . . [E]very people on this planet must have the right to life: the continued existence of its unique racial fabric and resulting culture. (*White Patriot,* no. 56, p. 6, quoted in Ferber, 1999)

Sounds reasonable, right? That's because the new language of white supremacy allows racists to move away from explicitly racist language (of biological inferiority, for example). Duke's NAAWP also co-opts civil rights discourse, as in the organization's original mission statement: "The NAAWP is a not for profit, nonviolent, civil rights educational organization, demanding equal rights for whites and special privileges for none."

Such examples demonstrate one possible outcome of the emergence of white studies: to politically empower extremists by giving them a legitimate language for their racist ends. Note, however, that this rhetoric does not acknowledge the advantages whites typically enjoy. The power of whiteness studies is that it exposes the social construction of a seemingly natural (and neutral) category, giving a sense of the unequal footing beneath the labels "white" and "black." (That is, whites can embrace ethnic identity, but blacks are stuck in a racial category.) But like any new "technology" such discourse can be used for many ends.

Minority–Majority Group Relations

What are the *social* consequences of race? Scholars have defined four broad forms that minority–majority group relations can take: assimilation, pluralism, segregation, and conflict.

In the 1920s, sociologist Robert Park began to wonder what, on the one hand, held together the diverse populations in major American cities and, on the other hand, sustained their cultural differences. He came up with a race relations cycle of four stages: contact, competition, accommodation, and assimilation. His model, called straight-line assimilation, was at first accepted as the universally progressive pattern in which immigrants arrive, settle in, mimic the practices and behaviors of the folks who were already there, and achieve full assimilation in a newly homogenous country.

Straight-line assimilation Robert Park's 1920s universal and linear model for how immigrants assimilate: they first arrive, then settle in, and achieve full assimilation in a newly homogenous country.

Milton Gordon (1964) tweaked Park's model by suggesting multiple kinds of assimilation outcomes. For Gordon, an immigrant population can pass through (or stall in) seven stages of assimilation: cultural, structural, marital, identificational, attitude receptional, behavior receptional, and civic assimilation (Table 9.1).

Table 9.1: Gordon's Stages of Assimilation

SON'S OCCUPATION	CHARACTERISTIC
Cultural assimilation	Change of cultural patterns to those of host society
Structural assimilation	Large-scale entrance into cliques
Marital assimilation	Large-scale intermarriage
Identification assimilation	Development of sense of collective identity based exclusively on host society
Attitude reception assimilation	Absense of prejudice
Behavior reception assimilation	Absense of discrimination
Civic assimilation	Absense of value and power conflict

With Park and Gordon in mind, let's do a thought experiment. Imagine yourself as a Polish immigrant arriving at Ellis Island in 1900. You don't have much money, and you've come to America in search of opportunity; this is the land of plenty, so you've been told. You settle into a Polish enclave of Manhattan, where you connect with friends and maybe some family. You do your best to learn English. You buy a pair of riveted denim pants, popular among American workmen. You secure work in a factory thanks to your connections in the Polish community. After an initial period of tension and conflict stemming from job competition and housing constraints, you eventually are accepted by your Anglo-American neighbors, first by being allowed to join the workers' union and then—and this probably only happens to your children—by being allowed to marry into an Anglo family. By this time, you think of yourself as an American. Congratulations, you have reached Milton Gordon's final stage of civic assimilation.

Harold Isaacs (1975) noticed something that these theories of assimilation could not explain: People did not so easily shed their ethnic ties. Ethnic identification, among white ethnics and everyone else, persisted even after a group attained certain levels of structural assimilation. Clifford Geertz (1973) explained this persistence as a matter of primordialism—that is, the strength of ethnic ties resides in deeply felt or primordial ties to one's culture. Ethnicity is, in a word, *fixed*. If not biologically rooted, it's rooted in some other intractable source that Geertz reasoned must be culture.

Primordialism Clifford Geertz's term to explain the strength of ethnic ties because they are fixed in deeply felt or primordial ties to one's homeland culture.

The flip side of this argument came from Nathan Glazer and Daniel P. Moynihan in *Beyond the Melting Pot* (1963). Far from being a deeply rooted structure that kept people bonded to their culture, ethnic identification, they reasoned, persisted because it was in individuals' best interests to maintain it. They saw ethnic groups as miniature interest groups—individuals uniting for instrumental purposes, to fend off job competition, for instance. Glazer and Moynihan believed that ethnicity was fluid and circumstantial. More recently, scholars have posited that ethnic identification is both a deeply felt attachment and an instrumental position that can change according to circumstance (Cornell & Hartmann, 1998).

Pluralism

For most people, however, assimilation into American society is not very easy, and acceptance varies systematically. At times a pressure cooker has been invoked as a more appropriate metaphor than a melting pot. Park's model was useful in shifting attention away from essentialist explanations of the so-called innate differences among immigrants, but it suffers from several shortcomings. Most obviously, it does not apply to nonwhite immigrants, many of whom are not fully accepted into all areas of American society. Park's model also does not apply to involuntary immigrants, notably African Americans and some refugees. Ernest Barth and Donald Noel (1972) noted that assimilation is not

Figure 9.2: Five Largest Foreign-Born Populations in the United States, 1850 to the Present (in thousands)

1850		1880		1900		1930	
FRANCE	54	SWEDEN	194	SWEDEN	582	POLAND	1,269
CANADA	148	CANADA	717	GREAT BRITAIN	1,168	CANADA	1,310
GREAT BRITAIN	379	GREAT BRITAIN	918	CANADA	1,180	UNITED KINGDOM	1,403
GERMANY	584	IRELAND	1,855	IRELAND	1,615	GERMANY	1,609
IRELAND	962	GERMANY	1,967	GERMANY	2,663	ITALY	1,790
TOTAL: 2.2 million		TOTAL: 6.7 million		TOTAL: 10.3 million		TOTAL: 14.2 million	

SOURCE: U.S. Census Bureau, 2011f.

necessarily the end result for immigrants. On the contrary, other outcomes such as exclusion, pluralism, and stratification are possibilities. And as others point out (Lieberson, 1961; Massey, 1995; Portes & Zhou, 1993), some immigrants assimilate more easily than others, depending on a variety of structural factors, like migration patterns, differences in contact with the majority groups, demographics such as fertility and mortality rates and age structure, and, ultimately, power differentials between groups. This is the case for the "new immigration," which, in comparison with the earlier era of European immigration (1901–30), is a large-scale influx of non-European immigration that began in the late 1960s and continues to the present (Figure 9.2).

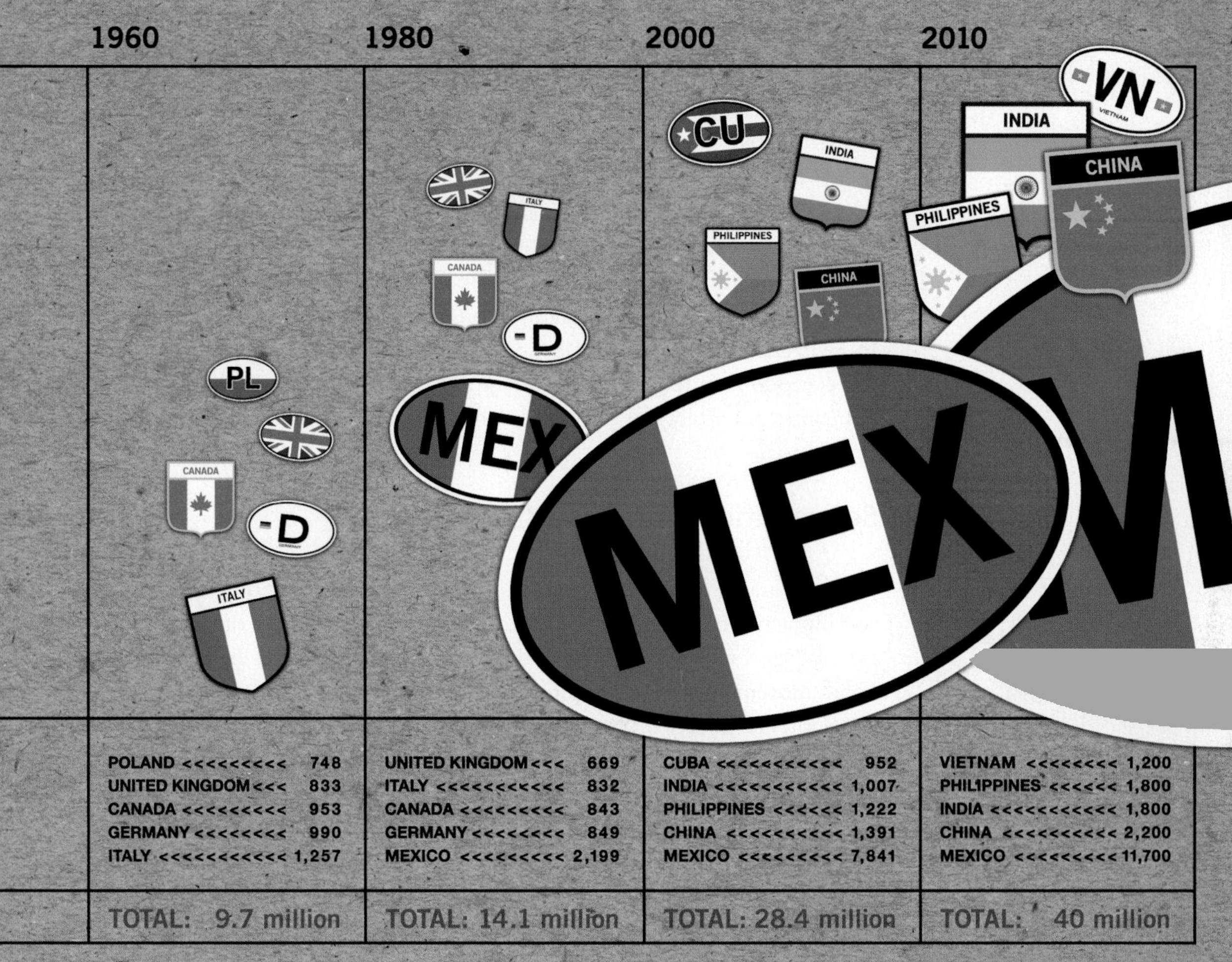

The new immigrants, largely from Hispanic and Asian countries, are racialized as nonwhites—even though Asians are widely considered a "model minority." They therefore are subject to a different set of conditions for assimilating and face greater obstacles to their upward mobility (Massey, 1995). For example, Portes and Zhou (1993) report that the children of Haitian immigrants living in Miami's Little Haiti are at high risk for downward mobility because they face social ostracism from their own ethnic community if they choose to adopt the outlook and cultural ways of native-born Americans. Among Haitian youth, a common message is the devaluation of mainstream norms, and anyone who excels at school or abides by mainstream rules runs the risk of being shunned for "acting white." This picture of assimilation is much more complex than Park's initial formulation.

Pluralism the presence and engaged coexistence of numerous distinct groups in one society.

A society with several distinct ethnic or racial groups is said to be a pluralism, meaning that a low degree of assimilation exists. A culturally pluralistic society has one large sociocultural framework with a diversity of cultures functioning within it. This is the premise of multiculturalism in America. Statistically speaking, in a pluralist country, no single group commands majority status. Switzerland, with its three linguistic groups—German, French, and Italian—is a striking example of ethnic autonomy and balance. The Census Bureau projects that whites will make up less than 53 percent of the population by 2050 (U.S. Census Bureau, 2010b). A broader definition of pluralism, however, is a society in which minority groups live separately but equally. Imagine America with no substantial stratification, no oppression, and no domination. In Switzerland, despite slight income differences among ethnic groups (with the exception of recent immigrant groups like the Turkish), no one group dominates politically, but the same cannot be said for America.

Segregation and Discrimination

Segregation the legal or social practice of separating people on the basis of their race or ethnicity.

A third paradigm for minority–majority relations is segregation, the legal or social practice of separating people on the basis of their race or ethnicity. An extreme case of segregation was the southern United States before the civil rights movement. Under the Jim Crow system of segregation, reinforced by the Supreme Court's 1896 ruling in *Plessy v. Ferguson,* a "separate but equal" doctrine ruled the South. Strictly enforced separation existed between blacks and whites in most areas of public life—from residence to health facilities to bus seats, classroom seats, and even toilet seats.

Black actor, singer, and civil rights leader Paul Robeson leads Oakland dockworkers in singing the national anthem in 1942.

Although the *Plessy* decision ruled that separate facilities for blacks and whites were constitutional as long as they were equal, in real life the doctrine legalized unequal facilities for blacks. The National Association for the Advancement of Colored People (NAACP) has long recognized that segregation and discrimination are inescapably linked. Nowhere is this clearer than in the case of education. Social science data consistently show that an integrated educational experience for minority children produces advantages over a non-integrated school experience. School segregation almost always entails fewer educational resources and lower quality for minority students, though the Harlem Children's Zone mentioned in Chapter 4

Elementary-school students in Ft. Myer, Virginia, face each other on the first day of desegregation.

provides an exception to this general rule. (See Chapter 13 for more on racial inequalities in schooling.)

As Anthony Marx (1998) has noted, concern over segregation grew during World War II as America was caught in the embarrassing contradiction of espousing antiracist rhetoric against its Nazi foes while upholding an egregiously racist doctrine at home. America emerged from the war as a global force with heightened stakes for its world reputation; this new status, along with growing public dissent, perhaps helped motivate the Supreme Court's landmark 1954 decision in *Brown v. Board of Education.* The Court's majority opinion that legally segregated public schools were "inherently unequal" is considered the ruling that struck down the "separate but equal" doctrine. It was also the spark that ignited the civil rights movement of the 1960s.

However, school desegregation has been under fire since several Supreme Court decisions in the 1990s (*Dowell,* 1991; *Pitts,* 1992; *Jenkins,* 1995). Two 2007 cases in Louisville, Kentucky, and Seattle, Washington, came the closest to overturning the spirit (if not the letter) of *Brown.* Meanwhile, former presidents Richard Nixon and Ronald Reagan both openly attacked desegregation initiatives, especially busing. In 1981, President Reagan's attorney general, William Bradford Reynolds, flatly proclaimed that the "compulsory busing of students in order to achieve racial balance in the public schools is not an acceptable remedy" (Orfield, 1996). Today most U.S. schools are only marginally less segregated than they were in the mid-1960s. Average white students in America attend a school where 78 percent of their classmates are also white. But in all this bickering over the effectiveness of busing the larger point is missed: School segregation is invariably linked to poverty, which is perpetuated by residential segregation, and perhaps that is the issue we should be addressing if we are concerned about mitigating racial disparities.

In 1968, under President Lyndon B. Johnson's initiative, the Kerner Commission reported that despite the civil rights movement sweeping the nation, America was split into two societies: "one black, one white—separate and unequal." The main reason for the fissure was residential segregation, what sociologist Lawrence Bobo has termed the "structural linchpin of American racial inequality" (Bobo, 1989). Residential segregation, scholars argue, maintains an urban underclass in perpetual poverty by limiting its ties to upwardly mobile social networks, which connect people to jobs and other opportunities. When you live in the ghetto, your chances of landing a good job through your social network are indeed slim (Wilson, 1987).

It has also been suggested that residential segregation inflicts poverty through a "culture of segregation" (Massey & Denton, 1993). According to this argument, you live in a ghetto that's extremely isolated from the outside world—no family restaurants like the Olive Garden, no mainstream bank branches, not even a chain grocery store that sells fresh vegetables. You're surrounded daily by the ills that accompany poverty: poor health, joblessness, out-of-wedlock children, welfare, educational failure, a drug economy, crime and violence, and, in general, social and physical deterioration. In the ghetto, the most extreme form of residential segregation, you come to believe that this is all there is to life; the social ills become normative. It's no big deal to sell drugs, drop out of school, depend on welfare, or run with a gang. You slide into the very behaviors that, in turn, reproduce the spiral of decline of your neighborhood.

Whether you buy this line of thought or not (and this viewpoint has been criticized as being overly deterministic), consider how a segregated neighborhood got that way in the first place. It didn't just pop up out of nowhere, nor was it always there. As Douglass Massey and Nancy Denton (1993) have argued, the ghetto was deliberately and systematically constructed by whites to keep blacks locked into their (unequal) place. Before 1900, blacks faced job discrimination but relatively little residential segregation. Blacks and whites lived side by side in urban centers, as the index of dissimilarity numbers in Figure 9.3 shows. The index of dissimilarity, the standard measure of segregation, captures the degree to which blacks and whites are evenly spread among neighborhoods in a given city. The index tells you the percentage of nonwhites who would have to move in order to achieve residential integration.

In 1942, a race riot broke out in Detroit, Michigan, during an attempt by white residents to force African Americans out of the neighborhood.

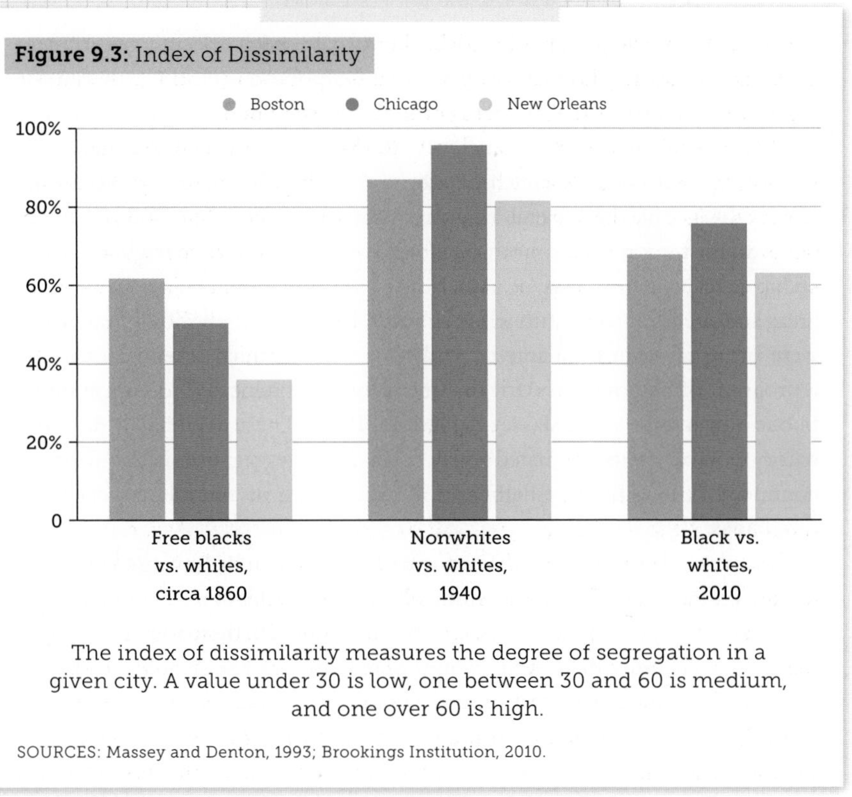

The index of dissimilarity measures the degree of segregation in a given city. A value under 30 is low, one between 30 and 60 is medium, and one over 60 is high.

SOURCES: Massey and Denton, 1993; Brookings Institution, 2010.

Various structural changes—industrialization, urbanization, the influx of southern blacks to the North who competed with huge waves of European immigrants—led to increased hostility and violence toward blacks, who found themselves shut out of both white jobs and white neighborhoods. The color line, previously more flexible and fuzzy, hardened into a rigid boundary between black and white.

The black ghetto was manufactured by whites through a set of deliberate, conscious practices. Boundaries separating black neighborhoods were policed by whites, first with the threat of violence and periphery bombings in the 1920s and then with "neighborhood associations" that institutionalized housing discrimination. Property owners signed secret agreements promising to not allow blacks into their domain. When a black family did move to a neighboring block, whites often adopted the strategy of flight instead of fight, and this process of racial turnover yielded the same result: black isolation. Even today, when a black family moves into a white neighborhood, the property value declines slightly, in subtle anticipation of the process of white flight, which leaves behind a run-down, undesirable black neighborhood—a veritable vicious circle. On the other hand, the formerly black neighborhood of Harlem in New York City is now no longer majority black, a consequence of the recent in-migration of whites and Hispanics (Roberts, 2010).

Also helping to create the black ghetto have been specific government policies, such as the Home Owners' Loan Corporation (HOLC), that in the early 1930s granted loans to home owners who were in financial trouble. The HOLC also instituted the practice of "redlining," which declared inner-city, black neighborhoods too much of a liability and ineligible for aid. Following the HOLC's lead, the Federal Housing Administration (FHA) and the Veterans Administration (VA)—both of which were designed to make home ownership a reality for struggling Americans—funneled funds away from black areas and predominantly into white suburbs. Finally, by the 1950s, urban slums were being razed in the name of "urban renewal," which essentially became a program of removal, as African Americans were relocated to concentrated public housing projects (Massey & Denton, 1993). These deliberately discriminatory policies are perpetuated today by de facto segregation in the form of continued suburban white flight and the splintering of school districts along racial lines.

Some scholars argue that a new form of segregation has emerged in America: the criminal justice system. During the 1960s, blacks were slightly overrepresented in the nation's prisons, but in absolute numbers, there were many more white felons because many more whites were in the total population. Today the racial distribution in jails and prisons is the reverse. Blacks and Latinos now make up the majority of incarcerated people. One in four black men in their twenties is in prison or jail, on probation, or on parole at any given moment (Pettit & Western, 2004). Is imprisonment just another means of confining the black population away from whites? Several scholars make this case, based on changes in drug laws that seem to affect minorities disproportionately (see Chapter 6 for more details, especially on the Rockefeller Drug Laws in New York State).

Ethnic Tutsi troops overlook a pile of skulls that will be reburied in a memorial to approximately 12,000 Tutsi massacred by Hutu militias.

Racial Conflict

The final paradigm of race relations is conflict relations, when antagonistic groups within a society live integrated in the same neighborhoods, hold the same jobs, and go to the same schools. This was the volatile scenario in Rwanda in 1994, when roughly 800,000 Tutsi were murdered by Hutu, mostly by machete, in the span of 100 days. That's about 333.3 killings per hour, or five and a half lives every second (Gourevitch, 1998). The killings, as well as the maiming and systematic rape of Tutsi women, were the culmination of more than a century of racial hostility that began with the Belgian colonization of Rwanda.

Belgian explorers, immersed in discourses of scientific racism, confronted two Rwandan tribes, the Hutu and the Tutsi, who for ages had been living and working together and intermarrying. Because of all their shared social, cultural, and genetic heritages, scientists today cannot distinguish Hutu and Tutsi into separate biological populations. But in the late nineteenth century, the Belgians gave preferential treatment to the Tutsi, whom they believed to be superior to the Hutu. What followed was a brutal system of oppression in which the Tutsi dominated the Hutu.

When Rwanda was granted independence in 1962, after a century of hatred brewing between the two groups, the Hutu took power under a dictatorship masked as a democracy, and their long-standing animosity simmered into an explosion in April 1994 after three years of failed crops. The result was genocide, the mass killing of a particular population based on racial, ethnic, or religious traits. The genocide, backed by the government and media, turned neighbors into murderers overnight: Friends killed friends, teachers killed students, and professionals killed coworkers. Rwanda was a stark reminder that when we speak of the myth or fiction of race, we cannot deny its reality in social life.

Genocide the mass killing of a group of people based on racial, ethnic, or religious traits.

Group Responses to Domination

There are several forms of response to oppression, four of which are briefly outlined below: withdrawal, passing, acceptance, and resistance. Although we tend to think of minority groups as being oppressed by majority groups, keep in mind that sometimes the majority are the oppressed group, as in South African apartheid, where 4.5 million white Afrikaners and British dominated 19 million indigenous people.

Withdrawal

An oppressed group may withdraw, as the Jewish population did after Nazi persecution in Poland. Before World War II, the Jewish population in Poland numbered 3.3 million, the second largest in the world. Eighty-five percent of Polish Jews died in the Holocaust, leaving roughly 500,000. After World War II, violence against Jews continued, and many moved. These conditions, plus the bitter taste of Polish complicity in the Holocaust itself, caused many Jews to leave for good. By 1947, Poland was home to just 100,000 Jews.

Another case of withdrawal was the Great Migration of the mid-twentieth century in the United States. Blacks streamed from the Jim Crow rural South in search of jobs and equality in the industrialized urban North and West; an estimated 1.5 million African Americans left per decade between 1940 and

1970. The North opened opportunities to blacks that previously had been violently denied them in the South, including economic and educational gains as well as the cultural freedom manifested in the Harlem Renaissance. But leaving the South did not always lead to immediate improvements. In their search for a better life, many African Americans found cramped shantytowns on the edge of urban centers, exploitation by factory owners looking for cheap black labor, and increasing hostility from white workers. Racialized competition for housing and employment sometimes led to violent clashes, such as the East St. Louis riots in the summer of 1917. The riots, principally involving white violence against blacks, raged for nearly a week, leaving nine whites and hundreds of African Americans dead. An estimated 6,000 black citizens, fearing for their lives, fled the city, another stark example of withdrawal.

Passing

Another response to racial oppression is passing, or blending in with the dominant group. During his early adulthood, Malcolm X, for example, attempted to look more like white men through the painful process of chemically straightening or "conking" his Afro. A more recent example was the pop star Michael Jackson. Passing is not necessarily about physical changes, though. One of the most common ways people have tried to pass has been to change their surnames. The single largest ethnic group in the United States today is German Americans. Not English, but German. Where, do you ask, are all the Schmidts and Muellers? They now go by Smith and Miller, after a huge wave of name changing among German Americans during the world wars—if not during the first one, then often by the second.

Acceptance versus Resistance

Subaltern describes a subordinate, oppressed group of people.

Another response is acceptance, whereby the oppressed group feigns compliance and hides its true feelings of resentment. In Erving Goffman's terms, members of this group construct a front stage of acceptance, often using stereotypes to their own advantage to "play the part" in the presence of the dominant group (see Chapter 4). Backstage, however, privately among their subaltern or oppressed group, they present a very different self. Sociologist Elijah Anderson refers to this as "code-switching," a strategy used by African Americans in the presence of dominant white society. In Anderson's ethnography of a black neighborhood in Philadelphia, blacks learn two languages, one of the street and one of mainstream society, and daily survival becomes a matter of knowing which one to speak at the right time. For an inner-city youth, an act of code-switching could be as simple as putting on a leather jacket and concealing his textbook beneath it for the walk home from school

(Anderson, 1999). (Code-switching is akin to the double consciousness that W. E. B. DuBois ascribed to African Americans who maintain two behavioral scripts; see Chapter 1.)

A more overt form of resistance, the fourth paradigm of group responses to domination, would be collective resistance through a movement such as revolution or genocide, or through nonviolent protest as in the U.S. civil rights movement (see Chapter 18 for a discussion of social movements).

Collective resistance an organized effort to change a power hierarchy on the part of a less-powerful group in a society.

Prejudice, Discrimination, and the New Racism

On the individual level, racism can manifest itself as prejudice or discrimination. Prejudice refers to thoughts and feelings about an ethnic or racial group, whereas discrimination is an act. Robert Merton developed a diagram for thinking about the intersections of prejudice and discrimination (Merton, 1949; Figure 9.4). One who holds prejudice and discriminates is an "active bigot." This is the prototypical racist who puts his money (or burning cross) where his (or her) mouth is. Those who are neither prejudiced nor discriminatory are "all-weather liberals," not only espousing ideologies of racial equality or talking the talk, but also walking the walk when faced with real choices.

Prejudice thoughts and feelings about an ethnic or racial group.

Discrimination harmful or negative acts (not mere thoughts) against people deemed inferior on the basis of their racial category without regard to their individual merit.

Many people fall between these two stances. A "timid bigot" is one who is prejudiced but does not discriminate—a closet racist perhaps, who backs down when confronted with an opportunity for racist action. Conversely, one who is not prejudiced but does discriminate is termed a "fair-weather liberal." Despite the fair-weather liberal's inner ideological stance in favor of racial equality, he or she still discriminates, perhaps without knowing it. For instance, a couple who consider themselves open minded about race relations may feel compelled to sell their home as soon as they are confronted with new black neighbors (white flight, as previously discussed here). Of course, they do not cite residential integration as their motivation for leaving, but instead offer an excuse that has embedded racist reasons, such as the differences in school districts. In fact, the prime time for families to move out of integrated neighborhoods happens to be around the time when the eldest child of the family turns five and begins school.

Figure 9.4: Merton's Chart of Prejudice and Discrimination

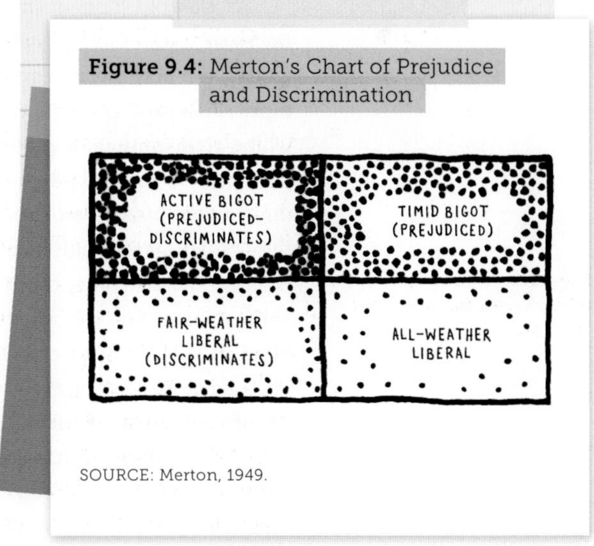

SOURCE: Merton, 1949.

Active bigots are hard to come by these days, because prejudicial viewpoints are largely

Right-wing National Democratic Party members protest German immigration and refugee policies. How is this an example of cultural racism?

unacceptable in the ostensibly antiracist West. But don't be fooled into thinking that race doesn't matter anymore. It does, and racism is still alive and going strong, although it's veiled in different terms. You just have to know how to look for it. Old-fashioned, overt racism tended to convey three basic ideas: Humans are separable into distinct types, they have essential traits that cannot be changed, and some types of people are just better than others. Not many people openly make such claims in America today, as they tend to be frowned on.

As this old kind of racism declines, race scholars are beginning to find traces of a new kind of racism gaining ground. According to Howard Winant (2001), the new racial hegemony comes with "race neutral" rhetoric and relies more on culture and nationality to explain differences between nonwhites and whites than immutable physical traits. The new line of thinking, called "laissez-faire racism," replaces biology with culture and presumes that there is something fixed, innate, and inferior about nonwhite cultural values. In America, this kinder, gentler antiblack ideology is characterized by the persistence of negative stereotyping, the tendency to blame nonwhites for their own problems, and resistance to affirmative action policy (Bobo et al., 1997). (We'll have more to say about the concept of affirmative action below and in Chapter 13 on education.) The irony is that since the civil rights triumphs of the 1960s, the official stance of formal equality has brought about subtler forms of prejudice and discrimination, making it harder to tackle racism and inequality. When a state proclaims racial equality, white privilege gets off the hook and goes unnoticed.

Likewise, in the new color-blind Europe, argues Neil MacMaster (2001), a "differentialist" or "cultural" racism has taken hold. Characteristic of cultural racism is the call to protect national (white) identity from "criminal" and polluting cultural outsiders, constructing an image of "fortress Europe." Anti-refugee commentary is one example of the new racist ideology. For example, in a televised speech in 1978, Margaret Thatcher made the following appeal to cultural purity in regard to 4 million immigrants from recently decolonized countries: "Now that is an awful lot, and I think it means that people are really rather afraid that this country might be swamped by people with a different culture" (MacMaster, 2001).

How Race Matters: The Case of Wealth

In *An American Dilemma* (1944), Gunnar Myrdal pointed out that blacks and whites think about equality in different but complementary ways. In his study, whites cared most about intimate relations—they were most adamant about maintaining personal distance from blacks, especially when it came to marriage, but they did not mind so much if blacks had equal chances of earning a living. Blacks valued equal employment and legal rights first; the freedom to marry whites was at the bottom of their list of concerns. These "rank orders of discrimination" gave Myrdal some hope; if economic discrimination was of least concern for whites and greatest for blacks, then maybe African Americans could catch up. But it has not worked out that way.

Nonwhites, especially African Americans, Latinos, and Native Americans, lag behind whites on a number of social outcomes, from income and educational attainment to crime rates and infant mortality rates. For example, blacks are half as likely as whites to graduate from college or hold a professional or managerial job, and are twice as likely to be unemployed and to die before their first year of life. As striking as the figures are, if there is one statistic that captures the persistence of racial inequality in the United States, it is net worth. If you want to determine your net worth, all you have to do is add up everything you own and subtract from this figure the total amount of your outstanding debt. When you do this for nonwhite and white families, the differences are glaring. So while most of America felt the impact of the housing market crash in 2006 and the 2007 to 2009 recession, African Americans and Latinos felt the blow far greater than whites. Median wealth for whites fell 16 percent, yet African Americans and Latinos experienced 53 and 66 percent losses, respectively (Pew Research Center, 2011b).

Latinos are a varied group but largely reflect African Americans on wealth measures. The median Latino family in 2009 had just $6,325 in assets and one third of these households had zero or negative net worth (Pew Research Center, 2011b). We know considerably less about Native Americans because reliable data are lacking, but given that they have a poverty rate of 32.2 percent (compared with just 13 percent for whites), their wealth is not likely to be high. Asian Americans, however, have low rates of poverty (12.1 percent) and high rates of home ownership, at about 60 percent (U.S. Census Bureau, 2011g).

This "equity inequality" has grown in the decades since the civil rights triumphs of the 1960s. What's more, the wealth gap cannot be explained by income differences alone. That is, the asset gap remains large even when we compare black and white families at the same income levels. Even among the often heralded new black middle class, the accumulated assets of a family earning $40,000 a year amount to less than $20,000; a similar white family has a nest egg of around $80,000. For many among the growing black and Latino middle classes, this lack of assets may mean living from paycheck to paycheck, being trapped in a job or neighborhood that is less beneficial in the long run, and not being able to send one's kids to top colleges. Parents' wealth is also a strong predictor of children's teenage and young adult outcomes—everything from teenage premarital childbearing to educational attainment to welfare dependency (Conley, 1999).

Equity inequality captures the historical disadvantage of minority groups and the way those disadvantages accrue over time. The institutional restraints on black property accumulation discussed above were one mechanism for hindering blacks' asset growth. Similar processes and policies have decimated the wealth of Native Americans, who went from living off the land (the entire U.S. territory) to being disproportionately impoverished and dispossessed over the course of a century by exploitative U.S. policies. One of the most telling examples of this sort of institutionalized dispossession happened to Japanese Americans. As skilled farmers, Japanese immigrants accrued enough wealth in the early twentieth century to attract resentment, culminating in the 1924 Alien Land Act, which prohibited noncitizens from owning land. Japanese immigrants then found success in business, running nurseries and selling cut flowers, and amassed considerable wealth by 1941, about $140 million cumulatively (Lui, 2004). When World War II broke out and panic spread over the possibility of a treacherous Japanese population in America, the Roosevelt administration mandated a program of internment by Executive Order 9066. Japanese American citizens were placed into camps in the western part of the United States. They were given a week to dispose of all assets, selling their homes and businesses to whites at scandalously low prices (Lui, 2004). The result was a huge forced transfer of wealth from Japanese to whites under discriminatory government policy.

What were the consequences of the Japanese internment camps? How are they an example of equity inequality?

The issue of race barely surfaced in all the discussion over George W. Bush's 2001 tax cuts. Amid his package of tax reductions was the proposed repeal of the federal estate tax, which had been in place since 1916 and affects only the richest 1.4 percent of the deceased. As the law stood at the time of the debate, the first $675,000 per individual ($1.35 million for couples) of net estate value was exempt from tax. Because of a 1997 change in the law, this exemption amount would rise steadily until it reached $1 million for individuals in 2006. The Bush estate tax repeal phased out the entire tax by 2010. When the tax returned in 2011 the exemption had been pushed to $5 million for an individual and $10 million for a couple. Because the number of African Americans who would benefit is extremely small, Bush's ultimate goal of eliminating the tax forever would likely exacerbate the already growing wealth gap between blacks and whites.

In summary, policies intending to address disparities between nonwhites and whites must take into account the extreme wealth gap and its historical trajectory. Affirmative action aimed at improving wages and increasing job openings for blacks, Latinos, and Native Americans can address only a piece of a larger cycle of equity inequality. Income from work provides for the day-to-day, week-to-week expenses; wealth is the stuff long-term upward mobility is made of.

Institutional Racism

Another cause of the asset inequality discussed above is the simple fact that property in black neighborhoods doesn't accrue value at the same rate as that in mostly white areas. Property reflects only the value accorded to it in the marketplace. In this vein, when a neighborhood's housing values precipitously decline as the proportion of black residents rises, the price changes provide a record of the economic value of "blackness." And it does not take any "active bigots" or otherwise racist individuals to generate this phenomenon. Namely, aside from any personal ideology, whites have an economic incentive to sell when they sense a neighborhood starting to integrate, since evidence shows that once a neighborhood reaches somewhere between 5 and 20 percent black, it quickly becomes predominantly black due to a rash of selling (with an accompanying drop in values) (Card et al., 2008). This expectation means that it is rational for whites to be the first to sell as blacks increase in numbers in a given area in order to prevent a loss of equity. This, of course, becomes a self-fulfilling prophecy and a vicious circle linking race and property values results—to the disadvantage of blacks. (Meanwhile, property value does not follow the same clear-cut pattern for other ethnic minorities, although minority enclaves generally have lower real estate value than exclusively white neighborhoods.)

The case of race and property values is an example of institutional racism—institutions and social dynamics that may seem color-neutral but

Institutional racism institutions and social dynamics that may seem race-neutral but actually disadvantage minority groups.

which end up disadvantaging minority groups. Another example is provided by sentencing laws for dealing or consuming cocaine. At the height of a period of panic over crack cocaine infiltrating neighborhoods, the United State passed the Anti-Drug Abuse Act of 1986. This law declared that for sentencing purposes, one gram of crack cocaine was equivalent to 100 grams of powdered cocaine. The result was the first time a possession charge for a typical user of crack resulted in a mandatory minimum sentence of five years. Since crack was cheaper and more prevalent in low-income, predominantly black communities, the result was a huge racial disparity in drug sentences by race. President Obama addressed this issue in 2010 by signing the Fair Sentencing Act, which reduced the ratio to 18-to-1. This ratio, while an improvement with respect to race, still leaves a significantly disparate impact by race (Davis, 2011).

Yet another example of institutional racism can be found in the case of hiring patterns by employers. With limited information about job applicants, employers may be rational to use social networks to recruit employees since informal ties (i.e., references) can provide more reliable information about individuals than can be gleaned from paper job applications. Since whites tend to hold more managerial positions and since social networks tend to be segregated by race, this need for additional information on the part of employers also perpetuates racial disparities with no racially explicit motivation.

A related dynamic is called statistic discrimination—a dynamic where firms use race as a short hand proxy for having attended poorer schools and having experienced other disadvantages that would lead to less productive performance. While this is not completely color blind, it is different than overt racism in that the motivation is not about race per se, but about underlying characteristics that tend to be associated with race. Finally, institutional racism can even be encoded into the educational system through test construction. There has been much debate about cultural bias in testing. Beyond that issue, however, is the effect of stereotypes on performance. The psychologists Claude Steele and Joshua Aronson, for example, have shown that they can drive black students' test scores down just by priming them with negative stereotypes before they sit for the exam (Steele & Aronson, 1998). These are just a few of the ways by which race can continue to disadvantage certain groups even in an age where overt racial animus may have waned in significance.

Figure 9.5: An Ethnic Snapshot of America Today

White, not Hispanic
63.7%

Each symbol represents 1% of the U.S. population.

SOURCE: U.S. Census Bureau, 2011f.

→ The Future of Race

This brief overview of the history of race and its present-day ramifications allows us to make some guesses about the future of race. For starters, racial and ethnic diversity in America will tend to increase (Figure 9.5). The 2010 Census data show a 134 percent increase in Americans who identify as multiracial, that is, 9 million people (Pew Research Center, 2011c). The number of foreign-born people in the United States surpassed 37 million (U.S. Census Bureau, 2010a). And according to the National Research Council projections, by the year 2050, largely thanks to the most recent wave of immigration (along with differential fertility rates), America's Latino and Asian populations will triple, making up about 25 percent and 8 percent of the United States, respectively (Smith & Edmonston, 1997). No longer black and white, America is now a society composed of multiple ethnic and racial groups with an ever-shifting color line marking fuzzy boundaries.

In 1996, there was a Multiracial March on Washington in which multiracial activists demanded a separate census category in order to bolster their political claims and recognition. Although the movement did not result in a multiracial identity category, for the first time ever, the 2000 Census allowed respondents to check off more than one box for racial identity. The resulting multiracial population is currently estimated to be about 5.16 million, and those are just the self-identified people who checked more than one race box in 2000. The latest census also asks separate questions about race and ethnicity, which means that census data can now be used to examine some of the racial diversity within the Hispanic population, as well as some ethnic diversity among African American and white populations (see Figure 9.6).

Figure 9.6: Race Questions from the 2010 U.S. Census

9. What is Person 1's race? ***Mark ☒ one or more boxes.***

☐ White
☐ Black, African Am., or Negro
☐ American Indian or Alaska Native — *Print name of enrolled or principal tribe.*

☐ Asian Indian ☐ Japanese ☐ Native Hawaiian
☐ Chinese ☐ Korean ☐ Guamanian or Chamorro
☐ Filipino ☐ Vietnamese ☐ Samoan
☐ Other Asian — *Print race. for example, Hmong, Laotian, Thai, Pakistani, Cambodian, and so on.*
☐ Other Pacific Islander — *Print race, for example, Fijian, Tongan, and so on.*

☐ Some other race — *Print race.*

Black alone
12.6%
Hispanic alone
16.3%
American Indian and Alaskan native
0.9%
Two or more races
2.9%
Some other race alone
6.2%
Asian alone
4.8%
Native Hawaiian
0.2%

This so-called browning of America brings us to a new crossroads. The white–black divide may become the white–nonwhite divide or the black–nonblack divide. Sociologist Jennifer Lee has looked at just this question and her research shows that the experience of first- and especially second-generation Asians and Latinos indicates the new color line is black–nonblack. What does this mean? In the simplest terms, it means that the biggest differences on demographic characteristics like income, educational attainment, and interracial marriage will be between blacks and all other groups while the distinctions between these other groups continue to narrow. Lee notes,

> If you look at rates of educational attainment or interracial marriage or multiracial reporting, Asians and Latinos, their disadvantage stems from their immigrant histories, and so with each generation you see outcomes improving. For African Americans, you see there's some progress, but it's not nearly at the same speed, and so what I see is [that] the divide is really blacks and everyone else. . . . The one caveat I would add is that those Latinos who have darker skin, who are more mistaken for African Americans or black Americans . . . will probably fall on the black side of the divide. In part because of their skin color, but also because their socioeconomic status is not on par with some of the other lighter skin Latino groups like Cubans. (Conley, 2009j)

Lee points out that the biggest losers in this new configuration of race in America are likely to be—no surprise—blacks, who may be blamed for their own poverty when compared to all these successful Latino and Asian immigrants. Lee cautions, "Someone will look at African Americans who have been here longer and who aren't attaining certain levels of mobility and say, why can't they make it? If race isn't an issue for Asians and Latinos it shouldn't matter for blacks. What I argue is that the stigma attached to blackness because of the history of blackness is so different; they are not immigrants. To compare African Americans to immigrants is never fair."

http://wwnorton.com/studyspace

To watch more of the interview with Jennifer Lee about the color line, visit wwnorton.com/studyspace.

How close are we to this new black–nonblack color line? At least four states (California, Texas, Hawaii, and New Mexico) are deemed "majority minority" states, where whites are not the majority of the population within major metropolitan areas (U.S. Census Bureau, 2010b). But let's not forget that racial categories are social constructions, not static entities. To claim a multiracial identity presupposes the existence of a monoracial identity, when we know no scientifically pure or distinct race of people exists. Similarly, the notion of a white minority presumes that whiteness is a fixed racial category, whereas whiteness has expanded to include groups that were considered nonwhite in the past and may continue to fold Asians and Latinos into a kind of whiteness that emphasizes symbolic ethnicity. Indeed, as Warren and Twine (1997) point out, as long as blacks are present, a back door is open for nonblacks to slip under the white umbrella. For example, the Asian success story as the "model minority" is made possible by Asians' ability to blend in with whites, because they are unequivocally not black. We are at a point in America when whiteness may be expanding again, as always with blacks serving as the counterweight.

Desegregation

In 2003, 118 firefighters in the New Haven Fire Department took promotion exams. When the city reviewed the results, it invalidated all of the candidates' tests because no black firefighter scored well enough to be promoted. The city worried that it would be sued over the test's disproportionate impact on minorities. Nineteen firefighters who passed the test—seventeen of whom are white and two of whom are Hispanic—sued the city, claiming that they were denied promotion because of their race. Ultimately, this case, *Ricci v. DeStefano*, went before the Supreme Court in 2009, and the Court ruled that New Haven's decision to ignore the examination's results violated the Civil Rights Act of 1964. Let's consider where this decision falls in the longer arc of affirmative action and the Civil Rights Act—almost half a century after its passage.

Two sections of Title VII of the Civil Rights Act of 1964 have long been in tension: Employees are protected from "disparate treatment"—that is, intentional actions that result in discriminatory outcomes. But they are also protected from "disparate impact"—that is, unintentional conditions, such as a biased test, if those conditions produce discriminatory outcomes. Affirmative action policies rest on the horns of this tension. Institutions—such as universities or employers—act intentionally on the basis of race in order to

Frank Ricci

compensate for an implicit disparate impact on racial minorities or other protected groups.

Justice Anthony Kennedy, writing the majority opinion, clarified that such efforts—like throwing out test results for the New Haven firefighter promotions—must be justified by the "strong-basis-in-evidence" standard; there has to be pretty powerful evidence that the test was unfair. The fact that no blacks made the competitive cut is not evidence in itself. That would be confusing the cart (the promotions) and the horse (the exam).

In light of this, we might reasonably ask ourselves: What would constitute evidence? Until this question is answered, Justice Kennedy's majority opinion gives us little clarity on how to ensure equal opportunity in America. Recall our discussion of equality in Chapter 7. Though simpler to administer, "equality of outcome"—what quotas seek to implement—has been rejected by U.S. courts and does not sit well with American ideology. So we are left with the tough job of figuring out whether someone's chances—that is, opportunities—have been adversely impacted by their race, rather than whether his or her outcomes were worsened. That's much harder.

What's more, the question of evidence of unintentional discrimination is harder to pin down in the case of employment opportunities than it is in the case of education—and especially hard for jobs like firefighting where outcomes are tough to measure. The difference lies in the fact that college is a preparation for the labor market—a means to an end, also known as a path to opportunity. We can measure the end results—how minorities and whites fare once they graduate—in order to ask whether affirmative action policies are rectifying an inherently unlevel admissions playing field or, rather, putting unqualified minorities in educational environments that they cannot handle at the expense of qualified whites.

For example, in *The Shape of the River*, authors William G. Bowen and Derek Bok (1998) demonstrate that minority students admitted with lower SAT scores than their nonminority counterparts go on to perform equally well as life marches on in a variety of contexts and measures, ranging from professional achievement to community service, and not as well in others, such as income. The results are mixed, depending on what you think the purpose of college is.

If it turns out to be fairly hard to measure disparate impact in college admissions, it's nearly impossible for employment. How would we measure the outcomes—that is, the productivity—of a lieutenant or captain in the New Haven Fire Department? Lives saved or fires prevented? Social cohesion in the firehouse or cleanliness? Money saved or dollars spent? It's impossible, of course, because many of the would-be indicators are in tension with each other.

It would be simpler to scrap our whole approach to discrimination—written in a bygone era of *de jure* discrimination—and start from scratch. Clearly there is a racially disparate impact in New Haven—but it's probably not on the exam, it's in life. Blacks in the area go to worse schools and come from families that are, on average, much more disadvantaged economically. African Americans and Latinos are much more likely to have one parent at home growing up and are exposed to more dangerous environments. By the time they take the promotion test, this disparate impact is buried under years—or even generations—of policies and conditions.

Expecting a single test to compensate for all that is unrealistic—silly, even. This is a symptom of a larger pathology in the American psyche where our deep and abiding belief in meritocracy clashes with our culture of individualism: We expect testing and schools to do the work of social policy when they can't really carry such a heavy load. Removing biased questions from an exam is usually much too little, way too late.

If we are sincere in our desire to ensure true equality of opportunity, we need to update our toolbox and focus on the disparate lives of disadvantaged groups—by race, class, and disability status, just to name a few—long before kids take the SATs or firefighters take an "externally validated" exam. Until then, *Ricci v. DeStefano* won't be the last we've heard on the issue of employment discrimination.

→ CONCLUSION

When you look at race using the sociological imagination, you'll recognize that it's hardly a cut-and-dried issue. You'll see the historical social construction of ideas and identities. You'll see the present-day realities—sometimes monstrosities—of an aspect of our lives so often called a myth or fiction. And you'll be equipped to look at the changing nature of race and race relations that will affect your future.

ASSIGNMENT

Ask three white people you know the following: "How would you describe yourself over the phone to someone who has never seen you before?" Ask three people who are not white the same question. Did the two groups differ at all in their descriptions? Did they use race or ethnicity as descriptors? How are the self-identifications consistent with (or different from) your expectations after reading this chapter?

QUESTIONS FOR REVIEW

1. What does the childhood anecdote from the beginning of the chapter, about not yet having learned the meaning of race, teach us regarding the nature of race? Would a nonwhite three-year-old have brought home a white "baby sister"? How does this question bring up the "invisible knapsack of privileges" that puts white people at an advantage?
2. What does real estate value have to do with school segregation? With this link in mind, how have inequalities in wealth contributed to long-term inequality between blacks and whites in the United States?
3. Although the validity of "race" is debatable, why do sociologists study race as it relates, for example, to the likelihood of going to prison? What does this mean about what is "real," the way people understand the world, and what sociologists should study?
4. How has science been informed by culture (including racist beliefs) and, in turn, how has science fueled racism?
5. As the saying goes, "You can't judge a book by its cover." How do eugenics and physiognomy contradict this saying (in regard to people)? Are the principles behind these pseudosciences still with us today?
6. What is "racialization" and how has it differed between Muslims and the Irish?
7. How is stating your ethnicity more similar to stating you like the Beatles than describing your race?
8. Which of the four forms of minority–majority group relations has recently been most prevalent in the United States and Rwanda, respectively? How have the minority groups in these countries responded quite differently to domination?
9. Thinking about the history of race, what do you predict for the future of "race" and "ethnicity" as social categories? Will they stay the same? What do demographic trends and history lessons suggest might happen in the coming decades in the United States?

PARADOX

RACE AS WE KNOW IT HAS NO DETERMINISTIC, BIOLOGICAL BASIS: ALL THE SAME, RACE IS SO POWERFUL THAT IT CAN HAVE LIFE-OR-DEATH CONSEQUENCES.

WATCH THE ANIMATED SHORT ABOUT THE RACE PARADOX AT

WWNORTON.COM/STUDYSPACE

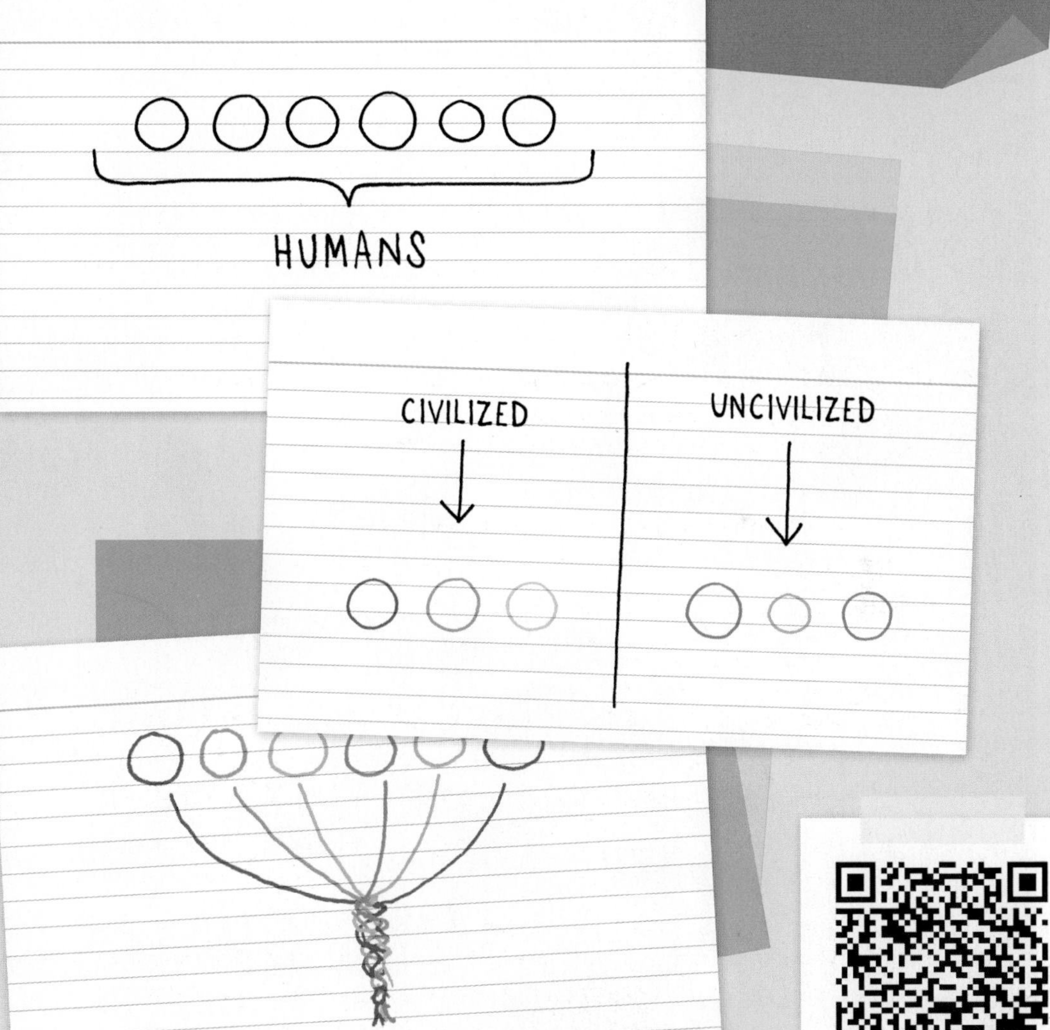

The Blue Birds, an Oglala Sioux family, live in a one-room house on the Pine Ridge Indian Reservation. They have been on a waiting list for more adequate housing for 17 years.

10 Poverty

PARADOX

HOW DO WE HELP THE POOR WITHOUT CREATING PERVERSE INCENTIVES THAT INDUCE MORE POVERTY IN THE LONG RUN?

Around the time President Lyndon Johnson delivered his first State of the Union address on January 8, 1964, declaring a "War on Poverty" in the United States, Marlin Card was conceived in a "real nice ride, parked at the top of a hill in Roslyn Heights in Long Island, New York." The car was parked behind Linden Court, one of a handful of public housing projects that pepper Nassau County's north shore. As Marlin's 19-year-old mother was experiencing the most intense part of morning sickness, toward the end of her first trimester, Johnson addressed a special session of Congress. On March 16, he declared, "Because it is right, because it is wise, and because, for the first time in our history, it is possible to conquer poverty, I submit, for the consideration of the Congress and the country, the Economic Opportunity Act of 1964." Johnson spoke with rhetorical flair and articulated a call for progressive policy that would be unheard of today, in an age where "big government" has been declared dead and buried: "It charts a new course. It strikes at the causes, not just the consequences of poverty."

Poverty can be defined as a condition of deprivation due to economic circumstances; this deprivation may be absolute or relative but is generally thought to be severe enough that the individual in this condition cannot live with dignity in his or her society. Intended to combat such deprivation, Johnson's legislation added new programs to old ones and brought them all under a single umbrella, the new Office of Economic Opportunity. This 1964 legislation introduced Head Start, College Work Study, and the Job Corps, to name just a few of its many programs. It wasn't merely a bureaucratic reorganization or incremental expansion of government programs, the new president

President Lyndon Johnson visits Imez, Kentucky, in 1964 to promote his War on Poverty and listen to resident Tom Fletcher describe some of the town's problems.

argued. "Rather, it is a commitment. It is a total commitment by this President, and this Congress, and this nation, to pursue victory over the most ancient of mankind's enemies" (1998/1964). Nearly fifty years later Johnson's words seem quaintly naïve—and yet somehow still moving.

Which brings us to a question that is so deceptively simple at first glance as to appear silly: Does poverty matter? More accurately, would raising the incomes of the least well off in the United States have any payback in terms of breaking the intergenerational cycle of poverty—making the American dream possible for more of our citizens and, in turn, saving society money in the long run? Or are such endeavors just a waste of money? Even worse, does aiding the poor create more problems than it solves through unintended consequences? In other words, is poverty cause or effect? Some would argue that we still don't know the answer to these questions long after Johnson promised to eradicate poverty as if it were smallpox. But perhaps poverty is neither cause nor effect but rather a proxy for an underlying social disease, namely, inequality and economic segregation. Significant new research suggests that this may, in fact, be the case.

This debate about whether poverty really hinders the life chances of low-income families or whether, instead, America is a land of opportunity and the poor are their own worst enemies has continued to rage through Republican and Democratic administrations, through welfare expansion and retrenchment, and through research study after research study. This debate has brought us such terms as the "culture of poverty," "welfare queens," and the "underclass"; it led Ronald Reagan to wave a copy of the help-wanted section of the *Washington Post* during the recession of 1983, asking why welfare recipients couldn't find work when there were so many job listings; it led to Bill Clinton's "end to welfare as we know it" in 1996, which prompted his assistant secretary of health and human services to resign in protest; and it led to George W. Bush's quixotic strategy of promoting marriage as economic policy.

After five decades, it seems appropriate to reflect on the impact of the War on Poverty and on the science that undergirded it, then and now. Usually, such evaluations are performed through objective analyses of statistics and economics. But there is also value in mapping onto social policy a human life—particularly one that has been directly affected by the policy. In many concrete ways, Marlin's life has reflected American social policy since his time in the womb: fed by food stamps, housed by the Department of Housing and Urban Development (HUD), and shuttled through the low end of the educational system before being interred in the ever-expanding prison-industrial complex. Faces like Marlin's appear on right-wing literature advocating lock-'em-up-and-throw-away-the-key sentencing policies. It's life histories like Marlin's that liberals prefer to ignore in favor of talking about "working families," but such histories must be confronted to illuminate the nature of poverty in America. Like the rest of us, Marlin is a complicated character whose life both challenges and fulfills many of the presumptions of both the left and the right.

Although Johnson's ambitious proposal and Marlin gestated together, the legislation beat Marlin into the world. On August 20, 1964, the Economic Opportunity Act of 1964 was born, about nine weeks before Marlin, on October 26. Thirty-eight years and much social policy later, I interviewed him for a book about sibling differences in economic success. He volunteered to participate in my study as a way to gain some intellectual stimulation beyond the legal research he was doing in the prison library for his upcoming parole hearing.

When I met Marlin, he was finishing a five-year sentence for burglary. He had been caught stealing from a stereo shop in Long Island. He has never carried a gun, never even hurt anyone, but has been a serial offender since his teens. Although born in rural Alabama, Marlin grew up in the public housing projects of New York City and neighboring Long Island. He had a younger sister who died days after her birth and a brother who died at 14 months. Marlin would have had an older sibling, too, if not for the backwoods abortion that Marlin claims made his mother go crazy from infection at age 16. According to Marlin, his mother Annie spent most of her days man hunting, sipping homemade "hooch" from a mayonnaise jar, and waiting in line in a welfare office. She had one other surviving child—a girl she bore in her mid-twenties, despite the pain of the rheumatoid arthritis that she had already developed and that was further exacerbated by her drinking. In short, Marlin is the product of the worst stereotypes of the urban American lower classes. Despite the fact that he suffered from a self-diagnosed case of attention-deficit/hyperactivity disorder (ADHD), he always received high praise in school and the neighborhood for his abilities. "Marlin, you're real smart," he was often told, "But you're bad as hell and C-R-A-Z-Y." Those same admirers would be quick to add that it wasn't his fault but his mother's.

Regardless of who was to blame, as Marlin grew older, the combination of his keen intellect and self-assessed attention-deficit tendencies caused him to become bored and restless in his low-achievement school environment, he explained. The "crazy" part overtook the "smart" side. The result of Marlin's erratic behavior was that rather than being placed in a gifted program or given medication to treat his hyperactivity, he was transferred to what was known as a "600" school—a special education program for problem kids. He eventually worked his way back to the regular education system, albeit to the lowest tracks in some of the worst-performing schools in New York, but by then the damage was done.

Before Marlin had entered middle school, he had cultivated his own taste for alcohol. By high school he had started using cocaine. He had lots of reasons to escape, plenty of direct emotional trauma apart from the daily stressors of poverty. In addition to his mother's debilitating illness, his baby brother Lew had just died.

To support his burgeoning drug habit, Marlin took to stealing, something he had learned from his mother. One Christmas, she told her kids to put on their winter coats and come shopping with her. Marlin wore a blue parka whose hood was trimmed with synthetic dog fur. The pockets had been torn out, which offered Marlin easy access to the space between the outer shell and the inner lining. His assignment then was to appropriate the sugar, catsup, and Kool Aid needed for the family's Christmas meal. His brother, who wore a brown tweed three-quarter-length coat, also with synthetic fur lining, was to steal a family-size can of Spam. Their mother meanwhile had $2 of food stamps to her name, with which she purchased a bag of onions and sack of potatoes, providing her two sons with a smooth exit in the process. That Christmas, she also announced that because of budgetary constraints, she had decided they would become Jehovah's Witnesses, who, as a matter of doctrine, don't believe in exchanging presents.

Stealing, Marlin learned from a young age, was what you did to eat on Christmas—or any other time you didn't have a dime to your name. He never wanted to get shot or hurt anyone, so he robbed businesses rather than residences; he did not want to confront someone in his or her own home. "I don't want to wake up some Clint Eastwood in the middle of the night," he explained. Furthermore, because he believed that most businesses carried insurance, his victims seemed less real and personalized to Marlin—after all, he claimed, "They all got insurance to the max. Hell, I thought I was helping them out when sales were slow." Even after he kicked his drug habit during a prison bid in New Jersey, Marlin continued to steal electronics equipment and similar items, fencing them on 125th Street in Harlem. It was hard for him to stop. Certainly, as he was a felon without much formal schooling, it would have been difficult for him to get a legitimate job, but he also liked the thrill—the rush of putting on black sweats and a mask, sneaking into a store in the middle of the night, running from the cops, and negotiating for the best prices when he sold his successful scores to other shops that didn't hesitate to do business with him.

Marlin's case puts the central question of poverty up front: If society had raised his mother's income, would he have fared any better? Could he have been lifted out of a life of crime if his mother's financial struggle had been any easier? Or would such an effort have been throwing good money after bad? Was poverty a cause or an effect in Marlin's life?

The Culture of Poverty

In 1966, when Marlin was two years old, the anthropologist Oscar Lewis published an article titled "The Culture of Poverty," which served as the capstone to a long career devoted to studying the lives of poor Mexicans (as well as some Puerto Ricans on the island and in New York City). The lives of Mexican peasants during the 1950s would have seemed to have little relevance to poverty in the United States, by then one of the richest nations in the world. But suddenly, the phrase "culture of poverty," which Lewis had used to describe a supposedly self-defeating set of practices of a few Mexican families, took root in the American public consciousness. The **culture of poverty** argument was that poor people adopt certain practices that differ from those of middle-class, "mainstream" society in order to adapt and survive in difficult economic circumstances. In the U.S. context, these practices might include illegal work, multigenerational living arrangements, multifamily households, serial relationships in place of marriage, and the pooling of community resources as a form of informal social insurance (otherwise known as "swapping"). Each of these cultural practices seems to be a rational response to a tenuous financial situation; according to the culture of poverty theory, once these survival adaptations are in place, they take on a life of their own, and in the long run they hold poor people back when they are no longer advantageous.

A Mexican peasant family near the volcano of Popocatepetl. How did anthropologist Oscar Lewis explain the ways that poor families adapt to difficult circumstances?

Culture of poverty the argument that poor people adopt certain practices that differ from those of middle-class, "mainstream" society in order to adapt and survive in difficult economic circumstances.

Let's take swapping as an example of an informal social safety net meant to make up for the sizable holes in the official one. Neighbors, friends, and relatives exchange time, money, and other resources when needed to make up for temporary shortfalls. If I have a job interview, you might watch my kids for a couple of hours, but I'll owe you one. Or when you're short on food at the end of the month, I might give you some of my food stamps if I have come into some extra cash that week. Swapping works when times are tough, but it also may hold people back from "making it," because it means that they are enmeshed in many cross-cutting obligations of reciprocity from which they cannot escape. If I finally secure a steady job, I will probably find many people coming to my door in need. So why strive to outdo the Joneses? I would just have to support them anyway.

Dating is another example. When I met with Marlin in the basement room in Hempstead, Long Island, he secured when released on parole, he showed me a photo of his new girlfriend. She was 10 years younger and beautiful, with long braided hair, smooth skin, and a slender figure. "On the physical tip, I never had a woman of her quality," he admitted. "I usually get the big mamas. Or even if they are small, then they're not in good shape. They're small because they're high or something." His new friend represented a marked improvement. Although she lived in the projects, she had a good job as a sales manager and health insurance for her children. Marlin explained that he had fallen for her in a way in which he had never fallen for anyone before. (She was not his prison-rebound lover, either; he had already been through another relationship

Becky De La Rosa (far left, on couch) and her best friend Malinda Puga (far right) sometimes watch several children, including their own, during the day to help out their friends and siblings. How is this an example of an informal safety net?

since getting out.) They had known each other only a few weeks, but already Marlin was smitten and anxious. "Usually I'm the one who says, 'Stop sweatin' me.' But this time, she is giving me a chill. I got to cool out." To make matters worse, Marlin explained that back in prison, he always preached to his fellow inmates that they should never get involved with a woman who has children. "Because, the daddy can always pop back into her life." And now he had ignored his own advice, he admitted, and laughed as he buried his smiling face in his calloused palm. And therein lies the catch-22. If men are afraid to become attached to women who already have children, for fear of getting burned, the instability of the household is perpetuated, particularly when the fathers themselves may be cycling in and out of marginal employment, prison, and the family.

Lewis's self-perpetuating cycle of poverty played right into the already raging debate over the state of the black family that had been ignited by Daniel Patrick Moynihan's controversial 1965 report on black families, in which he argued that a tangle of family pathology holds back the African American population (see Chapter 12). According to Moynihan, the cultural arrangement of the black family—matrifocal (where the mother assumes structural prominence) and multigenerational—is the cause, not the effect, of African American economic problems. The "tangle of pathology" and its ideological twin, the culture of poverty argument, engulfed much of sociology at the end of the 1960s, as actual fires spread across rioting urban America. This intellectual revolution, if it was that, peaked in 1970, when Harvard political scientist Edward Banfield wrote *The Unheavenly City*, a best-selling book that applied these ideas explicitly to the United States. Without undertaking field research, Banfield asserted that the lower class was unable to escape their own poverty because they were not future oriented. This lack of future orientation led to such troubles as an inability to delay gratification and save money, difficulty planning the right kind of families, and senseless knee-jerk violence. It was this instant-gratification mentality, he argued, that was keeping those in the lower class from moving up in the world. Those who did escape poverty did not disprove his point; rather, he noted that those folks were not really lower class; they were middle-class people who were just taking longer to reach their potential. You might start to see a problem here—the argument is that people in the lower class are in the lower class because they have the personality traits of people in the lower class. This is what we call a circular argument—like a dog chasing its tail, the directional arrow from cause to effect also points from effect to cause. At the time, many were relieved to embrace the notion that society was not to blame, rather that people in the lower class were responsible for their own pathological poverty.

It seems that Lyndon Johnson's War on Poverty had in a short time engendered a sizable backlash. Researchers who felt that poverty was the cause, not the effect, of the poor's ills spent much of the next few years rebutting contrary claims implicit in the culture of poverty thesis. During this time, Marlin was tagging along with his mother to various welfare offices in downtown Brooklyn for her "face-to-faces"—the humiliating rituals that public assistance recipients have to go through in order to stay on the welfare rolls. The two would have to get an early start the morning of their appointment day because, by then, Marlin's mother suffered from a severe case of rheumatoid arthritis. Marlin had to dress her before dawn so that they could secure a good spot in line. Even with such a jump-start, they often spent many hours standing in various lines to comply with regulations. These obstacles aside, their mood would lift dramatically once she had "busted her digit"—that is, cashed her check. Busting a digit meant the end of the preceding week of "hard times," as they called the last week of the month, when the previous check had long since run out and the only provisions remaining in the house were typically a box of Quaker Oats grits, a light bulb, and a gallon jug of ice water.

Welfare was one of the supposedly self-defeating cultural practices of the poor. The notion was that reliance on the government created a sense of helplessness and dependency, and hindered entry into the formal labor market when the economy picked up. It is fairly obvious that welfare did hinder work, but perhaps not through any complicated social-psychological dynamic of "learned helplessness" or the like. Rather, it could simply be that once you are on the dole, you have to spend considerable time and energy jumping through the hoops that the bureaucracy requires of you—not to mention making those Quaker Oats grits last through the week while attending to the full-time rigors of child care and housework. So it's not so easy to secure a decent job (even if there is one to be had) when you have to spend entire days keeping appointments to get your kids' food stamps that month. In addition, the government offices administering food stamps or the Supplemental Nutrition Program for Women, Infants, and Children (better known as WIC) are open for only limited hours and often are not located optimally to serve the poorest areas. This lack of accessibility could partly explain why the 45.3 million participants in the food stamp program (now renamed the Supplemental Nutrition Assistance Program or SNAP) translates to seven out of ten people eligible receiving the assistance (Food Research and Action Center, 2011).

Negative Income Tax

Minimizing the amount of time welfare programs require of their recipients was one of the many rationales behind the next idea in social policy: the negative income tax experiment. In the late 1960s and early 1970s, around the time that Marlin was dressing his mother to wait in line at public assistance offices, the United States conducted its most ambitious social experiment to date. At several sites around the country, scientists enrolled poor people in treatment and control groups. The control group got their welfare checks (and stood in line) or their wages as before, whereas the treatment group received a guaranteed check, as in social democracies such as Sweden. The government reclaimed the money through taxation until a certain crossover point at which households would start paying "positive" taxes—hence the term *negative income tax*. The research study began in 1968 across multiple sites in the state of New Jersey and then moved to Seattle and Denver in the early 1970s after some retooling.

The study's results confirmed the worst political fears of the left: In the treatment group, women left their marriages in droves because they were no longer financially dependent on a man, and unemployment spells increased in duration. (Of course, a number of feminists argued that providing some women with economic independence so they could escape bad or abusive marriages was a good thing; however, a policy that discourages marriage doesn't generally go over well in the United States.) For example, the Stanford Research Institute found that in Seattle and Denver, the treatment groups experienced an average work reduction of 9 percent for men and 18 percent for women. According to analyst Jodie T. Allen, who wrote about the program in "Designing Income Maintenance Systems" (1973), these statistics suggested that as much as 50 to 60 percent of the money paid to two-parent families under a negative income tax would replace earnings so that people would work less. We might not be able to lift families out of poverty, but we could give them a lot more leisure time.

The Underclass

For the next decade or so, as Marlin made his way through various public schools, there was silence from most poverty experts. In the meantime, however, real incomes had begun to stagnate (because of the 1973 energy crisis and a variety of other forces). By the late 1970s, inequality was sharply on the rise, welfare rolls swelled, and the crime rate had also turned sharply upward. By the 1980s, as Marlin started using crack cocaine, two more versions of the culture of poverty thesis had emerged. Writing in the *New Yorker* in 1981, journalist Ken Auletta inaugurated the concept of the underclass—the culture of poverty supersized for the 1980s. Not only are the poor different from the mainstream in their inability to take advantage of what society has to offer, went the underclass thesis, but also they are increasingly deviant and even dangerous to the rest of us.

Underclass the notion, building on the culture of poverty argument, that the poor not only are different from mainstream society in their inability to take advantage of what mainstream society has to offer but also are increasingly deviant and even dangerous to the rest of us.

Poverty researchers were slow to respond. In the meantime, social critic Charles Murray argued that the underclass thesis was flawed: The poor are no different from the rest of us; they respond rationally to economic incentives. According to Murray, poverty per se is not the culprit, nor is the so-called culture. The poor, he argued in *Losing Ground* (1984), were the victims of an ever-expanding welfare state that provided the wrong long-term incentives. Welfare regulations made work and marriage less attractive and rising welfare benefits more attractive. To make his case, Murray pointed to the expansion of welfare over the same period that showed a rise in crime, the proportion of out-of-wedlock births, and duration of unemployment. To bolster his claim, he rolled out the results of the negative income tax experiment. (See Chapter 15 for more on the modern welfare state.)

To watch more of my conversation with David Grusky, visit wwnorton.com/studyspace.

Social scientists who disagreed with both arguments found themselves trapped. To argue against the underclass concept, they had to show that the poor were no different from the rest of us but merely responding to a lack of opportunity. But that view played right into Murray's thesis about the perverse incentives of welfare. My conversation with Professor David Grusky, director of Stanford University's Center for the Study of Poverty and Inequality illustrates this dilemma (along with the opportunity that the 1996 welfare reform law provided):

Perverse incentives reward structures that lead to suboptimal outcomes by stimulating counterproductive behavior; for example, welfare—to the extent that it discourages work efforts—is argued to have perverse incentives.

> A long-standing argument against building a bigger safety net has been that it creates perverse incentives: that if we had an attractive alternative to the labor market, in the form of very substantial safety net resources, people would opt for the safety net instead of the labor market. It strikes me as highly implausible that anyone in a country like the United States that so values work, would choose the non-work alternative. I think that's implausible in the extreme. Now there were some situations in the old thinking of the past, in which perverse incentives were created and perhaps one could apply logic of that sort. But the Clinton Reforms, for whatever you think of them, the Clinton Welfare Reforms, eliminated most of those perverse incentives. And so I think it would be very old fashioned at this point in time to worry about perverse incentives built into the safety net. (Conley 2011c)

To pose an alternative to both positions—poor as deviant and poor as rational followers of perverse incentives—prominent sociologists such as William Julius Wilson argued that welfare was really a minor consideration with respect to the labor and marriage markets in inner cities. Deindustrialization,

Deindustrialization and globalization hit cities such as Detroit hard. There are more than 12,000 abandoned homes in the Detroit area, a by-product of the rapid depopulation of the city since the 1950s.

globalization, suburbanization, discrimination, gentrification, and other factors were the real culprits, according to Wilson and his supporters, and the lack of jobs created by these factors led to a dearth of employed men for women to marry (Wilson, 1978, 1996).

In the wake of Wilson's research, many poverty policy experts wanted to "make work pay." Hence, the abandonment of dreams of a Swedish-style welfare state in favor of targeted, work-friendly policies such as the expansion of the earned income tax credit, which eliminates the taxes that low-income workers have to pay. Politicians also pushed to raise the income limits on Medicaid, so that the poor would not lose their health insurance as they left welfare for the low-wage labor market. Finally, there was the 1996 Personal Responsibility and Work Opportunity Reconciliation Act (PRWORA), otherwise referred to as "the end of welfare as we know it." The PRWORA shifted more of the responsibilities of running welfare programs onto individual states, limited the number of months that a person can receive aid, and added other components to encourage two-parent families and discourage out-of-wedlock births.

Through these changes to welfare, all but forsaking poor adults in favor of the "deserving poor" or children, Democrats seemed to blunt the conservative critiques of perverse incentives in welfare. In lieu of universal health insurance, progressives pushed successfully for the Children's Health Insurance Program. Instead of more income support for families, Democrats would propose children's savings accounts that parents couldn't touch. As late as the 2000 presidential campaign, Al Gore argued for universal day care, the idea of making Head Start available to all American families, as was Social Security, and thus removing the stigma that derives from income requirements. After all, children shouldn't be held responsible for their parents' poor choices. Or should they?

About the same time that welfare reform went into effect, a third, almost fatal blow was dealt to leftists' arguments for an expanded safety net and a renewed focus on the well-being of poor children. It came from Susan Mayer, a sociologist who wrote *What Money Can't Buy: Family Income and Children's Life Chances* (1997). In it, she argued that the effects of income poverty on children have been vastly overstated. Study after study had showed that a childhood spent in poverty was associated with poor health, behavioral problems, bad grades, teenage pregnancy, dropping out of school, and ultimately continued poverty as an adult. But documenting an association between two factors is different from showing that poverty caused all these social ills. This logic was exactly what social scientists had used to debunk Murray a dozen years earlier: Just because you can draw a correlation between welfare expenditures and out-of-wedlock childbearing doesn't mean that one is driving the other. Rather, it may be a coincidence, or both may be caused jointly by something else. (In the case of the welfare-marriage link, some scholars have argued that good jobs are the missing third factor.)

Mayer did not simply argue that researchers with a political agenda may have been hasty in concluding that family poverty hurts children; she went one step better, making the case that the real impact of income on children was somewhere between trivial and minor. For example, she reasoned that if income really mattered in terms of school dropout rates, it should be family income before the age of dropping out that matters, not parental income afterward. But in her analysis, parents' income when a kid was in his or her twenties seemed to matter almost as much as parental income when that child was an adolescent, when he or she was at risk of leaving high school. Mayer smelled something fishy here. Likewise, when she compared different sources of income—from welfare, from earnings, and from investments—she found that earnings, the source most linked to successful parents, were more highly associated with positive outcomes for children, such as test scores and prosocial behavior. If it were truly the dollars that mattered for children, then investment income, gifts, and welfare dollars should have a positive effect, too, but they didn't seem to in her data. She also examined the association between parental income and certain purchases that are supposed to matter for young children. She found a relatively weak relationship between income and the standard measures that psychologists have used to rate the educational environment of the home, such as the presence of books, educational toys, and so on. Meanwhile, the household conditions that are highly responsive to income—such as money spent on food, eating out,

According to sociologist Susan Mayer, how does poverty affect children?

more spacious residences, and car ownership—were also weakly related to children's outcomes. In other words, what appears to matter for children is not money itself. Thus, giving money to poor parents would seem like an illogical policy prescription.

Mayer didn't begin this endeavor with a political agenda. She had assumed her research would document that poverty mattered for children, not that it would provide evidence to the contrary. She herself had been poor. As Mayer writes in the introduction of her book, "I've been poor and I've been not poor, and believe me, being not poor is much better."

The Bell Curve Thesis

In their best-selling book *The Bell Curve: Intelligence and Class Structure in American Life*, Richard Herrnstein and Charles Murray (1994) came to policy conclusions similar to Mayer's—that the same traits that make adults economically successful make them good parents—in a more polemical and less nuanced fashion. Mayer focused on the likelihood that the same skills both lead to higher incomes and make for good parenting; Herrnstein and Murray went a step further, arguing that what really matters is good genes. In an interview in *Skeptic,* Murray explained what he meant, using the example of child neglect:

> Well, as every parent knows without reading anything about I.Q., there is a plausible relationship between intelligence and child abuse. Which is to say, any parent knows if a child has had a fever for 24 hours and hasn't been taking in liquids, you make a calculation that this has gone on too long and we've got to get this kid to a doctor, etc. Any parent knows that childproofing a home takes foresight and thoughtfulness—it takes a certain amount of I.Q. With that plausible relationship in mind, the failure of social science and politicians alike to confront the possibility that low I.Q. is an important risk factor in child neglect is scandalous. Every single bit of evidence that does bear on this says that I.Q. is a great big factor in child neglect. (Miele, 1995)

And where does a low IQ come from? Genes, of course.

According to Hernnstein and Murray, successful parents have fortunate genes and pass them on to their kids—whether or not they buy books, educational toys, or Mozart CDs. They also claim that as the United States has become more meritocratic over the last half-century, fewer people with bad genes have risen to the top, and fewer with good ones have gotten stuck at the bottom. Thus, the poor are increasingly hopeless because it is increasingly their genes' fault that they remain at the bottom of the ladder. So why waste any money helping them climb out of poverty, as it's bound to be futile? If either Murray and Herrnstein or Mayer is correct, it means that the advocates for prenatal care, child care, and reductions in child poverty, who argue that a dollar spent on early-childhood services yields several dollars of savings in the long run, are way off the mark.

The poverty research community once again found itself on the ropes. Just showing an association between growing up poor and any adverse outcome was no longer good enough. The ultimate gauntlet had been thrown down: Was poverty just a side effect of biological conditions, or did it actually cause limited opportunities for children? Finally, some sociologists and economists have responded by conducting experiments. The last time researchers ventured into the world of socially engineered experiments, the result was disastrous for progressive arguments for expanded aid to the poor. Why would this time be different?

Moving to Opportunity

In 1966, when Marlin was two years old, Dorothy Gautreaux, a resident in a project on Chicago's South Side, took part in a class-action lawsuit that alleged public housing was serving as de facto government-sponsored segregation. *Gautreaux v. Chicago Housing Authority* dragged on for 10 years in federal courts, finally working its way up to the Supreme Court. Before the Court could rule, attorneys for the residents settled the suit with the U.S. Department of Housing and Urban Development (HUD). As a result of the lawsuit, the government undertook a new social experiment of sorts: a housing voucher plan to help 7,100 families in public housing secure homes in the private rental market in the more affluent Chicago suburbs. The goal was to disperse at least 75 percent of the families into neighborhoods with less than 30 percent minority residents. In addition to the vouchers, the participants received counseling and rental referral services to help them locate available units. Essentially, it represented an end-run to the years-long waiting list for the regular Section 8 program that provided poor families with subsidies in the private rental market.

The results of a study done decades later by Northwestern University sociologist James Rosenbaum (2000) found that those who moved out of the ghetto and into low-poverty areas had better employment situations, and their children improved on a number of indicators. The problem was that the Gautreaux Assisted Housing Program wasn't really an experiment: Families self-selected into the moving group, so there wasn't a fair comparison to a real control group. Furthermore, researchers tracked down only 60 percent of the original group who had relocated by the time of the second interview in 1989, so some suggested that the better outcomes might be attributable to the fact that the people interviewed were those most successful in their new homes.

A new study, "Moving to Opportunity" (MTO), attempted to pick up where Gautreaux left off. The sample of families was randomly assigned to

Dorothy Gautreaux

Tachon Evans and her daughter (left) moved from the Robert Taylor Homes (right) to the suburbs of Chicago through the Gautreaux Assisted Housing Program. The program helps move people from public housing to suburban homes in an effort to avoid segregation.

move to a low poverty area, or, for the control group, to wherever they wanted (usually a high-poverty neighborhood). All efforts were made to track them down whether they stayed put or continued to move. In 1994, Henry Cisneros, then secretary of HUD, picked Baltimore, Boston, Chicago, Los Angeles, and New York as the sites where this experiment would be carried out. Seventy million dollars was authorized for the study, and more funds would become available for a 10-year evaluation.

Of the families that agreed to participate, one-third received no housing voucher at all, another third received vouchers with no restrictions on where they moved, and the final treatment group received the vouchers and assistance in relocating to rental units in areas with less than 10 percent poverty rates plus tutorials in basic life skills ranging from balancing a checkbook to yard work to lease negotiation. It turned out that those in the treatment group reported experiencing less stress from violence and other factors and were generally happier and healthier. Among children, the effects were the most dramatic: Test scores increased, school truancy dropped, and health improved; most notably, the incidence of injuries and asthma episodes decreased. The bad news was that there was little in the way of short-run changes in welfare use between the treatment and control groups (although overall welfare rates did begin to drop in the late 1990s) or in employment and earnings, which also improved for all groups thanks to the economic boom of the 1990s. One limitation of the study was that it only yielded findings for families who had enrolled in the original study. We will never know about those families who would have been eligible for MTO but had either no knowledge of the program or no interest in it. Getting out of the ghetto may help only those poor families who want to leave and have the resources to remain informed about such opportunities.

MTO also didn't answer the poverty question, because incomes were held constant and the social environment had changed. So it really was the converse study to the negative income tax experiment of 25 years earlier, in which social conditions were not altered but incomes changed. In fact, MTO may be viewed as a direct test of the culture of poverty thesis. Better outcomes among those living in low-poverty neighborhoods can come about because of more opportunity or more tranquility or both. The results of MTO appear to suggest that uprooting families from high-poverty, high-risk neighborhoods produces greater tranquility, if not greater opportunity (at least initially). That is, the main return on investment seems to be the outcomes that are the most sensitive to social or cultural conditions and the behavior of peers: violence, fear, stress, and child development measures. The outcomes related to economic opportunity, such as parents' success in the labor force, seem less responsive. Read as a whole, the results suggest that when poor people live together, each family's risk of adverse outcomes increases. Isn't that the culture of poverty argument made more scientific and less anthropological? After all, what's so bad about living with poor people if not their own behavior? It's hard to argue that cleaner streets, better garbage service, backyards, lawns, and better-funded schools made the difference. Probably more important is not having to worry about your neighbors shooting you when you step outside your front door. MTO's results serve as an indictment both of the social problems rampant in poor neighborhoods and of the larger society that has invested in gated communities, suburban sprawl, and other forms of economic (and racial) segregation. MTO seems to imply that if income is not the main problem, social division is.

As for income itself, there has been no social engineering since the days of the negative income tax, just a series of smaller-scale experiments such as providing the poor with matching funds for savings accounts or offering private school vouchers through a lottery system. The best evidence about the impact of income comes not from purposive social experimentation but rather from accidental science—natural experiments that some researchers have exploited to examine the impact of income. Two recent studies that together form the best evidence on the impact of income concern gambling. Economists Guido Imbens, Donald Rubin, and Bruce Sacerdote surveyed lottery players in the mid-1980s and found that a modest prize ($15,000 a year for 20 years) did not have much effect on work behavior (Imbens et al., 2001). A larger prize (around $80,000 per year) did reduce work hours by about 20 percent (reproducing the negative income tax's results). Perhaps the most interesting results were those showing that people with zero earnings, who were not in the workforce at all before winning, increased their commitment to work after receiving their prize, even if it was modest. This could mean that those at the very bottom face significant financial obstacles to fully participating in the economy. Maybe they use their winnings to buy a car to get to work, to put down a deposit on a home, or to simply stop wasting time in welfare queues and spend that time looking for a job.

The second study (Costello et al., 2003) concerned the lives of Cherokee children who had experienced a windfall in income thanks to legalized gambling

To study the social effects of income, Imbens, Rubin, and Sacerdote surveyed lottery winners. What did they find? How does the survey of families receiving money from Cherokee casinos support their results?

on Native American reservations. Casino payouts in North Carolina lifted 14 percent of Cherokee families out of poverty. Among those families, children's behavioral problems decreased, largely as a result of the additional time that parents now had to supervise their children. Perhaps the negative income tax researchers were asking the wrong question 30 years ago; they should have focused on the children rather than the parents who received the checks.

The War on Poverty Today

Today Marlin does not drink, smoke, or use drugs. He gets up early each morning to report to his temporary agency for employment. (He makes $7.25 per hour gross, although the agency probably charges his actual employer, a public housing project where he does maintenance work, twice that amount.) On weekends Marlin often journeys into Manhattan to hit the wholesale district in search of designer bags that he resells to women on Long Island. This is really his last chance to go straight; if he is convicted of a felony again, he will likely be eligible for Social Security the next time he is released.

Over dinner at White Castle, I asked Marlin whether he believed that extra money when he was growing up would have made a difference in his life. "My mother would have just drunk the money away," he confessed, scoring one point for the right. Then what would have made a difference? I asked. He thought for a moment, leaning back in the plastic booth we occupied, lacing his fingers behind his neck. "The issue is not money, the issue is time," he explained. "It ain't just a ghetto thing; kids all across America are being raised by Nintendo and TV 'cause the parents have no time for them." He explained that his new girlfriend's children were in this situation as well. She worked six days a week, leaving her kids in the care of their great-grandmother, who used video games and the like to create some peace in the household.

"Everyone is working all the time," he claimed. What about welfare? I inquired. "Welfare doesn't make a difference, you still gotta work, you still gotta do everything they want." Why were Americans working so hard? "Prices are so high. And everyone thinks they need all these things—the Nintendo, et cetera—so they are always stressed about money. It's like a disease, and as I said, it ain't just a ghetto thing." I asked him if that meant raising the minimum wage and implementing other antipoverty policies that could lower economic stress would make a difference. People don't need more money, he countered, just more time: quality time with their children. Maybe the negative income tax and lottery results were not so bad after all. Maybe increased leisure and reduced work commitment would have paid off in the long run for kids.

On my way back to Manhattan—one of the most unequal counties in the continental United States (the borough is coterminous with New York County)—I turned over Marlin's comments in my mind. Back at White Castle, they seemed to make sense, and Marlin appeared to be almost a prophet about the state of America. But on the train, it dawned on me that his story didn't explain why rich kids still end up likely to be rich and poor kids more often grow up to be poor. So the next day, when he made his weekly trip to the wholesale district in the city, I asked him to elaborate. He claimed that it was because poor kids are not exposed to the horizon of possibilities: why they should go to college, what good jobs are like, and what living well actually means. Surrounded only by stress and frustrated expectations—made only worse by our society's corporate-manufactured needs—"ghetto kids just do what they are exposed to."

Cordillera, Colorado, an ultra-exclusive community for the very rich, overlooks a trailer park in Edwards, Colorado. Many of the domestic workers in Cordillera cannot find affordable housing in town and must make long commutes to their jobs.

Marlin and Susan Mayer may think along the same lines. *What Money Can't Buy* was about the impact of families' own money on their kids' life chances; her newest research addresses how "other people's money matters." Mayer says that we face a choice in rich societies: Do we prefer a society with lots of equality, leisure, and social cohesion or one with greater inequality, less leisure, less cohesion, and a higher level of creativity and more goods and services? She claims that no clear answer exists—for herself, for society, or even for the poorest citizens themselves.

In a personal interview with me a few years ago, Mayer concluded that "thinking about the meaning of money in a 'radical' capitalist nation like the U.S. is really very complicated and frustrating because it has so little to do with basic needs. The urge to want

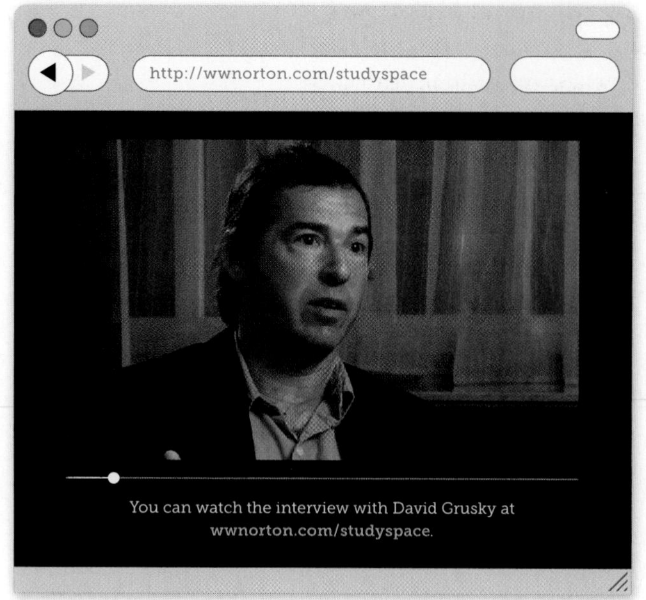

You can watch the interview with David Grusky at wwnorton.com/studyspace.

more seems so primal and the satisfaction from having more is so fleeting, and for most of us, no amount of understanding the essential irrationality of it makes us want less." If there is one thing that rubbing elbows with the rich has taught Mayer, it is the limits of what money can buy—at least at the top. For the rest of us, all that money of those at the top may be what matters the most, even if it isn't ours, because it structures our society and our desires in ways that we aren't even aware of. It is not just poverty but poverty in the midst of growing wealth, especially ostentatious consumerism (see Chapter 3), that really matters.

If this is true, as a society, we are moving backward with respect to economic opportunity by cutting taxes on the rich. Historically, high levels of income and wealth inequality mix with economic segregation (best embodied by the gated community or the exclusive apartment building) to create a noxious potion for the poor among us. It means that those at the bottom—and perhaps even the middle—have to travel farther and farther to reach their low-wage jobs servicing the needs of the wealthy. This intersection of inequality and real estate has reached absurd dimensions in Aspen, Colorado, where tourist industry workers often drive hours in their daily commutes to the ski resort—hence, economist Robert Frank's term the "Aspen effect" (2007). One of the security guards at my office wakes at 4:00 each morning to ride a bus through three states to reach his job by 8:00, so that he can own a home with a backyard and send his kids to decent schools. Of course, if time supervising children is what helps break the cycle of poverty, these daily marathons may do more harm than they are worth.

I am not alone in noticing the pernicious effect of economic segregation. Grusky shared with me a fantasy, so to speak:

> If one could wave with a magic wand [and] change one thing about American society, [the] one change that would have the biggest effect, in terms of reducing poverty and inequality [would] be to de-legitimate residential segregation. And, simply make it as part of the commitment that Americans take on that we should all live together, no matter how rich or poor we may be. And that segregating rich people in one neighborhood and poor people in another neighborhood is simply illegitimate. I think that one change would have major effects on, on how much poverty and inequality we see. It also would probably be one of the most difficult changes to undertake. (Conley, 2001c)

Where we live is only the most obvious way that gross inequality puts a strain on the lives of those at the bottom, however. There is also the more subtle issue of expectations and aspirations. A society with an extremely wealthy class—especially one that is socially isolated enough to lose the long-standing American taboo against conspicuous consumption—must constantly create new needs to soak up the luxury spending power of those at the top. Of course, these "needs" filter down to the rest of us through television and other such media. Marlin now supplements his paycheck with weekly runs to Manhattan to buy knockoff designer handbags in the wholesale district, which he sells for a small profit to working-class women on Long Island. In their conditions of production and distribution, the Chinese-made handbags act as a metaphor for the effects of growing inequality and consumerism. Marlin's customers are hardworking women who intentionally spend their disposable income on the counterfeit status symbols of the rich.

Poverty amid Plenty

The difficulties of conceptualizing poverty amid plenty are perhaps best illustrated by a speech given by one of *Forbes*'s 400 richest Americans, Tom Monaghan, who rose to great wealth from meager origins. "To me one of the most exciting things in the world is being poor," he began his lecture. To explain what he meant, Monaghan cited a study that concluded a family of four could survive on $68 per year around 1970 (equivalent to $256 today). "Now you're probably wondering how you can live on $68 a year. The first thing you do is go to the Farm Bureau and buy a hundred-pound bag of powdered milk. . . . While you're at the Farm Bureau, you buy yourself a bushel of oats or wheat or corn, and you mash that stuff up. . . . And you grow some vegetables and you get a few vitamin pills to supplement your diet. And I think that's exciting." He went on to talk about how cheaply he lived in a house trailer, calling it "the greatest living I ever did." He concluded his speech with a rhetorical appeal: "Oh gosh," Monaghan said, "I'd love to talk to all these people who say they can't get by" (Monaghan, 1990).

We could debate exactly how cheaply someone could survive in the contemporary United States or a similarly developed country, and we could question the hypocrisy of a man worth hundreds of millions of dollars castigating the poor for their implied whining, but that would miss the deeper point Monaghan raises. Namely, what does it mean to be poor in a country where starvation and death from the elements are rare? This question inevitably leads us to the debate over absolute versus relative measures of poverty. Monaghan's reasoning is not that far afield from a long tradition of absolute poverty measurement that has based its calculations on the cost of food.

How did Domino's Pizza CEO Tom Monaghan defend his views on poverty?

Absolute and Relative Poverty

Absolute poverty the point at which a household's income falls below the necessary level to purchase food to physically sustain its members.

Since the end of the eighteenth century, many individuals and institutions have tried to come up with a perfect measure of absolute poverty, the point at which a household's income falls below the necessary level to purchase food to physically sustain its members. (Note that such a concept fits very well with Karl Marx's notion of the physical reproduction of labor.) Attempts to establish such a minimal standard started in England in 1795 when the town of Speenhamland "instituted a relief program that made up the difference between a worker's wage and the cost of bread sufficient to feed him and his family" (Stone, 1994). In 1901, Benjamin Seebohm Rowntree attempted to devise a specific measure in York, England, when he documented an income level below which the necessities to maintain a person's physical efficiency could not be afforded. The results of this study were published in *Poverty, A Study of Town Life* (1910). Rowntree's approach was institutionalized in the United Kingdom by the Parliament's Beveridge Report in 1942, which became the platform for the welfare state of the Labour Party in 1945.

The most famous American version of the food-based measurement of poverty status was that of Mollie Orshansky in her 1963 article "Children of the Poor." To estimate the poverty line, she used a strategy not unlike that implicit in Monaghan's speech. She took the U.S. Department of Agriculture's recommendations for the minimum amount of healthy food, estimated the cost for a variety of family types (62 in all), and multiplied this figure by a factor of three (based on the results of the Consumer Expenditure Survey in the mid-1950s, which estimated that families spent an average of 35 percent of their household budgets on food). Soon, this became the official poverty line of the United States, and it has been the definition of poverty against which researchers have most frequently suggested alternatives. Figure 10.1 shows how this official poverty rate (and total numbers of "officially" poor Americans) has varied over a period of five decades.

Orshansky has been assailed from all sides for the choices she made in estimating the poverty line in the United States. Early criticism revolved around her choice of three as the multiplier. Some critics argued that three was too high because the poor often spent more than one-third of their income on food during the 1950s and early 1960s. However, this argument appears flawed as a result of its circularity: The poor may have been spending more of their resources on food because they were poor; because food is the most basic necessity of all, we do not know what other necessities the poor may have forsaken (such as medical care, adequate shelter, etc.) while spending over half their money to eat. Others argued that Orshansky's survey data from the 1950s overestimated the percentage of family income spent on food in the 1960s, suggesting that it had fallen to one-fourth, as indicated by the 1960–61 Consumer Expenditure Survey (Haber, 1966). The percentage of family income spent on food has steadily dropped since this period as well. Now housing

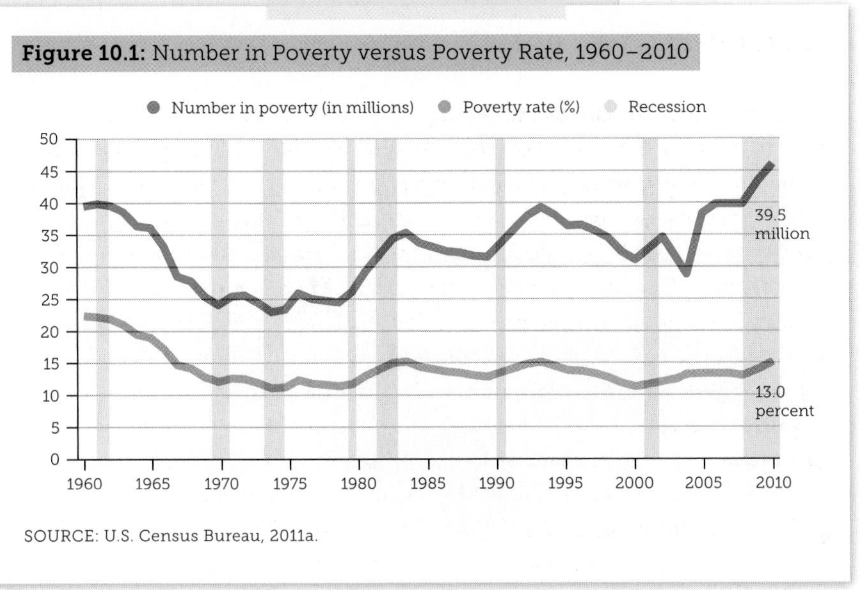

Figure 10.1: Number in Poverty versus Poverty Rate, 1960–2010

SOURCE: U.S. Census Bureau, 2011a.

makes up a much larger proportion of household budgets, and some scholars have called for housing to replace food as the basis for need calculations (Ruggles, 1990).

More recent criticisms have sought to change Orshansky's threshold by deemphasizing food expenditures as the basis of what are considered "necessities." Specifically, some researchers argue that the range of necessities has expanded since the early 1960s to include such items as indoor plumbing (which many of the rural poor did not have in the 1950s) and telephones. Is television a necessity? Are working heat and air conditioning? How about a computer? With these concerns in mind, many analysts have argued that it is impossible to adjust the poverty threshold over long periods of time based on the rate of inflation; instead, the poverty measure must be reformulated from scratch every so often because what is a necessity changes from period to period, from society to society. The U.S. poverty threshold has been further criticized because it does not take into account regional variation in the cost of living. Living on $8,000 a year in Mississippi is very different from trying to survive on that same income in New York City (see Figure 10.2).

Finally, there is the issue of assets and debts. Poverty is measured with respect to income alone. But income tells only part of the financial story for most American families. Significant variation in family wealth levels also exists. (Family wealth, often referred to as assets or net worth, equals total family debts, such as credit card debt or unpaid bills, subtracted from total salable assets, like a house or car.) This variation in net worth, over and above income levels, means that being poor can be a very different economic experience for families with the same income levels. This issue is particularly relevant to the

Figure 10.2: Cost of Living, 2011

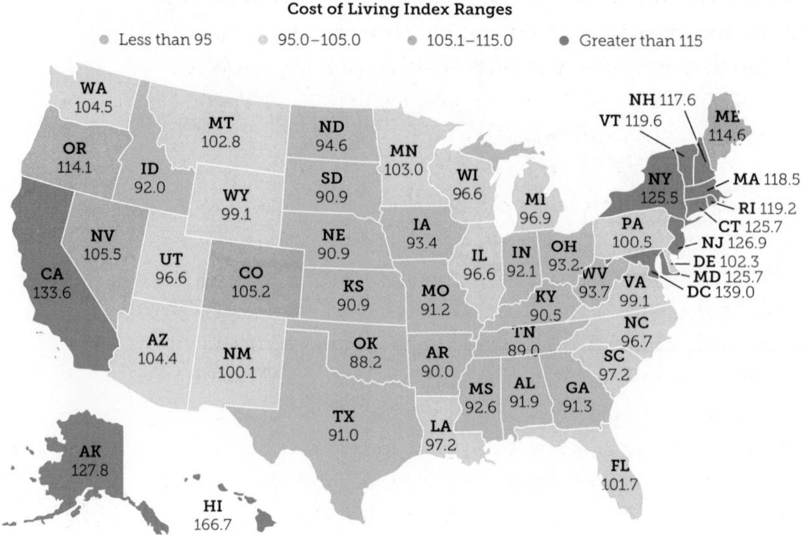

The cost of living index compares costs between regions using data on housing, transportation, utilities, health care, and groceries. An average score is 100, so states with numbers less than 100 are affordable, and those with scores above 100 are more expensive.

SOURCE: Missouri Economic Research and Information Center, 2012.

study of race, poverty, and life chances in America. As we saw in Chapter 9, there is significant disparity in net worth between different racial groups. The median African American family has about one-twentieth the net worth of a typical median white family (Pew Research Center, 2011b). This difference cannot be explained by income or other demographic characteristics (Oliver & Shapiro, 1995). This was very evident during the recent recession as net worth dropped for everyone. But the median white family's net worth in 2009 dropped 16 percent to $113,149, while African American families saw their net worth drop 66 percent to $5,677, with one third having zero or negative net worth (Pew Research Center, 2011b). So maybe additional income wouldn't have made a difference for Marlin (other than enabling his mother's drinking habit), but perhaps a nest egg might have. Because, as he points out, lacking time to spend with your kids isn't restricted to low-income families, it's possible that this discrepancy in levels of net worth goes a long way in explaining differential outcomes in children.

There are many potential ways to integrate income and wealth into a poverty measure (such as converting wealth levels to an annuity and adding that to annual income). However, policy makers stick to the traditional income-based poverty measure; given that many federal funds are allocated based on the proportion of a state's population that is poor, the Orshansky line has a political inertia difficult to alter. Similarly, researchers have just begun to take assets into account in explaining the impact of poverty on life chances, largely because good measures of family wealth have not been available until recent decades (as of 1984, when a number of reputable surveys started to ask about it).

All this criticism leads to the following question: Is it ever possible to arrive at an adequate absolute measure of poverty? Most scholars define necessities as what are required to live with dignity. Of course, if what is necessary to live with dignity in a given society is socially defined, then every measure of poverty is a relative measure; there will always be people who do not have those necessities in any market-based economy. The poor will always be with us, but to a greater or lesser degree depending on how unequally income and wealth are distributed. This is one of the ways that wealth creates poverty—by ratcheting up the social definition of necessity. Theorists who believe that all poverty is relational have argued for the implementation of measures identifying relative poverty, the determination of poverty based on a percentage of the median income in a given location. For instance, a relative measure might consider anyone with less than one-half the median income poor (Fuchs, 1967; Rainwater, 1974). This sort of measure has become standard in the literature on international comparisons of the poverty rate, because it provides an obvious yardstick across nations. However, it really measures income inequality at the bottom half of the distribution.

Relative poverty a measurement of poverty based on a percentage of the median income in a given location.

The Effects of Poverty on Children's Life Chances

There are three basic theories about why poverty is bad for kids. First, some researchers focus on the material deprivations that low socioeconomic status (SES) induces, such as poor nutrition, lack of adequate medical care, and unsafe environments (Callan et al., 1993; Mack & Lansley, 1985; McGregor & Borooah, 1992; Ringen, 1987). Food, for example, along with water, is the most basic necessity of all. Studies of severe famine in the Netherlands during World War II found that consuming fewer than 1,000 calories per day results in dramatic reductions in pregnant women's weight gain and infants' size at birth. Research in this tradition has gone beyond basic needs such as nutrition to show that low-income households experience other forms of material deprivation, which may explain part of the effect of poverty on childhood (Mayer, 1997). For instance, some work has shown that poor children are less likely to have educational toys or books in the household, and such items are positively associated with healthy cognitive development (Duncan et al., 1994; J. R. Smith et al., 1997; Zill, 1988; Zill et al., 1991). It is hard to imagine, however, that toys and books explain a very large share of the effect of low income on children.

Parenting stress hypothesis a paradigm in which low income, unstable employment, a lack of cultural resources, and a feeling of inferiority from social class comparisons exacerbate household stress levels; this stress, in turn, leads to detrimental parenting practices such as yelling and hitting, which are not conducive to healthy child development.

A second paradigm, often called the parenting stress hypothesis, sees low income, unstable employment, a lack of cultural resources (such as reliable social networks), and a feeling of inferiority from social class comparisons as exacerbating household stress levels; this stress, in turn, leads to detrimental parenting practices such as yelling and hitting, which are not conducive to healthy child development (Conger et al., 1992, 1994; Elder et al., 1995; Hanson et al., 1997; Hashima & Amato, 1994; Lempers et al., 1989; McLeod & Shanahan, 1993; Whitbeck et al., 1991). Furthermore, both home care and day care for low-income children generally involve fewer positive interactions between the child and the caregiver and less opportunity for play as compared with children in more affluent households (Howes & Olenick, 1986; Howes & Stewart, 1987; Phillips et al., 1987). Research does suggest that parents living in poverty are more likely than parents in better conditions to display punitive behaviors such as yelling and slapping and less likely to display love and warmth through behaviors such as cuddling and hugging (Conger et al., 1992, 1994; Elder et al., 1995). A great deal of evidence has connected such parenting practices to low IQ scores and to behavioral disorders in children (Conger et al., 1994).

What is notable about these two theories about the effects of poverty on children is how individualistic and behavioralist they are. Poverty, it seems, can either cause a family not to have enough material resources or cause the parents stress, which in turn leads to bad parenting practices. Either way, the causal arrow runs from the social condition of deprivation through the conditions of the home and the behavior of the parents and only then to the child. Parents are where the buck stops—either because they do not provide the resources their children need or because of their bad parenting practices. The bottom line is that poverty works through the family environment, so the family is ultimately responsible for mediating its impact on children. Poor heroic parents could blunt the deleterious effects by being savvy enough to provide a stimulating educational environment in the home on the cheap, or by not letting financial stress get between their children and them.

A third theory asserts that it is not poverty, lack of nonmonetary resources, or relative inequality that is so detrimental to child development as much as it is the differences between poor parents and higher-income parents (Mayer, 1997). Scholars in the "no effect" camp assert that the association between SES and child developmental outcomes is an illusion (that is, it is spurious). They claim that parental characteristics, ranging from parenting styles to genetic endowments that lead to low income, less education, and low occupational prestige, also lead to detrimental developmental outcomes for offspring. The "no effect" paradigm is similar to the material deprivation and parenting stress hypotheses in that it is a causal story about parents, but it is generally considered significantly more conservative. The difference is that the material deprivation and parenting stress models optimistically believe intervening factors can be measured and therefore manipulated, whereas the "no effect" camp

Children play on the Lower Brule Reservation in South Dakota. In what ways can poverty be damaging to children?

is less sanguine on the prospects of lessening the differences between poor and nonpoor families on child outcomes.

Let's return to Marlin for a moment—or, more accurately, Marlin's mother. According to the first model, things might have turned out differently if she had been able to provide more material resources to her children: more food, clothes, and educational stimuli. According to the second model, the important factor would have been a decrease in her stress. A reduction in the pressures she faced as an unemployed single mother would have resulted in more positive interactions with Marlin and his brother, perhaps even affecting her propensities for drinking and man hunting. In the third paradigm, she was both poor and a less-than-perfect parent for the same reasons, be they genetic or behavioral. So which assessment do we believe?

Why Is the United States So Different?

America—if you can make it here, you can make it anywhere, as the song goes: The rewards for success are staggering and unparalleled in any other democracy. The net worth of Bill Gates is an estimated $56 billion compared to the $49,445 median net worth of Americans as a whole (U.S. Census Bureau, 2011a). The average CEO earns $2.3 million per year (*Forbes*, 2011b). At the same time, the United States also has one of the highest poverty rates in the advanced world. A record 46.2 million people are living in poverty, the largest number ever recorded (U.S. Census Bureau, 2011a). Children are particularly hard hit: One in five American children lives in a household with income below the poverty line (Wright et al., 2010). Moreover, until the passage of the health care reform bill in 2010, many Americans had no health insurance, which was a leading cause of personal bankruptcy.

There are many ways to measure economic inequality, but they all arrive at the same answer: Economic rewards are far more lopsided here than in European countries such as social-democratic Sweden and union-driven France—and this inequality drives American poverty rates (see Chapter 7 on stratification and inequality). But the United States is also much more unequal than even our closest cousins, Great Britain and Canada. In fact, in terms of who gets what, we fall somewhere between Western European countries on the one hand and developing countries such as Pakistan, Mexico, and Nigeria on the other. Of course, Americans on average have higher incomes than people in developing nations, but the way their smaller pie is sliced is not that different from our own division of resources. For example, in the United States, the richest 10 percent of the population reaps incomes between five and six times greater than the poorest 10 percent. In Sweden, the comparable figure is about 2.5, in the Netherlands it is about 3, and in Great Britain it is approximately 4.5. In Mexico, however, it is somewhere between 9 and 12, depending on which year is examined. (On another measure, called the Gini coefficient, where a higher score means more inequality, the United States scores about 0.37, almost perfectly equidistant between Mexico's 0.49 on the high end and Sweden's 0.22 and Germany's 0.26 on the low side.) So while we have a way to go to reach third-world levels, the United States does not fit the model of most other industrialized nations either.

Direct comparisons of poverty rates tell a similar story: When the poverty line is set at 50 percent of the median income of a given country, a comparison of poverty rates among developed nations reveals that the United States indeed lags behind most of the developed world. In the United States, 17.3 percent of the population has incomes less than 50 percent of the median (Organization for Economic Co-operation and Development, 2012). The next closest countries are Australia, with a rate of 14.6 percent, and Canada at 12 percent (see Figure 10.3).

A lot of explanations exist for the unique position among advanced democracies in which the United States finds itself. First, there is the issue of timing. It seems as though the (continental) European countries that transitioned to free-market capitalism more recently did so when political institutions were better able to protect the weak through collective bargaining, welfare state transfers, and universal public services. Another explanation is institutional:

Figure 10.3: International Comparison of Poverty Rates among Wealthy Countries

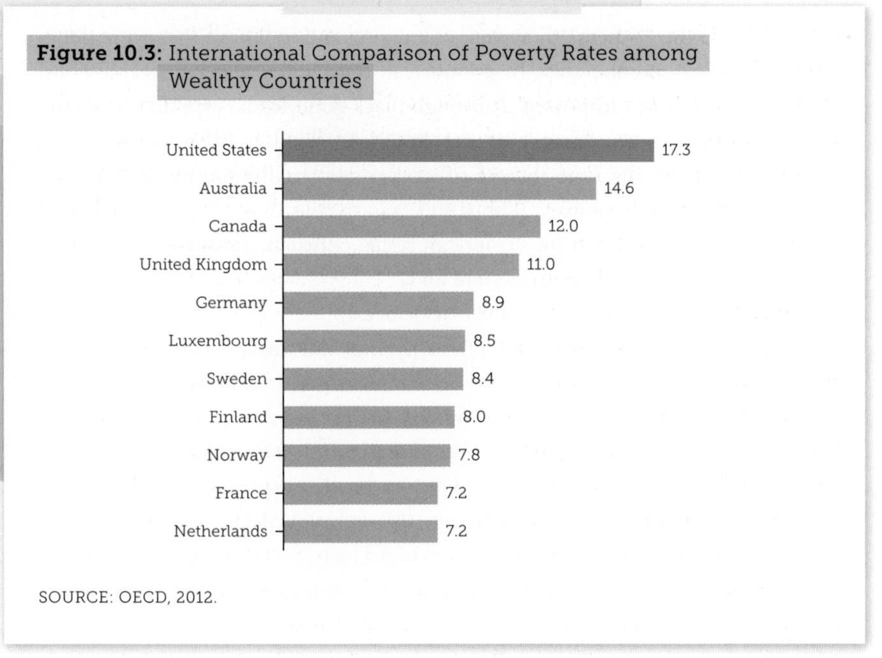

SOURCE: OECD, 2012.

The fragmented U.S. political system, which divides power between the federal government and the states and among three branches of government, makes it difficult to develop a comprehensive safety net in the same way that European countries with strong central governments and a parliamentary system of elections can. Another explanation claims that the key aspect of "American exceptionalism" is that we have no history of feudalism (with the exception of the South before the Civil War). This seems ironic at first glance: Feudalism, an oppressive form of political and economic oppression in which serfs toiled on the land of their lords, was far more unequal than the image of early America with its citizen-farmers and bountiful land (again, with the notable exception of slavery). Given such a history of inequality, it would seem that the European countries with this sort of social history should have more disparity through the present. But feudalism also developed a culture of state paternalism, in which the serfs received protection from their lord in return for working his land. Some argue that this arrangement metamorphosed into the modern welfare state, in which citizens pay higher taxes but can confidently expect their basic economic needs to be taken care of by the government, from cradle to grave. Without such a feudal history, the American cultural tradition of individualism has acted as a hindrance to such paternalism.

Finally, there is the looming shadow of race in America. Some scholars argue that although European powers racialized "others" in the form of colonized peoples, those "others" were typically outside the country itself and far away, with no prospect of full political rights. Therefore, providing a strong safety net became a way by which European nations defined themselves in opposition to the "others" they were colonizing and to whom they were denying full political membership. In contrast, in the United States a sizable colonized population was imported. Although black Americans were denied voting rights for much of the history of the American republic, they had begun to secure suffrage by the time the era of government redistribution had arrived in the mid-twentieth century. The result was that in order to prevent blacks from participating fully in the American social contract, authority was shifted from the federal government to state and local authorities, and these authorities could then choose to exclude blacks overtly or covertly. The result was a much weaker safety net, one that for a long time excluded minorities disproportionately. For example, to get Social Security through the congressional committees controlled by racist Southern Democrats, President Franklin D. Roosevelt had to agree to exclude agricultural and domestic workers from the old age insurance system. This exception was made purposely to exclude African Americans, who were disproportionately employed in these two sectors. It was not until the following decade, when Harry S. Truman addressed this gap in the safety net, that blacks became full participants in the social insurance system. Of course, that first, white-only generation reaped the windfall of Social Security, receiving payouts from day one without having paid a cent into the nascent system.

None of these explanations can account for all cases. Ireland, probably the latest and most rapidly developed northern European country, displays greater inequalities than, say, the Netherlands, Denmark, and the United Kingdom. Canada does not have a feudal past and it has a fractured, regional power structure (including semiautonomous provinces like Quebec), yet it enjoys a much more comprehensive safety net than the United States, its southern neighbor. Australia and New Zealand also lack feudal histories and have conquered racial minorities within their national borders, yet they still have much more progressive social policies than the United States. Therefore, the most probable answer is that timing, institutional structure, cultural history, and race were all necessary conditions for the unique position of the United States, but none alone was sufficient.

So maybe, ultimately, the story of poverty (in the United States) is really one of inequality. This is what David Grusky, at least, seemed to be implying with his own diagnosis when we spoke:

> I think, far too often, we give the labor market a free ride and assume that it's working perfectly and competitively. Rather [than just look at the safety net] we ought to often look at the more fundamental structural problems in [the] labor market that create such a need for a safety net. (Conley, 2011c)

Alas . . . Easier said than done.

Can the Poor Save?

In 2006, President George W. Bush signed the Pension Protection Act, a first step in trying to fix some of the problems with the employer-based retirement savings system in the United States. However, like health care, the main problem is one of coverage: Almost half of American employees work for an employer that does not offer a traditional pension or retirement savings plan. Especially in an age of frequent job change, we need a broader-based retirement security strategy that reaches people who will not be looked after by their former employer(s). The key is to make it easy for people to save.

With many likely to have a net negative private savings rate for much of the decade from 2000 through 2010, Americans need incentives to save now more than ever (see Figure 10.4). The hard part of saving, everyone knows, is being able to forget about all the seemingly unlimited needs and wants that arise each pay cycle and instead squirrel away part of our check. Those among the middle and working classes have it particularly rough in this regard: They have greater financial pressures and they often don't have an employer that is willing to make a matching contribution to a retirement account. In 2010 less than one third of workers were offered a pension plan. And for Southern states and other communities where there is less competition to draw workers, the number of benefits offered is even lower (Bureau of Labor Statistics, 2011c).

H&R Block recently conducted an experiment in which one group was offered a 50 percent match to divert some of their tax refund to an IRA. Only 14 percent of income tax filers took the company up on its offer (although this figure is dramatically higher than that recorded for those filers who were offered no match or a smaller one). This low figure may dumbfound economists as irrational, but it makes sense to sociologists. Much of H&R Block's clientele can barely make ends meet on a day-to-day basis. Plus, they are uncertain about the future, and rightly so: Who knows how long they will hold onto their present jobs in an age of employment instability? Who knows if they will live long enough to enjoy the fruits of their IRAs? They may estimate that $500 now is much more valuable than $750, plus compounded interest, 20 or 30 years in the future.

If it is true that future uncertainties combined with today's financial stresses put the squeeze on lower-income families' savings by raising what economists call their "discount rate" (the relative value of present consumption versus future savings), then one way exists to provide these families with an easy mechanism for savings commitment over the long haul: no money down, long-term matches. Instead of making repeated savings decisions to

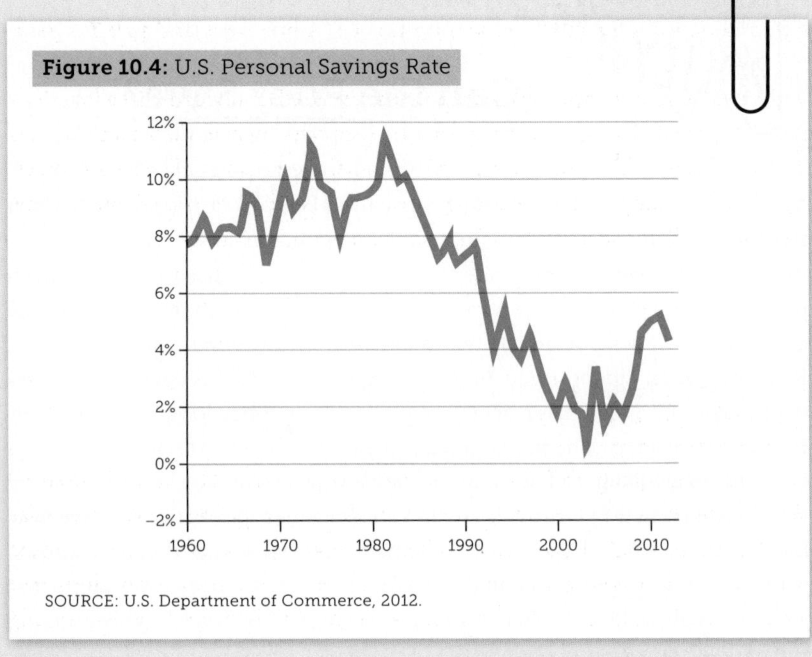

Figure 10.4: U.S. Personal Savings Rate

SOURCE: U.S. Department of Commerce, 2012.

fork over my tax refund year after year in order to qualify for a saver's credit (under the current policy) or an IRA match (under the H&R Block experiment or future policy), I would agree to give up future wages, say, 3 percent annually for 15 years. In return, I would receive a $1,000 initial deposit into my IRA and a 50 percent match for my 3 percent contribution over the course of the next 15 years. The key is that the government would be asking low-income earners to commit to saving future earnings, not current tax refunds. This commitment structure capitalizes on Americans' future uncertainty and high discount rate by giving them something now and asking them to pay later. Anyone who has succumbed to the lure of low-interest credit card deals and subsequently suffered crushing monthly payments when those rates increase knows the enticing logic of that deal.

The IRA plan probably sounds familiar to anyone with a 401(k). Most people who have an employer-sponsored retirement plan check a box once, usually at the time they first qualify for benefits, and then never think about saving again. They stop saving only if they actively opt out, and statistics show that very few people opt out once they opt in. Therefore, the Pension Protection Act takes a step in the right direction by encouraging (although not requiring) companies to make 401(k) deductions the default unless a participant completes the paperwork to withdraw. But for the increasing numbers of Americans who are self-employed, are unstably employed, or work for a company that does not offer a 401(k), we need to create the same structure of savings. The IRA would provide a mechanism by which those who don't have the option of a 401(k) at work can check a box once and save for years to come.

The plan might appeal to both political parties. Republicans have long lobbied for private savings accounts for all Americans (hence, their failed efforts at Social Security reform in 2005). Meanwhile, Democrats talk about protecting Social Security and augmenting it for those at the bottom of the income distribution. The incentivized IRA accomplishes both tasks.

→ CONCLUSION

What are we talking about when we refer to poverty? The term is used to describe villagers in the African country of Malawi struggling to live on a dollar a day when a drought leads to crop failure; it is also used to describe Americans who have little hope to realize their dreams but enjoy color televisions and indoor plumbing, and whose everyday lives involve perhaps more stress and depression than physical deprivation.

Poverty, then, is a state of absolute or relative deprivation based on economic conditions (as opposed to, say, political conditions). It has both geophysical roots—such as a high disease burden and shorter growing seasons in the tropical regions of the world—and social causes ranging from war to corruption, from segregation and ghettoization to the sometimes perverse incentives of social policies. Although poverty may be a many-faceted condition, one commonality holds true: Generally, we know it when we see it. But once we recognize its face, knowing what type of poverty it is (relative or absolute) and its root causes (social or environmental) can help us think clearly about how to tackle it without making the problem worse.

PRACTICE

ASSIGNMENT

There are many programs and agencies to help the poor. Locate one agency (or organization) that helps the poor in your community. Speak with a person who works or volunteers at that agency and gather information on what he or she does. How does that person help the poor? How many people does he or she help in a given year? How is the agency funded (government, church, private donors, etc.)? Are there any structural challenges you can perceive that might make it difficult for the poor to access the agency's benefits? Is there any way that this person might be doing more harm than good?

QUESTIONS FOR REVIEW

1. Poverty affected Marlin Card's life chances, although it is not completely clear how. What evidence does Marlin's life provide to support the material deprivation theory and parenting stress hypothesis? Apart from parenting, what other factors should we consider to best understand Marlin's path?
2. How does welfare help the poor? What are some characteristics of welfare that hinder work? How did the negative income tax experiment suggest that welfare creates perverse effects and how could the results be interpreted otherwise?
3. How does the "underclass" theory relate to the "culture of poverty"? How does William Julius Wilson's argument provide a very different perspective?
4. How does the neighborhood one calls home affect a poor person's life chances? How does the study "Moving to Opportunity" add to our understanding of poverty?
5. How do the studies on lottery and gambling winners test the impact of income on the behavior and outcomes of the poor? How do the words of Marlin and the work of Susan Mayer shift the focus to wealth and consumerism?
6. What is the difference between absolute and relative poverty? What are some of the challenges involved in setting a poverty line and keeping this measure accurate?
7. What is unique about the extent of poverty in the United States compared to other countries? How might race be an explanatory factor within the United States?

PARADOX

HOW DO WE HELP THE POOR WITHOUT CREATING PERVERSE INCENTIVES THAT INDUCE MORE POVERTY IN THE LONG RUN?

WATCH THE ANIMATED SHORT ABOUT THE POVERTY PARADOX AT

WWNORTON.COM/STUDYSPACE

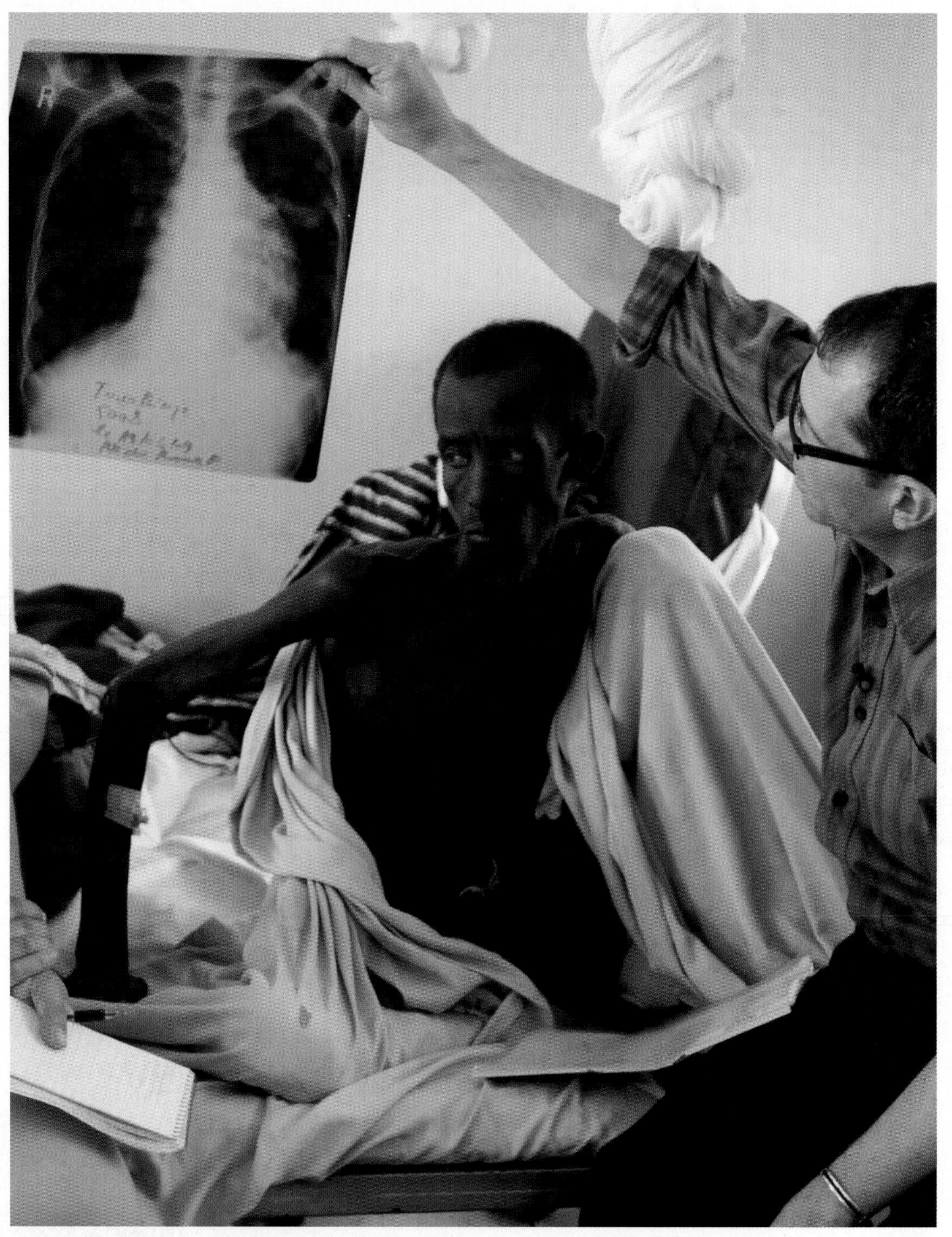

Michael Rich, a doctor with Partners in Health, treats a tuberculosis patient in Haiti.

11 Health and Society

PARADOX

WHAT CAUSES PEOPLE TO DIE CHANGES OVER TIME, BUT THE GROUP AT GREATEST RISK OF DYING FROM THESE AFFLICTIONS, THOSE LOW IN SOCIOECONOMIC STATUS, STAYS THE SAME.

Perhaps it's because Paul Farmer was born in North Adams, Massachusetts—a Berkshires mill town that died and was reborn as an electronics hub that also died when work went offshore and now is attempting to reincarnate itself yet again as the home of MASS MoCA, the Massachusetts Museum of Contemporary Art. Perhaps it's because he spent a good portion of his childhood living in a bus and on a houseboat in Florida. Whatever the reason, Dr. Farmer has been one to see hope and opportunity where others see only desperation and desolation.

Many doctors choose their career path because they want to help people. Some go further—volunteering for Doctors Without Borders, Smile Train, the International Committee of the Red Cross, or some other international organization meant to help sick and desperate peoples in the world's poorest countries. Many of these physicians and surgeons feel overwhelmed, as if they are mere Band-Aids on gushing wounds. Unsurprisingly, volunteers burn out quickly. But not Paul Farmer, who lives with his family in Rwanda and spends significant amounts of time in Haiti, where he works to improve the social and economic status of the country as well as offering medical care. Some days he treats 1,000 patients—that is, when he can step away from his teaching duties at Harvard Medical School.

Perhaps he has been able to keep at it ever since his student days because he is also trained to think like a social scientist. In addition to being an MD, Farmer is a PhD in medical anthropology. His experience as a social scientist allows him to make connections between invisible social forces and the patients he sees in Haiti (or Siberia or Peru or Rwanda or Boston, for that matter).

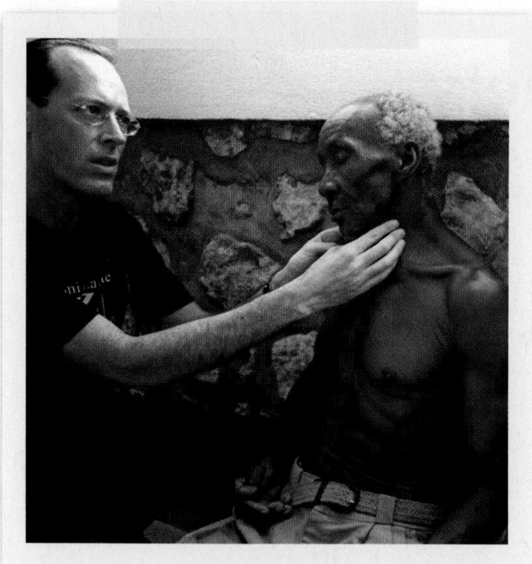

Paul Farmer with a patient in Haiti.

For example, not only does he provide treatment for AIDS and drug-resistant tuberculosis, he helped found an international nongovernmental organization, Partners in Health, to extend his work across the globe. Meanwhile, he also writes books such as *Infections and Inequalities* (1999) and *Haiti after the Earthquake* (2011), which demonstrate the linkages between poverty and illness. And he lobbies for cheaper drug prices for the developing world and for action and assistance on the part of rich Western societies—impatiently dismissing the claims that things are too far gone in the places he works to merit investment.

While doctors might feel justifiably overwhelmed by the constant onslaught of sickness they confront daily, at least there are some patients whose pain has been eased at the end of the day. Social scientists face a more difficult question: Is their work ever able to offer anyone any kind of relief from discomfort or suffering? After all, how does making the normal strange, documenting invisible social forces, or anticipating unintended consequences of a particular public policy help folks live longer, fuller, happier lives? It's all so abstract for many of us. Dr. Farmer, by contrast, seems to have found a sweet spot of synergy between his local, hands-on work with real, live human beings and his social scientific writing and advocacy.

Of course, as remarkable as Farmer is (some of his patients liken him to a god), he is just one person among many who sacrifice a comfortable lifestyle to help those who have drawn the shortest of straws in life. His world renown is partly due to a serendipitous meeting with Tracy Kidder, who went on to write the best-selling book about Farmer, *Mountains beyond Mountains*, with a title adapted from a Haitian phrase. So not only is he a remarkable story in his own right, his story is also an exemplar of the global media industry and a testament to the role of luck and chance in modern life. He would probably say the same is true for his poorest patients: There's little that separates his lot in life from theirs except the accident of birth.

The Rise (and Fall?) of the Medical Profession

Doctors have more power than any other professionals in America and most other societies. This, however, is a relatively recent phenomenon. Some scholars claim that doctors' power peaked in the 1980s and is now on the decline. Regardless, it might be worthwhile to examine why doctors gained so much influence over our lives in the first place.

Why We Think Doctors Are Special

Doctors have an enormous amount of social power, political power, and prestige; we defer to our doctors in ways that we do not defer to other people. The respect we feel for doctors may result in part from the scarcity of doctors in our society, the fact that it takes years of education to become one, and the apparent difficulty of mastering the skills involved. For example, there are about 271 doctors per 100,000 individuals in the United States (compared with 361 lawyers, 402 accountants, and 536 college teachers). It generally takes 20 years of formal schooling plus an internship and residency training to become a practicing physician. Plenty of other professions require talent and many years of training, but doctors are different from investment bankers, judges, or lawyers. For starters, there are no limits on the number of law or business schools in the United States, but the number of medical schools and medical graduates is strictly regulated. This regulation allows doctors to maintain the exclusiveness of their profession and contributes to their privileged position.

One very important reason doctors occupy a unique position in modern society is that they offer a universally valued product, health and longevity (or, at least, they claim to offer it). Their power and prestige derive largely from the fact that they offer something that everybody wants—to feel better and live a long life.

If you are on a subway and someone yells for a doctor, we generally believe that if one is present, he or she has a moral obligation not to inquire about the ill passenger's health insurance status or financial means but to help that person right away. Some doctors have "MD" on their license plates, perhaps as a status symbol or because it brings them special privileges if caught speeding or parking illegally, but the title also obligates them to help in cases of emergency. We believe that doctors must not only do no harm but also do what is in the best interests of the patient. In this way, doctors appear to be answering to a high moral calling as embodied by, for instance, the Hippocratic Oath.

One of the key traits of a profession (doctors included), as opposed to a job or even a career, is that the members of a given profession are oriented toward their peers, not their clients. While doctors are serving their patients, they are equally concerned with the approval of other doctors. In fact, the sociological definition of a "quack" is a professional who violates this unstated ethic by seeking to make a client—the customer or patient—happy at the expense of the esteem of his or her peers. Your professor could make most of you students (the clients) happy by canceling the final exam and giving an A to everyone. But this would not be looked on kindly by his or her colleagues; in fact, it might get your professor bounced out of the profession.

Greek physician Hippocrates (c. 460–377 BCE).

Another reason doctors have so much social prestige is their individualized objectivity, which gives them a certain power in their relationship with clients. They are simultaneously very intimate (think about a rectal exam or psychiatry session) and personal with you but also objective and highly technical. Doctors may have knowledge of your most personal and private affairs. Your gynecologist or urologist, for example, may need to know things about your sex life that you do not tell anyone else.

This individualized objectivity may be the reason patients put so much emphasis on trust in assessing their relationships with their doctors. Sociologists David Mechanic and Sharon Meyer (2000) found that patients consider interpersonal confidence the most important factor in rating their doctors. Technical and medical competence is important, but we tend to assume that most—if not all—doctors possess this skill. While mental health patients also heavily stress the importance of confidentiality (understandably, given the stigma attached to mental illness), patients suffering from a variety of illnesses were most concerned that they be able to trust their doctors to talk to them like human beings, to show care and compassion, to listen to them and take their concerns seriously. "Bedside manner," as we call it, matters most. If you had a serious illness, such as cancer, you would want your doctor to explain the diagnosis and treatment in terms you could understand. If you read about a new drug in the newspaper, you would want your doctor to listen to your questions and explain why that medication was or wasn't appropriate for you. If your insurance changed midway through your treatment, you would want to trust your doctor to explain what the new plan would and wouldn't cover.

Last but not least, doctors deploy specific props and scripts to assert their power. For instance, doctors set a front stage (offices with Latin diplomas on the wall, a large desk between the doctor and his or her patients) and a backstage (the examination room, where your paper gown exposes your backside). (See the discussion of Erving Goffman's dramaturgical theory in Chapter 4.) Have you ever arrived at a doctor's office and been seen right away? No matter if you are early, late, or right on time, you probably have to wait. We are socialized into accepting this wait as part of the drill, but it is yet another way the power dynamic is revealed in the doctor-patient relationship. If you miss an appointment, often you will still be charged the fee, even if your doctor had plenty of work to fill up the time. But if you must wait for two hours to be seen by your dermatologist, tough luck.

Actor Hugh Laurie as television physician Gregory House. Doctors are valued for their objectivity and technical knowledge. What other qualities do patients want in their doctors?

The power and prestige that doctors enjoy on account of their unique circumstances translate into other benefits and privileges. In the past, doctors set their own pay rates. They essentially billed what they wanted to charge for a procedure, using as a guide what was standard. Insurance was reimbursed on a "fee for service" basis: If the doctor took your insurance, there was a set billable rate. If there was a co-pay of 20 percent for a $100 office visit, you would pay $20, and the insurance company had to pay the rest. In this scenario, the doctor had an incentive to say, "Take two aspirin, make an appointment with my secretary for tomorrow, and then we'll follow up with you again in two weeks and run some tests." Each time the doctor did a procedure or met with you, he or she billed you and your insurance company. And because you paid only part of the total cost, because you cared about your health, and because you trusted your doctor thanks to the asymmetry of information (assuming that he or she knew more than you did about what's best), you said, "Sure, see you then." Doctors had most of the control in this situation, which created a problem called "supplier-induced demand": Doctors created excess demand for their services.

Another form of power that doctors have, besides setting their own pay rates and controlling demand for their services, is prescription authority. There are occupational battles over who can prescribe what and who can perform which procedures.

An additional sign of doctors' power is their self-regulation. The American Medical Association (AMA) and state medical boards are their judge, jury, and jailer. A doctor who amputates the wrong leg of a patient may still be able to get a new job because there is such a (self-induced) shortage of doctors. This may seem ludicrous—in any other profession, you would be prosecuted for criminal negligence. The AMA, however, is a very strong political body. They have a monopoly over the policing of their own, and they are reluctant to take away a doctor's license.

Finally, doctors have authority in areas beyond strict medicine. Medicalization is the process by which problems or issues not traditionally seen as medical come to be framed as such. Alcoholism is a classic example. People did not formerly think of addiction as a medical problem but as a sin of excess, a moral failing, a problem of self-control. Now many accept alcoholism as a disease and talk about its medical aspects—the genetic tendencies, the biochemical aspects. We know that the disease runs in families, and researchers continue in their efforts to identify the genes that may affect one's susceptibility to alcoholism. We can treat addiction itself and even the tendency toward addictive behavior with pharmaceuticals. Even the judicial process has become medicalized, giving medical doctors legal power. Often, they play the critical role of expert witnesses in court cases, testifying whether or not a defendant is mentally competent to know the difference between right and wrong and whether he or she is fit to stand trial. Or a doctor might attest that road rage is a syndrome with biomedical components.

Medicalization the process by which problems or issues not traditionally seen as medical come to be framed as such.

The Rise of the Biomedical Culture

Medical professionals currently hold a great deal of power, but it's important to realize that this hasn't always been the case. In fact, historically speaking, this is a relatively recent phenomenon. In ancient Rome, for instance, medicine

Ancient Roman surgical tools. Why did doctors have little prestige in ancient Rome?

was a low-level occupation. Physicians were either slaves or low-ranking freedmen or foreigners, often Turks or Arabs brought to Rome from the outlying provinces of the empire. Even in eighteenth-century England, physicians generally were at the margins of the gentry. They had higher status than in ancient Rome, but they were not considered an elite class. Surgeons had an even lower social status: The profession originally evolved from barbers, because barbers were good with straight razors and could cut people open and stitch them up. Today in the United Kingdom, surgeons are sometimes still referred to as "Mister," not "Doctor," thanks to their origins.

More recently, in the modern Soviet Union and even after its dissolution, Russian physicians were paid relatively little, earning less than three-quarters the average industrial wage. It is no coincidence that 70 percent of doctors in Soviet Russia were women, because the percentage of women in a profession has a robust negative correlation with the profession's pay and social status.

If doctors have not always been as socially prestigious and powerful as they are in contemporary America, how did this authority come about? Health is a universally valued product, but until recently, doctors could not offer health and longevity. In fact, they were rather incompetent. They used leeches or cutting to get rid of "bad" blood and hoped this would cure you of the "poison" causing your illness. Some historians believe that George Washington died as the result of a bloodletting treatment for a cold that drained five pints from his body. At best, doctors sympathetically watched you die. They did not have antibiotics or vaccines. Before gaining power and prestige, doctors had to become more effective through advances in technology and knowledge. In 1816, the stethoscope was invented, allowing doctors to hear inside living beings and giving them the means to examine patients rather than merely observe them.

During the nineteenth century, doctors also promoted a system of licensing, which began to exclude other forms of medicine practiced widely at this time. One of the more prominent forms was homeopathy. Homeopathy (derived from *homeo*, meaning "same," and *patho*, meaning "poison") is guided by the notion that the "poison is the cure." It's not unlike vaccination: You are given a little bit of the poison, a little bit of the disease, in order to cure or prevent an illness. Homeopathy was a widely followed medical practice in the nineteenth century until what we now call traditional medicine became the dominant paradigm with the assistance of state licensing boards.

In addition to constraining the types of doctors who were able to practice, licensing also gave doctors more economic clout. Until the mid-nineteenth century, medicine in England and the United States was essentially considered philanthropic: If you did not pay your physician's bill, he could not sue you for payment; doctors had no legal recourse. Licensing changed this system, as the orthodox medical practitioners convinced state legislatures to pass laws allowing physicians to sue for payment, but only if they were licensed. This legislation led to the development of the AMA and state licensing boards and marked the beginning of the end for homeopathic doctors. These boards also constrained the number of medical degrees awarded annually, thereby restricting the number of practicing physicians so as not to create a surplus. In this way they drove up wages and guaranteed constant employment for doctors.

Another concurrent historical development was the emergence of more important roles for large institutions. Hospitals, formerly places to die, became places to heal (at least sometimes). It took a long time before death rates within hospitals declined precipitously, but at least it was no longer a sure death sentence when you walked into a hospital. By the late nineteenth century, hospitals had become important social institutions, and doctors' relationships to hospitals changed. Previously, doctors were merely employees of hospitals, but they gained rights to admit patients to one or more hospitals—thereby obtaining a more powerful position in the relationship. Specifically, hospitals came to depend on doctors for their supply of customers, or patients; and the physician, who could easily send his or her patient to another facility, held the power.

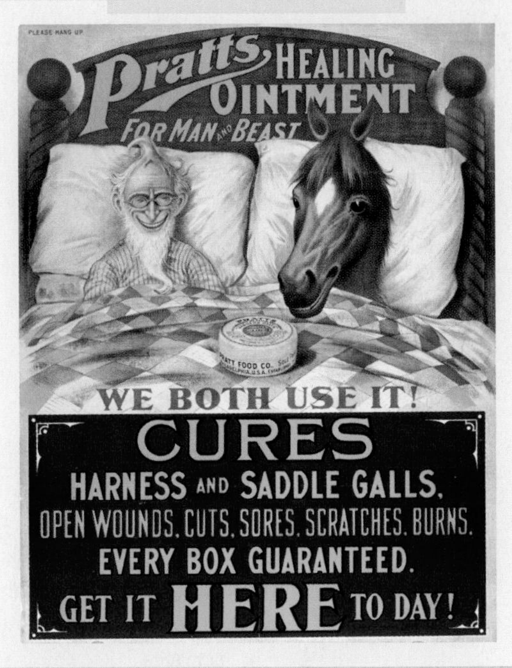

An 1880s advertisement for a homeopathic cure.

Doctors' Denouement?

By 1990 or so, doctors' authority began to decline for several reasons. First, market forces had infiltrated medicine. By 1990, concerns about the rising cost of health care had become a major political issue and led to changes in the way we pay for health care and, in particular, the rise of health maintenance organizations (HMOs). The different types of health insurance providers are discussed below.

Another sign of the declining authority of doctors was the rise of external regulation. No longer is the AMA the sole arbiter of what constitutes good medical practice. Medical "bills of rights" now exist. In 1998, President Bill Clinton signed into law a federal patients' bill of rights. Its main provision was no "drive-through deliveries," by requiring insurance companies to pay for a woman's stay in the hospital up to 48 hours after giving birth vaginally and 96 hours following a caesarean (doctors probably like this mandate, because it means more care, not less). The 1986 Emergency Medical Treatment and Active Labor Act (EMTALA) also requires emergency rooms to treat you, at

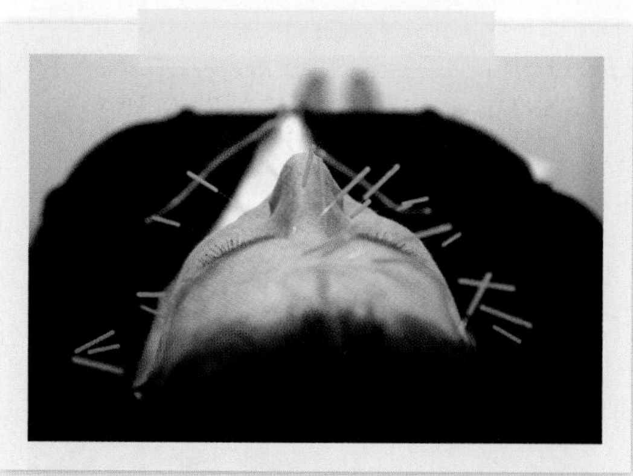

Alternative medical treatments such as acupuncture have become increasingly professionalized.

least enough to stabilize your condition, regardless of your ability to pay for services. Increasingly, emergency rooms have become money drains on hospitals, and consequently, many are being shut down.

Likewise, there are debates about whether the rise of heterodoxy, or nontraditional medicine, has challenged the authority of the traditional medical community. More and more people are exploring alternative medicines, such as biofeedback, massage therapy, acupuncture, chiropractics, and herbal medicine. Doctors' monopoly on treatment is starting to decline to some extent, although a growing number of doctors have responded by incorporating these nontraditional forms of medicine into their own practices. Some of the alternative practitioners are certified; others aren't. Learning from the history of the medical profession, some try to create certification, which not only increases their legitimacy but also represents an attempt to restrict the field, allowing for greater control over prices, knowledge, and services.

Ironically, the rise of technology, which contributed to the power and prestige of the medical profession, is the third force that has eroded the authority of doctors. Many procedures no longer require the steady, trained hand of a doctor. A nurse practitioner can swab your throat, dip the swab into a chemical solution, and tell in five minutes whether you have strep throat. Doctors have become, in a sense, victims of their own technological innovation and success. Developments in pharmaceuticals have given drug companies the chance to challenge the medical community, too.

The Internet has also changed the way medicine is practiced. Now you can do your own medical research online, learning about anything from pain in the lower right back to kidney stones. You can compile a list of potential causes for your symptoms and go to your doctor not as a passive patient but as an active consumer of health care, challenging and questioning his or her opinions and judgments.

What Does It Mean to Be Sick?

The Sick Role

Chapter 4 introduced the concept of role theory, which sees individuals as taking on certain roles in society, much like actors in a movie. In the 1950s, sociologist Talcott Parsons combined role theory with medical sociology to create the concept of the sick role (1951). According to Parsons, the sick role comes with two rights and two obligations. The sick person has the right (1) not to perform normal social roles (the degree of exemption from rights and responsibilities depends on the severity of the illness) and (2) not to be held accountable for his or her condition. The two obligations are (1) to try to get well and (2) to seek competent help and comply with doctors' orders. Those who have successfully adopted the sick role cannot be looked down on or morally judged if they do not work. But they may be the source of opprobrium if they fail to take their medicine, continue to eat fried foods after a heart attack, or smoke after a diagnosis of throat cancer.

Sick role concept describing the social rights and obligations of a sick individual.

Categorizing the sick role in such a way, however, puts the emphasis on the individual rather than on the social context and thus brings about a paradox. For example, because we know that certain behaviors are linked to specific diseases—smoking to emphysema and lung cancer, a high-fat diet to heart disease, and high sugar intake to type 2 diabetes—individuals are often seen as being at least partially responsible for their diseases, rather than unaccountable as is presumed under right (2) above. Also, how many patients have the ability to assess what constitutes competent help and the resources to obtain it? If you have unlimited time and money, you might see a preeminent dermatologist about a mole on your arm. If, however, you don't have insurance or can't take the time off from work to see a doctor, you might ignore the mole. If it turns out to be skin cancer, do you lose your rights as a sick person because you didn't fulfill your obligations?

Social Construction of Illness

In fact, what it means to be sick or healthy varies across time and place. *The Spirit Catches You and You Fall Down* (Fadiman, 1997) is the story of a Hmong immigrant family living in Southern California whose daughter Lia was diagnosed by her Western doctors as having epilepsy. Seizures, the main symptom of epilepsy, were viewed by her family as periods of time in which her soul was visiting the spirit world, a high honor in Hmong culture, one that carried a risk of failure to reunite body and soul. (It would be kind of like being able to take trips to heaven for Christians.) Author Anne Fadiman tries to give voice to both sides of the story—the doctors blame the parents for noncompliance with the prescribed medication regimen, whereas the parents blame the doctors for the medication's side effects. By examining the clash between modern Western and traditional Hmong culture, this story explores the different meanings of health and illness corresponding to the same phenomenon.

To use another example, alcoholism was not always seen as a disease, as mentioned earlier. Throughout much of history, it was seen as a moral weakness. What is seen as a personality flaw in one person (laziness) may be

You can watch my interview with Ka Liu at wwnorton.com/studyspace.

viewed as a legitimate medical condition in another (chronic fatigue syndrome) depending on that individual's sex, race, class background (and, therefore, access to medical care), religion, nationality, and the time period in which he or she lives.

Sometimes a new category is created by the medical profession. But other times there is a shift in diagnoses from one diagnosis to another thanks to different costs (such as stigma) and rewards (such as aid) attendant to those categories. I spoke with Ka Liu about her research with Marissa King and Peter Bearman on the rapid rise of autism diagnoses among U.S. children: "There has been a lot of increase on the high functioning end, but also, interestingly, at the low, most severe end. This is the diagnostic substitution between other [intellectual disabilities] and autism" (Conley, 2011d).

Further, like most social processes, this process of medicalization does not just happen to individuals in a random way, it can spread just like a virus does in a population. Liu described the "contagiousness" of autism as akin to the adoption of fashion or iPhones: "It is like the spreading of a new technology. People learn about certain ways of doing things [through] recognition of the symptoms" (Conley, 2011d). The "things" that parents "are doing" by recognizing the symptoms in their children is getting them resources from the educational and health systems of their state. This is not to say that there may be chemical or biological roots to the autism epidemic in the United States through, say, increased exposure to particular toxins in the environment; but ignoring the sociological perspective would lead to an incomplete understanding of the problem, so to speak.

The U.S. Health-Care System

Is health care a right or a privilege? The ongoing debates in Congress over the 2010 health-care reform act attest to the difficulty of answering that question. Many other wealthy industrialized nations—the United Kingdom, the Netherlands, France, Italy—have had universal health care for decades. Below we explore some of the social impacts of health-care costs and the impact the new health-care legislation may have on America.

Health Care in the United States: Who's Got You Covered?

The first growth spurt in the U.S. health-care industry occurred during the Great Depression in the 1930s. Established by the American Hospital Association, Blue Cross, and later Blue Shield, the health-care industry is characterized by the fee-for-service model of insurance discussed earlier. You go to the doctor for a sore throat and pay $25 for the visit. The insurance company pays for the rest—the lab work, the balance of the doctor's fees, and so on. Some commercial (for-profit) insurance companies also operate on the fee-for-service model but base the cost to the consumer on the risk the individual poses (PricewaterhouseCoopers, 2011). For example, if you have a history of cancer in your family, are a smoker, are overweight, or live in an area filled with toxic waste sites, the insurance company is going to charge you more money for the same amount of coverage than the person sitting next to you who works out, doesn't smoke or drink, or has four grandparents over the age of 90. In insurance parlance, this is called risk adjustment.

As discussed earlier, one of the main problems with the fee-for-service model is that doctors have the incentive to overtreat (supplier-induced demand)—to see you again and again and bill the insurance company. This, of course, drives up medical costs for everybody. Health maintenance organizations (HMOs) originally developed as an attempt to hold down costs by paying doctors a salary based on the number of patients they take on. Under HMOs, the medical provider receives a capitation, meaning fee per person as opposed to fee per treatment. The patients still pay a fee, called a co-pay, each time they go to the doctor. Under this system, doctors receive (more or less) the same amount of money whether they see a patient once a year or once a week; thus, the incentive for the doctor (from a strictly financial perspective) is to keep you healthy so that you require less treatment and reduce your number of visits to the doctor's office. Of course, this system creates the opposite problem: Doctors have an incentive to undertreat, because they generally don't get much extra money each time you come in.

Although the United States doesn't have a universal health-care system, the government does provide health care for some of the most vulnerable groups in the population. Medicare, for example, covers most people aged 65 or older and some younger people with disabilities. Medicaid is a joint federal and state program that helps cover medical costs for poor people with limited resources. Although this patchwork of programs provides medical coverage or assistance for some of society's most disadvantaged groups, the bureaucratic processes can

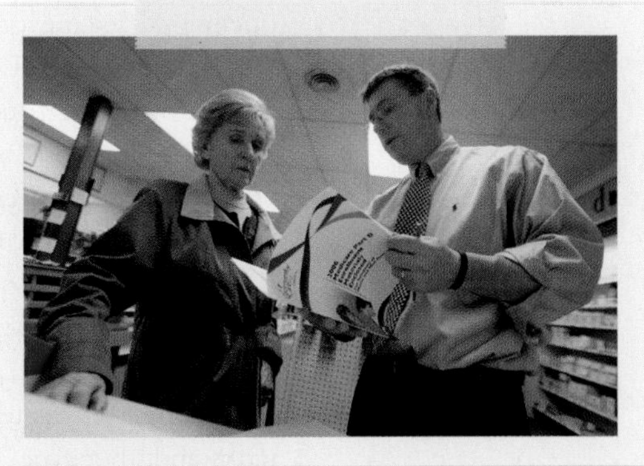

A pharmacist explains Medicare insurance options. Why do some poor and elderly patients decide not to take advantage of programs such as Medicaid and Medicare?

be difficult to navigate. These programs change constantly, and qualification criteria and benefit packages may vary widely by state. Because the individuals who most need these programs, the elderly and the poor, are the least likely to have access to up-to-date technology such as the Internet, it may be difficult for them to find the necessary information about what is covered, how to get reimbursed, or even where to find a doctor.

In addition to Medicare and Medicaid, aggressive measures have been taken to provide comprehensive health insurance for children in particular. The State Children's Health Insurance Plan (SCHIP) came into effect in the late 1990s to provide more money and state-level assistance for children's health care. It was meant to expand the number of children with coverage beyond what Medicaid provided. States can create separate insurance programs for children or combine SCHIP with general Medicaid funding. The federal government matches the funding states provide while allowing states to set their own criteria for eligibility and control the disbursement of funds.

For many uninsured Americans who do not qualify for government assistance, the cost of health care is truly prohibitive. A personal or family illness is the most common reason individuals (as opposed to companies) file for bankruptcy in the United States. In April 2006, Massachusetts passed into law a plan intending to lower the rate of uninsured people to less than 1 percent of the state's population. As of 2009, a total of 5 percent were uninsured and 3 percent of the state's children were uninsured (Kaiser Family Foundation, 2011).

The Social Determinants of Health and Illness

How does the position of doctors in society matter for our health? The dirty little secret is that doctors don't matter that much in determining who is healthy and when they are healthy. In Western societies, you usually go to the doctor only when you decide that you are sick. When was the last time you woke up in the morning and said, "I feel great today! I think I'll see if the doctor has an opening to see me after lunch"?

The truth is that health care and health-care systems are not very important in predicting outcomes like mortality rates, life expectancy, and quality of life. Much more important, it turns out, are factors such as nutrition, clean water, lifestyle choices, and social position. In 1967, British researchers began to study the health of civil servants in what is known as the Whitehall Study. By focusing on one occupational sector, the civil service, this study controlled for the differences *between* men in different occupations and examined the differences *among* men of different social classes in similar occupations. Over an initial period of ten years, the researchers found that men who held lower ranks and, therefore, lower status had much higher rates of common illnesses and ailments (including heart disease, diabetes, and stress) and higher mortality rates. The men in lower ranks had more risk factors—obesity, higher levels of stress, less physical activity. Not knowing whether this was a cause or effect of lower economic status, researchers tried to factor out prior health status and still found that men in the lowest rank were more than twice as likely as men in the highest rank to suffer from cardiovascular problems. The findings of the study were so important that the study has continued, expanding to include women and periodically looking at the impact of specific programs, such as smoking cessation, on health disparities. This study is conducted in a society where everyone has access to health care regardless of their socioeconomic status (SES). None of the participants are poor or undernourished, and they all have a sufficient salary to survive. So what does the Whitehall Study tell us about the role of social factors as determinants of who gets sick?

The Whitehall Study has shown that who you are, where you live, how much you earn, and what you do for a living all play a major role in determining your health. Along with similar research, it has shown how social forces affect our bodies, our morbidity, and our general risk of mortality. Morbidity means illness in a general sense—the absence of complete health. It could mean something like the chicken pox (an acute condition) or not being able to walk very well because you have lower back pain (a chronic condition). Mortality means death, so when we refer to mortality rates in this chapter, we're talking about the likelihood of an individual or groups of individuals dying. The Whitehall scholars speculated that the social stress resulting from lower rank in the hierarchy of social class led directly to poorer outcomes for those at the bottom—through the release of stress hormones, for example—as well as indirectly, through different behavioral responses (such as overeating and smoking as a result of their social position). These assertions, however, remain controversial in the field, because some researchers argue that Whitehall does not adequately address the possibility that underlying personality differences and skill sets led to both occupational and health differences or that health directly determined the rank to which the bureaucrats rose by virtue of its effect on productivity.

Morbidity illness in a general sense.

Mortality death.

What Can Height Tell Us about the Relationship between Health and Society?

The April 5, 2004, edition of the *New Yorker* magazine featured an article titled "The Height Gap" that discussed how tall men benefit from their height. Taller men have higher incomes, are more politically powerful ("only 5 of the 43 U.S. presidents have been shorter than average"), and are luckier in love.

The article spotlighted the anthropometric economist John Komlos. Komlos has been investigating why the Dutch are now the tallest population in the world. Sociologists are interested in height because it is determined both by genetics and by environmental conditions during infancy and childhood. African Pygmies, on the one hand, lack the necessary growth hormones and proteins for the population's average height to exceed five feet. However,

Pieter Gijselaar is seven feet tall. In the last 150 years the Dutch have become the tallest people on earth, and experts say they are still growing.

Anthropologist Barry Bogin (1995) studied two groups of Mayan Indians in Guatemala who came from the same place but then parted ways when some migrated to America as refugees. After 15 years, Bogin found that the Mayans living in the United States, where they had a better diet and access to healthier lifestyles, were an average of four inches taller than their Guatemalan counterparts.

But given that the United States is a relatively prosperous country even compared with other developed European states, why are the Dutch so much taller than we are? One theory holds that it's not just about wealth but also about equality. The United States is one of the wealthiest countries in the world, but a high, and increasing, gap also exists between the rich and the poor. In countries such as the Netherlands, which has a social-democratic government, wealth is distributed much more equally. The Netherlands provides excellent pre- and postnatal care to everyone at no or nominal cost. The U.S. population, until the recent health-care legislation was enacted, included about 40 million people (roughly 13 percent of the population) who did not have health insurance. As mentioned above, health care is a relatively minor factor in determining the health (and height) of populations. The psychological stress that inequality creates may exact a toll on our height directly through stress reactions and indirectly through social behavior. Even Americans who can afford to live healthier lifestyles may not necessarily do so. Human growth primarily takes place in three spurts—one in infancy, one around the ages of 6 to 8, and one in adolescence. If American tweens and teens are stocking up on French fries and hamburgers rather than apples and carrot sticks, they might not be getting the nutrients they need to maximize their growth potential. Wealth doesn't matter just for height, though, and in the following section we'll discuss some of the social factors that affect our life outcomes.

We're Not All Born Equal: Prenatal and Early Life Determinants

We know that a mother's health can affect the health of her baby. Advances in technology, however, now allow the diagnosis and even treatment of some conditions before birth. Likewise, reproductive technologies to combat infertility

Indian visitors to a New Delhi hospital stand next to a poster that reads, "Save the girl child, finding out the gender of a fetus is a sin." Because of the rampant practice of sex-selective abortions, India has a dearth of female babies.

allow for the manipulation of genetic factors before conception. Amniocentesis, the process of inserting a needle into the uterus to extract fluid from the amniotic sack surrounding the fetus, has been used since the beginning of the 1900s. Because the fluid contains the fetus's DNA, genetic screening can be done for certain diseases before birth. This technology provides an opportunity for improving health and decreasing infant mortality, but it also raises ethical issues. If a fetus has an incurable disease, should the mother abort it? What if the fetus is healthy but undesirable for some other reason? In countries such as China and India, where boys hold greater cultural value than girls, amniocentesis (and less-invasive ultrasound technology) can be used to determine the sex of the fetus early on. Particularly in rural areas where families live in poverty, if parents can give their resources to only one child, they will often choose a boy because there will likely be a better return on their investment. These considerations might lead to selective abortions of female fetuses.

Even without such procedures, more boys than girls are born worldwide, thanks to the lighter load of genetic material that male sperm carry. (The Y chromosome has hardly any genetic material compared with the X chromosome and, being lighter, tends to reach the egg more quickly.) In general, the sex ratio is usually around 1.05, meaning that for every 105 baby boys born, 100 baby girls are born. However, higher mortality rates for boys usually mean that this number evens out in adulthood and eventually flips, leaving more old women than old men. In India and China, however, the birth ratio is higher. Recent estimates put China's sex ratio at birth at 1.12. This might not seem like a big difference, but in a country with a population of 1.3 billion, this means

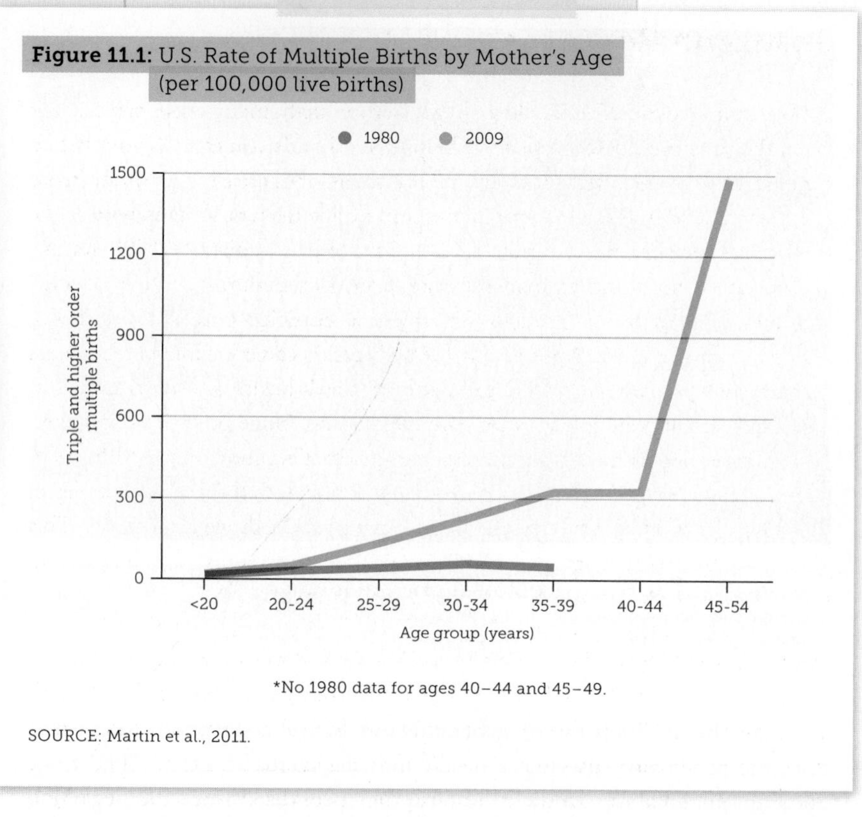

Figure 11.1: U.S. Rate of Multiple Births by Mother's Age (per 100,000 live births)

SOURCE: Martin et al., 2011.

that tens of millions of baby girls have gone "missing" since China's one-child policy was enacted in the early 1980s. This imbalance in the sex ratio leads to further social problems, including lack of marriage partners for young men, which may eventually lead to a change in the cultural valuation of women.

Another consequence of assisted reproductive technology (ART) has been the rise in the number of twins, triplets, and higher-order multiple births (see Figure 11.1). This happens in two ways. When a woman has in vitro fertilization, several pre-embryos (zygotes) may be inserted into her uterus in hopes of increasing the chance of implantation, which carries the associated risk that more than one may implant. Likewise, if a woman is taking ovulation-inducing drugs, either in hopes of getting pregnant or in preparation for in vitro fertilization, more eggs may be traveling down the tubes, and two or more eggs may merge with sperm. The increase in higher-order births has raised new ethical issues as women, their partners, and their doctors must decide whether to "reduce" (i.e., selectively abort some of the embryos) because risks sharply increase for the mother and the embryos as the number of embryos increases. Another concern is that in multiple births babies have a greater risk of low birth weight and prematurity. Babies who gestate in a crowded womb struggle to get what they need for nine months and illustrate how health inequality (and sibling rivalry) can begin even before birth.

Post-Birth Health Inequalities

As you can imagine, if inequalities begin before birth, many more can emerge from the time the doctor slaps your behind and hands you over to your proud parents. Low birth weight has become the focus of increasing attention from the medical and academic communities and policy makers. A baby with a low birth weight weighs five pounds, eight ounces or less at birth (<2,500 grams). Low birth weight results from either inadequate growth during gestation (called intrauterine growth restriction or IUGR) or a curtailed period of gestation, otherwise known as premature birth. Several factors can contribute to low birth weight, such as parental birth weight and mother's health and nutritional status, which are also associated with parental income. Once born, however, low-birth-weight babies have lower average educational attainment and SES, and a greater chance of giving birth to low-birth-weight babies themselves (Conley et al., 2003). In 2009 the rate of infants born with low birth weight was 8.2. This was only a 0.1 percent drop from 2006, which had the highest level reported in four decades (U.S. Department of Health and Human Services, 2011a).

Race In the United States, whites hold a significant advantage in health and longevity, having a life expectancy at birth of 78.9 years compared with African Americans' 73.8 (U.S. Census Bureau, 2009a). This discrepancy is seen as both a major social problem and a sign of social inequality. David Satcher, the surgeon general during much of Bill Clinton's presidency, made the reduction of health disparities by race one of his primary goals. By 2010 and then 2020, he wanted to reduce gaps in outcomes such as hypertension, cancer, and overall mortality. But things don't even start out equal. The infant mortality rate (per 1,000) by race is as follows: white, 5.6; black, 13.3; Latino, 5.5 (Kochanek et al., 2011; Figure 11.2). African American infants are more than twice as likely to die as their white counterparts, and compared with their middle-class white counterparts, middle-class black women still experience high rates of low-birth-weight babies (Kashef, 2003). Asian/Pacific Islanders have the lowest infant mortality rates, probably because, although a diverse group, they do better economically, on average. Indeed, with regard to health, racial inequalities historically have played out in a variety of ways. Heart disease and cancer are most prevalent among African Americans, cirrhosis of the liver and suicide most prevalent among Native Americans. Hispanics have higher rates of diabetes and HIV/AIDS than whites.

If we focus on health disparities between blacks and whites, because they are among the most extreme, what accounts for these differences? For starters, there's a high correlation between SES and race, but blacks have worse health than whites regardless of income or education level. There is evidence to suggest that racism in day-to-day life contributes to differences in health in several ways. Blacks are disproportionately poor in the United States, and being poor can be very stressful. The irony is that middle- and upper-class African Americans also

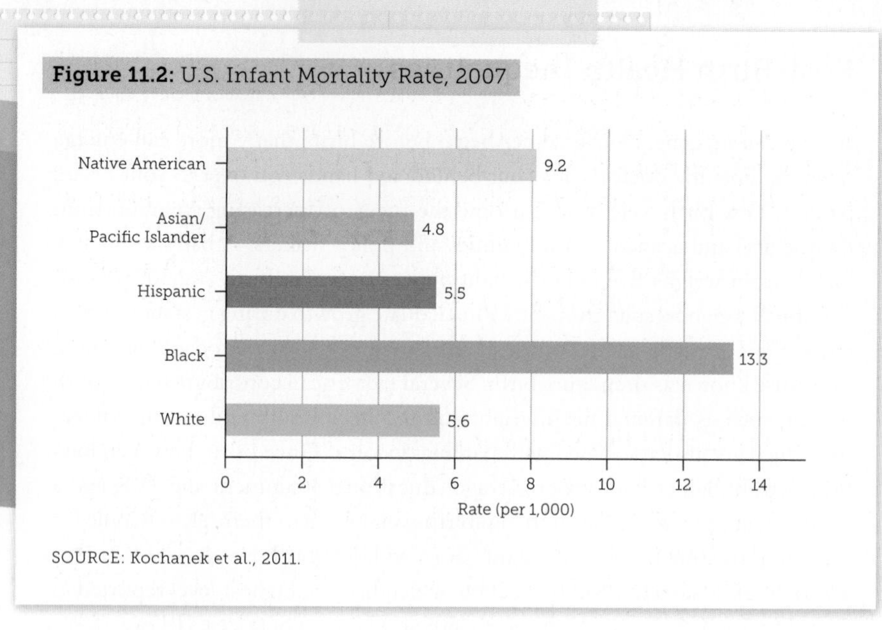

Figure 11.2: U.S. Infant Mortality Rate, 2007

SOURCE: Kochanek et al., 2011.

have high rates of hypertension, which is known to be linked to stress. One theory is that it is precisely the mismatch—the incongruity between what people assume their economic status to be, based on stereotypes, and what it actually is—that elevates stress levels. Also, middle- and upper-class blacks may face discrimination when they are perceived as "token" minorities in the workplace.

It's a vicious cycle. African Americans are more likely to be the victims of both overt and subtle forms of prejudice. Although specific acts, such as a violent attack, could clearly affect someone's health, so could the gradual accumulation of more minor injustices in the form of stress and high blood pressure, not to mention racism's psychological impacts. The hypothesis of "John Henryism" is another example of how discrimination and racial symbolism may affect health. John Henry, like Paul Bunyan, is a star of American folklore. As legend has it, he was a steel-driving man, working on the railroad. With the development of the steam engine, machinery threatened to replace his manpower. John Henry told his boss he could drive the stakes into the rail through the mountain faster than the steam engine. His story was immortalized in many folk and chain-gang songs:

> John Henry said to his Captain,
> "A man ain't nothin' but a man,
> And before I'll let your steam drill beat me down,
> Die with the hammer in my hand,
> Die with the hammer in my hand."

The good news is that John Henry won the race and beat the steam drill. The bad news is that he died from exhaustion afterward. He remains a legend and cultural symbol of the hardworking African American man. The social psychologist Sherman James and his associates (1987), drawing on the symbolism of John Henry, suggest a link between historical and cultural factors that lead to higher rates of hypertension among blacks. Americans value hard work and self-reliance, and these values combine with the history of slavery to make blacks likely to take a John Henry–like approach to dealing with the psychological, social, and environmental stressors they face (Conley et al., 2003). Specifically, as John Henry battled the steam engine, many African Americans battle the negative stereotypes in American society, working extra hard to prove themselves.

Socioeconomic Status It probably won't surprise you to hear that people with higher incomes live longer, but why is that the case? Is it that health insurance and health care in the United States are so expensive? Is it diet? What does income buy that decreases mortality? Likewise, more highly educated people enjoy longer life expectancies on average, and a number of straightforward explanations exist. Higher-educated people behave differently from people with less education. People with a college education smoke less, eat more healthily, and exercise more often. They often have more information and knowledge to work with when facing their own health choices and interactions with the health-care system. But perhaps their overall better health contributed to their high levels of educational attainment. If you battled a serious illness as a child or teenager, for example, you might have missed a lot of school or not been able to attend college (Marmot & Wilkinson, 1999).

So how do we explain the correlation between SES and health? There are three main theories that attempt to explain this association. The first theory, which we might call selection theory, says that the relationship between lower income and higher morbidity is spurious (that is, false or not really causal) because other factors such as genetics and biology affect both health and SES. A second theory, called the drift explanation, asserts that reverse causality exists, that health causes social position (as in the education example given in the previous paragraph). There is some logic behind this argument: If you don't have good health, you may not be able to work, so higher morbidity would result in lower SES.

Finally, one must consider the social determinants theory that social status position determines health (see Chapter 7). Being of a lower income level or SES causes higher morbidity and lower general health. What are the factors that could make this happen? Again, there are three general schools of thought for answering this question:

1. The psychosocial interpretation focuses on individuals' social class status relative to that of those around them. Feelings of inadequacy, low worth, and stigma cause people stress and wear down their bodies. If you have taken out tens of thousands of dollars in loans and work two jobs to

get through college while your roommate is independently wealthy, the persistent presence of that inequality could affect your health directly by making you feel stressed, depressed, or angry, or indirectly by causing poor health choices such as smoking, using drugs, failing to exercise, and eating badly.

2. The second theory, the materialist interpretation, asserts that the differential access to a healthy life—including all monetary, psychological, and environmental risk factors—is a result of socioeconomic factors. Buying organic may be healthy, for example, but it is also expensive. So is joining a health club or obtaining top-notch medical care. Poor neighborhoods meanwhile are more likely to have higher concentrations of toxic chemicals.

3. The final theory seeking to explain how lower SES causes lower mortality is called the fundamental causes interpretation. This theory focuses on examining how social factors shape illness and health to understand the pervasive link between SES and health. The crux of the argument is this: "Because resources are differentially distributed across the socioeconomic hierarchy, people of higher social position have more resources at their disposal than those below them and are, therefore, better able to maintain good health and avoid disability and death" (Carpiano et al., 2006). At bottom, the fundamental causes hypothesis states that multiple and ever-changing mechanisms exist by which SES (and other dimensions of power) affect health. What the causes have in common, however, is the greater ability of high-status individuals to make use of new information and health resources as they become available. For example, Figure 11.3 shows that the gradient for lung cancer, which is strongly

Figure 11.3: Brain and Lung Cancer Statistics

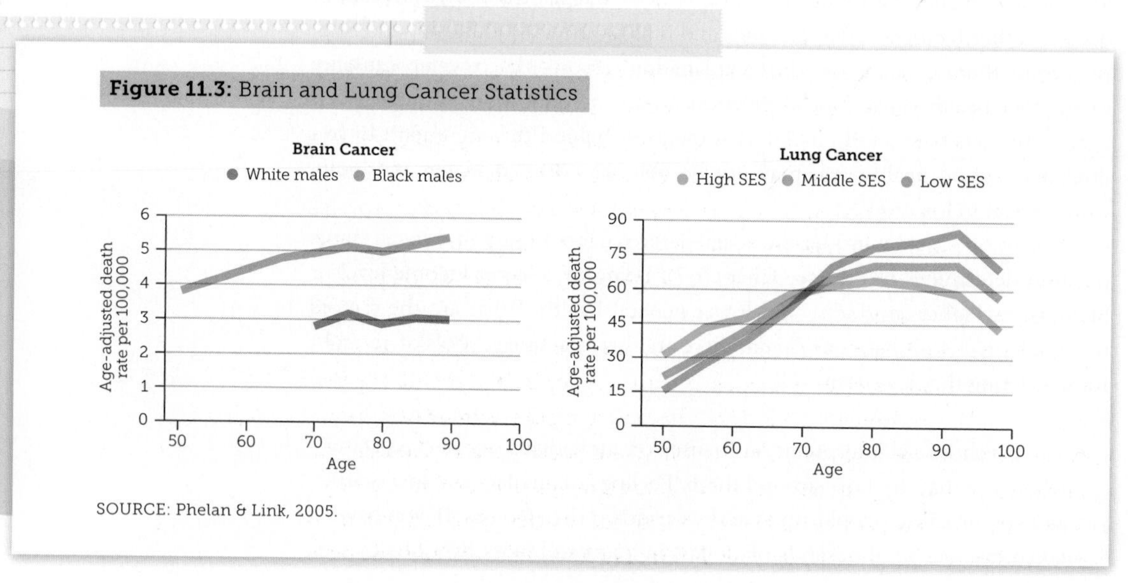

SOURCE: Phelan & Link, 2005.

impacted by health behaviors, is much steeper than that for brain cancer, which is generally viewed as less predictable or less preventable.

If the idea of fundamental causes seems a bit abstract, historical changes can help sort out what sociologists mean. For example, by today's standards, during the 1950s and 1960s, poor people ate a healthier diet than rich people. Low-income individuals ate more whole grains, legumes, and vegetables because they cost less. Wealthier people thought it was healthy to eat red meat for its iron and milk and eggs for their protein, and they could afford to do so more often. In the 1970s, a revolution in our understanding of nutrition occurred, shifting the emphasis from meats and eggs to a balanced diet of fruits, vegetables, grains, and moderate amounts of meat. What was considered a healthy diet essentially flipped. The moment new health information became available, it was the high-SES individuals who were able to take advantage of it. Perhaps because they can afford to buy fresh fruits and vegetables and high-quality, low-fat meats and because they are better informed about the benefits of such food choices, wealthier people now have much better diets on average. Likewise, before the surgeon general's famous 1964 report on the dangers of smoking, there wasn't much of a class gradient in tobacco use. However, immediately upon release of that report, the SES gradient widened and has continued to do so ever since. By contrast, outcomes about which we know little, such as a brain aneurism, show no apparent SES differences (Carpiano et al., 2006).

Changes in policy often provide "natural" experiments that social researchers can use to their advantage for teasing out cause and effect. Adriana Lleras-Muney, an economist at Princeton University, used changes in state-level compulsory education laws in the early to mid-1900s to examine the impact of education on health outcomes later in life. In a nutshell, she figured, "If compulsory schooling laws forced people to get more schooling than they would have chosen otherwise, and if education increases health, then individuals who spent their teens in states that required them to go to school for more years should be relatively healthier and live longer" (Lleras-Muney, 2005). Such a natural experiment offers a way to gather evidence that education influences health (and not vice versa). Lleras-Muney found that an extra year of schooling decreased individuals' chances of dying by 3.6 percentage points in a given ten-year period. (Recall our discussion in Chapter 10 of the effects of poverty on children's life chances.)

Another natural experiment testing the relationship between SES and health occurred with a sudden change in Social Security policy in 1977 mandating that people born before January 1, 1917, would receive higher retirement incomes than those born after this date. The people at the Social Security Administration had to choose an arbitrary cutoff date for the enactment of the agency's new policy, so there would be no reason to believe that people born right before and right after the date are any different except in the amount of Social

Security they received. Researchers used this natural experiment to explore the impact of income on elderly mortality. Their findings were counterintuitive: The people who received less Social Security lived longer. If income and mortality are negatively related, meaning that as your income increases, your chances of dying decrease, what happened here? What Stephen Snyder and William Evans found was that individuals who were receiving smaller Social Security packages compensated for the effects by working part-time longer (2002). Because social isolation is thought to increase mortality among the elderly, staying in the labor market had a positive impact on these individuals' longevity. Something about work is beneficial—mentally, physically, or both—to one's health, provided, of course, you're not working in a coal mine or on a deep-sea fishing boat. Such natural experiments are fortunate for researchers because they show more clearly what's cause, what's effect, and under what circumstances particular causes and effects occur.

Marital Status Married people tend to live longer, particularly married men. But can we say that being married causes you to live longer or enjoy better health? Remember that we are not randomly assigning people to marry or remain single. There is a marriage market, and as in all markets, different groups have varying levels of success in it. We already mentioned that taller men tend to have higher rates of marriage. Because height is a fairly good proxy for childhood health, maybe healthier people do better on the marriage market, thus suggesting the true causal story is that health leads to marriage. Do you want to marry someone who suffers from a hacking tuberculosis cough and therefore cannot work and has no money? All other things being equal, you might opt for a healthier partner. Likewise, if you're very ill and spend a lot of time in the hospital or are confined to your home by a disability or chronic condition, you might have difficulty meeting people. It might be that better health leads to better marriage prospects, not the other way around.

Perhaps, though, marriage actually has a salutary effect—maybe it benefits your health. This idea certainly seems plausible. After all, when you settle down, you probably do not go out as much or engage in the risky behaviors you might have when single. Ramen noodles and soda may no longer be acceptable dinner options. Does marriage have beneficial effects, or does who gets married tend to be special in some way? There's probably some truth to both explanations.

Gender Who lives longer, women or men? Women do, at least in the United States. According to the U.S. Census, in 2008 male life expectancy at birth was 75.5 years, but for women it was 80.5 years. Even the projected 2020 life expectancy statistics show women outliving men by 4.8 years (U.S. Census Bureau, 2011g; Figure 11.4). Many differences in mortality are linked to specific illnesses, such as heart disease and cancer, both of which are more likely to afflict men than women. In fact, heart disease is the number-one killer of both

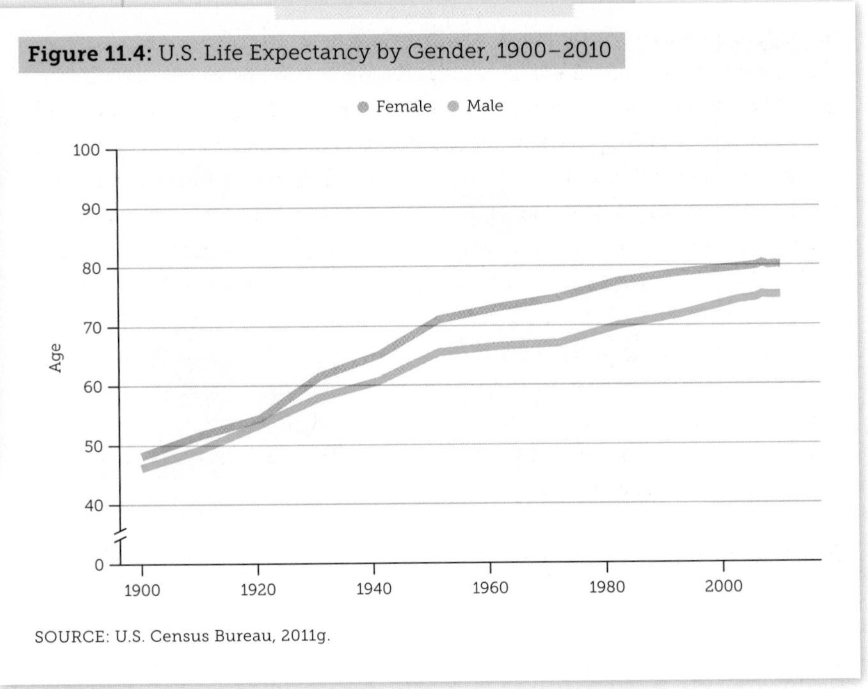

Figure 11.4: U.S. Life Expectancy by Gender, 1900–2010

SOURCE: U.S. Census Bureau, 2011g.

American men and women. As more women enter higher-level and consequently higher-stress jobs, their rates of hypertension, heart disease, and stroke are increasing. (See Chapter 14 for more about the impact of this change on the health of working mothers.) However, other reasons for higher mortality rates among men include the differences in health care–seeking behavior between men and women: Women are more likely to see the doctor for a persistent cough or an unexplained skin rash.

Interactions Between Race and Gender If whites live longer than blacks and women live longer than men, then how do the mortality rates of black men compare with those of white women? Although both race and sex affect mortality rates, their individual effects pale in comparison to their interactive (that is, multiplicative) effect. The average life expectancy at birth for white women is 81.3 years, compared with only 70.2 for black men (U.S. Census 2011g; Figure 11.5). As noted earlier in the discussion of "John Henryism," black men may be at much higher risk for stress, which is linked to heart disease and stroke—the two leading killers of African Americans. Nonwhites are more likely to face racism, have low SES, and work more dangerous jobs, and the presence of several of these factors can be a deadly combination (Xu et al., 2009).

Family Structure Family structure, family size, and birth order are also determinants of mortality. Larger families have higher child mortality rates.

Figure 11.5: U.S. Life Expectancy by Race, 2010

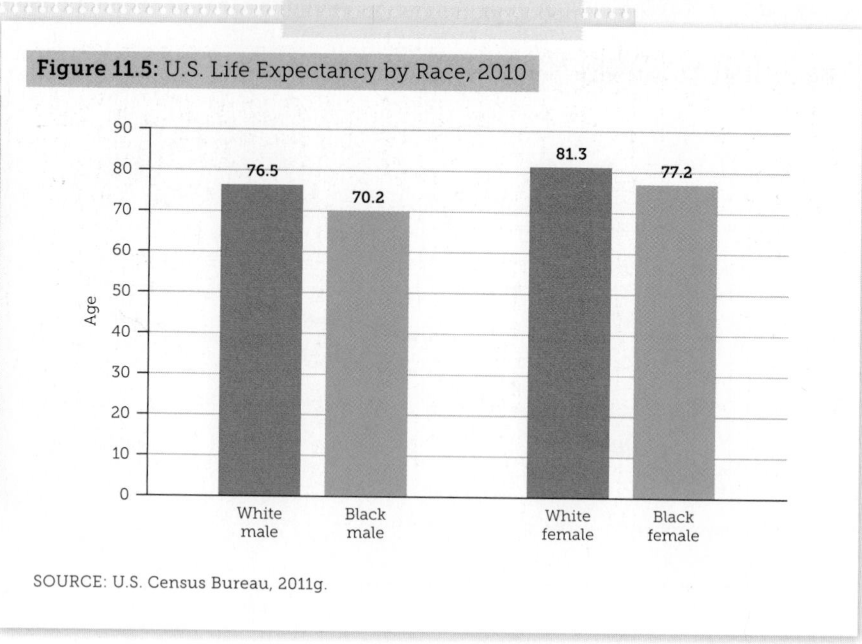

SOURCE: U.S. Census Bureau, 2011g.

When kids are spaced closer together, there is higher mortality. Why might this be the case? In developing countries in particular, resources key to survival (such as food) are stretched thinner in the household. If you have one pot of soup and eight mouths to feed instead of four, everyone gets half as much food, which translates into half the calories and nutrients. In our society, where food scarcity is less of an issue and accidental death is a greater cause of child mortality, supervision, or lack thereof, is the larger issue, because it's harder to supervise six children than two. The spacing of children also matters. Having three children in seven years is very different from having three children in three years. Parental resources are more taxed by rapid-fire spacing than by larger gaps between births.

Likewise, according to statistics, firstborn children are more likely to die young. One reason could be that parents are less experienced: The firstborn is an experiment in which parents learn through trial and (hopefully not too much) error. Another hypothesis is that firstborns are more often unintended pregnancies. Parents tend to be younger, and the mother may have been partying, drinking, smoking, or using drugs further into the pregnancy because she did not realize she was expecting a baby; thus, some of her actions early in the pregnancy may adversely affect the health of the fetus. It is also true, however, that the effect may run in the other direction: Child mortality creates firstborns or, to be more specific, only children. We can separate firstborn children into two groups, those who have younger siblings and those who are only children (first by default). It turns out that the higher risk of death occurs in the latter group. When we say that the direction of causation runs backward (that B causes A), what we mean is that if you have a traumatic experience with your firstborn child—if the baby

A poor farm family in Musala, Kenya. How do family size and structure affect life outcomes?

is severely ill or dies in infancy—you are less likely to have more children. It is not that firstborn children are at a higher risk for any real reason; rather, it is that people change their child-bearing history when something bad happens to their first child. (All the firstborns reading this passage can now breathe a sigh of relief.)

The Sociology of Mental Health

Mental illness is a tricky subject because its place in society has always been ambiguous. The label "mentally ill" was formerly reserved for individuals whose behaviors were considered bizarre or otherwise "unnatural." Asylums were used to house society's undesirables. With the work of Sigmund Freud and the advent of psychoanalysis, mental illness came to be seen, at least in the medical community, as one end of a continuum rather than one category in a dichotomy of "sane" versus "insane" persons. Diagnostic psychiatry, now the prevailing paradigm, treats mental illness much like any other illness, identifying its symptoms and prescribing treatment. Where does mental health fit into the larger health-care system?

Rise of Diagnostic Psychiatry

In 1952, the American Psychiatric Association (APA) published the first edition of the *Diagnostic and Statistical Manual of Mental Disorders (DSM)*, containing about 60 disorders. The social meanings of mental illness have always been contested, and the *DSM* is interesting because it represents the social construction of mental illness. In the nineteenth century, for example, women were frequently diagnosed as hysterical, and today the increasing diagnosis of borderline personality disorder, whose symptoms are analogous to those of hysteria, is a similar diagnosis under a different name. What the *DSM* did was standardize the canon of mental disorders and their definitions, such that a woman diagnosed with mania by one psychiatrist in Maine would (in theory) receive the same diagnosis from another psychiatrist in Texas (although it's never been that cut and dried, despite the APA's attempts at standardization). The second edition did not make sharp distinctions between normal and abnormal behavior; rather, behaviors were considered to exist on a continuum in reaction to various life circumstances. For example, if one of your parents was killed in an automobile accident, you might be depressed, but this was still considered a normal reaction. (The second edition of the *DSM* also included homosexuality as a psychiatric disorder, although this entry was removed in 1973.)

A major change occurred in 1980 with the publication of *DSM III*. This version was largely atheoretical, meaning that diseases were not attributed to certain causes (such as life events). In this way, it was primarily diagnostic and largely adopted a medical model (as opposed to a psychological one). You receive a diagnosis of "depressed" if you exhibit the associated symptoms for a period of two weeks or longer, much in the same way you might be diagnosed with chicken pox if you have a fever and red, itchy bumps. Unlike earlier editions, however, *DSM III* removed the social context in favor of the biomedical model. If you are depressed, it is presumed that you have a chemical imbalance. In the diagnosis criteria, no consideration is given to what life events, if any, may have triggered your feelings, although according to the manual, doctors were expected to take life factors into account.

Today the *DSM* is in its fourth edition and contains information on almost 400 distinct mental illnesses. Its use has increased, largely because of the bureaucratic requirements of the insurance industry: In order to get paid, mental health professionals must find a diagnosis category that "fits" you. Hence, the proliferation of new entries such as attention deficient/hyperactivity disorder (ADHD), generalized anxiety disorder, and premenstrual dysphoric disorder—all of which previously belonged to less medical, lay categories.

The major changes in the *DSM* that took place between its second and third editions reflect both changes in the field of psychiatry and our social understanding of mental illness. Dynamic psychiatry, which focused on identifying the internal conflicts that produced a mental illness, was usurped by diagnostic psychiatry, which seeks to identify the symptoms of specific underlying diseases. As noted above, this change marked a radical transformation in the field of psychiatry and has, in turn, had lasting effects on the social world. In trying to understand the current high rates of depression, for instance, sociologists Allan Horwitz and Jerome Wakefield ask whether our society is really more depressed than it used to be (2007). Maybe it's an artifact of how we measure depression. People may be more likely to report depression now because awareness about mental illness has increased. What was formerly thought of as being "blue" or "down in the dumps" because of specific life events may now (for better or worse) be treated as a much more serious problem. Or we may have better diagnostic tools. Depression was historically overdiagnosed in women, because the symptoms were more "female." Men's depression manifests itself differently, but this is not surprising given the different cultural scripts we have for emotion based on gender—yelling (male) versus crying (female), feeling angry (male) versus sad (female).

One of the larger shifts in the field of psychiatry in recent decades is the way we differentiate between sadness and depression. On its Web site, the National Alliance on Mental Illness (NAMI) notes that "the characterization of our emotional reactions to life's challenges as 'depression' is more than just a change in colloquial expression. It represents a transformation in psychiatric thinking." When multiple symptoms are present, symptoms last for more than two weeks, or symptoms interfere with someone's daily functioning, the patient may be diagnosed as clinically depressed.

The problem with our current measurements of depression, Horwitz and Wakefield argue, is that context is largely ignored. What if you experienced symptoms of depression for longer than two weeks right after September 11, 2001? Or what if you found out that your lifelong partner had left you for someone else? That's not depression, according to Horwitz and Wakefield; that's a normal emotional reaction to life's trauma, simply the human condition. Of course, because suicidal thoughts (ideation) or impulses are the hallmark of depressed individuals, identifying and treating these individuals are serious and necessary endeavors. However, overestimating the prevalence of depression, so that those with a serious mental illness are lumped into the same category as individuals with normal sadness, may dilute the attention and resources of public health officials, policy makers, and medical practitioners.

The Power of a Pill?

Once mental illness became medicalized, it wasn't long before pharmacological treatments overtook traditional "talk therapy." After all, once the social context is removed from the understanding of human behavior, all you need is a pill to fix the underlying organic disease, right?

Drugs can and do help people. If you have a headache, aspirin may help. Likewise, if you are clinically depressed, an antidepressant may alleviate some of your suffering. The availability of drugs may also help people seek treatment: If they felt helpless before, knowing that medication is available may inspire them to see a doctor. However, a negative side exists. Not all illnesses can be treated with drugs; some require talk therapy, which often is not covered as

Kathryn Orrick plays and teaches classical piano, something she couldn't do until antidepressant medications helped her out of depression. While she agrees the medicines should be closely monitored, especially with new patients, she credits her treatment for allowing her to live a full life.

comprehensively by insurance companies. Drugs may be over- or misprescribed, and there may be lethal results. Some studies have shown that certain antidepressants increase suicidal thoughts and tendencies in adolescents, although much controversy surrounds these claims. Drugs may also have the adverse social effect of increasing stigmatization, because pharmaceuticals might be seen as an indication of something seriously wrong. Prescriptions for antidepressants jumped 400 percent from 1988 to 2008 with approximately one in ten Americans over the age of twelve taking antidepressant medication (Pratt et al., 2011).

Pharmaceutical companies can market their drugs only to treat specific diseases, so they benefit from the diagnostic model of psychiatry. If your depression stems from a traumatic childhood marked by memories of abandonment by your alcoholic parents who were primarily concerned with their own needs, costly hours of therapy might be in order. If, however, your depression is caused by a chemical imbalance in your brain, your doctor can prescribe a drug covered by your insurance company. (Of course, it may be a childhood trauma that is causing a chemical imbalance, further complicating the sometimes flimsy distinction between biology and environment.) As you can imagine, adopting the biomedical model in psychiatry has both benefits and drawbacks. On the one hand, recognizing that mental illnesses are diseases with biological components can alleviate some of the stigma attached to them. (We don't say that people with cancer are crazy but that they're sick; why shouldn't the same hold for schizophrenics?) On the other hand, saying these diseases are completely biological may lead us to ignore important contexts and blame the sufferers when they aren't cured by a drug.

Global Health

Global Poverty and Health: Cause versus Effect

When we talk about the impact of SES on life expectancy in the United States, we're talking about differences of about five years on average (remember, though, that when we take into account race and sex, the difference is more than ten years). Although these differences are both real and important, they take on a whole new meaning when viewed in a global context. Ignoring differences in race, sex, and class, Americans are tied for 29th place (out of 176) with countries like Greece and Cuba for the highest life expectancy in the world

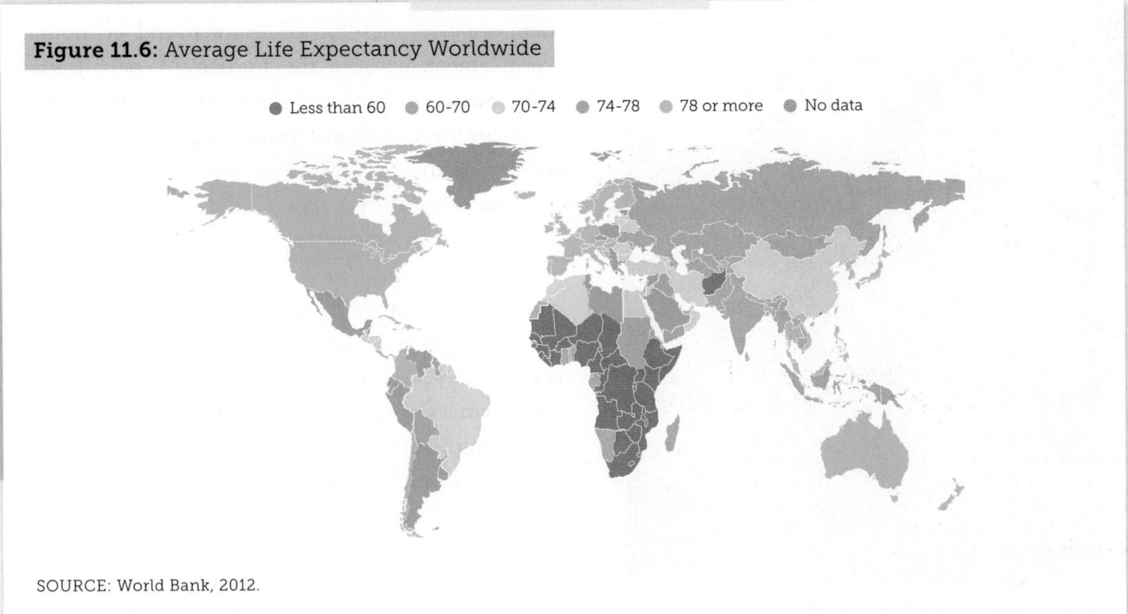

Figure 11.6: Average Life Expectancy Worldwide

SOURCE: World Bank, 2012.

(UN Statistics Division, 2010; Figure 11.6). In many countries in sub-Saharan Africa—one of the most economically depressed regions in the world—life expectancy remains below 50 years and is falling in some areas, largely because of AIDS.

What is the leading killer worldwide? Not AIDS. Cancer? Not yet. Heart disease? Diabetes? There are still plenty of regions in the world free of fast-food chains. Give up? Waterborne illness. Worldwide, more than one billion people don't have access to clean water (Poverty.com, 2008). Annually, 1.6 million people die from diarrhea alone, the majority under five years of age, because of unclean water (World Health Organization, 2008). So why is this a social issue? The technology and know-how for clean water exist. So does the money (worldwide at least). Many countries, however, don't have the funds or the infrastructure to handle these problems. As Kofi Annan, the former UN secretary-general, said, "We shall not finally defeat AIDS, tuberculosis, malaria, or any of the other infectious diseases that plague the developing world until we have also won the battle for safe drinking water, sanitation and basic health care" (United Nations, 2001). Even ethnic conflicts and turf wars may grow out of smaller disputes over scarce resources—clean water being a major one.

Do poorer countries have more health problems because they're poor, or are they poor because they have so many health problems? Well, both. It's not a simple matter of cause and effect; unfortunately, there's an effective feedback loop. Governments, communities, and individuals in the least developed areas must expend a great deal of their energy and resources on dealing with the problems of basic survival. Girls and women in particular are limited in

A Panama Canal worker sprays insecticide in an effort to control the spread of yellow fever and malaria.

their opportunities for educational and economic advancement because the burden of performing tasks such as collecting water—no small feat when the nearest well is miles away—falls disproportionately on them.

Like waterborne illness, the mosquito-borne disease malaria typically affects the least developed areas of the world (it's the number-four killer of children younger than five worldwide). Consider the problems malaria posed for the Western Hemisphere's development. During the construction of the Panama Canal, malaria, along with yellow fever, was a major cause of death and illness for workers. In 1906, 80 percent of all the employees working on the canal were hospitalized for malaria.

In fact, the U.S. Centers for Disease Control and Prevention (CDC) grew out of an agency called Malaria Control in War Areas (MCWA) that served the purpose of controlling and eliminating malaria in the areas surrounding U.S. military bases around the world. In the United States, particularly in the South, a campaign was waged during the first half of the twentieth century to drain swamps (where the parasite-carrying mosquitoes bred) and deploy window screens. By 1951, malaria was considered eradicated in the United States. In the 1950s, the World Health Organization (WHO) undertook an initiative to eradicate malaria worldwide. There were notable improvements in many areas thanks to the indoor spraying of the pesticide DDT, but once programs were discontinued (largely because of concerns about DDT's environmental effects), rates rose to their previous levels in some areas, most notably sub-Saharan Africa.

No malaria-endemic region of the world has ever developed economically, claims economist Jeffrey Sachs (2001). There are lots of infectious diseases and parasites out there, so what's the big deal with malaria? This was a question I posed to him in an interview and here's what he had to say.

> The *Anopheles* mosquito genus that carries malaria exists in a variety of species. The one that Africa has, the *Anopheles gambiae*, is different in its lethality because of the way it transmits the disease. There's this fascinating hypothesis that because Africa was simultaneously burdened by sleeping sickness which affected cattle spread by the tsetse fly, farmers in Africa didn't have a mixed animal crop system. So, when the malaria was transmitted from chimpanzees to humans in biological time, the mosquitoes learned to bite humans in Africa. By the time malaria came to Asia and especially to India millennia

> later, the Vedic farming system of ancient India was a cattle-based system. So [when] you look at the mosquitoes, the *Anopheles* mosquito in Africa bites people almost exclusively. In India, about 70 percent of the bites for the dominant kind of species are on cattle. (Conley, 2009g)

Malaria can be a fatal disease in humans; before the age of antibiotics, it had a very high morbidity rate, so high it could wipe out entire villages. As Sachs has explained, the particular situation in Africa encouraged the malaria-carrying mosquitoes to target humans rather than animals. Having malaria is a real drain on productivity, especially when it turns out to be fatal.

In other words, controlling and, ideally, eliminating malaria are a prerequisite for significant economic development. Steps are being taken to help the areas of the world that struggle with the most basic of public health issues, such as high malaria infection rates. If used consistently, insecticide-treated bed nets, which cost less than $10 apiece, can save lives in malaria-infested areas. African river blindness (onchocerciasis) is a scourge similar in its devastation to malaria. However, thanks to a concerted international effort since 1974, onchocerciasis has largely been eradicated from many areas, and this example illustrates the connection between health and economic development. One group estimates that 600,000 cases of blindness have been prevented in West Africa by the worldwide campaign. Furthermore, according to some estimates, about 100,000 square miles of land are now safe for settlement because of the eradication of the disease (World Bank, 2002).

Unfortunately, we are not making similar progress on the malaria front: Not only has the malaria problem yet to be solved in many of the world's poorer regions, but it's also reemerging in parts of the world where we believed we had conquered it. Malaria, along with tuberculosis, gonorrhea, and childhood ear infections, is one of the diseases that is becoming more difficult to treat because of antibiotic-resistant strains of the diseases. This problem, referred to as antimicrobial resistance, is thought to be the result of evolutionary adaptation on the part of bacteria and other infectious agents. Although antibiotics represent one of the greatest medical achievements ever made, nature is fighting back with bigger and badder antigens. Antimicrobial resistance has been exacerbated by the prescription of unnecessary antibiotics and the widespread use of mixing antibiotics into animal feed as a routine practice to

To see more of the conversation with Jeffrey Sachs, please go wwnorton.com/studyspace.

prevent herd death in the unnaturally close conditions of feedlots. Failing to finish a prescribed course of antibiotics can also contribute to the development of resistant strains. International efforts are underway to identify the most dangerous antibiotic-resistant strains, but as we come up with new and improved ways to treat illnesses, we need to consider what new and improved diseases we may simultaneously create.

Vaccines are another means of preventing disease that are standard in most developed countries but often rare in poorer nations. More than 20,000 cases of polio were reported each year in the United States before the vaccine for polio was introduced in 1955. Reported cases dropped to 2,525 by 1960 and to only 61 in 1965; almost no naturally occurring cases have been reported in the last 20 years (CDC, 2007a). The success of the vaccine in the United States sparked a worldwide initiative to eradicate the disease. However, in recent years, reports of polio have come from at least 15 countries that were thought to have eliminated it. In 2010, approximately 500,000 Americans died from vaccine-preventable diseases (Centers for Medicare and Medicaid Services, 2011). Although a vaccine for malaria does not yet exist, there is great promise for Africa from recently developed vaccines for other diseases, such as meningitis. Figure 11.7 shows the leading causes of death for young children worldwide.

Figure 11.7: Causes of Death in Children under Five, 2008

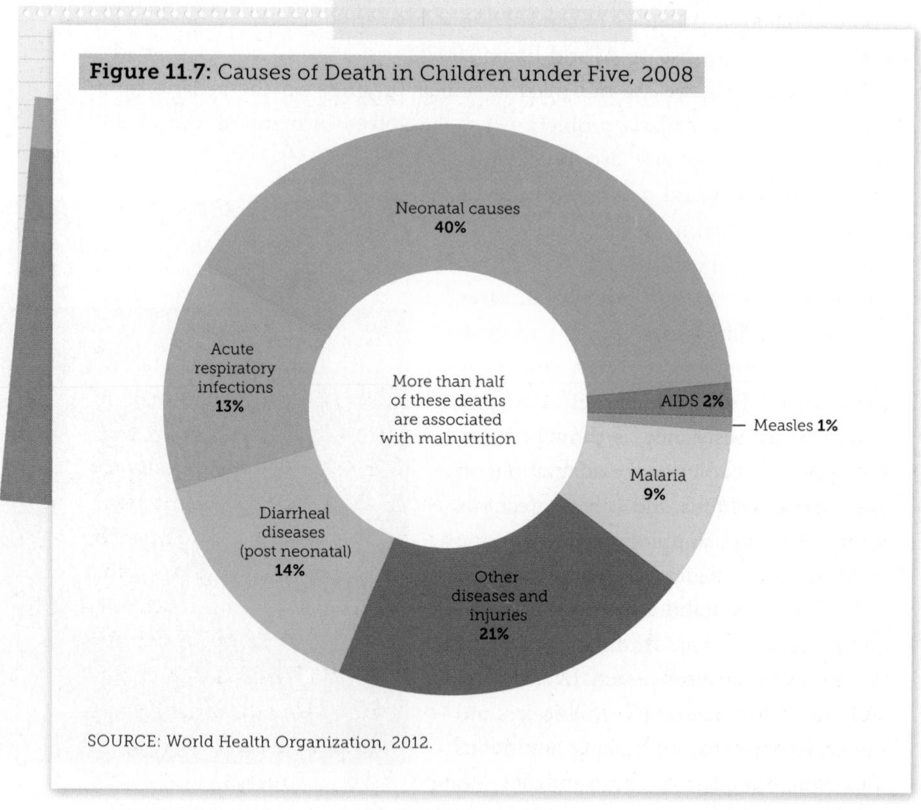

SOURCE: World Health Organization, 2012.

$H_2$0 To Go

Considering that there are one billion people in the world who still don't have access to clean drinking water, being able to buy safe drinking water is quite a luxury. Americans drank, on average, 29 gallons of bottled water per person in 2007, second only to soda. By volume, bottled water is often more expensive than gasoline; prices for water today range from less than $1 for a gallon jug of filtered water at the grocery store to more than $20 per gallon for high-end brands purchased in 9-ounce bottles. So why do we drink bottled water? Tastes vary by location, but generally in taste tests people can't tell the difference between tap and bottled water. Scientifically, it has not been proven that bottled water is better (in fact, your dentist may recommend that you switch back to tap if you're not getting enough fluoride), and the contents of tap water are more heavily regulated than those of bottled water. To put this information in a global context, according to the International Water Management Institute, for $1.7 billion a year in addition to what's already spent on water projects, everyone on earth could have access to clean water. For another $9.3 billion a year, everyone could have better sanitation (a major factor in preventing illness). In 2007, Americans alone spent $11.7 billion on bottled water (Mascha, 2008). You do the math.

The Age of AIDS

This chapter opened with the following paradox: What kills people (smallpox, the bubonic plague, polio) changes over time, but who is more likely to die (the poor, the uneducated, minorities) stays the same. An example of this on the global scale has been HIV/AIDS. When the first cases of what would later be termed acquired immunodeficiency syndrome (AIDS) were reported in 1981, it was thought to be a disease of gay men (dispelling this and other popular myths about HIV/AIDS has been a key component of educational programs). In fact, it has become very much a heterosexual disease in America. A quarter of a century after initial reports of cases, AIDS had killed more than 500,000 Americans and 25 million people worldwide. Currently, African American women have the highest rate of HIV contraction in the United States. Figure 11.8 breaks out the population living with HIV by region.

Figure 11.8: Population Living with HIV, 2010

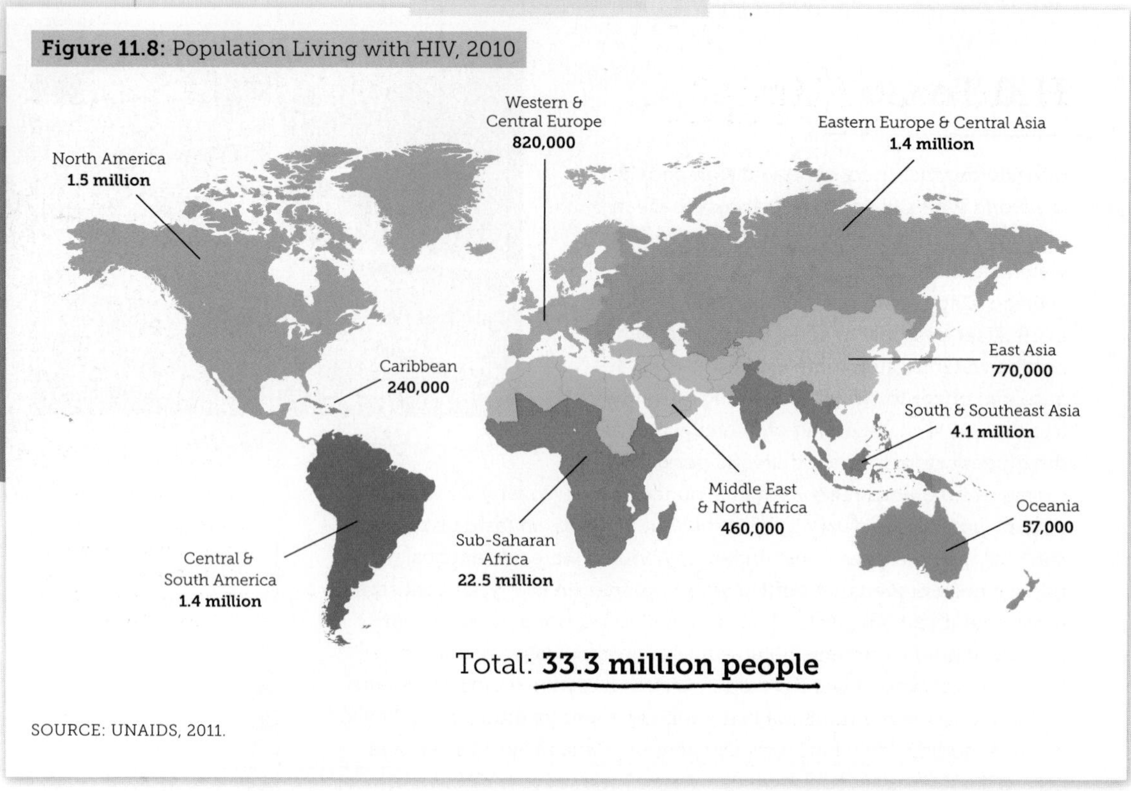

SOURCE: UNAIDS, 2011.

Nationally, AIDS has played a role in transforming doctor–patient relationships. AIDS took the form of a modern-day leprosy, bringing a huge stigma to those who had it. Because in its early years AIDS was most prevalent in gay communities, community groups such as ACT UP (AIDS Coalition to Unleash Power) and the Gay Men's Health Crisis (see Chapter 18) organized to challenge stereotypes about people living with AIDS and about HIV transmission—namely, that it is transmitted only through homosexual sex. HIV is carried in bodily fluids; shared intravenous needles, unprotected sexual activity (both heterosexual and homosexual), and mother-to-infant exchange are the most frequent modes of virus transmission. Like most diseases, AIDS is more prevalent among poorer populations, especially on the global scale. Although there have been huge advances in formulating drugs that stop HIV from evolving into full-blown AIDS, in preventing HIV transmission from mother to infant, and in prolonging the life expectancy of people with HIV/AIDS, access to these drugs is extremely limited. Poverty exacerbates international health inequalities. Even in countries where low-cost medications are increasingly available to people with HIV, if they don't have access to proper nutrition and clean water to take the medication, it will not be effective and in fact contributes to the problem of antiretroviral resistance to medication. Currently, the most promising strategy for combating AIDS is increasing awareness about prevention strategies such as using clean needles and condoms and, most recently, promoting male circumcision.

A Modern Plague?

A medical worker in Beijing, China, disinfects a railway waiting room as part of prevention measures in the fight against SARS.

HIV/AIDS, probably the most widely recognized pandemic of our age, is believed to have originated when an animal strain of the virus mutated and infected a human. Experts believe that avian or bird flu has the potential to mutate and spread in a similar way. There is no way to predict when or if this will happen, but world officials currently treat it as a highly likely scenario. Experts can try to predict which strains are most likely to mutate into human form, and pharmaceutical companies can try to produce vaccines for those strains. Such measures are intended to prepare us for something like severe acute respiratory syndrome (SARS), which seemingly came out of the blue in 2003; but the truth is, the occurrence of a health epidemic is somewhat of a crap shoot.

What we can control, however, is our social reaction to an outbreak. Sociologist Duncan Watts (2005) suggests that we can learn from SARS and use it as a model of reaction. What can a sociologist tell us that a health expert can't? Watts focuses on the social response by all groups involved:

> [P]eople in affected cities can mitigate the spread of the disease by avoiding work and school and not flooding to hospitals unless they are sick. Those in nearby regions can go about their lives but should avoid traveling into the affected cities or even out of the region. And people far from affected areas can maintain their distance (that is, more or less how they reacted to SARS). Airline travel should be discouraged, or even actively shut down until the extent of spread is ascertained; but other forms of transport, like rail and road, should also be treated warily.

Spreading an infection on a global scale takes just a few individuals moving from infected areas and transmitting the disease elsewhere. The actions of conscientious citizens and governments can mean the difference between fatal—yet contained—local outbreaks and a modern-day plague.

Sin Taxes

If you are overweight or obese—a category that now includes 72 percent of adult men and 64 percent of adult women—you might be unpatriotic. Michelle Obama announced that obesity is costing America billions of dollars in health-care expenditures—$147 billion to be exact—and poses a threat to national security (White House, Office of the First Lady, 2010). She stated in a briefing that "obesity is now one of the most common disqualifiers for military service." While the White House pledges to mount an awareness campaign, increase funding for healthy school lunch programs, and stock convenience stores with fresh fruits and vegetables, some state and city governments are taking a different approach.

They want to tax you toward healthy living, starting with soda. The average American drinks 50 gallons of the sugary stuff every year. A 1¢ per ounce tax is projected to curtail our consumption by 11 gallons a year. What's more, it could raise over $15 billion annually. Retail prices would rise from the $2.99 sale price for a 12-pack of Coca-Cola to $4.43. This would make a 12-pack of soda comparable to an equivalent amount of milk, still less than a carton of orange juice, and significantly more than a glass of tap water. Tap water costs about a penny for every 4–5 gallons.

This type of "sin tax" is controversial, but nothing new. The best example of this kind of tax is tobacco—a pack of cigarettes in New York City generates $5.26 in taxes for city, state, and federal governments with every sale. And the tax seems to be working. Lifelong smokers usually start in their teens. Teens are especially sensitive to high prices (that pack in New York City is likely to cost $12 at the corner store). Therefore, many teens failed to start smoking because they were priced out of the habit and most never bothered to pick it up when they were more flush. Today, Americans smoke at half the rate they once did and the numbers continue to decline.

So will a beverage tax make us healthier? Will it curtail consumption as predicted? Or will the tax be regressive, that is, put stress on poor families whose food budgets are already stretched thin while wealthier families barely notice it?

First, how do we know that eliminating soda from our diets will have an impact on our health? Opponents point out that all food has calories and it is calories, not calories from soda in particular, that make us fat. Many of these opponents happen to work for the beverage companies and they too nod toward patriotism, claiming that a beverage tax would limit personal freedom to consume as we choose without government interference. Perhaps unfortunately, nutritionists do not have an ironclad comeback. While soda does not offer anything of nutritive value, it has been difficult to prove that it is uniquely talented at contributing to expensive chronic health problems like type 2 diabetes and heart disease. Sure, extra calories make a person fat and liquid calories do add up more quickly because the stomach does not trigger a sense of satiation from beverage consumption. But candy bars are similarly far from broccoli on the healthful food scale, and so are French fries and many other foods. Maybe Mrs. Obama is right to tell people to get off the couch and spend more on school health rather than to try to tax soda out of our financial grasp. Then again, we've all been told to get off the sofa and put down the potato chips for decades, yet we're bigger than ever. Perhaps putting soda out of financial reach is harsh, but if gentle prods aren't working, can we afford to take the tax off the table?

→ CONCLUSION

In this chapter, you've learned how something that seems so fundamentally biological is shaped in important ways by social structure. We can decide what we eat, whether we smoke, and if we exercise, but we can't choose what sex or race we're born, what food we can afford, and whether our health insurance company will reimburse us for our gym membership or psychotherapist. What are some of the changes that could be made to the structure of our society that would improve health for everyone? Eradicating racial disparities in wealth, power, and status might solve many problems, but that, unfortunately, is probably a long way off. What feasible short-term changes could be made? Should we tax fast-food businesses for the unhealthy merchandise they proffer in order to defray the costs that society pays for the obesity epidemic? This money could be put toward healthier school lunches or toward physical education programs. If bird flu strikes, should we quarantine infected individuals in an effort to curtail the spread of the disease worldwide—while cutting off the victims from critical social support (such as their family members) in the process? A seemingly endless list of possible questions emerges when we recognize that health and biology, on the one hand, and social life, on the other hand, are not two distinct worlds but rather are intertwined.

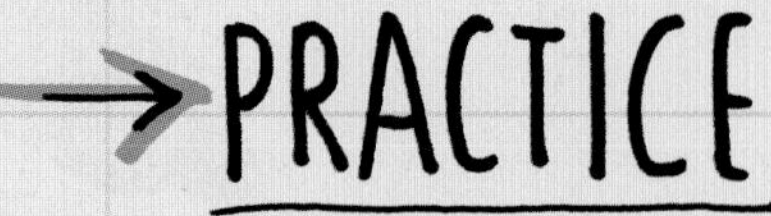

ASSIGNMENT

Health care is a major issue in national and local elections, and debates about medicine and the structure of the health-care system abound in the United States, yet nonmedical factors largely determine the social distribution of health and illness. What are some of the social causes and explanations for these leading causes of death in the United States: heart disease, cancer, stroke, chronic lower respiratory diseases, and diabetes?

QUESTIONS FOR REVIEW

1. How does the uniqueness of health as a "good" help explain the high status of doctors? How does this, in turn, help explain the discomfort around the commercialization of bodies?
2. What would be an argument in support of sin taxes on fast-food meals? Considering that fast-food meals are usually less expensive than healthier options and provide food quickly for underpaid and overworked Americans, how might sin taxes unintentionally reproduce class differences?
3. What are some of the ways in which people in the United States with fewer resources are at a greater health risk? According to the Whitehall Study, why are certain groups at a particular disadvantage?
4. How does licensing within the medical profession relate to the status of doctors? How does the AMA contribute to the power of doctors?
5. A student gets very sick the day before an exam and (thanks to a doctor's note) is allowed to take the test later. Describe Talcott Parsons's "sick role." How do this role's rights and obligations help explain this example?
6. How could the social construction of illness help us understand hypochondria?
7. Describe the way race and stress interact to create a higher health risk for African Americans. Do sex and higher socioeconomic status make a difference?
8. How has the way psychologists diagnose mental illnesses changed? How is the understanding of context related to the use of drugs to treat mental illness?

PARADOX

WHAT CAUSES PEOPLE TO DIE CHANGES OVER TIME, BUT THE GROUP AT GREATEST RISK OF DYING FROM THESE AFFLICTIONS, THOSE LOW IN SOCIOECONOMIC STATUS, STAYS THE SAME.

WATCH THE ANIMATED SHORT ABOUT THE HEALTH AND SOCIETY PARADOX AT

WWNORTON.COM/STUDYSPACE

HOW DOES SOCIOLOGY RELATE TO YOUR LIFE?

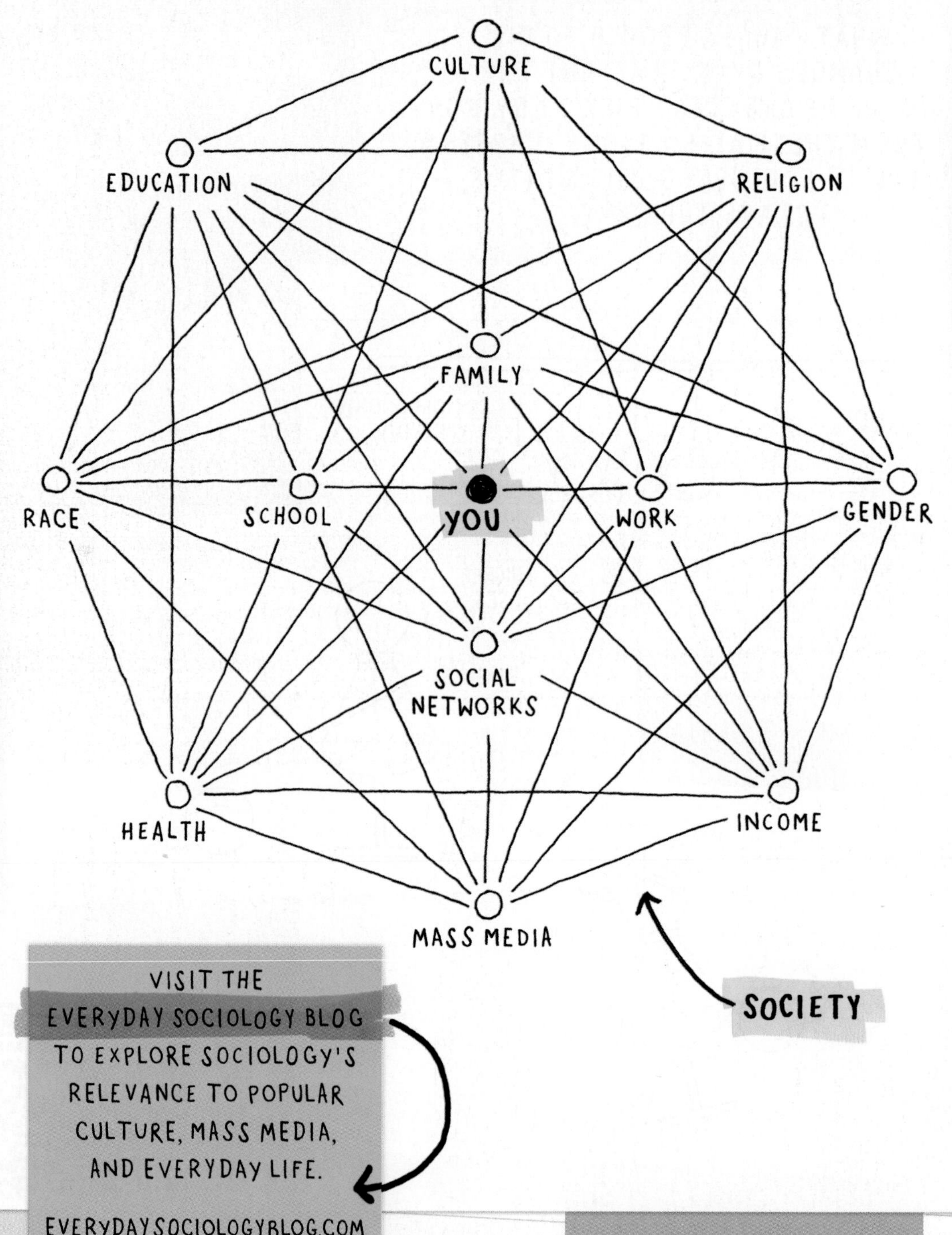

VISIT THE EVERYDAY SOCIOLOGY BLOG TO EXPLORE SOCIOLOGY'S RELEVANCE TO POPULAR CULTURE, MASS MEDIA, AND EVERYDAY LIFE.

EVERYDAYSOCIOLOGYBLOG.COM

WWNORTON.COM/SOC

PART III

BUILDING BLOCKS: INSTITUTIONS OF SOCIETY

Yossi and his two dads, Ken Bukowski and Peter Altman, relax at home.

12 Family

PARADOX

WE THINK OF THE FAMILY AS A HAVEN IN A HARSH WORLD, BUT IN FACT, INEQUALITY BEGINS AT HOME.

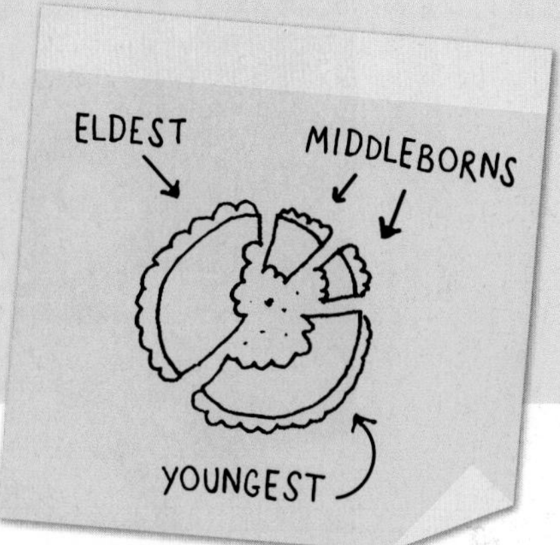

In many ways, Ozzie and Harry typify the American ideal of a family. They met while Harry was vacationing in Italy, and it was love at first sight. Harry was 31 and successful; Ozzie was 24, talented, and full of promise. The two quickly initiated a passionate monogamous relationship. Eight years later the couple owned a house in the Los Angeles area, where they lived with their two daughters. Harry worked as a literary agent, supporting Ozzie, a full-time homemaker, and the kids. Theirs is a fairy tale come true.

Yet the story of Ozzie and Harry brings the traditional concept of family into a modern perspective. The two could not come from more dissimilar backgrounds. Harry is white, Jewish, and Ivy League–educated; Ozzie is Afro-Brazilian, Catholic, and less formally schooled. Harry is well off; Ozzie grew up in a poor family and was raised without a father. The couple is "transracial, transnational, cross-class, [and] interfaith" (Stacey, 2004). In fact, they share only one demographic characteristic: They are both male.

Not only is the couple an against-all-odds success story, their story illustrates just how strong our notion of traditional family is. Even in this most progressive of arrangements, the two assume the historically gendered roles that we often associate with family units. Where do these notions of the traditional family come from? To examine this, let's start with the original Ozzie and Harriet: the Nelsons.

There is something inevitably comforting about watching family television shows from the 1950s. It is a glimpse into a foreign yet consoling world where growing boys like Ricky and David Nelson may be viewed dashing into a kitchen, with schoolbooks in hand and a cheerful "Hi, Mom. Hi, Pop!"

Why did the idea of traditional family—embodied here by the Nelsons from the television show The Adventures of Ozzie and Harriet—emerge after World War II?

Their loving parents, Ozzie and Harriet, together listen to their children's problems and together steer them on the right path to adulthood. *The Adventures of Ozzie and Harriet*—the situation comedy that first aired on ABC in 1952—typifies a familiar, traditional form of family that today evokes nostalgia and fuels political debates: the male breadwinner (although no one knows for sure what Ozzie did for a living); the kind, female homemaker; and their nurtured, well-socialized children.

The scenes of 1950s family life can overwhelm the unprepared viewer with a surge of sentiments, everything from the warm fuzzies to bleak loneliness to bitter cynicism. At first blush, the quality of family life today, with widespread divorce, out-of-wedlock births, dual incomes, and ever-increasing work hours, seems to have taken a nosedive. But if the domestic world of Ozzie and Harriet seems too good to be true, that's because, of course, it is. Anyone watching at the time readily acknowledged that such television shows did not reflect how Americans actually lived. Rather, they portrayed American families as people wanted to see them. Millions of viewers turned to the idealized life presented in *The Adventures of Ozzie and Harriet* to be entertained by the dramatization of mundane details of suburban life and soothed by the easy resolution of the day's problems by the end of the episode.

In the postwar era the traditional family—the idealized model of a male breadwinner, a female homemaker, and their dependent children—emerged as the dominant, normative, and mythical model for domestic life. It was dominant, because indeed many Americans took to it; in the 1950s, 86 percent of children lived in two-parent families, and 60 percent of children were born into homes with a male breadwinner and a female homemaker (Coontz, 2001). It was normative, because it has been hailed, then and now, as the proper form for families, the way things ought to be. Finally, the taken-for-grantedness of the traditional family is mythical, because its existence does not represent a natural, timeless, or universal approach to family arrangements.

In the sociological imagination the traditional family looks less like a universal norm and more like an ideological construct—and an unusual one at that. Arising out of unique social structural conditions of the 1950s, characters such as the Nelsons are exceptional, not just for their special Christmas décor and family picnics but also because they are, in fact, unique. That is, the so-called traditional family model deviates from both its predecessors and its successors. Yet many of us still idealize this model and miss it terribly. By studying cross-cultural variation in family forms, we'll see that this allegedly traditional family is not always the dominant model. By unpacking the historical development of the traditional family and its subsequent breakdown, we'll come to recognize that this idea of family is not a universal fact. And regardless of what kind of family ties you may deem worth forging, worth loving, and worth defending, as a sociologist your job will be to study all family forms without prejudgment.

Family Forms and Changes

Why do we fall for the people we do? At first thought this might seem like a simple question. You start by envisioning the personal qualities of your lover, perhaps something about his or her physique, personality, sense of humor, or charm. If you take a step back and really try to think about it, you might admit to more practical reasons as well—physical proximity, shared language, financial security—those everyday factors vital to functioning relationships. If you take yet another step back, you face the larger question of mate selection: the phenomenon of human partnering that is patterned by history, culture, and law.

I know this is an unromantic way to view your love life, but consider the host of cultural and legal codes that prohibit you from partnering with, say, your 14-year-old first cousin. In Victorian England or a modern-day Muslim tribe, however, a man's 14-year-old first cousin might be a perfectly good match. Historically, interracial partnerships have also been prohibited. In 1961, when President Obama's parents were married it was still illegal in 22 different states for a white and a nonwhite to be married. Then in *Loving vs. Virginia* (1967) the Supreme Court unanimously struck down America's antimiscegenation laws. (See Chapter 9 for a discussion of the one-drop rule.) Similar laws, aimed at

The Lovings embrace at a press conference the day after the Supreme Court ruled in their favor in *Loving v. Virginia*, June 13, 1967.

maintaining white "racial purity," existed in South Africa during apartheid as well as in Nazi Germany. In the contemporary world ethnically mixed couples are hardly shocking, but 50 years ago in the United States they were almost unthinkable. When a culture maintains either legal or normative sanctions against people marrying outside their race, class, or caste, we call it a rule of endogamy, meaning marriage from within. To some extent, we all practice endogamy—that is, on some level people tend to hook up with similar people, because it makes for easier relations if you and your partner share a social group. In other parts of the world, such as India, historically people haven't had much of a choice: The caste system of India is based on a rigid adherence to endogamy (see Chapter 7).

In much of the contemporary Western world, exogamy, or marriage to someone outside one's social group, is legally possible, if not always culturally acceptable. Consider the following unlikely pair: the African American son of a steel mill worker in Illinois and the only child and sole heir of a megamillionaire, white, chart-topping rock-and-roll star in Tennessee. The 1994 union of Lisa Marie Presley and Michael Jackson lasted less than two years, but it is an example of a couple who transgressed social, class, and racial groups. However, what is also telling is that by the time they met and fell for each other, they were already both celebrities and social equivalents, despite the gulf between their backgrounds. Total exogamy—when people from completely different social categories get together—is rare.

Endogamy marriage to someone within one's social group.

Exogamy marriage to someone outside one's social group.

In addition to codes of endogamy and exogamy, another basic social structure governs your love life: how many partners you're expected to have. In societies that practice monogamy a person can partner with only one other. In societies that practice polygamy people have more than one sexual partner or spouse at a time. This can take the form of a woman having several husbands, called polyandry, as happens in some rural areas of Asia. Or a man can take several wives, called polygyny, the most common form of polygamy, practiced in many contemporary Islamic and African cultures. Although the Mormon Church outlawed polygamy in 1890, some Mormon splinter groups, called fundamentalists, continue the practice of one man supporting several families at the same time (Lee, 2006).

Monogamy the practice of having only one sexual partner or spouse at a time.

Polygamy the practice of having more than one sexual partner or spouse at a time.

Polyandry the practice of having multiple husbands simultaneously.

Polygyny the practice of having multiple wives simultaneously.

The next time someone asks why you fell for your special someone, keep in mind that the answer could be quite long and sociologically involved. Cultural norms and state regulations play a fundamental, if invisible, role in your love life. These factors first set the limits as to who is even available on your romantic horizon. Once you find that person (or those persons, for you polygamists), your next move will be to form a relationship with him or her, probably in the shape of a family. But just what does the typical traditional family look like?

Malinowski and the Traditional Family

The normative "traditional family" is one in which a heterosexual couple lives with their dependent children in a self-contained, economically independent household. This family is typically a patriarchal one, governed by a male head with a dependent wife and children. In 1913 Bronislaw Malinowski put to rest a long-standing family debate among anthropologists about the universal existence of families. Scholars had argued that traditional tribal societies couldn't possibly have family units because of their egregious non-discriminating sexual promiscuity. Malinowski, based on his research of Australian Aboriginals (who seemed to have sex with everyone), suggested that these natives did, in fact, form ties indicative of familial arrangements. The Aboriginals, he found, recognized family relations and kept them distinct from other forms of social connection. They maintained a central place, the equivalent of a hearth and home, where the family gathered. And they bestowed feelings of love, affection, and care on each family member. Thus, the dispute was settled: The family was accepted as a universal human institution for most of the twentieth century, and this notion continues to endure today. It is so strong that scientists look for Malinowski's family ties even among rodents. Neurogeneticists have discovered a genetic basis for monogamous coupling in one species of prairie voles and are hard at work trying to determine whether or not humans share the same neurological mechanisms for partner preference (Young & Wang, 2004; Fink et al., 2006; Young & Hammock, 2007).

Malinowski argued that the family, in addition to being a universal phenomenon, was a necessary institution for fulfilling the task of child rearing in society. The influential structural-functional sociologist Talcott Parsons would expand on this notion in the 1950s. As we learned in Chapter 8, according to Parsons, the traditional nuclear family, consisting of a mother and father and their children, was a functional necessity in modern industrial society, because it was most compatible with fulfilling society's need for productive workers and child nurturers. And so the nuclear family reigned supreme, timeless, and universal. (Note that although the nuclear family is a particular form of the traditional model, in this chapter we will use the two terms synonymously.)

Nuclear family familial form consisting of a father, mother, and their children.

The problem with functionalist arguments such as these is that even if one social institution seems to perform some function for society, the function is not necessarily performed only by that particular institution.

Families come in all different forms. What are some of the ways that family groups can differ from culture to culture? For instance, how does an extended family in the United States (top) differ from the Na in China (middle) or Zambian families in Africa (bottom)?

A functional need is not sufficient cause for the development of an institution, especially not when other kinds of institutions can perform the function just as well. But when you have Western blinders on, as most social scientists following Malinowski did, it becomes difficult to see anything other than the kind of family life you expect to see. When properly fitted with your sociological lens, however, you can make the familiar strange, and you'll find some colorful variation among familial arrangements.

Take the Mandurucu villagers of South America, for instance. They give new meaning to the hearth-and-home feature of Malinowski's universal family. Mandurucu men and women live in separate houses at different ends of their village; they eat separate meals; they sleep apart. In fact, they only meet up with each other to have sex (Collier et al., 1997). Among the Na people of southern China, who have managed to retain their distinctive culture despite war, Communism, and the onset of quasi-capitalism, the institution of marriage doesn't exist. The Na do not have any practice like it, nor do they put much thought into fatherhood. Children grow up with uncles rather than fathers as the primary males in the home. Sex occurs in the middle of the night, when men visit women for anonymous and spontaneous encounters. There are no social rules restricting who can partner with whom. Yet the Na manage just fine, reproducing from generation to generation and maintaining a stable economy.

If the Na take hands-off fatherhood to the extreme, women in present-day Zambia implode our notions of caring motherhood. Zambian mothers don't nurture their daughters in the way Westerners would expect. When a Zambian girl needs advice, she is expected to seek out an older female relative as a confidante in preference to her mother (Collier et al., 1997). Mothers' "essential" nature has always been defined in the West as nurturing and connected to offspring—presumably ordained by women's biological birthing functions. However, the way motherhood is practiced in Zambian culture suggests that a mother's unconditional warmth, despite the rhetoric, is not necessarily a biological given.

The Family in the Western World Today

Even the modern Western family comes in a variety of forms. The typical American family today is not likely to resemble the Nelsons. In addition to nuclear families, one needs to count the extended family—kin networks that extend outside or beyond the nuclear family. Families with no children also exist (for instance, families that become "empty nest" couples after their children move out), as do two-wage-earner families (dual-income families), single-parent families, blended stepfamilies, and adopted families, to name just a few possibilities. Although the traditional family was the dominant model for a

Extended family kin networks that extend outside or beyond the nuclear family.

majority of people living in the 1950s, it never described home life for all Americans. And it's increasingly losing its edge today as families take on new shapes and sizes. As of 1986, fewer than 10 percent of U.S. families consisted of a male breadwinner, a female housewife, and their children (Stacey, 1996). Today a minority 23 percent of married-couple family groups fit that description (U.S. Census Bureau, 2010c).

In the face of soaring divorce rates, the Ozzie and Harriet way of life is indeed becoming a historical artifact. Nowadays, although the exact figure varies considerably from study to study, approximately 40 percent of all marriages end in divorce (Hurley, 2005). That doesn't seem to discourage too many people, though, because three of four divorced men and two of three divorced women try their hand again in remarriages. But alas, marriages are like dominos: One tends to topple after the next, and just 45 percent of remarriages remain intact (40 percent of those involving children). It's commonly perceived that divorce has skyrocketed since the 1950s, but actually the divorce rate has been steadily rising since the nineteenth century, as divorce became less and less of a social and religious taboo. Furthermore, rising divorce rates in the United States have not put marriage in any danger of extinction. According to the United Nations, approximately 90 percent of Americans marry at some point in their lives, more than in any other industrialized nation in the world.

Given the increased incidence of divorce and remarriage, families are taking on new shapes and sizes, such as single-parent and blended arrangements (see Figure 12.1). As of 2009, about 16 percent of children in America lived in a blended family (U.S. Census, 2011h), which reconfigures the aftermath of divorce into step-relations. (We'll have more to say about the effect of divorce on children below.) Cohabitation, living together in an intimate relationship without formal legal or religious sanctioning, has also emerged as a socially acceptable arrangement; roughly 7 percent of heterosexual American couples live together as opposed to legally tying the knot, a 13 percent increase from 2009 (Fry & Cohn, 2011). However, most cohabitations either dissolve or end in marriage. Furthermore, most cohabiters believe that living together is an effective means of curtailing future divorce. It's the commonsense notion that living together provides a sample of what married life is like and will inform and improve the couple's future marriage. On the opposite side of the debate, conservative supporters of "family values" point to studies showing a higher divorce rate among couples who cohabit before marriage than those who don't (Meckler, 2002). Conservative Christian counselors advise that "living in sin" sets up a rockier road for a marriage, but the actual reason for the higher divorce rate probably has to do more with selection bias: Most people who cohabit are also the kind of individuals who are more likely to flout social conventions and therefore divorce anyway.

Cohabitation living together in an intimate relationship without formal legal or religious sanctioning.

The single women are having their days as well, as proportions of women who never marry and never have children are on the rise. The Census Bureau estimates that 40 percent of women born in the 1980s will not marry or bear

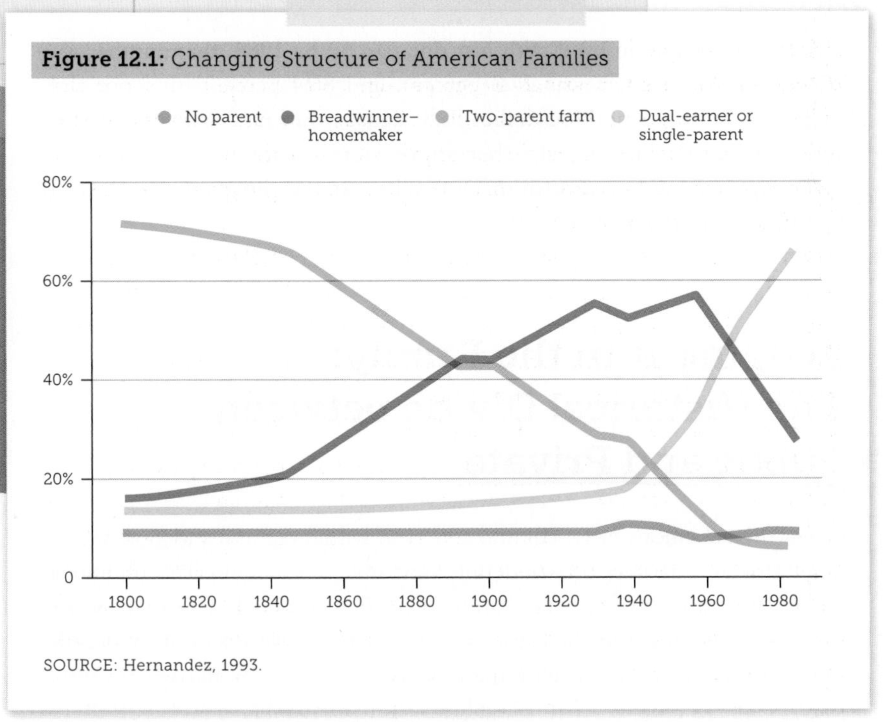

children. Childbirth seems less of a cultural imperative for women, and women who do have children are doing so at a later age than ever before. The average age of women during their first childbirth experience has increased from about 21 to 25 years since the 1970s (U.S. Census Bureau, 2010d). This varies by subgroup: White professional women, on average, postpone motherhood even longer. Another interesting new twist in American families is the rapid rise in the number of twins. Between the years 1980 and 1997, the number of twin births rose 52 percent (from 68,339 to 104,137), and triplet and other higher-order multiple births increased by a staggering 404 percent (from 1,337 to 6,737 births). This rise took place almost entirely among white women. As professional white women increasingly delay childbearing, they are biologically more likely to give birth to twins, and this trend is compounded by the more widespread use of fertility treatments, which increase the likelihood of a multiple birth (Martin et al., 2010). And then there is adoption. In 2008, approximately 2.5 percent of children in the United States were adopted (Federal Interagency Forum on Child and Family, 2011). This may sound negligible, but 2.5 percent is roughly 2.3 million children. International adoption rates, which had been climbing since the 1980s, peaked at 22,000 in 2004 and are now falling, in part because of more rigorous qualifications required of new parents by foreign countries as well as UN-sanctioned adoption bans on countries like Guatemala.

Single mother Melissa Ludtke holds adopted daughter Maya Xia. Why have stories like Ludtke's become more common over the last few decades?

Single-parent families, historically the result of death or desertion, are on the rise now as more parents never marry or end up divorced. In 1960,

9 percent of children lived with just one parent; by 1986, that number was 25 percent; by 2009, it was 27.3 percent, and 86.4 percent of those children lived in single-mother families (U.S. Census Bureau, 2011i). Worldwide, single-parent families are also becoming more common—as of the late 1990s, approximately one-fifth of all families around the globe were headed by women (UNICEF, 2007).

Keeping It In the Family: The Historical Divide between Public and Private

Given the enormous cross-cultural and even within-cultural variation among family forms, you may be wondering how and why the so-called traditional family ever came to be the standard marker of normalcy. The short answer is that the development of the family was tied to the development of modernity, state formation, and the rise of the modern economy. For starters, *traditional family* is a misleading term; this family structure is not characteristic of all tradition, just that of the 1950s. The nuclear model of stay-at-home mom and working father is itself deviant compared with American family arrangements both 50 years before it and 50 years after. It was a historically specific model in a unique era, in which many white city-dwellers moved to the suburbs, married young, and raised three or four children. It was a prosperous era, too: In the 1950s real wages grew more in any single year than they did in the 1980s as a whole. With just a high-school education, an average 30-year-old white man could earn enough at his manufacturing job to buy a median-priced home on 15 percent of his salary (Coontz, 2001). Today, with just a high-school education, an average 30-year-old man is likely to be tenuously positioned in the service sector, making about $15 an hour and probably lacking employer-provided health insurance. But it's not just money that set the 1950s apart. As Stephanie Coontz notes in *The Way We Never Were: American Families and the Nostalgia Trap* (1992), people long for the sense of simplicity, wholesomeness, and ease that 1950s families like the Nelsons are perceived to have enjoyed.

Early Modern Families

The traditional family is a relatively new phenomenon that developed only as complex, state-governed societies emerged. In the preindustrial family of the nineteenth century, each household unit operated like a small business—that is, as a miniature family economy. It was a site for both production and

Preindustrial families, such as these settlers, operated like a small business. The home was a site for work and the entire family was involved.

consumption, where work was done in the home and the home was a working unit. Families made and used their own food, clothes, and goods, and there was little if any surplus wealth.

Families tended to live near their kin and thus could rely for help and support on kinship networks, strings of relationships between people related by blood and co-residence (that is, marriage). Preindustrial communities didn't have huge savings banks, insurance companies, payday lenders, or government agencies to help in hard times; that was the role of family. For example, a down-and-out uncle might have a failed crop of wheat one summer. He could call in an IOU from his luckier cousin across the village, borrowing some of his crop and setting off a reciprocal exchange of food, clothing, and child care. Such families would have a grapevine structure, where more lateral kinship ties endured than vertical ones (usually, no more than three generations of one family were alive at a time). Communities cooperated in a noncash economy, using a barter system to swap goods. There was no significant accumulation of goods, no savings, no wealth, and not much beyond what individuals needed to survive. Minimal division of labor between the sexes also existed, such that men were involved in child care, and women and children often performed the same manual labor as men. Indeed, in the preindustrial family, children were thought of as "small adults," as Philippe Ariès argued in 1962. They didn't warrant any special treatment or consideration, and childhood was hardly the nurturing period we

Kinship networks strings of relationships between people related by blood and co-residence (that is, marriage).

think of today. In fact, some scholars argue that the whole notion of childhood, or children's special needs, is a relatively recent invention, as is that of motherhood as a full-time occupation. Both have emerged only since the middle of the nineteenth century and have been made possible through industrialization, the rise of the cash economy, formal schooling, and the establishment of privacy in the family.

Families in the Industrial Era

With the Industrial Revolution, the realms of the public and private—previously intertwined as one in the working family—split into separate spheres of work and home, as men left household production for wage work in factories. (See Chapter 14 for a brief history of capitalism and its impact on family life.) Families stopped being productive mini-economies for the barter system and instead became strictly sites for consumption. Out went household spinning and weaving, and in came the factory-made sweater. Food, clothing, furniture, decorations, appliances, cosmetics, pharmaceuticals: You name it, the family was there to consume it. Specifically, women made the choices of what and how much their families would consume.

Furthermore, "women's work," tending the home and raising children, became relegated to the private, domestic sphere, where it went unpaid as a woman relied on a man's wages, at least among the middle classes. All the extra money in the new wage economy passed through the hands of women, who remained in charge of running the home and doing the shopping. Such functions might seem like a move toward women "wearing the pants" in the family, but they, in fact, provided a point of emergence for a new form of gender inequality. Women were in charge of spending the family's money, not earning it, and in our society, work for money is the most highly valued form of labor. Women's work was the unpaid management of the home, and this distinction established unequal positions for men and women in society. At the very least, a man had the chance to spend his wages before they ever reached the other members of his family.

The results of these structural changes were far-reaching. First, a gendered division of labor arose in the household, where women now were in exclusive charge of maintaining the home and rearing children. Second, as the mobility of families searching for paid labor opportunities increased, they became separated from their kinship networks. Family structures changed from grapevine forms to "beanpole" families, where kinship ties are vertical. Because people didn't live near their siblings, aunts, and uncles, they could depend only on their children and parents who lived with them. As life expectancies increased, up to five generations may have been alive at any given time, but lateral ties (such as those existing between cousins) weakened because of longer distances separating these kin.

The beanpole family structure is particularly taxing on women today, who, because of delayed childbirth, are likely to find that their parents need assistance just as their own children are leaving home. As a result of declining fertility and longer life expectancies, the U.S. population is growing older, so the problem of elder care (and its disproportionate impact on women) will only get worse. In 2010 the median age in the United States was 37.2 years, with seven states having a median age of 40 or over (U.S. Census Bureau, 2011j).

A third fallout of the new cash economy and the resulting split between public and private realms was the creation of the cult of domesticity, the notion that true womanhood centers on domestic responsibility and child rearing. During the first half of the twentieth century, ideas sprang up surrounding woman's true nature—ideas meant to support her newly created role as housewife. These included the notion that women, more than men, are endowed with the innate emotional qualities required to provide warmth and comfort. According to this ideology, not only are women better suited for home life, their domesticity also comes to be seen as necessary for the survival of society. Women, so the argument goes, are needed to ensure that the home remains a safe haven in the otherwise cold seas of capitalist enterprise. As breadwinners, men struggle in the dog-eat-dog commercial world, whereas women provide the emotional shelter that anchors private life in human sentiment, emotion, care, and love.

This nineteenth-century painting illustrates the Victorian feminine domestic ideal. How did the Industrial Revolution transform the division of labor between men and women?

Cult of domesticity the notion that true womanhood centers on domestic responsibility and child rearing.

Families after World War II

By the 1950s the model nuclear family had already come to be idealized, although it was mostly attainable only by white middle- and upper-class families (see the section below on racial and ethnic differences in family structure). Most men's earnings were simply not great enough to afford a stay-at-home wife and dependent children. The gap between ideal and real narrowed as real wages (wages adjusted for inflation) increased in the 1950s, making the patriarchal tradition of a male breadwinner and a female homemaker a feasible arrangement for a greater number of families. Still, many nonwhite, non-middle-class families and individuals were excluded from the prosperity of the 1950s (see Chapter 9), and women worked outside the home throughout history, especially nonwhite women.

During the post–World War II economic boom, the manufacturing economy thrived with unionized jobs, real living wages, government housing subsidies, and job-training programs. It was a period of great optimism and for

Textile factory workers in 1949. Why did many women leave their jobs after World War II?

good reasons: The Depression was over, America and its allies had won the war, and the United States was now dominant on the world's economic stage. Americans moved en masse to the suburbs—often to homes that required little to no down payment. Meanwhile, many women quit their jobs, if they had them, and returned full time to cultivating domesticity; the divorce rate dropped to just over one in four marriages; and fertility rates soared during this "baby boom." The Ozzie and Harriet Nelson type of family was in its prime.

As family scholars are quick to point out, however, these trends in families were atypical. Although the divorce rate dipped in the 1950s, it had been on the rise since the end of the nineteenth century, so modern appeals to return to an age when divorce did not exist ring somewhat hollow. Furthermore, the fertility boom following World War II represented an unusual spike in family size, which had otherwise been on the decline since well before the turn of the century. What's more, the 1950s were also an era of rampant teen pregnancies: The teenage birthrate was twice as high in 1957 as in the 1990s. The difference was that pregnant teens in the postwar era had less access to abortion, and when they bore children, they more often got married. In fact, the 1950s marked the twentieth century's youngest national average for age at time of marriage—an average of 20 and 22 years old for women and men, respectively. Finally, the decline in women's workforce participation represented a dip in an otherwise upward trend, especially given women's labor power during World War II (when women were hired as temporary replacements for men serving in the armed forces).

Although the period was an anomaly in many ways, we tend to look back fondly (and sometimes bitterly) to the 1950s family as the normal and right way for families to be. But Stephanie Coontz found that while children's well-being and family economic security were at an all-time high toward the end of the 1960s, it was also a time of tumultuous struggle for racial and sexual equality (Coontz, 2001). What, then, do we really miss?

Family and Work: A Not-So-Subtle Revolution

Since the 1970s, American men and women have been caught up in what Kathleen Gerson (1985) calls a "subtle revolution" in our way of organizing work and home—even as we fantasize about an imagined time gone by.

Women's participation in the labor force has soared, whereas fertility rates have plummeted. By the end of the 1970s, more women were in, rather than out of, the labor force for the first time. In 1950, approximately 30 percent of women worked outside the home; that number more than doubled to 60 percent by 1999 (Francis, 2005). Today, even with high unemployment rates, 65 percent of all mothers, married or not, work (Joint Economic Committee, 2011; Figure 12.2).

At the same time, birthrates have dropped, sinking from a baby boom to a baby bust. In the mid-1950s the birthrate was about 106.2 births per 1,000 women. That rate had dropped to just 62.9 by 1980, and as of 2009 it was at 66.7 (CDC, 2011a). The National Center for Health Statistics reports that marriage rates since the 1960s have also declined, and many adults are postponing marriage to later in life. With the rising divorce rate, marriage is looking less and less like the stable force in women's lives that it was in the postwar era. In fact, by 2007, more Americans 15 and older were single than married for the first time in a century. The result is that the cult of domesticity is out of the picture for most women, and daughters since the 1970s have increasingly departed from their mother's paths.

The gender revolution in work and family is probably here to stay, and with notable effects on children. Research study after research study has hinged on one basic question: Is maternal employment good, bad, or neutral for kids? There's no shortage of hypotheses. A study published in *Child Development* (Brooks-Gunn et al., 2003) suggests that having a working mother in one's

Figure 12.2: Women in the Labor Force, 1970–2011

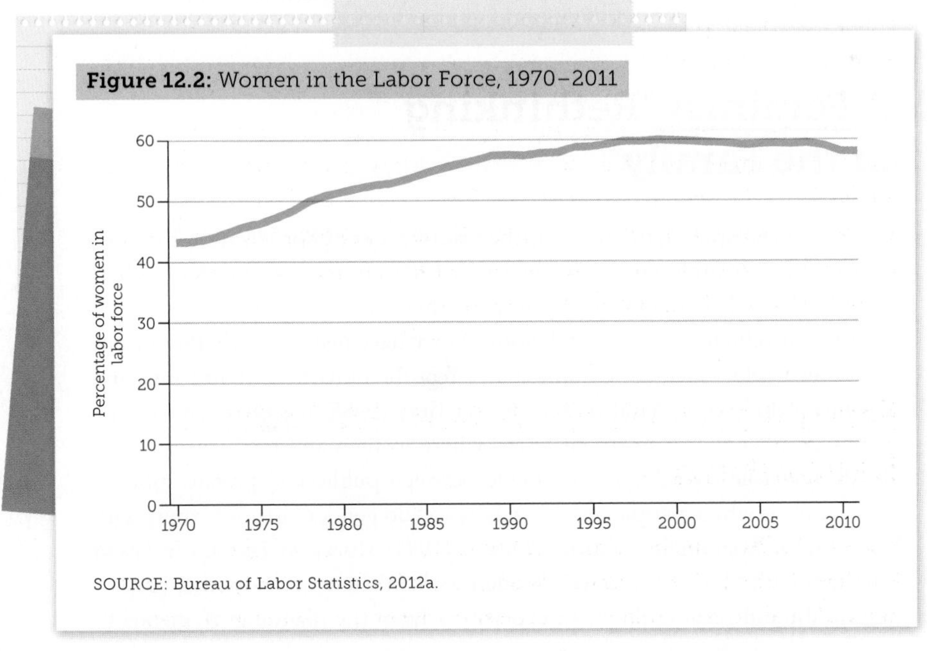

SOURCE: Bureau of Labor Statistics, 2012a.

A mother and her daughters prepare dinner. The family is where people first learn how to "do gender" and conform to social norms. What are some of the lessons that we might learn about gender at home?

early years can result in lower cognitive achievement and increased behavioral problems for a child. Yet another study published in the prestigious journal *Science* (Chase-Lansdale et al., 2003) claims the opposite: For moms with lower income levels, leaving kids in day care to enter the workforce is beneficial. Hundreds of studies fall on both sides of the argument, with mothers' employment being either disastrous or advantageous to their children. Family situations are just too complex and diverse to generalize. Perhaps, then, this mishmash of results is a consequence of asking the wrong question. Maybe we should instead ask, "How does maternal employment affect children differently within the family?"

In *The Pecking Order* (2004), I found that when a mother worked while raising her children, the adult daughters and sons eventually attained jobs that were more or less equivalent and made about the same income. But in families with a stay-at-home mom, the gender gap widens. When the mother does not work and thus cannot provide a same-sex parental role model in terms of career choices, daughters fare far worse than sons, earning roughly $8,000 less a year than their brothers later in life. And without a working-mother role model, daughters are 15 percent less likely to graduate from college than their brothers (whereas in the general population, more women than men earn college degrees).

A Feminist "Rethinking of the Family"

As noted in Chapter 4, the family is the primary unit of socialization for most of us. If family life is structured by larger forces in the social order, such as wage policy and gender inequality at work, then it is also simultaneously a site for the reproduction of these relations. As we have just seen, whether or not a mother works outside the home may affect the outcomes of her sons and daughters differently. Sarah Fenstermaker Berk (1985) has characterized the family as a "gender factory" of sorts, where women and men learn to take on distinct roles paralleling the divide between public and private spheres. The family is where people first learn how to "do gender" in conformity with social rules. Sociologist Marjorie Duvall (1991) shows in *Feeding the Family* that family ties are constructed through women's acts of shopping, preparing meals, and serving them. In everything from the planning of menus to accommodating a child's dislike of lima beans, women are doing gender. As Barbara Risman notes, "It is at home that most people come to believe that men and women are and should be essentially different" (1998). In the act of traditional marriage itself, rituals are gender-stratified: Brides are given away by their fathers, and they take the last name of a husband in patrilineal custom.

The idealized cult of domesticity, although a historical and cultural anomaly among many possibilities, has had powerful and lasting effects on many women's family ideals. Feminist consciousness, raised in the 1960s, led many women to question the ideology of domesticity, finding it "stultifying, infantilizing, and exploitative" of women (Stacey, 1987). In 1963, the feminist writer Betty Friedan led the assault against the limits of being a homemaker with her classic *The Feminine Mystique.* She writes in the introduction:

Betty Friedan at a National Organization for Women rally in 1970.

> The problem lay buried, unspoken, for many years in the minds of American women. It was a strange stirring, a sense of dissatisfaction, a yearning that women suffered in the middle of the twentieth century in the United States. Each suburban housewife struggled with it alone. As she made the beds, shopped for groceries, matched slipcover material, ate peanut butter sandwiches with her children, chauffeured Cub Scouts and Brownies, lay beside her husband at night—she was afraid to ask even of herself the silent question—"Is this all?" (1963/1997, p. 15)

Sociologists elaborated on Freidan's invocation, claiming that what really distinguishes the head of the family is power. The family, as they see it, is a battleground for the power to make collective decisions on everything from who does the laundry to what neighborhood to live in to what college fund to invest in. This is the case, argues sociologist Jessie Bernard in *The Future of Marriage* (1972), even in the comfortable living rooms of traditional nuclear families such Ozzie and Harriet Nelson's. Take, for instance, the tensions that arise from the different ways household members spend money. In studies of welfare recipients, women have been known to spend a greater portion of their welfare benefits on children than fathers do. And in a study of Japanese American families, working wives tended to keep their earnings separate from their husbands' income and even secret, in order to preserve their autonomy to spend it how they—and not their husbands—chose (Glenn, 1986).

Furthermore, money is not all the same within the family; rather, husbands', wives', and children's incomes are earmarked in distinctive ways. Women's earnings tend to be spent on extras, so-called luxury items, or otherwise nonessential expenses. Her money is devalued as "fun money." Men's earnings, on the other hand, are earmarked for essentials. When sociologist Margaret Nelson interviewed working wives, one woman explained, "What he makes there is mainly like insurance, taxes, and all that. What I make usually goes for food, clothing—whatever I find necessary . . . or just to take the kids once a week to Middlebury and blow it" (Nelson, 1990). So even a household's income is gendered. As Viviana Zelizer (2005) notes, the distinctions between household incomes help protect a man's status and sense of masculinity when a wife also takes on a breadwinner role in dual-income families. In this way, feminist rethinking of the family urges us not to view the family as a necessarily cohesive, unified whole but to recognize that the family is not immune from socially structured gender relations. And as gender relations change, so too do family forms. As women become less financially dependent on men, for example, more equality slowly develops in other areas of their relationships. Or does it?

When Home Is No Haven: Domestic Abuse

Family life is not always the warm, nurturing environment it appears to be on prime-time television, where moms and dads stand ready with hugs, siblings crack jokes, and grandma is strict but well intentioned. Abuse, neglect, and manipulation happen across all familial relationships—sibling "rivalry" becomes physically aggressive, husbands and wives with powerful tempers hit and control one another, adult children plunder their elderly parents' life savings. The most frequent form of family violence is sibling on sibling (Eriksen & Jensen, 2006). But before you assign all the blame for your current low self-esteem on that time your brother walloped you upside the head with a shoe, note that the strongest two predictors of sibling-on-sibling violence are dads with short tempers and moms who get physical when it comes to punishing the kids (Eriksen & Jensen, 2006). So is it your brother's fault that he learned how to solve problems by mimicking dad's anger management strategy and piggybacking on mom's heavy hand of authority? This monkey-see, monkey-do explanation has had a long history in the study of domestic violence. Studies have found that abuse transmission is not genetic and that only about one-third of people who are abused as children go on to have a seriously neglectful or abusive relationship with their own children (Oliver, 1993). Broad social factors like poverty, single-parent households, and low levels of educational attainment are associated with higher levels of all types of domestic abuse.

When violence occurs within a couple it's often called IPV, intimate partner violence. According to the Bureau of Justice Statistics, women account for 85 percent of the victims of IPV (2003). In 2007, IPV resulted in 2,340 deaths, 70 percent women and 30 percent men. In a given year the health care cost of IPV was an estimated $8.3 billion (CDC, 2011b).

Elder abuse is a relatively new field of study that investigates physical, verbal, and financial abuse intentionally or unintentionally perpetrated against folks (usually family members) who are at least 57 years old. Estimates suggest elder abuse is not particularly widespread; one-year prevalence was 4.6 percent for emotional abuse, 1.6 percent for physical abuse, 0.6 percent for sexual abuse, 5.1 percent for potential neglect, and 5.2 percent for current financial abuse by a family member (Acierno et al., 2010). The impact of mistreatment in intimate relationships can have serious and long-lasting financial, health, and emotional consequences for individuals, families, and communities.

The Chore Wars: Supermom Battles the Laundry

One of the main ways that gender is enacted within the family is with respect to the unpaid labor that needs to be done at home. In the case of housework and the chore wars, gender remains a salient social force that shapes family life. The cult of domesticity lingers on, such that even though 60 percent of women participated in the workforce in 2008, domestic duties, such as housework and child care, still fall disproportionately on their shoulders (Francis, 2005). Women return from the office to take up what Arlie Hochschild (1989) calls the **second shift**: responsibility for housework and child care—everything from cooking dinner to doing laundry, bathing children, reading bedtime stories, and sewing Halloween costumes. Despite women's gains in the public realm of work, the revolution at home has, as Hochschild described it, stalled. (Indeed, as we'll see in Chapter 14, many women view the workplace as a refuge from their harried domestic lives.)

Second shift women's responsibility for housework and child care—everything from cooking dinner to doing laundry, bathing children, reading bedtime stories, and sewing Halloween costumes.

Within a two-career household, parents are likely to spend their at-home time on separate—and unequal—tasks. One study from 1965 to 1966 found that working women averaged 3 hours each day on housework, whereas men put in a meager 17 minutes. When it comes to leisure activities, however, men surpass their working wives. Working fathers watch an hour more of television per day than working mothers. They also sleep a half hour longer (Hochschild, 2003). The resulting "leisure gap" can brew hostilities between exasperated, exhausted wives and their unresponsive husbands.

Using national studies on time use from the 1960s and 1970s, Hochschild counted the hours that women and men put in on the job in addition to their time spent on housework and child care. She determined that women worked roughly 15 hours longer each week than men (Hochschild, 2003). After 52 weeks, this added up to 780 hours more that women work than men—that's an extra month! This gap appears to be closing, however, as men do more and women do less housework (see Figure 12.3). Valerie A. Ramey and Neville Francis (2006) found that as of 2004, women spent roughly 9 hours more per week on what they termed "home production": housework along with child care and homework assistance.

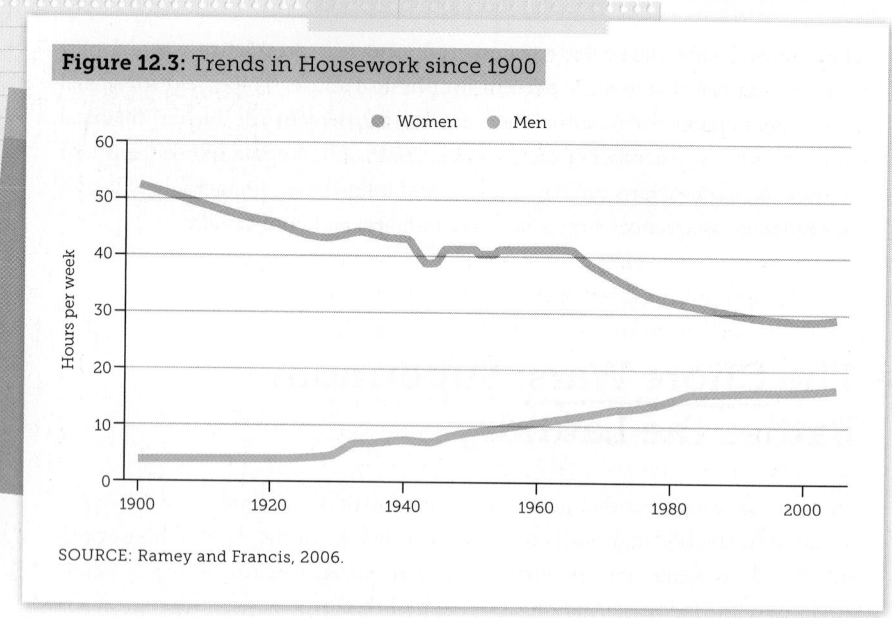

Figure 12.3: Trends in Housework since 1900

SOURCE: Ramey and Francis, 2006.

The division of labor in the home refers to not just who does how much but also who does what. As Viviana Zelizer (2005) shows, housework tasks are patterned around gender. When men do housework, their contribution is referred to as "helping out around the house," and their wives zealously thank them. Women who have "helping" husbands in the home consider themselves extremely lucky. Many men, however, never report feeling lucky or extremely thankful when their wives do the housework. And women *do* the housework; they don't simply "help out."

In addition, men are typically in charge of outdoor, stereotypically masculine activities, whereas women disproportionately do the work inside. Even cooking is broken down by gender: Men more often cook the meat for a meal when they share work in the kitchen. Men also have more control over when they help out, because they are more likely to be in charge of chores that don't require completion on a daily basis, such as changing the oil in the family car or mowing the lawn. Women are more likely to be locked into a fixed and harried housework routine: pick up the kids from day care, cook dinner, wash the dishes, administer the bath, and put the baby to bed (Zelizer, 2005).

Yet another male advantage in the division of household labor is that men get to do more of what they like to do, while women are often stuck with the most undesirable chores, such as scrubbing toilets and ironing. The time fathers spend with their children is more likely to be special recreational time, such as trips to the park, rather than more mundane daily baths and feedings. In fact, most of a father's child-care time occurs on the weekends, whereas mothers spend their time with children during the other five days of the week. Finally as children grow up, their care of aging parents takes on gendered patterns. Adult daughters are often the primary caregivers to parents, and they are more likely than their brothers to help an aging parent with housework. Adult sons, in contrast, assist aging parents with appliance repairs and yard work (Zelizer, 2005).

Neoclassical economists typically look at a member's power in the family as a direct expression of that member's utility to the family unit, and that tends to be measured in terms of his or her income. In such a formulation, money talks, and whoever earns the bacon doesn't have to cook it. This is not so for women, whose income goes only so far in increasing their power in the family. The more a wife contributes to the household income, the more her husband is likely to share, or "help out" with, the second shift. That seems to fit the bacon theory. But as soon as the wife's earnings start to overtake her husband's, he drops out of the shared domestic equation, leaving the entire second shift up to her (Bittman et al., 2003). Furthermore, when women earn more than their husbands, the perceived insult to masculinity may make for a tense home environment. Men, it seems, are not willing to let anyone else wear the proverbial pants in the household.

Sociologists have noted a chore gender gap: Men frequently perform intermittent tasks that they enjoy, such as grilling dinner, whereas women often take on undesirable everyday chores.

With all the advances in home cooking and cleaning technology over the past few decades, you might wonder why the second shift can't be handled a little more efficiently than in a whole extra month of labor a year. But, as Ruth Schwartz Cowan reports in *More Work for Mother: The Ironies of Household Technology from the Open Hearth to the Microwave* (1983), all those time-saving devices like the vacuum cleaner and the washing machine have paradoxically increased the amount of time women spend on housework. As Windex, dishwashers, and the Swiffer broom crowded the market, standards of cleanliness rose and even more cleaning was necessary than before. That said, as women have increased their hours in the formal labor market, the gender gap has declined in recent years: Women now do only 1.8 hours of household work for every hour a man completes, compared with the six-fold difference in the 1960s.

The entrepreneur Don Aslett, who built a business around domestic cleaning services, told one sociologist, "The whole mentality out there is that if you clean, you're a scumball" (Ehrenreich, 2001). Although not always so harshly spoken of, housework certainly is overlooked as a worthy or meaningful activity in America. For one thing, it's unpaid labor, and in a cash economy, it seems pretty, well, worthless. For another, it has been construed historically as women's work. A housewife, measured against modern criteria for success such as salaries, pensions, benefits, bonuses, and promotions, is just a housewife. Radical feminists in the 1960s argued that housework should be fairly compensated, because without a woman's labor, the American male workforce would not be able to keep going. This "reproductive labor" argument stressed the value of social reproduction, all the activities and tasks that women performed daily to keep their working husbands running smoothly. The movement for just compensation for women's household labor was one banner galvanizing early radical feminists.

This movement, you've probably figured out, did not catch on immediately. In fact, it took a good four decades and one tragedy. Zelizer (2005) showed that women's unpaid work commanded a price tag in the distribution of monetary rewards for surviving family members of those killed in the September 11, 2001, terrorist attacks. In the aftermath of 9/11, friends and family grappled with the shock and grief of losing loved ones. Some relatives of victims filed wrongful death suits against the airlines of the hijacked planes. To curb individual lawsuits and to spare the airlines from insurmountable litigations, the U.S. government established the September 11 Victim Compensation Fund. Attorney Kenneth Feinberg had the job of administering the $7 billion fund to settle 2,880 death claims and 2,680 personal injury claims (Chen, 2004). It was up to Feinberg to decide, among those injured and the families of those killed, who received what.

As Zelizer notes, at first the fund was distributed to surviving family members in the amount of the deceased's estimated future earnings and made no provision for compensating unpaid household work. Feminists organized and lobbied Feinberg on the issue, arguing that "ignoring the unpaid work performed by full-time workers raises sex discrimination concerns. . . . Women victims, especially mothers, are much more likely to have expended significant time on unpaid work" (Zelizer, 2005). In the end, the Victim Compensation Fund Final Rule allowed for a case-by-case review of compensation claims on the lost economic value of household services that would have been provided by the deceased. Perhaps it takes a national tragedy for people to reevaluate the importance of individual, daily life.

It also takes marginalization to appreciate the center, as Christopher Carrington's study of gay couples in San Francisco demonstrates. Blumstein and Schwartz (1983) have suggested that an egalitarian division of labor is much more likely to exist in the households of gay and lesbian couples. But as Carrington (1999) notes, they also pay much more care and attention to their household chores, spending about two times as long on cleaning as heterosexual couples. The explanation? Homosexual couples see housework as a means of legitimating their households; thus, it is a more central, validating activity for them than it is for the typical working wife.

If, as sociologists argue, the burden of the second shift falls on working mothers in dual-income families, we might expect some nasty consequences. Indeed, Hochschild found that in response to the stalled revolution, some women tried to do it all. This is the supermom strategy. She cooks, she cleans, she climbs the career ladder, all while being a devoted parent and loving partner. Supermoms, of course, don't really exist, but there is a perpetual myth that some women can do it all, and if other women can't, it's a result of some personal flaw.

Many women juggle full-time jobs with caring for their children and running their home with little help from their spouses. According to Arlie Hochschild, what are the consequences of the supermom strategy?

Women who buy into the supermom myth burn out quickly, and typically their marriages absorb the shock. In one study, Hochschild (1989) found that married women are more likely than men to think about divorce (30 percent of married women have considered divorce versus 22 percent of men), and wives contemplate divorce more often than husbands. Women are also likely to give a more comprehensive list of reasons for wanting a divorce. In her interviews of dual-income families, Hochschild encountered bitter women, fed up with doing all the work, and puzzled men, confused over their wives' hostilities, or bitter themselves at begrudgingly having to help out more.

Because women still earn less than men, about $0.77 for every dollar that a man earns, a disproportionate financial shock hits women after a divorce (U.S. Department of Labor, 2011). Given the rampant threat of divorce, some women bite the second shift bullet, just letting the hostilities simmer. Other women manage by cutting household corners where they can, allowing the dust to pile up and skimping on the children's evening story time. For them, hostilities linger beneath a growing sense of parental guilt.

In households where men and women genuinely share the second shift, marriages are much more likely to be stable and happy ones. Studies (for example, that conducted by Michael S. Kimmel in 2000) have found that when men share the housework, working wives experience less stress. Barbara Risman (1998) calls these "fair families," where husbands and wives equally split the roles of breadwinner and homemaker. In fair families, couples honor an ideology of gender equality, and both men and women benefit from such an arrangement. Women win the self-respect that comes with being economically independent, and they respond by regarding marriage less as a necessity and more as a voluntary, love-based relationship. Men, by sharing the breadwinner burden, are less stressed and feel freer to find jobs they enjoy. Perhaps most important, Risman speculates about a uniqueness in these sharing couples: They are more often close friends.

Despite these findings, most men simply don't budge on the issue of sharing the second shift. But they should, advises Dr. Benjamin Spock, and not just because it makes for a healthier, happier home environment. Dr. Spock's phenomenally successful parenting guide, *Baby and Child Care*, has sold more than 50 million copies in seven editions since 1946, making it second in sales only to the Bible. Among Spock's child-rearing tips was the suggestion that fathers should be involved parents. Studies consistently find that men who share child rearing and housework have happier marriages, better health, and longer lives (Kimmel, 2000). As Dr. Spock put it, "There is no reason why fathers shouldn't be able to do these jobs as well as mothers" (1946/1998). Furthermore, studies show that when left to their own devices, men are perfectly fine housekeepers, cooks, and primary parents (Gerson, 1993). Men just don't live up to their potential as often when a woman is around to handle the second shift.

Swimming and Sinking: Inequality and American Families

African American Families

For millions of American households, the idealized traditional family in *The Adventures of Ozzie and Harriet* never even came close to a lived reality. For African American families, who throughout history have combined work and family, the split between the public and private spheres has never made much sense. Neither has the ideal of exclusive, "isolationist" motherhood made sense for women lacking the resources that allow for full-time homemaking. More often, black and poor women have come to rely on extra-familial female networks in order to manage child-care and work responsibilities (Stack & Burton, 1994). If the average American woman has two shifts, then the typical black American mother has three—because she is more often the primary or only breadwinner. This greater importance of women in the black family has unfortunately been conflated with "backward" female domination or matriarchy.

Social scientists in the 1960s made heavy use of the matriarchal thesis to explain social problems in the African American community. In *The Negro Family: The Case for National Action* (1965), Daniel Patrick Moynihan found that 25 percent of black wives out-earned their husbands, versus only 18 percent of white wives. This "pathological" matriarchy, Moynihan argued, undercuts the role of the father in black families and leads to all sorts of problems later in life, such as domestic violence, substance abuse, crime, and degeneracy. You name it, the matriarch caused it. The root of matriarchy, Moynihan asserted, dated back to the days of slavery, which reversed roles for men and women and continued to haunt African Americans up to the time of his report. (See Chapter 10 for more on the Moynihan report.)

According to the Moynihan report and similar arguments, the matriarch is a stereotypically bad black mother. She's domineering and unfeminine, always wearing the pants in the family. She's hefty and gruff. She spends so much time away from the home that she can't supervise her own kids. And when she is at home, she's too bossy and strong; thus, she emasculates her man and drives him away. If only the matriarch could be a little more feminine, a little less strong, a little *whiter,* suggested the report, the black family could lift itself up out of poverty. The image of the matriarch makes it easier to lay the blame on African American families for their own problems—social ills such as neighborhood decay, stagnating wages, single motherhood, higher divorce rates, and lower school achievement. The matriarch is also a powerful reminder to all women of just what can go wrong when women challenge the patriarchal decree that they be submissive, dependent, and feminine. The Moynihan report's prescription for the social problems of black people was just this: Black women should aspire to the cult of true (white) womanhood.

Scholars like W. E. B. DuBois had argued all along, however, that African American female-headed families were the outcome, rather than the cause, of racial oppression and poverty. And in 1987 William Julius Wilson graphed a "marriageable Black male index," which highlighted the scarcity of employed, un-incarcerated black men (fewer than 50 marriageable black men per 100 black women back then). In such a context, if black women didn't work to pay the rent, put food on the table, and take care of the kids, who would? As Elaine Kamplain has pointed out, African American mothers were "damned if they worked to support their families and damned if they didn't" (Hochschild, 2003).

Matriarchy is one of many misreadings that social critics have imposed on the black family. But when critics hold fast to the idealized concept of the nuclear family, they are likely to see any model that differs from the traditional yardstick as deviant. The sociologist's trick is to view the traditional family, in which a heterosexual couple lives together with their dependent children in a self-contained, economically independent household, as just one of many potential family forms. After all, this particular kind of family evolved from the socially constructed separation of home and work—a separation rooted in the upper classes—and the experiences of most African American families stray from that norm. In fact, asserts Patricia Hill Collins (1990), women of color have never fit this model. Collins looks at the family with a different set of lenses on, what she calls an Afrocentric worldview, which allows for alternative concepts of family and community, for instance, as more of a collective effort with strong neighborhood support—the "It takes a village" model that we described in Chapter 10 on the culture of poverty.

Locating the traditional family as a specific historical phenomenon that has rarely applied to black families enables us to analyze the black community's unique characteristics in a less judgmental manner. African American communities tend to have an expanded notion of kinship, as denoted by the all-encompassing use of the words *brother* and *sister.* This may have developed out of blacks' historical experience with slavery. Because slaves were separated from their biological families at the auction block by white owners, blacks adapted by expanding the definition of *family* from immediate bloodlines to racial ones. Under slavery, black men and women occupied indistinct work

Many African American parents rely on extrafamilial community members to help raise children. What are some of the criticisms of the matriarchal thesis?

roles, often performing the same labor side by side in plantation fields. The legacy of their shared labor was incompatible with a nuclear family, a model predicated on the differentiation between male and female spheres (Collins, 1990).

As a result of segregation throughout the twentieth century, the particular African American notions of community and family continued to endure. But after World War II, the manufacturing economy took a downturn and many black workers, employed by shrinking industries, found themselves at risk of economic marginalization. Marital rates among blacks have been in decline since the 1960s, and female-headed households have been on the rise among both the poor and middle classes. Only 39.2 percent of black children lived in two-parent families, compared with 74.9 percent of white children (U.S. Census Bureau, 2011j). This statistic reflects, in part, the high rates of unemployment and incarceration and low rates of education among black men.

Latino Families

According to the 2010 U.S. census, Latinos are the largest minority group in America, making up 16 percent of the American population. The U.S. Census Bureau defines Latino as "a person of Cuban, Mexican, Puerto Rican, South or Central American, or other Spanish culture or origin regardless of race" (U.S. Census Bureau, 2011e). Latinos also live all over the United States, although they have clustered on the West Coast and in the South and Midwest (Hernandez et al., 2007). Given the diverse origins and geography of Latinos, how can we make general claims about the Latino family? Sociologists don't all agree that such a thing exists or that a generic Latino identity is even imaginable (Santa Ana, 2004). But there are a few common threads that run through many Latino families. Their family ties are strong, and family is a top priority to many Latinos—so important, in fact, that individual Latinos often define their self-worth in terms of their family's image and accomplishments (Ho, 1987). Like African American families, Latino families act as safety nets, and members take seriously their responsibilities to help one another, even in long chains of needy extended relations (Skogrand et al., 2004). They have a strong sense of community and allegiance to it (Hurtado, 1995). For example, so many Latino immigrants send remittances, or money, to family members back home that remittances are now one of the largest sources of cash to the Mexican and many other Central American economies.

Traditional rules of gender and authority also loom large in Latino culture. Women listen to their men, and children to their elders, in a clear-cut hierarchy. This should make sense to anyone who's taken a Spanish language class (or studied any other Romance language). The heavy use of titles and ranks in the everyday vocabulary shows that respect and formality are crucial (DeNeve, 1997). Most Latino families are also shaped by a tradition of devout Catholicism. Combine high religiosity with the importance of family honor, and you soon recognize a few tendencies: high rates of marriage and relatively low rates of divorce, high rates of marriage at a young age, and a lot of babies born out of wedlock. This third outcome may seem contradictory, but think about it: If a young Latina does have premarital sex and becomes pregnant without a marriage prospect in sight, she's less likely than her African American or white peers to have an abortion, a worse breach of Catholic culture than an out-of-wedlock birth. Add to that a tight-lipped stance on discussing sex at home, the dwindling of preventive sex education, and the difficulty (not to mention the embarrassment) teens face trying to get their hands on effective and affordable birth control, and you end up with a lot of babies born to single Latina moms. About 52.5 percent of all Latino babies are born to unwed mothers, compared with 28.6 percent of non-Hispanic white babies (those numbers are still lower than the nearly 72.3 percent of African American babies born outside of marriage) (CDC, 2011c).

Flat Broke with Children

Single mothers and poverty in America often go hand in hand, and these twin challenges plague nonwhite communities to a greater extent than white Americans. In a shrinking welfare state with widening economic gaps between the rich and the poor, single mothers are faced with tough trade-offs between mothering and work. Single mothers rely on a combination of welfare, family, lovers, luck, and creativity to make ends meet. At any given point in the past few decades, half of all mothers raising children by themselves have relied on welfare to get by. In contrast to the media myth of the "lazy welfare mother" who watches television and buys filet mignon with her food stamps, many of these mothers work hard (often off the books) and desperately want to escape poverty. Welfare critics might be surprised to read *Making Ends Meet: How Single Mothers Survive Welfare and Low-Wage Work* (1997), in which sociologists Kathryn Edin and Laura Lein find that all single mothers prefer self-reliance to welfare dependency. In fact, a majority get off the welfare rolls in two years, and hardly any stay on welfare for more than eight years.

In their study of 379 mothers across four U.S. cities, Edin and Lein traced what happens when poor single mothers are faced with the choice between welfare and work. The word *choice* here is misleading: It implies freedom, as though these women can easily move from dependency to self-sufficiency. Former president Ronald Reagan firmly believed as much in 1981, when he spoke about

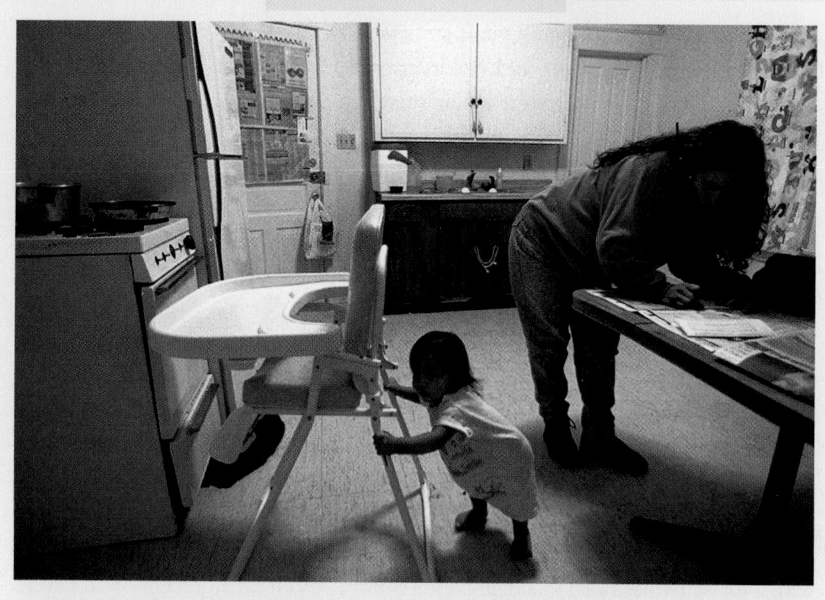

Jenni McGlaun talks on the phone while her 15-month-old son, Jesse, plays in their Milwaukee home. McGlaun has been on and off welfare for five years. What does Kathryn Edin and Laura Lein's research on single mothers reveal about the choices these women face between welfare and work?

unemployment and poverty problems. People who wanted to work could find it if only they would read the help-wanted ads, he reasoned. He even waved a newspaper in front of reporters, the "help-wanted" section circled in red, and proclaimed that there was obviously no shortage of jobs, just a shortage of personal responsibility and motivation on the part of lazy people. However, because single mothers are often unskilled or semi-skilled and have less education than average, their employment options are limited to low-wage work that rarely provides benefits (the kinds of jobs listed in the paper Reagan had flashed).

Edin and Lein found that mothers on welfare could cover about three-fifths of their expenses. In low-wage jobs, they faced a larger gap between earnings and expenses, in part to cover the costs of transportation, child-care arrangements, increased rent, and fewer food stamps. (Both the food stamp program and federal housing program consider income when determining benefits; even a father's child support can translate into a rent increase for a single mother.) This system makes a savings account virtually impossible for welfare recipients to maintain and is arguably the real culprit behind the trap of dependency. In fact, leaving welfare for work substantially increases these women's expenses, such that they can cover only two-thirds of those expenses on low wages alone. One working mother voiced her frustrations:

> Ask any politician to live off my budget. Live off my minimum wage job and just a little bit of food stamps—how can he do it? I bet he couldn't. I'd

> like him to try it for one month. Come home from work, cook dinner, wash clothes, do everything, everything, get up and go to work the next day, and then find you don't have enough money to pay for everything you need. (Edin & Lein, 1997, p. 149)

Barbara Ehrenreich, a sociologist and writer, tried to make ends meet with low-wage work in 1998. That was a year in which the Preamble Center for Public Policy estimated that the odds against a typical welfare recipient's landing a job at a living wage were about 97 to 1. Nationwide, it took an average hourly wage of $8.89 to afford a one-bedroom apartment. Currently, the federal minimum wage is $7.25, which amounts to a full-time yearly salary of $15,080. Only approximately 7 percent of the labor force makes the minimum wage, but about 30 percent of the workforce plugs away for $8 an hour or less, and Ehrenreich wanted to figure out just how they did it (Ehrenreich, 2001).

Ehrenreich traveled the country working for $6 or $7 an hour as a waitress, maid, and Wal-Mart salesperson. At these low wages, she had to pay high rates for rent by the week (because she lacked the required one-month security deposit). She had to eat for less than $9 a day, a budget that at best included canned beans, fast food, or noodle soup microwaved at a convenience store, and she supplemented this diet by sponging junk food from charities. All the while, Ehrenreich prayed for her health to keep up (low-wage jobs are often physically taxing), gave up clothes shopping, and juggled two or more jobs. She still could not afford to live off of her wages:

> I grew up hearing over and over, to the point of tedium, that "hard work" was the secret of success: "Work hard and you'll get ahead" or "It's hard work that got us where we are." No one ever said that you could work hard—harder than you ever thought possible—and still find yourself sinking ever deeper into poverty and debt. (2001, p. 220)

Most welfare recipients live with few extras, often in neighborhoods with high poverty concentration and elevated crime rates. Yet politicians and voters alike worry about the cycle of dependency, the so-called welfare trap, and taxpayers deeply resent any person—real or perceived—who gets a free ride. Welfare critic Charles Murray, author of the conservative classic *Losing Ground* (1984), believes welfare moms are staining the very moral fabric that holds the country together (see Chapter 10). As he sees it, all economic support should be pulled from under the feet of single mothers, and that would keep poor women and teens from having babies for whom they cannot care.

The 1996 Personal Responsibility and Work Opportunity Reconciliation Act, the national welfare reform enacted during the Clinton administration, didn't go as far as Murray would have liked, but it did make into policy the sentiment common among taxpayers that it was time for lazy welfare moms to get their act together, learn self-sufficiency, and take responsibility for themselves. But responsibility can take on several, often conflicting, meanings for mothers. Faced with either welfare

In *Flat Broke with Children*, Sharon Hays found that many women stayed in abusive relationships or married for financial support to escape poverty. For instance, Marcia Felts Wimberly weathered an abusive husband in order to get a surgery covered by his insurance. Now a single mom, she has no medical insurance and is struggling with debt.

or low-wage work, single mothers find that the government's definition of responsibility is narrowly defined as wage work. In *Flat Broke with Children: Women in the Age of Welfare Reform* (2003), Sharon Hays shows that many of these women are forced to take low-paying jobs with no future and little career stability. As a result, they are frequently driven to marry for financial support. All too often, Hays finds, single mothers (and their children) end up in poverty, homeless, or seeking alternatives to get by, including illicit sources of income.

Single mothers' paid labor often requires that they sacrifice responsible parenthood. By forcing welfare moms to enter the workforce while not providing adequate child care, the government encourages women to abandon their children in an unsupervised home. To the single mothers Hays interviewed, real responsibility meant taking care of and supervising their children, looking after their health, and providing them with a safe home environment. According to Hays, for the most desperate women in America, being a responsible worker requires being an irresponsible mother. To manage this tension between being a good worker or a good mother, single mothers may shoot for the nearly impossible strategy of self-reliance, but in reality they often end up depending on cash assistance from family or boyfriends. They barter with sisters, cousins, and kindly neighbors. They also take side jobs (again hiding their income to avoid rent increases or food stamp ineligibility) or go to relief agencies, although this last option proves too humiliating for most to bear. As a last resort, some single mothers turn to criminal activity such as prostitution or drug dealing, where the earnings are high but the moral costs "rob them of the self-respect they gained from trying to be good mothers" (Edin & Lein, 1997).

The Pecking Order: Inequality Starts at Home

By now, you can see that there's no universal family form and plenty of gender inequality exists in American families. But you might still think that, at least when it comes to the children, the home (no matter who makes up a family) is a haven of equality, altruism, and infinite love in an otherwise harsh world. In *Haven in a Heartless World* (1977), Christopher Lasch paints a rosy portrait of domestic life. To him, the home really is a haven where workers seek refuge from the cold winds of a capitalist public sphere. The family is sacred because it provides intimate privacy, managed by a caring woman who shields male workers from "the cruel world of politics and work." Building on the socially constructed split between the public and private spheres, this idea of the family as insulated from the outside world is deeply entrenched in America.

However, as you might have guessed by now, such ideas give a misleading sense of the family as a harmonious unit, its members altruistically sacrificing for one another to forge a healthy, hearty, and loving private world. As I found while researching my book *The Pecking Order* (2004), a compelling, but largely invisible, struggle also takes place in the home. In each American family, there exists a pecking order among siblings—a status hierarchy, if you will—that can ignite the family with competition, struggle, and resentment. Parents often abet such struggles, despite their protestations that they "love all their children equally."

Let me illustrate with the story of a future president, William Jefferson Blythe IV, born to a 23-year-old widow named Virginia. Childhood was rough for young Bill, especially after his mother married Roger Clinton, a bitter alcoholic who physically abused his wife. Bill cites the day that he stood up to his stepfather as the most important day in his transition to adulthood and perhaps his entire life. In 1962, when Bill was 16, Virginia finally left Roger, but by then there was another Roger Clinton in the family, Bill's younger half-brother.

Despite the fact that Bill despised his stepfather, he went to the Garland County courthouse and changed his last name to Clinton so that he would have the same surname as the younger brother he cherished. Although they were separated by ten years, were only half-siblings, and ran in very different circles, the brothers were close. The younger Roger probably hated his father more than Bill did, but he nonetheless took on some of the old man's traits as he came of age, most notably substance abuse. By age 18, he was heavily into marijuana. During Bill's first (unsuccessful) congressional run in 1974, Roger spent much of his time stenciling signs while smoking joints at campaign headquarters.

As Bill's political fortunes rose, Roger's prospects first stagnated and then sank. He tried his hand at a musical career, worked odd jobs, and eventually began dealing drugs—and not just pot. In 1984 the Arkansas state police informed then-Governor Bill Clinton that his brother was a cocaine dealer under investigation. After a sting operation, which the governor did not obstruct, Roger was arrested. He was beside himself in tears, threatening suicide for the shame he had brought on his family and especially his brother, the successful politician.

You might be wondering, as Clinton biographer David Maraniss has, "How could two brothers be so different: the governor and the coke dealer, the Rhodes scholar and the college dropout?" (1995). To be sure, a pair of brothers who are, respectively, a former president and an ex-con is a fairly extreme example. But the basic phenomenon of sibling differences in success that the Clintons represent is not all that unusual. In fact, in explaining economic inequality in America, sibling differences represent more than half of all the differences between individuals.

What do sibling disparities as large as these indicate? If asked to explain why one brother succeeded where the other failed miserably, most people will point to different individual characteristics, such as work ethic, responsibility, personal motivation, and discipline. To account for a sibling's failures, people also tend to cite personal reasons, such as "a bad attitude," "poor emotional or mental health," or, most commonly, "lack of determination" (Conley, 2004).

Other people will grapple for an explanation by suggesting the role of birth order. The commonly held idea is that firstborns are naturally more driven and successful, if just because they are most favored by their parents. But this is still a form of individual explanation—something unique to the biology or psychology of the sibling—that fails to take into account the role of sociological factors. For example, in families with two kids, birth order doesn't matter that much. Firstborns don't have too much advantage over one younger sibling. For example, slightly fewer than one-fourth of U.S. presidents were firstborns, about what we would expect from chance. Birth position matters only in the context of larger families and limited resources. When family resources are stretched thin, love really does become a pie, as they say. The children born first or last into a large family seem to fare better socioeconomically than those born in the middle. Middle kids feel the effects of a shrinking pie, as they tend to be shortchanged on resources like money for college and parental attention.

Taken as a whole, the facts about intrafamily stratification present a much darker portrait of American family life than we are accustomed to. Sure, we want to think of the home as a haven in a heartless world, but the truth is that inequality starts at home. These statistics also pose problems for media stories and politicians concerned with the erosion of the idealized nuclear family. In fact, they hint at a trade-off between economic opportunity and stable, cohesive families. The family is, in short, no shelter from the cold winds of capitalism; rather, it is part and parcel of that system.

A pecking order emerges during the course of childhood. It both reflects and determines siblings' positions in the overall status ordering that occurs within society. It is not just the will of parents or the "natural" abilities of children (or lack thereof); the pecking order is conditioned by the swirling winds of society, which in turn envelop the family. Furthermore, sibling disparities are much more common in poor families and single-parent homes than in rich, intact families. In fact, when families have limited resources, the success of one sibling often generates a negative backlash among the others. As the parents unwittingly put all their eggs—all their hopes and dreams—in just one basket, the other siblings inevitably are left out in the cold. Americans like to think that their behavior and destiny remain solely in their own hands. But the pecking order, like other aspects of the social fabric, ends up being shaped by social forces.

The Future of Families, and There Goes the Nation!

Divorce

Throughout this chapter we have examined the idealization of monogamous marriage as a key characteristic of American culture. Sociologist Andrew Cherlin writes in *The Marriage-Go-Round: The State of Marriage and the Family in America Today* (2009) about how the idealized conception of marriage is currently helping to delay age at first marriage and otherwise shape contemporary American marital patterns. He finds a paradox. On the one hand, Americans value marriage very highly—85 to 90 percent of us will eventually get married. On the other hand, America has the highest divorce rate of any comparable Western country. How does he explain this love-hate relationship? Cherlin suggests that both the drive to get married and the desire to divorce are rooted in our collective past,

> all the way to the Colonial days when marriage was the nexus of civil society that the early settlers established. It's very important here. . . . We want to be married. At the same time though, we're very individualistic, and that has deep cultural roots too. Think about the saying "Go west, young man." Think about the rugged individual. We're individualists. And so we want to be married, but we evaluate our marriages in very personal terms. Am I getting the personal growth that I need out of my marriage? And if you think the answer is no, you feel justified in leaving. (Conley, 2009k)

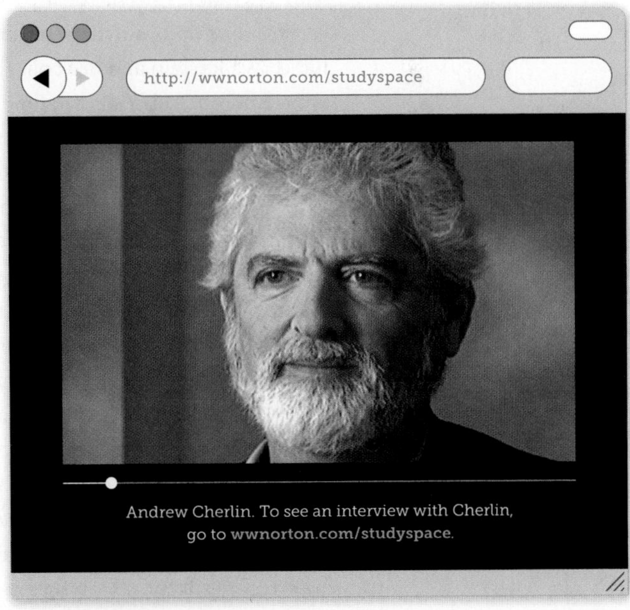

Andrew Cherlin. To see an interview with Cherlin, go to wwnorton.com/studyspace.

Social science research over the past couple of decades has struggled to establish just how high rates of divorce alter the social fabric. Figure 12.4 illustrates the divorce rate in America since 1920. Adding a layer to the American marriage paradox, it turns out that the most politically and religiously conservative states have the highest rates of divorce: "The states with the top ten divorce rates, eight out of ten of those, voted for John McCain in the 2008 election. All ten voted for George Bush in the 2004 election" (Conley, 2009k). Cherlin explains that personal economics, not personal values, may end up contributing to rocky marriages. The states with high divorce rates are relatively poor; a sizable number of their citizens struggle to find jobs with decent wages, which compromises the ideal vision of family as a haven protected from crass financial concerns. Couples who cannot provide themselves a middle-class lifestyle may begin to question the utility of marriage in the first place. They face all of the responsibility of looking out for each other without the means to live the ideal lifestyle to which they aspire. Cherlin also notes that younger people have even more difficulty finding good jobs because they have less work experience and this may delay their marriage plans (Conley, 2009k). Young couples may live together, even have children together, holding off on long-term personal relationships until after they have established long-term financial relationships with reliable employers.

Much of the debate about divorce follows the children of divorced parents through their educational careers and into their adult relationship choices. The moral and political debate surrounding the long-term consequences of divorce has largely treated its effects as uniform for all offspring. In *The Pecking Order* (2004), I paint a more nuanced picture, in which circumstances and context widely vary the impact of divorce on kids—even those in the same family. Everything from the timing of the divorce to a parent's hostility can influence a kid's educational attainment, future earnings, and socioeconomic success. Blanket condemnations of divorce are therefore dangerously naïve, as are those who say that it's no big deal.

For example, in their best seller *The Unexpected Legacy of Divorce* (2000), Judith Wallerstein and her colleagues claim that divorce almost universally damages children's self-esteem and developmental trajectories. Based on interviews with about 50 offspring of divorced parents, they conclude that adult children of divorce suffer from higher rates of depression, endure low self-esteem, and have difficulties forming fulfilling, lasting relationships of their own.

Sociologist Linda Waite and columnist Maggie Gallagher echo this view in *The Case for Marriage: Why Married People Are Happier, Healthier, and Better Off Financially* (2000). (The title, in this case, says it all.) They claim that married parents provide better homes for their children than divorced ones because they have more money and time to spend on the children, enjoy stronger emotional bonds with them, have more social capital (connections) that will be helpful to their children's chances for success, and are physically and mentally healthier. By contrast, they say, divorced families are likely to manifest more child abuse, neglect, and delinquency, and the children will probably attain less education.

On the flip side of the debate are research findings that suggest a less calamitous future for the children of single-parent families, finding that children from

Figure 12.4: U.S. Divorce Rate

SOURCE: U.S. Census Bureau, 2010e.

divorced households generally do not do much worse than other kids. In *For Better or for Worse: Divorce Reconsidered* (2002), psychologists E. Mavis Hetherington and John Kelly argue that the children of divorce, for the most part, do adjust well to the new reality. Under some conditions, but certainly not all, divorce produces in kids more stress and depression, and lower future socioeconomic success. Continued parental conflict and role reversals in which children "play parent," for example, make divorce potentially destructive. In other cases, however, parents who leave a high-conflict marriage probably spare their children from ongoing family feuds, hostilities, or abuse. At least one study shows that kids from high-conflict marriages that stay together may do worse than kids from high-conflict marriages that break up (Morrison & Coiro, 1999).

Too often, social science research is carelessly picked up in political debates as simple sound bites. Saying kids from divorced families fare worse than kids from intact families is one thing; saying that divorce caused those worse outcomes is quite another matter. That is, we can't really know for sure that had those parents stayed together, the kids would have been better off. We can only say that high levels of parental conflict are bad—with or without divorce in the picture.

Blended Families

As should be clear by this point, the dynamics involved in maintaining a family (both as a whole and in terms of the individual relationships within it) are complicated. This complexity increases drastically when two family units are integrated. As stated on **Helpguide.org**, "To a child who does not belong to one, stepfamily may suggest Cinderella's family or the Brady Bunch." However, if you are part of a blended family or know someone who is (there's a good chance you do, given that one-third of the children in the United States now fall into this category), you understand that neither extreme reflects reality. As divorce becomes more common, so too does the blended family form. Two people meet, fall in love, get married, have kids—we'll call them family A. Then they decide to split. Another pair does the same (family B). Some time later, Mom A encounters Dad B, and the process repeats. The result is a blended family or stepfamily, with stepparents, stepchildren, and sometimes step-siblings. Blended families are the result of not only divorce but also death. When either partner dies, remarriage is not uncommon. According to the 1990 U.S. census, 3.6 percent of grooms and 10 percent of brides had previously lost a spouse (Kreider & Ellis, 2011).

In fact, in his book, Cherlin estimates that over a quarter of American children today experience at least two maternal partner changes, and more than 8 percent experience three or more. Some developmental psychologists worry about this dynamic, as it impacts children's ability to form trusting, stable ties with adult figures in their lives. Others see children as robust and more or less adaptable to most changes that come their way.

Gay and Lesbian Couples

Marriage, divorce, remarriage. Stepfamilies, blended families. Another family arrangement on the rise, as we saw at the beginning of the chapter, is same-sex couples. At present, same-sex marriages are legal in the Netherlands, Belgium, Spain, Norway, Sweden, Canada, Portugal, Iceland, Argentina, Mexico, and the U.S. states of Massachusetts, New Hampshire, Vermont, Connecticut, Iowa, and New York. Thousands of gay and lesbian couples have sworn their marriage vows in these states, although their unions are not legally recognized at the federal level in the United States.

Such unions have been met with ardent opposition. Thus far 30 states have adopted constitutional amendments against same-sex marriages. In 1996 President Clinton signed into federal law the Defense of Marriage Act (DOMA), which stipulates that federally recognized marriages must be heterosexual. In addition, under DOMA, states are not required to recognize same-sex marriages conducted in other jurisdictions. Much of the support for such bills relies on the argument that the best way for children to be raised is by a heterosexual couple taking care of their own biological children. However, research consistently finds that lesbian and gay parents are at least as successful as heterosexuals in producing well-adjusted, successful offspring (Stacey, 1997).

Civil unions legally recognized unions explicitly intended to offer similar state-provided legal rights and benefits as marriage.

If met with such resistance, why don't gay and lesbian couples accept recognition instead through civil unions (legally recognized unions explicitly intended

Figure 12.5: Antidiscrimination Laws by State

UNITED STATES OF AMERICA

ANTIDISCRIMINATION CHECKLIST

State	Same-Sex Marriage	2nd Parent Adoption (Same-Sex Couples)	Job Antidiscrimination	Hate Crimes Protection	Civil Unions	Health Benefits (Same-Sex Partners)	Housing Antidiscrimination
~~ALABAMA~~							
~~ALASKA~~							
ARIZONA				✓			
ARKANSAS		✓					
CALIFORNIA		✓	✓	✓	✓	✓	✓
COLORADO		✓	✓	✓			✓
CONNECTICUT	✓	✓	✓	✓	✓	✓	✓
DELAWARE		✓	✓	✓	✓		✓
FLORIDA		✓		✓			
~~GEORGIA~~							
HAWAII		✓	✓	✓	✓		✓
~~IDAHO~~							
ILLINOIS		✓	✓	✓	✓	✓	✓
INDIANA		✓					
IOWA	✓	✓	✓	✓	✓	✓	✓
KANSAS				✓			
KENTUCKY				✓			
LOUISIANA				✓			
MAINE	✓	✓	✓	✓	✓	✓	✓
MARYLAND	✓	✓	✓	✓			✓
MASSACHUSETTS	✓	✓	✓	✓	✓	✓	✓
~~MICHIGAN~~							
MINNESOTA		✓	✓	✓			✓
~~MISSISSIPPI~~							
MISSOURI				✓			
MONTANA						✓	
NEBRASKA				✓			
NEVADA		✓	✓	✓	✓		✓
NEW HAMPSHIRE	✓	✓	✓	✓	✓		✓
NEW JERSEY		✓	✓	✓	✓	✓	✓
NEW MEXICO		✓	✓	✓		✓	✓
NEW YORK	✓	✓	✓	✓		✓	✓
~~NORTH CAROLINA~~							
~~NORTH DAKOTA~~							
OHIO		✓					
~~OKLAHOMA~~							
OREGON		✓	✓	✓	✓	✓	✓
PENNSYLVANIA				✓			
RHODE ISLAND		✓	✓	✓	✓	✓	✓
~~SOUTH CAROLINA~~							
~~SOUTH DAKOTA~~							
TENNESSEE				✓			
TEXAS				✓			
~~UTAH~~							
VERMONT	✓	✓	✓	✓	✓	✓	✓
~~VIRGINIA~~							
WASHINGTON	✓	✓	✓	✓	✓	✓	✓
~~WEST VIRGINIA~~							
WISCONSIN		✓	✓	✓			✓
~~WYOMING~~							

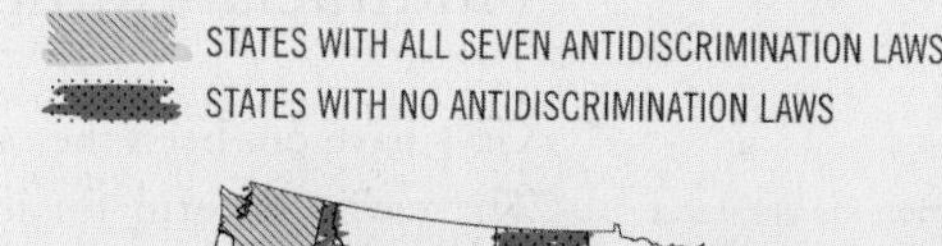

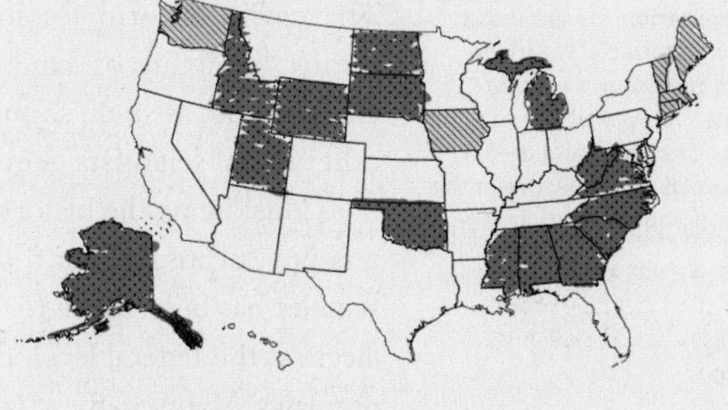

Domestic partnerships legally recognized unions that guarantee only select rights to same-sex couples.

to offer similar state-provided legal rights and benefits as marriage) and domestic partnerships (legally recognized unions that guarantee only select rights to same-sex couples), as indeed some states offer? Federal allowance and recognition, the ultimate goal of those advocating same-sex marriage, would open up a more comprehensive set of rights and responsibilities than is possible at the state level. These include joint tax filing, Social Security and survivor benefits, and tax-free transfers or inheritance. At the state level, the rights afforded married couples are primarily symbolic or related to employee benefits, but they are no less important. Married gay and lesbian couples in Massachusetts do not have any federal benefits, but each now possesses the ability to recognize legally the significant other as his or her husband or wife. Symbolically, this is of immense importance, as it lends a third-party legitimacy to the relationship. Figure 12.5 gives you an idea of the diversity among state laws governing same-sex marriage.

An old joke goes, "Gays and lesbians getting married—haven't they suffered enough?" That is, if homosexual couples want to marry, why not just let them do it? Opponents of gay marriage—many of whom are strongly religious, "social values" conservatives—argue that nontraditional familial arrangements will wreak social havoc. Let gays get married, so the argument goes, and you effectively destroy the family. Once the family goes, look out, the next step is chaos, no moral order. Furthermore, opponents of gay marriage claim that the purpose of a family is to procreate and raise children into functioning adults, and this is determined by biology. Because gay marriage does not produce the biological children of both parents, such people believe that it is not functional, right, or natural.

According to the Pew Research Center, views are steadily shifting. In 1996, 64 percent of Americans were opposed to gay and lesbian marriage. And by 2011, American views were divided, 45 percent in favor and 46 percent opposed. A general trend toward acceptance has also been on the rise. Currently, the majority of Americans (58 percent) believe homosexuality should be accepted by society (Pew Research Center, 2011d).

Multiracial Families

Miscegenation the technical term for interracial marriage, literally meaning "a mixing of kinds"; it is politically and historically charged—sociologists generally prefer the term *exogamy* or *outmarriage*.

Gays have not been the only ones who have faced obstacles to legal marriage. The technical term for interracial marriage is miscegenation, which literally means "a mixing of kinds." This term, however, is politically and historically charged and, as such, should be used with a degree of caution. Sociologists and other social scientists generally prefer the term *exogamy* or *outmarriage*.

Considering the history of race relations in the United States (see Chapter 9), it is not surprising that the idea (and even legality) of interracial marriages and families has been cause for controversy. Although interracial marriage was never illegal at the federal level, from 1913 to 1948, 30 states enforced antimiscegenation laws. Many of these laws lasted until 1967, when the Supreme Court finally declared them unconstitutional, reversing the restrictions in 16 remaining states.

We have undoubtedly come a long way since 1967. One year after the Supreme Court ruling (1968), a Gallup poll revealed that 80 percent of Americans were opposed to blacks and whites getting married. By 2007 that number had dropped to 25 percent. However, attitudes toward exogamy in the United States vary greatly by location, religion, and a host of other factors. And, of course, such polls capture only expressed attitudes, subject to social desirability bias, not actual behavior (i.e., actual intermarriage rates).

In 2008, 14.6 percent of new marriages were between people of different races or ethnic groups. Asian Americans had the highest rate of outmarriage at 31 percent, followed by 26 percent of Latinos, 16 percent of blacks, and 9 percent of whites. These percentages significantly change when gender is taken into account. For example, 40 percent of Asian American women marry someone outside of their race, unlike Asian American men with only a 20 percent rate of outmarriage. Black men have a 22 percent rate of outmarriage verses black women's rate of 9 percent.

American families are increasingly looking like the family of Taye Diggs and Idina Menzel, pictured above. How are attitudes about multiracial families changing?

Beyond Gay Marriage

When the poet Elizabeth Barrett Browning wrote, "How do I love thee? Let me count the ways," little did she know that a century and a half later the list would extend into the hundreds—at least for married couples. As of 2004, the U.S. General Accounting Office had identified more than 1,000 legal rights and responsibilities attendant to marriage (Shah, 2004). The era of big government is clearly not over when it comes to family policy.

These rights and responsibilities range from the continuation of water rights upon the death of a spouse to the ability to take funeral leave. And that's just the federal government. States and localities have their own marriage provisions. New York State, for example, grants a spouse the right to inherit a military veteran's peddler's license. And Hawaii extends to spouses of state residents lower fees for hunting licenses. No wonder gay and lesbian

Jeanne Fong (left) and Jennifer Lin, a same-sex couple from San Francisco, celebrate during a marriage equality rally in Washington, D.C.

activists put such a premium on access to marriage rights. Some gay marriage advocates want all spousal rights immediately and will settle for nothing less. Others take an incremental approach, aiming to secure first the most significant domestic partner rights, such as employer benefits.

But rather than argue about whether gay or lesbian couples should be allowed to tie the knot or be granted any marital rights at all, perhaps it is time to do an end run around the culture wars by breaking down or unbundling the marriage contract into its constituent parts. Then, applying free-market principles, we could allow each citizen to assign the various rights and responsibilities now connected to marriage as he or she sees fit. In addition to employer benefits, some of the key marital rights include the ability to pass property and income back and forth tax-free, spousal privilege (that is, the right not to testify against one's husband or wife), medical decision-making power, and the right to confer permanent residency to a foreigner, just to name a few. The mutual responsibilities of marriage include parenthood—a husband is the legal father of any child born to his wife regardless of biological paternity—and shared tort liability. Why not allow people to parcel out each of these marital privileges?

Take my own marriage as a case in point: My ex-wife is a foreigner who applied for citizenship, and her marriage to me made that possible. But as the law now stands, I, as a straight American man, theoretically could become a green card machine. As long as I can convince the overstretched Department of Homeland Security that my penchant for falling in love with foreign women is genuine, I can divorce and remarry as many times as I like, obtaining permanent residency for each of my failed loves along the way. Is that fair to the gay man who falls in love with a foreigner he can't sponsor? For that matter, is it fair to the many Americans who can't sponsor aging grandparents or, in some cases, even parents? Or even to straight Americans who are happy marrying other Americans and don't want to see the country fill up with my romantic baggage?

Why not instead give all Americans the right to sponsor one person in their lifetime—a right that they could sell, if they so desire? This would mean that if I wanted to marry a Kenyan after divorcing an Australian, I could, but I would need to purchase, perhaps on eBay, the right to confer citizenship from someone else who didn't need it. Similarly, why not let all Americans name one person (other than their lawyer, priest, or therapist) who can't be forced to testify against them in court? This zone of privacy could be transferred over the course of a lifetime, perhaps limiting such changes to once every five years.

While we are at it, how about allowing each of us to choose someone with whom we share our property, with all the tax (and liability) implications that choice would imply? We might even allow parenthood to become contractual, by letting people name those individuals they want to be the stepparents to their biological children.

We could go down the long list of rights and responsibilities embedded in the marriage contract. Ideally, most people would choose one person in whom to vest all these rights, but everyone would have the freedom to decide how to configure these domestic, business, legal, and intimate relationships in the eyes of the law.

Other people have proposed changing marriage by making it more flexible. A prominent group of queer activists (see **www.beyondmarriage.org**) continues to argue that the law should recognize a variety of households—from conjugal couples to groups of elderly people living collectively—as "legal families." But they have not specified the rights that should go along with such arrangements or addressed the problems and paradoxes that might arise if legal rights and responsibilities were extended to groups of more than two. Unbundling marital rights would achieve the same end without creating new inequities based on group size.

It might also take some of the vitriol out of the marriage debate. Marriage itself could stay in church (or in Las Vegas, as the case may be). And each couple could count their own ways to love.

→ CONCLUSION

By now you should be wary of any social institution that is hailed supreme because it is "more natural." You should be skeptical of any family arrangement that is deemed more functional than another, and you should hold the traditional family at a critical distance, especially considering the experiences of women, African Americans, gays and lesbians, the poor, the mainstream, and the marginalized.

Under the "postmodern family condition," as Judith Stacey calls it, clear rules no longer exist in our complex, diversified, and sometimes messy postindustrial society (1996). Gone are the ruling days of the normative Nelsons. Families today take on many shapes and sizes that best fit their members' needs, and they are defined not by blood ties but by the quality of relationships. Let us count the ways. . . .

ASSIGNMENT

To demonstrate the diversity of family forms, ask ten of your friends about their families. Are they part of nuclear families? Are any of their parents divorced, remarried, in a same-sex couple? List your own family arrangements and those of your friends—are the results surprising? What do these results suggest regarding the idea of a normative "traditional" family?

QUESTIONS FOR REVIEW

1. The case of Ozzie and Harry at the beginning of the chapter brings to mind the variety of family arrangements. Describe the "nuclear family" and three other family forms. Does sociological research suggest that one such arrangement is necessarily the right one?
2. Think about the discussion regarding rights for same-sex couples. How do the functionalist arguments by Bronislaw Malinowski (1913) and Talcott Parsons (1951) help explain the changes (or lack thereof) in the institution of marriage?
3. How do historical cultural ideals relate to current rates of marriage and divorce in the United States? Name one reason that the likelihood of being currently married might be lower among those with low incomes.
4. Sometimes what's considered "normal" is far from what's most prevalent currently or historically. How does this statement relate to perceptions about the "traditional" family?
5. Describe how a gendered division of labor arose after the Industrial Revolution. How was this change tied to kinship networks?
6. What is the cult of domesticity? How has it changed over the last century?
7. What is the second shift, and how does it relate to a leisure gap between husbands and wives?
8. Are mothers on welfare lazy? Use the findings by Kathryn Edin and Laura Lein (1997) to help answer this question.
9. What is a pecking order, and what does the term mean for children in a family? According to this concept, does your birth position in the family or number of siblings matter to your life chances for success in school and beyond?

PARADOX

WE THINK OF THE FAMILY AS A HAVEN IN A HARSH WORLD BUT IN FACT, INEQUALITY BEGINS AT HOME. →

WATCH THE ANIMATED SHORT ABOUT THE FAMILY PARADOX AT

WWNORTON.COM/STUDYSPACE

Topeka High School students hang out after class. Even after the Supreme Court outlawed segregation in Topeka, it still took more than 40 years for the schools to become fully integrated.

13 Education

PARADOX

ALTHOUGH SCHOOL IS SUPPOSED TO BE THE INSTITUTION IN SOCIETY THAT PROVIDES EQUAL OPPORTUNITY, IT ENDS UP SORTING AND STRATIFYING STUDENTS BY THE BACKGROUNDS FROM WHICH THEY COME.

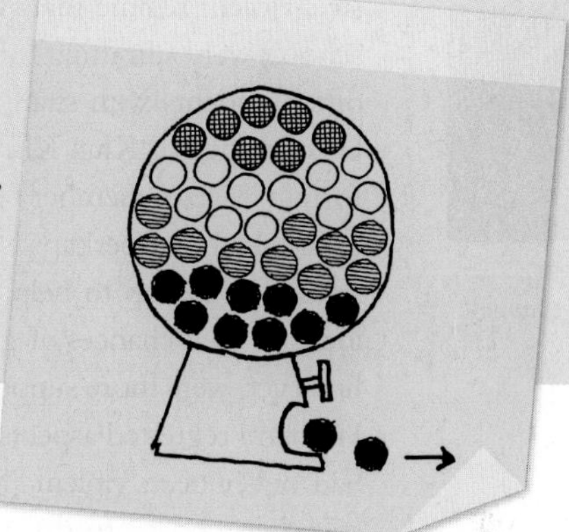

Like the other freshmen who entered the hallowed halls of Yale University for the first time in 2005, Sayed Rahmatullah Hashemi had to take some time to adjust to his new surroundings. A devout Muslim, he had to find the direction of Mecca and choose from limited offerings in the dining hall. (It wasn't until weeks into the fall semester, after he had lost 15 pounds, that a friend told him kosher meat was available at the Jewish dining hall.) Hashemi also had to adjust to other aspects of campus life, such as making new friends and trying out unfamiliar activities, like cricket. But Hashemi faced other obstacles as well—ones with which most freshmen did not have to contend. As an Afghani who spent most of his childhood in Pakistan, Hashemi had only a fourth-grade formal education, and despite speaking English well, it was his fourth language after Pashto, Urdu, and Persian. Furthermore, in order to receive an American education, Hashemi had left his wife and two children in Pakistan, and he missed them sorely. That said, perhaps the most striking difference between Hashemi and his fellow Yalies was that he had been, until just a few years before entering college, an active member of the Taliban regime in Afghanistan. In fact, Hashemi worked as a "roving ambassador" in the United States (a position that entailed representing the Taliban regime by giving interviews and speeches and meeting with American politicians) and was featured in Michael Moore's movie *Fahrenheit 9/11*. During one of the speeches Hashemi gave on his U.S. tour, a woman stood, lifted her burqa, and shouted that he had imprisoned women. He replied, "I'm really sorry to your husband. He might have a very difficult time with you." The exchange is immortalized in Moore's film.

Sayed Rahmatullah Hashemi

Until the *New York Times* ran an article profiling this unusual student in January 2006 (Brown, 2006), most Yale students had no idea that there was a former Taliban official in their midst. And, for that matter, neither did most Americans. But the revelation caused quite a commotion. Some questioned why the Ivy League university admitted Hashemi, who had only a fourth-grade education, when many highly qualified Americans had been turned away. Others, of course, questioned the logic of admitting a student who had represented an oppressive, violent regime that America was fighting hard to dismantle. If Ivy League schools were admitting former Taliban members, would they also start accepting other students with shady pasts—perhaps former terrorists and former members of the Ku Klux Klan? Some Americans also disagreed with the idea of a former Taliban member benefiting from the openness of our society. And some even joked that perhaps a Taliban summer camp or student-exchange program should be set up to help Americans pad their college applications in order to increase their chances of gaining acceptance into Ivy League universities. Others, however, were more supportive of Yale's decision. They pointed to evidence that Hashemi regretted aspects of his past and that his involvement with the Taliban had never been violent (his jobs were more administrative: translating, giving speeches, and so forth). Such supporters also suggested that he might benefit from an education that would teach him American values. Finally, they pointed out that his fellow students could learn a lot from his experiences.

Clearly, a former Taliban member's acceptance by an Ivy League university opened up a huge can of worms. In addition to the more obvious moral questions about how and why Yale selected Hashemi, I would suggest that the reactions to the story were so animated because they touched on larger questions about the American educational system. For example, the reactions reflect the American ideal of fairness and equal opportunity, particularly in terms of education. Although it is debatable whether admitting former Taliban members to American universities shows just how fair-minded Americans are, most would argue that all students, regardless of background, should have a shot at a good education. The reactions also address what we think schools should teach students. In this case, we assume that Hashemi will learn American values through his American education—and that these values are something worth acquiring. Finally, perhaps Americans were so inflamed precisely because Hashemi was admitted to an Ivy League university. This suggests two things: First, that Americans believe elite schools offer more opportunities to their graduates than less selective institutions do, and second, that given the advantages such a degree provides, Americans think those admitted to the most prestigious schools should be the most academically deserving. Thus, many have questioned the admission of Hashemi because of his scant educational background just as they would other students who appear underqualified.

A third issue, which might arise no matter which college we are talking about, is peer effects. Parents know that college isn't all about the coursework or professors. It's also about peers who socialize one another into becoming adult members of society. For many noncommuting students, college is the first time that they are living away from their families.

These topics not only are at the forefront of American thought but also play a prominent role in how sociologists study the educational system in the United States. Throughout history, sociologists have weighed in on all these issues. They have studied the values that schools and peers impart and what students gain from their experiences. They have also examined emerging trends in higher education, including the increasing competition to gain access to the most elite colleges. Sociologists have also researched the idea that not all schools provide the same quality of education. Finally, sociologists have paid considerable attention to how well the American educational system has lived up to its ideology of equal opportunity for all. Therefore, without necessarily intending to, the story of one former Taliban member touched on many educational issues that are of interest to the American public and sociologists alike.

Learning to Learn or Learning to Labor? Functions of Schooling

Let's start with the basics. Sociologists define education as the process through which academic, social, and cultural ideas and tools, both general and specific, are developed. First and foremost, schools are supposed to teach basic skills and impart knowledge. Thus, we expect students to leave school with at least the ability to read, write, and do arithmetic, as well as knowing who George Washington is. However, in reality, all schools do not achieve these goals. Functional illiteracy (the inability to read or write well enough to be a functioning member of society) plagues about 14 percent of the nation's population 16 years of age and older. Further, innumeracy, having insufficient mathematical skills to function in society, is experienced by 22 percent of the population ages 16 and older (Kutner et al., 2005).

Education the process through which academic, social, and cultural ideas and tools, both general and specific, are developed.

How do schools train us to be good workers? What are some of the other functions of education?

Schools may also teach more specific skills that students need for the workplace. Vocational programs might focus on carpentry or mechanical skills, whereas professional schools train doctors and lawyers. In fact, the skills you obtain from vocational and postsecondary schools can be considered an investment in your future. Just as we can upgrade a computer to run faster and more efficiently, people can deliberately invest in knowledge and skills, called human capital, that make them more productive and bankable (Thurow, 1970). You can invest in human capital in a number of ways: going to college, taking a night class, or learning a trade.

Socialization

As we saw in Chapter 4, another function of schooling is to socialize young people. Schools pass down the values, beliefs, and attitudes that are important in American society. For example, think about all the things we learn through the rules and structure of school that are valued by American culture. Bells ring to ensure that we learn how to get to places on time, we are punished for cheating to reinforce the consequences of being dishonest, and we are taught to obey authority in the form of teachers and administrators. What's especially important about universal schooling (the fact that American public schools are free and mandatory until high school) is that most students in the country go through more or less the same socialization processes. This gives them a common background that is useful when they enter the workforce or other institutions where they must function collectively. For example, consider how difficult it would be to maintain an efficient society if some schools taught students to be punctual and others didn't. At some point when these students got together, whether at college or in the workplace, these different socialization experiences would lead to inevitable conflicts. In 1968, sociologist Phillip Jackson coined the term hidden curriculum to describe these nonacademic and less overt socialization functions of schooling. According to Roland Meighan (1981), "The hidden curriculum is taught by the school, not by any teacher. . . . [S]omething is coming across to the pupils which may never be spoken in the English lesson or prayed about in assembly. They are picking up an approach to living and an attitude to learning."

Hidden curriculum the nonacademic and less overt socialization functions of schooling.

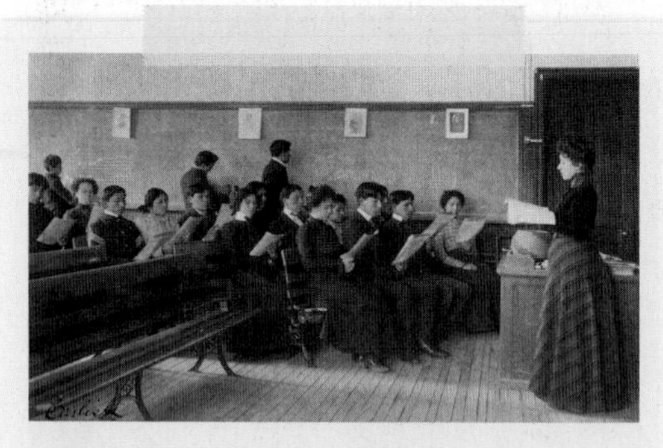

Boarding schools like the Carlisle Indian Industrial School were dedicated to inducing Native American children to abandon their traditional cultures.

Because of their ability to instill similar values in students, schools have been viewed as excellent places to integrate immigrants and other outsiders and instill dominant cultural values. Take, for example, the extreme case of the original inhabitants of this place: American Indians. As the country expanded westward in the 1800s, Americans racked their brains over how to best assimilate the people who populated those lands (after forced relocation, small-pox inoculation, and all-out warfare failed to eradicate tribal groups altogether). Their solution? Send them to school! Under the banner of "Kill the Indian, save the child," Americans set up boarding schools, such as the Carlisle Indian Industrial School in Pennsylvania, that took children as young as six away from their families to teach them more "civilized" ways of life. The prescribed regimen for assimilation included forbidding the children to speak their own language, placing the schools far from children's homes to prevent the continued influence of American Indian culture, disparaging native practices, encouraging Christianity, and generally praising the superiority of white ways. These schools flourished for some 60 years (from 1870 to the early 1930s) before Americans started to express discontent over the education American Indians were receiving, complaining that it was too expensive and encouraged dependency rather than self-sufficiency. Today, there are still seven federally funded boarding schools for elementary and secondary education that receive more applications than they can accommodate. Additionally, there are now tribally run schools on some reservations where students learn tribal languages and culture in small classes with other American Indian students (Bear, 2008).

Initiatives for educating native populations were not specific to the United States. Between 1910 and 1970 in Australia, an estimated 100,000 Aboriginal and "half-caste" children were taken from their families and made legal wards of the state. Most were subsequently placed in British-run camps or schools with the stated purpose of culturally assimilating the kids, collectively referred to as the "stolen generation," into white society (Human Rights and Equal Opportunity Commission, 1997). The plight of these Aboriginal families has been dramatized in the book *Follow the Rabbit-Proof Fence* (1996; later the 2002 movie *Rabbit-Proof Fence*), written by Doris Pilkington (Nugi Garimara), the daughter of a woman who had escaped one such residential school as a young girl (along with two others) and walked a remarkable 1,500 miles to rejoin her family. Ten years later the heroine was taken into custody a second time—and again she escaped and survived the same journey. In 2008, newly elected Prime Minister Kevin Rudd of Australia formally apologized for these policies but stopped short of promising compensation.

Homes Are Sought For These Children

A GROUP OF TINY HALF-CASTE AND QUADROON CHILDREN at the Darwin half-caste home. The Minister for the Interior (Mr Perkins) recently appealed to charitable organisations in Melbourne and Sydney to find homes for the children and rescue them from becoming outcasts.

I like the little girl in centre of group, but if taken by anyone else, any of the others would do, as long as they are strong

Six Aborigine girls are put up for adoption in a 1934 newspaper.

Although nothing this extreme would likely take place today in the West, using school to socialize students to accept dominant cultural values is still seen by some in a sinister light. According to certain Marxist theorists, schools are unwitting pawns of the capitalist classes and teach the skills that are conducive to maintaining dominant and subordinate positions in the workforce, such as self-discipline, obedience, punctuality, and dependability (Bowles & Gintis, 1976). And perhaps, to a certain extent, they do. However, you might point out that not all positions require the same skills: What if your job does not require you to be subordinate or obedient? In fact, what if it requires you to hold authority over others or pursue unconventional thinking?

Some theorists answer this question by suggesting that schools first sort students according to their future jobs and then teach them the skills necessary for those positions. In his influential work *Power and Morality* (Sorokin & Lunden, 1959), Pitirim Sorokin argued that schools are sorting machines: First they test students for ability, talent, and social and moral character. Then they eliminate students who aren't up to snuff while promoting the best and brightest. Once sorted, students are taught different skills and socialized in the ways deemed most appropriate for their likely future positions. Thus, if students show an aptitude for working with their hands, they may be placed in a vocational or mechanical program. Likewise, students who are intellectually exceptional may be placed in a school's gifted and talented program. Students, in their respective programs, then start learning the skills and behaviors necessary for success in their future careers.

If this were strictly the case, the sorting machine wouldn't be so bad: Schools would use students' talents, skills, and other aptitudes to place them in the programs that would best prepare them for the future. Unfortunately, however, some theorists suggest that schools don't sort students solely according to their merits; instead, they contend that schools divide them in ways that reproduce the kinds of inequalities we examined in Chapter 7. Thus, for example, schools may tend to disproportionately sort lower-class students into vocational classes that feed them into blue-collar positions. These positions essentially put them right back where they started from—the lower class.

A striking example of this sorting process was recounted by Jonathon Kozol, who toured public schools in several large American cities between 1988 and 1990 and then recounted his observations in *Savage Inequalities* (1991). In one school in New York City, he noticed that black students were disproportionately sorted into special education classes that focused on teaching vocational skills. According to the principal, in addition to learning woodworking, the "children learn to punch in time cards at the door . . . in order to prepare them for employment." Having been sorted, these students were taught the skills that educators thought would best prepare them for their specific futures. However, the fact that these students were mostly black and, tellingly, only in elementary school calls into question the extent to which these decisions were based solely on students' merits.

→ Do Schools Matter?

> The school is . . . in a former roller skating rink. . . . The lobby is long and narrow. . . . There are no windows. The principal . . . tells me that the school's "capacity" is 900 but that there are 1,300 children here. The size of

> classes for fifth and sixth grade children in New York, she says, is "capped" at 32, but she says that the class size in the school goes "up to 34." (I later see classes, however, as large as 37.) . . . Textbooks are scarce and children have to share their social studies books. . . . The carpets are patched and sometimes taped together to conceal an open space. . . . Two first grade classes share a single room without a window, divided only by a blackboard. . . . The library is a tiny, windowless and claustrophobic room. (Kozol, 1991, pp. 85–87)

> The dogwoods and magnolias on the lawn in front of P.S. 24 are in full blossom on the day I visit. . . . The school serves 825 students in the kindergarten through sixth grade. . . . This is . . . a great deal smaller than the 1,300 children packed into the former skating rink; but the principal . . . still regards it as excessive for an elementary school. . . . The district can't afford librarians but P.S. 24, unlike the poorer schools of District 10, can draw on educated parent volunteers who staff the room in shifts three days a week. A parent organization also raises independent funds to buy materials, including books. . . . There is a computer in each class [except in the special education classes]. (Kozol, 1991, pp. 92, 94–95)

The two public schools are both in New York City, the first in a poor section and the second in an affluent neighborhood. As these descriptions so vividly demonstrate, all schools are not created equal, and these differences are likely to affect educational outcomes. For example, after reading the descriptions of the elementary schools above, which students do you think will do better in school? Those in the "roller skating" school, who have to share textbooks and classrooms, or those in P.S. 24, where most classrooms have their own computers? Most of us would probably guess that students in schools with more advantages get a better education than those in less adequately equipped schools.

An overcrowded school in Brooklyn (left) and students in art class at an elite Manhattan private school.

The Coleman Report

What if I told you that while achievement differences most likely exist between the students at these two schools, research has determined that few, if any, of the differences described above actually affect educational outcomes? Such was the finding of a landmark sociological study known as the Coleman Report (Coleman et al., 1966). The study was conducted in 1964, nearly 10 years after *Brown v. Board of Education* (the Supreme Court ruling that mandated the desegregation of schools), and at a time when public schools throughout the nation were still highly segregated. Furthermore, achievement gaps between black and white schools remained high. Suspecting that these gaps could be explained by measurable differences between the schools blacks and whites attended (e.g., textbook availability and classroom size), the government commissioned a study. The results of the research were surprising even to James Coleman himself. To put it succinctly, the researchers found that differences in resources between schools didn't matter. Derived from surveys of 600,000 students in 4,000 schools and an examination of the facilities, school curricula, administration, and extracurricular activities at each school, the data indicated that school characteristics explained, if anything, only a tiny amount of the differences in educational outcomes among schools. Instead, the researchers determined that most of the differences in achievement among schools could be attributed to two factors: family background (which we'll come back to later in the chapter) and the other peers with whom students attended school (which is highly correlated with family background). Black students fared better in majority-white schools, and lower-income children did better in middle-class schools.

These findings were a bombshell in the education world. After all, American ideology tells us that schools are the place where students from all walks of life get a fair shot at obtaining a good education. And if they don't, we'd expect studies to pick up on the differences among schools that explain educational inequalities. But researchers couldn't deny the findings: Even those who reanalyzed Coleman's data arrived at similar results (e.g., Jencks et al., 1972). Schools entered an era of underappreciation, but researchers wouldn't let the issue drop. They just couldn't believe that schools, especially when they were so clearly different, didn't affect educational outcomes, so they refined their research methods and data collection tools. It did not take long for the new, improved studies to show links between students' achievement outcomes and school characteristics.

Class Size

Perhaps the most widely celebrated example of how schools affect educational achievement comes from the research conducted during Project STAR, a longitudinal, four-year study begun in 1985 by the Tennessee State

Department of Education. In the study, students and teachers from kindergarten through third grade were randomly assigned to small classes (13–17), regular-sized classes (22–26), or regular-sized classes with a teacher's aide. Various researchers then examined the short- and long-term consequences of smaller class size. The results provided evidence that schools with smaller classes significantly benefited their students compared to schools with larger classes.

Specifically, the researchers found that even after returning to regular classes, students in the study assigned to smaller classes experienced significantly fewer disciplinary problems and significantly higher achievement test scores than nonparticipants (Nye et al., 1994). The researchers also determined that these benefits were long lasting. Students who were placed in the smaller classes for all four years of the study had significantly higher graduation rates (Finn et al., 2005) and were more likely to take an ACT or SAT exam, which researchers used as a crude measure for determining whether students planned to attend college (Krueger & Whitmore, 2001). Finally, in terms of both the short- and long-term benefits, researchers found that the effects were particularly strong for minority students and those from low-income families.

Private Schools versus Public Schools

Aside from Project STAR, much of the newer evidence on the importance of school effects derives from studies comparing public schools with private schools. Although some parents send their children to private schools for non-educational (e.g., religious) reasons, many do so because they believe the quality of education is higher than in public schools, and they're willing to invest money in it. In fact, the costs of some private schools rival those of an Ivy League education. Many New York City private elementary and high schools charge over $37,000 a year, exceeding Harvard's tuition rates.

What do you get for 40 grand a year? Columbia University sociologist Shamus Khan studied one of the most elite boarding schools in the nation, St. Paul's (his own alma mater), by accepting a teaching position there in order to conduct ethnographic research. We spoke about the findings about elite educational institutions that he reports in his book, *Privilege: The Making of an Adolescent Elite at St. Paul's School* (2010):

> [One] way to think about a place like St. Paul's is that it converts birthright into credentials. It provides [advantaged students] with a degree of legitimacy. So people who didn't go to St. Paul's can look at that kid and say, "Well I know he came from a well-off background, but he worked really hard. He went to this amazing high school, and he went to this amazing college and that's why he is where he is." (Conley, 2011e)

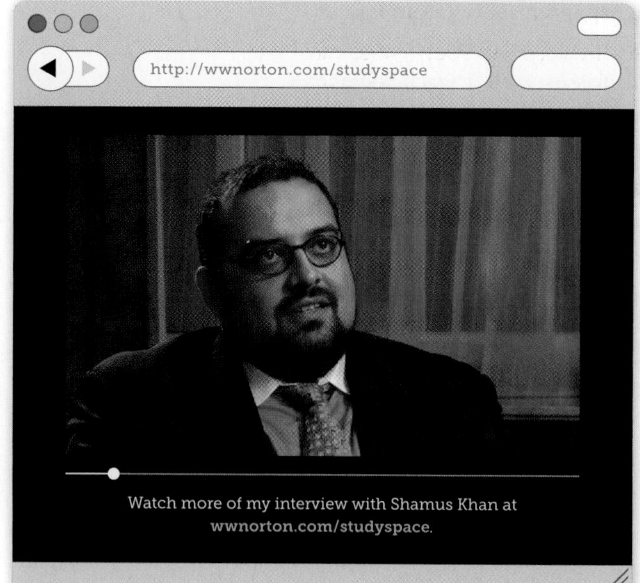

Watch more of my interview with Shamus Khan at wwnorton.com/studyspace.

According to Khan, however, the story is slightly more complicated. He elaborates:

> I've one big caution about thinking about them that way though: There're also lots of people who go to these institutions who aren't from families like [the typical] St. Paul's [students]. And so even if what St. Paul's does is convert the birthright of some people into credentials, that's not all [such schools] do. [They also] allow for advancement of many people at the institution who weren't born with such advantages, who do achieve a lot by going there. (Conley, 2011e)

Of course, the sociologist knows this dose of upward mobility and meritocracy is exactly what gives elite schools their "legitimating function"—otherwise they'd just be places for rich kids and known as such. Aside from whatever legitimating function they may serve, are private schools really better academically than public ones, or are wealthy parents ultimately deluding themselves and needlessly spending thousands of dollars per year in the process? Once we move beyond the benefits that Khan shows, the story is more complicated. Several studies (e.g., Bryk et al., 1993; Coleman & Hoffer, 1987; Coleman et al., 1982) have found that school sector (private versus public) is associated with educational outcomes even after students' different backgrounds are taken into account. However, the exact details of these effects are somewhat unexpected. After dividing the private institutions into Catholic and non-Catholic schools, researchers determined that Catholic schools (which are generally among the least expensive private schools) were the most successful in preparing students academically, particularly students from disadvantaged backgrounds (e.g., minority students and those from lower socioeconomic strata). For example, these studies found that Catholic school students scored the highest on achievement tests, followed by secular private school and public school students (Coleman et al., 1982), respectively. Thus, private schools may have an impact, but not necessarily according to how expensive they are.

How do we explain these sector differences? Are the plaid designs on some private school uniforms cognitively stimulating? According to researchers, a more plausible explanation is that certain academic and behavioral differences between private and public schools predict educational outcomes. For example, researchers determined that private school students did more homework, had a greater chance of being enrolled in academic programs, and took more college preparatory classes than public school students. Behaviorally, private school students had better attendance, became involved in fewer fights, and threatened teachers less than public school students. James S. Coleman and Thomas Hoffer (1987) also suggest that the strong effects of the Catholic schools stem from the large amounts of social capital in the community—that is, any relationship between people that can facilitate the actions of others (see Chapter 5). In the case of Catholic schools, Coleman and Hoffer (1987), as well as Anthony Bryk, Valerie Lee, and Peter Holland (1993), hypothesize that the closeness of the Catholic community reinforces among teachers, parents, and students behaviors and norms that are conducive to learning. Alternatively, it could just be that families who value education the most and are most able to get their kids into a private school are the families whose kids would succeed no matter what schools they attended; in this paradigm, schools again act as social sorting machines rather than having important effects of their own. In fact, recent evidence from private school scholarship lotteries suggests that this last explanation may indeed be the most accurate (see pp. 531–32). Hence, Khan's parents may only be getting the ideology of a better education for their money.

Social capital the information, knowledge of people, and connections that help individuals enter, gain power in, or otherwise leverage social networks.

However, as researchers studied these differences among schools, they came across another impressive finding: Differences among students *within* schools (e.g., in achievement scores) were significantly greater (as much as four times as large) than the differences among students *between* schools (Coleman et al., 1966; Jencks et al., 1972). Let's turn now to what goes on inside a school that could explain these extreme differences.

What's Going On Inside Schools?

The Sorting Machine Revisited: Tracking

Earlier we talked about schools as sorting machines, placing students such that existing social structures would be reproduced. If you attended a typical comprehensive American high school, it is likely that much of this sorting was achieved through tracking, a way of dividing students into different classes by ability or future plans. School subjects might be divided by the level of ability required (high or low) or the type of preparation (academic, vocational, or general). For example, if you are college-bound, you may be sorted into honors, or college preparation, classes. Dividing students into different tracks is instrumental in both preparing them for their future positions and explaining the large differences we observe among students within schools.

Tracking a way of dividing students into different classes by ability or future plans.

Tracking is intended to create a better learning environment, because students' goals are matched to their curricula. Sounds reasonable. And research has determined that tracking has significant impacts even after controlling

A second-grade teacher in Phoenix gives remedial help in English to students whose first language is not English. Creating separate remedial classes is an example of tracking. What are the benefits and consequences of tracking?

for background characteristics. For example, Adam Gamoran and Robert Mare (1989) found that students in their school's college track had significantly higher math achievement and were more likely to graduate from high school. Furthermore, James Rosenbaum (1980) determined that tracking significantly predicted whether students attended college. Finally, Richard Arum and Yossi Shavit (1995) ascertained that students who graduated from vocational tracks were less likely to be unemployed and more likely to enter the workforce as skilled laborers. Of course, we can't know for sure whether it was the lessons learned in the respective tracks that drove these results or whether the tracking system itself is merely good at sorting students by future promise.

But tracking has a dark side. First, notice that none of the positive benefits we've reviewed above involve the general track. This in-between track, preparing students for neither work nor college, seems to provide no benefits to students. Second, researchers have discovered that students from privileged backgrounds are significantly more likely to be in college tracks even after taking into account variables that should predict track placement, including achievement (Gamoran & Mare, 1989; Lucas, 1999). Furthermore, because race, ethnicity, and class are so intertwined, higher-class whites are usually overrepresented in academic tracks, and black, Hispanic, and lower-class students are overrepresented in noncollege tracks (O'Connor, 2009). But if privileged students aren't placed in the highest tracks based on merit, why are they so overrepresented in these classes? Qualitative research (e.g., Lareau, 2003) suggests that middle-class parents actively intervene in school matters to obtain the best advantages for their children. For example, they might request that their child be placed in the highest track despite mediocre achievement because they are more likely to be college graduates and know how important the college track is for their child's future. Or, in diverse schools, these parents might want to separate their children from the minority and lower-class students in the lower tracks (Oakes, 1985).

Steven Morgan looked at students in private Catholic schools to see if he could tease out the relationship between academic achievement, religiosity, and parental involvement. He chose Catholic schools because "what's interesting about Catholic schools in the US is there are quite a few non-Catholic students enrolled in them, and those are the students that seem to do particularly well in Catholic school" (Conley, 2009l) even though it might seem harder for non-Catholic students to fit in with disciplinary and cultural expectations at a Catholic school, thus making it harder for them to focus on their school work. Morgan attributes the success of the non-Catholic students to their parents' desire to see them succeed academically. These non-Catholic kids in Catholic schools are kids who, he says, "are particularly ambitious and they have a belief that the Catholic schools are better in a lot of areas and in fact they may have a more demanding curriculum" (Conley, 2009l). The evidence from non-Catholic students consistently outdoing their Catholic peers suggests that parents' goals for their children may play a large role in the kids' educational success, casting some doubt on just how much tracking benefits high-performing students. Maybe those in the higher track would have been equally successful had their school forgone tracking and kept all the students together.

http://wwnorton.com/studyspace

Steven Morgan. To see an interview with Morgan, go to **wwnorton.com/studyspace**.

The research conducted by Jeannie Oakes (1985) has suggested that tracking might actually be bad because there are stark differences in the quality of teaching and content of materials between tracks. This is best illustrated by the answers students gave Oakes when she asked them to identify the most important thing they had learned or done in their classes. Typical answers from students in the high tracks included the following:

> I have learned a lot about molecules and now am able to reason and figure out more things.
>
> Things in nature are not always what they appear to be or what seems to be happening is not what really is happening.

Responses from students in the lower track included the following:

> How to ride motorcycles and shoot trap. [I don't know what trap is either.]
>
> To be honest, nothing.
>
> The only thing I've learned is how to flirt with the chicks in class. This class is a big waste of time and effort.
>
> How to blow up light bulbs. (Oakes, 1985, pp. 70–71)

We can see, then, why some have accused tracking of being an important factor in increasing or reproducing inequality (Gamoran & Mare, 1989). Although tracking gives some students educational advantages, it disproportionately awards these advantages to those who are already privileged. Minority and lower-class students are often left behind as a result, receiving inferior instruction and learning less in their classes.

Many educational systems in Western Europe take tracking a step further, sorting students into different schools altogether, in some countries as early as age 10. In Germany, for example, all students are required to enter *Grundschule* (literally, "ground school") at age six and attend for four years. At the end of the fourth grade, teachers recommend which type of secondary schooling is most appropriate for each child based primarily on academic performance. Unlike in the United States, however, in Germany the ultimate decision lies with a student's parents. Austria, Hungary, and the Slovak Republic follow a similar tracking model. Other countries, such as Canada, Japan, Norway, and the United Kingdom, have a system more akin to the United States' (Hanushek & Wößmann, 2006).

The Classroom Pressure Cooker

In addition to shedding light on some of the negative aspects of tracking, Oakes's study also demonstrates the importance of teacher-student and peer-to-peer dynamics in student experiences. In the United States, where schooling is not nationally standardized, individual teachers appear to matter a lot more to the intellectual dynamics of the classroom (Amanda E. Lewis in her 2004 study, in fact, compares the classroom to an individual "fiefdom"), so students in different classrooms might obtain different types of instruction that vary widely in their quality.

Teachers not only rule in their classroom kingdoms but also do so in an atmosphere of intense contact. Let's say, to be conservative, that teachers spend about 5 of the 6.5 hours in a typical school day with students. This means that over the course of a 185-day school year, teachers and students have more than 900 hours of sustained contact. Phillip Jackson described such an intense climate in the following way:

> There is a social intimacy [in the classrooms] . . . that is unmatched elsewhere in our society. Buses and movie theaters may be more crowded than classrooms, but people rarely stay in such densely populated settings for extended periods of time and while there, they usually are not expected to concentrate on work or to interact with each other. . . . Only in schools do thirty or more people spend several hours each day literally side by side. (Jackson, 1968, p. 8)

What we have in a classroom is the potential for a powerful pressure cooker: Students and teachers spend hours of their days together under the teachers' jurisdictions. What goes on inside will therefore play an important role in student outcomes. Let's look at the components of a classroom that affect student experiences.

Researchers have found that some teachers are more effective than others. However, identifying what qualities make a good teacher has been much more difficult. What methods might a sociologist use to explain why award-winning teachers such as Clyde Hashimoto (left) and Linda Alston (right) succeed where other teachers fail?

First, of course, there is the teacher. We know that some teachers are more effective than others, and research backs up this notion (e.g., Murnane et al., 2005; Rockoff, 2004; Schacter & Thum, 2004). Although researchers have identified the general effects of teachers in their statistical analyses, they've had much less luck pinpointing the exact characteristics of teachers that affect student achievement. For example, some studies have found that teachers' experience is significantly related to student achievement, but only in the first few years of teaching (Hanushek et al., 1998, 2005; Murnane et al., 2005). Furthermore, although some studies (Murnane et al., 2005) have determined that teachers' own educational background is related to student achievement, others (Hanushek et al., 1998, 2005) indicated no systematic pattern between the two.

Perhaps these researchers have been unable to consistently pinpoint characteristics of teacher quality because such characteristics are hard to quantify. For example, it is difficult to measure the routines that make a class run smoothly, teachers' ability to quiet disruptive students, or the tendency to give extra encouragement that differentiates one teacher from another. Therefore, to understand what makes a teacher effective, we'll have to turn away from studies that measure teacher quality with quantitative variables and instead examine research that has either created sophisticated experiments to test these effects or gone inside the classroom to observe what works.

For example, we could imagine that teachers who expect a lot from their students motivate them to work harder, but of course, the problem lies in measuring these expectations. One pair of researchers succeeded in doing so through a creative research design. In the early 1960s Robert Rosenthal and Lenore Jacobson (1968) visited an elementary school at the beginning of the academic year and administered IQ (intelligence quotient) tests, which measure cognitive abilities such as verbal and numerical reasoning and knowledge, to all the students. They then randomly selected one-fifth of the students and told the teachers that these students were especially bright and had particular potential for growth. (Remember, though, that in reality they had been selected at random.) At the end of the school year, the researchers retested the students and found that those who had been labeled "bright" did significantly better on the new IQ test than their peers. Furthermore, teachers rated these children as being more intellectually curious and happier, and needing less social approval.

What the researchers accomplished in this study was a rough quantification of how teacher expectations can affect student achievement. They confirmed that when teachers held higher expectations for certain students (and likely changed their behavior toward those children accordingly), these students responded by meeting teacher expectations. This process is called the Pygmalion effect or more commonly the self-fulfilling prophecy.

Unfortunately, the power of teachers' expectations and the self-fulfilling prophecy can work both ways. Although students might benefit from high expectations, their outcomes can also be depressed by low expectations. Moreover, teachers seem to have low expectations for certain groups of students more frequently—for example, boys, minorities, and lower-income youths—even when they have the same cognitive ability as students in other groups (e.g., Clifton et al., 1986).

Another way that one teacher might be more effective than another is through his or her instructional methods. Some teachers may prefer more traditional teaching styles, whereas others continually try out the latest strategies for effective teaching. Still others may invent their own strategies. Take, for example, what happened daily in a class profiled by Amanda Lewis (2004) in her study of elementary schools. While most classes in the study spent the morning reviewing academic material, students in one teacher's class gathered in a circle during the same time period to give each other compliments. However, when the class became rowdy, they were instructed to offer insults instead:

> Mr. Ortiz starts put-downs with Julio. Julio begins by telling Robin she's fat and ugly. Robin tells Thompson he's ugly. . . . Catherine tells Rebecca she doesn't like her earrings. She has to tell Darnell—Mr. Ortiz gives her several suggestions, melon head, etc. . . . Luis tells Lisa that she stinks. She tells Daniel that he dresses like a rag. He tells Rose that she farts too much. (Lewis, 2004, p. 47)

Maybe the creative strategy of prompting children to share compliments and insults will benefit some of them, but it is more likely that these students will fall behind children who are studying a more traditional curriculum. In fact, as Lewis's ethnography proceeded, she reported that the same class would sometimes go days without any formal science, social studies, or math instruction, with the students then lagging behind on basic skills.

What are some of the best practices that Donald Langlois and Charlotte Rappe Zales identified in their research on effective teaching? Why might these teaching styles be more effective than others?

Other teachers may opt for teaching styles that have been found to positively affect achievement. Teaching methods supported by extensive research are called best practices. For example, after analyzing more than 700 research papers from the 1980s, Donald E. Langlois and Charlotte Rappe Zales (1992) came up with a list of the most effective teaching methods. These included such approaches as minimizing lost class time to activities other than instruction (Mr. Ortiz seems to have missed that memo), having clear expectations for acceptable behavior and consistent consequences for misbehavior, maintaining a fixed routine, and setting high standards for class work.

Teachers are clearly an important element of classroom life, but we can't forget the many other people who are in the classroom—peers. Who attends a class and how they behave set a tone for the classroom environment. For example, a classroom might be run by one of the best teachers in the school, but if the students continually disrupt class, that teacher will have to take time away from teaching to address such problems. In fact, David Figlio (2005a) determined that more behavior problems in a classroom significantly increase other students' disciplinary problems and reduce their test scores.

Recall one of the key findings of the Coleman Report: The composition of students in a school significantly affected student outcomes. Nowhere would this be more applicable than in a classroom, where contact is longer and more intense as compared to schoolwide social interaction. Therefore, researchers have examined, in particular, how the academic characteristics of classmates affect their peers. For example, if low-achieving students are placed in a classroom with mostly high-achieving students, will they fall even farther behind or rise to the challenge? Research from numerous studies suggests that when students are in a classroom with others of high ability, all students profit. For example, Caroline Hoxby (2000) found that increases in peers' reading scores were successful in raising individual student scores. In another study, Ron W. Zimmer and Eugenia F. Toma (2000) determined that raising average ability in classrooms increased individual student achievement, particularly for low-ability students. Unfortunately, this effect works both ways. If you are in a classroom with mostly low-achieving students, research suggests that you will make fewer gains than you would in a classroom with more high-achieving students (Leiter, 1983). And we are back around again, appearing to promote tracking within schools and justify parents' decisions to pursue external tracking by placing their children in private schools.

Higher Education

The Rise and Rise of Higher Education: Credentialism

Consider this set of facts: In 1910, fewer than 3 percent of men and women over age 25 had a college degree. By 2010 this number had jumped to 19.4 percent of the population (U.S. Census Bureau, 2011b). In a relatively short time, this country has experienced a virtual educational boom. How can we explain these dramatic increases?

Functionalist Perspectives According to functionalists (who believe that everything in a society exists to fulfill a function; see Chapter 1), the rise of education boils down to simple supply and demand. As industrialization took hold throughout the twentieth century, jobs became more technical and required a more educated workforce. By attaining more education, students were simply responding to employer demand.

As clear-cut as this explanation is, it is not well backed by data. In his review of the literature, Randall Collins (1971) concludes that although the demands of industrialization did play a role in expanding the educational system, industrialization alone can't account for the extreme trends we've witnessed. For example, in contrast to what we'd expect from traditional functionalist theory, Collins finds that much of what students learn in school isn't related to their work, that necessary skills tend to be acquired on the job, and that many Americans have more education than they need for their occupations. Therefore, we must look elsewhere for a plausible explanation.

Conflict Perspectives According to the theorists who subscribe to the conflict perspective of education, in contrast, the dramatic increase in college graduation may be traced to American views on education and the expansion of the school system in the twentieth century. (Recall our discussion of conflict theory in Chapter 1.) Since colonial times education in the United States has been a badge of elite status (whereas in Europe, where class systems are more rigid, a fancy lineage could be a more important factor in gaining entrance into the elite). High levels of education signal to employers that you have been indoctrinated in the dominant group's values; thus, education is often used as a screen for top positions. In 1910, when 24 percent of people over age 25 had completed fewer than 5 years of elementary school and only 14 percent had completed high school or more (Snyder & Tan, 2005), maintaining an elite status through schooling meant perhaps completing high school. However, as the American educational system expanded throughout the century, higher levels of education became universal (Figure 13.1). By 2004 only 1.5 percent of the population 25 and older had completed fewer than 5 years of elementary school and 85 percent had completed high school or more (Snyder & Tan, 2005). This trend means that as education expanded, members of the elite—and those who wanted to move into the elite—had to obtain more and more education to set themselves apart from others (Collins, 1979).

Credentialism an overemphasis on credentials (e.g., college degrees) for signaling social status or qualifications for a job.

The conflict perspective also provides an explanation for the rise of credentialism or an overemphasis on credentials (e.g., college degrees) for

Figure 13.1: A Century of Higher Education Rates

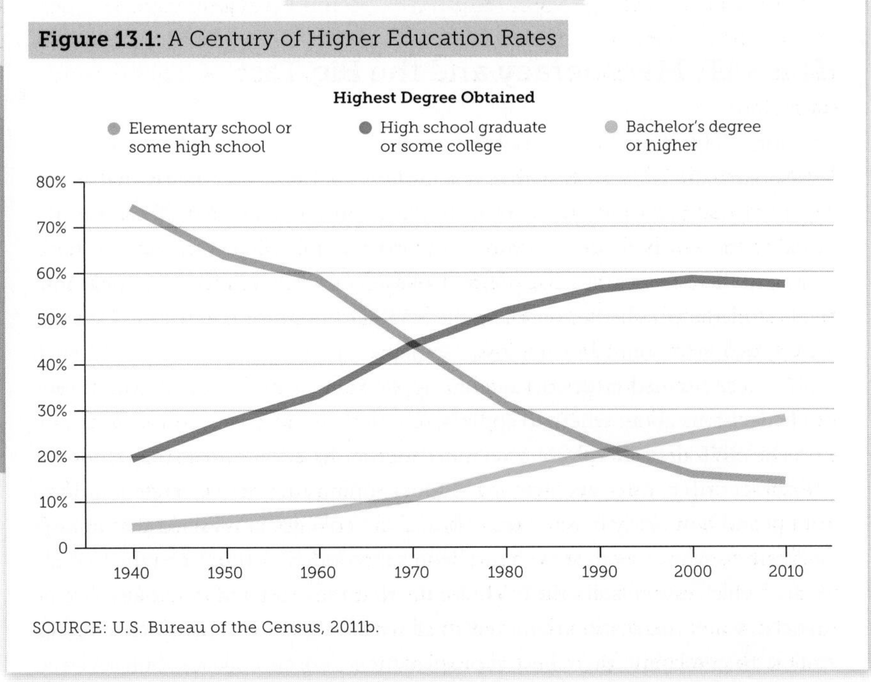

SOURCE: U.S. Bureau of the Census, 2011b.

signaling social status or job qualifications. When everybody attains so much education, employers tend to increase job requirements to screen out people. To do this, they rely more and more on credentials that signal both social status and area of specialty (the field in which your degree was awarded). According to Collins (1971, 1979), however, this upgrading does not reflect the increase in skills needed for particular jobs. The same jobs that 50 years ago required only a high-school diploma now require a college degree. Thus, people today often are overqualified for their jobs. (In fact, countless Web sites now exist that give advice on how to cope with being overqualified for your job.)

The upgrading of degree requirements by employers is a cycle reinforced by students who keep getting more education to meet employer minimum requirements. (Employers increase the requirements again when too many students reach this minimum level.) So how do we break the cycle? Clearly, students can't be expected to keep increasing their educational attainment, staying in school until their forties. Instead, trends point to people differentiating themselves academically not just through years of education but through quality of education, such as the selectivity or prestige of the college they attend. For example, Samuel R. Lucas and Aaron D. Good (2001) demonstrate that once education levels are saturated, members of the wealthier classes don't just move on to the next level of education: They also try to obtain the best education within that tier. Thus, at the high-school level, which is nearly universal, higher-class students attend private schools at higher rates or are placed in the highest tracks at school. Likewise, as the college tier becomes more saturated, there is more competition among students to get into the most selective schools.

The SAT: Meritocracy and the Big Test

In spring 2006 many high-school seniors' worst nightmare came true. The College Board, the organization that administers the SAT, announced that it had incorrectly scored more than 4,000 tests taken in October 2005. To add to the scandal, the errors tended toward the worst possible direction—underestimation, anywhere from 10 to 200 points. Colleges scrambled to reassess applicants, while students who hadn't yet taken the SAT signed up for two tests in case one was scored incorrectly. But for many students, the damage was done. Although colleges reexamined affected students' applications, some students had already made decisions about where to apply based on their incorrectly low scores.

The SAT debacle of 2006 reignited questions about a test that has been the subject of controversy for years. Questioning the merits of standardized testing and how fairly it assesses students, 731 colleges minimized the number of students who have to submit test scores (Setoodeh, 2006). Even the College Board, which administers the SAT, admits that the exam can provoke extreme anxiety, which the board attempted to alleviate in 2009 by giving students the option to send only their best scores to their chosen colleges. Still, even as more colleges gravitate away from the SAT, the test remains a pivotal part of the admissions process at most schools. Why?

According to the College Board, the SAT is a vital part of the admissions process because it helps predict a student's potential for college success above and beyond the typical measures, such as high-school GPA and class rank, which may vary widely among students from different schools. In particular, the SAT was designed to predict a student's grades freshman year. But does it live up to these promises? Apparently so. Research (Bowen & Bok, 1998; Zwick & Sklar, 2005) confirms that the SAT accurately predicts not only freshman year GPA but a variety of other outcomes, including class rank, likelihood of graduation, and a student's chance of obtaining an advanced degree.

Amanda Hecker, a high-school senior in New Jersey, was one of the students who learned that the College Board had scored her SAT incorrectly. Why do critics question the validity of tests like the SAT for judging college admissions?

If this is the case, why are critics so opposed to using these standardized tests for admissions? First, researchers note that the SAT does not, as the College Board asserts, predict college outcomes above and beyond high-school grades and class rank. For example, Rebecca Zwick and Jeffrey C. Sklar (2005) found that although the SAT was a significant predictor of freshman year GPA, one's high-school GPA was a stronger predictor. Other researchers (Crouse & Trusheim, 1988) have determined that if admissions counselors had looked only at high-school records to assess students, 84 percent of the time they would have made the same admissions decisions as when they used the SAT. In the 16 percent of cases that remained, low SAT scores were the determining factor in rejecting students, although they may not be the fairest way to eliminate candidates.

Second, even if the SAT generally predicts college outcomes pretty well, if we dig a little deeper, an intriguing pattern emerges. The SAT accurately predicts the college outcomes only for white students. It doesn't do as well in predicting outcomes such as college GPA for black and Hispanic students (Bowen & Bok, 1998; Pearson, 1993; Vars & Bowen, 1998; Zwick & Sklar, 2005).

Third, researchers question how meritocratic the SAT actually is. Do the scores reflect the abilities that *should* matter? Not necessarily. SAT scores are consistently correlated with race, ethnicity, and class. African Americans and Hispanics systematically score lower than white students, and higher-class students (who, among other things, can pay for SAT preparatory classes, which do increase scores) systematically score higher than lower-class students. Unless we're willing to believe that lower-class, black, and Hispanic students are inherently less intelligent, the SAT is biased toward certain groups of students. In fact, evidence exists that negative stereotypes of minority groups play an important role in explaining at least some of the differences in test scores—this is called stereotype threat, a particular form of test anxiety. At this point,

I am compelled to point out the extreme irony of this situation. The SAT was originally created to give the child who attends local public schools the chance to show that he or she is just as "able" as the kid who went to an elite, private high school. Back in 1933 Harvard sought to cast a wider net than the handful of elite private schools that had routinely provided most of its undergraduate population. The solution was to come up with a more "objective" standard, set by an institution external to the university itself. Thus, it was in this spirit of meritocracy that the SAT was born.

Finally, much of the predictive power of the SAT stems from the correlation between the test and family background. When studies control for family background (meaning that they calculate how much the SAT would predict if all students came from the same backgrounds), the SAT's predictive power diminishes. That is, the SAT might appear to predict college grades, but part of that effect derives from the fact that students from families with higher incomes generally get better grades *and* higher SAT scores. In fact, researchers have found that background characteristics map onto SAT scores so well that using them to predict outcomes instead of the SAT would work equally well. For example, economist Jesse Rothstein (2004) determined that high-school GPA and school and individual demographic information predict freshman year GPA just as well as using only the high-school GPA and SAT score. Thus, Rothstein (2004) points out that college admissions officers would choose the best-prepared class by explicitly admitting higher-class students from wealthier schools, rather than just using SATs as a proxy for these background characteristics. This solution would save everybody a lot of time, money, and anxiety, but, of course, it would cast a dark shadow over the SAT's purported meritocratic nature.

Given all the evidence against the predictive power of the SAT and its inability to assess students fairly, we return to our original question: Why do colleges use the SAT as an admissions practice? Part of the reason may be that for colleges that receive many applications, using a numerical cutoff substantially lessens their workload. Others (Crouse & Trusheim, 1988) suggest that the longevity of the SAT is merely a testament to the ability of the College Board to sell its product. In any event, the SAT debacle of 2006 put these issues on the table and may indeed spur a reassessment of the test's importance in the college admissions process.

Affirmative Action: Myths and Reality

In a study of admissions practices at elite schools, Thomas Espenshade, Chang Chung, and Joan Walling (2004) found that group A was four times as likely to be admitted as other students and that group B was three times as likely to be admitted. Not only were these groups more likely to gain admission to elite schools, but they did so despite having lower SAT scores than other applying students. Given all that we have heard about preferential admissions practices, you might assume that these preferences were given to minority students. Group A perhaps was made up of black students, and group B Latinos. This assumption, however, would be wrong. In this study, applicants in group A were athletes, whereas those in group B were legacies, children of alumni parents or close relatives. Both groups were disproportionately white.

A pair of future presidents: George Bush carries his infant son George W. Bush on his shoulders at the Yale University campus. George W. Bush would later attend Yale (like his father). Why do you think legacy students receive preferential treatment when applying for college?

As we saw in Chapter 9 on race, affirmative action refers to a set of policies that grant preferential treatment to a number of particular subgroups within the population. Affirmative action is intended to level the playing field for historically underrepresented groups, such as certain racial minorities and women (although women now make up a majority of American college students). Often, affirmative action is thought to be the only form of preferential treatment. As we have seen from the example above, this is a myth. In reality, schools give preferential treatment based on many characteristics, not just race or ethnicity. There are preferences not only for being a legacy or an athlete but also for exhibiting leadership experience, living in a certain place such as a rural community, or even having unusual life circumstances (Fetter, 1995; Freedman, 2003; Zwick, 2002). (Yale Taliban, anyone? He had a rural background and demonstrated leadership *and* unusual life circumstances, to say the least.) Furthermore, in many cases, these preferences are equal to or higher than those given to African American and Hispanic students (Bowen & Bok, 1998; Espenshade et al., 2004).

Affirmative action a set of policies that grant preferential treatment to a number of particular subgroups within the population—typically, women and historically disadvantaged racial minorities.

Another myth is that affirmative action takes away opportunities from deserving white students. To address this myth, we should first establish a little-known fact about which institutions are affected by affirmative action. Research (Kane, 1998) has found that affirmative action is an issue only at selective institutions that represent only one-fifth of American colleges. Why? Because the majority of schools in the United States admit just about everyone. Economist Thomas J. Kane (1998) determined that at the least selective colleges in his sample, being black or Hispanic gave little to no advantage in college admissions.

Does this mean that affirmative action takes away slots in elite schools from deserving white students? Not necessarily. Kane gives the following analogy:

> Suppose that one parking space in front of a popular restaurant is for disabled drivers. Many of the non-disabled drivers who pass by the space while circling the parking lot in search of a place to park may be tempted to think that they would have an easier time finding a space if the space had not

> been reserved. Although eliminating the space would have only a minuscule effect on the average parking search for non-disabled drivers, the cumulative cost perceived by each passing driver is likely to exceed the true cost simply because people have a difficult time thinking about small probability events. (Kane, 1998, p. 453)

What is the actual probability of the "small probability event," the increased chance that a white student would have in gaining admission to elite schools if affirmative action was abolished? According to Espenshade and Chung (2005), abolishing affirmative action would increase a white student's chances of acceptance by only 0.5 percent. The real gain would occur among Asian students, who are not considered part of a historically underrepresented minority group in colleges and whose grades and test scores tend to exceed those of whites. Asians' acceptance rates would increase from 18 to 23 percent.

A third myth is that African American and Hispanic students who gain entrance to selective schools through affirmative action are underprepared and will flounder in the competitive environment. The literature here presents mixed results. On the one hand, numerous researchers have found that black and Hispanic students whose background characteristics, SAT scores, and high-school GPAs are equivalent to those of white students have lower college GPAs (Bowen & Bok, 1998; Kane, 1998). However, these researchers also determined that the more selective the schools that blacks and Hispanics attended, the greater their chances of graduation. Students in more selective schools were also more likely to go on to earn professional or doctoral degrees (Bowen & Bok, 1998). An important question is how minority students fare once they leave school. Here again, the contrast with athletes and legacies is informative. In *The Shape of the River* (1998), William G. Bowen and Derek Bok demonstrate that minority students admitted with lower SAT scores than their nonminority counterparts perform equally well as life marches on in a variety of contexts and measures, ranging from professional achievement to community service, but not as well in others, such as income. By contrast, student athletes, James Shulman and William G. Bowen tell us in *The Game of Life: College Sports and Educational Values* (2002), are admitted with the lowest average SAT scores of all groups and perform worse than their higher-scoring, nonathlete counterparts in terms of educational outcomes, yet they end up earning more money. These disparities probably exist because there are many more determinants of post-schooling income than the kind of education people receive or how well they perform in school—namely, the class resources of their families. Minorities in elite colleges may disproportionately come from lower-class families, and athletes may, on average, come from more advantaged families.

Despite the amount of data that refute affirmative action myths, an ongoing belief in them has contributed to the recent dismantling of many affirmative action programs. How will this affect minority students if the trend continues? Presumably, fewer African American and Hispanics would be admitted to selective colleges. With systematically lower SAT scores than whites (the reasons for these test score gaps are explored in more detail in the next section), these students would be at an immediate disadvantage. According to Espenshade and Chung (2005), eliminating affirmative action would decrease black and Hispanic acceptance rates by one-half to two-thirds. The decreased presence of minority students on these campuses would limit diversity and the attendant opportunities for interaction and dispelling of stereotypes.

Intelligence or IQ?

Intelligence that is related to educational outcomes is generally measured using a standardized IQ test. But IQ is measured with a test, just like the SATs, and it is worth considering if IQ tests are plagued with difficulties, just like the SATs. Can we trust IQ tests to be reliable? In short, not really. First, the IQ test measures only one kind of intelligence. What about the ability to think creatively or understand complicated scientific concepts? These types of intelligence might also be relevant to academic achievement. Howard Gardner (1983) has even suggested the theory of multiple intelligences to account for such aptitudes, but we confront a roadblock when deciding how to accurately assess them.

Second, most sociologists have criticized IQ tests for being culturally biased toward those with white, middle-class knowledge. In other words, the test reflects the knowledge that the dominant group in a society deems worthy of being called intelligence. For example, in the 1960s the Stanford-Binet IQ test included a question that asked respondents to answer which of two females was prettier. The first image showed a woman with blond hair and blue eyes; the second a woman with darker skin and larger lips. Although such obviously biased cultural references have since been purged from most exams, more subtle ones may remain.

Finally, even the updated IQ tests we use don't measure innate (i.e., genetically determined) intelligence. By the time children are tested, they have interacted with their environment in ways that have affected their cognitive development. In fact, even if a test was developed that could be administered within the first few minutes of birth, it might not measure innate intelligence. If the proponents of "womb music" are right, mothers who sing or play music while pregnant stimulate their fetuses' brains, perhaps leading to higher IQ scores.

Inequalities in Schooling

Throughout this chapter I've demonstrated that numerous inequalities in schooling exist. Minority and lower-class students are disproportionately placed in low tracks, are the subject of less favorable teacher expectations, and consistently score lower on the SAT. However, we have yet to explore the reasons behind such inequalities. The following sections focus on some of the ways background characteristics, over which students themselves have no control, affect educational outcomes. Be warned that the strength of these effects is much greater than the American ideology of equal opportunity for all would suggest.

Class

Social class or **socioeconomic status (SES)** an individual's position in a stratified social order.

As we saw in Chapter 7, social class has long been thought to socialize students into different achievement profiles and distinct schooling trajectories. Social class or socioeconomic status (SES), an individual's position in a stratified social order, is composed of any combination of parental educational attainment, parental occupational status (e.g., janitor versus doctor), family income, and family wealth. Students whose parents have higher levels of any of these four measures of class generally enjoy better educational opportunities. Higher-class students obtain more years of schooling (Conley, 2001), get better grades (Arum, 2003), are more likely to complete high school before age 19 (Conley, 1999), score higher on cognitive tests (Chase-Lansdale et al., 1997), and, as mentioned earlier, are more likely to be placed in higher tracks (Gamoran & Mare, 1989; Lucas, 1999).

A high-school student meets with a private college admissions consultant. Children from wealthier families benefit from being able to devote additional resources to help position their children to succeed at school.

But how do these advantages work? Clearly, teachers don't receive a list with each student's social class in order to assign grades according to their ranking by social class. Instead, most of the effects of social class are mediated through other factors that affect educational achievement. For example, SAT scores are mediators between class and college outcomes. Class affects SAT scores, and SAT scores affect college admissions.

Let's start with some of the straightforward advantages, such as the benefits of money. If your parents have a higher income, they may be able to afford extra tutoring if you're lagging behind. They could pay for SAT prep courses (Kaplan, one of the largest test-prep services, charges about $1,000 per comprehensive course) and hand scoring ($50 for the essay section and $50 for the multiple choice section) to ensure that the College Board doesn't screw up again. They might even enlist the services of a college consultant, who may charge up to $40,000, according to Bloomberg Businessweek, to get you into the best college. Likewise, if your parents are wealthy, they can liquidate or borrow against stocks and bonds or mortgage their house to pay for your college education, buy another house in a better school district, or send you to a private school. The same goes for parental education. More educated parents may feel comfortable helping their children with homework through high school, whereas less educated parents may have difficulty with the assignments as they become more difficult. As you might imagine, these factors overlap and are cumulative; for example, parents with more income, wealth, and education can afford tutors and the best schools and provide more extensive help with homework.

Cultural Capital A more subtle way that social class is related to educational outcomes is through the importance of cultural capital, the symbolic and interactional resources that people use to their advantage in various situations (Bourdieu, 1977; Lareau, 1987, 2003). Pierre Bourdieu, who coined the term, recognized three distinct types of cultural capital: embodied, objectified, and institutionalized. In the first type, the skill rests in our body—hence, the term *embodied*. For example, if you learn to play the piano, that "competency" is a form of embodied cultural capital. The piano itself serves as an example of objectified cultural capital, because it required a significant investment of time and money to acquire. Cultural capital becomes institutionalized when it is legitimated through a formal system, such as education: for example, when you are accepted into an elite music conservatory because of your piano-playing ability.

Cultural capital symbolic and interactional resources that people use to their advantage in various situations.

Much cultural capital, however, is not as straightforward as piano playing. Some important aspects of embodied cultural capital include the ability to deal with bureaucracies (such as the school system itself), confidence in public social settings, and even a sense of entitlement. In a school setting, many of these advantages work in concert with the rewards that schools give to students with values and expectations aligned with those of the institution. For example, teachers tend to place a high emphasis on parental involvement (e.g., volunteering in classrooms or reading to children) because it improves students' educational outcomes (Lareau,

1987). However, research has found that middle- and upper-class parents have much higher levels of involvement than lower-class parents. This is not because higher-class parents have more desire for their children to succeed but because they agree with the idea that schooling responsibilities should be shared and they may have more time to be involved. In contrast, according to Annette Lareau (2003), working-class parents more often believe that educational responsibility falls solely on teachers, and thus they may not be as involved. This disparity may be compounded by the greater intimidation that lower-SES parents might experience in the face of bureaucracies (such as the educational system) and authorities (such as teachers and principals)—that is, their lower degree of cultural capital.

Numerous studies have pinpointed other ways that cultural capital from the home confers academic advantages. For example, Lareau determined that middle-class parents ask their children many questions, reason with them in the hope of persuading them to do certain things, elicit opinions, and, in general, speak more often using a wider vocabulary with their children. Conversely, lower-class families use more directives and fewer words. However, because schools value verbal ability and use middle-class speech patterns (eliciting opinions from students by following Socratic teaching methods), students accustomed to this verbal style generally enjoy advantages in school. Keep in mind that behaviors rewarded by schools are not necessarily what are "right" or "correct." Values about schooling vary according to the historical period (not long ago corporal punishment was considered a valid disciplinary tool for all students). In another period, children who quietly accepted directives and didn't share their opinions would have been considered respectful, a quality that may have been more valued by the school system at the time.

Similarly, schools tend to reward middle-class knowledge obtained outside school. Consider a game that took place in an elementary school class. The teacher gave clues about states, and students raised their hands to answer. White students dominated the game; few minority students ever raised their hands. Lewis (2004) attributed this not to differences in learning that occurred in the classroom but to the advantages that the white and middle-class students had carried over from their home life. In answering the questions, these students talked about the states as places they had visited, where relatives lived, or where parents had gone to college.

The cultural capital that derives from higher social class is also important to the interactions that parents and students have with schools. Lareau (2003) and Lewis (2004) have found that upper- and middle-class parents have more informal interactions with teachers and are much more comfortable during interactions than lower-class parents. Because middle- and upper-class parents' class positions are similar to teachers', both parties may feel more comfortable interacting with each other. It is also more likely that parents from these classes see teachers as their equals or even as inferiors, and this perception, among other factors, gives them a sense of entitlement to judge teachers and actively intervene in their children's schooling to gain advantages for them (as discussed in the section on tracking). For example, Lewis (2004) writes of a mother who went to a parent-teacher conference, challenged a particular grade the teacher had given her daughter, and successfully persuaded the teacher to increase it, whereas a lower-SES parent might not have felt empowered to intervene in this manner.

Race

Bill Cosby is angry. Gone are his days of colorful sweaters and Jell-O commercials. The new Cosby is on a mission: fighting against black underachievement in the American school system. In a controversial speech delivered on May 17, 2004, at the NAACP's gala to commemorate the fiftieth anniversary of *Brown v. Board of Education*, Cosby inflamed the crowd by blaming African American parents and students themselves for achievement gaps:

> And these people are not parenting. They're buying things for the kid—$500 sneakers—for what? They won't buy or spend $250 on *Hooked on Phonics*. . . . *Brown v. Board of Education* is no longer the white person's problem. We've got to take the neighborhood back. We've got to go in there. . . . *Brown v. Board of Education*—these people who marched and were hit in the face with rocks and punched in the face to get an education, and we got these knuckleheads walking around who don't want to learn English. (Cosby, 2004)

Bill Cosby speaking to parents at a Compton, California, high school. Why are his lectures about black underachievement controversial?

Cosby's words reignited a controversy that has been raging for decades about the educational gaps between black and white students (see Chapter 9 on race). Recent data continue to show that black students underperform compared with whites on various measures of educational achievement. Blacks score lower on cognitive achievement tests and experience higher rates of being left back, suspended, and expelled. These differences in school performance are reflected in measures of high-school and college graduation. In 2010, 84.2 percent of blacks ages 25 and older had at least a high-school diploma (or equivalency degree), compared with 87.6 percent of whites (see Figure 13.2). During the same year only 19.8 percent of blacks over the age of 25 had at least a college degree, as opposed to 30.3 percent of whites (U.S. Census Bureau, 2011b). Who is to blame for these differences? Does responsibility solely lie on the shoulders of African American parents and students, as Bill Cosby suggested? Or are larger societal forces more important contributors to these gaps?

In the last section, we reviewed the importance of social class in determining educational achievements, and it is a major contributor to the black–white achievement gap. On average, blacks have lower levels of each of the four social class indicators mentioned above. One way to illustrate the class differentials between blacks and whites is to compare poverty rates. In 2009, 25.8 percent of blacks lived below the poverty line, compared with 12.3 percent of whites. Think that's bad? It gets worse. In 2009, 35.3 percent of African American children under age 18 lived below the poverty line, compared with

Figure 13.2: Educational Attainment Based on Race, 2010

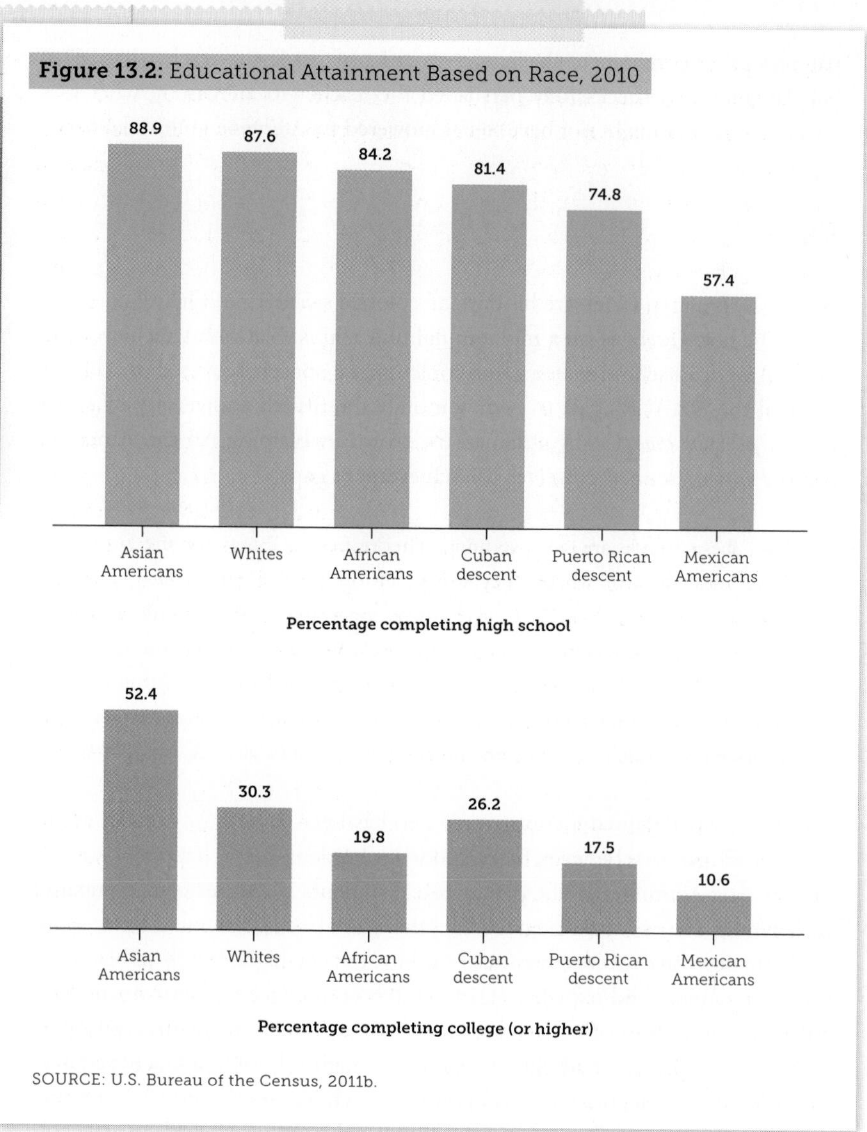

SOURCE: U.S. Bureau of the Census, 2011b.

17 percent of white children (U.S. Census Bureau, 2010e). Worse still, shifting from income poverty to wealth (net worth), we find that the typical black family has 5 cents to the typical white family's dollar of wealth (Taylor et al., 2011).

Class Intersections When researchers have controlled for SES, many of the black–white educational gaps are significantly narrowed; such findings attest to the importance of class differences in racial educational outcomes. For example, Christopher Jencks and Meredith Phillips (1998) found that one-third of the test score gap between young black and white children was removed once class was controlled for. Similarly, I determined that after factoring out class differences, African Americans had a greater chance of graduating from high school, were 44 percent less likely to be held back a grade, and were equally likely to be suspended or expelled from school as white students (Conley, 1999).

More evidence for the importance of background influences in black–white achievement gaps comes from research on summer setbacks. The idea behind this research is that during the school year it's hard to figure out how much learning is taking place in school and how much is occurring outside it (because students are exposed to both at the same time). To get around this, some researchers have compared increases in achievement that occur during the school year with those that take place during the summer. When comparing these test scores for a sample of first and second graders in Baltimore, Doris Entwisle and Karl Alexander (Alexander et al., 1994; Entwisle & Alexander, 1992) found that all the students had similar growth in the achievement test scores during the school year (even those from lower-class backgrounds, which indicates that schools do matter). However, during the summer, upper-class children continued to make gains, while the lower-class students lost ground. This suggests that the upper-class children were being exposed to educational opportunities in their homes, communities, and summer camps that encouraged learning and cognitive growth. By the time they returned to school the next fall, they were significantly ahead of their lower-class peers.

Strong evidence exists that many of the black–white achievement gaps can be explained by class and the advantages it brings. But class can't explain all the gaps. Therefore, researchers have turned to a variety of noneconomic theories to explain what class alone can't. One prominent theory suggests that a large portion of the achievement gap can be explained by African American students' hesitancy to excel in school for fear of being accused of "acting white" (Fordham & Ogbu, 1986). According to these researchers, years of oppression (specifically, their transport to this country against their will as slaves and involuntary immigrants) and questions about their innate intelligence have led blacks to doubt their own intellectual ability and associate book learning and school with being white. Not wanting to sell out, African Americans have disengaged from school or downplayed their academic achievements to avoid embracing what is seen as white behavior.

Although Signithia Fordham and John Ogbu (1986) uncovered extensive evidence of this phenomenon undermining achievement, a study by Karolyn Tyson, William Darity, Jr., and Domini Castellino (2005), also conducted using ethnographic methods (researchers observing firsthand what goes on in a school; see Chapter 2), found only limited evidence to support the theory. This corroborates results from survey-based studies, which have also found little support. Instead, evidence exists that the inversion of dominant values (achievement is bad, acting out is good) is prevalent among many groups of underprivileged youth regardless of race (MacLeod, 1985/1997; Willis, 1981). What's more, researchers have found that the association of academic achievement with "acting white" may be a recent phenomenon, existing only since the 1980s. The kicker is that the "acting white" dynamic, to the extent that it does exist, may be an ironic result of school desegregation and tracking. Because of desegregation, many blacks find themselves in majority-white schools now. That trend combined with tracking, especially unfair tracking, means that high-achieving blacks find themselves socially isolated in honors and advanced placement classes. The good news, Tyson and colleagues have found (2005), is that this does not deter blacks from efforts to achieve once they are in a rigorous academic track. The bad news is that carrying the "burden of the race" does stop some minority students from challenging themselves in an academic setting.

Stereotypes This last point leads to other explanations for black–white achievement differentials that entail more social psychological dynamics. One body of research suggests that underperformance is the result of African Americans' having internalized negative stereotypes. If you are told that you're lazy, ignorant, or stupid long enough, and treated this way, you might start to believe it. Furthermore, if you start to believe it and it affects your academic outcomes, you have become a self-fulfilling prophecy (recall the effects of teacher expectations examined earlier in this chapter).

Stereotype threat when members of a negatively stereotyped group are placed in a situation where they fear they may confirm those stereotypes.

A related psychological process that might contribute to black underachievement, particularly in high-stakes testing situations, is stereotype threat, which is when members of a negatively stereotyped group are placed in a situation where they fear that they may confirm those stereotypes. For example, when black students take the SAT, they may unconsciously worry that they will confirm negative stereotypes about African American intelligence. Support for this hypothesis comes from a series of experiments conducted by Claude Steele and Joshua Aronson (1998). Black and white Stanford undergraduates were randomly assigned to one of two groups. Both groups were given a verbal test similar to the SAT, but the first group was told it was a diagnostic test of intellectual ability, while the second group was told that it was simply a problem-solving task. After controlling for the participants' SAT scores, the researchers found that blacks taking the so-called diagnostic test scored significantly lower than the black students taking the nondiagnostic test in a more relaxed atmosphere and lower than all the white students. The culprit? The activation of negative stereotypes brought about by presenting the test as a measure of intelligence. In subsequent experiments, this "activation" concept was further supported by the lower performance of black students who were asked to check off their race on a demographic questionnaire before taking what was described as a nondiagnostic test.

The Gene Movement A final explanation for African American underachievement that refuses to die out despite masses of contrary evidence is the idea that racial differences in intelligence are genetic (see the discussion of eugenics in Chapter 9). In the 1920s researchers found that IQ, measured with biased and unsophisticated tools, varied according to skin color. According to their measures, whites had the highest IQ scores and blacks the lowest. They further claimed that black students with lighter skin scored higher than those with darker skin. (The researchers apparently tried to conduct the same study with Mexican students, but some students had spent more time out in the sun than others and their tans got in the way of measurement.) These findings were used to confirm the superiority of white skin as a marker for innate intelligence (Blanton, 2000).

A predominately Maori classroom in New Zealand. The Maori are an example of a stigmatized minority that has lower IQ test scores and lower educational and occupational outcomes. However, these outcomes vanish when these students move out of cultures that stigmatize them.

In the 1960s psychologist Arthur Jenson (1969) resuscitated this argument by claiming that the differences in IQ tests between blacks and whites likely resulted from genetic differences between the groups. His position was refuted by both sociological and biological evidence. Sociologists even pointed out that stigmatized minorities in all countries, even when they are of the same "race," have lower IQ test scores and lower educational and occupational outcomes. The Maori in New Zealand, for example, have lower school retention rates and qualification levels. In 1996, nearly 50 percent of the Maori population in New Zealand had no educational qualifications at all, compared with roughly 30 percent of non-Maori. The Burakumin in Japan (see Chapter 9) have also been the targets of stigmatization and discrimination since the beginning of the seventeenth century. Although the Buraku are physically indistinguishable from the non-Buraku, a huge discrepancy exists between the educational achievements of the two groups (Ikeda, 2001). These differential outcomes disappear altogether, however, when Buraku children attend schools in the United States, where they are perceived simply as Japanese (Spencer et al., 1987).

Unfortunately, such refutations haven't stopped the racialized genetics movement. Another round of attacks on black innate intelligence came in the form of *The Bell Curve* (1994), written by psychologist Richard J. Herrnstein and political scientist Charles Murray. In a nutshell, the authors claim that everyone is where they are because of their genes because America is a meritocracy. If you're poor or uneducated, blame it on your genes. If you're making lots of money and have a great job, lucky you for being in a successful gene pool. Likewise, if blacks do worse than whites in educational or occupational outcomes, it must be because of their genes. After the book created a stir among readers, researchers systematically negated Herrnstein and Murray's claims. For example, Claude S. Fischer and colleagues (1996) reanalyzed all of Herrnstein and Murray's data and found that, among other things, they had underestimated the impact of SES and used an intelligence test designed to measure what participants had learned in school, not innate intelligence. No doubt we will witness another incarnation of this same argument in the next few decades.

Ethnicity

Most research on achievement gaps has focused on black–white differences because of American history. However, there are notable differences between other minority groups and whites as well. For example, like African Americans, Hispanics score lower on the SATs, have a higher rate of repeating grades, and are suspended or expelled at higher rates than white students. Furthermore, Hispanic students have the highest high-school dropout rate of any minority group in the nation. Some of these differences can be attributed to language difficulties, but many of the same factors that apply to blacks apply to Hispanics. Hispanics, like African Americans, have lower social-class standings on average and are the target of numerous negative stereotypes that may depress achievement. They have also been the target of people who contend that inequalities stem from genetic differences between groups.

Asians, in contrast, have been touted in American culture as "model minorities" or the "immigrant success story." Asians first arrived in this country facing significant discrimination and oppression, and their continuing upward mobility has indeed been an impressive feat. In a relatively short time, Asians have gone from being characterized as the "yellow peril" to scoring consistently higher on tests of math ability, having higher GPAs, and going to college at higher rates than non-Asian students. How did they do it? One intriguing line of research (Portes & MacLeod, 1996) suggests that although some Asian groups are no more socioeconomically advantaged than other immigrants, their communities contain a high degree of social capital: Extremely close ties exist between adults, and they support each other's parenting rules.

Impending Crisis: Boy–Girl Achievement Gap

"Yes, we're sorry to say, there really is a crisis," lament Michael Gurian and Kathy Stevens (2005), authors of *The Minds of Boys: Saving Our Sons from Falling Behind in School and Life*. In recent years journalists, psychologists, and educators alike have brought attention to what they have termed the "boy crisis." The crisis may be described as follows: Whereas 30 years ago girls lagged behind boys in educational outcomes, it seems that "girl power" mantras, Title IX (which provided equal funding to girls in classrooms and for sports), and the feminist movement have made their mark. Girls are now surpassing boys in their educational outcomes.

How true are these assertions? In recent years girls have been less likely to repeat a grade or drop out of high school. In addition, girls outperform boys in national reading and writing tests (and score roughly equal to boys in math, contrary to popular belief). They also attend college in higher numbers and are more likely to graduate (Freeman, 2004). In 2010, 87.6 percent of women over age 25 had a high school degree as opposed to 86.6 percent of men. Furthermore, in 2009, 60.4 percent of the graduate degrees awarded were earned by women (U.S.

Census Bureau, 2010f). Note, however, that despite all the education that women attain, it does not pay off in the workplace. As recently as 2000, women earned only 80 percent of what men with an equal education do (BLS, 2009). (See Chapter 8 for a more thorough discussion of wage and employment differences by gender.)

On the flip side, while boys are more likely to engage in risky behaviors and experience serious problems at school (e.g., being identified as having a learning disorder or emotional disturbance), they also make up a larger proportion of those taking calculus and science AP tests, and, on average, they score higher on those tests than girls. In addition, boys score higher than girls on every AP test except foreign languages, though girls represent a larger proportion of those taking certain tests (Freeman, 2004). (The fact that a smaller, more select group of boys take such tests may contribute to their higher scores.) A male advantage is also apparent in SAT scores, with boys scoring higher than girls on the math and critical reading while females outperform males on the writing section (Institution of Education Sciences, 2010).

The question remains: Is there a crisis? Boys may perform better than girls on college entrance exams, but this appears to be the only advantage they enjoy at the moment (and one that hasn't affected the exceptional rates of girls' college entrance and graduation). However, before rendering a final verdict, let's bring in one more piece of evidence. While the media have been busy generating sensational headlines about the boy–girl achievement gap, researchers have been systematically examining trends and explanations for the differences. For example, Claudia Buchmann, Thomas A. DiPrete, and Troy A. Powell (2006) found that among students born before the mid-1960s, girls achieved as much education as boys only when both parents were college educated. Boys, however, seemed to do equally well in school regardless of their parents' education. But for students born after the mid-1960s, the opposite pattern emerged. Girls from all backgrounds started to do better in school. At the same time, boys living with single mothers or in households where the father had a high-school education or less started doing much worse.

This suggests that headlines about the boy crisis should really read something like "Girls Catch Up, While Boys from Lower-Class Backgrounds Lose Ground." It is not so much that girls are surpassing boys in educational achievement but that they have started doing equally well at the same time that boys from lower-class backgrounds have started doing worse. The boy crisis, then, has had only a limited effect on the middle- and upper-class children whose parents have been most vocal and concerned about the trend.

All in the Family

Most American parents assume that their homes are a haven from the harsh world. They like to believe that they send out each of their children into the world on identical footing. Oh, how parents delude themselves! As discussed in Chapter 12,

Why might the size of a family and the space between its children's ages affect achievement scores and grades?

inequality starts at home. Growing up in the same family with the same parents is no guarantee that siblings are going to end up with similar educational outcomes.

First, parents may not recognize the delicate balance that exists between the number of children they have, their spacing (e.g., three children one year apart versus three children all four years apart), and their gender composition. Yet all three factors have significant impacts on educational achievement. For example, research has consistently found that the bigger the family, the lower the children's achievement test scores and grades (Downey, 1995; Steelman & Powell, 1985). What's just as important as family size is how far apart the children are spread. For example, Brian Powell and Lala Carr Steelman (1990) determined that students with siblings spaced closer together had lower achievement scores and grades, even after the researchers controlled for SES and previous achievement. This research also found that while an additional sibling in the family is damaging to the other children's grades, additional brothers had a particularly negative impact.

Resource dilution model hypothesis stating that parental resources are finite and that each additional child dilutes them.

What brings about these effects? The most prominent hypothesis, the resource dilution model, suggests simply that parental resources are finite and each additional child gets a smaller amount of them. Furthermore, if children are spaced closer together, there is more competition for the same resources at the same time. This is the case not just for economic resources but also for the amount of interaction parents and children have. Research (Downey, 1995) has supported such a model, finding that the frequency of communication with parents, parents' educational expectations, the amount of money saved for college, and presence of educational materials in the home all successfully explain the effect of family size on educational performance. Only children, despite common stereotypes as an at-risk group, on average outperform those with siblings, because they enjoy a monopoly on family resources. (They also tend to come from more socioeconomically advantaged families.)

If sibling numbers and composition are important to educational achievement, what about what I've called the "pecking order" among siblings? Does the first child turn out to be a leader? Does the middle child always suffer? Although some researchers (e.g., Steelman & Powell, 1985) have found that birth order has no effects, my coauthor Rebecca Glauber and I (2006) uncovered evidence that middle children do suffer a crunch because of their family position. We determined that with the transition from two to three children, the middle child is the one who suffers from less parental monetary investment and runs a greater risk of being held back a grade—particularly boys. Meanwhile, Steelman and Powell (1989) found that later-born children had a better chance of getting parental financial support for college than older siblings did, perhaps because of their parents' improving financial status over the years.

Finally, research about differences in educational achievement within families has also taken on a biological bent. Specifically, studies have examined the effect of differences in sibling birth weight on educational attainment. Whether because of health problems, slowed cognitive development, or getting bullied for their smaller size, siblings with lower birth weight have lower educational outcomes than their heftier siblings. For example, my coauthor Neil G. Bennett and I (2000) found that low birth weight significantly decreases children's chances of graduating from high school by the age of 19. These poor educational outcomes may be related to another disadvantage: Low-birth-weight children have a greater tendency to exhibit poor classroom behavior. Pamela Kato Klebanov, Jeanne Brooks-Gunn, and Marie McCormick (1994) found that low-birth-weight children received lower attention and higher daydreaming and hyperactivity scores from their teachers than normal-birth-weight students.

Vouchers

Despite the findings of the Coleman Report and other research questioning the relevance of measurable aspects of school quality on student achievement, schools are still where the hot political debates about education are fought. One of the biggest fights centers on the question of school choice—specifically, private school vouchers. Basically, the idea behind the voucher movement is that for schooling to be equal, students should be able to choose where

Breanna Walton joins the line for recess at a Washington, D.C., private school. She is one of about 1,700 low-income students in Washington attending a private or parochial school through the nation's first federal voucher program.

they want to go to school, regardless of whether they can pay for it. To make this ideology a reality, school choice proponents endorse the use of vouchers, coupons administered by the government that may be redeemed at any school, private or public. Students take the dollar amount of whatever their public school would have spent on their education and apply it toward the tuition at another school.

Supporters of school choice argue that when families are able to choose schools, everybody benefits. First, students don't have to attend subpar schools. Second, competition among schools vying for students maintains the pressure to keep educational standards high all around. For example, if students leave the public school system in significant numbers, public schools will be forced to improve. Opponents of school choice point out that the reality of school choice is much more complicated: Not all parents could or would send their children to different schools. (What if the closest high-quality school is two hours away?) Further, what if the schools of choice did not have room for more children? And, if they started taking in all students, would their effectiveness diminish? How does choice square with the demonstrated importance of peer effects?

Despite these concerns, school choice backers were persuasive enough to convince several American cities, such as Milwaukee, Cleveland, and New York City, to test voucher programs. Therefore, some 20 years after the initial school choice debate, we can assess whether the voucher promises have come true. Unfortunately, the results of voucher programs have been mixed at best. For example, in Milwaukee, where low-income students received vouchers to the private or public schools of their choice, researchers found that after five years of the program, achievement test scores were not consistently different between those who used the vouchers and a control group of low-income public school students (Witte, 1998). Similarly, in New York City, a lottery determined which low-income children enrolled in kindergarten through fourth grade received vouchers for three years' tuition in private schools. When this group was compared with the control (students who had applied to the voucher program but were not chosen), the effects of the vouchers varied depending on how the research question was framed (Krueger & Zhu, 2002). However, researchers generally found that the test scores of students who used vouchers didn't differ from those of other children, except for an increase in black students' math scores in the first year of follow-up.

→ CONCLUSION

We've learned about the skills schools teach and their role in socializing (or brainwashing, depending on your point of view) students with American values. We've also examined how differences between and within schools can affect educational outcomes. After years of being underappreciated as a result of the findings in the Coleman Report, schools are finally receiving the attention they deserve. In fact, some research suggests that schools might do more than we realized for students, particularly for those from disadvantaged backgrounds (e.g., Alexander et al., 1994; Entwisle & Alexander, 1992). Within schools, we've looked at how tracking can inadvertently lead to reproducing inequalities and how certain factors in classrooms are instrumental in student outcomes.

In terms of higher education, we've examined trends indicating that the rise of college graduates has potentially contributed to a nation of overcredentialed workers. We've also questioned how much stock we should put in SAT scores for deciding college admissions (and if their poor predictive power weren't enough, now we have to add the possibility of future scoring mishaps to the list of problems). In addition, we've examined many of the myths about affirmative action that have led to its misrepresentation and subsequent dismantling.

Finally, we've taken a closer look at some of the background characteristics that affect educational outcomes and how they can be a powerful force in determining where you get to in life. Contrary to the American ideology of equal educational opportunity for all, schools are not the fairest places for students from disadvantaged backgrounds. This is especially unfortunate because school in America has historically been (and still is) the way for students to move up in the world.

In addition to learning what schools are all about, you should also have learned that not everything is as it seems. Scratch a little deeper and you see that the statistics paraded by the media, educators, and sometimes even sociologists may not tell the full story. For example, we've learned that the SAT might predict college GPA, but if we look more closely, it doesn't hold up to all its promises. Similarly, we've heard in the media about the impending "boy crisis" because of the achievement gap between boys and girls. However, after dissecting the trends, we know that girls have merely caught up with boys, whereas boys from lower-class families, not those from the middle- and upper-class families who are making all the fuss, are the students truly at risk.

Finally, I hope you've learned what sociology can do for educational policy. The most obvious example of this is the Coleman Report. The results of this study are among the most cited findings in educational literature. It also has had a significant impact on how the government decided to address differences in educational achievement. Thus, sociologists who study education don't just do it in isolation; much of what they find can be, and has been, applied to the real world.

ASSIGNMENT

Review the statistics on educational levels in the United States that appear on the National Center for Education Statistics Web site (**nces.ed.gov/programs/digest/d05/tables/dt05_008.asp**), then take a look at the historical summary of U.S. job categories available from the U.S. Bureau of Labor Statistics ftp site (**ftp://ftp.bls.gov/pub/suppl/empsit.ceseeb1.txt**). Pay particular attention to the decrease in manufacturing jobs (which usually don't require a college degree) as part of the total percentage of jobs in the U.S. economy. How might changes in the structure of the U.S. economy be linked to the rise of higher education? Do you notice any other potentially significant trends?

QUESTIONS FOR REVIEW

1. How does Sayed Rahmatullah Hashemi's admission to Yale fit within an affirmative action framework? How do the reactions to Hashemi's admission relate to or differ from myths surrounding affirmative action?
2. Describe the school voucher system. What do preliminary findings suggest regarding the importance of which school people attend?
3. "Through the meritocratic education system everyone has the chance to succeed in America." Do you agree with this statement? Find a theory or a research finding from this chapter that supports this assertion and another that challenges it. Do these theories or findings complicate your view of America as a meritocracy?
4. What is the "hidden curriculum" of education? In this light, how do Marxist theorists like Samuel Bowles and Herbert Gintis (1976) interpret the role of schools?
5. Why were the findings in the Coleman Report so surprising? How has research on achievement differences clarified the conclusions of the report?
6. How does research on the Pygmalion effect potentially support and reject the notion of "tracking" in schools?
7. You must complete a master's degree to get a job that your parents got with a bachelor's degree and your grandparents got with a high-school diploma. Use the work on credentialism to explain this phenomenon.
8. Why do people debate the use of SAT scores for college admission?
9. Describe the relative power of social class and genetics toward explaining inequalities in schooling.
10. How does family background—for example, cultural capital from the home (Lareau, 2003)—affect educational achievement? How do studies about family size and birth order complicate our understanding of the effect of family background?

PARADOX

ALTHOUGH SCHOOL IS SUPPOSED TO BE THE INSTITUTION IN SOCIETY THAT PROVIDES EQUAL OPPORTUNITY, IT ENDS UP SORTING AND STRATIFYING STUDENTS BY THE BACKGROUNDS FROM WHICH THEY COME.

WATCH THE ANIMATED SHORT ABOUT THE EDUCATION PARADOX AT

WWNORTON.COM/STUDYSPACE

Trade union representatives wear clockface masks and mingle with London commuters to mark Work Your Proper Work Hours Day. British and American employees work more hours than most Western nations but are less productive. Research suggests that this is because of workplace stress and absenteeism caused by overwork.

14 Capitalism and the Economy

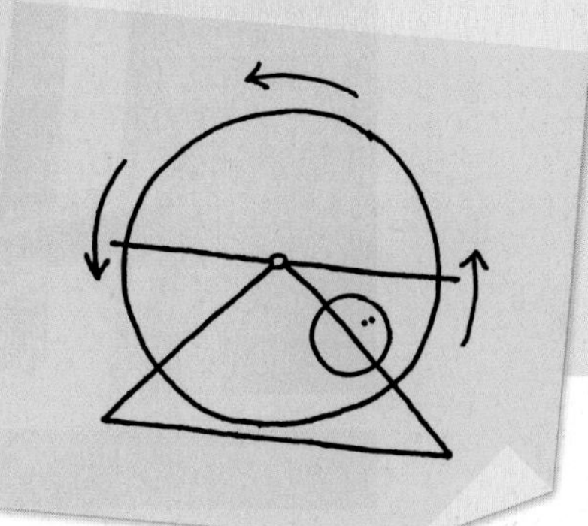

Whether we like him or not, we can all agree that Obama has made history. No, I'm not talking about being the first African American president. I am talking about the fact that he has been the first-ever BlackBerry president. President Obama won the first battle of his administration back in 2009 after having declared, "They're going [to have] to pry it out of my hands" (Krangel, 2009). While the Secret Service and intelligence agencies may still worry about the cyber security of all his mobile devices, for the rest of white-collar America, it's nice to see a first family that reflects how the rest of us live.

His dedication to a smartphone is but one way that the Obamas have embodied changes in the way we live and work. There's the fact, of course, that he has lived and worked in what could arguably be called the nation's first (and certainly most important) "home office"—otherwise known as the White House. More and more Americans are working from home.

Not without nostalgia, the family farm has almost completely receded into history. But the home office trend that started in the early 1960s, when urban artists who couldn't afford the rent on separate residences and studios started occupying postindustrial spaces, continues to blur the line between home space and workplace. By 1969, the home office movement gained steam with the publication of *The Home Office Guide,* by recent college graduate Leon Henry. Ten years later, the media latched onto the term, describing this strange new breed of accountants, sales reps, therapists, and the like who plied their trade out of a spare bedroom, on the kitchen table, or from any other nook of their residence. The complaints of home office professionals were the same

Barack Obama, the first BlackBerry president.

back then as they are now: a lack of privacy, too many distractions, blurred boundaries, and so forth. I am sure the Obamas could identify here.

With the birth of the personal computer, the number of folks who used their home as their principal place of business skyrocketed, increasing 56 percent over the 1980s and another 23 percent in the 1990s (Conley, 2009). Perhaps predictably, the IRS lagged behind society in this transformation and struggled with a series of court cases on how to draw an increasingly moot line between work life and everything else. Today, they are similarly trying to figure out how to treat company cell phones that are often used for both work and personal calls.

The Obama White House reflects how today's professionals live in other ways as well. Whereas George W. Bush—more akin to the man in the gray flannel suit of yesteryear—liked to call it quits by evening, Obama typically has taken a break to eat with his family and spend some "quality time" with them, but he often returned to work and has been known to dash off e-mails well after midnight. Bush's daughters were grown by the time Bush was in the White House, whereas Obama's younger girls present demands on Obama's time. The president has worn as a badge of fatherhood that he managed to attend their school events and parent-teacher meetings despite the constant demands of his political office. Bush was married to a longtime homemaker; the Obamas, in contrast, have had to undergo some role shifts as Mrs. Obama gave up her career as an attorney and hospital administrator to take on the full-time role of mother and First Lady.

So as the Obama household faces many of the same strains that millions of professional families do, they have shown leadership in how to handle these tensions: Instead of having outsourced their family needs to the growing market for nannies and other household labor, they turned back to the strong African American tradition of three-generation households. Namely, Michelle's mother moved into 1600 Pennsylvania Avenue. By having another adult family member to fill in the gaps and provide loving care to Malia and Sasha, the Obamas eased the stress of the intrusion of work into every moment of their day and night. And maybe President Obama feels less guilt when he has sneaked off another text message at the family dinner table.

For some individuals, the boundaries between work and home have eroded to the point that they resemble precapitalist, cottage industry modes of production more than anything seen since the Industrial Revolution. How did we get here? Perhaps we should start with a brief history of the capitalist system.

How have forces such as technological change and globalization transformed the work place and work hours?

A Brief History of Capitalism

In its purest form, capitalism is an economic system in which property and goods are primarily privately owned; investments are determined by private decisions; and prices, production, and the distribution of goods are determined primarily by competition in an unfettered marketplace. Various scholars place the early stages of modern capitalism somewhere between the fifteenth and nineteenth centuries in Europe. The dates are highly disputed because many elements of capitalism existed in earlier epochs. For example, the use of money (as opposed to barter) is seen as central to capitalism, and many ancient civilizations used money in one form or another. Likewise, private property existed to different degrees in various times and places. However, capitalism as a whole, most would agree, started to develop along with the agricultural and industrial revolutions in Europe.

Capitalism economic system in which property and goods are primarily owned privately; investments are determined by private decisions; and prices, production, and the distribution of goods are determined primarily by competition in an unfettered marketplace.

Before capitalism in Europe, the dominant economic system was feudalism, most simply characterized by the presence of lords, vassals, serfs, and fiefs. A lord was a nobleman who owned land, and a vassal was granted the land, termed a fief, by the lord. The fief remained the property of the lord, but it was left to the vassal to reap the harvests from it. In exchange, the vassal provided military protection for the lord. Serfs, who were of peasant origin, formed the lowest class in feudal society. Serfs were bound to the land and required to give the lord a portion of their production; they were, in turn, granted protection. They differed from slaves, however, in that they were allowed to own property and could not be sold. These relationships formed the basic framework for feudalism and arguably for the class structures that came into being in subsequent centuries upon the system's demise.

Feudalism precapitalist economic system characterized by the presence of lords, vassals, serfs, and fiefs.

During the early Tudor period in England (1485–1558), some of the open fields, often referred to as the commons (that is, they existed for the public good;

Fifteenth-century French peasants working the fields. What characterized work during the era of medieval feudalism?

anyone could graze livestock there), were "enclosed" or partitioned off. During this "enclosure movement," the lords often bounded the commons with hedges. Because this was land that had been publicly available for grazing and planting, the enclosures led to the eviction of many of the people working the land. The result was that they had little choice but to migrate to nearby cities in search of work, as one of their primary means of survival had been removed. These changes and dynamics would eventually lead to the rise of both the city and the wage system.

The evolution of capitalism was also heavily influenced by the development of technology. The history of social relations, according to Marxists, is a history of humankind's struggle to control and dominate nature through the use of technology. The technological conditions of a given epoch, in turn, determine our mode of social relationships. Around 1700, new farming technologies were introduced that directly increased food output; hence, this period is commonly termed the agricultural revolution. Innovations such as the seed drill, selective breeding, and crop rotation led to an immediate increase in food abundance. As a result, the land could support more people, allowing for increased population and further adding to the labor pool created by the enclosure movement.

Agricultural revolution the period around 1700 marked by the introduction of new farming technologies that increased food output in farm production.

Other changes occurred as well. For example, early colonial globalization established spice routes from colonial interests in India and the Far East and led to the development of new ways to store meat in England. Previously, livestock had to be slaughtered at the onset of winter, but these new preservation methods allowed that operation to be done at any time of year. This increased abundance, in turn, further spurred the enclosure movement, because land was now more productive and therefore more valuable.

The combination of the enclosure movement, more people, and technological improvements (which lowered the amount of labor needed per acre) led to the displacement of more and more peasants from agricultural labor. This growth of surplus peasant labor, in turn, led to mass migration to cities such as London and Manchester and to the rise of a wage-labor system. Here we can see the groundwork being laid for what we call industrial capitalism.

Of course, wage labor would not have become available unless new jobs had been created for these former peasants. At the end of the eighteenth century and the beginning of the nineteenth century, an economy once dominated by small-scale artisan labor (that is, handicrafts and subsistence farming) transitioned into one dominated by manufacturing, machinery, and unskilled factory work. This massive historical transition was also propelled by the development of new technologies. It began with the mechanization of textile industries—fabric manufacturing such as clothing, rugs, and upholstery.

Dramatic innovations in the textile industry made the manufacturing process more efficient and corresponded with the mass migration of rural workers into cities. What were some of the social consequences of the Industrial Revolution?

One major innovation for textile production was the power loom, a weaving machine powered by driving shafts, which made the manufacturing process much more efficient.

Another major innovation of the Industrial Revolution was the development of the steam engine, which opened up markets through its eventual use in railroads. For instance, water was often used in mining, and part of the workers' job was to remove the water in order to access the materials being extracted. Steam-powered pumps now did this, allowing the workers to focus on the extraction of the mineral itself.

With the rise of large-scale factory production, the influx of peasants to urban areas to find work, and the rise of a system of wage labor, along came monetization, the establishment of a legal currency. The barter system in villages allowed a peasant to trade livestock or produce, but in the context of large cities and wage labor, the need for a monetary system emerged. This led to the formation of new social institutions and organizations, such as the corporation. Corporations emerged as a way to limit the liability of investors, thus allowing corporations to attract a larger number of willing stockholders. In the United States, corporations are legally recognized persons and share many of the rights of an individual. For instance, corporations can act as legal entities by entering into contracts or owning property. The corporation can also sue (and be sued). This is where limited liability comes into the picture. Limited liability is a form of ownership that creates a division between the

Corporation a legal entity unto itself that has a legal personhood distinct from that of its members, namely, its owners and shareholders.

individual—that is, the shareholder or executive—and the business entity. It is, in this sense, a legal way to protect investors from personal responsibility for any liabilities beyond the value of the company itself. Many companies have abbreviations in their titles, such as LLP (limited liability partnership; most law firms are LLPs) and Inc. (incorporated), or, as in South America, SA (*sociedad anónima* or "anonymous society"). Today, many of the contracts that make business possible aren't between individual people but rather between legally recognized entities in the form of corporations.

Theorizing the Transition to Capitalism

Adam Smith

Adam Smith

Perhaps capitalism's greatest advocate was Adam Smith, the father of liberal economics. In *The Wealth of Nations* (1776/2003), Smith wondered how societies, groups of individuals pursuing their own self-interests, manage to stay intact and not fall into the chaos of civil strife. His answer was simple: Individual self-interest in an environment of others acting similarly will lead to a situation of competition, as long as basic laws and contracts are honored. Note the difference between competition (where rules constraining the game are followed) and conflict (where no holds are barred).

For Smith, individuals have "the propensity to truck, barter, and exchange one thing for another" (Smith, 1776/2003). This drive for exchange combines with an ever-increasing division of labor to produce greater wealth for all. Smith uses the example of a pin factory. If a craftsman has to fashion each pin from scratch, snipping the wire, honing the point, attaching a head, and polishing the pin, he can make only a few dozen a day, at best. However, once the job is broken into its constitutive parts and each portion of the process assigned to a separate worker, the same craftsman can produce hundreds or perhaps even thousands of pins a day. Of course, he would be now working with others to make the pins, but dividing by the total number of man-hours, his efficiency is still orders of magnitude greater. Why so? There are two reasons: First, if the task is broken down into parts, each part can be completed more quickly; second, and perhaps more important for Smith, once people specialize in this way, they are better able to innovate. If you spent your entire work life performing a single task, you would get pretty good at it, especially compared with someone who performs that task only once in a while as part of a wider sweep of work. What's more, in all that time thinking about sharpening pins, you might come up with some inventions to make your life easier and to help you become the best pin sharpener in London. You might even create a machine to do your job for you. You certainly would have the incentive, because you want to drive all other pin sharpeners out of business. According to Smith, this cycle of division of labor, innovation, and trade results in the production of goods that society desires, in the proportions that it desires, and at the price it is willing to pay.

To keep this metaphorical engine running, however, money is needed to grease the gears. Smith sings the praises of monetization or the "cash nexus," as it was dubbed by the Scottish essayist Thomas Carlyle (1839/1971). The barter system, says Smith, was often inefficient and unwieldy. For example, let's say that I have a certain number of cows and you have a large quantity of salt. I need salt to cure my meat, and you need a cow to slaughter. How much salt would I get for a cow? However much it is, I have a fairly good notion I don't need or want that much salt. I would probably have to involve the whole village and a good bit of time to coordinate such a trade. I may have to trade my cow for a huge amount of salt and then distribute that salt to each family in the village and try to collect what I need from each of them in return. People are not going to make a trade if it's inefficient, and therefore, many trades don't occur that would be optimal in economic terms—that is, trades that would make all of us better off.

With money, however, all any trade ever requires is two partners. I *think* I know exactly how much a cow is worth. (The more widespread a market is and the better circulated the information about trading prices, the more confidence we have that we know the right price for our cow or salt.) You give me that much money, and I will buy only as much salt from you as I need. In short, money allows us to get back change. And perhaps even more important, money can store value. It gives me the ability to save efficiently. In the barter system, every sale was a purchase and vice versa. If you wanted to unload your cow, you had to take something for it, often right away. Because money stores value, the actions of buying and selling can be staggered over time and across people. Finally, money develops, or at least relies on, trust. In the barter system you know what you are getting in return when you sell something. But if I accept dollars, pesos, pounds, or euros in exchange for my cow, I am taking a leap of faith. I am trusting that the currency will be accepted wherever I go. In this sense, Smith argues, money is inherently social; it facilitates social relations between humans.

Georg Simmel

The classical sociologist Georg Simmel—whose work on social groups we discussed in Chapter 5—also took a positive view of capitalism. Unlike Smith, however, Simmel (1900) didn't view money as an agent of social change. Instead, he saw the development of monetary payment systems as part of a historical evolution, the depersonalization of exchange. In a precapitalist system such as feudalism, a serf was treated more like an animal than a human being, according to Simmel. In return for his labor, the serf received in-kind payment in the form of items needed for survival—actual sustenance necessary to live and reproduce. In this sense, the payment was quite literally personal in nature. But with the arrival of capitalism, Simmel observes, payment forms evolved toward giving more and more freedom to the worker.

In the early days of capitalism, when craftsmen produced specific products from start to finish, most payment was in the form of payment per unit or piecework payment. This form of payment still exists in developed countries, although only on a smaller scale. For instance, you and a custom carpenter can agree on a design and a price for him to build some bookshelves. What happens if the wood turns out to be rotten? The craftsman is at risk. If he needs to start from scratch with a second batch of wood, he might not break even on the transaction. However, he is obligated to deliver a bookshelf that isn't rotten. Piecework payment is slightly better for the worker than in-kind payment because money carries with it a certain amount of freedom. Once a decent set of bookshelves is delivered and paid for, the carpenter can take the money and buy food or a car—do whatever he wants with the cash. The worker remains in control of the payment he receives and therefore has vastly more freedom than under the in-kind payment scheme.

A step up from this system, for Simmel, is wage labor. Simmel argues that under the system of wage labor, people are paid in money, and furthermore, this wage is not tied to the quality of the raw materials, accidents, or other exigencies in the production process. Let's say that you work for an hourly wage for a nongovernmental organization translating reports from Spanish into English. You have been working all day on a particularly long report, and 15 minutes before your day is about to end, the hard drive crashes and all your work for the day is lost. Despite the lost report, you still get paid for the eight hours you worked under the wage labor system; it's the role of the employer to shoulder the costs of the faulty computer and the lost work. In this sense, workers under capitalism are not completely dependent on the quality of the raw materials, the technology, or the production process. The worker sells his or her labor to the employer, and it is the employer's problem if the results do not live up to expectations.

Even better than wage labor, according to Simmel, is salary. Under a salary system, workers are paid not for a direct service but for the sum total of their services. For one year of employment, you are paid a set amount of money, and that figure is what you and your employer agreed would be acceptable for an average level of performance and an average amount of work over the course of an entire year. If you have a bad day or cannot come in, you still are paid. Both sick days and vacation days are allotted. Better still than a regular salary is a civil service salary, whereby payment is not tied to the productive value of the workers at all but related to the "appropriate standard of living" for someone at that particular grade level and amount of experience.

Finally, Simmel talks about the honorarium. An honorarium is seen as distinct from the product itself. For instance, if an institution asks you to give a speech or to provide some other service, it may offer you an honorarium. The notion is that you are giving the speech or providing the service independent of the money. You may care very much about the money, but a clear sociological distinction exists between the product and the payment. You agree to provide the service, and then you act pleasantly surprised when there is some monetary attachment to it. Likewise, the people who invited you to present the speech have to give you the honorarium just because you showed up, no matter what you end up saying. According to Simmel, a separation between the personal and the economic exists, just as there was in the development of limited liability.

Workers waiting in line for their wages. Why did Georg Simmel argue that wage labor was better than precapitalist work?

It is through these increasingly depersonalized forms of monetary payment, Simmel argues, that capitalism makes true friendship possible. By severing market relations from the personal, we now have a private sphere of pure sociability that is distinct from the economic or public sphere. Simmel argues that in precapitalist times, people traded with their neighbors and relied on each other to produce enough food and then fairly divide it up among the entire village. In this situation, business was mixed with pleasure, and people were distrustful of one another. Your friend is your business partner, and to top it off, your daughter may have married his son. But he is also your competitor.

In modern capitalist society, however, there is a strong norm against mixing business with pleasure. People keep these two worlds apart, or at least they attempt to do so. Simmel argues that it is only by maintaining a monetized, economic public sphere that we can enjoy a private sphere that truly is private, where we actively exclude market and monetary relations in order to experience pure sociability.

Karl Marx

Unlike Smith and Simmel, Marx considered capitalism both fundamentally flawed and inevitably doomed (see Chapter 1). Whereas Smith and Simmel saw the benefits of the division of labor, Marx saw alienation, which he considered the basic state of being in a capitalist society. Alienation is a condition in which people are dominated by forces of their own creation that then confront them as alien powers. Marx viewed alienation as taking four forms under capitalist production: alienation from the product, the process, other people, and one's self.

Alienation a condition in which people are dominated by forces of their own creation that then confront them as alien powers; according to Marx, the basic state of being in a capitalist society.

In the first sense, workers are alienated from the product that they produce. They do not know it or have complete knowledge of what they are producing. By contrast, the artisan fashioned products from start to finish, from raw materials to the packaged item on the shelf. If a woman desired a new pair of shoes, she would go to the local shoemaker, who would measure her foot and choose an appropriate *last* (or wooden form) around which to construct the shoe. The shoemaker would then cut and fit a pattern of leather to the size of the last. In the next phase, the shoemaker would stitch the upper sole to the inner sole with thread (which he might have made himself). He then attached the sole and a heel with some tacks. The result was a completed shoe. The point is that each craftsman was the master of his particular product, from start to finish. He knew every aspect of it, because he built it from scratch.

The situation in a modern factory is very different. The production process is now broken down among several people, sometimes several hundred—leading to greater efficiency and returns to scale, as Adam Smith celebrated. Factory work has become so specialized and their roles so interchangeable and devoid of skill, according to Marx, that most people working in shoemaking factories today probably do not know the entire process for making a shoe. Would they know how to spin the fabric for the shoe, dye the fabric, mold the sole, and sew it all together? It is doubtful. And we're just talking about a shoe! Imagine the process for building a car, a computer, or any of the many things around you. As a result of the same division of labor that Smith praises, capitalist workers are no longer masters of their products, in Marx's view. Rather, the product is the master of the worker. As Marx noted, "The object that labour produces, its product, now stands opposed to it as something alien, as a power independent of the producer" (1844/1932).

Workers in modern capitalism are also alienated from the process of production. For instance, if the precapitalist shoemaker woke up in the morning with a hangover from the night before, he could choose to sleep in and finish his work later. He knew, in this situation, that by the end of the week he had to produce a certain number of shoes for his customers and could budget his time as he saw fit. Thus, there was a certain freedom in the rhythm of work. The modern-day laborer, by contrast, has no choice but to swallow some aspirin and trudge off to the factory, fast-food restaurant, or computer terminal. This is especially true for laborers who work for subsistence wages and therefore need to work every day to survive. Think about the day laborers who stand on certain street corners in Los Angeles, San Francisco, Chicago, and many other American cities, hoping to find work that day. They do not control the process at all; it controls them. They are told when to go to work and when to go home; they are told when to leave early and when to stay late. For Marx, that is the nature of wage labor and salaried labor in the modern industrial capitalist system. Labor is, in a sense, forced by economic need, and its rhythm is controlled not by the individual producer but by some larger social force, institution, or individual. The result is alienation.

Why would Karl Marx have argued that the factory workers making shoes on the right were more alienated from their work than the shoemaker on the left?

But that's not all. In addition, workers are alienated from other people, according to Marx, because capitalism turns all relations into market relations (in contrast to Simmel, who believed that capitalism created a sphere separate from economic interactions). Marx notes, "What is true of man's relationship to his work, to the product of his work and to himself, is also true of his relationship to other men. . . . Each man is alienated from others. . . . [E]ach of the others is likewise alienated from human life" (1844/1932). But what does this mean exactly? Our relationships with others become conditioned by the ethic of capitalism: profit maximization. For instance, we start using the language of worth to describe the moral qualities of individuals. Time becomes monetized in a wage labor system. Men who do not make money are viewed by others as forsaking the sale of their time on the wage labor market and thus are morally suspect.

Finally, Marx argues, we are alienated from ourselves. This is a somewhat romantic notion about what makes humans unique from other animals: our ability to create objects for both affective and instrumental value—objects with inherent use value and objects that become tools to produce yet other things, respectively. (As it turns out, this ability is not uniquely human; chimpanzees and other animals also create tools and toys.) But what ultimately separates humans from other animals, according to Marx, is that humans can experience conception before execution; that is, we have the ability to create something in our minds before we fashion it in nature. Our actions aren't just hardwired like those of a bee constructing a honeycomb; we are creative beings. (Again, recent research on animals suggests that they have notions of advance planning and time, so we are not unique in this regard either.) However, Marx sees capitalism as stifling our species-being, our natural creativity. He states that "work is *external* to the worker. . . . It is not part of his nature; consequently he does not fulfill himself in his work but denies himself" (1844/1932).

Marx's critique does not cast capitalism in a good light. However, Marx also suggested that these problems will sooner or later pass because, in his view, capitalism will ultimately self-destruct. Specifically, Marx argued, the capitalist system faces crises of overproduction, in which the system is so efficient that it produces an abundance of goods; the problem arises when the competition is stiff and wages are driven down so low that nobody can afford to buy these goods. For a while, in Marx's view, the system can solve such periodic occurrences by destroying some capital (through war) or by conquering new markets. But eventually, when capitalism has spread to every nook and cranny and run out of new places to invade, and when the dynamic of competition reaches its logical conclusion (one capitalist taking over all his or her competitors), then it will face the crisis that will putatively destroy it. In the *Communist Manifesto,* Marx and Engels claimed:

> The development of modern industry . . . cuts from under its feet the very foundation on which the bourgeoisie [capitalist classes] produces and appropriates products. What the bourgeoisie therefore produces, above all, are its own gravediggers. Its fall and the victory of the proletariat are equally inevitable. (1848/1998, p. 9)

Socialism an economic system in which most or all the needs of the population are met through nonmarket methods of distribution.

Communism a political ideology of a classless society in which the means of production are shared through state ownership and in which rewards are tied not to productivity but to need.

Under capitalism, Marx believed, the working class would rise against the employing (or capitalist) class, and would eventually usher in a new mode of production termed socialism, in which most or all the needs of the population are met through nonmarket methods of distribution, followed swiftly by communism, a classless society in which the means of production are shared through state ownership and in which rewards are tied not to productivity but to need. But this has not happened, you counter? Marx might reply that there are still new markets to conquer in our increasingly globalized economy, and capitalists continue to compete with one another in many industries, so maybe it just hasn't happened yet.

Max Weber

Max Weber, whom we also met in Chapter 1, had plenty to say about how capitalism came about and why it spread in the places it did. The short version is that Weber, unlike Marx, believed that not just technology but also ideas in and of themselves generate social change. He claimed, in fact, that modern capitalism would not have arisen without the Protestant Reformation, which, according to Weber, created the necessarily social conditions for capitalism by promoting theological insecurity and instilling a doctrine of predestination (the notion that only the elect will go to heaven). This religious change, combined with an accounting advance (the rise of double-entry bookkeeping), laid the groundwork for economic development. Faced with uncertainty as to whether they would be saved (go to heaven) in the afterlife, people looked to monetary fortune in this life as a sign from God that they were indeed among the lucky ones. (More on this in Chapter 16 on religion.)

Although Weber shared Marx's negative view of capitalism, his reasons were different. Weber worried that capitalism ate at the soul in a way that was somewhat different from Marx's concept of alienation. For Weber, modern industry and its associated bureaucracy and rationality create an "iron cage" from which we cannot escape. Here we can see, in Weber's own words from 1904, this chapter's paradox in action:

> In the field of highest development, in the United States, the pursuit of wealth, stripped of its religious and ethical meaning, tends to become associated with purely mundane passions, which often give it the character of sport. . . . Couldn't the old man be satisfied with his $75,000 a year and rest? No! The frontage of the store must be widened to 400 feet. Why? That beats everything, he says. In the evening when his wife and daughter read together, he wants to go to bed. Sundays he looks at the clock every five minutes to see when the day will be over—what a futile life! (1904/2003, p. 283)

Recent Changes in Capitalism

In the time since Smith, Simmel, Marx, and Weber wrote about capitalism, world poverty has not been eliminated through the division of labor, new forms of exchange have emerged that are even more abstract than money, and capitalist-fueled development has arguably sacrificed the health of the planet for a dramatic improvement in quality of life, especially in advanced industrial and postindustrial economies. We don't directly manufacture as many goods anymore (in the United States, at least); instead, our economy is dominated by services. And we see the rise of all sorts of work arrangements in which the factory is a faint echo, and yet workers with no boss feel beholden to an abstract taskmaster of sorts and torn between the dual commitments of unpaid home labor and making a living in the formal world of work. Perhaps the greatest irony is that the better one does (gaining higher wages for her commissions), the greater the pressure one feels to work, because although higher earnings can theoretically be used to "purchase" leisure in what's called the income effect by economists, the same higher wages mean that the opportunity cost of not working—the amount of earnings she is missing out on if she declines work opportunities—has also risen (creating what economists call the substitution effect). Increasingly, in a 24/7 information economy, casual workers (those not employed full time but working on a contract-to-contract or freelance basis) choose to work more. Worries about job insecurity mean that they need to hoard work and wages when they have access to them, but the pressures of home don't go away, particularly for women. How did we get here?

You've Come a Long Way, Baby (or Have You?): Work, Gender, and Family

In 1914, automobile magnate Henry Ford announced a breakthrough policy at his Ford Motor Company: the $5 day. Ford's automobile factory workers were guaranteed a wage of $5 per day of work, equal to just over $113 in current dollars. The policy, designed to lower turnover rates among workers and justify faster production lines, was an effective tool thanks to its popular appeal. Male job candidates flooded the factory gates daily in hopes of being hired, and production workers thankfully conceded to the monotonous work of assembly lines (a technique of mass production that Ford played a major role in developing).

Family wage a wage paid to male workers sufficient to support a dependent wife and children

Ford, waving the banner of the family wage, or a wage paid to male workers sufficient to support a dependent wife and children, was heralded for both his generosity and his genius. Ford wrote in his autobiography: "The man does work in the shop, but his wife does the work in the home. The shop must pay them both. . . . Otherwise we have the hideous prospect of little children and their mothers being forced out to work" (Ford & Crowther, 1922/1973). In the context of his time, when few factory workers earned anything close to a living wage, Ford's policy was indeed arguably enlightened and progressive.

'GOLD RUSH' IS STARTED BY FORD'S $5 OFFER

Thousands of Men Seek Employment in Detroit Factory.

Will Distribute $10,000,000 in Semi-Monthly Bonuses.

No Employe to Receive Less Than Five Dollars a Day.

Why did Henry Ford offer the family wage? Why might a feminist sociologist criticize this policy?

The sociological analysis of the family wage, however, reveals the ways work and family are connected by gender inequality, both in the workplace (as discussed in Chapter 8) and at home (Chapter 12). Advocates for the family wage in the early twentieth century asserted that every worker had the right to a "living wage," so that children and wives need not work. (This was before the enactment of child labor laws.) Implied in their definition is women's dependence on men's wages. By assuming women's dependence, the family wage was denied to them, thus pushing women and children into the very dependency to which they were presumed to be naturally suited. It is from policies such as these that we get our idea of the traditional family model: a male breadwinner and his female dependent. The few women who did work for Ford still earned $2.30 a day in 1915. Unmarried men and married men without dependents were also ineligible for the $5 day. Meanwhile, eligible married men had to subject themselves to Ford's "sociology department": teams of scientists who dropped by unannounced to check on workers' private lives, everything from their health and sexual patterns, to household finances, to their drinking or gambling habits. Ford insisted that his workers, to receive the family wage, live in the "right" kind of families.

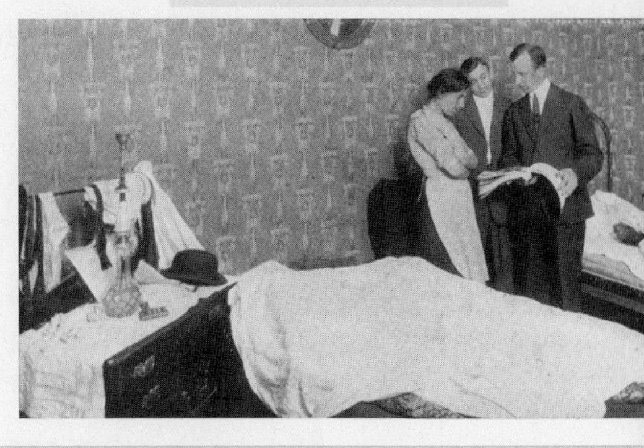

A company sociological department advisor visits the home of a Ford Motor Company employee in 1915. The scientist uses a book of photos to give the employee's wife housekeeping advice.

Feminist sociologists charge that the family wage is a patriarchal bargain. It is a living wage that provides a male breadwinner but at the cost of women's autonomy and freedom. The male breadwinner–female homemaker family, firmly entrenched as an ideal by the twentieth century, disadvantaged women in several ways. First, as Alice Kessler-Harris (1990) shows, a worker's wage reveals the social value we put on his or her worth. Rather than free-market supply of and demand for an employee's skills, expectations about gender roles were primary in determining the wages earned by men and women. A man's wage was viewed as a badge of honor; a woman's wage was just "pin money," to be used on luxuries and nonessentials. Rarely was a woman's wage expected to provide for her own livelihood, and never was it expected to support her children without the help of a father. This viewpoint justified a much lower wage for women, but it ignored the millions of unmarried, abandoned, and widowed women who worked to take care of themselves and their children. It was a particularly cruel disservice to black women, who were eight times as likely as white women during the early twentieth century to work for wages and more likely to live without the support of a male partner (Kessler-Harris, 1990). Figure 14.1 provides a comparison of men and women's wages over the last half-century or so.

When economists and politicians did consider single working women, they maintained that a woman's wage need meet only the barest of necessities, lest women turn away from the morality of family life, as enshrined in the cult of domesticity, and become enticed by the sinful and degrading world of work. Never mind that lower wages might also mean the need to work more hours outside the home in order to make ends meet. One policy maker justified lower wages with appeals to women's naturally high endurance of physical discomfort: "Her physical wants are simpler. The living wage for a woman is lower than the living wage for a man because it is possible for her as a result of traditional drudgery and forced tolerance of pain and suffering to keep alive upon less" (Kessler-Harris, 1990).

Thus, the different wages for men and women reflected deeply entrenched attitudes about gender and work that became self-confirming myths and enforced women's dependence. At the most basic level, the unfair family wage pushed heavy incentives on women to marry in order to survive economically. The family wage also impelled women to stay married, even when their marriages were oppressive, rife with conflict, or simply unhappy. As Barbara

Figure 14.1: Male and Female Median Earnings, 1959–2010

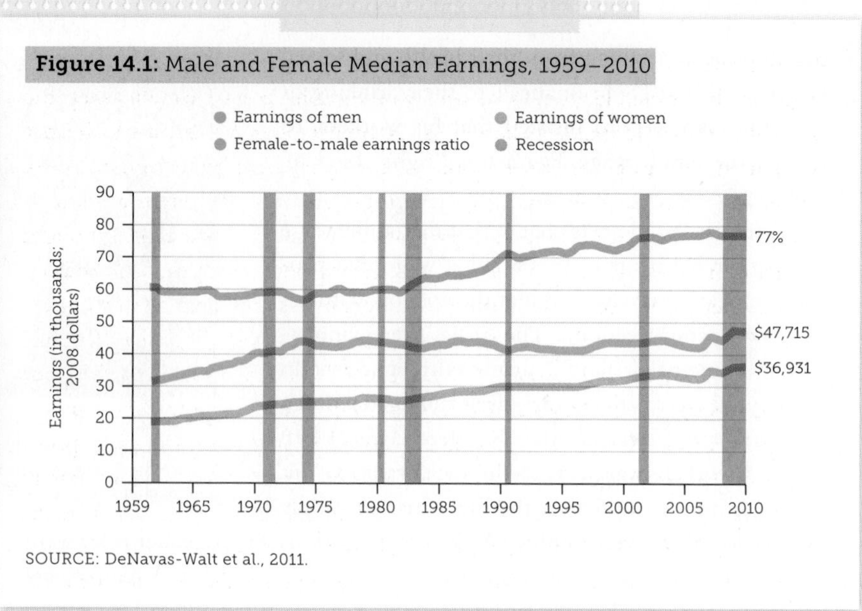

SOURCE: DeNavas-Walt et al., 2011.

Risman argues, marriage is one of the linchpins of inequality in American society:

> In what other institution are social roles, rights, and responsibilities based—even ideologically—on ascribed [i.e., birth] characteristics? When life options are tied to racial categories we call it racism at best and apartheid at worst. When life options are tied to gender categories we call it marriage. (1998, p. 36)

Surely, such an attitude no longer applies today, you're probably thinking, but the gender bias built into the family wage persists. Historical inertia of the family wage kept the average female wage at two-thirds that of the male wage through 1960. The gap is narrowing somewhat since 1960, as women now typically earn 77 cents to the male dollar, but pay inequity as a result of gender continues to hold tight the boundaries between the male public and female private spheres. It is hard to identify cause and effect when examining women's family responsibilities and their lower pay outside the home. Does lower work commitment (because of family responsibilities) lead to lower wages? Or do lower wages make it easier for women to prioritize unpaid home labor?

As feminist economist Heidi Hartmann (1976) has argued, men still have a vested interest in maintaining their privileged position as exclusive living-wage earners. They have a material advantage over women, they benefit from women's unpaid domestic labor in the home, and their advantage further gives them a superior sense of self. Nancy Folbre (1987), another economist, has argued that not just men but also employers and capitalist owners (predominantly male) stand to gain from women's weaker position in the labor market. Women, she contended, could be used as a flexible reserve army to keep the peace among white male workers. That is, by dangling the threat of cheaper women employees before male workers, employers were better able to break strikes, defy unionization, and assert control over labor. More recent research indicates that women are not "unorganizable." Where they were once thought to care more about their responsibilities at home than their careers and thus be uninterested or unable to invest time and effort in the unionization movement, by 2005, 43 percent of the unionized work force consisted of women (Cobble, 2007). Not only have union ranks grown more feminized since the 1970s, but women's participation has changed the typical bargaining framework. Unions, especially those dominated by women, now propose compensation packages that address wages, health care, and vacation time as well as paid family leave and better access to child care in their negotiations with management (Milkman, 2007). (We'll have more to say about unions below.)

Few families today, even among the upper middle classes, can afford a full-time stay-at-home mom. Dual-income families are now the majority. In 65.4 percent of all marriages with children, mothers work outside the home for pay (Bureau of Labor Statistics, 2011d). Women with young children have also increased in numbers in the workforce. In 2008, 77.5 percent of women with children under age 17 worked, compared with just 47.4 percent in 1975 (Bureau of Labor Statistics, 2011d). For mothers of infants age one and under, only 31 percent worked in 1976. In 2008, 56.4 percent worked, and almost two-thirds of those women were employed full-time (Bureau of Labor Statistics, 2009b). But attitudes about moms working full-time have recently shifted back to a more traditional perspective (at least among the moms themselves). The Pew Research Center reports that, "among working mothers with minor children (ages 17 and under), just one-in-five (21%) say full-time work is the ideal situation for them, down from the 32% who said this back in 1997" (Taylor et al., 2007).

Although family roles have changed drastically, workplace organization has failed to keep up and typical American parents have less disposable income now than they did in the 1960s, when a sole breadwinner could comfortably support a family of four (Warren & Warren Tyagi, 2003). Americans work longer hours than the citizens of most industrialized nations; we even put in two more weeks of work each year than our alleged "workaholic" German counterparts. Economist Juliet Schor reported, in *The Overworked American* (1991), that in the last two preceding decades, the average U.S. worker had added an extra 164 hours to his or her work year. That tallies to a whole month more of work completed in 1990 than in 1970. Until the Great Recession, which put a kink in the long-term trend, U.S. work hours had been on the rise. According to the U.S. Bureau of Labor Statistics, in 1970 the average full-time employee worked 42.7 hours per week; in 1988 this figure rose to 43.6 (Hochschild, 1997); by 2007 it was 45.9 (Bureau of Labor Statistics, 2007).

For such long hours, Americans receive little vacation compared with workers in other countries (Figure 14.2). German and Spanish workers average six weeks of paid vacation time; the British get about five. In contrast, the average American worker is entitled to eighteen days but uses only fourteen of those offered.

It's no surprise, then, that the demands of work infringe on home life. This is so even when parents experience one of the most revered and momentous events of family life—the birth of a child. A German mother, after giving birth, is federally entitled to at least 14 weeks of paid maternity leave at full pay. Italian mothers receive 20 paid weeks. Canadian mothers, since legislation

Figure 14.2: Annual Vacation Days and Holidays Worldwide

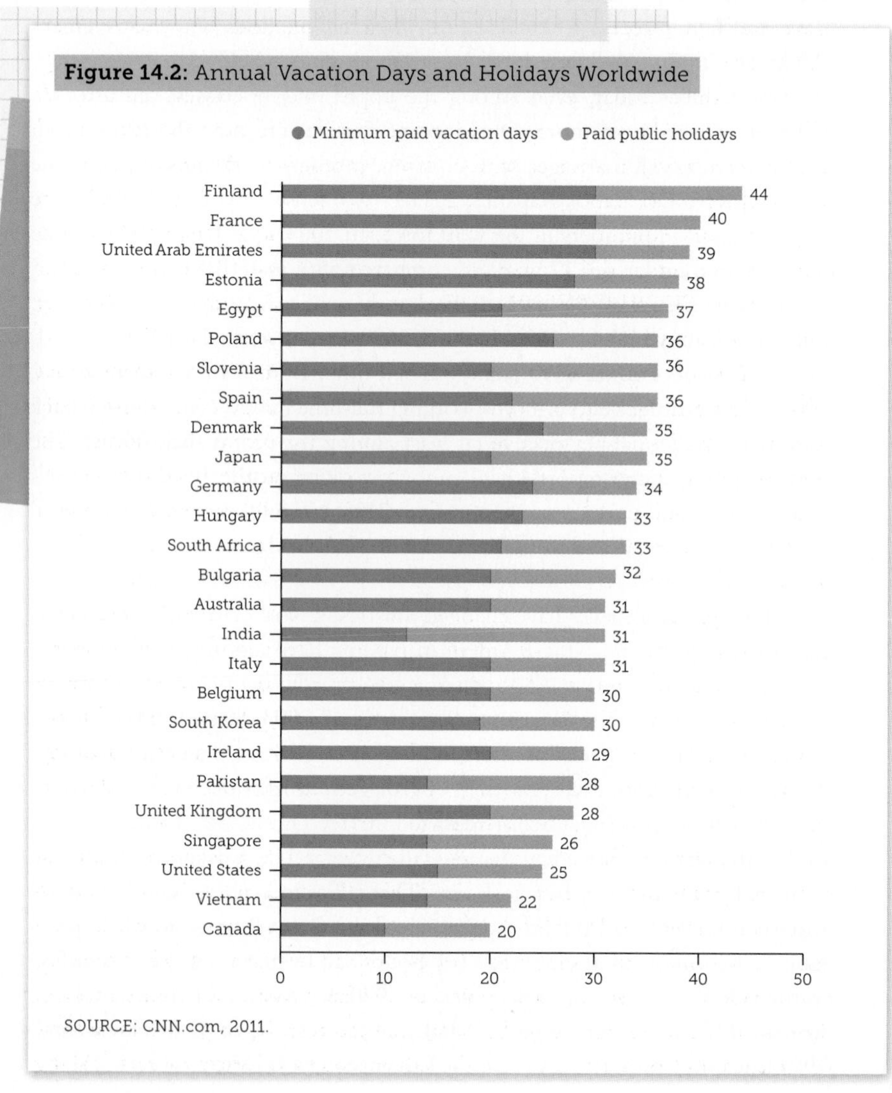

SOURCE: CNN.com, 2011.

in 2002, have the right to take a full year off from work after childbirth at 60 percent of their pay. Mothers in Norway get 80 percent of their salary for their child's first year. In Sweden half of all new fathers take 6 weeks of paid paternity leave. Around the globe, 127 countries, including almost every industrialized nation, guarantee some form of paid leave for parents. The United States is not among them. In 1993, President Bill Clinton signed the much celebrated Family and Medical Leave Act, giving American workers the right to 12 weeks of leave to care for a newborn baby or attend to a family emergency. However, the leave is not necessarily paid, and it applies only to the half of the nation who work for a company of more than 50 employees. The act also doesn't apply to part-timers, most of whom are women.

Curiously enough, when companies do implement family-friendly policies, workers often don't take advantage of them. In *The Time Bind: When Work Becomes Home and Home Becomes Work* (1997), Arlie Hochschild finds that people's lives increasingly center on the world of work, and as a result, families are suffering. The midwestern corporation Hochschild studied, fictitiously called "Amerco," offered generous pro-family policies, such as part-time hours and "flexplace," which allows workers to work from home. Amerco also offered "flextime," so that workers could adjust their schedules, early or late, as they needed. But despite a work environment that seemed family friendly, Hochschild found that most workers ended up working longer hours during the course of their employment. She asks, "Why don't working parents, and others too, take the opportunity available to them to reduce their hours at work?" (1997).

Her answer is surprising and differs from the economic argument about substitution effects. Working parents don't take advantage of family-friendly corporate policies, she asserts, because they prefer to avoid their homes and families. The workplace has become, in a strange departure from nineteenth-century formulations, a haven from the chaos and the emotional and physical disarray of the second shift at home. Hochschild suggests a reversal of the sacred and the profane, in which the home has fallen from grace, with its members seeking refuge and relief at the workplace. For the harried supermom, bombarded by the pressing demands of children, husbands, and housework, work increasingly becomes a safe place of comfort and ease. With too much to do at home and too little time to do it, "a tired parent flees a world of unresolved quarrels and unwashed laundry for the reliable orderliness, harmony, and managed cheer of work. The emotional magnets beneath home and workplace are in the process of being reversed" (1997).

If you find Hochschild's argument too narrowly focused on emotional concerns, you're not alone. In *The Time Divide: Work, Family, and Gender Inequality* (2004), sociologists Jerry Jacobs and Kathleen Gerson argue that workers do not take advantage of family-friendly policies for a number of other reasons: Under cultural and structural conditions that keep work and family divided, they are afraid of losing their jobs. Workers perceive a trade-off between family policies and opportunities for the advancement of their careers. Taking

Balancing work and family life puts a strain on most Americans. Angela drops her daughter off at her parents' house before taking her son to school and going to work at a hospital in Marshall, Missouri. She and her husband both work full time and are up as early as 4:30 a.m. and work as late as 7:30 p.m. during the week.

advantage of parental leave or part-time hours, working parents believe, sends a negative message to the boss that could lead to placement on the "mommy track" and a dead-end career.

Meanwhile, studies consistently show that working mothers are less depressed, have higher self-esteem, and report a greater sense of happiness than housewives. One study even suggests that women who work feel more valued at home than those who stay home (Hochschild, 2003). Women today share what Judith Stacey calls "post-feminist expectations" for family and work. They have "the desire to combine marriage to a communicative, egalitarian man with motherhood and a successful, engaging career" (Stacey, 1996). Such expectations only a few decades earlier would have sounded crazy. Although working mothers have higher self-esteem and better mental health than nonworking ones, studies also show that they are also more likely to feel anxious and tired. They get sick more often than their husbands. Their divorce rates have risen. The entrance of women into the workplace has increased their economic power, but in the absence of other social changes, this subtle revolution will have "stalled," in Hochschild's words.

The flip side of this story is that while the demands of work impinge on life at home, the growing cost of America's middle-class lifestyles means that many families feel they have no choice but to send both parents into the full-time workforce. Economist Elizabeth Warren suggests that it is not Americans' greedy consumer spending habits that are putting them in a financial bind but rather that they are pinched by the cost of safe housing in good school districts combined with the high cost of health care and destabilized career paths (Warren, 2007). It is hard to argue with parents who want their children to be safe and well educated. Yet not all public schools can guarantee either safety or high-quality education, thus increasing the demand for housing in safer, higher-test-scoring neighborhoods, which pushes housing prices beyond the reach of sole-breadwinner families. Mortgages, property taxes, and school tuitions are fixed costs that cannot easily be trimmed if families suffer unforeseen layoffs, medical emergencies, or divorce. In the past few years the personal bankruptcy rate in America has been higher than ever. Approximately one in ten families now find no other way out of their financial quagmires.

The Service Sector

Changing gender roles and work–family tensions are two important features of the current version of capitalism, but they are by no means the only ones. Perhaps the most important recent change in the American economy is that making money no longer exclusively relies on the creation of a tangible product. The service sector, the section of the economy that provides intangible services, has grown rapidly over the last 30 years. These services can range from restaurant work (the largest occupation for women without a college education), to health-care provision, to higher education, to legal or financial advice, to computer tech support, to deep-tissue massages.

Service sector the section of the economy that involves providing intangible services.

How does the new service economy challenge old theories? Does Marx's two-class model still make sense in such an era? How are we alienated differently in the service world than in the manufacturing world? Or is the story largely the same? Service work poses challenges to Smith's and Simmel's theories as well. Does the division of labor proceed apace or slow down with conversion to a service model? And does the evolution toward depersonalized relations of payment and exchange become complicated by occupations that require face-to-face interaction with a smile and a thank you and a receipt (or perhaps your meal is free)?

Globalization

Going hand in hand with the development of the service economy is the complicated and contested process of globalization, generally defined as a multidimensional set of social processes that create, multiply, stretch, and intensify worldwide social exchanges and interdependencies. This means that I can wake up in the morning and have a free video chat with my friend in New Delhi using Skype, buy commodities from a Jamaican company in the afternoon, and in the evening read the Parisian newspaper *Le Figaro* online. But what are the implications of globalization for capitalism? Essentially, it means an increase in trade and economic exchanges among individuals, corporations, and states in different areas of the globe.

Such processes are, however, not entirely new. In the last flush of the great European empires, between 1890 and 1914, for instance, the relative magnitude and geographical scale of trade flow and capital were higher than they are today. However, there are at least four recent phenomena that make the current period of globalization novel: new markets, new means of exchange, new players, and new rules.

First, new markets include financial markets where anyone with the proper equipment can participate. Second, new means of exchange, such as cellular phones, personal computers, e-mail, and the Web, allow for almost instantaneous transactions. (Recall the example of Kate Rich and the Feral Trade network, discussed in Chapter 5.) With these new forms of communication technology, a person in Buenos Aires, Argentina, can buy a commodity in Cape Town, South Africa, and sell it in Moscow, Russia, in a matter of minutes (or seconds, even). Third, there are new players. These new players are all transnational, which makes them unique to this epoch of globalization. The World Trade Organization (WTO), for example, acts as the regulation authority for trade. An increase in multinational corporations (corporations located in more than one country) and worldwide nongovernmental organizations (such as Doctors Without Borders, Oxfam, and Amnesty International) has also occurred. Fourth, new rules are at play. Although countries have always negotiated trade agreements, as of late there has been a proliferation of multilateral trade agreements, including the North American Free Trade Agreement (NAFTA) and, more recently, the Central American Free Trade Agreement (CAFTA). Multilateral means that they don't result from the negotiations between two nation-states, but rather are the end result of negotiations among multiple players and thus enforce rights, impose sanctions, or encourage business at a regional or worldwide level.

One thing that globalization has clearly exposed is the global divide between the haves and the have-nots. For instance, according to a 2011 Credit Suisse report 0.5 percent of the global adults hold more than a third of the world's wealth whereas the majority 68.4 percent of the world have only a collective 4.2 percent of global wealth. This type of unbalanced distribution is often referred to as a champagne-glass distribution of inequality (Credit Suisse, 2011; Figure 14.3). Furthermore, 925 million people are hungry in the world, 1 billion people do not have access to clean drinking water, and 2.3 million children die from preventable diseases (World Food Programme, 2011). On the other hand, these global poverty rates are substantially lower than they were a generation ago, partly as a result of the increased income globalization has brought to many. Debate continues to grow over whether trade and other

Champagne-glass distribution the unequal, global distribution of income, so named for its shape.

Figure 14.3: Champagne-Glass Distribution

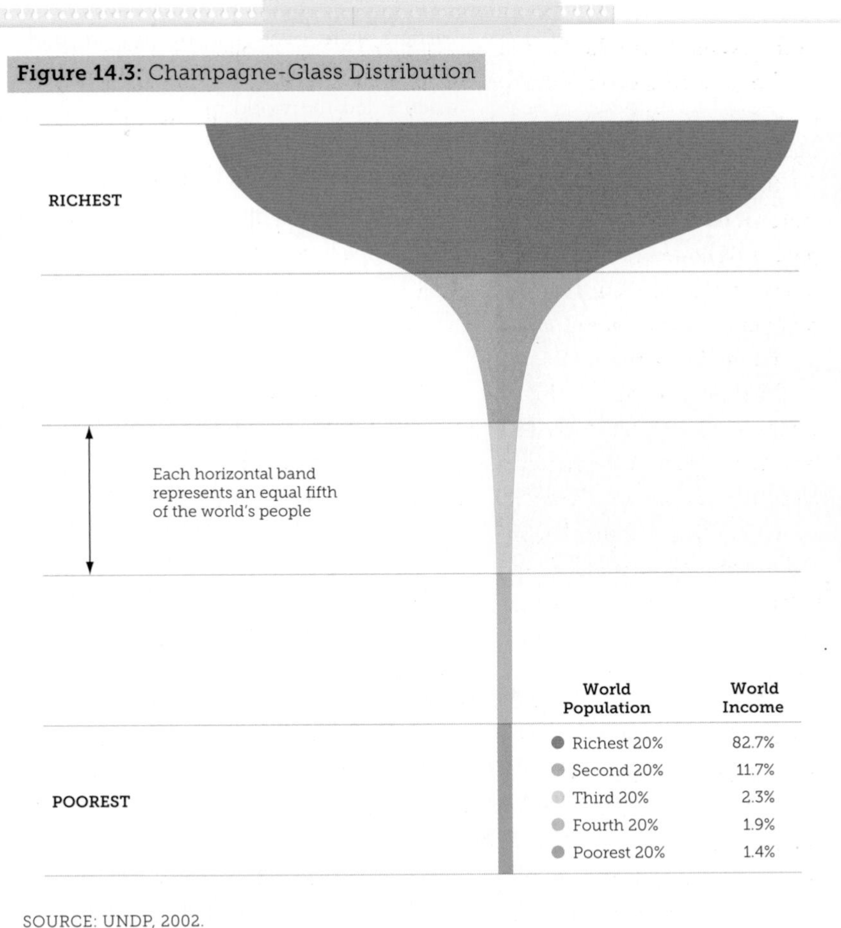

SOURCE: UNDP, 2002.

recent developments in globalization have ameliorated or intensified global income inequality (see Chapter 7 on stratification).

While it might seem like globalization is just the direction toward which history marches, it has come in ebbs and flows. Moreover, there is nothing inevitable about globalization, as Brown University professor Nitsan Chorev points out in her book *Remaking U.S. Trade Policy: From Protectionism to Globalization*, which she discussed with me. "Globalization is not inevitable. It's not only the result of the reduction of the price of transportation, for example. Even when companies each have an interest in [expanding global trade], they had to overcome [protectionist] political barriers that were in place." And, of course, not all industries favor open international markets. In the United States, for instance, the steel and textile industries bitterly opposed trade liberalization. Her book documents how, in the United States at least, those

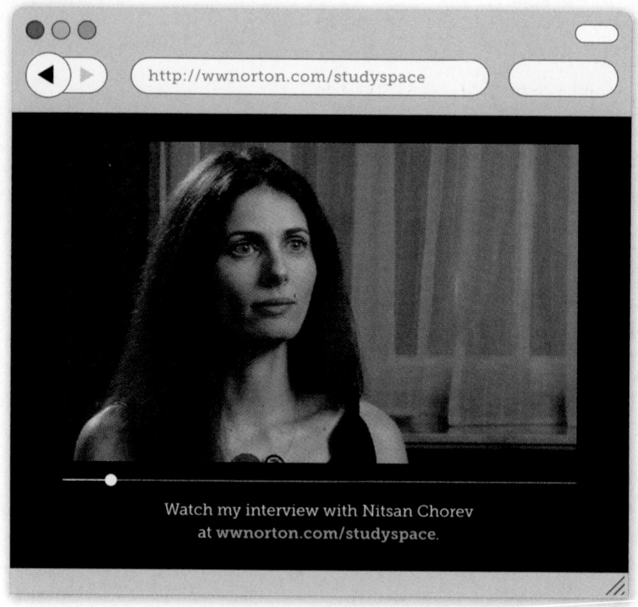

Watch my interview with Nitsan Chorev at wwnorton.com/studyspace.

barriers were overcome by the pro-trade sectors—ironically, the auto industry back when it led the world market—by shifting the locus of policy making from Congress (where members were incentivized to protect their district's businesses from competition even if the whole of the economy was worse off) to the executive and judicial branches (which were more immune to such pressures and, instead, had a national constituency).

Even if increasing globalization is not a law of nature—like gravity—the current wave shows no signs of abating anytime soon. So how can we manage the process so that the losers in this ongoing economic transformation do not suffer dire fates? Chorev has some thoughts here, too:

> So, the solution to the problems that globalization has brought has to be through regulation. And the question is whether the regulation should be at the national level or international. And possibly one could convincingly argue that at the moment, international regulation would be more effective. One possibility, which has been negotiated at the WTO for years now, is adding to trade negotiations agreements that protect labor and [the] environment. The US government does not push enough for it. [And] developing countries resist for obvious reasons: cheap labor is the comparative advantage and if they lose that, then they lose the globalization struggle, right? So, you have to think of other ways. Either through the WTO, or in other means to create a better balance. (Conley, 2011f)

The Reign of the Corporation

Nike, Wal-Mart, Apple, Kraft, Microsoft. These are the engines driving our globalizing economy. Corporations are the institutions that structure economic life in every corner of the planet, displacing the roles of powerful former ruling institutions such as monarchies, religions, and perhaps even governments. As I mentioned earlier, under American law, the corporation is legally an individual. Legal scholars call it a juristic person because it has all the formalized rights, duties, and responsibilities of a person. The Latin root of the term is *corpus*, meaning "body," and a corporation is a body of people that has authority to act as an individual.

Corporate personhood came about through a series of developments starting in the seventeenth century in Europe, at the start of the industrial age. Historically, state governments granted charters to corporations to expand trade and exploration, spawning corporate colonialism such as the massive power and spread of the Dutch and British East India Companies. Under the old ways of doing things, a state provided the charter, and the corporation's duty was to carry out whatever functions the state defined. But in 1886 the U.S. Supreme Court found that the Fourteenth Amendment, intended to protect the rights of freed slaves, also granted corporations the legal status of persons, thus establishing a distinction between corporations and their owners.

The Corporate Psychopath?

From anticorporate movements like the Seattle protests of the WTO in 2000 to everyday "culture jamming," as seen in activist media such as *Adbusters* magazine (see Chapter 3), corporations are vilified for their greed, injustices, and callous ecological devastation. In the award-winning 2003 documentary *The Corporation*, the filmmakers asked: If corporations are legal persons, what kind of personality do they have? Their answer: pathological. Corporations act like psychos, claimed FBI consultant Robert Hare in the film, because they show little regard, remorse, or guilt for harming others; they are unable to maintain long-term relationships; they lie all the time; and they fail to conform to social norms by obeying the law. That's because, like many psychopaths, corporations are solely self-interested—in their case, interested only in the relentless pursuit of profits for their shareholders.

However, as easy as it may be to stigmatize corporations, given the system in which corporations must operate, they're not necessarily pathological so much as rational. Forget the environment, forget workers' rights, forget morals and fairness. Unless these factors improve the bottom line—that is, "shareholder value"—they don't figure into corporate concerns. As the economist Milton Friedman remarked in a now famous *New York Times Magazine* essay, "There is one and only one social responsibility of business—to use its resources and engage in activities designed to increase its profits so long as it stays within the rules of the game, which is to say, engages in open and free competition without deception or fraud" (Friedman, 1970).

Through the rational pursuit of profit, good people can end up doing bad things. Max Weber made this observation about modern bureaucratic organizations, of which corporations are an exemplary form (see Chapter 15). In Weber's theory, bureaucracies flourish because of their efficiency and rational means to achieve profit-driven ends. But there's a cost that comes with the increased power of the specialized bureaucracy: People become alienated from

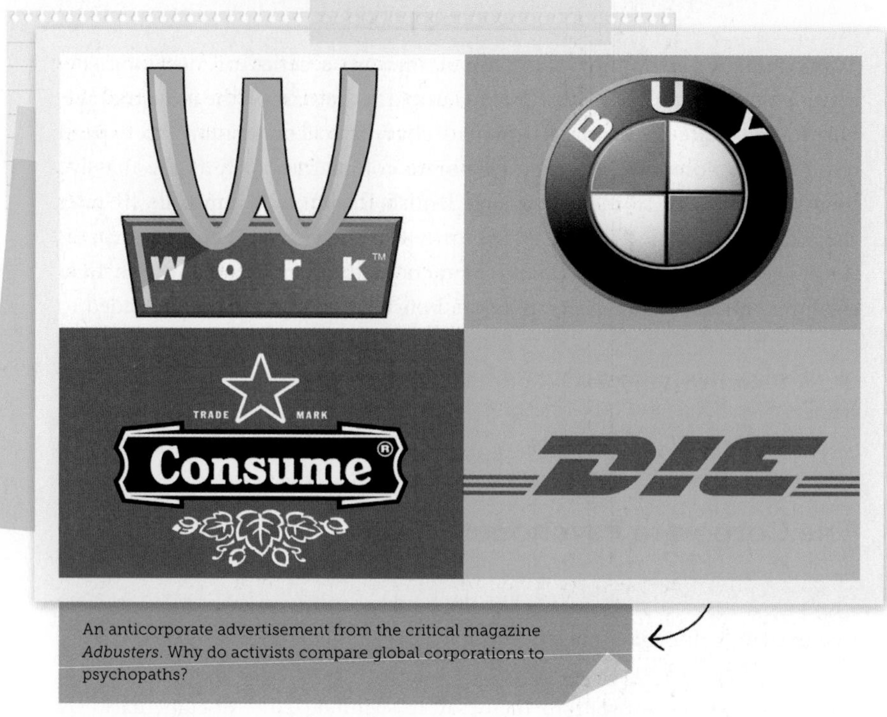

An anticorporate advertisement from the critical magazine *Adbusters*. Why do activists compare global corporations to psychopaths?

any sense of right and wrong and from a human connection, what Weber called the "parceling-out of the soul" (Weber, 1946).

If profit maximization is the nature of the corporation, the problem arises when corporations turn their backs on social responsibility. This involves various types of foul play, from obstructing open competition of the free market to engaging in willful fraud and deceit. When a business is not competitive, it may take the form of a monopoly or oligopoly. A monopoly occurs when one seller of a good or service dominates the market to the exclusion of others, potentially leading to zero competition. In an oligopoly, there are only a handful of sellers. Together, these firms often have enough market power to set prices through what economists call collusion (that is, coordination), such as a cartel. Again, this means effectively zero competition, which is great for the seller firms, because they can charge whatever they like for products or services, regardless of quality. The sellers can reduce supply (including reduction of service standards) to drive up demand and/or drive down costs and reel in huge profits. But this is bad news for consumers, of course, as they will have no close substitutes and are forced to either pay high prices or forgo sometimes vital products. This is also bad news for general social welfare, because without a competitive market, vast inefficiencies arise.

Monopoly the form of business that occurs when one seller of a good or service dominates the market to the exclusion of others, potentially leading to zero competition.

Oligopoly the condition when a handful of firms effectively control a particular market.

Just how competitive are corporations? To do well in the game, it is in their own interests to shut out their competitors from the market. Corporations can do this in a couple of ways without necessarily crossing the line into monopoly.

There's the Microsoft way: Microsoft has maintained its over 80 percent share of the market for personal computing operating systems in the past decades by continually upgrading with new standards that force all computer users to adopt its software to obtain certain computer services (Net Applications, 2011). In this type of extreme monopoly, either you get with the Microsoft program (literally) or you simply can't use a computer easily. Despite numerous lawsuits against Microsoft launched by the U.S. and European Union governments, Microsoft continues to enjoy market dominance and billions of dollars in profits.

Another way to beat the competition is to slide into an industry through the government back door. This is the preferred method of dominance for the Carlyle Group, a multibillion-dollar equity firm that invests in industries such as defense, telecommunications, energy, and health care. How does it achieve mammoth success in these heavily regulated industries? Critics charge that the Carlyle Group's secret is political arbitrage, the use of insider political knowledge to earn profits. By hiring former secretaries of defense, former presidents, and former heads of government regulatory commissions in order to gain access to current officials, the Carlyle Group can influence government decisions on spending and policy in its own favor (Briody, 2003).

Corporations can also dominate the market by offering the lowest prices, thereby attracting the most buyers. To do this, they may lower production costs in a variety of creative ways, such as cutting environmental corners, weakening labor unions, and telling good old-fashioned lies. Of course, they may have just built a better mousetrap and figured out how to manufacture it for a reasonable price. There is no single explanation for corporate profits.

The Environment One way of keeping costs low is to maintain efficient methods of production, which often means bypassing environmental concerns. Caring about the earth's sustainability can be expensive; it requires maintaining low levels of pollution, disposing of waste in safe ways, and maybe investing in costly eco-friendly technology. But helping the environment is not always cost-prohibitive. Some companies like Wal-Mart have found ways to help their bottom line and the environment by doing things like reducing packaging; Apple computer tries to use recyclable materials like glass and aluminum rather than nonrecyclable composites. As a general rule, though, whenever industry spreads to a developing nation, environmental damage ensues. Dumping, pollution, and toxic accidents—such are the costs of development when it occurs without adequate government oversight.

Even in countries with stricter environmental guidelines for industries, disasters happen. Consider the BP Deepwater Horizon drilling rig leak, the worst environmental disaster in U.S. history. While the oil leak was ostensibly caused by an accident, BP was long known for its shoddy safety record. Meanwhile, the government agency charged with overseeing offshore oil drilling, the Minerals Management Service, was stacked with industry executives and hence approved BP's request to drill without a full environmental impact study. And when things blew up (literally and figuratively), BP (and government) officials were caught without a plan to stem the flow of oil in the Gulf of Mexico, and didn't have the resources to clean up the spill's aftermath. In the case of Deepwater Horizon (or the Exxon *Valdez* spill of 1989, for that matter), everyone pays for the accident (especially oil-coated sea creatures), but who is really to blame when our collective lifestyle and policy choices rely on, and facilitate reliance on, imported oil?

Offshoring a business decision to move all or part of a company's operations abroad to minimize costs.

Labor: Sweat It or Bust It Another corporate strategy to reduce production costs is to lower labor costs. One publicly unfavorable way is offshoring labor, that is, moving all or part of a company's operations abroad, to developing nations with lower pay scales and lenient labor laws. By outsourcing production to sweatshops and call centers in the developing world, large companies can manufacture their products for a fraction of what it would cost to pay even minimum wages in the United States. In the globalized economy, offshoring gives corporations based in the developed world access to a comparatively cheap and pliable workforce, largely composed of women, youth, and uneducated rural migrants in search of a better life. This strategy can, however, land companies in hot water in the form of widespread public criticism—as did Kathie Lee Gifford's Kmart apparel line and Nike's use of Asian labor in the 1990s. Amid heightened public awareness, businesses are sometimes held accountable for offshore human rights violations such as starvation wages, intimidation of labor organizers, use of child labor, and inhumane working conditions. In 1991, Levi Strauss was among the first companies to adopt a corporate code of conduct regarding labor. Levi holds its contractors to good labor practices and will assess a nation's human rights record before setting up shop there. Hundreds of American companies now have similar codes. In such a scenario, power is held not by the poor laborers themselves, but by the wealthy first-world consumers who sometimes decide they are willing to pay a bit more in order to consume with a clear conscience.

Union an organization of workers designed to facilitate collective bargaining with employers.

Union busting a company's assault on its workers' union with the hope of dissolving it.

Sometimes, however, organized labor poses a threat to corporate profits. When a group of workers get together for collective bargaining, they form a union, which makes them better able to promote and protect their collective interests than each worker would be alone. When a company assaults its workers' union by, for example, refusing to negotiate or renew a union contract in the hope of breaking it up, it is called union busting. Unionization in America is protected under freedom of association, a right that is generally considered implicit in the First Amendment and was recognized as a human right by the Right to Organize and Collective Bargaining Convention in 1949. Despite legal protection, unionization has been on the decline in the United States since the 1950s, when 35 percent of workers in the private sector were covered by labor contracts compared with just 6.9 percent today Bureau of Labor Statistics, 2011e). The result, according to experts at the Economic Policy Institute, is that workers have taken a toll in the form of increasing income inequality

More than 2,500 employees work in this Haitian factory that produces Levi jeans and Hanes clothing. Why do large corporations like Levi Strauss offshore their manufacturing facilities?

and decreasing health and pension benefits; workers' wages have also failed to continue rising as they did during the postwar glory years (Eisenbrey, 2007). However, drawing a causal link between the two trends is tricky because so many other changes are occurring at the same time. Compare this set of developments with those facing our counterparts in Europe, where strong union contracts cover the majority of workers: 68 percent in Germany and more than 90 percent in Belgium, France, and Sweden (see Figure 14.4). Wage growth across the Atlantic has generally been better for the bottom half of employed earners, but unemployment has also been higher.

What accounts for the decline in U.S. unionization rates? There's a common perception, especially among political conservatives, that unions are outdated, corrupt, and a drag on business. Some complain that government is inefficient, hinting that the high rate of public-sector unionization, 36.8 percent, may be to blame. It's also a widespread notion that unions hurt productivity, in theory because they impose worker rules that obstruct the free market, thereby making employees less efficient. Although this might make theoretical sense, the evidence from industrial studies is mixed. A survey of the economics literature shows that unions are associated positively with productivity in the United States across sectors and particularly in manufacturing (Doucouliagos & Laroche, 2003). And when you look at the countries that have high rates of unionization, they also have correspondingly high rates of productivity (Eisenbrey, 2007). This is perhaps because, with collective bargaining efforts, unionized workers receive contract benefits, and contract benefits make for productive workers. After all, the better your health coverage, working conditions, and job security, the less likely you will be to worry about those things,

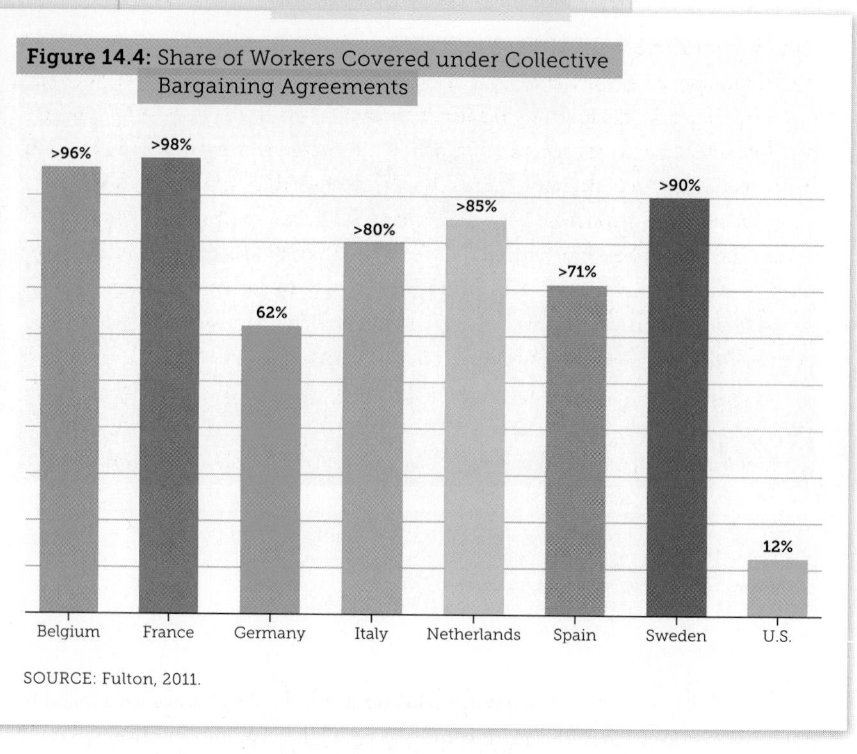

Figure 14.4: Share of Workers Covered under Collective Bargaining Agreements

SOURCE: Fulton, 2011.

and the more you can concentrate on doing your job well. On the other hand, it could be that the trades with enough clout to unionize tend to be those that are highly skilled and productive, making the fact that they are unionized irrelevant to their rewards.

Unions also are widely perceived as corrupt forces that the majority of workers don't want. However, according to several studies, workers today want to be part of a union more than ever before. The majority of workers surveyed in 2006, 85 to 90 percent of one representative sample, desire a greater collective say at the workplace than they had in the mid-1990s. According to a 2011 Gallup poll, 52 percent of Americans say they approve of unions (2011). Even among workers who don't necessarily favor a union, there are a considerable number who want some kind of worker representation that meets regularly with management.

Why don't workers unite if they want collective bargaining, especially given the protections of labor laws under the principle of freedom of association? According to other surveys, workers don't unionize because they are aware of management hostility to collective action (Freeman, 2007). Whether in the form of outright (and illegal) opposition such as intimidating and firing organizers or through subtler means like antiunion presentations on company time, workers get the hint that unions are not the best way to stay on their employer's good side. In fact, in one 2003 survey, workers claimed that the biggest disadvantage of having a union was worse relations between employees and management (Freeman, 2007). It is a vicious circle. Workers might have more security to speak up for their rights if they unionize, but often they never start down that road because they fear for their livelihood if they do. With the rise in global telecommunications and transportation, and a corresponding erosion of protectionist trade policies (such as tariffs designed to make domestic goods competitive with imported ones), companies' threats to pack up and move abroad have only become more realistic since the 1970s. On the other hand, new unionization efforts have increasingly been led by industries heavily represented by immigrants to America. In Los Angeles, janitors and drywallers have recently become unionized; in North Carolina, meatpackers formed a union in the face of management opposition (Milkman, 2006). All of these struggles relied on the support of Central American first- and second-generation immigrants who, recent studies have found, are at least as likely to be in unions as whites (Rosenfeld & Kleycamp, 2009).

Regulating Credit Default Swaps

As much as we might like to think of corporations as malevolent zombie psychopaths, their defenders would argue—as Milton Friedman does in the section above—that they are merely following the rules with one thing in mind: profit maximization. If the rules are broken, hey, blame the government, not the corporations.

While folks who assign evil motives to corporations have probably been watching too much Austin Powers, corporate defenders are telling only half the story: Not only do corporations seek profits by following the rules; often they work to rewrite the rules in their own favor. The results can be disastrous. Exhibit A: The 2008 financial meltdown.

If asked what single policy caused the credit bubble and bust of the 00s decade, most economists, policy analysts, and well-informed Americans might say it was the repeal of Glass-Steagall. The second Glass-Steagall act (officially the Banking Act of 1933) was signed into law in June 1933 after a run on Michigan's banks in January of that year. In addition to setting up the Federal Deposit Insurance Corporation (FDIC), which provided a government guarantee to depositors' accounts up to a certain limit, the law drew a clear distinction between investment banks and commercial banks. Commercial banks were protected from losses but also were restricted in the forms of investments they could make. Basically, they were forbidden from entering the securities

Henry Paulson, secretary of the U.S. Treasury, left, and Ben S. Bernanke, chairman of the U.S. Federal Reserve, testify before the U.S. Congress in 2008 about credit default swaps.

markets—trading in stocks, bonds, or derivatives. Its full repeal was effected by the Financial Services Modernization Act of 1999, which obliterated the distinction between commercial and investment banks by allowing your local Main Street bank, as well as industry behemoths like Bank of America, to leverage your deposit in the global securities markets. Whom do we have to thank for this "modernization" act? Yep, you guessed it: the banking lobby.

Of course, many other factors came into play in pumping up (and collapsing) the financial soufflé—ranging from the fact that the Fannie Mae and Freddie Mac corporations were privately owned, for-profit companies that gave loans to homebuyers with an implicit government backing to the rapid expansion of the subprime credit market. But one policy that gets remarkably little attention, despite its central role in the haywire credit markets of the naughts decade, was the decision, made by a midlevel bureaucrat in the New York State Insurance Department, that credit default swaps did not constitute insurance.

A credit default swap is a private contract between two parties in which one pays the other a "premium" so that if the underlying loan or bond defaults—the borrower does not pay back, goes bankrupt, or otherwise fails—then the entity that has been paying the premium gets a lump sum. Sounds a lot like insurance: You pay a premium to the company, and if you die or your house burns down, then you (or your beneficiary) get a lump sum.

While at one time insurance was illegal—it was considered gambling—today it is a regulated market where policy sellers are required to hold in reserve certain monies in order to make sure they can cover policies if the policies get called in at a reasonable rate. With a few major exceptions, that system has worked for the better part of the last century. But in the waning days of the Clinton administration, banking industry lobbyists, led by Federal Reserve Chairman Alan Greenspan, rushed to write and pass the Commodity Futures Modernization Act of 2000. This bill was buried within a budget act that ran longer than 10,000 pages. It was never debated (and probably not read by more than a handful of legislators) before it was passed on the eve of the congressional Christmas recess. The Commodity Futures Modernization Act exempted credit default swaps from federal oversight and gave the contracts immunity from state gambling laws.

Coincidentally, the final piece of groundwork for the disaster had already been laid six months earlier when a French-owned bond insurance company wrote the New York State Insurance Department to inquire whether it could enter the market for credit default swaps as part of its insurance business. Rochelle Katz, an associate attorney at the department, wrote back that it could not, because "[a]bsent . . . a contractual provision [for indemnification], the instrument is not an insurance contract" (Katz, 2000). The rest is history—financial history.

Seeing how policy gets made can be worse than seeing how sausage gets made.

→ CONCLUSION

This chapter has taken us through a rapid tour of modern capitalism. We started with the enclosure movement, wherein the commons were divided up into private parcels of land, marking the beginning of the end of the feudal way of life. Soon improved agricultural technology supported many more people, leading to industrialization, urbanization, and monetization. Legal structures, such as the rise of limited liability and corporate personhood, evolved to accommodate the new relations of production. And voilá, there you have modern industrial capitalism. Some scholars, such as Smith and Simmel, saw these developments as important steps forward, leading to greater wealth and personal freedom for all; others, such as Weber and Marx, took a darker view of the rise of capitalism, pointing to alienation and the "parceling out" of the soul. Modern capitalism has, as we have seen, undergone a number of changes since the period in which these folks were writing. We have witnessed a new era of globalization, a workforce composition gender change, the emergence of a large service sector, and the rise and fall of trade unionism. Where we go from here is anyone's guess. But you now have the tools to make as educated a guess as anyone.

PRACTICE

ASSIGNMENT

As discussed in this chapter, Americans are not guaranteed paid family leave (unlike the citizens of many other countries). However, there is some variation on this matter from state to state and from one employer to the next. Find out whether your school offers paid family leave to employees. If so, what kind of benefits does it provide? Are only certain types of employees eligible? Do your state and city have family leave programs that go beyond federal policies?

QUESTIONS FOR REVIEW

1. As we saw at the beginning of the chapter, people like President Obama are increasingly mixing work and home life. How might this trend be related to globalization and the decline in labor unions?
2. How are guest worker programs (temporary work visas for migrants) and offshoring labor potentially related? In your own words, provide two arguments for and against guest worker programs in the United States.
3. How do Arlie Hochschild's findings in *The Time Bind* differ from our understanding of the substitution effect? How do Jerry Jacobs and Kathleen Gerson build on Hochschild's work?
4. Barack Obama is known for many firsts, including being the first BlackBerry president. How has technology increasingly changed our relationship between work and home?
5. What is capitalism? How were the "enclosure movement" and "monetization" related to the advent of capitalism?
6. How does Adam Smith, in *The Wealth of Nations*, suggest that capitalism helps keep societies together? How do monopolies deviate from Smith's ideal view of capitalism?
7. Describe the concept of "alienation" as described by Karl Marx and illustrate two of its forms with examples. How does Max Weber's negative view of capitalism differ from Marx's?
8. How did the $5 per day wage at the Ford Motor Company shine a light on judgments about families and the role of women in society?

PARADOX

THE MORE ONE EARNS, THE MORE ONE CAN AFFORD LEISURE; HOWEVER, THE MORE ONE EARNS, THE MORE IT COSTS TO NOT WORK IN TERMS OF FORGONE WAGES.

WATCH THE ANIMATED SHORT ABOUT THE CAPITALISM AND THE ECONOMY PARADOX AT

WWNORTON.COM/STUDYSPACE

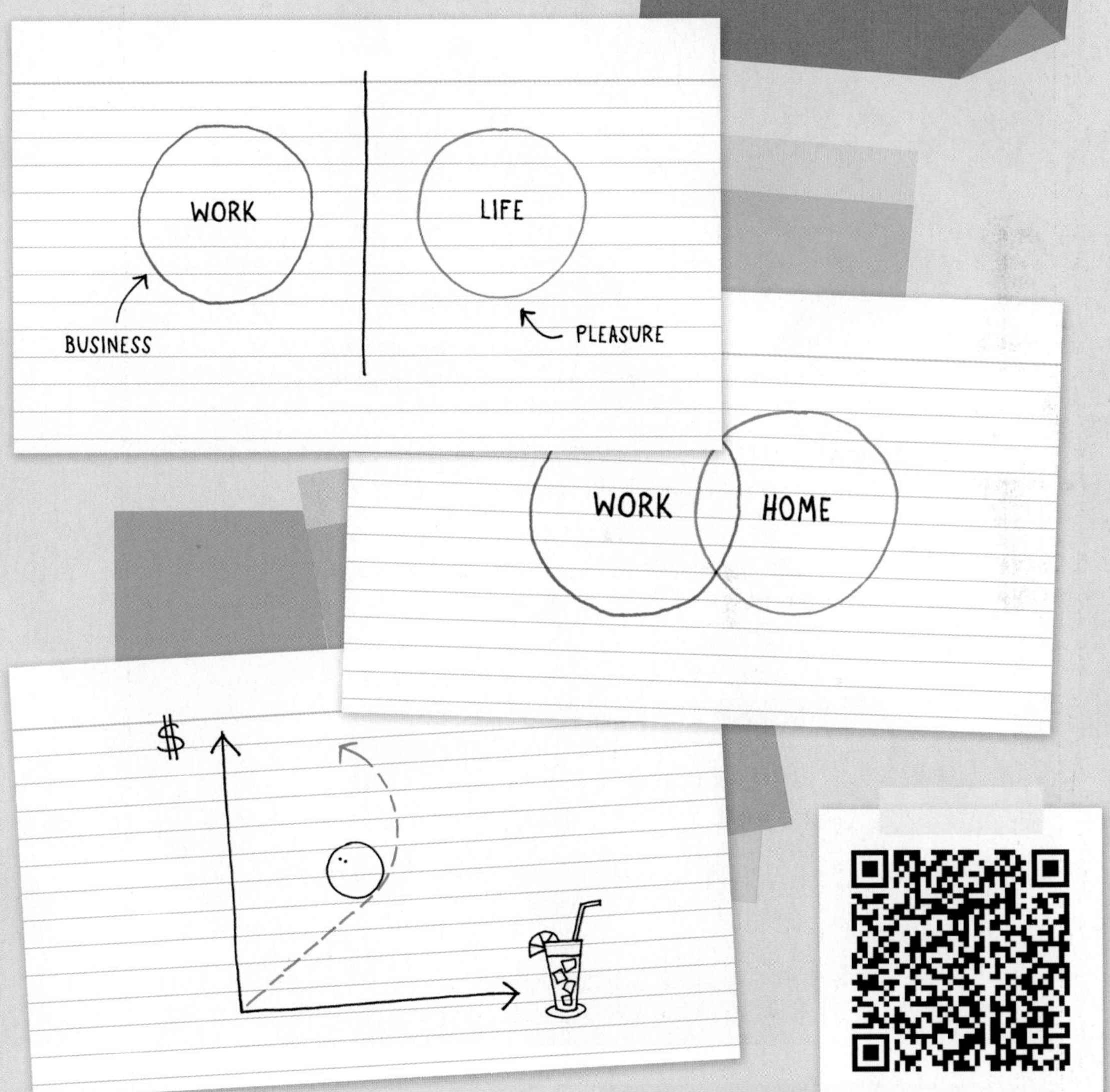

A passport, stamps, and coins from Sealand. Should we consider Sealand a state? Why or why not?

15 Authority and the State

PARADOX

AUTHORITY IS BASED ON THE IMPLICIT THREAT OF VIOLENCE, BUT THE MOMENT THAT FORCE IS USED, ALL AUTHORITY IS LOST.

Prince Roy of Sealand, formerly Paddy Roy Bates, is the sovereign ruler of the small, previously abandoned sea fort Roughs Tower off the coast of England. Built by the British during World War II to protect the English mainland, Fort Roughs Tower is a mere six nautical miles from shore and only a few thousand square feet. On September 2, 1967, capitalizing on the peculiarities of international law, Paddy Roy Bates and his family became the proud new owners of this principality. Roy of Sealand and his wife, the Princess of Sealand, were royalty overnight. The British government, of course, didn't quite agree.

According to Sealand's official Web site, in late 1968 the British navy "entered the territorial waters claimed by Roy of Sealand," and "as he was aware of his sovereignty, Roy of Sealand threatened the navy by undertaking defensive activity. Shots were fired from Sealand in warning." To translate, Prince Roy decided both to press his luck by engaging the British military and to test his claim of statehood by taking a couple of pot shots in defense of his small hunk of metal. Unimpressed by the prince, the British government summoned him to appear in court.

In a spectacular victory for hopeful nation builders everywhere, the British court found that Sealand was not subject to mainland law because it was located too far outside territorial waters. The royal Roy family stayed put and continued to inhabit the concrete-and-steel island for what has now been more than 40 years. Of course, the history of Sealand has not been without its share of conflict.

Ten years after his successful court battle, Prince Roy entered into talks with German businessmen over the prospect of building a casino on the fort, but the negotiations quickly went sour. Accurate details of the ensuing debacle are hard to come by. In one account, Sealand was occupied by 30 Germans who first imprisoned Prince Roy's son, the Prince Regent Michael, and then shipped him off to Holland on a passing fishing vessel. According to another version of the story, the Prince Regent was merely captured and locked in Sealand's kitchen (Crenson, 2005). Both stories, however, agree that, upon reports of Sealand's hostile takeover, Prince Roy flew back to the kingdom by helicopter, declaring that he would sooner blow the island to pieces than see it ruled by crooks. Depending on whose story you believe, Prince Roy retook the fort—either single-handedly or by enlisting the help of some 20 friends. He also rescued his son, who was either peacefully enjoying tea and crumpets in Sealand's kitchen or afloat somewhere off the coast of Holland.

At any rate, Prince Roy was again triumphant. Current Sealand official documents indicate that the nation now boasts its own state bank, weather service, and heliport (in case the country is again invaded by the Germans). Parties interested in claiming a piece of Sealand can purchase a royal title online for approximately U.S.$48.

If being a run-of-the-mill baron or baroness of Sealand won't suffice, and you find yourself with an extra few thousand dollars to spend, you might consider looking into your own alternative real estate opportunities in Earth's most expansive, untapped housing market: the open seas. The Seasteading Project (**www.seasteading.org**), a little-known aquatic investment opportunity, seeks to build permanent oceanic platforms for the adventurous nation builder for as little as $50 to $200 per square foot of sovereignty. The Seasteading Project is dedicated to "lower[ing] the barrier of entry to the market of government."

If you hope to be an effective ruler, read this chapter with an eye to the mechanics of statehood—what it means to be a state, how you might go about keeping your polity intact, and what functions your state is expected to perform. Although most of this chapter concerns the work of one social theorist, Max Weber, we will also look at more recent developments in state theory. By the end of this chapter, you should be well equipped to buy and rule your own sea kingdom, or at least to speak intelligently about states in the modern world.

Students, before reading this chapter, please turn to page 738 and read the passage there. When you have finished, continue reading this section.

Types of Legitimate Authority

Politics power relations among people or other social actors.

Authority the justifiable right to exercise power.

The case of Prince Roy's oceanic haven and the mechanics of statehood are areas of investigation in the subdiscipline of political sociology, which studies politics—power relations among people or other social actors, be it at a governmental level or an interpersonal level or any level in between. To pass judgment on whether Prince Roy's Sealand merits statehood, we need to define the term *state*. And before we can do that, we need to talk about authority, the justifiable right, not just the ability, to exercise power. Rulers have authority if they can persuade their subordinates that their claim to power is valid.

To classify the kinds of legitimate authority or domination, sociologist Max Weber used three accounts of a ruler's "superiority and fitness to rule" (Parkin, 1982). These explanations are sometimes referred to as "claims to legitimacy" or the legitimation of authority and domination. When you, as a kid, asked to stay up past your bedtime, your mom or dad may have invoked parental authority by denying your request with a simple "because I said so" or "because I'm the parent, that's why." Generally, Weber expects rulers to legitimate their claim to authority with better explanations.

Charismatic Authority

The first type of authority, charismatic authority, rests on the personal appeal of an individual leader. Have you ever met someone at school, at work, or in your group of friends who, for reasons that might have eluded you at the time, was referred to as a natural leader? This person may have had an uncanny way with people and was probably the center of attention, comfortable making decisions, responding to crises, and delivering orders with enviable panache. This "superhuman" aura and affective appeal are what Weber called charisma, specific qualities that inspire loyalty and obedience in others.

Charismatic authority authority that rests in the personal appeal of an individual leader.

Charismatic leaders such as Barack Obama succeed based largely on their personal appeal. What are the limitations of charismatic authority?

Think about presidential elections, when a candidate may be criticized for his insipid personality, poor sense of humor, or inadequate social grace—in other words, his lack of charisma. Note the ever-popular candidate charisma test: Would you rather have dinner with candidate X or candidate Y? The personal appeal of leaders has real consequences. In *Freakonomics* (2005), Steven Levitt and Stephen Dubner verify Weber's intuitions about charisma with cold, hard numbers, finding that no amount of campaign money will help a candidate win an election if the electorate just doesn't like him or her. (Of course, in this day and age, money—spent well—may help buy spin and, in turn, charisma; the relationship may be difficult to untangle.)

Because charismatic authority derives from the extraordinary attributes of a single individual, Weber anticipated that this form of legitimate authority would be particularly difficult to maintain or pass on. Imagine you are involved in a brand-new college club, for instance, with a hotshot leader who seems to be on top of everything from budget concerns to public relations. When your leader graduates, what happens to your club? Weber believes there are two options: Either you, as the club's new president, follow the hotshot's lead and try to do everything exactly as she did, or you write a constitution detailing the organization's rules and procedures. In the first case, hotshot's charismatic authority has become traditionalized; in the latter, it has been rationalized.

Traditional Authority

Traditional authority authority based on appeals to the past or traditions.

Traditional authority, as the name implies, rests on appeals to the past or traditions. Rule based on traditional authority dominates "by virtue of age-old rules and power," and leaders are "designated according to traditional rules and are obeyed because of their traditional status" (Weber, 1922/1968). Hereditary monarchies, whereby the crown passes down through a single family, are examples of traditional authority, as are the customs and ceremonies contained in the Jewish Torah. We consent to this type of legitimate domination because it is the way things have always been, the way our parents and grandparents did it, and the way we are expected to do it, too. For example, if you have ever attempted to improvise on your great-great-grandmother's cookie recipe, only to be reprimanded by your mother ("No, we have to make it the way grandma did!"), you are well acquainted with traditional authority.

Unlike charismatic authority, traditional authority does not suffer from problems of succession, but it has its own set of difficulties. Because all the decisions in a traditionalized club would be made with reference to what the former leader did in the now distant past, the club would not be very adaptable. In fact, it would be almost incapable of adapting to new circumstances unless something the first leader did or said established a clear precedent for action.

Legal-Rational Authority

How is a police officer following procedures an example of legal-rational authority?

Legal-rational authority—the brand of authority that is supposedly most pervasive in modern society—is based on legal, impersonal rules. The rules rule. Even individuals in positions of authority are subject to these ubiquitous, impersonal rules (Weber, 1922/1968). Formal roles and rules overshadow the personal attributes of individuals and traditional ways of doing things. If you are arrested on the street by a police officer for disorderly conduct, you obey not by virtue of the officer's charm and upstanding character but because the officer reminds you that "it's the law." Likewise, the police officer does not have the authority to dispense with you as he or she pleases but has to follow a given set of rules, reading you your Miranda rights and properly documenting the entire event for his or her superiors and for the court system. At the station, the officer is responsible for filing the required paperwork and reporting the incident in accordance with the rules. In this form of authority, rules and roles transcend individuals.

Legal-rational authority a system of authority based on legal, impersonal rules; the rules rule.

Legal-rational authority is highly routinized, based on a standard, regular procedure. In the context of authority, routinization refers to the clear, rule-governed procedures used repeatedly for decision making. For example, the police officer writes down an offender's violations of the law, handcuffs the offender, and then transports the offender to the police station. Legal authority is also highly rationalized or subject to ever-expanding modes of organization. That is, each step of a given process is rationalized to the extent that it is governed by considerations of efficiency. One last important aspect of legal-rational authority is that it is attached to roles, not individuals. Not just anyone has the authority to make you comply by putting your hands into metal cuffs and following orders. The police officer has that authority—but only if he or she is following proper procedure.

Routinization the clear, rule-governed procedures used repeatedly for decision making.

Rationalization an ever-expanding process of ordering or organizing.

A bureaucracy is a legal-rational organization or mode of administration that governs with reference to formal rules and roles and emphasizes meritocracy. For example, have you ever wanted to enroll in a course that was already filled to capacity? Maybe you needed that particular course to fulfill a requirement. If so, you might have visited the registrar's office to beg for permission to enroll in that course. Once there, you probably waited in a long line only to discover that the registrar would grant you no favors because "that's the rule." You might have tried to convince her that it would be very easy to enroll you, or you might have resorted to manipulation with a good, theatrical cry or a flirtatious smile. But, alas, you would be admitted to the class only if another rule exists permitting exceptions to enrollment limits.

Bureaucracy a legal-rational organization or mode of administration that governs with reference to rules and roles and emphasizes meritocracy.

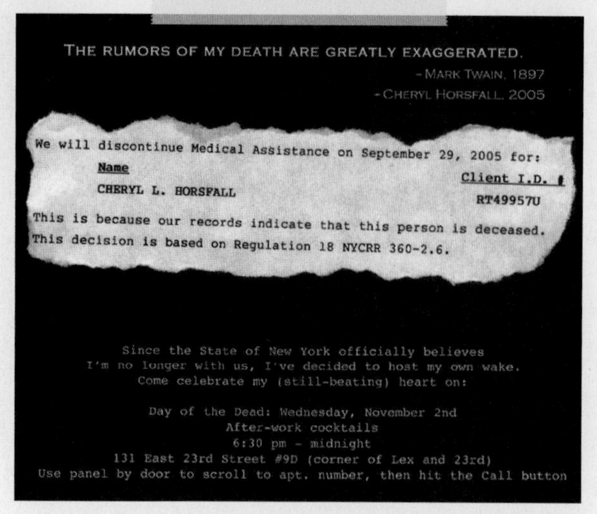

THE RUMORS OF MY DEATH ARE GREATLY EXAGGERATED.
- MARK TWAIN, 1897
- CHERYL HORSFALL, 2005

We will discontinue Medical Assistance on September 29, 2005 for:
Name
CHERYL L. HORSFALL
Client I.D. #
RT49957U
This is because our records indicate that this person is deceased.
This decision is based on Regulation 18 NYCRR 360-2.6.

Since the State of New York officially believes
I'm no longer with us, I've decided to host my own wake.
Come celebrate my (still-beating) heart on:

Day of the Dead: Wednesday, November 2nd
After-work cocktails
6:30 pm - midnight
131 East 23rd Street #9D (corner of Lex and 23rd)
Use panel by door to scroll to apt. number, then hit the Call button

A clerical error by the state of New York declared Cheryl Horsfall legally dead. On the left is the invitation to her "wake." On the right, Horsfall (holding a wine glass and very much alive) "mourns" with a friend.

No matter how infuriating the registrar's "red tape" (common parlance for the morass of bureaucratic rules), it would probably never compare with the red tape of a state bureaucracy. Take the case of Cheryl Horsfall, who was effectively killed by a state bureaucracy—not really murdered, but rather technically murdered. In 2005, a New York State agency sent Horsfall a letter stating that she was deceased, although it gave no details about the cause or date of her supposed death. Because Horsfall was dead in the eyes of New York State, her application for health insurance was denied. What could Cheryl do other than hold a wake for herself? So she did—complete with a shrine, candles, flowers, coconut cake, and guests, which included several ex-boyfriends (Wilkinson, 2006). To rejoin the living, Horsfall had to make numerous, unanswered phone calls and trek back and forth to various state agencies; she eventually received official documentation attesting to the fact that she was alive. How did this thing called bureaucracy manage to take the life of one innocent New Yorker?

Characteristics of Bureaucracies Bureaucracies seek to make routine tasks efficient and to provide order in a disorderly world. They have five defining characteristics. First, they are usually structured hierarchically, meaning that the bureaucratic organization has many levels, and there are frequently multiple people working at each level of administration. Each successive level is typically assigned different tasks, and higher levels supervise lower levels. Each successively higher level is also granted greater decision-making control. If you must get something done through a bureaucratic organization, you may need to work with people at more than one level, often starting at the bottom and working your way up.

Second, the positions within a bureaucracy are highly specialized. Specialization, the opposite of generalization, refers to the process of giving each person specific, delimited tasks. Instead of one worker in a bureaucracy having several functions, each worker has a small and related set of specific functions. Taylorism or scientific management is an example of the specialization or division of labor, referring to the methods of labor management introduced by Frederick Winslow Taylor to streamline the processes of mass production. Along a figurative or literal assembly line, one worker might insert screws, the next worker might tighten the screws, and the third worker might cover the screws with plastic caps. A worker in a state bureaucracy might spend all day entering information from timesheets into a database; checking the timesheets and tallying them would be the work of other bureaucrats. Similarly, the "deceased" Cheryl Horsfall might never have received her proof-of-life documentation if she hadn't found the right person to contact.

People waiting in line to submit their passport applications. As a result of changes in travel rules in 2007, the U.S. State Department was unable to keep up with the backlog of passport requests.

Specialization the process of making work consist of specific, delimited tasks.

Taylorism the methods of labor management introduced by Frederick Winslow Taylor to streamline the processes of mass production in which each worker repeatedly performs one specific task.

A bureaucracy is also distinguished by its impersonality: The person working in a bureaucracy is detached from the role he or she plays. Think back to your trip to the registrar to enroll in the full-to-capacity course. If you tried crying to convince the bureaucrat at the registrar's office that you should be allowed to enroll, it may not have worked because you appealed to the person, not the role, by using human empathy as a form of manipulation. Bureaucracies function by demanding that individual workers act only in accord with the designated tasks and responsibilities of their specific role. In fact, the authority of a given bureaucrat rests on the very fact that he or she "doesn't make the rules." The very fact that everyone has a superior all the way up the food chain is what legitimates authority at each rung. That is, of course, one of the dangers of bureaucracy: the lack of personal responsibility for one's moral decisions within the framework of the organization (think of Germany's Third Reich, for instance, and the now infamous Nuremburg defense, "I was only following orders").

This also means that workers' individual quirks, personality traits, and even human empathy are relatively unimportant to their functioning within a role. Likewise, promotions to higher levels within an idealized bureaucratic hierarchy are based on achievement, not personal attributes or favoritism, making a bureaucracy a meritocracy. Bureaucracies are also (in theory) highly efficient. The application of practical, specialized knowledge to specific goals is a trademark of bureaucratic administration.

Meritocracy a society that assigns social status, power, and economic rewards on achievement, not ascribed, personal attributes or favoritism.

Of course, there is no "perfect" bureaucracy. Indeed, crying in front of the registrar may have worked, because inherent to organizations are rules to allow for exceptions to rules. So, if the registrar was a savvy and empathetic bureaucrat, she might have thought up a solution that entailed enrolling you in an independent study with that same professor with the exact same course requirements. Officially, the rule about enrollment limits would have been respected, yet you can get what you need, the registrar can get you out of her office, and the entire legal-rational structure would not collapse into anarchy.

Weber once said that bureaucracy was the "iron cage" of modern life. (How must Cheryl Horsfall, supposedly deceased, have felt, being alive and well but trapped by the red tape of a state bureaucracy?) Weber criticized bureaucratic administration and its effects on individuals and modern society. He complained about specialization, hierarchy, and meritocracy, as the world becomes "filled with nothing but those little cogs, little men clinging to little jobs and striving toward bigger ones" (1946). He referred to bureaucracy as the "parceling-out of the soul," an allusion to its specialization and bloodless efficiency. Weber also believed that bureaucracy was an unstoppable, totalizing machine becoming ubiquitous in the modern world—even infecting the human soul.

Obedience to Authority

Earlier in the chapter, did you turn to the end of the chapter when instructed to do so? Why? You probably decided to obey my command because, as the author of a sociology textbook and as a college professor, I have some degree of authority. But why, although we've never met and you haven't experienced my charismatic appeal, did you obediently flip through a few hundred pages to find the correct page? The following case study shows that obedience to authority is an extraordinarily powerful mechanism of social control, capable of making perfectly rational people do otherwise unthinkable things. (Recall our discussion of social control in Chapter 6.)

The Milgram Experiment

Milgram experiment an experiment devised in 1961 by Stanley Milgram, a psychologist at Yale University, to see how far ordinary people would go to obey a scientific authority figure.

In 1961, Stanley Milgram, a psychologist at Yale University (whose work on social networks we examined in Chapter 5), devised a test, the so-called Milgram experiment, to see how far ordinary people would go to obey an authority figure. The experiment's participants, men of various backgrounds, were told that the experiment sought to test the effects of punishment on learning. As the "teacher," each participant was asked to administer an electric shock to a "learner" in another room when the learner gave an incorrect answer in a word-pairing exercise. With each wrong answer, the teacher was instructed to administer a higher-voltage electric shock to the learner. Unknown to the

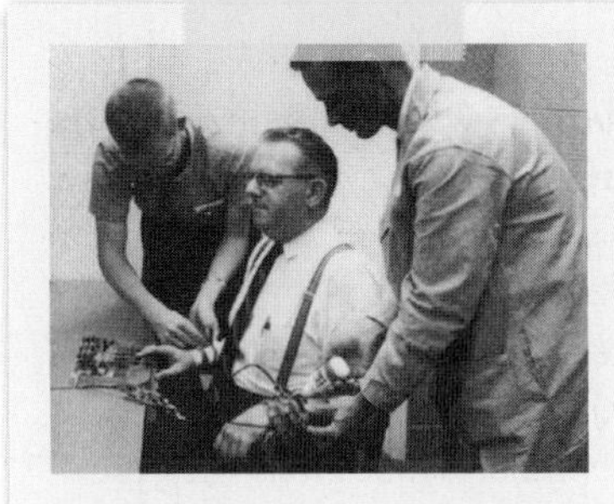

Scenes from the Milgram experiment. What does the experiment tell us about authority?

research subjects was the fact that the learner was not actually receiving electric shocks but was an actor employed by Milgram.

At the beginning of the experiment, the actor would set up a tape recorder with prerecorded sounds for each level of electrical shock. After an established number of wrong answers, the experiment's participants would hear the actor crying out in pain, begging the teacher to abort the test, and complaining of a serious heart condition. If the research subject expressed apprehension or refused to continue the experiment, Milgram's research team would issue a series of verbal prods, ordering him to continue. For example, the first time a participant hesitated, the researcher would say, "Please continue." After a second hesitation, the researcher would say, "It is essential that you continue." After a third hesitation, the researcher would urge, "You have no choice, you must continue." The white-coated member of the experimental team would assure the subject that the researcher would bear all responsibility. Many of the experiment's participants burst into fits of nervous laughter, expressed displeasure and anxiety, and threatened to stop the experiment. With the prodding of the Yale researchers, however, 65 percent of the research subjects went on shocking the learner to the highest voltage level, labeled "lethal."

Before the experiment, Milgram had asked a group of psychologists to estimate the percentage of research participants who would continue shocking an obviously distressed person to the maximum voltage level. The psychologists estimated that fewer than 10 percent would continue all the way up the voltage ladder. This experiment shed some light on how normal people could be complicit in war crimes like the Holocaust.

Authority, Legitimacy, and the State

Authority is key to our understanding of statehood; but before we define a state, we first have to talk about power. According to Weber's *Economy and Society*, a social actor has power if he or she is able to "carry out his own will *despite resistance*" (1922/1968). For instance, if you were a particularly difficult child and resisted your parents' attempt to impose a bedtime but your resistance was

Power the ability to carry out one's own will despite resistance.

futile, your parents had power. If over a cacophony of congressional support, the president vetoes a bill, the president has power. This definition of power may seem very simple and straightforward, but it is hard to pin down, because power may be based on "all conceivable qualities of a person and all conceivable combinations of circumstances" (1922/1968), such as the power of personal persuasion through rhetorical argument or the power of love. Weber, however, gives us some tools to describe certain types of social power.

Domination the probability that a command with specific content will be obeyed by a given group of people.

Domination is a "special case of power." Weber defines it as the "probability that a command with a given specific content will be obeyed by a given group of persons." There are two types of domination: domination by economic power and domination by authority. Domination by economic power, as defined by Weber, is control "by virtue of a constellation of interests" or "by virtue of a position of monopoly" (1922/1968). John D. Rockefeller's Standard Oil is an excellent example of domination by economic power: Until it was dissolved by the government in 1911 for violation of antitrust laws, the company was in a position to issue commands and dictate the price of oil to oil producers by virtue of its monopoly on oil refining. If the oil producers didn't like it, they were out of luck because Standard Oil was their only customer.

State as defined by Weber, "a human community that (successfully) claims the *monopoly of the legitimate use of physical force* within a given territory."

Domination by authority refers to a situation in which the will of the ruler influences the conduct of the ruled so they act as if the ruler's will were also their own (Weber, 1922/1968). In other words, it is the willing obedience of the ruled to the commands of legitimate authority. Your deference to your parents and professors and your obedience to the laws of the U.S. government are examples of domination by authority. Even though Weber acknowledges that domination by economic power is more common, he uses the term *domination* to refer only to domination by authority, of which the state is the ultimate example.

What makes Don Corleone, Marlon Brando's character in *The Godfather*, an example of a leader who dominates by authority?

In *Politics as a Vocation* (a 1919 lecture at Munich University), Weber issued one of the most succinct and oft-cited (though contested) definitions of the state: A state, he wrote, is "a human community that (successfully) claims the *monopoly of the legitimate use of physical force* within a given territory" (2004). What exactly does this statement mean? It means that hidden under any form of domination by authority—and, by extension, any state—is the threat of violence. A perfect illustration of Weber's claim is the film *The Godfather*. The Corleone family works in a manner analogous to a state: Its members kowtow before Don Corleone because they know that if they don't do what is asked of them, they'll disappear permanently. Don Corleone doesn't have to make threats to back up

Mary Ann Vecchio kneels by the body of fellow student Jeffrey Miller during the May 4, 1970, antiwar demonstration at Kent State University. How does the Kent State massacre illustrate the paradox of authority?

his orders; rather, it is implicit that there will be consequences if his orders are not followed and that he has the power to exact physical punishment if he is crossed. (However, he is not a one-man state, as he does not quite have a monopoly on the use of physical force and it is not seen as legitimate by many.)

Using Weber's terminology, we would say that Don Corleone wields authority over the Corleone crime family: the ability to convince others to do as he wishes without resorting to coercion (i.e., forcing them to). Just the implicit threat of physical force suffices. But what happens if one of the Corleones demands something—money, for example—from someone who isn't in the family and thus is not fully aware of Don Corleone's authority? He will likely resort to coercion, the use of force to get these outsiders to do what he wants. In the quaint parlance of another notorious crime family, the Sopranos, you can either "play nice" or get whacked. It is in the direct use of such threats that coercion differs from authority, in which the physical ability to back up one's power is *implicitly* understood.

Coercion the use of force to get others to do what you want.

Within this difference lies the paradox of authority. Even though the state's (or Tony Soprano's) authority derives from the implicit threat of physical force, as soon as the state resorts to physical coercion, all its legitimate authority is lost. In other words, having to resort to violence is proof that people are not listening to you. The annals of world history corroborate Weber's theory. Take,

Paradox of authority although the state's authority derives from the implicit threat of physical force, resorting to physical coercion strips the state of all legitimate authority.

for example, a tragic case from America's past. On May 4, 1970, a group of unarmed students at Kent State University in Ohio assembled peacefully to protest the Vietnam War. After unsuccessfully trying to disperse the crowd of protesters with tear gas, the National Guard fired at the students, killing four (two of whom were not even protesting) and wounding nine. Even though the state has a monopoly on the legitimate use of force, because it actually used that force (illegitimately, in the eyes of many), the incident sparked massive student protests across the country along with countless public debates and lawsuits, with citizens calling the government's authority into question. The state was forced to respond to the crisis. Then President Richard Nixon, in an effort to save the face of state authority, invited some of the Kent State students to the White House. The shootings are still sometimes referred to as the "Kent State massacre."

The International System of States

Weber takes it for granted that all states exercise a monopoly on the legitimate use of force within a given territory. But multiple states in Africa, including Angola, Congo, Rwanda, Sudan, Somalia, and Sierra Leone, to name a few, do not or have not exercised such a monopoly in recent times. In these countries, rebel or insurrectionist groups are in constant armed conflict with their respective governments. For example, since 2011, armed Islamist and

Not all states have a monopoly on the legitimate use of force within their borders. In Yemen, militia groups attacked government soldiers and civilians during Arab Spring.

tribal groups have attacked the government of Yemen. Not only did forces loyal to the regime battle these rebels, they fired upon peaceful demonstrators who were part of the "Arab Spring," and even shelled an army unit that had declared itself neutral in the conflict. Such a disintegration of a monopoly can even affect relations with other states. For example, in July 2006 Hezbollah, an Islamist rebel group and political party in Lebanon, began an armed conflict with the neighboring state Israel without the sanction of the "official" Lebanese government. Hezbollah's military conflicts with Israel and territorial claims within southern Lebanon led to Hezbollah's escription by the Lebanese prime minister as a "state within a state."

Like the insurrectionary groups of Sudan, Hezbollah, by its use of military might against Israel, challenges Weber's definition of statehood. If a state by definition maintains a monopoly on the use of force within a territory, how do we reconcile the cases where the local, legitimate authorities clearly do not exercise the requisite monopolies? The answer forces us to reach beyond Weber's terse formulation for an alternative, broader account of statehood.

Weber, being a German political theorist who lived in the late nineteenth and early twentieth centuries, no doubt had past and present European states in mind and used these states as templates for his conception of statehood. But the history of Europe is not the same as the history of the African and Asian continents. In fact, there are important differences in the historical trajectories of these continents, which Weber may have discounted or just plain missed. European states developed in a long series of fights over territorial boundaries, such as the Austro-Prussian War of 1866 and the Balkan Wars of 1912–13. European states came to exercise territorial monopolies on the use of force through a long history of conflict that coalesced into the borders we recognize today.

After all the war and other violence, the current European countries emerged as bona fide states (with striking exceptions such as the republics of the former Soviet Union and the former Yugoslavia). The relations among these European states led to the development of the international state system, through which each state is recognized as territorially sovereign by fellow states. Each state tacitly agrees to mind its own business when it comes to the internal affairs of other sovereign countries as long as borders are respected. This is the principle of noninterference. (Again, there are notable exceptions to this, such as the Bush administration's doctrine of preemptive war that was put into practice during the invasion of Iraq in 2003.)

International state system a system in which each state is recognized as territorially sovereign by fellow states.

Africa is likewise composed of territorially sovereign states. These states, however, are not necessarily the products of centuries of bloody internal land disputes, as in Europe, but instead are the products of the international state system and legitimating institutions such as the United Nations, which have transformed the very definition of statehood. Africa also has a history of European colonialism—the story of outside invaders controlling the lands and people of the African continent. After gaining independence from

THE CASE OF SOMALILAND

One afternoon in summer 2005, I was sitting in an office in Addis Ababa waiting to meet with the prime minister of Ethiopia, Meles Zenawi, as part of a delegation from the United Nations. Our meeting concerned the implementation of the UN Millennium Development Goals. While in the waiting room, I began chatting with a woman who was also waiting for a meeting with Prime Minister Zenawi. She introduced herself as the foreign minister of Somaliland. I had thought that I was pretty well versed in African geography by that point and only recalled Somaliland as the archaic, colonial name of present-day Somalia. "Excuse me?" I asked. "Don't you mean Somalia?" She handed me a pamphlet, explaining that she represented the government of Somaliland, a breakaway province in the north, bordering Southern Ethiopia and Djibouti (a small port city-state).

Then it all made sense: I had never heard of Somaliland because it was literally "not on the map"; that is, although it declared independence from Somalia in 1991, it was not recognized by any other nation and therefore did not exist in the international system of nation-states. (It still doesn't.) The people were, no doubt, working hard to gain recognition—hence, the foreign minister's visit to Ethiopia, the picture of their flag, and so on. But until they are recognized by other states and international institutions such as the United Nations, they remain merely a "self-proclaimed" nation-state.

What was most ironic, I later learned, was that only Somaliland, the northernmost of the three regions of Somalia, had a functional internal system of government in

A market in Somaliland. What role does the international system play in legitimizing state authority?

which a single entity had a monopoly over the legitimate use of force. In Mogadishu—the ostensible capital of all Somalia—violence was rampant and people had to bribe warlords merely to survive. There was no legitimacy and no functional state, but in the international system, this nonstate supposedly covered the entire geographic territory of Somalia, including the area Somaliland claimed as its own. Mogadishu today is still a violent city, but the sitting president of Somalia, Sheikh Sharif Sheikh Ahmed, has been recognized by Obama's administration (along with neighboring countries Uganda and Burundi and the rest of the African Union) as the legitimate ruler of Somalia even though the Bush administration was at one point contemplating what steps could be taken to rid Somalia of Sheikh Sharif because he was thought to be allied with Al Qaeda (Anderson, 2009).

But back in 2005, the foreign minister of Somaliland was still hopeful that her visit might persuade her western neighbor to recognize her administration as the legitimate authority in Somalia. Somaliland did not gain independence or legitimate rule, but is relatively calm compared to the southern portion of Somalia, where the moderate government of Sheikh Sharif is fighting the Islamist militant group Shaabab, which now controls the area. Within the international community, an unwritten rule exists that neighboring states must first recognize a new state's autonomy before more distant ones will do so. This convention is guided by the assumption that abutting nations are the most likely to be affected by the political upheaval caused by the emergence of a new state. For Somaliland, Ethiopia remains key, because its recognition of the new government could influence other countries to follow suit. In the case of Somalia, recognition of Sheikh Sharif's legitimacy by the African Union as well as Western states like the United States means not only legitimacy on paper and in diplomatic circles but also a reliable supply of arms and military power. The African Union stationed thousands of troops in Mogadishu; the United States sent forty tons of arms.

Berbera Port, Somaliland

Perhaps Weber focused too much on the internal workings of the state apparatus, to the neglect of external forces. For a state to have the critical monopoly on legitimate violence, it must have the consent of not only those within its territory but also important external actors. After all, what good is legitimacy among the Somalilanders if foreign tanks are going to roll in and flatten the entire region? Although it might make more sense to start from scratch and redraw the entire political map of Africa (not to mention the Middle East) with better motives at heart than when it was originally divided (Gambia, for example, was created in the middle of Senegal just to preserve an English route up the Gambia River), the inertia of the international state system prevents that from occurring. Competition over natural resources, different postcolonial interests, people of the same ethnicity in neighboring countries, and religious and ideological divisions all make it difficult to rationalize and correct territorial errors made in the past. In other words, political boundaries create stakes and interests, and once boundaries are in place, they take on a logic and force of their own.

their European colonizers, each of these African states became a full-fledged member of the international system of states with all the attendant rights and obligations of participating in the system. However, they had no guarantee of a monopoly on force within their territory because they often had been arbitrarily produced through the international system of states without ever really satisfying Weber's fundamental criterion of statehood. Sudan, Lebanon, Congo, and Sierra Leone are all states—if only because once an institution is set up, it has its own force of inertia. For example, once oil-rich southern Nigeria is connected to oil-poor northern Nigeria, it is certainly in the interests of the northern Nigerians to maintain the integrity of the nation-state, even if the religious and ethnic makeups of the two regions vary greatly. Likewise, even without such stark divisions, it is in the interests of political elites to control as much territory as possible. That said, perhaps the violent civil wars in places such as Iraq or Somalia today reflect a process similar to the one that largely occurred in Europe centuries ago.

New State Functions: The Welfare State

The state's role in developing social policies—policies developed to meet social needs—has prompted scholars to reconsider the definition of statehood. After the period of rapid industrialization that began in the late eighteenth century and culminated in the beginning of the twentieth century, many states began adopting variants of social insurance and pension programs such as disability, old age, and unemployment benefits (Skocpol & Amenta, 1986). The growth in these types of benefits continued in most advanced industrial nations throughout the twentieth century, especially following World War II, buffered by the logic of Keynesian economics. (John Maynard Keynes, a prominent British economist, postulated that government intervention in the form of social expenditures could pull the economy out of a recession by stimulating demand for products and services.) Perhaps, then, starting with the postwar years, it is more accurate to think of states as "organizations that extract resources through taxation *and* attempt to extend coercive control and political authority over particular territories and the people residing in them" (Skocpol & Amenta, 1986). Notice that this definition still includes a reference to coercion and political authority (that is, Weber's monopoly on legitimate force), but now states are concerned with another function, social provisions, and may rightly be called welfare states. A welfare state is a system in which the state is responsible for the well-being of its citizens. In practice, this usually entails providing a number of key necessities, such as food, health care, and housing, outside the economic marketplace. (See Chapter 10 for more on welfare and the welfare state in the realm of health care.)

Welfare state a system in which the state is responsible for the well-being of its citizens.

Why and how did the welfare state develop? One theory, sometimes called the logic of industrialism thesis, holds that nations develop social welfare benefits to satisfy the social needs created by industrialization. In this view, the state intervenes to take care of people who are not needed in the labor market: children, people with disabilities, and the elderly. Simply, "economic growth is the ultimate cause of welfare state development" (Wilensky, 1974). When a society's members all work constantly just to feed themselves, there is little surplus to serve as insurance or as alms for unproductive citizens. However, once a given community has some surplus, it can afford to insure against downturns and to take care of the sick, elderly, and people with disabilities. Social Security, for example, helps meet the needs of aging citizens who no longer work. Because modern industry generally doesn't depend on the labor of senior citizens, the state intervenes to help make sure these retirees have enough money for food, clothing, and shelter.

Another view of the development of the welfare state, called neo-Marxist theory, starts with the question of how democracy and capitalism can coexist. This theory is concerned with explaining the contradictions between formal legal equality and social class inequality. Specifically, when private property is held by a small section of the population, the democratic impulse (that is,

Workers from the Tennessee Valley Authority (TVA) install a turbine housing at the Cherokee Dam in Jefferson City, Tennessee. Why did economist John Maynard Keynes and President Franklin D. Roosevelt initiate New Deal projects like the TVA during the 1930s?

the wishes of the masses) might be to confiscate that property. To resolve this tension and maintain private property rights, the welfare state emerges. In this manner, the welfare state is seen as the mediator of class conflict, "granting concessions to both capitalists and workers" (Quadagno, 1987) to ensure the long-term health of society. To serve the interests of the rich owners of the means of production, the welfare state "buys off" the workers by providing necessities and a degree of economic security. For example, many Marxist scholars have pointed to the New Deal as an example of the state acting as a class mediator. During the New Deal, industry was forced to grant concessions to labor—shorter working hours, better working conditions, and union recognition, for instance—in order to maintain existing class relationships (i.e., to avoid a more radical revolution during the Great Depression that might have led to the abolition of private property through communism).

Third, state-centered approaches emphasize the role of state bureaucrats in formulating welfare state policies. Statist theories tie the development of the welfare state not to economic or political factors but to government bureaucrats who design policies based on perceived social conditions because bringing home the pork enhances their power in society. Theda Skocpol and Edwin Amenta (1986), two prominent exponents of the state-centered approach, argue that in some cases, the state may act autonomously to formulate social policy—meaning that state bureaucrats are solely or primarily responsible for creating or modifying social policy. For example, consider how a city might go about constructing housing units for low-income families. Assuming that the city council has already allocated funds to the project, control of the project would then probably be transferred to city planners for implementation. The city planners, as state bureaucrats fairly insulated from the whims of politicians or economic elites, run the project by designing the housing units, choosing their location, and rationing the project's budget. State bureaucrats may also play a role in drafting the budgets for other projects, providing further social policy recommendations and influencing the outcomes of policy proposals.

Citizenship rights the rights guaranteed to each law-abiding citizen in a nation-state.

Civil rights the rights guaranteeing a citizen's personal freedom from interference, including freedom of speech and the right to travel freely.

Political rights the rights guaranteeing a citizen's ability to participate in politics, including the right to vote and the right to hold an elected office.

Social rights the rights guaranteeing a citizen's protection by the state.

Another strand in studies of the welfare state concerns the types of social provisions offered by the state and to whom these provisions are granted. Specifically, what is a citizen's relationship to the state? The people living within a state, excluding noncitizens and felons, have certain rights called citizenship rights. Sociologist T. H. Marshall has defined three broad types of citizenship rights: civil rights, political rights, and social rights. Civil rights guarantee a citizen's personal freedom from interference, including freedom of speech and the right to travel freely. Political rights guarantee a citizen's rights to participate in politics, including the right to vote and the right to hold an elected office. And, last, social rights guarantee a citizen's protection by the state, including "protection from the free market in the areas of housing, employment, health, and education" (Hasenfeld et al., 1987). Marshall recognized that an inherent contradiction exists between civil rights, which guarantee freedom from state interference, and social rights, which make it the state's responsibility to interfere in the lives of citizens.

President Bill Clinton signs welfare reform legislation in 1996.

Social rights to public assistance may be of two broad types. The first type is the right to contributory programs, such as Social Security benefits in the United States. To be eligible for these programs, "citizens earn their rights through tax contributions" (Hasenfeld et al., 1987). Rights to means-tested programs, such as Temporary Assistance to Needy Families (TANF) and food stamps, are contingent on proof of insufficient financial resources. Rights to means-tested programs are subject to changes in how states define the concept of the "deserving poor." For example, in 1996, President Bill Clinton signed the Personal Responsibility and Work Opportunity Reconciliation Act, which drastically shortened the maximum allowable time during which citizens could claim welfare benefits and introduced multiple compliance requirements such as mandatory employment searches and job training. Because of these changes, the "deserving poor" no longer included those who weren't disabled yet were chronically unemployed.

Radical Power and Persuasion

Recall that Weber defined power as an actor's capacity to "carry out his own will *despite resistance*." Thus, Weber implies that where there is power, there must be resistance. But why should that be the case? Are we to believe that whenever and wherever power is at work, it presupposes (or elicits) resistance? Steven Lukes asks a similar question in *Power: A Radical View* (1974/2005) and suggests that power may be "at its most effective when least observable"; in such a situation, it may not generate resistance at all.

Lukes describes power as three-dimensional. The first dimension of power is visible when different agendas clash, conflict results, and one side prevails. For example, when you were a child and your parents insisted that you go to bed, you may have thrown temper tantrums, perhaps threatening to run away if they didn't allow you to watch more television. Your parents wanted you to go to bed because they preferred that you get a good night's rest. Your preference was for more television and less parental involvement. Your divergent preferences generated a conflict—perhaps in the form of shouting and a resultant spanking or time-out.

The second dimension of power is more complicated and occurs when the power is so formidable that no conflict results from competing interests because one side is convinced it's a losing battle. Let's say that one night, instead of throwing a temper tantrum before being put to bed, you went to bed without a fight. Once you were tucked in with the lights turned out and your parents were safely back in the living room, you hurled your stuffed bear at your bedroom door in protest. You and your parents still had divergent preferences, but in this scenario you didn't bother to throw a temper tantrum because you knew your parents would ultimately make the decision to put you to bed.

Lukes's novel contribution to the study of power is what he calls power's third dimension. It is the power not only to persevere despite overt or veiled resistance but to "prevent such conflict from arising in the first place." Conflict may be averted through "influencing, shaping, or determining" desires, wants, and preferences. In this scenario, still using our bedtime example, not only do you go to bed when your parents want you to and refrain from abusing any stuffed animals, but you actively want to go to bed at the appointed hour. Why? Lukes would say that your parents have manipulated your preferences. You don't fight with them at bedtime because you now believe that going to bed early is what *you* want to do.

Obviously, Lukes isn't talking about parents' power over children's bedtimes when he writes about three-dimensional power. His concern is with larger social groups, specifically, how "potential issues are kept out of politics" through means that do not generate conflict because they shape the desires of social actors. These desires may be shaped by familiar social forces such as processes of socialization (see Chapter 4) or by means of information control through the mass media (see Chapter 3).

One way to wield invisible power is by shaping the choice set. My sister, a staunch opponent of capital punishment, related a story dating back to the time period when she resided in Arizona, a state that had used capital punishment for as long as she had lived there. One year an initiative to switch from electrocution to lethal injection as the method of execution appeared on the election ballot. She was conflicted about how to vote. She departed from the voting booth troubled by the very choice she had faced. Why couldn't there be a referendum on execution itself? The answer lies in the fact that the choices had already been established by political actors. At that time in Arizona, if capital punishment itself had appeared on the ballot, it probably would have survived. But the power to frame the terms of the debate is one of the most important and invisible forms of power.

One reason that our choices are constrained is that it is impossible to decide among all alternatives at any given time. Even in democracies, choices tend to come down to yes-or-no, left-or-right votes. When more than two choices are offered, results can often become indeterminate and suboptimal for all. The economist Kenneth Arrow won the Nobel Prize for proving this "impossibility theorem," which states that there is no system of voting that will consistently yield the top choice of the most voters when there are more than two alternatives. It turns out that when faced with more than two options, no foolproof voting exists that is resistant to strategic voting (voters not voting in line with their underlying preferences in order to effect a desired outcome). Let's say you and your friends are trying to decide which movie to see. If there were only two movie screens, then you could just vote as a group. But imagine that a triplex

A shanty in Clear Fork, Tennessee, that coal miner Carl Miller, his wife, and their seven children called home in 1963.

comes to town. You would like to see *Drugstore Cowboy,* but only slightly more than *The Matrix*, which seems somewhat popular with the rest of the group. What you really want to avoid is seeing *Forrest Gump*, and you know that many of your friends do want to see that movie. So instead of voting for *Drugstore Cowboy*, you vote for *The Matrix* in the hope of defeating *Forrest Gump*. *The Matrix* could win in the end, even if it wasn't anyone's first choice. There are many ways to narrow down choices, but none of them guarantee that the will of the majority rules, so the importance of power lies in its ability to narrow the choice set and socialize desires, thereby generating consent. What's most unsettling about the entire process is that such a reduction of choices seems to be unavoidable to keep things moving along.

In a real-world example, John Gaventa, in *Power and Powerlessness* (1980), describes his investigation of the synergistic effects of power's three dimensions on the lives of coal miners in the Clear Fork Valley in central Appalachia. Many of the community's miners were desperately poor, working in unsafe mines and living in dilapidated company housing. Between 1960 and 1970, 34 percent of the area's residents lived without piped water and 60 percent did not have flush toilets. The workers often suffered from black lung disease and were left with "gnarled limbs from accidents." The coal company owned the miners' homes, controlled the local stores, and even monopolized health services. The company deducted "rent, services, goods purchased at the store, medical bills, even funeral expenses" directly from miners' wages, with the result that "misbehavior in the job could cause the loss of a home; failure to shop at the company store (where prices were often higher) could mean the loss of work; disobedience of a single rule could mean eviction from the game altogether."

Given such dire conditions, the miners might be expected to revolt, or at least strike, against the all-powerful mining corporation. But in a quintessential example of how the manipulation of needs, desires, and aspirations may cut against the apparently objective interests of social actors, the workers were prone to express loyalty, even affection, for their employers. Gaventa found that through the interrelated effects of power's three dimensions, conflict was squelched as preferences and desires were shaped through the local newspaper and other information outlets, as well as the education of the miners' children in the company-run school. On the other hand, we cannot know for sure that the miners and their families were not just acting rationally in a cold-eyed assessment of their objective alternatives. That is, they may have known that the mining corporation was manipulating them, but judged working there the best available option and thought little of their ability to alter the situation. There is no alternate social universe where we can see what would have happened if they had enjoyed other sources of information (i.e., an independent press) and had, in turn, engaged in mass revolt. The best we can do as social scientists is to find another similar community—perhaps one with an independent newspaper and school system—that pursued a different path and see if the workers there revolted, and if they were, indeed, better off in the end.

Power and International Relations

Other recent work on power has focused on international relations. Relations between states differ in important ways from relations within states. Does the paradox of state authority, in which a state's legitimate authority is contingent on not using force to secure obedience, hold true when one state is trying to influence the behavior of another state? Traditionally, scholars have highlighted the importance of "hard power," or the use of military or economic force to influence behavior, in international politics. During World War II the Allied Powers used military force (a lot of it) to influence the behavior of Germany, Japan, and Italy. The United States chose a similar strategy in 2003, when it attempted to exact political change in Iraq by overthrowing Saddam Hussein's Baathist regime and trying to squelch the resulting insurgency. In the international arena, where states struggle to influence other state actors, coercive power seems to be the rule instead of the exception.

Joseph Nye, a scholar at Harvard's Kennedy School of Government (as well as a former assistant secretary of defense), has proposed that the exclusive use of hard power in international politics is out of date. For one thing, states are now increasingly economically dependent on one another thanks to globalization, and this means that the use of force to influence the behavior of other states has become more costly. In 1945, we dropped an atomic bomb on the Japanese cities of Hiroshima and Nagasaki. Today Japan is consistently one of our top trading partners (not to mention the exporter of cultural products such as j-pop and manga).

The 1945 Allied bombing of Dresden (left) is an example of a hard power strategy. The cultural influence of soft power resources is seen in a billboard advertising Kentucky Fried Chicken in Damascus (right). How are these approaches different? Which is more effective?

If the United States opted to use force against Japan to influence its decisions or internal politics, it would risk losing valuable import and export markets.

Instead, Nye is a proponent of what he calls soft power. Soft or co-optive power is "getting others to want what you want" through "attraction rather than coercion or payments" (Ichihara, 2006; Nye, 1990). The idea behind soft power is similar to that behind Weber's concept of legitimate authority: Cultural myths or legitimizations can help persuade people (or entire nations) to obey. Nye hypothesizes that "if a state can make its power seem legitimate in the eyes of others, it will encounter less resistance to its wishes." So, for example, Hollywood movies might be an important soft power resource for America, just as anime is an important soft power resource for Japan. Hollywood films are often popular abroad simply because they're extravagant and entertaining, but at the same time they can be vehicles for some of the United States' favorite ideologies such as free trade or democratic political institutions. In either case, attraction is used to influence external state actors.

Soft power power attained through the use of cultural attractiveness rather than the threat of coercive action (hard power).

Take the Middle East as a case study in hard versus soft power. Syrian citizens' fascination with Big Macs, Whoppers, and all other things greasy and American is a perfect example of Nye's concept of soft power (see Chapter 3). It is not culinary excellence that attracts young Syrians to McDonald's and Burger King but the attractiveness of the wider American culture they embody. Since the U.S. invasion of Iraq, however, sales of Coca-Cola, Whoppers, and Big Macs have decreased as feelings of anti-Americanism have grown. America may be underestimating the power of persuasion, which, in turn, can be bad for business.

Dictatorship or Democracy? States of Nature and Social Contracts

What are the origins of the state, and how have those origins shaped the types of government we have? In *Leviathan* (1651/1981), Thomas Hobbes suggests that in the absence of an agreed-upon authority figure (a state), life would

The 1651 frontispiece of Thomas Hobbes's *Leviathan*.

be hideously chaotic and violent. The natural state of humanity is not peaceful; rather, individuals would seek to better themselves at the expense of all others. Every person would be an enemy to all other persons—it would be a war of all against all, to use Hobbes's phrasing. To achieve peace and avoid death, humans enter into a social contract and submit to an overarching sovereign authority charged with ensuring peace by threatening death for deviant behavior (the "leviathan," or sea monster). This leviathan is not an external force that comes in to quell the war of all against all and exact obedience but is composed of and created by the citizens themselves.

John Locke thought Hobbes was slightly off the mark. In his *Second Treatise of Government* (1690/1980), Locke says that before the emergence of a sovereign authority, individuals lived in a happy, conflict-free state of nature as equals. Each person had the executive power to punish offenses committed by wayward individuals (see the discussion of informal social norms in Chapter 6). Locke believed that the sovereign state emerged not because life without it was a disaster but because individuals needed help adjudicating discord, in particular, conflicts over personal property. For Locke, then, submitting to a centralized authority was not a matter of life or death but a matter of money.

Although they have some common features (namely, the idea of the state arising out of the self-interests of the citizenry), the two theories have different implications for social life and the role of state. According to Hobbes, we need a strong, central authority in order to live in peace and harmony with our neighbors. Human interaction is, by nature, rife with conflict and fear. According to Locke, the state of nature is primarily peaceful, as natural law regulates interpersonal relations without the interference of a cumbersome sovereign authority. The two conceptions of what it means to be in a state of nature dictate the proper and rightful functions of the sovereign authority. They may, in fact, help us understand the origins of democracy and dictatorship.

Democracy a system of government wherein power theoretically lies with the people; citizens are allowed to vote in elections, speak freely, and participate as legal equals in social life.

Dictatorship a form of government that restricts the right to political participation to a small group or even to a single individual.

In the world today, some states are organized as democracies: They have a system of government wherein power theoretically lies with the people, and therefore citizens are allowed to vote in elections, speak freely, and participate as legal equals in social life. Other states are dictatorships: forms of government that restrict the right to political participation to a small group or even to a single individual. Such states may limit suffrage, censor information to the public, and arrange the brutal "disappearances" of nonsubmissive subordinates. To Weber, the differences between democracy and dictatorship are irrelevant to statehood—these bona fide states and forms of domination differ only by the types of ideas the regimes produce about their own legitimacy. They are merely different breeds of the same underlying animal.

Bucking Weber, however, many scholars have tried to explain why some states end up as democracies and others become dictatorships. Barrington Moore's classic *Social Origins of Dictatorship and Democracy* (1966/1993) sets out to answer this question by investigating the history of several nations, including France, Great Britain, Japan, the United States, China, and India. Moore hypothesizes that the fate of each nation is determined by the struggle between social classes. Specifically, for democracy to emerge, the bourgeoisie (those who own businesses) must be strong enough to attenuate the control of the land-owning feudal lords. If the bourgeoisie, in the form of traders and merchants, is strong enough, a revolution takes place. The bourgeois revolution "attacks obstacles to a democratic version of capitalism that have been inherited from the past" (Moore, 1966/1993). Moore thus believes that the emergence of modern capitalism is important to the development of political democracy.

The economists Daron Acemoglu and James Robinson update Moore's thesis in their similarly titled book *The Economic Origins of Dictatorship and Democracy* (2006). Like Moore, they build a model explaining the variations in forms of government. They ask the same kind of questions (Why are some states more democratic than others, and how did they get that way?) but produce a different answer using game theory, the study of the decisions actors make in situations where there is uncertainty and where their success depends on the strategies of others. A game can be any situation where the outcome for one or more actors depends on the choices of another actor or actors.

Game theory the study of strategic decisions under conditions of uncertainty and interdependence.

Have you ever tried to guess when the bathroom will be free for your morning shower? Your decision to get up at 8:00 A.M. or 8:15 A.M. depends on the information you have about the actions of your roommates. If you wake up at 8:00 A.M., you lose 15 minutes of sleep but are fairly confident that your roommates will still be snoring away. If you sleep in until 8:15 A.M., you gain 15 minutes of shut-eye but risk losing the bathroom to one of your roommates. Your decision changes based on the anticipated actions of your roommates (the other game players), who may be making the very same calculations. Games can be anything from roommates fighting for control of the bathroom, to chess and checkers, to the maneuverings of state actors.

Acemoglu and Robinson use game theory to understand how some states wind up more democratic than other states. Pretend that each state is the site of an ongoing game between two players: the elite player and the mass citizenship player. The elites are, of course, the rulers, the oppressors, the pillagers of small and unarmed villages. The mass citizenship player is the conglomeration of ordinary people who want, for instance, greater representation within their respective governments and the right to vote on specific social policies. One day, all the ordinary people join together and revolt against the elite. The elites, fearing for their lives and, more pressingly, desiring to protect their privileged social positions, need to respond. Do they give in to the demands of the rabble-rousers?

Consider the possibilities (the "strategies" in game theory talk) of each player. The ordinary people want democratic reforms. They are moderately armed and are threatening to revolt. But they are also aware that they don't have the military resources or time to sustain a revolution forever. The elites, on the other hand, are scared and will say anything to avoid the rebellion and get what they want now, but will promptly (and conveniently) forget what they promised when the crisis has passed. So although the elites will promise democratic concessions when faced with imminent danger to life, limb, and social position, they have no good reason to give the ordinary people what they want after the threat of an uprising has dwindled and life has returned to normal. Thus, the ordinary people must find a way to transform "temporary opportunity into permanent advantage," and the elites must make their promises credible.

There are two basic outcomes, or solutions, to the game. The elites may promise to lower the ordinary people's taxes and give each of them a free car. However, in a few years the elites are back to exploiting the poor, oppressed population as tax rates creep up again. Alternatively, if the mass citizenship resists the temptations of a temporary concession, they may use the threat of a revolution to demand a change to the political institutions of the state, such as the right to vote or the establishment of a parliament. If the citizens can use their temporary opportunity—their credible threat of revolution—to induce a change in the existing political institutions, then the country is on the path to democratization, according to Acemoglu and Robinson. The ordinary people have used their fleeting advantage to change the underlying distribution of political power. Democracy is just one possible outcome of a strategic game played by competing social groups.

Collective action problem the difficulty in organizing large groups because of the tendency of some individuals to freeload or slack off.

To play the democratization game and make coherent demands of the elite, however, the ordinary people must first overcome a collective action problem. The theory of collective action, pioneered by Mancur Olson in *The Logic of Collective Action* (1965), asserts that it is harder to organize larger groups than smaller ones. (We'll take a closer look at collective action and social movements in Chapter 18.) For example, in most social systems, the ordinary people far outnumber the elite. Let's say that there are 3,000 ordinary people, and all of them agree that the present system of governance is abysmal, and they would like to change it. Here's the catch: A revolution takes work, and every ordinary person wants to reap its benefits but would rather not expend the time, energy, and resources necessary to coordinate it. If 3,000 ordinary people exist in the society, each individual represents only 1/3,000 or 0.033 percent of the total team effort. If each individual reasons that he or she is a very small and insignificant share of the total team effort, and it would be better to conserve precious time, energy, and resources and let someone else do the risky revolutionary work, then the mass of ordinary people is unlikely to come together as a team and secure concessions from the elite faction—especially when the price of failure is high (perhaps beheading) and when resources are few (i.e., most folks are just trying to scrape by and avoid starvation).

Small groups, like the elite player, are much better equipped to get what they want. Let's say the elite faction is composed of five wealthy families. All these wealthy families know each other fairly well, not only through business organizations but also by virtue of vacationing in shared destinations like the Alps or perhaps by sending their children to the same elite boarding schools. If five families make up the elite, each family counts as one-fifth or 20 percent of the total team effort. Because the elites have much more to lose through the inaction of just one family, each member reasons that his or her family's effort is very significant to the team's eventual victory and decides to spend the time, energy, and resources on coordinating their efforts. In addition, because all the members of a small group usually know each other, the social consequences of inaction are much greater—they risk being chastised by their associates and friends if they choose to not participate. (Among the ordinary people, each individual is less likely to know the other team members and therefore does not suffer the same social consequences of inaction.)

There is still more bad news for the ordinary people: Robert Michels, in his study of political parties (1915), concluded that even if they win the game and secure democratic governance, all organizations, no matter how democratic in principle, face coordination problems. True democracy means that each citizen is essentially a legislator. However, as the scale of democracy expands, high levels of mass participation become unsustainable. Direct deliberative democracy, like a town hall meeting, is pretty difficult to pull off when the populace grows beyond a few hundred citizens. In large and complex organizations (like a state), the power structure will inevitably begin to resemble an oligarchy, a form of government in which power lies with a small group of leaders. Michels called this inevitability "the iron law of oligarchy."

For example, let's say the ordinary people overcome their initial collective action problems, win the right to vote, and organize into a political party. How do you think this political party, which represents thousands of citizens, would be run? The answer, it turns out, takes us back to Weber. Once democracy prevails, simple coordination problems necessitate the creation of a bureaucracy to efficiently manage the political party. As we already know, a bureaucracy has certain immutable characteristics. For one, the decision-making process is both rationalized, meaning governed by calculations of efficiency, and routinized, meaning that the same rule-governed procedure is used over and over. A bureaucracy is also structured hierarchically, which guarantees that ultimate decision-making control is in the hands of a few elites at the top of the pyramid. So much for democratic control of the state. The ordinary people have earned a new relation of domination: life in the iron cage.

Who Rules in the United States?

If you have grown up in the United States, by now you have interacted with the state on many levels, starting the day you were born and issued a birth certificate. Bringing our discussion out of the hypothetical and into the real world, where does the United States fit in our newly acquired understanding of collective action and democratic representation? Who rules in the United States?

In the United States national-level legal authority is split among three branches of government, a system intended to maximize legitimacy by ensuring that each branch is "checked and balanced" by the other two. The executive branch is led by the president, who is also the head of state (meaning the official representative of government to other states). The legislative branch is composed of the House of Representatives and the Senate, which together make up the U.S. Congress. The U.S. Supreme Court and lower federal courts are the judicial branch. Elected officials select members of the judicial branch; the president and all senators and representatives are chosen in regularly held elections. The federal government, to the extent allowed by the U.S. Constitution, takes precedence over state and local governments.

Max Baucus, chairman of the Senate Finance Committee, surrounded by health-care lobbyists, staff, and fellow senators. What is the role of power elites in shaping federal policy?

That said, the United States is a fairly decentralized (i.e., federalist) state in many respects, and individual states make and enforce many of the laws with which we are familiar.

Knowing who officially makes the decisions, however, may say fairly little about how choices are actually made. For that, we need to understand how officials gain office and which voices are heard once officials assume power. Since the Civil War, American electoral politics have almost always been organized into a two-party system, whereby two political parties have such a monopoly on voters that any other party has a difficult time garnering enough votes to win an election (with some notable exceptions, usually at the state or local level). A political party is an organization that seeks to gain power in a government, generally by backing candidates for office who subscribe to the organization's ideals. The United States' two major parties, Democratic and Republican, tend to be fairly broad in the scope of interests they represent, although the Democratic Party is traditionally thought of as "left" or liberal, whereas the Republican Party represents the "right" or conservatives. Broadly, the Democrats seek a secular government with a relatively high level of economic and social intervention, and the Republicans seek a smaller, laissez-faire government and the upholding of religious ideals through state regulation of morality. In practice, however, both Republicans and Democrats often hold some combination of the two parties' stereotypical convictions, and many competing ideologies exist within each party.

Political party an organization that seeks to gain power in a government, generally by backing candidates for office who subscribe (to the extent possible) to the organization's political ideals.

Political parties are not the only organizations that try to affect policy in support of their goals. An interest group is an organization that seeks to gain power in government without directly campaigning for election or being appointed to office. Rather, such groups use a variety of other paths to influence policy, such as persuading elected officials to advocate for the group's agenda or working through the existing regulatory bureaucracy or the legal system. Examples of interest groups include trade unions representing the workers in particular job categories, corporations lobbying to win a government contract, and single-issue groups seeking to affect a particular policy (such as AIPAC, the American Israel Public Affairs Committee, which seeks to influence U.S. policy toward Israel). Interest groups represent yet another approach to making collective action work for a group of people with similar political goals.

Interest group an organization that seeks to gain power in government and influence policy without direct election or appointment to office.

Beyond Strawberry and Vanilla: Political Participation in Modern Democracies

Despite the extension of political rights in modern democracies, the United States has a voting rate of only around 60 percent in presidential elections and much lower in nonpresidential elections. News anchors and political pundits often pour verbal shame on the American public for a decline in voting rates. But are the rates really declining? When political scientists set out to get to the bottom of the question, they realized that while most polls look at the total voting age population, it would be more accurate to look only at the people who are actually eligible to vote. It is important to note that convicted felons are unable to vote; noncitizen permanent residents cannot vote either. So while it is true that the voting rate of the total population has fallen, it is not true that the voting rate of the eligible population has changed much (Figure 15.1). People don't vote like they used to not because they are too busy (or lazy) to get to the polls on election day but because they are prohibited from voting (McDonald & Popkin, 2001). Social scientists Christopher Uggen and Jeff Manza even suggest that if convicted felons—the vast majority of whom are not in prison—had been able to vote in 2000, Al Gore would have been elected president (Manza & Uggen, 2006)! However, political participation is not limited to voting in elections but rather includes a wide range of activities from voting to working on a candidate's political campaign to marching in the streets. Succinctly, political participation is any "activity that has the intent or effect of influencing government action" (Verba et al., 2004).

Political participation activity that has the intent or effect of influencing government action.

Why does political participation matter? For many, democracy is the promise of a voice in governance. Political participation is important then because it is the sum of that voice. Through political participation, citizens "inform governing elites of their needs and preferences." Participation matters "both for its own sake and for its role in bringing about equality in the other valued goods—life, liberty, and property—that are affected by government policies" (Verba et al., 2004). In short, no participation means no voice.

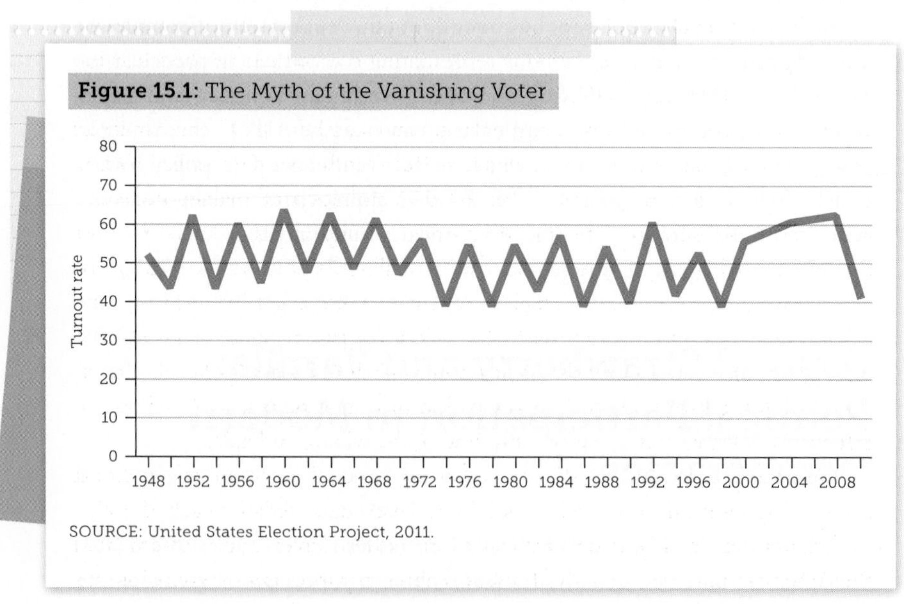

SOURCE: United States Election Project, 2011.

So who participates and who doesn't? Sociologists have consistently found striking disparities in rates and types of participation across social groups, as reflected in the numbers of people who register to vote (Figure 15.2). In keeping with these findings, voter turnout is much lower among the poor (those with incomes below or close to the family poverty line) than among the financially well off (those with family incomes over $75,000) (Verba et al., 2004). For other forms of political participation, such as working for or donating to a candidate's campaign, the participation gap is even wider between income groups. In monetary contributions to political campaigns, "the average donation from an affluent respondent is *fourteen times* the average contribution from a poor one" (Verba et al., 2004). If we decompose the population by socioeconomic status, a measure that includes both educational level and income, we find that political participation steadily declines as we go down the scale. Groups at the top of the socioeconomic scale nearly always participate more, whereas those on the bottom consistently participate less. Finally, research has found that citizens receiving means-tested benefits are the least likely to be politically active. Ironically, these citizens perhaps have the most to lose by not participating, because they are vulnerable to the changing political and policy definitions of what constitutes a social right and who is defined as belonging to the "deserving poor."

Largely prompted by the rapid decrease in political participation from the mid-1960s through the close of the twentieth century, academic inquiries into citizens' nonparticipation have produced a variety of explanations. The *civic voluntarism model* points to three components to explain political participation (or nonparticipation): political orientation, resources, and mobilization efforts. The first participatory factor, *political orientation,* is simply the strength of an individual's political commitments. If a citizen is strongly antiabortion, antigun, or pro something else, he or she is more likely to visit the polls or join a political campaign than another citizen who is apathetic about such political issues. *Resources* include money to donate to parties or causes as well as civic skills such as leadership, communications, and organizational abilities that "make it easier to get involved and enhance an individual's effectiveness as a participant" (Verba et al., 2004). If a citizen both is interested in politics and has the necessary resources, *mobilization efforts* by political parties or nonpartisan groups can boost political participation. These include mass mailings, phone calls, or door-to-door canvassing to encourage eligible citizens to vote or get involved in some other meaningful way. In summary, the civic voluntarism model suggests that individuals have certain preexisting attributes—civic skills and political orientations—that predispose them to participation or nonparticipation. Mobilization efforts can increase participation only among the willing and able.

Frances Fox Piven and Richard Cloward reject the notion that political nonparticipation can be traced to individual-level characteristics such as political orientation. In *Why Americans Don't Vote* (1988), Piven and Cloward hold the American party system—and political elites in particular—responsible for

Figure 15.2: Voter Registration Rates by Social Group, 2010

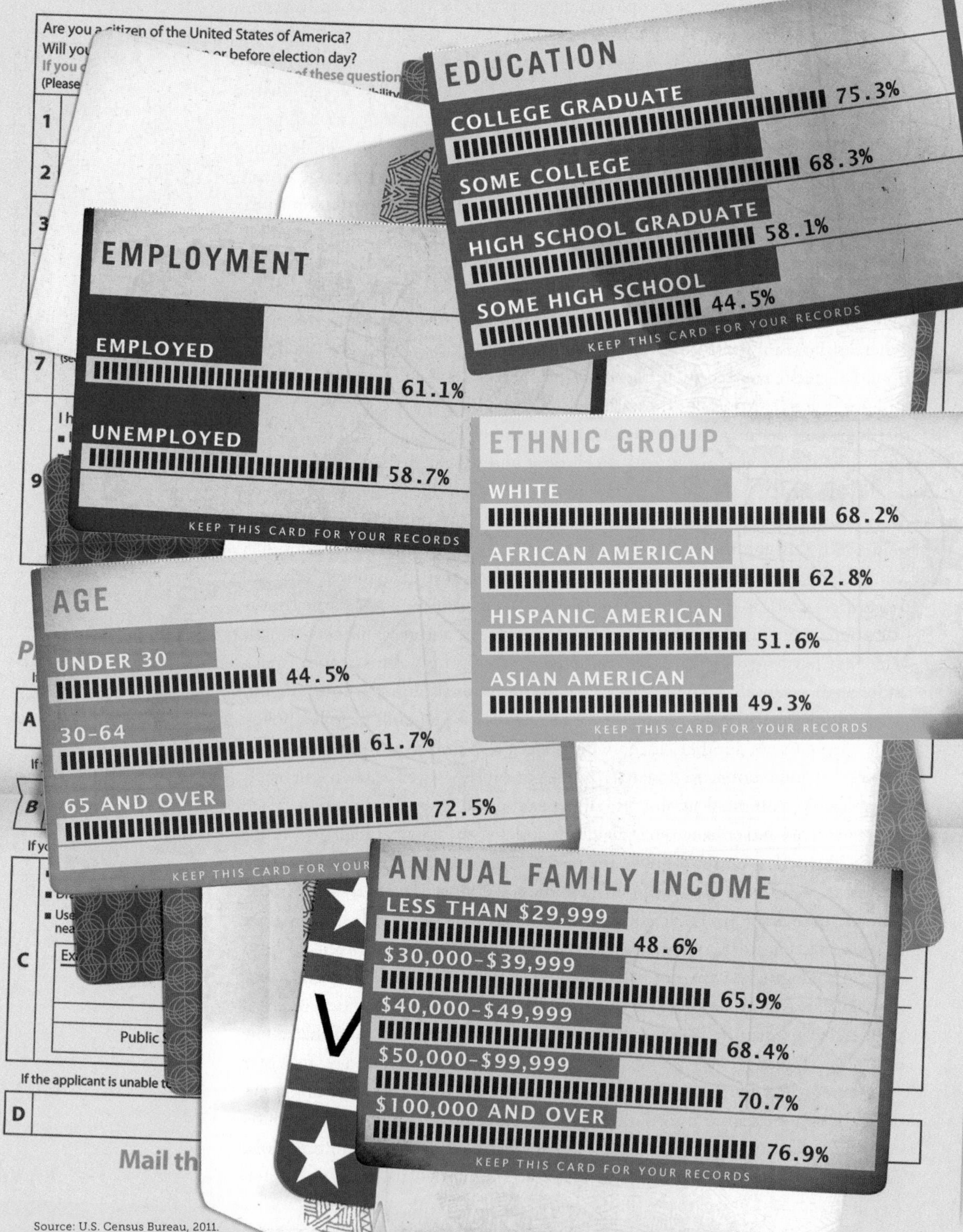

Source: U.S. Census Bureau, 2011.

Americans' low rate of political participation. They attribute "apathy and lack of political skill," the two individual-level components of the civic voluntarism model, to "party strategies and political culture . . . sustained by legal and procedural barriers to electoral participation" (Piven & Cloward, 1988). Such barriers have historically included "literacy tests, stricter naturalization procedures, and burdensome voter registration procedures." These obstacles prevent certain people from voting altogether and increase the time and effort required of those who remain eligible. "Voter rights" sounds like a dry bit of constitutional law that typically engages a few corporate lawyers and judges here and there. But Piven took up voting rights as a grassroots issue during the Reagan years (1981–89) after she revisited something she already knew, which is that the electoral system in the United States "over represents the better off and under represents the worse off." She recruited a team to go out in the community and "do mass registration of poor people, voter registration of poor people at the agencies where they received services." But there was trouble—"we quickly learned from our groundwork with our organizers, that they were just signing up for it, they weren't actually doing it. It was a real free rider problem." Piven thought the organizations serving the poor would logically want more of their constituents to get out and vote if for no other reason than to help these groups secure more government funding. But it turned out organizations were more interested in fighting for the interests of their wealthy board members. So then Piven's voter registration team "tried to get mayors, black mayors especially, to do voter registration in municipal agencies," so that voting would be "part of the infrastructure of the election system, not dependent on volunteers whose interest was sparked by a particular campaign or by the availability of a foundation grant." But even this fight was "rough going" (Conley, 2009m). For both parties the goal was to keep the electorate stable, not to bring in large numbers of minorities and poor people. So yet again, Piven's team set out to recruit a new group of decision makers. This time they went after the political allegiance of federal lawmakers and interest groups by forming what came to be known as the Motor Voter Coalition to fight for a bill tying voter registration in federal elections to the issuance or renewal of drivers' licenses or applications for certain social services. Piven describes how Motor Voter became law one year after Republican president George Bush vetoed it in 1992.

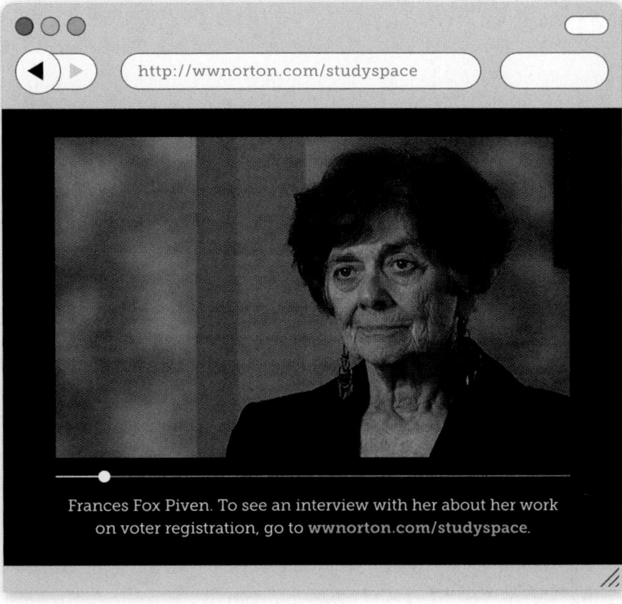

Frances Fox Piven. To see an interview with her about her work on voter registration, go to **wwnorton.com/studyspace**.

> During his campaign Bill Clinton promised Rock the Vote, one of the groups in the coalition, that he would support the bill. When he was elected and took office, there was a little window of opportunity because by '94 we [the Democrats] no longer had the House of Representatives. The bill went through. There were compromises required at the last minute. We got calls from Washington very late at night about we had to drop some program, you couldn't have welfare, 'cause we needed six in order to end the filibuster, we needed six Republican senators, and at the very last minute we dropped unemployment insurance because we reasoned that most of the unemployed would have driver's licenses. At any rate, the bill went through. (Conley, 2009m)

Victory at last! Or then again, no. Piven sighs, "Once the Democrats lost office, the implementation collapsed."

Although voting has recently become easier for eligible citizens, the United States still lags behind other industrialized nations in turnout. For example, whereas some European countries have chosen to schedule elections on weekends, elections in the United States take place on workdays, making it difficult for many working people to get to the polls. (Puerto Rico, a U.S. territory, makes election day a holiday and consequently enjoys higher voting rates.) In an interview following Obama's election (Conley, 2009m), Piven noted that "voting is not a silver bullet, but it's one of the aspects of our political system that can be democratized and we should protect it and expand voting rights to everyone." She went on to argue that access to voting rights is necessary but insufficient; political engagement after election day is required to force change in systems stymied by the significant inertia of the status quo.

National Voter Registration Act

Partly in response to Piven and Cloward's forceful critique and subsequent mobilization, President Bill Clinton signed the National Voter Registration Act (NVRA), commonly known as Motor Voter, into law in 1993. Under this legislation, local motor vehicle agencies and public assistance agencies (where citizens receive means-tested benefits) double as voter registration centers, thereby dismantling some of the procedural barriers to voting by making registration easier for eligible citizens. The hope was that these government sites would afford easy access to registration to some of the nation's subpopulations that are known to have low voting rates—specifically, those receiving welfare, the young, and the disabled.

As expected, Motor Voter has boosted voter turnout: Voter registration at motor vehicle offices alone was found to boost voter turnout by just over one percentage point (Fitzgerald, 2005). However, similar measures such as Post Office registration (a provision of Motor Voter) and unrestricted absentee voting have not proved as successful. The mixed results of studies on the effect of lowering the time and convenience costs of voting have led some scholars to inquire into other causes of nonparticipation. If it isn't about time and convenience, what is it about?

Students at the University of Alabama at Birmingham participate in the effort to register voters. Why don't more Americans vote?

There does not appear to be a single answer. Felon disenfranchisement is part of the story; so are polling hours, the lack of same-day registration options, the fact that we vote on a weekday that is not a holiday, and a widespread feeling that individual votes don't really count. Low voter turnout seems to be a many-headed monster that won't be vanquished by a single policy intervention. Some folks fear that low rates of political participation in the United States pose a fundamental threat to our democracy and the legitimacy of our political institutions. Others, however, suggest that we should stop worrying about low voter turnout, arguing that reduced participation in a democratic society is a sign of a contented population and a low degree of conflict.

→ CONCLUSION

In this chapter we have examined power, domination, authority, bureaucracy, states, organizations, and political institutions. We have seen how Weber conceptualized authority and how his insights into bureaucratic organizations and the process of rationalization continue to shape our daily lives. We have also examined some fundamental problems of modern-day political life, such as collective action problems and the iron law of oligarchy, which paint a somewhat pessimistic picture for the future of democracy and the cherished notion that everyone should have a voice in governance. Finally, as political sociologists, we are left to ponder how we might make democracy work better and how the most vulnerable members of society might be given a voice despite iron cages and oligarchies.

PRACTICE

ASSIGNMENT

On what kinds of authority does our national government draw? Is it purely legal-rational, or can you find examples of other types of authority in our system?

QUESTIONS FOR REVIEW

1. What is a "state" and how do the examples of Sealand and Somaliland clarify this definition?
2. Voter turnout in the United States is relatively low. Compare the civic voluntarism model and the position of Frances Fox Piven and Richard Cloward in explaining this phenomenon. How do the results from the National Voter Registration Act add to our understanding of voter turnout?
3. What is the difference between coercion and authority? Use an example to demonstrate this difference.
4. Choose a historical figure whose authority stemmed from his or her charisma. Describe why this person's authority was charismatic and how this form of legitimate authority changed over time (for example, describe whether it was traditionalized or rationalized).
5. Describe the concept of "domination" and its two types. How does this concept help us understand the results of the Milgram experiment?
6. What is a welfare state? Describe two theories that explain the development of the welfare state. Do these theories help us understand the way authority is maintained?
7. How are dictatorships and democracies different? How are the citizenship rights of the population (as defined by T. H. Marshall) different under these two kinds of political regimes?
8. In a democratic society, why is it possible for a small group of elites to get what it wants at the expense of the larger population? In your answer, consider the work on collective action.

PARADOX

AUTHORITY IS BASED ON THE IMPLICIT THREAT OF VIOLENCE, BUT THE MOMENT THAT FORCE IS USED, ALL AUTHORITY IS LOST.

WATCH THE ANIMATED SHORT ABOUT THE AUTHORITY AND THE STATE PARADOX AT

WWNORTON.COM/STUDYSPACE

Bobby Bible (left), born Robert Engel in Los Angeles, preaches while a Palestinian man passes the Church of the Nativity, considered the traditional birthplace of Jesus, in Bethlehem. Bible plans to bring his crusade to Jerusalem after Christmas Day to preach among the Jews.

16 Religion

PARADOX

THE RELIGIONS THAT DEMAND THE MOST FROM THEIR MEMBERS OFTEN GROW THE FASTEST, BUT AS RELIGIONS BECOME LARGE AND SUCCESSFUL, THEY TEND TO BECOME LESS STRICT. →

In 2008, a popular local journalist and builder won election to the city council in Asheville, North Carolina. Though he may have won the election, Cecil Bothwell's bid was heavily contested because of his religious beliefs (Schrader, 2009). Bothwell delicately skirts the label "atheist" because the stigma attached to the term leads people to think he worships Satan or is lacking a moral compass. He prefers the term *post-theist* and says that he practices the Golden Rule—to treat others with deference, respect, and caring consideration—but that it is irrelevant whether or not he believes in a particular deity. We learn in grade school that the U.S. Constitution guarantees a separation between church and state. You may be surprised to note that in North Carolina there is a law barring from office any person who denies "the being of Almighty God" no matter how many votes the person may have rightfully won. Unfortunately for the North Carolinians who wrote the law, it holds no weight against the federal Constitution.

Despite opponents' ongoing efforts to keep Bothwell out of office—including mailing a flyer accusing him of publishing a smear campaign against the televangelist Billy Graham—Bothwell assumed office as scheduled alongside two other new council members. While the other members were sworn into office with their hands on a Bible, Bothwell chose to "affirm" his acceptance and kept his hands to himself. Though Bothwell may be one of the first atheist (or post-theist) politicians to hold office in America, candidates' political backgrounds frequently threaten to keep them from office unless they are mainstream Protestants. John F. Kennedy was the first Catholic to serve as president of the United States; during the campaign, opponents claimed that

Cecil Bothwell "affirming his acceptance" of his new position on the Asheville city council.

a Kennedy win would be a victory for the pope. With great alarm they noted America might unwittingly fall under the control of the Vatican!

Following Bothwell's assumption of office, an unrelated federal court ruling in a nearby town abolished its custom of inviting religious leaders to open council meetings with prayer. In light of this decision, Bothwell and the Asheville city council are now discussing switching from an opening prayer to a moment of silence. The relationship between religion and culture in America is no trivial concern. An anonymous editorial published in Asheville's *Citizen Times* sums it up this way: "There's no overstating how serious these issues are to a great many in our community. Religious roots run deep here, and people who feel their faith is under siege are people who feel their very being is under siege" ("Religion and Politics Still a Volatile Mix," 2009). The tension in Asheville is indicative of the changing face of religion and religious practice in contemporary America. There are more atheists and agnostics now than ever before (nearly 10 percent of the population) but church membership is growing, especially at evangelical megachurches with congregations of 10,000 or more.

Fights have also erupted elsewhere over prayer in school, the words "in God we trust" on U.S. coinage, and the words "under God" in the Pledge of Allegiance. Concern over "playing God" was introduced into debates about health-care plans that would offer terminally ill patients counseling about end-of-life care, not to mention the abortion and stem cell research debates.

Civil religion a set of sacred beliefs so commonly accepted by most people that it becomes part of the national culture.

In America, the mingling of patriotism and piety takes on the form of what is called civil religion, a set of sacred beliefs so commonly accepted by most people that it becomes part of the national culture (Bellah, 1967). Americans are more religious than any other industrialized nation in the world, measured in terms of personal convictions and religious affiliations (see Figure 16.3 on page 625). Therefore, religion and politics mingle, and if the press is correct, the stakes are high in the "culture wars," in which two forces are pulling in opposite directions for a hold on the moral fabric of the nation. On the right, Christian conservatives want religion to play a stronger role in defining our national character. On the left, liberals argue for a secular political sphere, free to operate without religious intervention. Sociologists doubt just how raging this war really is, for Americans seem to agree on more moral issues than the media coverage suggests. Just look at Asheville. They are willing to swap prayer for a moment of silence, no contentious debates necessary.

The universal presence of religion can be found not just in politics but also in other social institutions such as the family, race and gender relations, and social movements. Religion plays a part in structuring inequality too. The sociology of religion looks beyond personal experiences of faith and seeks to uncover the ways that the personal is socially patterned by religion, sometimes in powerful and consequential ways. For instance, have you ever wondered why Protestants have a higher rate of suicide than Catholics (see Chapter 6)? Or why people are drawn to very strict religious bodies? And why is black church life on a Sunday sometimes just as vibrant as Friday nightlife? The sociological challenge is to take something as seemingly personal as faith and ask two things about it: First, how is faith influenced by the larger social world? Second, how does faith shape our social world? The sociologist Peter Berger (1967) noted that this is a dialectical relationship, one balanced by the opposition of religious doctrine on the one hand and the realities of the physical and social world on the other.

You might think that people follow a particular faith because it just rings true to their hearts. That's certainly a part of it, but it's not the whole sociological story. In fact, certain religions are more attractive to different types of people at different points in their lives. Even the level of strictness of a given faith matters in drawing followers, but in a paradoxical way: Typically, the stricter the religious institution, the better its chances of taking off than a faith that has fewer rules and more lenient practices. As a social institution, religion has the power to radically alter global contours, but at the same time, the structure of a given society influences the way religious ideas take shape. Whether or not you are a believer, you are undeniably a follower in the sense of being caught up in religious influences.

What Is Religion?

In broad terms, religion is the way people make sense of their world—the shared stories that guide how they live (McGuire, 2007). Our definition of religion is quite similar to the definition we used for culture in Chapter 3—"a set of beliefs, traditions, and practices; the sum total of social categories and concepts we embrace"—though this is admittedly more comprehensive than religion. The point is that religion and culture overlap. More specifically, religion is a system of beliefs and practices regarding sacred things. These beliefs keep us in line with expected behaviors, so religion serves as a kind of script for our actions, programming us to be able to distinguish right from wrong. The sacred realm refers to holy things that are put to special use for the worship of gods or supreme beings, things kept separate from the profane or everyday realm. The sacred realm is unknowable and mystical, so it inspires us with feelings of awe and wonder. Some combinations that offend many of us because they violate the separation of the sacred and the profane are commerce in religious places, swearing in a house of worship, and the presence of holy texts in toilets.

Religion a system of beliefs, traditions, and practices around sacred things, a set of shared "stories" that guide belief and action.

Sacred holy things meant for special use and kept separate from the profane; the sacred realm is unknowable and mystical, so it inspires us with feelings of awe and wonder.

Profane the things of mundane, everyday life.

This last one is no joke. In 2005, *Newsweek* broke the story that American prison guards at Guantánamo Bay had flushed a Qur'an (or Koran), a sacred Muslim text, down the toilet as part of interrogation tactics. The story was later retracted, but not before sparking anti-American protests and riots throughout the Islamic world (Seelye, 2005). Given some of the previous shocking scenes of torture and abuse in detainee camps, the alleged

Why do religions set aside certain objects, actions, or places as sacred? Whether it's praying in Mecca, receiving communion, or reading the Torah, what might be the social function of distinguishing the sacred from the profane?

desecration of the Qur'an may have at first seemed like small potatoes. But defacing the holy book is especially shocking to Muslims, explained one Pakistani man to *Newsweek* reporters: "We can understand torturing prisoners, no matter how repulsive. . . . But insulting the Qur'an is like deliberately torturing all Muslims. This we cannot tolerate" (Thomas, 2005). How can symbolic violence be more painful than physical violence? What makes the Muslim's Qur'an, the Christian's Bible, or the Jew's Torah so sacred?

Sacred things derive their power from the collective investment of the religious community. An affront on someone's religious symbols is therefore an insult to his or her whole social world, belief systems, and customs. This is a point the functionalist sociologist Émile Durkheim made—one that we'll come back to. But let's start with a brief introduction to the different belief systems around the world (Figure 16.1).

Theism the worship of a god or gods, as in Christianity, Islam, and Hinduism.

Ethicalism the adherence to certain principles to lead a moral life, as in Buddhism and Taoism.

Animism the belief that spirits roam the natural word, as in totemism.

Religion takes three major forms: theism, the worship of a god or gods as in Christianity, Islam, and Hinduism; ethicalism, the adherence to certain principles to lead a moral life, as in Buddhism and Taoism; and animism, the belief that spirits are part of the natural word, as in totemism.

Christianity is the most prevalent world religion: 33 percent of people in the world identify themselves as Christian, approximately 2.1 billion people (Figure 16.2). The largest Christian groups worldwide are Roman Catholics (17.3 percent), Protestants (5.8 percent), and Eastern Orthodox (3.4 percent), plus a slew of smaller groups like New Thought, Christian Scientists, and

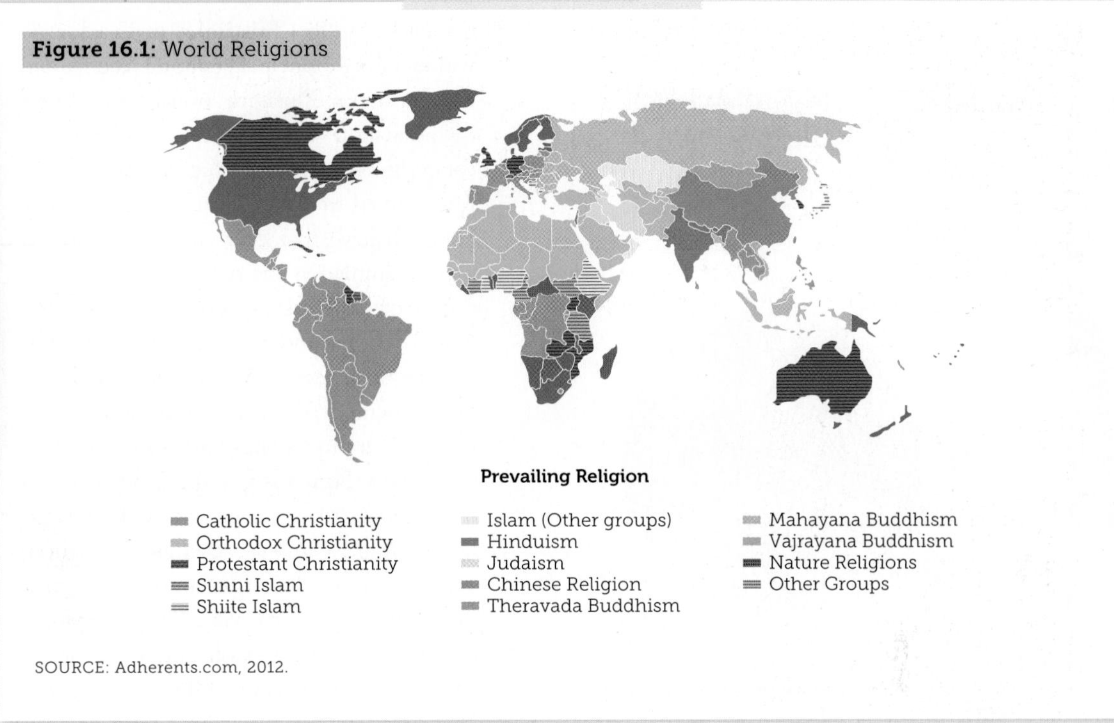

Figure 16.1: World Religions

Quakers (Adherents.com, 2012). Christianity is split among multiple denominations. Denominations are sets of congregations—groups of people who gather together, especially for worship—that share the same faith and are governed under one administrative umbrella. Christians are united by their belief that Jesus Christ was the son of God, born from a virgin named Mary, sent for the forgiveness of the sins of the world. They also believe that Christ will come once again to judge humanity and mark the end of time. Catholics follow the Roman Catholic Church and its head, the bishop of Rome, currently Pope Benedict XVI. Protestants broke from the Catholic Church during the sixteenth-century Reformation, upset with the decadence of the church and the extortion of money from parishioners that was supposedly necessary for moving the souls of their departed relatives from purgatory (also known as limbo) on to heaven.

Denominations big groups of congregations that share the same faith and are governed under one administrative umbrella.

Congregations groups of people who gather together, especially for worship.

Muslims follow Islam, the world's second largest religion (also the United States' second biggest), representing 22.5 percent of the world's population, approximately 1.5 billion people (Adherents.com, 2012). Its teachings center on the authority of the Qur'an, the revelations of God (Allah) as revealed to the prophet Muhammad in the seventh century. The Muslim population in the United States has grown since the 1960s because of immigration from Middle Eastern and South Asian countries such as Indonesia, India, Pakistan, and Bangladesh (Sheler, 2001). Estimates of the number of Muslims in the United States vary, although some reliable studies suggest that the number is around

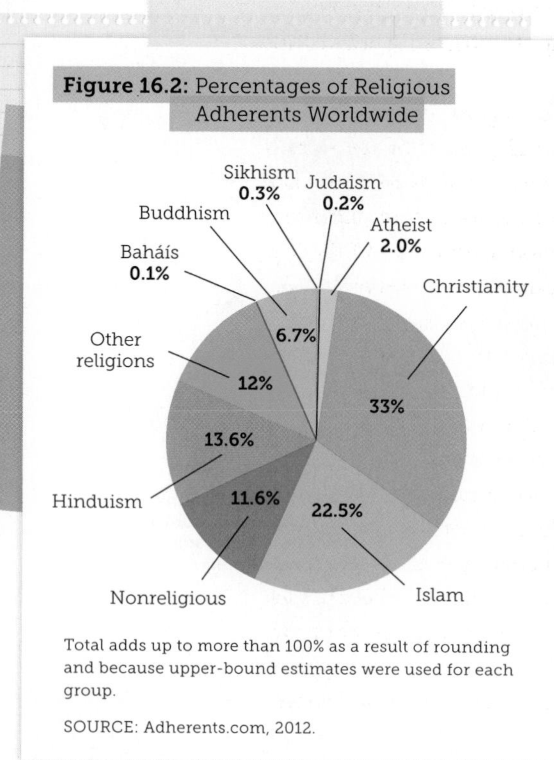

Figure 16.2: Percentages of Religious Adherents Worldwide

Total adds up to more than 100% as a result of rounding and because upper-bound estimates were used for each group.

SOURCE: Adherents.com, 2012.

6 million. As in Christianity, divisions exist within Islam, principally among Sunnis and Shiites. Sunni Muslims, by far the largest denomination of Islam, believe that the first four caliphs or leaders to succeed the Prophet Muhammad were legitimate spiritual leaders. Shiites believe that only Ali, the son-in-law of Muhammad, is the rightful and legitimate successor. Muslims are also split by their austerity of belief and practice. Those who follow liberal Islam—which includes believing in democracy, free expression, and gender equality—try to reconcile modern secularism with Islam. Secularism is the general movement away from religiosity and spiritual belief toward a rational, scientific orientation, a trend observed in Muslim and Christian industrialized nations alike. There is plenty of debate about how faith can be reconciled with modernity, science, and democracy, and liberal Muslims try to achieve such reconciliation. At the opposite end of the spectrum are Islamists or Islamic fundamentalists, a small minority, who reject secularism and democracy; in the extreme, they may use terrorist means to further their religious goals.

Secularism a general movement away from religiosity and spiritual belief toward a rational, scientific orientation, a trend adopted by industrialized nations in the form of separation of church and state.

Hindus make up the next largest group, 13.6 percent of the world's population, primarily in India (Adherents.com, 2012). Hinduism is a type of polytheism, the worship of many gods. There are countless gods according to Hindus, and all of them work to control nature, reproduction, crops, and other facets of life. A central tenet of Hinduism is the belief in reincarnation—the idea that each of us is born and reborn over and over again in a cycle which ends in salvation only by following the traditional rules of caste, decency, and prayer. Christians and Muslims believe that having faith in God will help them withstand the trials of life. While Hindus do not believe in faith, they do believe in a principle called karma. Karma literally means "act," but karma also includes thoughts and speech. Hindus believe that every person and element of the natural world has a role to fulfill. Proper fulfillment of that role will result in alignment with the rest of the world; improper fulfillment of that role results in a misalignment. The net value of a person's actions or karma is carried with them and will shape their fate in the future.

Buddhism is the most prevalent form of ethicalism, in which moral principles are the sacred sources of belief. About 7 percent of the world's population are Buddhist, primarily in Asia. Like Hindus, Buddhists adhere to a belief in karma. Furthermore, they hold "four noble truths": that all existence is suffering, that the cause of suffering is desire, that nirvana—a release of the soul from the body and karmic baggage—can be achieved only through giving up our cravings, and that this is achieved by following the Noble Eightfold Path of right living (with eight facets).

Judaism is the world's eleventh largest organized religion, with an estimated 14 million adherents, representing approximately 0.22 percent of the world's population. About 1.9 percent of the U.S. population profess to be Jewish. The Jewish faith, like Christianity and Islam, is not monolithic, meaning that it doesn't have just one form. Judaism's major denominations are Orthodox, Conservative (*Masorti*), and Reform. On the Orthodox and Conservative side, the emphasis is on tradition and strict adherence to Jewish law and custom, including the segregation of the sexes during worship. Reform Judaism is more relaxed, with the express aim of reconciling modernity and the Jewish faith. All denominations are united by a shared belief in God and the teachings of the Torah, God's revelations to the prophet Moses.

Finally, about 12 percent of the world's population is nonreligious or atheist (Adherents.com, 2012). This group makes up the third largest religious category in the world, but they are still far outnumbered by the 85 percent of religious believers worldwide. These people hold a wide range of beliefs, such as agnosticism, the belief that theological claims fundamentally are not provable. Also included in this group are humanists, those who embrace a type of ethical philosophy that puts faith in humanity's own rules of right and wrong. Atheists believe that no god exists.

Although the content of religious systems varies across cultures, the fact of religion is fairly stable and universal. How do sociologists make sense of such an omnipresent social fact?

Theory: Marx, Weber, and Durkheim

Karl Marx

In studying religion, Karl Marx used a conflict theoretical approach (see Chapter 1), the basis of his social theory called dialectic materialism, which is the struggle between contradictory, interacting forces that eventually results not in victory for one of the forces, but in the creation of a third force that replaces the two opposing forces. A major force of change throughout history, for Marx, was conflict. It was rooted in the tension between the owners of the means of production and the propertyless workers in society. This conflict was at the heart of all social facts of life: education, family, art, and religion. In his *Contribution to the Critique of Hegel's Philosophy of Right,* Marx (1844/1978) famously remarked that religion is the "opiate of the masses." To Marx, religion is a clever means of stratification, of allocating rewards such that some people benefit handsomely from the fruits of society while

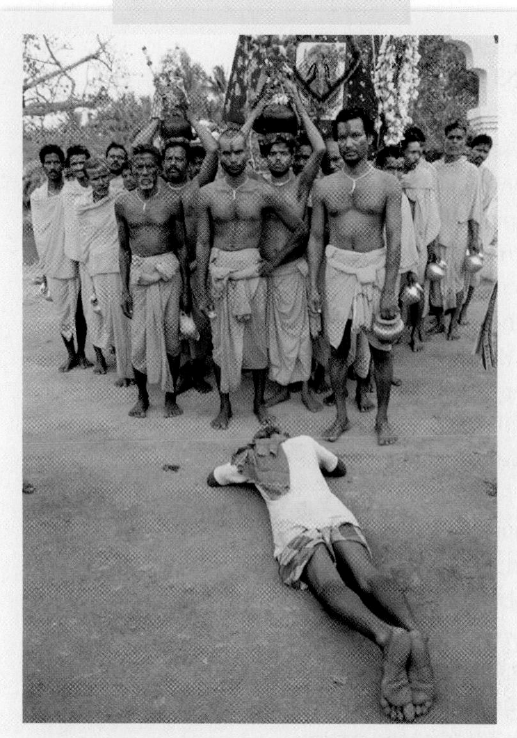

A Hindu man prostrate at the feet of members of the Brahmin caste during Dandajayatra, a festival dedicated to the Hindu deity Shiva.

many others suffer. Religious convictions, he claimed, hold sway over people with promises of happiness in the afterlife, keeping them duped into remaining exploited workers in oppressive, alienating factory jobs. The myth of salvation keeps men toiling in manufacture, scraping by on unfair wages with the hope of finding happiness in the afterlife, while the boss grows rich on their backs. Marx agreed with critiques of religion at the time that sought to remind the world that "man makes religion; religion does not make the man." His colleague Friedrich Engels (1878) explained, "All religion . . . is nothing but the fantastic reflection in men's minds of those external forces which control their daily lives." Marx's critique of religion was part of his broader agenda to expose the "illusory happiness of men." If only workers could see the real truth, they would overthrow their oppressors and demand real happiness with honest and just working conditions.

Marx's conflict theory of religion links two ideas that might seem at odds: inequality and faith. Because religion comes with a set of norms about how the world works, faith can keep the downtrodden in their places so long as religious norms make it seem just. Historically, there's something to conflict theory. Take India as an example, where religion justified the oppressive caste system for thousands of years (see Chapter 7). Castes are ranked statuses based on birth that determined life chances for Indians, everything from what type of education they received to what jobs they could hold and whom they might marry. Until an awareness movement in the 1990s, the caste system was believed to be the natural way of the world, ordained by the gods. To take another example, in Europe through the nineteenth century, Christianity was used as a justification to exploit what were considered barbarous and uncivilized groups of people around the world. The real motivation behind imperialism, of course, was economic—to pillage natural resources and profit from slave labor—but doing so in the name of Christ made it seem okay, even commendable, for hundreds of years.

Scholars have challenged many aspects of Marxist theory, especially its failure to take religion seriously. How can faith, something experienced by the overwhelming majority of the world, be reduced to a function of class oppression?

Max Weber

Max Weber took up the challenge by showing religious ideas as independent forces in their own right. In Weber's view, the best way to figure out what drives social action is to put oneself in another person's shoes and imagine that person's intentions and meanings. By emphasizing *Verstehen* (German for "understanding"), Weber gives credence to the power of ideas (see Chapter 1). Ideas are so powerful, Weber insists in *The Protestant Ethic and the Spirit of Capitalism* (1904/2003), that when enough people hold dearly a certain set of beliefs, the course of history is forever altered.

The Protestant Ethic starts with the idea that the Western world has changed since the 1850s, relative to the traditional societies that existed beforehand. Rationality is the driving force for action in the modern world, as opposed to tradition or habit, which was the reason people did things in the past. How, he wonders, did this modern world come into being?

To answer this question, Weber begins with the observation that different regions of Europe that counted greater or lesser proportions of Protestants in their populations had corresponding different rates of capitalist activity. In predominantly Protestant areas such as central Germany, people tended to own more capital. Protestant Germany also was one of the most economically successful regions of Europe, and workers were more likely to be highly educated and skilled, often employed in large industrial and commercial companies.

What was occurring in central Germany that wasn't happening in, say, northern Germany, which was predominantly Catholic? What motivated all this capitalist activity in central Germany? With these questions in mind, Weber visited America in 1904, touring the country for three months. Here he had the chance to observe a flourishing capitalistic economy in America and to read Benjamin Franklin's *Necessary Hints to Those That Would Be Rich* (1736) and *Advice to a Young Tradesman* (1748), written in the eighteenth century. Some key statements that came from Franklin's writings include "Time is money," "Credit is money," "Money begets money," and "A penny saved is a penny earned." These maxims have become commonsense in mainstream American culture, but in an earlier ethic where poverty was a virtue, this would have sounded like simple, dishonorable greed. In a capitalist society, however, Franklin's principles of thrift were praiseworthy for any man of honor. They included the duty to increase individual wealth, the moral duty to fulfill a calling and make money through a vocation, the validation of moneymaking as an end in itself, and the utilitarianism of values (that is, virtues are only virtuous if they are useful to the individual). In Franklin's new philosophy, Weber identified what he called the "spirit of capitalism." This spirit, he notes, sets forth a peculiar restraint: You work very hard, but you cannot enjoy the fruits of your labor. Accumulating piles of money for the mere sake of having piles of money seems irrational. How has greed become the ideal virtue of the honest man? How did people suddenly accept the idea of labor as an end in itself if it's not in their self-interests?

As we saw in Chapter 14, according to Weber, Protestantism was a necessary condition for the emergence of capitalism. Specifically, Calvinist teachings shaped the kind of personalities needed for capitalism to develop. The early

How were Max Weber's interpretations of capitalist axioms like those of Benjamin Franklin in Poor Richard's Almanack?

Protestant sects, especially Calvinism, believed that each person had a calling, which entailed fulfilling one's duty to God through day-to-day work in disciplined, rational labor. A person could fulfill his or her calling by choosing a vocation and then methodically completing its associated work for God's glory. Salvation entailed rigorous self-discipline, the rational application of one's labor.

Another key idea of the new Protestant faiths was predestination, the notion that only the elect are chosen by God for salvation. But the trick is that you don't know if you've been chosen or not. The best you can do is look for signs in this life of what awaits you in the next life. One such sign is success: If you're successful in this life, it's reasonable to assume you will be successful in the afterlife. Another sign is your self-discipline and simple lifestyle free from pleasures of the flesh and other luxuries. In other words, if you are successful in fulfilling your calling and you do not enjoy it, then all signs are looking good for your afterlife.

If Protestants want to be successful but can't enjoy their success, then a good Protestant is a rich one. As good Protestants sought profit, not pleasures, a new era characterized by rationalization, asceticism, and individualism began. Protestants were encouraged to earn, save, accumulate, and give to others, and as an unintended consequence, the system of capitalism took off. Thus, one of the unforeseen effects of early Protestant teachings, claimed Weber, was the capitalist system.

Weber and Marx present two very different theoretical approaches. Marx saw a causal chain moving from the economic base to the cultural and religious superstructure, in which religion is part of an ideology stemming from class interests. Weber offers a more complicated story, where ideas and beliefs are not mere reflections of a class base. To Weber, the causal connection works both ways, creating an "elective affinity" between the economic and the cultural: "It is not, of course, the intention here to set a one-sided spiritualistic analysis of the causes of culture and history in place of an equally one-sided 'materialistic' analysis. *Both are equally possible*" (Weber, 1904/2003, p. 125, emphasis added). If the history of our society can be envisioned as a train, moving along through eras of invention, war, disaster, and enlightenment, ideas are, in his words, the "switchmen" of the tracks. They hold the potential, when believed in enough and by the right people at the right time, to change the course of history in unexpected, counterintuitive ways.

Once the capitalist system took root, the Protestant ethic that had allowed it to spread began to fade away, dropping out of the new economic system. Capitalism, Weber believed, was able to sustain itself without the religious meanings crucial to its early development. In Ben Franklin's maxims, this spirit of capitalism already thrived without the religious undertones. The pursuit of money has become an end in itself, and the world has been overtaken by efficiency and rationalism. The English minister Richard Baxter claimed in 1681 that the desire for material goods should lie over people's shoulders "like a lightweight coat that could be thrown off at any time" (Weber, 1904/2003, p. 123). But, in Weber's terms, this desire has become in the modern rational world a "steel-hard casing" or an "iron cage," in which we are forever trapped, chasing after gain for the sake of gaining, caught in a rat race of increasing coldness, calculation, and disenchantment.

Weber thought the modern world had been deserted by the gods and remade into a clinical, predictable, and demystified place. Indeed, Protestantism is a modern faith that stands removed from the ancient elements of the sacred: mystery, miracle, and magic. In a roundabout way, Weber ends up sounding like Marx in predicting that the cold, impersonal winds of capitalism would intrude on all aspects of personal and spiritual life, erasing inefficient feelings such as religious devotion.

Weber's ideas have not gone uncontested. Daniel Chirot, for instance, argues that Protestantism was not the only or the most important driving force behind the spread of capitalism (Chirot, 1985). He finds that because of geography—climate, agriculture, natural barriers against invasion—certain parts of Europe were more apt to nurture capitalist enterprises than others.

How did the idea of predestination embraced by Dutch Protestants help early capitalism take root in Western Europe?

Why did Durkheim study Australian Aborigines in the early twentieth century? What did he see as the social function of religion?

Émile Durkheim

Émile Durkheim's functionalist approach (see Chapter 1) finds both purpose and power in modern religious belief. He tackled first the question of what religion is by studying totemism among Australian Aboriginal societies, which he wrote about in *Elementary Forms of the Religious Life* (1917/1995). Durkheim argued that he researched totemism not for the "sheer pleasure of recounting the bizarre and the eccentric" but to comprehend a more general religious nature, which he considered a "fundamental and permanent aspect of humanity."

The sociologist's task, according to Durkheim, is not to determine which religions are "true" and which are "false." Rather, the sociologist must treat every religion as real and find out what commonalities they share. He noted that it is a "fundamental postulate of sociology that a human institution cannot rest upon error and falsehood." Durkheim, in fact, came to argue that our very categories of thought—notions of time, space, cause, and effect—are created in and from religion.

Indeed, Durkheim believed that the "skeleton of thought" that every human must possess in order to function in the world is a product of religious thought. This insight led him to theorize that religion is an "eminently social thing." Its "representations are collective representations that express collective realities." As such, the sociologist must approach a rite like a rain dance or genital mutilation and "know how to reach beneath the symbol to grasp the reality it represents and that gives the symbol its true meaning." (Recall our discussion of cultural relativism in Chapter 3.) Be they wood carvings, chants, drawings, or holy days, our sacred symbols are not just the result of some wild mythological imaginations spawned under the deceptive guise of language. How could all of humanity be strung along for centuries under some kind of elaborate trickery? Durkheim gives people more credit than that: For him, sacred things acquire power because their owners have collectively invested them with it:

> The Arunta [a member of an Aboriginal tribe] who has properly rubbed himself with his *churinga* [a sacred stone or wooden object] feels stronger; he is stronger. The soldier who falls defending his flag certainly does not believe he has sacrificed himself to a piece of cloth. Such things happen because social thought, with its imperative authority, has a power that individual thought cannot possibly have. (1917/1995, p. 229)

Religious force is a feeling that the collectivity inspires in its individual members, which then is projected outside the individual and objectified as an external force. The power of the sacred is not felt as coercion; rather, "Each individual carries the whole in himself. It is part of him, so when he yields to its promptings, he does not think he is yielding to coercion but instead doing what his own nature tells him to do." When people conform to the rules of their religion, they are in effect yielding to the moral authority of society.

Social Solidarity Durkheim further argued that religions perform social functions. Specifically, religion perpetuates social unity or solidarity by strengthening the collective conscience: the shared beliefs and ideas, ways of thinking and knowing. Religion strengthens the bonds of people not only to their gods but also to their society, because God is a representation of society. Religious thought becomes not just the sum of individual parts but a distinctive whole that cannot be reduced to its parts. Social solidarity in modern societies is a force that has become larger than individuals, acting on and constraining them—although without them, the force would not exist.

One indication that religious participation strengthens social solidarity comes from deviance studies, in which research has shown that religiously active people are less likely to commit crimes. (See our discussion of social control and deviance in Chapter 6.) When you are busy raising money for church charity, you don't have time to be exposed to criminal activities, nor would you want your religious peer group to find out about your illegitimate behavior. Furthermore, the fear of divine punishment, called the "hellfire effect," is likely to keep you in line. However, moral communities are not insulated from their social context, and the solidarity of religion probably prevents crime most when it exists within a close-knit system such as a school or a homogeneous community, where everyone shares the same beliefs—an increasing rarity in heterogeneous modern society. (The Amish communities that we profiled in Chapter 5 are a conspicuous exception.)

There is also evidence of the positive effect of religion-induced social solidarity on individuals' well-being. In one study, for example, religious attendance and affiliation are inversely correlated with alcohol, tobacco, and substance use and therefore with the risks of developing chronic diseases (Koenig et al., 1994). On average, people who are religiously involved "live slightly longer lives and experience slightly lower levels of depressive symptoms" than people who are less religious (McCullough & Smith, 2003). Of course, we cannot know for sure if religion actually causes these positive outcomes or, rather, something about particular individuals predisposes them both to be religious and to live healthy

The house church movement offers an alternative to traditional churches, meeting in small congregations (often around 10 to 15 people) and focusing on community and mission work. Why might religious people live longer and suffer fewer cases of depression?

lifestyles. Perhaps folks who are religious gain intrinsic enjoyment from following rules, predisposing them to gain positive feelings both from religion and from following the surgeon general's recommendations for a healthy lifestyle.

Secularization or Speculation?

In the 1960s, the future of religion in America was in doubt. Social scientists of the day, touting secularization theory, predicted a future American social scene in which religious influence would be diminished. The waning power of religious ideas was associated with a 400-year-old worldwide trend of modernization and is evident in the separation of religion from institutions such as the state, economy, and family. It involves the rising importance of the everyday (the profane) and the diminishing significance of the sacred. It is equally visible in the shift of marriage counseling from the priest to the therapist and in the popularity of the crucifix as a fashion accessory. Secularization affects the organization of society—less church control over state policy, for example. It also means that religion weighs less and less upon our consciousness.

Secularization worried social scientists and theologians alike during the 1960s; many considered it not just a neutral parallel trend to modernization but a distinct force with which to be reckoned. Peter Berger (1967) considered secularization the result of a larger sociostructural crisis in religion caused by pluralism, the presence and engaged coexistence of numerous distinct groups in one society. Pluralism has widely been considered detrimental to religion. With diverse religions, so the argument goes, various churches offer their own answers to life's deep questions, often discrediting others' views. The result, fears Berger, is a "crisis of credibility," a loss of religious legitimacy and plausibility. Pluralism threatens to rip apart a unified faith's sacred canopy, a term Berger used to describe the entire set of religious norms, symbols, and beliefs which convey the feeling that life is worth living, reality is meaningful and ordered, and all is not just random chaos. When the sacred canopy rips and gives way to conflicting ideas about how the world works, Berger feared, we end up with religious disintegration, psychological malaise, and chaos. If every church claims to have the right answers and each doctrine seems plausible, how can you know which church to join and what to believe? Pluralism presents modern individuals with an unprecedented crisis: to figure out for themselves life's greater meaning (Berger, 1967). Faced with that daily challenge, why even get out of bed?

Pluralism the presence and engaged coexistence of numerous distinct groups in one society.

Sacred canopy Peter Berger's term to describe the entire set of religious norms, symbols, and beliefs that express the most important thing in life, namely, the feeling that life is worth living and that reality is meaningful and ordered, not just random chaos.

Despite many attempts, the mission to unite Christians has repeatedly failed. The reason, Roger Finke and Rodney Stark argue in *The Churching of America, 1776–1990* (1992), is that pluralism is a natural state of the unregulated religious sphere. Because different people look for different things in a religion—say, worldliness or otherworldliness, strictness or permissiveness—a plethora of churches naturally arises to satisfy people's religious tastes. Even states that mandate faiths for their citizens, as medieval and Renaissance Europe did, still end up with a considerable number of heretics and dissenters, as well as religious indifference.

Religious Pluralism in the United States

The United States is both highly religious and pluralistic, standing out among other industrialized and wealthy nations in this regard (Inglehart & Baker, 2000). About 86 percent of Americans claim a religious affiliation, although identifying, believing, and participating can mean quite different things (Fischer & Hout, 2006). In a random sample, people from 65 countries were asked to rate the importance of God in their lives on a scale from 1 to 10. The percentage of Americans who responded with a 10 was a whopping 50 percent (Figure 16.3).

In its level of religiosity, the United States is closer to some poor developing nations than to other wealthy democratic states. According to the General Social Survey, almost two-thirds of Americans believe in God, whereas only 2.2 percent do not. Approximately 77 percent believe in heaven, 63 percent in hell, and 58 percent in the devil. About one-third of Americans think the Bible is the actual word of God (Sherkat & Ellison, 1999). Yet American faith has tended to be more broad than deep, such that "of those Americans who say the Bible is either the actual or the inspired Word of God, only half can name the first book in the Bible" (Chaves, 2002).

Figure 16.3: Percentage of National Populations That Rated the Importance of God in Their Lives as "10"

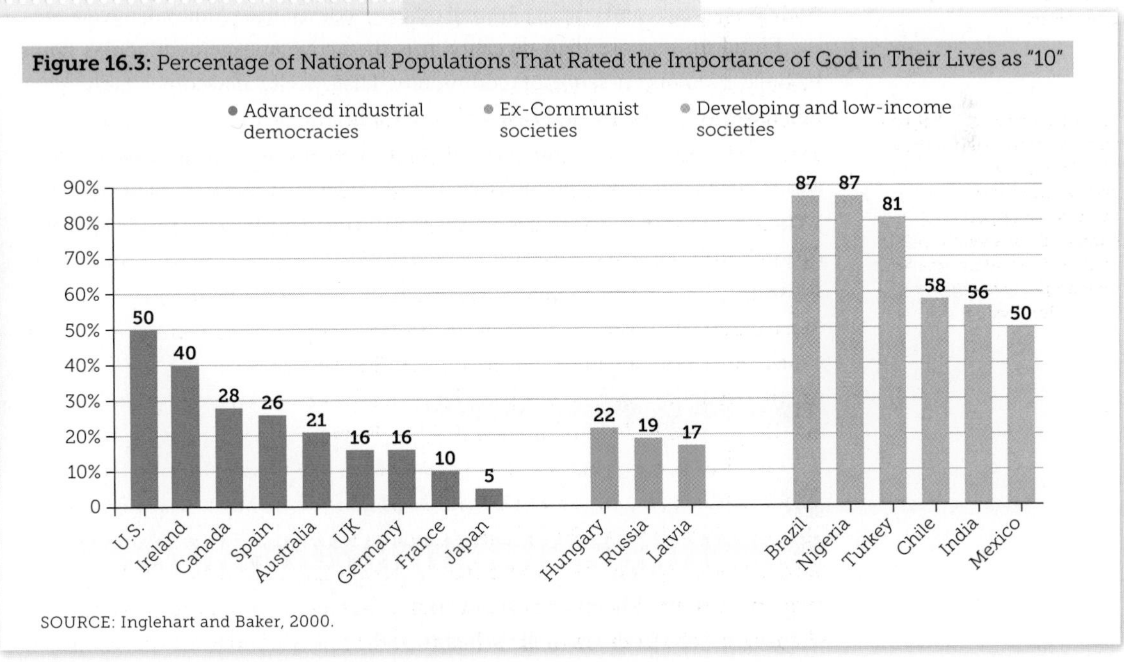

SOURCE: Inglehart and Baker, 2000.

The United States also stands out as a highly pluralistic religious society; more than 280 denominations and 300,000 congregations exist, not to mention the continuous flux of new cults and movements (Ammerman, 2005). Protestants outnumber Catholics, although since 1900 Protestantism has shrunk from a following of 80 percent of Americans to only 51.3 percent. Figure 16.4 provides a visual representation of the major American faiths.

According to a 2007 survey by the Pew Forum on Religion and Public Life, 26.3 percent of the U.S. population are white evangelicals (Pew Forum on Religious and Public Life, 2008). Evangelicals can be members of any denomination, but the term is typically reserved for groups distinguished by four main beliefs: The Bible is without error, salvation comes only through belief in Jesus Christ, personal conversion is the only path to salvation (the "born again" experience), and others must also be converted. Evangelicals try to proselytize, to win people over, by engaging with wider society.

Evangelicals members of any denomination distinguished by four main beliefs: the Bible is without error, salvation comes only through belief in Jesus Christ, personal conversion is the only path to salvation (the "born again" experience), and others must also be converted. They proselytize by engaging with wider society.

Fundamentalists religious adherents who follow a scripture (such as the Bible or Qur'an) using a literal interpretation of its meaning.

Fundamentalists also follow the Bible as a literal text but do not necessarily try to spread the gospel to the same extent that evangelicals do. The term *conservative Protestant* is often used to refer to evangelicals and fundamentalists, as well as Pentecostals, a nonmainstream group that believes in otherworldly phenomena such as speaking in tongues that they view as evidence of the miracle of receiving the Holy Ghost.

Taken together, conservative Protestants, mainline Protestants (denominations that do not interpret the Bible literally, such as Methodists, Lutherans, and Episcopalians), Catholics, and Orthodox Christians account for about 80 percent of all Americans. The remaining 16 percent who are non-Christians—Buddhists, Hindus, Jews, Jains, Muslims, Sikhs, Baha'is, Confucians, Pagans, Shintoists, Taoists, Zoroastrians, and atheists, among others—coexist in a pluralist United States.

Pluralism is more than diversity; it is the active engagement across faiths to build a common sense of community. Historically, newcomer faiths were greeted with suspicion and hostility, and Catholics, Mormons, Jews, and other minority religious adherents were all subject to social exclusion, harassment, and even church arson and violence. If not excluded, people of minority faiths were encouraged to assimilate to majority Anglo-Protestantism (Eck, 2006). More recently, however, pluralism, understood as engagement with and respect for other faiths, has become a social ideal.

Figure 16.4: One Nation, Many Faiths

Protestants
51.3%

Each symbol represents 1% of the U.S. population.

SOURCE: Pew Forum on Religious and Public Life, 2010.

That's not to say that religious difference is always a smooth matter of respect and communication. Jen'nan Read is a sociologist who writes about Muslims in America and has taken on "probably the most complicated topic in the Muslim community and outside of it because it's so misunderstood," which is the veil or hijab. She found that Muslim women in America who wear the veil tend to be highly educated and choose to veil in spite of their families' disapproval. They wear it "for their own individual identity, and for their own feelings of being American. Because part of being American for them is the freedom to choose, to wear this even if their families don't want them to" (Conley, 2009i). But America is not always as accepting of their choice as they might like. In Cape Henlopen, Delaware, a Muslim family sued their daughter's school district on the grounds that a fourth-grade teacher had initiated a campaign of harassment against the young Muslim student. The teacher allegedly taught class lessons on the evils of the Qur'an and associated the Muslim student with terrorists. Fellow students began ridiculing her at school as the "loser Muslim," and eventually she had to transfer to another school district (Spiegel, 2006). Following an investigation by the U.S. Department of Justice (2007), the school district now requires programs promoting religious tolerance and offers special training to teachers. Since September 11, 2001, reports of the harassment and bullying of Sikhs and Muslims, by fellow students and teachers alike, have continued to rise. These instances show the failures of pluralism and fly in the face of religious tolerance, a basic ideal of the Constitution.

According to Jen'nan Read, why is the hijab so misunderstood?

Religious Attendance in the United States

Identification with a religious denomination is currently high in America, and Finke and Stark (1992), in *The Churching of America,* find that religious participation

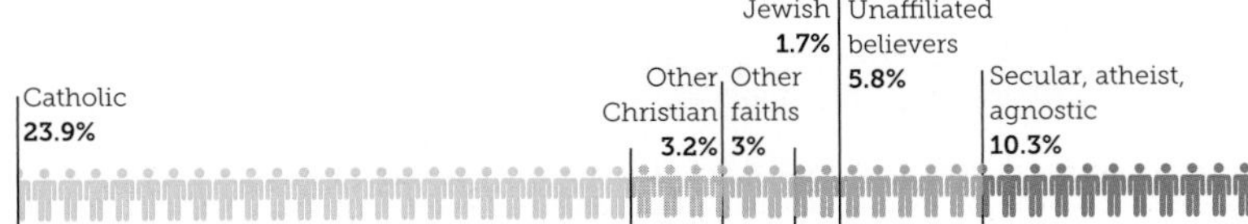

has increased over the course of our history, based on growing rates of church membership. They find, for instance, that church membership was only 10 percent in 1789, rising to 22 percent by 1890 and reaching 60 percent during the 1960s. Of course, the nature of churchgoing has changed as well, evolving from elite social clubs in the eighteenth century to today's informal communal gatherings.

Today, 40 percent of Americans report going to the service of a religious organization nearly every week (Pew Forum on Religious and Public Life, 2008). However, it's difficult to rely on the word of the average survey respondent, because Americans tend to over-report church attendance, a common problem social scientists call "social desirability bias." (Recall our discussion of survey research in Chapter 2.) When researchers have counted congregants at actual services and compared those counts to self-reports of attendance, they found that the self- reports were 10 to 30 percent higher than observational data (Fischer & Hout, 2006). Whether from guilt, embarrassment, or a desire to look good in front of social scientists, people tend to bend the truth on surveys when questions have a moral undertone. When researchers simply ask a random sample if they attend service once a month, they find that 60 percent do. But when study participants keep journals of their daily whereabouts, researchers find that rates of attendance are significantly lower (Hadaway et al., 1993). (See Figure 16.5.)

Service attendance, in fact, seems to be declining. Time-use records have shown that weekly attendance has dipped in the last 30 years, from 40 percent

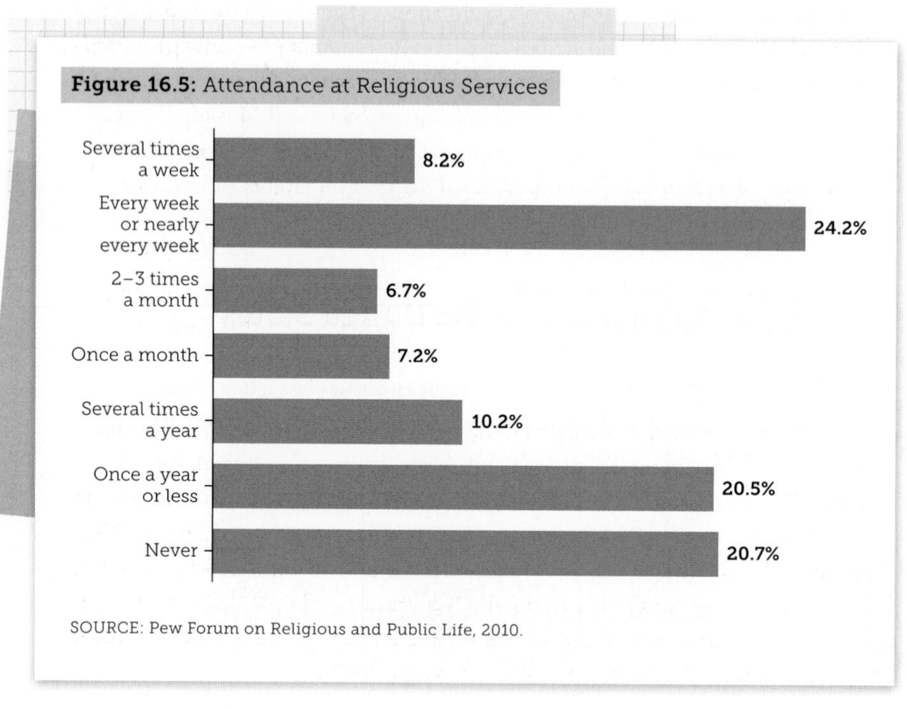
Figure 16.5: Attendance at Religious Services

SOURCE: Pew Forum on Religious and Public Life, 2010.

going to church once a week in 1965 to only 25 percent in 1994 (Chaves, 2002). This is not unique to the United States. In more than 20 advanced industrial countries, churchgoing is on the decline. (The opposite is happening in former Communist countries, where people attend church in greater numbers, perhaps to make up for lost time under Communism.) In contrast, there is a persistence of religious belief and even a rise in spirituality (Inglehart & Baker, 2000). That is, attendance and church membership rates may go up and down, but beliefs in the divine and the afterlife are here to stay.

Even if only about a quarter of Americans weekly attend church, as reported in the 2004 General Social Survey, religious service attendance far outnumbers involvement in other voluntary organizations. In addition to their time, Americans donate considerable amounts of money to religious organizations.

Given this muddled picture of a diverse religious nation, is all the concern over secularization warranted? Are there signs that pluralism is eroding faith? Given Weber's prediction that the gods fled in the face of rationalized economy and Marx's warning that modernization would wipe out all mystical thinking, why do people continue to hold religious beliefs in modern society? Secularization theory in the 1960s foretold the end of religion's importance in not just the social world but also our individual psyches. Religious commitment, the theorists told us, was waning, and the church was in a crisis. Indeed, great differentiation exists among faiths in America, and service attendance does not match followers' proclaimed conviction or even perhaps their best intentions. Overall, however, religion has proved a sturdy force. In 1997, Peter Berger backed away from his old claims, telling an interviewer in *Christian Century:*

> I think what I and most other sociologists of religion wrote in the 1960s about secularization was a mistake. Our underlying argument was that secularization and modernity go hand in hand. With more modernization comes more secularization. It wasn't a crazy theory. There was some evidence for it. But I think it's basically wrong. Most of the world today is certainly not secular. It's very religious. ("Epistemological Modesty," 1997, p. 972)

Although American engagement in formal religious life may have declined since the 1960s, Americans retain their beliefs in the supernatural. The otherworldly *Harry Potter* and *Twilight* franchises have grossed millions; advances in space travel inspire awe of the mysterious cosmos; even the decoding of DNA sequences is further proof of "intelligent design" to some believers. For all our scientific explanations and discoveries, modern people still turn to religion because some experiences—bafflement, suffering, and wonder—forever remain a part of the human condition (Chaves, 2002).

At the Micro Level: Is it a Great Big Delusion?

Right around 2007, the pages of prominent book reviews and more than a fair share of bloggers became involved in a heated debate over faith. The ruckus surrounded a few books by atheist academics that had been published back to back—namely, *The God Delusion* by Richard Dawkins (2006), an Oxford University evolutionary biologist; *God Is Not Great* by Christopher Hitchens (2007), a left-leaning public intellectual; and *Letter to a Christian Nation* by Sam Harris (2006), an American neuroscience student.

These best-selling authors take aim at religious belief as being factually inaccurate, irrational, and dangerous, and they use faith in science to try to disprove the existence of supernatural intelligence. They were vehemently criticized on a number of points, especially for not taking religious belief seriously. One reviewer noted that Dawkins simply dismissed belief as "base superstition" and that he equated followers with fundamentalists (Orr, 2007). What about religion's power to console people, to give guidance and strength, to give purpose and answers to these looming questions: Why am I here? What is the meaning of life? What comes after death?

Instead of criticizing religion in general, which is Dawkins's mission, sociologists of religion are more interested in another set of questions: Why do

Richard Dawkins poses in front of an ad campaign that he and the British Humanist Association posted on 800 buses around Great Britain.

people value their religious beliefs? How do they experience their faith in a way that makes them truly believe in something that an Oxford scientist has dismissed as factually inaccurate? To answer this set of questions, we turn to microsociology, an approach that examines everyday human interactions, practices, and beliefs on the small scale (see Chapter 1).

Religious experience an individual's spiritual feelings, acts, and experiences.

Religious experience, as the psychologist William James (1903/1982) defined it, involves "feelings, acts, and experiences of individual men in their solitude, so far as they apprehend themselves to stand in relation to whatever they may consider the divine." To the people who experience them, these feelings, acts, and experiences are very real, physical, and powerful. Achieving spiritual awakening (*Bodhi*) for a Buddhist or deep meditation (*dhyāna*) for a Hindu can alter how he or she perceives the world. In one interview study, a woman discussed an out-of-body experience, in which she was "whooshed" up into an astral plane to meet Jesus: "It's not a person, it's not a body, it's like a being of light. . . . And I feel like I've died and gone to heaven. I'm like ahh. And this deep booming, booming male voice says, 'Welcome home, Cathy,' and I start to sob" (Bender, 2007). Is this a fairly predictable neurological response to the lack of oxygen, as rational science critics would claim? To judge the authenticity of religious experience is not the job of sociology, says sociologist Nancy Ammerman (2005), echoing Durkheim; the job of sociologists is to better understand the meaning and uses of religion in people's lives. For example, Meredith McGuire focuses on how religion is physically felt in the body (2007). It is through "embodied practices"—touches, postures, gestures, and movements—that religion becomes constituted by some followers as authentic and real, according to McGuire. Even something as simple as breathing can be a religious practice, as in pranayama yoga, where slow and deliberate breaths are part of connecting to spirituality (McGuire, 2007). Dancing is a common embodied practice of religions, and by sharing rhythmic dance moves, a community of worshippers can express their connection to one another and to their spirituality. Inasmuch as breathing and dancing reflect spiritual experiences, they also reproduce it, strengthening believers' bonds to their faith with each breath or clap of the hands (McGuire, 2007).

Sociologists may also study the way people reconcile religion and rationality. For example, creationism as laid out in the book of Genesis in the Bible seems fundamentally at odds with theories of evolution. But people don't always accept literal interpretations of religion wholesale, as sociologist Kelly Besecke (2007) determined in her study of American Christians. Besecke found that people practice reflexive

How might sociologists study religious experiences like transcendental meditation?

Reflexive spirituality a contemporary religious movement that encourages followers to look to religion for meaning, wisdom, and profound thought and feeling rather than for absolute truths on how the world works.

spirituality—that is, they look to religion for meaning, wisdom, and profound thought and feeling rather than for absolute truths about how the world works. The reflexive spiritualists Besecke studied were also tired of swallowing the whole scientific story. They believed in logic and reasoning to help them get to the bottom of some of life's challenges but didn't trust science to provide them with transcendent truths, symbolic meanings, or inspirational metaphors. For reflexive spiritualists, the tensions between fact and faith become less compelling, and religion remains a sensible avenue for finding meaning in life.

The Power of Religion: Social Movements

The Reverend Simeon Jocelyn of New Haven, speaking in 1834 before a meeting of the American Anti-Slavery Society, condemned slavery as the nation's moral failing. "Resolved," he said, "That the American church is stained with the blood of 'the souls of poor innocents,' and holds the keys of the great prison of oppression; that while she enslaves, she is herself enslaved" (quoted in Young, 2002). Jocelyn, like most evangelicals of the day, was riding on a new crest of social action. The antislavery and temperance (anti-alcohol) campaigns were among the first major social movements in the United States. (See Chapter 18 for a broader discussion of social movements.)

The American landscape in the 1830s was in turmoil. In a time of rapid market expansion, when new canal and road networks offered unprecedented possibility for mobility, people were plucked from traditional life and plunged into urban, industrial, and sometimes remote places, such as the West. The U.S. population jumped from 3.8 million in 1790 to 12.8 million in 1830 (Young, 2002). Yet despite rapid growth, America of the early 1800s still lacked national institutions. The centralized post office had been established, making interregional communication possible, but no political institution existed that could put it to use for enacting sweeping social change. Such a context created difficulties for the abolitionist and temperance campaigns as they tried to disseminate their messages. It was nearly impossible to mobilize the kind of powerful political network that would persuade people to do anything about slavery and alcohol. Instead, they deployed religion.

Although the country enjoyed a limited national governmental apparatus—and no lobbyists, political action committees, or interest group think tanks—there were a readily available and sturdy evangelical ethos, a shared culture, and a blossoming network of religious organizations. In particular, the churches of elites such as Presbyterians and Congregationalists (to which about one-third of all regular churchgoers belonged) shared a spirit of "organized benevolence," the idea that God held high expectations for the new country. It was their mission to become the keepers of the new Promised Land, to protect it

Attendees at camp meetings, such as this Methodist revival in 1839, led many of the antislavery and temperance movements before the Civil War.

against national sins like slavery and alcohol. Meanwhile, other growing groups such as the Methodists and Baptists promoted the personal confession of sin, which soon grew into public spectacles. Public confessions and conversions became a widespread recruitment vehicle, bringing mass numbers to American churches. In 1780 perhaps 400 Baptist congregations and a handful of Methodist congregations existed; by 1820 these churches numbered 5,400 congregations (Gaustad, 1962).

These two elements, public confession and national sin, converged in no time into a public confession against the sins of the nation, or what sociologist Michael Young calls "confessional protest" (2002). In the face of particular sins like drinking and slavery, this religious infrastructure allowed the temperance and antislavery movements to resonate with the masses. In 1829 the American Temperance Society had just 200 branches, mostly clustered in Connecticut, Massachusetts, and New York; by 1834 there were more than 8,000 branches with 1.5 million members. The antislavery movement also boomed. The Anti-Slavery Society started in 1833 with the goal of "the abolition of slavery by the spirit of repentance." It grew from 75 auxiliaries to 1,340 by 1838. Its messages were disseminated in large part by women, who dominated the rosters of both the temperance and the antislavery societies. Because women lacked formal political power, the societies became socially acceptable places for them to exert influence outside the home.

These movements picked up momentum as mass spectacles of confession and conversion spread throughout the country. During public confessions in upstate New York, spirits merchants poured their stock into the streets, prompting hundreds of audience members to swear off booze. It was announced at one temperance convention in Boston, in 1836, that the entire nation was guilty if its citizens indulged a sin like drinking:

> That in the support of the wholesome laws of God and our country, we here pledge ourselves never to swerve from our purposes and efforts, while the monster intemperance is allowed to spread its withering influence abroad in our land. (Young, 2002, p. 681)

Similarly, in abolitionist meetings, slave owners and merchants renounced slavery as part of becoming born again.

It wasn't an easy road for members of these new movements, particularly the abolitionists, who were met with mob riots, threats, harassment, hurled eggs, stones, and in one case even bullets (Young, 2002). But they persevered, grew in number, and eventually won—a victory made possible not through state or national political institutions, the typical vehicles for enacting social change today, but through religion.

The significance of piety—dutiful adherence to religious doctrine in mind and body—in America lies not in religion's popularity but rather in its capacity to mold our social world. Religion and politics have mingled in many profound ways since the nineteenth century. Consider the civil rights movement led by the Reverend Dr. Martin Luther King, Jr., who has been immortalized in our national history with near sainthood status. (In its obituary of April 5, 1968, the *New York Times* exalted the Nobel Peace Prize winner as "a veritable hero," a "prophet," and the "voice of anguish.") We tend to put a lot of stock in the power of charismatic individuals such as King. However, even a leader as oratorically gifted and politically astute as he was needed the right set of circumstances. Those circumstances, it turns out, had already been put in place by a powerful force: religion. In *The Origins of the Civil Rights Movement,* Alden Morris (1984) contends that King's power was the result of a strong organizational base that was already in place in the 1960s in the black community, and its centerpiece was the church. Theorists of "resource mobilization" have argued that religion played a central role in the civil rights movement by providing organizational and symbolic resources, preparing African Americans and binding them into dense social networks, building coalitions, opening communication, and providing within-community funding. King was effective because he was backed by the Southern Christian Leadership Conference and the Student Nonviolent Coordinating Committee, both mobilized through the black church. In fact, argues David Garrow (1968), King was in the right place at exactly the moment when the movement needed an educated, inspiring spokesman.

Religion can be a means of gaining political momentum, strengthening group cohesion, and expressing group culture. It can work to the advantage of marginalized communities such as African Americans, but the reverse is also true: Religion can dismiss, oppress, or marginalize certain groups. For example, right-wing hate groups rely heavily on religiosity, citing the biblical determination of difference and inequality between races. White supremacists of the Kingdom Identity Ministries in Arkansas, for example, claim that the real difference between whites and blacks is preordained by the divine, and the knights of the Fiery Cross, otherwise known as the Ku Klux Klan, define themselves as "religious warriors," justifying their antiblack terrorist tactics in the name of God and religious values. After the Civil War, Reconstruction-era Klan members spread their message with exuberance and theatricality; many Klansmen committed their "holy" atrocities in squirrel-skin masks, masquerade costumes, and even women's dresses, incorporating the conventions of minstrelsy and the circus to get their message across (Parsons, 2005).

Spiritual conviction and religious organizations have been integral in shaping the social landscape—for better or for worse. Even when not put to use by competing groups as they jockey for social power, religion proves a powerful force in the day-to-day shaping of individual consciousness.

Martin Luther King, Jr., preaching at his church. What was religion's role in the U.S. civil rights movement?

Religion and the Social Landscape

Just as religion shapes social institutions like government and social movements, so too does it operate on small-scale perceptions and choices in everyday spheres, such as family life, voting choices, lifestyles, and racial attitudes. Sometimes implicitly, other times glaringly, faith is related to family structure, gender, social status, age, and educational attainment.

Families

In general, religion is seen to be associated with family. For example, religious individuals tend to have more children than their nonreligious counterparts and divorce less often (Sherkat, 1998; Hayford & Morgan, 2008). On average, studies show that nonreligious women have two children, moderately religious women have 2.31 children, and very religious women have 2.69 children. Differences in child-rearing styles do exist among faiths. Conservative Protestants are more likely than Catholics to embrace corporal punishment and hierarchal and authoritarian relationships between parents and children, but they also yell less frequently at their kids and give them more affection than other parents (Wilcox, 1999). Religious fathers spend more time one-on-one with their children and hug and praise them more often than fathers without a strong religious affiliation (Wilcox, 2004). That said, Nancy Nason-Clark (2000) has found that rates of domestic violence are no different in religious communities when contrasted to secular ones.

Evangelical Protestants, such as those belonging to the Southern Baptist Convention, tend to embrace a traditional patriarchal family structure, in which the wife submits to her provider husband (see Chapter 12). This family structure appears to work fairly well for many, as evangelical Protestants report high levels of marital happiness and accord, though it may be harder for members of religious families to admit the existence of domestic abuse. The lowest reported incidence of domestic violence in the United States among all religious groups occurs among churchgoing evangelical married men, but oddly, evangelical married men who don't go to church on a regular basis are associated with the highest rates of domestic violence (Wilcox, 2004). Nason-Clark has found that rates of abuse within religious families are about the same as rates in the general U.S. population but that there is a greater stigma attached to family discord in religious families, making it more difficult for them to report abuse. When they do report abuse, they may turn to clergy members who are not specifically trained to handle domestic abuse and who are invested in promoting family unity. On the other hand, some religious abuse victims find that their attempts to seek help outside the religious community are unsatisfying, because they do not draw on their faith or church doctrine to make sense of what happened to the victims, to comfort them, or to give them strength to heal (Nason-Clark, 2000).

Race

In 1963, the Reverend Dr. Martin Luther King, Jr. said in an interview, "We must face the fact that in America, the church is still the most segregated major institution in America. At 11:00 on Sunday morning when we stand and sing and Christ has no east or west, we stand at the most segregated hour in this nation." Is Sunday morning still the most segregated hour in America? Pretty much. While workplaces and neighborhoods have become more mixed, ongoing research has found that only 8 percent of churches are racially mixed, where no single race makes up more than 80 percent of the congregation. Catholic churches are more likely to be mixed, owing in part to Hispanic migration. Only 2 to 3 percent of Protestant churches are racially mixed (Dart, 2001).

The black church has long played an important role in the larger black community—Martin Luther King was both a religious and a political leader. Of course, religious organizations are just like other organizations in that they have to adapt to and cope with the external pressures of social change. The black church's role in black communities has been tempered by the changing social conditions of African Americans. Some scholars have argued that black and white churches operate in similar ways today—primarily as providers of mental health and psychological well-being. But others have argued that the black church does more than provide spiritual fixes (Chaves & Higgins, 1992). Historically, the church has played a more central role in the secular lives of black congregations than in those of white congregations. This resulted from three conditions. First, African Americans share a legacy of racial discrimination, violence, and injustice. Second, no other secular institution has ever organized and helped the black community as much as the church. Third, the black community has substantial social needs that necessitate an effective social helping hand. (See our discussion of racism and black-white inequality in Chapter 9.)

Religion has often been called a "free space" for African American churchgoers (Sherkat & Ellison, 1999), providing a psychological and social haven in the face of marginalization and hostility. In areas of life where other institutions may leave gaps, the black church provides a source of collective self-help, political activism, social networking, and community involvement. The black church remains a salient force in fighting for civil rights and easing poverty (Chaves & Higgins, 1992).

The black church was also at the forefront of the trend to liven up Sunday services with rousing music and even dance. Here again, we see that there are links

Members of the Praise Dance Ministry of Camden, New Jersey, perform at Gospelfest. The annual festival features choirs, steppers, and praise dancers.

between the black church and the wider black community. Gospel music that started in the church filtered out and continues to influence R&B musical styles. Furthermore, whereas dancing acquired a bad name in some Christian churches, seen as a gateway to sinful behavior or a sin in itself, since the late nineteenth century some black Southern Baptist churches have incorporated dance into worship. What was once called praise dancing and has now influenced liturgical dance (neither of which is still restricted to black churches) involves physical interpretations of songs and scripture. There is now a national Gospelfest, sponsored by McDonald's, in which praise groups from various churches compete in a spiritual dance-off.

Gender

Patterns of religious activity and affiliation also arise according to gender. Women are more active in religious organizations than men, either because they are socialized to be the more virtuous of the sexes or because they feel a greater need for the kind of social and financial support the church offers (Figure 16.6). There is a

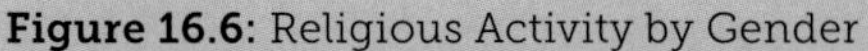

Figure 16.6: Religious Activity by Gender

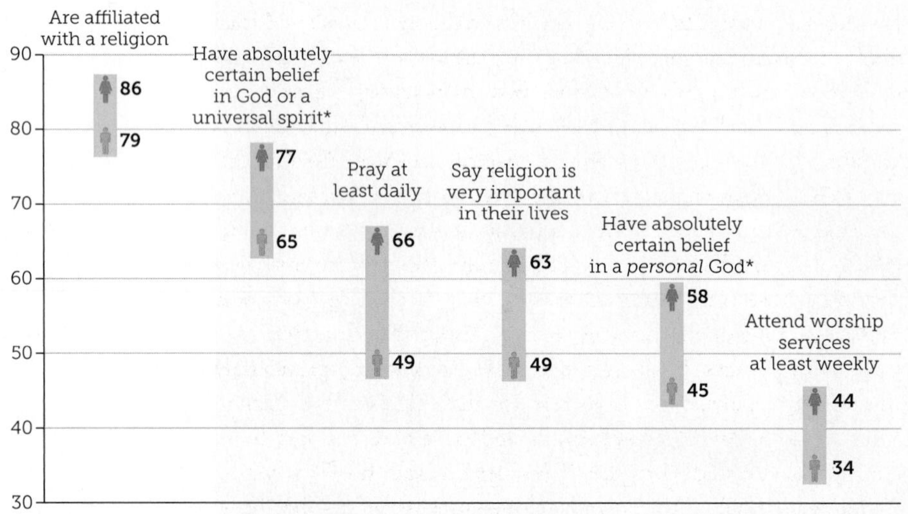

*Question wording: Do you believe in God or a universal spirit? [IF BELIEVE IN GOD, ASK]: How certain are you about this belief? Are you absolutely certain, fairly certain, not too certain, or not at all certain? [IF BELIEVE IN GOD, ASK]: Which comes closest to your view of God? God is a person with whom people can have a relationship or God is an impersonal force?

SOURCE: Pew Forum on Religious and Public Life, 2010.

women's group in nearly one of every three congregations but a men's group in just one of four (Ammerman, 2005). These women's groups, once called "ladies' aid" organizations, exist to help women experience spiritual growth as well as to lend a hand to congregation members in hard times, providing them with jobs, services, and food. They have been on the decline since women's mass entry into the labor force starting in the 1970s.

Conservative Protestant and Mormon women participate less in the labor force because traditional religious beliefs go hand in hand with more traditional beliefs about gender (see Chapter 8). Jennifer Glass and Jerry Jacobs (2005) show that evangelically reared women are less interested in their careers and more interested in their families, and get married and bear children earlier than other women do. Some sociologists interpret such findings as evidence that these conservative faiths breed gender inequality.

Class

A person's socioeconomic status is also linked to religion (see Chapter 7). Hindus, Jews, and Buddhists along with atheists and agnostics tend to be the most highly educated, while members of evangelical Protestant churches and historically black churches have less education (Pew Forum on Religious and Public Life, 2008). Interestingly, while people with more education have less attachment to some of the more traditional religious beliefs, higher education spurs increased participation in religious organizations (Iannaccone, 1997). Highly educated individuals are more likely to explore less traditional faiths and belief structures and/or to participate in religious organizations for the civic rewards of belonging. On college campuses, faculty members in the natural, physical, and engineering sciences are much more likely to belong to a church and to express religious commitment than are social scientists or those in law or the humanities (Steinberg, 1974). Higher-income earners donate more to religious organizations, but they also score lower on church participation than lower-income earners (in effect, offsetting their absence with larger donations to the collection plate). And people whose education level exceeds that of their religious peer group are likely to switch to a different, higher-brow group (Sherkat, 1991).

Historically, America has been dominated by Protestants, particularly Episcopalians, Presbyterians, and Congregationalists (called the United Church of Christ since 1957). So important and powerful was this trend that its influence was referred to as the "Episcopalianization of the whole upper class" (Baltzell, 1958). The reason, sociologists contend, is that Protestants were here first, so they had the upper hand in shaping social policies and institutions in line with their values and to their own advantage, making it hard for incoming religious groups such as Jews and Catholics to get a foothold in cultural and political arenas. In a study of *Who's Who in America,* sociologists found that those listed today are more religiously diverse than they were in the 1960s (Davidson et al., 1995). Jews and Catholics have made some gains in *Who's Who,* reflecting in part growing religious tolerance and the slight relative decline of Protestant power. Protestants have lost some ground, the authors conclude, but they are still overrepresented at the top of the status, class, and political hierarchy in America. In particular, Episcopalians have shown remarkable stability among the nation's powerful and cultural elites. With about 2.3 million members, the Episcopal Church in America is only the fifteenth largest, yet one of four U.S. presidents has been a member of this institution (Goodstein, 2007).

Aging

Both men and women tend to become more religious with age. Stark and Bainbridge (1987) believe this results because of the increased need for social support systems as well as the heightened search for answers to life's big questions. This increased religiousness is associated with increased levels of altruism and feelings of purposefulness in life's everyday activities, which help people age more gracefully (Dillon & Wink, 2003).

Types of Involvement

Associational involvement, according to Lenski (1961), refers to the frequency of church attendance, whereas communal involvement refers to how much of your primary group interactions are restricted to followers of your own faith, how isolated or enmeshed you are in the religious community. Associational and communal involvement varies by faith. For instance, Jews have weak associational involvement but strong communal ties. Catholics have strong associational involvement but weak communal ties. Both are weak for white Protestants; both are strong for black Protestants. Lenski, in agreement with Durkheim, argues that the pull of the congregation is much stronger and more influential on behavior and attitudes and outlook than the associational pull of the church. For example, African Americans tend to be more religiously active than whites, and African Americans who live in rural or suburban areas are more active than African Americans who live in cities. The reason is that alternative social networks and supports exist in cities, but the church is the main resource for black communal life outside urban centers (Nelsen, 1988).

Geography and Politics

Religious believers tend to be concentrated in certain parts of the country. Catholics are disproportionately located in the Northeast and Southwest.

Lutherans tend to live in the upper Midwest. Baptists dominate the South, and Mormons are most common in Utah (Bradley et al., 1992). Political affiliations overlap with religious ones, such that regional voting patterns correlate to religious beliefs. Thirty years ago, voting behavior and party affiliation were best predicted by a person's income. Today, however, religious attitudes are the best indicators. A high rate of agreement with the statement "AIDS is God's punishment for immoral sexual behavior," for instance, may be highly correlated with a state that goes Republican in an election (Varian, 2006). Why the shift? According to one study (Glaeser & Ward, 2006), Republican strategists such as Karl Rove (and Ronald Reagan before him) deliberately shifted their base to religious followers. Republicans' surest voter stronghold used to be the wealthy elites—a limited and fickle crowd—but these days the Republican Party speaks to everyone from poor evangelicals to everyday businessmen. In contrast, people who are more politically liberal tend to be less religious (Glock & Stark, 1965). This pattern holds internationally, too: Left-leaning liberal countries such as France and the Netherlands are relatively not very religious.

Selling God and Shopping for Faith: The Commercialization of Religious Life

On Easter Sunday 2006 in Atlanta, some 40,000 people converged in a worship spectacle in the famous sports and concert arena, the Georgia Dome. With the expressed aim of "giving the Devil his due," the Resurrection Sunday service of New Birth Missionary Baptist Church was heralded as the largest Easter service in the world. Indeed, the big-budget production presented four hours of religious entertainment, including a 500-member choir, a marching band, a rock group, a flag corps, several dance troupes, and a closing performance by Patti LaBelle (who did not fail to mention the release of her new album). The only thing this Sunday service appeared to be missing was silence. New Birth, not one for shying away from profits, is known for its dazzling productions that attract huge crowds as well as "corporate sponsors, politicians, and entertainers looking for a way to get their own good word out" (Goodman, 2006a).

Religion in the United States is big business. Americans donated $101.81 billion to religious organizations in 2010 (Giving USA, 2011). A study by the Hartford Institute for Religious Research found that the average annual income of a megachurch, which is typically a conservative Protestant church that attracts at least 2,000 worshippers per week, is $4.6 million (Twichell, 2004). Ministers of megachurches reportedly earned more than $100,000

Megachurch typically, a conservative Protestant church that attracts at least 2,000 worshippers per week.

Lee Esther Head and The Glory Group dance for some 35,000 worshippers gathered at the Georgia Dome for the New Birth Missionary Baptist Church's annual Easter Sunday service.

a year in the 1990s (Nussbaum, 2006). The fast-growing market for Christian products is also quite lucrative. Mel Gibson's controversial film *The Passion of the Christ,* for instance, grossed $370 million. (Apart from questions about its historical accuracy, the film was criticized as being anti-Semitic.) Christian music totals $700 million in sales annually. In 2002, evangelical pastor Rick Warren wrote *The Purpose-Driven Life,* which has sold more than 30 million copies—the largest sales figure for any nonfiction hardcover book ever published in the United States. Warren was subsequently chosen to deliver the invocation at President Barack Obama's historic inauguration. Christian products are estimated at $4.2 billion in annual sales. There's even a growing field of Christian public relations, which manages and markets particular "brands" of Christianity. Wal-Mart has caught on, expanding its Christian-themed merchandise, which currently grosses over $1 billion a year (Coolidge, 2011).

Among faith's consumers, plenty of "buy and return" activity exists. Approximately one-third of Americans switch religious affiliations, and nearly a third of those switch more than once (Roof, 1989). According to survey data, there is growth among conservative Protestant sects, Jehovah's Witnesses, and Mormons, whereas moderate and liberal Protestant churches are losing numbers (Sherkat & Ellison, 1999). Religion shopping is especially high among teens. In a 2002–03 survey of 13-to-17-year-olds, the National Study of Youth and Religion found that 16 percent of respondents participated in more than one congregation at a time. About 4 percent attend youth groups outside their congregations. Taking a consumerist approach to faith, teens report feeling more authentically connected to their religion after exploring the market for themselves (Banerjee, 2005).

Although it may make some people uncomfortable to use economic language to discuss faith, viewing religious choice through this lens of "the market" makes religious pluralism seem less like a crisis—as the old secularization theory held—and more like a strength (Sherkat & Ellison, 1999). Such a "rational choice," or economic, perspective on religion sees congregations as franchises and ministers as entrepreneurial salespeople. The churchgoer is a consumer who spends his or her time and money on religion in exchange for supernatural compensators (Stark & Bainbridge, 1985), or promises of future rewards, such as salvation or eternity in heaven. Shopping the church market for the best promises of salvation and answers about the meaning of life is no simple task, for there are inherent risk and uncertainty about the worth of these "goods." It's up to the ministers and religious leaders to market them to you in an attractive way so as to draw you in.

Supernatural compensators promises of future rewards, such as salvation or eternity in heaven.

Because each faith offers a different spin on the meaning of life, death, and the afterlife, the more religious diversity a society has, the less credible any one particular faith is. Secularization theory held that pluralism would undermine religion for this reason. In contrast, rational choice scholars like Stark and Finke (2000) borrowed an idea from the eighteenth-century economist Adam Smith that competition makes for better goods (see Chapter 14). In a highly pluralistic society such as the United States, where churches compete with one another to sustain a congregation, the quality of religion is better than what would exist under a state-controlled religious monopoly, as in Catholic medieval Europe (Finke & Stark, 1992). Competition makes all religions shape up and maintain high quality in order to attract consumers; therefore, pluralism results in high overall levels of religiosity. Thus, this long history of freedom and choice in the religious "marketplace" may be one explanation for America's high levels of religiosity, compared with countries such as England and Sweden (Stark & Finke, 2000). If the good news is that religious pluralism offers a range of choices among faiths, the bad news, some critics contend, is that religion is being marketed—which is ostensibly a profane act. Saddleback Church in Lake Forest, California, the church presided over by pastor and best-selling author Rick Warren, has been compared to megacorporations such as Google or Starbucks. Warren's church has become a brand; he even hires a public relations agent to manage it (Saroyan, 2006).

Just how does one go about selling God? A few lessons from American religious entrepreneurship.

Lesson 1: If You Can't Beat 'Em, Join 'Em

Youth groups appeal to teens by featuring rock bands, incorporating teen lingo (one T-shirt slogan reads, "Jesus is my homeboy"), and frank, open prayer that connects to issues of everyday life. Increasingly, churches offer secular activities such as health clinics, gyms, sports fields, and marriage and substance abuse counseling; in one Houston church, there's even a McDonald's (James, 2003). Many churches have stripped away the traditional dogma, revamping sermons with dramatic skit performances and hymns with rock or pop beats to cater to young crowds. The Message: Relent and give the video game generation what they want.

Lesson 2: Bigger Is Better

Witness the megachurch phenomenon that spread through many middle-class suburbs beginning in the mid-1990s. The average megachurch has Sunday worship attendance of 3,924. Sixty percent of them are in the American Sunbelt, mostly in California, Texas, Florida, and Georgia. Megachurch congregations

A group takes a break from listening to a rock concert to watch a live feed from Pastor Rick Warren. Warren's Saddleback Church in Lake Forest, California, averages over 20,000 in attendance each weekend and has more than 80,000 members. What is the allure of a megachurch?

run the gamut from Southern Baptist to liberal Protestant, though 54 percent of them are nondenominational (Bird & Thumma, 2011).

Willow Creek Community Church of Illinois, which draws around 20,000 people a week, had an annual budget of about $27.44 million in 2011. The House of Hope megachurch complex of Salem Baptist Church is a 10,000-seat, $50 million project built in 2005 to accommodate 22,000 members. Rick Warren, author of the best seller mentioned above, is also the pastor of Saddleback Church in California with five churches and 80,000 members (Ferran, 2009).

Megachurch ministries take their cues from business management, luring suburbanites with a theatrical experience complete with lighting rigs, electric bands playing contemporary music, dramatic skits, and sermons that draw lessons from daily living (Niebuhr, 1995). They stress family values above religious traditions and are known for being flexible and creative. At first glance, these don't even look like churches; they seem more like community centers or even colleges (Goldberger, 1995). Some churches, seeking venues with adequate parking, have moved into old warehouses, armories, and even sporting venues. With their ordinary facades, megachurches drive home the point that religion is an integral and relevant part of routine suburban living.

Megachurches are also appearing in black communities, particularly suburban, middle-class ones. In one of the country's most affluent African American communities, Prince Georges County in Maryland, the Ebenezer African Methodist Episcopal megachurch thrives. It even has valet parking and white-gloved ushers for its 12,000 members in its $18 million building ("Black Megachurches Surge," 1996).

Megachurches have filled a niche among urban and ethnic populations, too. Take, for example, the Promise Church in Queens, New York, which is home to a mostly Korean American Pentecostal congregation. It has more than 4,000 members, making it the largest of the four Korean megachurches in the city (Knafo, 2005). Featuring big-production plays, it hopes to win over young Korean Americans, who have largely abandoned Christianity over the last few years. The trend, known among Koreans as the "silent exodus," is a result of many prosperous Koreans moving out of Queens. The church was once the core source of social support and services, but as Korean businesses flourish, the church has withered. Enter megachurches like Promise, which offer pop cultural allure to win back worshippers.

Lesson 3: Speed Pleases

Many churches feature several quick services in one day—sometimes because the parking and seating just cannot accommodate the entire congregation. These events often get right down to the point, addressing frank issues and problems of daily living in 50 minutes or less with just enough time for one group of parishioners to file out while the next worshippers are filing in. But perhaps the epitome of speed is the so-called "drive-through" church. For its Memorial Day service in 2005, the Metropolitan Church of the Quad Cities in Iowa offered one that took just a few minutes (Baker, 2005).

Lesson 4: Sex Sells

Except for the Song of Solomon, the Bible simply is not very sexy. According to Bible publisher Thomas Nelson, Inc., which has been issuing Bibles for more than 200 years, the number one reason teens don't read the Bible is because it is "too big and freaky looking." To spice things up, some publishers have combined youth pop culture with the traditional Bible to engender a new genre of the New Testament: the Biblezine. Throughout the glossy pages of *Revolve* for girls, scripture appears next to color photographs and advice columns addressing boy problems, fashion questions, and the complications of friendship (Haskell, 2004). The cover looks like that of any

Publishers design Biblezines such as *Revolve* and *Refuel* to appeal to young Christians by emulating popular magazines. They even include fashion tips, quizzes, bios, and community basics. Why are some critical of these new kinds of Bibles?

other teen magazine, with fresh-faced models smiling behind headlines such as "Are You Dating a Godly Guy?" and "Beauty Secrets You've Never Heard Before."

Meanwhile, *Refuel,* for boys, features articles about rock music, sports, and sexuality, and the cover features headlines such as "How to Attract Godly Girls" and "What Is 'Radical Faith?' " This Biblezine has innovatively marketed the scripture as if it were a hot new video game, as something that is easily mastered, with immediate pay-off:

> **GOD'S WORD ROCKS . . . IN REVOLVE 2010!** Now in its sixth edition, the *Revolve* series has proven effective in reaching teenage girls by featuring **the complete Ne3w Testament** in a cool magazine design.
> **4Real:** Real teens share real stories of real faith
> **Guy 411: Chad Eastham** dishes the dirt on dudes
> **Backstage Pass:** Behind the scenes of *The Word of Promise Next Generation* with **Jordin Sparks, Cody Lindley, Emily Osment**, and more
> **Drama-Trauma with Stellar Kart! Tons of Quizzes! Free Music!** Snag free tunes from your artists like Group 1 Crew, Stellar Kart, and Britt Nicole!
> **Plus** devo articles, profiles, interviews, blogs, and more! (Thomas Nelson, Inc., 2010)

The value of Biblezines lies in their appeal to youth culture, but a danger may lie in their ease, speed, and slickness. Specifically, some skeptics ask what happens to religion's deep meanings and sense of greatness when they are subsumed by commercialization and marketing (Haskell, 2004). What secularizing effects might such "profane" business models have? For instance, the Christian publishing house Zondervan came under fire in 2002 for publishing a Bible translation with gender-neutral language and for bending, according to some evangelicals, to the secular influence of its parent company, HarperCollins (Kirkpatrick, 2002). Other critics fear the marketing of God, surmising that many megachurches serve their congregations "theology lite." For example, when several megachurches canceled normal services in favor of Christmas-themed services in 2005 when Christmas fell on a Sunday, it was seen as an affront to worship. Some contend that with contemporary church-marketing techniques—Christian public relations, marketing, and branding—the message gets lost in size and profits. After all, why should God need to be sold (Saroyan, 2006)?

Despite these concerns, faith and marketing have long been intertwined. In 1925, Bruce Barton portrayed Jesus as the original businessman in his best seller *The Man Nobody Knows.* The 1970 rock opera *Jesus Christ Superstar* became a Tony Award–winning musical and later a film though it was condemned by religious groups at the time. Today, there's a Christian Tattoo Association, founded in the mid-1990s, with over 100 Christian punk and Goth members across the country.

The Paradox of Popularity

In his popular book *The Social Sources of Denominationalism* (1929), H. Richard Niebuhr set out to explain why so many religious groupings exist under one faith, Christianity. He concluded that the reason for so many different denominations was that people had a diversity of needs, and indeed, in a highly pluralistic society such as America, there is something for everyone. But among the sea of choices, some churches fare better than others. Some come and go, catching barely any notice, whereas others ride a wave of success followed by an inevitable crash, only to then wash away. Others endure. To track the reasons behind the various successes and failures of churches, sociologists look not at the merits of any one faith but instead at the social patterns of religious organizations in general.

The Sect–Church Cycle

Churches religious bodies that coexist in a relatively low state of tension with their social surroundings. They have mainstream or "safe" beliefs and practices relative to those of the general population.

Sects or **sectarian groups** high-tension organizations that don't fit so well within the existing social environment. They are usually most attractive to society's least privileged—outcasts, minorities, or the poor—because they downplay worldly pleasure by stressing otherworldly promises.

Sociologists classify religious organizations as churches, sects, or cults. Churches are religious bodies that coexist in a relatively low state of tension with their social surroundings (Finke & Stark, 1992). They have mainstream, "safe" beliefs and practices relative to those of the general population. Because they are world-affirming more often than world-criticizing, they peacefully coexist (or at least try to) with the secular world, so they are low-tension organizations.

Sects or sectarian groups, by contrast, are high-tension bodies that don't fit so well within the existing social environment (Finke & Stark, 1992). These organizations are usually most attractive to society's least privileged—outcasts, minorities, or the poor—because they downplay worldly pleasure by stressing otherworldly promises. Sects can be an appealing alternative to engagement in secular life, because sectarian groups typically limit their contact to the outside world, keeping mainstream culture at a distance for fear of contamination. Material things don't matter as much as the supernatural world, which each sect purports to understand better than any other religious body.

Sects usually start out by splintering off an existing church, typically when church leaders become too involved in secular issues in some members' eyes. To distance themselves from what they see as worldly concerns and corruption, members may form their own sect. Over time, if the sect picks up a significant following, it almost inevitably transforms into its own church, ultimately becoming part of the mainstream. As this happens, a new splinter group, made up of new "true" radicals, may become discontent and branch off to form their own sect. Thus, the cycle continues.

This pattern is clear among Protestant denominations, which over the centuries have modernized their doctrines, embraced mainstream values, and thus lost much of their distinctiveness; they then often go into decline (Finke & Stark, 1992). With increased popularity, mainline faiths simply become too watered down, and intense religiosity decreases. For example, the United Methodist Church has over 12 million members world wide. While there has been an overall 25 percent increase in membership in the last decade, there has been an 8 percent decrease in membership in the United States (UMC.org, 2011). In the founding year of the United States, 1776, the Methodists were a tiny religious society with only 65 churches throughout the colonies and 4,921 members. By 1850 they dominated the nation with 13,302 congregations and more than 2.6 million members. In *Southern Cross: The Beginnings of the Bible Belt* (1997), historian Christine Leigh Heyman describes early Methodists as a radical bunch. They supported gender equality and the abolition of slavery, so it's no surprise that they faced difficulty drawing crowds in the South. To cement their initial popularity, Methodists shed some of their less popular beliefs and practices (such as extreme celibacy and the occasional castration of a minister). As they built seminaries, began paying full-time ministers, and developed a less radical, more systematic theology, they increasingly appealed to the mainstream and as a result soon became the most popular church. Meanwhile, sectarian splinter groups such as the Free Methodists and Holiness Churches broke off to bring the faith back to its old-time roots (Finke & Stark, 1992).

Heaven's Gate leader Marshall Herff Applewhite. What distinguishes a cult such as Heaven's Gate from a sect or a church?

A cult, on the other hand, is a religious movement that makes some new claim about the supernatural and therefore does not as easily fit within the sect–church cycle. A famous example was Heaven's Gate, formed in 1973 by two previously mainline Protestants, Marshall Herff Applewhite and Bonnie Nettles. Known as "The Two," they spread the word that civilization was doomed. Furthermore, they claimed that only the disciplined few could be saved by way of a spacecraft to be sent by God. In 1997, 39 members of the group, trying to reach God's U.F.O. behind the Hale-Bopp comet, committed mass suicide in California. Outrageously otherworldly as they were, Heaven's Gate was not successful in generating a mass following. A few better-known cults have been enormously successful, such as those started by Jesus, Buddha, Joseph Smith, and Muhammad. All religions begin as cults, and their leaders offer new insights, claiming that they are the word of God. Because they're so novel, cults are often high-tension movements that antagonize their social world and/or are antagonized by it. From the examples above, it should be clear that some cults evolve into low-tension organizations, whereas others destroy themselves with their own zealotry.

Cult religious movement that makes some new claim about the supernatural and therefore does not as easily fit within the sect–church cycle.

Contemporary evangelicals can be divided into several different camps. What distinguishes modernists from centrists or traditionalists? How do they appeal to different groups?

The sect–church cycle is currently playing out for evangelicals, the conservative Protestant congregations that blossomed in the South and have been growing steadily over the last two centuries (as compared to liberal Protestant congregations), while mainline Protestant churches have more recently seen declines in membership. In 2011, the United Methodist Church lost 7.8 million members, a 1 percent drop. The Presbyterian Church had a record loss of 2.7 million members, a 2.61 percent drop. Meanwhile, Jehovah's Witnesses had the highest overall growth, increasing their membership by 4.37 percent (Yeakley, 2011). Despite this growth, evangelicals are currently faced with the pressures of the sect–church cycle as they increasingly fracture on political issues. To make matters more unstable, one of the most prominent leaders of the evangelical movement, the Reverend Billy Graham, has retired, and the movement is struggling to define its identity. John C. Green, who studies religion, characterizes evangelicals as belonging to one of three camps: traditionalists, centrists, and modernists. Traditionalists and centrists each account for 40 to 50 percent of evangelicals; modernists make up the remaining minority (Luo, 2006).

As you can see, there is tension between traditionalists and centrists. In these fissures, a new style of church has arrived on the evangelical scene. "Emerging" or "postmodern" churches, also called "alt-worship," have tapped

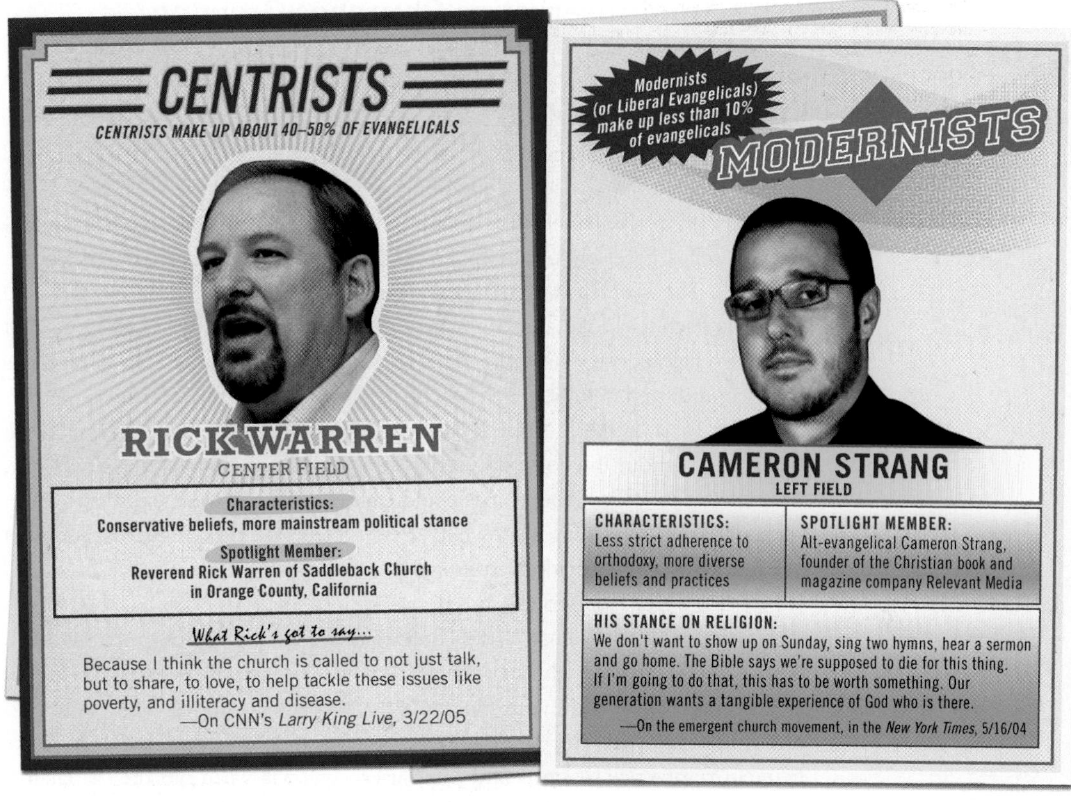

into a generation of religious dropouts, those with little or no formal attachment to the church. The disillusionment of these dropouts has arisen as part of a backlash against the enormous success of megafaiths. According to pastor Lee Rabe of Threads, an emerging church in Kalamazoo, Michigan, alt-worshipers want a church that provides an intense experience yet also makes sense within their daily lives, with theological relaxations such as reading the Bible as a narrative (that is, as not necessarily unerring) and a de-emphasis on individual salvation in favor of holistic world recovery (Luo, 2006). Emerging churches can be found in school gyms and storefronts, and some scholars predict that these small-scale sites will be the next big trend in evangelical worship (Leland, 2004).

Evangelicalism, since its very beginning, has been accustomed to friction. In the late 1940s the National Association of Evangelicals was founded with the goal of moving away from the strict fundamentalism that has always been intermingled with the evangelical Protestant tradition. The movement was initially intended to be a middle ground between what was seen as theological liberalism in mainline Protestantism and cultural separatism among fundamentalists (Luo, 2006). If evangelicalism was a middle road then, it is faced with forks and fissures of its own today.

Why Are Conservative Churches Growing?

How has evangelicalism cornered an increasing amount of the religious market? The secret to evangelicalism's success may lie in the strictness of its doctrine. Dean M. Kelley, an executive of the National Council of Churches, proposed this "strict church thesis" in his controversial *Why Conservative Churches Are Growing* (1972). Kelley claimed that conservative sects were outpacing mainline churches precisely because of their strictness: "Strong organizations are strict. . . . The stricter the stronger" (Finke & Stark, 1992). Rational choice theorists such as Finke and Stark have taken up Kelley's thesis to argue that when a religious body has a lot of low-commitment members, it will lose its highly committed members because of the problem of free riders (a more formal term for a shirker). Nobody likes free riders; they reap all the benefits of belonging without the costs of participating. Besides being just plain irksome, free riders can affect group morale and cause all the hardworking members to slack off as well, creating a snowball effect of freeloading until no one bothers any longer to do the work of running an organization.

To avoid free riders, Stark and Finke argue, a religious body has to charge a high entry fee (2000). This "strict church" thesis has been the source of much debate, but to anyone who has played on a sports team, it should make sense. If just anyone could show up on game day to play, the sports team would no doubt be swamped with freeloading jocks. But if you impose high costs like mandatory practice sessions and fundraisers, you will weed out the casual athletes from the committed ones and end up with a more devoted, and probably more effective, team. Exclusivity generates strength for organizations, including religious bodies. As a result of exclusivity, conservative denominations and sectarian groups are also better able to mobilize their resources for social action such as fundraising or political campaigning (Iannaccone et al., 1995).

It may seem paradoxical that stricter religious institutions are more likely to grow than easier faiths. After all, strictness is not something people necessarily seek from their religion. But people who have strong religious beliefs tend to build stronger congregations and stronger religious communities: The stronger the community, the better it works. The stronger the religious organization, the more it demands of you, the more you are likely to value it, and thus the greater chance you'll stick with it. Less restrictive churches, such as most mainline Protestant denominations, may be more reasonable in the amount of time and dedication they ask of you, but the trade-off is that you may value them less and defect more easily. Furthermore, because sectarian groups claim to hold the one and only religious truth, their devoted members get more out of their exclusive access to the truth than they do from being connected to and accepted in the wider secular world. Who needs a 401(k) individual retirement account when he or she is part of God's in-group?

An important caveat is that not all strict faiths are growing, nor can we expect, say, radical orthodox Jewish sects to boom in the next few years just because they demand a lot of time and effort from their constituents. In fact, orthodox Jews do not generally accept non-Jewish converts and care little about growing their congregations by new recruitment. All voluntary organizations have to find their niche, claim Stark and Finke (2000), and the market niche for radical faiths is relatively small compared with that for mainline or moderately conservative faiths. Although sectarian or fundamentalist groups may experience rapid growth, they are ultimately limited by how many people will find those niches attractive in the first place.

The thesis indeed fits with historical trends of the success of conservative, or strict, religious groups, such as Islamists. Islam is the world's second-largest religion, after Christianity. As a large religion, it too faces fractures and separatist movements from within. One movement that has gained the most attention in U.S. media and politics is Islamic fundamentalism, which—in common terminology—also refers to the political ideology of Islamism. Islamists call for the authority of Islamic law—known as shar'ia (often literal translations from the Qur'an)—over secular law. They also are more likely to support political violence in the name of holy war (jihad). Unfortunately, many mainstream Muslims are wrongly identified as Islamists, when in fact most Muslims oppose Islamists and their goals. Sociologist Jen'nan Read urges us to remember that "just like Christians in the United States, they're a diverse population. We've got very secular Arab Muslims who are basically Muslim in name only, attend the mosque maybe once a year or never. And then we've got very devout Muslims who are very religious and uphold the five pillars of Islam. Just like Christians, there is a difference between being a devout Christian and being an extremist. There is also a difference between being a devout Muslim and being an extremist" (Conley, 2009i). Read goes on to lament that devout Muslims and extremists became lumped together after 9/11. Americans have a tendency to think of all practicing Muslims as extremists, which can lead to bigotry, profiling, and harassment.

Because of their extreme beliefs and practices, Islamists face the same dilemmas as other radical religious movements. Should they water down their message to attract popular support? Or should they maintain a pure, radical vision among a small following (Kurzman, 2002)? Already, Islam is split along liberal, conservative, secular, fundamentalist, and even feminist lines. However, some commentators speculate that the U.S.-led wars in Iraq and Afghanistan have increased the popularity of Islamism, at least in the short run. More generally, the war on terror has increased, paradoxically, global identification with terrorists by opening up a niche for Islamist fundamentalism to define itself against the power of the United States.

The process of secularization that comes with a religion's successes does not weaken religiosity in general. On the contrary, with every church's falter, split, and demise, some sort of religious revival follows (Stark & Bainbridge, 1985, 1987). Likewise, as the fortunes of individual organizations fall, new ones rise in their place, and religion moves forward.

Teaching the Bible in School

Perhaps the most significant push to expand religious influence in the contemporary United States is the inclusion of creationism in public school curricula by way of the intelligent design movement. Intelligent design posits that biological life is too complex to have happened randomly, so it could only be the work of a higher being (Goodstein, 2005). The idea has its roots in creationism, the belief that humans and the universe were created by a supreme being. (In 1987, the Supreme Court ruled it unconstitutional to teach creationism in public schools.) In Pennsylvania in 2004 some parents of students in the town of Dover filed a lawsuit against the school board, which had voted that students must listen to a statement at the start of biology class explaining that evolution was a "flawed" theory and that an alternative existed, intelligent design (Goodstein, 2005). In December 2005, federal judge John E. Jones III determined that intelligent design was a "religious alternative masquerading as a scientific theory" and barred its instruction in the public schools. Dover is still recovering from the media hype and its stereotyping as a zone of "cultural warfare between liberal atheists and Bible-thumping fundamentalists" (Gately, 2005).

Negotiating the separation of church and state is an inherently tricky business in a highly religious, individualistic, and pluralistic country such as the United States, compared with a country with a relatively low level of religiosity and a high level of centralized authority such as France. To settle disputes about the appropriateness of religious icons in school, in 2004 the French government banned all students from wearing any religious garb or conspicuous symbols in its public schools. Students found in violation—those wearing Islamic veils, Jewish skullcaps, large Christian crosses, or Sikh turbans, for example—would be expelled. Although supported by many, such severe separation of church and state—seen as an attempt to uphold France's republican ideal of secularism to the extreme—has been criticized as biased by some, because its unofficial targets were seen to be female Muslim students who wore scarves and veils (Sciolino, 2004). But the reaction was nowhere near that which would ensue if such a policy were enacted in the United States.

Lawsuits and media hype abound in distinguishing between the constitutionally legitimate and the heartfelt. Tensions can be felt in football locker rooms, where pregame prayer is the norm for many top college players. Marcus Borden, a high-school football coach in East Brunswick, New Jersey, fueled a controversy when he resigned in 2005 after being ordered by the district to stop the practice of pregame prayer (Drape, 2005). In 2006, the Georgia state legislature passed an act requiring the Bible to be taught in public schools.

A photo of Charles Darwin sticks out of the snow in Dover, Pennsylvania. Parents of high school students in this small, rural town successfully sued the school board for trying to introduce intelligent design into the science curriculum.

Already about 1,000 public high schools nationwide use the Bible in their curriculum, which the Supreme Court allows so long as it is taught objectively and not as fact. Georgia was the first state to use the Bible as a teaching textbook, although in 2005, a federal judge ordered the state to remove stickers from one district's science textbooks that called evolution into question (Goodman, 2006b). And so the controversy goes on.

→ CONCLUSION

The force of religious beliefs can move social mountains. Ideas, beliefs, and convictions are, to echo Weber, the switchmen of the train tracks of history. They are powerful resources used to mobilize calls to social action like the civil rights movement. They anchor our outlook on the world, acting as the toolkit we deploy to make sense of our daily life. It is not up to the sociologist to deem these beliefs valid or untrue; rather, it is our task to understand their origins and effects in the social world. This inquiry has led us to unlikely places: from the temperance movement of the 1830s to the organizational backbone of the Reverend Dr. Martin Luther King, Jr.'s call for racial justice in the 1960s; from the glossy pages of a Biblezine to the local coffeehouse to talk rock and roll and Gospel. Religion has remained a powerful, constant backdrop in our society and often plays a starring role in social life.

PRACTICE

ASSIGNMENT

Research the history of a religious affiliation—the one into which you were born or now belong, or one you simply find intriguing. Did it begin as a cult or a sect that split off from another religious group? Has it become less strict over time? Is it active in politics? Was it founded by a charismatic leader? If so, was there a crisis of leadership when it came time to find a new leader?

QUESTIONS FOR REVIEW

1. How does Émile Durkheim's understanding of "the power of the sacred" and social solidarity help us understand the story of Cecil Bothwell and the Asheville city council described at the beginning of the chapter?
2. How does the inclusion of creationism and the Bible in school curricula shed light on the delicate balance between church and state?
3. What is the "sect–church cycle"? With this in mind, describe how we can understand religion as an engine of social change. How do the abolitionist and civil rights movements illustrate this point?
4. Explain how Karl Marx and Max Weber differ in the way they link religion and the economy.
5. According to Weber, what do Calvinism and predestination have to do with the emergence of capitalism? How has this theory been challenged?
6. Although it's unclear why religious people tend to live longer and experience fewer symptoms of depression, how could Peter Berger's concept of "sacred canopy" help explain this trend?
7. This chapter provided an overview of numerous religions. Describe why it is more sociologically significant to study the power of religion and how it is linked to other parts of society than, say, which religion is "right." Use the microsociological findings from this chapter to support your answer.
8. Why are religious attitudes such a strong predictor of voting behavior and political affiliation? How does this link relate to the geography of the United States?
9. After questioning one's religious beliefs and learning about other faiths, an individual changes religious affiliations. How does the theory of secularization explain or fail to explain this change?
10. What is the difference between the "sacred" and the "profane"? Come up with an example in which a table is sacred and another where it is profane. What does this mean about the way we interpret religion and the way religion helps us interpret the social world?

PARADOX

THE RELIGIONS THAT DEMAND THE MOST FROM THEIR MEMBERS OFTEN GROW THE FASTEST, BUT AS RELIGIONS BECOME LARGE AND SUCCESSFUL, THEY TEND TO BECOME LESS STRICT.

WATCH THE ANIMATED SHORT ABOUT THE RELIGION PARADOX AT

WWNORTON.COM/STUDYSPACE

A cyclist bikes through polluted air in Lanzhou, in China's western Gansu Province. China has recently passed the United States to become the world's largest national emitter of greenhouse gases.

17 Science, the Environment, and Society

PARADOX

SOCIETY INVENTS TECHNOLOGIES TO MINIMIZE DANGERS FROM NATURE BUT THOSE SAME INVENTIONS CREATE NEW RISKS THAT NEED TO BE MANAGED.

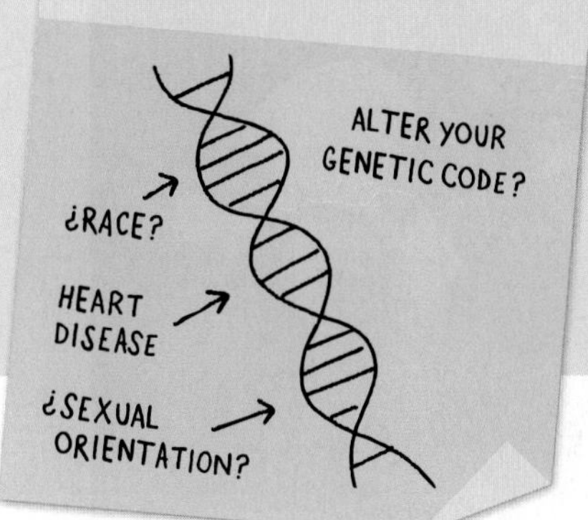

When Wangari Maathai was awarded the Nobel Peace Prize, she told the Nobel Prize Committee that environmental preservation was central to promoting international peace. In hearing about receiving the award, Maathai proclaimed:

> Many wars are fought over resources, which are becoming increasingly scarce across the earth. If we did a better job of managing our resources sustainably, conflicts over them would be reduced. So, protecting the global environment is directly related to securing peace. . . . [T]hose of us who understand the complex concept of the environment have the burden to act. We must not tire, we must not give up, we must persist. (Maathai, 2004)

From her humble upbringings on the slopes of Mount Kenya, Maathai recognized the importance of environmental sustainability. As a child, she wandered up and down Mount Kenya, gathering firewood for her mother. Although her educational pursuits brought her first to the United States and Germany and then to the University of Nairobi, where in 1971 she became the first woman in East and Central Africa to obtain a PhD, Maathai never forgot these childhood experiences.

In 1977, Maathai started the Green Belt Movement. She was concerned primarily with the effects of deforestation on rural communities. A report issued by the United Nations claimed that only 9 trees were replanted for every 100 cut down in Africa. This rapid rate of deforestation caused massive soil erosion and water pollution in many rural communities. It meant that

Wangari Maathai (left) and other activists plant trees during a 1999 campaign in Kenya's Karura Forest.

rural families had more and more trouble finding firewood. Maathai linked these environmental conditions to poverty in rural Africa and believed that efforts to sustain the environment would simultaneously help eliminate rural poverty.

Over the last 30 years, the Green Belt Movement has planted more than 30 million trees, helping to mitigate the effects of deforestation in rural communities. But planting trees throughout rural Kenyan communities has done more than improve environmental health. Restoring natural systems empowers local communities, which become the stewards of their environment. In particular, the movement has empowered women to take control of their local environment. Because environmental health is critical to reducing poverty in rural Africa, Maathai's organization has empowered local communities with greater control over their economic situation through environmental preservation.

Wangari Maathai and the Green Belt Movement demonstrate the important relationship between the environment and society. Maathai recognized that altering environmental conditions has serious impacts on the health and well-being of communities. The simple act of planting trees, according to the Green Belt Movement, has profound social effects for community empowerment, gender equality, and international peace.

Science and Society

Like Wangari Maathai, sociologists also recognize that scientific innovations, environmental change, and technological advances affect society. More specifically, sociologists of science are interested in the ways scientific communities study the objects of their research, in the way science changes how we live and interact with each other, and in the unexpected social consequences of scientific discoveries. What sociologists of science do is no different than what other sociologists do—they make the familiar strange, show hidden social structures, and connect the seemingly individual and personal to larger social and historical forces. It's just that science itself (including the social sciences and sociology itself) forms the object of study. The traditions in this field range broadly from ethnographic observation of how scientists make decisions and how users adopt (and adapt to) new technologies all the way to theoretical work that questions the very notion of a scientific "fact." Sociology of science emerges from training a sociological lens on the history and philosophy of science.

Thomas Kuhn and the Structure of Scientific Revolutions

The goal of science (including social science) is to learn new things about the world. Botanists and zoologists seek new information about plants and animals. Astronomers try to discover new things about the solar system. Sociologists try to learn new things about society. But how does new information come about? How does the process of scientific discovery translate into new information about the natural and social world? According to the scientist (and scientific historian) Thomas Kuhn, scientific discovery doesn't proceed along a linear path (a straight line) or simply accumulate little by little; rather, Kuhn (1962) believes, periods of "normal science" are ruptured every so often by scientific revolutions that shift the paradigm of a given science. But what is normal science, and what is a paradigm? And how do scientific revolutions happen?

According to Kuhn, a paradigm is the framework within which scientists operate. Cell biologists share a certain paradigm with other cell biologists. The equipment they use to study cells is the same, as is their understanding of how different parts of the cell (the cytoplasm, ribosomes, or mitochondria) operate. All mainstream cell biologists agree that ribosomes make protein in a cell and that electron microscopes are good instruments to study cells. They all share the knowledge that there are two methods by which cells reproduce themselves—meiosis and mitosis, depending on the type of cell.

Paradigm the framework within which scientists operate.

In each scientific field, scientists adhere to a particular set of paradigms to guide their research. The big bang, for instance, is a paradigm about the origins of the universe. Likewise, Charles Darwin's theory of evolution has become an accepted paradigm in biology. The helical structure of DNA famously described by James Watson and Francis Crick in 1953 has provided a paradigm for examining the human genome. Researchers working on the Human Genome Project adhere to this paradigm of the double helix discovered by Watson and Crick.

Now that we've defined a paradigm, what is normal science? If you were a cell biologist, you would probably work in a laboratory with other scientists. When you conducted experiments and obtained results, you would be conducting what Kuhn calls normal science: science that's conducted within an existing paradigm. Although you might learn new information about the process of meiosis or the protein-creating capabilities of ribosomes, you wouldn't be overturning existing knowledge of meiosis or ribosomes. Rather, you would gradually add to it through the process of scientific discovery. You might

Normal science science conducted within an existing paradigm, as defined by Thomas Kuhn.

Copernicus's sun-centered system (above) replaced the Ptolemaic Earth-centered model (left) in 1543.

clarify part of the existing paradigm or gather evidence to lend stronger support to the paradigm. This, Kuhn claims, is normal science.

During the practice of normal science, anomalies arise that don't fit neatly into the existing paradigm. Researchers may make discoveries that don't conform to their current assumptions about cell biology. When enough anomalies accrue to challenge the existing paradigm, showing that it is incomplete or inadequate to explain all observed phenomena, Kuhn calls this point a paradigm shift or scientific revolution. Keep in mind that such scientific revolutions are infrequent. When they do occur, they turn existing ways of thinking about science on their heads—think of Copernicus and the shift from earth-centered to sun-centered thinking. Thus, scientific revolutions represent major breaks in periods of normal science and are responsible for important scientific advancements.

Paradigm shift or **scientific revolution** when enough anomalies accrue to challenge the existing paradigm, showing that it is incomplete or inadequate to explain all observed phenomena.

Is Science a Social and Political Endeavor?

The scientific process as presented by Thomas Kuhn should occur outside the boundaries of the day-to-day world, so that social concerns and political interests don't enter into it. This is the traditional view of science: a value-neutral endeavor conducted by objective researchers. Although scientific researchers have particular moral, political, and religious beliefs, scientific method requires that they leave those "biases" at the laboratory door, because the process of discovering new knowledge requires scientists to remain uninfluenced by their personal views and political pressures. This is called the normative view of science, or the way science ought to be conducted.

Normative view of science the notion that science is unaffected by the personal beliefs or values of scientists but rather follows objective rules of evidence.

As a sociologist, you should recognize that this traditional view of science isn't entirely accurate. Science is constantly influenced by political and social factors. Such biases are manifested through the type of research that scientists decide to pursue. Why do some physicists study nuclear fusion, whereas others study thermodynamics? Why do some sociologists study patterns of international migration, whereas others study types of postmodern families? Why do some biologists research a vaccine for HIV/AIDS, whereas others try to find a cure for baldness? One answer is simply that different researchers are interested in different topics. One sociologist might believe that patterns of international migration are interesting and important, whereas another might be particularly interested in changing family patterns: Both sociologists' research topics are affected by their values and interests.

An alternative explanation, however, is that researchers select topics, in part, based on the funding available for their research. For example, after Hurricane Katrina in 2005, the National Science Foundation (NSF) funded Small Grants for Exploratory Research (SGER) for researchers in the fields of science, engineering, and education to rapidly gather research and collect data relevant to the causes and effects of the hurricane. Without funding from the NSF, some of the scientists would have been unable to conduct research on Hurricane Katrina. So the economic concerns of scientists, the NSF's ability to fund their livelihood, helped to determine the topics selected. And, of course, like any federal agency with congressional funding, the NSF sets its priorities by means of a political process, not a purely scientific one.

In this way, nonscientists often make decisions that affect the course of science. One example is President George W. Bush's involvement in the debate about embryonic stem cell research. Scientists agree that embryonic stem cell research may unlock the cures to major diseases, including Parkinson's disease and Alzheimer's disease. In 2001, President Bush decided to allow federal funding for existing embryonic stem cell lines, but he stipulated that the funds couldn't be used to develop new stem cells from existing human embryos. Bush announced his decision via a press release:

> As a result of private research, more than 60 genetically diverse stem cell lines already exist. . . . I have concluded that we should allow federal funds to be used for research on these existing stem cell lines, where the life and death decision has already been made. . . . This allows us to explore the promise and potential of stem cell research without crossing a fundamental moral line, by providing taxpayer funding that would sanction or encourage further destruction of human embryos that have at least the potential for life. (Bush, 2001)

Bush is no scientist, but his position as president of the United States empowered him to make decisions about funding for science. Limiting the availability of federal funding for stem cell research was clearly a political and moral decision. Politically, he sought to placate conservative religious groups. Morally, he sought to promote his personal beliefs about life and death and right and wrong. By limiting the availability of federal funding to the existing lines of embryonic stem cells, President Bush limited the possibility of

George W. Bush announces his decision to limit funding for embryonic stem cell research while surrounded by families who had adopted frozen embryos.

scientific research. (President Obama subsequently rescinded the Bush policy, although opponents of stem cell research continue to challenge its legality.) As this example demonstrates, the process and possibility of scientific discovery can be driven by political considerations.

Another example of science following the dictates of politics is the Manhattan Project. During World War II, some U.S. leaders feared that the Nazis were developing atomic weapons. In 1942, the United States therefore started research on the development of an atomic weapon under the leadership of the U.S. Army Corps of Engineers. Led by General Leslie R. Groves and physicist J. Robert Oppenheimer, the Manhattan Project was the code name given to the team of research scientists at work on developing atomic weapons for the United States. Although the details of the scientific pursuits are complicated (and probably better explained by a physicist than a sociologist), it is clear that the Manhattan Project was created for political and social reasons. The decision to pursue nuclear technologies and the rapid pace of research were both influenced by international geopolitical circumstances.

The Pursuit of Truth and the Boundaries of Science

All science claims to promote knowledge, but sometimes different sources of knowledge reveal different things. Imagine that on your morning walk to your introductory biology class, you encounter a man giving a loud public speech in the local park. Intrigued, you listen to the soapbox orator rant about the dangers of global warming, which is occurring at unprecedented rates, he reports. You continue to class, unconvinced by his arguments. Arriving a few minutes early, you start to read the morning newspaper, where there's an article about a report by government scientists stating that global warming is, in fact, a myth. According to the report, little change in atmospheric temperatures has occurred over the century. As you finish the article, your professor arrives and introduces today's topic: global warming. Already primed, you pay careful attention. According to your professor, a world-renowned climatologist, global warming is occurring at alarming rates, melting ice caps, raising ocean temperatures, and threatening the global ecosystem. As you leave the lecture, you begin to wonder whom you should believe about global warming: the soapbox orator, the government scientists, or your professor. Who is telling the truth? Who is presenting the facts?

Science holds a privileged place in our society in relation to knowledge and truth. We are taught to accept scientific findings as fact and to trust the knowledge gained through scientific research. As the sociologist Thomas Gieryn writes, "If 'science' says so, we are more often than not inclined to believe it or act on it—and to prefer it over claims lacking this epistemic seal of approval" (1999). You'd be more likely to believe your professor than the soapbox orator, right? That's because your professor has the credibility of a scientist, whereas the soapbox orator does not. Throughout your life, you've probably been taught to trust scientists and to be wary of people screaming in local parks. But the government report was also written by scientists. When faced with different stories by different scientists, how do we decide who is more credible? As Gieryn notes, the claims of science, scientists, and scientific discovery aren't nearly as clear-cut as you might think (1999).

Let's take a closer look at a real example from Dover, Pennsylvania, which we examined in a religious context in Chapter 16. In 1995, the Dover school board instituted a policy requiring that ninth-grade science teachers read their students a statement challenging Darwin's theory of evolution, which claims that the evolution of an organism occurs through a natural, competitive process that allows the specific, genetically based traits that are best adapted to local conditions to survive and reproduce at the expense of those organisms that are genetically less adapted to the particular conditions they face. Darwin calls this process of competition within the species natural selection, and very few scientists disagree with Darwin's theory.

The statement prepared by the Dover school board, however, was as follows:

> The Pennsylvania Academic Standards require students to learn about Darwin's theory of evolution and eventually to take a standardized test of which evolution is a part.

> Because Darwin's theory is a theory, it continues to be tested as new evidence is discovered. The theory is not a fact. Gaps in the theory exist for which there is no evidence. A theory is defined as a well-tested explanation that unifies a broad range of observations.
>
> Intelligent design is an explanation of the origin of life that differs from Darwin's view. The reference book, "Of Pandas and People," is available for students who might be interested in gaining an understanding of what intelligent design actually involves.
>
> With respect to any theory, students are encouraged to keep an open mind. The school leaves the discussion of the origins of life to individual students and their families. As [Dover is] a standards-driven district, class instruction focuses upon preparing students to achieve proficiency on standards-based assessments. (*Kitzmiller et al. v. Dover Area School District et al.*, 2005)

The statement introduces an alternative theory, called intelligent design, to explain the origin and evolution of species. Proponents of intelligent design claim that life is too complex to have evolved through natural selection. Rather, they propose that an "intelligent designer" had a hand in creating and selecting various species.

The debate about intelligent design offers a real-life example about the boundaries of science (Gieryn, 1999). Proponents of intelligent design, backed by a tenured professor of biochemistry at Lehigh University named Michael Behe, claim that it is a legitimate scientific theory. Opponents argue that the strong empirical support for Darwin's theory of evolution and the near-universal dismissal of intelligent design in the scientific community delegitimize it as a credible alternative to natural selection. The human eye, for instance, is "designed" in quite a suboptimal way with blood vessels and nerves covering the light-sensitive cells. The retina is, in essence, inside out—resulting in the blind spot—owing to the path-dependency of evolution. In fact, many biologists argue that if you don't accept natural selection, a domino effect would occur and much of what we know in biology would crumble, because the model of natural selection forms a foundation for other knowledge.

In the case of the Dover school board, a group of parents sued the board, claiming that the attempts to offer intelligent design as an alternative theory were akin to introducing religion into the classroom—a violation of the First Amendment. In December 2005, the U.S. district court sided with the parents and forbade the teaching of intelligent design in science classes. Meanwhile, the main proponents of intelligent design instruction on the school board were voted out of office in the 2005 local elections.

Boundary work work done to maintain the border between legitimate and nonlegitimate science within a specific scientific discipline or between legitimate disciplines.

The intelligent design debate demonstrates the type of boundary work being done to create a distinction between legitimate and nonlegitimate science within a specific scientific discipline. When sociologists such as Gieryn refer to boundary work, they mean "instances in which . . . divisions between fields of knowledge are created, advocated, attacked, or reinforced" (Gieryn, 1999).

Scientists perform boundary work when they engage in debates about the legitimacy of scientific theory. For instance, most scientists would consider the research on evolution in the journal Nature legitimate science, but they would not accept the alternate theories promoted by the Creation Museum in Petersburg, Kentucky (pictured above).

In this case, biologists are debating the boundaries of legitimate theories of evolution. Another kind of boundary work occurs between different scientific disciplines. In this boundary work, scientists in different disciplines reach different answers to the same scientific questions. Urban planners, nutritionists, and biologists might all be researching the causes of obesity in America (the same scientific question), but they may arrive at different answers because they're working through different frameworks.

As an urban planner, you might examine forms of urban sprawl and the car-dependent city. Certain trends, such as cities becoming less pedestrian-friendly and people being more reliant on the automobile, might help explain obesity for an urban planner. As a nutritionist, you'd probably research the caloric intake of obese Americans. You might also research the types of food eaten by different people and the dietary patterns that cause obesity. As a biologist, you might think that the key to unlocking the obesity mystery lies in people's genetics and biochemistry. You'd search for a gene for obesity, or a genetic condition that makes people prone to being obese. Urban planners, nutritionists, and biologists approach the question of obesity from their respective disciplines and reach different answers. Sometimes these are complementary, but other times they conflict.

The Laboratory as a Site for Knowledge

In 1979, anthropologists Bruno Latour and Steve Woolgar published *Laboratory Life,* an account of the process of scientific discovery in the laboratory. The researchers spent two years conducting ethnographic research of Nobel

Jonas Salk in his lab in Pittsburgh, Pennsylvania. What conclusions did Bruno Latour and Steve Woolgar make about the scientific process based on their observations of Salk?

Prize–winning physician Jonas Salk's laboratory. As uninvolved observers, they watched scientists conduct experiments, review papers, and interact with one another in this setting. Latour and Woolgar argue that ethnographic approaches had never before been used to look at reclusive (and exclusive) scientific laboratories largely because science holds such a privileged place in Western society. Nonetheless, they called Western scientists a "tribe" worthy of study by anthropologists and decried the lack of information about how this tribe of scientists behaved (1979).

The scientific laboratory is the primary site in which many scientific data are collected, researched, and analyzed. If you are a social scientist, your laboratory, so to speak, is the real world. If you want to understand how homeless people live, you're likely to conduct ethnography in a homeless shelter. You might also use data collected from surveys (like the U.S. Census) or through face-to-face interviews. Most natural scientists, in contrast, tend to extract elements from the natural world and bring them into their laboratory. Although some scientists do work or gather samples in the outside world, they usually return to their laboratories to analyze those samples. Biologists, for example, examine cells under the microscopes in their labs, whereas chemists might model the structure of proteins in computational laboratories. The laboratory therefore plays an important part in the scientific process.

Inside laboratories, Latour and Woolgar argue, there exists a unique process of scientific discovery—with its own language, its own system of promotion, and its own hierarchy. Their research traces the construction of scientific fact. Scientific facts don't just pop up from experiments. Instead, scientists debate research findings, discuss their results, and work through disagreements. Some findings make it out of the laboratory and into print; others don't. Latour and Woolgar pay particularly close attention to the circumstances of the laboratory. For example, power struggles within the hierarchy of the lab may determine which results or explanations of data receive more attention.

Latour and Woolgar's work on the social construction of scientific facts has been widely criticized in the scientific community. These critics argue that their claims undermine the purity of scientific pursuit and thereby weaken scientific claims to truth. In *Fashionable Nonsense* (1999), the physicists Alan Sokal and Jean Bricmont took Latour, specifically, to task over a particular claim about the death of Pharaoh Ramses II around 1213 B.C. Historians claim that Ramses died of tuberculosis, but Latour points out that tuberculosis wasn't discovered until 1882. If tuberculosis didn't exist as a scientific fact until 3,000 years after Ramses' death, Latour argues, how could it be considered the cause of his death? What allows Latour to make this argument is his notion that scientific facts are "created," not discovered. Most scientists dismiss this provocative claim as nonsense: Just because tuberculosis hadn't been discovered yet doesn't mean it didn't kill Ramses. Scientific facts, they argue, are not made but rather preexist in objective reality waiting to be discovered by truth-seeking researchers.

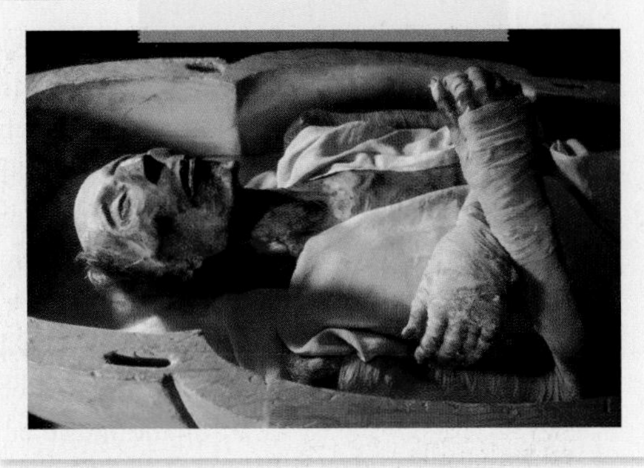

How did Ramses II become a flash point in the "science wars" between Latour and other scientists 3,000 years after he died?

These debates, often called the "science wars," have been taken up by philosopher Ian Hacking in *The Social Construction of What?* (1999). Hacking tries to mediate between constructionists such as Latour and scientists such as Sokal. He pushes for a middle ground, arguing that there's something legitimate in both social constructivism and scientific truth. On the one hand, cultural norms and social situations influence both what is discovered and how the discovery process proceeds. To argue that social norms aren't relevant is to ignore the realities of the social world. On the other hand, as Barbara Herrnstein Smith points out (2009), the scientific models of the way the world works are taken as fact because they often enable us to predict, shape, and intervene in the world more reliably than other ways of thinking.

The Matthew Effect

One example of how social life influences science that Hacking (and physical scientists) might be comfortable acknowledging is the Matthew effect, a term Robert Merton coined in 1968. The term refers to a passage in the Book of Matthew in the Christian Bible that reads, "For unto every one that hath shall be given, and he shall have abundance: but from him that hath not shall be taken away even that which he hath." Sociologists deploy the Matthew effect as a metaphor to describe how prestige is earned and rewards are distributed in the scientific community. In this context, the first half of the quotation means that prestige brings more prestige. A well-known scientist is more likely to be credited with a particular scientific discovery than lesser-known colleagues, even if they worked as a team to produce that knowledge. Scientists who have won major awards or written highly regarded books will be showered with further praise. The opposite holds true as well: Scientists without great prestige will have difficulty earning it. Graduate students often produce much of the work for which their professors become famous, running the chemistry experiments or reporting on the daily progress of plant growth and development,

Matthew effect a term used by sociologists to describe the notion that certain scientific results get more notoriety and influence based on the existing prestige of the researchers involved.

but the fame associated with scientific discovery is bestowed on the professor. What's more, a finding published by a famous scientist is more likely to influence the future course of research than one published by a lesser-known figure.

Sociologist John Evans (2002) has found, in a study of debates over human genetic engineering, that more prestigious, senior authors were cited more often than junior researchers. Evans tried to factor out the quality of the work but, of course, it is impossible to exactly measure something like quality. Duncan Watts, another sociologist, took an innovative approach to this question—albeit in the realm of culture, not science—when he set up an online music lab with free downloads and manipulated how the rankings of band popularity were presented (see Chapter 2). Indeed, he found that a system of cumulative advantage developed so that small initial differences in ranking often became solidified and magnified. Because his was an experiment, he knew that, although quality mattered, the effects he detected were distinct from those related to quality.

Agriculture and the Environment

The process of natural or physical science may be a subject of sociological study in itself, but sociologists also research the effects of the social world and the natural world on each other. Studies have examined how the environment affects and is affected by social institutions, how computer science is changing social relations, and how agricultural technologies affect human population growth. These are just a few examples of a potentially endless list of intersections between social science and natural science. Let's start with the sociology of the environment by way of example.

Sign indicating North Pole for tourists, among melting ice, Arctic Ocean.

Global Warming and Climate Change

Al Gore, the former vice president and presidential candidate, is one of the most visible crusaders raising awareness about climate change. In 2006, Gore starred in a film entitled *An Inconvenient Truth* that documented the impact of human activity on climate temperatures through a process called the greenhouse effect. According to this film, the effects of global warming are devastating. It is responsible for the increase in the number of deadly hurricanes, such as Hurricane Katrina. Global warming is shifting ice caps and melting glaciers, thereby increasing sea levels and threatening human communities living along coastal areas. Because of rising atmospheric temperatures, heat waves are becoming more intense, and tropical diseases are migrating to new climates. Malaria, a tropical disease, has been found in new places where the mosquitoes that carry the disease previously had been unable to live. Hundreds of species of animals and plants are responding to increasing temperatures by moving closer and closer to the North and South Poles.

So, what exactly is global warming? Carbon dioxide (CO_2) and other greenhouse gases such as methane are trapped in the atmosphere, naturally warming the temperature of the earth. This process enables the planet to remain at a temperature comfortable for human habitation. In recent years, however, scientists have observed rising atmospheric concentrations of these gases as well as higher average global temperatures. The growth rate of emissions was close to 1 percent in the 1990s and grew to an average 3 percent increase in the last decade. In 2009, there was a 1.4 percent drop reflecting the economic recession. Yet just one year later the highest increase in emissions since the industrial revolution was recorded at 5.9 percent. China is now the leading emitter of greenhouse gases, making the United States the second largest producer of greenhouse gases. Emissions from China rose 10 percent between 2009 and 2010, putting 2.2 billion tons of carbon into the atmosphere (Global Carbon Project, 2011). Global warming refers to these rising atmospheric temperatures (see Figure 17.1).

Global warming rising atmospheric concentrations of carbon dioxide and other greenhouse gases as well as higher global average temperatures.

Figure 17.1: Variations of Earth's Surface Temperature Over 140 Years

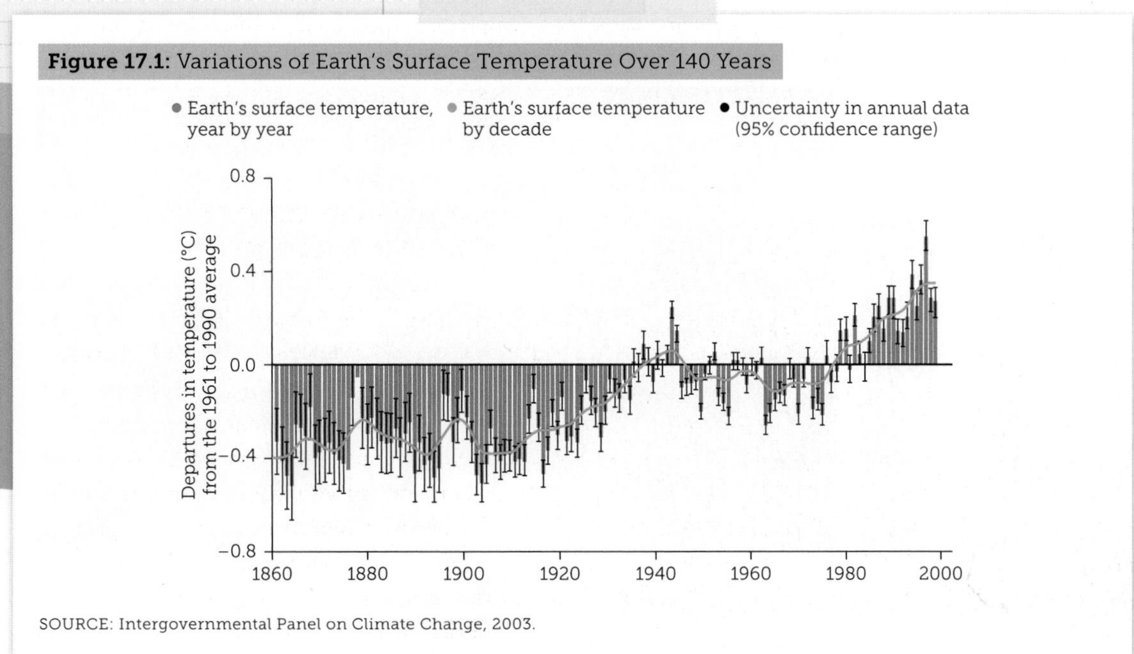

SOURCE: Intergovernmental Panel on Climate Change, 2003.

Although some disagreement exists in the scientific community about the exact causes of global warming, the vast majority of scientists acknowledge that the roots of global warming can be traced back to human activities. In particular, deforestation and the burning of coal, natural gas, and oil have caused atmospheric temperatures to creep upward. The burning of fossil fuels releases CO_2 and other greenhouse gases into the atmosphere. In particular, CO_2 emissions from cars, trucks, and airplanes are a primary cause of global warming. The United Nations Intergovernmental Panel on Climate Change estimates that 3.5 percent of global warming results from airplanes, and that figure could rise to 15 percent by 2050 (Penner et al., 1999). Traffic in major cities also accounts for a significant portion of climate change. Drivers around the world waste millions of gallons of gasoline sitting idly in traffic, adding CO_2 to the atmosphere. After CO_2 emissions from planes, trucks, and cars, scientists estimate that deforestation is the second largest contributor to rising temperatures. As environmental activists like Wangari Maathai have long argued, deforestation contributes to global warming in two ways: First, the burning of the forest releases CO_2 into the atmosphere, and second, the deforested trees are no longer around to sequester atmospheric carbon.

Just as the causes of climate change can be traced back to human societies, climate change will strongly affect human societies, too. Extreme weather patterns, such as prolonged heat waves and increasing numbers of hurricanes, portend drastic consequences for society. Sociologists have an interest in these topics. For example, in *Heat Wave: A Social Autopsy of Disaster in Chicago* (2002),

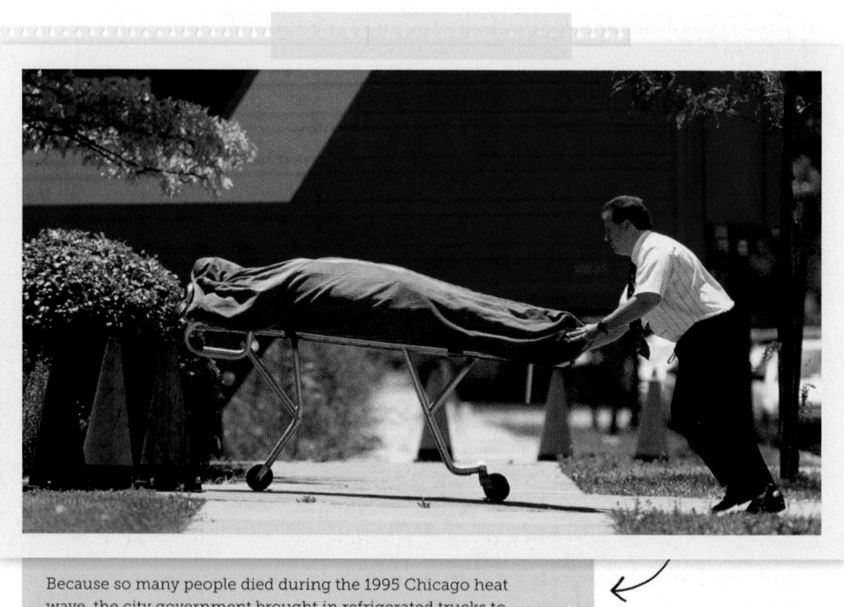

Because so many people died during the 1995 Chicago heat wave, the city government brought in refrigerated trucks to store the bodies.

Eric Klinenberg studied many of the effects of Chicago's 1995 heat wave on city residents. Through his research, he discovered that although the heat wave was certainly catastrophic, resulting in the deaths of 739 individuals (the human toll made it one of the worst disasters in the United States up to that point), the way that events played out had far more to do with social forces than natural ones. Specifically, most of the fatalities occurred among elderly, African American, and poor residents and largely resulted from social isolation.

Although Klinenberg didn't study global warming, the scientific community has warned that global warming will create prolonged heat waves like the one he studied as well as more frequent and severe weather events of all kinds, further exacerbating socioeconomic stratification, whereby certain groups of people are affected much more severely than others (see Chapter 7). Furthermore, researchers believe that global warming will affect agricultural production by changing regional temperatures and altering rainfall patterns, thereby forcing farmers to adjust to changing environmental conditions. As ocean levels rise, human societies may experience a massive migration away from shorelines and islands. Populations forced from coastal communities and isolated islands because of rising water levels could cause a significant refugee crisis worldwide. Although this list isn't exhaustive, you can begin to understand some of the social challenges that human societies will face as global temperatures continue to rise.

Organic Foods and Genetically Modified Organisms

As changing atmospheric temperatures affect human societies globally, their impact remains abstract. It may be difficult for us to pinpoint the effects of global warming on our everyday lives. So now we'll bring our discussion closer to home: your local supermarket. Imagine you're standing in the produce section trying to decide which apples to purchase, but the options are numerous and the decision becomes too complicated. Do you buy Fuji apples flown in from New Zealand? Or maybe you prefer Empire apples from upstate New York? There are two types of Granny Smith apples, both from Washington State. One is labeled organic; the other is not. As you continue through the grocery store, you arrive at the dairy coolers and recall a story you heard on National Public Radio about a protein hormone called rBST that is injected into cows. After listening to the radio segment, you decided that you didn't want to purchase products manufactured from hormone-injected cows, so you scour the dairy section, reading the fine print, in search of rBST-free products. Before heading to the checkout counter, you remember that you're supposed to pick up some cornmeal to bake cornbread for the Mexican-themed fiesta

What kind of apples do you buy? Organic? Local? Which one is more affordable? Which one is better for you or the environment? How can sociology help you answer these questions at the grocery store?

you and your roommate are hosting. As you grab the least expensive box of cornmeal, you notice a label informing you that the product in your hand "may contain genetically modified ingredients." Although it's the cheapest, you struggle to decide if you should purchase this brand and consume a lab experiment. Exhausted, you finally reach the checkout counter. Who knew grocery shopping could be so difficult? Let's take a closer look at the scenarios you encountered in your (hypothetical) grocery store trip in relation to the environment and society.

Organic Foods In recent years, supermarkets throughout the country have begun stocking "organic" foods, and entire stores dedicated to organic products are becoming commonplace. In Seattle, the Puget Consumers Coop is one of the city's largest organic grocery stores, actively partnering with local organic farms to bring fresh produce to consumers. Even in your local chain grocery store, there's probably a section in the produce aisle dedicated to organic foods. You may have a notion that organic equals healthier, but what exactly does organic mean? Is it really about the production of food, or is it a way of life? Is *organic* a scientific term or a cultural one?

For Michael Pollan, the author of *The Omnivore's Dilemma: A Natural History of Four Meals* (2006), the debate over organic foods is more than a question of agricultural production. It's both a political and a moral statement—even a quasi-religious statement. Pollan investigated food production at different levels. He notes that growing demand for organic foods prompted the National Organic Program of the U.S. Department of Agriculture (USDA) to release guidelines for commercial use of the word *organic* in 2002. Pollan examines the production of four meals: from fast-food megachains to straight-from-the-dirt salad. Like the book *Fast Food Nation* by Eric Schlosser (2001) and the documentary *Super Size Me* by Morgan Spurlock (2004), Pollan's work highlights the horrors of commercial slaughterhouses and the chemical components of mass-produced food. But by looking at the in-between stages, including food labeled "organic" purchased from one nationwide organic food store chain, Pollan shows that an organic label isn't simply a question of being chemical-free and straight from the land. In 2009, novelist Jonathan Safran Foer turned to nonfiction to write about the ethics of eating animals—in terms of animal suffering as well as the much greater environmental impact of consuming calories from animal sources rather than plant sources. Both Pollan and Foer have reached best-seller status—eating well is high on our collective consciousness.

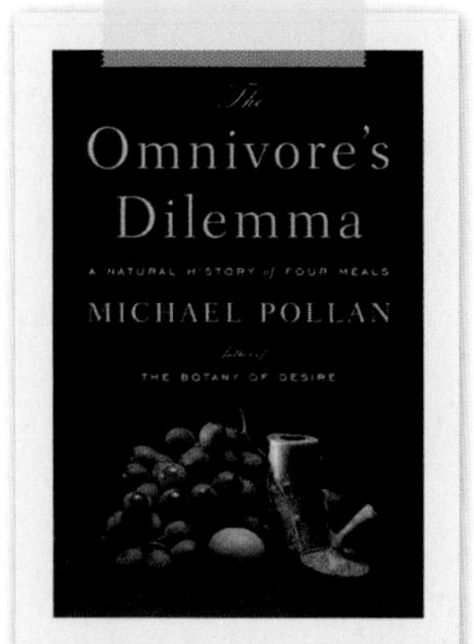

Organic foods are pesticide-free and don't contain genetically modified ingredients. Organic farms follow a strict set of guidelines outlined by the USDA. Some products are certified organic, meaning that they contain at least

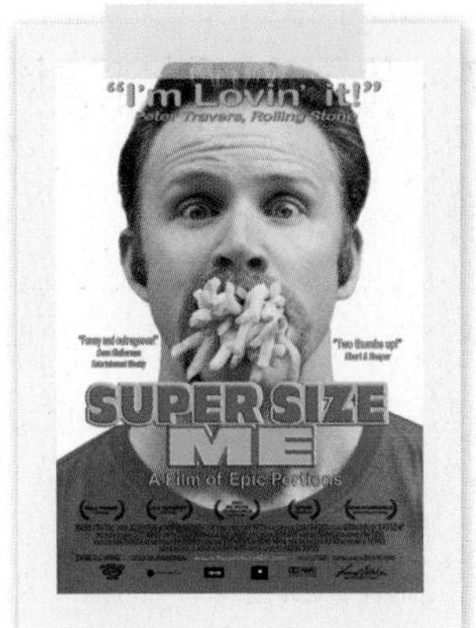

95 percent organic ingredients, whereas other products are labeled "made with organic ingredients," meaning that at least 70 percent of their ingredients are certified organic. Sometimes, meat and poultry aren't labeled organic even though they come from free-range animals raised without growth hormones or antibiotics. That's because maintaining an organic farm (with USDA certification) is expensive. Small farms often operate at a disadvantage—with smaller profits they may not be able to afford to comply with the costly certification requirements. Although megafarms in the Midwest might be certified organic, they still truck their produce across the country to put it in grocery stores—a process that isn't particularly friendly to the environment.

Eating organic has become a way of life, as well as a political statement about farming, food production, and consumerism. People often assume that organic also means healthier, for the environment, the human consumer, and the animals (in the case of dairy and meat). Sometimes, they assume that organic produce comes from small local farms, not megafarms owned by parent companies like Colgate Palmolive, which owns Tom's of Maine, and Dean Foods, which owns Horizon Organic. As organic becomes more and more popular, a number of social issues will come to the fore: First, big agrobusiness has the political clout to affect the FDA's definition of organic (and it has been lobbying as of late for a relaxation of the standards for this label) and the money to undergo the process of certification. So organic farming may be another way that stratification occurs between big and small farms—yet another force putting the squeeze on family farms. Likewise, on the consumer end, the availability of organic products may add to health stratification by income. Specifically, organic products are almost always more expensive than nonorganic ones, offering wealthier and more educated customers a health opportunity that may not be available as readily to those with limited resources. There is hardly a technological advance that does not play out unequally across existing social divisions in society.

Genetically Modified Foods Although organic foods have hit the grocery store shelves without much controversy, another product has been filling supermarket aisles amid some debate. Genetically modified foods (made with genetically modified organisms, GMOs) have been finding their way to grocery store shelves and dinner tables, creating increasing controversy about their environmental and health effects. GMOs are products whose genetic structures have been altered. In doing so, scientists have been able to make specific changes to various seeds and crops. By all accounts, GMOs are one of the most significant advances in agricultural technology over the last decade. But why, you might ask, would farmers want to alter the genetic makeup of their crops? What are the benefits of genetically modified crops, and what are the dangers?

According to proponents of GMOs, altering the genetic structure of particular crops has the potential to produce higher yields (Qaim & Zilberman,

2003). With higher yields, genetically modified crops could help make American farms (which are heavily subsidized by the government) more profitable and lower food prices for consumers. Genetically modified crops may also have better resistance to insects, diseases, and other problems, further improving yields (and perhaps quality). By modifying the genetic structure of crops and seeds in this way, farmers can avoid using pesticides and herbicides that might be toxic to humans. Rather, the plant's genetic structure would make it "naturally" resistant (maybe by tasting nasty to those pests). Also, genetic modifications may decrease the maturation time of crops or keep them riper and fresher longer in the stores, thereby reducing waste.

Genetically modified crops have also been hailed as the panacea for development woes around the world. In July 2000, *Time* magazine ran a cover with the words "This Rice Could Save a Million Kids a Year." The accompanying story was about Ingo Potrykus, a professor of plant sciences at the Federal Institute of Technology in Zurich, Switzerland, and the inventor of golden rice, which could help solve key health and nutritional problems for children in developing countries (Robinson & Nash, 2000). By inserting a particular bacterial gene into the genetic structure of rice, Potrykus and his colleagues worked to create rice with high levels of vitamin A. Their goal was to combat vitamin A deficiency, a condition that causes blindness in millions of children around the world. Because rice is a staple in many children's diets worldwide (particularly in Asia), Potrykus and others believe that genetically modified rice containing more vitamin A could be an answer to this debilitating condition. In Potrykus's vision, farmers in developing countries could substitute a genetically modified crop for their traditional one.

Ingo Potrykus's genetically modified golden rice might prevent health problems for millions of poor children. Why is it controversial?

Genetic modification is not without its problems, however. Opponents of genetically modified crops point to two primary risks: risks to the environment and risks to human health. Scientists know very little about how changes in the genetic structure of one organism may affect its relationship with other organisms and the ecosystem as a whole. For instance, one type of genetically modified corn in Canada was toxic to a particular caterpillar. Through the modification of the genetic structure of corn to keep away these predators, the Canadian corn crop has flourished. However, we don't know the consequences of reducing the caterpillar population by cutting off a primary food source for them. Will the birds that eat the caterpillars die out? What would the ripple effects of that be? Given the interconnectedness of ecological systems, it is hard to predict the outcome of an intervention at one point in the food chain. What's more, some researchers have argued that the Canadian corn modifications have also been harmful to the monarch butterfly, a cherished species that doesn't damage corn crops.

Opponents of genetically modified food also claim that the results are simply unnatural (think fish genes turning up in tomatoes) and that we simply don't know enough about this technology to ensure safety for human consumers (Bakshi, 2003). They fear that genetically modified foods may have unanticipated long-term, adverse health effects or that they may even cause new illnesses. That said, proponents argue that farmers have been genetically modifying food organisms for centuries already—first through selective breeding (apples have been cultivated over generations from a native fruit called a hawthorn) and more recently by the exposure of seeds to X-rays to induce random mutations in the hope that some will yield benefits.

Greenpeace activists dressed to symbolize the bul-ul, a traditional Ifugao rice guardian, protest genetically modified rice in April 2007, outside the Philippines' Department of Agriculture in Manila.

As with organic farming, the debates about the risks and rewards offered by genetically modified foods involve both natural science and social science. One framework for understanding them is Ulrich Beck's concept of the risk society (1992). Beck argues that risks can be grouped into two categories: external risks and manufactured risks. External risks derive from nature—hurricanes, floods, earthquakes, and the like—and have been a part of human history since long before the first machine was ever invented. However, with modernity comes manufactured risks, risks that result from human activity. These run the gamut from large-scale nuclear events (such as the meltdown at Japan's Fukushima Daiichi reactor in 2011) to the personal risks of riding a motorcycle at 100 miles per hour. A risk society both produces and is concerned with mitigating manufactured risks (like those from GMOs), and the risks, as we saw with Hurricane Katrina in Chapter 9, are unequally distributed by socioeconomic status and other dimensions of power. They sometimes inform how we make social decisions: For example, should we really rebuild New Orleans as it was before the disaster? Should we construct the Freedom Tower at Ground Zero as tall as the towers of the World Trade Center were? Should we attempt to preserve the "American way of life" by continuing to burn fossil fuels at our current rate, regardless of the irreparable harm it may do to the planet?

Risk society a society that both produces and is concerned with mitigating risks, especially manufactured risks (ones that result from human activity).

Charles Perrow, for one, would say no. In *The Next Catastrophe* (2007), he argues that disasters resulting from manufactured risks (as well as external risks) are an inevitable part of modern life. Although we cannot eliminate them, we can reduce their impact. Perhaps, he argues, it doesn't really make sense to have a city with a large population in a hurricane-prone area at an altitude below sea level. And maybe it doesn't make sense to build a huge tower piercing the sky when there is so much air traffic that will need to skirt by it. By dispersing risks—like storing hazardous materials in smaller quantities across wider areas—Perrow argues that disasters can be less disastrous, even as they remain inevitable. Perrow's analysis illuminates Beck's concept of risk society: Social scientists (and society as a whole) struggle to minimize risk even as human technology produces more of it with each new discovery.

The Green Revolution

The green revolution is another example that may shed light on the risk society concept. The umbrella term *green revolution* refers broadly to two agricultural trends: first, the introduction of high-yield crop varietals in developing countries, and second, improvements in agricultural technologies including irrigation systems, fertilizers, and pesticides. In 1945, the Rockefeller Foundation and the Mexican government established the Cooperative Wheat Research and Production Program (later CIMMYT, the International Maize and Wheat Improvement Center) to improve Mexico's agricultural output, especially its wheat yields. Norman Borlaug, who was instrumental to this effort, won the 1970 Nobel Peace Prize for his role.

By the mid-1960s, these same technologies were developed for use in other regions of the world, with help from many nongovernmental organizations (NGOs) and financing from the World Bank. In Asia, the International Rice Research Institute developed high-yield varieties of paddy rice. By the late 1990s, almost half of East Asian crops were planted with such high-yield varieties; more than two-thirds of South Asian farming is done with these seeds. The corresponding figure for sub-Saharan Africa is a mere 11 percent. Each extension of the green revolution technologies, from their home bases in Japan and the United States to Mexico, India, East Asia, Latin America, and Africa, has depended on local research to adapt high-yield technologies to local crops, pests, and farm systems (for example, rain-fed versus irrigated). Africa has been a late beneficiary of the green revolution because of its distinctive mix of crops and its very high dependence on rain-fed agriculture (whereas the first generation of high-yield varieties depended on irrigation).

The green revolution is widely credited with increasing agricultural productivity in countries throughout the developing world. Along with the introduction of fertilizers and pesticides, as well as the increased use of irrigation systems, new high-yield seeds have increased the quantity of food production. Through the green revolution, food production has kept pace with population growth. Meanwhile, as incomes have increased thanks to greater agricultural productivity, population growth has slowed (Conley et al., 2007). Likewise, because the new technologies require greater skills to realize their full benefit—coordinating irrigation with fertilizer inputs and so on—they have increased the value of formal schooling in many rural areas, particularly for women (Rosenzweig, 1982).

The green revolution has also rearranged the economic units of production. Because the costs of irrigation systems and fertilizer are sometimes prohibitively expensive for individual farms and households, new collectives and cooperatives have emerged to bring together household farmers. The results, therefore, not only have been agricultural and scientific but also have reshaped the social organization of farming. The green revolution has reduced the number of individual, family-owned farms and made farming a collective, community endeavor.

The green revolution is not without its critics, however. Because of its focus on boosting caloric output through the intensified production of staple foods such as wheat and rice, farmers are often encouraged to switch from local, indigenous crops to other high-yield crops distributed by the movement's proponents. The result, according to Vandana Shiva, an Indian scientist and anti–green revolution activist, is the sacrifice of micronutrients attained only through variety in a diet. In this way, she argues, the green revolution has depleted biodiversity in many areas. And by relying on fewer crops, farmers are more susceptible to disease or predators destroying their fields (Shiva, 1992a, 1992b, 2002).

Likewise, argues Shiva, the green revolution seed varieties emphasize higher yields but require a great deal of water. Although this switch to water-reliant varieties of wheat and paddy rice has been responsible for an increase in production, it has simultaneously created new environmental problems by overextending India's water supply and its reliance on irrigated as opposed to rain-fed agriculture. Writing for *YES! Magazine,* Shiva (2004) gave the following example:

> In the Deccan area of south India, sorghum was traditionally intercropped with pulses and oilseeds to reduce evaporation. The Green Revolution replaced this indigenous agriculture with monocultures. Dwarf varieties replaced tall ones, chemical fertilizers took the place of organic ones, and irrigation displaced rain-fed cropping. As a result, soils were deprived of vital organic material, and soil moisture droughts became recurrent.

Moreover, these new models of production have focused on the market-based distribution of water resources, at the expense of the traditional water management techniques of local communities. Shiva points to situations in which Indian women have to walk farther and farther to find water. She also argues that the use of fertilizers and pesticides has ruined local soils, depleting natural, organic ingredients. These results, she argues, should raise long-term concerns about the sustainability of the green revolution's agricultural techniques. Although Shiva doesn't dispute that the green revolution has increased agricultural output and household incomes, her criticisms raise questions about the costs of such changes as well as their sustainability—economic, cultural, and environmental.

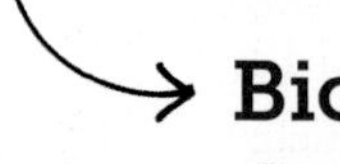

Biotechnology and the Human Genome

Since launching the Human Genome Project in 1990, scientists have sought to understand the building blocks of DNA, which consists of four nucleotide bases: adenine (A), thymine (T), cytosine (C), and guanine (G). At the start of the Human Genome Project, scientists believed that there were 90,000 genes in human DNA. After 13 years of research, however, they discovered that only between 20,000 and 25,000 human genes exist. The Human Genome Project has enabled scientists to crack the genetic code, helping us understand everything from disease to race.

This may sound like the realm of biological science, not sociology. Unraveling the mysteries of the genetic code is probably better left to hard scientists, right? As with the innovations in agricultural production, though, each new piece of scientific information raises important sociological questions. If scientists discover the genes for obesity, for instance, should we screen children for the obesity gene? If so, what kinds of social stigma might they face throughout their childhood? What if scientists locate a gene for Alzheimer's disease? Should people know, long before the condition manifests itself, that they're carrying a gene that increases their chances of eventually suffering from this debilitating disease?

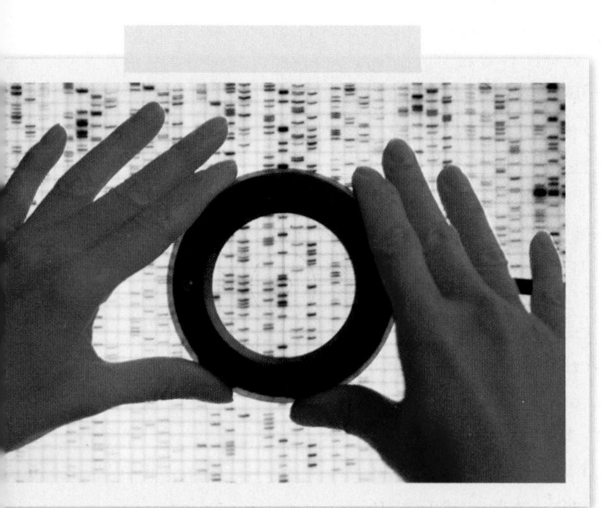

A scientist scans sections of DNA for subsequent computer analysis. What are the possible social consequences of decoding the human genome?

When scientists embarked on the Human Genome Project, their goal was to identify all of the genes in human DNA. Their project became one of the first major scientific endeavors to acknowledge and address the ethical, legal, and social issues that arose from its own process of scientific discovery. You'll find that newspapers increasingly print stories about genomic discoveries: the genes associated with breast cancer risk; the genes for homosexuality, depression, and alcoholism; the genes related to violent tendencies, assertiveness, worry, and sickle-cell anemia, to name just a few. Sometimes, these discoveries have been based on small samples and then fail to be replicated. Those debunking stories don't often make the headlines, however.

Many social concerns have arisen from the Human Genome Project, including privacy, stratification, and stigmatization. Concerns about privacy deal

Gattaca: Genetics and the Future of Society

The 1997 movie *Gattaca* presents a future divided between "those born of nature, and those engineered by science." In the futuristic world of *Gattaca*, embryos are genetically prescreened before implantation for their probable likelihood of various diseases and disabilities as well as their predicted life expectancy. Ethan Hawke plays Vincent Freeman, a "natural" person (conceived the old-fashioned way) born with a high genetic propensity for heart disease and a predicted life expectancy of only 34 years. Freeman's genetic profile—combined with "genoism," illegal but commonly practiced discrimination based on one's genetic code—prevents him from gaining admission to a training program for astronauts, but Freeman overcomes that obstacle by stealing someone else's identity, which he uses to pass a series of genetic tests required for his inclusion on a mission to Saturn.

Although *Gattaca* is fictitious, some of the implications for genetic testing seem much more real today than they were when *Gattaca* was produced more than a decade ago. In 1997, the Human Genome Project was underway, but the sequencing of the human genome hadn't yet been completed. Scientists didn't know what type of knowledge they'd gain from the human genome, nor had they considered all the ethical issues involved in sequencing it. *Gattaca* presents us with an extreme scenario—a society in which children are screened at birth for genetic mutations and where only those prenatally engineered for success are given a chance—but it also challenges us (via Hollywood) to consider some of the ways that genetic knowledge and testing might be used.

with access to the data. Your genetic structure might reveal information about your susceptibility to disease or about particular personal characteristics. Who should have access to this information? What if scientists discover a gene making people more prone to criminal behavior? Should the government have this information so they can track these people more closely? What if scientists discover a gene for learning disabilities? Should this information be given to schools? In time, you can imagine a market for genetic information emerging, just like the existing market for your credit history. If scientists find that your genetic code, like your credit history, reveals something about your behavior patterns, should they be able to sell this information commercially?

A second major sociological concern that has emerged from the Human Genome Project is stigmatization, which occurs when society marks someone as disgraceful or different. (See Chapter 6 for a discussion of stigma.) What if scientists discover a gene for intelligence? Would people lacking this gene be stigmatized as unintelligent? Stigmatization could occur as scientists discover genes for various conditions considered abnormal or threatening to society.

A third sociological concern resulting from the Human Genome Project is that knowledge of our genetic structure will increase stratification in society if we begin to label people as intelligent/unintelligent, beautiful/ugly, or healthy/unhealthy based on their genetic code. The Pygmalion study (discussed in Chapter 13) showed stigma's power to create its own reality, as such labels become self-fulfilling prophecies: When people expect a certain outcome, they tend to act in ways that bring about that outcome (otherwise known as the W. I. Thomas principle). What if we discover a gene for violence? As the example of *Gattaca* shows, Hollywood implies this could lead us to lock away people with the gene before they even commit a crime. In a more realistic scenario, many observers worry about the concentration of wealth, power, and control that may result from the rush to patent our genetic code for private purposes.

One controversy emerging from molecular genetics is the search for a "gay gene." A 1992 issue of *Science,* one of the leading scientific publications, reported the results of a recent study linking homosexuality with genetics. In an article entitled "Twin Study Links Genes to Homosexuality," Constance Holden wrote, "A new study of twins and adoptive brothers has turned up fresh evidence that genes play a strong role in the development of homosexuality." This discovery set off a search for a gay gene in the scientific community. In 2005, scientists reported further evidence of a link between homosexuality and genetics in the journal *Human Genetics* (Mustanski et al., 2005). By comparing the genetic structures of two gay brothers with that of two other brothers, only one of whom was gay, researchers located part of the genetic structure that they believe is a factor in determining homosexuality. These findings have failed to replicate with any consistency, however.

A big question mark surrounding the existence of the so-called gay gene revolves around the forces of natural selection: How and why would a gene that leads to reduced reproduction survive in a population? One answer is that gay uncles (and aunts) help raise their nieces and nephews and provide family solidarity. However, much evidence suggests that gays are no more involved with their families than are heterosexuals. Further, the idea of group selection—that some individuals make reproductive sacrifices for the sake of the wider community—is not widely accepted among biologists. A better explanation is what's called antagonistic pleiotropy in technical terms. That is, what if the same genes that caused women to be more fertile also as an unintended by-product caused men to be more likely to be gay? Indeed, a trio of Italian researchers found that the women in the families of gay men tended to have more children than those of straight men. Further, it was only on the maternal side—where men get their lone X-chromosome—and not on the paternal side. This helps rule out social explanations (such as large families causing homosexuality). However, it doesn't completely rule out a nongenetic explanation, because the mother's side might have more social influence than the dad's side (particularly in Italy, where the study was done).

The biological roots of sexual orientation need not be limited to genes. Prenatal hormones may also play a role. For example, research by Anthony F. Bogaert has also identified a positive relationship between the number of older biological brothers a boy has and his chance of being gay that could be the result of the mother's immune system's "remembering" her previous male pregnancies and altering the hormonal environment in utero for subsequent male fetuses (Blanchard & Bogaert, 1996; Bogaert, 2006). And what about lesbianism? Research indicates that increased exposure to testosterone in utero causes a number of physiological changes in female fetuses, some of which have been linked to homosexuality (Martin & Nguyen, 2004; Rahman et al., 2003).

The identification of a biological mechanism could cause further stigmatization of homosexuals in society if they are deemed to be "innately" different from heterosexuals. (See our discussion of homosexuality in Chapter 8 on gender.) Alternatively, as some gay activists hope, such a finding could promote tolerance by demonstrating that homosexuality is not a lifestyle or moral choice but a natural attribute like height or eye color. These discoveries also brush the cobwebs off old nature/nurture debates in the scientific community: Is homosexuality a product of nature (biological pathways triggered during development) or nurture (the social environment in which children are raised)? And what if there are people who did not experience the biological pathways scientists have recently discovered but still identify themselves as homosexual? What about firstborn sons who are gay? Will they be stigmatized as being "fake" gays?

Race and Genetics

As scientists continue to unravel the mystery of the human genome, some researchers are searching for information about the genetic basis of race. Race is an ambiguous concept (see Chapter 9)—the line between who's black and who's white, for instance, isn't clearly defined and has changed over the course of American history. But what if scientists locate a gene for racial difference buried in our genetic code? Would that clarify our understanding of race? Culling the human genome for clues about the scientific basis of race has reopened the question of whether race is a social or scientific concept.

Likewise, the search to understand race by digging into our genetic code has spawned an entire industry, with companies like DNA Print Genomics (see Chapter 9) and Family Tree DNA competing to help individuals trace their ancestral history. Family Tree DNA, which claims that "genealogy by genetics is the greatest addition to genealogy since the creation of the family tree," has started selling kits to consumers so they can allegedly trace their ancestry through their genetic code. For $119, men can take the "Y-DNA12 Test," which will tell them if they share ancestry with other males as well as the geographic and ethnic origin of that ancestry. More comprehensive (and expensive) tests can determine more recent paternal relationships. Women can purchase the "mt-DNA Universal Female Test," providing similar information, for $99. After you send Family Tree DNA your check, the company will mail you a simple form and a genetic testing kit. Just scrape the inside of your cheek to collect cells, fill out some paperwork, and wait to learn your ancestry as revealed by your DNA.

Harvard professor Henry Louis Gates, Jr. hosted a 2006 PBS documentary in which he, along with several other African American celebrities, publicly took such a DNA test to trace his personal lineage through the genes on his Y chromosome. Because the history of slavery in the United States was truncated, many African Americans have been unable to trace their heritage back to a particular African country: Records of slaves' origins weren't always complete or even maintained. Furthermore, to blunt the potential for revolutionary action on the part of slaves who shared a common language and sense of solidarity, slave owners purposefully erased Africans' tribal and national heritage by dispersing and remixing groups arriving on the shores of the New World. Genetic testing may thus help many African Americans re-create their currently unknown genealogical history. Having matched the DNA of various African American celebrities with various populations throughout Africa, scientists such as Rick Kittles, an associate professor at the University of Illinois at Chicago and the founder of the African Ancestry network, claim to be able to trace the lineage of African Americans back to their specific African roots. Of course, this technology for tracing ancestral roots is fraught with debate. Are the DNA samples from African populations collected in a database sufficiently exhaustive as to be able to

Henry Louis Gates, Jr. is one of the 460,000 people who have taken a DNA test to determine their ancestry.

trace someone's roots reliably to a particular place? What does it mean for someone to find out his or her genetic ancestry (or at least part of it), and what are the benefits and the risks? You might learn that your ancestors came from the area of West Africa now called Nigeria, but you probably couldn't pinpoint their origins much more specifically than that. Africa is, after all, a continent with more than 50 nations and 1,000 languages as well as a long history of internal migration.

As Charles Rotimi, a Nigerian geneticist living in the United States, points out, this technology can be a double-edged sword. Many people are concerned about confidentiality and accuracy. The tests can be faulty, and they require scientists to have access to people's genetic data. Other critics are simply unsure about the usefulness of such information. Rotimi gives the example of finding out that your ancestors were slave owners. What can you do with this knowledge? There could be unintended social, economic, or psychological consequences for you.

What's more, scientists have little basis to compare different racial groups. They don't have an exhaustive sample of all racial and ethnic groups in the world. Although your genetic information may be a close match to a sample in a database, it might be even closer to a population that's not included in the database. In addition, no definitive genetic markers for race exist. There's no single gene that separates people into different races—you're black if you have it, and white if you don't. Instead, scientists look for groups of similar outward traits in populations that society labels as one race or another. As we saw in Chapter 9, the concept of race emerges as both scientific and sociological.

Another PBS documentary, *The Lost Tribes of Israel* (2000), attempted to test the ancestral claims of the Lemba people of southern Africa, practicing Jews who claim to be direct descendants of Abraham, Isaac, and Jacob. Although some historians claim that the Lemba adopted their Jewish heritage through the work of missionaries centuries ago, the Lemba maintain they are one of the Lost Tribes of Israel. They claim that their Jewish heritage can be traced directly back to the ancient populations that occupied the geographic area of modern-day Palestine and Israel. To test this genetic relationship to the earliest Jews, scientists obtained DNA samples from the Cohanim—a small group of Jews who are said to have descended directly from Aaron, the brother of Moses. They compared samples of DNA from self-described Cohanim to samples of non-Cohanim or lay Jews in Israel to determine the genetic differences between the direct descendants of Aaron and other Jews. The scientists identified a distinctive set

Members of the Lemba community at the Rusape Jewish Tabernacle during a Rosh Hashanah service.

of genetic markers found in 50 percent of the Cohanim and seen in about 10 percent of lay Jews.

If the Lemba people possessed this set of genetic markers unique to Jewish populations, researchers believed, their claims of being one of the Lost Tribes of Israel would be validated. The same scientific team then collected DNA samples from Bantu (African), Yemeni (Arab), and Sephardic and Ashkenazi Jews (including Cohanim from both communities) to compare the degree of similarity that existed between each of these groups. Tests of DNA from the Lemba people revealed that the tribe shared a series of genetic markers (called the Cohen Modal Haplotype) with the Cohanim at a rate that closely matched that of the lay Jews. In one particular clan of the Lemba, the Buba, the Cohanim genetic marker was found in more than 50 percent of males (PBS, 2000). For many scientists, this confirmed that the Lemba were direct descendants of the original Israelites rather than Africans converted by missionaries long ago. Although the research may have helped to set the historical record straight, it raised a handful of other sociological questions about the intersections of race, ethnicity, religion, and geography.

Alondra Nelson has been asking tough questions about how genetic testing has pushed social scientists to refine their mantra that race is a social construction. Is race *either* a social construction *or* a biological one? Nelson responds,

> For social scientists, the coding of the human genome and the quick change in science around questions of race and ancestry really forced us to go back to the drawing board and think carefully about what we mean when we state that "race is a social construct." That statement is still true. What social scientists have not done so well over the last two decades or so, perhaps, is looked at the way in which biology becomes part of that process. So, it's not to say that race is social or biological. I would still suggest that race is a social construct and I think the ways that people negotiate the genetic genealogy tests really proves this point. They get the information, these hard genetic facts, and then these facts enter this whole process about "Who am I? Who was my family before? Does this change who I think my family is now?" And so that suggests that the biological is drawn into social understandings and practices of race and ethnicity. (Conley, 2009n)

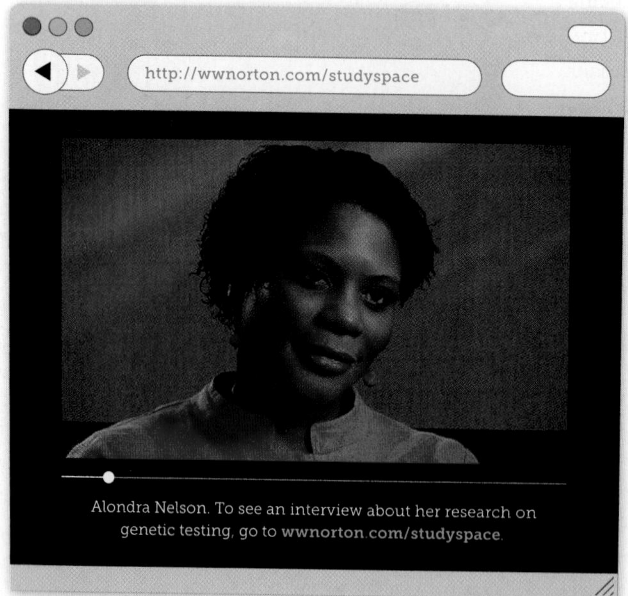

Alondra Nelson. To see an interview about her research on genetic testing, go to **wwnorton.com/studyspace**.

She goes on to note that the hard facts of genetics often impact the less-well-defined operations of family life. There are the obvious difficulties that could arise if genetic testing revealed the person whom you thought to be your biological father was actually not. There are also more subtle impacts of genetic testing on families. When one member of a family has DNA entered into a criminal database, that DNA submission is also exposing the genetic backgrounds of other family members who might then be at a higher risk of being apprehended by the criminal justice system. This shift toward DNA evidence disproportionately impacts poorer families who are more likely to encounter the criminal justice system in the first place and less likely to be able to afford high-quality lawyers to dispute these findings. And as Nelson points out, the sword doesn't cut the other way, because "courts are denying to people who are incarcerated the right to use DNA evidence to prove their innocence" (Conley, 2009n).

Cloning

As we increase our knowledge of the genetic code, some scientists have entered the field of cloning, the attempt to replicate an existing cell or organism. It involves taking DNA from the cell of a particular animal and inserting it into an egg cell that has had its nucleus—and therefore the important components of its own genetic material—removed. If this altered cell is allowed to mature, the resulting organism will be an exact genetic replica of the organism from which the DNA was originally taken (with the exception of any mutations and mitochondrial DNA). There are two primary types of cloning: reproductive cloning and research cloning. The goal of reproductive cloning is to make a genetic copy of an existing person or organism. The goal of research cloning is to reproduce cells that can be used for research purposes. Cells cloned for research are not allowed to mature into humans or other animals. Cells cloned through reproductive cloning, however, usually are allowed to develop into a mature person, animal, or other organism. Although cloning is a scientific process, the debate about cloning understandably crosses social, scientific, and religious boundaries.

In 1996, Dolly the sheep was the first animal cloned from DNA taken from an adult animal.

The cloning controversy began in earnest in 1996, when scientist Ian Wilmut at the Roslin Institute in Edinburgh, Scotland, cloned a sheep. The clone, named Dolly, was a genetically identical replica of the sheep from which her DNA was taken. The cloning of Dolly set off a wave of excitement in the United States. If scientists could clone a complex mammal such as a sheep, could they also clone a human being? If so, what would this mean for society? Would cloned humans be stigmatized? Or would cloning result in superhumans? Would the combination of cloning and genetic modification allow scientists to create new types of beings? Should policy makers legislate against cloning human beings?

Shortly after Wilmut's announcement that he had cloned Dolly, the bioethicist Leon Kass published an article questioning the wisdom of human cloning in the *New Republic* (1997). Kass's article opposed the advancement of human cloning, referring to it as repugnant, revolting, and grotesque. The process of creating genetically identical human beings, according to Kass, violates social norms and threatens important values. (Note that humans who are genetic copies already exist: identical twins.) Yet Kass acknowledges several social reasons that people might want to clone another human being. Cloning could replace a child who has died or provide a genetically identical source of organs for a dying individual. Cloning could allow same-sex couples or infertile couples the opportunity to have their own biological children. Despite his initial repugnance to the idea of human cloning, Kass also recognizes the potential benefits.

The ethical, legal, and social issues involved in human cloning are significant. Given political and ethical opposition to the process, it's unlikely that human cloning will progress with reckless abandon in the scientific community. But technologically, at least, it is now a reality, so it presents an opportunity for us to ask questions about how human cloning would affect society and social relations. For starters, cloning would probably reshape our understanding of the family. Traditional family structures are already changing, but cloning could hasten that change by allowing new forms of kinship, such as a son who is also a twin. Similarly, cloned individuals wouldn't have two genetic parents; rather, they'd be the product of one cloned cell. Americans have reported widespread disapproval of the process of human cloning, so cloned individuals might face social stigma. The parent of a clone might even react negatively. After all, there are many environmental factors that affect how we develop in the womb and afterward. How would parents process these differences when they expected an exact replica? Conversely, they might have an unexpected negative reaction to a child who is too similar. Twins grow up knowing someone exists who shares many of their traits. A clone's parent experiences that burden (or shock) all of a sudden. Might parents of clones be too invested in their offspring, thereby squelching the child's individuality as they try to get it right a second time around? Do the social benefits of human cloning outweigh some of the ethical controversies?

Computers and the Internet

One of the most important technical revolutions of the late twentieth and early twenty-first centuries has been the development and expansion of the Internet. Its history stretches back to the 1950s, when the United States was engaged in the Cold War with the Soviet Union. Although originally developed as a means for the United States to regain its technological supremacy, the

Internet as you know and use it today has been around only since the early 1990s, when it was made available for public use. Today researchers estimate that 2.1 billion people use the Internet. That's over 30 percent of the world's population and the number is growing (Internet World Stats, 2011).

Many aspects of the Internet that we take for granted today are relatively new developments, and the Internet continues to change rapidly. Although wireless connections (WiFi or wireless fidelity) have been available since 1994, they have become widely used only in recent years. Likewise, the rise of Google.com from a company started in founder Larry Page's Stanford dorm room to a publicly owned company worth billions of dollars happened in less than a decade. Google is now such an integral part of our society that the verb *google* has become part of our language. Terms such as *blog, twitter, cyberspace,* and *Facebook* have also made their way into the American lexicon as the Internet has assumed a central place in our everyday lives. (See Chapter 4 for a discussion of its impact on interpersonal relations.) Of course, the Internet, like other technological changes, has significant social implications and plays a role in the social stratification of our society.

The Digital Divide

Does the Internet reduce inequality by allowing more people to access the information and resources available online? Or does it increase inequality by allowing some well-connected people to exploit the resources of the Internet, while others lag behind? The subject of this debate about the Internet and inequality is often referred to as the digital divide. Imagine that several people are about to embark on a job search. The first is a college senior on a campus wired with WiFi, so she can access the Internet 24 hours a day. She has her own laptop, but in case it breaks, there are several computer labs in her dorm and a handful more in the library. The second person lives in a poorer community in a major American city. Although he doesn't have access to the Internet in his house, a public library with a high-speed Internet connection is located around the corner. The library is open from noon to 8:00 P.M. every day, so he has fairly regular access to the Internet. It's much easier for him to search for a job today than it was five years ago, although sometimes it's difficult for him to get to the library during its hours of operation, and often there is a line for the terminals, in which case his access time is limited to half-hour slots. The third person lives in a rural community. She has used the Internet before but doesn't do so regularly, because there are few places in her town where she can access it. Even if she could afford to establish an Internet connection at home, her options for doing this are limited by which (if any) services are available in her area, dial-up being the most likely option. For her, finding a job remains primarily a process of talking to neighbors, inquiring in person at businesses, and passing out résumés. As a result of these differing levels of Internet access, the process of looking for employment is an entirely different experience for each person.

Digital divide differential access to telecommunications and information technologies based on socioeconomic status.

Chris Brunson (left) and his brother Sean (right) are members of the first family to receive a computer as part of a $1 million pilot program, the Habitat for Humanity Digital Divide Initiative.

It's undeniable that someone with a computer and an Internet connection at home has more access to online information than someone who has to go to a local public library to log on. But the digital divide doesn't just refer to the frequency with which people can access the Internet. It also refers to people's knowledge of the Internet and its capabilities. Many infrequent users might not know the extent of information available to them on the Web. They might not know that www.craigslist.com is a good source for housing in many cities or that www.idealist.org is a good place to look for nonprofit jobs. Such information can be found quickly through a Google search. In addition to factual knowledge of what's available on the Web, a more fundamental issue in the digital divide is people's differing ability to efficiently search and evaluate information. People with limited knowledge of Internet resources might have a difficult time navigating to their local newspaper's Web site, finding the job postings section, and searching the listings. They might not know little tricks such as putting search terms in quotation marks or using Boolean operators (+, –, OR). But with a little ingenuity and patience, they could learn such strategies online, too. Apparently, some aspects of the digital divide are really more part of a general education or skills divide.

The Social Divide

When discussing the digital divide, researchers often distinguish between the social divide and the global divide. The former refers to differences in knowledge and access within countries; the latter refers to differences in knowledge and access between countries. As discussed above, in a single country like the United States, people have differential access and ability to harness the powers of the Internet. If this divide between users and nonusers (or those knowledgeable about Internet resources and those lacking full knowledge of these resources) is increasing stratification within countries, then the Internet is causing a wider social divide within society (Norris et al., 2001). Figure 17.2 charts some demographic aspects of current Internet use in the United States, illustrating the social divide.

According to a 2008 survey published on CNET, 18 percent of Americans do not have access to the Internet at home (Musil, 2008). Meanwhile, another research study found that after education level, one of the main cleavages in the digital divide within the United States was the split between rural and urban users. According to a 2009 report by the Pew Internet and American Life Project, 70 percent of rural households in America have Internet access at home, as

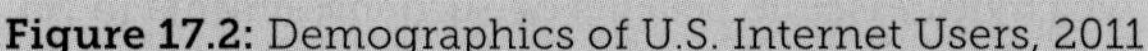

Figure 17.2: Demographics of U.S. Internet Users, 2011

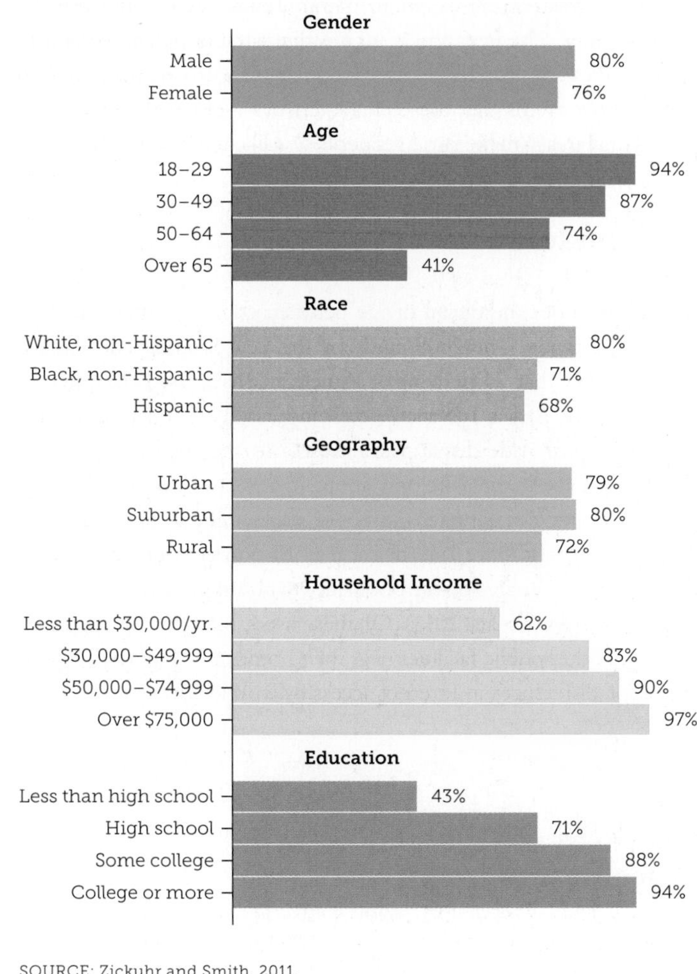

SOURCE: Zickuhr and Smith, 2011.

opposed to 74 percent of urban dwellers and 79 percent of suburbanites. In rural areas Internet access is less likely to be high-speed broadband. Grants from the USDA and from Obama's stimulus plan have targeted the development of broadband resources in rural areas.

What explains this difference between Internet use in rural and urban communities? Why are urban and suburban households more likely to have high-speed Internet connections than rural households? One answer could be that in rural communities there aren't as many companies able to install these connections, and as a result, rural communities don't have the physical infrastructure to become connected. This dynamic, in turn, results from the lower population densities in rural areas, which decrease the benefits of such investments to private or public Internet providers. This argument assumes that if rural communities had the same infrastructure as urban communities, they would use the Internet at the same rates. The Pew report argues that rural populations tend to be older, have less education, and have lower incomes than urban and suburban populations. The report claims that these characteristics—rather than the mere fact of living in a rural area—make rural residents less likely to use the Internet.

The Global Divide

When researchers talk about the digital divide between countries, they could be referring to the global divide. The 2009 study by the Pew Internet and American Life Project reported that 74 percent of Americans have used the Internet in their lifetime (2009). In Africa, Internet access and usage are much more limited. Recent surveys report wide disparities in access to the Internet in Africa, though even the highest access rates are only about 25 percent (Morocco, Egypt). In South Africa, the most developed country on the continent, approximately 9.4 percent of the population have Internet access. In poorer countries such as Malawi and Guinea, the percentage of the population with Internet access is closer to 0.9 percent (Internet World Stats, 2011). Of these users, many access the Internet at cyber cafés and other public facilities near their homes. See Figure 17.3 for a graphic illustration of differences in Internet access by world region.

Figure 17.3: Global Internet Usage, 2012

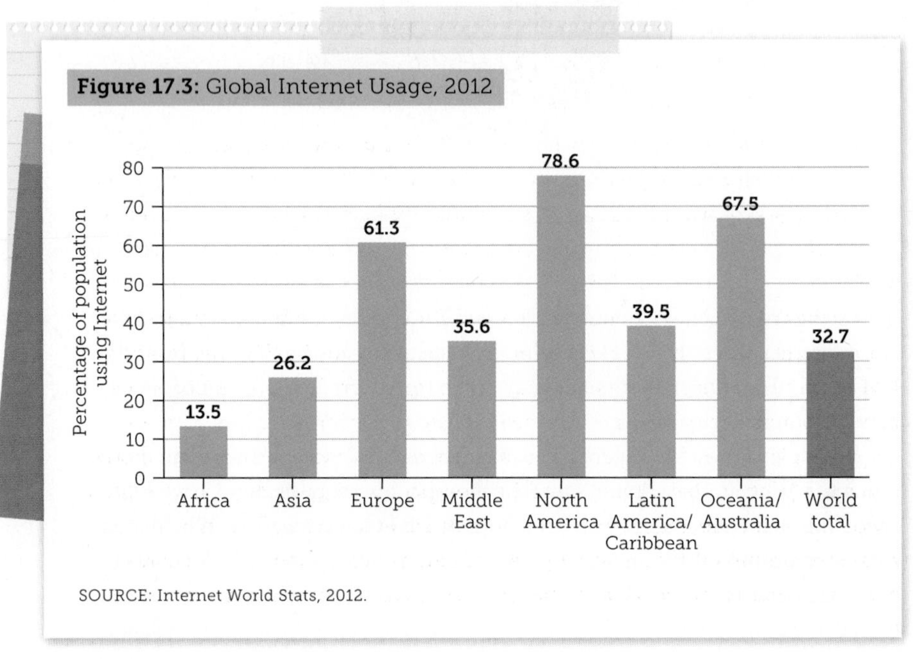

SOURCE: Internet World Stats, 2012.

Such divisions among countries may reinforce existing economic differences. If wealthy countries can harness the power of the Internet and related technologies, such as WiFi and personal digital assistants, to boost their economies while poor countries struggle just to get connected, the wealth disparity between rich countries and poor nations may grow. And as the gap grows, some scholars argue, it will become increasingly difficult for the poorer nations to catch up with wealthier ones. Others, however, argue that the digital age is just what the doctor ordered for poor countries, because landlocked nations or countries with few physical resources can participate in the globally enriching process of trade and development by becoming involved in the digital economy when distance and physical terrain are less relevant. Many New York City parking tickets are processed in West Africa, for example; Internet and phone-based troubleshooting centers for household products are increasingly located in India. The possibilities are seemingly limitless if a country can put the necessary infrastructure in place and develop the necessary human capital in the form of skills (and these are big "if's"). One of these skills is knowledge of English, because the Internet's origins in the United States have cemented English as the lingua franca or dominant language of world commerce.

Frankenfood v. No Nukes v. Abortion Politics

Nowhere is the intersection of science with politics more visible than when new technologies hit the public domain. Back in the 1970s, folks worried that microwave ovens would radiate their children. We kids were also warned not to sit too close to the television for fears of what the glowing phosphorous screen would do to our retinas. In the 1990s and 2000s concerns about a potential link between brain cancer and cell phones prompted a number of studies. The same was true for a theory about a link between vaccines (and/or the mercury-based preservatives in many of them) and rising autism rates. This last issue—driven by a constituency of concerned and angry parents—prompted not one but multiple studies by the National Academy of Sciences (an apolitical body of elite scientists that gets charged by Congress with assessing the scientific evidence on certain issues and delivering a consensus report). The vaccine worries even prompted Congress to pass legislation—alas, it was not the kind of law that parents would have hoped for. As part of the Patriot Act, House majority leader Dick Armey slipped in a provision that protected Eli Lily from any lawsuits on account of thimerisol (the preservative) in its vaccines.

Why do some technologies seem to evoke debate and even fierce political battles, while others—take the Internet or flat-screen televisions, for example—slip comfortably into our lives with little backlash? An interesting comparison in this regard is the relatively quiet reception that genetically modified food has received in the United States as compared with the concern and protests it has unleashed in Europe. Why the difference?

At first glance, we might simply say that we Americans tend to embrace new technologies more wholeheartedly. After all, aren't we a more future-oriented, newer country that embraces ingenuity and entrepreneurship? But that would ignore the fact that we actually lag behind our European counterparts with respect to adoption of many new technologies, such as cell phones, broadband, and high-speed rail, to name a few examples. Or we might argue that Europe simply has a more robust civil society—more geared to collective action than our individualistic American culture is. But that would ignore the fact that the 1970s and 1980s witnessed huge rallies in the United States against nuclear power (before and after the Three Mile Island reactor accident in 1979) that has basically shut down an entire industry for three decades. Meanwhile, France gets more than three-quarters of its wattage from nuclear power with nary a peep from its normally noisy citizens (even after the Chernobyl disaster that made Three Mile Island look like spilled milk).

The answer—at least in the view of sociologist of science John Evans—lies, ironically, in the more religious nature of the United States as compared to that of Europe. This answer is ironic in that we might at first think a more secular society such as those found in Western Europe would be more ready to embrace science and technology. "Well, in actuality from what I've studied of religious people in the United States, the idea of modifying plants, animals, and things is considered to be non-problematic," he explained to me during our conversation. "One of my interviewees might say to me," he elaborated, referring to his own study subjects, " 'Well, God has already given us that task to do.' Therefore, it doesn't particularly bother people to modify food forms" (Conley 2009o). If we already have dominion over nature as God's children, altering a few food-plants to be insect resistant or to pack in more nutrients is merely us fulfilling our divine role. (If we try to mess with the human form, Evans warned, that's an entirely different story.) In Europe, meanwhile, religion didn't really come into the picture and the underlying frame of debate was about environmental concerns.

Evans also emphasizes the role of professionalized bureaucrats. The more that debate is co-opted by professionals in the technocratic language of government agencies, like the FDA or the National Academy of Sciences, the less it becomes about moral value-laden questions and more about instrumental rationality (efficient means-to-ends). No longer do we ask if we should modify foods through genetic engineering, but rather—as Weber would have predicted—bureaucracy asks what is the safest, most cost-effective way to do so.

This last point doesn't explain the difference in GMO response across the Atlantic, as both the U.S. and Europe have large bureaucracies to deal with agricultural technologies, but it does provide some advice for those who would hope to depolarize some hot-button debates—say, gun safety or abortion: Create a federal agency to deal with the issue while somehow simultaneously turning down the volume on the debate going on outside the professional, scientific community (good luck with that!). "In the UK the abortion question was always tied in with essentially medical practice and part of the National Health Service," Evans explained. "Because abortion was always defined as part of medicine, it never had the same heat associated with it, whereas in the United States it was sort of semi-shunned by the medical profession, not brought into that framework, and remained in the public sphere as this divisive debate" (Conley, 2009o). So while we may continue to enjoy our Frankenfood with little indigestion, don't expect the abortion (or gun control) debates to go away anytime soon.

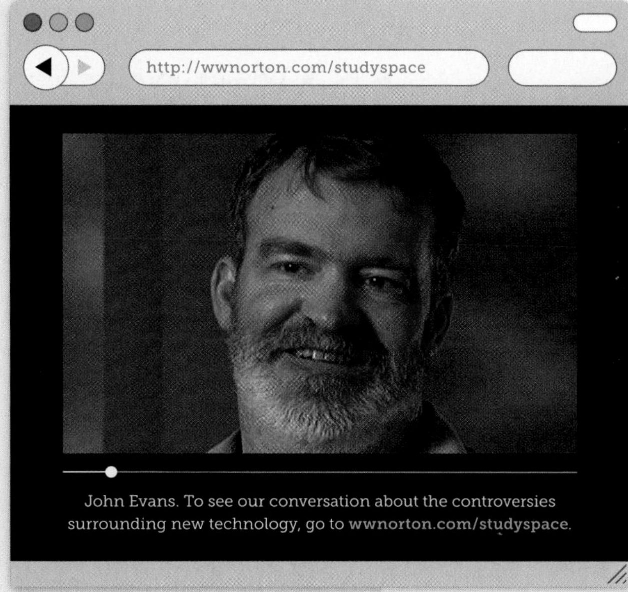

John Evans. To see our conversation about the controversies surrounding new technology, go to wwnorton.com/studyspace.

→ CONCLUSION

From genetics to nutrition to technology, scientific study is embedded in a social and political context. Progress in so-called natural science has strong implications for our social world and vice versa. As sociologists, we are interested in the effects that one has on the other. Important questions include how new technologies break down or reinforce existing social distinctions. For example, with the increasing prevalence and importance of the Internet, what will the digital divide mean in a few years? More important, what can we do about it? However, in addition to posing these empirical inquiries, we must also follow a more fundamental line of questioning. How do we know that we know? Are facts created, as Latour would suggest, or already in existence, just waiting to be discovered? Is the boundary between the natural and the social breaking down? As in the pursuit of science itself, in the study of science, the most important part of the entire endeavor is to ask the tough questions.

ASSIGNMENT

Select a scientific discovery or a technological innovation and research its impact on human societies. Your selection can be historical or contemporary. It can be major (like the automobile) or minor (like the pencil sharpener). Has it affected stratification in society? Has it reshaped patterns of family or community? Has it reduced poverty? Has it changed patterns of social control or deviance? Also, draw on material from other chapters when you think about the discovery or innovation.

QUESTIONS FOR REVIEW

1. How do both the Green Belt Movement and findings from Eric Klinenberg's *Heat Wave* demonstrate the relationship between the environment and society? What concerns and courses of action do these examples provide?
2. Describe the Human Genome Project and the green revolution. Using these examples, explain how policies that could yield desirable results sometimes have unintended negative consequences.
3. With new scientific discoveries and technologies come new questions and often new risks. How does Ulrich Beck describe "risk" and how does Charles Perrow's response direct us for the future?
4. According to Thomas Kuhn, what is a paradigm? Use Charles Darwin's theory of evolution to illustrate how paradigms affect the way scientists do research and describe a hypothetical paradigm shift.
5. Research is not conducted in a social vacuum. Can you provide two examples, one of them from this chapter, to show how scientific inquiry typically differs from the "traditional" view of science, including the way we choose what to study?
6. How do Thomas Gieryn's writings on the authority of science help us understand the concerns related to possible findings of the Human Genome Project? What is the potential link between science and stigmatization?
7. Why are sociologists interested in studying "the environment"? As an example, how would sociological attention to organic food result in a more profound understanding of inequality?
8. What is cloning? How do reactions to the cloning of humans (including embryonic cells) illustrate the link between scientific endeavors and social norms?
9. The editors at an academic journal decide what gets published (and therefore, what is "good" science). In this sense, how would the editors of a prestigious sociology journal be doing "boundary work" within their discipline and across others?

PARADOX

SOCIETY INVENTS TECHNOLOGIES TO MINIMIZE DANGERS FROM NATURE BUT THOSE SAME INVENTIONS CREATE NEW RISKS THAT NEED TO BE MANAGED. →

WATCH THE ANIMATED SHORT ABOUT THE SCIENCE, THE ENVIRONMENT, AND SOCIETY PARADOX AT

WWNORTON.COM/STUDYSPACE

"All the News We Hope to Print"

The New York Times

Special Edition
Today, clouds part, more sunshine, recent gloom passes. **Tonight,** strong leftward winds. **Tomorrow,** a new day. Weather map throughout.

VOL. CLVIV . . No. 54,631 NEW YORK, SATURDAY, JULY 4, 2009 FREE

IRAQ WAR ENDS

COURTESY ARMY.MIL

U.S. Army helicopters begin moving troops and equipment from Saddam Hussein's former Baghdad palace.

Nation Sets Its Sights on Building Sane Economy

True Cost Tax, Salary Caps, Trust-Busting Top List

By T. VEBLEN

The President has called for swift passage of the Safeguards for a New Economy (S.A.N.E.) bill. The omnibus economic package includes a federal maximum wage, mandatory "True Cost Accounting," a phased withdrawal from complex financial instruments, and other measures intended to improve life for ordinary Americans. (See highlights box on Page A10.) He also repeated earlier calls for passage of the "Ban on Lobbying" bill currently making its way through Congress.

Treasury Secretary Paul Krugman stressed the importance of the bill. "Markets make great servants, terrible leaders, and absurd religions," said Krugman, quoting Paul Hawken, an advocate of corporate responsibility and author of "Blessed Unrest, How the Largest Movement in the World Came into Being and Why No One Saw It Coming."

"At this point, the market is our leader and our religion. No wonder the median standard of living has been declining so much for so long."

Krugman said that the new Treasury bill seeks to ensure the prosperity of all citizens, rather than simply supporting large corporations and the wealthy. "The market is supposed to serve us. Unfortunately, we have ended up serving the market. That's very bad."

Much as Roosevelt, after the Great Depression, put the brakes on C.E.O. wages and irresponsible banking practices, administration officials claim that today we need to rein in the industry that has caused such chaos and misery.

"The building blocks of post-World War II American middle-class prosperity have all been swept away," said House Speaker Nancy Pelosi, who initially op-

Continued on Page A10

Troops to Return Immediately

By JUDE SHINBIN

WASHINGTON — Operation Iraqi Freedom and Operation Enduring Freedom were brought to an unceremonious close today with a quiet announcement by the Department of Defense that troops would be home within weeks.

"This is the best face we can put on the most unfortunate adventure in modern American history," Defense spokesman Kevin Sites said at a special joint session of Congress. "Today, we can finally enjoy peace — not the peace of the brave, perhaps, but at least peace."

As U.S. and coalition troops withdraw from Iraq and Afghanistan, the United Nations will move in to perform peacekeeping duties and aid in rebuilding. The U.N. will be responsible for keeping the two countries stable; coordinating the rebuilding of hospitals, schools, highways, and other infrastructure; and overseeing upcoming elections.

The Department of the Treasury confirmed that all U.N. dues owed by the U.S. were paid as of this morning, and that moneys previously earmarked for the war would be sent directly to the U.N.'s Iraq Oversight Body.

The president noted that the Iraq War had resulted in the burning of many bridges. "Yet our history with our allies runs deep," he said, "and we all know that friends forgive friends for anything. Or nearly." A spokesperson for the French Ministry of Defense confirmed that France would assist the U.S. withdrawal. "The U.S. helped the Soviet Union defeat Hitler. We do recognize that."

In conflict zones worldwide, leaders and rebels pledged peace. (See "In Conflict Zones Worldwide, Peace Moves," on Page A4.)

On Wall Street, reactions were mixed, with the Dow Jones Industrial Average up 84 points, to close at 4,212. While KBR stock was quickly downgraded to a "junk" rating of BBB-, defense contractors such as Lockheed Martin and Northrop Grummon started up.

Continued on Page A5

Maximum Wage Law Succeeds

Salary Caps Will Help Stabilize Economy

By J.K. MALONE

WASHINGTON — After long and often bitter debate, Congress has passed legislation, fiercely fought for by labor and progressive groups, that will limit top salaries to fifteen times the minimum wage. Tying the bill to a plan of overall reform of the U.S. economy, the bill echoes a similar effort enacted by President Franklin Roosevelt in 1942, which was followed by the longest period of growth for the middle class in U.S. history.

"When C.E.O. salaries remain stable thanks to high taxation of high salaries, there's little incentive to take big risks with shareholders' money, and the economy remains in a steady growth mode," said Senator Barney Frank, one of the bill's co-sponsors. "But when C.E.O. salaries can fly through the roof, there's a very strong incentive for C.E.O.s

Continued on Page A10

TREASURY ANNOUNCES "TRUE COST" TAX PLAN

By MARCUS S. DRIGGS

The long-awaited "True Cost" plan, which requires product prices to reflect their cost to society, has been signed into law.

Beginning next month, throwaway items like plastic water bottles and other items which are wasteful or damaging to the environment will be heavily taxed, as in many developed countries. Steep taxes will also apply to large cars and gasoline.

The new plan calls for a 200 percent tax on gasoline, comparable to the one long in effect in most European countries. Companies and consumers are already switching in droves from inefficient gas vehicles to new electric cars. "We suddenly have a waiting list 200 names long for the EV1," said Jake Cluber, the owner of Cluber Chevrolet in

Continued on Page A10

Recruiters Train for New Life
As a ban is imposed on recruiting minors, ex-recruiters nationwide look for new work. The Times follows one on his job-hunt odyssey through Manhattan and surrounding areas.

BY BARRY GLOAD, PAGE A12

Last to Die
Two proportional monuments — one to the Iraqi dead, 300 feet high, and one to the American dead, 15 feet high — are unveiled in Baghdad, and a five-year-old boy whose lifespan coincided with that of the Iraq War is remembered.

BY J. FINISTERRA, PAGE A5

USA Patriot Act Repealed
Eight years later, a shamefaced Congress quietly repeals the much-maligned USA Patriot Act, unanimously... or almost.

BY SYBIL LUDINGTON, PAGE A8

Evangelicals Open Homes to Refugees
Up to a million Iraqi exiles — nearly half of the total — will find sanctuary in Christian homes across the U.S., vows the National Association of Evangelicals. Other denominations are expected to follow.

BY W. WILBERFORCE, PAGE A7

Public Relations Industry Starts to Shut Down
The public relations industry has been criticized for misleading the American people, corrupting politicians, and even helping to start wars. Now, it's beginning the process of shutting down for good.

BY LOUIS BECK, PAGE A10

Ex-Secretary Apologizes for W.M.D. Scare

300,000 Troops Never Faced Risk of Instant Obliteration

By FRANK LARIMORE

Ex-Secretary of State Condoleezza Rice reassured soldiers that the Bush Administration had known well before the invasion that Saddam Hussein lacked weapons of mass destruction.

"Now that all of you brave servicemen and women are returning, it's important to us to reassure you, and the American people, that we were certain Hussein had no W.M.D.s and that he would never launch a first strike against the U.S.," Ms. Rice told a group of wounded soldiers at a Veterans' Administration hospital yesterday.

"I want you to know that if we had had the slightest suspicion that Saddam could use W.M.D.s against you, we never would have sent hundreds of thousands of you to be sitting ducks on the Iraqi border for several months."

Mr. Rice was referring to the fact that by August 2002, eight months before the ground invasion, the US had over 100,000 troops stationed in countries throughout the Gulf, a number that grew to over 300,000 shortly before the 2003 attack on Baghdad. Most of these were within range of the Scud missiles used by Mr. Hussein in the 1991 Gulf War, that could easily have been fitted with chemical or biological weapons if they had existed.

Rice noted that in the 1991 Gulf War, Hussein had used missiles to launch attacks on Israel, which made him popular with Arab citizens throughout the Middle East.

"Do you really think we would have given Saddam a major public relations coup by allowing him

Popular Pressure Ushers Recent Progressive Tilt

Study Cites Movements for Massive Shift in DC

By SAMUEL FIELDEN

The spate of reform initiatives undertaken by the Administration and both houses of Congress can be attributed directly to grassroots advocacy, according to a comprehensive study due out this month.

"In education and health care, most notably, but also in housing, banking, and the environment, we have documented unprecedented responsiveness on the part of political leaders," said Dr. Joyce Wellmon, director of the Plains Institute for Policy Analysis, a New York-based think tank. "Our data

The report includes extensive interviews with House and Senate staff, who speak of "unimaginable change," a "dramatic policy shift," and "a new era of accountability" since the elections.

"Not since the Great Depression has the interaction between popular movements and public leaders been so robust," said Jorge Lazaro, head of the U.S. Government Accountability Office. Lazaro cited, in particular, the Wagner Act, also known as the National Labor Relations Act of 1935, which recognized the right of workers to

Nationalized Oil To Fund Climate Change Efforts

By MARION K. HUBBERT

Congress has voted to place ExxonMobil, ChevronTexaco, and other major oil companies under public stewardship, with the bulk of the companies' profits put in a public trust administered by the United Nations, and used for alternative energy research and development in order to solve the global climate crisis.

While unusual, this is not the first time the government has chosen to take control of large corporations. From 1942 to 1944, U.S. car factories were retooled in order to produce tanks for the war effort.

18 Collective Action, Social Movements, and Social Change

PARADOX

WHAT MAKES YOU AN INDIVDUAL IS YOUR AFFILIATION WITH MULTIPLE GROUP IDENTITIES.

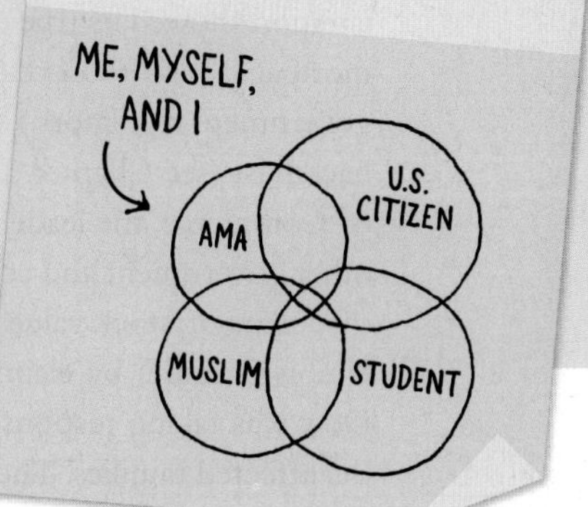

I first met Andy Bichlbaum and Mike Bonanno over a decade ago when they came to speak at Yale University on "21st Century Investing Strategies." As it turned out, the title was a tad misleading, as they actually showed slides of the Barbie Liberation Organization, which they had sponsored to switch the voice boxes of about 300 GI Joe and Barbie dolls and then restock them on sales shelves. They also spoke about the Web site they had just acquired, www.gwbush.com, in preparation for an antic disruption of the upcoming 2000 presidential campaign. I would quickly get used to—and in fact embrace—their deceptive ways. Andy and Mike aren't even their real names, so let's call them the Yes Men, which is how they are now known.

Their activism reinvented the tradition of political satire pioneered by Jonathan Swift in the eighteenth century. Over coffee after the lecture, we talked about their latest project: the co-optation of the Bush campaign Web site. I, in turn, told them about my idea for corporate criminal liability to go along with legal corporate personhood (bestowed by the Fourteenth Amendment to the Constitution—the very same amendment that guaranteed equal protection to former slaves after the Civil War—and recently reaffirmed by the Supreme Court's controversial *Citizens United* decision). I further explained that each shareholder would have to serve time in jail proportionate to their ownership stake, for crimes such as 10,000 counts of criminal manslaughter in the case of the Union Carbide chemical disaster in Bhopal, India. (See the policy box in Chapter 14 for a more detailed discussion of corporate criminal liability.) They loved it, apparently; before I realized anything was afoot, I was asked to speak at a law school on account of my role as a "Bush advisor on corporate crime."

After a little digging around, I found that I had been made a consultant to the presidential candidate on his corporate "tough love" stance—at least in the Yes Men's alternate universe. I panicked, asking them to expunge my name and university affiliation. And yes, I declined the law school invitation—something that Andy and Mike never do. But the damage was done without my assistance. The Bush folks pursued a cease and desist order against them, and in a public statement, Bush claimed that the Web site had gone too far in attacking him and that "there ought to be limits to freedom." (Subsequently, the Bush administration showed its true colors in allowing the Enron scandal and the subprime mortgage crisis to develop under the very noses of supposedly independent government regulators.) While that ended my brief stint as a "culture jamming" hacktivist (see Chapter 3), the duo went on to impersonate the U.S. Chamber of Commerce, the leadership of the World Trade Organization, and a host of other government and corporate officials. They even temporarily drove billions of dollars of stock value off the Dow Chemical company (which had acquired Union Carbide) by claiming on the BBC World Service television news that Dow was taking responsibility for the Bhopal disaster and would remunerate the affected families. The Yes Men went on to make two movies documenting their stunts and still seek social change through impersonation and satire with Web and other new-media tools that Jonathan Swift couldn't have dreamed of back in his day. I smiled a bit when I opened the "special edition" of the *New York Times* that they handed out on July 4, 2009. In the business section, "Carlton Donally" was the author of an article describing Senator John McCain's bold new plan to humanize corporations and get tough on corporate crime. Sometimes, you get swept up in a social movement whether you like it or not.

Collective Action: What is it Good For?

When you arrive at your sociology class, you probably sit in one of the chairs designated for students and take out your notebook. You perform these actions because you've been socialized as a student (as discussed in Chapter 4). If you were to arrive late, sit on the floor (assuming there are still seats available), or talk loudly during the lecture, this behavior would be called deviant (see Chapter 6). But what if every student sat on the floor? And as soon as the professor started to lecture, every student began to talk loudly? In that case, you would be engaged in collective action.

Collective action action that takes place in groups and diverges from the social norms of the situation.

Have you ever been involved in a protest march? Have you ever sent a letter or an e-mail to your congressional representatives? Have you ever signed a petition or attended a political rally? If so, you've been involved in collective action. This chapter introduces the interrelated concepts of collective action, social movements, and social change. We will examine the process through which collective action becomes a social movement and the way social movements promote social change. This chapter also delineates the broader premodern, modern, and postmodern periods of social transformation.

As mentioned above, for your behavior to count as collective action, you must act as part of a group and against the expected social norms of the situation. The type of behavior that counts as collective action also depends on both the number of people participating and the location of the behavior, however. If you started to speak in tongues in the middle of your sociology class, that behavior would probably be viewed as deviance. But if the entire class started to speak in tongues in the middle of the lecture, that could be called collective action. The same behavior in a Pentecostal Church, however, where it is normal to speak in tongues, wouldn't violate social expectations. Speaking in tongues at a Lutheran or an Episcopalian service, on the other hand, would again be considered deviance (or collective action, if you did it among a group).

University of California students march to protest sweatshops that manufacture college apparel. Why is this an example of crowd collective action?

There are two main types of collective action: crowd collective action and mass collective action (Granovetter, 1978). In crowd collective action, you must be face to face with the other members of your group. Collective action can also occur when people aren't physically together. Imagine the National Rifle Association (NRA) asking all its members to write letters to their senators protesting a particular law; such an initiative might produce tens of thousands of letters. This letter-writing campaign counts as collective action, too, but because the people writing letters live in different towns and cities, it is known as mass collective action. If all these letter writers travel to Washington, D.C., to march on the Capitol, then mass collective action becomes crowd collective action.

Theories of Collective Action

How does collective action come about? How do individuals decide to get together and violate social norms? Do they plan it on listservs or huddle in underground rooms late at night to plan their collective actions? Or does it happen spontaneously? Does collective action just erupt when certain people come together? How do they come to think of themselves as connected in some way?

Convergence Theory One theory of collective action, convergence theory, states that collective action happens when people with similar ideas and tendencies gather in the same place (Cantril, 1941). It doesn't necessarily require planning. The setting isn't particularly important, except that it attracts like-minded people. One example of convergent collective action is the riots that sometimes follow an English soccer (or, as the Brits call it, football) match. Who goes to football matches? Mostly zealous fans who are antagonistic toward their

Convergence theory theory of collective action stating that collective action happens when people with similar ideas and tendencies gather in the same place.

Greek soccer players cower behind riot police for protection from objects and flares thrown by rival fans after a championship game. How is a football riot an example of convergent collective action?

opponents (and who may have consumed a couple of pints of beer before and during the match). They probably don't plan to riot at the end of the game, but the convergence of like-minded (and drunk) people causes this collective action.

The main problem with convergence theory is that it's often reduced to the sum of its parts. If collective action results from drunken English football fans coming together, then why isn't there a riot every time they come together? Sometimes they go home peacefully. Other times they riot rancorously. Convergence theory doesn't explain the inconsistency of group action.

Contagion Theory A second theory of collective action, called contagion theory, claims that collective action arises because of people's tendency to conform to the behavior of others with whom they are in close contact (LeBon, 1895/2002). The mechanism by which movements grow is similar to the spread of a disease—adherents spread their enthusiasm infectiously among close contacts, who then become infected themselves, and so it goes. If you're peacefully protesting the city's decision to bulldoze your apartment building and suddenly the protester next to you starts chanting, "Two-Four-Six-Eight, We Will Not Negotiate," you'll be more likely to start chanting, too. Before long, every protester will be imitating the others, chanting slogans to save the apartment building. You might never have thought that you'd chant in a public protest, but the actions of other people influenced your behavior. If you've never been involved in a public protest, imagine yourself at a rock concert. As a particular song starts playing, some people begin to jump up and down. Soon, everyone is jumping up and down, imitating nearby concertgoers. Or if you're in the stands at an (American) football game and the fans start the "wave," when the wave comes around to your section of the stadium, you might feel as if you have little choice but to stand and wave your arms like everyone else. Contagion theory suggests that the behavior of other people in groups is contagious—especially under the encouraging influence of a charismatic leader.

Contagion theory theory of collective action claiming that collective action arises because of people's tendency to conform to the behavior of others with whom they are in close contact.

Although contagion theory helps explain how collective action spreads from one person throughout the entire group, it downplays individual agency (or, as we call it in everyday life, free will) and treats individuals as mindless sheep, thoughtlessly following the actions of their neighbors. Also, like convergence theory, it doesn't explain inconsistency. Why do some members of a group choose to chant, while others resist? Contagion theory doesn't explain why some situations are more conducive to collective action and why some people are more prone to imitating their neighbors than others.

Emergent Norm Theory The third theory of collective action, emergent norm theory (Turner & Killian, 1987), emphasizes the influence of "keynoters" in promoting new behavioral norms, especially in unusual situations for which already established norms are inadequate. Keynoters are not the same as leaders. They don't have to stand on podiums, shouting into megaphones. They can just be people whose actions become, either intentionally or not, the behavior copied by an entire group. Also, keynoters don't necessarily have to be the people in charge but can be anyone from whom other people take cues in a given context. If you have to evacuate an airplane using the emergency exits, one of your fellow passengers might start directing people out of the plane in an orderly manner. Even though she wasn't formally elected or appointed as the leader, people are taking cues from her in this situation which is highly unusual for most passengers. Imagine you're in a battalion of 800 soldiers, marching forward toward enemy lines. All of a sudden, a couple of soldiers in front start to scream and run back, which is uncharacteristic among troops who are trained not to defect. You're not sure what, if anything, has happened up ahead, but you, too, start running backward. Better safe than sorry, right? Those soldiers are the "keynoters," and their actions influence everyone's behavior as a new norm emerges on the battlefield. It isn't just that your neighbor is running, so you run too—that would be an illustration of contagion theory. Rather, it's that a novel situation has arisen in which collective behavior is determined, perhaps unwittingly, when the group copies the behavior of an individual or small group of individuals possibly for no other reason than that these folks were the first to be forced to react. The handful of keynoters within the group may be recognizable leaders, but more often than not they're just members of the group whose behavior sets the standard.

Emergent norm theory theory of collective action emphasizing the influence of keynoters in promoting particular norms.

Like contagion theory and convergence theory, emergent norm theory doesn't explain collective action perfectly (Aguirre et al., 1998). It doesn't always explain why particular people emerge as leaders. In some cases, like the soldiers in the battalion, it is fairly obvious, but in other situations why someone becomes a leader may not be so clear. In the airplane example, how did one woman emerge as the keynoter? Was it because she sat closest to the exit? Maybe the emergent leader had a particularly calm demeanor in the face of danger. Emergent norm theory says that new norms for behavior will emerge, but it doesn't suggest why particular people set the terms for this new behavior. The theory also doesn't explain why some actions emerge as norms within the group, whereas other actions don't. In the battalion of soldiers example, why did running away become the emergent norm? Why didn't the soldiers stay and fight, rather than turn away from their enemies? And why didn't the battalion take its cues from the other members in the front of the squad who continued marching forward? Emergent norm theory doesn't explain why one behavior rather than another emerges in collective action. It simply suggests that, in group situations, certain people in the crowd set the behavioral pattern that emerges as the norm for the group.

Value-Added Theory Neil Smelser (1962) borrowed the term *value-added* from economics to explain how social movements increase in value in a series of progressive stages. Value-added theory establishes six conditions that are required for a movement to coalesce and achieve a successful outcome. First, there must be a social strain present that existing power holders are unable or unwilling to alleviate. In New York in the 1970s an increasing number of pets were fouling the sidewalk with poop. This was a problem city leaders found rather trivial compared to all of the other troubles besetting the city. But pedestrians felt otherwise and they wanted action. The second requirement for a successful movement under the value-added theory is that folks must be able to agree on a definition of the problem. There was trouble early on in the movement for pooper scooper legislation because only some people felt that the problem was a lack of public decency on the part of dog owners, who should be made to pick up after their pooches. Others (mostly dog owners themselves) felt it was a lack of commitment on the part of the Department of Sanitation and asked for more street-sweeping. The third condition for value-added movements is that the folks must be free to act on their grievance. Awareness is nice, but the ability to act is critical. In the case of the aggrieved New York citizens, severe budgetary constraints made it impossible to increase the duties of the Sanitation Department, which curtailed the activism of those who were lobbying for sidewalk cleaners to scoop up the mess. Fourth, there must be a spark that ignites the controversy. In the case of New Yorkers lobbying for a pooper scooper law, they found their controversial episode when a young child was infected with a parasite found in dog poop. Too bad for the sick baby, but great for the movement that could now "prove" that public dog poop threatened the eyesight of babies citywide. The fifth requirement is mobilization for action: folks need to gather together in an organized fashion. For the pooper scooper law activists, already established mothers' groups took up the cause and later united with neighborhood groups on the issue of dog droppings. The sixth requirement necessary in the value-added theory is the failure of social control by established power holders. In the case of the poop scoop controversy, riots did not break out in the streets. In 1978, lawmakers maintained social control by passing a law requiring dog owners to scoop the poop or face a fine (Brandow, 2008). Had the law failed to pass, the steps of City Hall might have been lit up with flaming paper bags full of dog doo. (See Chapter 6 for more on social control.)

Identity and Collective Action

In Chapter 5, we examined the relationship of individuals and groups, and explored the way individual behavior is influenced by group behavior and vice versa. We also looked at network theory, examining how social networks develop and expand throughout society. In this section, we will build on individual–group interaction to examine the effect of collective action on the creation of individual identities.

Identity is simply a definition of who you are. How do you identify yourself? You might start by telling people that you're a student and stating the name of your school. If they ask for more details about you, you might tell them your religion, or maybe your race. If they continue asking for information, what other things could you use to identify yourself? The neighborhood where you live? Your political affiliations? Your sexual orientation? Your favorite baseball team? As we said in the paradox, what makes you an individual is your affiliation with multiple group identities.

Perhaps you're a white Catholic student at a particular university who lives in a particular neighborhood, is a Democrat, is straight, and is a Texas Rangers fan. To identify yourself, you have to refer to various group affiliations. In this case, you're associated with a group of Rangers fans, a group of students at a university, a group of people who are Catholic, and so on. Each of these groups contributes to your identity as an individual. If you add enough questions to the list above (What high school did you attend? What sport do you play at your university? To what extracurricular clubs do you belong?), you'll soon realize that you are probably the only person in the world who has that set of group affiliations. Your uniqueness as an individual comes from the collection of groups to which you belong.

Sharing a group affiliation with another person helps us develop emotional attachments to that person. If two people are members of Students Against Destructive Decisions, their identity as members of that group instantly gives them a connection. If nothing else, each person knows that the other believes strongly in stopping drunk driving and other risky behavior. Both may have experienced a life-altering tragedy that brought them to the group. This shared affiliation gives them an emotional connection from which to build their relationship.

Think about your best friend. Where did you meet him or her? Did you meet in a class at school or maybe on a sports team? Perhaps you met at a youth group or in your neighborhood? Unless you met randomly on the street and struck up a conversation, you probably met him or her in a context in which you already shared an affiliation, which became the basis of your current friendship. Thus, our collective associations (such as church groups, baseball teams, and high-school clubs) become the foundation on which we form emotional relationships with other people.

If you work the night shift at McDonald's, you might identify yourself as a fast-food employee or as someone who works late at night. You probably didn't start working at McDonald's because you identified as a fast-food employee; rather, you identify as a fast-food employee because you started to work at McDonald's. But you may have volunteered for the late shift because you already self-identified as a night owl. As you can see from these examples, not only does your identity determine the groups to which you belong, but the groups to which you belong also determine your identity. This back-and-forth process of identity and group association is an important part of collective action. If you grew up in a Jewish family and throughout your life have self-identified as Jewish, this is a stable, or static, aspect of your identity. But if in your early twenties you embrace a new religion and start to practice it, your religious identity will have changed, or become dynamic.

In addition to having both static and dynamic identities, you also have multiple identities because you belong to multiple groups. Although you think the Texas Rangers are the greatest team in baseball, you're more than just a Rangers fan. One of the difficulties of having multiple identities is that they can conflict with one another. If you identify as a Catholic but are also part of a pro-choice organization, you might find these identities difficult to resolve. As a result, one of the paradoxes of identity and collective action is that the lines between your multiple identities are often ambiguous and poorly defined. (Chapter 4 gives more information about role strain and role conflict for individuals in groups.)

→ Social Movements

Social movement collective behavior that is purposeful, organized, and institutionalized but not ritualized.

Collective action describes an event or a particular behavior. A march to protect a woman's right to make reproductive choices and a group of students spontaneously taking over a campus office to protest sweatshop labor are examples of collective action. But when this behavior becomes purposeful, organized, and institutionalized, collective action turns into a social movement. Social movements are not ritualized. They don't simply happen every year, like a Memorial Day parade or the New Year's Eve celebration at Times Square. Such rituals don't aim to change something about society; rather, they seek to celebrate a tradition of some sort.

Social movements, in contrast, are motivated by a social or political aim. They attempt to achieve these aims through conflict and action directed at particular opponents, not just through consensus and compromise. The participants in a social movement share a collective identity, but though they organize meetings and coordinate action, the tie that binds participants together in a social movement is a shared commitment to social change. In the initial stages of social movements, individuals generally participate primarily through informal social networks. As the movement develops, the institutions grow more formal and structured. Even in later phases, the movement is united through a common commitment to social or political change. But as Doug McAdam, a sociologist who has spent years examining social movements, pointed out in an interview for this book, "I still believe that social movement scholarship tends to be movement centric [so it focuses on movements], and invariably we overrate the causal significance or agency of those movements. Organized collective action is necessary, but not sufficient to generate a successful movement. . . . Some new threat or perceived opportunity in the broader social environment is a crucial component" (Conley, 2009p). Keep that in mind as you read through the following theories social scientists have developed to explain how social movements emerge and take shape.

Types of Social Movements

Social movements come in different shapes and sizes. Four main types exist: alterative, redemptive, reformative, and revolutionary (Table 18.1). They are distinguished by the people whose behavior they seek to change and the extent of societal change they hope to achieve.

Alterative social movements social movements that seek the most limited societal change and often target a narrow group of people.

Alterative Social Movements

Alterative social movements seek the most limited societal change; they often target a narrow group of people (Nicholas, 1973). They are usually issue oriented, focusing on a singular concern and seeking to change individuals' behaviors in relation to that issue. Mothers Against Drunk Driving (MADD) is one of the most successful alterative social movements. It targets a relatively small group of people (people who drink and drive) and seeks a specific behavioral change (getting people to stop drinking and driving). Despite the narrow scope of the group's efforts, MADD is largely responsible for the concept of the "designated driver," which has helped reduce alcohol-related motor vehicle fatalities in the United States.

MADD was founded by a mother, Cindy Lightner, whose daughter Cari had been killed by a drunk driver. Lightner founded MADD in her deceased daughter's bedroom, where she started to gather information about other victims of drunk driving. The organization expanded rapidly; many families of drunk-driving victims contacted MADD to become involved in the campaign. Soon MADD opened chapters in states throughout the nation and lobbied Congress and state legislatures for tougher drunk-driving laws. Among its successes, MADD was instrumental in raising the drinking age to 21 and lowering the legal blood alcohol content (BAC) to 0.08 percent across the country. MADD also aimed to change social behavior by raising awareness of the dangers of drinking and driving. Its publicity campaigns used real victims' names and faces to personalize the cause it was promoting. MADD's success came through both changing individual behavior and advocating for legal reforms. By 2000, one survey found that 97 percent of Americans knew that MADD

Table 18.1: Types of Social Movements

	LIMITED SOCIAL CHANGE	RADICAL SOCIAL CHANGE
Target particular subgroups	Alterative	Redemptive
Target entire society	Reformative	Revolutionary

Mothers Against Drunk Driving (MADD) volunteer Janet Priewe of Wisconsin holds up picture posters of drunk driving victims outside the U.S. Capitol. Why is an organization such as MADD an example of an alterative social movement?

stood for Mothers Against Drunk Driving—an astoundingly high level of name recognition for a social movement. Through its lobbying efforts, educational outreach, and publicity campaigns, MADD has successfully changed people's behavior about drinking and driving and, in doing so, has saved thousands of lives.

Another alterative social movement is the now-defunct Models with Conscience, run by Heather Chase, an organization that sought to recruit models who would agree only to accept modeling contracts for companies that were animal friendly and environmentally conscious. This is a good example of an alterative movement—it targeted only the subset of the population who were active models and only asked them to change a small part of their behavior. It's also a good example of the importance of leadership. When Chase left, her organization ceased to function. Models Against Fur has taken up the anti–animal cruelty cause, maintaining the spirit of at least some of Chase's original intentions in the modeling community despite her absence.

Redemptive social movements social movements that target specific groups but advocate for more radical change in behavior.

Redemptive Social Movements Like alterative social movements, redemptive social movements target specific groups; however, they advocate for more radical change in behavior. If you go to a specific organization—say, Covenant House—after you have run away from home and lived on the streets addicted to drugs, you're joining a redemptive social movement. Covenant House attempts to do more than change one particular behavior (such as drug use); it tries to help you reorganize your entire life. The social workers at Covenant House might help new residents find employment and open a bank account. They might then provide them with drug addiction counseling and bring together people with similar concerns to talk through their problems. At Covenant House, you'd be put on a fixed schedule. You'd probably wake up at a particular time, eat breakfast at a certain hour, and leave for work at the same time each day. This structured routine is aimed at reforming all your daily practices, not just a single behavior. This type of redemptive social movement seeks to return people to the normal routine of day-to-day society. Redemptive social movements such as Covenant House are often, although not always, affiliated with a religious group.

How is a redemptive social movement such as Covenant House different from alterative movements? In this picture, Covenant House volunteers serve meals to homeless, runaway, and at-risk young adults.

The Meadowlark Academy in Kansas for troubled teenage girls is another example of a redemptive social movement. The program at Meadowlark, which costs about $4,000 per month to attend, usually lasts for approximately 9 to 12 months and seeks to reform the girls' behavior. The girls remain on a rigid daily schedule that includes physical exercise, school activities, and group therapy sessions. The girls are usually sent to the academy by their legal guardians, sometimes against their will. The goal of the Meadowlark Academy is not to change one small aspect of the girls' lives (their grades or health) but rather to achieve a more holistic reformation of their way of life.

Reformative Social Movements Reformative social movements advocate for limited social change across an entire society (DellaCava et al., 2004). You might think that America, for the most part, is doing fairly well but would be a better place if everyone ate organic vegetables and biked to work. You might start by joining a group in your community like Critical Mass, which advocates for more bicycle-friendly commuting in Portland, Oregon; San Francisco; and hundreds of other global locations. Critical Mass is a loosely knit organization trying to make cities less dependent on cars. It encourages commuters to ride their bicycles to work and advocates for wider bicycle lanes on city streets. The movement is not limited to a small group of people; rather, it aims to change the transportation behavior of most of the Western world. However, the scope of change the group seeks is relatively minor (although its members might not agree). The group's not calling for a new system of government or an enormous change in people's approach to social interaction. The scope of its proposed change is limited to altering the way people commute to work, but members target pretty much everyone.

Reformative social movements social movements that advocate for limited social change across an entire society.

Another movement that falls under the category of reformative social movements is the slow food movement, whose proponents believe that it is healthier—for individuals, communities, and the environment—to eat locally grown food. Instead of importing cherries from Argentina, avocados from

Cyclists take part in a Critical Mass rally. What makes a movement such as Critical Mass reformative?

Mexico, and apples from New Zealand, the movement believes, it is healthier to eat food grown in one's own geographic region. The movement seeks to change a behavior across all of society, but the scope of that change is limited. The movement doesn't want to revolutionize our land ownership system or overthrow the government; it just wants people to be more thoughtful about the implications of their eating behavior for the environment, community well-being, and personal health. However, both Critical Mass and the slow food movement may believe that if we alter one aspect of our daily behavior, the ripples through our social structures will be so huge as to result in revolutionary change (and they may be right).

Revolutionary social movements social movements that advocate the radical reorganization of society.

Revolutionary Social Movements Revolutionary social movements are the final category of social movements. They advocate the radical reorganization of society (Goodwin, 2006). One example of a revolutionary social movement was that led by the Weather Underground during the Vietnam War. This group of students, a radical splinter group of Students for a Democratic Society, wanted to overthrow the American government through armed attacks. The Weather Underground bombed several government buildings (after issuing evacuation warnings), took part in jailbreaks and riots, and expressed solidarity with the Vietnamese who were experiencing the impact of U.S. military force. They believed that only revolutionary means, not political parties or processes, could bring about change. After the Vietnam War ended, most of the Weathermen surrendered, or were apprehended by the authorities, without having succeeded in their goals (Varon, 2004).

A more successful revolutionary movement took place in South Africa, where a coalition of political and labor groups, the United Democratic Front (UDF), sought to overthrow the apartheid government. The apartheid system in South Africa classified South Africans based on four "racial" categories: white, colored, Indian, and black. The government passed laws treating each racial group separately—and unequally. Blacks weren't allowed to enter cities without government-issued passes and were forced to live in separate homelands. The antiapartheid movement sought to change these racist laws, and in the early 1980s, it coalesced around the UDF. After the primary antiapartheid political party, the African National Congress (ANC), had been banned, the UDF quickly became the main antiapartheid organization. It incorporated black, Indian, and colored South Africans into a single movement aiming to overthrow the apartheid system. When the ANC was recognized as legal in South Africa, it took over the antiapartheid struggle, and the UDF faded into the background. This revolutionary social movement succeeded in ending the apartheid system. South Africa held its first democratic elections in 1994, electing the Nobel Peace Prize–winning Nelson Mandela, who had spent many years in prison as a political detainee under the apartheid regime.

Thousands of social movements exist throughout society at the local, national, and global levels. There are historical social movements that have achieved their goals, such as the antiapartheid movement in South Africa, and recent social movements that have just started advocating for social change, such as the slow food movement.

Two of the most famous recent social movements include the Tea Party movement and the Occupy Wall Street movement. Both could be considered revolutionary social movements, though, of course, the way they want to transform society differs dramatically. The Tea Partiers seek to radically reduce the role of government in American society by slashing regulations and cutting taxes back to a bare minimum. This characterization, however, is drawing a very diverse set of people, organizations, and viewpoints with a single broad stroke. Some self-proclaimed Tea Partiers want to impose socially conservative laws—such as anti-abortion statutes. Others are of a more libertarian ilk. Such diversity is inevitable for such a broad-based movement. However, unlike most revolutionary movements, the Tea Party organizations were seeded with money from very wealthy, politically active conservatives (most notably, the industrialist Koch brothers). As such, this movement has sometimes been called "Astroturf" as in false grass roots, though there is no question that

Members of the United Democratic Front (UDF) march in South Africa. The UDF sought to overthrow the apartheid regime that governed South Africa until 1994.

Occupy Wall Street members protest their eviction from Zuccotti Park, where the group had been encamped for nearly two months in 2011. What type of societal change do social movements such as Occupy hope to achieve?

the passage of the Affordable Care Act (a.k.a. Obamacare) health reform law precipitated a political uprising of sorts.

The Occupy Wall Street movement (OWS)—also known as the 99-percenters—represents an equally diverse set of social actors, though it was not seeded by wealthy donors. This is perhaps unsurprising, as the change OWS seeks to implement would not be in the interest of the wealthy. In fact, the very thing they are protesting is rising economic inequality. During the period in which they literally "occupied Wall Street" by camping out in Zuccotti Park in lower Manhattan, the participants went out of their way to make decisions through a deliberative process with no leadership cadre. This was, in fact, one of the reasons they never coalesced around a single message of change, though most 99-percenters would agree that marginal tax rates on the wealthy (the one percent) should be raised to address the needs of society, and independent of the revenue rationale, to lower inequality.

Both the Tea Party and Occupy movements face a choice moving forward: If they define key issues on which they seek change, then they lose some of their revolutionary appeal and become targeted, reformative social movements. The risk of such a narrowing is both success and failure. If, for example, Occupy focuses on raising taxes on the rich to redistribute revenue to the poor, then the group may very well fail in its efforts and lose steam. However, if the 99-percenters are successful in altering tax policy, then their raison d'etre has disappeared. But remaining devoid of concrete goals also poses challenges in the form of fatigue, frustration, and ineffectualness in getting *anything* changed.

Models of Social Movements: How Do They Arise?

To explain the emergence and sustenance of social movements, social scientists have developed several models. The earliest one is now known as the classical model and is based on a concept of structural weakness in society. This structural weakness results in the psychological disruption of individuals. When this disruption reaches a certain threshold, it gives rise to a social movement. Thus, social movements are a collective response to structural strain that has a psychological effect on individuals. In this model, political goals or achievements do not play a large role in the formation of movements.

Classical model model of social movements based on a concept of structural weakness in society that results in the psychological disruption of individuals.

There are several variations of this basic account. That is, strain can arise from different sources depending on the specific model. For example, society itself may create tension by engendering social isolation, which causes alienation and anxiety, thereby resulting in the form of discontent that leads to collective action and social movements. (Recall our discussion of capitalism and Marxism in Chapter 14.) Strain can also come from status inconsistency—when the rank orderings in society are somehow contradictory (for example, when the new merchant class has economic power but not political clout). The result within the individual is what psychologists call cognitive dissonance; this condition, in turn, may spur people to take action.

There are several problems with the classical model. How do we know what magnitude and type of systemic strain will give rise to a movement? Critics of this theory point out that strains of various types and impacts are always present in societies (McAdam, 1982). The theory cannot account for social movements arising in some circumstances and not in others. Another criticism is aimed at the way individuals are pathologized by this theory. In addition, the model completely removes the desire to attain specific, rational political goals while overemphasizing psychological tensions.

Social scientists subsequently tried to work through the weaknesses of the classical model by demonstrating that social movements are collective phenomena rather than symptoms of individual discontent. These revisions led to the resource-mobilization theory, which emphasizes political context and goals (McCarthy & Zald, 1973, 1977) but also states that social movements are unlikely to emerge without the necessary resources—or, if they do, are unlikely to succeed. Discontent and the availability of resources are the key factors that determine if a social movement will coalesce. From this perspective, it seems that the powerful or elite members of society have a greater chance of leading or contributing in other ways to a movement because they control more resources.

Resource-mobilization theory model of social movements that emphasizes political context and goals but also states that social movements are unlikely to emerge without the necessary resources.

Hundreds of students gather for a rally with Reverend Dr. Martin Luther King, Jr. (right) at the St. James Baptist Church in Birmingham, Alabama. Why were students and congregations key to the success of the civil rights movement?

Many theorists take issue with this account, because successful social movements like the anti-apartheid movement in South Africa are often led by those who are relatively powerless and have few monetary resources. Usually, these are the people who have most at stake in the success of the movement and in change. Theorists also point out that the involvement of the elite classes in a movement often results in its decline and eventual demise. If a movement becomes dependent on external sponsors, organizations within the movement can be easily co-opted by elite groups in cases of conflicting demands. Movements may have indigenous organizational strength (for example, the local churches and student organizations that nurtured the civil rights movement, as discussed in Chapter 16). It is not clear whether resource-mobilization theory includes this type of resource. Furthermore, what constitutes the grievances that lead to insurgencies is unclear.

Political process model model of social movements that focuses on the structure of political opportunities. When these are favorable to a particular challenger, the chances are better for the success of a social movement led by this challenger.

The most recent explanation of social movement theory is the political process model (McAdam, 1982), which focuses on the structure of political opportunities. When these are favorable to a particular challenger, the chances are better for the success of a social movement led by this challenger. This model combines variables internal and external to the movement (for example, indigenous organizational strength is internal to the movement, whereas the political context, such as the presence of political opportunities, is external). Three sets of conditions influence the development of insurgency according to this model: expanding political opportunities, indigenous organizational strength, and certain shared cognitions (for example, beliefs of injustice suffered and sense of self-empowerment) among a movement's proponents. Whether the movement is sustainable over time also depends on the responses of other groups in society. The political process model is not perfect, but it is widely accepted as the most useful model. Some criticisms of this model point to its structural bias (it focuses on political or economic structures), downplaying cultural or emotional components, which can sometimes play a major role (Morris, 2004).

No one model can predict movement outcomes in all cases. Why a movement succeeds or fails is not just about the resources available or how many political opportunities open up for movement participants. Some actors are better able to make use of the available resources and opportunities than others. Strategic thinking enables certain actors to make more of a situation than others who do not have such skills (Ganz, 2004). Moreover, what constitutes a favorable outcome for a movement is not always clear. A movement could win enormous gains but then lose them all over time. An example of this is the temperance movement in America, which achieved its ostensible goal of

Was the temperance movement a success? In the short term the prohibitionists achieved their goal, but what were the long-term consequences?

turning America into a dry nation, but only for about 13 years. Today few people would advocate prohibition, and many people suggest that, over the long term, prohibition resulted in a more irresponsible drinking culture in the United States (Gusfield, 1986).

What's more, sociologist Edwin Amenta claims that the success or failure of a movement cannot always be so easily measured. Amenta uses the Townsend Plan movement as an example. Conceived in the early 1930s, this movement organized about 2 million elderly Americans into Townsend Clubs to demand a pension from the government. By 1935, when President Franklin D. Roosevelt proposed Social Security legislation to the Congress, the force of the Townsend movement was palpable. The claims of the Townsend Plan's proponents were finally recognized by the welfare state. What seemed like a failure at the start actually created conditions for later success (Amenta, 2006).

Three Stages of Social Movements

Social movements are generally thought to evolve through three stages, assuming they survive long enough: emergence, coalescence, and routinization. The first stage, emergence, occurs when the social problem being addressed is first identified. As bicyclists realized that Americans' reliance on automobiles to commute to work was unhealthy for the environment, they began to raise

Emergence the first stage of a social movement, occurring when the social problem being addressed is first identified.

awareness of this social phenomenon. The problems of pollution and traffic congestion moved to the forefront, and bicycle commuting emerged as a transportation alternative. Likewise, in the early 1980s, a new deadly disease emerged among gay men in the United States. The disease would later be known as HIV/AIDS, but in the early stages, people didn't know what it was—they just knew that there was something askew within this particular community. Consciousness about this disease arose among a small population, and its members began raising awareness more broadly. In this early stage of social movements, a handful of people expend great effort merely to draw attention to a particular social issue that is otherwise not in the public consciousness.

Coalescence the second stage of a social movement, in which resources are mobilized (that is, concrete action is taken) around the problems outlined in the first stage.

In the second stage, coalescence, resources are mobilized (that is, concrete action is taken) around the problems outlined in the first stage. Through advocacy and education, more and more people become aware of the social problem. They organize meetings, start donating money, and begin lobbying elected political officials. New York bicycle advocates formed an organization called Transportation Alternatives and started encouraging their friends and coworkers to ride their bikes to work. They lobbied the city council for better laws and infrastructure to promote bicycle safety. Similarly, in 1981 advocates for HIV/AIDS awareness formalized an organization that started as a telephone hotline, the Gay Men's Health Crisis, and began distributing information to medical professionals and at-risk populations.

Because the formalization of organizations requires extensive resources, including money from donors and time commitments from members, some social movements simply fade away at this second stage. Social movement researchers disagree on the best ways to predict which social movements will make it through the second phase. Sometimes, organizations achieve their objectives before becoming formalized. If a social movement begins to form on a college campus to encourage divestment from a particular country and the university decides to divest, then the social movement might disappear before it takes on a formal organizational structure. Other social movements fade away because of a lack of support. Imagine a social movement with the goal of getting every person in a city to work on Saturdays. That social movement would probably disappear quickly, because few people would support it. In the process of formalizing their organization, participants in social movements might adopt new goals and abandon old ones. If you begin a social movement to halt the construction of a building, you may broaden your goals to improve zoning laws, building regulations, or development rights in your entire city.

Members of the World Wildlife Fund (WWF) demonstrate at the World Water Forum in Mexico City. Why might sociologists define the WWF as an institutionalized social movement?

The final stage in the formation of social movements is called routinization or institutionalization. In this stage, the social movement is institutionalized, and a formal structure develops to promote the cause. The organization may hire an executive director, a press secretary, and field organizers, for instance. It usually sets up a headquarters from which to organize its activities and coordinate its efforts. Social movements that have reached this final phase include NARAL (National Abortion Rights Action League), Pro-Choice America, a group that defends abortion rights, and Operation Rescue, an antiabortion organization. As each movement became effective and expanded its membership base, it became institutionalized.

Routinization or **institutionalization** the final stage of a social movement, in which it is institutionalized and a formal structure develops to promote the cause.

Social Movement Organizations

After social movements have been institutionalized, social movement organizations (SMOs) develop to recruit new members and coordinate participation. These groups also help raise money, clarify goals, and structure participation in the movement.

Social movement organization (SMO) a group developed to recruit new members and coordinate participation in a particular social movement; SMOs also often raise money, clarify goals, and structure participation in the movement.

One type of social movement organization, a professional movement organization, has a full-time leadership staff dedicated to the movement and a large membership base that plays a minor role in the organization. The professional leaders speak on behalf of their constituency and often attempt to influence public policy through lobbying efforts. For example, NARAL Pro-Choice America is an influential professional organization that evolved from a single mother's desire to effect change as a result of her own experience. It was founded as the National Association for the Repeal of Abortion Laws in 1969. In 1975, after the Supreme Court had preempted state law by declaring the right to abortion a part of the implicit constitutional right to privacy, the organization moved to Washington, D.C., to focus on national lobbying efforts in Congress. The organization is currently run by President Nancy Keenan and employs a full-time staff dedicated to organizing, lobbying, and communicating with its membership. The membership of NARAL Pro-Choice America plays a minor role in the organization other than financing personnel and activities. On occasion, however, members are called on to sign petitions, join marches, and contact their legislators about particular pro-choice issues.

Another type of social movement organization is called a participatory movement organization. In these organizations, unlike professional movement organizations, the rank-and-file membership is directly involved. (Recall our discussion of organizations as social networks in Chapter 5.) Participatory movement organizations can be further divided into two subgroups: mass protest organizations and grassroots organizations. A mass protest organization advocates for social change through protest and demonstration. Although it lacks the organizational structure of a professional movement organization, it

EMERGENCE, COALESCENCE, AND ROUTINIZATION IN THE HIV/AIDS MOVEMENT

In 1981, doctors began to identify a new disease among an otherwise healthy population of homosexual men. They didn't know what was causing the disease's symptoms or how to treat it, but they were able to identify that something was amiss within this subpopulation. Doctors initially called the disease "gay-related immune deficiency" or GRID. As awareness and fear mounted throughout the gay community in New York City, a group of 80 concerned men gathered in the apartment of writer Larry Kramer. They mobilized their social contacts and used the media to sound the alarm. Before long, the Centers for Disease Control (CDC) declared GRID an epidemic, and the gay community further mobilized to promote awareness of the disease and raise money for research. During this early period, the social movement that would later become the AIDS awareness movement in the United States was emerging from a small apartment in New York City.

As rates of infection grew, people rallied together to promote awareness of the disease and spread information about it. In 1981, concerned activists founded the Gay Men's Health Crisis (GMHC), around which the movement coalesced. The GMHC established an office on West 22nd Street in New York City and held its first fund-raiser in 1982. It began publishing a newsletter that was distributed to more than 50,000 doctors, hospitals, clinics, and libraries throughout the country. During this period, gay-related immune deficiency was renamed acquired immunodeficiency syndrome or AIDS. With the establishment of a formal organization, the AIDS awareness movement coalesced into a defined social movement.

Crowds visit the AIDS Memorial Quilt in Washington, D.C.

The activities of GMHC continued to grow. It funded the first AIDS discrimination lawsuit in 1983 and, two years later, organized the first international AIDS conference in Atlanta, Georgia. The following year, GMHC organized the first AIDS Walk—now an annual fund-raising event throughout the United States. Organizers also created the NAMES Project AIDS Memorial Quilt to memorialize individuals who have died from the disease. On December 1, 1988, GMHC promoted the first AIDS Day, and the federal government eventually passed laws to stop AIDS-related discrimination. President Bill Clinton was the first politician to run for national office with an explicit HIV/AIDS policy, illustrating his recognition of the serious threat the disease posed. In 2003, Mayor

A Gay Men's Health Crisis march during a 1985 gay pride parade in New York City.

Michael Bloomberg of New York City appointed a citywide coordinator of AIDS policy.

Although GMHC coalesced into a formal, organized social movement, the usual tensions inherent in a burgeoning social movement took root. One major challenge GMHC faces is broadening the focus of its work. Although the AIDS crisis started in a community of mostly white gay men in New York, its reach has spread to other communities. GMHC has been challenged to respond to the needs of communities of color, especially African American men, as well as those of infected women. In the mid-1990s, tensions erupted within GMHC about its ability to serve growing African American populations in need of HIV/AIDS awareness education, counseling, and testing. When the media mogul David Geffen donated $2.5 million to GMHC, its board of directors decided to use the money to open a facility in Chelsea, a predominantly white neighborhood with a large gay population in Manhattan. Three African American GMHC board members—Richard Dudley, Doug Robinson, and Billy Jones—walked out of a GMHC meeting in a highly publicized protest of the organization's refusal to consider expanding facilities into neighborhoods of color. Rather than expand to include women and straight men infected with HIV, the organization recently launched a campaign to curtail the use of methamphetamine, a drug used disproportionately by men who have sex with men.

relies on high levels of member participation to achieve its goals. The protesters involved in global justice and antiglobalization movements have often been associated with mass protest organizations. Rather than attempt to effect social change through organized political channels or political lobbying, participants in global justice movements take to the streets to promote their cause.

Critical Mass, the cyclist organization discussed earlier in the chapter (page 709), is another example of a mass protest organization. Once a month, hundreds of members of Critical Mass meet and ride their bikes through urban areas. Their goal is to disrupt traffic flow as a form of protest against the car-centered culture in cities. They aren't highly organized—they don't have an executive director, they don't lobby city councils, they don't even maintain an official Web site. Instead, they rely on high levels of participation: To disrupt the flow of traffic, hundreds of cyclists must participate. If only 15 cyclists participated, they wouldn't be very effective at drawing attention to their cause.

Other mass protests form in response to particular events. When the Republican National Convention was held in New York City in 2004, thousands of protesters converged on various parts of the city to denounce the gathering. To develop into a mass protest, they simply needed to agree on a meeting location. There wasn't a particular group that sponsored, organized, and arranged these protests against the convention but rather a loose network of activists who coordinated their efforts. Similarly, many protests against Arizona's draconian crackdown on illegal immigrants popped up in cities across the nation when the law passed in 2010. Although some professional organizations helped coordinate the protests, their success required large numbers of participants but very little organizational structure.

Grassroots organization a type of social movement organization that relies on high levels of community-based membership participation to promote social change. It lacks a hierarchical structure and works through existing political structures.

A grassroots organization also relies on high levels of community-based membership participation to promote social change. Like a mass protest organization, it lacks the hierarchical structure of a professional movement organization. Unlike a mass protest organization, however, such a group works through existing political structures to promote social change. Grassroots organizations are often involved in letter-writing campaigns and local political organizing to achieve their goals. They tend to focus on local issues and concerns, coordinating ideologically committed members through informal networks.

Grassroots social movements often develop around specific projects in specific places. A common example of such a movement is NIMBYism ("Not In My Back Yard"), when local communities oppose the placement of undesirable facilities in their neighborhoods. Such facilities range from power plants to low-income housing to prisons and drug treatment centers. In Harpswell, Maine, a group of concerned residents protested an attempt by ConocoPhillips Company to construct a liquefied natural gas (LNG) terminal off the coast of central Maine. The community believed that the LNG plant would ruin the quality of the natural environment, as well as damage the delicate local economy based on the lobster industry. There wasn't a formal organization to protest the terminal's construction, but the residents of Harpswell organized on their own to protect their environment and lifestyle. The citizens of Harpswell produced materials protesting the LNG terminal and started a petition drive. They contacted television stations and local officials. Their organization was spontaneous, and their approach wasn't radical. Nonetheless, they succeeded in stopping the construction of the LNG terminal, demonstrating the powerful potential of grassroots social movements.

A fishing family in Harpswell, Maine, protests the construction of a liquefied natural gas terminal. Can you think of an example of a NIMBY movement in your hometown?

In Florida, NIMBY forces opposed the establishment of oil pipes and drilling that might damage sea-bottom marine habitats. But often NIMBYism can be hypocritical and selfish. For example, in Cape Cod in 2001, community dissent delayed the construction of a large wind farm in Nantucket Sound. Some members of the community made claims of ecological damage, but mostly they were unhappy about the farm's likely obstruction of their very expensive views. (The protesters included the Wampanoag Indian tribe, which claimed the wind turbines would violate their rights by interfering with their views of the sunrise in sacred ceremonies.) The Massachusetts electorate generally votes in favor of wind power, but many Cape Cod residents opposed it when they would bear the aesthetic cost personally. Likewise, most Americans recognize the need for jails and homeless shelters, but they don't want to live next to them. When each locality pursues its own interests, sometimes the greater good is lost in the shuffle and the results are suboptimal from the perspective of society as a whole.

Voluntary Organizations: Why Is America a "Land of Joiners"?

In the 1830s, Alexis de Tocqueville wrote *Democracy in America* based on his visit to the United States from France. Tocqueville was surprised to find that America was, in his words, a "land of joiners." By this, Tocqueville meant that Americans frequently came together to join voluntary associations. "Americans of all ages, all conditions, all minds constantly unite," Tocqueville wrote. "Not only do they have commercial and industrial associations in which all take part, but they also have a thousand other kinds: religious, moral, grave, futile, very general and very particular, immense and very small." In democratic societies such as the United States, Tocqueville observed that citizens enjoyed greater equality than citizens in aristocratic societies. Although Tocqueville praised this equality, he also believed that it made democratic citizens independent and weak, so that they were politically powerless without voluntary organizations. After all, what good is one vote? He wrote that democratic citizens "can do almost nothing by themselves, and none of them can oblige those like themselves to lend them their cooperation. They therefore all fall into impotence if they do not learn to aid each other freely" (Tocqueville, 1835). Voluntary associations in Tocqueville's land of joiners were a way for independent citizens to assist one another.

The propensity of Americans to join voluntary groups—the Parent Teacher Association (PTA) at your high school, the local softball league, or a knitting club—has puzzled sociologists, historians, and political scientists since Tocqueville first wrote about America as a land of joiners. Why are Americans so likely to join groups? Our participation in elections and formal political processes is one of the lowest in the world, which makes the question all the more intriguing. Numerous social scientists have attempted to explain this American tendency to "join." Some, like Tocqueville, suggest that the uniquely egalitarian nature of American democracy has made Americans more likely than Europeans to enlist in voluntary organizations (Doyle, 1977). Because Americans are, in theory, relatively classless and individualistic and thus lack a hierarchical structure through which to seek change,

When they are not driving little cars in parades, Shriners raise money to help children with orthopedic conditions, burns, and spinal cord injuries. Why do volunteer organizations such as the Shriners play such a major role in American communities?

so the argument goes, they need voluntary organizations to gain political power. Other scholars suggest that America's unique pattern of settlement is responsible for high levels of voluntary organizations. In particular, the town square culture of early New England—in which people came together in town squares to discuss and debate current civic issues—created a long-lasting culture of voluntary association (J. Baker, 1997). Still others point to America's identity as a land of immigrants who formed voluntary organizations to unite with other immigrants who shared similar cultural or political values (Gamm & Putnam, 1999).

Although there is no single reason why America became a land of joiners, widespread agreement exists that the nation has had uniquely high levels of civic associations. There is some evidence that this tradition is on the decline, however, as the greater number of Americans joining associations may be merely writing checks and visiting Web sites rather than attending face-to-face meetings (see Chapter 5 for a discussion of declining social capital in America). A possible explanation for this trend is the rise of online associations. We may be joining (and organizing) more and showing up less because the Internet makes it easy to form new groups whenever we feel the need. It also allows for social connection (of some form) without requiring face-to-face contact. The explosion of Web sites like Facebook, MySpace, and Friendster is an important example of this phenomenon. Political activism has moved online as well, with the Obama and Howard Dean campaigns leading successful Web-based fundraising efforts that brought new donors into the political process. What's more, activist fundraisers intent on rapidly providing aid and relief to Haitians following the January 2010 earthquake invited donations via text messaging. The American Red Cross was able to raise more than $22 million through text messaging alone (Strom, 2010).

Social Movements and Social Change

The aim of all social movements is to change society. Of course, change happens whether social movements cause it or not. The past hundred years in the United States provide several good examples of social evolution. The beginning of the twentieth century was a time of high immigration to American urban centers. Garment factories in major cities like New York and San Francisco employed many new immigrants, whereas today the factories have moved abroad where salaries are lower. One hundred years ago, most of the immigrants to New York City came from Europe, but today most of the immigrants are from Latin America and Asia.

Fifty years later, in the years following World War II, the American suburb started to develop rapidly. These were also the years of the baby boom, in which many families had larger numbers of children. (This blip in birth rates 50 years ago has had huge implications for society today.) This was also the time when the civil rights movement emerged. And in 1965, the door to immigration was opened once again, remaking the demographics of the country. (See Chapter 5 for more on the social impact of the Hart-Cellar Act.)

Our society has changed drastically even since the early 1980s, when the United States was still engaged in the Cold War with the now-defunct Soviet Union. Very few households had personal computers, and the Internet hadn't been invented yet. The car phone, a precursor to the cell phone, was introduced so people could make calls while on the road. As these examples show, society has changed in innumerable ways in the last 100, 50, or even just 25 years.

Some changes in society affect the demographic structures of cities, states, and nations. In 1900, for instance, the average American household had 4.60 people, according to the U.S. Census. By 1970, the average American household size had declined to 3.14 people. In 2008, the average household size was recorded as 2.61 people (U.S. Census Bureau, 2010b). This dramatic fall in the size of the average household in the United States represents a major change in society over the past century. Of course, the change in household size wasn't the direct result of a social movement. Although many social movements did affect family size indirectly—such as the women's rights movement and the movement to promote birth control and legalize abortion—there wasn't a letter-writing campaign or a major protest march calling for fewer children to be born.

Other social changes have political implications. Fifty years ago, African Americans faced widespread discrimination and segregation in public facilities across some parts of the country. Since the civil rights movement of the 1950s and 1960s, legalized, overt discrimination has largely been eliminated (although other forms of discrimination remain). The civil rights movement was one of America's largest social movements—one that effected major social change.

Still other changes have to do with fashion, culture, and style. Although social movements don't generally coalesce around fashion issues, styles often become associated with various social movements. Think about those who advocated peace during the Vietnam War. Not everyone opposed to that war was a hippie, but hippie fashions such as tie-dyed t-shirts and macramé vests came into vogue

thanks to their prominence in the peace movement. Although the movement existed to spread peace, not fashion, certain styles of dress and behavior took front stage.

When sociologists talk about social change, they are referring to transformations in social institutions, political organizations, and cultural norms across time. Some changes are planned; others are not. The civil rights movement was a planned, organized attempt to change the way African Americans were treated in the United States. Hoping to implement social change, leaders and rank-and-file members of the movement organized events, planned sit-ins, and lobbied politicians. Smaller changes in society, such as changes in clothing fashion or hairstyles, are usually unplanned and simply happen.

Social change can be major or minor. In the eyes of different folks, it can be either important or trivial. Most people would agree that the strides made by African Americans in the civil rights movement represented an important social change, transforming social and political relations in the United States. On the other hand, the dwindling popularity of a particular brand of clothing is a trivial change, having little effect on people's lives. Also, some social changes affect everyone in society, whereas others are limited to a specific group of people. Laws about putting your feet on the seats in New York City subway cars affect the residents there but probably have minimal effect on the residents of Seattle, Washington. Other social changes, such as changes in the federal tax code, may affect everyone in the United States.

Premodern, Modern, and Postmodern Societies

Whereas social movements and collective action both respond to and create societal changes across short periods of time, the terms *premodern*, *modern*, and *postmodern* refer to social change across longer periods of time. Unlike specific

Compare these families from 1908, 1972, and today. How has life changed over the last 100 years?

social movements, which may span 10, 30, or 50 years, these terms express more fundamental societal reorganizations across broader historical periods—and may not even refer to specific periods of time. Rather, they are meant to indicate particular ways of understanding, framing, and conceptualizing society.

Premodern Societies

Premodernity social relations characterized by concentric circles of social affiliation, a low degree of division of labor, relatively undeveloped technology, and traditional social norms.

Modernity social relations characterized by rationality, bureaucratization, and objectivity—as well as individuality created by nonconcentric, but overlapping, group affiliations.

Premodern societies are what used to be called "primitive" societies: individuals live in small groups such as tribes or villages, there is a low degree of literacy, there is not much division of labor, and technology is relatively undeveloped. According to the sociologist Georg Simmel, such premodern societies are characterized by concentric circles of social affiliation (Figure 18.1). In this type of community, I am in the middle of my social world. Around me is my family; one circle beyond my family is my village; one circle beyond my village is my kingdom, perhaps. Each group is embedded—or set within—the groups around it: All the people in my family live in my village; all the people in my village belong to my kingdom. Because Simmel was concerned with social networks and affiliation, this model of concentric circles was useful to him for describing premodern social relations and the period of premodernity.

In premodern societies, individuals are the source of authoritative knowledge. Villages may have a spiritual leader, who passes knowledge along from the gods to the people. Tradition is very important in premodern society; customs passed down through the generations help guide everyday life. Without science or technology, premodern societies rely largely on myths to explain the world around them. These myths or stories are also passed down through generations. Basically, any society that has not industrialized or urbanized is living in a premodern mode, but in today's interconnected world, it is difficult to find an entire society that is premodern—although some tribal cultures deep in the rain forest of South America or located in other remote rural areas still socially distant from the rest of the world might fit the bill.

Figure 18.1: Premodern Society

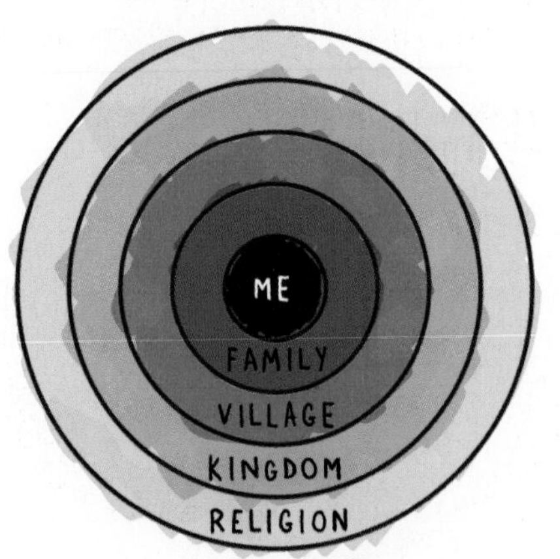

Modernity

The term modernity is used in many fields, including art history, literature, and sociology, with little agreement about what it means. One relatively uncontested notion, however, is that the modern way of life replaced the premodern period with the rise of science and objectivity. Although it is impossible to pinpoint an exact transition from premodernity to modernity in the West, some scholars point to the early fifteenth century, the beginning of the Renaissance, as the origins of modernity; others use the Enlightenment, and still others point to the Industrial Revolution as the key moment. No matter when it started, modernism has generally been characterized as an era of rationality, bureaucratization, and objectivity. As scientific knowledge gained prominence throughout society, it competed with religion as the primary method of knowing, culminating in the eighteenth-century Enlightenment. New political structures developed, with the rise of the modern nation-state and the process of urbanization. Technological advances revolutionized agricultural production and forms of mass communication. Increased industrialization and the specialization of labor revolutionized economic production.

For Simmel, modernity is characterized by the birth of the individual through a web of group affiliations (see Chapter 5). No longer does everyone in my family live in my village and everyone in my village share the same religion. As noted in our discussion of identity earlier in this chapter, each person is a unique combination of overlapping group affiliations (Figure 18.2). This happens by necessity when a society urbanizes, because city dwellers often come from various parts of the country and live side-by-side although they do not have a common background or set of group affiliations.

According to the sociologist Max Weber, modernity emerged from the Protestant Reformation, which introduced concepts of rationality and bureaucracy. It established a legal-rational system as the basis for authority in society, and it concretized structures of bureaucracy throughout society (see Chapters 15 and 16). This rational, logical system extended to literature, architecture, and art. The rise of the novel in literature, for example, reflected these forces by imposing a logical, linear flow on the narrative. The modern affinity for linearity and order extends to public space as well. It was the modern era that saw the rise of urban planning as embodied by Pierre-Charles L'Enfant's layout of Washington, D.C., and Georges-Eugène Haussmann's planning of Paris. As these examples suggest, modernity refers to a mode of social organization, not just a period of time. A common theme in modernity is the notion of progress—itself a rational, linear notion of advancement in a single direction of betterment. And central to progress is man's management of nature through technological innovation.

Figure 18.2: Modern Society

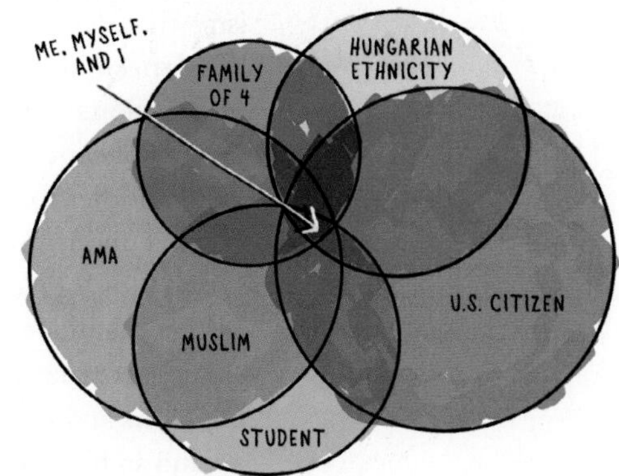

Since the 1960s, many scholars have claimed that the modern period is drawing to a close. Some point to the demolition of the Pruitt-Igoe Houses in St. Louis, a symbol of modernity, as the end of the modern period. They were one of St. Louis's largest public housing projects. According to many critics, they also demonstrated that

An aerial view of the Pruitt-Igoe housing project (left) and the exterior of the Centre Georges Pompidou. How does Pruitt-Igoe embody the modern period? What makes the Pompidou an example of postmodernism?

the modern, bureaucratic approach to public housing that concentrated low-income communities in high-rise public projects had failed. In 1972, the city of St. Louis decided to demolish the 33 buildings. The towering brick structures (characteristic of modern architecture) and the planned community of the projects (representative of the modernist faith in rational, organized government solutions to social problems) came to destruction at the hands of the St. Louis Housing Authority.

Postmodernism

Postmodernity social relations characterized by a questioning of the notion of progress and history, the replacement of narrative with pastiche, and multiple, perhaps even conflicting, identities resulting from disjointed affiliations.

Over the last three decades, many academics have claimed that we have entered a period of postmodernity. In the modern and premodern periods, people believed that society was always progressing forward and each new invention built on previous inventions. History was driven by clashes between opposing forces—such as communism and capitalism—and always ended with one side emerging victorious. Society progressed along the victorious path toward some ultimate endpoint that was presumed to be better than what preceded it.

Postmodernity, by contrast, has been characterized by a questioning of this linear progression. The grand struggles (like communism versus capitalism) that defined the modern period have been abandoned. In their place have arisen ideas about multiculturalism and the blending of different narratives. Some people have said that the postmodern condition is embodied by the concept of pastiche, taking a little bit from one culture and a little bit from another to form a sort of collage.

Like modernity, postmodernity isn't a specific time period but a form of societal (dis)organization. In many ways, the postmodern period is a reaction against the modern period. Postmodern critics often suggest that science and logic, the cornerstones of modernist thinking, have failed to answer important questions and have been abandoned. You may have encountered postmodern art and architecture, which don't follow the formal rigidities of modern art and architecture. Rather, they experiment with new mediums, new techniques, and new forms. Rap music—with its tradition of sampling rather than of sole authorship—is the archetypal postmodern music genre. The architect Philip Johnson's Seagram Building in New York City (completed in 1958) is often cited as an early example of postmodern architecture, because its beams are placed on the outside of the building, thereby inverting and challenging the notion of boundaries between inside and outside. A similar yet more blatant strategy may be seen in the Centre Georges Pompidou in Paris, constructed in the 1970s.

Simmel's group affiliation model if adapted to postmodernity might look like a series of nonconcentric, nonoverlapping, and sometimes even contradictory identities and affiliations (Figure 18.3). The individual seems to have disintegrated into fragments and multiple, postmodern selves.

Figure 18.3: Postmodern Society

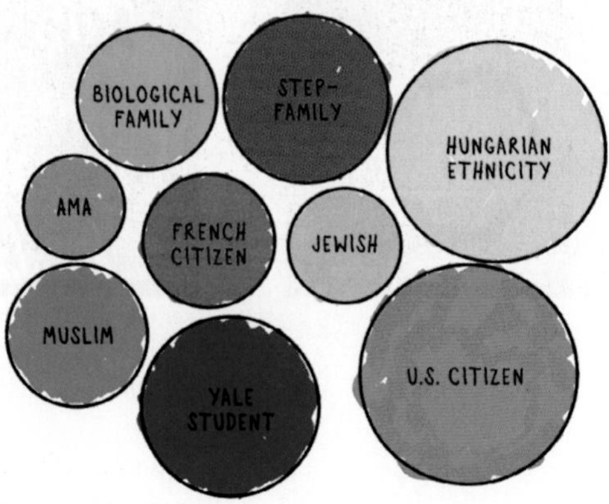

The Causes of Social Change

What drives social change, be it over 20 years or two millennia? What, besides social movements, that is? The short answer is that social change can result from technological innovation, the emergence of new ideas, changes in cultural identities, and conflict between social actors.

Technology and Innovation

As we saw in Chapter 17, technological innovation has been a major contributor to social change. The invention of computers and the Internet has brought about major changes in society. People can live in Milan, Italy, and hold telephone conferences with a company in San Francisco, California. Managers carrying BlackBerrys can communicate with their employees or clients 24 hours a day. People can work from home, so their homes may be farther away from their offices. Companies can locate their headquarters outside cities, where costs may be cheaper, because technology allows them to communicate instantaneously. Technology has a huge influence on the organization of social and economic life.

New Ideas and Identities

The emergence of new ideas and information has also contributed to social change. For example, in recent years, researchers have presented studies suggesting that the daily consumption of red wine lowers a person's risk of heart

Many social changes occurred in the wake of World War II, such as the founding of the United Nations, the Marshall Plan, and the conflict that resulted in the creation of Israel.

disease. This information has changed some people's behavior and therefore has brought about social change. Likewise, new information about the dangers of pollution, climate change, and global warming is altering people's driving behavior, increasing the demand for hybrid cars in the United States. As fully electric cars gain in popularity and the dangers of climate change become clearer, this information may serve as a major source of social change. Finally, ideas from political leaders have caused social change in many societies. The rising importance of Green Parties in many European countries has shifted social behavior and attitudes.

The examples above all involve information flowing from experts to the general public who then make changes for themselves or their families. But change can also arise without the help of professional experts like scientists or politicians. Changes in the cultural identities of groups of people need not be the result of findings from research studies or political movements. The secularization of some Jewish communities in America has not been the result of a top-down plan within the Jewish community or any other expert opinion. Intermarriage rates between Jews and non-Jews have slowly ticked up as Judaism has come to be seen increasingly as an ethnicity and a religion, allowing nonreligious Jews to maintain a Jewish identity without strict adherence to religious doctrine.

Social Change and Conflict

Other social changes are the result of conflict. The division of Germany in the aftermath of World War II was a direct result of the conflict itself. East and West Germany developed very differently during the postwar period, largely because of the political systems implemented at the end of the conflict. World War II was also responsible for the Cold War, the establishment of the State of Israel, and the founding of the United Nations, just to mention a few of the enduring legacies of the global reorganization after the war. When ideas or institutions clash, new patterns of social organization emerge from their resolution. This version of history was originally championed by the German philosopher Georg Wilhelm Friedrich Hegel (1770–1831), who, in his theory of dialectics, argued that conflict was the motor of history. Each idea (or thesis) has an opposite (or antithesis). The thesis and the antithesis come into conflict, eventually resulting in their resolution (or synthesis). The synthesis, however, becomes a new thesis, which then evinces a new antithesis and eventually necessitates a new synthesis. This process of conflict and resolution, according to Hegel, is how history proceeds.

Is Activism Dead?

The buildup to the U.S. invasion of Iraq in 2003 triggered the largest antiwar rallies since the Vietnam War era, both in America and abroad. Yet the chants of millions of protesters—"Regime change starts at home" and "Support our troops, bring them home"—seemed to fall on deaf ears in Washington.

One way of interpreting the failure of the peace movement to affect U.S. foreign policy is that it failed strategically. Street marches may be the peace movement's equivalent of heavy armor and infantry—which has been supplanted by high-tech weaponry that supposedly requires fewer troops. Maybe rather than taking to the public square, protesters should have taken to the new commons: the Internet.

Indeed, activists have started using the Internet to mobilize new forms of social movements. From straightforward petitioning drives (like those found on the clearinghouse site www.thepetitionsite.com) to more innovative sites (like www.voteswap.com, which enabled voters in hotly contested states who wished to vote for Ralph Nader in the 2000 election but didn't want to tip their state into the Bush column to trade their votes with Gore voters in a state where the election wasn't hotly contested), social movements have taken the Internet by storm. But how effective are these new online social movements? How do they compare to traditional approaches to organizing, raising money, and effecting change?

On the one hand, online social movements profit from a relatively inexpensive form of organization and action. E-mailing members is cheaper than sending letters, and maintaining Web sites is certainly cheaper than maintaining offices. On the other hand, politicians and policy makers can easily ignore online social movements. They know that e-mail is cheap and easy, and therefore they value it less. In the 2004 election, presidential candidate Howard Dean capitalized on the innovative use of the Internet to raise money for his campaign. While other candidates were holding fund-raising dinners and traveling across the country to raise money from major donors, Dean relied on hundreds of thousands of small contributions made through the click of a button on his Web site. In fact, the average contribution made to the Dean campaign through the Internet was $80. Throughout the campaign, Dean raised millions of dollars and, using the Web site www.meetup.com, mobilized more than 25,000 supporters to attend monthly meetings in about 225 cities across the country. Now the Internet is the primary way national politicians raise money.

Sociologist Doug McAdam points out that though the "information wants to be free" ethos of the Internet makes it easy for nascent social movements to disseminate their messages quite broadly, the connections between e-friends may not be as sticky as the connections between members of face-to-face organizations. McAdam noted that "successful movements, movements that take off very quickly, emerge within established communities and essentially the members of that community are threatened with the loss of member benefits for failure to go along. It's not clear that the electronic communities have the same capacity to monitor people's compliance with the new line of action. In an information sense, there's no question that these new technologies disseminate information, create all sorts of opportunities for new and original framings" (Conley, 2009p). But electronically based movements may not be able to take advantage of existing interpersonal relationships to mobilize behavioral change. If some long-lost friend of yours on Facebook sends out a mass e-mail about how she has decided to donate money to save Arctic seals, you are more likely to know about her choice and become aware of the plight of the seals than you would have been pre-Internet, but you may not feel compelled to do much. Yet if your roommate decides to go 100 percent organic and gives you a dirty look and a lecture every time you fill the refrigerator with conventional products, you may be more likely to make changes in your behavior just to maintain the otherwise good vibes in your relationship.

http://wwnorton.com/studyspace

Doug McAdam. To see our conversation about social movements, visit wwnorton.com/studyspace.

The most interesting uses of Internet technology for political protest are even more innovative and radical than voteswap

.com and meetup.com, however. We already learned about the Yes Men at the beginning of this chapter. Another example is Electronic Disturbance Theater (EDT), a group that organizes virtual sit-ins by publicly distributing an applet called FloodNet that, when activated, sends automatic browser "reload" requests to the targeted Web site every few seconds. EDT then organizes specific times when certain Web sites will be hit by thousands of protesters. The hope is to bring down the site. In 1998, in support of the Zapatista autonomy movement in Chiapas, Mexico, EDT targeted the servers of the Pentagon and Mexico's then president Ernesto Zedillo. In January 2002, 160,000 people downloaded FloodNet from the EDT Web site and deluged the World Economic Forum site; its server failed after a few hours and stayed down for the rest of the week. Ricardo Dominguez, EDT's cofounder, claims that the official goal of such sit-ins is not necessarily to disable servers but merely to disturb them. In fact, EDT calls its actions "performances." Of course, the distinction between disturbing and hacking is a fine line.

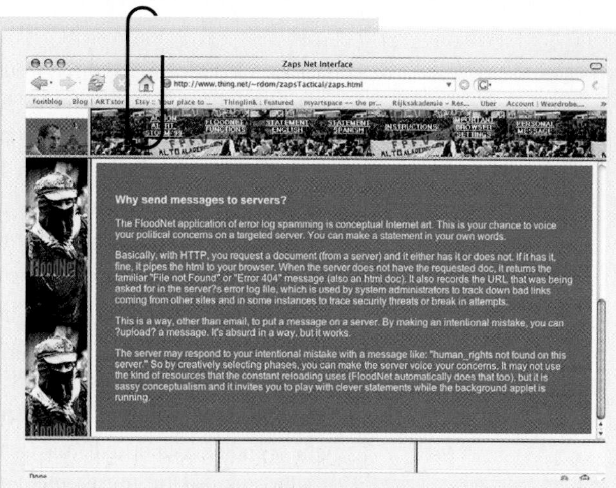

The Electronic Disturbance Theater (EDT) FloodNet Web page. Now that you are familiar with the different types of social movements, how would you categorize EDT?

Another fairly radical group is the Bureau of Inverse Technology (at www.bureauit.org) or BIT. Like many groups, BIT is an anonymous organization that straddles the line between activism and art, billing itself as an "information agency serving the information age." One of BIT's latest projects is the antiterror line. This is a phone number—actually two, one in the United States and one in Britain—to monitor infringements on civil rights by government authorities in the wake of antiterror legislation. The principle is simple: You, the user, program the number into your cell phone; if you are ever confronted by the police, dial the number, and the machine at the other end of the line will record the interaction as evidence. Marchers going to a protest might gear up their phones; blacks who are likely to experience racial profiling might also want one-touch dialing; and, of course, other populations that are highly vulnerable under the USA Patriot Act, such as foreigners, particularly those from Islamic countries, might want to be at the ready. If you are not able to record the interaction (after all, it might be difficult to get your cell phone to work if you are being bludgeoned by a policeman's billy club), then you can call the phone number after the fact to report the event. In this way, the web server will build an archive of information about the government that, in its public accessibility, stands in stark contrast to the way the government is increasingly collecting secret information about the population.

A common thread in the online activist and arts community is the use of "kits" to enlist other activists. A kit can be as simple as EDT's FloodNet program or as complicated as BIT Radio, which provides instructions on how to build a transmitter to jam local radio programming, replacing it with an activist message. BIT did this in New York City during the World Economic Forum, broadcasting environmental information over National Public Radio's frequency. The brevity of the illicit broadcasts prevents the transmitter stations from being found out. Anyone in the world can theoretically set up a BIT Radio station by following the downloadable instructions at the BIT site.

To varying degrees, what EDT, BIT, and the Yes Men have in common is the ability to generate media attention for their actions and to draw together like-minded individuals across vast spaces, thereby reducing the need to generate a crowd in any particular locality. One BIT engineer calls this "scale." Besides unifying a geographically diverse protesting community, another benefit of this kind of networked activism is that—for the most part—the police cannot shut you down with horses, water hoses, rubber bullets, and mass lockups. They can merely reregister your domain name or take down your server—and you, in turn, can find another in due time.

Whereas Ricardo Dominguez claims that street protest is a relic of a bygone era, the Yes Men and BIT demur. "There is nothing that can replace the generative power, the connections that are made in face-to-face contact during protests," claims a BIT spokesperson. Says "Andy," one of the Yes Men, in an e-mail interview: "It's clear that traditional forms of protest are still the most powerful. It's always hard to measure the effects of such things, but we know that people taking to the streets helped shut down the [WTO's] Seattle Ministerial [meeting], forced [British prime minister] Tony Blair to stop pretending he was representing the majority, etc.—lots of signs that it works." So in the end, the largest payoffs may be in the linkage of the Internet to live protest marches. After all, the peace marches of February 15, 2003, represented the largest worldwide protests ever recorded. And although they had been coordinated by many Internet activists, they still required people to show up, shout, beat drums, and in some cases risk arrest. It happened that they did not achieve their goal, but maybe they were just the beginning.

→ CONCLUSION

Social movements have changed the landscape of U.S. history. In the near future, the influence of movements may grow in scope. The increasing use of technology has brought together participants from all corners of the world. When protests were being organized for the 1999 WTO summit in Seattle, complete strangers got in touch and coordinated their efforts over the Internet.

Additionally, social change that resulted from previous movements—namely, the civil rights and women's movements—means that new categories of people have the opportunity to participate in new movements. On the other hand, as movements grow, do they weaken? That is, are we more likely to click on a link and less likely to take to the streets? Are the emotional satisfaction and sense of identity that we draw from social movements thinner as such movements broaden? To understand movements, let's return to the paradox at the beginning of the chapter. Affiliation with multiple group identities is central to an individual identity. Identity and its emotional impulses both result from and form the basis of collective action. An important type of collective action, directed at social change, is a social movement. Organizations of movement activists are crucial to social movements and the resulting social change.

One of the important points in this chapter is that movements are not individual efforts, and they take place when people are resourceful—not just when they have resources. Movement culture, solidarity among participants, and indigenous organizations go a long way in nurturing a movement. Although social change may be a product of social movements, immediate social change does not prove conclusively that a movement is successful, because the change may be temporary (for instance, the temperance movement). In contrast, a movement that does not produce immediate social change cannot necessarily be termed a failure. Another irony is that a successful social movement often puts itself out of business (think of the woman suffrage movement). So . . .

Because this is the final chapter, you get a bonus paradox:

PARADOX

A SUCCESSFUL SOCIAL MOVEMENT SHOULD END UP DESTROYING ITSELF, BECAUSE IT WILL HAVE SOLVED THE PROBLEM THAT MOTIVATED ITS VERY EXISTENCE.

The same is true for textbooks, so congratulations, sociologists, my job is done!

ASSIGNMENT

Historically, colleges are places in which many social movements have been born. Find a social movement on your campus and figure out when the movement was started, who started it, what its goals are, and who is an active participant. Can you match this social movement with any of the four main "types" of social movements described in this chapter? Document some of the major turning points in your social movement. Were there major victories that emboldened your movement or major defeats that damaged it? Determine if the movement you've identified follows (or followed) the typical stages of a social movement outlined in this chapter. Can you identify the emergence phase? What were the characteristics of the coalescence phase? Has the movement become institutionalized?

QUESTIONS FOR REVIEW

1. Pick a social movement discussed in the chapter to research on the Internet. Does it illustrate the three stages of social movements? Moreover, of the various types of social movement organizations, to which does it best correspond and why?
2. How has activism changed since the advent of the Internet? How has the line blurred between legally allowed activism and illegal behavior?
3. How are individuals' affiliations linked to identity? How has this relationship likely changed from premodern to modern to postmodern times?
4. What is the difference between "collective action" and behavior that is simply deviant? Describe this contrast through examples of both "crowd collective action" and "mass collective action."
5. A group of students suddenly marches out of the classroom shortly after their professor makes an inappropriate comment. Voters send an e-mail through an antiwar organization's Web site to their local official. Half of the population watches the season finale of a popular television show. How do the examples above demonstrate the difference between collective action, a social movement, and behavior that corresponds to neither?
6. How does the "resource-mobilization theory" build on a weakness of the "classical model" in the effort to theorize on the way social movements arise?
7. How is Alexis de Tocqueville's theory about America as a "land of joiners" consistent with the existence of various grassroots organizations?
8. Use an example from this chapter to describe some of the possible links between technology and innovation, social movements, and social change. How do information and the way it is circulated affect social movements and, in turn, social change?

PARADOX

WHAT MAKES YOU AN INDIVIDUAL IS YOUR AFFILIATION WITH MULTIPLE GROUP IDENTITIES.

WATCH THE ANIMATED SHORT ABOUT THE COLLECTIVE ACTION, SOCIAL MOVEMENTS, AND SOCIAL CHANGE PARADOX AT

WWNORTON.COM/STUDYSPACE

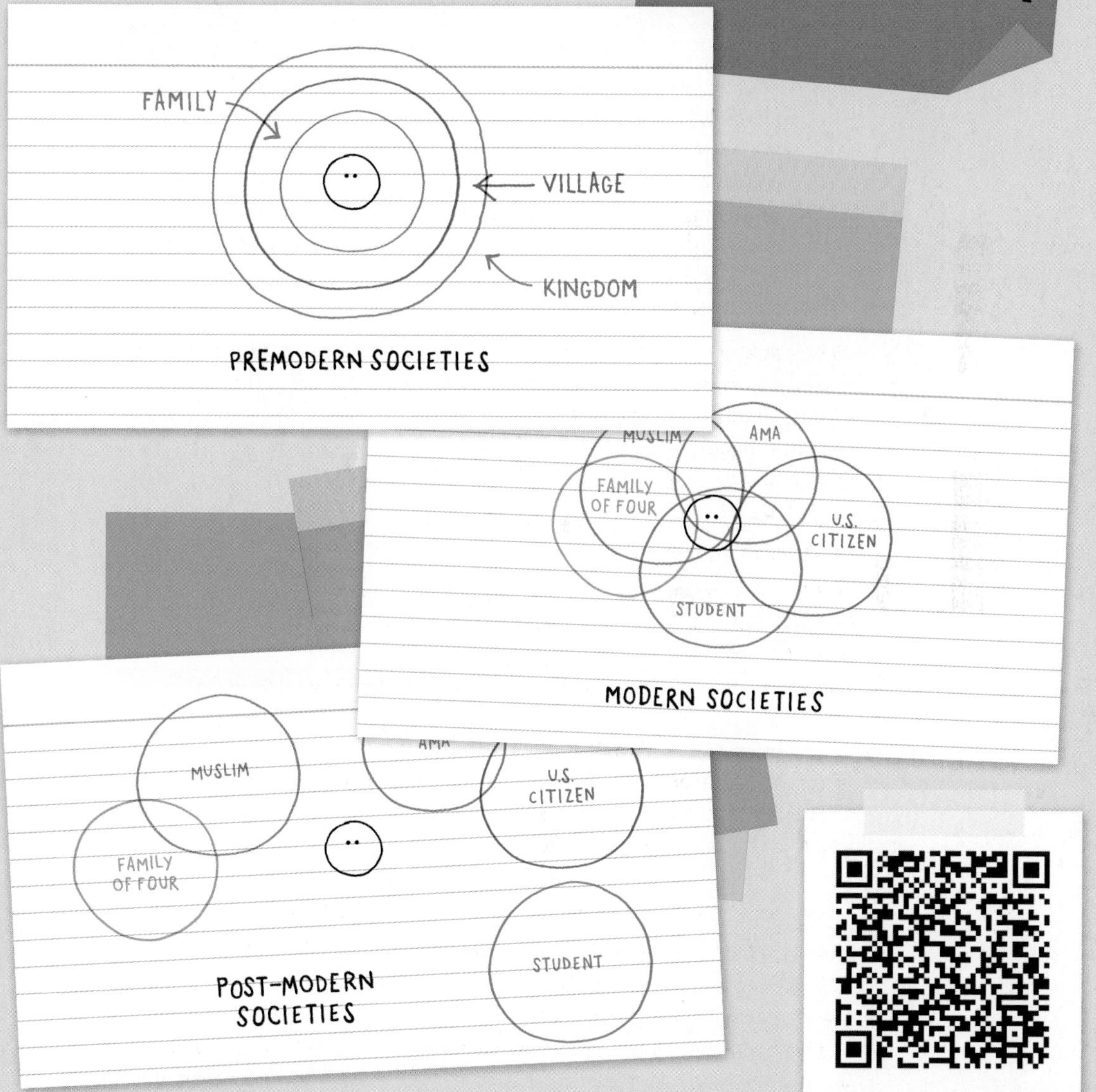

Thank you, readers of Chapter 15, for turning, as instructed, to this page. Why did you do it? That is, why did you follow instructions? You may have been curious, as when you turn to the last page of a novel to see how it ends. That would be an emotional or affective reason. But as much as I would like to think that this textbook is as exciting as a mystery novel, you probably were not dying of curiosity about the surprise ending of this chapter. It is more likely that you were just following orders. But you don't follow all orders indiscriminately, do you? You followed this order (or request—after all, I was careful to say please) because this book, or the voice of the author, has some sort of *legitimate authority*. Feel free to return to Chapter 15, where you left off. A systematic explanation of authority and legitimacy awaits you.

GLOSSARY

A

Absolute poverty the point at which a household's income falls below the necessary level to purchase food to physically sustain its members.

Achieved status a status into which one enters; voluntary status.

Affirmative action a set of policies that grant preferential treatment to a number of particular subgroups within the population—typically, women and historically disadvantaged racial minorities.

Agricultural revolution the period around 1700 marked by the introduction of new farming technologies that increased food output in farm production.

Alienation a condition in which people are dominated by forces of their own creation that then confront them as alien powers; according to Marx, the basic state of being in a capitalist society.

Alterative social movements social movements that seek the most limited societal change and often target a narrow group of people.

Altruistic suicide suicide that occurs when one experiences too much social integration.

Animism the belief that spirits roam the natural word, as in totemism.

Anomic suicide suicide that occurs as a result of insufficient social regulation.

Anomie a sense of aimlessness or despair that arises when we can no longer reasonably expect life to be predictable; too little social regulation; normlessness.

Ascribed status a status into which one is born; involuntary status.

Association *see* correlation.

Authority the justifiable right to exercise power.

B

Biological determinism a line of thought that explains social behavior in terms of who you are in the natural world.

Boundary work work done to maintain the border between legitimate and nonlegitimate science within a specific scientific discipline or between legitimate disciplines.

Bourgeois society a society of commerce (modern capitalist society, for example) in which the maximization of profit is the primary business incentive.

Bourgeoisie the capitalist class.

Broken windows theory of deviance theory explaining how social context and social cues impact whether individuals act deviantly; specifically, whether local, informal social norms allow deviant acts.

Bureaucracy a legal-rational organization or mode of administration that governs with reference to rules and roles and emphasizes meritocracy.

C

Capitalism economic system in which property and goods are primarily owned privately; investments are determined by private decisions; and prices, production, and the distribution of goods are determined primarily by competition in an unfettered marketplace.

Caste system religion-based system of stratification characterized by no social mobility.

Causality the notion that a change in one factor results in a corresponding change in another.

Champagne-glass distribution the unequal, global distribution of income, so named for its shape.

Charismatic authority authority that rests in the personal appeal of an individual leader.

Churches religious bodies that coexist in a relatively low state of tension with their social surroundings. They have mainstream or "safe" beliefs and practices relative to those of the general population.

Citizenship rights the rights guaranteed to each law-abiding citizen in a nation-state.

Civil religion a set of sacred beliefs so commonly accepted by most people that it becomes part of the national culture.

Civil rights the rights guaranteeing a citizen's personal freedom from interference, including freedom of speech and the right to travel freely.

Civil unions legally recognized unions explicitly intended to offer similar state-provided legal rights and benefits as marriage.

Class system an economically based hierarchical system characterized by cohesive oppositional groups and somewhat loose social mobility.

Classical model model of social movements based on a concept of structural weakness in society that results in the psychological disruption of individuals.

Coalescence the second stage of a social movement, in which resources are mobilized (that is, concrete action is taken) around the problems outlined in the first stage.

Coercion the use of force to get others to do what you want.

Cohabitation living together in an intimate relationship without formal legal or religious sanctioning.

Collective action action that takes place in groups and diverges from the social norms of the situation.

Collective action problem the difficulty in organizing large groups because of the tendency of some individuals to freeload or slack off.

Collective resistance an organized effort to change a power hierarchy on the part of a less-powerful group in a society.

Communism a political ideology of a classless society in which the means of production are shared through state ownership and in which rewards are tied not to productivity but to need.

Comparative research a methodology by which two or more entities (such as countries), which are similar in many dimensions but differ on one in question, are compared to learn about the dimension that differs between them.

Conflict theory the idea that conflict between competing interests is the basic, animating force of social change and society in general.

Conformist individual who accepts both the goals and strategies to achieve them that are considered socially acceptable.

Congregations groups of people who gather together, especially for worship.

Consumerism the steady acquisition of material possessions, often with the belief that happiness and fulfillment can thus be achieved.

Contagion theory theory of collective action claiming that collective action arises because of people's tendency to conform to the behavior of others with whom they are in close contact.

Content analysis a systematic analysis of the content rather than the structure of a communication, such as a written work, speech, or film.

Contradictory class locations the idea that people can occupy locations in the class structure that fall between the two "pure" classes.

Convergence theory theory of collective action stating that collective action happens when people with similar ideas and tendencies gather in the same place.

Corporate crime a particular type of white-collar crime committed by the officers (CEOs and other executives) of a corporation.

Corporation a legal entity unto itself that has a legal personhood distinct from that of its members, namely, its owners and shareholders.

Correlation or **association** simultaneous variation in two variables.

Credentialism an overemphasis on credentials (e.g., college degrees) for signaling social status or qualifications for a job.

Crime the violation of laws enacted by society.

Cult religious movement that makes some new claim about the supernatural and therefore does not as easily fit within the sect–church cycle.

Cult of domesticity the notion that true womanhood centers on domestic responsibility and child rearing.

Cultural capital symbolic and interactional resources that people use to their advantage in various situations.

Cultural relativism taking into account the differences across cultures without passing judgment or assigning value.

Cultural scripts modes of behavior and understanding that are not universal or natural.

Culture a set of beliefs, traditions, and practices; the sum total of social categories and concepts we embrace in addition to beliefs, behaviors (except instinctual ones), and practices; that which is not the natural environment around us.

Culture jamming the act of turning media against themselves.

Culture of poverty the argument that poor people adopt certain practices that differ from those of middle-class, "mainstream" society in order to adapt and survive in difficult economic circumstances.

D

Deductive approach a research approach that starts with a theory, forms a hypothesis, makes empirical observations, and then analyzes the data to confirm, reject, or modify the original theory.

Democracy a system of government wherein power theoretically lies with the people; citizens are allowed to vote in elections, speak freely, and participate as legal equals in social life.

Denominations big groups of congregations that share the same faith and are governed under one administrative umbrella.

Dependent variable the outcome that the researcher is trying to explain.

Deterrence theory philosophy of criminal justice arising from the notion that crime results from a rational calculation of its costs and benefits.

Dialectic a two-directional relationship, one that goes both ways.

Dictatorship a form of government that restricts the right to political participation to a small group or even to a single individual.

Digital divide differential access to telecommunications and information technologies based on socioeconomic status.

Discrimination harmful or negative acts (not mere thoughts) against people deemed inferior on the basis of their racial category without regard to their individual merit.

Divide et impera the role of a member of a triad who intentionally drives a wedge between the other two actors in the group.

Domestic partnerships legally recognized unions that guarantee only select rights to same-sex couples.

Domination the probability that a command with specific content will be obeyed by a given group of people.

Double-blind study an experimental study where neither the subjects nor the researchers know who is in the treatment group and who is in the control (placebo) group.

Double consciousness a concept conceived by W. E. B. DuBois to describe the two behavioral scripts, one for moving through the world and the other incorporating the external opinions of prejudiced onlookers, which are constantly maintained by African Americans.

Dramaturgical theory the view (advanced by Erving Goffman) of social life as essentially a theatrical performance, in which we are all actors on metaphorical stages, with roles, scripts, costumes, and sets.

Dyad a group of two.

E

Education the process through which academic, social, and cultural ideas and tools, both general and specific, are developed.

Egoistic suicide suicide that occurs when one is not well integrated into a social group.

Elite-mass dichotomy system system of stratification that has a governing elite, a few leaders who broadly hold power in society.

Embeddedness the degree to which ties are reinforced through indirect paths within a social network.

Emergence the first stage of a social movement, occurring when the social problem being addressed is first identified.

Emergent norm theory theory of collective action emphasizing the influence of keynoters in promoting particular norms.

Endogamy marriage to someone within one's social group.

Equality of condition the idea that everyone should have an equal starting point.

Equality of opportunity the idea that everyone has an equal chance to achieve wealth, social prestige, and power because the rules of the game, so to speak, are the same for everyone.

Equality of outcome a position that argues each player must end up with the same amount regardless of the fairness of the "game."

Essentialism a line of thought that explains social phenomena in terms of natural ones.

Estate system politically based system of stratification characterized by limited social mobility.

Ethicalism the adherence to certain principles to lead a moral life, as in Buddhism and Taoism.

Ethnicity one's ethnic quality or affiliation. It is voluntary, self-defined, nonhierarchal, fluid, and multiple, and based on cultural differences, not physical ones per se.

Ethnocentrism the belief that one's own culture or group is superior to others and the tendency to view all other cultures from the perspective of one's own.

Ethnomethodology literally "the methods of the people," this approach to studying human interaction focuses on the ways in which we make sense of our world, convey this understanding to others, and produce a shared social order.

Eugenics literally meaning "well born;" the theory of controlling the fertility of populations to influence inheritable traits passed on from generation to generation.

Evangelicals members of any Protestant denomination distinguished by four main beliefs: the Bible is without error, salvation comes only through belief in Jesus Christ, personal conversion is the only path to salvation (the "born again" experience), and others must also be converted. They proselytize by engaging with wider society.

Exchange mobility mobility in which, if we hold fixed the changing distribution of jobs, individuals trade jobs not one-to-one but in a way that ultimately balances out.

Exogamy marriage to someone outside one's social group.

Experimental methods methods that seek to alter the social landscape in a very specific way for a given sample of individuals and then track what results that change yields; often involve comparisons to a control group that did not experience such an intervention.

Extended family kin networks that extend outside or beyond the nuclear family.

F

Face the esteem in which an individual is held by others.

Family wage a wage paid to male workers sufficient to support a dependent wife and children.

Fatalistic suicide suicide that occurs as a result of too much social regulation.

Female circumcision the removal of a woman's sexually sensitive clitoris.

Feminism a consciousness-raising movement to get people to understand that gender is an organizing principle of life. The underlying belief is that women and men should be accorded equal opportunities and respect.

Feminist methodology a set of systems or methods that treat women's experiences as legitimate empirical and theoretical resources, that promote social science *for* women (think public sociology, but for a specific half of the public), and that take into account the researcher as much as the overt subject matter.

Feudalism precapitalist economic system characterized by the presence of lords, vassals, serfs, and fiefs.

Formal social sanctions mechanisms of social control by which rules or laws prohibit deviant criminal behavior.

Free rider problem the notion that when more than one person is responsible for getting something done, the incentive is for each individual to shirk responsibility and hope others will pull the extra weight.

Functionalism the theory that various social institutions and processes in society exist to serve some important (or necessary) function to keep society running.

Fundamentalists religious adherents who follow a scripture (such as the Bible or Qur'an) using a literal interpretation of its meaning.

G

Game theory the study of strategic decisions under conditions of uncertainty and interdependence.

Gender a social position; the set of social arrangements that are built around normative sex categories.

Gender roles sets of behavioral norms assumed to accompany one's status as a male or female.

Generalizability the extent to which we can claim our findings inform us about a group larger than the one we studied.

Generalized other an internalized sense of the total expectations of others in a variety of settings—regardless of whether we've encountered those people or places before.

Genocide the mass killing of a group of people based on racial, ethnic, or religious traits.

Glass ceiling an invisible limit on women's climb up the occupational ladder.

Glass escalator the promotional ride men take to the top of a work organization, especially in feminized jobs.

Global warming rising atmospheric concentrations of carbon dioxide and other greenhouse gases as well as higher global average temperatures.

Grassroots organization a type of social movement organization that relies on high levels of community-based participation to promote social change. It lacks a hierarchical structure and works through existing political structures.

H

Hegemonic masculinity the condition in which men are dominant and privileged, and this dominance and privilege is invisible.

Hegemony a condition by which a dominant group uses its power to elicit the voluntary "consent" of the masses.

Hidden curriculum the nonacademic and less overt socialization functions of schooling.

Historical methods research that collects data from written reports, newspaper articles, journals, transcripts, television programs, diaries, artwork, and other artifacts that date to a prior time period under study.

Homosexual the social identity of a person who has sexual attraction to and/or relations with other persons of the same sex.

Hypothesis a proposed relationship between two variables.

I

I one's sense of agency, action, or power.

Ideology a system of concepts and relationships, an understanding of cause and effect.

Income money received by a person for work, from transfers (gifts, inheritances, or government assistance), or from returns on investments.

Independent variable a measured factor that the researcher believes has a causal impact on the dependent variable.

Inductive approach a research approach that starts with empirical observations and then works to form a theory.

Informal social sanctions the usually unexpressed but widely known rules of group membership; the unspoken rules of social life.

In-group another term for the powerful group, most often the majority.

Innovator social deviant who accepts socially acceptable goals but rejects socially acceptable means to achieve them.

Institutionalization *see* routinization.

Institutional racism institutions and social dynamics that may seem race-neutral but actually disadvantage minority groups.

Interest group an organization that seeks to gain power in government and influence policy without direct election or appointment to office.

International state system a system in which each state is recognized as territorially sovereign by fellow states.

Isomorphism a constraining process that forces one unit in a population to resemble other units that face the same set of environmental conditions.

K

Kinship networks strings of relationships between people related by blood and co-residence (that is, marriage).

L

Labeling theory the belief that individuals subconsciously notice how others see or label them, and their reactions to those labels, over time, form the basis of their self-identity.

Large group a group characterized by the presence of a formal structure that mediates interaction and, consequently, status differentiation.

Legal-rational authority a system of authority based on legal, impersonal rules; the rules rule.

M

Macrosociology generally concerned with social dynamics at a higher level of analysis—that is, across the breadth of a society.

Master status one status within a set that stands out or overrides all others.

Material culture everything that is a part of our constructed, physical environment, including technology.

Matthew effect a term used by sociologists to describe the notion that certain scientific results get more notoriety and influence based on the existing prestige of the researchers involved.

Me the self as perceived as an object by the "I"; the self as one imagines others perceive one.

Mechanical or **segmental solidarity** social cohesion based on sameness.

Media any formats or vehicles that carry, present, or communicate information.

Mediator member of a triad who attempts to resolve conflict between the two other actors in the group.

Medicalization the process by which problems or issues not traditionally seen as medical come to be framed as such.

Megachurch typically, a conservative Protestant church that attracts at least 2,000 worshippers per week.

Meritocracy a society where status and mobility are based on individual attributes, ability, and achievement; a society that assigns social status, power, and economic rewards on achievement, not ascribed, personal attributes or favoritism.

Microsociology sociology that seeks to understand local interactional contexts; its methods of choice are ethnographic, generally including participant observation and in-depth interviews.

Middle class a term commonly used to describe those individuals with nonmanual jobs that pay significantly more than the poverty line—though this is a highly debated and expansive category, particularly in the United States, where broad swathes of the population consider themselves middle class.

Midrange theory a theory that attempts to predict how certain social institutions tend to function.

Milgram experiment An experiment devised in 1961 by Stanley Milgram, a psychologist at Yale University, to see how far ordinary people would go to obey a scientific authority figure.

Miscegenation the technical term for multiracial marriage; literally meaning "a mixing of kinds"; it is politically and historically charged—sociologists generally prefer *exogamy* or *outmarriage.*

Modernity social relations characterized by rationality, bureaucratization, and objectivity—as well as individuality created by nonconcentric, but overlapping, group affiliations.

Monogamy the practice of having only one sexual partner or spouse at a time.

Monopoly when one seller of a good or service dominates the market to the exclusion of others, potentially leading to zero competition.

Morbidity illness in a general sense.

Mortality death.

N

Narrative the sum of stories contained in a set of ties.

Nativism movement to protect and preserve indigenous land or culture from the allegedly dangerous and polluting effects of new immigrants.

Nonmaterial culture values, beliefs, behaviors, and social norms.

Normal science science conducted within an existing paradigm, as defined by Thomas Kuhn.

Normative view of science the notion that science is unaffected by the personal beliefs or values of scientists but rather follows objective rules of evidence.

Norms how values tell us to behave.

Nuclear family familial form consisting of a father, mother, and their children.

O

Offshoring a business decision to move all or part of a company's operations abroad to minimize costs.

Oligopoly the condition when a handful of firms effectively control a particular market.

One-drop rule the belief that "one drop" of black blood makes a person black, a concept that evolved from U.S. laws forbidding miscegenation.

Ontological equality the philosophical and religious notion that everyone is created equal at birth.

Operationalization the process of assigning a precise method for measuring a term being examined for use in a particular study.

Organic solidarity social cohesion based on difference and interdependence of the parts.

Organization any social network that is defined by a common purpose and has a boundary between its membership and the rest of the social world.

Organizational culture the shared beliefs and behaviors within a social group; often used interchangeably with *corporate culture.*

Organizational structure the ways in which power and authority are distributed within an organization.

Other someone or something outside of oneself.

Out-group another term for the stigmatized or less powerful group, the minority.

P

Panopticon a circular building composed of an inner ring and an outer ring designed to serve as a prison in which the guards, housed in the inner ring, can observe the prisoners without the detainees knowing whether they are being watched.

Paradigm the framework within which scientists operate.

Paradigm shift or **scientific revolution** when enough anomalies accrue to challenge the existing paradigm, showing that it is incomplete or inadequate to explain all observed phenomena.

Paradox of authority although the state's authority derives from the implicit threat of physical force; resorting to physical coercion strips the state of all legitimate authority.

Parenting stress hypothesis low income, unstable employment, a lack of cultural resources, and a feeling of inferiority from social class comparisons exacerbate household stress levels; this stress, in turn, leads to detrimental parenting practices such as yelling, shouting, and hitting, which are not conducive to healthy child development.

Participant observation a qualitative research method that seeks to uncover the meanings people give their behavior by observing social actions in practice.

Party a group that is similar to a small group but multifocal.

Patriarchy a nearly universal system involving the subordination of femininity to masculinity.

Perverse incentives reward structures that lead to suboptimal outcomes by stimulating counterproductive behavior; for example, welfare—to the extent that it discourages work efforts—is argued to have perverse incentives.

Placebo a simulated treatment given to a control group in an experimental study to factor out the effect of merely being in an experiment from the effect of the actual treatment under consideration.

Pluralism the presence and engaged coexistence of numerous distinct groups in one society.

Political participation activity that has the intent or effect of influencing government action.

Political party an organization that seeks to gain power in a government, generally by backing candidates for office who subscribe (to the extent possible) to the organization's political ideals.

Political process model model of social movements that focuses on the structure of political opportunities. When these are favorable to a particular challenger, the chances are better for the success of a social movement led by this challenger.

Political rights the rights guaranteeing a citizen's ability to participate in politics, including the right to vote and the right to hold an elected office.

Politics power relations among people or other social actors.

Polyandry the practice of having multiple husbands simultaneously.

Polygamy the practice of having more than one sexual partner or spouse at a time.

Polygyny the practice of having multiple wives simultaneously.

Population an entire group of individual persons, objects, or items from which samples may be drawn.

Positivist sociology a strain within sociology that believes the social world can be described and predicted by certain describable relationships (akin to a social physics).

Postmodernism a condition characterized by a questioning of the notion of progress and history, the replacement of narrative within pastiche, and multiple, perhaps even conflicting, identities resulting from disjointed affiliations.

Postmodernity social relations characterized by a questioning of the notion of progress and history, the replacement of narrative with pastiche, and multiple, perhaps even conflicting, identities resulting from disjointed affiliations.

Power the ability to carry out one's own will despite resistance.

Prejudice thoughts and feelings about an ethnic or racial group.

Premodernity social relations characterized by concentric circles of social affiliation, a low degree of division of labor, relatively undeveloped technology, and traditional social norms.

Primary deviance the first act of rule-breaking that may incur a label of "deviant" and thus influence how people think about and act toward you.

Primary groups social groups, such as family or friends, composed of intimate face-to-face relationships that strongly influence the attitudes and ideals of those involved.

Primordialism Clifford Geertz's term to explain the strength of ethnic ties because they are fixed in deeply felt or primordial ties to one's homeland culture.

Profane the things of mundane, everyday life.

Proletariat the working class.

Public sociology the practice of sociological research, teaching, and service that seeks to engage a wide audience for a normative, productive end.

Q

Qualitative methods methods that attempt to collect information about the social world that cannot be readily converted to numeric form.

Quantitative methods methods that seek to obtain information about the social world that is already in or can be converted to numeric form.

R

Race a group of people who share a set of characteristics—typically, but not always, physical ones—and are said to share a common bloodline.

Racialization the formation of a new racial identity, in which ideological boundaries of difference are drawn around a formerly unnoticed group of people.

Racism the belief that members of separate races possess different and unequal traits.

Rationalization an ever-expanding process of ordering or organizing.

Rebel individual who rejects both traditional goals and traditional means and wants to alter or destroy the social institutions from which he or she is alienated.

Recidivism when an individual who has been involved with the criminal justice system reverts back to criminal behavior.

Redemptive social movements social movements that target specific groups but advocate for more radical social change in behavior.

Reference group a group that helps us understand or make sense of our position in society relative to other groups.

Reflection theory the idea that culture is a projection of social structures and relationships into the public sphere, a screen onto which the film of the underlying reality or social structures of our society is projected.

Reflexive spirituality a contemporary religious movement that encourages followers to look to religion for meaning, wisdom, and profound thought and feeling rather than for absolute truths on how the world works.

Reflexivity analyzing and critically considering our own role in, and effect on, our research.

Reformative social movements social movements that advocate for limited social change across an entire society.

Relative poverty a measurement of poverty based on a percentage of the median income in a given location.

Reliability likelihood of obtaining consistent results using the same measure.

Religion a system of beliefs, traditions, and practices around sacred things, a set of shared "stories" that guide belief and action.

Religious experience an individual's spiritual feelings, acts, and experiences.

Research methods approaches that social scientists use for investigating the answers to questions.

Resocialization the process by which one's sense of social values, beliefs, and norms are reengineered, often deliberately through an intense social process that may take place in a total institution.

Resource dilution model hypothesis stating that parental resources are finite and that each additional child dilutes them.

Resource-mobilization theory model of social movements that emphasizes political context and goals but also states that social movements are unlikely to emerge without the necessary resources.

Retreatist one who rejects both socially acceptable means and goals by completely retreating from, or not participating in, society.

Reverse causality a situation in which the researcher believes that A results in a change in B, but B, in fact, is causing A.

Revolutionary social movements social movements that advocate the radical reorganization of society.

Risk society a society that both produces and is concerned with mitigating risks, especially manufactured risks (ones that result from human activity).

Ritualist individual who rejects socially defined goals in order to live within his or her own means.

Role the duties and behaviors expected of someone who holds a particular status.

Role conflict the tension caused by competing demands between two or more roles pertaining to different statuses.

Role strain the incompatibility among roles corresponding to a single status.

Routinization or **institutionalization** the final stage of a social movement, in which it is institutionalized and a formal structure develops to promote the cause; the clear, rule-governed procedures used repeatedly for decision making.

S

Sacred holy things meant for special use and kept separate from the profane; the sacred realm is unknowable and mystical, so it inspires us with feelings of awe and wonder.

Sacred canopy Peter Berger's term to describe the entire set of religious norms, symbols, and beliefs that express the most important thing in life, namely, the feeling that life is worth living and that reality is meaningful and ordered, not just random chaos.

Sample the subset of the population from which you are actually collecting data.

Scientific racism nineteenth-century theories of race that characterize a period of feverish investigation into the origins, explanations, and classifications of race.

Scientific revolution *see* paradigm shift.

Second shift women's responsibility for housework and child care—everything from cooking dinner, to doing laundry, bathing children, reading bedtime stories, and sewing Halloween costumes.

Secondary deviance subsequent acts of rule-breaking that occur after primary deviance and as a result of your new deviant label and people's expectations of you.

Secondary groups groups marked by impersonal, instrumental relationships (those existing as a means to an end).

Sects or **sectarian groups** high-tension organizations that don't fit so well within the existing social environment. They are usually most attractive to society's least privileged—outcasts, minorities, or the poor—because they downplay worldly pleasure by stressing otherworldly promises.

Secularism a general movement away from religiosity and spiritual belief toward a rational, scientific orientation, a trend adopted by industrialized nations in the form of separation of church and state.

Segmental solidarity *see* mechanical solidarity.

Segregation the legal or social practice of separating people on the basis of their race or ethnicity.

Self the individual identity of a person as perceived by that same person.

Service sector the section of the economy that involves providing intangible services.

Sex the biological differences that distinguish males from females.

Sex role theory Talcott Parsons's theory that men and women perform their sex roles as breadwinners and wives/mothers, respectively, because the nuclear family is the ideal arrangement in modern societies, fulfilling the function of reproducing workers.

Sexism occurs when a person's sex or gender is the basis for judgment, discrimination, and hatred against him or her.

Sexual harassment an illegal form of discrimination, involving everything from inappropriate jokes on the job to outright sexual assault to sexual "barter"—all intended to make women feel uncomfortable and unwelcome, particularly on the job.

Sexuality desire, sexual preference, sexual identity, and behavior.

Sick role concept describing the social rights and obligations of a sick individual.

Small group a group characterized by face-to-face interaction, a unifocal perspective, lack of formal arrangements, and a certain level of equality.

Social capital the information, knowledge of people, and connections that help individuals enter, gain power in, or otherwise leverage social networks; any relationship between people that can facilitate the actions of others.

Social class or **socioeconomic status (SES)** an individual's position in a stratified social order.

Social cohesion social bonds; how well people relate to each other and get along on a day-to-day basis.

Social construction an entity that exists because people behave as if it exists and whose existence is perpetuated as people and social institutions act in accordance with the widely agreed upon formal rules or informal norms of behavior associated with that entity.

Social control those mechanisms that create normative compliance in individuals.

Social Darwinism the application of Darwinian ideas to society, namely, the evolutionary "survival of the fittest."

Social deviance any transgression of socially established norms.

Social equality a condition whereby no differences in wealth, power, prestige, or status based on nonnatural conventions exist.

Social institution a complex group of interdependent positions that perform a social role and reproduce themselves over time; also defined in a narrow sense as any institution in a society that works to shape the behavior of the groups or people within it.

Social integration how well you are integrated into your social group or community.

Social mobility the movement between different positions within a system of social stratification in any given society.

Social movement collective behavior that is purposeful, organized, and institutionalized but not ritualized.

Social movement organization (SMO) a group developed to recruit new members and coordinate participation in a particular social movement; SMOs also often raise money, clarify goals, and structure participation in the movement.

Social network a set of relations—essentially, a set of dyads—held together by ties between individuals.

Social regulation the number of rules guiding your daily life and, more specifically, what you can reasonably expect from the world on a day-to-day basis.

Social rights the rights guaranteeing a citizen's protection by the state.

Socialism an economic system in which most or all the needs of the population are met through nonmarket methods of distribution.

Socialization the process by which individuals internalize the values, beliefs, and norms of a given society and learn to function as members of that society.

Socioeconomic status (SES) *see* social class.

Sociological imagination the ability to connect the most basic, intimate aspects of an individual's life to seemingly impersonal and remote historical forces.

Sociology the study of human society.

Soft power power attained through the use of cultural attractiveness rather than the threat of coercive action (hard power).

Specialization the process of making work consist of specific, delimited tasks.

State as defined by Weber, "a human community that (successfully) claims the *monopoly of the legitimate use of physical force* within a given territory."

Status a recognizable social position that an individual occupies.

Status hierarchy system a system of stratification based on social prestige.

Status set all the statuses one holds simultaneously.

Status-attainment model approach that ranks individuals by socioeconomic status, including income and educational attainment, and seeks to specify the attributes characteristic of people who end up in more desirable occupations.

Stereotype threat when members of a negatively stereotyped group are placed in a situation where they fear they may confirm those stereotypes.

Stigma a negative social label that not only changes others' behavior toward a person but also alters that person's own self-concept and social identity.

Straight-line assimilation Robert Parks's 1920 universal and linear model for how immigrants assimilate: they first arrive, then settle in, and achieve full assimilation in a newly homogenous country.

Strain theory Merton's theory that deviance occurs when a society does not give all its members equal ability to achieve socially acceptable goals.

Stratification structured social inequality or, more specifically, systematic inequalities between groups of people that arise as intended or unintended consequences of social processes and relationships.

Street crime crime committed in public and often associated with violence, gangs, and poverty.

Strength of weak ties the notion that relatively weak ties often turn out to be quite valuable because they yield new information.

Structural functionalism theoretical tradition claiming that every society has certain structures (the family, the division of labor, or gender) that exist in order to fulfill some set of necessary functions (reproduction of the species, production of goods, etc.).

Structural hole a gap between network clusters, or even two individuals, if those individuals (or clusters) have complementary resources.

Structural mobility mobility that is inevitable from changes in the economy.

Subaltern describes a subordinate, oppressed group of people.

Subculture the distinct cultural values and behavioral patterns of a particular group in society; a group united by sets of concepts, values, symbols, and shared meaning specific to the members of that group distinctive enough to distinguish it from others within the same culture or society.

Supernatural compensators promises of future rewards, such as salvation or eternity in heaven.

Survey an ordered series of questions intended to elicit information from respondents.

Symbolic ethnicity a nationality, not in the sense of carrying the rights and duties of citizenship but identifying with a past or future nationality. For later generations of white ethnics, something not constraining but easily expressed, with no risks of stigma and all the pleasures of feeling like an individual.

Symbolic interactionism a micro-level theory in which shared meanings, orientations, and assumptions form the basic motivations behind people's actions.

T

Taylorism the methods of labor management introduced by Frederick Winslow Taylor to streamline the processes of mass production in which each worker repeatedly performs one specific task.

Tertius gaudens the new third member of a triad who benefits from conflict between the other two members of the group.

Theism the worship of a god or gods, as in Christianity, Islam, and Hinduism.

Tie a set of stories that explains our relationship to the other members of our network.

Total institution an institution in which one is totally immersed and that controls all the basics of day-to-day life; no barriers exist between the usual spheres of daily life, and all activity occurs in the same place and under the same single authority.

Tracking a way of dividing students into different classes by ability or future plans.

Traditional authority authority based on appeals to the past or traditions.

Triad a group of three or more.

U

Underclass the notion, building on the culture of poverty argument, that the poor not only are different from mainstream society in their inability to take advantage of what mainstream society has to offer but also are increasingly deviant and even dangerous to the rest of us.

Union an organization of workers designed to facilitate collective bargaining with employers" follows "organization.

Union busting a company's assault on its workers' union with the hope of dissolving it.

Upper class a term for the economic elite.

V

Validity the extent to which an instrument measures what it is intended to measure.

Values moral beliefs.

Verstehen German: understanding. The concept of *Verstehen* forms the object of inquiry for interpretive sociology—to study how social actors understand their actions and the social world through experience.

W

Wealth a family's or individual's net worth (that is, total assets minus total debts).

Welfare state a system in which the state is responsible for the well-being of its citizens.

White-collar crime offense committed by a professional (or professionals) against a corporation, agency, or other institution.

BIBLIOGRAPHY

Abramsky, S. (2002, August 19). The prison bloom. *Gotham Gazette*. Retrieved from www.gothamgazette.com/iotw/prisons/abramsky.shtml

Acemoglu, D., et al. (2001, December). The colonial origins of comparative development: An empirical investigation. *The American Economic Review, 91*(5), 1369–1401.

Acemoglu, D., & Robinson, J. A. (2006). *The economic origins of dictatorship and democracy*. New York: Cambridge University Press.

Acierno, R., et al. (2010). Prevalence and correlates of emotional, physical, sexual, and financial abuse and potential neglect in the United States: The National Elder Mistreatment Study. *American Journal of Public Health, 100*(2), 292–297.

Adherents.com. (2012). Major religions of the world ranked by number of adherents. http://www.adherents.com/Religions_By_Adherents.html

Aguirre, B. E., et al. (1998). A test of the emergent norm theory of collective behavior. *Sociological Forum, 13*(2), 301–320.

Allegretto, S. A. (2011, March 23). State of working America's wealth. *Economic Policy Institute*. Retrieved from www.epi.org/page/-/BriefingPaper292.pdf

Allen, F. A. (1981). *The decline of the rehabilitative ideal: Penal policy and social purpose*. New Haven: Yale University Press.

Allen, J. T. (1973). Designing income maintenance systems: The income accounting problem. *Studies in Public Welfare*, paper no. 5. Washington, DC: Government Printing Office.

Amenta, E. (2006). *When movements matter: The Townsend Plan and the rise of Social Security*. Princeton, NJ: Princeton University Press.

American Association of University Professors (AAUP). (2007). *Financial inequality in higher education: The annual report on the economic status of the profession, 2006–07*. Retrieved from www.aaup.org/NR/rdonlyres/B25BFE69-BCE7-4AC9-A644-7E84FF14B883/0/zreport.pdf

AFL-CIO. (2011). Trends in CEO pay. http://www.aflcio.org/Corporate-Watch/CEO-Pay-and-the-99/Trends-in-CEO-Pay

American Society for Aesthetic Plastic Surgery (ASAPS). (2011, April 4). Demand for plastic surgery rebounds by almost 9%. Retrieved from www.surgery.org/media/news-releases/demand-for-plastic-surgery-rebounds-by-almost-9%25

Ammerman, N. T. (2005). *Pillars of faith: American congregations and their partners*. Berkeley: University of California Press.

Anderson, E. (1999). *Code of the street: Decency, violence, and the moral life of the inner city*. New York: W. W. Norton.

Anderson, J. L. (2009). The most failed state: Letter from Mogadishu. *The New Yorker, 85*(41), 64.

Anderson, S., et al. (2010, September). Executive excess 2010: CEO pay and the great recession. *Institute for Policy Studies*. Retrieved from www.ips-dc.org/reports/executive_excess_2010

Arab American Institute. (2011). Demographics. Webpage. Retrieved from www.aaiusa.org/pages/demographics/

Arnold, M. (1869). *Culture and anarchy*. London: Smith, Elder & Co.

Arum, R. (2003). *Judging school discipline: The crisis of moral authority*. Cambridge, MA: Harvard University Press.

Arum, R., & Shavit, Y. (1995). Secondary vocational education and the transition from school to work. *Sociology of Education, 68*(3), 187–204.

Asch, S. E. (1956). Studies of independence and conformity: A minority of one against a unanimous majority. *Psychological Monographs, 70*(9, Whole No. 416).

Atlas, J. (2005, February 27). The battle behind the battle at Harvard. *The New York Times*. Retrieved from http://query.nytimes.com/gst/fullpage.html?res=950DE3D8143DF934A15751C0A9639C8B63&sec=&spon=

Aughinbaugh, A. (2001). Does Head Start yield long-term benefits? *Journal of Human Resources, 36*(4), 641–665.

Auletta, K. (1981, November 16). I—the underclass. *The New Yorker*, p. 63.

Babbie, E. R. (2007). *The practice of social research* (11th ed.). Belmont, CA: Wadsworth.

Baker, D. C. (2005, May 26). Church hosts "drive-thru" Sunday services. *Quad-City Times*. Retrieved from www.qctimes.com/articles/2005/05/26/local/export93493.txt

Bakshi, A. (2003). Potential adverse health effects of genetically modified crops, part B. *Journal of Toxicology and Environmental Health, 6*, 211–255.

Baltzell, E. D. (1958). *Philadelphia gentlemen.* New York: Free Press.

Banerjee, N. (2005, December 30). Going to church to find a faith that fits. *The New York Times*, pp. 1a, 18. Retrieved from http://query.nytimes.com/gst/fullpage.html?res=9906E6D81330F933A05751C1A9639C8B63

Banfield, E. (1970). *The unheavenly city* . Boston: Little, Brown.

Barth, E. A. T., & Noel, D. L. (1972). Conceptual frameworks for the analysis of race relations: An evaluation. *Social Forces, 50*, 333–348.

Bear, C. (2008, May 13). American Indian school a far cry from the past. *Morning Edition.* National Public Radio.

Bearman, P. S., & Brückner, H. (2001). Promising the future: Virginity pledges and the transition to first intercourse. *American Journal of Sociology, 106*(4), 859–912.

Bearman, P. S., et al. (2004). Chains of affection: The structure of adolescent romantic and sexual networks. *American Journal of Sociology, 110*(1), 44–91.

Beauvoir, S. de. (1952). *The second sex.* New York: Knopf.

Beck, U. (1992). *Risk society: Towards a new modernity* (Mark Ritter, Trans.). London: Sage.

Becker, H. S. (1953, November). Becoming a marihuana user. *American Journal of Sociology, 59*, 235–243.

Becker, H. S. (1963). *Outsiders: Studies in the sociology of deviance.* New York: The Free Press.

Bellah, R. N. (1967). Civil religion in America. *Daedalus, 96*, 1–21.

Bellah, R. N. (1985). *Habits of the heart: Individualism and commitment in American life.* Berkeley: University of California Press.

Bender, C. J. (2007). Touching the transcendent: Rethinking religious experience in the sociological study of religion. In N. Ammerman (Ed.), *Everyday religion: Observing modern religious lives* (Chapter 11, pp. 201–219). New York: Oxford University Press. Retrieved from www.oxfordscholarship.com/oso/private/content/religion/9780195305418/p050.html#acprof-9780195305418-chapter-11

Benedict, H. (2007, March 7). The private war of women soldiers. *Salon.com.* Retrieved from www.salon.com/news/feature/2007/ 03/07/women_in_military/print.html

Benedict, R. (1934). *Patterns of culture.* New York: Mentor Books.

Berbrier, M. (2000). The victim ideology of white supremacists and white separatists in the United States. *Sociological Focus, 33*, 175–191.

Berger, P. L. (1967). *The sacred canopy: Elements of a sociological theory of religion.* Garden City, NY: Anchor Books.

Berk, S. F. (1985). *The gender factory: The apportionment of work in American households.* New York: Plenum Press.

Bernard, J. S. (1972). *The future of marriage.* New York: World Publishers.

Berry, B. (1963). *Almost white.* New York: Macmillan.

Bertrand, M., & Mullainathan, S. (2003). *Are Emily and Greg more employable than Lakisha and Jamal? Afield experiment on labor market discrimination* (NBER Working Paper No. W9873).

Besecke, K. (2007). Beyond literalism: Reflexive spirituality and religious meaning. In N. Ammerman (Ed.), *Everyday religion: Observing modern religious lives* (pp. 169–186). New York: Oxford University Press. Retrieved from www.oxfordscholarship.com/oso/private/content/religion/9780195305418/p009.html

Bianchi, S., & Robinson, J. (1997). What did you do today? Children's use of time, family composition, and the acquisition of social capital. *Journal of Marriage and the Family, 59*(2), 332–344.

Bird, W., & Thumma, S. (2011). A new decade of megachurches. Retrieved from http://hirr.hartsem.edu/megachurch/New-Decade-of-Megachurches-2011Profile.pdf

Bittman, M., et al. (2003). When does gender trump money? Bargaining and time in household work. *American Journal of Sociology, 109*, 186–214.

Bixler, M. T. (1992). *Winds of freedom: The story of the Navajo Code Talkers of World War II.* Darien, CT: Two Bytes.

Black megachurches surge. (1996). *Christian Century, 113*(21), 686–687. Retrieved from www.christiancentury.org

Blanchard, R., & Bogaert, A. F. (1996). Homosexuality in men and number of older brothers. *American Journal of Psychiatry, 153*, 27–31.

Blanton, C. K. (2000). "They cannot master abstractions, but they can often be made efficient workers": Race and class in the intelligence testing of Mexican Americans and African Americans in Texas during the 1920's. *Social Science Quarterly, 81*(4), 1014–1026.

Blau, P. M., & Duncan, O. D., with collaboration of A. Tyree. (1967). *The American occupational structure.* New York: Wiley.

Blumenbach, J. F. (1775). De generis humani varietate native. Göttingen: Apud viduam Abr. Vandenhoek.

Blumer, H. (1969). *Symbolic interactionism: Perspective and method.* Englewood Cliffs, NJ: Prentice-Hall.

Blumstein, A., & Beck, A. J. (1999). Population growth in U.S. prisons, 1980–1996. In M. Tonry & J. Petersilia

(Eds.), *Prisons: Crime and justice 26* (pp. 17–61). Chicago: University of Chicago Press.

Blumstein, P. W., & Schwartz., P. (1983). *American couples: Money, work, and sex.* New York: Morrow.

Bobo, L. (1989). Keeping the linchpin in place: Testing the multiple sources of opposition to residential integration. *Revue Internationale de Psychologie Sociale, 2,* 306–323.

Bobo, L., et al. (1997). Laissez-faire racism: The crystallization of a kinder, gentler, antiblack ideology. In S. A. Tuch & J. K. Martin (Eds.), *Racial attitudes in the 1990s: Continuity and change* (pp. 15–42). Westport, CT: Praeger.

Bogaert, A. F. (2006). Biological versus nonbiological older brothers and men's sexual orientation. *Proceedings of the National Academy of Sciences of the United States of America, 103*(28), 10771–10774.

Bogin, B. (1995). Plasticity in the growth of Mayan refugee children living the United States. In C. G. N. Mascie-Taylor and B. Bogin (Eds.), *Human variability and plasticity* (pp. 46–74). Cambridge: Cambridge University Press.

Bordo, S. (1990). Feminism, postmodernism, and gender skepticism. In L. J. Nicholson (Ed.), *Feminism/postmodernism* (pp. 133–156). New York: Routledge.

Bourdieu, P. (1977). Cultural reproduction and social reproduction. In J. Karabel & A. H. Halsey (Eds.), *Power and ideology in education* (pp. 487–511). New York: Oxford University Press.

Bowen, W., et al. (2009). *Crossing the finish line: Completing college at America's public universities.* Princeton, NJ: Princeton University Press.

Bowen, W. G., & Bok, D. (1998). *The shape of the river: Long-term consequences of considering race in college and university admissions.* Princeton, NJ: Princeton University Press.

Bowles, S., & Gintis, H. (1976). *Schooling in capitalist America: Educational reform and the contradictions of economic life.* New York: Basic Books.

Bozorgmehr, M., et al. (1996). Middle Easterners: A new kind of immigrant. In R. Waldinger & M. Bozorgmehr (Eds.), *Ethnic Los Angeles* (pp. 347–378). New York: Russell Sage Foundation.

Bradley M. B., et al. (1992). *Churches and church membership in the United States, 1990.* Atlanta: Glenmary Research Center.

Brandow, M. (2008). *New York's poop scoop law: Dogs, the dirt and due process.* West Lafayette, IN: Purdue University Press.

Briody, D. (2003). *The iron triangle: Inside the secret world of the Carlyle Group.* Hoboken, NJ: Wiley.

Brookings Institution. (2010). 2010 Racial and ethnic distributions of 100 largest metropolitan and 2000–2010 change. Retrieved from www.brookings.edu/%7E/media/Files/rc/papers/2011/0831_census_race_frey/0831_census_race_appendixa.pdf

Brooks-Gunn, J., et al. (2003). Maternal employment and child cognitive outcomes in the first three years of life: The NICHD study of early child care. *Child Development, 73*(4), pp. 1052–1072.

Brown, C. (2006, February 26). The freshman. *The New York Times Magazine,* p. 55.

Brubaker, R. (1992). *Citizenship and nationhood in France and Germany.* Cambridge, MA: Harvard University Press.

Brückner, H., & Bearman, P. S. (2005). After the promise: The STD consequences of adolescent virginity pledges. *Journal of Adolescent Health, 36,* 271–278.

Bryk, A., et al. (1993). *Catholic schools and the common good.* Cambridge, MA: Harvard University Press.

Buchmann, C., et al. (2006). The growing female advantage in higher education: The role of family background and academic achievement? *American Sociological Review, 71*(4), 515–541.

Bureau of Justice Statistics. (2002). Recidivism of Prisoners Released in 1994. www.ojp.usdoj.gov/bjs/reentry/recidivism.htm#returned

Bureau of Justice Statistics. (2003). Brief on intimate partner violence. Retrieved from www.bjs.gov/content/pub/pdf/ipv01.pdf

Bureau of Justice Statistics. (2010). Correctional populations in the United States, 2009. Office of Justice Programs (December). Retrieved from http://bjs.ojp.usdoj.gov/content/pub/pdf/cpus09.pdf

Bureau of Labor Statistics (BLS), U.S. Department of Labor. (2006, September). *Highlights of women's earnings in 2005.* Retrieved from www.bls.gov/cps/cpswom2005.pdf

Bureau of Labor Statistics (BLS), U.S. Department of Labor. (2007). Working and work-related activities done by men and women in 2007. *American time use survey.* Retrieved from www.bls.gov/tus/current/work.htm#a1

Bureau of Labor Statistics (BLS), U.S. Department of Labor. (2009a). Highlights of women's earnings in 2008. Retrieved from www.bls.gov/cps/cpswom2008.pdf

Bureau of Labor Statistics (BLS), U.S. Department of Labor. (2009b). Labor force participation of mothers with infants in 2008. Retrieved from http://stats.bls.gov/opub/ted/2009/may/wk4/art04.htm

Bureau of Labor Statistics (BLS), U.S. Department of Labor. (2011a). Education pays. . . . Retrieved from www.bls.gov/emp/ep_chart_001.htm

Bureau of Labor Statistics (BLS), U.S. Department of Labor. (2011b). Women in the labor force: A databook. Retrieved from www.bls.gov/cps/wlf-databook2011.htm.

Bureau of Labor Statistics (BLS), U.S. Department of Labor. (2011c). National Compensation Survey. Retrieved from www.bls.gov/news.release/ebs2.t01.htm

Bureau of Labor Statistics (BLS), U.S. Department of Labor. (2011d). Share of married-couple families with an employed mother at its lowest, 1994–2010. Retrieved from www.bls.gov/opub/ted/2011/ted_20110506.htm

Bureau of Labor Statistics (BLS), U.S. Department of Labor. (2011e). Union members summary. Retrieved from www.bls.gov/news.release/union2.nr0.htm

Bureau of Labor Statistics (BLS), U.S. Department of Labor. (2012a). Labor force characteristics: Employment status of the civilian noninstitutional population by age, sex, and race. Retrieved from www.bls.gov/cps/cpsaat03.pdf

Burt, R. (1992). *Structural holes.* Cambridge, MA: Harvard University Press.

Bush, G. W. (2001, August 9). President discusses stem cell research [Press release]. *The White House: President George W. Bush.* Retrieved from http:// georgewbush-whitehouse.archives.gov/news/releases/2001/08/20010809-2.html

BusinessWeek. (1971, June 19). Executive compensation scorecard. *BusinessWeek*, 58–78.

BusinessWeek. (1981, May 11). Executive compensation scorecard. *BusinessWeek*, 58–78.

BusinessWeek. (1991, May 6). Executive compensation scorecard. *BusinessWeek*, 96–112.

BusinessWeek. (2001, April 16). Executive compensation scorecard. *BusinessWeek*, 82–109.

Calhoun, C. (2002). *Dictionary of the social sciences.* New York: Oxford University Press.

Callan, T., et al. (1993). Resources, deprivation and the measurement of poverty. *Journal of Social Policy*, *22*, 141–172.

Cantril, H. (1941). *The psychology of social movements.* New York: Wiley.

Card, D. et al. (2008). Tipping and the Dynamics of Segregation. *The Quarterly Journal of Economics* 123, no. 1 (2008): 177-218.

Carlyle, T. (1971). *Selected writings* (A. Shelston, Ed.). Harmondsworth: Penguin Books. (*Chartism* originally published 1839.)

Carpiano, R. M., et al. (2006). Social inequality and health: Future directions for the fundamental cause explanation for class differences in health. Presented at the Russell Sage Foundation–sponsored conference "Social Class: How Does It Work?" New York.

Carrington, C. (1999). *No place like home: Relationships and family life among lesbians and gay men.* Chicago: University of Chicago Press.

Carroll, J. (2007, August 16). Most Americans approve of interracial marriages. Gallup News Service. Retrieved from www.gallup.com/poll/28417/most-americans-approve-interracial-marriages.aspx

Centers for Disease Control and Prevention. (2007a, April 6). Polio disease—Questions and answers. Retrieved from www.cdc.gov/vaccines/vpd-vac/polio/dis-faqs.htm

Centers for Disease Control and Prevention (CDC), National Center for Health Statistics. (2008, December). Prevalence of overweight, obesity, and extreme obesity among adults: United States, trends 1960–62 through 2005–2006. Data from the National Health and Nutrition Examination Survey (NHANES). Retrieved from www.cdc.gov/nchs/data/hestat/overweight/overweight_adult.htm#table1

Centers for Disease Control and Prevention. (2010a). Surveillance summaries: Youth risk behavior surveillance. Retrieved from www.cdc.gov/mmwr/pdf/ss/ss5905.pdf

Centers for Disease Control and Prevention. (2010b). Suicide: Facts at a glance. Retrieved from www.inthesetimes.com/working/entry/6801/the_state_of_native_america_very_unemployed_and_mostly_ignored/

Centers for Disease Control and Prevention. (2011a). National Vital Statistics System: Birth data. Retrieved from www.cdc.gov/nchs/births.htm

Centers for Disease Control and Prevention. (2011b). Understanding intimate partner violence: Fact sheet 2011. Retrieved from www.cdc.gov/violenceprevention/pdf/ipv_factsheet-a.pdf

Centers for Disease Control and Prevention. (2011c). National Vital Statistics Report: Births: Preliminary data for 2008, Table 1 (April 6). Retrieved from www.cdc.gov/nchs/data/nvsr/nvsr58/nvsr58_16.pdf

Centers for Medicare and Medicaid Services. (2011). Immunizations: An overview. Retrieved from www.cms.gov/Immunizations/

Central Intelligence Agency (CIA). (2010). *The world factbook.* Retrieved from www.cia.gov/library/publications/the-world-factbook/geos/xx.html

Chase-Lansdale, P. L., et al. (1997). Neighborhood and family influences on the intellectual and behavioral competence of preschool and early school-age children.

In J. Brooks-Gunn et al. (Eds.), *Neighborhood poverty: Vol. 1* (pp. 79–118). New York: Russell Sage Foundation.

Chase-Lansdale, P. L., et al. (2003). Mothers' transitions from welfare to work and the well-being of preschoolers and adolescents. *Science, 299*(5612), 1548–1552.

Chauncey, G. (1994). *Gay New York: Gender, urban culture, and the makings of the gay male world, 1890–1940.* New York: Basic Books.

Chaves, M. (2002, Summer). Abiding faith. *Context Magazine, 1*(2).

Chaves, M., & Higgins, L. M. (1992). Comparing the community involvement of black and white congregations. *Journal for the Scientific Study of Religion, 31*(4), 425–440.

Chen, D. W. (2004, November 18). $7 billion for the grief of Sept. 11. *The New York Times.* Retrieved from www.nytimes.com/2004/11/18/ntregion/18fund.html

Cherlin, A. J. (2009). *The marriage-go-round: The state of marriage and the family in America today.* New York: Knopf.

Chirot, D. (1985, April). The rise of the West. *American Sociological Review, 50,* 181–195.

Chodorow, N. (1978). *Reproduction of mothering: Psychoanalysis and the sociology of gender.* Berkeley: University of California Press.

Chorev, N. (2007). *Remaking U.S. trade policy: From protectionism to globalization.* Ithaca, NY: Cornell University Press.

Clifton, R. A., et al. (1986). Effects of ethnicity and sex on teachers' expectations of junior high school students. *Sociology of Education, 59*(1), 58–67.

Cloward, R., & Ohlin, L. (1960). *Delinquency and opportunity.* New York: Free Press.

Cobble, D. S. (2007). *The sex of class: Women transforming American labor.* Ithaca, NY: Cornell University Press.

Colapinto, J. (2000). *As nature made him: The boy who was raised as a girl* (1st ed.). New York: HarperCollins.

Coleman, J., et al. (1966). *Equality of educational opportunity.* Washington, DC: U.S. Government Printing Office.

Coleman, J., & Hoffer, T. (1987). *Public and private high schools.* New York: Basic Books.

Coleman, J., et al. (1982). *High school achievement: Public, Catholic and private schools compared.* New York: Basic Books.

Collier, J., et al. (1997). Is there a family? New anthropological views. In R. N. Lancaster & M. di Lionardo (Eds.), *The gender/sexuality reader: Culture, history, political economy* (pp. 71–81). New York: Routledge.

Collins, P. H. (1990). Work, family, and black women's oppression. In *Black feminist thought: Knowledge, consciousness and the politics of empowerment* (pp. 45–68). New York: Routledge.

Collins, R. (1971). Functional and conflict theories of educational stratification. *American Sociological Review, 36*(6), 1002–1019.

Collins, R. (1979). *The credential society: A historical sociology of education and stratification.* New York: Academic Press.

Comisi, C. (2011). Landmark partnership between the Coalition of Immokalee Workers and Bon Appétit Management Company. *WhyHunger.* Retrieved from www.whyhunger.org/news-and-alerts/48-why-reporter/807-landmark-partnership-between-the-coalition-of-immokalee-workers-and-bon-appetit-management-company.html

Conger, R., et al. (1992). A family process model of economic hardship and adjustment of early adolescent boys. *Child Development, 63,* 526–541.

Conger, R., et al. (1994). Economic stress, coercive family process and developmental problems of adolescence. *Child Development, 65,* 541–561.

Conley, D. (1999). *Being black, living in the red: Race, wealth, and social policy in America.* Berkeley: University of California Press.

Conley, D. (2001). Capital for college: Parental assets and postsecondary schooling. *Sociology of Education, 74,* 59–72.

Conley, D. (2004). *The pecking order: Which siblings succeed and why.* New York: Pantheon Books.

Conley, D. (2009). *Elsewhere, U.S.A.: How we got from the company man, family dinners and the affluent society to the home office, BlackBerry moms and economic anxiety.* New York: Pantheon.

Conley, D. (2009a). Interview with Mitchell Duneier. New York, NY, October 8.

Conley, D. (2009b). Interview with Duncan Watts. New York, NY, October 8.

Conley, D. (2009c). Interview with C. J. Pascoe. 104th Annual Meeting of the American Sociological Association, San Francisco, CA, August 8.

Conley, D. (2009d). Interview with Paula England. 104th Annual Meeting of the American Sociological Association, San Francisco, CA, August 8.

Conley, D. (2009e). Interview with Victor Rios. 104th Annual Meeting of the American Sociological Association, San Francisco, CA, August 9.

Conley, D. (2009f). Interview with Devah Pager. New York, NY, October 8.

Conley, D. (2009g). Interview with Jeffrey Sachs. New York, NY, October 8.

Conley, D. (2009h). Interview with Michael Hout. 104th Annual Meeting of the American Sociological Association, San Francisco, CA, August 9.

Conley, D. (2009i). Interview with Jen'nan Read. 104th Annual Meeting of the American Sociological Association, San Francisco, CA, August 9.

Conley, D. (2009j). Interview with Jennifer Lee. 104th Annual Meeting of the American Sociological Association, San Francisco, CA, August 9.

Conley, D. (2009k). Interview with Andrew Cherlin. 104th Annual Meeting of the American Sociological Association, San Francisco, CA, August 8.

Conley, D. (2009l). Interview with Steven Morgan. 104th Annual Meeting of the American Sociological Association, San Francisco, CA, August 8.

Conley, D. (2009m). Interview with Frances Fox Piven. 104th Annual Meeting of the American Sociological Association, San Francisco, CA, August 9.

Conley, D. (2009n). Interview with Alondra Nelson. New York, NY, October 8.

Conley, D. (2009o). Interview with John Evans. 104th Annual Meeting of the American Sociological Association, San Francisco, CA, August 8.

Conley, D. (2009p). Interview with Doug McAdam. 104th Annual Meeting of the American Sociological Association, San Francisco, CA, August 8.

Conley, D. (2010). Interview with Kate Rich. E-mail interview, January.

Conley, D. (2011a). Interview with Allison Pugh. 106th Annual Meeting of the American Sociological Association, Las Vegas, NV, August 21.

Conley, D. (2011b). Interview with Annette Lareau. 106th Annual Meeting of the American Sociological Association, Las Vegas, NV, August 21.

Conley, D. (2011c). Interview with David Grusky. 106th Annual Meeting of the American Sociological Association, Las Vegas, NV, August 21.

Conley, D. (2011d). Interview with Ku Lia. 106th Annual Meeting of the American Sociological Association, Las Vegas, NV, August 21.

Conley, D. (2011e). Interview with Shamus Khan. 106th Annual Meeting of the American Sociological Association, Las Vegas, NV, August 21.

Conley, D. (2011f). Interview with Nitsan Chorev. 106th Annual Meeting of the American Sociological Association, Las Vegas, NV, August 21.

Conley, D., & Bennett, N. G. (2000). Is biology destiny? Birth weight and life chances. *American Sociological Review, 65*(3), 458–467.

Conley, D., & Glauber, R. (2006). Parental educational investment and children's academic risk: Estimates of the impact of sibship size and birth order from exogenous variation in fertility. *Journal of Human Resources, 41*(4), 722–737.

Conley, D., et al. (2003). *The starting gate: Birth weight and life chances.* Berkeley: University of California Press.

Conley, D., et al. (2007). *Africa's lagging demographic transition: Evidence from exogenous impacts of malaria ecology and agricultural technology.* Cambridge, MA: National Bureau of Economic Research.

Connell, R. (1987). *Gender and power.* Stanford, CA: Stanford University Press.

Cookson, Jr., P. W., & Persell, C. (1985). *Preparing for power.* New York: Basic Books.

Cooley, C. H. (1909). *Social organization: A study of the larger mind.* New York: Scribner's.

Cooley, C. H. (1922; orig. 1902). *Human nature and the social order.* New York: Scribner's.

Coolidge, C. (2011, September 16). Christian goods big seller for Wal-Mart. *ABC News.* Retrieved from http://abcnews.go.com/Business/story?id=86290&page=1#.Tt-3dXPZuoA

Coontz, S. (1992). *The way we never were: American families and the nostalgia trap.* New York: Basic Books.

Coontz, S. (Ed.). (2001). *Historical perspectives on family diversity. Shifting the center: Understanding contemporary families.* Mountain View, CA: Mayfield Publishing Company.

Corbett, S. (2007, March 18). The women's war. *The New York Times.* Retrieved from www.nytimes.com/2007/03/18/magazine/18cover.html?scp=1&sq=&st=cse

Cornell, S. (1988). *The return of the native: American Indian political resurgence.* New York: Oxford University Press.

Cornell, S., & Hartmann, D. (1998). Fixed or fluid? Alternative views of ethnicity and race. In *Ethnicity and race: Making identities in a changing world* (pp. 39–71). Thousand Oaks, CA: Pine Forge Press.

Correctional Association of New York. (2007, February). *Drop the rock: Repeal the Rockefeller Drug Laws.* Retrieved from www.correctionalassociation.org/PPP/publications/-Repeal%20the%20RDL%20February%202007.pdf

Cosby, B. (2004). *Pound cake speech.* Presented at Constitution Hall, Washington, DC. Retrieved from www.americanrhetoric.com/speeches/billcosbypoundcakespeech.htm

Costello, E. J., et al. (2003). Relationships between poverty and psychopathology: A natural experiment. *Journal of the American Medical Association, 290,* 2023–2029.

Covert, B. (2011, March 8). Prepare for a possible "womancession." *National Public Radio.* Retrieved from www.npr.org/2011/03/08/134357162/the-nation-prepare-for-a-possible-womancession

Cowan, R. S. (1983). *More work for mother: The ironies of household technology from the open hearth to the microwave.* New York: Basic Books.

Credit Suisse. (2011). Global wealth report. Retrieved from https://infocus.credit-suisse.com/data/_product_documents/_shop/323525/2011_global_wealth_report.pdf

Crenson, M. (2005, July 17). They pledge allegiance to own countries; Dreamers claim islands for invented nations, or even an old offshore artillery platform. New homeland can be merely a state of mind. *Los Angeles Times*, p. A16.

Crouse, J., & Trusheim, D. (1988). The case against the SAT. *Public Interest, 93*, 97–110.

Currie, D. H. (1999). *Girl talk: Adolescent magazines and their readers.* Toronto: University of Toronto Press.

Currie, J. (2000). *Early childhood intervention programs: What do we know?* Chicago: Joint Center for Poverty Research.

Currie, J., & Thomas, D. (1995). Does Head Start make a difference? *American Economic Review, 85*(3), 341–364.

Currie, J., & Thomas, D. (1999). Does Head Start help Hispanic children? *Journal of Public Economics, 74*(2), 235–262.

Daniels, G., & Kaling, M. (Writers), & Feig, P. (Director). (2009). Niagara [Television series episode]. In B. Silverman et al. (Executive producers), *The Office.* New York, NY: NBC.

Dart, J. (2001, February 28). Hues in the pews: Racially mixed churches an elusive goal. *Christian Century.* Retrieved from http://hirr.hartsem.edu/cong/articles_huesinthepews.html

Davidson, J. D, et al. (1995). Persistence and change in the Protestant establishment, 1930–1992. *Social Forces, 74*(1), 157–175.

Davis, F. J. (1991). *Who is black? One nation's definition.* University Park: Pennsylvania State University Press.

Davis, G. F. (2003). American cronyism. *Contexts, 2*(3).

Davis, K. (1940). Extreme social isolation of a child. *The American Journal of Sociology, 45*, 554–565.

Davis, K., & Moore, W. E. (1944). Some principles of stratification. *American Sociological Review, 10*(2), 242–249.

Davis, L. (2011). Race, Gender, and Class at a Crossroads: A survey of their intersection in employment, economics, and the law. *The Journal of Gender, Race & Justice.*

Dawkins, R. (2006). *The god delusion.* Boston: Houghton Mifflin.

Death Penalty Information Center. (2012). Facts about the Death Penalty. Retrieved from http://www.deathpenaltyinfo.org/documents/FactSheet.pdf

De Baca, L. C. (2011, May 23). Labor trafficking in troubled economic times: Protecting American jobs and migrant human rights. Office to Monitor and Combat Trafficking in Persons Statement before the Commission on Security and Cooperation in Europe (U.S. Helsinki Commission), Washington, DC. Retrieved from www.state.gov/g/tip/rls/rm/2011/164657.htm

DellaCava, F. A., et al. (2004). Adoption in the U.S.: The emergence of a social movement. *Journal of Sociology and Social Welfare, 31*(4), 141–160.

DeNavas-Walt, C., et al. (2011). Income, poverty, and health insurance coverage in the United States: 2010. Retreived from www.census.gov/prod/2011pubs/p60-239.pdf

DeNeve, C. (1997, Winter). Hispanic presence in the workplace. *The Diversity Factor*, 14–21.

Denizet-Lewis, B. (2004, May 30). Friends, friends with benefits, and the benefits of the local mall. *The New York Times Magazine.* Retrieved from www.nytimes.com/2004/05/30/magazine/30NONDATING.html?ex=1216353600&en=68ca79c485d7e207&ei=5070

DeParle, J. (2004). *American dream: Three women, ten kids and a nation's drive to end welfare.* New York: Viking.

De Vos, G., & Wagatsuma, H. (1966). *Japan's invisible race: Caste in culture and personality.* Berkeley: University of California Press.

Dillon, S. (2009, October 8). Study finds high rate of imprisonment among dropouts. *The New York Times.* Retrieved from www.nytimes.com/2009/10/09/education/09dropout.html

Dillon, M., and Wink, P. (2003). Religiousness and spirituality: Trajectories and vital involvement in late adulthood. In M. Dillon (Ed.), *Handbook of the sociology of religion* (pp. 179–189). Cambridge: Cambridge University Press.

DiMaggio, P. J. & Powell, W. (1983). The iron cage revisited: Institutional isomorphism and collective rationality in organizational fields. *American Sociological Review, 48*, 149.

Dinnerstein, L., et al. (1996). *Native and strangers: A multicultural history of Americans.* New York: Oxford University Press.

Dobbie, W., & Fryer, R. G., Jr. (2009, April). Are high quality schools enough to close the achievement gap?

Evidence from a bold social experiment in Harlem (NBER Working Paper No. 15473). Unpublished.

Domhoff, G. W. (2010). Wealth, income, and power. *Who rules America?* Retrieved from www2.ucsc.edu/whorulesamerica/power/wealth.html

Doucouliagos, C., & Laroche, P. (2003). What do unions do to productivity? A meta-analysis. *Industrial Relations, 42*(4).

Dove. (2006). *Real women have real curves.* Retrieved from www.campaignforrealbeauty.com/flat3.asp?id=2287&src=InsideCampaign_firming

Dowd, M. (2005, October 30). What's a modern girl to do? *The New York Times.* Retrieved from www.nytimes.com/2005/10/30/magazine/30feminism.html?scp=1&sq=&st=cse

Downey, D. B. (1995). When bigger is not better: Family size, resources, and children's educational performance. *American Sociological Review, 60*(5), 746–761.

Doyle, D. H. (1977). The social functions of voluntary associations in a nineteenth-century American town. *Social Science History, 1*(3), 333–355.

Drape, J. (2005, October 30). Increasingly, football's playbooks call for prayers. *The New York Times.* Retrieved from www.nytimes.com/2005/10/30/sports/football/30religion.html?scp=1&sq=&st=cse

DuBois, W. E. B. (1903). *The souls of black folk.* Paris: A.C. McClurg & Co.

Duncan, G., et al. (1994). Economic deprivation and early childhood development. *Child Development, 65*(2), 296–318.

Durkheim, E. (1951; orig. 1897). *Suicide: A study in sociology* (G. Simpson & J. A. Spaulding, Trans.). New York: The Free Press.

Durkheim, E. (1972). The forced division of labor. In A. Giddens (Ed.), *Selected writings* (p. 181). Cambridge: Cambridge University Press.

Durkhiem, E. (1995; orig. 1917). *The elementary forms of religious life* (K. E. Fields, Trans. and Intro.). New York: Free Press.

Durkheim, E. (1997; orig. 1893). *The division of labor in society* (Intro. by Lewis A. Coser; W. D. Halls, Trans.). New York: Free Press.

Duvall, M. L. (1991). *Feeding the family: The social organization of caring as gendered work.* Chicago: University of Chicago Press.

Dyer, G. (1985). *War.* New York: Crown.

Easterly, W., & Levine, R. (2002). *Tropics, germs, and crops: How endowments influence economic development* (NBER Working Paper No. W9106).

Eck, D. L. (2006). From diversity to pluralism. In *On common ground: World religions in America* [CD-ROM]. Cambridge: The Pluralism Project.

Edgerton, R. (1995). "Bowling alone": An interview with Robert Putnam about America's collapsing civic life. *American Association for Higher Education Bulletin, 48*(1).

Edin, K., & Lein, L. (1997). *Making ends meet: How single mothers survive welfare and low-wage work.* New York: Russell Sage Foundation.

Ehrenreich, B. (2001). *Nickel and dimed: On (not) getting by in America.* New York: Metropolitan Books.

Ehrenreich, B., & Hochschild, A. R. (Eds.). (2004). Global woman: Nannies, maids and sex workers in the global economy. New York: Macmillan Holt.

Eisenbrey, R. (2007). *Strong unions, strong productivity: Snapshot for June 20.* Economic Policy Institute. Retrieved from www.epi.org/content.cfm/webfeatures_snapshots_20070620

Elder, G., et al. (1995). Linking family hardship to children's lives. *Child Development, 56*, 361–375.

Engels, F. (1878, May–July). *Herrn Eugen Dühring's Umwälzung des Sozialismus* in the supplement to *Vorwärts.*

Enloe, C. H. (2000). *Maneuvers: The international politics of militarizing women's lives.* Berkeley: University of California Press.

Entwisle, D. R., & Alexander, K. L. (1992, February). Summer setback: Race, poverty, school composition, and mathematics achievement in the first two years of school. *American Sociological Review, 57*(1), 72–84.

Epistemological modesty: An interview with Peter Berger. (1997, October 29). *The Christian Century.* Retrieved from www.christiancentury.org

Epstein, C. F. (1988). *Deceptive distinctions: Sex, gender, and the social order.* New Haven: Yale University Press.

Eriksen, S., & Jensen, V. (2006). All in the family? Family environment factors in sibling violence. *Journal of Family Violence, 21*(8), 497–507.

Erikson, K. (2005). *Wayward puritans: A study in the sociology of deviance* (Rev. ed.). Boston: Pearson/Allyn & Bacon.

Espenshade, T. J., & Chung, C. Y. (2005). The opportunity cost of admission preferences at elite universities. *Social Science Quarterly, 86*(2), 293–305.

Espenshade, T. J., et al. (2004). Admission preferences for minority students, athletes, and legacies at elite universities. *Social Science Quarterly, 85*(5), 1422–1446.

Essman, E. (2007). The American people: Social classes. *Life in the USA: The complete guide for immigrants and Americans.* Retrieved from www.lifeintheusa.com

Estabrook, B. (2009, March). Politics of the plate: The price of tomatoes. *Gourmet.* Retrieved from www.gourmet.com/magazine/2000s/2009/03/politics-of-the-plate-the-price-of-tomatoes.

Evans, J. (2002). *Playing God? Human genetic engineering and the rationalization of public bioethical debate.* Chicago: University of Chicago Press.

Eyerman, R. (2001). *Cultural trauma: Slavery and the formation of African American identity.* Cambridge: Cambridge University Press.

Fadiman, A. (1997). *The spirit catches you and you fall down: A Hmong child, her American doctors, and the collision of two cultures.* New York: Farrar, Straus, and Giroux.

Fagan, J., et al. (2003, March 31). Reciprocal effects of crime and incarceration in New York City neighborhoods. *Fordham Urban Law Journal, 30,* 1551–1602. Retrieved from SSRN: http://ssrn.com/abstract=392120 or doi:10.2139/ssrn.392120

Farmer, P. (1999). *Infections and inequalities: The modern plagues.* Berkeley: University of California Press.

Farmer, P. (2011). *Haiti after the earthquake* (A. Gardner & C. Van Der Hoof Holstein, Eds.). New York: PublicAffairs.

Fausto-Sterling, A. (2000). *Sexing the body: Gender politics and the construction of sexuality* (1st ed.). New York: Basic Books.

Federal Bureau of Investigation (FBI). (2002, October 28). *Crime in the United States 2001.* Retrieved from www.fbi.gov/pressrel/pressrel02/cius2001.htm

Federal Bureau of Investigation (FBI). (2003). *Facts and figures 2003.* Retrieved from www.fbi.gov/libref/factsfigure/wcc.htm

Federal Bureau of Investigation (FBI). (2011a). *Uniform Crime Reports: Crime in the United States.* http://www.fbi.gov/about-us/cjis/ucr/crime-in-the-u.s/2010/crime-in-the-u.s.-2010

Federal Interagency Forum on Child and Family Statistics. (2011). America's children: Key national indicators of well-being. Retrieved from www.childstats.gov/americaschildren/special1.asp

Ferber, A. L. (1999). *White man falling: Race, gender, and white supremacy.* Lanham, MD: Rowman & Littlefield.

Ferran, L. (2009, December 31). Megachurch asks for nearly $1M in 48 hours: Pastor Rick Warren of Saddleback Church asks members for $900,000 before New Year. In *Good Morning America,* ABCnews.com. Retrieved from http://abcnews.go.com/GMA/church-asks-mil-48-hours/story?id=9455589

Fetter, J. H. (1995). *Questions and admissions: Reflections on 100,000 admissions decisions at Stanford.* Stanford, CA: Stanford University Press.

Figlio, D. N. (2005a). *Boys named Sue: Disruptive children and their peers* (NBER Working Paper No. W11277). Retrieved from http://palm.nber.org/papers/w11277

Fink, S., et al. (2006). Mammalian monogamy is not controlled by a single gene. *Proceedings of the National Academy of Sciences of the United States of America, 103*(20), 10956–10960. Retrieved from www.pnas.org/content/103/29/10956

Finke, R., & Stark, R. (1992). *The churching of America, 1776–1990: Winners and losers in our religious economy.* New Brunswick, NJ: Rutgers University Press.

Finn, J. D., et al. (2005). Small classes in the early grades, academic achievement, and graduating from high school. *Journal of Educational Psychology, 97*(2), 214–223.

Fischer, C., & Hout, M. (2006). How Americans prayed: Religious diversity and change. In C. Fischer & M. Hout (Eds.), *A century of difference: How America changed in the last one hundred years* (pp. 186–211). New York: Russell Sage Foundation.

Fischer, C. S., et al. (1996). *Inequality by design: Cracking the bell curve myth.* Princeton, NJ: Princeton University Press.

Fischer, P. M., et al. (1991, December). Brand logo recognition by children aged 3 to 6 years: Mickey Mouse and old Joe the Camel. *Journal of the American Medical Association, 266,* 3145–3148.

Fitzgerald, M. (2005). Greater convenience but not greater turnout: The impact of alternative voting methods on electoral participation in the United States. *American Politics Research, 33*(6), 842–867.

Foer, J. S. (2009). *Eating animals.* New York: Little, Brown.

Folbre, N. (1987). *A field guide to the U.S. economy.* New York: Pantheon Books.

Food Research and Action Center. (2011). SNAP/Food stamp monthly participation data. Retrieved from http://frac.org/reports-and-resources/snapfood-stamp-monthly-participation-data/

Forbes. (2011a). America's highest paid chief executives. *Forbes.* Retrieved from www.forbes.com/lists/2011/12/ceo-compensation-11_land.html

Forbes. (2011b). The world's billionaires. *Forbes.* Retrieved from www.forbes.com/wealth/billionaires/list

Ford, H., & Crowther, S. (1973; orig. 1922). *My life and work, by Henry Ford.* New York: Arno Books.

Fordham, S., & Ogbu, J. (1986). Black students' school success: Coping with the "burden of acting white." *Urban Review, 18,* 176–206.

Foss, R. J. (1994). The demise of homosexual exclusion: New possibilities for gay and lesbian immigration. *Harvard Civil Rights–Civil Liberties Law Review, 29* 439–475.

Foster, D. (2006, February 19). Mind over splatter. *The New York Times*. Retrieved from www.nytimes.com/2006/02/19/opinion/19foster.html?scp=1&sq=february+19%2C+2006+foster&st=nyt

Foucault, M. (1977). *Discipline and punish: The birth of the prison*. New York: Pantheon Books.

Foucault, M. (1978). *The history of sexuality*. New York: Pantheon Books.

Foucault, M. (1980). *Power/knowledge: Selected interviews and other writings, 1972–1977* (C. Gordon, Ed.). New York: Pantheon Books.

Fragile Families. (2004, July). Racial and ethnic differences in marriage among new, unwed parents. *Fragile Families Research Brief, 25*. Retrieved from www.fragilefamilies.princeton.edu/briefs/ResearchBrief25.pdf

Francis, D. R. (2005, November). Changing work behavior of married women. *NBER Digest*. Retrieved from www.nber.org/digest/nov05/w11230.html

Frank, R. H. (2007). *Falling behind: How rising inequality harms the middle class*. Berkeley: University of California Press.

Franklin, B. (1736). Necessary hints to those that would be rich.

Franklin, B. (1748). Advice to a young tradesman.

Franklin, J. H. (1980). *From slavery to freedom* (5th ed.). New York: Knopf.

Fredrickson, G. M. (2002). *Racism: A short history*. Princeton, NJ: Princeton University Press.

Freedman, J. O. (2003). *Liberal education and the public interest*. Iowa City: University of Iowa Press.

Freeman, C. E. (2004, November 19). *Trends in educational equity of girls and women: 2004* (NCES 2005-016). U.S. Department of Education, National Center for Education Statistics. Washington, DC: U.S. Government Printing Office. Retrieved from http://nces.ed.gov/pubsearch/pubsinfo.asp?pubid=2005016

Freeman, R. B. (2007, February 22). *Do workers still want unions? More than ever* (Briefing Paper No. 182). Economic Policy Institute, Agenda for Shared Prosperity. Retrieved from www.sharedprosperity.org/bp182.html

Friedan, B. (1997; orig. 1963). *The feminine mystique*. New York: W. W. Norton.

Friedman, M. (1970, September 13). A Friedman doctrine—The social responsibility of business is to increase its profits. *The New York Times Magazine*. Retrieved from http://select.nytimes.com/gst/abstract.html?res=F10F11FB3E5810718EDDAA0994D1405B808BF1D3&scp=1&sq=The+social+responsibility+of+business+is+to+increase+its+profits&st=p

Fry, R., & Cohn, D. (2011). Living together: The economics of cohabitation. Pew Research Center. Retrieved from http://pewresearch.org/pubs/2034/cohabitation-rate-doubled-since-mid-90s-only-more-educated-benefit-economically

Fryer, R. G., & Levitt, S. D. (2003). *The causes and consequences of distinctly black names* (NBER Working Paper No. W9938).

Fuchs, V. (1967). Redefining poverty and redistributing income. *Public Interest, 8*, 88–95.

Fulton, L. (2011). Worker representation in Europe. Labour Research Department and ETUI. Retrieved from www.worker-participation.eu/National-Industrial-Relations/Across-Europe/Collective-Bargaining2

Gamm, G., & Putnam, R. D. (1999). The growth of voluntary associations in America, 1840–1940. Patterns of social capital: Stability and change in comparative perspective: Part II. *Journal of Interdisciplinary History, 29*(4), 511–557.

Gamoran, A., & Mare, R. D. (1989). Secondary school tracking and educational inequality: Compensation, reinforcement or neutrality? *American Journal of Sociology, 94*(5), 1146–1186.

Gans, H. (1979a). *Deciding what's news: A study of CBS Evening News, NBC Nightly News, Newsweek and Time*. New York: Vintage.

Gans, H. (1979b). Symbolic ethnicity: The future of ethnic groups and cultures in America. *Ethnic and Racial Studies, 2*, 1–19.

Ganz, M. (2004). Why David sometimes wins: Strategic capacity in social movements. In J. Goodwin & J. M. Jasper (Eds.), *Rethinking social movements: Structure, meaning, and emotion* (pp. 177–198). Lanham, MD: Rowman & Littlefield.

Garces, E., et al. (2002, September). Longer term effects of Head Start. *American Economic Review, 92*, 999–1012.

Gardner, H. (1983). *Frames of mind: The theory of multiple intelligences*. New York: Basic Books.

Garfinkel, H. (1967). *Studies in ethnomethodology*. Englewood Cliffs, NJ: Prentice-Hall.

Garrett, J. T. (1994). Health. In M. B. Davis (Ed.), *Native Americans in the 20th century* (pp. 233–237). New York: Garland.

Garrow, D. (1968). *Bearing the cross: Martin Luther King, Jr. and the Southern Christian Leadership Conference—A personal portrait*. New York: Morrow.

Gately, G. (2005, December 31). A town in the spotlight wants out of it. *The New York Times*. Retrieved from www.nytimes.com/2005/12/21/education/21dover

.html?scp=1&sq=A%20town%20in%20the%20spotlight%20wants%20out%20of%20it.&st=cse

Gates, G. J. (2011, April). How many people are lesbian, gay, bisexual, and transgender?. The Williams Institute, UCLA School of Law. Retrieved from http://services.law.ucla.edu/williamsinstitute/pdf/How-many-people-are-LGBT-Final.pdf

Gaustad, E. (1962). *Historical atlas of American religion.* New York: Harper and Row.

Gaventa, J. (1980). *Power and powerlessness: Quiescence and rebellion in an Appalachian valley*. Urbana: University of Illinois Press.

Geertz, C. (1973). *The interpretation of cultures*. New York: Basic Books.

Gerson, K. (1985). *Hard choices: How women decide about work, career, and motherhood.* Berkeley: University of California Press.

Gerson, K. (1993). *No man's land: Men's changing commitments to family and work*. New York: Basic Books.

Gieryn, T. F. (1999). *Cultural boundaries of science: Credibility on the line*. Chicago: University of Chicago Press.

Gilbert, D. (1998). *The American class structure in an age of growing inequality*. Belmont, CA: Wadsworth.

Gilligan, C. (1982). *In a different voice: Psychological theory and women's development.* Cambridge, MA: Harvard University Press.

CNN.com. (2011). "Give me a break." *Having it all: Work/life balance. CNN.com.* Retrieved from www.cnn.com/SPECIALS/2007/work.life.balance/chart/

Giving USA. (2011). The annual report on philanthropy for the year 2010. Retrieved from www.givingusareports.org/products/GivingUSA_2011_ExecSummary_Print.pdf

Glaeser, E. L., & Ward, B. A. (2006, January). *Myths and realities of American political geography* (Harvard Institute of Economic Research Discussion Paper No. 2100). Retrieved from http://ssrn.com/abstract=874977

Glass, J., & Jacobs, J. (2005). Childhood religious conservatism and adult attainment among black and white women. *Social Forces, 84*, 555–579.

Glassner, B. (1999). *The culture of fear: Why Americans are afraid of the wrong things.* New York: Basic Books.

Glazer, N., & Moynihan, D. P. (1963). *Beyond the melting pot: The Negroes, Puerto Ricans, Jews, Italians, and Irish of New York City*. Cambridge, MA: M.I.T. Press.

Glenn, E. N. (1986). *Issei, Nisei, war bride: Three generations of Japanese American women in domestic service.* Philadelphia: Temple University Press.

Global Carbon Project. (2011). Carbon budget. Retrieved from www.globalcarbonproject.org/carbonbudget/10/hl-full.htm

Glock, C., & Stark, R. (1965). *Religion and society in tension.* Chicago: Rand McNally.

Goffman, E. (1959). *The presentation of self in everyday life.* New York: Doubleday.

Goffman, E. (1961). *Asylums: Essays on the social situation of mental patients and other inmates*. New York: Doubleday Anchor.

Goffman, E. (1963). *Stigma: Notes on the management of spoiled identity*. Englewood Cliffs, NJ: Prentice-Hall.

Goldberger, P. (1995, April 20). The gospel of church architecture, revised. *The New York Times*, pp. C1, 5. Retrieved from http://query.nytimes.com/gst/fullpage.html?res=990CE0DC123FF933A15757C0A963958260&sec=&spon=&&scp=1&sq=+Megachurches:%20User-friendly%20architecture+&st=cse

Goodman, B. (2006a, April 17). People stand, the spirit walks: Easter at the Georgia Dome. *The New York Times.* Retrieved from www.nytimes.com/2006/04/17/us/17easter.html?scp=1&sq=People+stand%2C+the+spirit+walks%3A+Easter+at+the+Georgia+Dome.&st=nyt

Goodman, B. (2006b, March 29). Teaching the Bible in Georgia's public schools. *The New York Times.* Retrieved from www.nytimes.com/2006/03/29/education/29bible.html?scp=1&sq=Teaching%20the%20Bible%20in%20Georgia%E2%80%99s%20public%20schools.&st=cse

Goodstein, L. A. (2007, February 25). A divide, and maybe a divorce. *New York Times*, p. 1. Retrieved from www.nytimes.com/2007/02/25/weekinreview/25goodstein.html?scp=1&sq=A%20divide,%20and%20maybe%20a%20divorce&st=cse

Goodwin, J. (2006). *No other way out: States and revolutionary movements*. New York: Cambridge University Press.

Gordon, M. M. (1964). *Assimilation in American life: The role of race, religion, and national origins*. New York: Oxford University Press.

Gourevitch, P. (1998). *We wish to inform you that tomorrow we will be killed with our families: Stories from Rwanda.* New York: Farrar, Straus & Giroux.

Graetz, M. J., & Shapiro, I. (2005). *Death by a thousand cuts: The fight over taxing inherited wealth.* Princeton, NJ: Princeton University Press.

Gramsci, A. (1971). *Selections from the prison notebooks.* London: Lawrence and Wishart.

Granovetter, M. (1973). The strength of weak ties. *American Journal of Sociology, 78*, 1360–1380.

Granovetter, M. (1974). *Getting a job: A study of contacts and careers*. Chicago: University of Chicago Press.

Granovetter, M. (1978). Threshold models of collective behavior. *American Journal of Sociology, 83*(6), 1420–1443.

Grant, M. (1936; orig. 1916). *The passing of the great race* (4th rev. ed.). New York: Charles Scribner's Sons. Retrieved from www.archive.org/stream/passingofgreatra00granuoft/passingofgreatra00granuoft_djvu.txt.

Gray, J. (1992). *Men are from Mars, women are from Venus: A practical guide for improving communication and getting what you want in your relationships.* New York: HarperCollins.

Greer, C. (2006, April). *Black ethnicity: Political attitudes, identity, and participation in New York City.* Institute for Social and Economic Research and Policy, Columbia University. Retrieved from www.iserp.columbia.edu/news/articles/black_ethnicity.html

Grosz, E. A. (1994). *Volatile bodies: Toward a corporeal feminism.* Bloomington: Indiana University Press.

Guerino, P., et al. (2012). Prisoners in 2010. U.S. Department of Justice, Bureau of Justice Statistics. http://bjs.ojp.usdoj.gov/content/pub/pdf/p10.pdf

Gurian, M., & Stevens, K. (2005). *The minds of boys: Saving our sons from falling behind in school and life.* San Francisco: Jossey-Bass.

Gusfield, J. (1986). *Symbolic crusade: Status politics and the American temperance movement* (2nd ed.). Champaign: University of Illinois Press.

Haber, A. (1966). Poverty budgets: How much is enough? *Asia Pacific Journal of Human Resources, 1*(3), 5–22.

Hacker, J. (2006). *The great risk shift: The assault on American jobs, families, health care and retirement and how.* New York: Oxford University Press.

Hacking, I. (1999). *The social construction of what?* Cambridge, MA: Harvard University Press.

Hadaway, K. C., et al. (1993). What the polls don't show: A close look at U.S. church attendance. *American Sociological Review, 58*, 741–752.

Haley, A. (1976). *Roots: The saga of an American family.* New York: Doubleday.

Haney, L. (1996). Homeboys, babies, men in suits: The state and the reproduction of male dominance. *American Sociological Review, 61*, 759–778.

Haney López, I. F. (1995). White by law. In R. Delgado (Ed.), *Critical race theory: The cutting edge* (pp. 542–550). Philadelphia: Temple University Press.

Hannaford, I. (1996). *Race: The history of an idea in the West.* Washington, DC: The Woodrow Wilson Center Press.

Hanson, T. L., et al. (1997). Economic resources, parental practices and children's well-being. In G. Duncan & J. Brooks-Gunn (Eds.), *Consequences of growing up poor* (pp. 190–238). New York: Russell Sage Foundation.

Hanushek, E. A., et al. (2005). *The market for teacher quality* (NBER Working Paper No. 11154).

Hanushek, E. A., et al. (1998). *Teachers, schools, and academic achievement* (NBER Working Paper No. 6691).

Hanushek, E. A. & Wößmann, L. (2006). Does educational tracking affect performance and inequality? Differences-indifferences evidence across countries. *The Economic Journal, 116*(510), C63–76.

Harding, S. (1987). *Feminism and methodology: Social science issues.* Bloomington: Indiana University Press.

Harlem Children's Zone, Inc. (2011). History. *The Harlem Children's Zone Project.* Retrieved from www.hcz.org/about-us/history

Harris, A. R., et al. (2002). Murder and medicine: The lethality of criminal assault 1960–1999. *Homicide Studies, 6,* 128.

Hartmann, H. (1976). Capitalism, patriarchy, and job segregation by sex. *Signs, 1*(2), 137–169.

Hartmann, H. (1981). The unhappy marriage of Marxism and feminism. In L. Sargent (Ed.), *Women and revolution: A discussion of the unhappy marriage between Marxism and feminism* (pp. 1–43). Boston: South End Press.

Hasenfeld, Y., et al. (1987). The welfare state, citizenship, and bureaucratic encounters. *Annual Review of Sociology, 13*, 387–415.

Hashima, P. Y., & Amato, P. R. (1994). Poverty, social support and parental behavior. *Child Development, 65*, 394–403.

Haskell, K. (2004, May 16). Revelation plus make-up advice. *The New York Times.* Retrieved from http://query.nytimes.com/gst/fullpage.html?res=9906E2D7173FF935A25756C0A9629C8B63

Hawley, A. (1968). Human ecology. In D. Sills (Ed.), *International encyclopedia of the social sciences* (pp. 327–337). New York: Macmillan.

Hayford, S. R., & Morgan, P. S. (2008). Religiosity and fertility in the United States: The role of fertility intentions. *Sociological Forces, 86*(3), 1163–1188.

Hays, S. (2003). *Flat broke with children: Women in the age of welfare reform.* New York: Oxford University Press.

Heilbroner, R. L. (1999). *The worldly philosophers.* New York: Simon & Schuster.

Henry, L. (1969). *The home office guide.* New York: Arc Books.

Herbert, W. (2011, June 7). Virginity and promiscuity: Evidence for the very first time. *Association for Psychological Science.* Retrieved from www.psychologicalscience.org/index.php/news/

full-frontal-psychology/virginity-and-promiscuity-evidence-for-the-very-first-time.html

Herdt, G. H. (1981). *Guardians of the flutes: Idioms of masculinity.* New York: McGraw-Hill.

Hernandez, D. J. (1993). Figure 2.2, Percentage of children aged 0–17 living in four types of families, 1790–1989. In D. J. Hernandez, *America's children: Resources from family, government, and the economy.* New York: Russell Sage Foundation.

Hernandez, D. J., et al. (2007, April). Children in immigrant families in the U.S. and 50 states: National origins, language, and early education. *Children in America's newcomer families.* Child Trends and the Center for Social and Demographic Analysis, State University at Albany, SUNY 2007 Research Brief Series.

Herrnstein, R. J., & Murray, C. (1994). *The bell curve: Intelligence and class structure in American life.* New York: Free Press.

Hetherington, E. M., & Kelly, J. (2002). *For better or for worse: Divorce reconsidered.* New York: W. W. Norton.

Heyman, C. L. (1997) *Southern cross: The beginnings of the Bible belt.* New York: Knopf.

Hitchens, C. (2007). *God is not great: How religion poisons everything.* New York: Twelve Books, Hachette Book Group.

Ho, M. K. (1987). *Family therapy with ethnic minorities.* Newbury Park, CA: Sage.

Ho, V. (2009, March 12). Native American death rates soar as most people are living longer. *Seattlepi.com.* Seattle, Washington. Retrieved from www.seattlepi.com/local/403196_tribes12.html

Hobbes, T. (1981; orig. 1651). *Leviathan.* New York: Penguin Books.

Hochschild, A. R. (1989). *The second shift: Working parents and the revolution at home.* New York: Viking.

Hochschild, A. R. (1997). *The time bind: When work becomes home and home becomes work.* New York: Metropolitan Books.

Hochschild, A. R. (2003). *The commercialization of intimate life: Notes from home and work.* Berkeley: University of California Press.

hooks, b. (1984). Black women: Shaping feminist theory and feminism: A movement to end sexist oppression and the significance of the feminist movement. *Feminist theory from margin to center* (pp. 1–17). Boston: South End Press.

Horwitz, A. V., & Wakefield, J. C. (2007). *The loss of sadness: How psychiatry transformed normal sorrow into depressive disorder.* New York: Oxford University Press.

Hout, M. (1983). *Mobility tables: Quantitative applications in the social sciences.* Beverly Hills, CA: Sage.

How to tell your friends from the Japs. (1941, December 22). *Time.* Retrieved from www.time.com/time/magazine/article/0,9171,932034,00.html

Howe, L. K. (1977). *Pink collar workers: Inside the world of women's work.* New York: Putnam.

Howes, C., & Olenick, M. (1986). Family and child influences on toddlers' compliance. *Child Development, 26,* 292–303.

Howes, C., & Stewart, P. (1987). Child's play with adults, toys, and peers: An examination of family and child care influences. *Developmental Psychology, 23,* 423–430.

Hoxby, C. (2000, August). *Peer effects in the classroom: Learning from gender and race variation* (NBER Working Paper No. 7867).

Human Rights Watch. (2006). Building towers, cheating workers. Report. Retrieved from www.hrw.org/sites/default/files/reports/uae1106webwcover.pdf

Human Rights and Equal Opportunity Commission (HREOC). (1997, April). *Bringing them home: Report of the national inquiry into the separation of Aboriginal and Torres Strait Islander children from their families.* Retrieved from www.hreoc.gov.au/social_justice/bth_report/report/index.html

Hurley, D. (2005, April 19). The divorce rate: It's not as high as you think. *The New York Times.* Retrieved from www.nytimes.com/2005/04/19/health/19divo.html?scp=1&sq=&st=cse

Hurtado, A. (1995). Variations, combinations, and evolutions: Latino families in the United States. In R. E. Zambrana (Ed.), *Understanding Latino families: Scholarship, policy, and practice* (pp. 40–61). Thousand Oaks, CA: Sage.

Hymowitz, K. S. (2004, Autumn). Dads in the "hood." *City Journal.* Retrieved from www.city-journal.org/html/14_4_dads_hood.html

Iannaccone, L. R. (1997). Skewness explained: A rational choice model of religious giving. *Journal of the Scientific Study of Religion, 36,* 141–157.

Iannoccone, L. R., et al. (1995). Religious resources and church growth. *Social Forces, 74,* 705–731.

Ichihara, M. (2006). Making the case for soft power. *SAIS Review, 26*(1), 197–200.

Ikeda, H. (2001). Buraku students and cultural identity: The case of a Japanese minority. In K. Shimahara (Ed.), *Ethnicity, race, and nationality in education: A global perspective* (pp. 81–100). Mahwah, NJ: Erlbaum.

Imbens, G. W., et al. (2001, September). Estimating the effect of unearned income on labor earnings, savings, and consumption: Evidence from a survey of lottery players. *American Economic Review, 91*(4), 778–794.

Inglehart, R., & Baker, W. (2000, February). Modernization, cultural change and the persistence of traditional values. *American Sociological Review.*

Institution of Educations Sciences (IES), National Center for Education Statistics (NES). (2010). Digest of education Statistics: Table 144. SAT mean scores of college-bound seniors by sex: 1966–67 through 2008–09. U.S. Department of Education. Retrieved from http://nces.ed.gov/programs/digest/d09/tables/dt09_144.asp

Intergovernmental Panel on Climate Change. (2003). *Climate Change 2001: Working Group I: The Scientific Basis.* www.grida.no/climate/ipcc_tar/wg1/005.htm

Internet World Stats. (2011). Usage and population statistics. Retrieved from www.internetworldstats.com/stats.htm

Internet World Stats. (2012). World Internet users and population stats. Retrieved from www.internetworldstats.com/stats.htm

Intersex Society of North America (ISNA). (2006). *What's wrong with the way intersex has traditionally been treated?* Retrieved from www.isna.org/faq/concealment

Isaacs, H. (1975). *Idols of the tribe: Group identity and political change.* New York: Harper & Row.

Jackson, P. (1968). *Life in classrooms.* New York: Holt, Reinhart, & Winston.

Jackson, R. M. (1998). *Destined for equality.* Cambridge, MA: Harvard University Press.

Jacobs, J. (1961). *The death and life of great American cities.* New York: Random House.

Jacobs, J., & Gerson, K. (2004). *The time divide: Work, family, and gender inequality.* Cambridge, MA: Harvard University Press.

Jacobson, M. F. (1998). Anglo-Saxons and others, 1840–1924. In *Whiteness of a different color: European immigrants and the alchemy of race* (pp. 39–90). Cambridge, MA: Harvard University Press.

James, G. (2003, June 29). Exurbia and God: Megachurches in New Jersey. *The New York Times,* pp. 1, 17. Retrieved from http://query.nytimes.com/gst/fullpage.html?res=9406E0D71439F93AA15755C0A9659C8B63

James, S. A., et al. (1987). Socioeconomic status, John Henryism, and hypertension in blacks and whites. *American Journal of Epidemiology, 126,* 664–673.

James, W. (1982; orig. 1903). *The varieties of religious experience.* New York: Penguin.

Jencks, C., & Phillips, M. (Eds.). (1998). *The black-white test score gap.* Washington, DC: Brookings Institution Press.

Jencks, C., et al. (1972). *Inequality: A reassessment of the effect of family and schooling in America.* New York: Basic Books.

Jenson, A. R. (1969). How much can we boost IQ and scholastic achievement? *Harvard Educational Review, 39,* 1–123.

Johnson, L. (1998, July; orig. March 16, 1964). Proposal for a nationwide war on the sources of poverty. In P. Halsall (Ed.), *Internet modern history sourcebook.* Retrieved from www.fordham.edu/halsall/mod/1964johnson-warpoverty.html.

Johnson, M. P. (1995). Patriarchal terrorism and common couple violence: Two forms of violence against women. *Journal of Marriage and the Family, 57,* 283–295.

Johnston, D. C. (2003). *Perfectly legal: The covert campaign to rig our tax system to benefit the super rich—and cheat everybody else.* New York: Portfolio.

Johnston, D. C. (2005, June 5). Richest are leaving even the rich far behind. *The New York Times.* Retrieved from www.-nytimes.com/2005/06/05/national/class/HYPER-FINAL.html?scp=1&sq=Richest%20are%20leaving%20even%20the%20rich%20far%20behind&st=cse

Joint Economic Committee Majority Staff. (2011, May). Understanding the economy: Working mothers in the Great Recession. Retrieved from http://jec.senate.gov/public/?a=Files.Serve&File_id=c8242af9-a97b-4a97-9a9d-f7f7999911ab

Kaiser Family Foundation. (2011). State Health Facts. Retrieved from http://statehealthfacts.org/comparecat.jsp?cat=3&rgn=23&rgn=1

Kane, T. J. (1998). Racial and ethnic preferences in college admissions. In C. Jencks & M. Phillips (Eds.), *The black-white test score gap* (pp. 431–456). Washington, DC: Brookings Institution Press.

Kanter, R. M. (1977). *Men and women of the corporation.* New York: Basic Books.

Kaplan, E. A. (2003, October 3–9). Black like I thought I was: Race, DNA, and a man who knows too much. *L.A. Weekly.* Retrieved from www.alternet.org/story.html?StoryID=16917

Kashef, Z. (2003). Persistent peril: Why African American babies have the highest infant mortality rate in the developed world. *RaceWire* (February). Retrieved from www.arc.org/racewire/030210z_kashef.html

Kass, L. R. (1997, June 2). The wisdom of repugnance. *The New Republic.*

Katz, R. (2000, June 16). Re: Credit default option facility [Letter to B. Lundkvist]. State of New York Insurance Department.

Kelley, D. M. (1972). *Why conservative churches are growing: A study in sociology of religion.* San Francisco: Harper & Row.

Kelling, G. L., & Sousa, Jr., W. H. (2001). Do police matter? An analysis of the impact of New York City's police reforms. *Civic Report, 22.*

Kennedy, S., & Bumpass, L. (2008). Cohabitation and children's living arrangements: New estimates from the United States. *Demographic Research, 19*(47), 1663–1692. Retrieved from www.demographic-research.org/Volumes/V0119/47/

Kessler-Harris, A. (1990). *A woman's wage: Historical meanings and social consequences.* Lexington: University Press of Kentucky.

Khan, S. R. (2010). *Privilege: The making of an adolescent elite at St. Paul's School.* Princeton, NJ: Princeton University Press.

Kidder, T. (2003). *Mountains beyond mountains: Healing the world: The quest of Dr. Paul Farmer.* New York: Random House.

Kilbourne, J. (1979). *Killing us softly: Advertising's image of women* [Videorecording]. Belmont, MA: Cambridge Documentary Films.

Kim, S. (2001). Hegemony and cultural resistance. In N. J. Smelser & P. B. Baltes (Eds.), *International encyclopedia of the social & behavioral sciences.* New York: Elsevier.

Kimmel, M. S. (1996). *Manhood in America: A cultural history.* New York: Free Press.

Kimmel, M. S. (2000). *The gendered society.* New York: Oxford University Press.

Kinsey, A. C. (1948). *Sexual behavior in the human male.* Philadelphia: Saunders.

Kirkpatrick, D. (2002, June 8). Evangelical sales are converting publishers. *The New York Times.* Retrieved from http://query.nytimes.com/gst/fullpage.html?res=9C03EFD6153DF93BA35755C0A9649C8B63

Kitzmiller, et al. v. Dover Area School District, et al., 400 F. Supp. 2d 707 (M.D. Pa. 2005). Retrieved from www.pamd.uscourts.gov/kitzmiller/kitzmiller_342.pdf

Klebanov, P. K., et al. (1994). Classroom behavior of very low birth weight elementary school children. *Pediatrics, 94*(5), 700–708.

Klein, M. (1949). *The psycho-analysis of children* (3rd ed.). London: Hogarth Press.

Klein, N. (2000). *No logo: Taking aim at the brand bullies.* New York: Picador.

Klinenberg, E. (2002). *Heat wave: A social autopsy of disaster in Chicago.* Chicago: University of Chicago Press.

Knafo, S. (2005, December 25). Praise the Lord and raise the curtain. *The New York Times.* Retrieved from http://query.nytimes.com/gst/fullpage.html?res=9402E6DB1530F936A15751C1A9639C8B63

Knobel, D. T. (1986). *Paddy and the republic: Ethnicity and nationality in antebellum America.* Middletown, CT: Wesleyan University Press.

Kochanek, K. D., et al. (2011). National vital statistics reports. Deaths: Preliminary data for 2009. Retrieved from www.cdc.gov/nchs/data/nvsr/nvsr59/nvsr59_04.pdf

Koenig, H. G., et al. (1994). Religious practices and alcoholism in a southern adult population. *Hospital Communication Psychiatry, 45,* 225–231.

Kohn, M. L., & Schooler, C. (1983). *Work and personality: An inquiry into the impact of social stratification.* Norwood, NJ: Ablex.

Kozol, J. (1991). *Savage inequalities: Children in America's schools.* New York: Crown.

Krakauer, J. (1997). *Into the wild.* New York: Anchor Books.

Krangel, E. (2009, January 8). Obama on BlackBerry: "They're going to pry it out of my hands." *Business Insider.* Retrieved from www.businessinsider.com/2009/1/obama-on-blackberry-theyre-going-to-pry-it-out-of-my-hands

Krantz, M. (2002, November 24). Web of board members ties together corporate America. *USA Today.* Retrieved from www.usatoday.com/money/companies/management/2002-11-24-interlock_x.htm

Kraybill, D. B. (Ed.). (1993). *The Amish and the state.* Baltimore, MD: Johns Hopkins University Press.

Kraybill, D. B., & Nolt, S. (1995). *Amish enterprise: From plows to profits.* Baltimore, MD: Johns Hopkins University Press.

Kreider, R., & Ellis, R. (2011). Number, timing, and duration of marriages and divorces: 2009. Current population reports, U.S. Census Bureau. Retrieved from www.census.gov/prod/2011pubs/p70-125.pdf

Krueger, A. B., & Whitmore, D. M. (2001). The effect of attending a small class in the early grades on college test-taking and middle school test results: Evidence from Project STAR. *Economic Journal, 111*(468), 1–28.

Krueger, A. B., & Zhu, P. (2002). *Another look at the New York City school voucher experiment* (NBER Working Paper No. 9418).

Krugman, P. (2005, September 16). Not the new deal. *The New York Times.* Retrieved from www.nytimes.com/2005/09/16/opinion/16krugman.html?scp=6&sq=Not%20the%20new%20deal%20krugman&st=cse

Kuhn, T. (1962). *The structure of scientific revolutions.* Chicago: University of Chicago Press.

Kulick, D. (1998). *Travesti: Sex, gender, and culture among Brazilian transgendered prostitutes.* Chicago: University of Chicago Press.

Kuruvil, M. C. (2006, September 3). 9/11: Five years later. Typecasting Muslims as a race. *San Francisco Chronicle.* Retrieved from www.sfgate.com/cgi-bin/article.cgi?f=/c/a/2006/09/03/MNG4FKUMR71.DTL

Kurzman, C. (2002, December). Bin Laden and other thoroughly modern Muslims. *Contexts Magazine, 1*(4), 13–20.

Kutner, M., et al. (2005). *A first look at the literacy of America's adults in the 21st century* (NCES 2006-470). U.S. Department of Education, National Assessments of Adult Literacy. Washington, DC: U.S. Government Printing Office.

Lamont, M. (1992). *Money, morals, and manners.* Chicago: University of Chicago Press.

Langlois, D. E., & Zales, C. R. (1992). Anatomy of a top teacher. *Education Digest, 57*(5), 31–34.

Laqueur, T. (1990). *Making sex: Body and gender from the Greeks to Freud.* Cambridge, MA: Harvard University Press.

Lareau, A. (1987). Social class differences in family-school relationships: The importance of cultural capital. *Sociology of Education, 60*, 33–85.

Lareau, A. (2002). Invisible inequality: Social class and child-rearing in black families and white families. *American Sociological Review, 67*, 747–776.

Lareau, A. (2003). *Unequal childhoods: Class, race, and family life.* Berkeley: University of California Press.

Lareau, A., et al. (2006, July). *Social class and children's time use* (working paper). University of Maryland Department of Sociology.

Lasch, C. (1977). *Haven in a heartless world: The family besieged.* New York: Basic Books.

Lasch, C. (1991). *The true and only heaven: Progress and its critics.* New York: W. W. Norton.

Latour, B., & Woolgar, S. (1979). *Laboratory life: The social construction of scientific facts.* Los Angeles: Sage.

LeBon, G. (2002; orig. 1895). *La psychologie des foules.* (*The crowd: A study of the popular mind.*) Mineola, NY: Dover.

Lee, F. R. (2006, March 28). In Utah, Hollywood seems oversexed. *The New York Times.* Retrieved from http://query.nytimes.com/gst/fullpage.html?res=9806E3D91430F93BA15750C0A9609C8B63&sec=&spon=&pagewanted=2

Leiter, J. (1983). Classroom composition and achievement gains. *Sociology of Education, 56*(3), 126–132.

Leland, J. (2004, May 16). Alt-worship. *The New York Times.* Retrieved from http://query.nytimes.com/gst/fullpage.html?res=9E00E4DC123DF93BA25751C0A9629C8B63

Lempers, J. D., et al. (1989). Economic hardship, parenting and distress in adolescence. *Child Development, 60*, 25–39.

Lenski, G. (1961). *The religious factor: A sociological study of religion's impact on politics, economics, and family life.* New York: Doubleday.

Lever, J. (1976). Sex differences in the games children play. *Social Problems, 23*, 478–487.

Levitt, S. D., & Dubner, S. J. (2005). *Freakonomics: A rogue economist explores the hidden side of everything.* New York: Morrow.

Lewis, A. E. (2004). *Race in the schoolyard: Negotiating the color line in classrooms and communities.* New Brunswick, NJ: Rutgers University Press.

Lewis, C., et al. (1992). Sex stereotyping of infants: A re-examination. *Journal of Reproductive and Infant Psychology, 10*, 53–61.

Lewis, O. (1966). The culture of poverty. *Scientific American, 215*(4), 19–25.

Lieberson, S. (1961). A societal theory of race and ethnic relations. *American Sociological Review, 26*, 902–910.

Lieberson, S., et al. (2000). The Instability of Androgynous Names: The Symbolic Maintenance of Gender Boundaries. *American Journal of Sociology, 105, 5,* 1249–1287.

Lleras-Muney, A. (2005). The relationship between education and adult mortality in the United States. *Review of Economic Studies, 72*, 189–221.

Locke, J. (1980; orig. 1690). *Second treatise of government.* Indianapolis, IN: Hackett.

Lorber, J. (1994). *Paradoxes of gender.* New Haven: Yale University Press.

Lucas, S. R. (1999). *Tracking inequality: Stratification and mobility in American high schools.* New York: Teachers College Press.

Lucas, S. R., & Good, A. D. (2001). Race, class, and tournament track mobility. *Sociology of Education, 74*, 139–156.

Lui, M. (2004). Doubly divided: The racial wealth gap. In C. Collins et al. (Eds.), *The wealth inequality reader.* Cambridge, MA: Economic Affairs Bureau.

Lukes, S., & British Sociological Association. (2005; orig. 1974). *Power: A radical view.* New York: Palgrave Macmillan.

Luo, M. (2006, April 16). Evangelicals debate the meaning of "evangelical." *The New York Times*, pp. 4, 5. Retrieved from www.nytimes.com/2006/04/16/

weekinreview/16luo.html?scp=1&sq=Evangelicals%20debate%20the%20meaning%20of%20%E2%80%9Cevangelical&st=cse

Maathai, W. (2004, October 10). Statement on the occasion of receiving the 2004 Nobel Peace Prize. *The Green Belt Movement.* Retrieved from www.greenbeltmovement.org/w.php?id=10

Mack, J., & Lansley, S. (1985). *Poor Britain.* London: Allen & Unwin.

MacKinnon, C. (1983). Feminism, Marxism, method and the state: Toward feminist jurisprudence. *Signs: Journal of Women in Culture and Society, 8*, 635.

MacLeod, J. (1995; orig. 1987). *Ain't no makin' it: Aspirations and attainment in a low-income neighborhood.* Boulder, CO: Westview Press.

MacMaster, N. (2001). *Racism in Europe 1870–2000.* Basingstoke, Hampshire: Palgrave.

Malinowski, B. (1913). *The family among the Australian Aborigines.* London: University of London Press.

Maltz, M. D. (2001). *Recidivism.* Orlando, FL: Academic Press. (Original work published 1984.) Retrieved from www.uic.edu/depts/lib/forr/pdf/crimjust/recidivism.pdf

Manza, J., & Uggen, C. (2006). *Locked out: Felon disenfranchisement and American democracy.* New York: Oxford University Press.

Maraniss, D. (1995). *First in his class: The biography of Bill Clinton.* New York: Simon & Schuster.

Marmot, M., & Wilkinson, R. G. (Eds). (1999). *Social determinants of health.* New York: Oxford University Press.

Martin, J. A., et al. (2010). National vital statistics reports. National Center for Health Statistics. Births: Final Data for 2008. Division of Vital Statistics. Retrieved from www.cdc.gov/nchs/data/nvsr/nvsr59/nvsr59_01.pdf

Martin, J. A., et al. (2011). National vital statistics reports. National Center for Health Statistics. Births: Final Data for 2009. Division of Vital Statistics. Retrieved from www.cdc.gov/nchs/data/nvsr/nvsr60/nvsr60_01.pdf

Martin, J. T., & Nguyen, D. H. (2004). Anthropometric analysis of homosexuals and heterosexuals: Implications for early hormone exposure. *Hormones and Behavior, 45*(1), 31–39.

Martineau, H. (1837). *Theory and practice of society in America.* London: Saunders & Otley.

Martineau, H. (1838). *How to observe morals and manners.* London: Charles Knight & Company.

Marx, A. W. (1998). To bind up the nation's wounds: The United States after the Civil War. In *Making race and nation: A comparison of South Africa, the United States, and Brazil* (pp. 120–157). Cambridge: Cambridge University Press.

Marx, K. (1932; orig. 1844). Estranged labor. *Economic and Philosophical Manuscripts of 1844.* Retrieved from www.marxists.org/archive/marx/works/1844/manuscripts/labour.htm.

Marx, K. (1978; orig. 1844). Contribution to the critique of Hegel's philosophy of right: Introduction. In R. Tucker (Ed.), *The Marx-Engels reader* (pp. 53–65). New York: W. W. Norton.

Marx, K. (1999; orig. 1890–91). Critique of the Gotha programme. In *Marxists Internet archive.* Retrieved from www.marxists.org/archive/marx/works/1875/gotha/index.htm.

Marx, K., & Engels, F. (1998; orig. 1848). *The communist manifesto.* New York: Penguin Group.

Mascha, M. (2008, March 31). 2007 US bottled water sales statistics. *The Water Connoisseur.* Retrieved from www.finewaters.com/Newsletter/The_Water_Connoisseur_Archive/2007_US_Bottled_Water_Sales_Statistics.asp

Massey, D. S. (1995). The new immigration and ethnicity in the United States. *Population and Development Review, 21*, 631–652.

Massey, D. S., & Denton, N. A. (1993). *American apartheid: Segregation and the making of the underclass.* Cambridge, MA: Harvard University Press.

Mayer, S. (1997). *What money can't buy: Family income and children's life chances.* Cambridge, MA: Harvard University Press.

McAdam, D. (1982). *Political process and the development of black insurgency, 1930–1970.* Chicago: University of Chicago Press.

McCarthy, J. D., & Zald, M. N. (1973). *The trend of social movements in America: Professionalization and resource mobilization.* Morristown, NJ: General Learning Press.

McCarthy, J. D., & Zald, M. N. (1977). Resource mobilization and social movements: A partial theory. *American Journal of Sociology, 82*(6), 1212–1241.

McCloskey, D. (1999). *Crossing: A memoir.* Chicago: University of Chicago Press.

McCullough, M., & Smith, T. (2003). Religion and health: Depressive symptoms and mortality as case studies. In M. Dillon (Ed.), *Handbook of sociology of religion* (pp. 190–206). Cambridge: Cambridge University Press.

McDonald, M., & Popkin, S. (2001). The myth of the vanishing voter. *American Political Science Review, 95*(4), 963–974.

McGregor, P.P.L., & Borooah, V. K. (1992). Is low spending or low income a better indicator of whether or not a household is poor: Some results from the 1985 Family Expenditure Survey. *Journal of Social Policy*, *21*(1), 53–69.

McGuire, M. (2007). Embodied practices: Negotiation and resistance. In N. Ammerman (Ed.), *Everyday religion: Observing modern religious lives* (pp. 187–200). New York: Oxford University Press. Retrieved from www.oxfordscholarship.com/oso/public/content/religion/9780195305418/toc.html?q=Embodied `practices:`Negotiation`resistance

McIntosh, P. (1988). *White privilege and male privilege: A personal account of coming to see correspondences through work in women's studies.* Wellesley, MA: Wellesley College Center for Research on Women.

McLeod, J. D., & Shanahan, M. J. (1993). Poverty, parenting and children's mental health. *American Sociological Review*, *58*, 351–366.

Mead, G. H. (1934). *Mind, self, and society from the standpoint of a social behaviorist* (C. W. Morris, Ed.). Chicago: University of Chicago Press.

Mead, M. (1928). *Coming of age in Samoa.* New York: Morrow.

Mechanic, D., & Meyer, S. (2000). Concepts of trust among patients with serious illness. *Social Science and Medicine*, *51*(5), 657–668.

Meckler, L. (2002, July 24). Divorce, American style. Study: Certain couples more likely to split up than others. *CBS News.* Retrieved from www.cbsnews.com/stories/2002/07/24/national/main516165.shtml

Media Matters for America. (2005). *The "truth" according to Limbaugh.* Retrieved from www.mediamatters.org/items/200508160001

Meier, R. F. (1982). Perspectives on the concept of social control. *Annual Review of Sociology*, *8*, 35–55.

Meighan, R. (1981). *A sociology of educating.* New York: Holt, Reinhart, & Winston.

Merton, R. (1938). Social structure and anomie. *American Sociological Review*, *3*, 672–682.

Merton, R. (1949). Discrimination and the American creed. In R. M. MacIver (Ed.), *Discrimination and national welfare; a series of addresses and discussion* (pp. 99–126). New York: Institute for Religious and Social Studies.

Merton, R. (1949). *Social theory and social structure.* Glencoe, IL: Free Press.

Michels, R. (1915). *Political parties: A sociological study of the oligarchical tendencies of modern democracy* (E. and C. Paul, Trans.). New York: Hearst's International Library.

Miele, F. (1995). For whom the bell curve tolls: Interview with Charles Murray. *Skeptic*, *3*(2), 34–41. Retrieved from www.prometheism.net/articles/interview01.html

Milkman, R. (1987). *Gender at work: The dynamics of job segregation by sex during World War II.* Urbana: University of Illinois Press.

Milkman, R. (2006). *LA Story: Immigrant workers and the future of the US labor movement.* New York: Russell Sage Foundation.

Milkman, R. (2007). Unions fight for work and family policies. In Dorothy Sue Cobble (Ed.), *The sex of class: Women transforming American labor* (pp. 63–80). Ithaca, NY: Cornell University Press.

Mills, C. W. (1959). *The sociological imagination.* New York: Oxford University Press.

Mills, C. W. (2000; orig. 1956). *The power elite.* New York: Oxford University Press.

Missouri Economic Research and Information Center. (2012). Cost of living data series 4th quarter 2011. Retrieved from www.missourieconomy.org/indicators/cost_of_living/index.stm.

Molnar, A., & Sawicky, M. B. (1998, April). *The hidden costs of Channel One: Estimates for the 50 states.* Tempe, AZ: Commercialism in Education Research Unit.

Monaghan, T. (1990, August). The thrill of poverty. *Harpers Magazine*, p. 22.

Montesquieu, C., Baron de. (1750; orig. 1748). *The spirit of the laws* (Vols. 1–2, Thomas Nugent et al., Trans.), 1777.

Moore, B. (1993; orig. 1966). *Social origins of dictatorship and democracy: Lord and peasant in the making of the modern world.* Boston: Beacon Press.

Morning, A. (2004). *The nature of race: Teaching and learning about human difference.* Ph.D. dissertation, Department of Sociology, Princeton University.

Morris, A. (1984). *The origins of the civil rights movement.* New York: Free Press.

Morris, A. (2004). Reflections on social movement theory: Criticisms and proposals. In J. Goodwin & J. M. Jasper (Eds.), *Rethinking social movements: Structure, meaning, and emotion* (pp. 233–246). Lanham, MD: Rowman & Littlefield.

Morrison, D. R., & Coiro, M. J. (1999). Parental conflict and marital disruption: Do children benefit when high-conflict marriages are dissolved? *Journal of Marriage and the Family*, *61*, 626–637.

Moskovitz, D. (2006, September 8). Anti-Muslim incidents on rise in state, watchdog group says. *Miami Herald.* Retrieved from www.miami.com/mld/miamiherald/15465296.htm

Moynihan, D. P. (1965). *The Negro family: The case for national action*. Washington, DC: Office of Policy Planning and Research United States Department of Labor.

Murnane, R. J., et al. (2005). Learning why more learning takes place in some classrooms than others. *German Economic Review*, *6*(3), 309–330.

Murray, C. A. (1984). *Losing ground: American social policy, 1950–1980*. New York: Basic Books.

Murray, S. (2009, May 9). The curse of the Class of 2009. *The Wall Street Journal*. Education section. Retrieved from http://online.wsj.com/article/SB124181970915002009.html#

Musil, Steven. (2008, May 18). Survey: One-fifth of Americans have never used e-mail. CNET NewsBlog. Retrieved from http://news.cnet.com/8301-10784_3-9946706-7.html

Mustanski, B. S., et al. (2005, March). A genomewide scan of male sexual orientation. *Human Genetics, 116*(4), 272–278. doi:10.1007/s00439-004-1241-4. PMID 15645181. Retrieved from http://mypage.iu.edu/~bmustans/Mustanski_etal_2005.pdf

Myrdal, G. (1944). *An American dilemma: The Negro problem and modern democracy*. New York: Harper & Brothers.

Nanda, S. (1990). *Neither man nor woman: The hijras of India*. New York: Wadsworth. [second edition published in 1999].

Nason-Clark, N. (2000). Making the sacred safe: Woman abuse and communities of faith. *Sociology of Religion, 61*(4), 349–368.

National Center for Education Statistics (NCES). (2009). Table 3: Percentage distribution of school teacher by age category, average and median age of teachers, and percentage distribution of teachers, by sex, school type, and selected school characteristics, 2007–2008. *Characteristics of public, private, and Bureau of Indian Education elementary and secondary school teachers in the United States: Results from the 2007–2008 schools and staffing survey*. U.S. Department of Education, Institute of Education Sciences. Retrieved from http://nces.ed.gov/pubsearch/pubsinfo.asp?pubid=2009324

Nelsen, H. M. (1988). Unchurched black Americans: Patterns of religiosity and affiliation. *Review of Religious Research*, *29*, 398–412.

Nelson, D. J., & Rogers, D. C. (2004). *A national analysis of diversity in science and engineering faculties at research universities*. Retrieved from www.now.org/issues/diverse/diversity_report.pdf

Nelson, M. K. (1990). *Negotiated care: The experience of family day care providers*. Philadelphia: Temple University Press.

Net Applications. (2011). Market share for mobile and desktop. Retrieved from http://marketshare.hitslink.com/operating-system-market-share.aspx?qprid=8

New York City Department of Public Health. (2009). Don't drink yourself fat [Public service poster]. Retrieved from www.nytimes.com/imagepages/2009/09/01/nyregion/01fat.ready.html

New York State Division of Parole (2007, September). *New York State parole handbook* (NYSPH). Retrieved from http://parole.state.ny.us/Handbook.pdf

Nicholas, R. W. (1973). Social and political movements. *Annual Review of Anthropology*, *2*, 63–84.

Niebuhr, G. (1995, April 18). The gospels of management. The minister as marketer: Learning from business. *The New York Times,* p. 1. Retrieved from http://query.nytimes.com/gst/fullpage.html?res=990CE7DB113FF93BA25757C0A963958260&scp=1&sq=Megachurches:%20The%20gospels%20of%20management.%20The%20minister%20as%20marketer:%20Learning%20from%20business&st=cse

Niebuhr, H. R. (1929). *The social sources of denominationalism*. New York: Holt.

Nissle, S., & Bshor, T. (2002). Winning the jackpot and depression: Money cannot buy happiness. *International Journal of Psychiatry in Clinical Practice*, *6*(3), 183–186.

Norris, P., et al. (2001). *Digital divide: Civic engagement, information poverty, and the Internet worldwide*. Cambridge: Cambridge University Press.

Nussbaum, P. (2006, January 21). A global ministry of "muscular Christianity." *The Washington Post*. Retrieved from www.washingtonpost.com/wp-dyn/content/article/2006/01/21/AR2006012100284_pf.html

Nye, B. A., et al. (1994). Small is far better. *Research in the Schools*, *1*(1), 9–20.

Nye, J. (1990). Soft power. *Foreign Policy*, *80*, 153–171.

Oakes, J. (1985). *Keeping track: How schools structure inequality*. New Haven: Yale University Press.

Oakley, A. (1972). *Sex, gender, and society*. London: Maurice Temple Smith.

Obama, B. (2008). Changing the odds on urban poverty (campaign speech). Retrieved from www.youtube.com/watch?v=Xh5QRMaa_KE

Obama, B. (2009, July 24). Promoting innovation, reform, and excellence in America's public schools. The White House: Office of the Press Secretary.

Retrieved from www.whitehouse.gov/the-press-office/fact-sheet-race-top

O'Barr, W. (1995). *Linguistic evidence: Language, power and strategy—The courtroom.* San Diego, CA: Academic Press.

O'Connor, N. (2009, April). Hispanic origin, socio-economic status, and community college enrollment. *Journal of Higher Education, 80*(2), 121–145.

Oliver, J. E. (1993). Intergenerational transmission of child abuse: Rates, research and clinical implications. *American Journal of Psychiatry, 150,* 1315–1324.

Oliver, M., & Shapiro, T. (1995). *Black wealth, white wealth: A new perspective on racial inequality.* London: Routledge.

Olson, M. (1965). *The logic of collective action.* Cambridge, MA: Harvard University Press.

Oreopoulos, P., & Salvanes, K. (2009). How large are returns to schooling? Hint: Money isn't everything. *NBER Working Paper Series.* Cambridge, MA: National Bureau of Economic Research. Retrieved from www.nber.org/papers/w15339.pdf

Orfield, G. (1996). Turning back to segregation. In G. Orfield & S. E. Eaton (Eds.), *Dismantling desegregation: The quiet reversal of* Brown v. Board of *Education* (pp. 1–22). New York: The New Press.

Organization for Economic Co-operation and Development (OECD). (2012). Income distribution: Poverty. Retrieved from http://stats.oecd.org/Index.aspx?QueryId=11554&QueryType=View.

Orr, A. H. (2007). A mission to convert. *The New York Review of Books, 54*(1). Retrieved from www.nybooks.com/articles/19775

Orshansky, M. (1963). *Children of the poor* (Social Security bulletin). Washington, DC: U.S. Department of Labor.

Ortner, S. (1974). Is female to male as nature to culture? In M. Z. Rosaldo & L. Lamphere (Eds.), *Woman, culture, and society* (pp. 67–88). Stanford, CA: Stanford University Press.

Oyěwùmí, O. (1997). *The invention of women: Making an African sense of Western gender discourses.* Minneapolis: University of Minnesota Press.

Pager, D. (2003). Blacks and ex-cons need not apply. *Contexts, 2*(4), 58–59.

Pareto, V. (1983; orig. 1935). *The mind and society* (A. Livingston, Ed., A. Bongiorno & A. Livingston, Trans.). New York: AMS Press.

Pareto, V., & Finer, S. E. (1966). *Sociological writings.* New York: Praeger Sociology.

Parker, I. (2007, July 30). Our far flung correspondents: Swingers. *The New Yorker.* Retrieved from www.newyorker.com/reporting/2007/07/30/070730fa_fact_parker

Parkin, F. (1982). *Max Weber.* London: Tavistock.

Parsons, E. F. (2005). Midnight rangers: Costume and performance in the reconstruction-era Ku Klux Klan. *The Journal of American History, 92*(3), 811.

Parsons, T. (1951). *The social system.* Glencoe, IL: Free Press.

Pascoe, C. J. (2007). *Dude, you're a fag: Masculinity and sexuality in high school.* Berkeley: University of California Press.

PBS. (2000, February 22). Lost tribes of Israel. *Nova.* Retrieved from www.pbs.org/wgbh/nova/transcripts/2706israel.html

Pearson, B. Z. (1993). Predictive validity of the scholastic aptitude test (SAT) for Hispanic bilingual students. *Hispanic Journal of Behavioral Sciences, 15*(3), 342–356.

Penner, J. E., et al. (Eds.). (1999). *Aviation and the global atmosphere.* Cambridge: Cambridge University Press. Retrieved from www.ipcc.ch/ipccreports/sres/aviation/index.php?idp=64

Perrow, C. (2007). *The next catastrophe: Reducing our vulnerabilities to natural, industrial, and terrorist disasters.* Princeton, NJ: Princeton University Press.

Pettit, B., & Western, B. (2004). Mass imprisonment and the life course: Race and class inequality in U.S. incarceration. *American Sociological Review, 69*(2), 151–169.

Pew Center on the States. (2008). Appendix A-6: 1 in X incarceration rates by sex, race/ethnicicy, age & state. *One in 100: Behind Bars in America 2008.*

Pew Forum on Religious and Public Life. (2008, February). US religious landscape survey: Religious affiliation: Diverse and dynamic. Washington, DC: The Pew Forum on Religion and Public Life.

Pew Forum on Religious and Public Life. (2010). U.S. religious landscape survey. Retrieved from http://religions.pewforum.org/reports

Pew Internet & American Life Project. (2009). *Home broadband adoption 2009.* Retrieved from http://pewresearch.org/pubs/1254/home-broadband-adoption-2009

Pew Research Center. (2007). U.S. religious landscape survey. Retrieved from http://religions.pewforum.org/reports

Pew Research Center. (2011a). Muslim American survey. Retrieved from www.people-press.org/2011/08/30/section-1-a-demographic-portrait-of-muslim-americans/

Pew Research Center. (2011b). Pew Research Center's social & demographic trends (July 26). Wealth gaps rise to record highs between whites, blacks and

Hispanics. Retrieved from http://pewresearch.org/pubs/2069/housing-bubble-subprime-mortgages-hispanics-blacks-household-wealth-disparity

Pew Research Center. (2011c). Multi-race Americans and the 2010 Census (April 5). Retrieved from www.pewsocialtrends.org/2011/04/05/multi-race-americans-and-the-2010-census/

Pew Research Center. (2011d). Most say homosexuality should be accepted by society. (May 13). Retrieved from http://pewresearch.org/pubs/1994/poll-support-for-acceptance-of-homosexuality-gay-parenting-marriage

Phelan, C., & Link, B. G. (2005). Controlling disease and creating disparities: A fundamental cause perspective. *Journals of Gerontology, 60B,* 30, 31.

Phillips, D., et al. (1987). Child care quality and children's social development. *Developmental Psychology, 23,* 537–543.

Pierce, J. L. (1995). *Gender trials: Emotional lives in contemporary law firms* (Intro. and Chap. 3–6). Berkeley: University of California Press.

Pilkington, D. (1996). *Follow the rabbit-proof fence.* St. Lucia: University of Queensland Press.

Pipher, M. B. (1994). *Reviving Ophelia: Saving the selves of adolescent girls.* New York: Putnam.

Piven, F. F., & Cloward, R. A. (1988). *Why Americans don't vote: And why politicians want it that way.* Boston: Beacon Press.

Plath, S. (1971; orig. 1963). *The bell jar.* New York: Harper and Row.

Pollan, M. (2006). *The omnivore's dilemma: A natural history of four meals.* New York: Penguin Press.

Portes, A. (1969). Dilemmas of a golden exile: Integration of Cuban refugee families in Milwaukee. *American Sociological Review, 34,* 505–518.

Portes, A., et al. (1985). After Mariel: A survey of the resettlement experiences of 1980 Cuban refugees in Miami. *Estudios Cubanos* (Cuban studies), *15,* 37–59.

Portes, A., & MacLeod, D. (1996). Educational progress of children of immigrants: The roles of class, ethnicity and school context. *Sociology of Education, 69*(4), 255–275.

Portes, A., & Zhou, M. (1993). The new second generation: Segmented assimilation and its variants. *Annals of the American Academy of Political and Social Science, 530,* 74–96.

Posner, R. A. (1992). *Sex and reason.* Cambridge, MA: Harvard University Press.

Powell, B., & Steelman, L. C. (1990). Beyond sibship size: Sibling density, sex composition, and educational outcomes. *Social Forces, 69*(1), 181–206.

Pratt, L. A., et al. (2011, October). *Antidepressant use in persons aged 12 and over: United States, 2005–2008.* National Center for Health Statistics data brief no. 76. Retrieved from www.cdc.gov/nchs/data/databriefs/db76.htm

PricewaterhouseCoopers. (2011). Health and well-being Touchstone survey results. Retrieved from www.pwc.com/en_US/us/hr-management/assets/PwC_2011_Health_and_Wellbeing_Touchstone_Survey_Results.pdf

Putnam, R. D. (2000). *Bowling alone: The collapse and revival of American community.* New York: Simon & Schuster.

Qaim, M., & Zilberman, D. (2003). Yield effects of genetically modified crops in developing countries. *Science, 299,* 900–902.

Quadagno, J. (1987). Theories of the welfare state. *Annual Review of Sociology, 13,* 109–128.

Quadagno, J. (1996). *The color of welfare: How racism undermined the war on poverty.* New York: Oxford University Press.

Radway, J. (1987). *Reading the romance: Women, patriarchy, and popular literature.* Chapel Hill: University of North Carolina Press.

Rahman, Q., et al. (2003). Sexual orientation–related differences in prepulse inhibition of the human startle response. *Behavioral Neuroscience, 117*(5), 1096–1102.

Rainwater, L. (1974). *What money buys: Inequality and the social meanings of income.* New York: Basic Books.

Ralli, T. (2005, September 5). Who's a looter? In storm's aftermath, pictures kick up a different kind of tempest. *The New York Times.* Retrieved from www.nytimes.com/2005/09/05/business/05caption.html

Ramey, V. A., & Francis, N. (2006). *A century of work and leisure.* Cambridge, MA: National Bureau of Economic Research.

Read, J. (2008, February). Muslims in America. *Contexts.* Retrieved from http://contexts.org/articles/fall-2008/muslims-in-america/

Reddy, G. (2005). *With respect to sex: Negotiating hijra identity in South India.* Chicago: University of Chicago Press.

Religion and politics still a volatile mix. (2009, December 9). *Asheville Citizen-Times,* p. A10. Retrieved from www.citizen-times.com/apps/pbcs.dll/article?AID=200991208030

Remez, L. (2000). Oral sex among adolescents: Is it sex or is it abstinence? *Family Planning Perspectives, 23*(6). Retrieved from www.guttmacher.org/pubs/journals/3229800.html

Reskin, B., & Roos, P. (1990). *Job queues, gender queues.* Philadelphia: Temple University Press.

Rich, A. (1980). Compulsory heterosexuality and lesbian existence. *Signs: Journal of Women in Culture and Society, 5*, 631–660.

Ringen, S. (1987). *The possibility of politics.* New York: Oxford University Press.

Rios, V. (2011). *Punished: Policing the lives of black and Latino boys.* New York: NYU Press.

Risman, B. J. (1998). *Gender vertigo: American families in transition.* New Haven: Yale University Press.

Roberts, S. (2010, January 5). No longer majority black, Harlem is in transition. *New York Times.* NY/Region section. Retrieved from www.nytimes.com/2010/01/06/nyregion/06harlem.html

Robinson, S. & Nash, J. M. (2000, July 31). Grains of hope. *Time, 156*(5). Retrieved from www.time.com/time/magazine/article/0,9171,997586,00.html

Rock, L. M., & Lipari, R. N. (2011, March). 2010 workplace and gender relations survey of active duty members overview report on sexual assault, DMDC Report No. 2010-025. *Defense Manpower Data Center Human Resources Strategic Assessment Program.* Retrieved from www.sapr.mil/media/pdf/research/DMDC_2010_WGRA_Overview_Report_of_Sexual_Assault.pdf

Rockoff, J. E. (2004). The impact of individual teachers on student achievement: Evidence from panel data. *The American Economic Review, 94*(2), 247–252.

Roof, W. C. (1989). Multiple religious switching. *Journal for the Scientific Study of Religion, 28*, 530–535.

Rosaldo, M. Z. (1974). Woman, culture and society: A theoretical overview. In M. Z. Rosaldo & L. Lamphere (Eds.), *Woman, culture, and society* (pp. 17–42). Stanford, CA: Stanford University Press.

Rosenbaum, J. E. (1980). Track misperceptions and frustrated college plans: An analysis of the effects of track perception in the National Longitudinal Survey. *Sociology of Education, 53*(2), 74–88.

Rosenbaum, J., with L. S. Rubinowitz. (2000). *Crossing the class and color lines: From public housing to white suburbia.* Chicago: University of Chicago Press.

Rosenfeld, J., & Kleykamp, M. (2009). Hispanics and organized labor. *American Sociological Review, 74*(4), 916–937.

Rosenhan, D. L. (1973). On being sane in insane places. *Science, 179*, 25–58.

Rosenthal, R., & Jacobson, L. (1968). *Pygmalion in the classroom: Teacher expectation and pupils' intellectual development.* New York: Rinehart & Winston.

Rosenzweig, M. R. (1982). Educational, subsidy, agricultural development and fertility change. *Quarterly Journal of Economics, 97*(1), 67–88.

Rothstein, J. M. (2004). College performance predictions and the SAT. *Journal of Econometrics, 121*(1–2), 297–317.

Rousseau, J. J. (2004; orig. 1754). A dissertation on the origin and foundation of the inequality of mankind. In *Discourse on inequality.* Whitefish, MT: Kessinger Publishing.

Rowntree, B. S. (1910). *Poverty, A study of town life.* London: Macmillan.

Rubin, G. (1975). The traffic in women: Notes on the "political economy" of sex. In R. R. Reiter (Ed.), *Toward an anthropology of women* (pp. 157–210). New York: Monthly Review Press.

Ruggles, P. (1990). *Drawing the line: Alternative poverty measures and their implications for public policy.* Washington, DC: Urban Institute Press.

Sachs, J. D. (2001.) *Macroeconomics and health: Investing in health for economic development.* Report of the Commission on Macroeconomics and Health. Geneva: World Health Organization.

Sadker, M., & Sadker, D. (1994). *Failing at fairness: How America's schools cheat girls.* New York: Touchstone.

Sadler, A. G., et al. (2003). Factors associated with women's risk of rape in the military environment. *American Journal of Industrial Medicine, 43*(3), 262–273.

Saez, E. (2010). Striking it richer: The evolution of top incomes in the United States. Retrieved from http://elsa.berkeley.edu/~saez/saez-UStopincomes-2008.pdf

Sahr, R. C. (2010, September 30). Inflation conversion factors 1774 to estimated 2019. Retrieved from http://oregonstate.edu/cla/polisci/sahr/sahr

Salai-i-Martin, X. (2002). *The disturbing "rise" of global income inequality* (NBER Working Paper No. 8904). Retrieved from www.nber.org/papers/w8904

Salganik, M. J., et al. (2006, 10 February). Experimental study of inequality and unpredictability in an artificial cultural market. *Science, 311*(5762), 854–856.

Sanday, P. R. (1990). *Fraternity gang rape: Sex, brotherhood, and privilege on campus.* New York: New York University Press.

Sander, T. H., & Putnam, R. D. (2005, September 10). Sept. 11th as a civics lesson. *The Washington Post,* p. A23. Retrieved from www.washingtonpost.com/wp-dyn/content/article/2005/09/09/AR2005090901821.html

Sander, T. H., & Putnam, R. D. (2010). Still bowling alone? The post-9/11 split. *Journal of Democracy, 21*(1), 9–16.

Santa Ana, O. (2004). Is there such a thing as Latino identity? *American family: Journey of dreams.* Retrieved from www.pbs.org/americanfamily/latino2.html

Saroyan, S. (2006, April 16). Christianity, the brand. *The New York Times.* Retrieved from http://query.nytimes.com/gst/fullpage.html?res=9807E0DA1E30F935A25757C0A9609C8B63

Schackner, B. (2002, September 27). College course focuses on the wealthy minority. *Post-Gazette.* Retrieved from www.post-gazette.com/localnews/20020929wealthy6.asp

Schacter, J., & Thum, Y. M. (2004). Paying for high- and low-quality teaching. *Economics of Education Review, 23*(4), 411–430.

Scharf, S. A., & Flom, B. A. (2010, October). Report of the fifth annual national survey on retention and promotion of women in law firms. *National Association of Women Lawyers.* Retrieved from www.aauw.org/learn/research/upload/NewVoicesPayEquity_NAWL.pdf

Schlosser, E. (2001). *Fast food nation: The dark side of the all-American meal.* Boston: Houghton Mifflin.

Schor, J. (1991). *The overworked American: The unexpected decline of leisure.* New York: Basic Books.

Schrader, J. (2009, December 8). Bothwell seating opposed. *Asheville Citizen-Times,* p. A1. Retrieved from www.citizen-times.com/

Sciolino, E. (2004, October 22). France turns to tough policy on students' religious garb. *The New York Times.* Retrieved from www.nytimes.com/2004/10/22/international/europe/22france.html?scp=1&sq=&st=cse

Scott, J. W. (1988). Women's history and gender: A useful category of analysis. *Gender and the politics of history* (pp. 28–50). New York: Columbia University Press.

Seelye, K. Q. (2005, May 16). *Newsweek* apologizes for report of Koran insult. *The New York Times,* p. A1. Retrieved from www.nytimes.com/2005/05/16/international/asia/16koran.html?scp=1&sq=Newsweek%20apologizes%20for%20report%20of%20Koran%20insult&st=cse

Setoodeh, R. (2006, March 20). Troubles by the score. *Newsweek.* Retrieved from www.msnbc.msn.com/id/11788171/site/newsweek

Shaheen, J. G. (1984). *The TV Arab.* Bowling Green, OH: Bowling Green State University Popular Press.

Sheler, J. (2001, October 29). Muslim in America. *U.S. News and World Report,* 50–52.

Sherkat, D. E. (1991). Leaving the faith: Testing theories of religious switching using survival models. *Social Science Research, 20,* 171–187.

Sherkat, D. E. (1998). Counterculture or continuity? Competing influences on baby boomers. Religious orientations and participation. *Social Forces, 76,* 1087–1115.

Sherkat, D. E., & Ellison, C. G. (1999). Recent developments and current controversies in the sociology of religion. *Annual Review of Sociology, 25,* 363–394.

Shiva, V. (1992a). Recovering the real meaning of sustainability. In D. E. Cooper & J. A. Palmer (Eds.), *The environment in question: Ethics in global issues* (pp. 187–193). London: Routledge.

Shiva, V. (1992b). Women's indigenous knowledge and biodiversity conservation. In G. Sen (Ed.), *Indigenous vision* (pp. 205–214). New Delhi: Sage.

Shiva, V. (2002). *Water wars: Privatization, pollution and profit.* Cambridge, MA: South End Press.

Shiva, V. (2004). Turning scarcity into abundance. *Yes! Magazine.* Retrieved from www.yesmagazine.org/article.asp?ID=698

Shore, B. (1998, October 1). *Culture in mind: Cognition, culture, and the problem of meaning.* New York: Oxford University Press.

Shulman, J., & Bowen, W. G. (2002). *The game of life: College sports and educational values.* Princeton, NJ: Princeton University Press.

Simmel, G. (1900). *Philosophie der Geldes* (The philosophy of money). Leipzig: Duncker & Humblot.

Simmel, G. (1950). Quantitative aspects of the group. In Kurt Wolff (Comp. and Trans.), *The sociology of Georg Simmel* (pp. 87–180). Glencoe, IL: Free Press.

Simon, S. (Host). (2008, January 12). Researcher studies gangs by leading one [Interview with Sudhir Venkatesh]. *Weekend Edition Saturday.* Washington, DC: NPR. Retrieved from www.npr.org/templates/story/story.php?storyId=18003654

Skocpol, T. (2004). Civic transformation and inequality in the contemporary United States. In K. Neckerman (Ed.), *Social Inequality* (pp. 731–769). New York: Russell Sage Foundation.

Skocpol, T., & Amenta, E. (1986). States and social policies. *Annual Review of Sociology, 12,* 131–157.

Skogrand, L., et al. (2004, July). Understanding Latino families: Implications for family education family resources. *Family Resources.* Retrieved from http://extension.usu.edu/diversity/files/uploads/Latino02-7-05.pdf

Smedley, A. (1999). *Race in North America: Origin and evolution of a worldview.* Boulder, CO: Westview Press.

Smelser, N. (1962). *Theory of collective behavior.* New York: Free Press.

Smith, A. (2003; orig. 1776). *The wealth of nations.* New York: Penguin.

Smith, B. H. (2009). *Natural reflections: Human cognition at the nexus of science and religion.* New Haven, CT: Yale University Press.

Smith, J. P., & Edmonston, B. (1997). *The new Americans.* Washington, DC: National Academic Press.

Smith, J. R., et al. (1997). Consequences of living in poverty for young children's cognitive and verbal ability and early school achievement. In J. G. Duncan & J. Brooks-Gunn (Eds.), *Consequences of growing up poor* (pp. 132–189). New York: Russell Sage Foundation.

Snowden, F. M. (1983). *Beyond color prejudice: The ancient view of blacks.* Cambridge, MA: Harvard University Press.

Snyder, S., & Evans, W. (2002). *The impact of income on mortality: Evidence from the social security notch* (NBER Working Paper No. W9197). Retrieved from www.nber.org/papers/w9197

Snyder, T. D., & Tan, A. G. (2005). *Digest of education statistics, 2004* (NCES 2006-005). U.S. Department of Education, National Center for Education Statistics. Washington, DC: U.S. Government Printing Office.

Social Security Administration. (2011, June 3). Popular baby names. *Social Security Online.* Retrieved from www.ssa.gov/oact/babynames/

Sokal, A., & Bricmont, J. (1999). *Fashionable nonsense: Postmodern intellectuals' abuse of science.* London: Picador.

Sommers, C. H. (2000). *The war against boys: How misguided feminism is harming our young men.* New York: Simon & Schuster.

Sorokin, P. (1959; orig. 1927). *Social and cultural mobility.* New York: Free Press.

Sorokin, P., & Lunden, W. A. (1959). *Power and morality: Who shall guard the guardians?* Boston, MA: Porter Sargent.

Spector, M. (2009, January 24). Bear market for charities. *The Wall Street Journal.* Retrieved from http://online.wsj.com/article/SB123275804805311965.html

Spencer, M. B., et al. (1987). Double stratification and psychological risk: Adaptational processes and school achievement of black children. *Journal of Negro Education, 56*(1), 77–87.

Spiegel, A. (Producer). (2006, December 15). Shouting across the divide, Act one: Which one of them is not like the other? [Radio broadcast]. On *This American life.* Retrieved from www.thisamericanlife.org/Radio_Episode.aspx?episode=322

Spock, B. (1998). *Baby and child care.* New York: Pocket Books. (Original work published 1946.)

Spohn, C., & Holleran, D. (2002). The effects of imprisonment on recidivism rates of felony offenders: A focus on drug offenders. *Criminology, 40*(2), 329–358.

Spurlock, M. (Director). (2004). *Super size me* [Motion picture]. United States: Sony Pictures.

Spurlock, M. (2008). *30 days with Muslim Americans* [Television show]. FX network.

Stacey, J. (1987). Sexism by a subtler name? Postindustrial conditions and postfeminist consciousness in the Silicon Valley. *Socialist Review, 96*, 7–28.

Stacey, J. (1996). *In the name of the family: Rethinking family values in the postmodern age.* Boston: Beacon Press.

Stacey, J. (1997). Neo-family-values campaign. In R. N. Lancaster & M. di Lionardo (Eds.), *The gender/sexuality reader: Culture, history, political economy* (pp. 453–472). New York: Routledge.

Stacey, J. (2004). Cruising to familyland: Gay hypergamy and rainbow kinship. *Current Sociology, 52*(2), 181–197.

Stacey, J., & Biblarz, T. (2001). (How) does the sexual orientation of parents matter? *American Sociological Review, 66*(2), 159–183.

Stacey, J., & Thorne, B. (1985). The missing feminist revolution in sociology. *Social Problems, 32*, 301–316.

Stack, C. B. (1974). *All our kin: Strategies for survival in a Black community.* New York: Harper & Row.

Stack, C. B., & Burton, L. M. (1994). Kinscripts: Reflections on family, generation and culture. In E. N. Glenn et al. (Eds.), *Mothering: Ideology, experience, and agency* (pp. 33–44). New York: Routledge.

Stark, R., & Bainbridge, W. S. (1985). *The future of religion: Secularization, revival, and cult formation.* Berkeley: University of California Press.

Stark, R., & Bainbridge, W. S. (1987). *A theory of religion.* Toronto: Lang.

Stark, R., & Finke, R. (2000). *Acts of faith: Explaining the human side of religion.* Berkeley: University of California Press.

Steele, C. M., & Aronson, J. (1998). Stereotype threat and the test performance of academically successful African Americans. In C. Jencks and M. Phillips (Eds.), *The black-white test score gap* (pp. 401–427). Washington, DC: Brookings Institution Press.

Steelman, L. C., & Powell, B. (1985). The social and academic consequences of birth order: Real, artifactual or both? *Journal of Marriage and the Family, 47*(1), 117–124.

Steelman, L. C., & Powell, B. (1989). Acquiring capital for college: The constraints of family configuration. *American Sociological Review, 54*(5), 844–855.

Steinberg, S. (1974). *The academic melting pot.* New York: McGraw-Hill.

Stevens, J. (2006). Pregnancy envy and the politics of compensatory masculinities. *Gender and Politics, 1,* 265–294.

Stoler, L. A. (2002). *Carnal knowledge and imperial power: Race and the intimate in colonial rule* (Intro. and Chap. 3). Berkeley: University of California Press.

Stone, B. (2009, July 31). YouTube wedding video spurs music sales. *The New York Times, Bits Blog.* Retrieved from http://bits.blogs.nytimes.com/2009/07/30/youtube-trumpets-popularity-of-viral-wedding-dance/

Stone, D. A. (1994). Making the poor count. *American Prospect, 17,* 84–88.

Story, L. (2005, September 20). Many women at elite colleges set career path to motherhood. *The New York Times.* Retrieved from www.nytimes.com/2005/09/20/national/20women.html?_r=1&scp=1&sq=Many%20women%20at%20elite%20colleges%20set%20career%20path%20to%20motherhood.&st=cse&oref=slogin

Strom, S. (2010, January 18). A deluge of donations via text messages. *New York Times.* Retrieved from www.nytimes.com/2010/01/19/us/19charity.html

Sum, A., et al. (2009, October). The consequences of dropping out of high school: Joblessness and jailing for high school dropouts and the high cost for taxpayers. Retrieved from www.clms.neu.edu/publication/documents/The_Consequences_of_Dropping_Out_of_High_School.pdf

Swanson, S. A., et al. (2011, March 7). Prevalence and correlates of eating disorders in adolescents: results from the National Comorbidity Survey Replication Adolescent Supplement. *Archives of General Psychiatry.* Retrieved from www.nimh.nih.gov/science-news/2011/most-teens-with-eating-disorders-go-without-treatment.shtml

Taylor, M. (2009, July 31). YouTube declares wedding video a financial success. *The Wall Street Journal, Digits Blog.* Retrieved from http://blogs.wsj.com/digits/2009/07/31/youtube-declares-wedding-video-a-financial-success/

Taylor, P., et al. (2007, July 12). From 1997 to 2007: Fewer mothers prefer full-time work. Pew Research Center. Retrieved from http://pewresearch.org/pubs/536/working-women

Taylor, P., et al. (2011, July 26). Wealth gaps rise to record highs between whites, blacks, Hispanics twenty-to-one. *Pew Research Center.* Retrieved from www.pewsocialtrends.org/2011/07/26/wealth-gaps-rise-to-record-highs-between-whites-blacks-hispanics/

TheKheinz. (2009, July 19). JK wedding entrance dance [YouTube Video]. Retrieved from www.youtube.com/watch?v=4–94JhLEiN0

Thomas, E. (2005, May 23). How a fire broke out. *Newsweek.* Retrieved from www.msnbc.msn.com/id/7857407/site/newsweek

Thomas, W. I., & Thomas, D. S. (1928). *The child in America: Behavior problems and programs.* New York: Knopf.

Thomas Nelson, Inc. (2010). Refuel: The complete New Testament (2nd ed.), NCV [Catalog blurb]. Retrieved from www.thomasnelson.com/consumer/-product_detail.asp?dept_id=190900&sku=0718013026

Thurow, L. (1970). *Investment in human capital.* Belmont, CA: Wadsworth.

Tocqueville, A. de (1835). *Democracy in America.* Retrieved from http://xroads.virginia.edu/~HYPER/DETOC/toc_indx.html

Tough, P. (2008). *Whatever it takes: Geoffrey Canada's quest to change Harlem and America.* New York: Houghton Mifflin Harcourt.

Triester, R. (2005, July 22). "Real beauty"—or real smart marketing? Salon.com. Retrieved from http://dir.salon.com/mwt/feature/2005/07/22/dove/indexl.html

Truth, S. (1851). Ain't I a woman? (speech delivered at the Women's Convention in Akron, Ohio). *Feminist.com.* Retrieved from www.feminist.com/resources/artspeech/genwom/sojour.htm

Turner, R., & Killian, L. M. (1987). *Collective behavior* (3rd ed.). Englewood Cliffs, NJ: Prentice-Hall.

Twichell, J. (2004). *Branded nation*: The marketing of Megachurch, College, Inc., and Museumworld. New York: Simon & Schuster.

Tyson, K., et al. (2005). It's not "a black thing": Understanding the burden of acting white and other dilemmas of high achievement. *American Sociological Review, 70*(4), 582–605.

UMC.org. (2011). 2011 state of the church: The people. Retrieved from www.umc.org/site/c.lwL4KnN1LtH/b.6765229/k.D5ED/2011_State_of_the_Church_The_People.htm

Unah, I., & Boger, J. C. (2001, April 16). *Race and the death penalty in North Carolina.* Retrieved from www.common-sense.org/pdfs/NCDeathPenaltyReport2001.pdf

UNAIDS. (2011). 2010 global report. Retrieved from www.unaids.org/globalreport/Global_report.htm

UNICEF. (2007). *The state of the world's children 2007: Women and children: The double dividend of gender equality.* New York: UNICEF.

United Nations. (2001, May 17). Poverty biggest enemy of health in developing world, secretary-general tells World Health Assembly [Press Release SM/SG/78 of Statement made before the 54th World Health Assembly in Geneva]. Retrieved from www.un.org/News/Press/docs/2001/sgsm7808.doc.htm

United Nations Development Program (UNDP). (2002). *Human development report 2002*. New York: Oxford University Press for the United Nations Human Development Program.

United Nations Statistics Division. (2010). Social indicators: Indicators on health [Table]. Retrieved from http://unstats.un.org/unsd/demographic/products/socind/health.htm

U.S. Census Bureau. (1993). We the First Americans. U.S. Department of Commerce Economics and Statistics Administration. Retrieved from www.census.gov/apsd/wepeople/we-5.pdf

U.S. Census Bureau. (2009a). Births, deaths, marriages, & divorces: Life expectancy. Table 102. Expectation of life at birth, 1970 to 2006, and projections, 2010 to 2020. In *The 2010 statistical abstract*. Retrieved from www.census.gov/compendia/statab/2010/tables/10s0102.pdf

U.S. Census Bureau. (2010a). Nation's foreign-born population nears 37 million (October 19). Retrieved from www.census.gov/newsroom/releases/archives/foreignborn_population/cb10-159.html

U.S. Census Bureau. (2010b). Population Finder fact sheet. 2006–2008 American Community Survey 3-Year Estimates. Data Profile Highlights. Retrieved from http://factfinder.census.gov/servlet/ACSSAFFFacts?_sse=on

U.S. Census Bureau. (2010c). America's families and living arrangements: 2010. Retrieved from www.census.gov/newsroom/releases/archives/families_households/cb10-174.html

U.S. Census Bureau. (2010d). Facts for Features: Mother's Day. Retrieved from www.census.gov/newsroom/releases/pdf/cb10-ff09.pdf

U.S. Census Bureau. (2010e). 2012 statistical abstract: Income, poverty, & wealth. Retrieved from www.census.gov/compendia/statab/cats/income_expenditures_poverty_wealth.html

U.S. Census Bureau. (2010f). Educational attainment by race, Hispanic origin, and sex: 1970 to 2010. Retrieved from www.census.gov/compendia/statab/2012/tables/12s0230.pdf

U.S. Census Bureau. (2011a). Income, poverty and health insurance coverage in the United States: 2010. Retrieved from www.census.gov/newsroom/releases/archives/income_wealth/cb11-157.html

U.S. Census Bureau. (2011b). Educational attainment by selected characteristics: 2010. Retrieved from www.census.gov/compendia/statab/2012/tables/12s0231.pdf

U.S. Census Bureau. (2011c). Native American/Alaskan and Native Hawaiian populations show growth. Retrieved from www.nativelegalupdate.com/2011/05/articles/census-2010-native-americanalaskan-and-native-hawaiian-populations-show-growth/

U.S. Census Bureau. (2011d). The black population: 2010 (September). Retrieved from www.census.gov/prod/cen2010/briefs/c2010br-06.pdf

U.S. Census Bureau. (2011e). The Hispanic population: 2010. 2010 Census briefs. (May). Retrieved from www.census.gov/prod/cen2010/briefs/c2010br-04.pdf

U.S. Census Bureau. (2011f). Overview of race and Hispanic origin: 2010. 2010 Census briefs (March). Retrieved from www.census.gov/prod/cen2010/briefs/c2010br-02.pdf

U.S. Census Bureau. (2011g). The 2012 statistical abstract: Births, deaths, marriages, & divorces: Life expectancy. Retrieved from www.census.gov/compendia/statab/cats/births_deaths_marriages_divorces/life_expectancy.html

U.S. Census Bureau. (2011h). Race and Hispanic origin of the foreign-born population in the United States: 2010. American Community Survey reports (January). Retrieved from www.census.gov/prod/2010pubs/acs-11.pdf

U.S. Census Bureau. (2011i). Census Bureau reports families with children increasingly face unemployment. Retrieved from www.census.gov/newsroom/releases/archives/families_households/cb10-08.html

U.S. Census Bureau. (2011j). Age and sex composition: 2010 Census brief (May). Retrieved from www.census.gov/prod/cen2010/briefs/c2010br-03.pdf

U.S. Census Bureau. (2011k). Voting and registration in the election of November 2010: Detailed tables. Retrieved from www.census.gov/hhes/www/socdemo/voting/publications/p20/2010/tables.html

U.S. Census Bureau. (2011l). America's families and living arrangements: 2010. Retrieved from www.census.gov/population/www/socdemo/hh-fam/cps2010.html

U.S. Census Bureau. (2012). Table 229: Educational attainment by race and Hispanic origin, 1970–2010. Retrieved from www.census.gov/compendia/statab/2012/tables/12s0229.pdf

U.S. Department of Commerce, Bureau of Economic Analysis. (2012). Personal income and outlays. Retrieved from http://research.stlouisfed.org/fred2/series/PSAVERT/

U.S. Department of Health and Human Services. (2011a). Child health USA 2011. Retrieved from http://mchb.hrsa.gov/chusa11/

U.S. Department of Health and Human Services, Assistant Secretary for Planning and Evaluation. (2011b). Annual update of the HHS poverty guidelines. Retrieved from http://aspe.hhs.gov/poverty/11fedreg.shtml

U.S. Department of Justice, Civil Rights Division. (2007). *Enforcement and outreach following the September 11 terrorist attacks.* Retrieved from www.usdoj.gov/crt/legalinfo/discrimupdate.htm

U.S. Department of Labor. (2011). White House fact sheet: Closing the gender wage gap. Retrieved from www.dol.gov/wb/equal-pay/WH-Equal-Pay-fact-sheet.pdf

United States Election Project. (2011). 2010 general election turnout rates. Retrieved from http://elections.gmu.edu/Turnout_2010G.html

U.S. Equal Employment Opportunity Commission. (2011). Written testimony of Algernon Austin, Ph.D., director of the Program on Race, Ethnicity, and the Economy. Economic Policy Institute. Retrieved from www1.eeoc.gov//eeoc/meetings/2-16-11/austin.cfm?renderforprint=1

U.S. Senate, Subcommittee on Immigration and Naturalization of the Committee on the Judiciary. (1965, February 10). Washington, D.C., pp. 1–3.

Van Buskirk, E. (2009, July 30). Hard "Boyled": Sony, Chris Brown cash in on viral wedding video. *Wired, Epicenter Blog.* Retrieved from www.wired.com/epicenter/2009/07/we-wont-get-boyled-again-sony-chris-brown-monetize-wedding-dance-video/

Varian, H. R. (2006, May 4). Red states, blue states: New labels for long-running differences. *The New York Times*, p. 3. Retrieved from www.nytimes.com/2006/05/04/business/04scene.html?scp=1&sq=Red%20states,%20blue%20states:%20New%20labels%20for%20long-running%20differences&st=cse

Varon, J. (2004). *Bringing the war home: The Weather Underground, the Red Army Faction, and revolutionary violence in the sixties and seventies.* Berkeley: University of California Press.

Vars, F. E., & Bowen, W. G. (1998). Scholastic aptitude test scores, race, and academic performance in selective colleges and universities. In C. Jencks and M. Phillips (Eds.), *The black-white test score gap* (pp. 457–479). Washington, DC: Brookings Institution Press.

Venkatesh, S. (2008). *Gang leader for a day: A rogue sociologist takes to the streets.* New York: The Penguin Press.

Verba, S., et al. (2004). Political inequality: What do we know about it? In K. M. Neckerman (Ed.), *Social inequality* (pp. 635–666). New York: Sage.

Waite, L., & Gallagher, M. (2000). *The case for marriage: Why married people are happier, healthier, and better off financially.* New York: Doubleday.

Wallerstein, J., et al. (2000). *The unexpected legacy of divorce.* New York: Hyperion.

Walsh, P. (2009, July 31). Wedding video now a tool to fight violence. *Star Tribune.* Retrieved from www.startribune.com/lifestyle/52201597.html

Wang, W., & Parker, K. (2011, August 17). Women see value and benefits of college; men lag on both fronts, survey finds. *Pew Research Center.* Retrieved from http://pewsocialtrends.org/2011/08/17/women-see-value-and-benefits-of-college-men-lag-on-both-fronts-survey-finds/

Warren, E. (2007). Unsafe at any rate. *Democracy: A Journal of Ideas, 5.* Retrieved from www.democracyjournal.org/article2.php?ID=6528&limit=0&limit2=1500&page=1

Warren, E., & Warren Tyagi, A. (2003). *The two-income trap: Why middle-class mothers and fathers are going broke.* New York: Basic Books.

Warren, J. W., & Twine, F. W. (1997). White Americans, the new minority? Non-blacks and the ever-expanding boundaries of whiteness. *Journal of Black Studies, 28*, 200–218.

Washington, E. (2008). Female socialization: How daughters affect their legislator fathers' voting on women's issues. *American Economic Review, 98*(1), 311–332.

Watts, D. (2003). *Six degrees: The science of a connected age.* New York: W. W. Norton.

Watts, D. J., et al. (2005). Multiscale, resurgent epidemics in a hierarchical metapopulation model. PNAS. Retrieved from www.pnas.org/content/102/32/11157.full.

Weber, M. (1946). *From Max Weber: Essays in sociology* (H. H. Gerth & C. W. Mills, Trans. & Ed.). New York: Oxford University Press.

Weber, M. (1968; orig. 1922). *Economy and society: An outline of interpretive sociology* (G. Rothe & C. Wittich, Eds.; E. Fischoff et al., Trans.). New York: Bedminster Press.

Weber, M. (2003; orig. 1904). *The Protestant ethic and the spirit of capitalism.* Oxford: Blackwell.

Weber, M. (2004). *The vocation lectures: Science as a vocation, politics as a vocation* (D.S. Owen et al., Eds.). Indianapolis, IN: Hackett.

Wegener, B. (1991). Job mobility and social ties: Social resources, prior job, and status attainment. *American Sociological Review, 56*(1), 60–71.

Welsh, B., & Farrington, D. (2008). Effects of Closed Circuit Television surveillance on crime. *Campbell Systematic Reviews:* 17. Oslo, Norway: The Campbell Collaboration.

West, C., & Zimmerman, D. (1987). Doing gender. *Gender & Society, 1*(2), 125–151.

Whitbeck, L. B., et al. (1991). Family economic hardship, parental support, and adolescent self-esteem. *Social Psychology Quarterly, 54*, 353–363.

White House, Office of the First Lady. (2010, February 9). First Lady Michelle Obama launches Let's Move: America's move to raise a healthier generation of kids [Press release]. Retrieved from www.whitehouse.gov/the-press-office/first-lady-michelle-obama-launches-lets-move-americas-move-raise-a-healthier-genera

Wilcox, W. B. (1999). *Religion and paternal involvement: Product of religious commitment or American convention?* Paper presented at Annual Meeting of the American Sociological Association, Chicago.

Wilcox, W. B. (2004). *Soft patriarchs, new men: How Christianity shapes fathers and husbands.* Chicago: University of Chicago Press.

Wilensky, H. L. (1974). *The welfare state and equality: Structural and ideological roots of public expenditures.* Berkeley: University of California Press.

Wilgoren, J. (2003, March 28). A nation at war: Women in the military: A new war brings new role for women. *The New York Times.* Retrieved from http://query.nytimes.com/gst/fullpage.html?res=9B01E2D61F30F93BA15750C0A9659C8B63

Wilkinson, A. (2006, July 24). Hell and back: Cheryl lives! *The New Yorker*, pp. 23, 82.

Williams, C. (1995). *Still a man's world: Men who do women's work.* Berkeley: University of California Press.

Williams, S. (2005). Million dollar blocks. Public service announcement. Digital presentation. Columbia University: Spatial Information Design Lab. Retrieved from www.spatialinformationdesignlab.org/movie.php?url=MEDIA/PSA_01.avi

Willis, P. (1981). *Learning to labor: How working class kids get working class jobs.* New York: Columbia University Press. (Original work published 1977.)

Wilson, A. D. (2000, August 7). *Rockefeller Drug Laws information sheet.* Partnership for Responsible Drug Information. Retrieved from www.prdi.org/rocklawfact.html

Wilson, J. Q., & Kelling, G. L. (1982). Broken windows: The police and neighborhood safety. *The Atlantic Monthly, 249*(3), 29–37.

Wilson, W. J. (1978). *The declining significance of race: Blacks and changing American institutions.* Chicago: University of Chicago Press.

Wilson, W. J. (1987). *The truly disadvantaged: The inner city, the underclass, and public policy.* Chicago: University of Chicago Press.

Wilson, W. J. (1996). *When work disappears: The world of the new urban poor.* New York: Knopf.

Wilson, W. J. (1998). Engaging publics in sociological dialogue through the media. *Contemporary Sociology, 27*(5), 435–438.

Winant, H. (2001). *The world is a ghetto: Race and democracy since World War II.* New York: Basic Books.

Wirth, L. (1938). Urbanism as a way of life. *American Journal of Sociology, 44*(1), 1–24.

Witte, J. F. (1998). The Milwaukee voucher experiment. *Educational Evaluation and Policy Analysis, 20*(4), 229–251.

Wood, W., et al. (2002). Sources of information about dating and their perceived influence on adolescents. *Journal of Adolescent Research, 17*, 401–417.

World Bank. (2002). Global partnership to eliminate riverblindness. Retrieved from www.worldbank.org/afr/gper/

World Bank. (2012). World development indicators & global development finance. Average life expectancy. Retrieved from http://databank.worldbank.org

World Food Programme. (2011). Hunger stats. Retrieved from www.wfp.org/hunger/stats

World Health Organization (WHO). (2008). Household water treatment and safe storage. Retrieved from www.who.int/household_water/en/

World Health Organization (WHO). (2012). Fact sheet: Children: Reducing mortality. Retrieved from www.who.int/mediacentre/factsheets/fs178/en/index.html

Wright, L. (2009, June 1). Slim's time. *The New Yorker.*

Wright, V., et al. (2010, January). Who are America's poor children? National Center for Children in Poverty, Columbia University, Mailman School of Public Health. Retrieved from www.nccp.org/publications/pub_912.html

Wuthnow, R. (1998). *Loose connections: Joining together in America's fragmented communities.* Cambridge, MA: Harvard University Press.

X, Malcolm, with assistance of A. Haley. (1965). *The autobiography of Malcolm X.* New York: Grove Press.

Xu, J., et al. (2009, August 19). Deaths: Preliminary data for 2007. *National Vital Statistics Reports, 58*(1). U.S. Department of Health and Human Services, Centers for Disease Control, National Center for Health Statistics. Retrieved from www.cdc.gov/nchs/data/nvsr/nvsr58/nvsr58_01.pdf

Yeakley, R. (2011, February 5). Evangelical churches still growing, mainline Protestantism in decline. *Huffington Post.* Retrieved from www.huffingtonpost.com/2011/02/15/report-us-churches-contin_n_823701.html

Young, L., & Hammock, E. (2007). On switches and knobs, microsatellites and monogamy. *Trends in Genetics, 23*(5), 209–212.

Young, L., & Wang, Z. (2004). The neurobiology of pair bonding. *Nature Neuroscience, 7*(10), 1048–1054. Retrieved from www.ecfs.org/projects/pchurch/AT%20BIOLOGY/PAPERS%5CNeurobiology%200f%20Pair%20Bonding.pdf

Young, M. P. (2002). Confessional protest: The religious birth of U.S. national social movements. *American Sociological Review, 67*, 660–688.

Zelizer, V. A. (2005). *The purchase of intimacy*. Princeton, NJ: Princeton University Press.

Zernike, K. (2006, April 23). College, my way. *The New York Times.* Retrieved from http://query.nytimes.com/gst/fullpage.html?res=9E01E1DB1F30F930A15757C0A9609C8B63

Zickuhr, K., & Smith, A. (2011). Digital differences, Pew Internet & American Life Project. Retrieved from www.pewinternet.org/Reports/2012/Digital-differences.aspx

Zill, N. (1988). Behavior, achievement, and health problems among children in stepfamilies: Findings from a national survey of child health. In E. M. Hetherington & J. Arasteh (Eds.), *Impact of divorce, single parenting and stepparenting in children* (pp. 325–368). Hillsdale, NJ: Erlbaum.

Zill, N., et al. (1991). *The life circumstances and development of children in welfare families: A profile based on national survey data.* Washington, DC: Child Trends, Inc.

Zimbardo, P. (1971). *Stanford prison experiment: A simulation study of the psychology of imprisonment conducted at Stanford University.* Retrieved from www.prisonexp.org

Zimbardo, P. (2007). *The Lucifer effect: Understanding how good people turn evil.* New York: Random House.

Zimmer, R. W., & Toma, E. F. (2000). Peer effects in private and public schools across countries. *Journal of Policy Analysis and Management, 19*(1), 75–92.

Zukin, S. (2003). *Point of purchase: How shopping changed American culture.* New York: Routledge.

Zwick, R. (2002). *Fair game? The use of standardized admissions tests in higher education.* New York: Routledge.

Zwick, R., & Sklar, J. C. (2005). Predicting college grades and degree completion using high school grades and SAT scores: The role of student ethnicity and first language. *American Educational Research Journal, 42*(3), 439–465.

CREDITS

TEXT

Chapter 1: From the book *Pulp Fiction*: A Quentin Tarantino Screenplay by Quentin Tarantino. Copyright © 1994 Quentin Tarantino. Reprinted by permission of Miramax Books. All Rights Reserved.

FIGURES & TABLES

Chapter 2: **Figure 2.4**: From Babbie, *The Practice of Social Research*, 11E. © 2007 Wadsworth, a part of Cengage Learning, Inc. Reproduced by permission. www.cengage.com/permissions.

Chapter 3: **Figure 3.1**: Graph of name "Kim" from "The Instability of Androgynous Names: The Symbolic Maintenance of Gender Boundaries" by Stanley Lieberson, Susan Dumais, and Shyon Baumann, *American Journal of Sociology*, Vol. 105, No. 5, March 2000, pp. 1249-1287. Copyright © 2000, The University of Chicago Press. Reprinted by permission of the publisher.

Chapter 5: **Figure 5.3**: Asch, S.E. "Studies of independence and conformity: A minority of one against a unanimous majority." *Psychological Monographs* 70 (9, Whole No. 416), 1956. We have made diligent efforts to contact the copyright holder to obtain permission to reprint this selection. If you have information that would help us, please write to Permissions Department, W. W. Norton & Company, Inc., 500 Fifth Avenue, New York, NY 10110. **Figure 5.5**: Figure 2, "Structure of Romantic and Sexual Contact at Jefferson" from "Chains of Affection: The Structure of Adolescent Romantic and Sexual Networks" by Peter S. Bearman, James Moody, and Katherine Stovel, *American Journal of Sociology*, Vol. 110, No. 1, July 2004, pp. 44-91. Copyright © 2004, The University of Chicago Press. Reprinted by permission of the publisher.

Chapter 6, p. 212 map: Prison Admissions Density Map, Brooklyn, NY 2003. Image Copyright: Spatial Information Design Lab, GSAPP, Columbia University. From: Architecture and Justice, Kurgan et al., 2006. Reprinted with permission.

Chapter 7: **Figure 7.1**: Figure from "Power in America: Wealth, Income, and Power" by G. William Domhoff. September 2005. Reprinted by permission of G. William Domhoff—www.whorulesamerica.net. **Table 7.2**: Figure from *Mobility Tables: Quantitative Applications in the Social Sciences* by Michael Hout. Copyright © 1983 by Sage Publications, Inc. Books. Reproduced with permission of Sage Publications, Inc. Books in the format Textbook via Copyright Clearance Center.

Chapter 9: **Table 9.2**: Figure "Gordon's Stages of Assimilation," *Assimilation in American Life: The Role of Race, Religion, and National Origins* by Milton M. Gordon, p. 71. Copyright © 1964, Oxford University Press, Inc. Reprinted by permission of Oxford University Press, Inc.

Chapter 12: **Figure 12.1**: Hernandez, Donald J. Figure 2.2, "Percentage of Children Aged 0–17 Living in Four Types of Families, 1790-1989." In *America's Children: Resources from Family, Government, and the Economy* by Donald J. Hernandez. © 1993 Russell Sage Foundation, 112 East 64th Street, New York, NY 10065. Reprinted with permission.

Chapter 16: **Figure 16.2**: Figure: "Major Religions of the World Ranked by Number of Adherents". Copyright © 2005 www.adherents.com. Reprinted by permission. **Figure 16.6**: Pew Research Center's Forum on Religion & Public Life, © 2009, Pew Research Center. http://pewforum.org/. Reprinted with permission.

PHOTOS

Chapter 1: **p. 1** Vincent Laforet/The New York Tmes/Redux; **p. 2** Katrina Wittkamp/Getty Images; **p. 5** Yaroslava Mills; **p. 7** Miramax/Photofest; **p. 11 left** Paul Sakuma/AP/Corbis; **p. 11 right** Daily Mail/Rex/Alamy; **p. 14 left** Spencer Platt/Getty Images; **p. 14 right** Getty Images;

p. 16 center Granger Collection, NY; **p. 16 left** SuperStock; **p. 16 right** Granger Collection, NY; **p. 17 lower left** Bridgeman Art Library; **p. 17 lower right** Bridgeman Art Library; **p. 17 top** Granger Collection, NY; **p. 18 left** Underwood & Underwood/Corbis; **p. 18 right** Corbis; **p. 19 left** Bridgeman Art Library; **p. 19 center left** Granger Collection, NY; **p. 19 center right** Bentley Historical Library The University of Michigan; **p. 19 right** Getty Images; **p. 20 left** Granger Collection, NY; **p. 20 right** Granger Collection, NY; **p. 21 left** Granger Collection, NY; **p. 21 center left** Granger Collection, NY; **p. 21 center right** Granger Collection, NY; **p. 21 right** Getty Images; **p. 22 top** Getty Images; **p. 22 left** University of Pennsylvania University Archives Digital Image Collection. Photo by Frederick A. Meyer; **p. 22 center** Time Life Pictures/Getty Images; **p. 22 right** Courtesy Ann Oakley; **p. 23 left** Newscom; **p. 23 center left** American Sociological Association; **p. 23 center right** Courtesy Anthony Giddens; **p. 23 right** Newscom; **p. 27** Underwood & Underwood/Corbis; **p. 30** Bettmann/Corbis; **p. 31** Bob Krist/Corbis; **p. 33** Fox Photos/Getty Images; **p. 35** Alamy.

Chapter 2: p. 42 AP Photo/John Swart; **p. 48** AP Photo/Julie Jacobson; **p. 53** Ovie Carter; **p. 56** AP Photo; **p. 57** Time Life Pictures/Getty Images; **p. 58** Michael Smyth; **p. 60** Joseph Rodriguez/Redux; **p. 64** Time Life Pictures/Getty Images; **p. 65** Ducklau/dpa/Corbis; **p. 66** Courtesy Matthew Salganik; **p. 70** © Jeff Lutes.

Chapter 3: p. 74 AP Photo/Yossi Aloni; **p. 76 (all)** Permission granted by Jill Peterson and Kevin Heinz; **p. 78** Granger Collection, NY; **p. 79 top left** Greg Gawlowski/Lonely Planet Images/Getty Images; **p. 79 top right** Lester Lefkowitz/The Image Bank/Getty Images; **p. 79 bottom left** Rose Hartman/Corbis; **p. 79 bottom right** Werner Forman/Corbis; **p. 80** Réunion des Musées Nationaux/Art Resource, NY; **p. 82 left** Mitch Kezar/Stone/Getty Images; **p. 82 center** Dolores Marat/Photonica/Getty Images; **p. 82 right** Rudy Sulgan/Corbis; **p. 85** Reprinted with permission of THE ONION. Copyright © 2007, by ONION, INC. www.theonion.com; **p. 86** Library of Congress; **p. 87** Wolfgang Kaehler/Corbis; **p. 88** Paramount Pictures/Photofest; **p. 89** Bettmann/Corbis; **p. 90 left** Peter Endig/dpa/Corbis; **p. 90 right** Christian Kober/Robert Harding World Imagery/Corbis; **p. 92** Images Distribution/Newscom; **p. 93 left** Corbis; **p. 93 right** John Springer Collection/Corbis; **p. 95 left** Bridgeman Art Library/Getty Images; **p. 95 center** Corbis; **p. 95 right** CNN via Getty Images; **p. 96** AP Photo; **p. 99** AP Photo/Ric Feld; **p. 100** Bettmann/Corbis; **p. 101 top** CBS/Photofest; **p. 101 bottom** ABC/Photofest; **p. 104** Newscom; **p. 105 left** AP Photo; **p. 105 right** Chris Graythen/Getty Images; **p. 106 top** Media Education Foundation; **p. 106 bottom** Ruby Washington/The New York Times/Redux; **p. 109** Courtesy of Erica Rothman, Nightlight Productions and Dalton Conley; **p. 110 left** Adbusters; **p. 110 right** Adbusters; **p. 112** Uriel Sinai/Getty Images.

Chapter 4: p. 116 Joe Fornabaio/The New York Times/Redux; **p. 119** Jose Luis Pelaez/Iconica/Getty Images; **p. 121** Jose Luis Pelaez, Inc./Corbis; **p. 123** Steve Skjold/Alamy; **p. 125** Red Images, LLC/Alamy; **p. 126** Courtesy of Erica Rothman, Nightlight Productions and Dalton Conley; **p. 129** Darren McCollester/Newsmakers/Getty Images; **p. 130** Courtesy Everett Collection; **p. 131** Scott Olson/Getty Images; **p. 132 left** http://helloblueivy-carter.tumblr.com/; **p. 132 right** John Ricard/FilmMagic/Getty Images; **p. 133** AFP/Getty Images/Newscom; **p. 134** Mark Peterson/Redux; **135** Courtesy of Erica Rothman, Nightlight Productions and Dalton Conley; **p. 137 top** AP Photo/Courtesy Zucker Public Relations; **p. 137 bottom** Photo: Jacqueline Hyde. CNAC/MNAM/Dist Réunion des Musées Nationaux/Art Resource, NY. © 2012 The Pollock-Krasner Foundation/Artists Rights Society (ARS), New York; **p. 138** Alamy; **p. 139 top** Reuters; **p. 139 right** Alamy; **p. 139 bottom** ERIC VIDAL/AFP/Getty Images; **p. 141** Wenner Media LLC; **p. 144** 20th Century Fox/Photofest; **p. 147** Courtesy of Harlem Children's Zone; **p. 149** Steve Meyers/AP.

Chapter 5: p. 152 Benoit Decout/REA/Redux; **p. 154** Kate Rich/Feral Trade; **p. 157** Mark Leong/Redux; **p. 158** Dawn Villella/The New York Times/Redux; **p. 161 left** Kelly-Mooney Photography/Corbis; **p. 161 right** Zefa RF/Alamy; **p. 162** Newscom; **p. 167** Mark Peterson/Redux; **p. 169** Courtesy of Erica Rothman, Nightlight Productions and Dalton Conley; **p. 170** Lee Celano/The New York Times/Redux; **p. 171** Richard Perry/The New York Times/Redux; **p. 172** AP Photo/The Ledger Independent, Terry Prather; **p. 173** AP Photo/Patriot-News, Paul Chaplin; **p. 174** Doug Pensinger/Getty Images for AFL; **p. 176** AP/Mandatory Credit: Lauren Greenfield/VII.

Chapter 6: p. 186 Agefotostock; **p. 188** Courtesy of Erica Rothman, Nightlight Productions and Dalton Conley; **p. 190 left** Rare Books Division of the New York Public Library, Astor, Lenox, and Tilden Foundations; **p. 190 right** AP Photo/David J. Phillip; **p. 191** Bettmann/Corbis; **p. 192 left** Bettmann/Corbis; **p. 192 right** Bettmann/Corbis; **p. 193** Three Lions/Getty Images;

p. 194 AP Photo/Greg Wahl-Stephens; **p. 196** SuperStock; **p. 200** Granger Collection, NY; **p. 203 top left** Jack Hollingsworth/Corbis; **p. 203 top right** Anthony-Masterson/ Riser/ Getty Images; **p. 203 bottom left** Seth Wenig/ Reuters/Corbis; **p. 203 bottom center** Buddy Mays/ Corbis; **p. 203 bottom right** Joseph Scherschel//Time Life Pictures/Getty Images; **p. 206** Ruth Fremson/The New York Times/Redux; **p. 208** PGZimbardo Inc; **p. 209** AP Photo; **p. 210** Allied Artists/Photofest; **p. 212** Courtesy of Erica Rothman, Nightlight Productions and Dalton Conley; **p. 213** PGZimbardo Inc; **p. 216** TIMOTHY A. CLARY/AFP/Getty Images; **p. 220** Richard Pell/Institute for Applied Autonomy; **p. 221** George Steinmetz/Corbis; **p. 223** Columbia University Graduate School of Architechure, Planning and Preservation; **p. 224** Q. Sakamaki/ Redux; **p. 226** Alamy; **p. 228** Bettmann/Corbis.

Chapter 7: **p. 237** © Tuca Vieira; **p. 238** Olgu Aytac; **p. 240** AP Photo/Jason DeCrow; **p. 241** Bridgeman Art Library/Getty Images; **p. 244** AP Photo/Themba Hadebe; **p. 245** AP Photo/Kevork Djansezian; **p. 248** Ted Streshinsky/Corbis; **p. 249** Ben Stechschulte/Redux; **p. 250** Reuters/Corbis; **p. 252** AFP/Getty Images; **p. 253** AP Photo; **p. 258** Roger L. Wollenberg/UPI/Newscom upiphotostwo109659; **p. 265** Courtesy of Erica Rothman, Nightlight Productions and Dalton Conley; **p. 268** Courtesy of Erica Rothman, Nightlight Productions and Dalton Conley; **p. 269** Q. Sakamaki/Redux; **p. 275 top** AP Photo; **p. 275 bottom** Granger Collection, NY.

Chapter 8: **p. 278** Abbie Trayler-Smith/Panos; **p. 280** Wikimedia Commons; **p. 282** Time Life Pictures/Getty Images; **p. 285** Reuters/Corbis; **p. 287** M. C. Escher Foundation; **p. 289** SAM PANTHAKY/AFP/Getty Images; **p. 290** SuperStock; **p. 293** Getty Images; **p. 295** Alamy; **p. 297** Corbis; **p. 298** AP Photo; **p. 301** Ashmolean Museum, University of Oxford/Bridgeman Art Library; **p. 303** Alamy; **p. 305** Reuters; **p. 306** Alamy; **p. 307** Courtesy of Erica Rothman, Nightlight Productions and Dalton Conley; **p. 309** Andy Kropa/Redux; **p. 312** Illustration, p. 69 from GUESS WHO by William S. Gray, A. Sterl Artley and Lillian Grey. Copyright 1951 by Scott, Foresman and Company. Reprinted by permission of Pearson Education, Inc.; **p. 315** AP Photo/Fremont Tribune, Matt Gade; **p. 318** Ted Banks/U.S. Navy via Getty Images; **p. 319** Granger Collection, NY; **p. 321** Time Life Pictures/Getty Images.

Chapter 9: **p. 324** SuperStock; **p. 327** UC Davis History Project/Thomas Nast; **p. 329** Reproduced by courtesy of Mauricio Hatchwell Toledano. www.facsimile-editions .com; **p. 331** SPL/Photo Researchers; **p. 332** Hulton-Deutsch Collection/Corbis; **p. 333** National Park Service, Statue of Liberty National Monument; **p. 334** Wikimedia Commons; **p. 335** Keith Bedford/The New York Times/ Redux; **p. 337** Simon Rawles/Alamy; **p. 338** Courtesy of Erica Rothman, Nightlight Productions and Dalton Conley; **p. 339** Reuters; **p. 340** Reuters; **p. 342** REUTERS/ Jonathan Ernst; **p. 343** Mario Villafuerte/Redux; **p. 346** Cheryl Senter for the Boston Globe; **p. 349** AP Photo/ The Sun Herald, Sean Loftin; **p. 354** National Archives; **p. 355** Bettmann/Corbis; **p. 356** Bettmann/Corbis; **p. 358** Reuters; **p. 362** Getty Images; **p. 364** Library of Congress; **p. 368** Courtesy of Erica Rothman, Nightlight Productions and Dalton Conley; **p. 370** AP Photo/Charles Dharapak.

Chapter 10: **p. 374** Reuters; **p. 376** Bettmann/Corbis; **p. 379** Hulton-Deutsch Collection/Corbis; **p. 380** Jill Johnson/Fort Worth Star- Telegram/Newscom; **p. 383** Courtesy of Erica Rothman, Nightlight Productions and Dalton Conley; **p. 384** Jeff Haynes/AFP/Getty Images; **p. 385** Viviane Moos/Corbis; **p. 387** Business and Professional People for the Public Interest; **p. 388 left** Photo by © Todd Buchanan 1993; **p. 388 right** Photo by © Todd Buchanan; **p. 390 left** Reuters; **p. 390 right** Newscom; **p. 391** AP Photo/E Pablo Kosmicki; **p. 392** Courtesy of Erica Rothman, Nightlight Productions and Dalton Conley; **p. 393** Peter Yates/Corbis; **p. 399** Danny Wilcox Frazier/Redux.

Chapter 11: **p. 408** Rwinkwavu, Rwanda. Laurie Wen/ Partners in Health; **p. 410** Gilles Peress/Magnum; **p. 411** Hulton Archive/Getty Images; **p. 412** Fox Broadcasting/ Photofest; **p. 414** Bridgeman Art Library; **p. 415** Granger Collection, NY; **p. 416** Reuters; **p. 418** Courtesy of Erica Rothman, Nightlight Productions and Dalton Conley; **p. 419** Joe Raedle/Getty Images; **p. 422** AP Photo/Peter Dejong; **p. 423** AFP/Getty Images; **427** Blank Archives/ Getty Images; **433** Andrea Kuenzig/laif/Redux; **p. 436** Newscom; **p. 438** Newscom; **p. 439** Courtesy of Erica Rothman, Nightlight Productions and Dalton Conley; **p. 441** Newscom; **p. 443** Xinhua/Xinhua Photo/Corbis; **p. 445** NYC Department of Health and Mental Hygiene.

Chapter 12: **p. 449** Jessica McGowan/The New York Times/Redux; **p. 450** Tomas Van Houtryve/VII Photo; **p. 452** ABC/Photofest; **p. 454** Time Life Pictures/Getty Image; **p. 456 top** Reed Kaestner/Corbis; **p. 456 center** Tami Blumenfield; **p. 456 bottom** Alamy; **p. 459** Time Life Pictures/Getty Images; **p. 461** Bettmann/Corbis; **p. 463** Louis Edmond Pomey/Fine Art Photographic/Getty Images; **p. 464** Bert Hardy/Getty Images; **p. 466** Alamy;

p. 467 JP Laffont/Sygma/Corbis; **p. 471** Getty Images; **p. 473** Sean Justice/Taxi/Getty Images; **p. 476** Ozier Muhammad/The New York Times/Redux; **p. 478** AP Photo; **p. 480** Ed Kashi/Corbis; **p. 483** Courtesy of Erica Rothman, Nightlight Productions and Dalton Conley; **p. 489** Photo by Alberto E. Rodriguez/Getty Images; **p. 490** Alex Wong/Getty Images.

Chapter 13: **p. 494** Ozier Muhammad/The New York Times/Redux; **p. 496** Newscom; **p. 497 left** Ariel Skelley/Corbis; **p. 497 right** Getty Images; **p. 498** Corbis; **p. 499** Corbis; **p. 501 left** Stephen Ferry/Redux; **p. 501 right** Mark Peterson/Corbis; **p. 504** Courtesy of Erica Rothman, Nightlight Productions and Dalton Conley; **p. 506** Mark Peterman/The New York Times/Redux; **p. 507** Courtesy of Erica Rothman, Nightlight Productions and Dalton Conley; **p. 509 left** AP Photo/The Garden Island, Dennis Fujimoto; **p. 509 right** AP Photo/Ed Andrieski; **p. 511** Greg Ruffing/Redux; **p. 515** Laura Pedrick/The New York Times/Redux; **p. 517** Corbis; **p. 520** Cindy Karp/The New York Times/Redux; **p. 523** AP Photo/Reed Saxon; **p. 527** Paul A. Souders/Corbis; **p. 530** Getty Images; **p. 532** Andrew Cutraro/The New York Times/Redux.

Chapter 14: **p. 536** Sion Touhig/Corbis; **p. 538** Official White House Photo by Pete Souza; **p. 539** Alamy; **p. 540** Granger Collection, NY; **p. 541** Granger Collection, NY; **p. 542** Granger Collection, NY; **p. 545** Hulton-Deutsch Collection/Corbis; **p. 547 left** Time Life Pictures/Getty Images; **p. 547 right** Crack Palinggi/Reuters/Corbis; **p. 550** Benson Ford Research Center; **p. 551** Benson Ford Research Center; **p. 556** Danny Wilcox Frazier/Redux; **p. 560** Courtesy of Erica Rothman, Nightlight Productions and Dalton Conley; **p. 565** AFP/Getty Images; **p. 568** Joshua Roberts/Bloomberg via Getty Images.

Chapter 15: **p. 572** Jonathan Lodge/GAMMA/Eyedea Presse; **p. 575** Joe Raedle/Getty Images; **p. 577** Michael Nagle/Redux; **p. 578 left, right** Courtesy Cheryl Horsfall; **p. 579** David Paul Morris/Getty Images; **p. 581 (all)** Alexandra Milgram; **p. 582** Silver Screen Collection/Hulton Archive/Getty Images; **p. 583** John Filo/Getty Images; **p. 584** AHMAD GHARABLI/AFP/Getty Images/Newscom; **p. 586** Stuart Freedman/Panos Pictures; **p. 587** Chris Sattlberger/Panos Pictures; **p. 589** AP Photo; **p. 591** AP Photo/J. Scott Applewhite; **p. 593** Bettmann/Corbis; **p. 595 left** Walter Hahn/AFP/GettyImages/Newscom; **p. 595 right** AP Photo/Saleh Rifai; **p. 596** Granger Collection, NY; **p. 600** Melina Mara/The Washington Post via Getty Images; **p. 605** Courtesy of Erica Rothman, Nightlight Productions and Dalton Conley; **p. 607** Landov.

Chapter 16: **p. 610** Reuters/Corbis; **p. 612** AP Photo/Asheville Citizen-Times, Erin Brethauer; **p. 614 top** Mohamed Messara/epa/Corbis; **p. 614 right** Pascal Deloche/Godong/Corbis; **p. 614 bottom** AFP/Getty Images; **p. 618** Christophe Boisvieux/Corbis; **p. 620** Time Life Pictures/Getty Images; **p. 621** SuperStock; **p. 622** Penny Tweedie/Getty Images; **p. 623** Bartram Nason; **p. 627** TANNEN MAURY/EPA/Landov; **p. 630** Leon Neal/AFP/Getty Images; **p. 631** Joshua Lutz/Redux; **p. 633** Old Dartmouth Historical Society–New Bedford Whaling Museum; **p. 635** Time Life Pictures/Getty Images; **p. 637** AP Photo/Diane Bondareff; **p. 642** © The Atlanta Journal-Constitution; **p. 644** Jehad Nga/Corbis; **p. 646 left** Revolve/Getty Images; **p. 646 right** Newscom; **p. 649** AP Photo/APTV; **p. 650** AP Photo/Gene J. Puskar; **p. 651 left** AP Photo/Vincent Yu; **p. 651 right** Relevant Media Group; **p. 655** Newscom.

Chapter 17: **p. 658** AP Photo/EyePress; **p. 660** Antony Njuguna/Reuters/Corbis; **p. 662 left** Sheila Terry/Photo Researchers; **p. 662 right** Stefano Bianchetti/Corbis; **p. 664** Alex Wong/Getty Images; **p. 667 left** Reprinted by permission from Macmillan Publishers Ltd: Nature. 423, 6941 (June 12 2003) © 2003; **p. 667 right** Tom Uhlman/The New York Times/Redux; **p. 668** Bettmann/Corbis; **p. 669** Patrick Landmann/Getty Images; **p. 670** Marketa Jirouskova/Oxford Scientific/Getty Images; **p. 672** Ralf-Finn Hestoft/Corbis; **p. 674 top** JEFF HAYNES/AFP/Getty Images; **p. 674 bottom** design & logo from THE OMNIVORE'S DILEMMA by Michael Pollan, copyright © 2006 by Michael Pollan. Used by permission of The Penguin Press, a division of Penguin Group (USA) Inc.; **p. 675** Roadside Attractions/Photofest; **p. 676** Time Life Pictures/Pars Int'l; **p. 677** Newscom; **p. 680** Peter Menzel/Photo Researchers; **p. 681** Columbia Pictures/Photofest; **p. 684** Librado Romero/The New York Times/Redux; **p. 685** AP Photo; **p. 686** Courtesy of Erica Rothman, Nightlight Productions and Dalton Conley; **p. 687** Najlah Feanny/Corbis SABA; **p. 690** AP Photo/Chuck Burton; **p. 695** Courtesy of Erica Rothman, Nightlight Productions and Dalton Conley.

Chapter 18: **p. 698** Steve Lambert/Because We Want It; **p. 701** Newscom; **p. 702** AFP/Getty Images; **p. 708** Michael Smith/Newsmakers/Getty Images; **p. 709** Mario Tama/Getty Images; **p. 710** Szilard Koszticsak/epa/Corbis; **p. 711** William F. Campbell/Timepix/Time Life Pictures/Getty Images; **p. 712** Robert Stolarik/The New York

Times/Redux; **p. 714** Bettmann/Corbis; **p. 715** Peter Stackpole//Time Life Pictures/Getty Images; **p. 716** AFP/Getty Images; **p. 718** Corbis; **p. 719** Owen Franken/Corbis; **p. 721** Anchor Publishing, Inc.; **p. 722** Todd Gipstein/Corbis; **p. 724 left** Corbis; **p. 724 right** Justin Geoffrey/Stone/Getty Images; **p. 725** Amy Eckert/Getty Images; **p. 728 left** Bettmann/Corbis; **p. 728 right** Derek Croucher; **p. 730 left** Time Life Pictures/Getty Images; **p. 730 center** Photo12/The Image Works; **p. 730 right** AFP/Getty Images; **p. 732** Courtesy of Erica Rothman, Nightlight Productions and Dalton Conley; **p. 733** Ricardo Domínguez.

INDEX